Intermediate Microeconomics and Its Application

Walter Nicholson
Amherst College

Christopher Snyder
Dartmouth College

12e

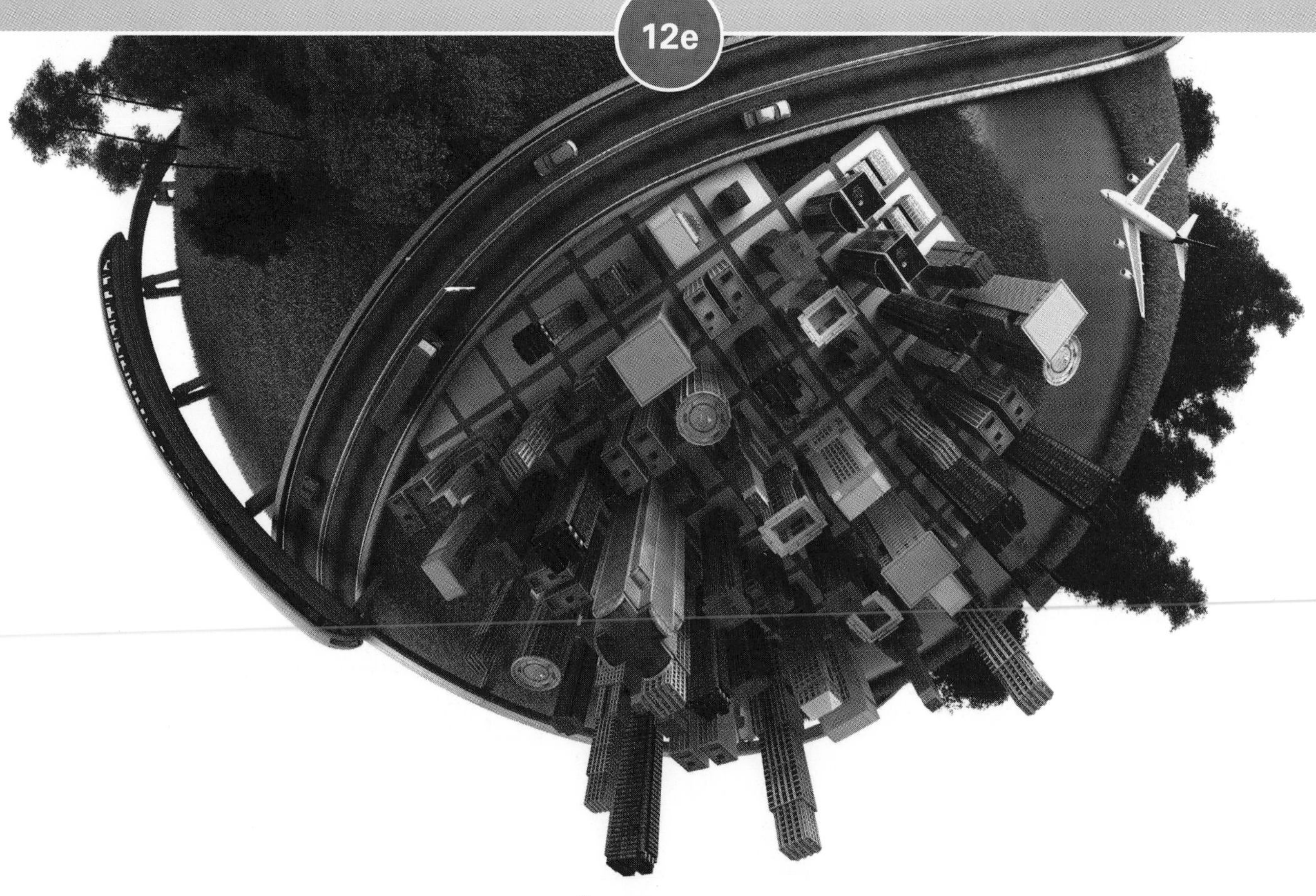

CENGAGE Learning®

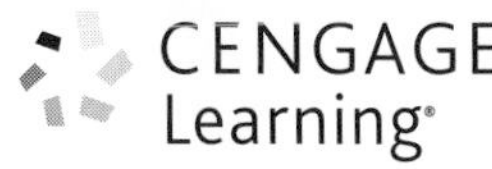

Australia • Brazil • Mexico • Singapore • United Kingdom • United States

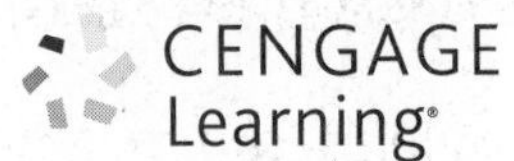

Intermediate Microeconomics and Its Application, Twelfth Edition
Walter Nicholson and Christopher Snyder

Vice President, General Manager, Social Science & Qualitative Business: Erin Joyner

Product Director/Executive Editor or Publisher: Michael Worls

Senior Product Manager: Steven Scoble

Content Developer: Daniel Noguera

Product Assistant: Mary Umbarger

Senior Brand Manager: Robin Lefevre

Market Development Manager: John Carey

Art and Cover Direction, Production Management, and Composition: Lumina Datamatics, Inc

Media Developer: Anita Verma

Intellectual Rights Acquisition Specialist, Text and Image: Amber Hosea

Manufacturing Planner: Kevin Kluck

Cover & Internal Image: © Pablo Scapinachis/Shutterstock

Library of Congress Control Number: 2014938973

Student Edition ISBN: 978-1-133-18903-9

Student Edition with PAC ISBN: 978-1-133-18902-2

Cengage Learning
20 Channel Center Street
Boston, MA 02210
USA

Cengage Learning is a leading provider of customized learning solutions with office locations around the globe, including Singapore, the United Kingdom, Australia, Mexico, Brazil, and Japan. Locate your local office at **www.cengage.com/global**

Cengage Learning products are represented in Canada by Nelson Education, Ltd.

To learn more about Cengage Learning Solutions, visit **www.cengage.com**

Purchase any of our products at your local college store or at our preferred online store **www.cengagebrain.com**

Printed in the United States of America
Print Number: 01 Print Year: 2014

Dedication

To my grandchildren: Elizabeth, Sarah, David, Sophia, Abigail, Nathaniel, Christopher, and Ava

Walter Nicholson

To my daughters: Clare, Tess, and Meg

Christopher Snyder

About the Authors

Walter Nicholson Walter Nicholson is the Ward H. Patton Professor of Economics, *Emeritus*, at Amherst College and a Visiting Professor at Ave Maria University. He received a B.A. in mathematics from Williams College and a Ph.D. in economics from the Massachusetts Institute of Technology. Professor Nicholson's primary research interests are in the econometric analyses of labor market problems and of policies to address them including unemployment compensation, job training programs, welfare policies, and trade adjustment assistance. Professor Nicholson is also a Senior Fellow at Mathematica Policy Research and an advisor on labor market policies to the U.S. and Canadian governments. He and his wife Susan live in Naples, Florida and Montague, Massachusetts.

Christopher Snyder Christopher Snyder is the Joel Z. and Susan Hyatt Professor of Economics at Dartmouth College, where he pursues research and teaching interests in microeconomic theory, industrial organization, and law and economics. He is a Research Associate in the National Bureau of Economic Research, serves on the board of the Industrial Organization Society, and is an Associate Editor of the *International Journal of Industrial Organization* and *Review of Industrial Organization*. Snyder received his B.A. in mathematics and economics from Fordham University and his Ph.D. in economics from the Massachusetts Institute of Technology. His recent research has appeared in leading journals in and outside of economics including the *Journal of Political Economy* and *Journal of the American Medical Association*. He lives in Hanover, New Hampshire, with his wife, who also teaches economics at Dartmouth, and three daughters.

Brief Contents

Contents

departure from the paradigm used throughout the rest of the book. We realize that many instructors may not have the time or inclination to cover this additional topic. For those that do, one suggestion would be to cover it at the end of the term, providing students with an appreciation of the fact that economics is not cut-and-dried but is continually evolving as new ideas are proposed, tested, and refined. Another suggestion would be to sprinkle a few behavioral topics into the relevant places in the chapters on consumer choice, uncertainty, and game theory.

Some of the new digital content should be a big help for instructors who adopt the electronic version for their classes. One set of videos contains a step-by-step solution to a problem from the end of the chapter hand-picked to best capture the core ideas from the chapter. Other videos select a more difficult problem, the sort that sometimes leads to a line in front of the instructor's door during office hours. These and the other videos should save the instructor time in office hours and lecture, time that can be used to carry on deeper discussions of applications or to more easily "flip" the classroom ensuring the students continue to master the basics.

Both of us have thoroughly enjoyed the correspondence we have had with users of our books over the years. If you have a chance, we hope you will let us know what you think of this edition and how it might be improved. Our goal is to provide a book that meshes well with each instructor's specific style. The feedback that we have received has really helped us to develop this edition and we hope this process will continue.

To The Student

We believe that the most important goal of any microeconomics course is to make this material interesting so that you will want to pursue economics further and begin to use its tools in your daily life. For this reason, we hope you will read most of our applications and think about how they might relate to you. But we also want you to realize that the study of economics is not all just interesting "stories." There is a clear body of theory in microeconomics that has been developed over more than two hundred years in an effort to understand the operations of markets. If you are to "think like an economist" you will need to learn this theoretical core. We hope that the attractive format of this book together with its many learning aids will help you in that process. As always, we would be happy to hear from any student who would care to comment on our presentation. We believe this book has been improved immeasurably over the years by replying to students' opinions and criticisms. We hope you will keep these coming. Words of praise would also be appreciated, of course.

Supplements To The Text

A wide and helpful array of supplements is available with this edition to both students and instructors.

- An Instructor's Manual with Test Bank, by Walter Nicholson and Christopher Snyder, contains summaries, lecture and discussion suggestions, a list of glossary terms, solutions to problems, a multiple-choice test bank, and suggested test problems. The Instructor's Manual with Test Bank is available on the text Web site at http://www.cengage.com/ to instructors only.
- Microsoft PowerPoint Slides, revised by Philip S. Heap, James Madison University, are available on the text Web site for use by instructors for enhancing their lectures.

- CourseMate, a powerful on-line resource center, contains quizzes, student resources, solutions to odd numbered problems, and more.
- Cognero, an on-line assessment system, supports the computerized Test Bank. Cognero allows instructors to create and assign tests, deliver tests through a secure on-line test center, and have the complete reporting and data dissemination at their fingertips.

Acknowledgments

Once again it was the professional staff at Cengage and its contractors that made this edition possible. We are grateful to Daniel Noguera and Steven Scoble for helping determine the scope of the revision, for setting up a time line, and for managing the whole process to ensure the deadlines were met. Their vision, encouragement, and advice were instrumental in moving this edition into the digital age with the addition of the video and other digital assets. We owe a special thanks to Malcolm Joseph, who guided the copyediting and production of the book. He took great care to make sure the flurry of handwritten, embedded, and emailed changes all made it into the final manuscript, and made sure the notation, grammar, and tone was maintained across 17 chapters and two authors. Michelle Kunkler managed to devise ways to incorporate the many elements of the book into an attractive whole. We also thank our media editor, Leah Wuchnick, and the marketing team, lead by Katie Jergens, for their respective contributions. Several Dartmouth students provided excellent research assistance. Paulina Karpis reviewed all the applications and helped us update all the facts and figures. Rex Woodbury provided a fresh set of eyes for reviewing the page proofs, ensuring that the text said what we wanted it to say and that all the i's were dotted in the equations.

We certainly owe a debt of gratitude to our families for suffering through another edition of our books. For Walter Nicholson, most of the cost has been born by his wife of 47 years Susan (who should know better by now). Fortunately, his ever expanding set of grandchildren has provided her with a well-deserved escape. The dedication of the book to them is intended both as gratitude to their being here and a feeble attempt to get them to be interested in this ever-fascinating subject.

Christopher Snyder is grateful to his wife Maura for accommodating the long hours needed for this revision and for providing economic insights from her teaching of the material. He is grateful to his daughters, to whom he has dedicated this edition, for expediting the writing process by behaving themselves and for generally being a joy around the house. He also thanks his Dartmouth colleagues for their understanding and for helpful discussions, in particular, with Erin Mansur, John Scott, Josh Schwartzstein, and Jon Zinman.

Walter Nicholson
Amherst, Massachusetts
June 2014

Christopher Snyder
Hanover, New Hampshire
June 2014

PART 1

Introduction

"Economics is the study of mankind in the ordinary business of life."

—Alfred Marshall, Principles of Economics, 1890

Part 1 includes only a single background chapter. In it, we will review some basic principles of supply and demand, which should look familiar from your introductory economics course. This review is especially important because supply and demand models serve as a starting point for most of the material covered later in this book.

Mathematical tools are widely used in practically all areas of economics. Although the math used in this book is not especially difficult, the appendix to Chapter 1 provides a brief summary of what you will need to know. Many of these basic principles are usually covered in an elementary algebra course. Most important is the relationship between algebraic functions and the graphs of these functions. Because we will be using graphs heavily throughout the book, it is important to be sure you understand this material before proceeding.

1 Economic Models

You have to deal with prices every day. When planning air travel, for example, you face a bewildering array of possible prices and travel-time restrictions. A cross-country flight can cost anywhere from $200 to $1,200, depending on where you look. How can that be? Surely the cost is the same for an airline to carry each passenger; so why do passengers pay such different prices?

Or, consider buying beer or wine to go with your meal at a restaurant (assuming you meet the unwarranted age restrictions). You will probably have to pay at least $5.95 for wine or beer that would cost no more than $1.00 in a liquor store. How can that be? Why don't people balk at such extreme prices, and why don't restaurants offer a better deal?

Finally, think about prices of houses. During the years 2004–2007, house prices rose dramatically. Annual gains of 25 percent or more were common in areas of high demand, such as California and south Florida. But these increases were not sustainable. Starting in late 2007, housing demand stalled, partly in connection with much higher interest rates on mortgages. By mid-2012, house prices had fallen precipitously. Declines of more than 50 percent occurred in many locations. How can you explain such wild gyrations? Are economic models capable of describing these rapid price moves, or would it be better to study these in a class on the psychology of crowds?

If these are the kinds of questions that interest you, microeconomics is the right course to take. As the quotation in the introduction to this part states, economics (especially microeconomics) is the study of "the ordinary business of life." That is, economists take such things as airfares, house prices, or restaurants' menus as interesting topics, worthy of detailed study. Why? Because understanding these everyday features of our world goes a long way toward understanding the welfare of the actual people who live here. The study of economics cuts through the garble of television sound bites and the hot air of politicians that often obscure rather than enlighten these issues. Our goal here is to help you to understand the market forces that affect all of our lives.

1-1 What Is Microeconomics?

Economics
The study of the allocation of scarce resources among alternative uses.

As you probably learned in your introductory course, **economics** is formally defined as the "study of the allocation of scarce resources among alternative uses." This definition stresses that there simply are not enough basic resources (such as land, labor, and capital equipment) in the world to produce everything that people want. Hence, every society must choose, either explicitly or implicitly, how its resources will be used. Of course, such "choices" are usually not made by an all-powerful dictator who specifies every citizen's life in minute detail. Instead, the way resources get allocated is determined by the actions of many people who engage in a bewildering variety of economic activities. Many of these activities involve participation in some sort of market transaction. Flying in airplanes, buying houses, and purchasing meals are just three of the practically infinite number of things that people do that have market consequences for them and for society as a whole. **Microeconomics** is the study of all of these choices and of how well the resulting market outcomes meet basic human needs.

Microeconomics
The study of the economic choices individuals and firms make and of how these choices create markets and affect welfare.

Obviously, any real-world economic system is far too complicated to be described in detail. Just think about how many items are available in the typical hardware store (not to mention in the typical Home Depot megastore). Surely it would be impossible to study in detail how each hammer or screwdriver was produced and how many were bought in each store. Not only would such a description take a very long time, but it seems likely no one would care to know such trivia, especially if the information gathered could not be used elsewhere. For this reason, all economists build simple **models** of various activities that they wish to study. These models may not be especially realistic, at least in terms of their ability to capture the details of how a hammer is sold; but, just as scientists use models of the atom or architects use models of what they want to build, economists use simplified models to describe the basic features of markets. Of course, these models are "unrealistic." But maps are unrealistic too—they do not show every house or parking lot. Despite this lack of "realism," maps help you see the overall picture and get you where you want to go. That is precisely what a good economic model should do. The economic models that you will encounter in this book have a wide variety of uses, even though, at first, you may think that some of them are unrealistic. The applications scattered throughout the book are intended to illustrate such practical uses. But they can also suggest the many ways in which the study of microeconomics can help you understand the economic events that affect your life.

Models
Simple theoretical descriptions that capture the essentials of how the economy work.

1-2 A Few Basic Principles

Much of microeconomics consists of simply applying a few basic principles to new situations. We can illustrate some of these by examining an economic model with which you already should be familiar—the **production possibility frontier**. This graph shows the various amounts of two goods that an economy can produce during some period (say, one year). Figure 1.1, for example, shows all the combinations of two goods (say, food and clothing) that can be produced with this economy's resources. For example, 10 units of food and 3 units of clothing can be made, or 4 units of food and 12 units of clothing. Many other combinations of food and clothing can also be produced, and Figure 1.1 shows all of them. Any combination on or inside the frontier can be produced, but combinations of food and clothing outside the frontier cannot be made because there are not enough resources to do so.

Production Possibility Frontier
A graph showing all possible combinations of goods that can be produced with a fixed amount of resources.

MICRO QUIZ 1.1

Consider the production possibility frontier shown in Figure 1.1:

1. Why is this curve called a "frontier"?
2. This curve has a "concave" shape. Would the opportunity cost of clothing production increase if the shape of the curve were convex instead?

This simple model of production illustrates six principles that are common to practically every situation studied in microeconomics:

- *Resources are scarce.* Some combinations of food and clothing (such as 10 units of food together with 12 units of clothing) are impossible to make given the resources available. We simply cannot have all of everything we might want.

Figure 1.1 Production Possibility Frontier

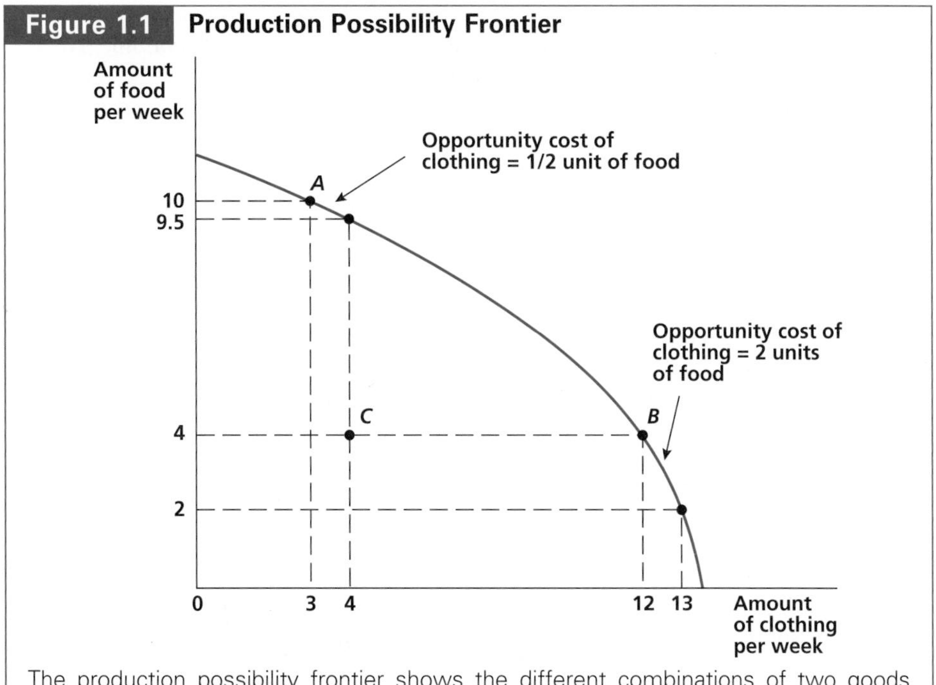

The production possibility frontier shows the different combinations of two goods that can be produced from a fixed amount of scarce resources. It also shows the opportunity cost of producing more of one good as the quantity of the other good that cannot then be produced. The opportunity cost at two different levels of production of a good can be seen by comparing points *A* and *B*. Inefficiency is shown by comparing points *B* and *C*.

- *Scarcity involves **opportunity costs**.* That is, producing more of one good necessarily involves producing less of something else. For example, if this economy produces 10 units of food and 3 units of clothing per year at point *A*, producing 1 more unit of clothing would "cost" one-half unit of food. In other words, to increase the output of clothing by 1 unit means the production of food would have to decrease by one-half unit.

Opportunity cost
The cost of a good as measured by the alternative uses that are foregone by producing it.

- *Opportunity costs are increasing.* Expanding the output of one particular goodwill usually involves increasing opportunity costs as diminishing returns set in. Although the precise reasons for this will be explained later, Figure 1.1 shows this principle clearly. If clothing output were expanded to 12 units per year (point *B*), the opportunity cost of clothing would rise from one-half a unit of food to 2 units of food. Hence, the opportunity cost of an economic action is not constant but varies with the circumstances.
- *Incentives matter.* When people make economic decisions, they will consider opportunity costs. Only when the extra (marginal) benefits from an action exceed the extra (marginal) opportunity costs will they take the action being considered. Suppose that the economy is operating at a place on its production possibility frontier where the opportunity cost of 1 unit of clothing is 1 unit of food. Then any person could judge whether he or she would prefer more clothing or more food and trade at this ratio. But if, say, there were a 100 percent tax on clothing, it would seem as if you could get only one-half a unit of clothing in exchange for giving up food—so you might choose to eat more and dress in last year's apparel. Or, suppose a rich uncle offers to pay one-half

your clothing costs. Now it appears that additional clothing costs only one-half unit of food, so you might choose to dress much better, even though true opportunity costs (as shown on the production possibility frontier) are unchanged. Much of the material in this book looks at the problems that arise in situations like these, when people do not recognize the true opportunity costs of their actions and therefore take actions that are not the best from the perspective of the economy as a whole.

- *Inefficiency involves real costs.* An economy operating inside its production possibility frontier is said to be performing "inefficiently"—a term we will be making more precise later. Producing, say, 4 units of clothing and 4 units of food (at point *C* in Figure 1.1) would constitute an inefficient use of this economy's resources. Such production would involve the loss of, say, 8 units of clothing that could have been produced along with the 4 units of food. When we study why markets might produce such inefficiencies, it will be important to keep in mind that such losses are not purely conceptual, being of interest only to economic researchers. These are real losses. They involve real opportunity costs. Avoiding such costs will make people better off.
- *Whether markets work well is important.* Most economic transactions occur through markets. As we shall see, if markets work well, they can enhance everyone's well-being. But, when markets perform poorly, they can impose real costs on the real economy—that is, they can cause the economy to operate inside its production possibility frontier. Sorting out situations where markets work well from those where they don't is one of the key goals of the study of microeconomics.

In the next section, we show how applying these basic concepts helps in understanding some important economic issues. First, in Application 1.1: Economics in the Natural World? we show how the problem of scarcity and the opportunity costs it entails are universal. It appears that these basic principles can even help explain the choices made by wolves or hawks.

1-3 Uses of Microeconomics

Microeconomic principles have been applied to study practically every aspect of human behavior. The insights gained by applying a few basic ideas to new problems can be far-reaching. For example, in Chapter 11, we see how one economist's initial fascination with the way prices were set for the attractions at Disneyland opened the way for understanding pricing in such complex areas as air travel or the bundling and pricing of Internet connections. In Chapter 15, we look at another economist's attempt to understand the pricing of used cars. The resulting model of the pricing of "lemons" offers surprising insights about how the information available in markets can affect the pricing of such important products as health care and legal services. One must, therefore, be careful in trying to list the ways in which microeconomics is used because new uses are being discovered every day.

One way to categorize the uses of microeconomics is to look at the types of people who use it. At the most basic level, microeconomics has a variety of uses for people in their own lives. An understanding of how markets work can help you make decisions about future jobs, about the wisdom of major purchases (such as houses), or about important financial decisions (such as retirement). Of course, economists are not much better than anyone else in predicting the future. There are legendary examples of economists who in fact made disastrous decisions—perhaps best illustrated by the financial collapse of a "hedge fund" run by two Nobel Prize–winning economists. But the study

APPLICATION 1.1

Economics in the Natural World?

Scarcity is a dominant fact of nature. Indeed, the effect of scarcity is often easier to study in natural environments because they are less complex than modern human societies. In trying to understand the pressures that scarcity imposes on actions, economists and biologists have used models with many similarities. Charles Darwin, the founder of modern evolutionary biology, was well acquainted with the writings of the major eighteenth- and nineteenth-century economists. Their thinking helped to sharpen his insights in *The Origin of Species*. Here we look at the ways in which economic principles are illustrated in the natural world.

Foraging for Food

All animals must use time and energy in their daily search for food. In many ways, this poses an "economic" problem for them in deciding how to use these resources most effectively. Biologists have developed general theories of animal-foraging behavior that draw largely on economic notions of weighing the (marginal) benefits and costs associated with various ways of finding food.[1]

Two examples illustrate this "economic" approach to foraging. First, in the study of birds of prey (eagles, hawks, and so forth), biologists have found that the length of time a bird will hunt in a particular area is determined both by the prevalence of food in that area and by the flight time to another location. These hunters recognize a clear trade-off between spending time and energy looking in one area and using those same resources to go somewhere else. Factors such as the types of food available and the mechanics of the bird's flight can explain observed hunting behavior.

A related observation about foraging behavior is the fact that no animal will stay in a given area until all of the food there is exhausted. For example, once a relatively large portion of the prey in a particular area has been caught, a hawk will go elsewhere. Similarly, studies of honeybees have found that they generally do not gather all of the nectar in a particular flower before moving on. To collect the last drop of nectar is not worth the time and energy the bee must expend to get it. Such weighing of marginal benefits and costs is precisely what an economist would predict.

Scarcity and Human Evolution

Charles Darwin's greatest discovery was the theory of evolution. Later research has tended to confirm his views that species evolve biologically over long periods of time in ways that adapt to their changing natural environments. In that process, scarcity plays a major role. For example, many of Darwin's conclusions were drawn from his study of finches on the Galápagos Islands. He discovered that these birds had evolved in ways that made it possible to thrive in that rather inhospitable locale. Specifically, they had developed strong jaws and beaks that made it possible for them to crack open nuts that are the only source of food during droughts.

It may even be the case that the evolution of economic-type activities led to the emergence of human beings. About 50,000 years ago *Homo sapiens* were engaged in active competition with Neanderthals. Although the fact that *Homo sapiens* eventually won out is usually attributed to their superior brainpower, some research suggests that this dominance may have derived instead from superior economic organization. Specifically, it appears that our forerunners were better at specialization in production and in trade than were Neanderthals. *Homo sapiens* made better use of the resources available than did Neanderthals.[2] Hence, Adam Smith's observation that humans have "the propensity to truck, barter, and trade one thing for another"[3] may indeed reflect an evolutionarily valuable aspect of human nature.

TO THINK ABOUT

1. Does it make sense to assume that animals consciously choose an optimal strategy for dealing with the scarcity of resources (see the discussion of Friedman's pool player later in this chapter)?
2. Why do some companies grow whereas others decline? Name one company for which the failure to adapt to a changing environment was catastrophic.

[1] See, for example, David W. Stephens and John R. Krebs, *Foraging Theory* (Princeton, NJ: Princeton University Press, 1986).

[2] See R. D. Horan and E. H. Bulte, and J. F. Shogren, "How Trade Saved Humanity from Biological Exclusion: An Economic Theory of Neanderthal Extinction," *Journal of Economic Behavior and Organization* (2005): 1–29.

[3] Adam Smith, *The Wealth of Nations* (New York: Random House, 1937), 13. Citations are to the Modern Library edition.

of microeconomics can help you to conceptualize the important economic decisions you must make in your life and that can often lead to better decision making. For example, Application 1.2: Is It Worth Your Time to Be Here? illustrates how notions of opportunity cost can clarify whether college attendance is really a good investment. Similarly, our discussion of home ownership in Chapter 7 should be of some help in deciding whether owning or renting is the better option.

Businesses also use the tools of microeconomics. Any firm must try to understand the nature of the demand for its product. A firm that stubbornly continues to produce a good or service that no one wants will soon find itself in bankruptcy. Application 1.3: The Rise and Fall of Blockbuster illustrates how one firm has had to constantly reorganize its methods of doing business in order to meet competition. As the example shows, some of the most elementary concepts from microeconomics can aid in understanding whether the changes worked and why the firm may ultimately disappear.

Firms must also be concerned with their costs; for this topic, too, microeconomics has found many applications. For example, in Chapter 7 we look at some of the research on airline company costs, focusing especially on why Southwest Airlines has been able to make such extensive inroads into U.S. markets. As anyone who has ever flown on this airline knows, the company's attention to keeping costs low verges on the pathological; though passengers may feel a bit like baggage, they certainly get to their destinations on time and usually at very attractive prices. Microeconomic tools can help to understand such efficiencies. They can also help to explore the implications of introducing these efficiencies into such notoriously high-cost markets as those for air travel within Europe.

Microeconomics is also often used to evaluate broad questions of government policy. At the deepest level, these investigations focus on whether certain laws and regulations contribute to or detract from overall welfare. For example, the 2008 financial crisis caused a major rethinking of how financial markets work and whether new forms of government regulation may be needed. As we see in later chapters, economists have devised a number of imaginative ways of addressing questions like this by modeling how such regulations may affect consumers, workers, and firms. These models often play crucial roles in the political debate surrounding the adoption or repeal of major policies. Later in this book, we look at many examples. Of course, there are usually two sides to most policy questions, and economists are no more immune than anyone else from the temptation to bend their arguments to fit a particular point of view. Knowledge of microeconomics provides a basic framework—that is, a common language—in which many such discussions are conducted, and it should help you to sort out good arguments from self-serving ones. In many of our applications we include a "Policy Challenge" that we hope will provide a succinct summary of the key economic issues that must be considered in making government decisions.

1-4 The Basic Supply-Demand Model

Supply-demand model
A model describing how a good's price is determined by the behavior of the individuals who buy the good and of the firms that sell it.

As the saying goes, "Even your pet parrot can learn economics—just teach it to say 'supply and demand' in answer to every question." Of course, there is often more to the story. But economists tend to insist that market behavior can usually be explained by the relationship between preferences for a good (demand) and the costs involved in producing that good (supply). The basic **supply-demand model** of price determination is a staple of all courses in introductory economics—in fact, this model may be the first thing you studied in your introductory course. Here we provide a quick review, adding a bit of historical perspective.

APPLICATION 1.2

Is It Worth Your Time to Be Here?

Those of you who are studying microeconomics as part of your college education are probably paying quite a bit to be in school. It is reasonable to ask whether this spending is somehow worth it. Of course, many of the benefits of college (such as the better appreciation of culture, and friendship) do not have monetary value. In this application, we ask whether the cost is worth it purely in dollar terms.

Measuring Costs Correctly

The typical U.S. college student pays about $22,000 per year for in-state tuition, fees, and room and board charges. So one might conclude that the "cost" of four years of college is about $88,000. But this would be incorrect for at least three reasons—all of which derive from a simple application of the opportunity cost idea:

- Inclusion of room and board fees overstates the true cost of college because most of these costs would likely be incurred whether you were in college or not.
- Including only out-of-pocket costs omits the most important opportunity cost of college attendance—foregone earnings you might make on a job.
- College costs are paid over time, so you cannot simply add 4 years of costs together to get the total.

The costs of college can be adjusted for these factors as follows. First, room and board costs amount to about $9,000 annually, so tuition and fees alone come to $13,000. To determine the opportunity cost of lost wages, we must make several assumptions, one of which is that you could earn about $20,000 per year if you were not in school and can make back only about $2,000 in odd jobs. Hence, the opportunity cost associated with lost wages is about $18,000 per year, raising the total annual cost to $31,000. For reasons to be discussed in Chapter 14, we cannot simply multiply $4 \cdot \$31{,}000$ but must allow for the fact that some of these dollar payments will be made in the future. In all, this adjustment would result in a total present cost figure of about $114,000.

The Earnings Gains to College

A number of recent studies have suggested that college graduates earn much more than those without such an education. A typical finding is that annual earnings for otherwise identical people are about 50 percent higher if one has attended college. Again, using our assumption of $20,000 in annual earnings for someone without a college education, this would imply that earnings gains from graduation might amount to $10,000 per year. Looked at as an investment, going to college yields about 9 percent per year (that is, $10/114 \approx 0.09$). This is a relatively attractive real return, exceeding that on long-term bonds (about 2 percent) and on stocks (about 7 percent). Hence, being here does seem worth your time.

Will the Payoffs Last?

These calculations are not especially surprising—most people know that college pays off. Indeed, college attendance in the United States has been expanding rapidly, presumably in response to such rosy statistics. What is surprising is that this large increase in college-educated people does not seem to have reduced the attractiveness of the investment, even in the weak labor markets that prevailed after the 2008–2009 recession. It must be the case that for some reason the demand for college-educated workers has managed to keep up with the supply. Possible reasons for this have been the subject of much investigation.[1] One likely explanation is that some jobs have become more complex over time. This process has been accelerated by the adoption of computer technology. Another explanation is that trade patterns in the United States may have benefited college-educated workers because they are employed disproportionately in export industries. Whatever the explanation, one effect of the increased demand for such workers has been a trend toward greater wage inequality in the United States and other countries (see Application 13.3).

POLICY CHALLENGE

The U.S. government offers loans and grants to many students so that they can attend college. Why are such loans necessary if college is such a good investment? Should the government provide larger loans to students who attend private schools where tuitions can be up to three times those charged for in-state students at public universities? From our calculations it seems that the return to attending a private college would be much smaller than from attending a public school because of these higher tuitions. Do you believe that actually is true? Should the promised rate of return determine how much the government will lend?

[1]For a discussion, see D. Acemoglu, "Technical Change, Inequality, and the Labor Market," *Journal of Economic Literature* (March 2002): 7–72.

APPLICATION 1.3

The Rise and Fall of Blockbuster

For many years, Blockbuster was the largest video rental company in the world, operating retail outlets in nearly 2,000 locations in the United States and in many foreign countries. The rapid growth of the company in the 1980s and early 1990s can be attributed both to the increased availability of VCRs and DVD players and to the related changes in the ways people watched movies. By the late 1990s, however, the company began to face increasingly complex challenges as the technology for delivering entertainment content to households evolved. Ultimately the company filed for bankruptcy in 2010 and was completely absorbed by Dish Network in 2011. In this application, we look at how the microeconomics of households' demands for entertainment (in combination with changing technology) made it impossible for Blockbuster to continue in the business model it had chosen.

Challenge 1: Content Availability

The first challenge Blockbuster faced arose directly out of the nature of consumer demand for movies and related entertainment products. The advent of VCRs and DVDs significantly increased the possibilities for home viewing. But consumers were obviously sensitive to the costs of doing so. At first content providers (that is, movie studios and television networks) were reluctant to provide very much of their copyright material to Blockbuster, fearing that such a move would substantially reduce what they could make from consumers directly. As a consequence, providers charged large fees for tapes and DVDs and offered relatively few copies to Blockbuster. This resulted in a high cost to consumers both because of direct rental charges and because of the frustration experienced by finding little content available. To meet these problems, in the mid-1990s Blockbuster negotiated "revenue-sharing" contracts with major providers. These encouraged the providers to offer more copies of popular offerings at much reduced prices. Demand for rentals grew rapidly as consumers discovered that the costs to them of renting had fallen dramatically.

Revenue-sharing contracts did pose a major danger to Blockbuster, however. With such contracts, content providers had every incentive to offer similar deals to other rental firms. The company had helped to establish a licensing contract that was indeed preferable for the ultimate consumer, but also established the route to increased competition.

Challenge 2: The Netflix Innovation

Perhaps the firm that initially derived the most benefit from Blockbuster-type revenue-sharing contracts was the fledgling rent-by-mail firm, Netflix. Renting by mail again reduced costs to consumers by two ways. First, time costs were significantly reduced because DVDs arrived at the doorstep. The need to go to the video rental "store" was eliminated. A second advantage Netflix had was that it provided DVDs from a few central locations. That meant that it could have a much larger inventory than was possible in any one Blockbuster store. Consumers could easily search this inventory with their home computers, so the costs of such search were dramatically lower. Blockbuster tried to compete with Netflix by establishing a rent-by-mail option, but this option was never very successful, in part because the firm itself feared that the mail option would undercut the positions of its own stores.

Challenge 3: Streaming

The widespread availability of high-speed internet service provided a third, and final, challenge to the Blockbuster rental model. Once movies or TV shows could be streamed directly into homes, the time costs for consumers acquiring films or TV shows essentially fell to zero. On-screen search options further reduced the costs of finding what one wanted. In addition, new competitors such as Amazon and Hulu threatened the established video outlets. For example, Netflix tried to split its rent-by-mail from its streaming operations in 2011, presumably with the ultimate goal of ending the mail option. But consumer opposition led the company to an embarrassing reversal after only a few weeks. Blockbuster was even slower to respond to the new streaming technology and ultimately filed for bankruptcy in September 2010. But that did not end the evolving saga of the company. Dish Network must have had some reason for buying the company, so it is likely that Blockbuster may reemerge in some form that combines retail outlets, streaming, and delivery of content by satellite.

TO THINK ABOUT

1. Joseph Schumpeter used the term "creative destruction" to refer to the constantly changing relationship between consumers' demands and the firms that successfully meet those demands in a market economy. There is no better illustration of this process than the 25-year history of Blockbuster. In general, do you think that this process improved overall economic welfare or not?
2. Many of the changes discussed in this example arose because the time costs involved to acquiring rentals were reduced for consumers. How would you put a value on such costs? How would consideration of time costs affect the overall relative prices of rentals? If time costs differ among consumers, how should this affect the ways in which consumers would spread themselves among the various rental alternatives?

Adam Smith and the Invisible Hand

The Scottish philosopher Adam Smith (1723–1790) is generally credited with being the first true economist. In *The Wealth of Nations* (published in 1776), Smith examined a large number of the pressing economic issues of his day and tried to develop economic tools for understanding them. Smith's most important insight was his recognition that the system of market-determined prices that he observed was not as chaotic and undisciplined as most other writers had assumed. Rather, Smith saw prices as providing a powerful "invisible hand" that directed resources into activities where they would be most valuable. Prices play the crucial role of telling both consumers and firms what goods are "worth" and thereby prompt these economic actors to make efficient choices about how to use them. To Smith, it was this ability to use resources efficiently that provided the ultimate explanation for a nation's "wealth."

Because Adam Smith placed great importance on the role of prices in directing how a nation's resources are used, he needed to develop some theories about how those prices are determined. He offered a very simple and only partly correct explanation. Because in Smith's day (and, to some extent, even today), the primary costs of producing goods were costs associated with the labor that went into a good, it was only a short step for him to embrace a labor-based theory of prices. For example, to paraphrase an illustration from *The Wealth of Nations*, if it takes twice as long for a hunter to catch a deer as to catch a beaver, one deer should trade for two beavers. The relative price of a deer is high because of the extra labor costs involved in catching one.

Smith's explanation for the price of a good is illustrated in Figure 1.2(a). The horizontal line at P^* shows that any number of deer can be produced without affecting the relative cost of doing so. That relative cost sets the price of deer (P^*), which might be measured in beavers (a deer costs two beavers), in dollars (a deer costs \$200, whereas a beaver costs \$100), or in any other units that this society uses to indicate exchange value. This value will change only when the technology for producing deer changes. If, for example, this society developed better running shoes (which would aid in catching deer but be of little use in capturing beavers), the relative labor costs associated with hunting deer would fall. Now a deer would trade for, say, 1.5 beavers, and the supply curve illustrated in the figure would shift downward. In the absence of such technical changes, however, the relative price of deer would remain constant, reflecting relative costs of production.

David Ricardo and Diminishing Returns

The early nineteenth century was a period of considerable controversy in economics, especially in England. The two most pressing issues of the day were whether international trade was having a negative effect on the economy and whether industrial growth was harming farmland and other natural resources. It is testimony to the timelessness of economic questions that these are some of the same issues that dominate political discussions in the United States (and elsewhere) today. One of the most influential contributors to the earlier debates was the British financier and pamphleteer David Ricardo (1772–1823).

Ricardo believed that labor and other costs would tend to rise as the level of production of a particular good expanded. He drew this insight primarily from looking at the way in which farmland was expanding in England at the time. As new and less-fertile land was brought into use, it would naturally take more labor (say, to pick out the rocks in addition to planting crops) to produce an extra bushel of grain. Hence, the relative price of grain would rise. Similarly, as deer hunters exhaust the stock of deer in a given area, they must spend more time locating their prey, so the relative price of deer

Figure 1.2 Early Views of Price Determination

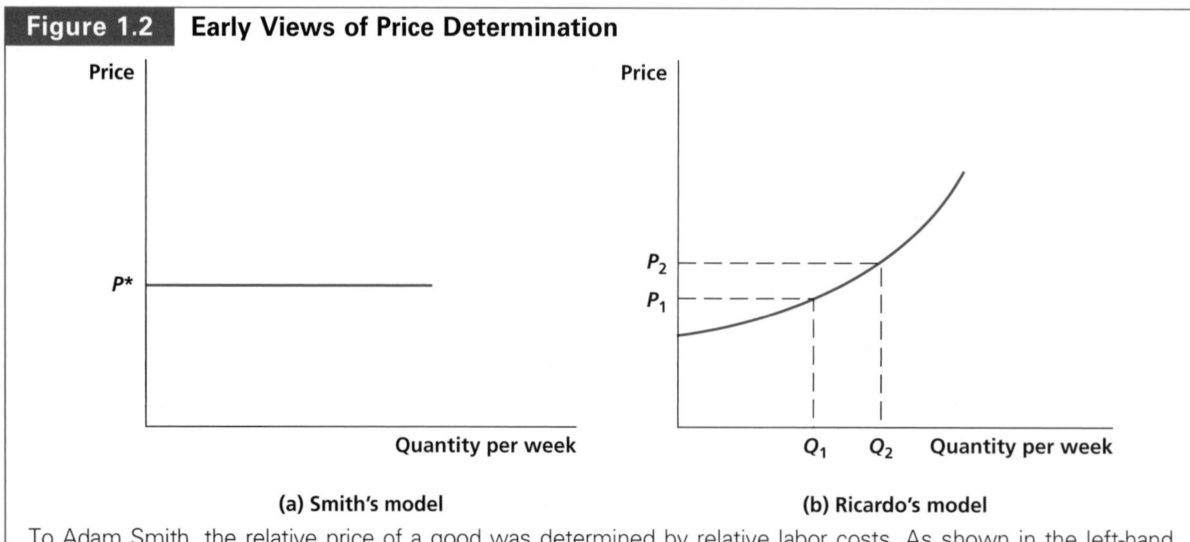

To Adam Smith, the relative price of a good was determined by relative labor costs. As shown in the left-hand panel, relative price would be P^* unless something altered such costs. Ricardo added the concept of diminishing returns to this explanation. In the right-hand panel, relative price rises as quantity produced rises from Q_1 to Q_2.

Diminishing returns Hypothesis that the cost associated with producing one more unit of a good rises as more of that good is produced.

would also rise. Ricardo believed that the phenomenon of increasing costs was quite general, and today we refer to his discovery as the law of **diminishing returns**. This generalization of Smith's notion of supply is reflected in Figure 1.2(b), in which the supply curve slopes upward as quantity produced expands.

The problem with Ricardo's explanation was that it really did not explain how relative prices are determined. Although the notion of diminishing returns improved Smith's model, it did so by showing that relative price was not determined by production technology alone. Instead, according to Ricardo, the relative price of a good can be practically anything, depending on how much of it is produced.

To complete his explanation, Ricardo relied on a subsistence argument. If, for example, the current population of a country needs Q_1 units of output to survive, Figure 1.2(b) shows that the relative price would be P_1. With a growing population, these subsistence needs might expand to Q_2, and the relative price of this necessity would rise to P_2. Ricardo's suggestion that the relative prices of goods necessary for survival would rise in response to diminishing returns provided the basis for much of the concern about population growth in England during the 1830s and 1840s. It was largely responsible for the application of the term "dismal science" to the study of economics.

Marginalism and Marshall's Model of Supply and Demand

Contrary to the fears of many worriers, relative prices of food and other necessities did not rise significantly during the nineteenth century. Instead, as methods of production improved, prices tended to fall and well-being improved dramatically. As a result, subsistence became a less plausible explanation of the amounts of particular goods consumed, and economists found it necessary to develop a more general theory of demand. In the latter half of the nineteenth century, they adapted Ricardo's law of diminishing returns to this task. Just as diminishing returns mean that the cost of producing one more unit of a good rises as more is produced, so too, these economists argued, the willingness of people to pay for that last unit declines. Only if individuals are offered a lower price for a good will they be willing to consume more of it. By focusing on the value to buyers of the last, or *marginal,* unit purchased, these economists had at last developed a comprehensive theory of price determination.

The clearest statement of these ideas was provided by the English economist Alfred Marshall (1842–1924) in his *Principles of Economics,* first published in 1890. Marshall showed how the forces of demand and supply *simultaneously* determine price. Marshall's analysis is illustrated by the familiar cross diagram shown in Figure 1.3.

As before, the amount of a good purchased per period (say, each week) is shown on the horizontal axis and the price of the good appears on the vertical axis. The curve labeled "Demand" shows the amount of the good people want to buy at each price. The negative slope of this curve reflects the marginalist principle: Because people are willing to pay less and less for the last unit purchased, they will buy more only at a lower price. The curve labeled "Supply" shows the increasing cost of making one more unit of the good as the total amount produced increases. In other words, the upward slope of the supply curve reflects *increasing* marginal costs, just as the downward slope of the demand curve reflects *decreasing* marginal value.

Market Equilibrium

In Figure 1.3, the demand and supply curves intersect at the point P^*, Q^*. At that point, P^* is the **equilibrium price**. That is, at this price, the quantity that people want to purchase (Q^*) is precisely equal to the quantity that suppliers are willing to produce. Because both demanders and suppliers are content with this outcome, no one has an incentive to alter his or her behavior. The equilibrium P^*, Q^* will tend to persist unless something happens to change things. This illustration is the first of many we encounter in this book about the way in which a balancing of forces results in a sustainable equilibrium outcome. To conceptualize the nature of this balancing of forces, Marshall used the analogy of a pair of scissors: Just as both blades of

Equilibrium price
The price at which the quantity demanded by buyers of a good is equal to the quantity supplied by sellers of the good.

Figure 1.3 The Marshall Supply-Demand Cross

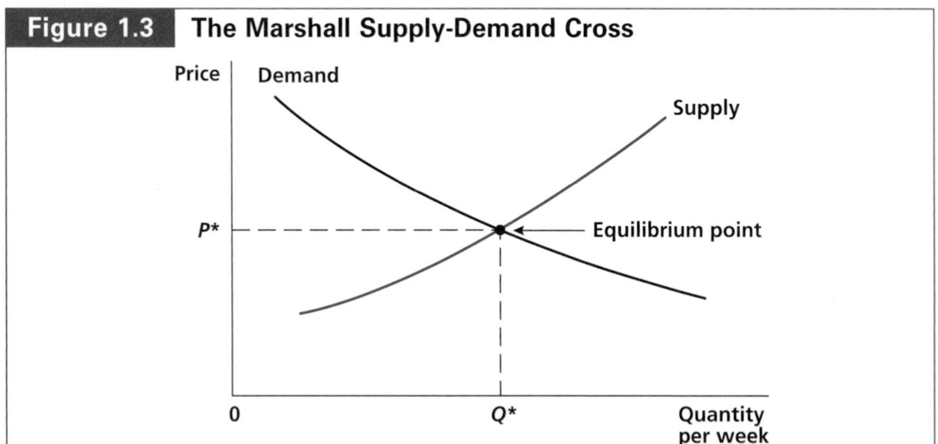

Marshall believed that demand and supply together determine the equilibrium price (P^*) and quantity (Q^*) of a good. The positive slope of the supply curve reflects diminishing returns (increasing marginal cost), whereas the negative slope of the demand curve reflects diminishing marginal usefulness. P^* is an equilibrium price. Any other price results in either a surplus or a shortage.

MICRO QUIZ 1.2

Another way to describe the equilibrium in Figure 1.3 is to say that at P^*, Q^* neither the supplier nor the demander has any incentive to change behavior. Use this notion of equilibrium to explain:

1. Why the fact that P^*, Q^* occurs where the supply and demand curves intersect implies that both parties to the transaction are content with this result?
2. Why no other P, Q point on the graph meets this definition of equilibrium?

the scissors work together to do the cutting, so too the forces of demand and supply work together to establish equilibrium prices.

Nonequilibrium Outcomes

The smooth functioning of market forces envisioned by Marshall can, however, be thwarted in many ways. For example, a government decree that requires a price to be set in excess of P^* (perhaps because P^* was regarded as being the result of "unfair, ruinous competition") would prevent the establishment of equilibrium. With a price set above P^*, demanders would wish to buy less than Q^*, whereas suppliers would produce more than Q^*. This would lead to a surplus of production in the market—a situation that characterizes many agricultural markets. Similarly, a regulation that holds a price below P^* would result in a shortage. With such a price, demanders would want to buy more than Q^*, whereas suppliers would produce less than Q^*. In Chapter 9, we look at several such situations where this occurs.

Change in Market Equilibrium

The equilibrium pictured in Figure 1.3 can persist as long as nothing happens to alter demand or supply relationships. If one of the curves were to shift, however, the equilibrium would change. In Figure 1.4, people's demand for the good increases. In this case, the demand curve moves outward (from curve D to curve D'). At each price, people now want to buy more of the good. The equilibrium price increases (from P^* to P^{**}). This higher price both tells firms to supply more goods and restrains individuals' demand for the good. At the new equilibrium price of P^{**}, supply and demand again balance—at this higher price, the amount of goods demanded is exactly equal to the amount supplied.

Figure 1.4 An Increase in Demand Alters Equilibrium Price and Quality

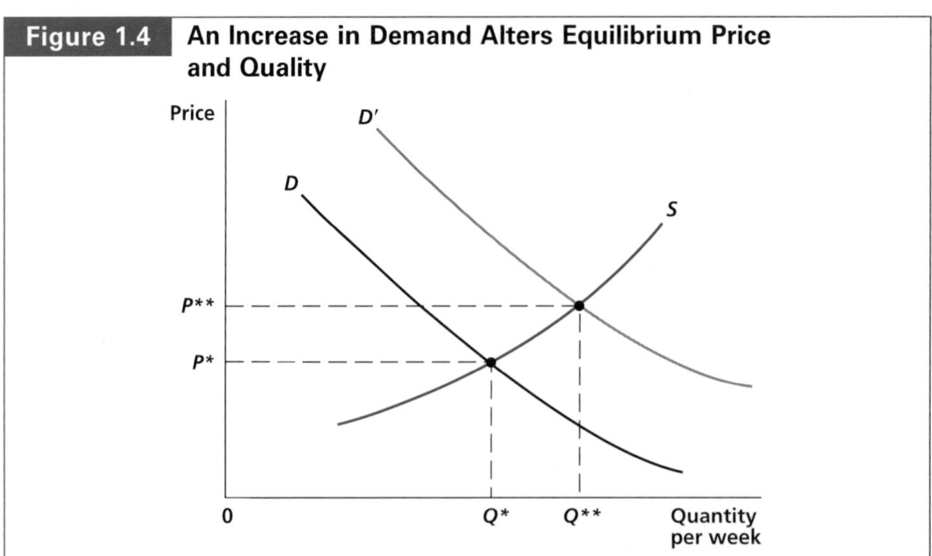

If the demand curve shifts outward to D' because there is more desire for the product, P^*, Q^* will no longer be at equilibrium. Instead, equilibrium occurs at P^{**}, Q^{**}, where D' and S intersect.

Figure 1.5 A Shift in Supply Alters Equilibrium Price and Quality

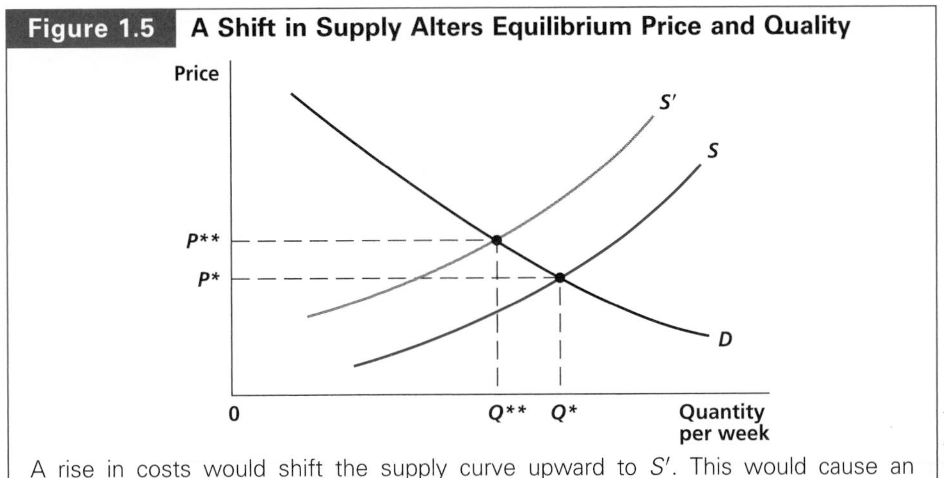

A rise in costs would shift the supply curve upward to S'. This would cause an increase in equilibrium price from P^* to P^{**} and a decline in quantity from Q^* to Q^{**}.

A shift in the supply curve also affects market equilibrium. In Figure 1.5, the effects of an increase in supplier costs (for example, an increase in wages paid to workers) are illustrated. For any level of output, marginal costs associated with the supply curve S' exceed those associated with S. This shift in supply causes the price of this product to rise (from P^* to P^{**}), and consumers respond to this price rise by reducing quantity demanded (from Q^* to Q^{**}) along the demand curve, D. As for the case of a shift in demand, the ultimate result of the shift in supply depicted in Figure 1.5 depends on the shape of both the demand curve and the supply curve.

MICRO QUIZ 1.3

Supply and demand curves show the relationship between the price of a good and the quantity supplied or demanded when other factors are held constant. Explain:

1. What factors might shift the demand or supply curve for, say, personal computers?
2. Why would a change in the price of personal computers shift neither curve? Indeed, would this price ever change if all of the factors identified previously did not change?

Marshall's model of supply and demand should be quite familiar to you, since it provides the principal focus of most courses in introductory economics. Indeed, the concepts of marginal cost, marginal value, and market equilibrium encountered in this model provide the starting place for most of the economic models you will learn about in this book. Application 1.4: Supply and Demand According to Bono shows that even rock stars can sometimes get these concepts right.

1-5 How Economists Verify Theoretical Models

Testing assumptions
Verifying economic models by examining the validity of the assumptions on which they are based.

Testing predictions
Verifying economic models by asking if they can accurately predict real-world events.

Not all models are as useful as Marshall's model of supply and demand. An important purpose of studying economics is to sort out bad models from good ones. Two methods are used to provide such a test of economic models. **Testing assumptions** looks at the assumptions upon which a model is based; **testing predictions**, on the other hand, uses the model to see if it can correctly predict real-world events. This book uses both approaches to try to illustrate the validity of the models that are presented. We now look briefly at the differences between the approaches.

APPLICATION 1.4

Supply and Demand According to Bono

The unlikely 2002 trip to Africa by the Irish rock star Bono in the company of U.S. Treasury Secretary Paul O'Neill sparked much interesting dialogue about economics.[1] Especially intriguing was Bono's claim that recently expanded agricultural subsidies in the United States were harming struggling farmers in Africa—a charge that O'Neill was forced to attempt to refute at every stop. A simple supply-demand analysis shows that, overall, Bono did indeed have the better of the arguments, though he neglected to mention a few fine points.

Graphing African Exports

Figure 1 shows the supply and demand curves for a typical crop that is being produced by an African country. If the world price of this crop (P^*) exceeds the price that would prevail in the absence of trade (P_D), this country will be an exporter of this crop. The total quantity of exports is given by the distance $Q_S - Q_D$. That is, exports are given by the difference in the quantity of this crop produced and the quantity that is demanded domestically. Such exporting is common for many African countries because they have large agrarian populations and generally favorable climates for many types of food production.

In May 2002, the United States adopted a program of vastly increased agricultural subsidies to U.S. farmers. From the point of view of world markets, the main effect of such a program was to reduce world crop prices. This is shown in Figure 1 as a drop in the world price to P^{**}. This fall in price would be met by a reduction in quantity produced of the crop to Q'_S and an increase in the quantity demanded to Q'_D. Crop exports would decline significantly.

So, Bono's point is essentially correct—U.S. farm subsidies do harm African farmers, especially those in the export business. But he might also have pointed out that African consumers of food also benefit from the price reduction. They are able to buy more food at lower prices. Effectively, some of the subsidy to U.S. farmers has been transferred to African consumers. Hence, even disregarding whether farm subsidies make any sense for Americans, their effects on the welfare of Africans is ambiguous.

Other Barriers to African Agricultural Trade

Agricultural subsidies by the United States and the European Union amount to over $500 billion per year. Undoubtedly, they have a major effect in thwarting African exports. Perhaps even more devastating are the large number of special measures adopted in various developed countries to protect favored domestic industries such as peanuts in the United States, rice in Japan, and livestock and bananas in the European Union. Because expanded trade is one of the major avenues through which poor African economies might grow, these restrictions deserve serious scrutiny.

Figure 1 U.S. Subsidies Reduce African Exports

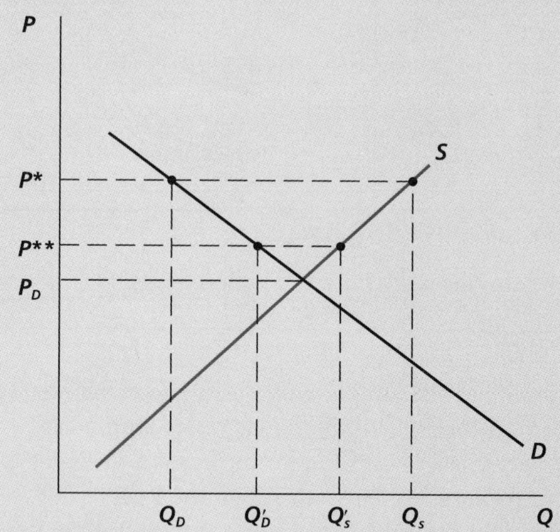

U.S. farm subsidies reduce the world price of this crop from P^* to P^{**}. Exports from this African country fall from $Q_S - Q_D$ to $Q'_S - Q'_D$.

POLICY CHALLENGE

Why do the United States and European countries subsidize farm output? What goals do these countries seek to achieve by such programs (possibly lower food prices or higher incomes for farmers)? Is the subsidization of crop prices the best way to achieve these goals?

[1] For a blow-by-blow description of this trip, see various issues of *The Economist* during May 2002.

Testing Assumptions

One approach to testing the assumptions of an economic model might begin with intuition. Do the model's assumptions seem reasonable? Unfortunately, this question is fraught with problems, since what appears reasonable to one person may seem preposterous to someone else (try arguing with a noneconomics student about how markets work, for example).

Assumptions can also be tested with empirical evidence. For example, economists usually assume that firms are in business to maximize profits—in fact, much of our discussion in this book is based on that assumption. Using the direct approach to test this assumption with real-world data, you might send questionnaires to managers asking them how they make decisions and whether they really do try to maximize profits. This approach has been used many times, but the results, like those from many opinion polls, are often difficult to interpret.

Testing Predictions

Some economists, such as Milton Friedman, do not believe that a theory can be tested by looking only at its assumptions. They argue that all theories are based on unrealistic assumptions—the very nature of theorizing demands that we make unrealistic assumptions.[1] Such economists believe that, in order to decide if a theory is valid, we must see if it is capable of explaining and predicting real-world events. The ultimate test of any economic model is whether it is consistent with events in the economy itself.

Friedman gives a good example of this idea by asking what theory explains the shots an expert pool player will make. He argues that the laws of velocity, momentum, and angles from physics make a suitable theoretical model, because the pool player certainly shoots *as if* he or she followed these laws. If we asked the players whether they could state these physical principles, they would undoubtedly answer that they could not. That does not matter, Friedman argues, because the physical laws give very accurate predictions of the shots made and are therefore useful as theoretical models.

Going back to the question of whether firms try to maximize profits, the indirect approach would try to predict the firms' behavior by assuming that they do act *as if* they were maximizing profits. If we find that we can predict firms' behavior, then we can believe the profit-maximization hypothesis. Even if these firms said on questionnaires that they don't really try to maximize profits, the theory will still be valid, much as the pool players' disclaiming knowledge of the laws of physics does not make these laws untrue. The ultimate test in both cases is the theory's ability to predict real-world events.

The Positive-Normative Distinction

Related to the question of how the validity of economic models should be tested is the issue of how such models should be used. To some economists, the only proper analysis is "positive" in nature. As in the physical sciences, they argue, the correct role for theory is to explain the real world as it is. In this view, developing "normative" theories about how the world *should be* is an exercise for which economists have no more special skills than anyone else. For other economists, this **positive-normative distinction** is not so clear-cut. They argue that economic models invariably have normative consequences that should be recognized. Application 1.5: Do Economists Ever Agree on Anything? shows that, contrary to common perceptions, there is considerable agreement among economists about issues

Positive-normative distinction
Distinction between theories that seek to explain the world as it is and theories that postulate the way the world should be.

[1]Milton Friedman, *Essays in Positive Economics* (Chicago: University of Chicago Press, 1953), Chapter 1. Another view stressing the importance of realistic assumptions can be found in H. A. Simon, "Rational Decision Making in Business Organizations," *American Economic Review* (September 1979): 493–513.

APPLICATION 1.5

Do Economists Ever Agree on Anything?

To the general public, economists seem to be completely confused. In many conversations, they bear the brunt of pointed jokes. Some of our favorites are:

1. If all economists in the world were laid end-to-end, they would never reach a decision.
2. How many economists does it take to change a lightbulb? Two—one to turn the bulb and one to say repeatedly, "Turn it the other way."

Positive Versus Normative Economics

These jokes convey the perception that economists never agree on anything. But that perception arises in part from an inability to differentiate between the positive and normative arguments that economists make. Economists (like everyone else) often disagree over political questions. They may, therefore, find themselves on opposite sides of controversial policy questions. Economists may also differ on empirical matters. For instance, they may disagree about whether a particular effect is large or small. But on basic theoretical questions, there is far less disagreement. Because most economists use the same tools, they tend to "speak the same language" and disagreements on positive questions are far less frequent.

Survey Results

This conclusion is supported by surveys of economists, a sample of which is described in Table 1. The table shows a high degree of agreement among U.S., Swiss, and German economists about positive questions such as the effects of tariffs or of rent controls.[1] There is considerably less agreement about broad normative questions, such as whether the government should redistribute income or act as the employer of last resort. For these types of policy questions, economists' opinions are affected by the same sort of political forces as are those of other citizens.[2]

TO THINK ABOUT

1. The 2012 presidential election featured much discussion about tax policy. Especially prominent were discussions of raising the maximum tax rate on capital income (that is, dividends and capital gains). Economists differed significantly among themselves about the wisdom of such an increase. List some statements regarding this increase about which you might expect most economists to agree. Then list some statements about which you might expect considerable disagreement. Can you find any evidence to support your conclusions?
2. As Table 1 shows, a significant majority of economists believe that tariffs reduce economic welfare. Yet many economists from low-income countries argue that without tariff protection their home industries will never develop to be competitive with the rest of the world. How can you reconcile these two views? Are these economists disagreeing about positive issues or normative ones?

Table 1 Percentage of Economists Agreeing with Various Propositions in Three Nations

PROPOSITION	UNITED STATES	SWITZERLAND	GERMANY
Tariffs reduce economic welfare	95	87	94
Flexible exchange rates are effective for international transactions	94	91	92
Rent controls reduce the quality of housing	96	79	94
Government should redistribute income	68	51	55
Government should hire the jobless	51	52	35

Source: B. S. Frey, W. W. Pommerehue, F. Schnieder, and G. Gilbert, "Consensus and Dissension Among Economists: An Empirical Inquiry," *American Economic Review* (December 1984): 986–994. Percentages represent the fraction that "Generally Agree" or "Agree with Provisions."

[1]Surveys also tend to show considerable agreement over the likely size of many economic effects. For a summary, see Victor R. Fuchs, Alan B. Krueger, and James M. Poterba, "Economists' Views about Parameters, Values, and Policy," *Journal of Economic Literature* (September 1998): 1387–1425.
[2]See Daniel B. Klein and Charlotta Stern, "Economists' Policy Views and Voting," *Public Choice* (2006): 331–342.

that are suitable for positive scientific analysis. There is far less agreement about normative questions related to what should be done. In this book, we take primarily a positive approach by using economic models to explain real-world events. The book's applications pursue some of these explanations in greater detail. You should feel free to adapt these models to whatever normative goals you believe are worth pursuing.

SUMMARY

This chapter provides you with some background to begin your study of microeconomics. Much of this material will be familiar to you from your introductory economics course, but that should come as no surprise. In many respects, the study of economics repeatedly investigates the same questions with an increasingly sophisticated set of tools. This course gives you some more of these tools. In establishing the basis for that investigation, this chapter reminds you of several important ideas:

- Economics is the study of allocating scarce resources among possible uses. Because resources are scarce, choices have to be made on how they will be used. Economists develop theoretical models to explain these choices.
- The production possibility frontier provides a simple illustration of the various output options that can be supplied in an economy. The curve clearly shows the limits imposed on the economy because resources are scarce. Producing more of one good means that less of something else must be produced. This reduction in output elsewhere measures the opportunity cost involved in such additional production.
- The most commonly used model of the allocation of resources is the model of supply and demand first fully described by Alfred Marshall in the latter part of the nineteenth century. The model shows how prices are determined by creating an equilibrium between the amount people want to buy and the amount firms are willing to produce. If supply and demand curves shift, new prices are established to restore equilibrium to the market.
- Proving the validity of economic models is difficult and sometimes controversial. Occasionally, the validity of a model can be determined by whether it is based on reasonable assumptions. More often, however, models are judged by how well they explain actual economic events.

REVIEW QUESTIONS

1. "To an economist, a resource is 'scarce' only if it has a positive price. Resources with zero prices are, by definition, not scarce." Do you agree? Or does the term *scarce* convey some other meaning?
2. The Production Possibility Frontier (PPF) shown in Figure 1.1 has a "concave" shape (you can remember that this shape is called "concave" because it resembles part of the entrance to a cave). Explain in words why this shape is consistent with the concept of diminishing returns to increasing clothing production—that is, describe why the opportunity cost of producing more unit of clothing increases as more is produced. How would the PPF look if there were no diminishing returns to clothing production? How might the PPF look if clothing production experienced "increasing returns" because bigger weaving machines could be used as clothing production expands?
3. Why do honeybees find it in their interest to leave some nectar in each flower they visit? Can you think of any human activities that yield a similar result?
4. Classical economists struggled with the "Water-Diamond Paradox," which seeks an explanation for why water (which is very useful) has a low price, whereas diamonds (which are not particularly important to life) have a high price. How would Smith explain the relative prices of water and diamonds? Would Ricardo's concept of diminishing returns pose some problem for this explanation? Can you resolve matters by using Marshall's model of supply and demand? If water is "very useful" to the demanders in Marshall's model, how would you know?
5. Marshall's model pictures price *and* quantity as being determined simultaneously by the interaction of supply and demand. Using this insight, explain the fallacies in the following paragraph:

   A rise in the price of oranges reduces the number of oranges people want to buy. This reduction by itself reduces growers' costs by allowing them to use only their best trees. Price, therefore, declines along with costs, and the initial price rise cannot be sustained.
6. "Gasoline sells for $4.00 per gallon this year, and it sold for $3.00 per gallon last year. But consumers bought more gasoline this year than they did last year. This is clear proof that the economic theory that people buy less when the price rises is incorrect." Do you agree? Explain.

7. "A shift outward in the demand curve always results in an increase in total spending (price times quantity) on a good. On the other hand, a shift outward in the supply curve may increase or decrease total spending." Explain.
8. Housing advocates often claim that "the demand for affordable housing vastly exceeds the supply." Use a supply-demand diagram to show whether you can make any sense out of this statement. In particular, show how a proper interpretation may depend on precisely how the word *affordable* is to be defined.
9. A key concept in the development of positive economic theories is the notion of "refutability"—a "theory" is not a "theory" unless there is some evidence that, if true, could prove it wrong. Use this notion to discuss whether one can conceive of evidence with which the following theories might be refuted:
   - Friedman's claim that pool players play as if they were using the rules of physics
   - The theory that firms operate so as to maximize profits
   - The theory that demand curves slope downward
   - The theory that adoption of capitalism makes people who are poor more miserable
10. The following conversation was heard among four economists discussing whether the minimum wage should be increased:

    Economist A. "Increasing the minimum wage would reduce employment of minority teenagers."

    Economist B. "Increasing the minimum wage would represent an unwarranted interference with private relations between workers and their employers."

    Economist C. "Increasing the minimum wage would raise the incomes of some unskilled workers."

    Economist D. "Increasing the minimum wage would benefit higher-wage workers and would probably be supported by organized labor."

Which of these economists are using positive analysis and which are using normative analysis in arriving at their conclusions? Which of these predictions might be tested with empirical data? How might such tests be conducted?

PROBLEMS

Note: These problems focus on the material from the Appendix to Chapter 1. Hence they are primarily numerical.

1.1. The following data represent five points on the supply curve for orange juice:

PRICE ($ PER GALLON)	QUANTITY (MILLIONS OF GALLONS)
1	100
2	300
3	500
4	700
5	900

and these data represent 5 points on the demand curve for orange juice:

PRICE ($ PER GALLON)	QUANTITY (MILLIONS OF GALLONS)
1	700
2	600
3	500
4	400
5	300

a. Graph the points of these supply and demand curves for orange juice. Be sure to put price on the vertical axis and quantity on the horizontal axis.
b. Do these points seem to lie along two straight lines? If so, figure out the precise algebraic equation of these lines. (Hint: If the points do lie on straight lines, you need only consider two points on each of them to calculate the lines.)
c. Use your solutions from part b to calculate the "excess demand" for orange juice if the market price is zero.
d. Use your solutions from part b to calculate the "excess supply" of orange juice if the orange juice price is $6 per gallon.

1.2. Marshall defined an equilibrium price as one at which the quantity demanded equals the quantity supplied.
a. Using the data provided in problem 1.1, show that $P = 3$ is the equilibrium price in the orange juice market.
b. Using these data, explain why $P = 2$ and $P = 4$ are not equilibrium prices.
c. Graph your results and show that the supply-demand equilibrium resembles that shown in Figure 1.3.
d. Suppose the demand for orange juice were to increase so that people want to buy 300 million

more gallons at every price. How would that change the data in problem 1.1? How would it shift the demand curve you drew in part c?

e. What is the new equilibrium price in the orange juice market, given this increase in demand? Show this new equilibrium in your supply-demand graph.

f. Suppose now that a freeze in Florida reduces orange juice supply by 300 million gallons at every price listed in problem 1.1. How would this shift in supply affect the data in problem 1.1? How would it affect the algebraic supply curve calculated in that problem?

g. Given this new supply relationship together with the demand relationship shown in problem 1.1, what is the equilibrium price in this market?

h. Explain why $P = 3$ is no longer an equilibrium in the orange juice market. How would the participants in this market know $P = 3$ is no longer an equilibrium?

i. Graph your results for this supply shift.

1.3. The equilibrium price in problem 1.2 is $P = 3$. This is an equilibrium because at this price, quantity demanded is precisely equal to quantity supplied ($Q = 500$). One might ask how the market is to reach this equilibrium point. Here we look at two ways:

a. Suppose an auctioneer calls out prices (in dollars per gallon) in whole numbers ranging from \$1 to \$5 and records how much orange juice is demanded and supplied at each such price. He or she then calculates the difference between quantity demanded and quantity supplied. You should make this calculation and then describe how the auctioneer will know what the equilibrium price is.

b. Now suppose the auctioneer calls out the various quantities described in problem 1.1. For each quantity, he or she asks, "What will you demanders pay per gallon for this quantity of orange juice?" and "How much do you suppliers require per gallon if you are to produce this much orange juice?" and records these dollar amounts. Use the information from problem 1.1 to calculate the answers that the auctioneer will get to these questions. How will he or she know when an equilibrium is reached?

c. Can you think of markets that operate as described in part a of this problem? Are there markets that operate as described in part b? Why do you think these differences occur?

1.4. In several places, we have warned you about the decision of Marshall to "reverse the axes" by putting price on the vertical axis and quantity on the horizontal axis. This problem shows that it makes very little difference how you choose the axes. Suppose that quantity demanded is given by $Q_D = -P + 10,\ 0 \leq P \leq 10$, and quantity is supplied by $Q_S = P - 2,\ P \geq 2$.

a. Why are the possible values for P restricted as they are in this example? How do the restrictions on P also impose restrictions on Q?

b. Graph these two equations on a standard (Marshallian) supply-demand graph. Use this graph to calculate the equilibrium price and quantity in this market.

c. Graph these two equations with price on the horizontal axis and quantity on the vertical axis. Use this graph to calculate equilibrium price and quantity.

d. What do you conclude by comparing your answers to parts a and b?

e. Can you think of any reasons why you might prefer the graph in part a to that in part b?

1.5. This problem involves solving demand and supply equations together to determine price and quantity.

a. Consider a demand curve of the form

$$Q_D = -2P + 20,$$

where Q_D is the quantity demanded of a good and P is the price of the good. Graph this demand curve. Also draw a graph of the supply curve

$$Q_S = 2P - 4,$$

where Q_S is the quantity supplied. Be sure to put P on the vertical axis and Q on the horizontal axis. Assume that all the Q_S and Ps are nonnegative for parts a, b, and c. At what values of P and Q do these curves intersect—that is, where does $Q_D = Q_S$?

b. Now, suppose at each price that individuals demand four more units of output—that the demand curve shifts to

$$Q'_D = -2P + 24.$$

Graph this new demand curve. At what values of P and Q does the new demand curve intersect the old supply curve—that is, where does $Q'_D = Q_S$?

c. Now finally, suppose the supply curve shifts to

$$Q'_S = 2P - 8.$$

Graph this new supply curve. At what values of P and Q does $Q'_D = Q'_S$? You may wish to refer to this simple problem when we discuss shifting supply and demand curves in later sections of this book.

1.6. Taxes in Oz are calculated according to the formula

$$T = .01I^2,$$

where T represents thousands of dollars of tax liability and I represents income measured in thousands of dollars. Using this formula, answer the following questions:

a. How much in taxes is paid by individuals with incomes of \$10,000, \$30,000, and \$50,000? What are the average tax rates for these income levels? At what income level does tax liability equal total income?

b. Graph the tax schedule for Oz. Use your graph to estimate marginal tax rates for the income levels specified in part a. Also show the average tax rates for these income levels on your graph.

c. Marginal tax rates in Oz can be estimated more precisely by calculating tax owed if persons with the incomes in part a get one more dollar. Make this computation for these three income levels. Compare your results to those obtained from the calculus-based result that, for the Oz tax function, its slope is given by $.02I$.

1.7. The following data show the production possibilities for a hypothetical economy during one year:

OUTPUT OF *X*	OUTPUT OF *Y*
1000	0
800	100
600	200
400	300
200	400
0	500

a. Plot these points on a graph. Do they appear to lie along a straight line? What is that straight line's production possibility frontier?

b. Explain why output levels of $X = 400$, $Y = 200$ or $X = 300$, $Y = 300$ are inefficient. Show these output levels on your graph.

c. Explain why output levels of $X = 500$, $Y = 350$ are unattainable in this economy.

d. What is the opportunity cost of an additional unit of X output in terms of Y output in this economy? Does this opportunity cost depend on the amounts being produced?

1.8. Suppose an economy has a production possibility frontier characterized by the equation

$$X^2 + 4Y^2 = 100.$$

a. In order to sketch this equation, first compute its intercepts. What is the value of X if $Y = 0$? What is the value of Y if $X = 0$?

b. Calculate three additional points along this production possibility frontier. Graph the frontier and show that it has a general elliptical shape.

c. Is the opportunity cost of X in terms of Y constant in this economy, or does it depend on the levels of output being produced? Explain.

d. How would you calculate the opportunity cost of X in terms of Y in this economy? Give an example of this computation.

1.9. Suppose consumers in the economy described in problem 1.8 wished to consume X and Y in equal amounts.

a. How much of each good should be produced to meet this goal? Show this production point on a graph of the production possibility frontier.

b. Assume that this country enters into international trading relationships and decides to produce only good X. If it can trade 1 unit of X for 1 unit of Y in world markets, what possible combinations of X and Y might it consume?

c. Given the consumption possibilities outlined in part b, what final choice will the consumers of this country make?

d. How would you measure the costs imposed on this country by international economic sanctions that prevented all trade and required the country to return to the position described in part a?

1.10. Consider the function $Y = X \cdot Z$, $X, Z \geq 0$.

a. Graph the $Y = 4$ contour line for this function. How does this line compare to the $Y = 2$ contour line in Figure 1A.5? Explain the reasons for any similarities.

b. Where does the line $X + 4Z = 8$ intersect the $Y = 4$ contour line? (Hint: Solve the equation for X and substitute into the equation for the contour line. You should get only a single point.)

c. Are there any points on the $Y = 4$ contour line other than the point identified in part b that satisfy this linear equation? Explain your reasoning.

d. Consider now the equation $X + 4Z = 10$. Where does this equation intersect the $Y = 4$ contour line? How does this solution compare to the one you calculated in part b?

e. Are there points on the equation defined in part d that would yield a value greater than 4 for Y? (Hint: A graph may help you explain why such points exist.)

f. Can you think of any economic model that would resemble the calculations in this problem?

Mathematics Used in Microeconomics

Mathematics began to be widely used in economics near the end of the nineteenth century. For example, Marshall's *Principles of Economics*, published in 1890, included a lengthy mathematical appendix that developed his arguments more systematically than the book itself. Today, mathematics is indispensable for economists. They use it to move logically from the basic assumptions of a model to deriving the results of those assumptions. Without mathematics, this process would be both more cumbersome and less accurate.

This appendix reviews some of the basic concepts of algebra and discusses a few issues that arise in applying those concepts to the study of economics. We will use the tools introduced here throughout the rest of the book.

A1-1 Functions of One Variable

The basic elements of algebra are called **variables**. These can be labeled X and Y and may be given any numerical value. Sometimes the values of one variable (Y) may be related to those of another variable (X) according to a specific functional relationship. This relationship is denoted by the **functional notation**

$$Y = f(X). \tag{1A.1}$$

This is read, "Y is a function of X," meaning that the value of Y depends on the value given to X. For example, if we make X calories eaten per day and Y body weight, then Equation 1A.1 shows the relationship between the amount of food intake and an individual's weight. The form of Equation 1A.1 also shows causality. X is an **independent variable** and may be given any value. On the other hand, the value of Y is completely determined by X; Y is a **dependent variable**. This functional notation conveys the idea that "X causes Y."

The exact functional relationship between X and Y may take on a wide variety of forms. Two possibilities are:

1. Y is a *linear function* of X. In this case

   $$Y = a + bX, \tag{1A.2}$$

   where a and b are constants that may be given any numerical value. For example, if $a = 3$ and $b = 2$, this equation would be written as

   $$Y = 3 + 2X. \tag{1A.3}$$

   We could give Equation 1A.3 an economic interpretation. For example, if we make Y the labor costs of a firm and X the number of labor hours hired, then the equation could record the relationship between costs and workers hired. In this case, there is

Variables
The basic elements of algebra, usually called X, Y, and so on, that may be given any numerical value in an equation.

Functional notation
A way of denoting the fact that the value taken on by one variable (Y) depends on the value taken on by some other variable (X) or set of variables.

Independent variable
In an algebraic equation, a variable that is unaffected by the action of another variable and may be assigned any value.

Dependent variable
In algebra, a variable whose value is determined by another variable or set of variables.

Table 1A.1 Values of X and Y for Linear and Quadratic Functions

LINEAR FUNCTION		QUADRATIC FUNCTION	
X	$Y = f(X)$ $= 3 + 2X$	X	$Y = f(X)$ $= -X^2 + 15X$
−3	−3	−3	−54
−2	−1	−2	−34
−1	1	−1	−16
0	3	0	0
1	5	1	14
2	7	2	26
3	9	3	36
4	11	4	44
5	13	5	50
6	15	6	54

a fixed cost of \$3 (when $X = 0$, $Y = \$3$), and the wage rate is \$2 per hour. A firm that hired 6 labor hours, for example, would incur total labor costs of $\$15[= 3 + 2(6) = 3 + 12]$. Table 1A.1 illustrates some other values for this function for various values of X.

2. Y is a *nonlinear function* of X. This case covers a number of possibilities, including quadratic functions (containing X^2), higher-order polynomials (containing X^3, X^4, and so forth), and those based on special functions such as logarithms. All of these have the property that a given change in X can have different effects on Y depending on the value of X. This contrasts with linear functions for which any specific change in X always changes Y by a precisely predictable amount no matter what X is.

   To see this, consider the quadratic equation

$$Y = -X^2 + 15X. \qquad \textbf{(1A.4)}$$

Y values for this equation for values of X between -3 and $+6$ are shown in Table 1A.1. Notice that as X increases by 1 unit, the values of Y go up rapidly at first but then slow down. When X increases from 0 to 1, for example, Y increases from 0 to 14. But when X increases from 5 to 6, Y increases only from 50 to 54. This looks like Ricardo's notion of diminishing returns—as X increases, its ability to increase Y diminishes.[2]

A1-2 Graphing Functions of One Variable

When we write down the functional relationship between X and Y, we are summarizing all there is to know about that relationship. In principle, this book, or any book that uses mathematics, could be written using only these equations. Graphs of some of these functions, however, are very helpful. Graphs not only make it easier for us to understand certain arguments; they also can take the place of a lot of the mathematical notation that must be developed. For these reasons, this book relies heavily on graphs to develop its basic economic models. Here we look at a few graphic techniques.

[2]Of course, for other nonlinear functions, specific increases in X may result in increasing amounts of Y (consider, for example, $X^2 + 15X$).

Figure 1A.1 Graph of the Linear Function $Y = 3 + 2X$

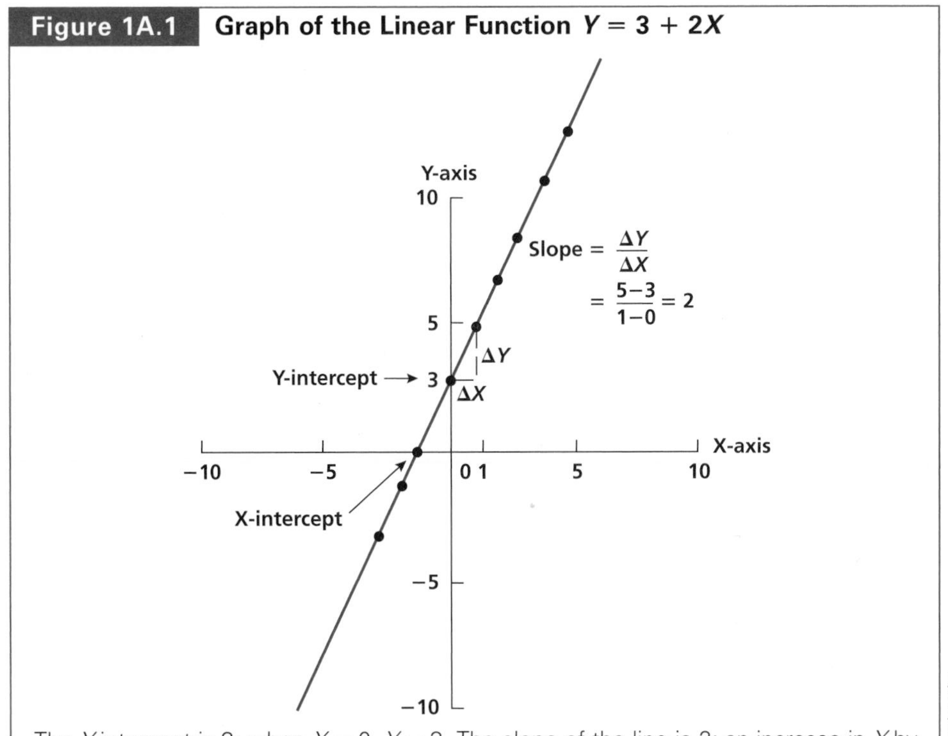

The Y-intercept is 3; when $X = 0$, $Y = 3$. The slope of the line is 2; an increase in X by 1 will increase Y by 2.

A graph is simply one way to show the relationship between two variables. Usually, the values of the dependent variable (Y) are shown on the vertical axis and the values of the independent variable (X) are shown on the horizontal axis.[3] Figure 1A.1 uses this form to graph Equation 1A.3. Although we use heavy dots to show only the points of this function that are listed in Table 1A.1, the graph represents the function for every possible value of X. The graph of Equation 1A.3 is a straight line, which is why this is called a **linear function**. In Figure 1A.1, X and Y can take on both positive and negative values. The variables used in economics generally take on only positive values, and therefore we only have to use the upper-right-hand (positive) quadrant of the axes.

Linear function
An equation that is represented by a straight-line graph.

Linear Functions: Intercepts and Slopes

Two important features of the graph in Figure 1A.1 are its slope and its **intercept** on the Y-axis. The Y-intercept is the value of Y when X is equal to 0. For example, as shown in Figure 1A.1, when $X = 0$, $Y = 3$; this means that 3 is the Y-intercept.[4] In the general linear form of Equation 1A.2,

Intercept
The value of Y when X equals zero.

$$Y = a + bX,$$

the Y-intercept will be $Y = a$, because this is the value of Y when $X = 0$.

[3]In economics, this convention is not always followed. Sometimes a dependent variable is shown on the horizontal axis as, for example, in the case of demand and supply curves. In that case, the independent variable (price) is shown on the vertical axis and the dependent variable (quantity) on the horizontal axis. See Example 1A.1.

[4]One can also speak of the X-intercept of a function, which is defined as that value of X for which $Y = 0$. For Equation 1A.3, it is easy to see that $Y = 0$ when $X = -3/2$, which is then the X-intercept. The X-intercept for the general linear function in Equation 1A.2 is given by $X = -a/b$, as may be seen by substituting that value into the equation.

Slope
The direction of a line on a graph; shows the change in *Y* that results from a unit change in *X*.

We define the **slope** of any straight line to be the ratio of the change in Y to the change in X for a movement along the line. The slope can be defined mathematically as

$$\text{Slope} = \frac{\text{Change in } Y}{\text{Change in } X} = \frac{\Delta Y}{\Delta X}, \qquad \textbf{(1A.5)}$$

where the Δ ("delta") notation simply means "change in." For the particular function shown in Figure 1A.1, the slope is equal to 2. You can clearly see from the dashed lines, representing changes in X and Y, that a given change in X is met by a change of twice that amount in Y. Table 1A.1 shows the same result—as X increases from 0 to 1, Y increases from 3 to 5. Consequently

$$\text{Slope} = \frac{\Delta Y}{\Delta X} = \frac{5-3}{1-0} = 2. \qquad \textbf{(1A.6)}$$

It should be obvious that this is true for all the other points in Table 1A.1. Everywhere along the straight line, the slope is the same. Generally, for any linear function, the slope is given by b in Equation 1A.2. The slope of a straight line may be positive (as it is in Figure 1A.1), or it may be negative, in which case the line would run from upper left to lower right.

A straight line may also have a slope of 0, which is a horizontal line. In this case, the value of Y is constant; changes in X will not affect Y. The function would be $Y = a + 0X$, or $Y = a$. This equation is represented by a horizontal line (parallel to the X-axis) through point a on the Y-axis.

Interpreting Slopes: An Example

The slope of the relationship between a cause (X) and an effect (Y) is one of the most important things that economists try to measure. Because the slope (or the related concept of elasticity) shows, in quantitative terms, how a small (marginal) change in one variable affects some other variable, this is a valuable piece of information for building most every economic model. For example, a researcher discovered that the quantity of oranges (Q) a typical family eats during any week can be represented by the equation:

$$Q = 12 - 0.2P, \qquad \textbf{(1A.7)}$$

where P is the price of a single orange, in cents. Hence, if an orange costs 20 cents, this family would consume eight oranges per week. If the price rose to 50 cents, orange consumption would fall to only two per week.[5] On the other hand, if oranges were given away ($P = 0$), the family would eat 12 each week. With this sort of information, it would be possible for an agricultural economist to assess how families might react to factors such as winter freezes or increased imports of oranges that might affect their price.

Slopes and Units of Measurement

Notice that in introducing Equation 1A.7, we were careful to state precisely how the variables Q and P were measured. In the usual algebra course, this issue does not arise because Y and X have no specific physical meaning. But in economics, this issue is crucial—the slope of a relationship will depend on how variables are measured. For example, if orange prices were measured in dollars, the same behavior described in Equation 1A.7 would be represented by

$$Q = 12 - 20P. \qquad \textbf{(1A.8)}$$

[5]Notice that this equation only makes sense for $P \leqq 60$ because it is impossible to eat negative numbers of oranges.

Notice that at a price of \$0.20, the family still eats eight oranges per week. With a price of \$0.50, they eat only two. The slope here is 100 times the slope in Equation 1A.7, however, because of the change in the way P is measured.

Changing the way that Q is measured will also change the relationship. If orange consumption is now measured in boxes of 10 oranges each, and P represents the price for such a box, Equation 1A.7 would become:

$$Q = 1.2 - 0.002P. \qquad \textbf{(1A.9)}$$

This equation still says that the family will consume eight oranges (that is, 0.8 of a box) each week if each box of oranges costs 200 cents and two oranges (0.2 of a box) if each box costs 500 cents. Notice that, in this case, changing the units in which Q is measured changes both the intercept and the slope of this equation.

Because slopes of economic relationships depend on the units of measurement used, they are not a very convenient concept for economists to use to summarize behavior. Instead, they usually use elasticities, which are unit-free. This concept is introduced in Chapter 3 and then used throughout the remainder of the book.

MICRO QUIZ 1A.1

Suppose that the quantity of flounder caught each week off New Jersey is given by $Q = 100 + 5P$ (where Q is the quantity of flounder measured in thousands of pounds and P is the price per pound in dollars). Explain:

1. What are the units of the intercept and the slope in this equation?
2. How would this equation change if flounder catch were measured in pounds and price measured in cents per pound?

KEEP *in* MIND

Marshall's Trap

In Chapter 1, we described how the English economist Alfred Marshall chose to put price on the vertical axis and quantity on the horizontal axis when graphing a demand relationship. This decision, although sensible for many economic purposes, has posed nightmares for students for more than a century because they are used to seeing the "independent variable" (in this case, price, P) on the horizontal axis. Of course, it is easy to solve Equation 1 A.7 for P as:

$$P = 60 - 5Q. \qquad \textbf{(1A.10)}$$

This equation even has an economic meaning—it shows the family's "marginal willingness to pay" for one more orange, given that they are already consuming a certain amount. For example, this family is willing to pay 20 cents per orange for one more orange if consumption is eight per week. But making price the dependent variable is not the customary way we think about demand, even though this is how Marshall graphed the situation. It is usually far better to stick to the original way of writing demand (that is, Equation 1A.7), but keep in mind that the axes have been reversed, and you need to think carefully before making statements about, say, changing slopes or intercepts.

Changes in Slope

Quite often in this text we are interested in changing the parameters (that is, a and b) of a linear function. We can do this in two ways: We can change the Y-intercept, or we can change the slope. Figure 1A.2 shows the graph of the function

$$Y = -X + 10. \qquad \textbf{(1A.11)}$$

Figure 1A.2 Changes in the Slope of a Linear Function

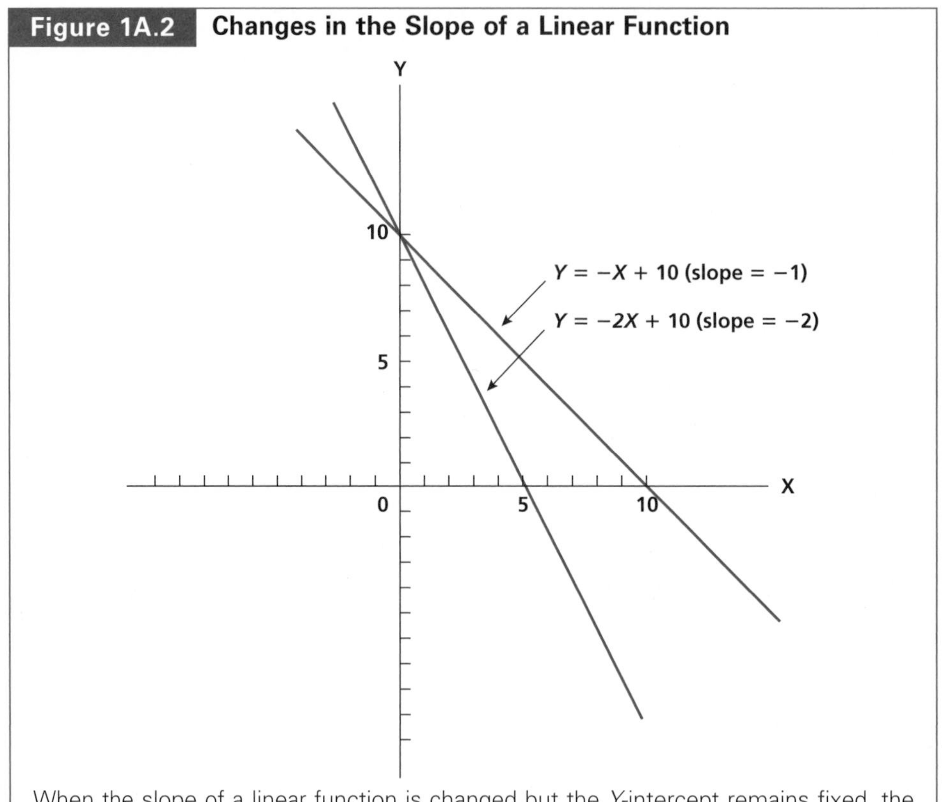

When the slope of a linear function is changed but the Y-intercept remains fixed, the graph of the function rotates about the Y-intercept.

This linear function has a slope of -1 and a Y-intercept of $Y = 10$. Figure 1A.2 also shows the function

$$Y = -2X + 10. \tag{1A.12}$$

We have doubled the slope of Equation 1A.11 from -1 to -2 and kept the Y-intercept at $Y = 10$. This causes the graph of the function to become steeper and to rotate about the Y-intercept. In general, a change in the slope of a function will cause this kind of rotation without changing the value of its Y-intercept. Since a linear function takes on the value of its Y-intercept when $X = 0$, changing the slope will not change the value of the function at this point.

Changes in Intercept Figure 1A.3 also shows a graph of the function $Y = -X + 10$. It shows the effect of changes in the constant term, that is, the Y-intercept only, while the slope stays at -1. Figure 1A.3 shows the graphs of

$$Y = -X + 12 \tag{1A.13}$$

and

$$Y = -X + 5. \tag{1A.14}$$

All three lines are parallel; they have the same slope. Changing the Y-intercept only makes the line shift up and down. Its slope does not change. Of course, changes in the Y-intercepts also cause the X-intercepts to change, and you can see these new intercepts.

Figure 1A.3 Changes in the *Y*-Intercept of a Linear Function

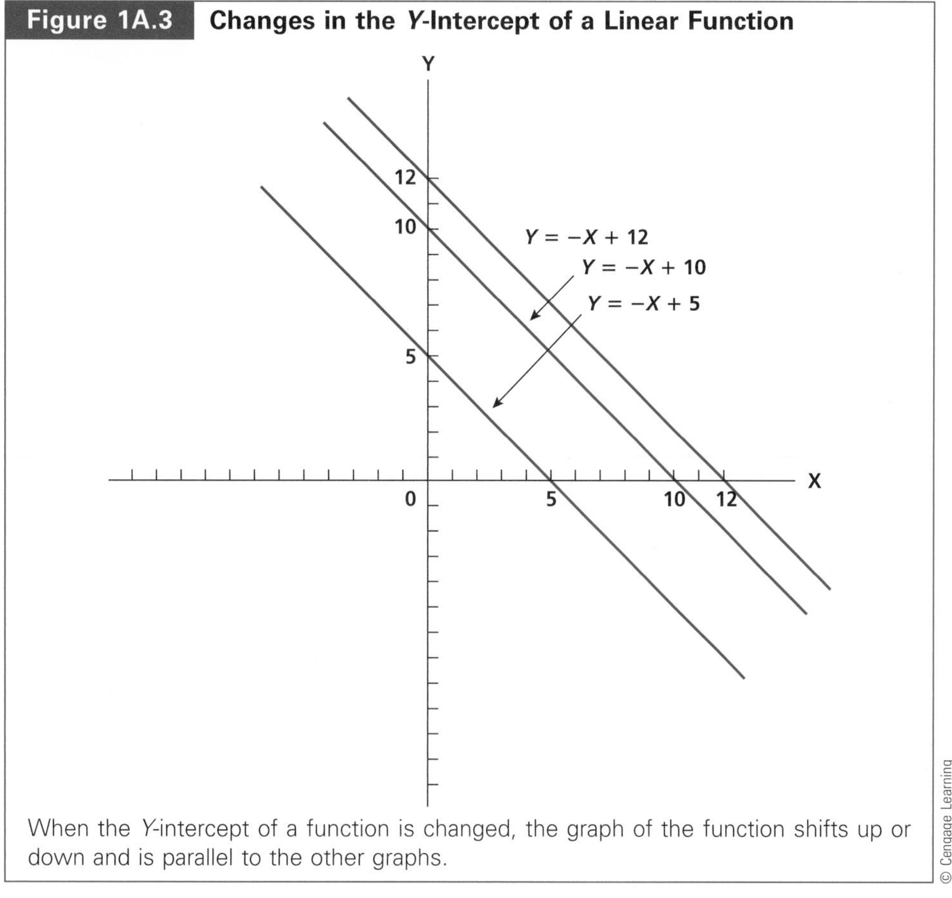

When the *Y*-intercept of a function is changed, the graph of the function shifts up or down and is parallel to the other graphs.

In many places in this book, we show how economic changes can be represented by changes in slopes or in intercepts. Although the economic context varies, the mathematical form of these changes is of the general type shown in Figure 1A.2 and Figure 1A.3. Application 1A.1: How Does Zillow.com Do It? employs these concepts to illustrate one way in which linear functions can be used to value houses.

> **MICRO QUIZ 1A.2**
>
> In Figure 1A.2, the *X*-intercept changes from 10 to 5 as the slope of the graph changes from −1 to −2. Explain:
>
> 1. What would happen to the *X*-intercept in Figure 1A.2 if the slope changed to −5/6?
> 2. What do you learn by comparing the graphs in Figure 1A.2 to those in Figure 1A.3?

Nonlinear Functions

Graphing nonlinear functions is also straightforward. Figure 1A.4 shows a graph of

$$Y = -X^2 + 15X, \qquad \textbf{(1A.15)}$$

for relatively small, positive values of *X*. Heavy dots are used to indicate the specific values identified in Table 1A.1, though, again, the function is defined for all values of *X*. The general concave shape of the graph in Figure 1A.4 reflects the nonlinear nature of this function.

APPLICATION 1A.1

How Does Zillow.com Do It?

The website Zillow.com (founded in 2006) provides estimated values for practically every residential home in the United States. Because this amounts to more than 70 million homes, there is no way that the company can study the details of each house as a traditional real estate appraiser might. Instead, the company uses public data on homes that recently sold together with statistical techniques to estimate a relationship between the price of a house (P) and those characteristics of a house that can be obtained from public sources (such as the number of square feet, X).

A Simple Example

For example, Zillow might determine that houses in a particular area obey the relationship:

$$P = \$50{,}000 + \$150X. \tag{1}$$

This equation says that a house in this location costs $50,000 (for the lot, say) plus $150 for each square foot. So, a 2,000 square foot house would be worth $350,000, and a 3,000 square foot house would be worth $500,000. Figure 1A shows this linear relationship. Using this relationship, Zillow can predict a value for every house in its database.

Figure 1A Relationship between the Floor Area of a House and Its Market Value

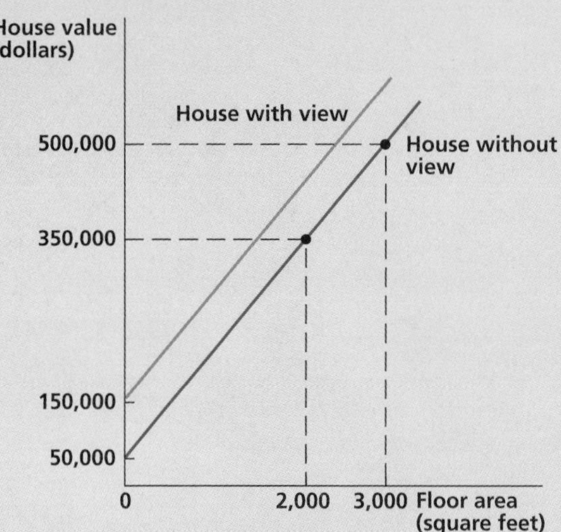

Using data on recent house sales, Zillow.com can calculate a relationship between floor area (X, measured in square feet) and market value (P). The entire relationship shifts upward by $100,000 if a house has a nice view.

Location, Location, Location

One factor that Zillow must pay close attention to is the location of the houses it is pricing. As any real estate agent will tell you, location is often all that matters in a home price. Hence, it would not be appropriate to estimate a relationship such as Equation 1A.1 for the entire United States or even for a fairly large city. Instead, the firm must narrow its focus on localities where the square foot value of a house might reasonably be expected to be constant. In especially desirable locations, houses might sell for $500–$1,000 per square foot or more, and lots would cost much more than $50,000.

What Zillow Can't See

A second problem with the Zillow estimates is that actual house prices may depend on factors about which Zillow has no information. For example, real estate databases may have no information about whether a house has a nice view or not. If having a view would raise a typical lot price by $100,000, for example, the relationship for houses with views should be the one shown by the upper line in Figure 1A. Zillow would systematically underestimate the values of such houses.

How Accurate Is Zillow?

Zillow has been upfront in noting that their estimates may not be accurate and, in fact, their website regularly analyzes accuracy by comparing their estimates to actual sales prices. For late 2012, for example, their data show that typically about 30 percent of all sales are within 5 percent of their Zillow estimates and 80 percent are within 20 percent. Reported accuracy varies considerably across U.S. cities, in part because of differences in data availability. For example, the company reports that its estimates for Boston are usually quite accurate, whereas those for Miami show considerable errors.

TO THINK ABOUT

1. Should Zillow eliminate from their calculations any house which seems to sell for an especially high price or an especially low price?
2. Can you think of any reasons why Zillow's recent estimates would be more accurate for Boston than for Miami?

Figure 1A.4 **Graph of the Quadratic Function $Y = -X^2 + 15X$**

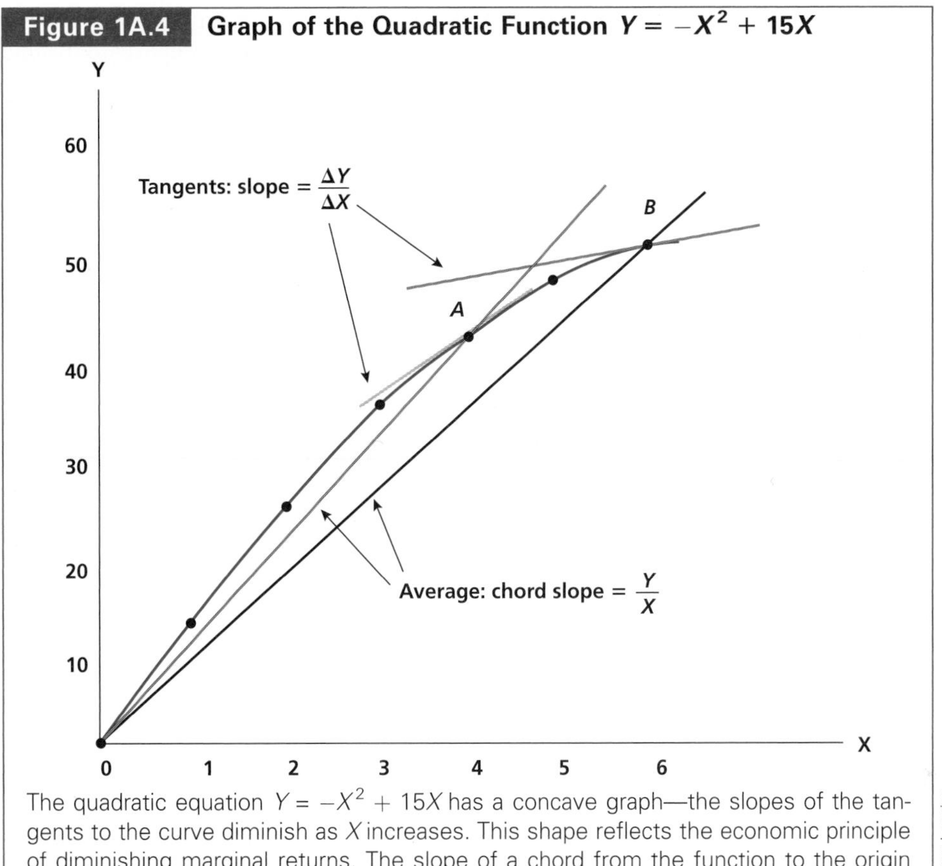

The quadratic equation $Y = -X^2 + 15X$ has a concave graph—the slopes of the tangents to the curve diminish as X increases. This shape reflects the economic principle of diminishing marginal returns. The slope of a chord from the function to the origin shows the ratio Y/X.

The Slope of a Nonlinear Function

Because the graph of a nonlinear function is, by definition, not a straight line, it does not have the same slope at every point. Instead, the slope of a nonlinear function at *a particular point* is defined to be the slope of the straight line that is tangent to the function at that point. For example, the slope of the function shown in Figure 1A.4 at point B is the slope of the tangent line illustrated at that point. As is clear from the figure, in this particular case, the slope of this function gets smaller as X increases. This graphical interpretation of "diminishing returns" to increasing X is simply a visual illustration of the fact already pointed out in the discussion of Table 1A.1.

Marginal and Average Effects

Marginal effect
The change in Y brought about by a one unit change in X at a particular value of X (Also the slope of the function.)

Economists are often interested in the size of the effect that X has on Y. There are two different ways of making this concept precise. The most usual is to look at the **marginal effect**—that is, how does a small change in X change Y? For this type of effect, the focus is on $\Delta Y/\Delta X$, the slope of the function. For the linear equations illustrated in Figure 1A.1 to Figure 1A.3, this effect is constant—in economic terms, the marginal effect of X on Y is constant for all values of X. For the nonlinear equation graphed in Figure 1A.4, this marginal effect diminishes as X gets larger. Diminishing returns and diminishing marginal effects amount to the same thing.

Average effect
The ratio of Y to X at a particular value of X (Also the slope of the ray from the origin to the function.)

Sometimes economists speak of the **average effect** of X on Y. By this, they simply mean the ratio Y/X. For example, as shown in Chapter 6, the average productivity of labor in, say, automobile production is measured as the ratio of total auto production (say, 10 million cars per year) to total labor employed (say, 250,000 workers). Hence, average productivity is 40 (= 10,000,000 ÷ 250,000) cars per year per worker.

Showing average values on a graph is more complex than showing marginal values (slopes). To do so, we take the point on the graph that is of interest (say, point A in Figure 1A.4 whose coordinates are $X = 4$, $Y = 44$) and draw the chord OA. The slope of OA is then $Y/X = 44/4 = 11$—the average effect we seek to measure. By comparing the slope of OA to that of OB ($= 54/6 = 9$), it is easy to see that the average effect of X on Y also declines as X increases in Figure 1A.4. This is another reflection of the diminishing returns in this function. In later chapters, we show the relationship between marginal and average effects in many different contexts. Application 1A.2: Can a "Flat" Tax Be Progressive? shows how the concepts arise in disputes about revising the U.S. personal income tax.

Calculus and Marginalism

Although this book does not require that you know calculus, it should be clear that many of the concepts that we cover were originally discovered using that branch of mathematics. Specifically, many economic concepts are based on looking at the effect of a small (marginal) change in a variable X on some other variable Y. You should be familiar with some of these concepts (such as marginal cost, marginal revenue, or marginal productivity) from your introductory economics course. Calculus provides a way of making the definitions for these ideas more precise. For example, in calculus, mathematicians develop the idea of the *derivative* of a function, which is simply defined as the limit of the ratio $\Delta Y/\Delta X$ as ΔX gets very small. This limit is denoted as dY/dX and is termed the derivative of Y with respect to X. In graphical terms, the derivative of a function is identical to its slope. For linear functions, the derivative has a constant value that does not depend on the value of X being used. But for nonlinear functions, the value of the derivative varies, depending on which value of X is being considered. In economic terms, the derivative provides a convenient shorthand way of noting the *marginal* effect of X on Y.

MICRO QUIZ 1A.3

Suppose that the relationship between grapes harvested per hour (G, measured in pounds) and the number of workers hired (L, measured in worker hours) is given by $G = 100 + 20L$:

1. How many additional grapes are harvested by the 10th worker? The 20th worker? The 50th worker?
2. What is the average productivity when 10 workers are hired? When 20 workers are hired? When 50 workers are hired?

Perhaps the most important use of calculus in microeconomics is to study the formal conclusions that can be derived from the assumption that an economic actor seeks to maximize something. All such problems reach the same general conclusion—that the dependent variable, Y, reaches its maximum value (assuming there is one) at that value of X for which $dY/dX = 0$. To see why, assume that this derivative (slope) is, say, greater than zero. Then Y cannot be at its maximum value because an increase in X would, in fact, succeed in increasing Y. Alternatively, if the derivative (slope) of the function were negative, decreasing X would increase Y. Hence, only if the derivative is 0 can X be at its optimal value. Similar comments apply when one is seeking to find that value of X, which yields a minimum value for Y.

APPLICATION 1A.2

Can a "Flat" Tax Be Progressive?

Ever since the U.S. federal income tax (FIT) was first enacted in 1913, there has been a running debate about its fairness, particularly about whether the rates of taxation fairly reflect a person's ability to pay. Historically, the FIT had steeply rising tax rates, though these were moderated during the 1970s and 1980s. Recently, a flat tax with a single tax rate has been proposed as a solution to some of the complexities and adverse economic incentives that arise with multiple rates. These ideas have been attacked as unfair in that they would eliminate the prevailing increasing rate structure.

Progressive Income Taxation

Advocates of tax fairness usually argue that income taxes should be "progressive"—that is, they argue that richer people should pay a *higher fraction* of their incomes in taxes because they are "more able to do so." Notice that the claim is that the rich should pay *proportionally* more, not just *more*, taxes. To achieve this goal, lawmakers have tended to specify tax schedules with increasing marginal rates. That is, an extra dollar of income is taxed at a higher rate the higher a person's income is. Figure 1A illustrates these increasing rates[1] by the line *OT*. The increasing slope of the various segments of *OT* reflects the increasing marginal tax rate structure.

Flat Taxes

Progressive rate structures are very hard to administer. For example, progressive rates make it difficult to withhold income tax from people because it is not often clear what rate to use. Also, a progressive rate structure usually requires some type of multiyear averaging to be fair to people whose incomes fluctuate a lot. One way to avoid problems like these and still have a "progressive" tax is to use a single rate system (a so-called flat tax) together with an initial personal exemption. The line *OT′* in Figure 1A shows such a tax. In this case, the tax schedule provides an initial exemption of $25,000 and then applies a flat rate of 25 percent on remaining income. Although this structure does not have rising marginal tax rates, it still is a progressive tax structure. For example, people who make $50,000 per year pay 12.5 percent of their income in taxes (0.25(50,000 − 25,000)/50,000 = 0.125), whereas people who make $150,000 pay nearly 21 percent of their income in taxes (0.25(150,000 − 25,000)/150,000 = 0.208).

Figure 1A Progressive Rates Compared to a Flat Tax Schedule

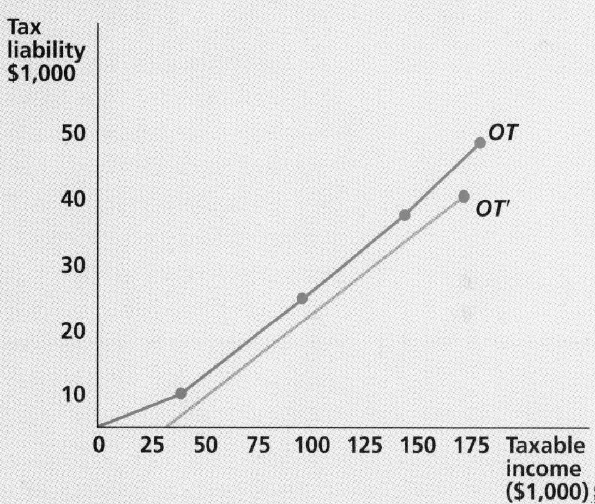

The line *OT* shows tax liabilities under the current rate schedule. *OT′* shows tax liabilities under one flat tax proposal.

Flat Tax Popularity

Many eastern European countries have recently introduced flat taxes. Estonia led the way in 1994 and was soon followed by Lithuania and Latvia. More recently many other countries have followed suit, including Russia, Georgia, Serbia, and Ukraine. What is unique about these countries is that they have all had recent major changes in their government structures, making it possible to do some fresh thinking about how income should be taxed.

POLICY CHALLENGE

The United States already has a flat tax. The "Alternative Minimum Tax" (AMT) allows an exemption of about $45,000 from income with the remainder being taxed at a flat 28 percent. The AMT also has far fewer special deductions and credits than does the regular income tax. Would it be a good idea to use the AMT to replace the current income tax? Would this tax be "progressive enough"? What groups do you think would support such a replacement? Who would oppose it?

[1]The tax does permit various deductions in calculating "taxable income." Hence, Figure 1A does not reflect the relationship between total income and taxes paid.

Consider the most well-known application of this principle. Let X be the quantity of output a firm produces. The profits a firm receives from selling this output depend on how much is produced and are denoted by (X). But profits are defined as the difference between revenue and cost [that is, $\pi(X) = R(X) - C(X)$]. Now applying the maximizing principle to profits yields:

$$\frac{d\pi(X)}{dX} = \frac{dR(X)}{dX} - \frac{dC(X)}{dX} = 0 \quad \text{or} \quad \frac{dR(X)}{dX} = \frac{dC(X)}{dX}. \qquad \textbf{(1A.16)}$$

In words, this says that for profits to be at a maximum, the firm should produce that level of output for which the derivative of revenue with respect to output (that is, *marginal revenue*) is equal to the derivative of costs with respect to output (that is, *marginal cost*). This calculus-based approach to profit maximization was first employed by the French economist A. Cournot in the early nineteenth century. It represents both a simpler and more elegant approach to showing the "marginal revenue equals marginal cost" implication of profit maximization than the combination of graphs and intuition that you probably encountered in your introductory economics course. Although we will not use many calculus-based explanations in this book, such mathematical tools are the primary way in which modern-day economists construct most of their models.

A1-3 Functions of Two or More Variables

Economists are usually concerned with functions of more than just one variable because there is almost always more than a single cause of an economic outcome. To see the effects of many causes, economists must work with functions of several variables. A two-variable function might be written in functional notation as

$$Y = f(X, Z). \qquad \textbf{(1A.17)}$$

This equation shows that Y's values depend on the values of two independent variables, X and Z. For example, an individual's weight (Y) depends not only on calories eaten (X) but also on how much the individual exercises (Z). Increases in X increase Y, but increases in Z decrease Y. The functional notation in Equation 1A.17 hints at the possibility that there might be trade-offs between eating and exercise. In Chapter 2, we start to explore such trade-offs because they are central to the choices that both individuals and firms make. The next example provides a first step in this process.

Trade-Offs and Contour Lines: An Example

As an illustration of how many variable functions can show trade-offs, consider the function

$$Y = \sqrt{X \cdot Z} = X^{0.5}Z^{0.5}, \quad X \geq 0, \quad Z \geq 0. \qquad \textbf{(1A.18)}$$

Choosing to look at this function is, of course, no accident—it will turn out that this function (or a slight generalization of it) will be used throughout this book whenever we need to illustrate trade-offs in a simple context.[6] Here, however, we will look only

[6]Formally, this function is a particular form of the "Cobb-Douglas" function that we will use to examine the choices of both consumers and firms.

at some of the function's mathematical properties. Table 1A.2 shows a few values of X and Z together with the resulting value for Y predicted by this function. Two interesting facts about the function are shown in the table. First, notice that if we hold X constant at, say, $X = 2$, increasing Z also increases Y. For example, increasing Z from 1 to 2 increases the value of Y from 1.414 to 2. Increasing Z further, to 3, increases Y further to 2.449. But the sizes of these increases get smaller as Z continues to increase further. In economic terms, this shows that the marginal gains from further Z are decreasing for this function if we hold X constant. Hence, if we were concerned about the cost of Z, we might be careful in buying more of it and instead think about increasing X to achieve gains in Y. This is precisely the sort of intuition that will guide our discussions of trade-offs in households' and firms' optimizing behavior.

Table 1A.2 Values of X, Z, and Y That Satisfy the Relationship $Y = \sqrt{X \cdot Z}$

X	Z	Y
1	1	1.000
1	2	1.414
1	3	1.732
1	4	2.000
2	1	1.414
2	2	2.000
2	3	2.449
2	4	2.828
3	1	1.732
3	2	2.449
3	3	3.000
3	4	3.464
4	1	2.000
4	2	2.828
4	3	3.464
4	4	4.000

Contour Lines

A second fact that is illustrated by the calculations in Table 1A.2 is that a number of different combinations of X and Z yield the same value for Y. For example, $Y = 2$ for $X = 1$, $Z = 4$, or for $X = 2$, $Z = 2$, or for $X = 4$, $Z = 1$. Indeed, it seems there are probably an infinite number of combinations of X and Z that would yield a value of $Y = 2$. Studying all of these combinations would appear to be a valuable way of learning about trade-offs between X and Z.

There are two ways in which we might make progress in examining such trade-offs. The first approach is algebraic—if we set $Y = 2$, we can solve Equation 1A.18 for the kind of relationship that X and Z must have to yield this outcome

$$Y = 2 = \sqrt{X \cdot Z} \text{ or } 4 = X \cdot Z \text{ or } X = \frac{4}{Z}. \quad \text{(1A.19)}$$

All of the combinations we just illustrated satisfy this relationship, as do many others. In fact, Equation 1A.19 shows precisely how we have to change the values of X and Z to keep Y at 2.

Another way to see the trade-offs in a multivariable function is to graph its **contour lines**. These show the various combinations of X and Z that yield a given value of Y. The term "contour lines" is borrowed from mapmakers who also use such lines to show altitude on a two-dimensional map. For example, a contour labeled "1,500 feet" shows the locations on the map that are precisely 1,500 feet above sea level. Similarly, a contour

MICRO QUIZ 1A.4

Consider the contour line "$Y = 3$" in Figure 1A.5:

1. If Z is reduced from 9 to 3, by how much will X have to be increased to keep Y at 3?
2. If Z is further reduced from 3 to 1, by how much will X have to increase to keep Y at 3?
3. Show the numerical reasoning behind your answers to Questions 1 and 2. Then calculate the values that X must take on to keep Y at 3 if Z takes on every unit value between 9 and 1.

Contour lines
Lines in two dimensions that show the sets of values of the independent variables that yield the same value for the dependent variable.

Figure 1A.5 **Contour Lines for $Y = \sqrt{X \cdot Z}$**

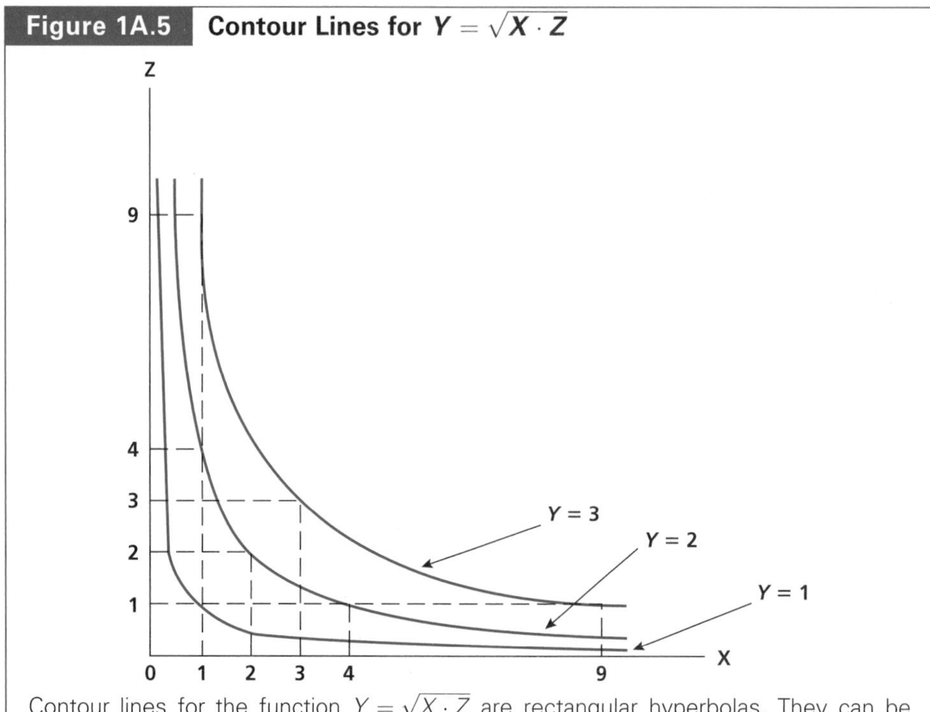

Contour lines for the function $Y = \sqrt{X \cdot Z}$ are rectangular hyperbolas. They can be represented by making Y equal to various supplied values (here, $Y = 1$, $Y = 2$, $Y = 3$) and then graphing the relationship between the independent variables X and Z.

labeled $Y = 2$ shows all those combinations of X and Z that yield a value of 2 for the dependent variable Y. Three such contour lines are shown in Figure 1A.5, for $Y = 1$, $Y = 2$, and $Y = 3$. In this particular case, the contour lines are hyperbolas, as can be seen from Equation 1A.19, which represents the contour line for $Y = 2$.

KEEP *in* MIND

Trade-offs Vary Along a Contour Line

The calculations in Micro Quiz 1A.4 show that the extra X that must be added to keep Y at 3 as Z is reduced keeps changing as one moves along the "$Y = 3$" contour line. When Z goes from 9 to 8, very little extra X is needed whereas when Z goes from 2 to 1 a lot of extra X is needed. This result is quite general—trade-offs are constantly changing along a contour line (unless it is a straight line). Consequently you need to be very careful to state where you are starting when you calculate trade-offs in most economic problems.

Simultaneous equations
A set of equations with more than one variable that must be solved together for a particular solution.

A1-4 Simultaneous Equations

Another mathematical concept that is often used in economics is **simultaneous equations.** When two variables (say, X and Y) are related by two different equations, it is sometimes, though not always, possible to solve these equations together for a single set of values of

X and Y that satisfies both of the equations. For example, it is easy to see that the two equations

$$\begin{aligned} X + Y &= 3 \\ X - Y &= 1 \end{aligned} \quad \text{(1A.20)}$$

have a unique solution of

$$\begin{aligned} X &= 2 \\ Y &= 1. \end{aligned} \quad \text{(1A.21)}$$

These equations operate "simultaneously" to determine the solutions for X and Y. One of the equations alone cannot determine a specific value for either variable—the solution depends on both of the equations.

Changing Solutions for Simultaneous Equations

It makes no sense in these equations to ask how a change in, say, X would affect the solution for Y. There is only one solution for X and Y from these two equations. As long as both equations must hold, the solution values for neither X nor Y can change. Of course, if the equations themselves are changed, then their solution will also change. For example, the equation system

$$\begin{aligned} X + Y &= 5 \\ X - Y &= 1 \end{aligned} \quad \text{(1A.22)}$$

is solved as

$$\begin{aligned} X &= 3 \\ Y &= 2. \end{aligned} \quad \text{(1A.23)}$$

Changing just one of the numbers in Equation Set 1A.20 yields an entirely different solution set.

MICRO QUIZ 1A.5

Economists use the *ceteris paribus* assumption to hold "everything else" constant when looking at a particular effect. How is this assumption reflected in simultaneous equations? Specifically:

1. Explain how the changes illustrated in Figure 1A.6 represent a change in "something else."
2. Explain how the changes illustrated in Figure 1A.6 might occur in a supply-demand context in the real world.

Graphing Simultaneous Equations

These results are illustrated in Figure 1A.6. The two equations in Equation Set 1A.20 are straight lines that intersect at the point (2,1). This point is the solution to the two equations, since it is the only one that lies on both lines. Changing the constant in the first equation of this system provides a different intersection for Equation Set 1A.22. In that case, the lines intersect at point (3,2), and that is the new solution. Even though only one of the lines shifted, both X and Y take on new solutions.

The similarity between the algebraic graph in Figure 1A.6 and the supply and demand graphs in Figure 1A.3 and Figure 1A.4 is striking. The point of intersection of two curves is called a "solution" in algebra and an "equilibrium" in economics, but in both cases we are finding the point that satisfies both relationships. The shift of the demand curve in Figure 1A.4 clearly resembles the change in the simultaneous equation set in Figure 1A.6. In both cases, the shift in one of the curves results in new solutions for both of the variables. If we could figure out the algebraic form for the supply and demand curves for a product, this example shows how we might make predictions about markets. Application 1A.3: Can Supply and Demand Explain Changing World Oil Prices? provides a glimpse of this sort of analysis.

Figure 1A.6 Solving Simultaneous Equations

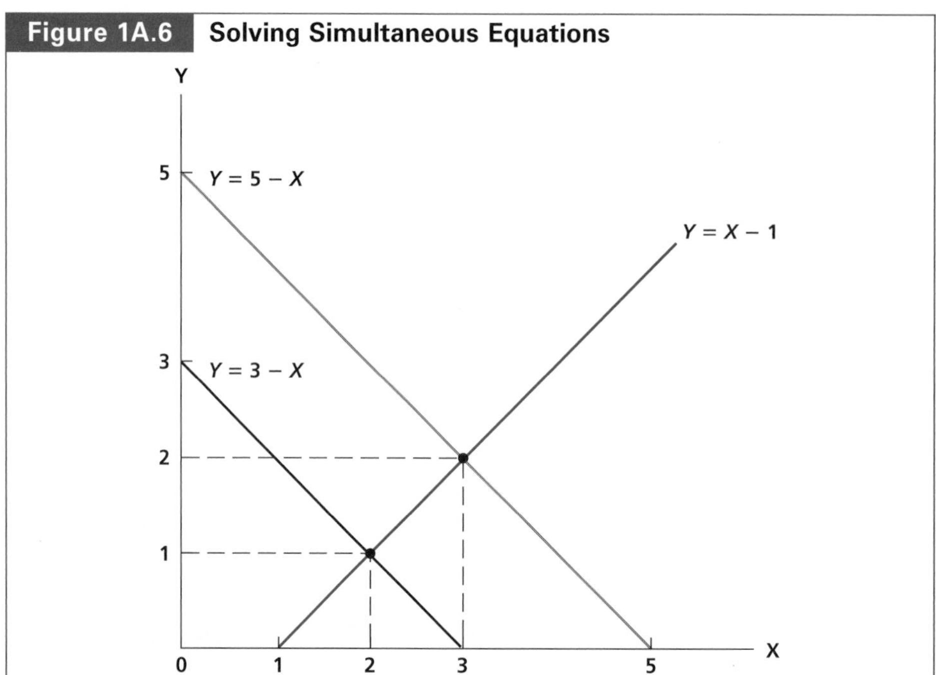

The linear equations $X + Y = 3$ ($Y = 3 - X$) and ($X - Y = 1$) can be solved simultaneously to find $X = 2$, $Y = 1$. This solution is shown by the point of intersection of the graphs of the two equations. If the first equation is changed (to $Y = 5 - X$), the solution will also change (to $X = 3$, $Y = 2$).

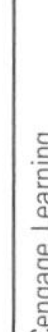

A1-5 Empirical Microeconomics and Econometrics

As we discussed in Chapter 1, economists are not only concerned with devising models of how the economy works. They must also be concerned with establishing the validity of those models, usually by looking at data from the real world. The tools used for this purpose are studied in the field of *econometrics* (literally, "economic measuring"). Because many of the applications that appear in this book are taken from econometric studies, and because econometrics has come to play an increasingly important role in all of economics, here we briefly discuss a few aspects of this subject. Any extended treatment is, of course, better handled in a full course on econometrics; but discussion of a few key issues may be helpful in understanding how economists draw conclusions about their models. Specifically, we look at two topics that are relevant to all of econometrics: (1) random influences, and (2) imposing the *ceteris paribus* assumption.

Random Influences

If real-world data fit economic models perfectly, econometrics would be a very simple subject. For example, an economist hypothesizes that the demand for pizza (Q) is a linear function of the price of pizza (P) of the form

$$Q = a - bP, \tag{1A.24}$$

where the values for a and b were to be determined by the data. Because any straight line can be established by knowing only two points on it, all the researcher would have to do is (1) find two places or time periods where "everything else" was the same (a topic we take up next), (2) record the values of Q and P for these observations, and (3) calculate the line passing through the two points. Assuming that the demand Equation 1A.24 holds in other times or places, all other points on this curve could be determined with perfect accuracy.

In fact, however, no economic model exhibits such perfect accuracy. Instead, the actual data on Q and P will be scattered around the "true" demand curve because of the huge variety of random influences (such as whether people get a yearning for pizza on a given day) that affect demand. This situation is illustrated in Figure 1A.7. The true demand curve for pizza is shown by the blue line, D. Researchers do not know this line. They can "see" only the actual points shown in color. The problem the researcher faces then is how to infer what the true demand curve is from these scattered points.

Technically, this is a problem in **statistical inference**. The researcher uses various statistical techniques in an attempt to see through all of the random things that affect the demand for pizza and to *infer* what the relationship between Q and P actually is. A discussion of the techniques actually used for this purpose is beyond the scope of this book, but a glance at Figure 1A.7 makes clear that no technique will find a straight line that fits the points perfectly. Instead, some compromises will have to be made in order to find a demand curve that is "close" to most of the data points. Careful consideration of the kinds of random influences present in a problem can help in devising which technique to use.[7] A few of the applications in this text describe how researchers have adapted statistical techniques to their purposes.

Statistical inference
Use of actual data and statistical techniques to determine quantitative economic relationships.

The *Ceteris Paribus* Assumption

All economic theories employ the assumption that "other things are held constant." In the real world, of course, many things do change. If the data points in Figure 1A.7 come

Figure 1A.7 Inferring the Demand Curve from Real-World Data

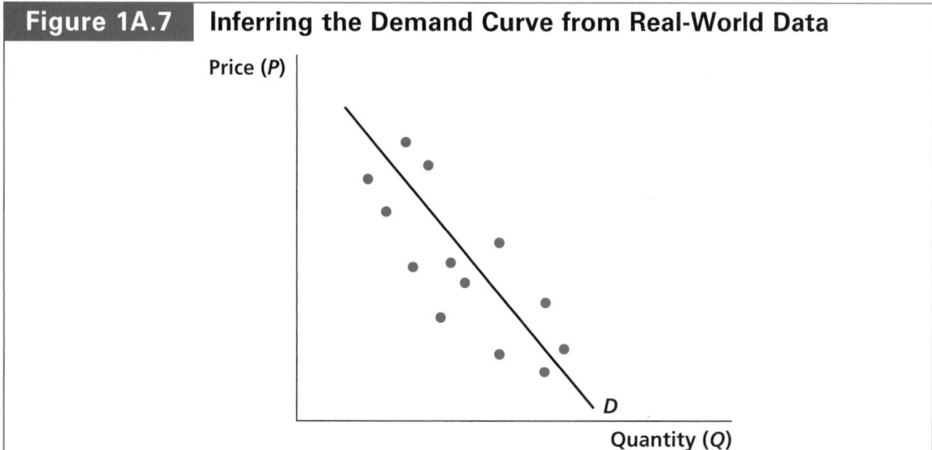

Even when the ceteris paribus assumption is in force, actual data (shown by the points) will not fit the demand curve (D) perfectly because of random influences. Statistical procedures must be used to infer the location of D.

[7] In many problems, the statistical technique of "ordinary least squares" is the best available. This technique proceeds by choosing the line for which the sum of the squared deviations from the line for all of the data points is as small as possible.

APPLICATION 1A.3

Can Supply and Demand Explain Changing World Oil Prices?

The price of crude oil fluctuates quite a bit on world markets. Since 2000 prices have been below \$30 per barrel at times and above \$130 per barrel at other times. Such wild gyrations have led many people to charge that oil prices are being "manipulated" by "speculators" and criminal investigations are launched when oil prices rise. Economists have generally not been especially sympathetic to the claim that the oil market is "rigged" and have instead tried to see how price movements might be explained by standard supply-demand analysis. In this application we take a look at this sort of analysis. We conclude with some thoughts about the effects of speculation.

A Simple Model

In prior editions of this book, we introduced a simple supply/demand model of the world market for crude oil. A starting point for the model is the recognition that the market for crude oil is indeed worldwide. Because the commodity being traded is basically the same everywhere, various sorts of arbitrage activities should ensure that this good trades for a single "world price." If we let this price be represented by P (in dollars per barrel) and the quantity of crude oil traded by Q (measured in millions of barrels per day), our model for the year 2001 took the form:

$$\begin{aligned} \text{Demand: } Q &= 85 - 0.4P \\ \text{Supply: } Q &= 55 + 0.6P. \end{aligned} \qquad (1)$$

Solving these equations simultaneously yields:

$$85 - 0.4P = 55 + 0.6P \Rightarrow P^* = 30, Q^* = 73. \qquad (2)$$

These are approximately the values that prevailed in 2001—crude oil traded at \$30 per barrel and a total of about 73 million barrels per day were produced.[1]

Increased Demand for Crude Oil

Between 2001 and 2008, the price of crude oil rose steadily. Probably the single most important cause was increasing world demand for petroleum products around the world, especially from rapidly developing economies such as China, India, and Brazil. This increase in demand can be accommodated into our simple model by just shifting the demand curve. If we assume world demand was growing at 4 percent per year, the demand curve in 2008 would have shifted outward to

$$Q = 112 - 0.6P. \qquad (3)$$

Notice that we can accomplish this shift by just changing the constant term in the original demand equation. This shift is shown in Figure 1. If we now solve again for supply-demand equilibrium we get $P^* = 57$, $Q^* = 87$. These values form our predictions of how the model of supply and demand would have estimated how the increase in demand should have affected the world market in 2008.

Figure 1 World Oil Market

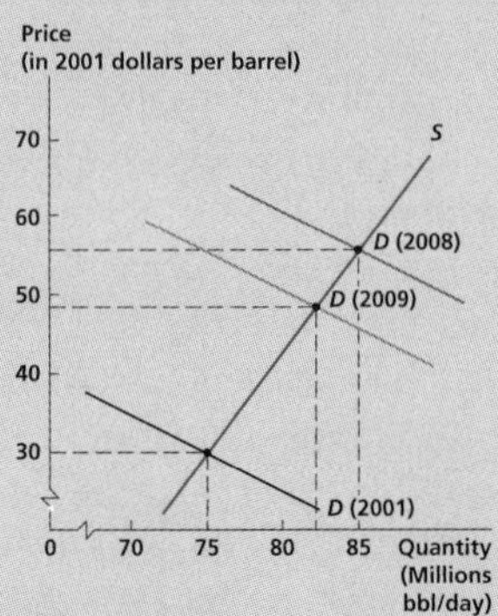

Model predicts that increasing demand between 2001 and 2008 raises relative price from \$30 to \$57. The recession of 2008–2009 reduced demand somewhat.

Assessing the Predictions

Our estimate for crude oil production in 2008 is remarkably close to its actual value—our model predicts a quantity of 87 million barrels per day whereas actual production was about 86 million barrels per day. At first glance, however, our price prediction seems well wide of the mark—our model predicts a price of \$57 whereas the actual price was about \$40 higher (\$97 per barrel).Before discarding our prediction, however, we need to be sure what our price means. As in all microeconomic models, the price variable shown on the vertical axis should be the "real" price—that is, it should record the price of the item being modeled relative to other prices. Because the initial specification of our model was from 2001, the price of \$57 in "2001 prices" not in the "2008 prices" reflected in the \$97 price recorded in the newspaper. Because of the worldwide nature of the crude oil market, we must take two factors into account if we are to compare predicted price to the actual one. First, overall inflation in the United States was about 23 percent between 2001 and 2008. Second, because oil prices are stated in dollars, we must also take account of the fact that the world value of the dollar declined by about 35 percent between 2001 and 2008. Ultimately therefore we should adjust the \$97 price downward by about 40 percent (because $1/1.23 \cdot 1.35 \approx 0.60$) to phrase it in the 2001 prices that characterize our model. Making this adjustment yields a real price in 2008 of about \$58 per barrel—very close to our predicted value of \$57.

Oil Prices During the Great Recession

The worldwide recession that started with the financial crisis of 2008 caused a significant contraction in the demand for crude oil. Still, this contraction should not have changed the situation illustrated in Figure 1 by very much. For example, the demand for crude oil fell by 5 percent in 2009. That should have shifted the demand curve to $Q = 106 - 0.4P$ and (as Figure 1 shows) the new market equilibrium would be $P^* = 49$, $Q^* = 84$. Again the prediction for quantity is very close to the value that prevailed in 2009, but the price seems off. We only predicted a decline of \$8 whereas the nominal price of crude oil in 2009 fell to by more than \$35 to about \$60 per barrel. Undoubtedly, part of the decline can be explained by the strengthening of the dollar in 2009 as the U.S. currency became a haven for people worried about the economy. But the size of the decline seems larger than might have been anticipated by the simple application of supply and demand logic.

Speculation in the Crude Oil Market

As for many commodities, the prices for crude oil fluctuate more than might be expected on the basis of supply and demand considerations only. For example, although the average price of crude oil was about \$94 per barrel in 2012, the price was as high as \$110 and as low as \$79 during the year. Because the factors that determine the location of supply and demand curves (costs of drilling or consumer incomes) change only slowly over time, something else must be going on. One possibility is that prices in this market are being affected by "speculation." Giving a precise definition to this term is difficult, but at its heart speculation consists of placing bets on the price of a commodity rather than buying or selling the commodity for its usefulness. For example, someone who thinks the price of crude oil will rise over the next six months could buy a tankful of oil today and hold it for sale later.

Speculation, Equilibrium Prices and Political Posturing

Economists generally doubt that these sorts of speculative activity can affect equilibrium prices over the long term. In Chapter 9, we will briefly examine the reasons for this belief. The main point we will make is that, while there is no doubt that speculation can cause prices to fluctuate around their equilibrium values, there is no reason to expect such activity to push prices in any particular direction. Still, politicians and other pundits cannot refrain from blaming "speculators" every time the price for a major commodity rises (though they seldom blame speculators for declines in price). For example, following the recession-induced decline in oil prices in 2009, the market gradually returned to its earlier equilibrium price of about \$94 per barrel in 2012. Because this price rise was occurring in an election year, politicians once again blamed "speculators" for the increase. One widely reported study made the (preposterously precise) claim that speculation added \$23.39 to the price of a barrel[2] of crude oil in early 2012. Numerous Congressional committees began investigations, hoping to catch speculators in the act of speculating. If the past is any guide, it is likely that they will find that speculative activity in the crude oil market was quite legal and had little, if any, impact on long-term prices.

TO THINK ABOUT

1. About half of the world's production of crude oil is controlled by nations that belong to the Organization of Petroleum Exporting Countries (OPEC). How can the operations of this organization be taken into account in our simple model of supply and demand?
2. The demise of the Gaddafi regime in Libya in 2010 briefly reduced world crude oil production by about 1.5 million barrels per day. How would you use the simple model of demand and supply to predict the effect that this reduction in supply would have on the world oil market?

[1]At this equilibrium, the price elasticity of demand for crude oil is -0.16 [$= -0.4(30/73)$] and the price elasticity of supply is 0.25 [$= 0.6(30/73)$]. Both of these figures are generally consistent with what has been found in empirical studies of the world market for crude oil.
[2]This prediction is discussed in the February 27, 2012, issue of *Forbes* Magazine.

MICRO QUIZ 1A.6

You have been hired by Dominos Pizza to estimate the demand curve for pizza using 24 months of data on price and quantity in ten major cities. Here are two methods you might use to determine this demand curve. Explain why each is probably incorrect.

Method 1: Plot all 240 data points on a single graph and draw a carefully fit line through these points.

Method 2: Plot 10 different demand curve graphs, one for each city. Carefully fit a demand curve to the data for each city. Calculate the average slope for these ten graphs and use that as your estimate of how pizza demand relates to price.

from different weeks, for example, it is unlikely that conditions such as the weather or the prices of pizza substitutes (hamburgers?) have remained unchanged over these periods. Similarly, if the data points in the figure come from, say, different towns, it is unlikely that all factors that may affect pizza demand are exactly the same in every town. Hence, a researcher might reasonably be concerned that the data in Figure 1A.7 do not reflect a single demand curve. Rather, the points may lie on several different demand curves, and attempting to force them into a single curve would be a mistake.

To address this problem, two things must be done: (1) Data should be collected on all of the other factors that affect demand, and (2) appropriate procedures must be used to control for these measurable factors in analysis. Although the conceptual framework for doing this is fairly straightforward,[8] many practical problems arise. Most important, it may not in fact be possible to measure all of the other factors that affect demand. Consider, for example, the problem of deciding how to measure the precise influence of a pizza advertising campaign on pizza demand. Would you measure the number of ads placed, the number of ad readers, or the "quality" of the ads? Ideally, one might like to measure people's perceptions of the ads—but how would you do that without an elaborate and costly survey? Ultimately, then, the researcher will often have to make some compromises in the kinds of data that can be collected, and some uncertainty will remain about whether the *ceteris paribus* assumption has been imposed faithfully. Many controversies over testing the reliability of economic models arise for precisely this reason.

Exogenous and Endogenous Variables

In any economic model, it is important to differentiate between variables whose values are determined by the model and those that come from outside the model. Variables whose values are determined by a model are called **endogenous variables** ("inside variables"), and those whose values come from outside the model are called **exogenous variables** ("outside" variables). In many microeconomic models, price and quantity are the endogenous variables, whereas the exogenous variables are factors from outside the particular market being considered, often variables that reflect macroeconomic conditions. To illustrate this distinction, we return to the simultaneous model specified in Equation 1A.22 but change the notation so that P and Q represent the price and quantity of some good. The values of these two variables are determined simultaneously by the operations of supply and demand. The market equilibrium is also affected by two exogenous variables, W and Z. W reflects factors that positively affect demand (such as consumer

[8]To control for the other measurable factors (X) that affect demand, the demand curve given in Equation 1A.22 must be modified to include these other factors as $Q = a - bP + cX$. Once the values for a, b, and c have been determined, this allows the researcher to hold X constant (as is required by the ceteris paribus assumption) while looking at the relationship between Q and P. Changes in X shift the entire Q-P relationship (that is, changes in X shift the demand curve).

income), whereas Z reflects factors that shift the supply curve upward (such as workers' wages). Our economic model of this market can be written as:

$$\begin{aligned} Q &= -P + W \\ P &= Q + Z. \end{aligned} \quad \textbf{(1A.25)}$$

After we specify values for W and Z, this becomes a model with two equations and two unknowns and can be solved for (equilibrium) values of P and Q. For example, if $W = 3$, $Z = -1$, this is identical to the model in Equation 1A.22, and the solution is $P = 1$, $Q = 2$. Similarly, if $W = 5$, $Z = -1$, the solution to this model is $P = 2$, $Q = 3$. Notice the solution strategy here. First, we must know the values for the exogenous variables in the model. We then plug these into the model and proceed to solve for the values of the endogenous variables. This is how practically all economic models work.

The Reduced Form

There is a shortcut to solving these models if you need to do so many times that involves solving for the endogenous variables in terms of the exogenous variables. By plugging the second equation in 1A.25 into the first, we get

$$\begin{aligned} 2Q = W - Z \quad &\text{or} \quad Q = (W - Z)/2 \\ P = Q + Z \quad &\text{or} \quad P = (W + Z)/2. \end{aligned} \quad \textbf{(1A.26)}$$

You should check that inserting the values for W and Z used previously into Equation 1A.26 will yield precisely the same values for P and Q that we found in the previous paragraph.

The equations in 1A.26 are called the **reduced form** of the "structural" model in Equations 1A.25. Not only is expressing all the endogenous variables in a model in terms of the exogenous variables a useful procedure for making predictions, but also there may be econometric advantages of estimating reduced forms rather than structural equations. We will not pursue such issues in this book, however.

KEEP *in* MIND

How to Know When a Problem Is Solved

A frustration experienced by many students who are beginning their study of microeconomics is that they cannot tell when they have arrived at a suitable solution to a problem. Making the distinction between endogenous and exogenous variables can help you in this process. After you identify which variables are being specified from outside a model and which are being determined within a model, your goal is usually to solve for the endogenous variables (that is, price and quantity). If you are given explicit values for the exogenous variables in the model (that is, prices for firms' input costs), a solution will consist of explicit numerical values for all of the endogenous variables in the model. On the other hand, if you are just given symbols for the exogenous variables, a solution will consist of a reduced form in which each endogenous variable is a function only of these exogenous variables. Any purported "solution" that fails to solve for each of the endogenous variables in a model is not complete. Throughout this book, we will point out situations where students sometimes make this sort of mistake.

SUMMARY

This appendix reviews material that should be familiar to you from prior math and economics classes. The following results will be used throughout the rest of this book:

- Linear equations have graphs that are straight lines. These lines are described by their slopes and by their intercepts with the Y-axis.
- Changes in the slope cause the graph of a linear equation to rotate about its Y-intercept. Changes in the X- or Y-intercept cause the graph to shift in a parallel way.
- Nonlinear equations have graphs that have curved shapes. Their slopes change as X changes.
- Economists often use functions of two or more variables because economic outcomes have many causes. These functions can sometimes be graphed in two dimensions by using contour lines. These lines show trade-offs that can be made while holding the value of the dependent variable constant. This is especially difficult in the case of simultaneous equations that determine the values of endogenous variables.
- Simultaneous equations determine solutions for two (or more) variables that satisfy all of the equations. An important use of such equations is to show how supply and demand determine equilibrium prices.
- Testing economic models usually requires the use of real-world data together with appropriate econometric techniques. An important problem in all such applications is to ensure that the *ceteris paribus* assumption has been imposed correctly.

PART 2

Demand

"There is one general law of demand.... The amount demanded increases with a fall in price and diminishes with a rise in price."

—Alfred Marshall, Principles of Economics, 1890

Part 2 examines how economists model people's economic decisions. Our main goal is to develop Marshall's demand curve for a product and to show why this demand curve is likely to be downward sloping. This "law of demand" (that price and quantity demanded move in opposite directions) is a central building block of microeconomics.

Chapter 2 describes how economists treat a consumer's decision problem. We first define the concept of utility, which represents a consumer's preferences. The second half of the chapter discusses how people decide to spend their limited incomes on different goods to get the greatest satisfaction possible—that is, to maximize their utility.

Chapter 3 investigates how people change their choices when their income changes or as prices change. This allows us to develop an individual's demand curve for a product. These individual demand curves can then be added up to yield the familiar market demand curve. Chapter 3 also looks at ways to use elasticities to measure how responsive market demand is to changes in income or prices.

2 Utility and Choice

Every day you must make many choices: when to wake up; what to eat; how much time to spend working, studying, or relaxing; and whether to buy something or save your money. Economists investigate all these decisions because they all affect the way any economy operates. In this chapter, we look at the general model used for this purpose.

The economic **theory of choice** begins by describing people's preferences. This amounts to a complete cataloging of how a person feels about all the things he or she might do. But people are not free to do anything they want—they are constrained by time, income, and many other factors in the choices open to them. Our model of choice must therefore describe how these constraints affect the ways in which individuals actually are able to make choices based on their preferences.

Theory of choice
The interaction of preferences and constraints that causes people to make the choices they do.

2-1 Utility

Economists model people's preferences using the concept of **utility**, which we define as the satisfaction that a person receives from his or her economic activities. This concept is very broad, and in the next few sections we define it more precisely. We use the simple case of a single individual who receives utility from just two commodities. We will eventually analyze how that person chooses to allocate income between these two goods, but first we need to develop a better understanding of utility itself.

Utility
The pleasure or satisfaction that people get from their economic activity.

Ceteris Paribus Assumption

Identifying all the factors affecting a person's feelings of satisfaction would be a lifelong task for an imaginative psychologist. To simplify matters, economists focus on basic, quantifiable economic goods and look at how people choose among them. Economists clearly recognize that all sorts of elements (aesthetics, love, security, envy, and so forth) affect behavior, but they develop models in which these are held constant and are not specifically analyzed.

Much economic analysis is based on this ***ceteris paribus*** (other things being equal) **assumption**. We can simplify the analysis of a person's consumption decisions by assuming that satisfaction is affected only by choices made among the goods being considered. All other effects on satisfaction are assumed to remain constant. In this way, we can isolate the economic influences that affect consumption behavior. This narrow focus is not intended to imply that other things that affect utility are unimportant; we are conceptually holding these other factors constant so that we may study choices in a simplified setting. In Chapter 17, we will take a somewhat broader view by looking at some of behavioral issues that may affect consumption choices.

***Ceteris paribus* assumption**
In economic analysis, holding all other factors constant so that only the factor being studied is allowed to change.

Utility from Consuming Two Goods

This chapter concentrates on an individual's problem of choosing the quantities of two goods (which for most purposes we will call simply "X" and "Y") to consume. We assume that the person receives utility from these goods and that we can show this utility in functional notation by

$$\text{Utility} = U(X, Y; \text{other things}) \tag{2.1}$$

This notation indicates that the utility an individual receives from consuming X and Y over some period of time depends on the quantities of X and Y consumed and on "other things." These other things might include easily quantifiable items such as the amounts of other kinds of goods consumed, the number of hours worked, or the amount of time spent sleeping. They might also include such unquantifiable items such as love, security, and feelings of self-worth. These other things appear after the semicolon in Equation 2.1 because we assume that they do not change while we look at the individual's choice between X and Y. If one of the other things should change, the utility from some particular amounts of X and Y might be very different than it was before.

For example, several times in this chapter we consider the case of a person choosing how many hamburgers (Y) and soft drinks (X) to consume during one week. Although our example uses trivial commodities, the analysis is quite general and will apply to any two goods. In analyzing the hamburger–soft drink choices, we assume that all other factors affecting utility are held constant. The weather, the person's basic preferences for hamburgers and soft drinks, the person's exercise pattern, and everything else are assumed not to change during the analysis. If the weather, for instance, were to become warmer, we might expect soft drinks to become relatively more desirable, and we wish to eliminate such effects from our analysis, at least for the moment. We usually write the utility function in Equation 2.1 as

$$\text{Utility} = U(X, Y) \tag{2.2}$$

with the understanding that many other things are being held constant. All economic analyses impose some form of this *ceteris paribus* assumption so that the relationship between a selected few variables can be studied.

Measuring Utility

You might think that economists would try to measure a basic concept such as utility, perhaps enlisting psychologists in the process. About 100 years ago, a number of economists did indeed pursue this issue, but they encountered several difficulties. The most important of these problems arose from trying to compare utility measures among people. Economists (and psychologists too) just could not manage to come up with a single scale of well-being that seemed to fit most people. In Application 2.1: Can Money Buy Health and Happiness? we look at some recent attempts to solve this problem. But, ultimately, it seems that there is no general way to compare the utility that a particular choice provides to one person to the utility that it provides to someone else. Today, economists have largely abandoned the search for a common utility scale and have instead come to focus on explaining actual observed behavior using simple models that do not require them to measure utility. That is the approach we will take in this book.

APPLICATION 2.1

Can Money Buy Health and Happiness?

Although measuring utility directly may be impossible, economists have been quite willing to explore various approximations. Perhaps the most widely used measure is annual income. As the old joke goes, even if money can't buy happiness, it can buy you any kind of sadness you want. Still, economists remain interested in developing some more alternative measures of well-being, and this application looks at some of that research.

Income and Health

An individual's health is certainly one aspect of his or her utility, and the relationship between income and health has been intensively studied. Virtually all of these studies conclude that people who have higher incomes enjoy better health. For example, comparing men of equal ages, life expectancy is about seven years shorter for those with incomes in the bottom quarter of the population than for those in the top quarter. Similar differences show up in the prevalence of various diseases—rates of heart disease and cancer are much lower for those in the upper-income group. Clearly it appears that money can "buy" good health.

There is less agreement among economists about why more income "buys" good health.[1] The standard explanation is that higher incomes allow people greater access to health care. But this hypothesis is contradicted by the fact that the connection between income and health persists in countries with extensive national health insurance systems. Such findings have led some economists to question the precise causality in the income-health linkage. Is it possible that the health is affecting income rather than vice versa? For example, health may affect the kinds or amount of work that a person can do. Similarly, large health-related expenses can prevent a person from accumulating both financial and human capital, thereby reducing income from such wealth. As in many economic situations, sorting out the precise relationship between income and health from the available data can be difficult.

Income and Happiness

A more general approach to the relationship between income and utility asks people to rank how happy they are on a numerical scale. Although people's answers show considerable variability, the data do show certain regularities. People with higher incomes report that they are happier than are those with lower incomes in virtually every survey. For example, the economic historian Richard Easterlin reports on measured happiness in the United States on a 4-point scale. He finds that people with incomes above $75,000 per year have an average happiness ranking of 2.8, whereas those with incomes below $20,000 per year have a ranking below 2.0.[2] Surveys from other countries show much the same result.

One peculiarity of the data on happiness is that people do not seem to get all that much happier as their own economic circumstances improve. Easterlin argues that this happens mainly because people's aspirations rise as they become richer.

Declining Happiness for Women

Much research on happiness has focused on the puzzling fact that the happiness of women seems to have declined in recent years despite the increased social and economic opportunities that have been opened to them. For example, Stevenson and Wolfers show that women's feelings of subjective well-being have declined significantly relative to those of men in a wide variety of surveys from both the United States and the European Union.[3] These authors examine a number of possible reasons for the decline, but find that most proposed explanations are not supported by the data. One possibility they raise is similar to Easterlin's—as opportunities have opened for women in many different domains, their aspirations have also expanded. Hence, the welfare implications of the measured decline in subjective well-being are ambiguous.

TO THINK ABOUT

1. Because a higher income makes it possible for a person to consume bundles of goods that were previously unaffordable, he or she must necessarily be better off. Isn't that all we need to know about well-being?
2. A wide variety of indices of well-being are used in recent years to rank countries. These range from the Human Development Index (on which the United States ranks 4th) to the Happy Planet Index (on which the United States ranks 114th). Can you make any sense out of these vastly different rankings? Look up some of these on the Internet and develop your own opinion about which, if any, are reliable indicators of the well-being of the citizens of a country.

[1] For a more complete discussion of the issues raised in this section, see James P. Smith, "Healthy Bodies and Thick Wallets: The Dual Relationship between Health and Economic Status," *Journal of Economic Perspectives* (Spring 1999): 145–166.

[2] Richard A. Easterlin, "Income and Happiness: Toward a Unified Theory," *Economic Journal* (July 2001): 465–484.

[3] See Betsey Stevenson and Justin Wolfers, "The Paradox of Declining Female Happiness," *American Economic Journal Economic Policy* (2009), 1:2, 190–225.

2-2 Assumptions about Preferences

In order to provide a foundation for our study of utility, we need to make three assumptions about behavior that seem quite reasonable. These are intended to provide a simple framework for what we mean when we say people make choices in a rational and consistent way.

Completeness

When faced with two options, A or B, it seems reasonable that a person can say whether he or she prefers A to B, or B to A, or finds them equally attractive. In other words, we assume that people are not paralyzed by indecision—that they can actually state what they prefer. This assumption rules out the situation of the mythical jackass who, finding himself halfway between a bale of hay and a sack of oats, starved to death because he was unable to decide which one to choose.

We can extend this example a bit by assuming that people can make such preference judgments about any possible options presented to them. That is, we will assume preferences are **complete**. For any two options presented, a person always is able to state which is preferred.

Complete preferences
The assumption that an individual is able to state which of any two options is preferred.

Transitivity

In addition to assuming that people can state their preferences clearly and completely, we also might expect these preferences to exhibit some sort of internal consistency. That is, we would not expect a person to say contradictory things about what he or she likes. This presumption can be formalized by the assumption that preferences are **transitive.** If a person states, "I prefer A to B" and "I prefer B to C," we would expect that he or she would also say, "I prefer A to C." A person who instead stated the contrary ("I prefer C to A") would appear to be hopelessly confused. Economists do not believe people suffer from such confusions at least not on a consistent basis. Of course, in some cases the options that people confront may be very complicated so making transitive choices may be beyond any person's mental ability. In Chapter 17 we look at a few such situations.

Transitivity of preferences
The property that if *A* is preferred to *B*, and *B* is preferred to *C*, then *A* must be preferred to *C*.

More Is Better: Defining an Economic "Good"

A third assumption we make about preferences is that a person prefers more of a good to less. In Figure 2.1, all points in the darkly shaded area are preferred to the amounts of X^* of good X and Y^* of good Y. Movement from point X^*, Y^* to any point in the dark shaded area is an unambiguous improvement, since in this area this person gets more of one good without taking less of another. This idea leads us to define an "economic good" as an item that yields positive benefits to people.[1] That is, more of a good is, by definition, better. Combinations of goods in the lightly shaded area of Figure 2.1 are definitely inferior to X^*, Y^* since they offer less of *both* goods.

These three assumptions about preferences are about enough to justify our use of the simple utility function that we introduced earlier. That is, if people obey these assumptions, they will make choices in a way consistent with using such a function. Notice that economists do not claim that people actually consult a utility function

[1]Later in this chapter, we briefly describe a theory of "bads"—items for which less is preferred to more. Such items might include toxic wastes, mosquitoes, or, for your authors, lima beans.

Figure 2.1 More of a Good Is Preferred to Less

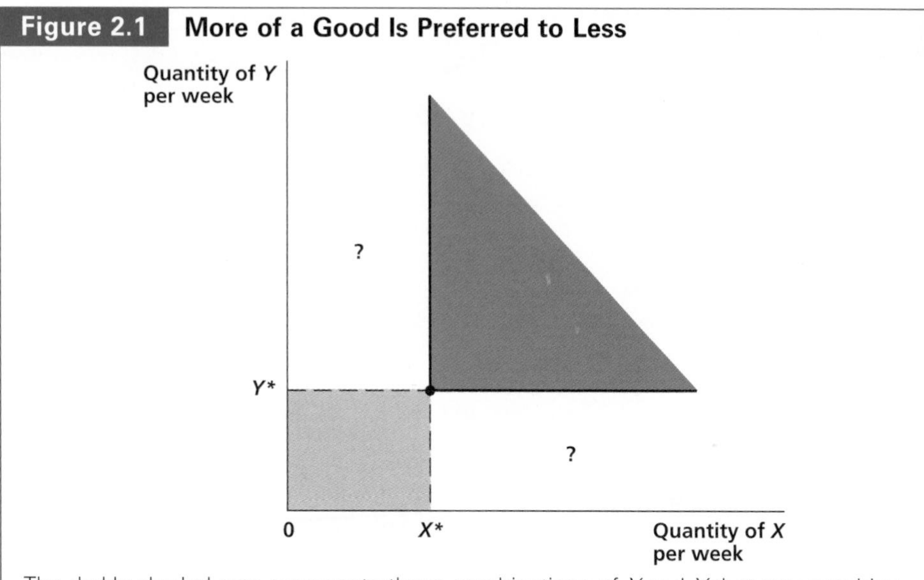

The darkly shaded area represents those combinations of X and Y that are unambiguously preferred to the combination X^*, Y^*. This is why goods are called "goods"; individuals prefer having more of any good rather than less. Combinations of X and Y in the lightly shaded area are inferior to the combination X^*, Y^*, whereas those in the questionable areas may or may not be superior to X^*, Y^*.

when deciding, say, what brand of toothpaste to buy. Instead, we assume that people have relatively well-defined preferences and make decisions *as if* they consulted such a function. Remember Friedman's pool player analogy from Chapter 1—the laws of physics can explain his or her shots even though the player knows nothing about physics. Similarly, the theory of utility can explain economic choices even though no one actually has a utility function embedded in his or her brain. Whether economists actually have to consider exactly what does go on in the brains of people has become a topic of some debate in recent years. In Application 2.2: Should Economists Care about How the Mind Works? we provide a first look at that debate.

2-3 Voluntary Trades and Indifference Curves

How people feel about getting more of some good when they must give up an amount of some other good is probably the most important reason for studying preferences and utility. The areas identified with question marks in Figure 2.1 are difficult to compare to X^*, Y^* because they involve more of one good and less of the other. Whether a move from X^*, Y^* into these areas would increase utility is not clear. To be able to look into this situation, we

MICRO QUIZ 2.1

How should the assumption of completeness and transitivity be reflected in Figure 2.1? Specifically:

1. What does the assumption of completeness imply about all of the points in the figure?
2. If it were known that a particular point in the "?" area in Figure 2.1 was preferred to point X^*, Y^*, how could transitivity be used to rank some other points in that area?

APPLICATION 2.2

Should Economists Care about How the Mind Works?

The theory of utility is a pure invention of economists. When noneconomists think about the decisions of people to buy things or take jobs, they are very unlikely to describe these in utility-maximizing terms. Rather, noneconomists believe that peoples' choices are influenced by a wide variety of social and psychological forces, and sometimes it may be simply impossible to explain certain decisions. Some scientists even believe that decisions are mainly influenced by chemical interactions in the brain and that these bear no particular relationship to economists' models.

Arguments about Utility Are Long-Standing

Economists have argued over the meaning of utility and utility maximization for over 100 years. For example, the nineteenth-century economist F. Y. Edgeworth believed that eventually psychologists would develop a machine that could measure pleasure (he called the device a "hedonimeter") and that the readings from this machine would provide a clear foundation for explaining choices. Other economists scoffed at the hedonimeter idea, stating that it was both impractical and unnecessary. For them, the utility model did a perfectly good job of predicting the economic behavior of people, and developing a more complete theory of the psychology underlying that behavior was totally unnecessary.[1] Building Edgeworth's machine ultimately proved to be impossible, and the utility theorists seemed to have won out. But concerns that it might be important to understand a bit more about the psychology and neurology of economic behavior lingered on.

After many years of neglect, interest in studying the relationship between psychology and economic behavior has begun a return, primarily because economists have found it difficult to explain some types of behavior using simple utility models. In Chapter 17, we will study some of these challenges in detail. Here, we just look at two examples.

Self-Control and Gym Memberships

It seems that people pay far more than they need to for using the local gym. In a 2006 paper, DellaVigna and Malmendier[2] look at the behavior of 7,000 health club members over a three-year period. They conclude that most of those who buy annual memberships would be much better off paying separately for each visit to the gym. Overall, people would save nearly 60 percent by opting for such a pay-as-you-go contract. Traditional theory would find it hard to explain why people choose a wasteful annual contract. Seemingly, only by introducing psychological ideas such as shortsightedness (perhaps people with annual memberships think they will go to the gym more often than they do) or the need for self-control (the annual membership may force people to go) can this type of behavior be explained. Adapting utility models to do this is an important area of current research.

Inattention to Full Prices

There is a lot of evidence that people don't really pay much attention when they make some economic choices. Often, decisions must be made in a hurry, or a consumer's thoughts may be focused on other things when he or she makes a purchase. For example, in an experimental study of purchases of CDs on eBay, Hossain and Morgan[3] found that buyers paid far less attention to shipping and handling costs than they did to the price of a good at auction, even when those other costs were a high fraction of a good's overall price. A similar lack of attention to all aspects of the price of a good has been noted for such diverse goods as alcoholic beverages, hospital services, and vacation packages. Clear thinking about prices can sometimes be difficult for people—it may involve real costs in getting and assessing the relevant information. How utility models should be modified to take such costs into account is a subject of increasing amounts of research.

TO THINK ABOUT

1. Positioning items on grocery store shelves is an important job for managers—they try to place profitable goods where they will draw attention. Doesn't this seem to be a waste of time if people are true utility maximizers in their shopping behavior?
2. What kinds of "irrational" economic decisions do you make? Why do you make these decisions? Can you develop a "rational" explanation for them?

[1]For a discussion, see D. Colander, "Edgeworth's Hedonimeter and the Quest to Measure Utility," *Journal of Economic Perspectives* (Spring 2007): 215–225.
[2]S. DellaVigna and U. Malmendier, "Paying Not to Go to the Gym," *American Economic Review* (June 2006): 694–719.
[3]T. Hossain and J. Morgan, "… Plus Shipping and Handling: Revenue (Non) Equivalence in Field Experiments on eBay," *Advances in Economic Analysis and Policy* (2006), 2: 1–27.

need some additional tools. Because giving up units of one commodity (for example, money) to get back additional units of some other commodity (say, candy bars) is what gives rise to trade and organized markets, these new tools provide the foundation for the economic analysis of demand.

Indifference Curves

To study voluntary trades, we use the concept of an **indifference curve**. Such a curve shows all those combinations of two goods that provide the same utility to an individual; that is, a person is *indifferent* about which particular combination of goods on the curve he or she actually has. Figure 2.2 records the quantity of soft drinks consumed by a person in one week on the horizontal axis and the quantity of hamburgers consumed in the same week on the vertical axis. The curve U_1 in Figure 2.2 includes all those combinations of hamburgers and soft drinks with which this person is equally happy. For example, the curve shows that he or she would be just as happy with six hamburgers and two soft drinks per week (point *A*) as with four hamburgers and three soft drinks (point *B*) or with three hamburgers and four soft drinks (point *C*). The points on U_1 all provide the same level of utility; therefore, he or she does not have any reason for preferring any point on U_1 to any other point.

Indifference curve
A curve that shows all the combinations of goods or services that provide the same level of utility.

The indifference curve U_1 is similar to a contour line on a map (as discussed in the Appendix to Chapter 1). It shows those combinations of hamburgers and soft drinks that provide an identical "altitude" (that is, amount) of utility. Points to the northeast of U_1 promise a higher level of satisfaction and are preferred to points on U_1. Point *E* (five soft drinks and four hamburgers) is preferred to point *C* because it provides more of

Figure 2.2 Indifference Curve

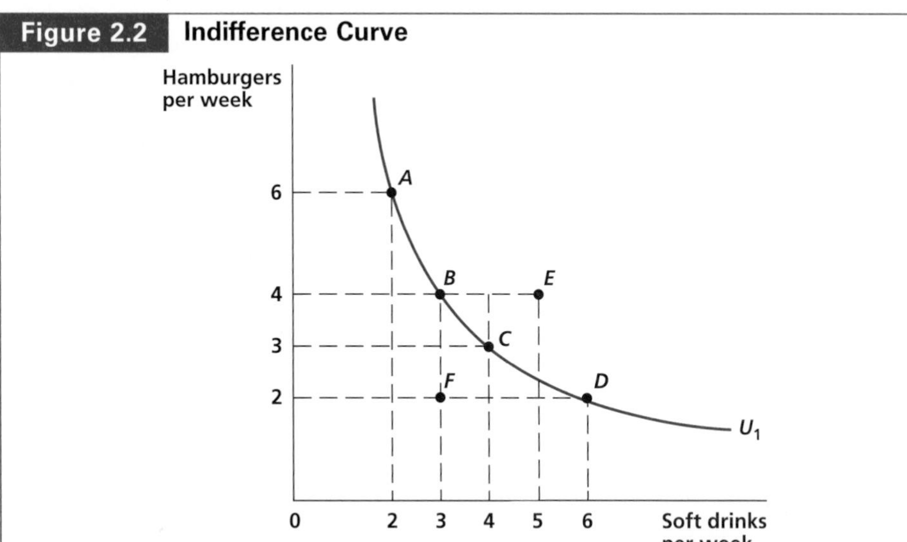

The curve U_1 shows the combinations of hamburgers and soft drinks that provide the same level of utility to an individual. The slope of the curve shows the trades an individual will freely make. For example, in moving from point *A* to point *B*, the individual will give up two hamburgers to get one additional soft drink. In other words, the marginal rate of substitution is approximately 2 in this range. Points below U_1 (such as *F*) provide less utility than points on U_1. Points above U_1 (such as *E*) provide more utility than U_1.

both goods. As in Figure 2.1, our definition of economic goods assures that combination E is preferred to combination C. Similarly, the assumption of transitivity assures that combination E is also preferred to combinations A, B, and D and to all other combinations on U_1.

Combinations of hamburgers and soft drinks that lie below U_1, on the other hand, are less desirable because they offer less satisfaction. Point F offers less of both goods than does point C. The fact that the indifference curve U_1 has a negative slope (that is, the curve runs from the upper-left portion of the figure to the lower-right portion) indicates that if a person gives up some hamburgers, he or she must receive additional soft drinks to remain equally well-off. This type of movement along U_1 represents those trades that a person might freely make. Knowledge of U_1 therefore eliminates the ambiguity associated with the questionable areas we showed in Figure 2.1.

Indifference Curves and the Marginal Rate of Substitution

What happens when a person moves from point A (six hamburgers and two soft drinks) to point B (four hamburgers and three soft drinks)? This person remains equally well-off because the two commodity bundles lie on the same indifference curve. He or she will voluntarily give up two of the hamburgers that were being consumed at point A in exchange for one additional soft drink. The slope of the curve U_1 between A and B is therefore approximately $-2/1 = -2$. That is, Y (hamburgers) declines two units in response to a one-unit increase in X (soft drinks). We call the absolute value of this slope the **marginal rate of substitution (MRS)**. Hence, we would say that the MRS (of soft drinks for hamburgers) between points A and B is 2: Given his or her current circumstances, this person is willing to give up two hamburgers in order to get one more soft drink. In making this trade, this person is substituting soft drinks *for* hamburgers in his or her consumption bundle. That is, by convention, we are looking at trades that involve more X and less Y.

Marginal rate of substitution (MRS)
The rate at which an individual is willing to reduce consumption of one good when he or she gets one more unit of another good. The absolute value of the slope of an indifference curve.

Diminishing Marginal Rate of Substitution

The MRS varies along the curve U_1. For points like A, this person has quite a few hamburgers and is relatively willing to trade them away for soft drinks. On the other hand, for combinations such as those represented by point D, this person has a lot of soft drinks and is reluctant to give up any more hamburgers to get more soft drinks. The increasing reluctance to trade away hamburgers reflects the notion that the consumption of any one good (here, soft drinks) can be pushed too far. This characteristic can be seen by considering the trades that take place in moving from point A to B, from point B to C, and from point C to D. In the first trade, two hamburgers are given up to get one more soft drink—the MRS is 2 (as we have already shown). The second trade involves giving up one hamburger to get one additional soft drink. In this trade, the MRS has declined to 1, reflecting an increased reluctance to give up hamburgers to get more soft drinks. Finally, for the third trade, from point C to D, this person is willing to give up a hamburger only if two soft drinks are received in return. In this final trade, the MRS is 1/2 (the individual is willing to give up one-half of a hamburger to get one more soft drink), which is a further decline from the MRS of the previous trades. Hence, the MRS steadily declines as soft drinks (shown on the X-axis) increase.

Balance in Consumption

MICRO QUIZ 2.2

The slope of an indifference curve is negative.

1. Explain why the slope of an indifference curve would not be expected to be positive for economic "goods."
2. Explain why the MRS (which is the absolute value of the slope of an indifference curve) cannot be calculated for point *E* in Figure 2.2 without additional information.

The conclusion of a diminishing MRS is based on the idea that people prefer balanced consumption bundles to unbalanced ones.[2] This assumption is illustrated precisely in Figure 2.3, where the indifference curve U_1 from Figure 2.2 is redrawn. Our discussion here concerns the two extreme consumption options *A* and *D*. In consuming *A*, this person gets six hamburgers and two soft drinks; the same satisfaction could be received by consuming *D* (two hamburgers and six soft drinks). Now consider a bundle of commodities (say, *G*) "between" these extremes. With *G* (four hamburgers and four soft drinks), this person obtains a higher level of satisfaction (point *G* is northeast of the indifference curve U_1) than with either of the extreme bundles *A* or *D*.

The reason for this increased satisfaction should be geometrically obvious. All of the points on the straight line joining *A* and *D* lie above U_1. Point *G* is one of these points (as the figure shows, there are many others). As long as the indifference curve obeys the assumption of a diminishing MRS, it will have the type of convex shape shown in Figure 2.3. Any consumption bundle that represents an "average" between two equally attractive extremes will be preferred to those extremes. The assumption of a diminishing MRS (or convex indifference curves) reflects the notion that people prefer variety in their consumption choices.

2-4 Indifference Curve Maps

Although Figures 2.2 and 2.3 each show only one indifference curve, the positive quadrant contains infinitely many such curves, each one corresponding to a different level of utility. Because every combination of hamburgers and soft drinks must yield some level of utility, every point must have one (and only one)[3] indifference curve passing through

[2]If we assume utility is measurable, we can provide an alternative analysis of a diminishing MRS. To do so, we introduce the concept of the marginal utility of a good *X* (denoted by MU_X). "Marginal utility" is defined as the extra utility obtained by consuming one more unit of good *X*. The concept is meaningful only if utility can be measured and so is not as useful as the MRS. If the individual is asked to give up some $Y(\Delta Y)$ to get some additional $X(\Delta X)$, the change in utility is given by

$$\text{Change in utility} = MU_Y \cdot \Delta Y + MU_X \cdot \Delta X. \qquad \{\text{i}\}$$

It is equal to the utility gained from the additional *X* less the utility lost from the reduction in *Y*. Since utility does not change along an indifference curve, we can use Equation i to derive

$$\frac{-\Delta Y}{\Delta X} = \frac{MU_X}{MU_Y}. \qquad \{\text{ii}\}$$

Along an indifference curve, the negative of its slope is given by MU_X/MU_Y. That is, by definition, the MRS. Hence we have

$$\text{MRS} = MU_X/MU_Y. \qquad \{\text{iii}\}$$

As a numerical illustration, suppose an extra hamburger yields two utils (units of utility; $MU_Y = 2$) and an extra soft drink yields four utils ($MU_X = 4$). Now MRS = 2 because the individual will be willing to trade away two hamburgers to get an additional soft drink. If we can assume that MU_X falls and MU_Y increases as *X* is substituted for *Y*, Equation iii shows that MRS will fall as we move counterclockwise along U_1.

[3]One point cannot appear on two separate indifference curves because it cannot yield two different levels of utility. Each point in a map can have only a single altitude.

Figure 2.3 Balance in Consumption Is Desirable

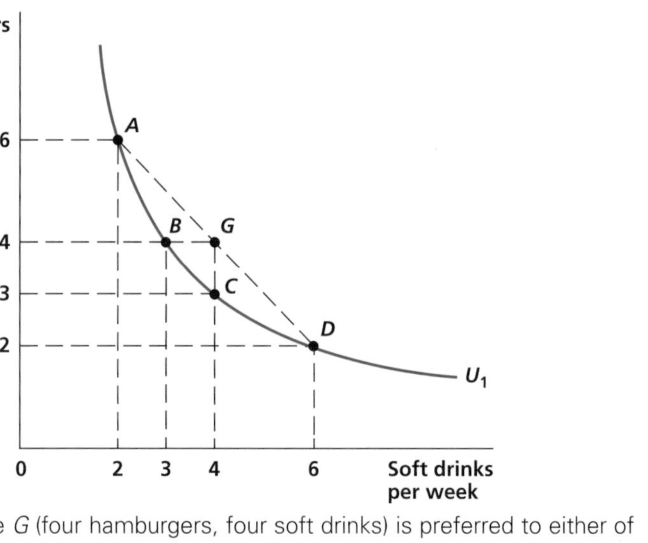

The consumption bundle *G* (four hamburgers, four soft drinks) is preferred to either of the extreme bundles *A* and *D*. This is a result of the assumption of a diminishing MRS. Because individuals become progressively less willing to give up hamburgers as they move in a southeasterly direction along U_1, the curve U_1 will have a convex shape. Consequently, all points on a straight line joining two points such as *A* and *D* will lie above U_1. Points such as *G* will be preferred to any of those on U_1.

Indifference curve map A contour map that shows the utility an individual obtains from all possible consumption options.

it. These curves are, as we said earlier, similar to the contour lines that appear on topographical maps, in that they each represent a different altitude of utility. In Figure 2.4, three indifference curves have been drawn and are labeled U_1, U_2, and U_3. These are only three of the infinite number of curves that characterize an individual's entire **indifference curve map**. Just as a map may have many contour lines (say, one for each inch of altitude), so too the gradations in utility may be very fine, as would be shown by very closely spaced indifference curves. For graphic convenience, our analysis generally shows only a few indifference curves that are relatively widely spaced.

The labeling of the indifference curves in Figure 2.4 has no special meaning except to indicate that utility increases as we move from combinations of good on U_1 to those on U_2 and then to those on U_3. As we have pointed out, there is no precise way to measure the level of utility associated with, say, U_2. Similarly, we have no way of measuring the amount of extra utility an individual receives from consuming bundles on U_3 instead of U_2. All we can say is that utility increases as this person moves to higher indifference curves. That is, he or she would prefer to be on a higher curve rather than on a lower one. This map tells us all there is to know about this person's preferences for these two goods. Although the utility concept may seem abstract, marketing experts have made practical use of these ideas, as Application 2.3: Product Positioning in Marketing shows.

2-5 Illustrating Particular Preferences

To illustrate some of the ways in which indifference curve maps might be used to reflect particular kinds of preferences, Figure 2.5 shows four special cases.

Figure 2.4 **Indifference Curve Map for Hamburgers and Soft Drinks**

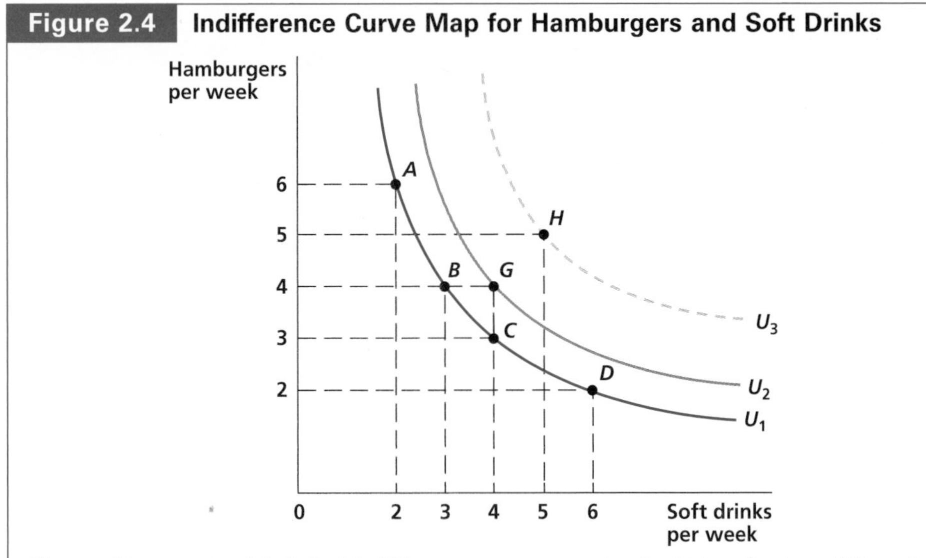

The positive quadrant is full of indifference curves, each of which reflects a different level of utility. Three such curves are illustrated. Combinations of goods on U_3 are preferred to those on U_2, which in turn are preferred to those on U_1. This is simply a reflection of the assumption that more of a good is preferred to less, as may be seen by comparing points *C*, *G*, and *H*.

A Useless Good

Figure 2.5(a) shows an individual's indifference curve map for food (on the horizontal axis) and smoke grinders (on the vertical axis). Because smoke grinders are completely useless, increasing purchases of them does not increase utility. Only by getting more food does this person enjoy a higher level of utility. The vertical indifference curve U_2, for example, shows that utility will be U_2 as long as this person has 10 units of food no matter how many smoke grinders he or she has.

An Economic Bad

The situation illustrated in Figure 2.5(a) implicitly assumes that useless goods cause no harm—having more useless smoke grinders causes no problem since one can always throw them away. In some cases, however, such free disposal is not possible, and additional units of a good can cause actual harm. For example, Figure 2.5(b) shows an indifference curve map for food and houseflies. Holding food consumption constant at 10, utility declines as the number of houseflies increases. Because additional houseflies reduce utility, an individual might even be willing to give up some food (and buy flypaper instead, for example) in exchange for fewer houseflies.

Perfect Substitutes

The illustrations of convex indifference curves in Figures 2.2 through 2.4 reflected the assumption that diversity in consumption is desirable. If, however, the two goods we were examining were essentially the same (or at least served identical functions), we could not make this argument. In Figure 2.5(c), for example, we show an individual's indifference curve map for Exxon and Chevron gasoline. Because this buyer is

APPLICATION 2.3

Product Positioning in Marketing

A practical application of utility theory is in the field of marketing. Firms that wish to develop a new product that will appeal to consumers must provide the good with attributes that successfully differentiate it from its competitors. A careful positioning of the good that takes account of both consumers' desires and the costs associated with product attributes can make the difference between a profitable and an unprofitable product introduction.

Graphic Analysis

Consider, for example, the case of breakfast cereals. Suppose only two attributes matter to consumers—taste and crunchiness (shown on the axes of Figure 1). Utility increases for movements in the northeast direction on this graph. Suppose that a new breakfast cereal has two competitors—Brand *X* and Brand *Y*. The marketing expert's problem is to position the new brand in such a way that it provides more utility to the consumer than does Brand *X* or Brand *Y*, while keeping the new cereal's production costs competitive. If marketing surveys suggest that the typical consumer's indifference curve resembles U_1, this can be accomplished by positioning the new brand at, say, point *Z*.

Introduction of the iPad

Apple's introduction of the iPad in 2010 (and the iPad2 in 2011) represents one of the most successful marketing efforts in history. Suppose that consumers of portable computing equipment value two characteristics: (1) portability and (2) comprehensiveness. Prior to the iPad's introduction, such consumers had two polar choices. They could choose large and relatively bulky laptop computers that provided comprehensive computer applications but were hard to lug around. Or consumers could choose smartphones that were easy to carry, but had small screens and offered a limited number of applications. The iPad fits neatly between these two options. It was relatively portable (especially since it could be connected to cell phone networks), it had a large screen, and, in short order, it offered thousands of nice applications. The tablet computer was an immediate success selling 300,000 units on its first day and over 50 million in the next two years. Clearly, the product was well positioned.

Figure 1 Product Positioning

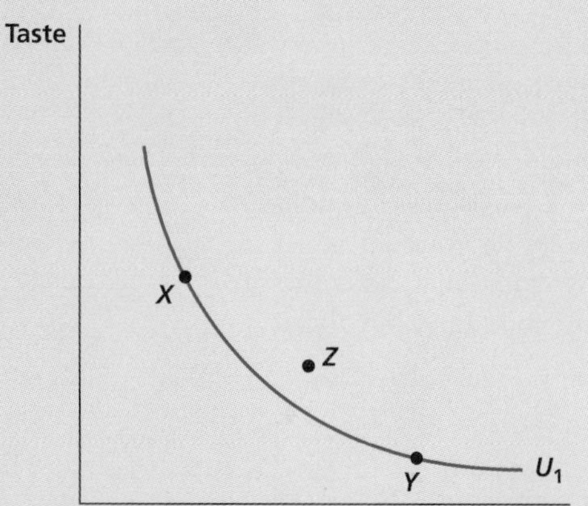

Market research indicates consumers are indifferent between the characteristics of cereals *X* and *Y*. Positioning a new brand at *Z* offers good market prospects.

Subway

With about 35,000 outlets worldwide, Subway (whose main product is, naturally enough, submarine sandwiches) is the largest restaurant chain in the world. The company's growth in the last 15 years has far eclipsed its older rivals, McDonalds and Burger King. This success is, in part, attributable to changing consumer valuation of the characteristics of fast-food franchises. Again, a two-characteristic illustration should suffice. When thinking about eating at a fast-food restaurant, suppose consumers value two characteristics: (1) speed of service and (2) quality of food. Although Subway usually cannot meet the speed of service promised by McDonalds, it has benefited significantly from a change in consumer attitudes toward quality. Specifically, Subway's "Eat Fresh" slogan together with its large assortment of vegetable toppings has led many consumers to believe it offers more healthy fare than the traditional burger emporium. By positioning itself between the major burger franchises and conventional sit-down restaurants, Subway has managed to provide utility-improving choices for many consumers.

TO THINK ABOUT

1. Our discussion of product positioning in this application paid no attention to the costs of providing various characteristics to consumers. Assuming that consumers will have to pay the costs associated with the various characteristics discussed, how would you develop a theory of which positioning choices will be successful?
2. Automobile manufacturers provide "options packages" to their buyers. Most offer relatively few specific packages, each of which offers a pre-defined set of added accessories. For example, an "interior package" may include leather seating, enhanced interior trim, special sound or video systems, and additional motor-controlled seats. Why do auto companies provide their options in packages rather than allowing consumers to choose whatever specific options each person wants?

Figure 2.5 Illustrations of Specific Preferences

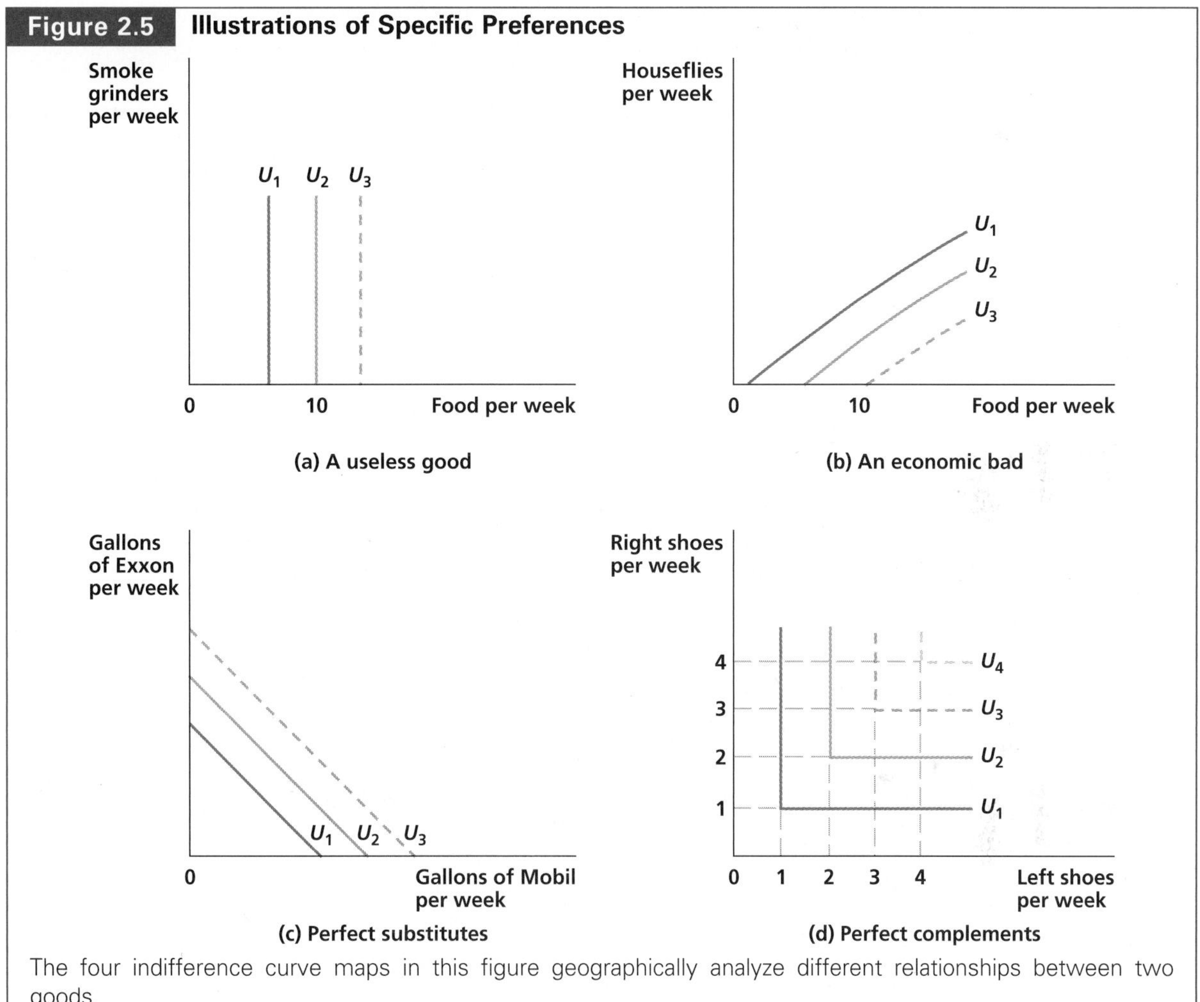

The four indifference curve maps in this figure geographically analyze different relationships between two goods.

unconvinced by television advertisements that stress various miracle ingredients, he or she has adopted the sensible proposition that all gallons of gasoline are pretty much the same. Hence, he or she is always willing to trade 1 gallon of Exxon for a gallon of Chevron—the MRS along any indifference curve is 1.0. The straight-line indifference curve map in Figure 2.5(c) reflects the perfect substitutability between these two goods.

Perfect Complements

In Figure 2.5(d), on the other hand, we illustrate a situation in which two goods go together. This person (quite naturally) prefers to consume left shoes (on the horizontal axis) and right shoes (on the vertical axis) in pairs. If, for example, he or she currently has three pairs of shoes, additional right shoes provide no more utility (compare this to the situation in panel a). Similarly, additional left shoes alone provide no additional utility. An extra pair of shoes, on the other hand, does increase utility (from U_3 to U_4)

because this person likes to consume these two goods together. Any situation in which two goods have such a strong complementary relationship to one another would be described by a similar map of L-shaped indifference curves.

Of course, these simple examples hint only at the variety in types of preferences that we can show with indifference curve maps. Later in this chapter, we encounter other, more realistic, examples that help explain observed economic behavior. Because indifference curve maps reflect people's basic preferences about the goods they might select, these graphs provide an important first building block for studying demand.

2-6 Utility Maximization: An Initial Survey

Economists assume that when a person is faced with a choice from among a number of possible options, he or she will choose the one that yields the highest utility—we call this assumption "utility maximization." As Adam Smith remarked more than two centuries ago, "We are not ready to suspect any person of being defective in selfishness."[4] In other words, economists assume that people know their own minds and make choices consistent with their preferences. This section surveys in general terms how such choices are made.

Choices Are Constrained

The most important feature of the utility maximization problem is that people are constrained in what they can buy by the size of their incomes. Of those combinations of goods that a person can afford, he or she will choose the one that is most preferred. This most preferred bundle of goods may not provide complete bliss; it may even leave this person in misery. It will, however, reflect the best (utility-maximizing) use of limited income. All other combinations of goods that can be bought with that limited income would leave him or her even worse off. It is the limitation of income that makes the consumer's choice an economic problem of allocating a scarce resource (the limited income) among alternative end uses.

An Intuitive Illustration

Consider the following problem: How should a person choose to allocate his or her spending among two goods (hamburgers and soft drinks) in order to obtain the highest level of utility possible? Answering this question provides fundamental insights into all of microeconomics. The basic result can easily be stated at the outset. In order to maximize utility given a fixed amount of income to spend on two goods, this person should spend the entire amount and choose a combination of goods for which the marginal rate of substitution between the two goods is equal to the ratio of those goods' market prices.

The reasoning behind the first part of this proposition is straightforward. Because we assume that more is better, a person should obviously spend the entire amount budgeted for the two items. The alternative here is throwing the money away, which is obviously less desirable than buying something. If the alternative was saving the money,

[4]Adam Smith, *The Theory of Moral Sentiments* (1759; reprint, New Rochelle, NY: Arlington House, 1969), 446.

we would have to consider savings and the decision to consume goods in the future. We will take up this more complex problem in Chapter 14.

The reasoning behind the second part of the proposition is more complicated. Suppose that a person is currently consuming some combination of hamburgers and soft drinks for which the MRS is equal to 1; he or she is willing to do without one hamburger in order to get an additional soft drink. Assume, on the other hand, that the price of hamburgers is \$3.00 and that of soft drinks is \$1.50. The ratio of their prices is $\$1.50/\$3.00 = 1/2$. This person is able to afford an extra soft drink by doing without only one-half of a hamburger. In this situation, the individual's MRS is not equal to the ratio of the goods' market prices, and we can show that there is some other combination of goods that provides more utility.

Suppose this person consumes one less hamburger. This frees \$3.00 in purchasing power. He or she can now buy one more soft drink (at a price of \$1.50) and is now as well-off as before, because the MRS was assumed to be 1. However, another \$1.50 remains unspent that can now be spent on either soft drinks or hamburgers (or some combination of the two). This additional consumption clearly makes this person better off than in the initial situation.

These numbers were purely arbitrary. Whenever a person selects a combination of goods for which the MRS (which shows trades this person is willing to make) differs from the price ratio (which shows trades that can be made in the market), a similar utility-improving change in spending patterns can be made. This reallocation will continue until the MRS is brought into line with the market-determined price ratio, at which time maximum utility is attained. We now present a more formal proof of this.

2-7 Showing Utility Maximization on a Graph

To show the process of utility maximization on a graph, we will begin by illustrating how to draw an individual's **budget constraint**. This constraint shows which combinations of goods are affordable. It is from among these combinations that a person can choose the bundle that provides the most utility.

Budget constraint
The limit that income places on the combinations of goods that an individual can buy.

The Budget Constraint

Figure 2.6 shows the combinations of two goods (which we will call simply X and Y) that a person with a fixed amount of money to spend can afford. If all available income is spent on good X, the number of units that can be purchased is recorded as X_{max} in the figure. If all available income is spent on Y, Y_{max} is the amount that can be bought. The line joining X_{max} and Y_{max} represents the various mixed bundles of goods X and Y that can be purchased using all the available funds. Combinations of goods in the shaded area below the budget line are also affordable, but these leave some portion of funds unspent, so these points will not be chosen.

The downward slope of the budget line shows that any person can afford to buy more X only if Y purchases are reduced. The precise slope of this relationship depends on the prices of the two goods. If Y is expensive and X is cheap, the line will be relatively flat because choosing to consume one less Y will permit the purchasing of many more units of X (an individual who decides not to purchase a new designer suit can instead choose to purchase many pairs of socks). Alternately, if Y is relatively cheap per unit and X is expensive, the budget line will be steep (doing without a doughnut will allow

Figure 2.6 Individual's Budget Constraint for Two Goods

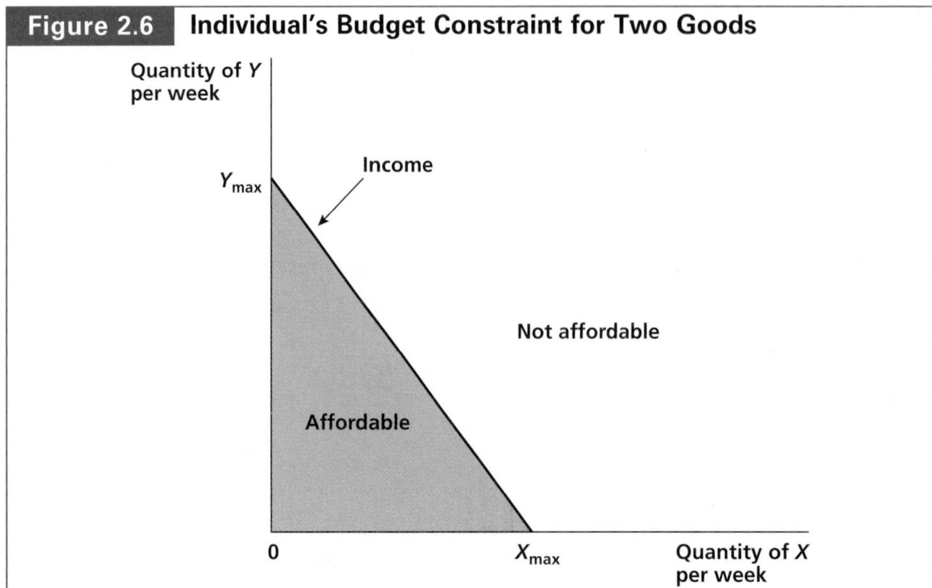

Those combinations of X and Y that the individual can afford are shown in the shaded triangle. If, as we usually assume, the individual prefers more than less of every good, the outer boundary of this triangle is the relevant constraint where all of the available funds are spent on either X or Y. The slope of this straight boundary is given by $-P_X/P_Y$.

you to buy only a small fraction of a gourmet meal). All of these relationships can be made more precise by using a bit of algebra.

Budget-Constraint Algebra

Suppose that a person has I dollars to spend on either good X or good Y. Suppose also that P_X represents the per-unit price of good X and P_Y the per-unit price of good Y. The total amount spent on X is given by the price of X times the amount purchased $(P_X \cdot X)$. Similarly, $(P_Y \cdot Y)$ represents total spending on good Y. Because the available income must be spent on either X or Y, we have

$$\text{Amount spent on } X + \text{Amount spent on } Y = I$$

or

$$P_X \cdot X + P_Y \cdot Y = I \tag{2.3}$$

Equation 2.3 is an algebraic statement of the budget line shown in Figure 2.6. To study the features of this constraint, we can solve this equation for Y so that the budget line has the standard form for a linear equation $(Y = a + bX)$. This solution gives

$$Y = -\left(\frac{P_X}{P_Y}\right)X + \frac{I}{P_Y} \tag{2.4}$$

Although Equations 2.3 and 2.4 say exactly the same thing, the relationship between Equation 2.4 and its graph is a bit easier to describe. First, notice that the Y-intercept of the budget constraint is given by I/P_Y. This shows that if $X = 0$, the maximum amount of Y that can be bought is determined by the income this person has and by the price of Y. For example, if $I = \$100$, and each unit of Y costs \$5, the maximum amount that can be bought is 20 $(= I/P_Y = \$100/\$5)$.

Now consider the slope of the budget constraint in Equation 2.4, which is $-P_X/P_Y$. This slope shows the opportunity cost (in terms of good Y) of buying one more unit of good X. The slope is negative because this opportunity cost is negative—because this person's choices are constrained by his or her available budget, buying more X means that less Y can be bought. The precise value of this opportunity cost depends on the prices of the goods. If $P_X = \$4$ and $P_Y = \$1$, the slope of the budget constraint is $-4\ (= -P_X/P_Y = -\$4/\$1)$—every additional unit of X bought requires that Y purchases be reduced by four units. With different prices, this opportunity cost would be different. For example, if $P_X = \$3$ and $P_Y = \$4$, the slope of the budget constraint is $-\$3/\$4 = -0.75$. That is, with these prices, the opportunity cost of one more unit of good X is now -0.75 units of good Y.

A Numerical Example

Suppose that a person has \$30 to spend on hamburgers (Y) and soft drinks (X) and suppose also that $P_Y = \$3$ and $P_X = \$1.50$. This person's budget constraint would then be

$$P_X X + P_Y Y = 1.5X + 3Y = I = 30 \tag{2.5}$$

Solving this equation for Y yields

$$3Y = 30 - 1.5X \quad \text{or} \quad Y = 10 - 0.5X. \tag{2.6}$$

Notice that this equation again shows that this person can buy a maximum of 10 hamburgers with his or her \$30 income because hamburger costs \$3. The equation also shows that the opportunity cost of buying one more soft drink is that hamburger purchases must be reduced by one-half.

KEEP *in* MIND

Memorizing Formulas Leads to Mistakes

When encountering algebra in economics for the first time, it is common for students to think that they have to memorize formulas. That can lead to disaster. For example, if you were to try to memorize that the slope of the budget constraint is $-P_X/P_Y$, there is a significant likelihood that you could confuse which good is good X and which good is Y. You will be much better off to remember to write the budget constraint in the form of Equation 2.5, and then solve for the quantity of one of the goods. As long as you remember to put the good you have solved for on the vertical (Y) axis, you will avoid much trouble.

Utility Maximization

A person can afford all bundles of X and Y that satisfy his or her budget constraint. From among these, he or she will choose the one that offers the greatest utility. The budget constraint can be used together with the individual's indifference curve map to show this utility maximization process. Figure 2.7 illustrates the procedure. This person would be irrational to choose a point such as A; he or she can get to a higher utility level (that is, higher than U_1) just by spending some of the unspent portion of his or her income. Similarly, by reallocating expenditures he or she can do better than point *B*. This is a case in which the MRS and the price ratio differ, and this person can move to a higher indifference curve (say, U_2) by choosing to consume less *Y* and more *X*. Point *D* is out of the question because income is not large enough to permit the purchase of that combination of goods. It is clear that the position of maximum utility will be at point *C* where the combination X^*, Y^* is chosen. This is the only point on indifference curve U_2 that can be bought with *I* dollars, and no higher utility level can be bought. *C* is the single point of tangency between the budget constraint and the indifference curve. Therefore, all funds are spent and

MICRO QUIZ 2.3

Suppose a person has $100 to spend on Frisbees and beach balls.

1. Graph this person's budget constraint if Frisbees cost $20 and beach balls cost $10.
2. How would your graph change if this person decided to spend $200 (rather than $100) on these two items?
3. How would your graph change if Frisbee and beach ball prices doubled to $40 and $20, respectively, with total spending of $200?

$$\text{Slope of budget constraint} = \text{Slope of indifference curve or (adjusting for the fact that both slopes are negative)} \tag{2.7}$$

$$P_X/P_Y = \text{MRS} \tag{2.8}$$

The intuitive example we started with is proved as a general result. For a utility maximum, the MRS should equal the ratio of the prices of the goods. The diagram shows that if this condition is not fulfilled, this person could be made better off by

Figure 2.7 Graphic Demonstration of Utility Maximization

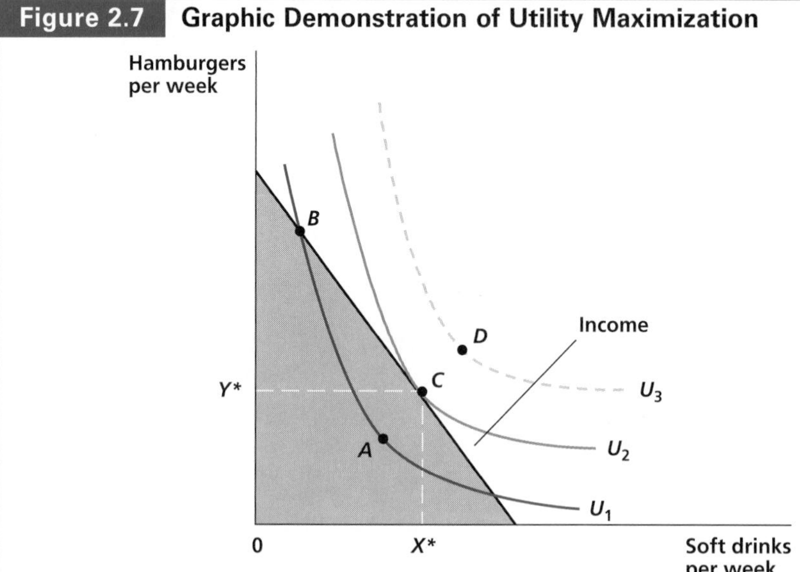

Point *C* represents the highest utility that can be reached by this individual, given the budget constraint. The combination *X**, *Y** is therefore the rational way for this person to use the available purchasing power. Only for this combination of goods will two conditions hold: All available funds will be spent, and the individual's psychic rate of trade-off (marginal rate of substitution) will be equal to the rate at which the goods can be traded in the market (P_X/P_Y).

reallocating expenditures.[5] You may wish to try several other combinations of X and Y that this person can afford to show that all of them provide a lower utility level than does combination C. That is why C is a point of tangency—it is the only affordable combination that allows this person to reach U_2. For a point of non-tangency (say B), a person can always get more utility because the budget constraint passes through the indifference curve (see U_1 in the figure). In Application 2.4: Ticket Scalping, we examine a case in which a shortage can lead to a situation in which this condition does not hold and therefore sets up the possibility of gains from additional trades.

2-8 Using the Model of Choice

This model of utility maximization can be used to explain a number of common observations. Figure 2.8, for example, provides an illustration of why people with the same income choose to spend this in different ways. In all three panels of Figure 2.8, the budget constraint facing each person is the same. However, Hungry Joe in panel a of the figure has a clear preference for hamburgers. He chooses to spend his \$30 almost exclusively on burgers. Thirsty Teresa, on the other hand, chooses to spend most of her \$30 on soft drinks. She does buy two hamburgers, however, because she feels some need for solid food. Extra-Thirsty Ed, whose situation is shown in panel c, wants a totally liquid diet. He gets the most utility from spending his entire \$30 on soft drinks. Even though he would, with more to spend, probably buy hamburgers, with his current limited income he is so thirsty that the opportunity cost of giving up a soft drink is just too high.

Figure 2.9 again shows the four special kinds of indifference curve maps that were introduced earlier in this chapter. Now we have superimposed a budget constraint on each one and indicated the utility-maximizing choice by E. Some obvious

MICRO QUIZ 2.4

Simple utility maximization requires MRS $= P_X/P_Y$.

1. Why does the price ratio P_X/P_Y show the rate at which any person can trade Y for X in "the market"? Illustrate this principle for the case of music CDs (which cost \$10 each) and movie DVDs (which cost \$17 each).
2. If an individual's current stock of CDs and DVDs yields him or her an MRS of 2 for 1 (that is, he or she is willing to trade two CDs for one DVD), how should consumption patterns be changed to increase utility?

[5]If we use the results of note 2 on the assumption that utility is measurable, Equation 2.6 can be given an alternative interpretation. Because

$$P_X/P_Y = \text{MRS} = MU_X/MU_Y \quad \{i\}$$

for a utility maximum, we have

$$\frac{MU_X}{P_X} = \frac{MU_Y}{P_Y}. \quad \{ii\}$$

The ratio of the extra utility from consuming one more unit of a good to its price should be the same for each good. Each good should provide the same extra utility per dollar spent. If that were not true, total utility could be raised by reallocating funds from a good that provided a relatively low level of marginal utility per dollar to one that provided a high level. For example, suppose that consuming an extra hamburger would yield 5 utils (units of utility), whereas an extra soft drink would yield 2 utils. Then each util costs \$.60 (= \$3.00 ÷ 5) if hamburgers are bought and \$.75 (= \$1.50 ÷ 2) if soft drinks are bought. Clearly hamburgers are a cheaper way to buy utility. So this person should buy more hamburgers and fewer soft drinks until each good becomes an equally costly way to get utility. Only when this happens will utility be as large as possible because it cannot be raised by further changes in spending.

APPLICATION 2.4

Ticket Scalping

Tickets to major concerts or sporting events are not usually auctioned off to the highest bidder. Instead, promoters tend to sell most tickets at "reasonable" prices and then ration the resulting excess demand either on a first-come-first-served basis or by limiting the number of tickets each buyer can purchase. Such rationing mechanisms create the possibility for further selling of tickets at much higher prices in the secondary market—that is, ticket "scalping."

A Graphical Interpretation

Figure 1 shows the motivation for ticket scalping for, say, Super Bowl tickets. With this consumer's income and the quoted price of tickets, he or she would prefer to purchase four tickets (point *A*). But the National Football League has decided to limit tickets to only one per customer. This limitation reduces the consumer's utility from U_2 (the utility he or she would enjoy with tickets freely available) to U_1. Notice that this choice of one ticket (point *B*) does not obey the tangency rule for a utility maximum—given the actual price of tickets, this person would prefer to buy more than one. In fact, this frustrated consumer would be willing to pay more than the prevailing price for additional Super Bowl tickets. He or she would not only be more than willing to buy a second ticket at the official price (since point *C* is above U_1) but also be willing to give up an additional amount of other goods (given by distance *CD*) to get this ticket. It appears that this person would be more than willing to pay quite a bit to a "scalper" for the second ticket. For example, tickets for major events at the 1996 Atlanta Olympics often sold for five times their face prices, and resold tickets for the 2012 Super Bowl went for nearly $4,000 each to die-hard Giants and Patriots fans.

Figure 1 Rationing of Tickets Leads to Scalping

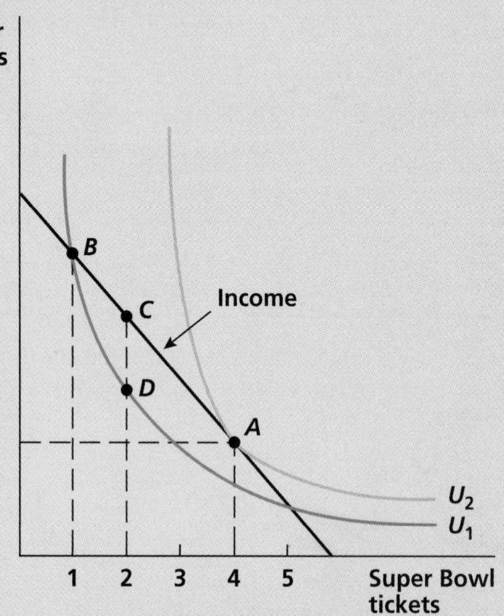

Given this consumer's income and the price of tickets, he or she would prefer to buy four. With only one available, utility falls to U_1. This person would pay up to distance *CD* in other goods for the right to buy a second ticket at the original price.

Antiscalping Laws

Most economists hold a relatively benign view of ticket scalping. They look at the activity as being a voluntary transaction between a willing buyer and a willing seller. State and local governments often seem to see things differently, however. Many have passed laws that seek either to regulate the prices of resold tickets or to outlaw ticket selling in locations near the events. The generally cited reason for such laws is that scalping is "unfair"—perhaps because the scalper makes profits that are "not deserved." This value judgment seems excessively harsh, however. Ticket scalpers provide a valuable service by enabling transactions between those who place a low value on their tickets and those who would value them more highly. The ability to make such transactions can itself be valuable to people whose situations change. Forbidding these transactions may result in wasted resources if some seats remain unfilled. The primary gainer from antiscalping laws may be ticket agencies that can gain a monopoly-like position as the sole source of sought-after tickets.

POLICY CHALLENGE

Antiscalping laws are just one example of a wide variety of laws that prevent individuals from undertaking voluntary transactions. Other examples include banning the sale of certain drugs, making it illegal to sell one's vote in an election, or forbidding the selling of human organs. One reason often given for precluding certain voluntary transactions is that such transactions may harm third parties. Is that a good reason for banning such transactions? Does the possibility for harmful third-party effects seem to explain the various examples mentioned here? If not, why are such transactions banned?

Figure 2.8 Differences in Preferences Result in Differing Choices

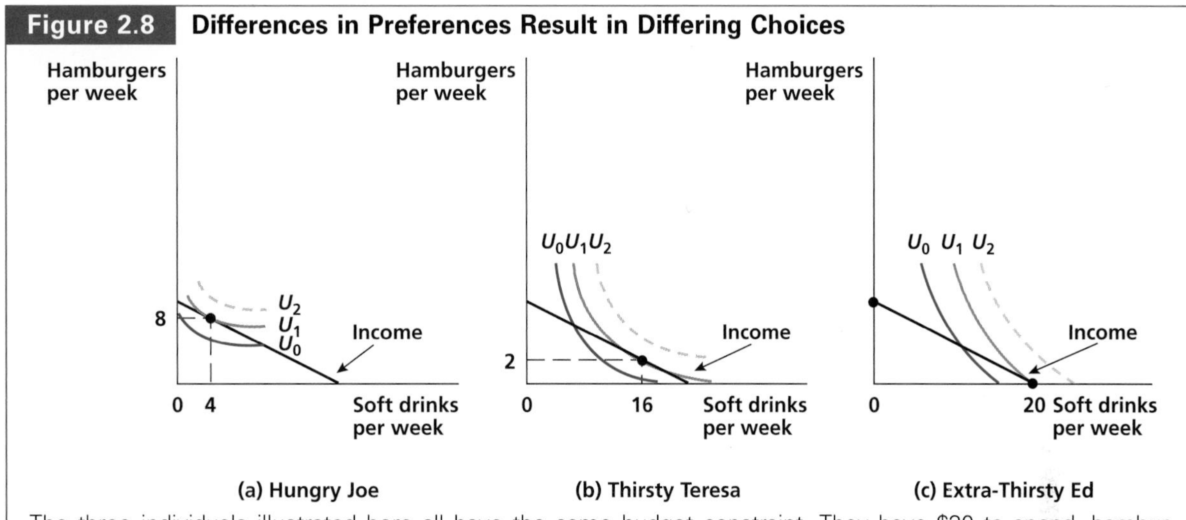

The three individuals illustrated here all have the same budget constraint. They have \$30 to spend, hamburgers cost \$3, and soft drinks cost \$1.50. These people choose very different consumption bundles because they have differing preferences for the two goods.

implications can be drawn from these illustrations. Panel a makes clear that a utility-maximizing individual will never buy a useless good. Utility is as large as possible by consuming only food. There is no reason for this person to incur the opportunity cost involved in consuming any smoke grinders. A similar result holds for panel b—there is no reason for this person to spend anything on houseflies (assuming there is a store that sells them).

In panel c, the individual buys only Exxon, even though Exxon and Chevron are perfect substitutes. The relatively steep budget constraint in the figure shows that Chevron is the more expensive of the two brands, so this person opts to buy only Exxon. Because the goods are identical, the utility-maximizing decision is to buy only the less expensive brand. People who buy only generic versions of prescription drugs or who buy all their brand-name household staples at a discount supermarket are exhibiting a similar type of behavior.

Finally, the utility-maximizing situation illustrated in Figure 2.9(d) shows that this person will buy shoes only in pairs. Any departure from this pattern would result in buying extra left or right shoes, which alone provide no utility. In similar circumstances involving complementary goods, people also tend to purchase those goods together. Other items of apparel (gloves, earrings, socks, and so forth) are also bought mainly in pairs. Most people have preferred ways of concocting the beverages they drink (coffee and cream, gin and vermouth) or making sandwiches (peanut butter and jelly, ham and cheese); and people seldom buy automobiles, stereos, or washing machines by the part. Rather, they consume these complex goods as fixed packages made up of their various components.

MICRO QUIZ 2.5

Figures 2.8 and 2.9 show that the condition for utility maximization should be amended sometimes to deal with special situations.

1. Explain how the condition should be changed for "boundary" issues such as those shown in Figures 2.8(c) and 2.9(c), where people buy zero amounts of some goods. Use this to explain why your authors never buy any lima beans.
2. How do you interpret the utility-maximizing conditions when goods are perfect complements, such as those shown in Figure 2.9(d)? If left and right shoes were sold separately, would any price ratio make you depart from buying pairs?

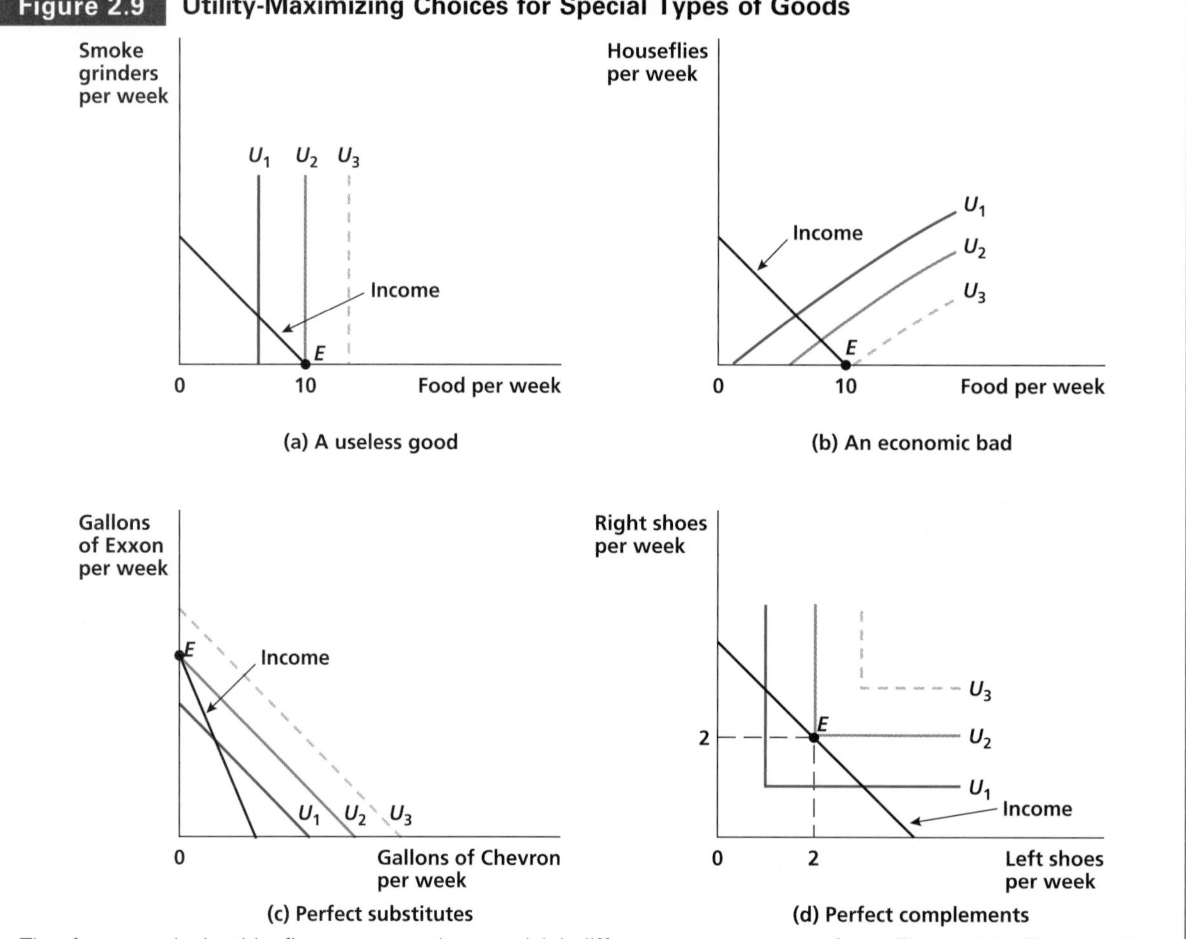

Figure 2.9 Utility-Maximizing Choices for Special Types of Goods

The four panels in this figure repeat the special indifference curve maps from Figure 2.5. The resulting utility-maximizing positions (denoted by *E* in each panel) reflect the specific relationships among the goods pictured.

Overall then, the utility-maximizing model of choice provides a very flexible way of explaining why people make the choices that they do. Because people are faced with budget constraints, they must be careful to allocate their incomes so that they provide as much satisfaction as possible. Of course, they will not explicitly engage in the kinds of graphic analyses shown in the figures for this chapter. But this model seems to be a good way of making precise the notion that people "do the best with what they've got." We look at how this model can be used to illustrate a famous court case in Application 2.5: What's a Rich Uncle's Promise Worth?

A Few Numerical Examples

Graphs can be helpful in conceptualizing the utility maximization process, but to solve problems, you will sometimes need to use algebra. This section provides a few ideas on how to solve such problems.

APPLICATION 2.5

What's a Rich Uncle's Promise Worth?

One of the strangest legal cases of the nineteenth century was the New York case of *Hamer v. Sidway*, in which nephew Willie sued his uncle for failing to carry through on the promise to pay him $5,000 if he did not smoke, drink, or gamble until he reached the age of 21. No one in the case disagreed that the uncle had made this deal with Willie when he was about 15 years old. The legal issue was whether the uncle's promise was a clear "contract," enforceable in court. An examination of this peculiar case provides an instructive illustration of how economic principles can help clarify legal issues.

Graphing the Uncle's Offer

Figure 1 shows Willie's choice between "sin" (that is, smoking, drinking, and gambling) on the *X*-axis and his spending on everything else on the *Y*-axis. Left to his own devices, Willie would prefer to consume point *A*—which involves some sin along with other things. This would provide him with utility of U_2. Willie's uncle is offering him point *B*—an extra $5,000 worth of other things on the condition that sin = 0. In this graph, it is clear that the offer provides more utility (U_3) than point *A*, so Willie should take the offer and spend his teenage years sin-free.

Figure 1 Willie's Utility and His Uncle's Promises

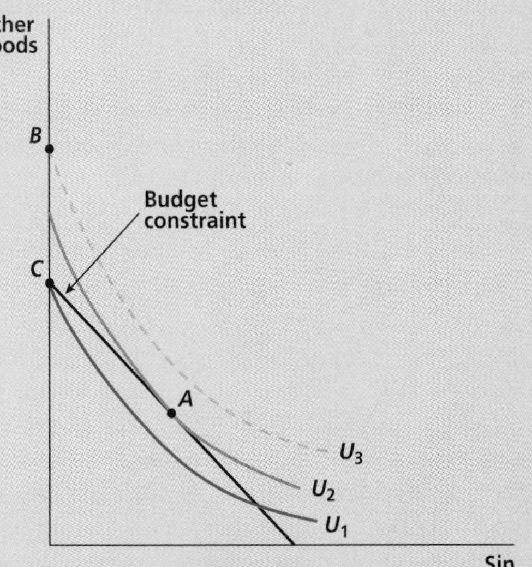

Left to his own devices, Willie consumes point *A* and gets utility U_2. His uncle's offer would increase utility to U_3. But, when his uncle reneges, Willie gets U_1 (point *C*).

When the Uncle Reneges

When Willie came to collect the $5,000 for his abstinence, his uncle assured him that he would place the funds in a bank account that Willie would get once he was "capable of using it wisely." But the uncle died and left no provision for payment in his will. So Willie ended up with no money. The consequences of being stiffed for the $5,000 can be shown in Figure 1 by point *C*—this is the utility Willie would get by spending all his income on non-sin items.

Willie Goes to Court

Not willing to take his misfortune lying down, Willie took his uncle's estate to court, claiming, in effect, that he had made a contract with his uncle and deserved to be paid. The primary legal question in the case concerned the issue of "consideration" in the purported contract between Willie and his uncle. In contract law the promise of party A to do something for party B is enforceable only if there is evidence that an actual bargain was reached. One sign that such an agreement has been reached is the payment of some form of consideration from B to A that seals the deal. Although there was no explicit payment from Willie to his uncle in this case, the court ultimately ruled that Willie's six years of abstinence itself played that role here. Apparently the uncle derived pleasure from seeing a "sin-free" Willie so this was regarded as sufficient consideration in this case. After much wrangling, Willie finally got paid.

TO THINK ABOUT

1. Suppose that the uncle's heirs had offered to settle by making Willie as well-off as he would have been by acting sinfully in his teenage years. In Figure 1, how could you show the amount they would have to pay?
2. Would the requirement that the uncle make Willie "whole" by paying the amount suggested in question 1 provide the right incentives for the uncle to stick to the original deal? (This is an example of how the choice of "damage rules" may affect the willingness of contracting parties to complete the deal.)

Perfect Substitutes Problems involving perfect substitutes are the easiest to solve—all you have to do is figure out which good is least expensive given the utility provided. When the goods are identical (Exxon and Chevron), this is easy—the consumer will choose to spend all of his or her budget on the good with the lowest price.[6] If Exxon costs $3 per gallon, and Chevron is $3.25, he or she will buy only Exxon. If the gasoline budget is $30, 10 gallons will be bought.

When goods are perfect substitutes, but not identical, the story is a bit more complicated. Suppose a person regards apple juice (A) and grape juice (G) as perfect substitutes for his or her thirst, but each ounce of apple juice provides four units of utility, whereas each ounce of grape juice provides three units of utility. In this case, the person's utility function would be

$$U(A, G) = 4A + 3G \tag{2.9}$$

The fact that this utility function is linear means that its indifference curves will be straight lines as in Figure 2.9(c). If the price of apple juice is 6 cents per ounce, and the price of grape juice is 5 cents per ounce, it might at first seem that this person will buy only grape juice. But that conclusion disregards the difference in utility provided by the drinks. To decide which drink is really least expensive, suppose this person has 30 cents to spend. If he or she spends it all on apple juice, 5 ounces can be bought, and Equation 2.9 shows that these will yield a utility of 20. If the person spends the 30 cents all on grape juice, 6 ounces can be bought, and utility will be 18. So, apple juice is actually the better buy after utility differences are taken into account.[7]

Perfect Complements Problems involving perfect complements are also easy to solve so long as you keep in mind that the good must be purchased in a fixed ratio to one another. If left shoes and right shoes cost $10 each, a pair will cost $20, and a person will spend all of his or her shoe budget on pairs. With $60 to spend, three pairs will be bought.

When the complementary relationship is not one to one, the calculations are slightly more complicated. Suppose a person always buys two bags of popcorn at $2.50 each at the movie theater. If the theater ticket itself costs $10, the combination "movie + popcorn" costs $15. With a monthly movie budget of $30, this person will attend two movies each month.

Let's look at the algebra of the movie situation. First, we need a way to phrase the utility function for movies (M) and popcorn (C). The way to do this is with the function

$$U(M, C) = \min(2M, C) \tag{2.10}$$

where "min" means that utility is given by the smaller of the two terms in parentheses. If, for example, this person attends a movie but buys no popcorn, utility is zero. If he or she attends a movie and buys three bags of popcorn, utility is 2—the extra bag of popcorn does not raise utility. To avoid such useless spending, this person should only consume bundles for which $C = 2M$—that is, two bags of popcorn for each movie. To find

[6] If the goods cost the same, the consumer is indifferent as to which is bought. He or she might as well flip a coin.

[7] Another way to see this uses footnote 5. Here, $MU_A = 4$, $MU_G = 3$, $P_A = 6$, $P_G = 5$. Hence, $MU_A/P_A = 4/6 = 2/3$, $MU_G/P_G = 3/5$. Since $2/3 > 3/5$, apple juice provides more utility per dollar spent than does grape juice.

out how much will actually be bought, you can now substitute this into this person's budget constraint:

$$30 = 10M + 2.5C \text{ or } 10M + 5M = 15M = 30 \text{ so } M = 2, C = 4 \qquad \textbf{(2.11)}$$

Notice that this solution assures utility maximization because we have first imposed the fixed relationship between the two goods. That allows us to treat movies and popcorn as a single item in the budget constraint, so finding the solution is easy.

A Middle-Ground Case Most pairs of goods are neither perfect substitutes nor perfect complements. Rather, the relationship between them allows some substitutability but not the sort of all-or-nothing behavior shown in the Exxon-Chevron example. One of the challenges for economists is to figure out ways of writing utility functions to cover these situations. Although this can become a very mathematical topic, here we can describe one simple middle-ground case. Suppose that a person consumes only X and Y and utility is given by the function we examined in the Appendix to Chapter 1:

$$U(X, Y) = \sqrt{X \cdot Y} \qquad \textbf{(2.12)}$$

We know from our previous discussion that this function has reasonably shaped indifference curves, so it may be a good example to study. To show utility maximization with this function, we need first to figure out how the MRS exhibited by an indifference curve depends on the quantities of each good consumed. Unfortunately, for most functions, figuring out the slope of an indifference curve requires calculus. So, often you will be given the MRS. In this case, the MRS is given by[8]

$$\text{MRS}(X, Y) = Y/X \qquad \textbf{(2.13)}$$

Utility maximization requires that Equation 2.8 hold. Let's again assume that Y (hamburgers) costs \$3 and X (soft drinks) costs \$1.50. The utility maximization requires that

$$\text{MRS}(X, Y) = Y/X = P_X/P_Y = \$1.50/\$3 = 0.5 \text{ so } Y = 0.5X \qquad \textbf{(2.14)}$$

To get the final quantities bought, we need to introduce the budget constraint, so let's again assume that this person has \$30 to spend on fast food. Substituting the utility-maximizing condition in Equation 2.13 into the budget constraint (Equation 2.5) yields

$$30 = 1.5X + 3Y = 1.5X + 3(0.5X) = 3X \text{ so } X = 10,\ Y = 5 \qquad \textbf{(2.15)}$$

One feature of this solution is that this person spends precisely half his or her budget (\$15) on X and half on Y. This will be true no matter what income is and no matter what the prices of the two goods are. Consequently, this utility function is a very special case and may not explain consumption patterns in the real world. The function (which, as we pointed out before, is called a "Cobb-Douglas" function) can be generalized a bit, as we show in Problem 2.10, but for most actual studies of consumer behavior, much more complicated functions are used.

[8]This can be derived by noting that marginal utilities are just the (partial) derivatives of this function. Hence, $MU_X = \partial U/\partial X = 0.5\sqrt{Y/X}$ and $MU_Y = \partial U/\partial Y = 0.5\sqrt{X/Y}$. So, $\text{MRS}(X, Y) = MU_X/MU_Y = Y/X$.

KEEP *in* MIND

You Must Use Both Utility Maximization and the Budget Constraint to Solve Problems

In all of these numerical examples, we described the relationship between goods and their prices that utility maximization requires and then incorporated that relationship into the individual's budget constraint to get final consumption amounts. Most problems in utility maximization must be solved in this way. Referring only to the utility function or only to the budge constraint will never yield a real solution because an important part of the consumer's problem will be missing. So, you should always check that you have ensured that your answers both imply utility maximization and satisfy the budget constraint.

2-9 Generalizations

The basic model of choice that we have been examining can be generalized in several ways. Here we look briefly at three of these.

Many Goods

Of course people buy more than two goods. Even if we were to focus on very large categories such as food, clothing, housing, or transportation, it is clear that we would need a theory that includes more than two items. Once we looked deeper into the types of food that people might buy or how they might spend their housing dollars, the situation would become very complex indeed. But the basic findings of this chapter would not really be changed in any major way. People who are seeking to make the best of their situations would still be expected to spend all of their incomes (because the only alternative is to throw it away—saving is addressed in Chapter 14). The logic of choosing combinations of goods for which the MRS is equal to the price ratio remains true too. Our intuitive proof showed that any choice for which the slope of the indifference curve differs from the slope of the budget constraint offers the possibility for improvement. This proof would not be affected by situations in which there are more than two goods. Hence, although the formal analysis of the many-good case is indeed more complicated,[9] there is not much more to learn from what has already been covered in this chapter.

Complicated Budget Constraints

The budget constraints discussed in this chapter all had a very simple form—they could all be represented by straight lines. The reason for this is that we assumed that the price a person pays for a good is not affected by how much of that good he or she buys. We assumed there were no special deals for someone who purchased many hamburgers or who opted for "super" sizes of soft drinks. In many cases, people do not face such simple budget constraints. Instead, they face a variety of inducements to buy larger quantities or complex bundling arrangements that give special deals only if other items are also bought. For example, the pricing of cable television offerings has

[9]For a mathematical treatment, see W. Nicholson and C. Snyder, *Microeconomic Theory: Basic Principles and Extensions*, 11th ed. (Mason, OH: Cengage, 2012), Chapter 4.

become very complicated. What you pay will depend of which channel packages you choose, whether you get high-speed Internet service or not, and whether the cable company also provides you with telephone service. Describing precisely the budget constraint faced by a consumer in such situations can sometimes be quite difficult. But a careful analysis of the properties of such complicated budget constraints and how they relate to the utility-maximizing model can be revealing in showing why people behave in the ways they do. Application 2.6: Loyalty Programs provides some illustrations.

Composite Goods

Another important way in which the simple two-good model in this chapter can be generalized is through the use of a **composite good**. Such a good is constructed by combining spending on many individual items into one aggregated whole. One way such a good is used is to study the way people allocate their spending among such major items as food and housing. For example, in the next chapter, we show that the fraction of income spent on food tends to fall as people get richer, whereas spending on housing is, more or less, a constant fraction of income. Of course, these spending patterns are in reality made up of individual decisions about what kind of breakfast cereal to buy or whether to paint your house; but adding many things together can often help illuminate important questions.

Composite good Combining expenditures on several different goods whose relative prices do not change into a single good for convenience in analysis.

Probably the most common use of the composite good idea is in situations where we wish to study decisions to buy one specific item such as airline tickets or gasoline. In this case, a common procedure is to show the specific item of interest on the horizontal (X) axis and spending on "everything else" on the vertical (Y) axis. This is the procedure we used in the applications in this chapter, and we use it many other times later in this book. Taking advantage of the composite good idea can greatly simplify many problems.

There are some technical issues that arise in using composite goods, though those do not detain us very long in this book. A first problem is how we are to measure a composite good. In our seemingly endless hamburger–soft drink examples, the units of measurement were obvious. But the only way to add up all of the individual items that constitute "everything else" is to do so in dollars (or some other currency). Looking at dollars of spending on everything else will indeed prove to be a very useful graphical device. But one might have some lingering concerns that, because such adding up requires us to use the prices of individual items, we might get into some trouble when prices change. This then leads to a second problem with composite goods—what is the "price" of such a good. In most cases, there is no need to answer this question because we assume that the price of the composite good (good Y) does not change during our analysis. But, if we did wish to study changes in the price of a composite good, we would obviously have to define that price first.

In our treatment we will not be much concerned with these technical problems associated with composite goods. If you are interested in the ways that some of the problems are solved, you may wish to do some reading on your own.[10]

[10] For an introduction, see W. Nicholson and C. Snyder, *Microeconomic Theory: Basic Principles and Extensions,* 11th ed. (Mason, OH: Cengage, 2012), Chapter 6.

APPLICATION 2.6

Loyalty Programs

These days, everyone's wallet is bulging with affinity cards. A quick check reveals that your authors regularly carry cards for Ace Hardware, Best Buy, Blockbuster, Costco, Delta Airlines, and Dick's Sporting Goods—and that is only the first four letters of the alphabet. These cards usually promise some sort of discount when you buy a lot of stuff. Why do firms push them?

Quantity Discounts and the Budget Constraint

The case of a quantity discount is illustrated in Figure 1. Here consumers who buy less than X_D pay full price and face the usual budget constraint. Purchases in excess of X_D entitle the buyer to a lower price (on the extra units), and this results in a flatter budget constraint beyond that point. The constraint, therefore, has a "kink" at X_D. Effects of this kink on consumer choices are suggested by the indifference curve U_1, which is tangent to the budget constraint at both point *A* and point *B*. This person is indifferent between consuming relatively little of *X* or a lot of it. A slightly larger quantity discount could tempt this consumer definitely to choose the larger amount. Notice that such a choice entails not only consuming low-price units of the good but also buying more of it at full price (up to X_D) in order to get the discount.[1]

Figure 1 Kinked Budget Constraint Resulting from a Quantity Discount

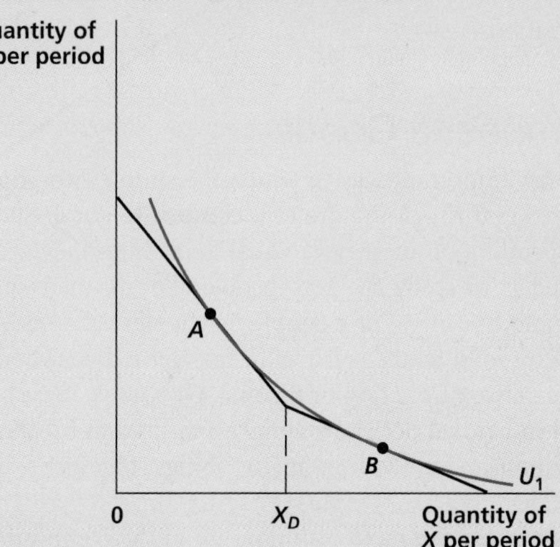

A quantity discount for purchases greater than X_D results in a kinked budget constraint. This consumer is indifferent between consuming relatively little *X* (point *A*) or a lot of *X* (point *B*).

Frequent-Flier Programs

All major airlines sponsor frequent-flier programs. These entitle customers to accumulate mileage with the airline at reduced fares. Because unused-seat revenues are lost forever, the airlines utilize these programs to tempt consumers to travel more on their airlines. Any additional full-fare travel that the programs may generate provides extra profits for the airline. One interesting side issue related to frequent-flier programs concerns business travel. When travelers have their fares reimbursed by their employers, they may have extra incentives to chalk up frequent-flier miles. In such a case airlines may be especially eager to lure business travelers (who usually pay higher fares) with special offers such as business class service or airport-based clubs. Because a traveler pays the same zero-price no matter which airline is chosen, these extras may have a big influence on actual choices made. Of course travel departments of major companies recognize this and may adopt policies that seek to limit travelers' choices.

Other Loyalty Programs

Most other loyalty programs work in the same way—credits accrued from prior purchases allow you to earn discounts on future ones. The effects of the programs on the sales of retailers may not be as significant as in the case of airlines, however, because many times customers may not understand how the discounts actually work. Retailers may also impose restrictions on discounts (that is, they may expire after a year), so their actual value is more apparent that real. Whether such programs really do breed consumer loyalty is much debated by marketing executives.

TO THINK ABOUT

1. How do the details of loyalty programs affect consumer purchasing decisions? What kinds of constraints do the programs you participate in impose? How do they affect your buying behavior?
2. Suppose frequent-flier coupons were transferable among people. How would this affect Figure 1 and, more generally, the overall viability of the program?

[1]For a more complete discussion of the kinds of pricing schemes that can be shown on a simple utility maximization graph, see J. S. DeSalvo and M. Huq, "Introducing Nonlinear Pricing into Consumer Theory," *Journal of Economic Education* (Spring 2002): 166–179.

SUMMARY

This chapter covers a lot of ground. We have seen how economists explain the kinds of choices people make and the ways in which those choices are constrained by economic circumstances. The chapter has been rather tough going in places. The theory of choice is one of the most difficult parts of any study of microeconomics, and it is unfortunate that it usually comes at the very start of the course. But that placement clearly shows why the topic is so important. Practically every model of economic behavior starts with the tools introduced in this chapter.

The principal conclusions in this chapter are as follows:

- Economists use the term "utility" to refer to the satisfaction that people derive from their economic activities. Usually only a few of the things that affect utility are examined in any particular analysis. All other factors are assumed to be held constant, so that a person's choices can be studied in a simplified setting.
- Utility can be shown by an indifference curve map. Each indifference curve identifies those bundles of goods that a person considers to be equally attractive. Higher levels of utility are represented by higher indifference curve "contour" lines.
- The slope of indifference curves shows how a person is willing to trade one good for another while remaining equally well-off. The absolute value of this slope is called the "marginal rate of substitution" (MRS), because it shows the degree to which an individual is willing to substitute one good for another in his or her consumption choices. The value of this trade-off depends on the amount of the two goods being consumed.
- People are limited in what they can buy by their "budget constraints." When a person is choosing between two goods, his or her budget constraint is usually a straight line because prices do not depend on how much is bought. The absolute value of the slope of this line represents the price ratio of the two goods—it shows what one of the goods is worth in terms of the other in the marketplace.
- If people are to obtain the maximum possible utility from their limited incomes, they should spend all the available funds and should choose a bundle of goods for which the MRS is equal to the price ratio of the two goods. Such a utility maximum is shown graphically by a tangency between the budget constraint and the highest indifference curve that this person's income can buy.

REVIEW QUESTIONS

1. The notion of utility is an "ordinal" one for which it is assumed that people can rank combinations of goods as to their desirability, but that they cannot assign a unique numerical (cardinal) scale for the goods that quantifies "how much" one combination is preferred to another. For each of the following ranking systems, describe whether an ordinal or a cardinal ranking is being used: (a) military or academic ranks; (b) prices of vintage wines; (c) rankings of vintage wines by the French Wine Society; (d) press rankings of the "Top Ten" football teams; (e) results of the U.S. Open Golf Championships (in which players are ranked by the number of strokes they take); (f) results of the NCAA basketball tournament (which is conducted using a draw that matches teams against one another until a final winner is found).

2. How might you draw an indifference curve map that illustrates the following ideas?
   a. Margarine is just as good as the high-priced spread.
   b. Things go better with Coke.
   c. A day without wine is like a day without sunshine.
   d. Popcorn is addictive—the more you eat, the more you want.
   e. It takes two to tango.

3. Inez reports that an extra banana would increase her utility by two units and an extra pear would increase her utility by six units. What is her MRS of bananas for pears—that is, how many bananas would she voluntarily give up to get an extra pear? Would Philip (who reports that an extra banana yields 100 units of utility, whereas an extra pear yields 400 units of utility) be willing to trade a pear to Inez at her voluntary MRS?

4. Oscar consumes two goods, wine and cheese. His weekly income is $500.
   a. Describe Oscar's budget constraints under the following conditions:
      i. Wine costs $10/bottle, cheese costs $5/pound;
      ii. Wine costs $10/bottle, cheese costs $10/pound;
      iii. Wine costs $20/bottle, cheese costs $10/pound;
      iv. Wine costs $20/bottle, cheese costs $10/pound, but Oscar's income increases to $1,000/week.
   b. Describe why budget constraints ii and iii will probably provide less utility than does budget constraint i. Are there any situations where this would not be the case?

c. Describe why budget constraint iv provides precisely the same options to Oscar as does budget constraint i. What income (in euros, €) would Oscar need if he is to afford these same options if wine costs €15 per bottle and cheese costs €7.50 per pound? How about a situation in England where wine costs £4 per bottle and cheese costs £2 per pound? What general conclusions can you draw by comparing all the budget constraints mentioned in this part?

5. While standing in line to buy popcorn at your favorite theater, you hear someone behind you say, "This popcorn isn't worth its price—I'm not buying any." How would you graph this person's situation?

6. A careful reader of this book will have read footnotes 2 and 5 in this chapter. Explain why these can be summarized by the commonsense idea that a person is maximizing his or her utility only if getting an extra dollar to spend would provide the same amount of extra utility no matter which good he or she chooses to spend it on. (Hint: Suppose this condition were not true—is utility as large as possible?)

7. Most states require that you purchase automobile insurance when you buy a car. Use an indifference curve diagram to show that this mandate reduces utility for some people. What kinds of people are most likely to have their utility reduced by such a law? Why do you think that the government requires such insurance?

8. As we showed in this chapter, utility maximization requires that a person equate the marginal rate of substitution (MRS) to the ratio of the goods' prices (P_X/P_Y). When asked to explain the reasoning behind this condition, students gave the following answers:

   Student A: Because the MRS shows the ratio of good Y to good X that this person wishes to consume, he or she must equate this ratio to the price ratio because the price ratio shows how much Y he or she can buy if one less X is bought.

   Student B: Because the MRS shows how this person is willing to trade good X for good Y he should choose prices that also reflect this ratio.

   Student C: Because the MRS shows how this person is willing to trade good X for good Y, he or she must adjust purchases so that this ratio is equal to the ratio of the goods' prices.

   Which of these students is stating the result correctly? What errors are the other two making?

9. Suppose that an electric company charges consumers \$.10 per kilowatt hour for electricity for the first 1,000 kilowatt hours used in a month but \$.15 for each extra kilowatt hour after that. Draw the budget constraint for a consumer facing this price schedule, and discuss why many individuals may choose to consume exactly 1,000 kilowatt hours.

10. Suppose an individual consumes three items: steak, lettuce, and tomatoes. If we were interested only in examining this person's steak purchases, we might group lettuce and tomatoes into a single composite good called "salad." Suppose also that this person always makes salad by combining two units of lettuce with one unit of tomato.
    a. How would you define a unit of salad to show (along with steak) on a two-good graph?
    b. How does the price of salad (P_S) relate to the price of lettuce (P_L) and the price of tomatoes (P_T)?
    c. What is this person's budget constraint for steak and salad?
    d. Would a doubling of the price of steak, the price of lettuce, the price of tomatoes, and this person's income shift the budget constraint described in part c?
    e. Suppose instead that the way in which this person made salad depended on the relative prices of lettuce and tomatoes. Now could you express this person's choice problem as involving only two goods? Explain.

PROBLEMS

2.1. Suppose a person has \$8.00 to spend only on apples and bananas. Apples cost \$.40 each, and bananas cost \$.10 each.
   a. If this person buys *only* apples, how many can be bought?
   b. If this person buys *only* bananas, how many can be bought?
   c. If the person were to buy 10 apples, how many bananas could be bought with the funds left over?
   d. If the person consumes one less apple (that is, nine), how many more bananas could be bought? Is this rate of trade-off the same no matter how many apples are relinquished?
   e. Write down the algebraic equation for this person's budget constraint, and graph it showing the points mentioned in parts a through d (using graph paper might improve the accuracy of your work).

2.2. Suppose the person faced with the budget constraint described in Problem 2.1 has preferences for apples (A) and bananas (B) given by

$$\text{Utility} = \sqrt{A \cdot B}$$

a. If $A = 5$ and $B = 80$, what will utility be?
b. If $A = 10$, what value for B will provide the same utility as in part a?
c. If $A = 20$, what value for B will provide the same utility as in parts a and b?
d. Graph the indifference curve implied by parts a through c.
e. Given the budget constraint from Problem 2.1, which of the points identified in parts a through c can be bought by this person?
f. Show through some examples that every other way of allocating income provides less utility than does the point identified in part b. Graph this utility-maximizing situation.

2.3. Paul derives utility only from CDs and DVDs. His utility function is

$$U = \sqrt{C \cdot D}$$

a. Sketch Paul's indifference curves for $U = 5$, $U = 10$, and $U = 20$.
b. Suppose Paul has \$200 to spend and that CDs cost \$5 and DVDs cost \$20. Draw Paul's budget constraint on the same graph as his indifference curves.
c. Suppose Paul spends all of his income on DVDs. How many can he buy and what is his utility?
d. Show that Paul's income will not permit him to reach the $U = 20$ indifference curve.
e. If Paul buys five DVDs, how many CDs can he buy? What is his utility?
f. Use a carefully drawn graph to show that the utility calculated in part e is the highest Paul can achieve with his \$200.

2.4. Sometimes it is convenient to think about the consumer's problem in its "dual" form. This alternative approach asks how a person could achieve a given target level of utility at minimal cost.

a. Develop a graphical argument to show that this approach will yield the same choices for this consumer as would the utility maximization approach.
b. Returning to Problem 2.3, assume that Paul's target level of utility is $U = 10$. Calculate the costs of attaining this utility target for the following bundles of goods (all of which yield $U = 10$):
   i. $C = 100, D = 1$
   ii. $C = 50, D = 2$
   iii. $C = 25, D = 4$
   iv. $C = 20, D = 5$
   v. $C = 10, D = 10$
   vi. $C = 5, D = 20$.
c. Which of the bundles in part b provides the least costly way of reaching the $U = 10$ target? How does this compare to the utility-maximizing solution found in Problem 2.3?

2.5. Ms. Caffeine enjoys coffee (C) and tea (T) according to the function $U(C, T) = 3C + 4T$.

a. What does her utility function say about her MRS of coffee for tea? What do her indifference curves look like?
b. If coffee and tea cost \$3 each and Ms. Caffeine has \$12 to spend on these products, how much coffee and tea should she buy to maximize her utility?
c. Draw the graph of her indifference curve map and her budget constraint, and show that the utility-maximizing point occurs only on the T-axis where no coffee is bought.
d. Would this person buy any coffee if she had more money to spend?
e. How would her consumption change if the price of coffee fell to \$2?

2.6. Vera is an impoverished graduate student, who has only \$100 a month to spend on food. She has read in a government publication that she can assure an adequate diet by eating only peanut butter and carrots in the fixed ratio of 2 pounds of peanut butter to 1 pound of carrots, so she decides to limit her diet to that regime.

a. If peanut butter costs \$4 per pound and carrots cost \$2 per pound, how much can she eat during the month?
b. Suppose peanut butter costs rise to \$5 because of peanut subsidies introduced by a politically corrupt government. By how much will Vera have to reduce her food purchases?
c. How much in food aid would the government have to give Vera to compensate for the effects of the peanut subsidy?
d. Explain why Vera's preferences are of a very special type here. How would you graph them?

2.7. Assume consumers are choosing between housing services (H) measured in square feet and consumption of all other goods (C) measured in dollars.

a. Show the equilibrium position in a diagram.
b. Now suppose the government agrees to subsidize consumers by paying 50 percent of their housing cost. How will their budget line change? Show the new equilibrium.
c. Show in a diagram the minimum amount of income supplement the government would have to give individuals instead of a housing subsidy to make them as well-off as they were in part b.
d. Describe why the amount shown in part c is smaller than the amount paid in subsidy in part b.

2.8. Suppose a person consumes only two goods, food (F) and other goods (X). This person's budget constraint can be written as

$$PF + X = I$$

where P is the relative price of food and X and I are measured in terms of prices of non-food items (that is, say inflation-adjusted dollars).

a. Explain why the budget constraint for this person can be written in this way and graph the constraint. Also show this person's utility-maximizing choices for F and X.

b. Suppose that the government provides a food subsidy to this person that allows him or her to consume all the food desired at half price. How would that shift this person's budget constraint? How would it affect food and non-food purchases?

c. Suppose now that the government requires that in order to buy food at half price this person must pay C dollars for a food credit card. Show graphically the maximum amount C could be in order to get this person to buy the card.

d. With C set at the amount described in the previous part, will this person consume more or less food than he or she did initially in part a?

2.9. Suppose that people derive utility from two goods—housing (H) and all other consumption goods (C).

a. Show a typical consumer's allocation of his or her income between H and C.

b. Suppose that the government decides that the level of housing shown in part a (say, H^*) is "substandard" and requires that all people buy $H^{**} > H^*$ instead. Show that this law would reduce this person's utility.

c. One way to return this person to the initial level of utility would be to give him or her extra income. On your graph, show how much extra income this would require.

d. Another way to return this person to his or her initial level of utility would be to provide a housing subsidy that reduces the price of housing. On your graph, show this solution as well.

2.10. A common utility function used to illustrate economic examples is the Cobb-Douglas function where $U(X, Y) = X^{\alpha}Y^{\beta}$, where α and β are decimal exponents that sum to 1.0 (for example, 0.3 and 0.7).

a. Explain why the utility function used in Problems 2.2 and 2.3 is a special case of this function.

b. For this utility function, the MRS is given by $\text{MRS} = MU_X/MU_Y = \alpha Y/\beta X$. Use this fact together with the utility-maximizing condition (and that $\alpha + \beta = 1$) to show that this person will spend the fraction of his or her income on good X and the fraction of income on good Y—that is, show $P_X X/I = \alpha$, $P_Y Y/I = \beta$.

c. Use the results from part b to show that total spending on good X will not change as the price of X changes so long as income stays constant.

d. Use the results from part b to show that a change in the price of Y will not affect the quantity of X purchased.

e. Show that with this utility function, a doubling of income with no change in prices of goods will cause a precise doubling of purchases of both X and Y.

3 Demand Curves

In this chapter, we will use the model of utility maximization to derive demand curves. We begin by showing how that model permits us to draw conclusions about the ways people respond to changes in their budget constraints—that is, to changes in their incomes or in the prices they face. An individual's demand curve for a product is just one example of such responses. The curve shows the relationship between the price of a good and how much of that good a person chooses to consume when all other factors are held constant. Later in the chapter, we discuss how all of these individual demand curves can be added up to get a market demand curve—the first basic building block of the price determination process.

3-1 Individual Demand Functions

Chapter 2 concluded that the quantities of X and Y that a person chooses depend on that person's preferences and on the details of his or her budget constraint. If we knew a person's preferences and all the economic forces that affect his or her choices, we could predict how much of each good would be chosen. We can summarize this conclusion using the **demand function** for some particular good, say, X:

Demand function
A representation of how quantity demanded depends on prices, income, and preferences.

$$\text{Quantity of } X \text{ demanded} = d_X(P_X, P_Y, I;\ \text{preferences}). \tag{3.1}$$

This function contains the three elements that determine what the person will buy—the prices of X and Y and the person's income (I)—as well as a reminder that choices are also affected by preferences for the goods. These preferences appear to the right of the semicolon in Equation 3.1 because, for most of our discussion, we assume that preferences do not change. People's basic likes and dislikes are developed through a lifetime of experience. They are unlikely to change as we examine their reactions to relatively short-term changes in their economic circumstances caused by changes in commodity prices or incomes.

The quantity demanded of good Y depends on these same general influences and can be summarized by

$$\text{Quantity of } Y \text{ demanded} = d_Y(P_X, P_Y, I;\ \text{preferences}). \tag{3.2}$$

Preferences again appear to the right of the semicolon in Equation 3.2 because we assume that the person's taste for good Y will not change during our analysis.

Homogeneity

One important result that follows directly from Chapter 2 is that if the prices of X and Y and income (I) were all to double (or to change by any identical percentage), the amounts of X and Y demanded by this person would not change. The budget constraint

$$P_X X + P_Y Y = I \quad (3.3)$$

is the same as the budget constraint

$$2P_X X + 2P_Y Y = 2I. \quad (3.4)$$

Graphically, these are exactly the same lines. Consequently, both budget constraints are tangent to a person's indifference curve map at precisely the same point. The quantities of X and Y the individual chooses when faced by the constraint in Equation 3.3 are exactly the same as when the individual is faced by the constraint in Equation 3.4.

This is an important result: The amounts a person demands depend only on the relative prices of goods X and Y and on the "real" value of income. Proportional changes both in the prices of X and Y and in income change only the units we count in (such as dollars instead of cents). They do not affect the quantities demanded. Individual demand is said to be **homogeneous** (of degree zero) for proportional changes in all prices and income. People are not hurt by general inflation of prices if their incomes increase in the same proportion. They will be on exactly the same indifference curve both before and after the inflation. Only if inflation increases some incomes faster or slower than price changes does it have an effect on budget constraints, on the quantities of goods demanded, and on people's well-being.

Homogeneous demand function
Quantity demanded does not change when prices and income increase in the same proportion.

3-2 Changes in Income

As a person's total income rises, assuming prices do not change, we might expect the quantity purchased of each good also to increase. This situation is illustrated in Figure 3.1.

Figure 3.1 Effect of Increasing Income on Quantities of X and Y Chosen

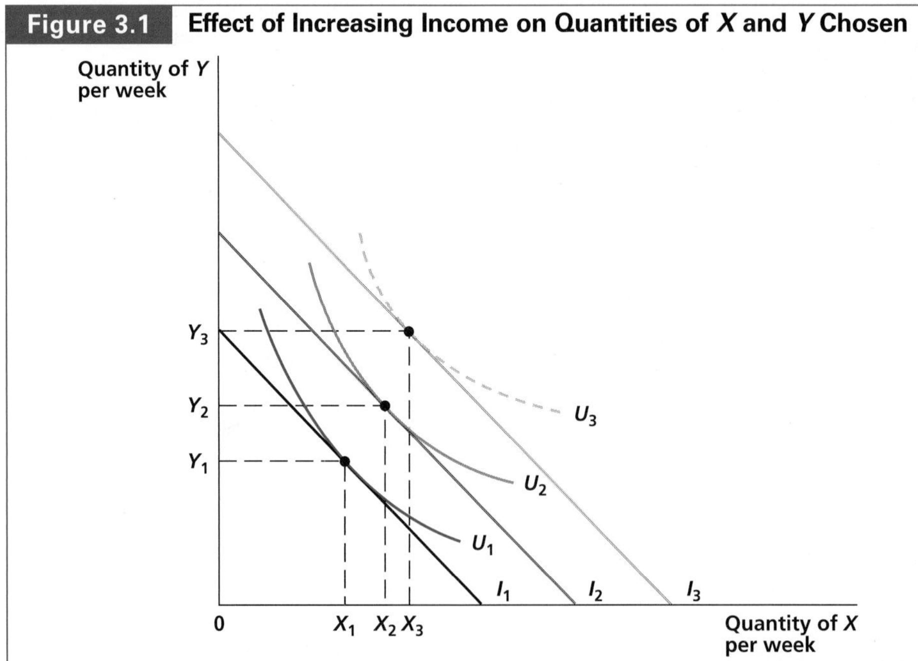

As income increases from I_1 to I_2 to I_3, the optimal (utility-maximizing) choices of X and Y are shown by the successively higher points of tangency. The budget constraint shifts in a parallel way because its slope (given by the ratio of the goods' prices) does not change.

As income increases from I_1 to I_2 to I_3, the quantity of X demanded increases from X_1 to X_2 to X_3 and the quantity of Y demanded increases from Y_1 to Y_2 to Y_3. Budget lines I_1, I_2, and I_3 are all parallel because we are changing only income, not the relative prices of X and Y. Remember, the slope of the budget constraint is given by the ratio of the two goods' prices, and these prices are not changing in this figure. Increases in income do, however, make it possible for this person to consume more; this increased purchasing power is reflected by the outward shift in the budget constraint and an increase in overall utility.

MICRO QUIZ 3.1

The relationship between a person's income and what he or she buys can sometimes be quite complicated. But there are also some simple cases that are very easy to study. Here are two examples of the relationship between housing demand and income:

1. Suppose that a person's MRS of housing (X) for other goods (Y) depends only on the ratio X/Y. Show that the quantity of housing purchased will always be a constant fraction of income so long as the price of housing relative to other goods does not change.
2. Suppose people have a point at which they have enough housing (say X^*). Up to X^* the MRS follows the pattern in case 1, but beyond X^* the MRS becomes zero. What would the relationship between income and housing demand look like in this case?

Normal Goods

In Figure 3.1, both good X and good Y increase as income increases. Goods that follow this tendency are called **normal goods**. Most goods seem to be normal goods—as their incomes increase, people tend to buy more of practically everything. Of course, as Figure 3.1 shows, the demand for some "luxury" goods (such as Y) may increase rapidly when income rises, but the demand for "necessities" (such as X) may grow less rapidly. The relationship between income and the amounts of various goods purchased has been extensively examined by economists, as Application 3.1: Engel's Law shows.

Normal good
A good that is bought in greater quantities as income increases.

Inferior Goods

The demand for a few unusual goods may decrease as a person's income increases. Some proposed examples of such goods are rotgut whiskey, potatoes, and secondhand clothing. This kind of good is called an **inferior good**. How the demand for an inferior good responds to rising income is shown in Figure 3.2. The good Z is inferior because the individual chooses less of it as his or her income increases. Although the curves in Figure 3.2 continue to obey the assumption of a diminishing MRS, they exhibit inferiority. Good Z is inferior only because of the way it relates to the other goods available (good Y here), not because of its own qualities. Purchases of rotgut whiskey decline as income increases, for example, because an individual is able to afford more expensive beverages (such as French champagne). Although, as our examples suggest, inferior goods are relatively rare, the study of them does help illustrate a few important aspects of demand theory.

Inferior good
A good that is bought in smaller quantities as income increases.

3-3 Changes in a Good's Price

Studying how a price change affects the quantity demanded of a good is more complex than looking at the effect of a change in income. Changing the price geometrically involves not only changing an intercept of the budget constraint but also changing its slope. Moving to the new utility-maximizing choice means moving to another indifference curve and to a point on that curve with a different MRS.

When a price changes, it has two different effects on people's choices. There is a **substitution effect** that occurs even if the individual stays on the same indifference

Substitution effect (in consumption)
The part of the change in quantity demanded that is caused by substitution of one good for another. A movement along an indifference curve.

APPLICATION 3.1

Engel's Law

One of the most important generalizations about consumer behavior is that the fraction of income spent on food tends to decline as income increases. This finding was first discovered by the Prussian economist Ernst Engel (1821–1896) in the nineteenth century and has come to be known as Engel's Law. Table 1 illustrates the data that Engel used. They clearly show that richer families spent a smaller fraction of their income on food.

Table 1 Percentage of Total Expenditures on Various Items in Belgian Families in 1853

EXPENDITURE ITEM	ANNUAL INCOME		
	$225–$300	$450–$600	$750–$1,000
Food	62.0%	55.0%	50.0%
Clothing	16.0	18.0	18.0
Lodging, light, and fuel	17.0	17.0	17.0
Services (education, legal, and health)	4.0	7.5	11.5
Comfort and recreation	1.0	2.5	3.5
Total	100.0	100.0	100.0

Source: Based on A. Marshall, *Principles of Economics*, 8th ed. (London: Macmillan, 1920), 97. Some items have been aggregated.

Recent Data

Recent data for U.S. consumers (see Table 2) tend to confirm Engel's observations. Affluent families devote a smaller proportion of their purchasing power to food than do poor families. Comparisons of the data from Tables 1 and 2 also confirm Engel's Law—even current low-income U.S. consumers are much more affluent than nineteenth-century Belgians and, as might be expected, spend a much smaller fraction of their income on food.

Table 2 Percentage of Total Spending by U.S. Consumers on Various Items, 2009

ITEM	ANNUAL TOTAL SPENDING		
	<$70,000	$70,000–$100,000	>$100,000
Food	14.1%	13.1%	11.4%
Housing	37.0	33.2	31.6
Health care + pensions	13.9	18.2	20.1
Other	35.0	35.5	36.9
Total	100.0	100.0	100.0

Source: *Statistical Abstract of the United States*, 2012 (available at http://www.census.gov/compendia/statab/), Table 688.

Are There Other Laws?

Table 2 also shows a tendency for the share of spending on housing to fall as income rises and a tendency for spending on health and pensions to rise with income. Whether these trends have the same generality as Engel's Law is open to question, however. Spending on these items can be affected in important ways by the business cycle (2009 was a year of major recession) and by the availability of public programs providing the same goods (such as Medicare or Medicaid). More detailed studies that seek to control for such influences have generally failed to identify regularities as significant as those identified by Engel over 150 years ago.

TO THINK ABOUT

1. How do you think the availability of Food Stamps for low-income people would affect the figures in Table 2?
2. Critics of local property taxes often claim these taxes are "regressive" (that is, low-income people pay a higher fraction of income on them than do higher-income people). According to the data in Table 2, do these critics have a point? Would it matter that many low-income people live in rental housing?

Figure 3.2 Indifference Curve Map Showing Inferiority

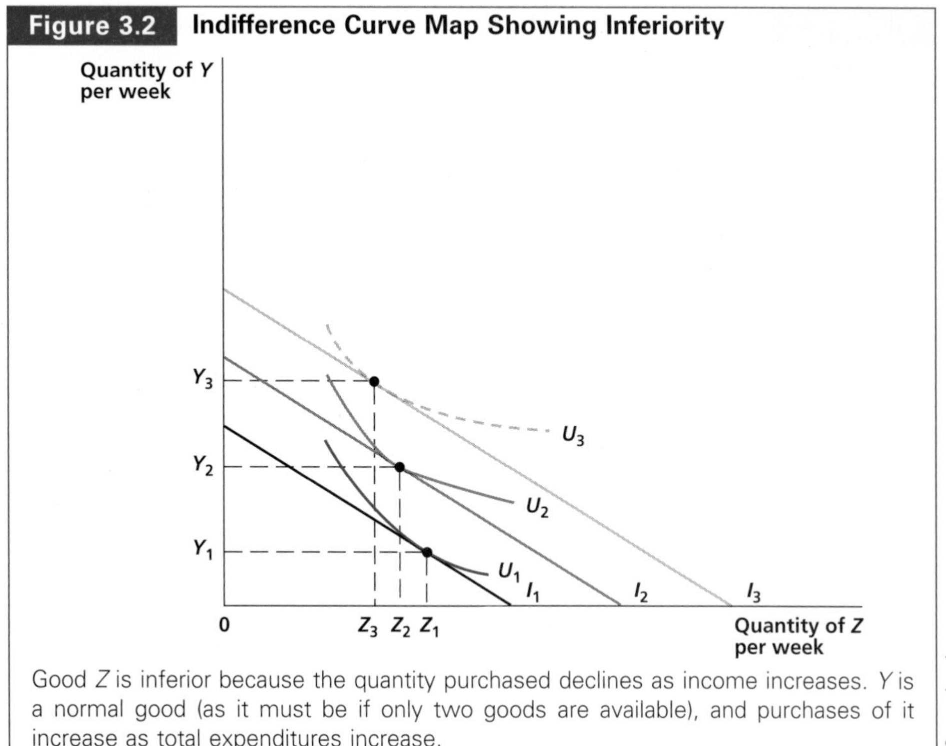

Good Z is inferior because the quantity purchased declines as income increases. Y is a normal good (as it must be if only two goods are available), and purchases of it increase as total expenditures increase.

curve because consumption has to be changed to equate the MRS to the new price ratio of the two goods. There is also an **income effect** because the price change also changes real purchasing power. People will have to move to a new indifference curve that is consistent with their new purchasing power. We now look at these two effects in several different situations.

Income effect
The part of the change in quantity demanded that is caused by a change in real income. A movement to a new indifference curve.

Substitution and Income Effects from a Fall in Price

Let's look first at how the quantity consumed of good X changes in response to a fall in its price. This situation is illustrated in Figure 3.3. Initially, the person maximizes utility by choosing the combination X^*, Y^* at point A. When the price of X falls, the budget line shifts outward to the new budget constraint, as shown in the figure. Remember that the budget constraint meets the Y-axis at the point where all available income is spent on good Y. Because neither the person's income nor the price of good Y has changed here, this Y-intercept is the same for both constraints. The new X-intercept is to the right of the old one because the lower price of X means that, with the lower price, this person could buy more X if he or she devoted all income to that purpose. The flatter slope of the budget constraint shows us that the relative price of X to Y (that is, P_X/P_Y) has fallen.

Substitution Effect

With this change in the budget constraint, the new position of maximum utility is at X^{**}, Y^{**} (point C). There, the new budget line is tangent to the indifference curve U_2. The movement to this new set of choices is the result of two different effects. First, the

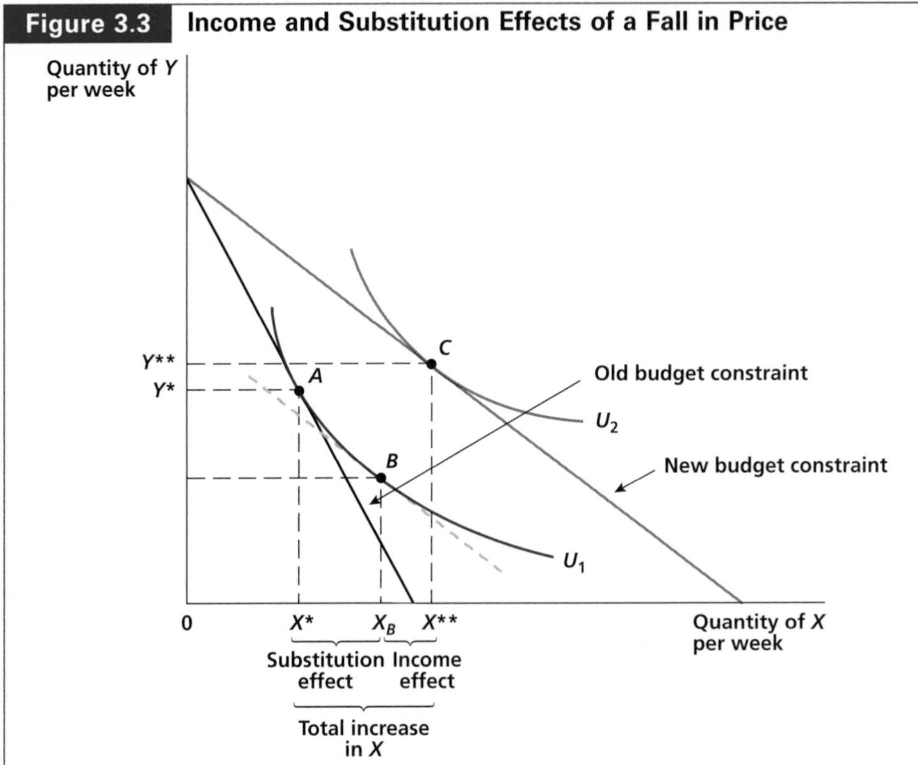

Figure 3.3 Income and Substitution Effects of a Fall in Price

When the price of *X* falls, the utility-maximizing choice shifts from *A* to *C*. This movement can be broken down into two effects: first, a movement along the initial indifference curve to point *B*, where the MRS is equal to the new price ratio (the substitution effect); and, second, a movement to a higher level of utility, since real income has increased (the income effect). Both the substitution and income effects cause more *X* to be bought when its price declines.

change in the slope of the budget constraint would have motivated this person to move to point *B* even if the person had stayed on the original indifference curve U_1. The dashed line in Figure 3.3 has the same slope as the new budget constraint, but it is tangent to U_1 because we are holding real income (that is, utility) constant. A relatively lower price for *X* causes a move from *A* to *B* if this person does not become better off as a result of the lower price. This movement is a graphic demonstration of the substitution effect. Even though the individual is no better off, the change in price still causes a change in consumption choices.

Another way to think about the substitution effect involved in the movement from point *A* to point *B* is to ask how this person can get to the indifference curve U_1 with the least possible expenditures. With the initial budget constraint, point *A* does indeed represent the least costly way to reach U_1—with these prices every other point on U_1 costs more than does point *A*. When the price of *X* falls, however, commodity bundle *A* is no longer the cheapest way to obtain the level of satisfaction represented by U_1. Now this person should take advantage of the changed prices by substituting *X* for *Y* in his or her consumption choices if U_1 is to be obtained at minimal cost. Point *B* is now the least costly way to reach U_1. With the new prices, every other point on U_1 costs more than point *B*.

Income Effect

The further move from B to the final consumption choice, C, is identical to the kind of movement we described in Figure 3.1 for changes in income. Because the price of X has fallen but nominal income (I) has stayed the same, this person has a greater real income and can afford a higher utility level (U_2). If X is a normal good, he or she will now demand more of it. This is the income effect. Notice that for normal goods this effect also causes price and quantity to move in opposite directions. When the price of X falls, this person's real income is increased and he or she buys more X because X is a normal good. A similar statement applies when the price of X rises. Such a price rise reduces real income and, because X is a normal good, less of it is demanded. Of course, as we shall see, the situation is more complicated when X is an inferior good. But that is a rare case, and ultimately it will not detain us very long.

The Effects Combined: A Numerical Example

People do not actually move from A to B to C when the price of good X falls. We never observe the point B; only the two actual choices of A and C are reflected in this person's behavior. But the analysis of income and substitution effects is still valuable because it shows that a price change affects the quantity demanded of a good in two conceptually different ways.

To get some intuitive feel for these effects, let's look again at the hamburger–soft drink example from Chapter 2. Remember that the person we are looking at has \$30 to spend on fast food, and hamburgers sell for \$3 and soft drinks for \$1.50. With this budget constraint, this person chose to buy 5 hamburgers and 10 soft drinks. Suppose now that there is a half-price sale on hamburgers because the seller must compete with a new taco stand—hamburgers now sell for \$1.50. This price change obviously increases this person's purchasing power. Previously, his or her \$30 would buy 10 hamburgers, and now it will buy 20. Clearly, the price change shifts the budget constraint outward and increases utility. The price decline also leaves this person with unspent funds. If he or she continues to buy 5 hamburgers and 10 soft drinks, spending will only be \$22.50 and there will be \$7.50 unspent.

Determining precisely how this person will change his or her spending is not possible unless we know the form of his or her utility function. But, even in the absence of a precise prediction, we can outline the forces that will come into play. First, he or she will buy more hamburgers with the increased purchasing power. This is the income effect of the fall in hamburger prices. Second, this person must recognize that hamburgers now are much cheaper relative to soft drinks. This will cause him or her to substitute hamburgers for soft drinks. Only by making such a substitution can this person's MRS be brought into line with the new price ratio (now $\$1.50/\$1.50 = 1$). This is the substitution effect.

Both of these effects then predict that hamburger purchases will increase in response to the lower sale price. For example, they might increase from 5 to 10, whereas soft drink sales stay at 10. This would exactly exhaust the \$30 fast-food budget. But many other outcomes are possible depending on how willing this person is to substitute the (now cheaper) hamburgers for soft drinks in his or her consumption choices.

The Importance of Substitution Effects

Any price change induces both substitution and income effects. In general, economists believe that substitution effects are more important in determining how people respond to price changes. One reason for the relative importance of substitution effects is that in most cases income effects will be small because we are looking at goods that constitute only a small portion of people's spending. Changes in the price of chewing gum or bananas have little impact on purchasing power because these goods make up much less than 1 percent of total spending for most people. Of course, in some cases income effects may be large—changes in the price of energy, for example, can have important effects on real incomes. But in most situations that will not be the case.

A second reason the economists tend to focus mainly on the substitution effects of price changes is that the sizes of these effects can be quite varied, depending on which specific goods are being considered. Figure 3.4 illustrates this observation by returning to some of the cases we looked at in Chapter 2. Panel a of Figure 3.4 illustrates the left shoe–right shoe example. When the price of left shoes falls, the slope of the budget constraint becomes flatter, moving from I to I'. But, because of the shape of the U_1 indifference curve in the figure, this causes no substitution effect at all—the initial bundle of goods (A) and the bundle illustrating the substitution effect (B) are the same point. As long as this person stays on the U_1 indifference curve, he or she will continue to buy the same number of pairs of shoes, no matter how the relative price of left shoes changes.

This situation is very different when two goods are close substitutes. Panel b of Figure 3.4 returns to the Exxon-Chevron example from Chapter 2. Suppose initially that the price of Exxon gasoline is lower than that of Chevron. Then the budget constraint (I) will be steeper than the indifference curve U_1 (which has a slope of -1 because the two brands are perfect substitutes), and this person will buy only Exxon (point A). When the price of Chevron falls below that of Exxon, the budget constraint will become flatter (I') and this person can achieve U_1 most cheaply by purchasing only Chevron (point B). The substitution effect in this case is huge, causing this person to completely alter the preferred gasoline choice.

Of course, the examples illustrated in Figure 3.4 are extreme cases. But they do show the wide range of possible substitution responses to a price change. The size of such responses in the real world will ultimately depend on whether the good being considered

Figure 3.4 Relative Size of Substitution Effects

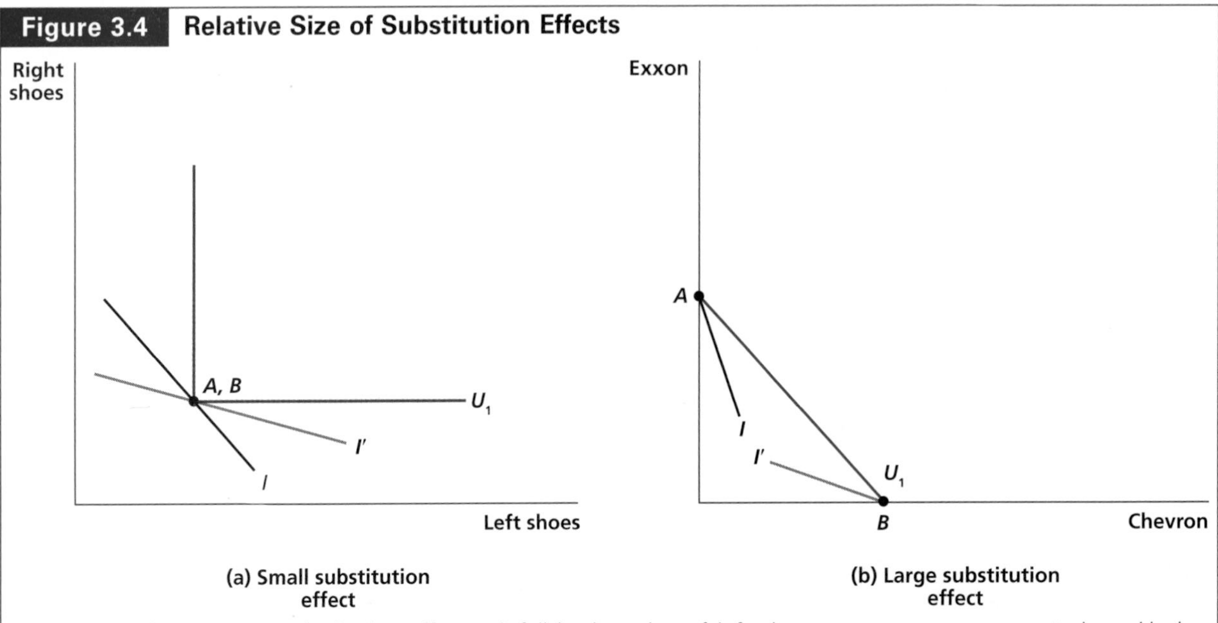

In panel a, there are no substitution effects. A fall in the price of left shoes causes no movement along U_1. In panel b, a fall in the relative price of Chevron causes this person to completely alter which brand is bought.

has many close substitutes. Application 3.2: The Consumer Price Index and Its Biases illustrates the importance of substitution effects in assessing measurement of inflation.

MICRO QUIZ 3.2

Use the discussion of substitution effects to explain:

1. Why most gasoline stations along a particular stretch of road charge about the same price;
2. Why the entry of big-box retailers like Target or Walmart into a market causes prices at small local retailers to fall.

Substitution and Income Effects for Inferior Goods

For the rare case of inferior goods, substitution and income effects work in opposite directions. The net effect of a price change on quantity demanded will be ambiguous. Here we show that ambiguity for the case of an increase in price, leaving it to you to explain the case of a fall in price.

Figure 3.5 shows the income and substitution effects from an increase in price when *X* is an inferior good. As the price of *X* rises, the substitution effect causes this person to choose less *X*. This substitution effect is represented by a movement from *A* to *B* in the initial indifference curve, U_2. Because price has increased, however, this person now has a lower real income and must move to a lower indifference curve, U_1. The individual will choose combination *C*. At *C*, more *X* is chosen than at point *B*. This happens because good *X* is an inferior good: As real income falls, the quantity demanded of *X* increases rather than declines as it would for a normal good. In our example here, the substitution effect is strong enough to outweigh the "perverse" income effect from the price change of this inferior good—so quantity demanded still falls as a result of the price rise.

Figure 3.5 Income and Substitution Effects for an Inferior Good

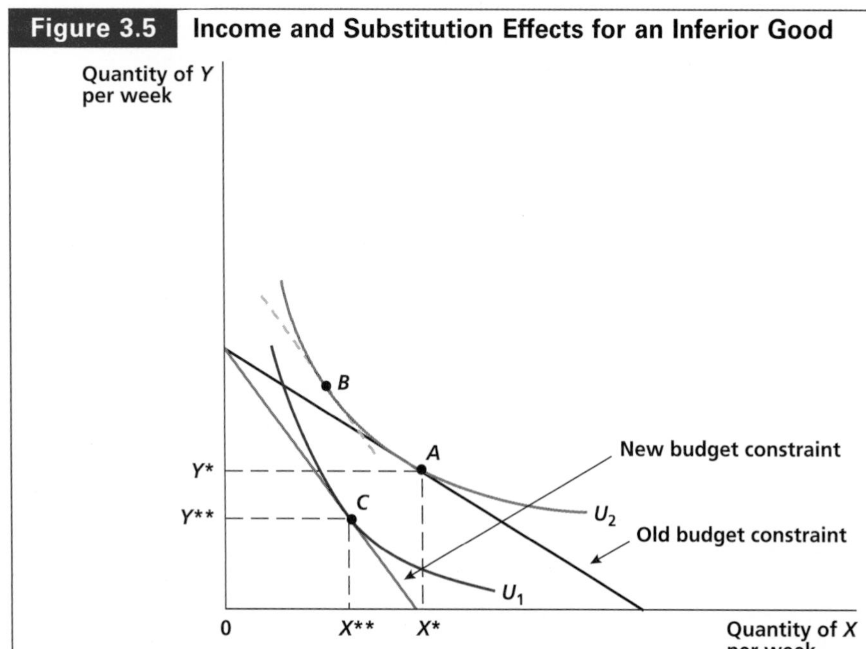

When the price of *X* increases, the substitution effect causes less *X* to be demanded (as shown by a movement to point *B* on the indifference curve U_2). However, because good *X* is inferior, the lower real income brought about by its price increase causes the quantity demanded of *X* to increase (compare point *B* and point *C*). In this particular example, the substitution effect outweighs the income effect and *X* consumption still falls (from X^* to X^{**}).

APPLICATION 3.2

The Consumer Price Index and Its Biases

One of the principal measures of inflation in the United States is provided by the Consumer Price Index (CPI), which is published monthly by the U.S. Department of Labor. To construct the CPI, the Bureau of Labor Statistics first defines a typical market basket of commodities purchased by consumers in a base year (1982 is the year currently used). Then data are collected every month about how much this market basket of commodities currently costs the consumer. The ratio of the current cost to the bundle's original cost (in 1982) is then published as the current value of the CPI. The rate of change in this index between two periods is reported to be the rate of inflation.

An Algebraic Example

This construction can be clarified with a simple two-good example. Suppose that in 1982 the typical market basket contained X_{82} of good X and Y_{82} of good Y. The prices of these goods are given by P^X_{82} and P^Y_{82}. The cost of this bundle in the 1982 base year would be written as

$$\text{Cost in 1982} = B_{82} = P^X_{82}X_{82} + P^Y_{82}Y_{82}. \quad \textbf{(1)}$$

To compute the cost of the same bundle of goods in, say, 2012, we must first collect information on the goods' prices in that year (P^X_{12}, P^Y_{12}) and then compute

$$\text{Cost in 2012} = B_{12} = P^X_{12}X_{82} + P^Y_{12}Y_{82}. \quad \textbf{(2)}$$

Notice that the quantities purchased in 1982 are being valued at 2012 prices. The CPI is defined as the ratio of the costs of these two market baskets multiplied by 100:

$$\text{CPI}_{12} = \frac{B_{12}}{B_{82}} \cdot 100 \quad \textbf{(3)}$$

The rate of inflation can be computed from this index. For example, if the same market basket of items that cost \$100 in 1982 costs \$230 in 2012, the value of the CPI would be 230 and we would say there had been a 130 percent increase in prices over this 30-year period. It might (probably incorrectly) be said that people would need a 130 percent increase in nominal 1982 income to enjoy the same standard of living in 2012 that they had in 1982. Cost-of-living adjustments (COLAs) in Social Security benefits and in many job agreements are calculated in precisely this way. Unfortunately, this approach poses a number of problems.

Substitution Bias in the CPI

One conceptual problem with the preceding calculation is that it assumes that people who are faced with year 2012 prices will continue to demand the same basket of commodities that they consumed in 1982. This treatment makes no allowance for substitutions among commodities in response to changing prices. The calculation may overstate the decline in purchasing power that inflation has caused because it takes no account of how people will seek to get the most utility for their incomes when prices change.

In Figure 1, for example, a typical individual initially is consuming X_{82}, Y_{82}. Presumably, this choice provides maximum utility (U_1), given his or her budget constraint in 1982 (which we call I). Suppose that by 2012 relative prices have changed in such a way that good Y becomes relatively more expensive. This would make the budget constraint flatter than it was in 1982. Using these new prices, the CPI calculates what X_{82}, Y_{82} would cost. This cost would be reflected by the budget constraint I', which is flatter than I (to reflect the changed prices) and passes through the 1982 consumption point. As the figure makes clear, the erosion in purchasing power that has occurred is overstated. With I', this typical

Figure 1 Substitution Bias of the Consumer Price Index

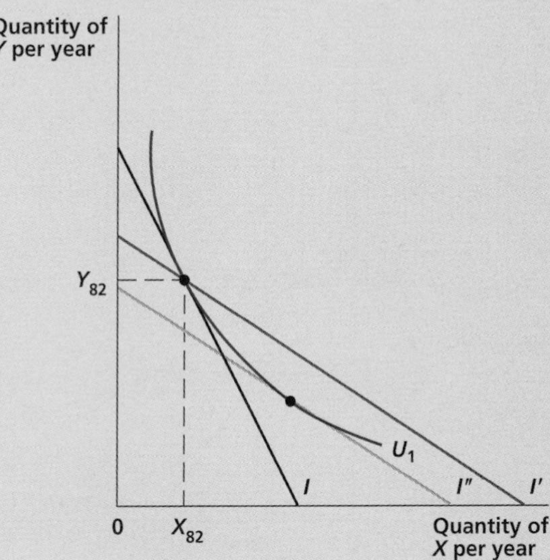

In 1982 with income I the typical consumer chose X_{82}, Y_{82}. If this market basket has different relative prices, the basket's cost will be given by I'. This cost exceeds what is actually required to permit the consumer to reach the original level of utility, I''.

person could now reach a higher utility level than could have been attained in 1982. The CPI overstates the decline in purchasing power that has occurred.

A true measure of inflation would be provided by evaluating an income level, say, I'', which reflects the new prices but just permits the individual to remain on U_1. This would take account of the substitution in consumption that people might make in response to changing relative prices (they consume more X and less Y in moving along U_1). Unfortunately, adjusting the CPI to take such substitutions into account is a difficult task—primarily because the typical consumer's utility function cannot be measured accurately.

New Product and Quality Bias

The introduction of new or improved products introduces a similar bias in the CPI. New products usually experience sharp declines in prices and rapidly growing rates of acceptance by consumers (consider cell phones or DVDs, for example). If these goods are not included in the CPI market basket, a major source of welfare gain for consumers will have been omitted. Of course, the CPI market basket is updated every few years to permit new goods to be included. But that rate of revision is often insufficient for rapidly changing consumer markets. See Application 3.4: Valuing New Goods for one approach to how new goods might be valued.

Adjusting the CPI for the improving quality poses similar difficulties. In many cases, the price of a specific consumer good will stay relatively constant from year to year, but more recent models of the good will be much better. For example, a good-quality laptop computer has had a price in the \$500–\$1,500 price range for many years. But this year's version is much more powerful than the models available, say, five or ten years ago. In effect, the price of a fixed-quality laptop has fallen dramatically, but this will not be apparent when the CPI shoppers are told to purchase a "new laptop." Statisticians who compute the CPI have grappled with this problem for many years and have come up with a variety of ingenious solutions (including the use of "hedonic price" models—see Application 1A.1: How Does Zillow.com Do It?). Still, many economists believe that the CPI continues to miss many improvements in goods' quality.

Outlet Bias

Finally, the fact that the Bureau of Labor Statistics sends buyers to the same retail outlets each month may overstate inflation. Actual consumers tend to seek out temporary sales or other bargains. They shop where they can make their money go the farthest. In recent years, this has meant shopping at giant discount stores such as Sam's Club or Costco rather than at traditional outlets. The CPI as currently constructed does not take such price-reducing strategies into account.

Consequences of the Biases

Measuring all these biases and devising a better CPI to take them into account is no easy task. Indeed, because the CPI is so widely used as "the" measure of inflation, any change can become a very hot political controversy. Still, there is general agreement that the current CPI may overstate actual increases in the cost of living by as much as 0.75 percent to 1.0 percent per year.[1] By some estimates, correction of the index could reduce projected federal spending by as much as a half trillion dollars over a 10-year period. Hence, some politicians have proposed caps on COLAs in government programs. These suggestions have been very controversial, and none has so far been enacted. In private contracts, however, the upward biases in the CPI are frequently recognized. Few private COLAs provide full offsets to inflation as measured by the CPI.

POLICY CHALLENGE

There are many aspects of government policy where it is necessary to adjust for inflation. Some of these include (1) adjusting Social Security benefits, (2) changing cutoff points for income tax brackets, and (3) adjusting the values of "inflation-protected" bonds. How should the government choose a price index to make all of these adjustments? For example, many economists have suggested using a "chained" price index in which commodity bundles are changed every month to address substitution bias. According to some estimates this would reduce adjustments for inflation by about 0.25 percent per year. Would this be fair to elderly Social Security recipients who typically spend much more on (highly inflationary) medical care than do younger consumers?

[1]For a nice graphical (and mathematical) discussion of many of the topics in this application, see Jerry Hausman, "Sources of Bias and Solutions to Bias in the Consumer Price Index," *Journal of Economic Perspectives* (Winter 2003): 23–44.

Giffen's Paradox

Giffen's paradox
A situation in which an increase in a good's price leads people to consume more of the good.

If the income effect of a price rise for an inferior good is strong enough, the rise in price could cause quantity demanded to *increase*. Legend has it that the English economist Robert Giffen observed this paradox in nineteenth-century Ireland—when the price of potatoes rose, people consumed more of them. This peculiar result might be explained by looking at the size of the income effect of a change in the price of potatoes. Potatoes not only were inferior goods but also used up a large portion of the Irish people's income. An increase in the price of potatoes therefore reduced real income substantially. The Irish were forced to cut back on other food consumption in order to buy more potatoes. Even though this rendering of events is economically implausible, the possibility of an increase in the quantity demanded in response to the price increase of a good has come to be known as **Giffen's paradox.**[1]

3-4 An Application: The Lump-Sum Principle

Economists have had a long-standing interest in studying taxes. We look at such analyses at many places in this book. Here we use our model of individual choice to show how taxes affect utility. Of course, it seems obvious (if we don't consider the value of the government services that taxes provide) that paying taxes must reduce a person's utility because purchasing power is reduced. But, through the use of income and substitution effects, we can show that the size of this welfare loss will depend on how a tax is structured. Specifically, taxes that are imposed on general purchasing power will have smaller welfare costs than will taxes imposed on a narrow selection of commodities. This "lump-sum principle" lies at the heart of the study of the economics of optimal taxation.

A Graphical Approach

A graphical proof of the lump-sum principle is presented in Figure 3.6. Initially, this person has I dollars to spend and chooses to consume X^* and Y^*. This combination yields utility level U_3. A tax on good X alone would raise its price, and the budget constraint would become steeper. With that budget constraint (shown as line I' in the figure), a person would be forced to accept a lower utility level (U_1) and would choose to consume the combination X_1, Y_1.

Suppose now that the government decided to institute a general income tax that raised the same revenue as this single-good excise tax. This would shift the individual's budget constraint to I''. The fact that I'' passes through X_1, Y_1 shows that both taxes raise the same amount of revenue.[2] However, with the income tax budget

[1] A major problem with this explanation is that it disregards Marshall's observations that both supply and demand factors must be taken into account when analyzing price changes. If potato prices increased because of a decline in supply due to the potato blight, how could *more* potatoes possibly have been consumed? Also, since many Irish people were potato farmers, the potato price increase should have increased real income for them. For a detailed discussion of these and other fascinating bits of potato lore, see G. P. Dwyer and C. M. Lindsey, "Robert Giffen and the Irish Potato," *American Economic Review* (March 1984): 188–192.

[2] Algebra shows why this is true. With the sales tax (where the per-unit tax rate is given by t), the individual's budget constraint is

$$I = I' = (P_X + t)X_1 + P_Y Y_1.$$

Total tax revenues are given by

$$T = tX_1.$$

With an income tax that collected the same revenue, after-tax income is

$$I'' = I - T = P_X X_1 + P_Y Y_1,$$

which shows that I'' passes through the point X_1, Y_1 also. That is, the bundle X_1, Y_1 is affordable with either tax, but it provides less utility than another bundle (X_2, Y_2) affordable with the income tax.

Figure 3.6 The Lump-Sum Principle

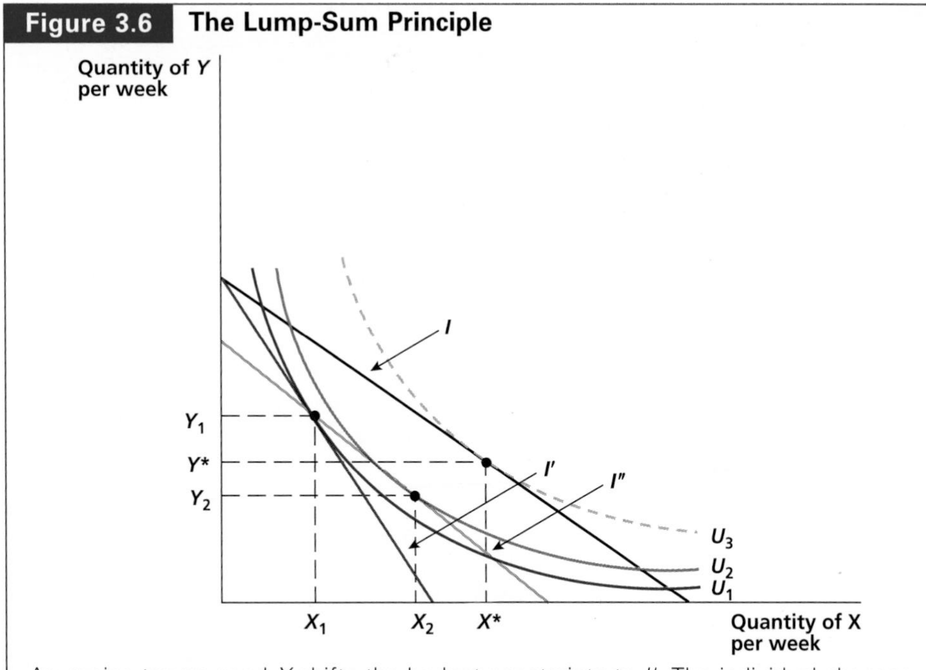

An excise tax on good X shifts the budget constraints to I'. The individual chooses X_1, Y_1 and receives utility of U_1. A lump-sum tax that collects the same amount shifts the budget constraint to I''. The individual chooses X_2, Y_2 and receives more utility (U_2).

constraint I'', this person will choose to consume X_2, Y_2 (rather than X_1, Y_1). Even though this person pays the same tax bill in both instances, the combination chosen under the income tax yields a higher utility (U_2) than does the tax on a single commodity.

An intuitive explanation of this result is that a single-commodity tax affects people's well-being in two ways: It reduces general purchasing power (an income effect), and it directs consumption away from the taxed commodity (a substitution effect). An income tax incorporates only the first effect, and, with equal tax revenues raised, individuals are better off under it than under a tax that also distorts consumption choices.

Generalizations

More generally, the demonstration of the lump-sum principle in Figure 3.6 suggests that the utility loss associated with the need to collect a certain amount of tax revenue can be kept to a minimum by taxing goods for which substitution effects are small. By doing so, taxes will have relatively little welfare effect beyond their direct effect on purchasing power. On the other hand, taxes on goods for which there are many substitutes will cause people to alter their consumption plans in major ways. This additional distortionary effect raises the overall utility cost of such taxes to consumers. In Application 3.3: The Inefficiency of In-kind Programs, we look at a few implications of these observations for welfare policy.

APPLICATION 3.3

The Inefficiency of In-kind Programs

Most countries operate a wide variety of programs to help low-income people. Some of these programs provide simple cash payments, but the most of these are "in-kind" programs that subsidize the prices of food, housing, or medical care. These types of programs have expanded greatly in recent years, while cash assistance has tended to lag. This sort of expansion, while perhaps made with noble intentions, has created two major problems in actually increasing the welfare of the low-income populations served: (1) The programs do not provide nearly as much utility gain per dollar spent as cash programs; and (2) the cumulative effect of the programs may create a situation where low-income people have very little incentive to work. In this application, we look at both of these issues.

The Lump-Sum Principle, Again

The inefficiency of in-kind programs is just a simple application of the lump-sum principle. In Figure 1, we show the budget constraint of a typical low-income person. A subsidy on good X (say food) would shift the budget constraint from I to I'. This would raise this person's utility from U_1 to U_2. The new utility-maximizing point would be at B. An income grant that cost the same amount as the in-kind subsidy is shown by budget line I''. With this budget, this person could have achieved a utility level of U_3. Because the in-kind program provides less utility than would an equally costly cash grant, the in-kind subsidy might be regarded as an inefficient way to provide assistance.

Figure 1 Superiority of an Income Grant

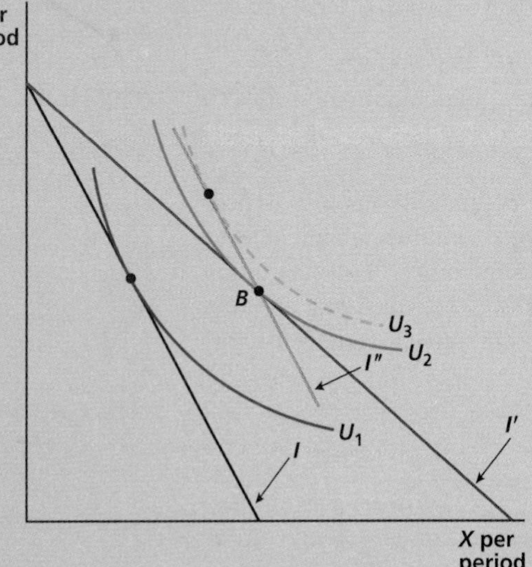

A subsidy on good X (constraint I') raises utility to U_2. For the same funds, a pure income grant (I'') raises utility to U_3.

Studying the inefficiency of in-kind programs when there are many such programs available can be quite complicated. Because each program distorts consumption along one particular dimension (say, encouraging the purchase of more food), the effects on other subsidized items (say, housing) can actually reduce inefficiencies. In a 1994 study, Michael Murray studied such interactions among three major in-kind programs (those for food, housing, and medical care) in the United States.[1] He concluded that the inefficiencies from multiple programs were somewhat less than those that would be estimated for each program individually. Still, in combination, all such programs yielded benefits to consumers that were worth (in terms of utility) only about 68 percent of what would have been provided by a simple cash grant costing the same.

The "Welfare Wall"

All welfare-type programs must reduce the benefits they provide as people's incomes rise. This effect creates an "implicit tax" on earning more. When there are multiple programs, each with its own implicit tax, these rates can accumulate to quite high levels. Some economists use the term "welfare wall" to refer to the barrier that such high rates create. For example, C. Eugene Steuerle finds that combined marginal tax rates can approach nearly 100 percent for single individuals in the United States who earn about $25,000 per year.[2] Although the precise effects on choices low-income people make about working are difficult to estimate, it would not be surprising if such effects were large.

TO THINK ABOUT

1. Why has spending on in-kind programs (such as food, housing, or medical care) grown so much more rapidly than spending on cash assistance to low-income people over the past three decades?
2. Why is it so difficult to structure the formulas for in-kind benefits programs in ways that avoid the welfare wall?

[1]Michael P. Murray, "How Inefficient Are Multiple In-kind Transfers?" *Economic Inquiry*, (April 1994): 209–225.

[2]C. Eugene Steuerle, Statement on "Marginal Tax Rates, Work, and the Nation's Real Tax System." U.S. Congress, Subcommittee on Human Resources, June 27, 2012.

3-5 Changes in the Price of Another Good

If you look carefully at Figures 3.3–3.6 you will see that a change in the price of X will also affect the quantity demanded of the other good (Y). In Figure 3.3, for example, a decrease in the price of X causes not only the quantity demanded of X to increase but the quantity demanded of Y to increase as well. We can explain this result by looking at the substitution and income effects on the demand for Y associated with the decrease in the price of X.

First, as Figure 3.3 shows, the substitution effect of the lower X price caused less Y to be demanded. In moving along the indifference curve U_1 from A to B, X is substituted for Y because the lower ratio of P_X/P_Y required an adjustment in the MRS. In this figure, the income effect of the decline in the price of good X is strong enough to reverse this result. Because Y is a normal good and real income has increased, more Y is demanded: The individual moves from B to C. In Figure 3.3 then Y^{**} exceeds Y^*, and the total effect of the fall in the price of X is to increase the demand for Y.

A slightly different set of indifference curves (that is, different preferences) could have shown different results. Figure 3.7 shows a relatively flat set of indifference curves where the substitution effect from a decline in the price of X is very large. In moving from A to B, a large amount of X is substituted for Y. The income effect on Y is not strong enough to reverse this large substitution effect. In this case, the quantity of Y finally chosen (Y^{**}) is smaller than the original amount. The effect of a decline in the price of one good on the

Figure 3.7 Effect on the Demand for Good *Y* of a Decrease in the Price of Good *X*

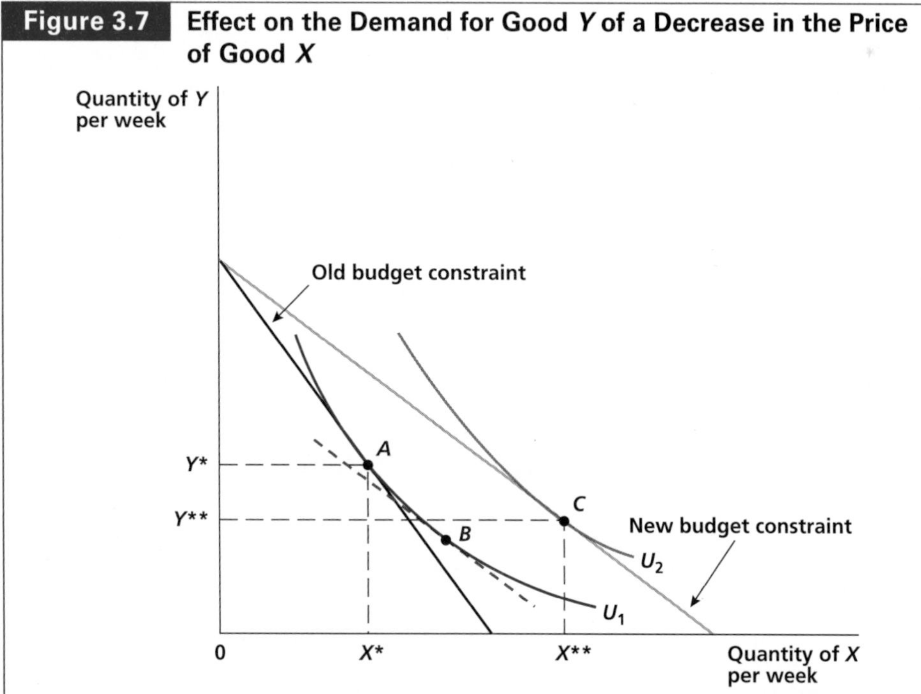

In contrast to Figure 3.3, the quantity demanded of Y now declines (from Y^* to Y^{**}) in response to a decrease in the price of X. The relatively flat indifference curves cause the substitution effect to be very large. Moving from A to B means giving up a substantial quantity of Y for additional X. This effect more than outweighs the positive income effect (from B to C), and the quantity demanded of Y declines. So, purchases of Y may either rise or fall when the price of X falls.

quantity demanded of some other good is ambiguous; it all depends on what the person's preferences, as reflected by his or her indifference curve map, look like. We have to examine carefully income and substitution effects that (at least in the case of only two goods) work in opposite directions.

Substitutes and Complements

Complements
Two goods such that when the price of one increases, the quantity demanded of the other falls.

Substitutes
Two goods such that if the price of one increases, the quantity demanded of the other rises.

Economists use the terms "substitutes" and "complements" to describe the relationships among goods. Complements are goods that go together in the sense that people will increase their use of both goods simultaneously. Examples of complements might be coffee and cream, fish and chips, peanut butter and jelly, or gasoline and automobiles. Substitutes, on the other hand, are goods that can replace one another. Tea and coffee, Hondas and Toyotas, or owned versus rented housing are some goods that are substitutes for each other.

Whether two goods are substitutes or complements of each other is primarily a question of the shape of people's indifference curves. The market behavior of individuals in their purchases of goods can help economists discover these relationships. Two goods are **complements** if an increase in the price of one causes a decrease in the quantity consumed of the other. For example, an increase in the price of coffee might cause not only the quantity demanded of coffee to decline but also the demand for cream to decrease because of the complementary relationship between cream and coffee. Similarly, coffee and tea are **substitutes** because an increase in the price of coffee might cause the quantity demanded of tea to increase as tea replaces coffee in use.

How the demand for one good relates to the price increase of another good is determined by both income and substitution effects. It is only the combined gross result of these two effects that we can observe. Including both income and substitution effects of price changes in our definitions of substitutes and complements can sometimes lead to problems. For example, it is theoretically possible for X to be a complement for Y and at the same time for Y to be a substitute for X. This perplexing state of affairs has led some economists to favor a definition of substitutes and complements that looks only at the direction of substitution effects.[3] We do not make that distinction in this book, however.

MICRO QUIZ 3.3

Changes in the price of another good create both income and substitution effects in a person's demand for, say, coffee. Describe those effects in the following situations and state whether they work in the same direction or in opposite directions in their impact on coffee purchases.

1. A decrease in the price of tea
2. A decrease in the price of cream

3-6 Individual Demand Curves

We have now completed our discussion of how the individual's demand for good X is affected by various changes in his or her economic circumstances. We started by writing the demand function for good X as

$$\text{Quantity of } X \text{ demanded} = d_X(P_X, P_Y, I;\ \text{preferences}).$$

Then we examined how changes in each of the economic factors P_X, P_Y, and I might affect an individual's decision to purchase good X. The principal purpose of this

[3]For a more extended treatment for this subject, see Walter Nicholson and Christopher Snyder, *Microeconomic Theory: Basic Principles and Extensions*, 11th ed. (Mason, OH: Cengage Learning, 2012), 184–188. The initial treatment of these effects was developed by J. R. Hicks in his classic work *Value and Capital* (London: Cambridge University Press, 1939), Chapter 3 and the mathematical appendix.

examination has been to permit us to derive individual demand curves and to be precise about those factors that might cause a demand curve to change its position. This section shows how a demand curve can be constructed. The next section looks at why this curve might shift.

An **individual demand curve** shows the *ceteris paribus* relationship between the quantity demanded of a good (say, X) and its own price (P_X). Not only are preferences held constant under the *ceteris paribus* assumption (as they have been throughout our discussion in this chapter), but the other factors in the demand function (that is, the price of good Y and income) are also held constant. In demand curves, we are limiting our study to only the relationship between the quantity of a good chosen and changes in its price.

Individual demand curve
A graphic representation of the relationship between the price of a good and the quantity of it demanded by a person, holding all other factors constant.

Figure 3.8 shows how to construct a person's demand curve for good X. In panel a, this person's indifference curve map is drawn using three different budget constraints in

Figure 3.8 Construction of an Individual's Demand Curve

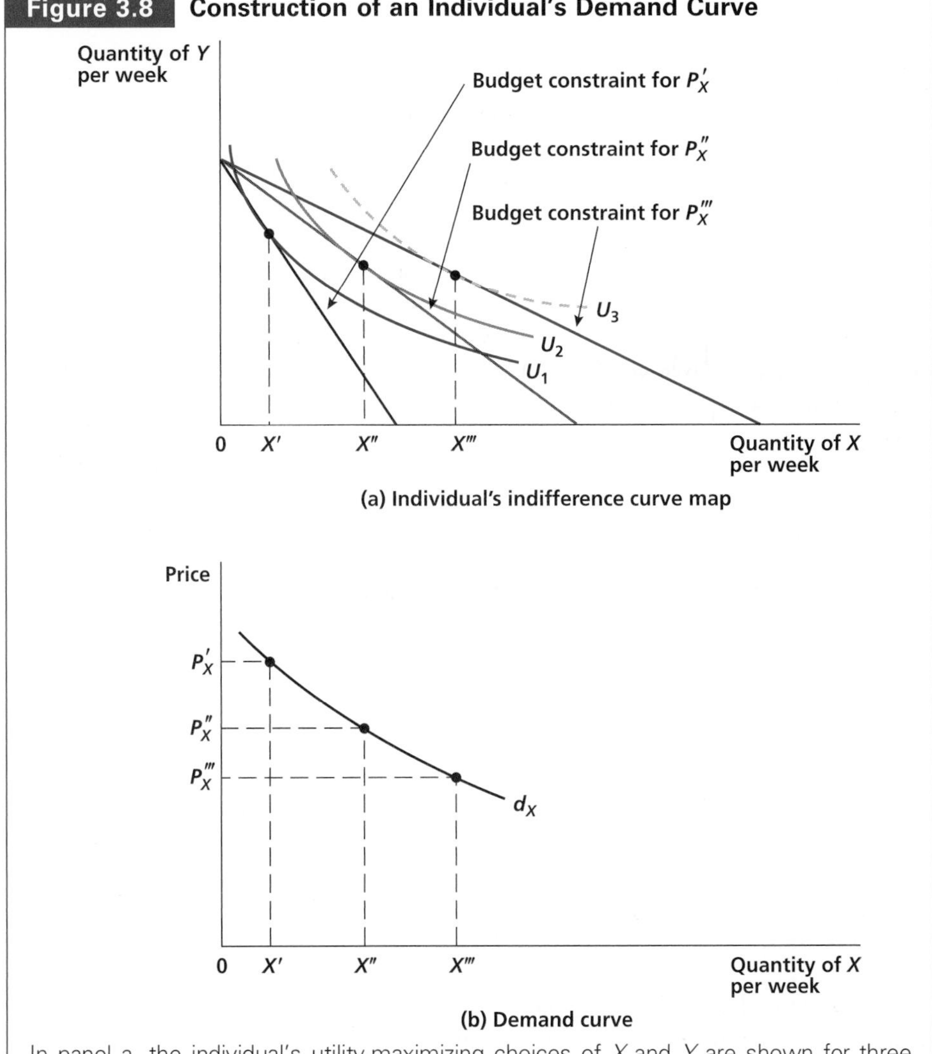

In panel a, the individual's utility-maximizing choices of X and Y are shown for three successively lower prices of X. In panel b, this relationship between P_X and X is used to construct the demand curve for X. The demand curve is drawn on the assumption that the price of Y and nominal income remain constant as the price of X varies.

which the price of X decreases. These decreasing prices are P'_X, P''_X, and P'''_X. The other economic factors that affect the position of the budget constraint (the price of good Y and income) do not change. In graphic terms, all three constraints have the same Y-intercept. The successively lower prices of X rotate this constraint outward. Given the three separate budget constraints, this person's utility-maximizing choices of X are given by X', X'', and X'''. These three choices show that the quantity demanded of X increases as the price of X falls on the presumption that substitution and income effects operate in the same direction.

The information in panel a in Figure 3.8 can be used to construct the demand curve shown in panel b. The price of X is shown on the vertical axis, and the quantity chosen continues to be shown on the horizontal axis. The demand curve (d_X) is downward sloping, showing that when the price of X falls, the quantity demanded of X increases. This increase represents both the substitution and income effects of the price decline.

Shape of the Demand Curve

The precise shape of the demand curve is determined by the size of the income and substitution effects that occur when the price of X changes. A person's demand curve may be either rather flat or quite steeply sloped, depending on the nature of his or her indifference curve map. If X has many close substitutes, the indifference curves will be nearly straight lines (such as those shown in panel b in Figure 3.4), and the substitution effect from a price change will be very large. The quantity of X chosen will increase substantially in response to a fall in its price; consequently, the demand curve will be relatively flat. For example, consider a person's demand for one particular brand of cereal (say, the famous Brand X). Because any one brand has many close substitutes, the demand curve for Brand X will be relatively flat. A fall in the price of Brand X will cause people to shift easily from other kinds of cereal, and the quantity demanded of Brand X will be increased significantly.

On the other hand, a person's demand curve for some goods may be steeply sloped. That is, price changes will not affect consumption very much. This might be the case if the good has no close substitutes. For example, consider a person's demand for water. Because water satisfies many unique needs, it is unlikely that it would have any substitutes when the price of water rose, and the substitution effect would be very small. However, since water does not use up a large portion of a person's total income, the income effect of the increase in the price of water would also not be large. The quantity demanded of water probably would not respond greatly to increases in its price; that is, the demand curve would be nearly vertical.

As a third possibility, consider the case of food. Because food as a whole has no substitutes (although individual food items obviously do), an increase in the price of food will not induce important substitution effects. In this sense, food is similar to our water example. However, food is a major item in a person's total expenditures, and an increase in its price will have a significant effect on purchasing power. It is possible, therefore, that the quantity demanded of food may be reduced substantially in response to a rise in food prices because of this income effect. The demand curve for food might be flatter (that is, quantity demanded reacts more to price) than we might expect if we thought of food only as a "necessity" with few, if any, substitutes.[4]

[4]For this and other reasons, sometimes it is convenient to talk about demand curves that reflect only substitution effects. We do not study such "compensated" demand curves in this book, however.

3-7 Shifts in an Individual's Demand Curve

An individual's demand curve summarizes the relationship between the price of X and the quantity demanded of X when all the other things that might affect demand are held constant. The income and substitution effects of changes in that price cause the person to move along his or her demand curve. If one of the factors (the price of Y, income, or preferences) that we have so far been holding constant were to change, the entire curve would shift to a new position. The demand curve remains fixed only while the *ceteris paribus* assumption is in effect. Figure 3.9 shows the kinds of shifts that might take place. In panel a, the effect on good X of an increase in income is shown. Assuming that good X is a normal good, an increase in income causes more X to be demanded at each price. At P_1, for example, the quantity of X demanded rises from X_1 to X_2. This is the kind of effect we described early in this chapter (Figure 3.1). When income increases, people buy more X even if its price has not changed, and the demand curve shifts outward. Panels b and c in Figure 3.9 record two possible effects that an increase in the price of Y might have on the demand curve for good X. In panel b, X and Y are assumed to be substitutes—for example, coffee (X) and tea (Y). An increase in the price of tea causes the individual to substitute coffee for tea. More coffee (that is, good X) is demanded at each price than was previously the case. At P_1, for example, the quantity of coffee demanded increases from X_1 to X_2.

On the other hand, suppose X and Y are complements—for example, coffee (X) and cream (Y). An increase in the price of cream causes the demand curve for coffee to shift inward. Because coffee and cream go together, less coffee (that is, good X) will now be demanded at each price. This shift in the demand curve is shown in panel c—at P_1, the quantity of coffee demanded falls from X_1 to X_2.

Changes in preferences might also cause the demand curve to shift. For example, a sudden warm spell would shift the entire demand curve for cold drinks outward. More drinks would be demanded at each price because now each person's desire for them has increased. Similarly, increased environmental consciousness during the 1980s and 1990s vastly increased the demand for such items as recycling containers and organically grown

Figure 3.9 **Shifts in an Individual's Demand Curve**

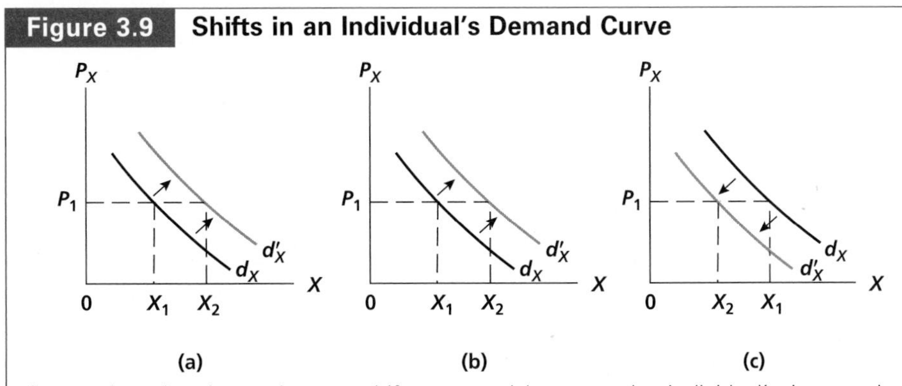

In panel a, the demand curve shifts outward because the individual's income has increased. More X is now demanded at each price. In panel b, the demand curve shifts outward because the price of Y has increased, and X and Y are substitutes for the individual. In panel c, the demand curve shifts inward because of the increase in the price Y; that is, X and Y are complements.

> **MICRO QUIZ 3.4**
>
> The following statements were made by two reporters describing the same event. Which reporter (if either) gets the distinction between shifting a demand curve and moving along it correct?
>
> **Reporter 1.** The freezing weather in Florida will raise the price of oranges, and people will reduce their demand for oranges. Because of this reduced demand, producers will now get lower prices for their oranges than they might have, and these lower prices will help restore orange purchases to their original level.
>
> **Reporter 2**. The freezing weather in Florida raises orange prices and reduces the demand for oranges. Orange growers should therefore accustom themselves to lower sales even when the weather returns to normal.

food. Similarly, fear that tomatoes or peanuts may have been tainted with salmonella in 2008 sharply reduced demand throughout the United States.

Be Careful in Using Terminology

It is important to be careful in making the distinction between the shift in a demand curve and movement along a stationary demand curve. Changes in the price of X lead to movements along the demand curve for good X. Changes in other economic factors (such as a change in income, a change in another good's price, or a change in preferences) cause the entire demand curve for X to shift. If we wished to see how a change in the price of steak would affect a person's steak purchases, we would use a single demand curve and study movements along it. On the other hand, if we wanted to know how a change in income would affect the quantity of steak purchased, we would study the shift in the position of the entire demand curve.

To keep these matters straight, economists must speak carefully. The movement downward along a stationary demand curve in response to a fall in price is called an **increase in quantity demanded**. A shift outward in the entire curve is an **increase in demand**. A rise in the price of a good causes a **decrease in quantity demanded** (a move along the demand curve), whereas a change in some other factor may cause a **decrease in demand** (a shift of the entire curve to the left). It is important to be precise in using those terms; they are not interchangeable.

Increase or decrease in quantity demanded
The increase or decrease in quantity demanded caused by a change in the good's price. Graphically represented by the movement along a demand curve.

Increase or decrease in demand
The change in demand for a good caused by changes in the price of another good, in income, or in preferences. Graphically represented by a shift of the entire demand curve.

3-8 Two Numerical Examples

Let's look at two numerical examples that use a person's preferences to derive his or her demand curve for a product.

Perfect Complements

In Chapter 2, we encountered a person who always buys two bags of popcorn (C) at each movie (M). Given his or her budget constraint of $P_C C + P_M M = I$, we can substitute the preferred choice of $C = 2M$ to get

$$P_C(2M) + P_M M = (2P_C + P_M)M = I \text{ or } M = I/(2P_C + P_M). \quad (3.5)$$

This is the demand function for movies. If we assign specific values for I and P_C, we can get the form for the movie demand curve. For example, if $I = 30$ and $P_C = \$2.50$, the equation for the demand curve is

$$M = 30/(5 + P_M). \quad (3.6)$$

Notice that if $P_M = 10$, this person will choose to attend two movies, which is precisely the result we got in Chapter 2. The impact of any other price can also be determined from Equation 3.6 (assuming you can attend fractions of a movie). Because the price of movies is in the denominator here, the demand curve will clearly slope downward—that is, higher movie prices will cause the number of movies attended to fall. Notice also that a higher income would shift the movie demand curve outward, whereas a higher popcorn price would shift it inward.

Some Substitutability

In Chapter 2, we also looked at a person who always spends half of his or her fast-food budget on hamburgers (Y) and half on soft drinks (X). This can be stated in terms of this person's budget constraint as $P_X X = P_Y Y = 0.5I$. So, here it is very simple to compute the demand function for, say, soft drinks, as

$$P_X X = 0.5I \text{ or } X = 0.5I/P_X. \tag{3.7}$$

If $I = 30$, the specific form for the soft drink demand curve would be

$$X = 15/P_X. \tag{3.8}$$

So, again, increases in price reduce the quantity demanded, and an increase in income will shift this demand curve outward. In this particular case, however, changes in the price of hamburgers do not shift the demand curve for soft drinks at all because this person has already decided to spend half of his or her budget on hamburgers regardless of their price.

KEEP *in* MIND

Demand Curves Show Only Two Variables

To graph any demand curve you must calculate the relationship between the quantity of that good demanded and its price. All other things that affect demand must be held constant. In particular, if a demand function contains income or prices of other goods, you must first assign specific values to these variables before attempting to graph a demand curve.

3-9 Consumer Surplus

Demand curves provide a considerable amount of information about the willingness of people to make voluntary transactions. Because demand curves are in principle measurable, they are much more useful for studying economic behavior in the real world than are utility functions. One important application uses demand curves to study the consequences of price changes for people's overall welfare. This technique relies on the concept of *consumer surplus*—a concept we examine in this section. The tools developed here are widely used by economists to study the effects of public policies on the welfare of consumers.

Demand Curves and Consumer Surplus

In order to understand the consumer surplus idea, we begin by thinking about an individual's demand curve for a good in a slightly different way. Specifically, each point on the demand curve can be regarded as showing what a person would be willing to pay for *one more unit* of the good. Demand curves slope downward because this "marginal willingness to pay" declines as a person consumes more of a given good. On the demand curve for T-shirts in Figure 3.10, for example, this person chooses to consume 10 T-shirts when

Figure 3.10 Consumer Surplus from T-Shirt Demand Price ($/Shirt)

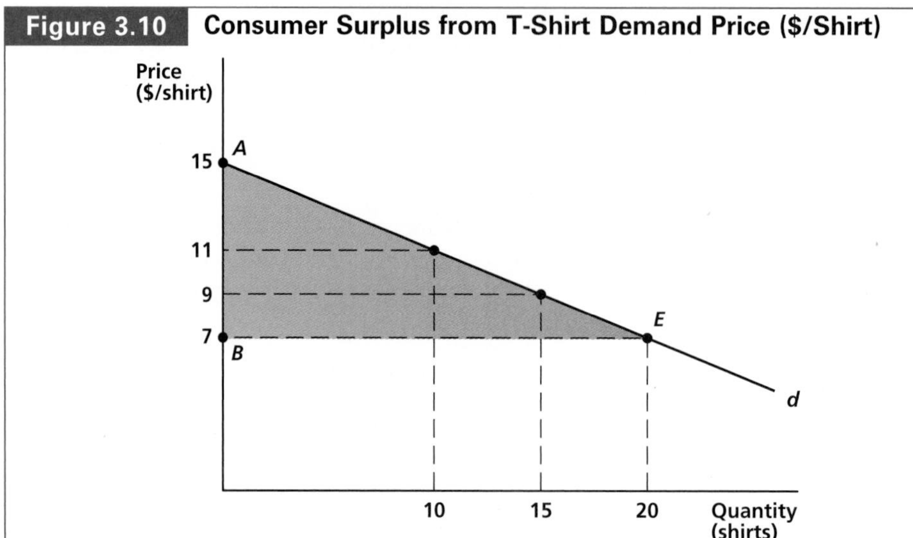

The curve *d* shows a person's demand for T-shirts. He or she would be willing to pay $11 for the 10th shirt and $9 for the 15th shirt. At a price of $7, he or she receives a surplus of $4 for the 10th shirt and $2 for the 15th shirt. Total consumer surplus is given by area *AEB* ($80).

the price is $11. In other words, this person is willing to pay $11 for the 10th T-shirt he or she buys. With a price of $9, on the other hand, this person chooses 15 T-shirts, so, implicitly, he or she values the 15th shirt at only $9. Viewed from this perspective, then, a person's demand curve tells us quite a bit about his or her willingness to pay for different quantities of a good.

Because a good is usually sold at a single market price, people choose to buy additional units of the good up to the point at which their marginal valuation is equal to that price. In Figure 3.10, for example, if T-shirts sell for $7, this person will buy 20 T-shirts because the 20th T-shirt is worth precisely $7. He or she will not buy the 21st T-shirt because it is worth less than $7 (once this person already has 20 T-shirts). Because this person would be willing to pay more than $7 for the 10th or the 15th T-shirt, it is clear that this person gets a "surplus" on those shirts because he or she is actually paying less than the maximal amount that would willingly be paid. Hence, we have a formal definition of **consumer surplus** as the difference between the maximal amounts a person would pay for a good and what he or she actually pays. In graphical terms, consumer surplus is given by the area below the demand curve and above the market price. The concept is measured in monetary values (dollars, euros, yen, and so on).

Consumer surplus
The extra value individuals receive from consuming a good over what they pay for it. What people would be willing to pay for the right to consume a good at its current price.

Because the demand curve in Figure 3.10 is a straight line, the computation of consumer surplus is especially simple. It is just the area of triangle *AEB*. When the price of T-shirts is $7, the size of this area is $0.5 \cdot 20 \cdot (\$15 - \$7) = \$80$. When this person buys 20 T-shirts at $7, he or she actually spends $140 but also receives a consumer surplus of $80. If we were to value each T-shirt at the maximal amount this person would pay for that shirt, we would conclude that the total value of the 20 T-shirts he or she consumes is $220, but they are bought for only $140.

A rise in price would reduce this person's consumer surplus from T-shirt purchases. At a price of $11, for example, he or she buys 10 T-shirts and consumer surplus would be computed as $0.5 \cdot 10 \cdot (\$15 - \$11) = \$20$. Hence, $60 of consumer surplus has been lost because of the rise in the price of T-shirts from \$7 to \$11. Some of this loss in consumer surplus went to shirt-makers because this person must pay \$40 more for the 10 T-shirts he or she does buy than was the case when the price was \$7. The other \$20 in consumer surplus just disappears. In later chapters, we see how computations of this type can be used to judge the consequences of a wide variety of economic situations in which prices change.

Consumer Surplus and Utility

The concept of consumer surplus can be tied directly to the theory of utility maximization we have been studying. Specifically, consumer surplus provides a way of putting a monetary value on the effects that changes in the marketplace have on people's utility. Consumer surplus is not really a new concept but just an alternative way of getting at the utility concepts with which we started the study of demand.

Figure 3.11 illustrates the connection between consumer surplus and utility. The figure shows a person's choices between a particular good (here again we use the T-shirt example) and "all other" goods he or she might buy. The budget constraint shows that with a \$7 price and a budget constraint given by line *I*, this person would choose to consume 20 T-shirts along with \$500 worth of other items. Including the \$140 spent on T-shirts, total spending on all items would be \$640. This consumption plan yields a utility level of U_1 to this person.

Now consider a situation in which T-shirts were not available—perhaps they are banned by a paternalistic government that objects to slogans written on the shirts. In this situation, this person requires some compensation if he or she is to continue to remain on the U_1 indifference curve. Specifically, an extra amount of income given by distance *AB* would just permit this person to reach U_1 when there are no T-shirts

Figure 3.11 Consumer Surplus and Utility

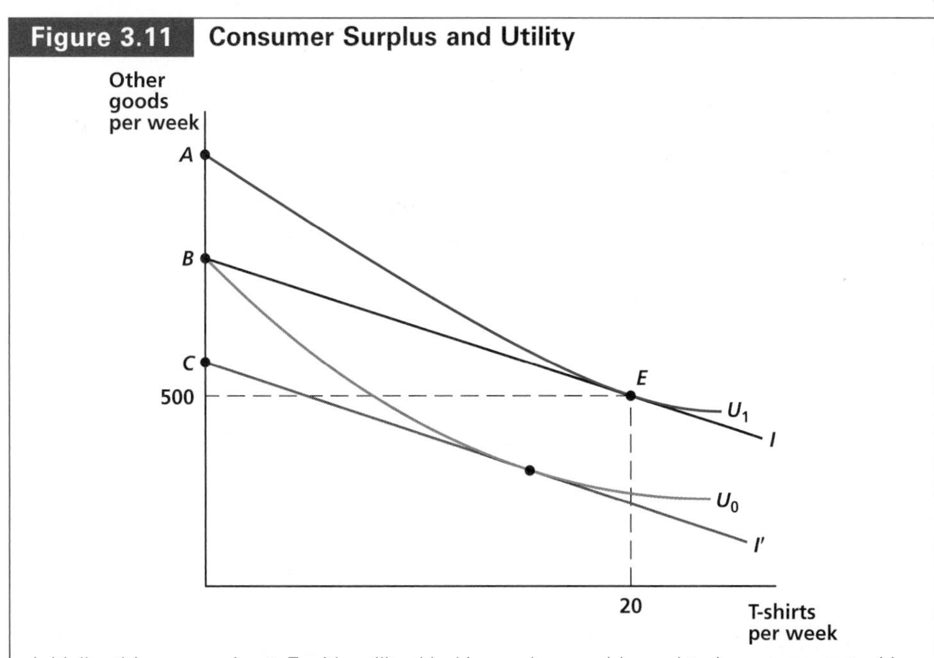

Initially, this person is at *E* with utility U_1. He or she would need to be compensated by amount *AB* in other goods to get U_1 if T-shirts were not available. He or she would also be willing to pay *BC* for the right to consume T-shirts rather than spending *I* only on other goods. Both distance *AB* and distance *BC* approximate the consumer surplus area in Figure 3.10.

MICRO QUIZ 3.5

Throughout this book, we see that consumer surplus areas are often triangular.

1. Explain why this area is measured in monetary values such as dollars. (Hint: What are the units of the height and width of the consumer surplus triangle?)
2. Suppose that the price of a product rose by 10 percent. Would you expect the size of the consumer surplus triangle to fall by more or less than 10 percent?

available. It is possible to show that this dollar value is approximately equal to the consumer surplus figure computed in the previous section—that is, distance *AB* is approximately $80. Hence, consumer surplus can also be interpreted as measuring the amount one would have to compensate a person for withdrawing a product from the marketplace.

A somewhat different way to measure consumer surplus would be to ask how much income this person would be willing to pay for the right to consume T-shirts at $7 each. This amount would be given by distance *BC* in Figure 3.11. With a budget constraint given by I', this person can achieve that same utility level (U_0) that he or she could obtain with budget constraint I if no T-shirts were available. Again, it is possible to show[5] that this amount also is approximately equal to the consumer surplus figure calculated in the previous section ($80). In this case, the figure represents the amount that a person would voluntarily give up in exchange for dropping a no-T-shirt law. Hence, both approaches reach the same conclusion—that consumer surplus provides a way of putting a dollar value on the utility people gain from being able to make market transactions. Application 3.4: Valuing New Goods shows how using a demand curve can solve an important problem in devising cost-of-living statistics.

3-10 Market Demand Curves

Market demand
The total quantity of a good or service demanded by all potential buyers.

Market demand curve
The relationship between the total quantity demanded of a good or service and its price, holding all other factors constant.

The **market demand** for a good is the total quantity of the good demanded by all buyers. The **market demand curve** shows the relationship between this total quantity demanded and the market price of the good, when all other things that affect demand are held constant. The market demand curve's shape and position are determined by the shape of individuals' demand curves for the product in question. Market demand is nothing more than the combined effect of economic choices by many consumers.

Construction of the Market Demand Curve

Figure 3.12 shows the construction of the market demand curve for good X when there are only two buyers. For each price, the point on the market demand curve is found by summing the quantities demanded by each person. For example, at a price of P_X^*, individual 1 demands X_1^*, and individual 2 demands X_2^*. The total quantity demanded at the market at P_X^* is therefore the sum of these two amounts: $X^* = X_1^* + X_2^*$. Consequently, the point X^*, P_X^* is one point on the market demand curve *D*. The other points on the curve are plotted in the same way. The market curve is simply the horizontal sum of each person's demand curve. At every possible price, we ask how much is demanded by each person, and then we add up these amounts to arrive at the quantity demanded by the whole market. The demand curve summarizes the *ceteris paribus* relationship between the quantity demanded of X and its price. If other things that influence demand do not change, the position of the curve will remain fixed and will reflect how people as a group respond to price changes.

[5]For a theoretical treatment of these issues, see R. D. Willig, "Consumer's Surplus without Apology," *American Economic Review* (September 1976): 589–597. Willig shows that distance *AB* in Figure 3.12 (which is termed the "compensating income variation") exceeds total consumer surplus, whereas distance *BC* (termed the "equivalent income variation") is smaller than consumer surplus. All three measures approach the same value if income effects in the demand for the good in question are small.

APPLICATION 3.4

Valuing New Goods

Estimating how consumers value a new good poses problems both for the firms that might wish to sell the good and for the government agencies that have to assess the impact of such goods on overall welfare. One way that has been used for this purpose is illustrated in Figure 1. In the figure, the typical person's demand curve for a newly introduced good is given by *d*. After introduction of the product, this typical person consumes X^* at a price of P_X^*. This is the only point observed on the demand curve for this product because the good did not exist previously. However, some authors have proposed using the information in Figure 1 to draw a tangent to *d* at this initial point and thereby calculate the "virtual price" at which demand for this good would have been zero (P_X^{**}).[1] This price is then taken to be the price before the new good was marketed. The welfare gain from introducing the new good is given by the consumer surplus triangle $P_X^{**}EP_X^*$. This is an approximation to the gain that consumers experience by being able to consume the new good at its current market price relative to a situation where the good did not exist. In some cases, the size of this gain can be quite large.

Figure 1 Valuing a New Good

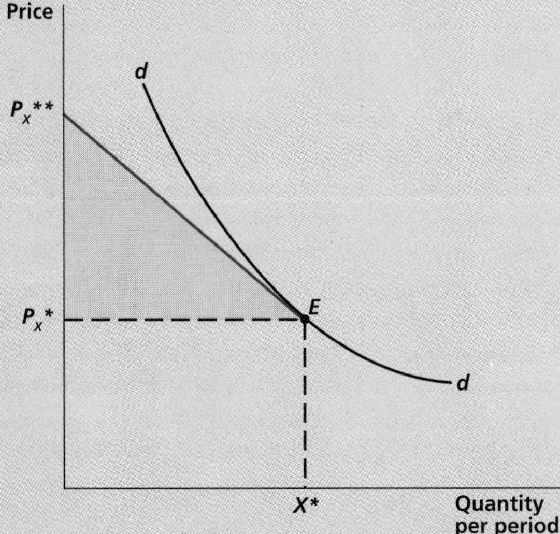

The virtual price P_X^{**} estimates the price at which demand for a new good would be zero. Being able to consume this good at a price of P_X^* yields consumer surplus given by area $P_X^{**}EP_X^*$.

The Value of Cell Phones

Jerry Hausman used this approach in an influential series of papers to estimate the value of cell phones to consumers. He found very large gains indeed, amounting to perhaps as much as $50 billion. Apparently, people really value the freedom of communication that cell phones provide. A major advantage of Hausman's work was to reiterate the notion that the standard methods used to calculate the Consumer Price Index (see Application 3.2: The Consumer Price Index and Its Biases) significantly understate the welfare gains consumers experience from new products. In the case of cell phones, for example, these goods did not enter the CPI until 15 years after they were introduced in the United States. Once cell phones were considered part of the CPI "market basket," no explicit account was taken of the benefits they provided to consumers relative to prior versions of mobile phones.

High-Speed Internet

Although some limited Internet connections were available in the 1980s, it was not until the advent of web browsers in 1993 that the demand for high-speed services began to grow rapidly. Prior to this time most Internet access was through dial-up modems that offered quite limited access. The advent of broadband and the experiences it provided ushered in an entirely new and different product. Internet access fees were first introduced into the Consumer Price Index in 1997. Subsequent research[2] developed better way to control for the quality of this service (speed, reliability, and so forth). Results of this research show that consumers have benefited significantly from a decline in the effective price of broadband services, though the degree of price decline seems to have slowed in recent years.

TO THINK ABOUT

1. The size of the welfare gain triangle in Figure 1 would seem to depend on the slope of the demand curve at point *E*. Can you provide an intuitive reason for this? (See also the discussion of price elasticity later in this chapter.)
2. Figure 1 seems to disregard Marshall's observation that prices are determined by demand *and* supply. How would you add supply curves to this graph? In what ways would adding a supply curve change the story?

[1]See J. Hausman, "Cellular Telephone, New Products, and the CPI," *Journal of Business and Economic Statistics* (April 1999): 188–194. Hausman shows how information from micro sales data on the new product can be used to estimate the slope of *d* at the initial market equilibrium.

[2]See Brendan Williams, "A Hedonic Model for Internet Access Service in the Consumer Price Index." *Monthly Labor Review* (July 2008): 33–48.

Figure 3.12 Constructing a Market Demand Curve from Individual Demand Curves

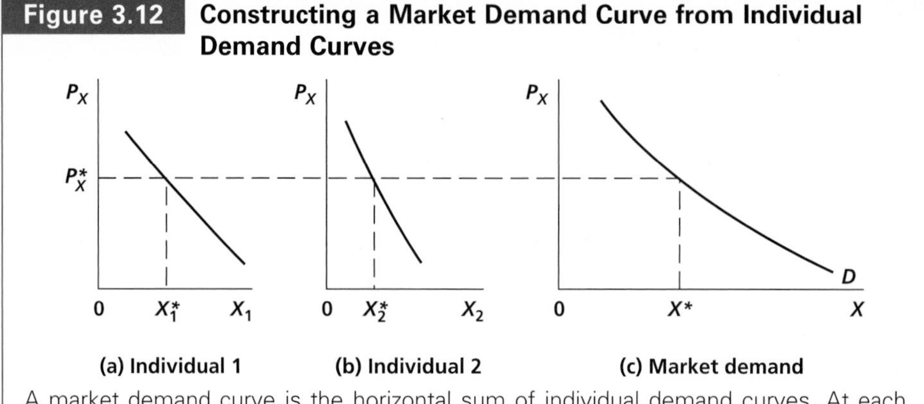

A market demand curve is the horizontal sum of individual demand curves. At each price, the quantity in the market is the sum of the amounts each person demands. For example, at P_X^* the demand in the market is $X_1^* + X_2^* = X^*$.

Shifts in the Market Demand Curve

Why would a market demand curve shift? We already know why individual demand curves shift. To discover how some event might shift a market demand curve, we must, obviously, find out how this event causes individual demand curves to shift. In some cases, the direction of a shift in the market demand curve is reasonably predictable. For example, using our two-buyer case, if both of the buyers' incomes increase and both regard X as a normal good, then each person's demand curve would shift outward. Hence, the market demand curve would also shift outward. At each price, more would be demanded in the market because each person could afford to buy more.

A change in the price of some other good (Y) will also affect the market demand for X. If the price of Y rises, for example, the market demand curve for X will shift outward if most buyers regard X and Y as substitutes. On the other hand, an increase in the price of Y will cause the market demand curve for X to shift inward if most people regard the two goods as complements. For example, an increase in the price of corn flakes would shift the demand curve for wheat flakes outward because these two cereals are close substitutes for each other. At every price, people would now demand more boxes of wheat flakes than they did before corn flakes became more expensive. On the other hand, an increase in the price of strawberries might shift the demand curve for wheat flakes inward because some people like the taste of wheat flakes only if they have strawberries on top. Higher-priced strawberries result in people demanding fewer boxes of wheat flakes at each price.

Numerical Examples

Earlier in this chapter, we derived the form of two specific individual demand curves. Constructing the market demand curve in these cases is especially easy as long as we assume all people are identical and that everyone faces the same price for the good in question. For example, in Equation 3.6, we found that an individual's demand for movies was given by $M = 30/(5 + P_M)$. If there are 1,000 moviegoers in town, each with the same demand, the market demand for attendance would be

$$\text{Total } M = 1{,}000M = 30{,}000/(5 + P_M). \tag{3.9}$$

At a price of \$10, movie attendance would be 2,000 (per week), whereas at a price of \$15 (with no change in the amount of income devoted to movies or in popcorn prices), attendance would fall to 1,500. An increase in the funds the typical person allocates to movies would shift this demand curve outward, whereas an increase in popcorn prices would shift it inward.

The story is much the same for our fast-food example. If 80 people stop by the restaurant each week, and each has a demand for soft drinks of the form $X = 15/P_X$, market demand would be

$$\text{Total } X = 80[15/P_X] = 1{,}200/P_X. \tag{3.10}$$

At a price of $1.50 per drink, 800 would be demanded each week, whereas a half-price sale would double this quantity demanded to 1600 per week. Again, an increase in fast-food funding would shift this demand curve outward, and, in this case, a change in the price of hamburgers (*Y*) would have no effect on the demand curve.

KEEP *in* MIND

Demanders Are Price Takers

In these examples, we assume that every person faces the same price for the product being examined and that no person can influence that price. These assumptions make market demand functions and their related market demand curves especially easy to calculate. If buyers faced different prices, or if some buyers could influence prices, the derivations would be much more complicated.

A Simplified Notation

Often in this book we look at only one market. In order to simplify the notation, we use the letter *Q* for the quantity of a good demanded (per week) in this market, and we use *P* for its price per unit. When we draw a demand curve in the *Q*, *P* plane, we assume that all other factors affecting demand are held constant. That is, income, the price of other goods, and preferences are assumed not to change. If one of these factors happened to change, the demand curve would shift to a new location. As was the case for individual demand curves, the term "change in quantity demanded" is used for a movement along a given market demand curve (in response to a price change), and the term "change in demand" is used for a shift in the entire curve.

3-11 Elasticity

Economists frequently need to show how changes in one variable affect some other variable. They ask, for example, how much does a change in the price of electricity affect the quantity of it demanded, or how does a change in income affect total spending on automobiles? One problem in summarizing these kinds of effects is that goods are measured in different ways. For example, steak is typically sold per pound, whereas oranges are generally sold per dozen. A $0.10 per pound rise in the price of steak might cause national consumption of steak to fall by 100,000 pounds per week, and a $0.10 per dozen rise in the price of oranges might cause national orange purchases to fall by 50,000 dozen per week. But there is no good

MICRO QUIZ 3.6

A shift outward in a demand curve can be described either by the extent of its shift in the horizontal direction or by its shift in the vertical direction. How would the following shifts be shown graphically?

1. News that nutmeg cures the common cold causes people to demand 2 million pounds more nutmeg *at each price*.
2. News that nutmeg cures the common cold causes people to be willing to pay $1 more per pound of nutmeg *for each total quantity demanded*.

way to compare the change in steak sales to the change in orange sales. When two goods are measured in different units, we cannot make a simple comparison between the demand for them to determine which demand is more responsive to changes in its price.

Use Percentage Changes

Economists solve this measurement problem in a two-step process. First, they practically always talk about changes in percentage terms. Rather than saying that the price of oranges, say, rose by \$0.10 per dozen, from \$2.00 to \$2.10, they would instead report that orange prices rose by 5 percent. Similarly, a fall in orange prices of \$0.10 per dozen would be regarded as a change of minus 5 percent.

Percentage changes can, of course, also be calculated for quantities. If national orange purchases fell from 500,000 dozen per week to 450,000, we would say that such purchases fell by 10 percent (that is, they changed by minus 10 percent). An increase in steak sales from 2 million pounds per week to 2.1 million pounds per week would be regarded as a 5 percent increase.

The advantage of always talking in terms of percentage changes is that we don't have to worry very much about the actual units of measurement being used. If orange prices fall by 5 percent, this has the same meaning regardless of whether we are paying for them in dollars, yen, euros, or pesos. Similarly, an increase in the quantity of oranges sold of 10 percent means the same thing regardless of whether we measure orange sales in dozens, crates, or boxcars full.

Linking Percentages

The second step in solving the measurement problem is to link percentage changes when they have a cause-effect relationship. For example, if a 5 percent fall in the price of oranges typically results in a 10 percent increase in quantity bought (when everything else is held constant), we could link these two facts and say that each percent fall in the price of oranges leads to an increase in sales of about 2 percent. That is, we would say that the "elasticity" of orange sales with respect to price changes is about 2 (actually, as we discuss in the next section, *minus* 2 because price and quantity move in opposite directions). This approach is quite general and is used throughout economics. Specifically, if economists believe that variable A affects variable B, they define the **elasticity** of B with respect to A as the percentage change in B for each percentage point change in A. The number that results from this calculation is unit-free. It can readily be compared across different goods, between different countries, or over time.

Elasticity
The measure of the percentage change in one variable brought about by a 1 percent change in some other variable.

3-12 Price Elasticity of Demand

Although economists use many different applications of elasticity, the most important is the **price elasticity of demand**. Changes in P (the price of a good) will lead to changes in Q (the quantity of it purchased) by moving along the demand curve. The price elasticity of demand measures this relationship. Specifically, the price elasticity of demand ($e_{Q,P}$) is defined as the percentage change in quantity in response to a 1 percent change in price (while holding other determinants of demand constant). In mathematical terms,

Price elasticity of demand
The percentage change in the quantity demanded of a good in response to a 1 percent change in its price while holding other determinants of demand constant.

$$\text{Price elasticity of demand} = e_{Q,P} = \frac{\text{Percentage change in } Q}{\text{Percentage change in } P}. \qquad \textbf{(3.11)}$$

This elasticity records how Q changes in percentage terms in response to a percentage change in P. Because P and Q move in opposite directions (except in the rare case of

Giffen's paradox), $e_{Q,P}$ will be negative.[6] For example, a value of $e_{Q,P}$ of -1 means that a 1 percent rise in price leads to a 1 percent decline in quantity, whereas a value of $e_{Q,P}$ of -2 means that a 1 percent rise in price causes quantity to decline by 2 percent.

It takes a bit of practice to get used to speaking in elasticity terms. Probably the most important thing to remember is that the price elasticity of demand looks at movements along a given demand curve and tells you how much (in percentage terms) quantity changes for *each* one percent change in price. You should also keep in mind that price and quantity move in opposite directions, which is why the price elasticity of demand is negative. For example, suppose that studies have shown that the price elasticity of demand for gasoline is -2. That means that every 1 percent rise in price will cause a movement along the gasoline demand curve reducing quantity demanded by 2 percent. So, if gasoline prices rise by, say, 6 percent, we know that (if nothing else changes) quantity will fall by 12 percent ($= 6 \times [-2]$). Similarly, if the gasoline price were to fall by 4 percent, this price elasticity could be used to predict that gasoline purchases would rise by 8 percent ($= [-4] \times [-2]$). Sometimes price elasticities take on decimal values, but this should pose no problem. If, for example, the price elasticity of demand for aspirin were found to be -0.3, this would mean that each percentage point rise in aspirin prices would cause quantity demanded to fall by 0.3 percent (that is, by three-tenths of 1 percent). So, if aspirin prices rose by 15 percent (and everything else that affects aspirin demand stayed fixed), we could predict that the quantity of aspirin demanded would fall by 4.5 percent ($= 15 \times [-0.3]$).

Values of the Price Elasticity of Demand

A distinction is usually made among values of $e_{Q,P}$ that are less than, equal to, or greater than -1. Table 3.1 lists the terms used for each value. For an elastic curve ($e_{Q,P}$ is less than -1),[7] a price increase causes a more than proportional quantity decrease. If $e_{Q,P} = -3$, for example, each 1 percent rise in price causes quantity to fall by 3 percent. For a unit elastic curve ($e_{Q,P}$ is equal to -1), a price increase causes a decrease in quantity of the same proportion. For an inelastic curve ($e_{Q,P}$ is greater than -1), price increases proportionally more than quantity decreases. If $e_{Q,P} = -1/2$, a 1 percent rise in price causes quantity to fall by only 1/2 of 1 percent. In general, then, if a demand curve is elastic, changes in price along the curve affect quantity significantly; if the curve is inelastic, price has little effect on quantity demanded.

Price Elasticity and the Substitution Effect

Our discussion of income and substitution effects provides a basis for judging what the size of the price elasticity for particular goods might be. Goods with many close substitutes (brands of breakfast cereal, small cars, brands of electronic calculators, and so on) are subject to large substitution effects

Table 3.1 Terminology for the Ranges of $e_{Q,P}$

VALUE OF $e_{Q,P}$ AT A POINT ON DEMAND CURVE	TERMINOLOGY FOR CURVE AT THIS POINT
$e_{Q,P} < -1$	Elastic
$e_{Q,P} = -1$	Unit elastic
$e_{Q,P} > -1$	Inelastic

[6]Sometimes the price elasticity of demand is defined as the absolute value of the definition in Equation 3.11. Using this definition, elasticity is never negative; demand is classified as elastic, unit elastic, or inelastic, depending on whether $e_{Q,P}$ is greater than, equal to, or less than 1. You need to recognize this distinction as there is no consistent use in economic literature.

[7]Remember, numbers like -3 are *less than* -1, whereas -1/2 is *greater than* -1. Because we are accustomed to thinking only of positive numbers, statements about the size of price elasticities can sometimes be confusing.

from a price change. For these kinds of goods, we can presume that demand will be elastic ($e_{Q,P} < -1$). On the other hand, goods with few close substitutes (water, insulin, and salt, for example) have small substitution effects when their prices change. Demand for such goods will probably be inelastic with respect to price changes ($e_{Q,P} > -1$; that is, $e_{Q,P}$ is between 0 and -1). Of course, as we mentioned previously, price changes also create income effects on the quantity demanded of a good, which we must consider to completely assess the likely size of overall price elasticities. Still, because the price changes for most goods have only a small effect on people's real incomes, the existence (or nonexistence) of substitutes is probably the principal determinant of price elasticity.

Price Elasticity and Time

Making substitutions in consumption choices may take time. To change from one brand of cereal to another may only take a week (to finish eating the first box), but to change from heating your house with oil to heating it with electricity may take years because a new heating system must be installed. Similarly, trends in gasoline prices may have little short-term impact because people already own their cars and have relatively fixed travel needs. Over a longer term, however, there is clear evidence that people will change the kinds of cars they drive in response to changing real gasoline prices. In general, then, it might be expected that substitution effects and the related price elasticities would be larger the longer the time period that people have to change their behavior. In some situations, it is important to make a distinction between short-term and long-term price elasticities of demand, because the long-term concept may show much greater responses to price change. In Application 3.5: Brand Loyalty, we look at a few cases where this distinction can be important.

Price Elasticity and Total Expenditures

The price elasticity of demand is useful for studying how total expenditures on a good change in response to a price change. Total expenditures on a good are found by multiplying the good's price (P) times the quantity purchased (Q). If demand is elastic, a price increase will cause total expenditures to fall. When demand is elastic, a given percentage increase in price is more than counterbalanced in its effect on total spending by the resulting large decrease in quantity demanded. For example, suppose people are currently buying 1 million automobiles at \$10,000 each. Total expenditures on automobiles amount to \$10 billion. Suppose also that the price elasticity of demand for automobiles is -2. Now, if the price increases to \$11,000 (a 10 percent increase), the quantity purchased would fall to 800,000 cars (a 20 percent fall). Total expenditures on cars are now \$8.8 billion (\$11,000 times 800,000). Because demand is elastic, the price increase causes total spending to fall. This example can be easily reversed to show that, if demand is elastic, a fall in price will cause total spending to increase. The extra sales generated by a fall in price more than compensate for the reduced price in this case. For example, a number of computer software producers have discovered that they can increase their total revenues by selling software at low, cut-rate prices. The extra users attracted by low prices more than compensate for those low prices.

If demand is unit elastic ($e_{Q,P} = -1$), total expenditures stay the same when prices change. A movement of P in one direction causes an exactly opposite proportional movement in Q, and the total price-times-quantity stays fixed. Even if prices fluctuate substantially, total spending on a good with unit elastic demand never changes.

Finally, when demand is inelastic, a price rise will cause total expenditures to rise. A price rise in an inelastic situation does not cause a very large reduction in quantity demanded, and total expenditures will increase. For example, suppose people buy

APPLICATION 3.5

Brand Loyalty

One reason that substitution effects are larger over longer periods than over shorter ones is that people develop spending habits that do not change easily. For example, when faced with a variety of brands consisting of the same basic product, you may develop loyalty to a particular brand, purchasing it on a regular basis. This behavior makes sense because you don't need to reevaluate products continually. Thus, your decision-making costs are reduced. Brand loyalty also reduces the likelihood of brand substitutions, even when there are short-term price differentials. Over the long term, however, price differences can tempt buyers into trying new brands and thereby switch their loyalties.

Automobiles

The competition between American and Japanese automakers provides a good example of changing loyalties. Prior to the 1980s, Americans exhibited considerable loyalty to U.S. automobiles. Repeat purchases of the same brand were a common pattern. In the early 1970s, Japanese automobiles began making inroads into the American market on a price basis. The lower prices of Japanese cars eventually convinced Americans to buy them. Satisfied with their experiences, by the 1980s many Americans developed loyalty to Japanese brands. This loyalty was encouraged, in part, by differences in quality between Japanese and U.S. cars, which became especially large in the mid-1980s. Although U.S. automakers have worked hard to close some of the quality gap, lingering loyalty to Japanese autos has made it difficult to regain market share. By one estimate, U.S. cars would have to sell for approximately $1,600 less than their Japanese counterparts in order to encourage buyers of Japanese cars to switch.[1]

Licensing of Brand Names

The advantages of brand loyalty have not been lost on innovative marketers. Famous trademarks such as Coca-Cola, Harley-Davidson, or Disney's Mickey Mouse have been applied to products rather different from the originals. For example, Coca-Cola for a period licensed its famous name and symbol to makers of sweatshirts and blue jeans, in the hope that this would differentiate the products from their generic competitors. Similarly, Mickey Mouse is one of the most popular trademarks in Japan, appearing on products both conventional (watches and lunchboxes) and unconventional (fashionable handbags and neckties).

The economics behind these moves are straightforward. Prior to licensing, products are virtually perfect substitutes and consumers shift readily among various makers. Licensing creates somewhat lower price responsiveness for the branded product, so producers can charge more for it without losing all their sales. The large fees paid to Coca-Cola, Disney, Michael Jordan, or Major League Baseball provide strong evidence of the strategy's profitability.

Overcoming Brand Loyalty

A useful way to think about brand loyalty is that people incur "switching costs" when they decide to depart from a familiar brand. Producers of a new product must overcome those costs if they are to be successful. Temporary price reductions are one way in which switching costs might be overcome. Heavy advertising of a new product offers another route to this end. In general, firms would be expected to choose the most cost-effective approach. For example, in a study of brand loyalty to breakfast cereals M. Shum[2] used scanner data to look at repeat purchases of a number of national brands such as Cheerios or Rice Krispies. He found that an increase in a new brand's advertising budget of 25 percent reduced the costs associated with switching from a major brand by about $0.68—a figure that represents about a 15 percent reduction. The author showed that obtaining a similar reduction in switching costs through temporary price reductions would be considerably more costly to the producers of a new brand.

TO THINK ABOUT

1. Does the speed with which price differences erode brand loyalties depend on the frequency with which products are bought? Why might differences between short-term and long-term price elasticities be much greater for brands of automobiles than for brands of toothpaste?
2. Why do people buy licensed products when they could probably buy generic brands at much lower prices? Does the observation that people pay 50 percent more for Nike golf shoes endorsed by Tiger Woods than for identical no-name competitors violate the assumptions of utility maximization?

[1]F. Mannering and C. Winston, "Brand Loyalty and the Decline of American Automobile Firms," *Brookings Papers on Economic Activity, Microeconomics* (1991): 67–113.

[2]M. Shum, "Does Advertising Overcome Brand Loyalty? Evidence from the Breakfast Cereals Market," *Journal of Economics and Management Strategy* (Summer, 2004): 241–272.

100 million bushels of wheat per year at a price of \$3 per bushel. Total expenditures on wheat are \$300 million. Suppose also that the price elasticity of demand for wheat is −0.5 (demand is inelastic). If the price of wheat rises to \$3.60 per bushel (a 20 percent increase), quantity demanded will fall by 10 percent (to 90 million bushels). The net result of these actions is to increase total expenditures on wheat from \$300 million to \$324 million. Because the quantity of wheat demanded is not very responsive to changes in price, total revenues are increased by a price rise. This same example could also be reversed to show that, in the inelastic case, total revenues are reduced by a fall in price. Application 3.6: Price Volatility shows how an inelastic demand curve can result in wild price swings when supply conditions change. When demand is elastic, prices are much more stable when supply conditions change.

MICRO QUIZ 3.7

The relationship between the price elasticity of demand and total spending can also be used "in reverse"—elasticities can be inferred from changes in spending.

1. Use the two panels of Figure 3.13 to show how the response of total spending to a *fall* in price can indicate what the price elasticity of demand is.
2. Suppose a researcher could measure the percentage point change in total spending for each percentage point change in market price. How could he or she use this information to infer the precise value of the price elasticity of demand?

The relationship between price elasticity and total expenditures is summarized in Table 3.2. To help you keep the logic of this table in mind, consider the rather extremely shaped demand curves shown in Figure 3.13. Total spending at any point on these demand curves is given by the price shown on the demand curve times the quantity associated with that price. In graphical terms, total spending is shown by the rectangular area bounded by the specific price-quantity combination chosen on the curve. In each case shown in Figure 3.13, the initial position on the demand curve is given by P_0, Q_0. Total spending in each graph is initially given by the area P_0Q_0. Now suppose price rises to P_1 causing quantity bought to fall to Q_1. Total spending is now given by area P_1Q_1. In both cases there are two effects: an increase in total spending (because price is higher on the goods actually bought) and a decrease in total spending (because the quantity of goods bought is smaller). For the case of the inelastic demand curve shown in panel a, the increase in total spending from the higher price on goods bought (light blue) is larger than the decrease resulting from the decline in quantity sold (gray). Hence, total spending rises. For the case of elastic demand shown in panel b, the increase in spending from the higher price on the goods actually bought (light blue) is smaller than the decrease in total spending from the reduction in quantity purchased (gray). Hence, total spending falls. Keeping a mental picture of the relatively extreme cases shown in Figure 3.13 can therefore be a good way of remembering the results summarized in Table 3.2.

Table 3.2 Relationship between Price Changes and Changes in Total Expenditure

IF DEMAND IS	IN RESPONSE TO AN INCREASE IN PRICE, EXPENDITURES WILL	IN RESPONSE TO A DECREASE IN PRICE, EXPENDITURES WILL
Elastic	Fall	Rise
Unit elastic	Not change	Not change
Inelastic	Rise	Fall

APPLICATION 3.6

Price Volatility

To an economist, price changes can almost always be explained by looking at supply and demand factors in a market. If you can assume that demand for a product is relatively stable, the effects of shifts in supply conditions can also tell us quite a bit about the price elasticity of demand. This possibility is illustrated in Figure 1 for two different kinds of products. For product *X*, demand is relatively inelastic (D_X), whereas for product *Y*, demand is quite elastic (D_Y). Consider now the effects of a very volatile supply situation in which the supply curve shifts back and forth among several possible positions. As Figure 1 shows, these shifts in supply will have very different consequences for changing prices depending on the nature of the demand curve. For good *X*, prices change dramatically when supply shifts. However, because demand is inelastic, the quantities bought are relatively stable. For good *Y*, this situation is reversed. In this case prices are relatively stable, whereas quantities change by a lot. Hence, evidence on prices in response to supply shifts can tell us quite a bit about the price elasticity of demand.

Farm Prices

Supply conditions for most agricultural products are highly volatile, primarily because weather conditions in growing areas can affect crop yields dramatically. Because the demand for products such as corn or wheat is relatively inelastic, this can lead to highly variable prices for farm products. For example, between 2005 and 2013 an index of crop prices was as low as 110 and as high as 250, even though prices for most other products were quite stable during the period.

This inelasticity of the demand curve for farm crops leads to what is called "The Paradox of Agriculture." During periods of bad weather, crop prices rise dramatically and total spending on crops actually increases (see Table 3.2). This causes total farm income to rise—so bad weather ends up being good for many farmers. On the other hand, good weather leads to bumper crops, a large fall in crop prices, and a decline in overall farm income. Hence, TV reporters who focus on the impact of localized droughts on farm output in one area (where the farmers really are harmed) largely miss the important benefit that this confers on other farmers who have been less affected by drought conditions.

Figure 1 Effect of a shift in supply depends on price elasticity of demand

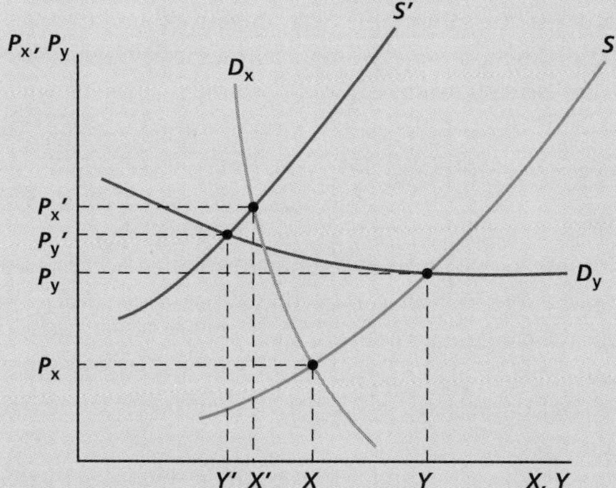

When supply shifts from S to S′, the effect on price and quantity depends on the elasticity of demand. If demand is inelastic (D_X) the largest changes are in prices ($P'_X - P_X$ is large). When demand is elastic (D_Y) the largest changes are in quantity ($Y - Y'$ is large).

Temporary Sales

When markets are relatively competitive, the demand curve facing any one seller will be quite elastic. Consider, for example, the situation of the McDonald's restaurant chain. The chain faces many competitors, who both produce similar hamburgers (Burger King) and other closely substitutable fast foods (Kentucky Fried Chicken). When McDonald's initiates a special sales campaign (as it did in 2012 with its "dollar meals"), it can gain a large quantity of extra sales with only a small price drop. A similar situation occurs when a particular service station offers a small price reduction in gasoline prices—everyone flocks to the gas station with the lowest posted price. Of course, such effects can only last until competitors respond to these temporary sales prices. Analyzing that possibility in detail must await our modeling of market equilibrium in later chapters. But it seems clear that with such elastic demand curves, prices for fast food will be relatively stable.

TO THINK ABOUT

1. Why is it important that the demand curves in Figure 1 stay in a fixed position? If demand were to shift when supply shifts, could we conclude anything about the elasticity of demand? Can you think of situations where a shift in supply is usually also accompanied by a shift in demand?
2. The volatility of farm prices often leads to requests to adopt price "stabilization" policies (such as holding buffer stocks of grains to smooth out supply disruptions). Would such a scheme benefit farmers?

Figure 3.13 Relationship between Price Elasticity and Total Revenue

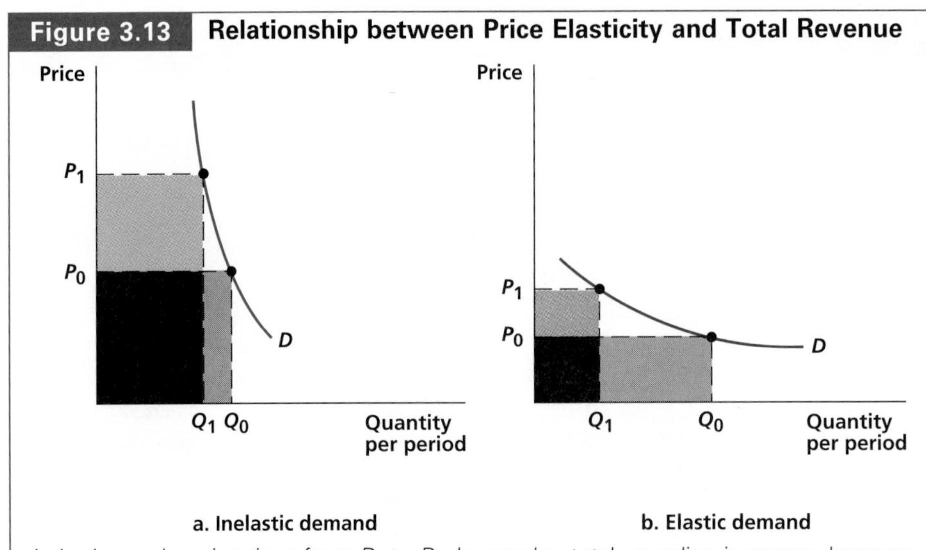

In both panels, price rises from P_0 to P_1. In panel a, total spending increases because demand is inelastic. In panel b, total spending decreases because demand is elastic.

3-13 Demand Curves and Price Elasticity

The relationship between a particular demand curve and the price elasticity it exhibits is relatively complicated. Although it is common to talk about *the* price elasticity of demand for a good, this usage conveys the false impression that price elasticity necessarily has the same value at every point on a market demand curve. A more accurate way of speaking is to say that "at current prices, the price elasticity of demand is…." and, thereby, leave open the possibility that the elasticity may take on some other value at a different point on the demand curve. In some cases, this distinction may be unimportant because the price elasticity of demand has the same value over a relatively broad range of a demand curve. In other cases, the distinction may be important, especially when large movements along a demand curve are being considered.

Linear Demand Curves and Price Elasticity: A Numerical Example

Probably the most important illustration of this warning about elasticities occurs in the case of a linear (straight-line) demand curve. As one moves along such a demand curve, the price elasticity of demand is always changing value. At high price levels, demand is elastic; that is, a fall in price increases quantity purchased more than proportionally. At low prices, on the other hand, demand is inelastic; a further decline in price has relatively little proportional effect on quantity.

This result can be most easily shown with a numerical example. Figure 3.14 illustrates a straight-line (linear) demand curve for, say, iPods. In looking at the changing elasticity of demand along this curve, we will assume it has the specific algebraic form

$$Q = 100 - 2P, \tag{3.12}$$

where Q is the quantity of iPods demanded per week and P is their price in dollars. The demonstration would be the same for any other linear demand curve we might choose.

Figure 3.14 Elasticity Varies along a Linear Demand Curve

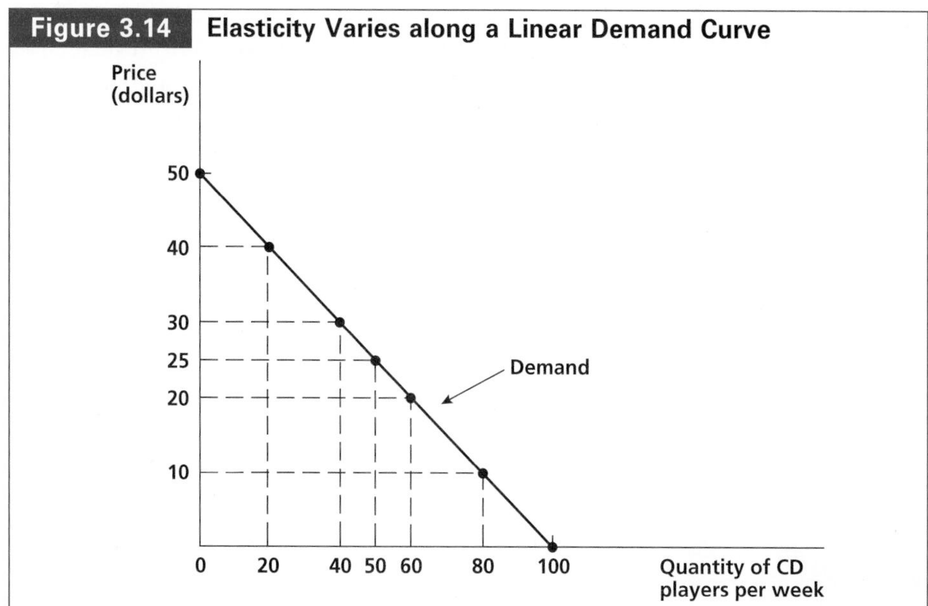

A straight-line demand curve is elastic in its upper portion and inelastic in its lower portion. This relationship is illustrated by considering how total expenditures change for different points on the demand curve.

Table 3.3 shows a few price-quantity combinations that lie on the demand curve, and these points are also reflected in Figure 3.14. Notice, in particular, that the quantity demanded is zero for prices of \$50 or greater.

Table 3.3 also records total spending on iPods ($P \cdot Q$) represented by each of the points on the demand curve. For prices of \$50 or above, total expenditures are \$0. No matter how high the price, if nothing is bought, expenditures are \$0. As price falls below \$50, total spending increases. At $P =$ \$40, total spending is \$800 (\$40 · 20), and for $P =$ \$30, the figure rises to \$1,200 (\$30 · 40).

For high prices, the demand curve in Figure 3.14 is elastic; a fall in price causes enough additional sales to increase total spending. This increase in total expenditures begins to slow as price drops still further. In fact, total spending reaches a maximum at a price of \$25. When $P =$ \$25, $Q = 50$, and total spending on iPods is \$1,250. For prices

Table 3.3 Price, Quantity, and Total Expenditures of iPods for the Demand Function

PRICE (P) (\$)	QUANTITY (Q)	TOTAL EXPENDITURES ($P \times Q$) (\$)
50	0	0
40	20	800
30	40	1,200
25	50	1,250
20	60	1,200
10	80	800
0	100	0

below \$25, reductions in price cause total expenditures to fall. At $P = \$20$, expenditures are \$1,200 ($\$20 \cdot 60$), whereas at $P = \$10$, they are only \$800 ($\$10 \cdot 80$). At these lower prices, the increase in quantity demanded brought about by a further fall in price is simply not large enough to compensate for the price decline itself, and total spending falls.

More generally, the price elasticity of demand at any point (P^*, Q^*) on a linear demand curve is given by

$$e_{Q,P} = b\frac{P^*}{Q^*}, \tag{3.13}$$

where b is the slope of the demand curve (for a proof, see Problem 3.10). So, at the point $P^* = 40$, $Q^* = 20$ in Figure 3.14, we can compute $e_{Q,P} = (-2)(40/20) = -4$. As expected, demand is very elastic at such a high price. On the other hand, at the point $P^* = 10$, $Q^* = 80$, the price elasticity is given by $e_{Q,P} = (-2)(10/80) = -0.5$. At this low price, the demand curve is inelastic. Interestingly, the price elasticity of demand on a linear curve is precisely -1 (that is, unit elastic) at the middle price (here, $P^* = 25$). You should be able to show this for yourself.

KEEP *in* MIND

Price Elasticity May Vary

An equation similar to Equation 3.13 applies to any demand curve, not only linear ones. This makes clear that, in most cases, price elasticity is not a constant but varies in a specific way along most demand curves. Consequently, you must be careful to compute the elasticity at the point that interests you. Applying calculations from one portion of a curve to another often will not work.

A Unit Elastic Curve

There is a special case where the warning about elasticity is unnecessary. Suppose, as we derived in Equation 3.10, that the weekly demand for soft drinks is

$$Q = \frac{1{,}200}{P}. \tag{3.14}$$

As shown in Figure 3.15, this demand curve has a general hyperbolic shape—it is clearly not a straight line. Notice that in this case, $P \cdot Q = 1{,}200$ regardless of the price. This can be verified by examining any of the points identified in Figure 3.15. Because total expenditures are constant everywhere along this hyperbolic demand curve, the price elasticity of demand is always -1. Therefore, this is one simple example of a demand curve that has the same price elasticity along its entire length.[8] Unlike the linear case, for this curve, there is no need to worry about being specific about the point

[8] More generally, if demand takes the form

$$Q = aP^b \ (b < 0), \tag{i}$$

the price elasticity of demand is given by b. This elasticity is the same everywhere along such a demand curve. Equation 3.3 is a special case of equation i for which

$$e_{Q,P} = b = -1 \text{ and } a = 1{,}200. \tag{ii}$$

Taking logarithms of equation i yields

$$\ln Q = \ln a + b \ln P, \tag{iii}$$

which shows that the price elasticity of demand can be found by studying the relationship between the natural logarithms of Q and P.

Figure 3.15 A Unitary Elastic Demand Curve

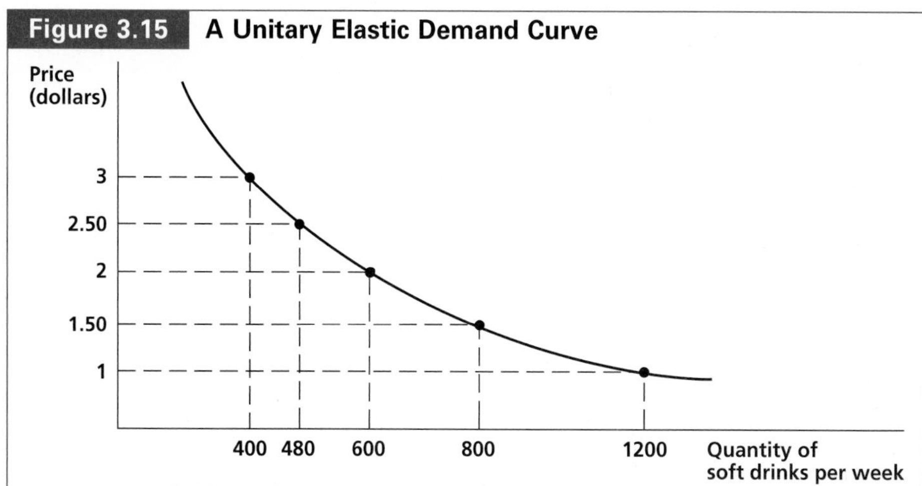

This hyperbolic demand curve has a price elasticity of demand of –1 along its entire length. This is shown by the fact that total spending on soft drinks is the same ($1,200) everywhere on the curve.

at which elasticity is to be measured. Application 3.7: An Experiment in Health Insurance illustrates how you might calculate elasticity from actual data and why your results could be very useful in discussions of actual economic policies.

3-14 Income Elasticity of Demand

Another type of elasticity is the **income elasticity of demand** ($e_{Q,I}$). This concept records the relationship between changes in income and changes in quantity demanded (holding other determinants of demand constant):

Income elasticity of demand
The percentage change in the quantity demanded of a good in response to a 1 percent change in income holding other determinants of demand constant.

$$\text{Income elasticity of demand} = e_{Q,I} = \frac{\text{Percentage change in } Q}{\text{Percentage change in } I}. \quad (3.15)$$

For a normal good, $e_{Q,I}$ *is* positive because increases in income lead to increases in purchases of the good. Among normal goods, whether $e_{Q,I}$ is greater than or less than 1 is a matter of some interest. Goods for which $e_{Q,I}>1$ might be called "luxury goods," in that purchases of these goods increase more rapidly than income. For example, if the income elasticity of demand for automobiles is 2, then a 10 percent increase in income will lead to a 20 percent increase in automobile purchases. Auto sales would therefore be very responsive to business cycles that produce changes in people's incomes. On the other hand, Engel's Law suggests that food has an income elasticity of much less than 1. If the income elasticity of demand for food were 0.5, for example, then a 10 percent rise in income would result in only a 5 percent increase in food purchases. Considerable research has been done to determine the actual values of income elasticities for various items, and we discuss the results of some of these studies in the final section of this chapter.

Possible values for the income elasticity of demand are restricted by the fact that consumers are bound by budget constraints. Use this fact to explain that:

1. Not every good can have an income elasticity of demand greater than 1? Can every good have an income elasticity of demand less than 1?
2. If a set of consumers spend 95 percent of their incomes on housing, the income elasticity of demand for housing cannot be much greater than 1?

APPLICATION 3.7

An Experiment in Health Insurance

The provision of health insurance is one of the most universal and expensive social policies throughout the world. National health insurance schemes can range from completely government-controlled enterprises (the National Health Service in the United Kingdom) to quite complex combinations of government and private insurance (the United States). In recent years most nations have experienced sharply rising costs for these schemes, and this has led to a number of reforms such as the passage of the Affordable Care Act in 2009 in the United States. To evaluate whether such changes will have any impact on reigning in costs, it is important to understand the problems that all health insurance programs encounter.

Moral Hazard

One such important problem is that insurance coverage of health care needs tends to increase the demand for services. Because insured patients pay only a small fraction of the costs of the services they receive, they will demand more than they would have if they had to pay market prices. This tendency of insurance coverage to increase demand is (perhaps unfortunately) called "moral hazard," though there is nothing especially immoral about such behavior.

The Rand Experiment

The Medicare program was introduced in the United States in 1965, and the increase in demand for medical services by the elderly was immediately apparent. In order to understand better the factors that were leading to this increase in demand, the government funded a large-scale experiment in four cities. In that experiment, which was conducted by the Rand Corporation, people were assigned to different insurance plans that varied in the fraction of medical costs that people would have to pay out of their own pockets for medical care.[1] In insurance terms, the experiment varied the "coinsurance" rate from zero (free care) to nearly 100 percent (patients pay everything).

Results of the Experiment

Table 1 shows the results from the experiment. People who faced lower out-of-pocket costs for medical care tended to demand more of it. A rough estimate of the elasticity of demand can be obtained by averaging the percentage changes across the various plans in the table. That is,

$$e_{Q,P} = \frac{\text{Percentage change in } Q}{\text{Percentage change in } P} = \frac{+12}{-66} = -0.18.$$

So, as might have been expected, the demand for medical care is inelastic, but it clearly is not zero. In fact, the Rand study found much larger price effects for some specific medical services such as mental health care and dental care. It is these kinds of services for which new insurance coverage would be expected to have the greatest impact on market demand.

TO THINK ABOUT

1. The data in Table 1 show average spending for families who faced differing out-of-pocket prices for medical care. Why do these data accurately reflect the changes in *quantity* (rather than spending) that are required in the elasticity formula?
2. Three ways to mitigate the effects of moral hazard on the demand for medical care are:
   - Inclusion of provisions that require people to pay a portion of their medical expenses (coinsurance and deductibles);
   - Incentives to get physicians to take costs into account when treating patients; and
   - Limits on the quantities of certain medical treatments that people can consume.

   What role, if any, do these provisions play in the Affordable Care Act (or in any other reform of national health insurance with which you are familiar)?

Table 1 Results of the Rand Health Insurance Experiment

COINSURANCE RATE	PERCENTAGE CHANGE IN PRICE	AVERAGE TOTAL SPENDING ($)	PERCENTAGE CHANGE IN QUANTITY
0.95		540	
0.50	-47	573	+6.1
0.25	-50	617	+7.7
0.00	-100	750	+21.6
Average	-66		+12.0

Source: Manning et al., Table 2.

[1] Details of the experiment are reported in W. G. Manning, J. P. Newhouse, E. B. Keeler, A. Liebowitz, and M. S. Marquis, "Health Insurance and the Demand for Medical Care: Evidence from a Randomized Experiment," *American Economic Review* (June 1987): 251–277.

3-15 Cross-Price Elasticity of Demand

Earlier, we showed that a change in the price of one good will affect the quantity demanded of many other goods. To measure such effects, economists use the **cross-price elasticity of demand**. This concept records the percentage change in quantity demanded (Q) that results from a 1 percentage point change in the price of some other good while holding other determinants of demand constant (call this other price is P'). That is,

Cross-price elasticity of demand
The percentage change in the quantity demanded of a good in response to a 1 percent change in the price of another good holding other determinants of demand constant.

$$\text{Cross-price elasticity of demand} = e_{Q,P'} = \frac{\text{Percentage change in } Q}{\text{Percentage change in } P'}. \tag{3.16}$$

If the two goods in question are substitutes, the cross-price elasticity of demand will be positive because the price of one good and the quantity demanded of the other good will move in the same direction. For example, the cross-price elasticity for changes in the price of tea on coffee demand might be 0.2. Each 1 percentage point increase in the price of tea results in a 0.2 percentage point increase in the demand for coffee because coffee and tea are substitutes in people's consumption choices. A fall in the price of tea would cause the demand for coffee to fall also, since people would choose to drink tea rather than coffee.

If two goods in question are complements, the cross-price elasticity will be negative, showing that the price of one good and the quantity of the other good move in opposite directions. The cross-price elasticity of doughnut prices on coffee demand might be, say, –1.5. This would imply that each 1 percent increase in the price of doughnuts would cause the demand for coffee to fall by 1.5 percent. When doughnuts are more expensive, it becomes less attractive to drink coffee because many people like to have a doughnut with their morning coffee. A fall in the price of doughnuts would increase coffee demand because, in that case, people will choose to consume more of both complementary products. As for the other elasticities we have examined, considerable empirical research has been conducted to try to measure actual cross-price elasticities of demand.

Suppose that a set of consumers spend their incomes only on beer and pizza.

1. Explain why a fall in the price of beer will have an ambiguous effect on pizza purchases.
2. What can you say about the relationship between the price elasticity of demand for pizza, the income elasticity of demand for pizza, and the cross-price elasticity of the demand for pizza with respect to beer prices? (Hint: Remember the demand for pizza must be homogeneous.)

3-16 Some Elasticity Estimates

Table 3.4 gathers a number of estimated income and price elasticities of demand. As we shall see, these estimates often provide the starting place for analyzing how activities such as changes in taxes or import policy might affect various markets. In several later chapters, we use these numbers to illustrate such applications.

Although interested readers are urged to look up some original studies of price and income elasticity for themselves, here we just point out a few general conclusions from those in Table 3.4. With regard to the price elasticity figures, most estimates suggest that product demands are relatively inelastic (between 0 and −1). For the groupings of commodities listed, substitution effects are not especially large, although they may be large

Table 3.4 Representative Price and Income Elasticities of Demand

ITEM	PRICE ELASTICITY	INCOME ELASTICITY
Food		
High-income country	−0.20	+0.40
Low-income country	−0.50	+0.78
Medical care	−0.18	+0.50
Housing	−0.40	+1.20
Automobiles (new)	−0.87	+1.70
Electricity	−0.75	+0.80
Natural gas	−0.65	+0.60
Transatlantic air travel	−1.30	+1.40
Beer	−0.30	+0.40
Cigarettes	−0.35	+0.50
Marijuana	−1.50	0.00

Sources: Food: Andrew Muhammad, James I. Seale, Jr., Birgit Meade, and Anita Regmi, *International Evidence on Food Consumption Patterns*, Economic Research Service, U.S. Department of Agriculture, 2012. Medical care: Manning et al., "Health Insurance and the Demand for Medical Care: Evidence from a Randomized Experiment," *American Economic Review* (June 1987): 251–277. Housing—price elasticity: Eric A. Hanushek and John M. Quigley, "What Is the Price Elasticity of Housing Demand?" *Review of Economics and Statistics* (April 1980): 449–454. Housing—income elasticity: F. de Leeuw, "The Demand for Housing," *Review of Economics and Statistics* (February 1971): 1–10. Automobiles: Patrick S. McCarthy, "Market Price and Income Elasticities of New Vehicle Demand," *Review of Economics and Statistics* (August 1996): 543–547. Electricity and natural gas: Anna Alberini, Will Gans, and Daniel Velez-Lopez, "Residential Consumption of Gas and Electricity and Natural Gas in the U.S.: The Role of Prices and Income," *Energy Economics* (September 2011): 870–881. Transatlantic air travel: J. M. Cigliano, "Price and Income Elasticities for Airline Travel," *Business Economics* (September 1980): 17–21. Beer: Christopher J. Ruhm, "What U.S. Data Should Be Used to Measure the Price Elasticity of Demand for Alcohol?" *Journal of Health Economics* (December 2012): 851–862. Cigarettes: F. Chalemaker, "Rational Addictive Behavior and Cigarette Smoking," *Journal of Political Economy* (August 1991): 722–742, Marijuana: T. C. Misket and F. Vakil, "Some Estimates of Price and Expenditure Elasticities among UCLA Students," *Review of Economics and Statistics* (November 1972): 474–475.

within these categories. For example, substitutions between beer and other commodities may be relatively small, though substitutions among brands of beer may be substantial in response to price differences. Still, all the estimates are less than 0, so there is clear evidence that people do respond to price changes for most goods.[9]

As expected, virtually all of the income elasticities in Table 3.4 are positive and are roughly centered about 1.0. Luxury goods, such as new automobiles or transatlantic travel ($e_{Q,I} > 1$), tend to be balanced by necessities, such as food or medical care ($e_{Q,I} < 1$). Because none of the income elasticities is negative, it is clear that both the existence of inferior goods and the occurrences of Giffen's paradox must be very rare.

[9]Although the estimated price elasticities in Table 3.4 incorporate both substitution and income effects, they predominantly represent substitution effects. To see this, note that the price elasticity of demand ($e_{Q,P}$) can be disaggregated into substitution and income effects by

$$e_{Q,P} = e_S - s_i e_i,$$

where e_s is the "substitution" price elasticity of demand representing the effect of a price change holding utility constant, s_i is the share of income spent on the good in question, and e_i is the good's income elasticity of demand. Because s_i is small for most of the goods in Table 3.4, $e_{Q,P}$ and e_S have values that are reasonably close.

SUMMARY

In this chapter, we showed how to construct the market demand curve for a product—a basic building block in the theory of price determination. Because market demand is composed of the reactions of many consumers, we began this study with a description of how individuals react to price changes. The resulting analysis of substitution and income effects is one of the most important discoveries of economic theory. This theory provides a fairly complete description of why individual demand curves slope downward, and this leads directly to the familiar downward sloping market demand curve. Because this derivation is fairly lengthy and complicated, there are quite a few things to keep in mind:

- Proportionate changes in all prices and income do not affect individuals' economic choices because these do not shift the budget constraint. That is, demand is homogeneous of degree zero for changes in all prices and income.
- A change in a good's price will create substitution and income effects. For normal goods, these work in the same direction—a fall in price will cause more to be demanded, and a rise in price will cause less to be demanded.
- A change in the price of one good will usually affect the demand for other goods as well. That is, it will shift the other good's demand curve. If the two goods are complements, a rise in the price of one will shift the other's demand curve inward. If the goods are substitutes, a rise in the price of one will shift the other's demand curve outward.
- Consumer surplus measures the area below a demand curve and above market price. This area shows what people would be willing to pay for the right to consume a good at its current market price.
- Market demand curves are the horizontal sum of all individuals' demand curves. This curve slopes downward because individual demand curves slope downward. Factors that shift individual demand curves (such as changes in income or in the price of another good) will also shift market demand curves.
- The price elasticity of demand provides a convenient way of measuring the extent to which market demand responds to price changes—it measures the percentage change in quantity demanded (along a given demand curve) in response to a 1 percent change in price.
- There is a close relationship between the price elasticity of demand and changes in total spending on a good. If demand is inelastic $(0 > e_{Q,P} - 1)$, a rise in price will increase total spending, whereas a fall in price will reduce it. Alternatively, if demand is elastic $(e_{Q,P} < -1)$, a rise in price will reduce total spending, but a fall in price will in fact increase total spending because of the extra sales generated.
- The price elasticity of demand is not necessarily constant along a demand curve, so some care must be taken in making calculations when prices change by significant amounts.

REVIEW QUESTIONS

1. Monica always buys one unit of food together with three units of housing, no matter what the prices of these two goods. If food and housing start with equal prices, decide whether the following events would make her better off or worse off or leave her welfare unchanged.
   a. The prices of food and housing increase by 50 percent, with Monica's income unchanged.
   b. The prices of food and housing increase by 50 percent, and Monica's income increases by 50 percent.
   c. The price of food increases by 50 percent, the price of housing remains unchanged, and Monica's income increases by 25 percent.
   d. The price of food remains unchanged, the price of housing increases by 50 percent, and Monica's income increases by 25 percent.
   e. How might your answers to parts c and d change if Monica were willing to alter her mix of food and housing in response to price changes?
2. When there are only two goods, the assumption of a diminishing MRS requires that substitution effects have price and quantity move in opposite directions for any good. Explain why this is so. Do you think the result holds when there are more than two goods?
3. George has rather special preferences for streaming TV shows. As his income rises, he will increase his streaming until he reaches a total of seven shows per week. After he is streaming seven shows per week, however, further increases in his income will not cause him to stream more than seven shows (because he has no more time for watching).
   a. Provide a simple sketch of George's indifference curve map.
   b. Explain how George will respond to a fall in the price of streamed TV shows.
4. Is the following statement true or false? Explain. "Every Giffen good must be inferior, but not every inferior good exhibits the Giffen paradox."

5. Explain whether the following events would result in a move along an individual's demand curve for popcorn or in a shift of the curve. If the curve would shift, in what direction?
   a. An increase in the individual's income
   b. A decline in popcorn prices
   c. An increase in prices for pretzels
   d. A reduction in the amount of butter included in a box of popcorn
   e. The presence of long waiting lines to buy popcorn
   f. A sales tax on all popcorn purchases
6. In the construction of the market demand curve shown in Figure 3.12, why is a horizontal line drawn at the prevailing price P_x^*? What does this assume about the price facing each person? How are people assumed to react to this price?
7. "Gaining extra revenue is easy for any producer—all it has to do is raise the price of its product." Do you agree? How will the success of the firm's decision to raise price depend on the elasticity of demand for its product? How would this success depend on the availability of close substitutes for the firm's product? (This topic is pursued in much more detail in Parts 3 and 4 of this book).
8. Suppose that the market demand curve for pasta is a straight line of the form $Q = 300 - 50P$, where Q is the quantity of pasta bought in thousands of boxes per week and P is the price per box (in dollars).
   a. At what price does the demand for pasta go to 0? Develop a numerical example to show that the demand for pasta is elastic at this point.
   b. How much pasta is demanded at a price of $0? Develop a numerical example to show that demand is inelastic at this point.
   c. How much pasta is demanded at a price of $3? Develop a numerical example that suggests that total spending on pasta is as large as possible at this price.
9. J. Trueblue always spends one-third of his income on American flags. What is the income elasticity of his demand for such flags? What is the price elasticity of his demand for flags?
10. Table 3.4 reports an estimated price elasticity of demand for electricity of -1.14. Explain what this means with a numerical example. Does this number seem large? Do you think this is a short- or long-term elasticity estimate? How might this estimate be important for managers of electric utilities or for bodies that regulate them?

PROBLEMS

3.1. Elizabeth M. Suburbs makes $200 a week at her summer job and spends her entire weekly income on new running shoes and designer jeans, because these are the only two items that provide utility to her. Furthermore, Elizabeth insists that for every pair of jeans she buys, she must also buy a pair of shoes (without the shoes, the new jeans are worthless). Therefore, she buys the same number of pairs of shoes and jeans in any given week.
   a. If jeans cost $20 and shoes cost $20, how many will Elizabeth buy of each?
   b. Suppose that the price of jeans rises to $30 a pair. How many shoes and jeans will she buy?
   c. Show your results by graphing the budget constraints from parts a and b. Also draw Elizabeth's indifference curves.
   d. To what effect (income or substitution) do you attribute the change in utility levels between parts a and b?
   e. Now we look at Elizabeth's demand curve for jeans. First, calculate how many pairs of jeans she will choose to buy if jeans prices are $30, $20, $10, or $5.
   f. Use the information from part e to graph Ms. Suburbs's demand curve for jeans.
   g. Suppose that her income rises to $300. Graph her demand curve for jeans in this new situation.
   h. Suppose that the price of running shoes rises to $30 per pair. How will this affect the demand curves drawn in parts b and c?

3.2. Currently, Paula is maximizing utility by purchasing five TV dinners (T) and four Lean Cuisine meals (L) each week.
   a. Graph Paula's initial utility-maximizing choice.
   b. Suppose that the price of T rises by $1 and the price of L falls by $1.25. Can Paula still afford to buy her initial consumption choices? What do you know about her new budget constraint?
   c. Use your graph to show why Paula will choose to consume more L and less T given her new budget constraint. How do you know that her utility will increase?
   d. Some economists define the "substitution effect" of a price change to be the kind of change shown in part c. That is, the effect represents the change in consumption when the budget constraint rotates about *the initial consumption bundle.* Precisely how does this notion of a substitution effect differ from the one defined in the text?
   e. If the substitution effect were defined as in part d, how would you define "the income effect" in order to get a complete analysis of how a person responds to a price change?

3.3. David gets \$3 per month as an allowance to spend any way he pleases. Because he likes only peanut butter and jelly sandwiches, he spends the entire amount on peanut butter (at \$0.05 per ounce) and jelly (at \$0.10 per ounce). Bread is provided free of charge by a concerned neighbor. David is a picky eater and makes his sandwiches with exactly 1ounce of jelly and 2ounces of peanut butter. He is set in his ways and will never change these proportions.

a. How much peanut butter and jelly will David buy with his \$3 allowance in a week?
b. Suppose the price of jelly were to rise to \$0.15 per ounce. How much of each commodity would be bought?
c. By how much should David's allowance be increased to compensate for the rise in the price of jelly in part b?
d. Graph your results of part a through part c.
e. In what sense does this problem involve only a single commodity—peanut butter and jelly sandwiches? Graph the demand curve for this single commodity.
f. Discuss the results of this problem in terms of the income and substitution effects involved in the demand for jelly.

3.4. Irene's demand for pizza is given by

$$Q = \frac{0.3I}{P},$$

where Q is the weekly quantity of pizza bought (in slices), I is weekly income, and P is the price of one slice of pizza. Using this demand function, answer the following:

a. Is this function homogeneous in I and P?
b. Graph this function for the case $I = 200$.
c. One problem in using this function to study consumer surplus is that Q never reaches zero, no matter how high P is. Hence, suppose that the function holds only for $P \leq 10$ and that $Q = 0$ for $P > 10$. How should your graph in part b be adjusted to fit this assumption?
d. With this demand function (and $I = 200$), it can be shown that the area of consumer surplus is approximately $CS = 198 - 6P - 60\ \ln(P)$, where "ln(P)" refers to the natural logarithm of P. Show that if $P = 10$, consumer surplus (CS) is approximately zero.
e. Suppose $P = 3$. How much pizza is demanded, and how much consumer surplus does Irene receive? Give an economic interpretation to this magnitude.
f. If P were to increase to 4, how much would Irene demand and what would her consumer surplus be? Give an economic interpretation to why the value of CS has fallen.

3.5. The demand curves we studied in this chapter were constructed holding a person's nominal income constant—hence, changes in prices introduced changes in real income (that is, utility). Another way to draw a demand curve is to hold utility constant as prices change. That is, the person is "compensated" for any effects that the prices have on his or her utility. Such *compensated demand curves* illustrate only substitution effects, not income effects. Using this idea, show that:

a. For any initial utility-maximizing position, the regular demand curve and the compensated demand curve pass through the same price-quantity point.
b. The compensated demand curve is generally steeper than the regular demand curve.
c. Any regular demand curve intersects many different compensated demand curves.
d. If Irving consumes only pizza and chianti in fixed proportions of one slice of pizza to one glass of chianti, his regular demand curve for pizza will be downward sloping but his compensated demand curve(s) will be vertical.

3.6. The residents of Uurp consume only pork chops (X) and Coca-Cola (Y). The utility function for the typical resident of Uurp is given by

$$\text{Utility} = U(X, Y) = \sqrt{X \cdot Y}.$$

In 2012, the price of pork chops in Uurp was \$1 each; Cokes were also \$1 each. The typical resident consumed 40 pork chops and 40 Cokes (saving is impossible in Uurp). In 2013, swine fever hit Uurp and pork chop prices rose to \$4; the Coke price remained unchanged. At these new prices, the typical Uurp resident consumed 20 pork chops and 80 Cokes.

a. Show that utility for the typical Uurp resident was unchanged between the two years.
b. Show that using 2012 prices would show an increase in real income between the two years.
c. Show that using 2013 prices would show a decrease in real income between the years.
d. What do you conclude about the ability of these indexes to measure changes in real income?

3.7. Suppose that the market demand curve for garbanzo beans is given by

$$Q = 20 - P,$$

where Q is thousands of pounds of beans bought per week and P is the price in dollars per pound.

a. How many beans will be bought at $P = 0$?
b. At what price does the quantity demanded of beans become 0?
c. Calculate total expenditures ($P \cdot Q$) for beans of each whole dollar price between the prices identified in parts a and b.
d. What price for beans yields the highest total expenditures?

e. Suppose the demand for beans shifted to $Q = 40 - 2P$. How would your answers to parts a through d change? Explain the differences intuitively and with a graph.

3.8. Tom, Dick, and Harry constitute the entire market for scrod. Tom's demand curve is given by

$$Q_1 = 100 - 2P$$

for $P \leq 50$. For $P > 50$, $Q_1 = 0$. Dick's demand curve is given by

$$Q_2 = 160 - 4P$$

for $P \leq 40$. For $P \leq 40$, $Q_2 = 0$. Harry's demand curve is given by

$$Q_3 = 150 - 5P$$

for $P \leq 30$. For $P > 30$, $Q_3 = 0$. Using this information, answer the following:

a. How much scrod is demanded by each person at $P = 50$? $P = 35$? $P = 25$? $P = 10$? and $P = 0$?
b. What is the total market demand for scrod at each of the prices specified in part a?
c. Graph each individual's demand curve.
d. Use the individual demand curves and the results of part b to construct the total market demand for scrod.

3.9. In this chapter we showed how the "consumer surplus" that people receive from being able to consume a good at its current price is given by the area below the demand curve and above that price. In this problem we look at the relationship between consumer surplus and the price elasticity of demand:

a. Show graphically that the loss in consumer surplus from a given increase in price is smaller for an elastic demand curve than for an inelastic demand curve (assuming that price and quantity are the same on both curves before the price increase).
b. Suppose that the price increase described in part a came about because of the imposition of a tax per unit on purchases of these goods. Would the amount of tax revenue collected be greater with the elastic demand curve or with the inelastic demand curve? Explain your result both graphically and intuitively.
c. The "excess burden" of a tax is defined as the loss in consumer surplus from the imposition of the tax less the tax revenue actually collected. Is the excess burden of the tax described in part b larger with the elastic demand curve or with the inelastic demand curve? Explain your answer both graphically and intuitively.
d. Suppose the government wanted to choose between two taxes that *raised the same amount of revenue.* Should it tax the good with an elastic demand curve or the one with the inelastic demand curve? Explain.

3.10. Consider the linear demand curve shown in the following figure. There is a geometric way of calculating the price elasticity of demand for this curve at any arbitrary point (say point E). To do so, first write the algebraic form of this demand curve as $Q = a + bP$.

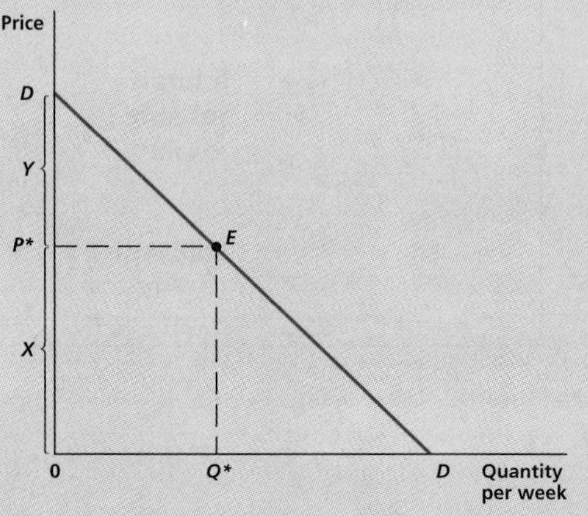

a. With this demand function, what is the value of P for which $Q = 0$?
b. Use your results from part a together with the fact that distance X in the figure is given by the current price, P^*, to show that distance Y is given by $-Q^*/b$ (remember, P^* is negative here, so this really is a positive distance).
c. To make further progress on this problem, we need to prove Equation 3.13 in the text. To do so, write the definition of price elasticity as

$$e_{Q,P} = \frac{\%\text{ change in } Q}{\%\text{ change in } P} = \frac{\Delta Q/Q}{\Delta P/P} = \frac{\Delta Q}{\Delta P} \cdot \frac{P}{Q}.$$

Now use the fact that the demand curve is linear to prove Equation 3.13.
d. Use the result from part c to show that $|e_{Q,P}| = X/Y$. We use the absolute value of the price elasticity here because that elasticity is negative, but the distances X and Y are positive.
e. Explain how the result of part d can be used to demonstrate how the price of elasticity of demand changes as one moves along a linear demand curve.
f. Explain how the results of part c might be used to approximate the price elasticity of demand at any point on a nonlinear demand curve.

PART 3

Uncertainty and Strategy

"It is a world of change in which we live ... the problems of life arise from the fact that we know so little."

—Frank H. Knight, Risk, Uncertainty and Profit, 1921

In Part 2, we looked at the choices people make when they know exactly what will happen. This study left us with a quite complete theory of demand and of how prices affect decisions. In this part, we expand our scope a bit by looking at how people make decisions when they are not certain what will happen. As is the case for the simple theory of demand, the tools developed here to deal with such uncertainty are used in all of economics.

Part 3 has only two chapters. The first (Chapter 4) focuses on defining the notion of "risk" and showing why people generally do not like it. Most of the chapter is concerned with methods that people may use to reduce the risks to which they are exposed. Uses of insurance, diversification, and options are highlighted as ways in which various risks can be reduced.

Chapter 5 then looks at a somewhat different kind of uncertainty—the uncertainty that can arise in strategic relationships with others. The utility-maximizing decision is no longer clear-cut because it will depend on how others behave. The chapter introduces the formal topic of game theory and shows, through increasingly complex formulations, how games can capture the essence of many strategic situations. We will learn to solve for the equilibrium of a game. In such an equilibrium, once it is established, no player has an incentive to change what he or she is doing because it is best for each given others' equilibrium behavior.

4 Uncertainty

So far, we have assumed that people's choices do not involve any degree of uncertainty; once they decide what to do, they get what they have chosen. That is not always the way things work in many real-world situations. When you buy a lottery ticket, invest in shares of common stock, or play poker, what you get back is subject to chance. In this chapter, we look at three questions raised by economic problems involving uncertainty: (1) How do people make decisions in an uncertain environment? (2) Why do people generally dislike risky situations? and (3) What can people do to avoid or reduce risks?

4-1 Probability and Expected Value

The study of individual behavior under uncertainty and the mathematical study of probability and statistics have a common historical origin in games of chance. Gamblers who try to devise ways of winning at blackjack and casinos trying to keep the game profitable are modern examples of this concern. Two statistical concepts that originated from studying games of chance, *probability* and *expected value,* are very important to our study of economic choices in uncertain situations.

The **probability** of an event happening is, roughly speaking, the relative frequency with which it occurs. For example, to say that the probability of a head coming up on the flip of a fair coin is 1/2 means that if a coin is flipped a large number of times, we can expect a head to come up in approximately one-half of the flips. Similarly, the probability of rolling a "2" on a single die is 1/6. In approximately one out of every six rolls, a "2" should come up. Of course, before a coin is flipped or a die is rolled, we have no idea what will happen, so each flip or roll has an uncertain outcome.

Probability
The relative frequency with which an event occurs.

The **expected value** of a gamble with a number of uncertain outcomes (or prizes) is the size of the prize that the player will win on average. Suppose Jones and Smith agree to flip a coin once. If a head comes up, Jones will pay Smith \$1; if a tail comes up, Smith will pay Jones \$1. From Smith's point of view, there are two prizes or outcomes (X_1 and X_2) in this gamble: if the coin is a head, $X_1 = +\$1$; if a tail comes up, $X_2 = -\$1$ (the minus sign indicates that Smith must pay). From Jones's point of view, the gamble is exactly the same except that the signs of the outcomes are reversed. The expected value of the gamble is then

Expected value
The average outcome from an uncertain gamble.

$$\frac{1}{2}X_1 + \frac{1}{2}X_2 = \frac{1}{2}(\$1) + \frac{1}{2}(-\$1) = 0. \quad \textbf{(4.1)}$$

The expected value of this gamble is zero. If the gamble were repeated a large number of times, it is not likely that either player would come out very far ahead.

MICRO QUIZ 4.1

What is the actuarially fair price for each of the following gambles?

1. Winning $1,000 with probability 0.5 and losing $1,000 with probability 0.5
2. Winning $1,000 with probability 0.6 and losing $1,000 with probability 0.4
3. Winning $1,000 with probability 0.7, winning $2,000 with probability 0.2, and losing $10,000 with probability 0.1

Now suppose the gamble's prizes were changed so that, from Smith's point of view, $X_1 = \$10$, and $X_2 = -\$1$. Smith will win $10 if a head comes up but will lose only $1 if a tail comes up. The expected value of this gamble is $4.50:

$$\begin{aligned}\frac{1}{2}X_1 + \frac{1}{2}X_2 &= \frac{1}{2}(\$10) + \frac{1}{2}(-\$1) \\ &= \$5 - \$0.50 = \$4.50.\end{aligned} \tag{4.2}$$

If this gamble is repeated many times, Smith will certainly end up the big winner, averaging $4.50 each time the coin is flipped. The gamble is so attractive that Smith might be willing to pay Jones something for the privilege of playing. She might even be willing to pay as much as $4.50, the expected value, for a chance to play. Gambles with an expected value of zero (or equivalently gambles for which the player must pay the expected value up front for the right to play, here $4.50) are called **fair gambles.** If fair gambles are repeated many times, the monetary losses or gains are expected to be rather small. Application 4.1: Blackjack Systems looks at the importance of the expected-value idea to gamblers and casinos alike.

Fair gamble
Gamble with an expected value of zero.

4-2 Risk Aversion

Risk aversion
The tendency of people to refuse to accept fair gambles.

Economists have found that when people are faced with a risky situation that would be a fair gamble, they usually choose not to participate.[1] A way to understand this **risk aversion** was first identified by the Swiss mathematician Daniel Bernoulli in the eighteenth century.[2] In his early study of behavior under uncertainty, Bernoulli theorized that it is not the monetary payoff of a gamble that matters to people. Rather, it is the utility (what Bernoulli called the *moral value*) associated with the gamble's prizes that is important for people's decisions. If differences in a gamble's money prizes do not completely reflect utility, people may find that gambles that are fair in dollar terms are in fact unfair in terms of utility. Specifically, Bernoulli (and most later economists) assumed that the utility associated with the payoffs in a risky situation increases less rapidly than the dollar value of these payoffs. That is, the extra (or marginal) utility that winning an extra dollar in prize money provides is assumed to decline as more dollars are won.

Diminishing Marginal Utility

This assumption is illustrated in Figure 4.1, which shows the utility associated with possible prizes (or incomes) from $0 to $50,000. The concave shape of the curve reflects the assumed diminishing marginal utility of these prizes. Although additional income always

[1]The gambles we discuss here are assumed to yield no utility in their play other than the prizes. Because economists wish to focus on the purely risk-related aspects of a situation, they must abstract from any pure consumption benefit that people get from gambling. Clearly, if gambling is fun to someone, he or she will be willing to pay something to play.

[2]For an English translation of the original 1738 article, see D. Bernoulli, "Exposition of a New Theory on the Measurement of Risk," *Econometrica* (January 1954): 23–36. In honor of their work formalizing Bernoulli's idea—see J. von Neumann and O. Morgenstern, *The Theory of Games and Economic Behavior* (Princeton, NJ: Princeton University Press, 1944)—the function reflecting utility under uncertainty is now called the von Neumann–Morgenstern utility function.

APPLICATION 4.1

Blackjack Systems

The game of blackjack (or twenty-one) provides an illustration of the expected-value notion and its relevance to people's behavior in uncertain situations. Blackjack is a very simple game. Each player is dealt two cards (with the dealer playing last). The dealer asks each player if he or she wishes another card. The player getting a hand that totals closest to 21, without going over 21, is the winner. If the receipt of a card puts a player over 21, that player automatically loses.

Played in this way, blackjack offers a number of advantages to the dealer. Most important, the dealer, who plays last, is in a favorable position because other players can go over 21 (and therefore lose) before the dealer plays. Under the usual rules, the dealer has the additional advantage of winning ties. These two advantages give the dealer a margin of winning of about 6 percent on average. Players can expect to win 47 percent of all hands played, whereas the dealer will win 53 percent of the time.

Card Counting

Because the rules of blackjack make the game unfair to players, casinos have gradually eased the rules in order to entice more people to play. At many Las Vegas casinos, for example, dealers must play under fixed rules that allow no discretion depending on the individual game situation; and, in the case of ties, rather than winning them, dealers must return bets to the players. These rules alter fairness of the game quite a bit. By some estimates, Las Vegas casino dealers enjoy a blackjack advantage of as little as 0.1 percent, if that. In fact, in recent years a number of systems have been developed by players that they claim can even result in a net advantage for the player. The systems involve counting face cards, systematic varying of bets, and numerous other strategies for special situations that arise in the game.[1] Computer simulations of literally billions of potential blackjack hands have shown that careful adherence to a correct strategy can result in an advantage to the player of as much as 1 or 2 percent. Actor Dustin Hoffman illustrated these potential advantages in his character's remarkable ability to count cards in the 1989 movie *Rain Man.*

Casino versus Card Counter

It should come as no surprise that players' use of these blackjack systems is not particularly welcomed by those who operate Las Vegas casinos. The casinos made several rule changes (such as using multiple card decks to make card counting more difficult) in order to reduce system players' advantages. They have also started to refuse admission to known system players. Such care has not been foolproof, however. For example, in the late 1990s a small band of MIT students used a variety of sophisticated card-counting techniques to take Las Vegas casinos for more than $2 million.[2] Their clever efforts did not amuse casino personnel, however, and the students had a number of unpleasant encounters with security personnel.

All of this turmoil illustrates the importance of small changes in expected values for a game such as blackjack that involves many repetitions. Card counters pay little attention to the outcome on a single hand in blackjack. Instead, they focus on improving the average outcome after many hours at the card table. Even small changes in the probability of winning can result in large cumulative winnings.

Expected Values of Other Games

The expected-value concept plays an important role in all of the games of chance offered at casinos. For example, slot machines can be set to yield a precise expected return to players. When a casino operates hundreds of slot machines in a single location, it can be virtually certain of the return it can earn each day even though the payouts from any particular machine can be quite variable. Similarly, the game of roulette includes 36 numbered squares together with squares labeled "0" and "00." By paying out 36-to-1 on the numbered squares, the casino can expect to earn about 5.3 cents ($= 2 \div 38$) on each dollar bet. Bets on Red or Black or on Even or Odd are equally profitable. The game of baccarat has the lowest expected return for casinos according to some experts, though in this case the game's high stakes may still make it quite profitable.

TO THINK ABOUT

1. If blackjack systems increase people's expected winnings, why doesn't everyone use them? Who do you expect would be most likely to learn how to use the systems?
2. How does the fact that casinos operate many blackjack tables, slot machines, and roulette tables simultaneously reduce the risk that they will lose money? Is it more risky to operate a small casino than a large one?

[1]The classic introduction to card-counting strategies is in Edward O. Thorp, *Beat the Dealer* (New York: Random House, 1962).

[2]Their experience was dramatized in the 2008 movie "21," based on the book by Ben Merzich, *Bringing Down The House* (New York: Free Press, 2002).

Figure 4.1 **Risk Aversion**

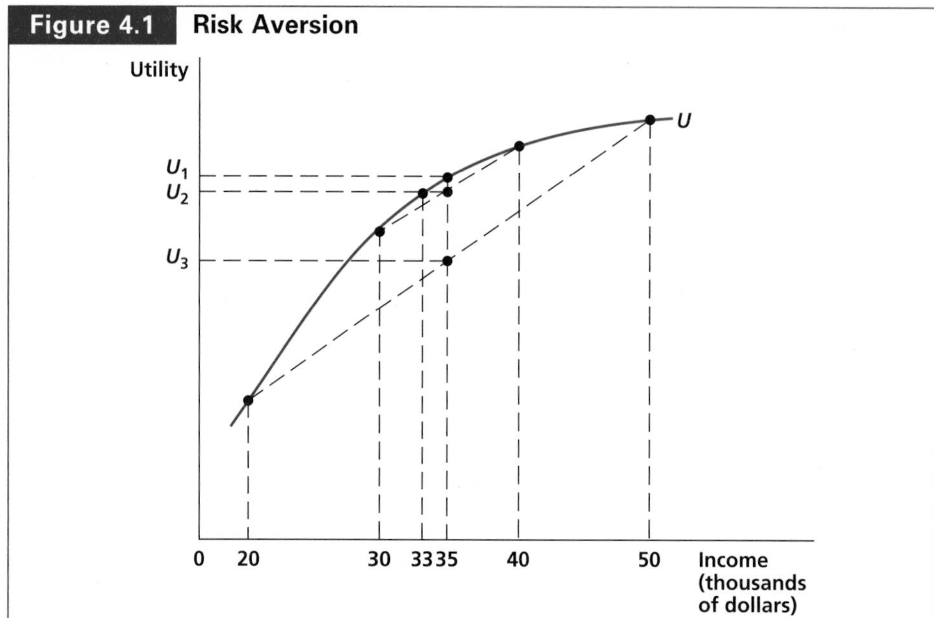

An individual characterized by the utility-of-income curve U will obtain a higher expected utility (U_1) from a risk-free income of \$35,000 than from a 50-50 chance of winning or losing \$5,000 (U_2). He or she will be willing to pay up to \$2,000 to avoid having to take this bet. A fair bet of \$15,000 provides even less expected utility (U_3) than the \$5,000 bet.

raises utility, the increase in utility resulting from an increase in income from \$1,000 to \$2,000 is much greater than the increase in utility that results from an increase in income from \$49,000 to \$50,000. It is this assumed diminishing marginal utility of income (which is in some ways similar to the assumption of diminishing marginal rate of substitution (MRS) introduced in Chapter 2) that gives rise to risk aversion.

A Graphical Analysis of Risk Aversion

Figure 4.1 illustrates risk aversion. The figure assumes that three options are open to this person. He or she may (1) retain the current level of income (\$35,000) without taking any risk, (2) take a fair bet with a 50-50 chance of winning or losing \$5,000, or (3) take a fair bet with a 50-50 chance of winning or losing \$15,000. To examine the person's preferences among these options, we must compute the expected utility available from each.

The utility received by the first option of staying at the current \$35,000 income is given by U_1. The U curve shows directly how the individual feels about this current income. The expected utility from the second option, the \$5,000 bet, is simply the average of the utility of \$40,000 (which the individual will end up with by winning the gamble) and the utility of \$30,000 (which he or she will end up with when the gamble is lost). This average utility is given by U_2.[3] Because it falls short of U_1, we can assume that the person will refuse to make the \$5,000 bet. Finally, the utility of the third option, the \$15,000 bet, is the average of the utility from \$50,000 and the utility from \$20,000.

[3]This average utility can be found by drawing the chord joining $U(\$40{,}000)$ and $U(\$30{,}000)$ and finding the midpoint of that chord. Because the vertical line at \$35,000 is midway between \$40,000 and \$30,000, it will also bisect the chord.

This is given by U_3, which falls below U_2. In other words, the person likes the risky \$15,000 bet even less than the \$5,000 bet.

KEEP *in* MIND

Choosing among Gambles

To solve problems involving a consumer's choice over gambles, you should proceed in two steps. First, using the formula for expected values, compute the consumer's expected utility from each gamble. Then choose the gamble with the highest value of this number.

Willingness to Pay to Avoid Risk

Diminished marginal utility of income, as shown in Figure 4.1, means that people will be averse to risk. Among outcomes with the same expected dollar values (\$35,000 in all of our examples), people will prefer risk-free to risky ones because the gains such risky outcomes offer are worth less in utility terms than the losses. In fact, a person would be willing to give up some amount of income to avoid taking a risk. In Figure 4.1, for example, a risk-free income of \$33,000 provides the same expected utility as the \$5,000 gamble (U_2). The individual is willing to pay up to \$2,000 to avoid taking that risk. There are a number of ways this person might spend these funds to reduce the risk or avoid it completely, which we will study later. Saying that someone is "very risk averse" is the same as saying that he or she is willing to spend a lot to avoid risk.

The shape of the utility-of-income curve, such as U in Figure 4.1, provides some idea of how risk averse the individual is. If U bends sharply, then the utility the individual obtains from a certain outcome will be well above the expected utility from an uncertain gamble with the same expected payoff. The less U bends (that is, the more linear U is), the less risk averse is the person. In the extreme, if U is a straight line, then the person will be indifferent between a certain outcome and a gamble with the same expected payoff. In other words, he or she would accept any fair gamble. A person with these risk preferences is said to be **risk neutral**.

What would the utility-of-income curve U be shaped like for someone who prefers risky situations?

Risk neutral
Willing to accept any fair gamble.

Even for a very risk-averse person with a utility-of-income curve that is sharply bent as in Figure 4.1, if we took a small piece of the curve, say that between incomes \$33,000 and \$35,000, and magnified it to be able to see it better, this piece looks almost like a straight line. Because straight lines are associated with risk-neutral individuals, this graphical exercise suggests that even people who are risk averse over large gambles (with, say, thousands of dollars at stake) will be nearly risk neutral over small gambles (with only a few dollars at stake). People are not very averse to small risks because even the worst case with a small risk does not reduce the person's income appreciably.

4-3 Methods for Reducing Risk and Uncertainty

In many situations, taking risks is unavoidable. Even though driving your car or eating a meal at a restaurant subjects you to some uncertainty about what will actually happen, short of becoming a hermit, there is no way you can avoid every risk in your life. Our analysis in the previous section suggests, however, that people are generally willing to pay something to reduce these risks. In this section, we examine four methods for doing so—insurance, diversification, flexibility, and information acquisition.

Insurance

Each year, U.S. insurance companies take in nearly $2 trillion in premiums for insurance of all types. Most commonly, consumers buy coverage for their own life, for their home and automobiles, and for their health care costs. But insurance can be bought (perhaps at a very high price) for practically any risk imaginable. For example, many people in California buy earthquake insurance, outdoor swimming pool owners can buy special coverage for injuries to falling parachutists, and surgeons or basketball players can insure their hands. In all of these cases, people are willing to pay a premium to an insurance company in order to be assured of compensation if something goes wrong.

The underlying motive for insurance purchases is illustrated in Figure 4.2. Here, we have repeated the utility-of-income curve from Figure 4.1, but now we assume that during the next year this person with a $35,000 current income (and consumption) faces a 50 percent chance of having $15,000 in unexpected medical bills, which would reduce his or her consumption to $20,000. Without insurance, this person's expected utility would be U_1—the average of the utility from $35,000 and the utility from $20,000.

Fair insurance
Insurance for which the premium is equal to the expected value of the loss.

Fair Insurance This person would clearly be better off with an actuarially **fair insurance** policy for his or her health care needs. This policy would cost $7,500—the expected value of what insurance companies would have to pay each year in health claims. A person who bought the policy would be assured of $27,500 in consumption. If he or she bought the

Figure 4.2 Insurance Reduces Risk

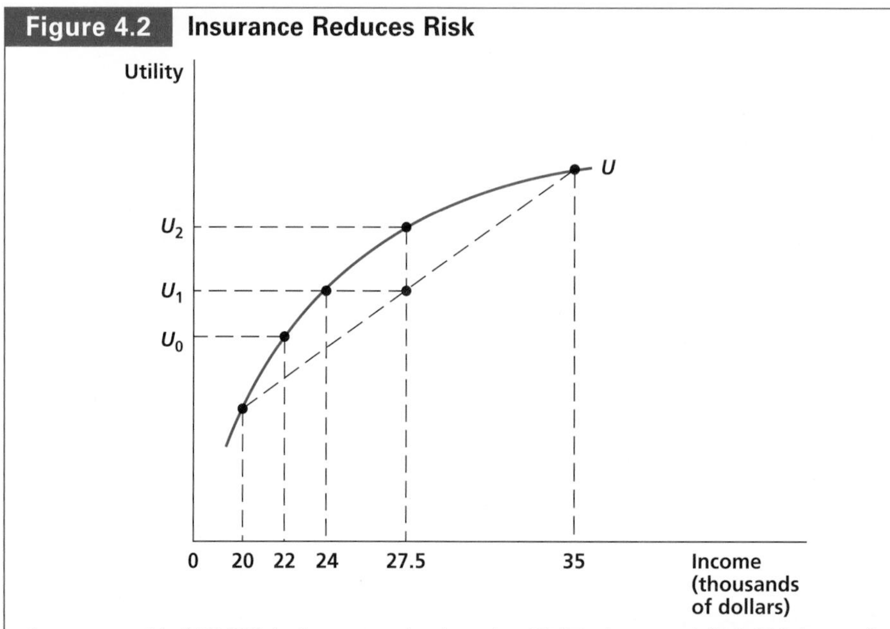

A person with $35,000 in income who faced a 50-50 chance of $15,000 in medical bills would have an expected utility of U_1. With fair insurance (which costs $7,500), utility would be U_2. Even unfair insurance costing $11,000 would still yield the same expected utility (U_1) as facing the world uninsured. But a premium of $13,000, which provides a utility of only U_0, would be too costly.

policy and stayed well, income would be reduced by the $7,500 premium. If this person suffered the illness, the insurance company would pay the $15,000 in medical bills, but this person would have paid the $7,500 premium, so consumption would still be $27,500. As Figure 4.2 shows, the utility from a certain income of $27,500 ($U_2$) exceeds that attainable from facing the world uninsured, so the policy represents a utility-enhancing use for funds.

Unfair Insurance No insurance company can afford to sell insurance at actuarially fair premiums. Not only do insurance companies have to pay benefits, but they must also maintain records, collect premiums, investigate claims to ensure they are not fraudulent, and perhaps return a profit to shareholders. Hence, a would-be insurance purchaser can always expect to pay more than an actuarially fair premium. Still, a buyer may decide that the risk reduction that insurance provides is worth the extra charges. In the health care illustration in Figure 4.2, for example, this person would be willing to pay up to $11,000 for health insurance because the risk-free consumption stream of $24,000 that buying such "unfair" insurance would yield provides as much expected utility (U_1) as does facing the world uninsured. Of course, even a desirable product such as insurance can become too expensive. At a price of $13,000, the expected utility provided with full insurance (U_0) falls short of what would be obtained from facing the world uninsured. In this case, this person is better off taking the risk of paying his or her own medical bills than accepting such an unfair insurance premium. In Application 4.2: Deductibles in Insurance, we look at one way to avoid unfair insurance associated with small risks.

Uninsurable Risks The preceding discussion shows that risk-averse individuals will always buy insurance against risky outcomes unless insurance premiums exceed the expected value of a loss by too much. Three types of factors may result in such high premiums and thereby cause some risks to become uninsurable. First, some risks may be so unique or difficult to evaluate that an insurer may have no idea how to set the premium level. Determining an actuarially fair premium requires that a given risky situation must occur frequently enough so that the insurer can both estimate the expected value of the loss and rely on being able to cover expected payouts with premiums from individuals who do not suffer losses. For rare or very unpredictable events such as wars, nuclear power plant mishaps, or invasions from Mars, would-be insurers may have no basis for establishing insurance premiums and therefore refrain from offering any coverage.

Two other reasons for absence of insurance coverage relate to the behavior of the individuals who want to buy insurance. In some cases, these individuals may know more about the likelihood that they will suffer a loss than does an insurer. Those who expect large losses will buy insurance, whereas those who expect small ones will not. This *adverse selection* results in the insurer paying out more in losses than expected unless the insurer finds a way to control who buys the policies offered. As we will see later, in the absence of such controls, no insurance would be provided even though people would willingly buy it.

The behavior of individuals after they are insured may also affect the possibility for insurance coverage. If having insurance makes people more likely to incur losses, insurers' premium calculations will be incorrect, and again, they may be forced to charge premiums that are too unfair in an actuarial sense. For example, after buying insurance for ski equipment, people may begin to ski more recklessly and treat the equipment more roughly because they no longer bear the cost of damage. To cover this increased chance of damage, insurance premiums may have to be very high. This *moral hazard* in people's behavior means that insurance against accidental losses of cash will not be available on any reasonable terms. In Chapter 15, we explore both adverse selection and moral hazard in much more detail.

APPLICATION 4.2

Deductibles in Insurance

A "deductible" provision in an insurance policy is the requirement that the insured pay the first *X* dollars in the event of a claim; after that, insurance kicks in. With automobile insurance policies, for example, a $500 deductible provision is quite standard. If you have a collision, you must pay the first $500 in damages, and then the insurance company will pay the rest. Most other casualty insurance policies have similar provisions.

Deductibles and Administrative Costs

The primary reason for deductible provisions in insurance contracts is to deter small claims. Because administrative costs to the insurance company of handling a claim are about the same regardless of a claim's size, such costs will tend to be a very high fraction of the value of a small claim. Hence, insurance against small losses will tend to be actuarially "unfair." Most people will find that they would rather incur the risks of such losses (such as scratches to the finish of their cars) themselves rather than paying such unfair premiums. Similarly, increasing the deductible in a policy may sometimes be a financially attractive option.

These features of deductibles in insurance policies are illustrated by the choices your authors make. For example, both of their automobile policies offer either a $500 or a $1,000 deductible associated with collision coverage. The $500 deductible policy costs about $100 more each year. Both authors have opted for the $1,000 policy on the principle that paying $100 for an extra $500 coverage each year seems like a bad deal.

Deductibles in Health Insurance

Although the logic of a deductible applies to health insurance too, the presence of such features has proven to be quite controversial.[1] For example, in 1988 Congress passed the Medicare Catastrophic Coverage Act. This act provided extra coverage for Medicare recipients, with a large annual deductible being required before coverage began. This policy proved unpopular for two reasons: (1) People argued that it was unfair to ask elderly people suffering "catastrophic" illnesses to pay the initial portion of their costs; and (2) the premium for the policy was to be paid by the elderly themselves rather than by the working population (as is the case for a major portion of the rest of the Medicare program). The uproar over the program was so large that it was repealed after only one year.

Arguments over deductibles surrounded the adoption of a Medicare Part D drug benefit in 2003. The plan's initial design confronted elderly consumers of prescription drugs with a complex deductible scheme: (1) the first $250 spent annually on drugs is not covered by the drug benefit, (2) 75 percent of annual spending on drugs between $250 and $2,100 is covered by Medicare, (3) no spending between $2,100 and $5,100 annually is covered by Medicare, and (4) 95 percent of annual spending over $5,100 is reimbursed by Medicare. Observers have had a difficult time trying to find a rationale for such a complex scheme—especially for the odd "doughnut hole" of coverage between $2,100 and $5,100 in annual spending. Clearly, the provision cannot have much to do with the administrative cost issue. The $250 deductible at the bottom of the schedule prevents the filing of claims for every aspirin bought. It may be that the hole is intended mainly to save money so that available funds can be focused on the most needy elderly (those with drug expenses over $5,100), but whether it has a rationale in the theory of insurance is anyone's guess.

Concerns about the ballooning U.S. budget deficit have renewed interest in saving government resources by raising deductibles. Over the last 15 years, the deductible for Medicare Part A (covering hospital stays) has increased over 50 percent, to $1,184 in 2013. Not only do government-provided health programs such as Medicare add to the deficit, but privately provided health insurance does too because employers get a tax break for the insurance benefit provided to employees. Some employers have taken advantage of this favorable tax treatment by offering extremely generous, "Cadillac" insurance plans to employees, placing few restrictions on what procedures are covered and low or no deductibles. One of the provisions of the 2010 Affordable Care Act (commonly called "Obamacare" after the president who signed it into law) was to reduce the tax break for Cadillac plans.

TO THINK ABOUT

1. In some cases, you can buy another insurance policy to cover a deductible in your underlying insurance. That is the case, for example, when you rent a car and for "Medigap" policies that cover Medicare deductibles. Does buying such a policy make sense?
2. Why are deductibles usually stated on an annual basis? If losses occur randomly, wouldn't a "lifetime" deductible be better?

[1]Many health insurance policies also have "co-payment" provisions that require people to pay, say, 25 percent of their claim's cost. Co-payments increase the price people pay for health care at the *margin*. Deductibles reduce the average price paid, but, after the deductible is met, the marginal price of added care is zero. For a discussion of co-payments in health (and other) insurance, see Chapter 15.

Diversification

A second way for risk-averse individuals to reduce risk is by diversifying. This is the economic principle underlying the adage, "Don't put all your eggs in one basket." By suitably spreading risk around, it may be possible to raise expected utility above that provided by following a single course of action. This possibility is illustrated in Figure 4.3, which shows the utility of income for an individual with a current income of $35,000 who must invest $15,000 of that income in risky assets.

For simplicity, assume there are only two such assets, shares of stock in company A or company B. One share of stock in either company costs $1, and the investor believes that the stock will rise to $2 if the company does well during the next year; if the company does poorly, however, the stock will be worthless. Each company has a 50-50 chance of doing well. How should this individual invest his or her funds? At first, it would seem that it does not matter since the two companies' prospects are identical. But, if we assume the company's prospects are unrelated to one another, we can show that holding both stocks will reduce this person's risks.

Suppose this person decides to plunge into the market by investing only in 15,000 shares of company A. Then he or she has a 50 percent chance of having $50,000 at the end of the year and a 50 percent chance of having $20,000. This undiversified investment strategy will therefore yield an expected utility of U_1.

Figure 4.3 Diversification Reduces Risk

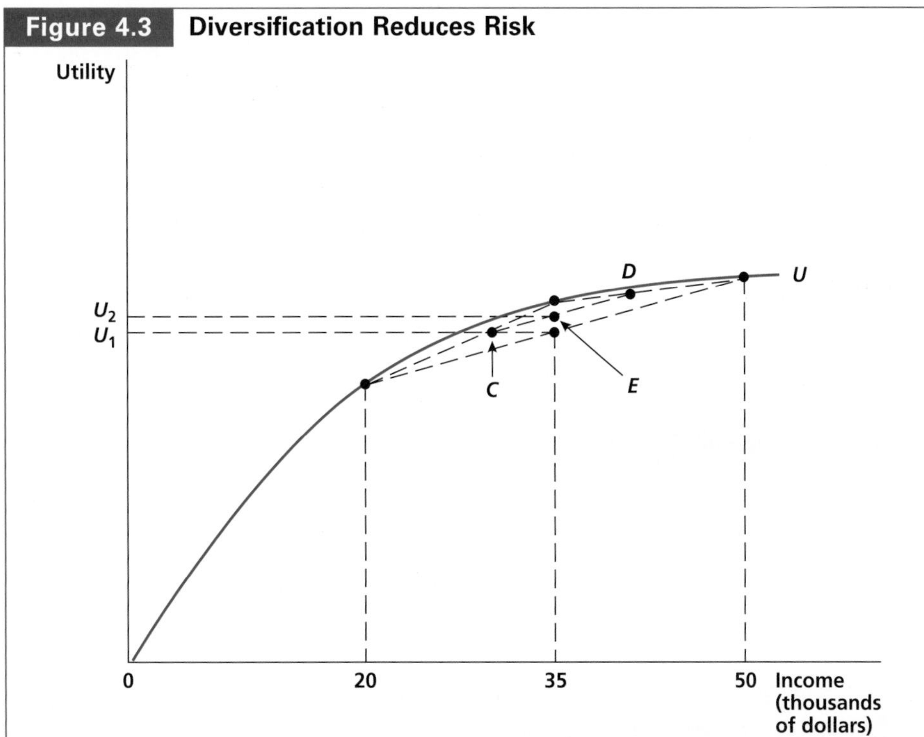

Here, an investor must invest $15,000 in risky stocks. If he or she invests in only one stock, expected utility will be U_1. Although two unrelated stocks may promise identical returns, investing in both of them can, on average, reduce risk and raise expected utility to U_2.

Table 4.1 Possible Outcomes from Investing in Two Companies

		COMPANY B'S PERFORMANCE	
		POOR	GOOD
Company A's Performance	Poor	$20,000	$35,000
	Good	35,000	50,000

Let's consider a diversified strategy in which the investor buys 7,500 shares of each stock. There are now four possible outcomes, depending on how each company does. These are illustrated in Table 4.1 together with the individual's income in each of these eventualities. Each of these outcomes is equally likely. Notice that the diversified strategy achieves very good or very bad results only when both companies do well or poorly, respectively. In half the cases, the gains in one company's shares balance the losses in the other's, and the individual ends up with the original $35,000. The diversified strategy, although it has the same expected value ($\$35{,}000 = 0.25 \cdot \$20.000 + 0.50 \cdot \$35{,}000 + 0.25 \cdot \$50{,}000$) as the single-stock strategy, is less risky.

Illustrating the utility gain from this reduction in risk requires a bit of ingenuity because we must average the utilities from the four outcomes shown in Table 4.1. We do so in a two-step process. Point *C* in Figure 4.3 represents the average utility for the case where company B does poorly (the average of the utility from $20,000 and $35,000), whereas point *D* represents the average utility when company B does well ($35,000 and $50,000). The final average of points *C* and *D* is found at point *E*, which represents an expected utility level of U_2. Because U_2 exceeds U_1, it is clear that this individual has gained from diversification.

Diversification
The spreading of risk among several alternatives rather than choosing only one.

The conclusion that spreading risk through **diversification** can increase expected utility applies to a number of situations. The reasoning in our simple illustration can be used, for example, to explain why individuals opt to buy mutual funds that invest in many stocks rather than choosing only a few stocks on their own (see Application 4.3: Mutual Funds). It also explains why people invest in many kinds of assets (stocks, bonds, cash, precious metals, real estate, and durable goods such as automobiles) rather than in only one. The principle of diversification applies to spheres other than financial markets. Students entering college who are unsure of where their interests or talents lie are well advised to register for a diverse set of classes rather than exclusively technical or artistic ones. By planting a variety of tree species, the groundskeeper can ensure that the campus is not laid bare by a single pest or weather conditions favoring certain trees over others. In all of these cases, our analysis shows that individuals will not only obtain higher expected utility levels because of the risk reduction from diversification but that they might even be willing to pay something (say, mutual fund fees, additional college tuition, or a less-than-perfectly-uniform tree canopy) to obtain these gains.

MICRO QUIZ 4.3

Explain why the following are examples of diversification—that is, explain why each choice specified offers the same expected value, though the preferred choice is lower in risk.

1. Preferring to bet $100 on each of 10 coin flips over $1,000 on a single flip
2. Preferring single feed lines at banks to lines for each teller
3. Preferring basketball to soccer if a single gamble is to determine the best team (this example may reflect a peculiarity of your authors)

APPLICATION 4.3

Mutual Funds

One of the most convenient ways for individuals to invest in common stocks is by purchasing mutual fund shares. Mutual funds pool money from many investors to buy shares in several different companies. For this service, individuals pay an annual management fee of about 0.5 to 1.5 percent of the value of the money they have invested.

Diversification and Risk Characteristics of Funds

Although mutual fund managers often sell their services on the basis of their supposed superiority in picking stocks, the diversification that funds offer probably provides a better explanation of why individuals choose them. Any single investor who tried to purchase shares in, say, 100 different companies would find that most of his or her funds would be used for brokerage commissions, with little money left over to buy shares. Because mutual funds deal in large volume, brokerage commissions are lower. It then becomes feasible for an individual to own a proportionate share in the stocks of many companies. For the reasons illustrated in Figure 4.3, this diversification reduces risk.

Still, investing in stocks generally is a risky enterprise, so mutual fund managers offer products that allow investors to choose the amount of risk they are willing to tolerate. Money market and short-term bond funds tend to offer little risk; balanced funds (which consist of both common stocks and bonds) are a bit riskier; growth funds offer the greatest risk. On average, the riskier funds have tended to yield a somewhat higher return for investors. For example, one well-known study of mutual fund performance during the 1960s found that each 10 percent increase in risk resulted in an increase in average total yield from the funds of about one percentage point.[1]

Portfolio Management

Managers of mutual funds can reduce risk further by the choices they make when purchasing specific stocks. Our numerical illustration of the benefits of diversification assumed that the returns on the shares of the two companies were independent of each other; it was that fact that resulted in the benefits from diversification. Further benefits in terms of risk reduction can be achieved if mutual fund managers find investments whose returns tend to move in opposite directions (that is, when one does well, the other does not, and vice versa). For example, some fund managers may choose to hold some of their funds in mining companies because precious metal prices tend to rise when stock prices fall. Another way to achieve this balancing of risk is to purchase stocks from companies in many countries. Such global mutual funds and international funds (which specialize in securities from individual countries) have grown rapidly in recent years. More generally, fund managers may even be able to develop complex strategies involving short sales or stock options that allow them to hedge their returns from a given investment even further. Recent financial innovations such as standardized put and call options, stock index options, interest rate futures, and a bewildering variety of computer-program trading schemes illustrate the increasing demand for such risk-reduction vehicles.

Index Funds

Index funds represent a more systematic approach to diversification. These funds, which were first introduced in the 1970s, seek to mimic the performance of an overall market average. Some of the most popular funds track the Standard and Poor's 500 Stock Market index, but funds that track market indices such as the Dow Jones Industrial Average or the Wilshire 5,000 Stock Average are also available. There are also index funds that mimic foreign stock market indices, such as the Nikkei Stock Average (Japan) or the *Financial Times* Index (United Kingdom). Managers of these index funds use complex computer algorithms to ensure that they closely track their underlying index. The primary advantage of these funds is their very low management cost. Most large index funds have annual expenses of less than 0.25 percent of their assets, whereas actively managed funds have expenses that average about 1.3 percent of assets. Historically, few managed funds have been able to overcome this cost disadvantage.[2]

TO THINK ABOUT

1. Most studies of mutual fund performance conclude that managers cannot consistently exceed the average return in the stock market as a whole. Why might you expect this result? What does it imply about investors' motives for buying managed mutual funds?
2. Mutual funds compute the net asset value of each share daily. Should the fund's shares sell for this value in the open market?

[1]M. Jensen, "Risk, the Pricing of Capital Assets, and the Evaluation of Investment Performance," *Journal of Business* (April 1969).

[2]One of the staunchest advocates of indexed over managed funds is Burton Malkiel. See, for example, B. G. Malkiel, "You're Paying Too Much for Investment Help," *Wall Street Journal*, May 29, 2013, page A15.

Flexibility

Diversification is a useful strategy to reduce risk for a person who can subdivide a decision by allocating small amounts of a larger quantity among a number of different choices. For example, an investor can diversify by allocating a pool of funds among a number of different financial assets. A student can diversify by subdividing the total number of courses he or she will take over a college career among several different subjects.

In some cases, a decision cannot be subdivided. It must be all or nothing. For example, a college student usually does not have permission to take each course at a different college; typically, he or she takes most courses on a single campus. Choosing which college to attend is an all-or-nothing decision. Other situations also involve all-or-nothing decisions, such as a consumer's decision regarding which winter coat to buy. He or she cannot buy half of a mild-weather jacket and half of a mountaineer's parka. Firms typically build huge factories to take account of efficiencies of a large-scale operation. It may be much less efficient for the firm to diversify into three different technologies by building three small factories a third of the size of the large one.

With all-or-nothing decisions, the decision maker can obtain some of the benefits of diversification by making flexible decisions. Flexibility allows the person to adjust the initial decision, depending on how the future unfolds. In the presence of considerable uncertainty and, thus, considerable variation in what the future might look like, flexibility becomes all the more valuable. Flexibility keeps the decision maker from being tied into one course of action and instead provides a number of options. The decision maker can choose the best option to suit later circumstances.

A numerical illustration of the value of flexibility is provided in Table 4.2. A person must decide on which coat to buy for an overnight hike in the face of uncertainty about what the weather conditions will be. Suppose the temperature is equally likely to be either bitter cold or mild. Put aside prices for now and just think about the benefits a consumer derives from different coats measured in utility terms. A parka is more suitable for cold conditions, providing utility of 100 in the bitter cold, but is less suitable for mild conditions, providing utility of only 50 because it becomes overly hot and heavy. A windbreaker has the opposite utility pattern, providing the shivering wearer with a utility of only 50 in the bitter cold but providing utility of 100 in mild conditions. The consumer has a third choice, a 2-in-1 coat, which provides more flexibility. The two layers can be zipped together to provide the insulation of a parka, or the outer liner can be worn alone as a windbreaker.

The 2-in-1 coat is a better choice than either of the other two coats alone because it provides more options than the other coats, allowing it to better adapt to the weather conditions. Given equal chances of cold or mild weather, the expected utility provided by the 2-in-1 is 100 but only 75 for the other two coats. If the three coats sold for the same price, the consumer would buy the 2-in-1, and depending on the utility value of money, the consumer would possibly be willing to pay considerably more for the 2-in-1.

Table 4.2 Utility Provided by Coats in Different Weather

	WEATHER CONDITIONS	
COATS	BITTER COLD	MILD
Parka	100	50
Windbreaker	50	100
2-in-1	100	100

Options We noted that the 2-in-1 coat is better than either of the others in the presence of uncertain weather conditions because it provides more options. Students are probably familiar with the notion that options are valuable from another context where the term is frequently used: financial markets where one hears about stock options and other forms of option contracts. There is a close connection between the coat example and these option contracts that we will investigate in more detail. Before discussing the similarities between the options arising in different contexts, we introduce some terms to distinguish them. An **option contract** is a financial contract offering the right, but not the obligation, to buy or sell an asset (say, a share of stock) during some future period at a certain price. Options that arise in settings involving uncertainty outside of the world of finance (our coat example is but one case) are called **real options**. Real options involve the allocation of tangible resources, not just the transfer of money from one person to another. In the coat example, the 2-in-1 coat can be viewed as a parka with a real option to convert the parka into a windbreaker if the wearer wants (it can also be viewed as a windbreaker with a real option to convert it into a parka).

Option contract
Financial contract offering the right, but not the obligation, to buy or sell an asset over a specified period.

Real option
Option arising in a setting outside of finance.

Attributes of Options There are many different types of option contracts, some of which can be quite complex. There are also many different types of real options, and they arise in many different settings, sometimes making it difficult to determine exactly what sort of option is embedded in the situation. Still, all options share three fundamental attributes.

1. **Specification of the underlying transaction.** Options must include details of the transaction being considered. This includes what is being bought or sold, at what price the transaction will take place, and any other details that are relevant (such as where the transaction will occur). With a stock option, for example, the contract specifies which company's stock is involved, how many shares will be transacted, and at what price. With the real option represented by the 2-in-1 coat, the underlying transaction is the conversion of a parka into a windbreaker.
2. **Definition of the period during which the option may be exercised.** A stock option may have to be exercised within two years or it will expire, but the parties to an option contract could agree on any exercise period, ranging from the very specific (the option may be exercised only on June 5 at 10:00 am) to the very general (the option may be exercised anytime). With the real option in the coat example, the decision was which coat to bring on a hiking trip, so the implicit exercise period is during the hike.
3. **The price of an option.** In some cases, the price of an option is explicit. A stock option might sell for a price of \$70. If this option is later traded on an exchange, its price might vary from moment to moment as the markets move. Real options do not tend to have explicit prices, but sometimes implicit prices can be calculated. For example, in the coat example, the option to convert a parka into a windbreaker could be measured as the price difference between the coat with the option (the 2-in-1) and the coat without (the parka). If the 2-in-1 sells for \$150 and the parka for \$120, the implicit price of the option is \$30. If the 2-in-1 is not as good an insulator in the cold as the parka, then the loss from this disadvantage adjusted by the probability that the disadvantage will be apparent (the probability that the weather is cold) would need to be added to the implicit price of the real option.

To understand any option, you need to be able to identify these three components. Whether the option is worth its price will depend on the details of the underlying transaction and on the nature of the option's exercise period. Let's look at how these details might affect an option's value to a would-be buyer.

How the Value of the Underlying Transaction Affects Option Value The value of the underlying transaction in an option has two general dimensions: (1) the expected value of the transaction and (2) the variability of the value of the transaction. An option to buy a share of Google stock at a price of $700 in the future is more valuable if Google's stock is presently trading at $900 than if it is trading at $500. The real option provided by the 2-in-1 coat to convert it into a windbreaker is more valuable if the material in the outer shell that will form the windbreaker is high quality and well suited to the mild weather for which it is designed.

The logic of why an option is more valuable if underlying conditions are more variable goes back to the definition of an option—that it gives the holder the right but not the obligation to exercise it. The holder can benefit from having an option to deal with certain extremes, and the fact that the option is increasingly poorly suited for other extremes is not harmful because the holder can simply choose not to exercise the option in these cases. A numerical example can help make the point clearer. Returning to the coat example, suppose that the weather conditions are more extreme, with the bitter cold even colder and the mild weather even warmer. The parka provides even more utility in the cold but less in the mild, and the reverse for the windbreaker. The new utility numbers are provided in Table 4.3. Under the original conditions, the expected utility from the 2-in-1 coat was 25 units higher than either of the other two coats: 100 compared to $(1/2)(100) + (1/2)(50) = 75$. Under more variable conditions, now the expected utility is 75 units higher: 150 compared to $(1/2)(150) + (1/2)(0) = 75$. The hiker would pay an even higher price premium for the 2-in-1 over the other coats than before. The real option of being able to convert the 2-in-1 coat into a windbreaker becomes more valuable as the mild conditions become warmer, and the fact that the windbreaker is worse suited to the colder conditions does not matter because the hiker will keep the 2-in-1 coat as a parka in that case.

Similarly, an option giving the holder the right to buy Google stock at a price of $700 in the future is worthless if the stock currently sells for less than $700 and does not vary at all. The stock option is valuable only if there is some chance the stock price will rise above $700. The more variability, the greater the chance the stock price rises well above the $700 threshold. More variability also means that there is a greater chance the price of Google stock will decline steeply. But the option holder does not care how steep the decline is because he or she will simply not exercise the option in that case. The holder of an option to buy Google shares is insulated against price declines but shares in all the benefits of price increases. Application 4.4: Puts, Calls, and Black-Scholes delves into more of the details on valuing stock options.

Table 4.3 Utility Provided by Coats under More Extreme Conditions

	WEATHER CONDITIONS	
COATS	BITTER COLD	MILD
Parka	150	0
Windbreaker	0	150
2-in-1	150	150

How the Duration of an Option Affects Its Value The effect of the duration of an option on its value is much easier to understand. Simply put, the longer an option lasts, the more valuable it is. Intuitively, the more time you have to take advantage of the flexibility an option offers, the more

APPLICATION 4.4

Puts, Calls, and Black-Scholes

Options on financial assets are widely traded in organized markets. Not only are there options available on most company's stocks, but there are also a bewildering variety of options on such assets as bonds, foreign exchange, and commodities, or even on indexes based on groups of these assets. Probably the most common options are those related to the stock of a single company. The potential transactions underlying these options are simply promises to buy or sell the stock at a specific ("strike") price over some period in the future. Options to buy a stock at a certain strike price are termed "call" options because the buyer has the right to "call" the stock from someone else if he or she wishes to exercise the option. Options to sell a stock at a certain price are called "put" options (perhaps because you have the option to put the stock into someone else's hands).

Suppose that Microsoft stock is currently selling at $30 per share. A call option might give you the right (but, again, not the obligation) to buy Microsoft in one month at, say, $32 per share.[1] Suppose you also believe there is a 50-50 chance that Microsoft will sell for either $35 or $25 in one month's time. Clearly the option to buy at $32 is valuable—the stock might end up at $35. But how much is this option worth?

An Equivalent Portfolio

One way that financial economists evaluate options is by asking whether there is another set of assets that would yield the same outcomes as would the option. If such a set exists, one can then argue that it should have the same price as the option because markets will ensure that the same good always has the same price. So, let's consider the outcomes of the Microsoft option. If Microsoft sells for $25 in a month's time, the option is worthless—why pay $32 when the stock can readily be bought for $25? If Microsoft sells for $35, however, the option will be worth $3. Could we duplicate these two payouts with some other set of assets? Suppose we borrow some funds (L) from a bank (with no interest, to make things simple) and buy a fraction (k) of a Microsoft share. After a month, we will sell the fractional share of Microsoft and pay off the loan. In this example, L and k must be chosen to yield the same outcomes as the option. That is,

$$k(\$25) - L = 0 \text{ and } k(\$35) - L = 3. \quad \textbf{(1)}$$

These two equations can easily be solved as $k = 0.3$, $L = 7.5$. That is, buying 0.3 of a Microsoft share and taking a loan of $7.50 will yield the same outcomes as buying the option. The net cost of this strategy is $1.50–$9 to buy 0.3 of a Microsoft share at $30 less the loan of $7.50 (which in our simple case carries no interest). Hence, this also is the value of the option.

The Black-Scholes Theorem

Of course, valuing options in the real world is much more complicated than this simple example suggests. Three specific complications that need to be addressed in developing a more general theory of valuation are as follows: (1) there are far more possibilities for Microsoft stock's price in one month than just the two we assumed; (2) most popular options can be exercised at any time during a specified period, not just on a specific date; and (3) interest rates matter for any economic transaction that occurs over time. Taking account of these factors proved to be very difficult, and it was not until 1973 that Fischer Black and Myron Scholes developed an acceptable valuation model.[2] Since that time, the Black-Scholes model has been widely applied to options and other markets. In one of its more innovative applications, the model is now used in reverse to calculate an "implied volatility" expected for stocks in the future. The Chicago Board Options Exchange Volatility Index (VIX) is widely followed in the financial press, where it is taken as a good measure of the current uncertainties involved in stock market investing.

TO THINK ABOUT

1. For every buyer of, say, a call option, there must of course also be a seller. Why would someone sell a call option on some shares he or she already owned? How would this be different than buying a put option on this stock?
2. The Black-Scholes model assumes that stock returns are random and that they follow a bell-shaped (normal) distribution. Does this seem a reasonable assumption?

[1]Options with a specific exercise date are called "European" options. "American" options can be exercised at any time during a specified time interval.
[2]F. Black and M. Scholes, "The Pricing of Options and Corporate Liabilities" *Journal of Political Economy* (May–June 1973): 637–654. This is a very difficult paper. Less-difficult treatments (together with some criticisms of Black-Scholes) can be found in most corporate finance texts.

likely it is that you will want to do so. An option that lets you buy a gallon of gasoline tomorrow at today's price isn't worth very much because the price is unlikely to change by very much over the next 24 hours. An option that lets you buy a gallon of gasoline at today's price over the next year is valuable because prices could explode over such a long period.

The level of interest rates can also affect the value of an option, but this is usually a relatively minor concern. Because buying an option gives you the right to make a transaction in the future, a correct accounting must consider the "present value" of that transaction (see Chapter 14). In that way, the return to being able to invest your other funds (say, in a bank) between the time you buy the option and when it is exercised can be taken into account. With normal levels of interest rates, however, only for options that are very long-lasting will this be a major element in the value of an option.

MICRO QUIZ 4.4

George Lucas has offered to sell you the option to buy his seventh *Star Wars* feature for $100 million should that film ever be made.

1. Identify the underlying transaction involved in this option. How would you decide on the expected value of this transaction? How would you assess the variability attached to the value of the transaction? What is the duration of this option?
2. How would you decide how much to pay Mr. Lucas for this option?

Options Are Valuable for Risk-Neutral People, Too True, options can be used to help risk-averse people mitigate uncertainty. For example, the option to convert the 2-in-1 coat into a windbreaker eliminates any payoff uncertainty, providing utility of 100 (Table 4.2 payoffs), regardless of the weather conditions.

But options also have value for risk-neutral people. We could assume that the utility numbers in the coat example are all monetary payoffs and that the risk-neutral hiker wants to maximize the expected value of these payoffs. All the calculations go through just as before to show that this risk-neutral hiker would prefer the 2-in-1 coat to the others (if the price is close to the price of the others). Having more options to fit uncertain future conditions is beneficial, regardless of risk attitudes.

Strategic Interaction Can Reverse Our Conclusions Adding more options can never harm an individual decision maker (as long as he or she is not charged for them) because the extra options can always be ignored. This insight may no longer be a strategic setting with multiple decision makers. In a strategic setting, economic actors may benefit from having some of their options cut off. This may allow a player to commit to a narrower course of action that he or she would not have chosen otherwise, and this commitment may affect the actions of other parties, possibly to the benefit of the party making the commitment.

A famous illustration of this point is provided by one of the earliest treatises on military strategy, by Sun Tzu, a Chinese general writing in 400 BC. It seems crazy for an army to destroy all means of retreat, burning bridges behind itself and sinking its own ships, among other measures. Yet, this is what Sun Tzu advocated as a military tactic. If the second army observes that the first cannot retreat and will fight to the death, it may retreat itself before engaging the first. We will discuss the strategic benefit of moving first and cutting off one's options more formally in the next chapter on game theory.

Information

The fourth and final way that we will discuss of coping with uncertainty and risk is to acquire more information about the situation. In the extreme, if people had full information allowing them to perfectly predict the future, there would be no uncertainty at all and thus no risk to be averse to.

People obviously would benefit from having more information about the future. A gambler could win a lot of money if he or she knew the outcome of the spin of the roulette wheel. An investor would benefit from knowing which stocks were likely to perform poorly and which were likely to perform well over the coming year. He or she could sell holdings of the poorly performing stocks and invest more in the ones expected to do well. In the example of a hiker's decision regarding which coat to buy for a weekend trip, a parka, a windbreaker, or a 2-in-1 coat, the hiker could benefit from having a good forecast of the weekend weather. If the 2-in-1 coat is more expensive than the others, the hiker could save the extra expense and still have a coat that is well suited to the conditions if he or she knew whether the temperature would still be bitter cold or mild.

People would even be willing to pay to get more information about the future. The savings in not having to pay for the expensive 2-in-1 and still having the right coat to fit the weather conditions are worth something to the hiker. He or she would be willing to invest real resources—time and money—into finding a good weather forecast. To the extent that they can profit from supplying good forecasts, weather forecasters would be willing to invest in better technologies to improve the accuracy of their forecast and the horizon. It is common for news programs on television stations to compete over which one has the newest radar system and the most up-to-date forecasts. The gambler would certainly pay to learn what the next spin of the roulette wheel will be, although there is really no way of learning this truly random outcome. The stock investor would also pay a considerable sum to an economist who could forecast which sectors of the economy will likely do well and thus which stocks will have large returns in the coming year. If stock markets are efficient, it may be almost as difficult to forecast future stock returns as to forecast the spin of a roulette wheel, although this does not reverse the conclusion that such information would be valuable in either case.

Whether and how much additional information should be obtained can be modeled as a maximizing decision. The person will continue to acquire information as long as the gain from the information exceeds the cost of acquiring it. In the next section, we will provide more details on gains and costs of information and how the decision maker should balance them.

Gains and Costs of Information A numerical example of the gains from information can be provided by returning to the coat example, in particular, the utility payoffs from different coats (parka, windbreaker, and 2-in-1) listed in Table 4.2. Recall that the hiker had considerable uncertainty about the upcoming weekend's weather, only knowing that there is an equal chance of either bitter cold or mild conditions. We will think about the gain to the hiker from having more precise information about the weather.

If all three coats sell for the same price, there is no value from a more precise forecast. The 2-in-1 coat is as good or better than the other two in all cases, so the right decision would be to buy it. Suppose, though, that the 2-in-1 coat is prohibitively expensive for this consumer to buy. Suppose the two remaining choices, the parka or windbreaker, sell for the same price. Then, the consumer would benefit from a more precise forecast. If the hiker could learn the weather perfectly, he or she would know exactly what coat to buy. The hiker's expected utility (not accounting for the price of the coat or the cost of the weather information) would equal 100 compared to only 75 in the situation of uncertainty, a gain of 25. If the weather forecast did not perfectly predict the weekend's weather, the expected utility gain would be positive but less than 25. How much less depends on how imprecise the forecast is.

The more uncertain the situation, the more valuable additional information is. Consider the utility payoffs from different coats in the more extreme example in Table 4.3. Again, suppose the hiker has a choice only between the parka and the windbreaker because the 2-in-1 is too expensive for him or her. Then, the hiker's gain from a perfect forecast of the upcoming weekend's weather would increase. To compute the expected utility increase, if the hiker has full information, he or she would be able to select the right coat for the conditions, providing utility of 150 in all cases. Without additional information, the parka and the windbreaker both provide expected utility $(1/2)(150) + (1/2)(0) = 75$ because both are ill-suited to one outcome. The gain from the perfect weather forecast is $150 - 75 = 75$ units of expected utility.

Information Is Valuable to Risk-Neutral People, Too We saw that options have value for both risk-neutral and risk-averse people. The same is true for information: information has value for risk-neutral people because they also benefit from being able to choose a better decision in light of more information. In the example with the hiker choosing between buying a parka and a windbreaker, we could reinterpret the utility payoffs as monetary payoffs, implying that the hiker is risk neutral, and all of our earlier conclusions would still hold. The risk-neutral hiker would gain a surplus of \$25 from a perfect weather forecast given the payoffs in Table 4.2 and a surplus of \$75 given the payoffs in Table 4.3. Risk-averse people might benefit a bit more from information because they can use the information to reduce the risk.

Balancing the Gains and Costs of Information A person can use information to better his or her situation. The key question, of course, is whether the gain is worth the time, effort, and expense that gathering information would entail. Consulting the newspaper or Internet weather forecast might make sense before packing a coat for a weekend hiking trip because the cost is low (may only take a few minutes), and the potential gains may be moderate (allowing one to pack light or to wear the suitable coat for the conditions). Similarly, reading *Consumer Reports* to learn about repair records before buying a car or making a few phone calls to discount stores to find out which has the lowest price for a new television might provide valuable enough information to be worth the fairly minimal cost. On the other hand, visiting every store in town to find the lowest-priced candy bar clearly carries the information search too far.

Information Differences among Economic Actors

This discussion suggests two observations about acquiring information. First, the level of information that an individual acquires will depend on how much the information costs. Unlike market prices for most goods (which are usually assumed to be the same for everyone), there are many reasons to believe that information costs may differ significantly among individuals. Some people may possess specific skills relevant to information acquisition (they may be trained mechanics, for example), whereas others may not possess such skills. Some individuals may have other types of experiences that yield valuable information, while others may lack that experience. For example, the seller of a product will usually know more about its limitations than will a buyer because the seller knows precisely how the good was made and what possible problems might arise. Similarly, large-scale repeat buyers of a good may have greater access to information about it than do first-time buyers. Finally, some individuals may have invested in some types of information services (for example, by having a computer link to a brokerage firm or by subscribing to *Consumer Reports*) that make the cost of obtaining additional information lower than for someone without such an investment.

Differing preferences provide a second reason why information levels may differ among buyers of the same good. Some people may care a great deal about getting the best buy. Others may have a strong aversion to seeking bargains and will take the first model available. As for any good, the trade-offs that individuals are willing to make are determined by the nature of their preferences.

The possibility that information levels will differ among people raises a number of difficult problems about how markets operate. Although it is customary to assume that all buyers and sellers are fully informed, in a number of situations this assumption is untenable. In Chapter 15, we will look at some of the issues that arise in such situations.

Procrastination May Be a Virtue Society seems to frown on procrastinators. "Do not put off to tomorrow what you can do today" and "A stitch in time saves nine" are familiar adages. Yet, lessons we have learned about option and information value can be applied to identify a virtue in procrastination. There may be value in delaying a big decision that is not easily reversed later. Such decisions might include a hiker's choice between a parka and a windbreaker when the coat cannot be returned later after having been worn, the decision by a firm to build a large factory to build a certain make of automobile that would be difficult to convert into the production of other makes or other goods, and the decision to shut down an existing factory. Delaying these big decisions allows the decision maker to preserve option value and gather more information about the future. To the outside observer, who may not understand all the uncertainties involved in the situation, it may appear that the decision maker is too inert, failing to make what looks to be the right decision at the time. In fact, delaying may be exactly the right choice to make in the face of uncertainty. After the decision is made and cannot be reversed, this rules out other courses of action. The option to act has been exercised. On the other hand, delay does not rule out taking the action later. The option is preserved. If circumstances continue to be favorable or become even more so, the action can be taken later. But if the future changes and the action is unsuitable, the decision maker may have saved a lot of trouble by not making it.

Consider the decision to build a factory to produce fuel-efficient cars. Such a decision might be justified by an increase in gasoline prices that might cause a jump in the demand for fuel-efficient cars. Yet, the auto maker may not want to jump right into the market. Gasoline prices may fall again, and consumers may be drawn to larger, more powerful cars, turning the investment in a factory for fuel-efficient cars into a money-losing proposition. The auto maker may want to wait until gasoline prices and demand for fuel-efficient cars are fairly certain to remain high. Delay does not preclude building the factory in the near future. However, if hundreds of millions have been sunk into a large factory and demand dries up for the product, there is little hope of recovering this investment. Uncertainty about future energy prices may explain consumers' reluctance to

APPLICATION 4.5

The Energy Paradox

Consumers seem to be too slow in adopting conservation measures such as energy-efficient appliances, low-wattage fluorescent light bulbs, and upgraded insulation. That is the conclusion economists and environmentalists arrive at using "cost–benefit analysis," a method for determining whether an investment is worth making. Generally speaking, cost–benefit analysis involves comparing the up-front cost of the investment against the future flow of benefits (converted into present values using appropriate discount rates—see Chapter 14 for more on discounting). If the discounted flow of benefits more than covers the cost of investment, then the analysis says the investment should be undertaken. Cost–benefit analysis has been applied to many situations, from malaria eradication in Africa to bridge projects in the United States. Applied to consumer conservation investments, the analysis typically suggests that the long-term flow of energy savings can be expected to more than cover the investment and provide a healthy return besides, much more than the consumer could get from the stock market, say.

Why, then, are consumers reluctant to adopt these conservation measures? This puzzle has been labeled the energy paradox by scholars who have studied it. Are consumers unaware of the conservation advances? Do they have problems borrowing the funds for the up-front investment? Or are they simply incapable of looking ahead to the future?

Cost–Benefit Analysis Ignores Option Value

K. A. Hassett and G. E. Metcalf explain the energy paradox as a problem with cost–benefit analysis (at least as it is sometimes naively applied) rather than with consumer rationality.[1] True, if the consumer's choice is restricted to investing now or never, then cost–benefit analysis will give the right answer. But the consumer often has a third choice: delaying investment and making the decision later. By delaying investment, the consumer can wait until he or she is surer that energy prices will remain high. The consumer can avoid the outcome in which energy prices fall and the conservation measure turns out to have been a bad investment.

The authors find strong incentives for delay. In a world of perfect certainty, cost–benefit analysis might suggest that the consumer should go ahead and invest immediately if he or she can expect a positive return of 10 percent on the conservation investment. However, given historical fluctuations in energy prices, this same consumer would need a much higher return, on the order of 40 to 50 percent, to induce him or her to invest immediately rather than wait. To an outside observer who ignored the option value of delay, the consumer would look excessively inert.

How Many Consumers Does It Take to Change a Light Bulb?

To make these ideas more concrete, consider a simple example of the decision of whether to replace a conventional light bulb with a low-wattage fluorescent. The price of a fluorescent bulb is \$3.50. Electricity savings from the new bulb are certain to be \$1 in the first year. Because of the uncertainty in energy prices, savings for the second and later years are uncertain. Suppose there is an equal chance that the savings for the second and later years is either \$1 or \$5.

Replacing the light bulb at the outset of the period would provide an additional return of 50 cents. Expected savings equal the \$1 from the first year and $(1/2)(\$1) + (1/2)(\$5) = \$3$ in the second and later years for a total of \$4. Subtracting off the \$3.50 initial cost of the fluorescent bulb shows that the return on immediate investment is 50 cents. So, immediate replacement looks like a good idea. But let's compute the return from delay. If the consumer delays for a period and then replaces the bulb at the start of the second year only if savings turn out to be \$5, the consumer earns an expected return equal to the probability 1/2 of the high future savings of \$5, times the net return over and above the cost of the bulb if savings are high $(\$5 - \$3.50 = \$1.50)$, for a grand total of $(1/2)(\$1.50) = 75$ cents. Therefore, delay is actually better than immediate investment (by an expected value of 25 cents). Although delay forces the consumer to give up the \$1 of certain savings in the first year, it allows the consumer the option of not replacing the bulb if high future savings of \$5 do not pan out.

POLICY CHALLENGE

1. U.S. politicians have been touting the need for "energy independence" (reducing reliance on imported foreign oil) achieved in part by the use of alternative fuels and in part by consumer conservation. Suppose reluctance of consumers to make investments in conservation is due to lack of information or foresight. What sort of government policies might work to increase conservation?
2. Suppose instead that the energy paradox is due to consumers' sophisticated valuation of the options provided by waiting. How would this affect government conservation policy?

[1] K. A. Hassett and G. E. Metcalf, "Energy Conservation Investment: Do Consumers Discount the Future Correctly?" *Energy Policy* (June 1993): 710–716.

adopt energy-saving technologies that on the surface look like good investments, as discussed further in Application 4.5: The Energy Paradox. Rather than being ignorant of the benefits and costs of the new technology, the procrastination of consumers may be a sophisticated response to uncertainty.

4-4 Pricing of Risk in Financial Assets

Because people are willing to pay something to avoid risks, it seems as if one should be able to study this process directly. That is, we could treat "risk" like any other commodity and study the factors that influence its demand and supply. One result of such a study would be to be able to say how much risk there is in the economy and how much people would be willing to pay to have less of it. Although, as we shall see, there are several problems with this approach, financial markets do indeed provide a good place to get useful information about the pricing of risk.

With financial assets, the risks people face are purely monetary and relatively easy to measure. One can, for example, study the history of the price of a particular financial asset and determine whether this price has been stable or volatile. Presumably, less volatile assets are more desirable to risk-averse people, so they should be willing to pay something for them. Economists are able to get some general idea of people's attitudes toward risk by looking at differences in financial returns on risky versus non-risky assets.

Investors' Market Options

Figure 4.4 shows a simplified illustration of the market options open to a would-be investor in financial assets. The vertical axis of the figure shows the expected annual return that the investor might earn from an asset, whereas the horizontal axis shows the level of risk associated with each asset. The points in the figure represent the various kinds of financial assets available. For example, point A represents a risk-free asset such as money in a checking account. Although this asset has (practically) no risks associated with its ownership, it promises a very low annual rate of return. Asset B, on the other hand, represents a relatively risky stock—this asset promises a high expected annual rate of return, but any investor must accept a high risk to get that return. All of the other points in Figure 4.4 represent the risks and returns associated with assets that an investor might buy.

Because investors like high annual returns but dislike risk, they will choose to hold combinations of these available assets that lie on their "northwest" periphery. By mixing various risky assets with the risk-free asset (A), they can choose any point along the line AC. This line is labeled the **market line** because it shows the possible combinations of annual returns and risk that an investor can achieve by taking advantage of what the market offers.[4] The slope of this line shows the trade-off between annual returns and risk that is available from financial markets. By studying the terms on which such trade-offs can be made in actual financial markets, economists can learn

Market line
A line showing the relationship between risk and annual returns that an investor can achieve by mixing financial assets.

[4]The actual construction of the market line is relatively complicated. For a discussion, see W. Nicholson and C. Snyder, *Microeconomic Theory: Basic Principles and Extensions*, 11th ed. (Mason, OH: South-Western, Cengage Learning, 2012), 244–248.

Figure 4.4 Market Options for Investors

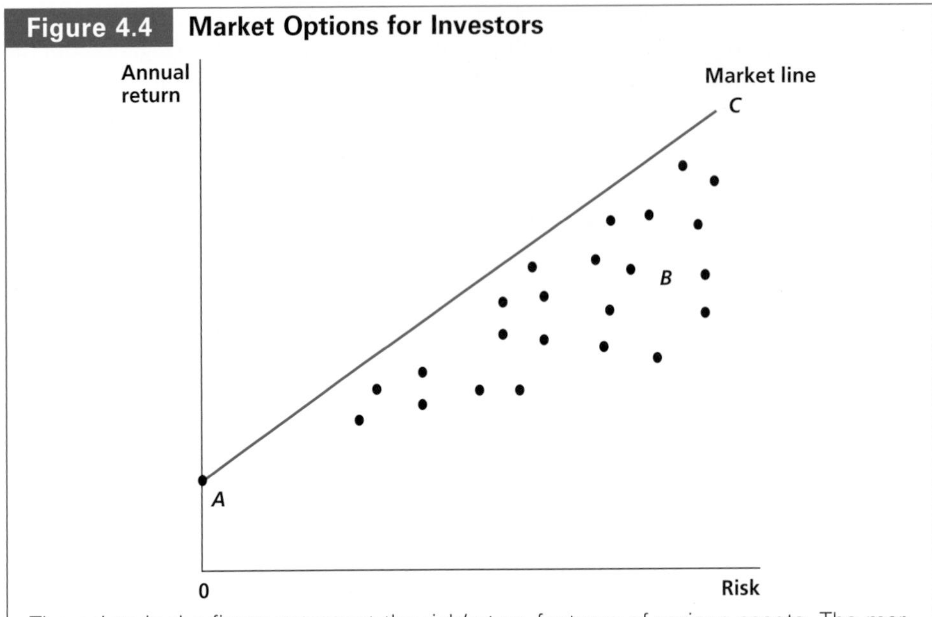

The points in the figure represent the risk/return features of various assets. The market line shows the best options a risk-averse investor can obtain by mixing risk assets with the risk-free asset *A*.

something about how those markets price risks. Application 4.6: The Equity Premium Puzzle illustrates these calculations but also highlights some of the uncertainties that arise in making them.

Choices by Individual Investors

The market line shown in Figure 4.4 provides a constraint on the alternatives that financial markets provide to individual investors. These investors then choose among the available assets on the basis of their own attitudes toward risk. This process is illustrated in Figure 4.5. The figure shows a typical indifference curve for three different types of investors. Each of these indifference curves has a positive slope because of the assumption that investors are risk averse—they can be induced to take on more risk only by the promise of a higher return. The curves also have a convex curvature on the presumption that investors will become increasingly less willing to take on more risk as the overall riskiness of their positions increases.

The three investors illustrated in Figure 4.5 have different attitudes toward risk. Investor I has a very low tolerance for risk. He or she will opt for a mix of investments that includes a lot of the risk-free option (point *L*). Investor II has a modest toleration for risk, and he or she will opt for a combination of assets that is reasonably representative of the overall market (*M*). Finally, investor III is a real speculator. He or she will accept a very risky combination of assets (*N*)—more risky than the overall market. One way for this investor to do that is to borrow to invest in stocks. The impact of any fluctuations in stock prices will then be magnified in its impact on this investor's wealth. Actual financial markets therefore accommodate a wide variety of risk preferences by providing the opportunity to choose various mixes of asset types.

APPLICATION 4.6

The Equity Premium Puzzle

As shown in Figure 4.4, differences in the rates of return of financial assets reflect, in part, the differing risks associated with those assets. The historical data show that stocks also called equities have indeed had higher returns than bonds to compensate for that risk. In fact, returns on common stock have been so favorable that they pose a puzzle to economists.

Historical Rates of Return

Table 1 cites some of the most widely used rate of return data for U.S. financial markets, compiled by Ibbotson Associates. These data show that over the period 1926–2012, common stocks of large companies provided average annual rates of return which exceeded those on long-term bonds by 5 percent per year, whether the bonds of corporations or the government are considered. The equity premium is even larger if the set of common stocks is expanded to include small companies, the average return on which was a whopping 16.5 percent over the period. The equity premium is larger still if rather than long term, we look at short-term government bonds: the average return on one-year treasury bills was a measly 3.1 percent over the period, essentially no better than inflation.

One way to measure the risk associated with various assets uses the "standard deviation" of their annual returns. This measure shows the range in which roughly two-thirds of the returns fall. For the case of, say, common stocks, the average annual return was 11.8 percent, and the standard deviation shows that in two-thirds of the years the average was within ±20.2 percent of this figure. In other words, in two-thirds of the years, common stocks returned more than −8.4 percent and less than +32.0 percent. Rates of return on stocks were much more variable than those on bonds.

Table 1 **Total Annual Returns, 1926–2012**

FINANCIAL ASSET	AVERAGE ANNUAL RATE OF RETURN (%)	STANDARD DEVIATION OF RATE OF RETURN (%)
Large company stocks	11.8	20.2
Long-term corporate bonds	6.4	8.3
Long-term government bonds	6.1	9.7

Source: Selected statistics from Table 6-7, *2013 Ibbotson Stocks, Bonds, Bills, and Inflation (SBBI) Classic Yearbook* (Chicago: Morningstar, Inc., 2013).

The Excess Return on Common Stocks

Although the qualitative findings from data such as those in Table 1 are consistent with risk aversion, the quantitative nature of the extra returns to common stock holding are inconsistent with many other studies of risk. These other studies suggest that individuals would accept the extra risk that stocks carry for an extra return of around 1 percent per year—significantly less than the 5 percent extra actually provided.

One set of explanations focuses on the possibility that the figures in Table 1 understate the risk of stocks. The risk individuals really care about is changes in their consumption plans. If returns on stocks were highly correlated with the business cycle, then they might pose extra risks because individuals would face a double risk from economic downturns—a fall in income and a fall in returns from investments. Behavioral economists have offered another explanation: individuals may experience extra psychological pain from losing money on investments in any given period beyond any consequences for their ultimate wealth. (For more on this type of behavioral bias, see the section entitled "Prospect Theory" in Chapter 17.) A recent explanation of the equity premium hinges on catastrophes (wars, riots, depressions, and so on) that have the potential of wiping out much of the value of stocks but so rare that they are seldom experienced, if at all, even in a long period spanning decades. The United States may have experienced an unusually tranquil period during 1926–2102 compared to other periods or countries; subtracting catastrophic losses that might have occurred in a less tranquil period would bring down the average for the return on stocks. Work remains to convince the economics profession that any of these explanations can account for the large equity premium on its own.[1]

TO THINK ABOUT

1. Holding stocks in individual companies probably involves greater risks than are reflected in the data for all stocks in Table 1. Do you think these extra risks are relevant to appraising the extra rate of return that stocks provide?
2. The real return on short-term government bonds implied by Table 1 is less than 1 percent per year. Why do people save at all if this relatively risk-free return is so low?

[1]For an extensive discussion, see J. B. DeLong and K. Magin, "The U.S. Equity Return Premium: Past, Present, and Future," *Journal of Economic Perspectives* (Winter 2009): 193–208.

Figure 4.5 Choices by Individual Investors

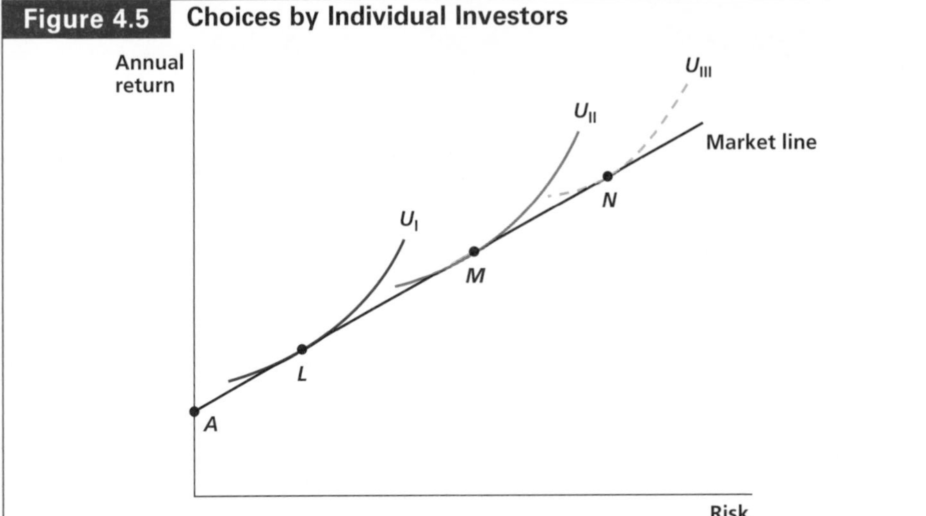

Points L, M, and N show the investment choices made by three different investors. Investor I is very risk averse and has a high proportion of the risk-free asset. Investor II has modest toleration for risk and chooses the "market" portfolio. Investor III has a great toleration for risk and leverages his or her position.

SUMMARY

In this chapter, we have briefly surveyed the economic theory of uncertainty and information. From that survey, we reached several conclusions that have relevance throughout the study of microeconomics.

- In uncertain situations, individuals are concerned with the expected utility associated with various outcomes. If individuals have a diminishing marginal utility for income, they will be risk averse. That is, they will generally refuse bets that are actuarially fair in dollar terms but result in an expected loss of utility.
- Risk-averse individuals may purchase insurance that allows them to avoid participating in fair bets. Even if the premium is somewhat unfair (in an actuarial sense), they may still buy insurance in order to increase utility.
- Diversification among several uncertain options may reduce risk. Such risk spreading may sometimes be costly, however.
- Buying options is another way to reduce risk. Because the buyer has the right, but not the obligation, to complete a market transaction on specified terms, such options can add flexibility to the ways people plan in uncertain situations. Options are more valuable when the expected value of the underlying market transaction is more valuable, the value of that transaction is more variable, and the duration of the option is longer.
- A final way to reduce risk is to obtain more precise information about the future. When to stop acquiring information is a maximizing decision, just like how much of a good to buy.
- Financial markets allow people to choose the risk-return combination that maximizes their utility. These markets therefore provide evidence on how risk is priced.

REVIEW QUESTIONS

1. What does it mean to say we expect a fair coin to come up heads about half the time? Would you expect the fraction of heads to get closer to exactly 0.5 as more coins are flipped? Explain how this law of large numbers applies to the risks faced by casinos or insurance companies.
2. Why does the assumption of diminishing marginal utility of income imply risk aversion? Can you think of other assumptions that would result in risk-averse behavior (such as the purchase of insurance) but would not require the difficult-to-verify notion of diminishing marginal utility?

3. Gamble 1 provides you with an expected value of 50 and an expected utility of 5, while gamble 2 provides you with an expected value of 75 and an expected utility of 4.3. Is it even possible for the gambles to be ranked one way based on expected values and the other way based on expected utilities? Which gamble would you chose, and on what basis?
4. "Risk-averse people should only be averse to big gambles with a lot of money at stake. They should jump on any small gamble that is unfair in their favor." Explain why this statement makes sense. Use a utility-of-income graph like Figure 4.1 to illustrate the statement.
5. "The purchase of actuarily fair insurance turns an uncertain situation into a situation where you receive the expected value of income with certainty." Explain why this is true. Can you think of circumstances where it might not be true?
6. Suppose that historical data showed that returns of Japanese stocks and returns on U.S. stocks tended to move in opposite directions. Would it be better to own only one country's stocks or to hold a mixture of the two? How would your answer change if the Japanese stock market always precisely mirrored the U.S. stock market?
7. As discussed in Application 4.4: Puts, Calls, and Black-Scholes, a call option provides you with the option to buy a share of, say, Microsoft stock at a specified price of $60. Suppose that this option can be exercised only at exactly 10:00 am on June 1, 2009. What will determine the expected value of the transaction underlying this option? What will determine the variability around this expected value? Explain why the greater this expected variability, the greater is the value of this option.
8. College students are familiar with the real option of being able to drop a course before the end of the term. The text provided a list of factors affecting the value of any option (value of underlying opportunity, variation in the situation, duration, price). What is meant by each one of these factors in the context of the decision to drop a course? How do the factors affect the value of this option? Given that options are valuable, how would you explain why some colleges put certain limits on the ability of students to drop courses?
9. Our analysis in this chapter suggests that individuals have a utility-maximizing amount of information. Explain why some degree of ignorance is optimal.
10. Explain why the slope of the market line in Figures 4.4 and 4.5 shows how risk is "priced" in this market. How might the data in Application 4.4: Puts, Calls, and Black-Scholes be plotted to determine this slope?

PROBLEMS

4.1. Wen, who has current wealth of $10,000, decides to take advantage of a free trip to Las Vegas to play roulette. His utility function over the wealth he ends up with after the trip Y (which equals his current wealth adjusted by any amount he ends up winning or losing) is $U(Y) = \sqrt{Y}$. He can take one of two gambles at the roulette table:

Gamble 1: Wager $1,000 on red. If red comes up, which happens with probability 18/38, he wins $1,000; otherwise he loses his $1,000 wager.

Gamble 2: Wager $500 on the single number 00. If 00 comes up, which happens with probability 1/38, he wins 35 times his wager ($17,500); otherwise he loses his $500 wager.

a. Are these fair gambles?
b. If Wen is forced to take one of the two gambles, which would he prefer?
c. If Wen isn't forced to play roulette, would he take a gamble?

4.2. Suppose a person must accept one of three bets:

Bet 1: Win $100 with probability 1/2; lose $100 with probability 1/2.

Bet 2: Win $100 with probability 3/4 lose $300 with probability 1/4.

Bet 3: Win $100 with probability 9/10; lose $900 with probability 1/10.

a. Show that all of these are fair bets.
b. Graph each bet on a utility-of-income curve similar to Figure 4.1.
c. Explain carefully which bet will be preferred and why.

4.3. Mr. Fogg is planning an around-the-world trip. The utility from the trip is a function of how much he spends on it (Y) given by

$$U(Y) = \log Y.$$

Mr. Fogg has $10,000 to spend on the trip. If he spends all of it, his utility will be

$$U(10{,}000) = \log 10{,}000 = 4.$$

(In this problem, we are using logarithms to the base 10 for ease of computation.)

a. If there is a 25 percent probability that Mr. Fogg will lose $1,000 of his cash on the trip, what is the trip's expected utility?
b. Suppose that Mr. Fogg can buy insurance against losing the $1,000 (say, by purchasing traveler's checks) at an actuarially fair premium of $250. Show that his utility is higher if he purchases this insurance than if he faces the chance of losing the $1,000 without insurance.
c. What is the maximum amount that Mr. Fogg would be willing to pay to insure his $1,000?
d. Suppose that people who buy insurance tend to become more careless with their cash than those who don't, and assume that the probability of their losing $1,000 is 30 percent. What will be the actuarially fair insurance premium? Will Mr. Fogg buy insurance in this situation? (This is an example of the moral hazard problem in insurance theory.)

4.4. Sometimes economists speak of the *certainty equivalent* of a risky stream of income. This problem asks you to compute the certainty equivalent of a risky bet that promises a 50-50 chance of winning or losing $5,000 for someone with a starting income of $50,000. We know that a certain income of somewhat less than $50,000 will provide the same expected utility as will taking this bet. You are asked to calculate precisely the certain income (that is, the certainty equivalent income) that provides the same utility as does this bet for three simple utility functions:

a. $U(I) = \sqrt{I}$.
b. $U(I) = \ln(I)$. (where "ln" means "natural logarithm")
c. $U(I) = \frac{-1}{I}$.

What do you conclude about these utility functions by comparing these three cases?

4.5. Suppose Molly Jock wishes to purchase a high-definition television to watch the Olympic wrestling competition in London. Her current income is $20,000, and she knows where she can buy the television she wants for $2,000. She had heard the rumor that the same set can be bought at Crazy Eddie's (recently out of bankruptcy) for $1,700 but is unsure if the rumor is true. Suppose this individual's utility is given by

$$\text{Utility} = \ln(Y)$$

where Y is her income after buying the television.

a. What is Molly's utility if she buys from the location she knows?
b. What is Molly's utility if Crazy Eddie's really does offer a lower price?
c. Suppose Molly believes there is a 50-50 chance that Crazy Eddie does offer the lower-priced television, but it will cost her $100 to drive to the discount store to find out for sure (the store is far away and has had its phone disconnected). Is it worth it to her to invest the money in the trip? (Hint: To calculate the utility associated with part c, simply average Molly's utility from the two states: [1] Eddie offers the television; [2] Eddie doesn't offer the television.)

4.6.  A person purchases a dozen eggs and must take them home. Although making trips home is costless, there is a 50 percent chance that all of the eggs carried on one trip will be broken during the trip. This person considers two strategies:

Strategy 1: Take the dozen eggs in one trip.

Strategy 2: Make two trips, taking six eggs in each trip.

a. List the possible outcomes of each strategy and the probabilities of these outcomes. Show that, on average, six eggs make it home under either strategy.
b. Develop a graph to show the utility obtainable under each strategy.
c. Could utility be improved further by taking more than two trips? How would the desirability of this possibility be affected if additional trips were costly?

4.7. Sophia is a contestant on a game show and has selected the prize that lies behind door number 3. The show's host tells her that there is a 50 percent chance that there is a $15,000 diamond ring behind the door and a 50 percent chance that there is a goat behind the door (which is worth nothing to Sophia, who is allergic to goats). Before the door is opened, someone in the audience shouts, "I will give you the option of selling me what is behind the door for $8,000 if you will pay me $4,500 for this option."

a. If Sophia cares only about the expected dollar values of various outcomes, will she buy this option?
b. Explain why Sophia's degree of risk aversion might affect her willingness to buy this option.

4.8. The option on Microsoft stock described in Application 4.4: Puts, Calls, and Black-Scholes gave the owner the right to buy one share at $32 one month from now. Microsoft currently sells for $30 per share, and investors believe there is a 50-50 chance that it could become either $35 or $25 in one month. Now let's see how various features of this option affect its value:

a. How would an increase in the strike price of the option, from $32 to $33, affect the value of the option?
b. How would an increase in the current price of Microsoft stock, from $30 to $31 per share, affect the value of the original option?

c. How would an increase in the volatility of Microsoft stock, so that there was a 50–50 chance that it could sell for either \$40 or \$20, affect the value of the original option?

d. How would a change in the interest rate affect the value of the original option? Is this an unrealistic feature of this example? How would you make it more realistic?

4.9. This problem will help you understand why Application 4.6: The Equity Premium Puzzle" really is a puzzle. Suppose that a person with \$100,000 to invest believes that stocks will have a real return over the next year of 7 percent. He or she also believes that bonds will have a real return of 2 percent over the next year. This person believes (probably contrary to fact) that the real return on bonds is certain—an investment in bonds will definitely yield 2 percent. For stocks, however, he or she believes that there is a 50 percent chance that stocks will yield 16 percent, but also a 50 percent chance they will yield -2 percent. Hence stocks are viewed as being much riskier than bonds.

a. Calculate the certainty equivalent yield for stocks using the three utility functions in Problem 4.6. What do you conclude about whether this person will invest the \$100,000 in stocks or bonds?

b. The most risk-averse utility function economists usually ever encounter is $U(I) = -I^{-10}$. If your scientific calculator is up to the task, calculate the certainty equivalent yield for stocks with this utility function. What do you conclude?

(Hint: The calculations in this problem are most easily accomplished by using outcomes in dollars—that is, for example, those that have a 50-50 chance of producing a final wealth of \$116,000 or \$98,000. If this were to yield a certainty equivalent wealth of, say, \$105,000, the certainty equivalent yield would be 5 percent.)

4.10. This problem is based on the two-state model in the appendix to this chapter. Leah, who recently graduated from college, is deciding whether to purchase renter's insurance, which insures one's personal property in an apartment against accidents or theft, from Gecko Insurance. The following questions direct you to use diagrams to analyze her decision.

a. Use a two-state diagram along the lines of Figure 4A.3 to explain why Leah could benefit from renter's insurance.

b. Suppose Leah is risk neutral. Use a diagram to determine whether she would buy fair insurance. Would she buy unfair insurance in her favor? Would she buy insurance that provides Gecko Insurance with a profit margin above what is needed to offset the expected loss (in other words, unfair insurance in Gecko's favor)?

c. Suppose again that Leah is risk averse but that now the chance of accident or theft is extremely remote. Use a diagram to explain why she would not be inclined to buy unfair insurance in Gecko's favor.

APPENDIX 4A

Two-State Model of Uncertainty

In this appendix, we provide a model that will allow us to discuss all of the previous material in this chapter in a single, unified framework. Although it takes a bit of work to understand this new model, the payoff will be to draw even more connections among the concepts in this chapter and to show how the tools developed in Chapter 2 to study utility maximization under certainty can be used to study decision making under uncertainty.

A4-1 Model

The basic outline of the model is presented in Figure 4A.1. For this model, an individual is assumed to face two possible outcomes (sometimes called states of the world), but he or she does not know which outcome will occur. The individual's income (and also consumption) in the two states is denoted by C_1 and C_2, and possible values for these are recorded on the axes in Figure 4A.1. In some applications, the states might correspond to the possibilities of an accident or no accident. In another application, the states might correspond to different weather conditions (cold or mild temperatures). In yet another

Figure 4A.1 Expected Utility Maximization in a Two-State Model

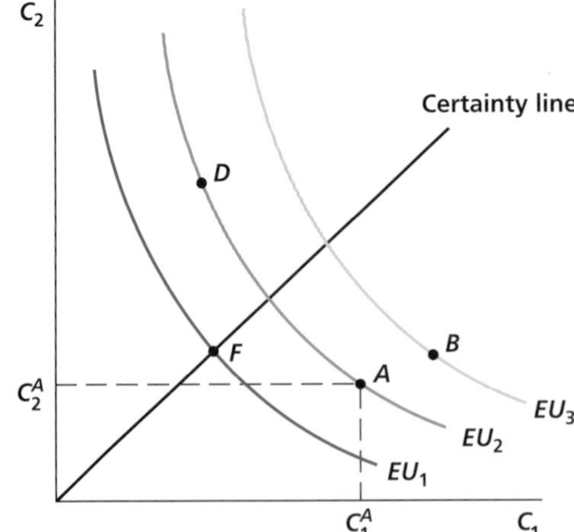

The individual faces two possible states of the world, and the axes record consumption under each of them. Offered various gambles such as *A*, *B*, *C*, and *D*, the individual will select the one on the highest indifference curve, here *B*, which provides the highest expected utility.

application, the states might correspond to the health of the overall economy (boom or bust). In real-world applications, there may be many more than two possible uncertain outcomes, perhaps even a continuum of them, but two is the minimum needed to represent uncertainty and makes drawing a graph easier. For obvious reasons, the model is called a two-state model.

Points on the graph such as *A, B, C,* and *D* represent possible choices under uncertainty, which we referred to earlier as gambles. For example, point *A* is the gamble providing consumption C_1^A if state 1 occurs and C_2^A if state 2 occurs. The certainty line indicates choices involving the same consumption in both states. The gamble illustrated as point *A* is well below the certainty line, indicating considerably more consumption in state 1 than in state 2. Point *A* could embody the prospects of an accident that reduces the person's income in state 2 and no accident in state 1. The colored curves are indifference curves familiar from utility maximization under certainty. Each curve shows all the gambles that the person would be equally well off taking. The one difference with consumer choice under certainty is that the indifference curves here link bundles providing the same level of *expected* utility rather than plain utility. This is indicated by the labels EU_1, EU_2, and so forth, indicating increasing levels of expected utility. Of the four gambles—*A, B, C,* and *D*—the one maximizing expected utility is *B,* appearing on the highest indifference curve.

KEEP *in* MIND

Preferences and Probabilities

As can be seen in the formula for expected values, expected utility combines two elements: the utility of consumption in each state and the probability each state occurs. Therefore, the indifference curves in Figure 4A.1 reflect both preferences and probabilities. Changes in the probabilities of the different states will shift the indifference curves, just as will changes in the utility function. In our analysis, we will keep the utility function and probabilities constant, allowing us to fix the indifference curves as drawn.

Each of the next several sections will return to a concept introduced previously in the chapter and show how the concept can be captured in a graph like Figure 4A.1.

A4-2 Risk Aversion

Figure 4A.2 shows how the shape of individuals' indifference curves varies with their attitudes toward risk. A risk-averse person will have indifference curves that look like graph (a). Compared to gambles *A* and *B,* which provide relatively variable consumption combinations (gamble *A* providing a lot of consumption in state 1 and little in state 2 and vice versa for gamble *B*), the individual would prefer more even consumption across the two states, such as gamble *D,* reflected in the appearance of *D* on a higher indifference curve than *A* and *B.* The individual dislikes variable consumption because deprivation in the "lean" (low-consumption) state is more costly than can be compensated by an equal amount of extra consumption in the "fat" (high-consumption) state. A substantial risk premium would have to be paid for the consumer to be willing to accept deprivation in the "lean" state.

It is the convexity of the indifference curves in graph (a), the bowing in toward the origin, that captures risk aversion. We also encountered convex indifference curves in our earlier study of choice under certainty in Chapter 2. There, the convexity of

Figure 4A.2 Risk Aversion in the Two-State Model

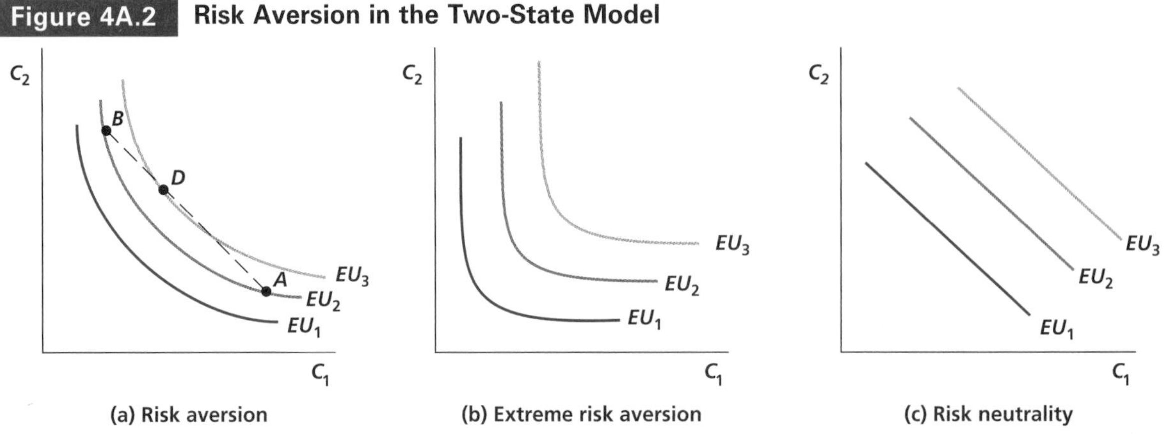

A risk-averse individual has convex indifference curves, shown in graph (a). Greater risk aversion shows up as a sharper bend in the indifference curves, as in graph (b). A risk-neutral individual has linear indifference curves, as in graph (c).

indifference curves reflected the preference of consumers for balance in consumption. Consumers preferred bundles with average amounts of the two goods to bundles with an extreme amount of either. Similar logic underlies risk aversion in the present setting involving uncertainty. A risk-averse consumer prefers balance in consumption, not necessarily between two goods in a bundle but between consumption in uncertain states.

Individuals with more sharply bent indifference curves—compare graph (b) to graph (a)—are even more risk averse. More risk-averse individuals are more reluctant to trade off less consumption in "lean" states for more consumption in "fat" states. Again, we have an analogy to the setting of choice under certainty in Chapter 2. There, consumers with sharply bent indifference curves (L-shaped in the extreme) regarded the goods as perfect complements and were unwilling to substitute from their preferred fixed proportions.

At the opposite extreme of very risk-averse individuals are risk-neutral ones, with linear indifference curves shown in graph (c). Risk-neutral people regard consumption in the two states as perfect substitutes. They care only about expected consumption, not how evenly consumption is divided between the states of the world. This is analogous to the case of perfect substitutes in the setting of consumer choice under certainty; we saw in Chapter 2 that consumers who regarded the goods in the bundle as perfect substitutes had linear indifference curves.

A4-3 Insurance

Figure 4A.3 shows how to analyze insurance in the two-state model. Consider the case of insurance against a possible car accident. In state 1, no accident occurs; the accident occurs in state 2. Each state has some chance of occurring. Point *A* represents the situation the individual faces without insurance. His or her consumption in state 2 is lower than in state 1 because some income has gone for car repairs and medical bills (and the person's pain and suffering may also be represented by a reduction in consumption).

This person might jump at the chance to give up some consumption from state 1 to increase consumption in state 2. He or she could then avoid the possibility of deprivation in state 2. Insurance can be used for this purpose. By buying insurance, this person

Figure 4A.3 **Insurance: A Two-State Model**

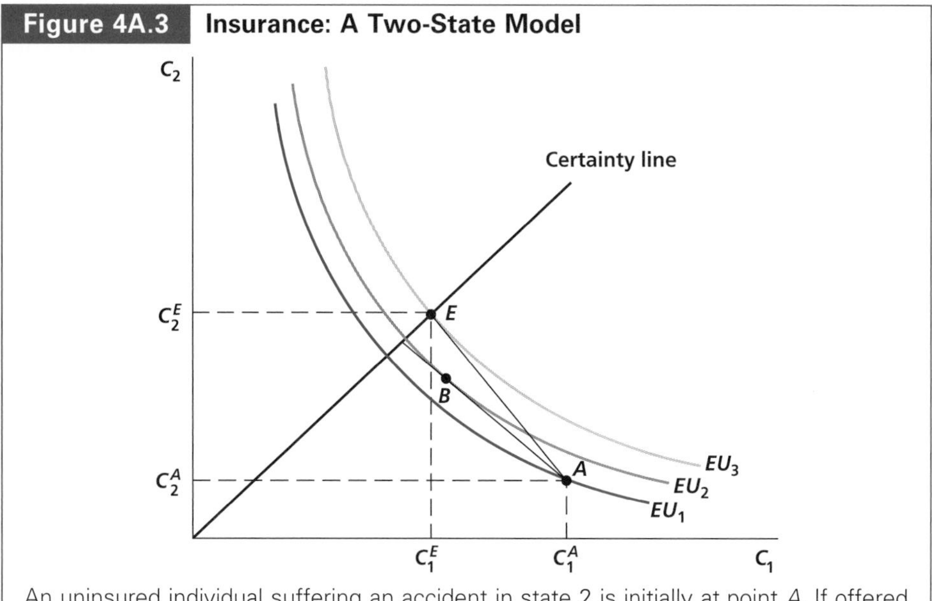

An uninsured individual suffering an accident in state 2 is initially at point *A*. If offered fair insurance, the individual would choose to become fully insured, moving to point *E* on the certainty line. If offered unfair insurance, he or she would buy only partial insurance, moving to a point such as *B*.

could even out consumption between the two states. The insurance premium reduces C_1 (consumption in the no-accident state) in return for a payment if an accident occurs, which increases C_2. Suppose that fair insurance is available on the market. Recall that the premium on fair insurance equals the expected insurance payment in case of an accident. The slope of line *AE* will represent the terms of fair insurance. The person can increase expected utility from EU_1 to EU_3 by purchasing complete insurance and moving to point *E*, where $C_1 = C_2$. This outcome is similar to the complete insurance solution examined in Figure 4.2. In other words, by paying a premium of $C_1^A - C_1^E$, this person has assured enough additional consumption when the accident happens $(C_2^E - C_2^A)$ that consumption is the same no matter what happens.

> **MICRO QUIZ 4A.1**
>
> Let's examine Figure 4A.3 more closely.
>
> 1. Why do choices along the "certainty line" imply that there is no risk?
> 2. If the probability of state 1 is 0.6 and the probability of state 2 is 0.4, what is the actuarially fair slope for the line *AE*?
> 3. In general, what determines the slope of the indifference curve EU_3?
> 4. Given your answer to part 2, can you explain why *AE* and EU_3 have the same slope at point *E*? (This question is relatively hard.)

Insurance does not have to be fair to be worth buying. If insurance were more costly than indicated by the slope of the line *AE*, some improvement in expected utility might still be possible. In this case, the budget line would be flatter than *AE* (because more expensive insurance means that obtaining additional C_2 requires a greater sacrifice of C_1), and this person could not attain expected utility level EU_3. For example, the slope of line *AB* might represent the terms of this unfair insurance. The individual would no longer opt for complete insurance but only partial insurance, selecting a point such as *B* below the certainty line. The person is at least a little better off with insurance than without, attaining expected utility EU_2. If the premium on the unfair insurance becomes too high, though, the person would prefer to remain uninsured, staying at point *A*.

Notice that the insurance line functions very much like the budget constraint from Chapter 2. Indeed, both represent market options among which the individual can choose. The slopes have different interpretations, in the case of budget constraint given by the prices of the two goods and here given by the terms of the insurance contract (premium relative to payment in case of an accident). But the certainty and uncertainty cases are similar, in that in both cases, the maximizing choice for the decision maker is the market option attaining the highest indifference curve. In both cases, this maximizing choice will be a point of tangency. In the insurance example, the tangency with fair insurance occurs at point *E*, and the tangency with unfair insurance occurs at point *B*. So, these points reflect the individual's insurance demand under different terms that insurance companies might offer.

MICRO QUIZ 4A.2

1. Without looking at Figure 4A.3, see if you can draw your own diagram to illustrate the benefits of, say, health insurance.
2. Use a separate diagram to analyze whether a risk-neutral person would ever want to purchase health insurance and under what conditions if so.

A4-4 Diversification

Figure 4A.4 captures the benefits of diversification in a two-state model. Suppose there are two financial assets, 1 and 2 (these could be stocks, bonds, gold, and so on). In state 1, asset 1 has a better return than asset 2. The opposite happens in state 2. Each state has some chance of occurring. Investing all of one's wealth in asset 1 leads to point A_1 and

Figure 4A.4 Diversification in a Two-State Model

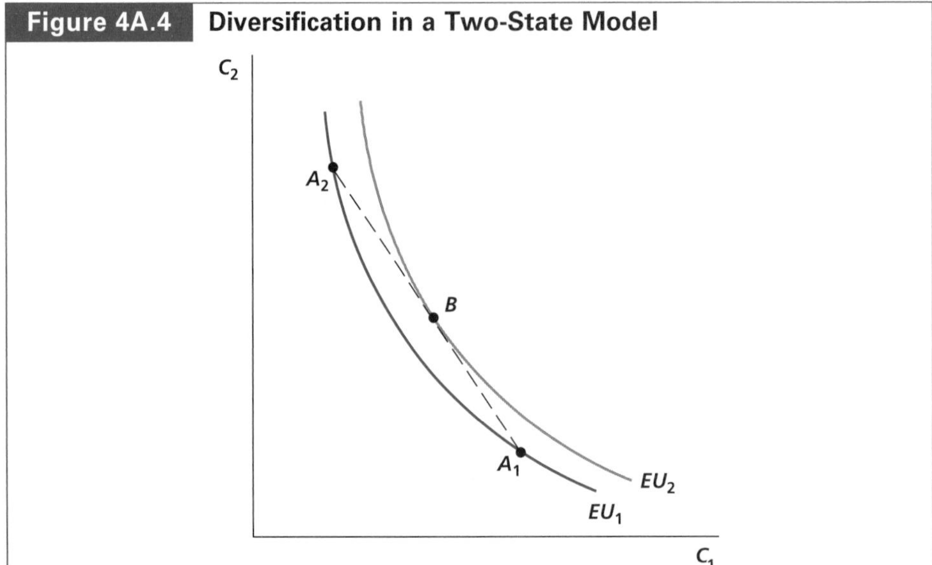

Investing exclusively in asset 1 leads to point A_1 and exclusively in asset 2 to point A_2. Points on the dotted line A_1A_2 represent varying amounts of diversification, with point *B* being the best for the individual.

all in asset 2 to point A_2. Rather than "putting all the eggs in one basket," the individual can diversify by investing in some of each asset. By varying the mix of assets in this diversified portfolio, the individual can attain any point on the line between A_1 and A_2. The best mix of assets is given by B. The consumer is better off after diversifying, obtaining expected utility EU_2.

A4-5 Option Value

Figure 4A.5 illustrates the value of an option in a two-state model. The individual's initial situation is given by point A. If the individual is given an additional option, B, he or she will then select what is best in the state that ends up occurring. In the graph, A is best in state 1 (because it provides more consumption than B in that state), and B is best in state 2. For example, A could represent wearing a parka, and B could represent the option of converting the coat into a windbreaker provided by a 2-in-1 coat that could be converted into either depending on the weather conditions. State 1 could be bitter cold, and state 2, mild weather. The individual could obtain consumption C_1^A in the bitter cold by wearing the 2-in-1 coat as a parka and C_1^B in mild weather by wearing it as a windbreaker. So, the highest combination of consumptions possible with the 2-in-1 coat is given by point O_1, the intersection of the dotted lines. The consumer could move from A to O_1 if he or she was not charged for option B. In the coat example, the individual could move to point O_1 if the 2-in-1 coat sold for the same price as the parka. If the individual is charged for the option up front (or in the coat example if the 2-in-1 is more expensive than the parka), this expense reduces consumption in both states, shifting O_1 down to O_2. As long as the option's price is not too high, the individual still is better off with the option, indicated on the graph by O_2's lying above the indifference curve through the starting point, A.

Figure 4A.5 Option Value in a Two-State Model

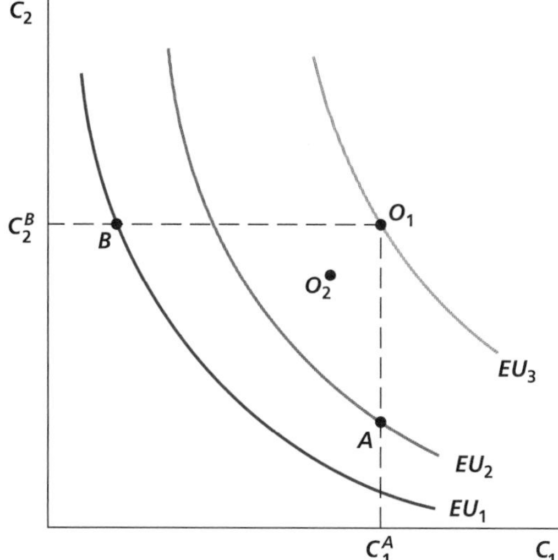

If an individual initially at A is given B as an option as well, he or she would stick with A in state 1 but would exercise option B in state 2. The individual's consumption possibilities would improve from A to O_1. The individual is better off with the option even if he or she has to pay a moderate price for it up front that shifts O_1 back to O_2.

The indifference curves in Figure 4A.5 are convex, implying that the individual is risk averse. The analysis could be repeated for a risk-neutral individual with straight lines for indifference curves. The conclusion that O_1 and O_2 are on higher indifference curves than A—implying the individual benefits from having an additional option, B—would continue to hold under risk neutrality.

We will leave the analysis of the two-state model there. The model is useful for understanding a range of topics related to uncertainty in addition to those presented earlier. And though there is a bit of reinterpretation involved, the model is almost identical to utility maximization under certainty from Chapter 2.

SUMMARY

This appendix revisited all of the topics from the chapter, analyzing them in a unified framework of the two-state model. The two-state model combines indifference curves and market opportunities in a way that looks very similar to utility maximization under certainty from Chapter 2.

5 Game Theory

A central assumption in this text is that people make the best choices they can, given their objectives. For example, in the theory of choice in Chapter 2, a consumer chooses the affordable bundle maximizing his or her utility. The setting was made fairly simple by considering a single consumer in isolation, justified by the assumption that consumers are price takers, small enough relative to the market that their actions do not measurably impact others.

Many situations are more complicated in that they involve strategic interaction. The best one person can do may often depend on what another does. How loud a student prefers to play his or her music may depend on how loud the student in the next dorm room plays his or hers. The first student may prefer soft music unless louder music is needed to tune out the sound from next door. A gas station's profit-maximizing price may depend on what the competitor across the street charges. The station may wish to match or slightly undercut its competitor.

In this chapter, we will learn the tools economists use to deal with these strategic situations. The tools are quite general, applying to problems anywhere from the interaction between students in a dorm or players in a card game, all the way up to wars between countries. The tools are also particularly useful for analyzing the interaction among oligopoly firms, and we will draw on them extensively for this purpose later in the book.

5-1 Background

Game theory was originally developed during the 1920s and grew rapidly during World War II in response to the need to develop formal ways of thinking about military strategy.[1] One branch of game theory, called cooperative game theory, assumes the group of players reaches an outcome that is best for the group as a whole, producing the largest "pie" to be shared among them; the theory focuses on rules for how the pie should be divided. We will focus mostly on the second branch, called noncooperative game theory, in which players are guided instead by self-interest. We focus on noncooperative game theory for several reasons. Self-interested behavior does not always lead to an outcome that is best for the players as a group (as we will see from the Prisoners' Dilemma to follow), and such outcomes are interesting and practically relevant. Second, the assumption of self-interested behavior is the natural extension of our analysis of single-player decision problems in earlier chapters to a strategic setting. Third, one can analyze attempts to cooperate using noncooperative game theory. Perhaps most importantly, noncooperative game

[1]Much of the pioneering work in game theory was done by the mathematician John von Newmann. The main reference is J. von Neumann and O. Morgenstern, *The Theory of Games and Economic Behavior* (Princeton, NJ: Princeton University Press, 1944).

theory is more widely used by economists. Still, cooperative game theory has proved useful to model bargaining games and political processes.

5-2 Basic Concepts

Game-theory models seek to portray complex strategic situations in a simplified setting. Like previous models in this book, a game-theory model abstracts from many details to arrive at a mathematical representation of the essence of the situation. Any strategic situation can be modeled as game by specifying four basic elements: (1) players, (2) strategies, (3) payoffs, and (4) information.

Players

Each decision maker in a game is called a *player*. The players may be individuals (as in card games), firms (as in an oligopoly), or entire nations (as in military conflicts). The number of players varies from game to game, with two-player, three-player, or n-player games being possible. In this chapter, we primarily study two-player games since many of the important concepts can be illustrated in this simple setting. We usually denote these players by A and B.

Strategies

A player's choice in a game is called a *strategy*. A strategy may simply be one of the set of possible *actions* available to the player, leading to the use of the terms "strategy" and "action" interchangeably in informal discourse. But a strategy can be more complicated than an action. A strategy can be a contingent plan of action based on what another player does first (as will be important when we get to sequential games). A strategy can involve a random selection from several possible actions (as will be important when we get to mixed strategies). The actions underlying the strategies can range from the very simple (taking another card in blackjack) to the very complex (building an anti-missile defense system). Although some games offer the players a choice among many different actions, most of the important concepts in this chapter can be illustrated for situations in which each player has only two actions available. Even when the player has only two actions available, the set of strategies may be much larger once we allow for contingent plans or for probabilities of playing the actions.

Payoffs

The returns to the players at the conclusion of the game are called *payoffs*. Payoffs include the utilities players obtain from explicit monetary payments plus any implicit feelings they have about the outcome, such as whether they are embarrassed or gain self-esteem. It is sometimes convenient to ignore these complications and take payoffs simply to be the explicit monetary payments involved in the game. This is sometimes a reasonable assumption (for example, in the case of profit for a profit-maximizing firm), but it should be recognized as a simplification. Players seek to earn the highest payoffs possible.

Information

To complete the specification of a game, we need to specify what players know when they make their moves, called their *information*. We usually assume the structure of the game is common knowledge; each player knows not only the "rules of the game" but also that the other player knows, and so forth. Other aspects of information vary from game to game, depending on timing of moves and other issues. In simultaneous-move games, neither player knows the other's action when moving. In sequential move games, the first mover does not know the second's action but the second mover knows what the first did. In some games, called games of incomplete information, players may have an opportunity to learn things that others don't know. In card games, for example, players see the cards in their own hand but not others'. This knowledge will influence play; players with stronger hands may tend to play more aggressively, for instance.[2]

The chapter will begin with simple information structures (simultaneous games), moving to more complicated ones (sequential games), leaving a full analysis of games of incomplete information until Chapter 15. A central lesson of game theory is that seemingly minor changes in players' information may have a dramatic impact on the equilibrium of the game, so one needs to pay careful attention to specifying this element.

5-3 Equilibrium

Students who have taken a basic microeconomics course are familiar with the concept of market equilibrium, defined as the point where supply equals demand. (Market equilibrium is introduced in Chapter 1 and discussed further in Chapter 9.) Both suppliers and demanders are content with the market equilibrium: Given the equilibrium price and quantity, no market participant has an incentive to change his or her behavior. The question arises whether there are similar concepts in game-theory models. Are there strategic choices that, once made, provide no incentives for the players to alter their behavior given what others are doing?

The most widely used approach to defining equilibrium in games is named after John Nash for his development of the concept in the 1950s (see Application 5.1: A Beautiful Mind for a discussion of the movie that increased his fame). An integral part of this definition of equilibrium is the notion of a best response. Player A's strategy a is a **best response** against player B's strategy b if A cannot earn more from any other possible strategy given that B is playing b. A **Nash equilibrium** is a set of strategies, one for each player, that are mutual best responses. In a two-player game, a set of strategies (a^*, b^*) is a Nash equilibrium if a^* is player A's best response against b^* and b^* is player B's best response against a^*. A Nash equilibrium is stable in the sense that no player has an incentive to deviate unilaterally to some other strategy. Put another way, outcomes that are not Nash equilibria are unstable because at least one player can switch to a strategy that would increase his or her payoffs given what the other players are doing.

Best response
A strategy that produces the highest payoff among all possible strategies for a player given what the other player is doing.

Nash equilibrium
A set of strategies, one for each player, that are each best responses against one another.

Nash equilibrium is so widely used by economists as an equilibrium definition because, in addition to selecting an outcome that is stable, a Nash equilibrium exists for all games. (As we will see, some games that at first appear not to have a Nash equilibrium will end up having one in mixed strategies.) The Nash equilibrium concept does have some problems. Some games have several Nash equilibria, some of which may be more plausible than others. In some applications, other equilibrium concepts may be more plausible than the Nash equilibrium. The definition of the Nash equilibrium leaves out the process by which players arrive at strategies they are prescribed to play. Economists have devoted a great deal of recent research to these issues, and the picture is far from settled. Still, Nash's concept provides an initial working definition of equilibrium that we can use to start our study of game theory.

[2]We can still say that players share common knowledge about the "rules of the game" in that they all know the distribution of cards in the deck and the number that each will be dealt in a hand even though they have incomplete information about some aspects of the game, in this example the cards in others' hands.

APPLICATION 5.1

A Beautiful Mind

In 1994, John Nash won the Nobel Prize in economics for developing the equilibrium concept now known as the Nash equilibrium. The publication of the best-selling biography *A Beautiful Mind* and the Oscar award-winning movie of the same title have made him world famous.[1]

A Beautiful Blond

The movie dramatizes the development of the Nash equilibrium in a single scene in which Nash is in a bar talking with his male classmates. They notice several women at the bar, one blond and the rest brunette, and it is posited that the blond is more desirable than the brunettes. Nash conceives of the situation as a game among the male classmates. If they all go for the blond, they will block each other and fail to get her, and indeed fail to get the brunettes because the brunettes will be annoyed at being second choice. He proposes that they all go for the brunettes. (The assumption is that there are enough brunettes that they do not have to compete for them, so the males will be successful in getting dates with them.) While they will not get the more desirable blond, each will at least end up with a date.

Confusion about the Nash Equilibrium?

If it is thought that the Nash character was trying to solve for the Nash equilibrium of the game, he is guilty of making an elementary mistake! The outcome in which all male graduate students go for brunettes is not a Nash equilibrium. In a Nash equilibrium, no player can have a strictly profitable deviation given what the others are doing. But if all the other male graduate students went for brunettes, it would be strictly profitable for one of them to deviate and go for the blond because the deviator would have no competition for the blond, and she is assumed to provide a higher payoff. There are many Nash equilibria of this game, involving various subsets of males competing for the blond, but the outcome in which all males avoid the blond is not one of them.[2]

Nash versus the Invisible Hand

Some sense can be made of the scene if we view the Nash character's suggested outcome not as what he thought was the Nash equilibrium of the game but as a suggestion for how they might cooperate to move to a different outcome and increase their payoffs. One of the central lessons of game theory is that equilibrium does not necessarily lead to an outcome that is best for all. In this chapter, we study the Prisoners' Dilemma, in which the Nash equilibrium is for both players to Rat when they could both benefit if they could agree to be Silent. We also study the Battle of the Sexes, in which there is a Nash equilibrium where the players sometimes show up at different events, and this failure to coordinate ends up harming them both. The payoffs in the Beautiful Blond game can be specified in such a way that players do better if they all agree to ignore the blond than in the equilibrium in which all compete for the blond with some probability.[3] Adam Smith's famous "invisible hand," which directs the economy toward an efficient outcome under perfect competition, does not necessarily operate when players interact strategically in a game. Game theory opens up the possibility of conflict, miscoordination, and waste, just as observed in the real world.

TO THINK ABOUT

1. How would you write down the game corresponding to the bar scene from *A Beautiful Mind*? What are the Nash equilibria of your game? Should the females be included as players in the setup along with the males?
2. One of Nash's classmates suggested that Nash was trying to convince the others to go after the brunettes so that Nash could have the blond for himself. Is this a Nash equilibrium? Are there others like it? How can one decide how a game will be played if there are multiple Nash equilibria?

[1]The book is S. Nasar, *A Beautiful Mind* (New York: Simon & Schuster, 1997), and the movie is *A Beautiful Mind* (Universal Pictures, 2001).

[2]S. P. Anderson and M. Engers, "Participation Games: Market Entry, Coordination, and the Beautiful Blond," *Journal of Economic Behavior and Organization* (May 2007): 120–137.

[3]For example, the payoff to getting the blond can be set to 3, getting no date to 0, getting a brunette when no one else has gotten the blond to 2, and getting a brunette when someone else has gotten the blond to 1. Thus there is a loss due to envy if one gets the brunette when another has gotten the blond.

5-4 Illustrating Basic Concepts

We can illustrate the basic components of a game and the concept of the Nash equilibrium in perhaps the most famous of all noncooperative games, the Prisoners' Dilemma.

The Prisoners' Dilemma

First introduced by A. Tucker in the 1940s, its name stems from the following situation. Two suspects, *A* and *B*, are arrested for a crime. The district attorney has little evidence in the case and is anxious to extract testimony against each other. She separates the suspects and privately tells each, "If you testify against your partner and he or she doesn't against you, I can promise you a reduced (one-year) sentence, and on the basis of your testimony, your partner will get four years. If you both testify against each other, you will each get a three-year sentence." Each suspect also knows that if neither of them testifies, the lack of evidence will cause them to be tried for a lesser crime for which they will receive two-year sentences.

The Game in Normal Form

The players in the game are the two suspects, *A* and *B*. (Though a third person, the district attorney, plays a role in the story, once she sets up the payoffs from confessing she does not make strategic decisions, so she does not need to be included in the game.) The players can choose one of two possible actions, Rat (a colorful term for testifying against one's partner in crime) or Silent. The payoffs, as well as the players and actions, can be conveniently summarized, as shown in the matrix in Table 5.1. The representation of a game in a matrix like this is called the **normal form**. In the table, player *A*'s strategies, Rat or Silent, head the rows and *B*'s strategies head the columns. Payoffs corresponding to the various combinations of strategies are shown in the body of the table. To ensure positive payoffs, the sentences have been converted into years of freedom over the next four years. We will adopt the convention that the first payoff in each box corresponds to the row player (player *A*) and the second corresponds to the column player (player *B*). To make this convention even clearer, *A*'s strategies and payoffs are a different color than *B*'s. For an example of how to read the table, if *A* is Rats and *B* is Silent, *A* earns 3 (for one year of prison, so three years of freedom over the next four years) and *B* earns 0 (for four years of prison, so no years of freedom). The fact that the district attorney approaches each separately indicates that the game is simultaneous: A player cannot observe the other's action before choosing his or her own action.

Normal form
Representation of a game using a payoff matrix.

Table 5.1 Prisoners' Dilemma in Normal Form

		B	
		Rat	**Silent**
A	**Rat**	1, 1	3, 0
	Silent	0, 3	2, 2

The Game in Extensive Form

The Prisoners' Dilemma game can also be represented as a game tree as in Figure 5.1, called the **extensive form**. Action proceeds from top to bottom. Each dark circle is a decision point for the player indicated there. The first move belongs to *A*, who can choose Rat or Silent. The next move belongs to *B*, who can also choose Rat or Silent. Payoffs are given at the bottom of the tree.

Extensive form
Representation of a game as a tree.

Figure 5.1 Prisoners' Dilemma in Extensive Form

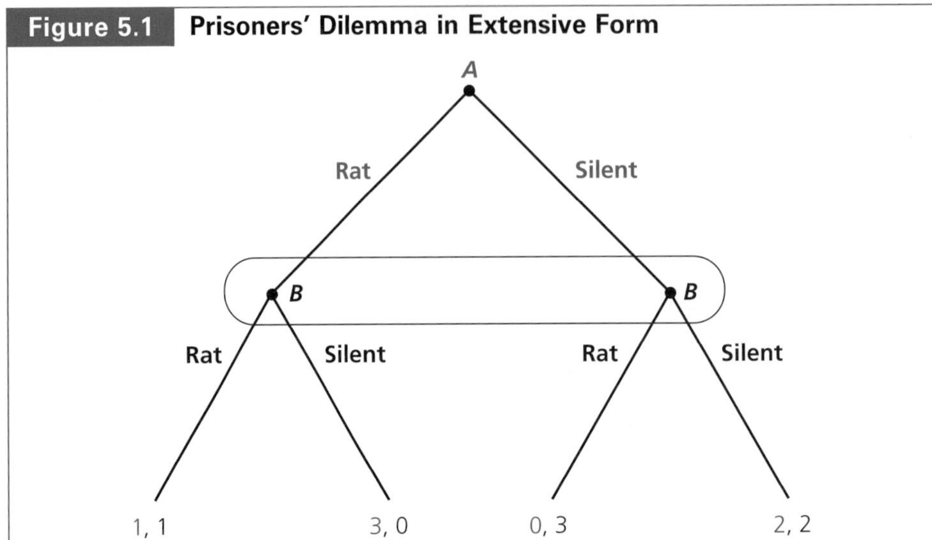

A chooses Rat or Silent, and *B* makes a similar choice. The oval surrounding *B*'s decision points indicates that *B* cannot observe *A*'s choice when *B* moves, since the game is simultaneous. Payoffs are listed at the bottom.

To reflect the fact that the Prisoners' Dilemma is a simultaneous game, we would like the two players' moves to appear in the same level in the tree, but the structure of a tree prevents us from doing that. To avoid this problem, we can arbitrarily choose one player (here *A*) to be at the top of the tree as the first mover and the other to be lower as the second mover, but then we draw an oval around *B*'s decision points to reflect the fact that *B* does not observe which action *A* has chosen and so does not observe which decision point has been reached when he or she makes his or her decision.

The choice to put *A* above *B* in the extensive form was arbitrary: We would have obtained the same representation if we put *B* above *A* and then had drawn an oval around *A*'s decision points. As we will see when we discuss sequential games, having an order to the moves only matters if the second mover can observe the first mover's action. It usually is easier to use the extensive form to analyze sequential games and the normal form to analyze simultaneous games. Therefore, we will return to the normal-form representation of the Prisoners' Dilemma to solve for its Nash equilibrium.

Solving for the Nash Equilibrium

Return to the normal form of the Prisoners' Dilemma in Table 5.1. Consider each box in turn to see if any of the corresponding pairs of strategies constitute a Nash equilibrium. First consider the lower right box, corresponding to both players choosing Silent. There is reason to think this is the equilibrium of the game since the sum of the payoffs, 4, is greater than the sum of the payoffs in any of the other three outcomes. However, both playing Silent is in fact not a Nash equilibrium. To be a Nash equilibrium, both players' strategies must be best responses to each other. But given that *B* plays Silent, *A* can increase his or her payoff from 2 to 3 by deviating from Silent to Rat. Therefore, Silent is not *A*'s best response to *B*'s playing Silent. (It is also true that *B*'s playing Silent is not a best response to *A*'s playing Silent, although demonstrating that at least one of the two players was not playing his or her best response was enough to rule out an outcome as

being a Nash equilibrium.) Next consider the top right box, where *A* plays Rat and *B* plays Silent. This is not a Nash equilibrium either. Given that *A* plays Rat, *B* can increase his or her payoff from 0 to 2 by deviating from Silent to Rat. Similarly, the bottom left box, in which *A* plays Silent and *B* plays Rat, can be shown not to be a Nash equilibrium since *A* is not playing a best response.

KEEP *in* MIND

Specify Equilibrium Strategies

The temptation is to say that the Nash equilibrium in the Prisoners' Dilemma is (1, 1). This is not technically correct. Recall that the definition of the Nash equilibrium involves a set of strategies, so it is proper to refer to the Nash equilibrium as "both players choose Rat." True, each outcome corresponds to unique payoffs in this game, so there is little confusion in referring to an equilibrium by the associated payoffs rather than strategies. However, we will come across games later in the chapter in which different outcomes have the same payoffs, so referring to equilibria by payoffs leads to ambiguity.

The remaining upper left box corresponds to both playing Rat. This is a Nash equilibrium. Given *B* plays Rat, *A*'s best response is Rat since this leads *A* to earn 1 rather than 0. By the same logic, Rat is *B*'s best response to *A*'s playing Rat.

Rather than going through each outcome one by one, there is a shortcut to finding the Nash equilibrium directly by underlining payoffs corresponding to best responses. This method is useful in games having only two actions having small payoff matrices but becomes extremely useful when the number of actions increases and the payoff matrix grows. The method is outlined in Table 5.2. The first step is to compute *A*'s best response to *B*'s playing Rat. *A* compares his or her payoff in the first column from playing Rat, 1, to playing Silent, 0. The payoff 1 is higher than 0, so Rat is *A*'s best response, and we underline 1. In step 2, we underline 3, corresponding to *A*'s best response, Rat, to *B*'s playing Silent. In step 3, we underline 1, corresponding to *B*'s best response to *A*'s playing Rat. In step 4, we underline 3, corresponding to *B*'s best response to *A*'s playing Silent.

For an outcome to be a Nash equilibrium, both players must be playing a best response to each other. Therefore, both payoffs in the box must be underlined. As seen in step 5, the only box in which both payoffs are underlined is the upper left, with both players choosing Rat. In the other boxes, either one or no payoffs are underlined, meaning that one or both of the players are not playing a best response in these boxes, so they cannot be Nash equilibria.

Dominant Strategies

Referring to step 5 in Table 5.2, not only is Rat a best response to the other players' equilibrium strategy (all that is required for Nash equilibrium), but Rat is also a best response to all strategies the other player might choose, called a **dominant strategy**. When a player has a dominant strategy in a game, there is good reason to predict that this is how the player will play the game. The player does not need to make a strategic calculation, imagining what the other might do in equilibrium. The player has one strategy that is best, regardless of what the other does. In most games, players do not have dominant strategies, so dominant strategies would not be a generally useful equilibrium definition (while the Nash equilibrium is, since it exists for all games).

Dominant strategy
Best response to all of the other player's strategies.

Table 5.2 Finding the Nash Equilibrium of the Prisoners' Dilemma Using the Underlining Method

Step 1: Underline payoff for *A*'s best response to *B*'s playing Rat.

		B Rat	*B* Silent
A	Rat	1, 1	3, 0
	Silent	0, 3	2, 2

Step 2: Underline payoff for *A*'s best response to *B*'s playing Silent.

		B Rat	*B* Silent
A	Rat	1, 1	3, 0
	Silent	0, 3	2, 2

Step 3: Underline payoff for *B*'s best response to *A*'s playing Rat.

		B Rat	*B* Silent
A	Rat	1, 1	3, 0
	Silent	0, 3	2, 2

Step 4: Underline payoff for *B*'s best response to *A*'s playing Silent.

		B Rat	*B* Silent
A	Rat	1, 1	3, 0
	Silent	0, 3	2, 2

Step 5: Nash equilibrium in box with both payoffs underlined.

		B Rat	*B* Silent
A	Rat	(1, 1)	3, 0
	Silent	0, 3	2, 2

The Dilemma

The game is called the Prisoners' "Dilemma" because there is a better outcome for both players than the equilibrium. If both were Silent, they would each only get two years rather than three. But both being Silent is not stable; each would prefer to deviate to Rat. If the suspects could sign binding contracts, they would sign a contract that would have them both choose Silent. But such contracts would be difficult to write because the district attorney approaches each suspect privately, so they cannot communicate; and even if they could sign a contract, no court would enforce it.

Situations resembling the Prisoners' Dilemma arise in many real world settings. The best outcome for students working on a group project together might be for all to work hard and earn a high grade on the project, but the individual incentive to shirk, each relying on the efforts of others, may prevent them from attaining such an outcome. A cartel agreement among dairy farmers to restrict output would lead to higher prices and profits if it could be sustained, but may be unstable because it may be too tempting for an individual farmer to try to sell more milk at the high price. We will study the stability of business cartels more formally in Chapter 12.

Mixed Strategies

To analyze some games, we need to allow for more complicated strategies than simply choosing a single action with certainty, called a **pure strategy**. We will next consider **mixed strategies**, which have the player randomly select one of several possible actions. Mixed strategies are illustrated in another classic game, Matching Pennies.

Pure strategy
A single action played with certainty.

Mixed strategy
Randomly selecting from several possible actions.

Matching Pennies

Matching Pennies is based on a children's game in which two players, *A* and *B*, each secretly choose whether to leave a penny with its head or tail facing up. The players then reveal their choices simultaneously. *A* wins B's penny if the coins match (both Heads or both Tails), and *B* wins *A*'s penny if they do not. The normal form for the game is given in Table 5.3 and the extensive form in Figure 5.2. The game has the special property that the two players' payoffs in each box add to zero, called a zero-sum game. The reader can check that the Prisoner's Dilemma is not a zero-sum game because the sum of players' payoffs varies across the different boxes.

To solve for the Nash equilibrium, we will use the method of underlining payoffs for best responses introduced previously for the Prisoners' Dilemma. Table 5.4 presents the results from this method. *A* always prefers to play the same action as *B*. *B* prefers to play a different action from *A*. There is no box with both payoffs underlined, so we have not managed to find a Nash equilibrium. It is tempting to say that no Nash equilibrium exists for this game. But this contradicts our earlier claim that all games have Nash equilibria. The contradiction can be resolved by noting that Matching Pennies does have a Nash equilibrium, not in pure strategies, as would be found by our underlining method, but in mixed strategies.

Table 5.3 Matching Pennies Game in Normal Form

		B	
		Heads	**Tails**
A	**Heads**	1, −1	−1, 1
	Tails	−1, 1	1, −1

Figure 5.2 Matching Pennies Game in Extensive Form

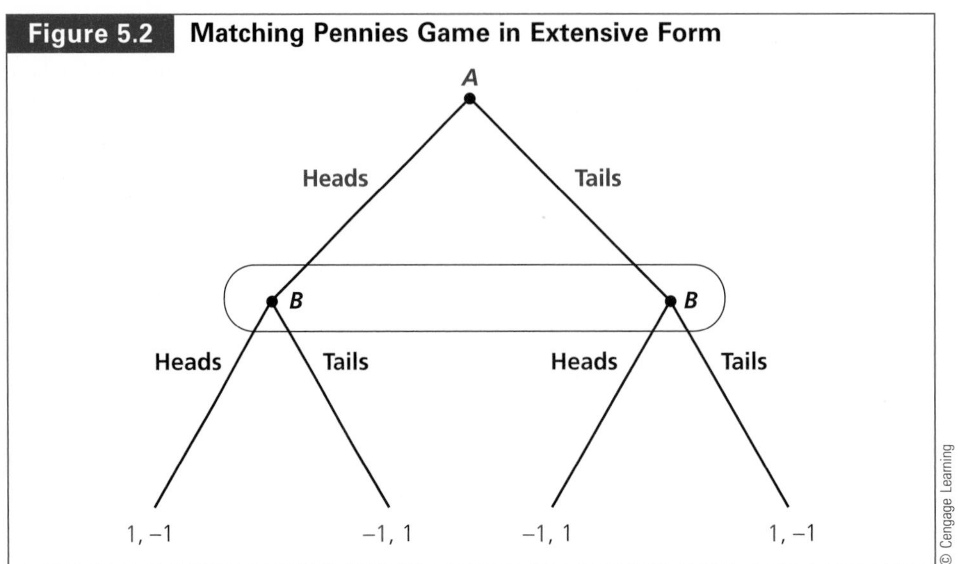

Solving for a Mixed-Strategy Nash Equilibrium

Rather than choosing Heads or Tails, suppose players secretly flip the penny and play whatever side turns up. The result of this strategy is a random choice of Heads with probability 1/2 and Tails with probability 1/2. This set of strategies, with both playing Heads or Tails with equal chance, is the mixed-strategy Nash equilibrium of the game. To verify this, we need to show that both players' strategies are best responses to each other.

In the proposed equilibrium, all four outcomes corresponding to the four boxes in the normal form in Table 5.3 are equally likely to occur, each occurring with probability 1/4. Using the formula for expected payoffs from the previous chapter, *A*'s expected payoff equals the probability-weighted sum of the payoffs in each outcome:

$$(1/4)(1) + (1/4)(-1) + (1/4)(-1) + (1/4)(1) = 0.$$

Similarly, *B*'s expected payoff is also 0. The mixed strategies in the proposed equilibrium are best responses to each other if neither player can deviate to a strategy that produces a strictly higher payoff than 0. But there is no such profitable deviation. Given that *B* plays Heads and Tails with equal probabilities, the players' coins will match exactly half the time, whether *A* chooses Heads or Tails (or indeed even some random combination of the two actions); so *A*'s payoff is 0 no matter what strategy it chooses. *A* cannot earn more than the 0 it earns in equilibrium. Similarly, given *A* is playing Heads and Tails with equal probabilities, *B*'s expected payoff is 0 no matter what strategy it uses. So neither player has a strictly profitable deviation. (It should be emphasized here that if a deviation produces a tie with the player's

Table 5.4 Solving for Pure-Strategy Nash Equilibrium in Matching Pennies Game

		B	
		Heads	Tails
A	Heads	<u>1</u>, −1	−1, <u>1</u>
	Tails	−1, <u>1</u>	<u>1</u>, −1

equilibrium payoff, this is not sufficient to rule out the equilibrium; to rule out an equilibrium, one must demonstrate a deviation produces a strictly higher payoff.)

Both players playing Heads and Tails with equal probabilities is the only mixed-strategy Nash equilibrium in this game. No other probabilities would work. For example, suppose *B* were to play Heads with probability 1/3 and Tails with probability 2/3. Then *A* would earn an expected payoff of $(1/3)\ (1) + \ = (2/3)(-1) = -1/3$ from playing Heads and $(1/3)(-1) + (2/3)(1) = 1/3$ from playing Tails. Therefore, *A* would strictly prefer to play Tails as a pure strategy rather than playing a mixed strategy involving both Heads and Tails, and so *B*'s playing Heads with probability 1/3 and Tails with probability 2/3 cannot be a mixed-strategy Nash equilibrium.

MICRO QUIZ 5.1

In Matching Pennies, suppose *B* plays the equilibrium mixed strategy of Heads with probability 1/2 and Tails with probability 1/2. Use the formula for expected values to verify that A's expected payoff equals 0 from using any of the following strategies.

1. The pure strategy of Heads
2. The pure strategy of Tails
3. The mixed strategy of Heads with probability 1/2 and Tails with probability 1/2
4. The mixed strategy of Heads with probability 1/3 and Tails with probability 2/3

KEEP *in* MIND

Indifferent among Random Actions

In any mixed-strategy equilibrium, players must be indifferent between the actions that are played with positive probability. If a player strictly preferred one action over another, the player would want to put all of the probability on the preferred action and none on the other action.

Interpretation of Random Strategies

Although at first glance it may seem bizarre to have players flipping coins or rolling dice in secret to determine their strategies, it may not be so unnatural in children's games such as Matching Pennies. Mixed strategies are also natural and common in sports, as discussed in Application 5.2: Mixed Strategies in Sports. Perhaps most familiar to students is the role of mixed strategies in class exams. Class time is usually too limited for the professor to examine students on every topic taught in class. But it may be sufficient to test students on a subset of topics to get them to study all of the material. If students knew which topics are on the test, they may be inclined to study only those and not the others, so the professor must choose which topics to include at random to get the students to study everything.

5-5 Multiple Equilibria

The Nash equilibrium is a useful solution concept because it exists for all games. A drawback is that some games have several or even many Nash equilibria. The possibility of multiple equilibria causes a problem for economists who would like to use game theory

APPLICATION 5.2

Mixed Strategies in Sports

Sports provide a setting in which mixed strategies arise quite naturally, and in a simple enough setting that we can see game theory in operation.

Soccer Penalty Kicks

In soccer, if a team commits certain offenses near its own goal, the other team is awarded a penalty kick, effectively setting up a game between the kicker and the goalie. Table 1 is based on a study of penalty kicks in elite European soccer leagues.[1] The first entry in each box is the frequency the penalty kick scores (taken to be the kicker's payoff), and the second entry is the frequency it does not score (taken to be the goalie's payoff). Kickers are assumed to have two actions: aim toward the "natural" side of the goal (left for right-footed kickers and right for left-footed players) or aim toward the other side. Kickers can typically kick harder and more accurately to their natural side. Goalies can try to jump one way or the other to try to block the kick. The ball travels too fast for the goalie to react to its direction, so the game is effectively simultaneous. Goalies know from scouting reports what side is natural for each kicker, so they can condition their actions on this information.

Table 1 Soccer Penalty Kick Game

		Goalie: Natural side for kicker	Goalie: Other side
Kicker	Natural side for kicker	.64, <u>.36</u>	<u>.94</u>, .06
	Other side	<u>.89</u>, .11	.44, <u>.56</u>

Do Mixed Strategies Predict Actual Outcomes?

Using the method of underlining payoffs corresponding to best responses, as shown in Table 1, we see that no box has both payoffs underlined, so there is no pure-strategy Nash equilibrium.

Following the same steps used to compute the mixed-strategy Nash equilibrium in the Battle of the Sexes, one can show that the kicker kicks to his natural side 3/5 of the time and 2/5 of the time to his other side; the goalie jumps to the side that is natural for the kicker 2/3 of the time and the other side 1/3 of the time.

This calculation generates several testable implications. First, both actions have at least some chance of being played. This is borne out in the Chiappori et al. data: Almost all of the kickers and goalies who are involved in three or more penalty kicks in the data choose each action at least once. Second, players obtain the same expected payoff in equilibrium regardless of the action taken. This is again borne out in the data, with kickers scoring about 75 percent of the time, whether they kick to their natural side or the opposite, and goalies being scored on about 75 percent of the time, whether they jump to the kicker's natural side or the opposite. Third, the goalie should jump to the side that is natural for the kicker more often. Otherwise, the higher speed and accuracy going to his natural side would lead the kicker to play the pure strategy of always kicking that way. Again, this conclusion is borne out in the data, with the goalie jumping to the kicker's natural side 60 percent of the time (note how close this is to the prediction of 2/3 we made above).

TO THINK ABOUT

1. Verify the mixed-strategy Nash equilibrium computed above for the penalty-kick game following the methods used for the Battle of the Sexes.
2. Economists have studied mixed strategies in other sports, for example whether a tennis serve is aimed to the returner's backhand or forehand.[2] Can you think of other sports settings involving mixed strategies? Can you think of settings outside of sports and games and besides the ones noted in the text?

[1] P.-A. Chiappori, S. Levitt, and T. Groseclose, "Testing Mixed-Strategy Equilibria When Players Are Heterogeneous: The Case of Penalty Kicks in Soccer," *American Economic Review* (September 2002): 1138–1151.

[2] M. Walker and J. Wooders, "Minimax Play at Wimbledon," *American Economic Review* (December 2001): 1521–1538.

to make predictions, since it is unclear which of the Nash equilibria one should predict will happen. The possibility of multiple equilibria is illustrated in yet another classic game, the Battle of the Sexes.

Table 5.5 Battle of the Sexes in Normal Form

		B (Husband)	
		Ballet	Boxing
A (Wife)	Ballet	2, 1	0, 0
	Boxing	0, 0	1, 2

Battle of the Sexes

The game involves two players, a wife (*A*) and a husband (*B*) who are planning an evening out. Both prefer to be together rather than apart. Conditional on being together, the wife would prefer to go to a Ballet performance and the husband to a Boxing match. The normal form for the game is given in Table 5.5, and the extensive form in Figure 5.3.

To solve for the Nash equilibria, we will use the method of underlining payoffs for best responses introduced previously. Table 5.6 presents the results from this method. A player's best response is to play the same action as the other. Both payoffs are underlined in two boxes: the box in which both play Ballet and also in the box in which both play Boxing. Therefore, there are two pure-strategy Nash equilibria: (1) both play Ballet and (2) both play Boxing.

The problem of multiple equilibria is even worse than it first appears. Besides the two pure-strategy Nash equilibria, there is a mixed-strategy one. How does one know this? One could find out for sure by performing all of the calculations necessary to find a mixed-strategy Nash equilibrium. Even without doing any calculations, one could guess that there would be a mixed-strategy Nash equilibrium based on a famous but peculiar result that Nash equilibria tend to come in odd numbers. Therefore, finding an even number of pure-strategy Nash equilibria (two in this game, zero in Matching Pennies) should lead one to suspect that the game also has another Nash equilibrium, in mixed strategies.

Figure 5.3 Battle of the Sexes in Extensive Form

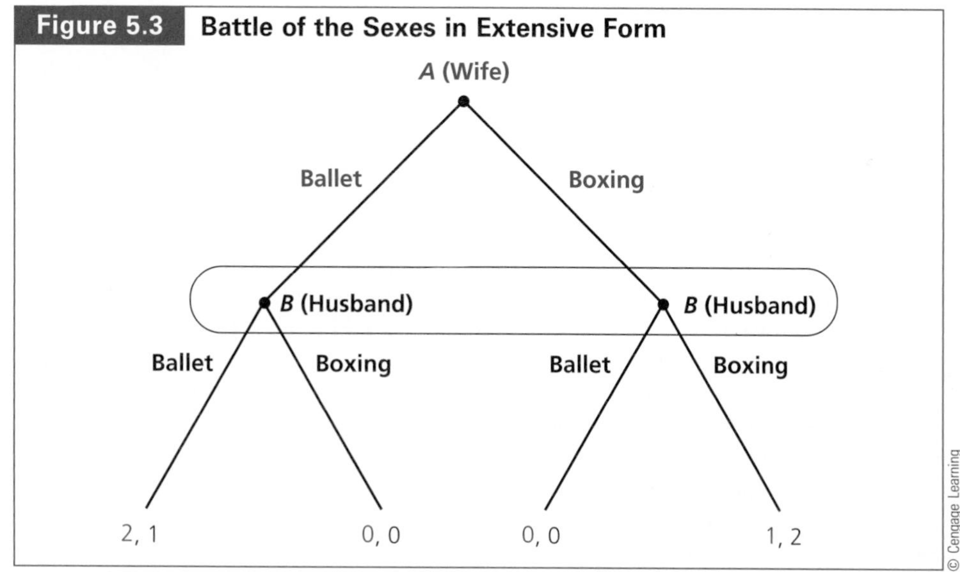

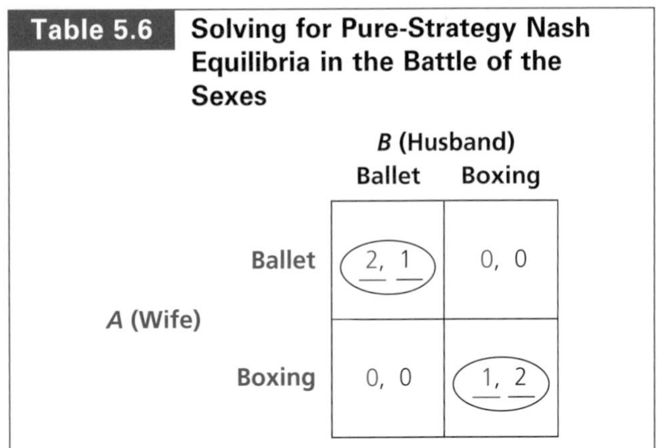

Table 5.6 Solving for Pure-Strategy Nash Equilibria in the Battle of the Sexes

		B (Husband)	
		Ballet	Boxing
A (Wife)	Ballet	2, 1	0, 0
	Boxing	0, 0	1, 2

Computing Mixed Strategies in the Battle of the Sexes

It is instructive to go through the calculation of the mixed-strategy Nash equilibrium in the Battle of the Sexes since, unlike in Matching Pennies, the equilibrium probabilities do not end up being equal (1/2) for each action. Let w be the probability the wife plays Ballet and h the probability the husband plays Ballet. Because probabilities of exclusive and exhaustive events must add to one, the probability of playing Boxing is $1 - w$ for the wife and $1 - h$ for the husband; so once we know the probability each plays Ballet, we automatically know the probability each plays Boxing. Our task then is to compute the equilibrium values of w and h. The difficulty now is that w and h may potentially be any one of a continuum of values between 0 and 1, so we cannot set up a payoff matrix and use our underlining method to find best responses. Instead, we will graph players' **best-response functions.**

Best-response function
Function giving the payoff-maximizing choice for one player for each of a continuum of strategies of the other player.

Let us start by computing the wife's best-response function. The wife's best-response function gives the w that maximizes her payoff for each of the husband's possible strategies, h. For a given h, there are three possibilities: she may strictly prefer to play Ballet, she may strictly prefer to play Boxing, or she may be indifferent between Ballet and Boxing. In terms of w, if she strictly prefers to play Ballet, her best response is $w = 1$. If she strictly prefers to play Boxing, her best response is $w = 0$. If she is indifferent about Ballet and Boxing, her best response is a tie between $w = 1$ and $w = 0$; in fact, it is a tie among $w = 0$, $w = 1$, and all values of w between 0 and 1!

To see this last point, suppose her expected payoff from playing both Ballet and Boxing is, say, 2/3, and suppose she randomly plays Ballet and Boxing with probabilities w and $1 - w$. Her expected payoff (this should be reviewed, if necessary, from Chapter 5) would equal the probability she plays Ballet times her expected payoff if she plays Ballet plus the probability she plays Boxing times her expected payoff if she plays Boxing:

$$(w)(2/3) + (1 - w)(2/3) = 2/3.$$

This shows that she gets the same payoff, 2/3, whether she plays Ballet for sure, Boxing for sure, or a mixed strategy involving any probabilities w, $1 - w$ of playing Ballet and Boxing. So her best response would be a tie among $w = 0$, $w = 1$, and all values in between.

Returning to the computation of the wife's best-response function, suppose the husband plays a mixed strategy of Ballet probability h and Boxing with probability $1 - h$. Referring to Table 5.7, her expected payoff from playing Ballet equals h (the probability the husband plays Ballet, and so they end up in Box 1) times 2 (her payoff in Box 1) plus $1 - h$ (the probability he plays Boxing, and so they end up in Box 2) times 0 (her payoff in Box 2), for a total expected payoff, after simplifying, of $2h$. Her expected payoff from playing Boxing equals h (the probability the husband plays Ballet, and so they end up in Box 3) times 0 (her payoff in Box 3) plus $1 - h$ (the probability he plays Boxing, and so they end up in Box 4) times 1 (her payoff in Box 4) for a total expected payoff, after simplifying, of $1 - h$.

Comparing these two expected payoffs, we can see that she prefers Boxing if $2h < 1 - h$ or, rearranging, $h < 1/3$. She prefers Ballet if $h > 1/3$. She is indifferent between Ballet and Boxing if $h = 1/3$. Therefore, her best response to $h < 1/3$ is $w = 0$, to $h > 1/3$ is $w = 1$, and to $h = 1/3$ includes $w = 0$, $w = 1$, and all values in between.

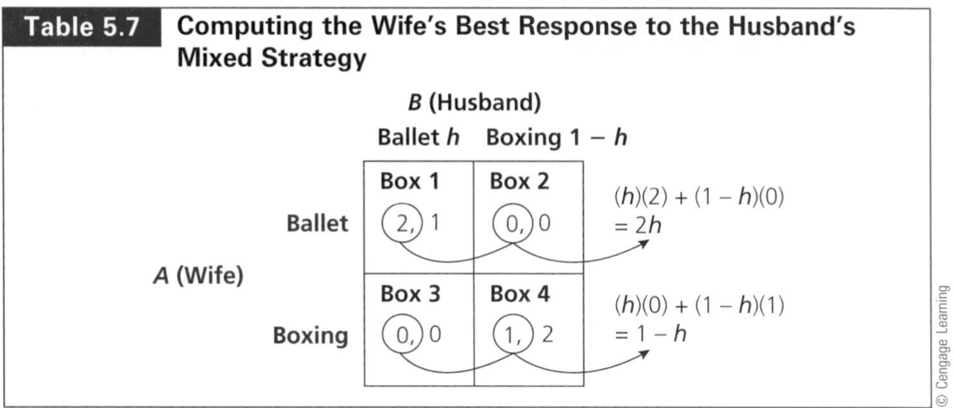

Table 5.7 Computing the Wife's Best Response to the Husband's Mixed Strategy

		B (Husband) Ballet h	B (Husband) Boxing $1-h$	
A (Wife)	Ballet	Box 1: (2,) 1	Box 2: (0,) 0	$(h)(2) + (1-h)(0) = 2h$
A (Wife)	Boxing	Box 3: (0,) 0	Box 4: (1,) 2	$(h)(0) + (1-h)(1) = 1-h$

Figure 5.4 graphs her best-response function as the light-colored curve. Similar calculations can be used to derive the husband's best-response function, the dark-colored curve. The best-response functions intersect in three places. These intersections are mutual best responses and hence Nash equilibria. The figure allows us to recover the two pure-strategy Nash equilibria found before: the one in which $w = h = 1$ (that is, both play Ballet for sure) and the one in which $w = h = 0$ (that is, both play Boxing for sure). We also obtain the mixed-strategy Nash equilibrium $w = 1/3$ and $h = 1/3$. In words, the mixed-strategy Nash equilibrium involves the wife's playing Ballet with probability 2/3 and Boxing with probability 1/3 and the husband's playing Ballet with probability 1/3 and Boxing with probability 2/3.

At first glance, it seems that the wife puts more probability on Ballet because she prefers Ballet conditional on coordinating and the husband puts more probability on Boxing because he prefers Boxing conditional on coordinating. This intuition is misleading. The wife, for example, is indifferent between Ballet and Boxing in the mixed-strategy Nash equilibrium given her husband's strategy. She does not care what probabilities she

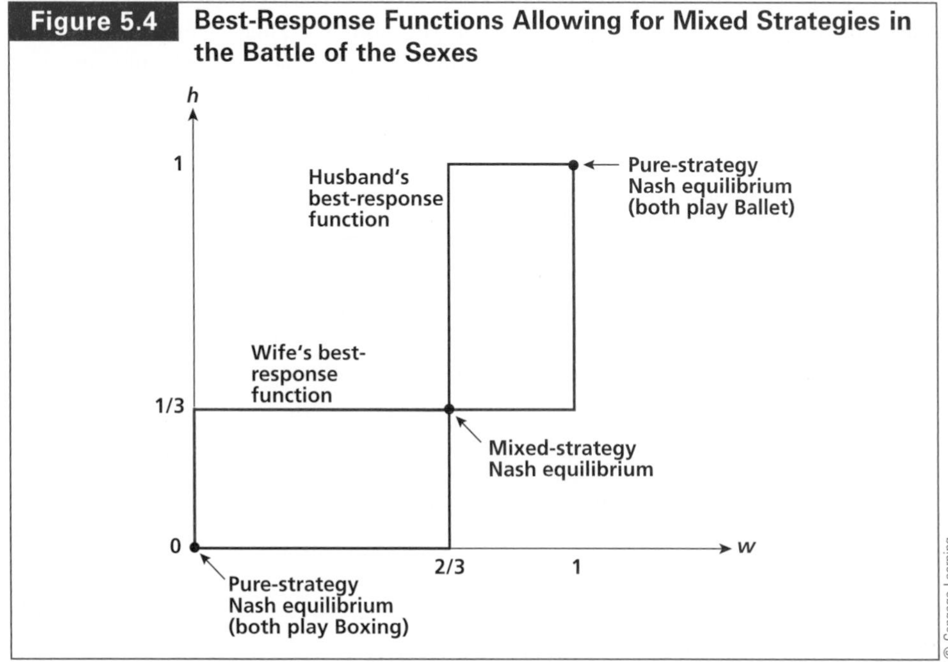

Figure 5.4 Best-Response Functions Allowing for Mixed Strategies in the Battle of the Sexes

MICRO QUIZ 5.2

1. In the Battle of the Sexes, does either player have a dominant strategy?
2. In general, can a game have a mixed-strategy Nash equilibrium if a player has a dominant strategy? Why or why not?

plays Ballet and Boxing. What pins down her equilibrium probabilities is not her payoffs but her husband's. She has to put less probability on the action he prefers conditional on coordinating (Boxing) than on the other action (Ballet) or else he would not be indifferent between Ballet and Boxing and the probabilities would not form a Nash equilibrium.

The Problem of Multiple Equilibria

Given that there are multiple equilibria, it is difficult to make a unique prediction about the outcome of the game. To solve this problem, game theorists have devoted a considerable amount of research to refining the Nash equilibrium concept, that is, coming up with good reasons for picking out one Nash equilibrium as being more "reasonable" than others. One suggestion would be to select the outcome with the highest total payoffs for the two players. This rule would eliminate the mixed-strategy Nash equilibrium in favor of one of the two pure-strategy equilibria. In the mixed-strategy equilibrium, we showed that each player's expected payoff is 2/3 no matter which action is chosen, implying that the total expected payoff for the two players is $2/3 + 2/3 = 4/3$ In the two pure-strategy equilibria, total payoffs, equal to 3, exceed the total expected payoff in the mixed-strategy equilibrium.

A rule that selects the highest total payoff would not distinguish between the two pure-strategy equilibria. To select between these, one might follow T. Schelling's suggestion and look for a **focal point**.[3] For example, the equilibrium in which both play Ballet might be a logical focal point if the couple had a history of deferring to the wife's wishes on previous occasions. Without access to this external information on previous interactions, it would be difficult for a game theorist to make predictions about focal points, however.

Focal point
Logical outcome on which to coordinate, based on information outside of the game.

Another suggestion would be, absent a reason to favor one player over another, to select the symmetric equilibrium. This rule would pick out the mixed-strategy Nash equilibrium because it is the only one that has equal payoffs (both players' expected payoffs are 2/3).

Unfortunately, none of these selection rules seems particularly compelling. The Battle of the Sexes is one of those games for which there is simply no good way to solve the problem of multiple equilibria. Application 5.3: High-Definition Standards War provides a real-world example with multiple equilibria. The difficulty in using game theory to determine the outcome in this market mirrors the difficulty in predicting which standard would end up dominating the market.

5-6 Sequential Games

In some games, the order of moves matters. For example, in a bicycle race with a staggered start, the last racer has the advantage of knowing the time to beat. With new consumer technologies, for example, high-definition video disks, it may help to wait to buy until a critical mass of others have and so there are a sufficiently large number of program channels available.

Sequential games differ from the simultaneous games we have considered so far in that a player that moves after another can learn information about the play of the game up to that point, including what actions other players have chosen. The player can use this information to form more sophisticated strategies than simply choosing an action;

[3]T. Schelling, *The Strategy of Conflict* (Cambridge, MA: Harvard University Press, 1960).

APPLICATION 5.3

High-Definition Standards War

A stark example of strategic behavior is the "war" over the new standard for high-definition video disks.[1] After spending billions in research and development, in 2006, Toshiba launched its HD-DVD player with six times the resolution of DVDs it was designed to replace. Within months, Sony launched its Blu-Ray player, offering similar features but in an incompatible format. The war was on. Sony and Toshiba engaged in fierce price competition, in some cases reducing prices for the player below production costs. They also raced to sign exclusive contracts with major movie studios (Disney signing on to the Blu-Ray format and Paramount to HD-DVD).

Game among Consumers

In a sense, the outcome of the standards war hinged more on the strategic behavior of consumers than the firms involved. Given that the two formats had similar features, consumers were mainly interested in buying the one expected to be more popular. The more popular player would afford more opportunities to trade movies with friends, more movies would be released in that format, and so forth. (Larger networks of users are also beneficial in other cases including cell phones, computer software, and even social-networking websites.)

Table 1 shows a simple version of a game between two representative consumers. The game has two pure-strategy Nash equilibria in which the consumers coordinate on a single standard. It also has a mixed-strategy Nash equilibrium in which consumers randomize with equal probabilities over the two formats. The initial play of the game is probably best captured by the mixed-strategy equilibrium. Neither standard dominated at first. Payoffs remained low as little content was provided in high definition, and this was divided between the two formats.

Table 1 **Standards Game**

		Consumer *B*	
		Blue-Ray	HD-DVD
Consumer *A*	Blue-Ray	1, 1	0, 0
	HD-DVD	0, 0	1, 1

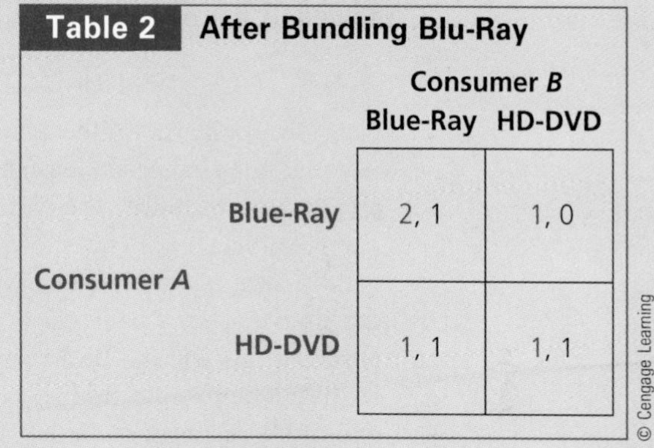

Table 2 **After Bundling Blu-Ray**

		Consumer *B*	
		Blue-Ray	HD-DVD
Consumer *A*	Blue-Ray	2, 1	1, 0
	HD-DVD	1, 1	1, 1

Victory for Blu-Ray

In 2008, Toshiba announced that it would stop backing the HD-DVD standard, signaling Sony's victory with Blu-Ray. Why did Sony eventually win? One theory is that Sony gained an enormous huge head start in developing an installed base of consumers by bundling a free Blu-Ray player in every one of the millions of Playstation 3 video-game consoles it sold. Lacking a game console of its own, Toshiba sought a deal to bundle HD-DVD with Microsoft's Xbox, but only succeeded in having it offered as an expensive add-on.

Table 2 shows how the game might change if a free Blu-Ray player is bundled with *A*'s Playstation. *A* receives a one-unit increase in the payoff from Blu-Ray because this strategy no longer requires the purchase of an expensive machine. The players coordinate even if *A* chooses HD-DVD and *B* chooses Blu-Ray because *A* can play Blu-Ray disks on his or her Playstation. The two pure-strategy Nash equilibria remain, but the mixed-strategy one has been eliminated. It is plausible that the Blu-Ray equilibrium would be the one played because consumers are as well or better off in that outcome as any other.

TO THINK ABOUT

1. Think about other standards wars. Can you identify factors determining the winning standard?
2. It was claimed that Nash equilibria tend to come in odd numbers, yet Table 2 has an even number. The resolution of this seeming contradiction is that Nash equilibria come in odd numbers *unless there are ties between payoffs in rows or columns.* Show that an odd number of Nash equilibria result in Table 2 if some of certain payoffs are tweaked to break ties.

[1] M. Williams, "HD DVD vs. Blu-Ray Disc: A History," *PC World* online edition, February 2008, http://www.pcworld.com/article/id,142584-c,dvddrives-media/article.html, accessed on October 6, 2008.

the player's strategy can be a contingent plan, with the action played depending on what the other players do.

To illustrate the new concepts raised by sequential games, and in particular to make a stark contrast between sequential and simultaneous games, we will take a simultaneous game we have discussed already, the Battle of the Sexes, and turn it into a sequential game.

The Sequential Battle of the Sexes

Consider the Battle of the Sexes game analyzed previously with all the same actions and payoffs, but change the order of moves. Rather than the wife and husband making a simultaneous choice, the wife moves first, choosing Ballet or Boxing, the husband observes this choice (say the wife calls him from her chosen location), and then the husband makes his choice. The wife's possible strategies have not changed: She can choose the simple actions Ballet or Boxing (or perhaps a mixed strategy involving both actions, although this will not be a relevant consideration in the sequential game). The husband's set of possible strategies has expanded. For each of the wife's two actions, he can choose one of two actions, so he has four possible strategies, which are listed in Table 5.8. The vertical bar in the second equivalent way of writing the strategies means "conditional on," so, for example, "Boxing | Ballet" should be read as "the husband goes to Boxing conditional on the wife's going to Ballet." The husband still can choose a simple action, with "Ballet" now interpreted as "always go to Ballet" and "Boxing" as "always go to Boxing," but he can also follow her or do the opposite.

Given that the husband has four pure strategies rather than just two, the normal form, given in Table 5.9, must now be expanded to have eight boxes. Roughly speaking, the normal form is twice as complicated as that for the simultaneous version of the game in Table 5.5. By contrast, the extensive form, given in Figure 5.5, is no more complicated than the extensive form for the simultaneous version of the game in Figure 5.3. The only difference between the extensive forms is that the oval around the husband's decision points has been removed. In the sequential version of the game, the husband's decision points are not gathered together in an oval because the husband observes his wife's action and so knows which one he is on before moving. We can begin to see why the extensive form becomes more useful than the normal form for sequential games, especially in games with many rounds of moves.

To solve for the Nash equilibria, we will return to the normal form and use the method of underlining payoffs for best responses introduced previously.

Table 5.8 Husband's Contingent Strategies

Contingent strategy	Same strategy written in conditional format
Always go to Ballet	Ballet | Ballet, Ballet | Boxing
Follow his wife	Ballet | Ballet, Boxing | Boxing
Do the opposite	Boxing | Ballet, Ballet | Boxing
Always go to Boxing	Boxing | Ballet, Boxing | Boxing

Table 5.9 Sequential Version of the Battle of the Sexes in Normal Form

		B (Husband)			
		Ballet | Ballet Ballet | Boxing	Ballet | Ballet Boxing | Boxing	Boxing | Ballet Ballet | Boxing	Boxing | Ballet Boxing | Boxing
A (Wife)	Ballet	2, 1	2, 1	0, 0	0, 0
	Boxing	0, 0	1, 2	0, 0	1, 2

Figure 5.5 Sequential Version of the Battle of the Sexes in Extensive Form

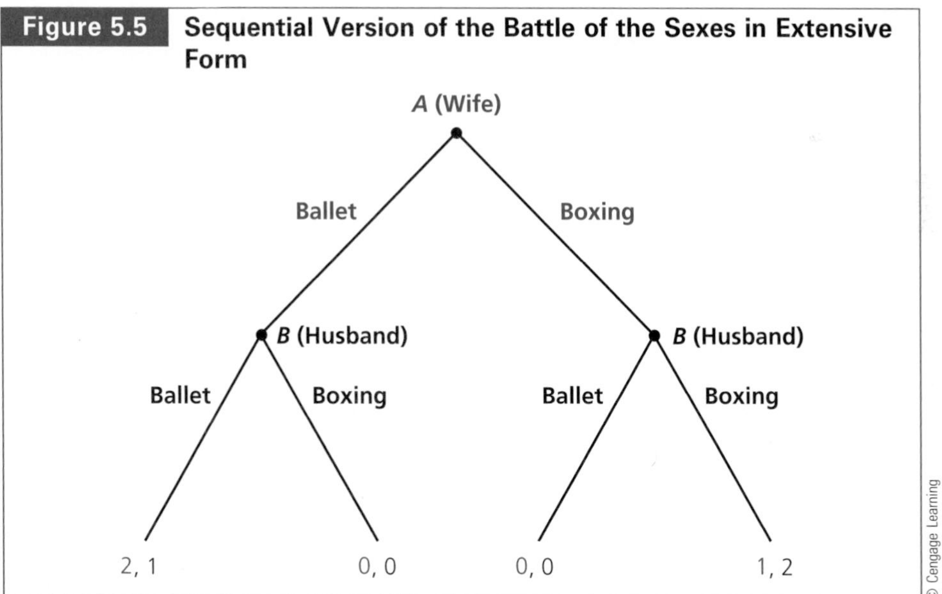

Table 5.10 presents the results from this method. One complication that arises in the method of underlining payoffs is that there are ties for best responses in this game. For example, if the husband plays the strategy "Boxing | Ballet, Ballet | Boxing," that is, if he does the opposite of his wife, then she earns zero no matter what action she chooses. To apply the underlining method properly, we need to underline both zeroes in the third column. There are also ties between the husband's best responses to his wife's playing Ballet (his payoff is 1 if he plays either "Ballet | Ballet, Ballet | Boxing" or "Ballet | Ballet, Boxing | Boxing") and to his wife's playing Boxing (his payoff is 2 if he

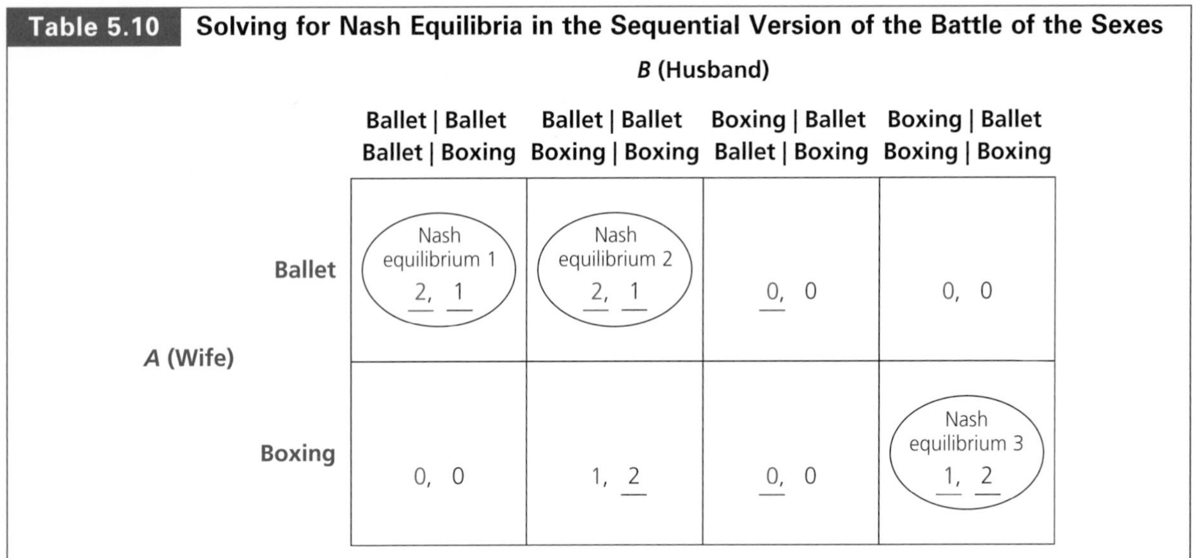

Table 5.10 Solving for Nash Equilibria in the Sequential Version of the Battle of the Sexes

		B (Husband)			
		Ballet | Ballet Ballet | Boxing	**Ballet | Ballet Boxing | Boxing**	**Boxing | Ballet Ballet | Boxing**	**Boxing | Ballet Boxing | Boxing**
***A* (Wife)**	**Ballet**	Nash equilibrium 1 2, 1	Nash equilibrium 2 2, 1	0, 0	0, 0
	Boxing	0, 0	1, 2	0, 0	Nash equilibrium 3 1, 2

plays either “Ballet | Ballet, Boxing | Boxing” or “Boxing | Ballet, Boxing | Boxing”). Again, as shown in the table, we need to underline the payoffs for all the strategies that tie for the best response. There are three pure-strategy Nash equilibria:

1. Wife plays Ballet, husband plays “Ballet | Ballet, Ballet | Boxing.”
2. Wife plays Ballet, husband plays “Ballet | Ballet, Boxing | Boxing.”
3. Wife plays Boxing, husband plays “Boxing | Ballet, Boxing | Boxing.”

MICRO QUIZ 5.3

Refer to the normal form of the sequential Battle of the Sexes.

1. Provide examples in which referring to equilibria using payoffs is ambiguous but with strategies is unambiguous.
2. Explain why “Boxing” or “Ballet” is not a complete description of the second mover’s strategy.

As with the simultaneous version of the Battle of the Sexes, with the sequential version we again have multiple equilibria. Here, however, game theory offers a good way to select among the equilibria. Consider the third Nash equilibrium. The husband’s strategy, “Boxing | Ballet, Boxing | Boxing,” involves an implicit threat that he will choose Boxing even if his wife chooses Ballet. This threat is sufficient to deter her from choosing Ballet. Given she chooses Boxing in equilibrium, his strategy earns him 2, which is the best he can do in any outcome. So the outcome is a Nash equilibrium. But the husband’s strategy involves an empty threat. If the wife really were to choose Ballet first, he would be giving up a payoff of 1 by choosing Boxing rather than Ballet. It is clear why he would want to threaten to choose Boxing, but it is not clear that such a threat should be believed. Similarly, the husband’s strategy, “Ballet | Ballet, Ballet | Boxing,” in the first Nash equilibrium also involves an empty threat, the threat that he will choose Ballet if his wife chooses Boxing. (This is an odd threat to make since he does not gain from making it, but it is an empty threat nonetheless.)

Subgame-Perfect Equilibrium

Game theory offers a formal way of selecting the reasonable Nash equilibria in sequential games using the concept of subgame-perfect equilibrium. Subgame-perfect equilibrium rules out empty threats by requiring strategies to be rational even for contingencies that do not arise in equilibrium.

Before defining subgame-perfect equilibrium formally, we need to say what a subgame is. A **subgame** is a part of the extensive form beginning with a decision point and including everything that branches out below it. A subgame is said to be **proper** if its topmost decision point is not connected to another in the same oval. Conceptually, this means that the player who moves first in a proper subgame knows the actions played by others that have led up to that point. It is easier to see what a proper subgame is than to define it in words. Figure 5.6 shows the extensive forms from the simultaneous

Proper subgame
Part of the game tree including an initial decision not connected to another in an oval and everything branching out below it.

Figure 5.6 Proper Subgames in the Battle of the Sexes

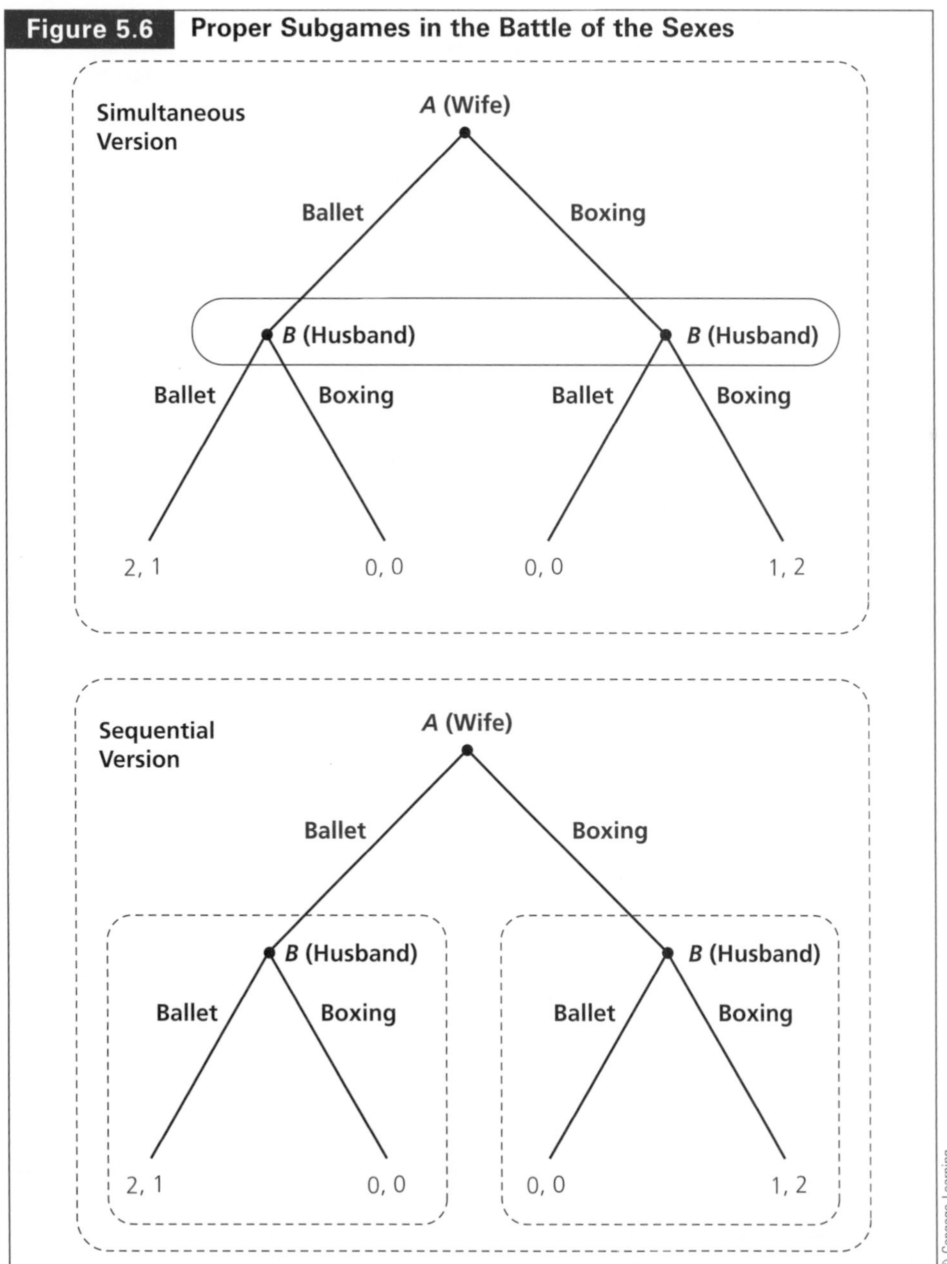

and sequential versions of the Battle of the Sexes, with dotted lines drawn around the proper subgames in each. In the simultaneous Battle of the Sexes, there is only one decision point that is not connected to another in an oval, the initial one. Therefore, there is only one proper subgame, the game itself. In the sequential Battle of the Sexes, there are three proper subgames: the game itself, and two lower subgames starting with decision points where the husband gets to move.

Subgame-perfect equilibrium Strategies that form a Nash equilibrium on every proper subgame.

A **subgame-perfect equilibrium** is a set of strategies, one for each player, that form a Nash equilibrium on every proper subgame. A subgame-perfect equilibrium is always a Nash equilibrium. This is true since the whole game is a proper subgame of itself, so a subgame-perfect equilibrium must be a Nash equilibrium on the whole game. In the simultaneous version of the Battle of the Sexes, there is nothing more to say since there are no other subgames besides the whole game itself.

In the sequential version of the Battle of the Sexes, the concept of subgame-perfect equilibrium has more bite. In addition to constituting a Nash equilibrium on the whole game, strategies must constitute Nash equilibria on the two other proper subgames. These subgames are simple decision problems, and so it is easy to compute the corresponding Nash equilibria. In the left-hand subgame, following his wife's choosing Ballet, the husband has a simple decision between Ballet, which earns him a payoff of 1, and Boxing, which earns him a payoff of 0. The Nash equilibrium in this subgame is for the husband to choose Ballet. In the right-hand subgame, following his wife's choosing Boxing, he has a simple decision between Ballet, which earns him 0, and Boxing, which earns him 2. The Nash equilibrium in this subgame is for him to choose Boxing. Thus we see that the husband has only one strategy that can be part of a subgame-perfect equilibrium: "Ballet | Ballet, Boxing | Boxing." Any other strategy has him playing something that is not a Nash equilibrium on some proper subgame. Returning to the three enumerated Nash equilibria, only the second one is subgame-perfect. The first and the third are not. For example, the third equilibrium, in which the husband always goes to Boxing, is ruled out as a subgame-perfect equilibrium because the husband would not go to Boxing if the wife indeed went to Ballet; he would go to Ballet as well. Subgame-perfect equilibrium thus rules out the empty threat of always going to Boxing that we were uncomfortable with in the previous section.

More generally, subgame-perfect equilibrium rules out any sort of empty threat in any sequential game. In effect, Nash equilibrium only requires behavior to be rational on the part of the game tree that is reached in equilibrium. Players can choose potentially irrational actions on other parts of the game tree. In particular, a player can threaten to damage both of them in order to "scare" the other from choosing certain actions. Subgame-perfect equilibrium requires rational behavior on all parts of the game tree. Threats to play irrationally, that is, threats to choose something other than one's best response, are ruled out as being empty.

Subgame-perfect equilibrium does not reduce the number of Nash equilibria in a simultaneous game because a simultaneous game has no proper subgames other than the game itself.

Backward Induction

Backward induction Solving for equilibrium by working backward from the end of the game to the beginning.

Our approach to solving for the equilibrium in the sequential Battle of the Sexes was to find all the Nash equilibria using the normal form, and then to sort through them for the subgame-perfect equilibrium. A shortcut to find the subgame-perfect equilibrium directly is to use **backward induction**. Backward induction works as follows: identify all of the subgames at the bottom of the extensive form; find the Nash equilibria on these subgames; replace the (potentially complicated) subgames with the actions and payoffs resulting from Nash equilibrium play on these subgames; then move up to the next level of subgames and repeat the procedure.

Figure 5.7 illustrates the use of backward induction to solve for the subgame-perfect equilibrium of the sequential Battle of the Sexes. First compute the Nash equilibria of the bottom-most subgames, in this case the subgames corresponding to the husband's decision problems. In the subgame following his wife's choosing Ballet, he would choose Ballet, giving payoffs 2 for her and 1 for him. In the subgame following his wife's choosing Boxing, he would choose Boxing, giving payoffs 1 for her and 2 for him. Next, substitute the husband's equilibrium strategies for the subgames themselves. The resulting game is a simple decision problem for the wife, drawn in the lower panel of the figure, a choice between Ballet, which would give her a payoff of 2 and Boxing, which would

Figure 5.7 Backward Induction in the Sequential Battle of the Sexes

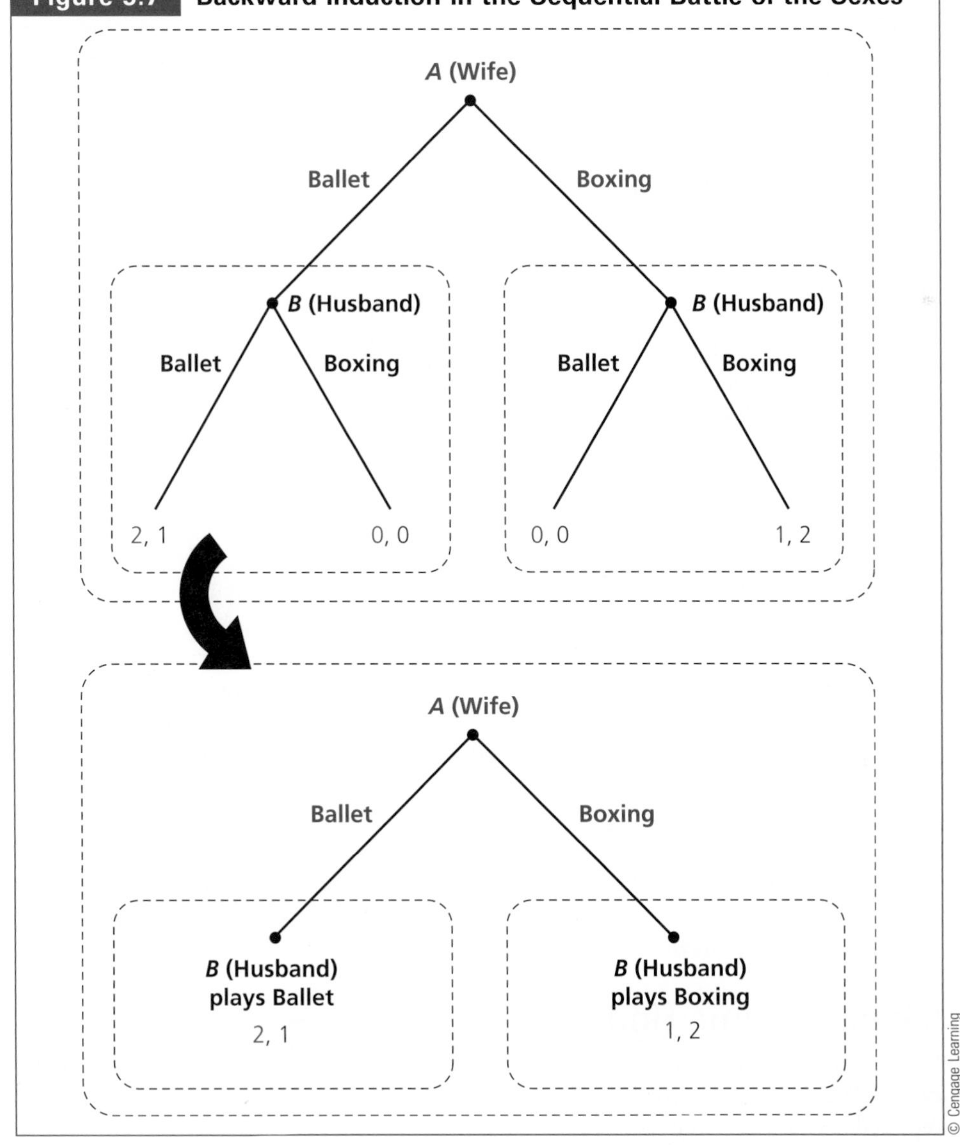

give her a payoff of 1. The Nash equilibrium of this game is for her to choose the action with the higher payoff, Ballet. In sum, backward induction allows us to jump straight to the subgame-perfect equilibrium, in which the wife chooses Ballet and the husband chooses "Ballet | Ballet, Boxing | Boxing," and bypass the other Nash equilibria.

Backward induction is particularly useful in games in which there are many rounds of sequential play. As rounds are added, it quickly becomes too hard to solve for all the Nash equilibria and then to sort through which are subgame-perfect. With backward induction, an additional round is simply accommodated by adding another iteration of the procedure.

Application 5.4: Laboratory Experiments discusses whether human subjects play games the way theory predicts in experimental settings, including whether subjects play the subgame-perfect equilibrium in sequential games.

Repeated Games

Stage game
Simple game that is played repeatedly.

So far, we have examined one-shot games in which each player is given one choice and the game ends. In many real-world settings, the same players play the same **stage game** several or even many times. For example, the players in the Prisoners' Dilemma may anticipate committing future crimes together and thus playing future Prisoners' Dilemmas together. Gas stations located across the street from each other, when they set their prices each morning, effectively play a new pricing game every day.

Trigger strategy
Strategy in a repeated game where the player stops cooperating to punish another player's break with cooperation.

As we saw with the Prisoners' Dilemma, when such games are played once, the equilibrium outcome may be worse for all players than some other, more cooperative, outcome. Repetition opens up the possibility of the cooperative outcome being played in equilibrium. Players can adopt **trigger strategies**, whereby they play the cooperative outcome as long as all have cooperated up to that point, but revert to playing the Nash equilibrium if anyone breaks with cooperation. We will investigate the conditions under which trigger strategies work to increase players' payoffs. We will focus on subgame-perfect equilibria of the repeated games.

Definite Time Horizon

For many stage games, repeating them a known, finite number of times does not increase the possibility for cooperation. To see this point concretely, suppose the Prisoners' Dilemma were repeated for 10 periods. Use backward induction to solve for the subgame-perfect equilibrium. The lowest subgame is the one-shot Prisoners' Dilemma played in the 10th period. Regardless of what happened before, the Nash equilibrium on this subgame is for both to play Rat. Folding the game back to the ninth period, trigger strategies that condition play in the 10th period on what happens in the ninth are ruled out. Nothing that happens in the ninth period affects what happens subsequently because, as we just argued, the players both Rat in the 10th period no matter what. It is as if the ninth period is the last, and again the Nash equilibrium on this subgame is again for both to play Rat. Working backward in this way, we see that players will Rat each period; that is, players will simply repeat the Nash equilibrium of the stage game 10 times. The same argument would apply for any definite number of repetitions.

Indefinite Time Horizon

If the number of times the stage game is repeated is indefinite, matters change significantly. The number of repetitions is indefinite if players know the stage game will be repeated but are uncertain of exactly how many times. For example, the partners in

APPLICATION 5.4

Laboratory Experiments

Experimental economics tests how well economic theory matches the behavior of experimental subjects in laboratory settings. The methods are similar to those used in experimental psychology—often conducted on campus using undergraduates as subjects—the main difference being that experiments in economics tend to involve incentives in the form of explicit monetary payments paid to subjects. The importance of experimental economics was highlighted in 2002, when Vernon Smith received the Nobel prize in economics for his pioneering work in the field.

Prisoners' Dilemma

There have been hundreds of tests of whether players Rat in the Prisoners' Dilemma, as predicted by Nash equilibrium, or whether they play the cooperative outcome of Silent. In the experiments of Cooper et al.,[1] subjects played the game 20 times, against different, anonymous opponents. Play converged to the Nash equilibrium as subjects gained experience with the game. Players played the cooperative action 43 percent of the time in the first five rounds, falling to only 20 percent of the time in the last five rounds.

Ultimatum Game

Experimental economics has also tested to see whether subgame-perfect equilibrium is a good predictor of behavior in sequential games. In one widely studied sequential game, the Ultimatum Game, the experimenter provides a pot of money to two players. The first mover (Proposer) proposes a split of this pot to the second mover. The second mover (Responder) then decides whether to accept the offer, in which case players are given the amount of money indicated, or reject the offer, in which case both players get nothing. As one can see by using backward induction, in the subgame-perfect equilibrium, the Proposer should offer a minimal share of the pot and this should be accepted by the Responder.

In experiments, the division tends to be much more even than in the subgame-perfect equilibrium.[2] The most common offer is a 50–50 split. Responders tend to reject offers giving them less than 30 percent of the pot. This result is observed even when the pot is as high as $100, so that rejecting a 30 percent offer means turning down $30. Some economists have suggested that money may not be a true measure of players' payoffs, which may include other factors such as how fairly the pot is divided.[3] Even if a Proposer does not care directly about fairness, the fear that the Responder may care about fairness and thus might reject an uneven offer out of spite may lead the Proposer to propose an even split.

Dictator Game

To test whether players care directly about fairness or act out of fear of the other player's spite, researchers experimented with a related game, the Dictator Game. In the Dictator Game, the Proposer chooses a split of the pot, and this split is implemented without input from the Responder. Proposers tend to offer a less-even split than in the Ultimatum Game, but still offer the Responder some of the pot, suggesting Responders had some residual concern for fairness. The details of the experimental design are crucial, however, as one ingenious experiment showed.[4] The experiment was designed so that the experimenter would never learn which Proposers had made which offers. With this element of anonymity, Proposers almost never gave an equal split to Responders and, indeed, took the whole pot for themselves two-thirds of the time. The results suggest that Proposers care more about being thought of as fair rather than truly being fair.

TO THINK ABOUT

1. As an experimenter, how would you choose the following aspects of experimental design? Are there any trade-offs involved?
   a. Size of the payoffs
   b. Ability of subjects to see opponents
   c. Playing the same game against the same opponent repeatedly
   d. Informing subjects fully about the experimental design
2. How would you construct an experiment involving the Battle of the Sexes? What theoretical issues might be interesting to test with your experiment?

[1]R. Cooper, D. V. DeJong, R. Forsythe, and T. W. Ross, "Cooperation without Reputation: Experimental Evidence from Prisoner's Dilemma Games," *Games and Economic Behavior* (February 1996): 187–218.

[2]For a review of Ultimatum Game experiments and a textbook treatment of experimental economics more generally, see D. D. Davis and C. A. Holt, *Experimental Economics* (Princeton, NJ: Princeton University Press, 1993).

[3]See, for example, M. Rabin, "Incorporating Fairness into Game Theory and Economics," *American Economic Review* (December 1993): 1281–1302.

[4]E. Hoffman, K. McCabe, K. Shachat, and V. Smith, "Preferences, Property Rights, and Anonymity in Bargaining Games," *Games and Economic Behavior* (November 1994): 346–380.

crime in the Prisoners' Dilemma may know that they will participate in many future crimes together, sometimes be caught, and thus have to play the Prisoners' Dilemma game against each other, but may not know exactly how many opportunities for crime they will have or how often they will be caught. With an indefinite number of repetitions, there is no final period from which to start applying backward induction, and thus no final period for trigger strategies to begin unraveling. Under certain conditions, more cooperation can be sustained than in the stage game.

Suppose the two players play the following repeated version of the Prisoners' Dilemma. The game is played in the first period for certain, but for how many more periods after that the game is played is uncertain. Let g be the probability the game is repeated for another period and $1 - g$ the probability the repetitions stop for good. Thus, the probability the game lasts at least one period is 1, at least two periods is g, at least three periods is g^2, and so forth.

Suppose players use the trigger strategies of playing the cooperative action, Silent, as long a no one cheats by playing Rat, but that players both play Rat forever afterward if either of them had ever cheated. To show that such strategies constitute a subgame-perfect equilibrium, we need to check that a player cannot gain by cheating. In equilibrium, both players play Silent and each earns 2 each period the game is played, implying a player's expected payoff over the course of the entire game is

$$(2)(1 + g + g^2 + g^3 + \cdots). \tag{5.1}$$

If a player cheats and plays Rat, given the other is playing Silent, the cheater earns 3 in that period, but then both play Rat every period, from then on, each earning 1 each period, for a total expected payoff of

$$3 + (1)(g + g^2 + g^3 + \cdots). \tag{5.2}$$

For cooperation to be a subgame-perfect equilibrium, Equation 5.1 must exceed Equation 5.2. Subtracting the second from the first equation, we see that the first exceeds the second if $-1 + g + g^2 + g^3 + \cdots > 0$, or in other words if

$$g + g^2 + g^3 + \cdots > 1. \tag{5.3}$$

To proceed further, we need to find a simple expression for the series $g + g^2 + g^3 + \cdots$. A standard mathematical result[4] is that the series $g + g^2 + g^3 + \cdots$ equals $g/(1 - g)$. Substituting this result in Equation 5.3, we see that the inequality holds, and so cooperation on Silent can be sustained, if g is greater than 1/2.[5]

This result means that players can cooperate in the repeated Prisoners' Dilemma only if the probability of repetition g is high enough. Players are tempted to cheat on the cooperative equilibrium, obtaining a short-run gain (3 rather than 2) by Ratting. The threat of the loss of future gains from cooperating deters cheating. This threat only works if the probability the game is continued into the future is high enough.

Other strategies can be used to try to elicit cooperation in the repeated game. We considered strategies that had players revert to the Nash equilibrium of Rat each period forever. This strategy, which involves the harshest possible punishment for deviation, is

---

[4]Let $S = g + g^2 + g^3 + \cdots$. Multiplying both sides by g, $gS = g^2 + g^3 + g^4 + \cdots$. Subtracting gS from S, we have $S - gS = (g + g^2 + g^3 + \cdots) - (g^2 + g^3 + g^4 + \cdots) = g$ because all of the terms on the right-hand side cancel except for the leading g. Thus $(1 - g)S = g$, or, rearranging, $S = g/(1 - g)$.

[5]The mathematics are the same in an alternative version of the game in which the stage game is repeated with certainty each period for an infinite number of periods, but in which future payoffs are discounted according to a per-period interest rate. One can show that cooperation is possible if the per-period interest rate is less than 100 percent.

called the grim strategy. Less harsh punishments include the so-called tit-for-tat strategy, which involves only one round of punishment for cheating. Since it involves the harshest punishment possible, the grim strategy elicits cooperation for the largest range of cases (the lowest value of g) of any strategy. Harsh punishments work well because, if players succeed in cooperating, they never experience the losses from the punishment in equilibrium. If there were uncertainty about the economic environment, or about the rationality of the other player, the grim strategy may not lead to as high payoffs as less-harsh strategies.

MICRO QUIZ 5.4

Consider the indefinitely repeated Prisoners' Dilemma.

1. For what value of g does the repeated game become simply the stage game?
2. Suppose that at some point while playing the grim strategy, players relent and go back to the cooperative outcome (Silent). If this relenting were anticipated, how would it affect the ability to sustain the cooperative outcome?

One might ask whether the threat to punish the other player (whether forever as in the grim strategy or for one round with tit-for-tat) is an empty threat since punishment harms both players. The answer is no. The punishment involves reverting to the Nash equilibrium, in which both players choose best responses, and so it is a credible threat and is consistent with subgame-perfect equilibrium.

5-7 Continuous Actions

Most of the insight from economic situations can often be gained by distilling the situation down to a game with two actions, as with all of the games studied so far. At other times, additional insight can be gained by allowing more actions, sometimes even a continuum. Firms' pricing, output or investment decisions, bids in auctions, and so forth are often modeled by allowing players a continuum of actions. Such games can no longer be represented in the normal form we are used to seeing in this chapter, and the underlining method cannot be used to solve for Nash equilibrium. Still, the new techniques for solving for Nash equilibria will have the same logic as those seen so far. We will illustrate the new techniques in a game called the Tragedy of the Commons.

Tragedy of the Commons

The game involves two shepherds, A and B, who graze their sheep on a common (land that can be freely used by community members). Let s_A and s_B be the number of sheep each grazes, chosen simultaneously. Because the common only has a limited amount of space, if more sheep graze, there is less grass for each one, and they grow less quickly. To be concrete, suppose the benefit A gets from each sheep (in terms of mutton and wool) equals

$$120 - s_A - s_B. \tag{5.4}$$

The total benefit A gets from a flock of s_A sheep is therefore

$$s_A(120 - s_A - s_B). \tag{5.5}$$

Although we cannot use the method of underlining payoffs for best responses, we can compute A's best-response function. Recall the use of best-response functions in computing the mixed-strategy Nash equilibrium in the Battle of the Sexes game. We resorted to best-response functions because, although the Battle of the Sexes game has only two actions, there is a continuum of possible mixed strategies over those two actions. In the Tragedy of the Commons here, we need to resort to best-response functions because we start off with a continuum of actions.

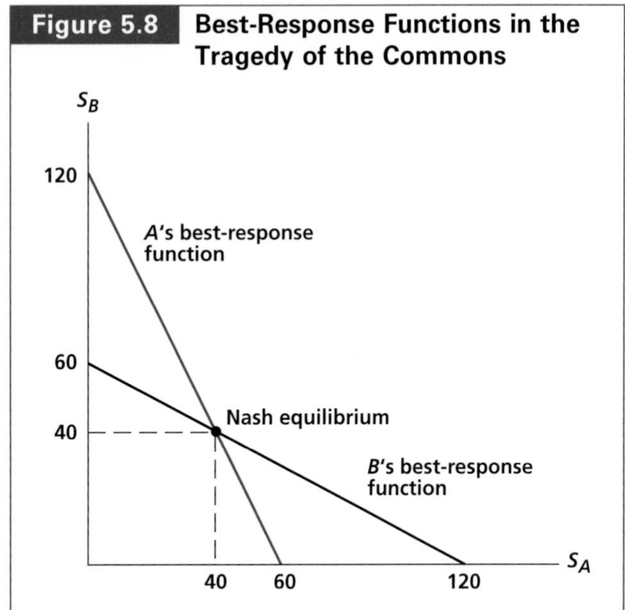

Figure 5.8 Best-Response Functions in the Tragedy of the Commons

A's best-response function gives the s_A that maximizes A's payoff for any s_B. *A*'s best response will be the number of sheep such that the marginal benefit of an additional sheep equals the marginal cost. His marginal benefit of an additional sheep is[6]

$$120 - 2s_A - s_B. \tag{5.6}$$

The total cost of grazing sheep is 0 since they graze freely on the common, and so the marginal cost of an additional sheep is also 0. Equating the marginal benefit in Equation 5.6 with the marginal cost of 0 and solving for s_A, A's best-response function equals

$$s_A = 60 - \frac{s_B}{2}. \tag{5.7}$$

By symmetry, *B*'s best-response function is

$$s_B = 60 - \frac{s_A}{2}. \tag{5.8}$$

For actions to form a Nash equilibrium, they must be best responses to each other; in other words, they must be the simultaneous solution to Equations 5.7 and 5.8. The simultaneous solution is shown graphically in Figure 5.8. The best-response functions are graphed with s_A on the horizontal axis and s_B on the vertical (the inverse of *A*'s best-response function is actually what is graphed). The Nash equilibrium, which lies at the intersection of the two functions, involves each grazing 40 sheep.

The game is called a tragedy because the shepherds end up overgrazing in equilibrium. They overgraze because they do not take into account the reduction in the value of other's sheep when they choose the size of their flocks. If each grazed 30 rather than 40 sheep, one can show that each would earn a total payoff of 1,800 rather than the 1,600 they each earn in equilibrium. Overconsumption is a typical finding in settings where multiple parties have free access to a common resource, such as multiple wells pumping oil from a common underground pool or multiple fishing boats fishing in the same ocean area, and is often a reason given for restricting access to such common resources through licensing and other government interventions.

Shifting Equilibria

One reason it is useful to allow players to have continuous actions is that it is easier in this setting to analyze how a small change in one of the game's parameters shifts the equilibrium. For example, suppose *A*'s benefit per sheep rises from Equation 5.4 to

$$132 - s_A - s_B. \tag{5.9}$$

A's best-response function becomes

$$s_A = 66 - \frac{s_B}{2}. \tag{5.10}$$

B's stays the same as in Equation 5.8. As shown in Figure 5.9, in the new Nash equilibrium, increases his flock to 48 sheep and *B* decreases his to 36. It is clear why the size of

[6]One can take the formula for the marginal benefit in (5.6) as given or can use calculus to verify it. Differentiating the benefit function (5.5), which can be rewritten $120s_A - s_A^2 - s_As_B$, term by term with respect to s_A (treating s_B as a constant) yields the marginal benefit (5.6).

A's flock increases: The increase in *A*'s benefit shifts his best-response function out. The interesting strategic effect is that—while nothing about *B*'s benefit has changed, and so *B*'s best-response function remains the same as before—having observed A's benefit increasing from Equation 5.4 to Equation 5.8, *B* anticipates that it must choose a best response to a higher quantity by *A*, and so ends up reducing the size of his flock.

Games with continuous actions offer additional insights in other contexts, as shown in Application 5.5: Terrorism.

Figure 5.9 Shift in Equilibrium When *A*'s Benefit Increases

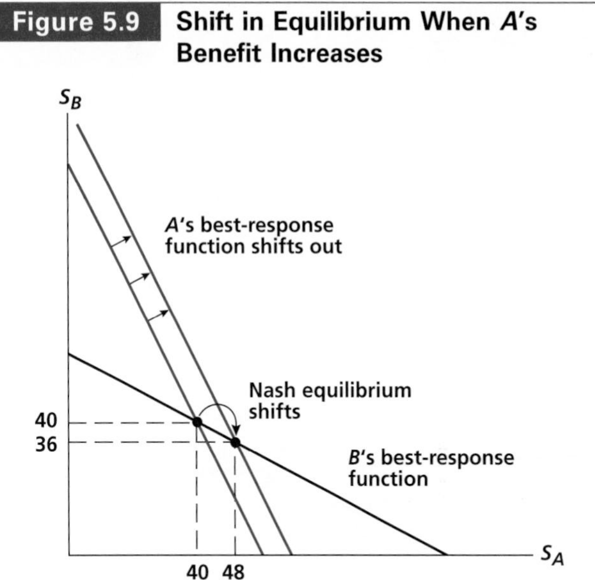

An increase in *A*'s benefit per sheep shifts his best-response function out. Though *B*'s best-response function remains the same, his equilibrium number of sheep falls in the new Nash equilibrium.

5-8 *N*-Player Games

Just as we can often capture the essence of a situation using a game with two actions, as we have seen with all the games studied so far, we can often distill the number of players down to two as well. However in some cases, it is useful to study games with more than two players. This is particularly useful to answer the question of how a change in the number of players would affect the equilibrium (see, for example, Micro Quiz 5.5). The problems at the end of the chapter will provide some examples of how to draw the normal form in games with more than two players.

MICRO QUIZ 5.5

Suppose the Tragedy of the Commons involved three shepherds (*A*, *B*, and *C*). Suppose the benefit per sheep is $120 - s_A - s_B - s_C$ implying that, for example, *A*'s total benefit is $s_A(120 - s_A - s_B - s_C)$ and marginal benefit is $120 - 2s_A - s_B - s_C$.

1. Solve the three equations that come from equating each of the three shepherds' marginal benefit of a sheep to the marginal cost (zero) to find the Nash equilibrium.
2. Compare the total number of sheep on the common with three shepherds to that with two.

5-9 Incomplete Information

In all the games studied so far, there was no private information. All players knew everything there was to know about each others' payoffs, available actions, and so forth. Matters become more complicated, and potentially more interesting, if players know something about themselves that others do not know. For example, one's bidding strategy in a sealed-bid auction for a painting would be quite different if one knew the valuation of everyone else at the auction compared to the (more realistic) case in which one did not. Card games would be quite different, and certainly not as fun, if all hands were played face up. Games in which players do not share all relevant information in common are called games of **incomplete information**.

Incomplete information
Some players have information about the game that others do not.

We will devote most of Chapter 17 to studying games of incomplete information. We will study signaling games, which include students choosing how much education to obtain in order to signal their underlying aptitude, which might be difficult to observe directly, to prospective employers. We will study screening games, which include the design of deductible policies by insurance companies in order to deter high-risk

APPLICATION 5.5

Terrorism

Few issues raise as much public-policy concern as terrorism, given the continued attacks in the Middle East and Europe and the devastating attack on the World Trade Center and Pentagon in the United States on September 11, 2001. In this application, we will see that game theory can be usefully applied to analyze terrorism and the best defensive measures against it.

Defending Targets against Terrorism

Consider a sequential game between a government and a terrorist. The players have the opposite objectives: The government wants to minimize the expected damage from terrorism, and the terrorist wants to maximize expected damage. For simplicity, assume the terrorist can attack one of two targets: target 1 (say, a nuclear power plant) leads to considerable damage if successfully attacked; target 2 (say, a restaurant) leads to less damage. The government moves first, choosing s_1, the proportion of its security force guarding target 1. The remainder of the security force, $1-s_1$, guards target 2. (Note that the government's action is a continuous variable between 0 and 1, so this is an application of our general discussion of games with continuous actions in the text.) The terrorist moves second, choosing which target to attack. Assume the probability of successful attack on target 1 is $1 - s_1$ and on target 2 is s_1, implying that the larger the security force guarding a particular target, the lower the probability of a successful attack.

To solve for the subgame-perfect equilibrium, we will apply backward induction, meaning in this context that we will consider the terrorist's (the second mover's) decision first. The terrorist will compute the expected damage from attacking each target, equal to the probability of a successful attack multiplied by the damage caused if the attack is successful. The terrorist will attack the target with the highest expected damage. Moving backward to the first mover's (the government's) decision, the way for the government to minimize the expected damage from terrorism is to divide the security force between the two targets so that the expected damage is equalized. (Suppose the expected damage from attacking target 1 were strictly higher than target 2. Then the terrorist would definitely attack target 1, and the government could reduce expected damage from this attack by shifting some of the security force from target 2 to target 1.) Using some numbers, if the damage from a successful attack on target 1 is 10 times that on target 2, the government should put 10 times the security force on target 1. The terrorist ends up playing a mixed strategy in equilibrium, with each target having a positive probability of being attacked.

Bargaining with Terrorists

Terrorism raises many more issues than those analyzed above. Suppose terrorists have taken hostages and demand the release of prisoners in return for the hostages' freedom. Should a country bargain with the terrorists?[1] The official policy of countries, including the United States and Israel, is no. Using backward induction, it is easy to see why countries would like to commit not to bargain because this would preclude any benefit from taking hostages and deter the terrorists from taking hostages in the first place. But a country's commitment to not bargain may not be credible, especially if the hostages are "important" enough, as was the case when the Israeli parliament voted to bargain for the release of 21 students taken hostage in a high school in Maalot, Israel, in 1974. (The vote came after the deadline set by the terrorists, and the students ended up being killed.) The country's commitment may still be credible in some scenarios. If hostage incidents are expected to arise over time repeatedly, the country may refuse to bargain as part of a long-term strategy to establish a reputation for not bargaining. Another possibility is that the country may not trust the terrorists to free the hostages after the prisoners are released, in which case there would be little benefit from bargaining with them.

TO THINK ABOUT

1. The U.S. government has considered analyzing banking transactions to look for large, suspicious movements of cash as a screen for terrorists. What are the pros and cons of such a screen? How would the terrorists respond in equilibrium if they learned of this screen? Would it still be a useful tool?
2. Is it sensible to model the terrorist as wanting to maximize expected damage? Instead, the terrorist may prefer to attack "high-visibility" targets, even if this means lower expected damage, or may prefer to maximize the sum of damage plus defense/deterrence expenditures. Which alternative is most plausible? How would these alternatives affect the game?

[1] See H. E. Lapan and T. Sandler, "To Bargain or not to Bargain: That Is the Question," *American Economic Review* (May 1988): 16–20.

consumers from purchasing. As mentioned, auctions and card games also fall in the realm of games of incomplete information. Such games are at the forefront of current research in game theory.

SUMMARY

This chapter provided an overview of game theory. Game theory provides an organized way of understanding decision making in strategic environments. We introduced the following broad ideas:

- The basic building blocks of all games are players, actions, payoffs, and information.
- The Nash equilibrium is the most widely used equilibrium concept. Strategies form a Nash equilibrium if all players' strategies are best responses to each other. All games have at least one Nash equilibrium. Sometimes the Nash equilibrium is in mixed strategies, which we learned how to compute. Some games have multiple Nash equilibria, and it may be difficult in these cases to make predictions about which one will end up being played.
- We studied several classic games, including the Prisoners' Dilemma, Matching Pennies, and Battle of the Sexes. These games each demonstrated important principles. Many strategic situations can be distilled down to one of these games.
- Sequential games introduce the possibility of contingent strategies for the second mover and often expand the set of Nash equilibria. Subgame-perfect equilibrium rules out outcomes involving empty threats. One can easily solve for subgame-perfect equilibrium using backward induction.
- In some games such as the Prisoners' Dilemma, all players are worse off in the Nash equilibrium than in some other outcome. If the game is repeated an indefinite number of times, players can use trigger strategies to try to enforce the better outcome.

REVIEW QUESTIONS

1. In game theory, players maximize payoffs. Is this assumption different from the one we used in Chapters 2 and 3?
2. What is the difference between an action and a strategy?
3. Why are Nash equilibria identified by the strategies rather than the payoffs involved?
4. Which of the following activities might be represented as a zero-sum game? Which are clearly not zero sum?
   a. Flipping a coin for $1
   b. Playing blackjack
   c. Choosing which candy bar to buy from a vendor
   d. Reducing taxes through various "creative accounting" methods and seeking to avoid detection by the IRS
   e. Deciding when to rob a particular house, knowing that the residents may adopt various countertheft strategies
5. Why is the Prisoners' Dilemma a "dilemma" for the players involved? How might they solve this dilemma through pregame discussions or post-game threats? If you were arrested and the D.A. tried this ploy, what would you do? Would it matter whether you were very close friends with your criminal accomplice?
6. The Battle of the Sexes is a coordination game. What coordination games arise in your experience? How do you go about solving coordination problems?
7. In the sequential games such as the sequential Battle of the Sexes, why does the Nash equilibrium allow for outcomes with noncredible threats? Why does subgame-perfect equilibrium rule them out?
8. Which of these relationships would be better modeled as involving repetitions and which not, or does it depend? For those that are repeated, which are more realistically seen as involving a definite number of repetitions and which an indefinite number?
   a. Two nearby gas stations posting their prices each morning
   b. A professor testing students in a course
   c. Students entering a dorm room lottery together
   d. Accomplices committing a crime
   e. Two lions fighting for a mate
9. In the Tragedy of the Commons, we saw how a small change in *A*'s benefit resulted in a shift in *A*'s best response function and a movement along *B*'s best-response function. Can you think of other factors that might shift *A*'s best-response function? Relate this discussion to shifts in an individual's demand curve versus movements along it.
10. Choose a setting from student life. Try to model it as a game, with a set number of players, payoffs, and actions. Is it like any of the classic games studied in this chapter?

PROBLEMS

5.1. Consider a simultaneous game in which player A chooses one of two actions (Up or Down), and B chooses one of two actions (Left or Right). The game has the following payoff matrix, where the first payoff in each entry is for A and the second for B.

		B Left	*B* Right
A	Up	3, 3	5, 1
A	Down	2, 2	4, 4

a. Find the Nash equilibrium or equilibria.
b. Which player, if any, has a dominant strategy?

5.2. Suppose A can somehow change the game in Problem 5.1 to a new one in which his payoff from Up is reduced by 2, producing the following payoff matrix.

		B Left	*B* Right
A	Up	1, 3	3, 1
A	Down	2, 2	4, 4

a. Find the Nash equilibrium or equilibria.
b. Which player, if any, has a dominant strategy?
c. Does A benefit from changing the game by reducing his or her payoff in this way?

5.3. Return to the game given by the payoff matrix in Problem 5.1.
a. Write down the extensive form for the simultaneous-move game.
b. Suppose the game is now sequential move, with A moving first and then B. Write down the extensive form for this sequential-move game.
c. Write down the normal form for the sequential-move game. Find all the Nash equilibria. Which Nash equilibrium is subgame-perfect?

5.4. Consider the war over the new format for high-definition video disks discussed in Application 5.3, but shift the focus to the game (provided in the following table) between the two firms, Sony and Toshiba.

		Toshiba Invest heavily	Toshiba Slacken
Sony	Invest heavily	0, 0	3, 1
Sony	Slacken	1, 3	2, 2

a. Find the pure-strategy Nash equilibrium or equilibria.
b. Compute the mixed-strategy Nash equilibrium. As part of your answer, draw the best-response function diagram for the mixed strategies.
c. Suppose the game is played sequentially, with Sony moving first. What are Toshiba's contingent strategies? Write down the normal and extensive forms for the sequential version of the game.
d. Using the normal form for the sequential version of the game, solve for the Nash equilibria.
e. Identify the proper subgames in the extensive form for the sequential version of the game. Use backward induction to solve for the sub-game-perfect equilibrium. Explain why the other Nash equilibria of the sequential game are "unreasonable."

5.5. Two classmates A and B are assigned an extra-credit group project. Each student can choose to Shirk or Work. If one or more players choose Work, the project is completed and provides each with extra credit valued at 4 payoff units each. The cost of completing the project is that 6 total units of effort (measured in payoff units) is divided equally among all players who choose to Work and this is subtracted from their payoff. If both Shirk, they do not have to expend any effort but the project is not completed, giving each a payoff of 0. The teacher can only tell whether the project is completed and not which students contributed to it.
a. Write down the normal form for this game, assuming students choose to Shirk or Work simultaneously.
b. Find the Nash equilibrium or equilibria.
c. Does either player have a dominant strategy? What game from the chapter does this resemble?

5.6. Return to the Battle of the Sexes in Table 5.5. Compute the mixed-strategy Nash equilibrium under the following modifications and compare it to the one computed in the text. Draw the corresponding best-response-function diagram for the mixed strategies.
   a. Double all of the payoffs.
   b. Double the payoff from coordinating on one's preferred activity from 2 to 4 but leave all other payoffs the same.
   c. Change the payoff from choosing one's preferred activity alone (that is, not coordinating with one's spouse) from 0 to 1/2 for each but leave all the other payoffs the same.

5.7. The following game is a version of the Prisoners' Dilemma, but the payoffs are slightly different than in Table 5.1.

		B	
		Rat	Silent
A	Rat	0, 0	3, −1
	Silent	−1, 3	1, 1

   a. Verify that the Nash equilibrium is the usual one for the Prisoners' Dilemma and that both players have dominant strategies.
   b. Suppose the stage game is played an indefinite number of times with a probability g the game is continued to the next stage and $1 - g$ that the game ends for good. Compute the level of g that is required for a subgame-perfect equilibrium in which both players play a trigger strategy where both are Silent if no one deviates but resort to a grim strategy (that is, both play Rat forever after) if anyone deviates to Rat.
   c. Continue to suppose the stage game is played an indefinite number of times, as in b. Is there a value of g for which there exists a subgame-perfect equilibrium in which both players play a trigger strategy where both are Silent if no one deviates but resort to tit-for-tat (that is, both play Rat for one period and go back to Silent forever after that) if anyone deviates to Rat? Remember that g is a probability, so it must be between 0 and 1.

5.8. Find the pure-strategy Nash equilibrium or equilibria of the following game with three actions for each player.

		B		
		Left	Center	Right
A	Up	4, 3	5, −1	6, 2
	Middle	2, 1	7, 4	3, 6
	Down	3, 0	9, 6	0, 8

5.9. Three department stores, A, B, and C, simultaneously decide whether or not to locate in a mall that is being constructed in town. A store likes to have another with it in the mall since then there is a critical mass of stores to induce shoppers to come out. However, with three stores in the mall, there begins to be too much competition among them and store profits fall drastically. Read the payoff matrix as follows: the first payoff in each entry is for A, the second for B, and the third for C; C's choice determines which of the bold boxes the other players find themselves in.

		C Chooses Mall		C Chooses Not Mall	
		B		B	
		Mall	Not Mall	Mall	Not Mall
A	Mall	−2, −2, −2	2, 0, 2	2, 1, 0	−1, 0, 0
	Not Mall	0, 1, 2	0, 0, −1	0, −1, 0	0, 0, 0

   a. Find the pure-strategy Nash equilibrium or equilibria of the game. You can apply the underlying method from the text as follows. First, find the best responses for A and B, treating each bold box corresponding to C's choice as a separate game. Then find C's best responses by comparing corresponding entries in the two boxes (the two entries in the upper-left corners of both, the upper-right corners of both, etc.) and underlining the higher of the two payoffs.
   b. What do you think the outcome would be if players chose cooperatively rather than non-cooperatively?

5.10. Consider the Tragedy of the Commons game from the chapter with two shepherds, A and B, where s_A and s_B denote the number of sheep each grazes on the common pasture. Assume that the benefit per sheep (in terms of mutton and wool) equals

$$300 - s_A - s_B$$

implying that the total benefit from a flock of s_A sheep is

$$s_A(300 - s_A - s_B)$$

and that the marginal benefit of an additional sheep (as one can use calculus to show or can take for granted) is

$$300 - 2s_A - s_B.$$

Assume the (total and marginal) cost of grazing sheep is zero since the common can be freely used.

a. Compute the flock sizes and shepherds' total benefits in the Nash equilibrium.
b. Draw the best-response-function diagram corresponding to your solution.
c. Suppose A's benefit per sheep rises to $330 - s_A - s_B$. Compute the new Nash equilibrium flock sizes. Show the change from the original to the new Nash equilibrium in your best-response-function diagram.

PART 4

Production, Costs, and Supply

"The laws and conditions of production partake of the character of physical truths. There is nothing arbitrary about them."

—J. S. Mill, Principles of Political Economy, 1848

Part 4 describes the production and supply of economic goods. The organizations that supply goods are called *firms.* They may be large, complex organizations, such as Microsoft or the U.S. Defense Department, or they may be quite small, such as mom-and-pop stores or self-employed farmers. All firms must make choices about what inputs they will use and the level of output they will supply. Part 4 looks at these choices.

To be able to produce any output, firms must hire many inputs (labor, capital, natural resources, and so forth). Because these inputs are scarce, they have costs associated with their use. Our goal in Chapter 6 and Chapter 7 is to show clearly the relationship between input costs and the level of the firm's output. In Chapter 6, we introduce the firm's production function, which shows the relationship between inputs used and the level of output that results. Once this physical relationship between inputs and outputs is known, the costs of needed inputs can be determined for various levels of output. This we show in Chapter 7.

Chapter 8 uses the cost concepts developed in Chapter 7 to discuss firms' supply decisions. It provides a detailed analysis of the supply decisions of profit-maximizing firms. Later, in Chapter 15, we will look at problems in modeling the internal organization of firms, especially in connection with the incentives faced by the firms' managers and workers.

6

Production

In this chapter, we show how economists illustrate the relationship between inputs and outputs using production functions. This is the first step in showing how input costs affect firms' supply decisions.

6-1 Production Functions

The purpose of any **firm** is to turn inputs into outputs: Toyota combines steel, glass, workers' time, and hours of assembly line operation to produce automobiles; farmers combine their labor with seed, soil, rain, fertilizer, and machinery to produce crops; and colleges combine professors' time with books and (hopefully) hours of student study to produce educated students. Because economists are interested in the choices that firms make to accomplish their goals, they have developed a rather abstract model of production. In this model, the relationship between inputs and outputs is formalized by a **production function** of the form

Firm
Any organization that turns inputs into outputs.

Production function
The mathematical relationship between inputs and outputs.

$$q = f(K, L, M...), \tag{6.1}$$

where q represents the output of a particular good during a period, K represents the machine (that is, capital) use during the period, L represents hours of labor input, and M represents raw materials used. The form of the notation indicates the possibility of other variables affecting the production process. The production function summarizes what the firm knows about mixing various inputs to yield output.

For example, this production function might represent a farmer's output of wheat during one year as being dependent on the quantity of machinery employed, the amount of labor used on the farm, the amount of land under cultivation, the amount of fertilizer and seeds used, and so forth. The function shows that, say, 100 bushels of wheat can be produced in many different ways. The farmer could use a very labor-intensive technique that would require only a small amount of mechanical equipment (as tends to be the case in China). The 100 bushels could also be produced using large amounts of equipment and fertilizer with very little labor (as in the United States). A great deal of land might be used to produce the 100 bushels of wheat with less of the other inputs (as in Brazil or Australia); or relatively little land could be used with great amounts of labor, equipment, and fertilizer (as in British or Japanese agriculture). All of these combinations are represented by the general production function in Equation 6.1. The important question about this production function from an economic point of view is how the firm chooses its levels of q, K, L, and M. We take this question up in detail in the next three chapters.

Two-Input Production Function

We simplify the production function here by assuming that the firm's production depends on only two inputs: capital (K) and labor (L). Hence, our simplified production function is now

$$q = f(K, L). \quad \textbf{(6.2)}$$

The decision to focus on capital and labor is for convenience only. Most of our analysis here holds true for any two inputs that might be investigated. For example, if we wish to examine the effects of rainfall and fertilizer on crop production, we can use those two inputs in the production function while holding other inputs (quantity of land, hours of labor input, and so on) constant. In the production function that characterizes a school system, we can examine the relationship between the "output" of the system (say, academic achievement) and the inputs used to produce this output (such as teachers, buildings, and learning aids). The two general inputs of capital and labor are used here for convenience, and we frequently show these inputs on a two-dimensional graph. Application 6.1: Every Household Is a Firm shows how the production function idea can yield surprising insights about quite ordinary behavior.

6-2 Marginal Product

Marginal product
The additional output that can be produced by adding one more unit of a particular input while holding all other inputs constant.

The first question we might ask about the relationship between inputs and outputs is how much extra output can be produced by adding one more unit of an input to the production process. The marginal physical productivity or, more simply, **marginal product** of an input is defined as the quantity of extra output provided by employing one additional unit of that input while holding all other inputs constant. For our two principal inputs of capital and labor, the marginal product of labor (MP_L) is the extra output obtained by employing one more worker while holding the level of capital equipment constant. Similarly, the marginal product of capital (MP_K) is the extra output obtained by using one more machine while holding the number of workers constant.

As an illustration of these definitions, consider the case of a farmer hiring one more person to harvest a crop while holding all other inputs constant. The extra output produced when this person is added to the production team is the marginal product of labor input. The concept is measured in physical quantities such as bushels of wheat, crates of oranges, or heads of lettuce. We might, for example, observe that 25 workers in an orange grove are able to produce 10,000 crates of oranges per week, whereas 26 workers (with the same trees and equipment) can produce 10,200 crates. The marginal product of the 26th worker is 200 crates per week.

Diminishing Marginal Product

We might expect the marginal product of an input to depend on how much of it used. For example, workers cannot be added indefinitely to the harvesting of oranges (while keeping the number of trees, amount of equipment, fertilizer, and so forth fixed) without the marginal product eventually deteriorating. This possibility is illustrated in Figure 6.1. The top panel of the figure shows the relationship between output per week and labor input during the week when the level of capital input is held fixed. At first, adding new workers also increases output significantly, but these gains diminish as even more labor is added and the fixed amount of capital becomes overutilized. The concave shape of the total output curve in panel a therefore reflects the economic principle of diminishing marginal product.

APPLICATION 6.1

Every Household Is a Firm

Turning inputs into outputs is something we all do every day without thinking about it. When you drive somewhere, you are combining labor (your time) with capital (the car) to produce economic output (a trip). Of course, the output from this activity is not traded in organized markets; but there is not very much difference between providing "taxi services" to yourself or selling them to someone else. In both cases, you are performing the economic role that economists assign to firms. In fact, "home production" constitutes a surprisingly large segment of the overall economy. Looking at people as "firms" can yield some interesting insights.

The Amount of Home Production

Economists have tried to estimate the amount of production that people do for themselves. By including such items as child care, home maintenance, commuting, physical maintenance (for example, exercise), and cooking, they arrive at quite substantial magnitudes—perhaps more than half of traditionally measured GDP. To produce this large amount of output, people employ significant amounts of inputs. Time-use studies suggest that the time people spend in home production is only slightly less than time spent working (about 30 percent of total time in both cases). Also, people's investment in home-related capital (such as houses, cars, and appliances) is probably larger than business firms' investment in buildings and equipment.

Production of Housing Services

Some of the more straightforward things produced at home are what might be called "housing services." People combine the capital invested in their homes with some purchased inputs (electricity, natural gas) and with their own time (cleaning the gutters) to produce living accommodations. In this respect, people are both producers of housing services and consumers of those same services; and this is precisely how housing is treated in U.S. GDP accounts. In 2012, for example, people spent $1.3 trillion in (implicitly) renting houses from themselves. They also spent $460 billion on furnishings, household equipment, and routine household maintenance even if we do not assign any value to the time they spent in household chores. Whether people change their production of housing services over the business cycle (do they fix the roof when they are laid off, for example) is an important question in macroeconomics because the decline in output during recessions may not be as large as it appears in the official statistics.

Production of Health

The production function concept is also used in thinking about health issues. People combine inputs of purchased medical care (such as medicines or physicians' services) together with their own time to "produce" health. An important implication of this approach is that people may to some extent find it possible to substitute their own actions for purchased medical care while remaining equally healthy. Whether current medical insurance practices give them adequate incentives to do that is widely debated. The fact that people may know more than their physicians do about their own health and how to produce it also raises a number of complex questions about the doctor-patient relationship (as we shall see in Chapter 15).

Production of Children

A somewhat more far-fetched application of the home production concept is to view families as producers of children. One of the most important observations about this "output" is that it is not homogeneous—children have both "quantity" and "quality" dimensions, and families will choose which combination of these to produce. Clearly, significant amounts of inputs (especially parental time) are devoted to this process—by some estimates the input costs associated with children are second only to housing for typical families. From an economic point of view, one of the more interesting issues involved in producing children concerns the fact that such investments are irreversible (unlike, say, housing, where one can always opt for a smaller house). This may cause some people to view this production as quite risky, as any parent of a surly teen can attest.

TO THINK ABOUT

1. If people produce goods such as housing services and health for their own consumption, how should we define the "prices" of these goods in the model of utility maximization used in prior chapters?
2. How does a family with more than one adult decide how to allocate each person's work time between home production and work in the market?

Figure 6.1 Relationship between Output and Labor Input, Holding Other Inputs Constant

Output per week

Total output

L* Labor input per week

(a) Total output

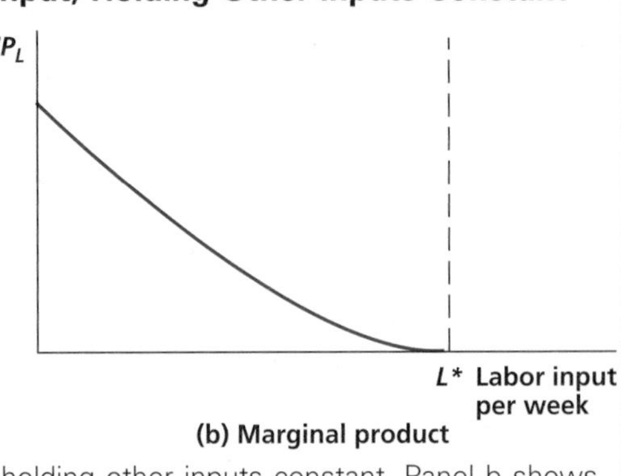

(b) Marginal product

Panel a shows the relationship between output and labor input, holding other inputs constant. Panel b shows the marginal product of labor input, which is also the slope of the curve in panel a. Here, MP_L diminishes as labor input increases. MP_L reaches zero at L^*.

Marginal Product Curve

A geometric interpretation of the marginal product concept is straightforward—it is the slope of the total product curve,[1] shown in panel a of Figure 6.1. The decreasing slope of the curve shows diminishing marginal product. For higher values of labor input, the total curve is nearly flat—adding more labor raises output only slightly. The bottom panel of Figure 6.1 illustrates this slope directly by the marginal product of labor curve (MP_L). Initially, MP_L is high because adding extra labor results in a significant increase in output. As labor input expands, however, MP_L falls. Indeed, at L^*, additional labor input does not raise total output at all. It might be the case that 50 workers can produce 12,000 crates of oranges per week, but adding a 51st worker (with the same number of trees and equipment) fails to raise this output at all. This may happen because he or she has nothing useful to do in an already crowded orange grove. The marginal product of this new worker is therefore zero.

Average Product

When people talk about the productivity of workers, they usually do not have in mind the economist's notion of marginal product. Rather, they tend to think in terms of "output per worker." In our orange grove example, with 25 workers, output per worker is $400(= 10{,}000 \div 25)$ crates of oranges per week. With 50 workers, however, output per worker falls to $240(= 12{,}000 \div 50)$ crates per week. Because the marginal productivity of each new worker is falling, output per worker is also falling. Notice, however, that the output-per-worker figures give a misleading impression of how productive an extra worker really is. With 25 workers, output per worker is 400 crates of oranges per week, but adding a 26th worker only adds 200 crates per week. Indeed, with 50 workers, an extra worker adds no additional output even though output per worker is a respectable 240 crates per week.[2]

---

[1]In mathematical terms, the MP_L is the derivative of the production function with respect to L. Because K is held constant in defining the MP_L, this derivative should be a "partial" derivative.

[2]Output per worker can be shown geometrically in the top panel of Figure 6.1 as the slope of a chord from the origin to the relevant point in the total product curve. Because of the concave shape of the total product curve, this slope too decreases as labor input is increased. Unlike the marginal product of labor, however, average productivity will never reach zero under ordinary circumstances with the firm producing some positive output.

Because most economic analysis involves questions of adding or subtracting small amounts of an input in a given production situation, the marginal product idea is clearly the more important concept. Figures on output per worker (that is, "average product") can be quite misleading if they do not accurately reflect these marginal ideas.

Appraising the Marginal Product Concept

The concept of marginal product itself may sometimes be difficult to apply because of the *ceteris paribus* assumption used in its definition. Both the levels of other inputs and the firm's technical knowledge are assumed to be held constant when we perform the conceptual experiment of, say, adding one more worker to an orange grove. But, in the real world, that is not how new hiring would likely occur. Rather, additional hiring would probably also necessitate adding additional equipment (ladders, crates, tractors, and so forth). From a broader perspective, additional hiring might be accompanied by the opening up of entirely new orange groves and the adoption of improved methods of production. In such cases, the *ceteris paribus* assumptions incorporated in the definition of marginal productivity would be violated, and the combinations of q and L observed would lie on many different marginal product curves. For this reason, it is more common to study the entire production function for a good, using the marginal product concept to help understand the overall function. Application 6.2: What Did U.S. Automakers Learn from the Japanese? provides an illustration of why such an overall view may be necessary.

MICRO QUIZ 6.1

Average and marginal productivities can be derived directly from the firm's production function. For each of the following cases, discuss how the values of these measures change as labor input expands. Explain why the cases differ.

Case 1. Apples harvested (q) depend on hours of labor employed (L) as $q = 10 + 50L$.

Case 2. Books dusted (q) depend on minutes spent dusting (L) as $q = -10 + 5L$.

6-3 Isoquant Maps

To picture an entire production function in two dimensions, we need to look at its **isoquant map**. We can again use a production function of the form $q = f(K, L)$, using capital and labor as convenient examples of any two inputs that might happen to be of interest. To show the various combinations of capital and labor that can be employed to produce a particular output level, we use an **isoquant** (from the Greek *iso*, meaning "equal"). For example, all the combinations of K and L that fall on the curve labeled $q = 10$ in Figure 6.2 are capable of producing 10 units of output per period. This single isoquant records the many alternative ways of producing 10 units of output. One combination is represented by point A. A firm could use L_A and K_A to produce 10 units of output. Alternatively, the firm might prefer to use relatively less capital and more labor and would therefore choose a point such as B. The isoquant demonstrates that a firm can produce 10 units of output in many different ways, just as the indifference curves in Part 2 showed that many different bundles of goods yield the same utility.

Isoquant map
A contour map of a firm's production function.

Isoquant
A curve that shows the various combinations of inputs that will produce the same amount of output.

There are infinitely many isoquants in the K–L plane. Each isoquant represents a different level of output. The isoquants record successively higher levels of output as we move in a northeasterly direction because using more of each of the inputs will permit output to increase. Two other isoquants (for $q = 20$ and $q = 30$) are also shown in Figure 6.2. They record those combinations of inputs that can produce the specified

APPLICATION 6.2

What Did U.S. Automakers Learn from the Japanese?

Average labor productivity in the U.S. automobile industry increased dramatically between 1980 and 1995. In 1980, each worker in the U.S. auto industry produced an average of about 40 cars annually. Fifteen years later the figure had grown to nearly 60 cars per worker—a 50 percent increase. One intriguing potential explanation for this pattern is that the entry of Japanese producers into the United States in the early 1980s may have spurred all firms to increase productivity. Between 1983 and 1986 Honda, Nissan, and Toyota all opened automobile assembly plants in the United States. These firms introduced a variety of production practices that had been developed for making cars in Japan over the prior 20 years. American firms also seem to have found these practices attractive.

The Development of "Lean" Technology

Henry Ford is generally credited with the invention of the automobile assembly line early in the twentieth century. This process allowed automakers to achieve significant cost reductions through the standardization of work tasks and specialization in producing a single model. Detroit came to lead the world in auto production through the use of such mass-production techniques.

The Japanese arrived somewhat later on the scene in automobile production. The industry did not achieve large-scale production until the early 1960s. Because Japan was still recovering from the ravages of World War II, companies were forced to develop production techniques that economized on capital and stressed flexibility. Although this "lean" approach to assembling cars arose out of necessity, it ultimately proved to be a significant advance in the way cars are made. Because machines and teams of workers were more flexible, it became easier to produce multiple models and complex accessory packages on the same assembly line. In addition, firms were better able to make use of emerging technical improvements in numerical and computer control of machinery than was possible on mass-production assembly lines. By the early 1980s, some economists believe, Japanese workers have been as much as 30 percent more productive than Americans in assembling cars.

Learning from the Japanese

The arrival of Japanese automakers in the United States gave American firms a major shake-up. Production methods that had remained little changed for 50 years came under increased scrutiny. Most new assembly plants built after the arrival of the Japanese tended to adopt lean technologies (and other Japanese innovations such as reducing parts' inventories). Existing plants were increasingly transformed into more flexible Japanese-type arrangements. By one estimate, as many as half of mass-production assembly lines were converted to Japanese-type lean technology over a 10-year period.[1] This adoption of new assembly techniques, in combination with other advances in the ways cars were made, explained a large part of the increase in worker productivity in the auto industry.

Industrial Relations Practices

In addition to these differences in production techniques, some people have suggested that differences in industrial relations practices between Japanese and U.S. automobile firms may explain some part of the productivity differences. Whereas U.S. auto firms often take adversarial positions *vis-à-vis* their unionized workers, most unions in Japan are company-specific. In addition, a large proportion of Japanese autoworkers cannot be fired and most obtain a significant fraction of their pay in the form of end-of-year bonuses. All of these features may make Japanese workers feel a greater allegiance to their firms than do their American counterparts. Some evidence from Toyota and Honda assembly plants in the United States suggests that such allegiance may pay off in terms of lower worker turnover and, perhaps, greater effort on the job. Quantifying such effects by comparing worker behavior in Japan and the United States has proven to be difficult, however, because of important cultural differences between the two nations.

TO THINK ABOUT

1. Why did it take so long for U.S. automakers to adopt Japanese techniques? Couldn't they just have visited Japan during the 1970s, say, and brought what they saw home? Why did it take the arrival of Japanese assembly plants in the United States to prompt the changes?
2. If Japanese industrial relations practices were also important in making Japanese auto firms more efficient, why didn't U.S. firms adopt these aspects of the Japanese "model"?

[1]See J. van Biesebroeck, "Productivity Dynamics with Technological Choice: An Application to Automobile Assembly," *Review of Economic Studies* (January 2003): 167–198.

Figure 6.2 Isoquant Map

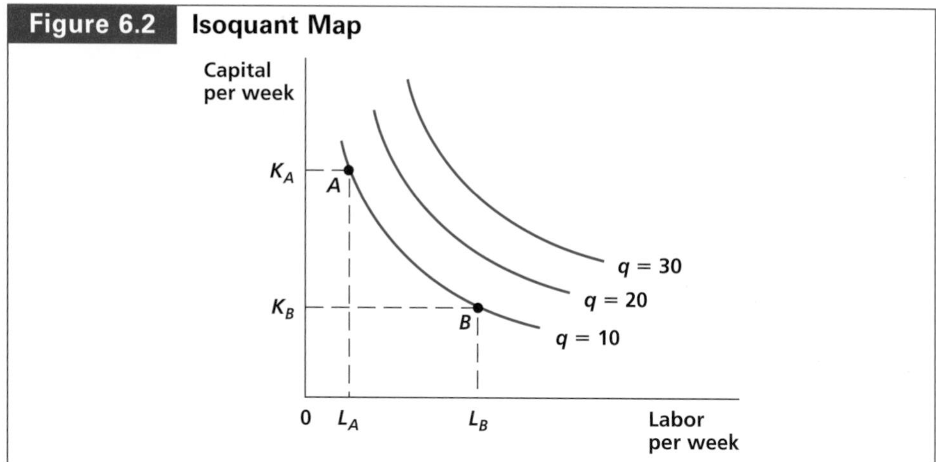

Isoquants record the alternative combinations of inputs that can be used to produce a given level of output. The slope of these curves shows the rate at which L can be substituted for K while keeping output constant. The negative of this slope is called the (marginal) rate of technical substitution (RTS). In the figure, the RTS is positive, and it is diminishing for increasing inputs of labor.

level of output. You should notice the similarity between an isoquant map and the individual's indifference curve map discussed in Part 2. Both are "contour" maps that show the "altitude" (that is, of utility or output) associated with various input combinations. For isoquants, however, the labeling of the curves is measurable (an output of 10 units per week has a precise meaning), and we are more interested in the characteristics of these curves than we were in determining the exact shape of indifference curves.

Rate of Technical Substitution

The slope of an isoquant shows how one input can be traded for another while holding output constant. Examining this slope gives some information about the technical possibilities for substituting labor for capital—an issue that can be quite important to firms. The slope of an isoquant (or, more properly, its negative) is called the marginal rate of technical substitution of labor for capital. Often, the "marginal" is dropped and the term is shortened to **rate of technical substitution**, abbreviated RTS. Specifically, the RTS is defined as the amount by which capital input can be reduced while holding quantity produced constant when one more unit of labor input is used. Mathematically,

Rate of technical substitution (RTS)
The amount by which one input can be reduced when one more unit of another input is added while holding output constant. The negative of the slope of an isoquant.

$$\begin{aligned}\text{Rate of technical substitution}&\\ \text{(of labor for capital)} &= \text{RTS(of } L \text{ for } K)\\ &= -(\text{Slope of isoquant})\\ &= -\frac{\text{Change in capital input}}{\text{Change in labor input}},\end{aligned} \tag{6.3}$$

where all of these changes refer to a situation in which output (q) is held constant. The particular value of this trade-off rate will depend not only on the level of output but also on the quantities of capital and labor being used. Its value depends on the point on the isoquant map at which the slope is to be measured. At a point such as A in Figure 6.2, relatively large amounts of capital can be given up if one more unit of labor is employed—at point A, the RTS is a high positive number. On the other hand, at point B, the availability of an additional unit of labor does not permit much of a reduction in capital input, and the RTS is relatively small.

RTS and Marginal Products

We can use the RTS concept to discuss the likely shape of a firm's isoquant map. Most obviously, it seems clear that the RTS should be positive; that is, each isoquant should have a negative slope. If the quantity of labor employed by the firm increases, the firm should be able to reduce capital input and still keep output constant. Because labor presumably has a positive marginal product, the firm should be able to get by with less capital input when more labor is used. If increasing labor actually required the firm to use more capital, it would imply that the marginal product of labor is negative, and no firm would be willing to pay for an input that had a negative effect on output.

We can show this result more formally by noting that the RTS is precisely equal to the ratio of the marginal product of labor to the marginal product of capital. That is,

$$\text{RTS (of } L \text{ for } K) = \frac{MP_L}{MP_K}. \quad \textbf{(6.4)}$$

Suppose, for example, that $MP_L = 2$ and $MP_K = 1$. Then, if the firm employs one more worker, this will generate two extra units of output if capital input remains constant. Put another way, the firm can reduce capital input by two when there is another worker and output will not change—the extra labor adds two units of output, whereas the reduced capital reduces output by two. Hence, by definition, the RTS is 2—the ratio of the marginal products.

Now, applying Equation 6.4, it is clear that if the RTS is negative, one of the marginal products must also be negative. But no firm would pay anything for an input that reduced output. Hence, at least for those portions of isoquants where firms actually operate, the RTS must be positive (and the slope of the isoquant negative).

Diminishing RTS

The isoquants in Figure 6.2 are drawn not only with negative slopes (as they should be) but also as convex curves. Along any one of the curves, the RTS is *diminishing*. For a high ratio of K to L, the RTS is a large positive number, indicating that a great deal of capital can be given up if one more unit of labor is employed. On the other hand, when a lot of labor is already being used, the RTS is low, signifying that only a small amount of capital can be traded for an additional unit of labor if output is to be held constant. This shape seems intuitively reasonable: The more labor (relative to capital) that is used, the less able labor is to replace capital in production. A diminishing RTS shows that use of a particular input can be pushed too far. Firms will not want to use "only labor" or "only machines" to produce a given level of output.[3] They will choose a more balanced input mix that uses at least some of each input. In Chapter 7, we see exactly how an optimal (that is, minimum cost) mix of inputs might be chosen. Application 6.3: Engineering and Economics illustrates how isoquant maps can be developed from actual production information.

MICRO QUIZ 6.2

A hole can be dug in one hour with a small shovel and in half an hour with a large shovel.

1. What is the RTS of labor time for shovel size?
2. What does the "one hole" isoquant look like? How much time would it take a worker to dig a hole if he or she used a small shovel for half the hole, then switched to the large shovel?

[3]An incorrect, but possibly instructive, argument based on Equation 6.4 might proceed as follows. In moving along an isoquant, more labor and less capital are being used. Assuming that each factor exhibits a diminishing marginal product, we might say that MP_L would decrease (because the quantity of labor has increased) and that MP_K would increase (because the quantity of capital has decreased). Consequently, the RTS ($= MP_L/MP_K$) should decrease. The problem with this argument is that *both* inputs are changing together. It is not possible to make such simple statements about changes in marginal productivities when two inputs are changing, because the definition of the marginal product of any one input requires that the level of all other inputs be held constant.

APPLICATION 6.3

Engineering and Economics

One approach that economists use to derive production functions for a specific good is through the use of information provided by engineers. An illustration of how engineering studies might be used is provided in Figure 1. As a start, assume that engineers have developed three processes (*A*, *B*, and *C*) for producing a given good. Process *A* uses a higher ratio of capital to labor than does process *B*, and process *B* uses a higher capital-to-labor ratio than does process *C*. Each process can be increased as much as desired by duplicating the basic machinery involved. The points a, b, and c on each such expansion ray through the origin show a particular output level, say q_0. By joining these points, we obtain the q_0 isoquant. Points on this isoquant between the single technique rays reflect proportionate use of two techniques.

Figure 1 Construction of an Isoquant from Engineering Data

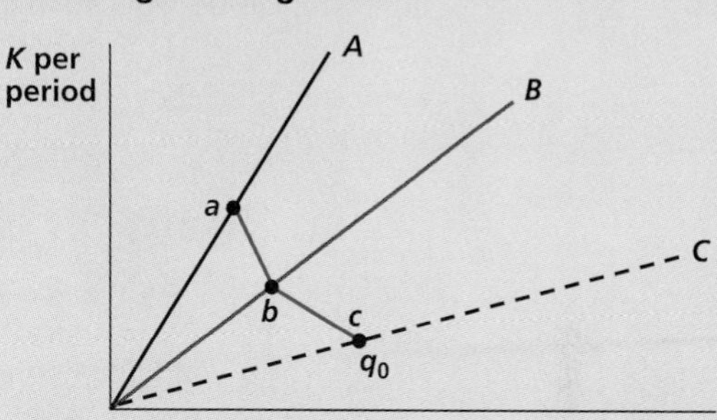

The rays *A*, *B*, and *C* show three specific industrial processes. Points *a*, *b*, and *c* show the level of operation of each process necessary to yield q_0. The q_0 isoquant reflects various mixtures of the three processes.

Solar Water Heating

This method was used by G. T. Sav to examine the production of domestic hot water by rooftop solar collectors.[1] Because solar systems require backup hot water generators for use during periods of reduced sunlight, Sav was especially interested in the proper way to integrate the two processes. The author used engineering data on both solar and backup heating to develop an isoquant map showing the trade-off between fuel use and solar system capital requirements. He showed that isoquant maps differ in various regions of the United States, with the productivity of solar collectors obviously depending upon the amount of sunlight available in the different regions. Solar collectors that work very efficiently in Arizona may be quite useless in often-cloudy New England.

Measuring Efficiency

One interesting application of the engineering isoquant shown in Figure 1 is to assess whether a firm (or an entire economy) is operating in a technically efficient manner. If q_0 is being produced using an input combination that lies northwest of the *abc* isoquant shown in the figure, we might conclude that this firm is not being as technically efficient as it might be given the available engineering data. For example, Zofio and Prieto use this approach to study the relative efficiency of various sectors in the Canadian, Danish, and UK economies.[2] They conclude that services are produced relatively inefficiently in both Canada and the United Kingdom and that construction is very inefficient in Denmark. Potential savings from moving onto the efficient engineering isoquant are quite large in the authors' model, amounting to 5% of GDP in some cases.

POLICY CHALLENGE

Over the past 30 years, the government has offered a wide variety of incentives for people to install alternative energy devices such as solar collectors or wind power generators. In many cases, these incentives can reduce peoples' out-of-pocket costs for such devices to less than one-third of their actual market price. What effect do such subsidies have on the adoption of such alternative technologies? Is this the best way to foster such alternatives? How might the fact that a particular technology is subsidized affect whether peoples' choices of technologies are efficient in the sense described in Figure 1?

[1] G. T. Sav, "The Engineering Approach to Production Functions Revisited: An Application to Solar Processes," *The Journal of Industrial Economics* (September 1984): 21–35.

[2] Jose L. Zofio and Angel M. Prieto, "Measuring Productive Inefficiency in Input-Output Models by Means of Data Envelopment Analysis." *International Review of Applied Economics* (September 2007): 519–537.

6-4 Returns to Scale

Because production functions represent actual methods of production, economists pay considerable attention to the characteristics of these functions. The shape and properties of a firm's production function are important for a variety of reasons. Using such information, a firm may decide how its research funds might best be spent on developing technical improvements. Or, public policy makers might study the form of production functions to argue that laws prohibiting very large-scale firms would harm economic efficiency. In this section, we develop some terminology to aid in examining such issues.

Adam Smith on Returns to Scale

Returns to scale
The rate at which output increases in response to proportional increases in all inputs.

The first important issue we might address about production functions is how the quantity of output responds to increases in all inputs together. For example, suppose all inputs were doubled. Would output also double, or is the relationship not quite so simple? Here we are asking about the **returns to scale** exhibited by a production function, a concept that has been of interest to economists ever since Adam Smith intensively studied (of all things) the production of pins in the eighteenth century. Smith identified two forces that come into play when all inputs are doubled (for a doubling of scale). First, a doubling of scale permits a greater "division of labor." Smith was intrigued by the skill of people who made only pin heads, or who sharpened pin shafts, or who stuck the two together. He suggested that efficiency might increase—production might more than double—as greater specialization of this type becomes possible.

Smith did not envision that these benefits to large-scale operations would extend indefinitely, however. He recognized that large firms may encounter inefficiencies in managerial direction and control if scale is dramatically increased. Coordination of production plans for more inputs may become more difficult when there are many layers of management and many specialized workers involved in the production process.

A Precise Definition

Which of these two effects of scale is more important is an empirical question. To investigate this question, economists need a precise definition of returns to scale. A production function is said to exhibit *constant returns to scale* if a doubling of all inputs results in a precise doubling of output. If a doubling of all inputs yields less than a doubling of output, the production function is said to exhibit *decreasing returns to scale.* If a doubling of all inputs results in more than a doubling of output, the production function exhibits *increasing returns to scale.*

Graphic Illustrations

These possibilities are illustrated in the three graphs of Figure 6.3. In each case, production isoquants for $q = 10, 20, 30,$ and 40 are shown, together with a ray (labeled A) showing a uniform expansion of both capital and labor inputs. Panel a illustrates constant returns to scale. There, as both capital and labor inputs are successively increased from 1 to 2, and 2 to 3, and then 3 to 4, output expands proportionally. That is, output and inputs move in unison. In panel b, by comparison, the isoquants get farther apart as output expands. This is a case of decreasing returns to scale—an expansion in inputs does not result in a proportionate rise in output. For example, the doubling of both capital and labor inputs from 1 to 2 units is not sufficient to increase output from 10 to 20.

Figure 6.3 Isoquant Maps Showing Constant, Decreasing, and Increasing Returns to Scale

(a) Constant returns to scale

(b) Decreasing returns to scale

(c) Increasing returns to scale

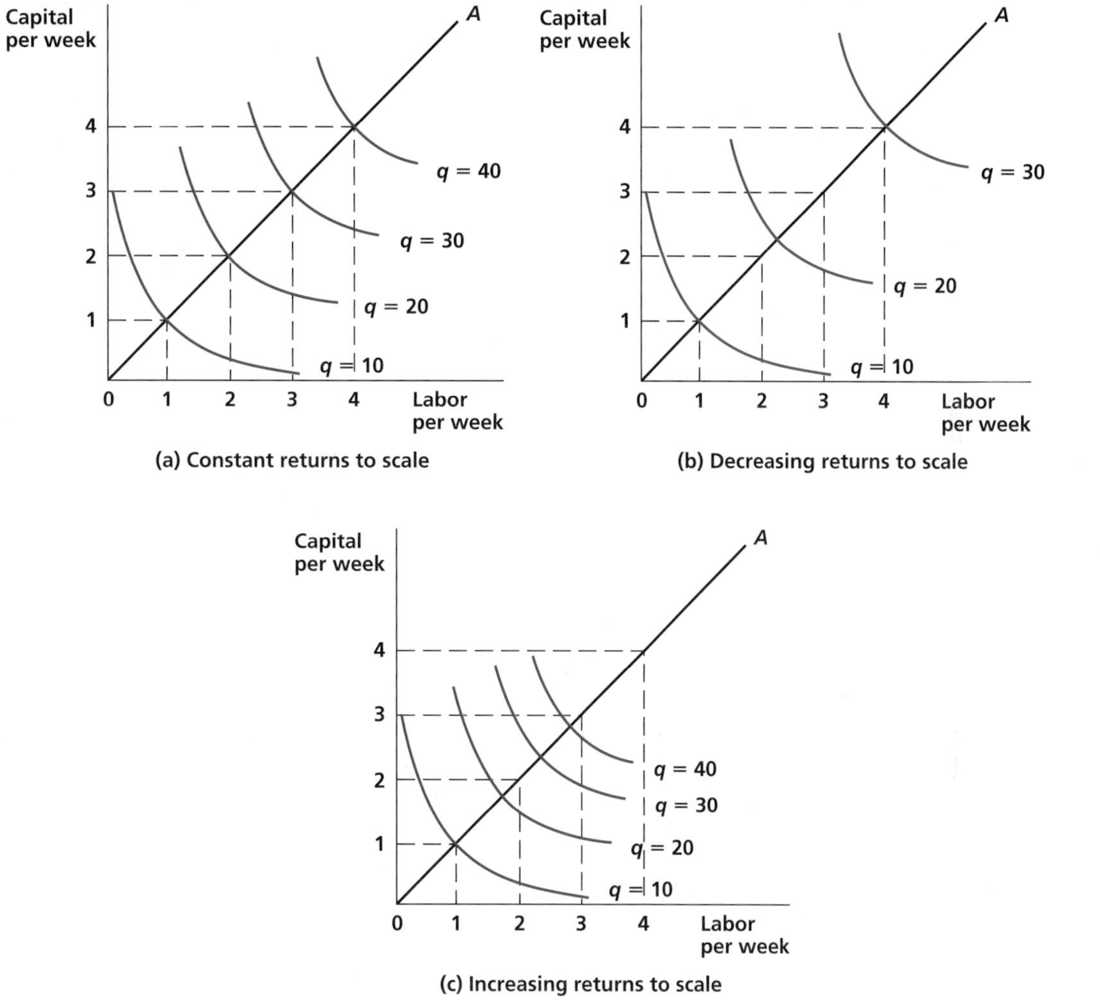

In panel a, an expansion in both inputs leads to a similar, proportionate expansion in output. This shows constant returns to scale. In panel b, an expansion in inputs yields a less-than-proportionate expansion in output, illustrating decreasing returns to scale. Panel c shows increasing returns to scale—output expands proportionately faster than inputs.

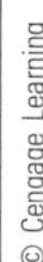

That increase in output would require more than a doubling of inputs. Finally, panel c illustrates increasing returns to scale. In this case, the isoquants get closer together as input expands—a doubling of inputs is more than sufficient to double output. Large-scale operation would in this case appear to be quite efficient.

The types of scale economies experienced in the real world may, of course, be rather complex combinations of these simple examples. A production function may exhibit increasing returns to scale over some output ranges and decreasing returns to scale over other ranges. Or, some aspects of a good's production may illustrate scale economies, whereas other aspects may not. For example, the production of computer chips can be highly automated; but the assembly of chips into electronic components is more difficult to automate and may exhibit few such scale economies. Application 6.4: Returns to Scale in Beer and Wine illustrates similar complex possibilities. Problems 6.7 and 6.8 at the end of this chapter show how the

APPLICATION 6.4

Returns to Scale in Beer and Wine

Returns to scale have played an important role in the evolution of the beer and wine industries in the United States and elsewhere. In principle, both of these industries exhibit increasing returns to scale as a result of the geometry of their production methods. Because both beverages are produced by volume but the capital involved in production (brewing kettles, aging casks, and so forth) has costs that are proportional to surface area, larger-scale producers are able to achieve significant cost savings. Of course, there are differences between beer and wine in the nature of the raw material used (wine grapes are much more variable in quality than are the ingredients of beer) and in the nature of demand. These have produced rather significant differences in the evolution of each industry.

Increasing Concentration in Beer Production

Prior to World War II, beer tended to be produced on a local level because of high transportation costs. Most large cities had three or more local breweries. Improvements in shipping beer together with national marketing of major brands on television caused a sharp decline in the number of breweries after the war. Between 1945 and the mid-1980s, the number of U.S. brewing firms fell by more than 90 percent—from 450 to 44. Major brewers such as Anheuser-Busch, Miller, and Coors took advantage of scale economies by building very large breweries (producing over 4 million barrels of beer per year each) in multiple locations throughout the country. Budweiser became the largest-selling beer in the world, accounting for more than one-third of industry output.

Product Differentiation and Microbreweries

Expansion of the major brewing companies left one significant hole in their market penetration—premium brands. Beginning in the 1980s, firms such as Anchor (San Francisco), Redhook (Seattle), and Sam Adams (Boston) began producing significant amounts of niche beers. These firms found that some beer consumers were willing to pay much higher prices for such products, thereby mitigating the higher costs associated with relatively small-scale production. The 1990s saw a virtual explosion of even smaller-scale operators. Soon even small towns had their own breweries. A similar course of events unfolded in the United Kingdom with the "real ale" movement. Still, national brewers continued to hold their own in terms of their total shares of the market, mainly because of their low costs.

Wine: Product Differentiation to the Extreme

Although wine production might have followed beer production and taken advantage of economies of scale and national marketing to become increasingly concentrated, that did not happen. In part, this can be explained by production technology. Maintaining quality for high volumes of production has been a recurring problem for winemakers, even though there are cost advantages. Most production problems arise because wine grapes can have widely different characteristics depending on precisely when they are harvested, how much rainfall they have had, and the nature of the soil in which they are grown. Blending grapes from many areas together can be technically difficult and will often result in a wine that represents a "lowest common denominator."

The impact of these difficulties in large-scale wine production are exacerbated by the nature of the demand for wine. Because wine has a relatively high income elasticity of demand, most wine is bought by people with above average incomes. These consumers seem to place a high value on variety in their choices of wine and are willing to pay quite a bit for a high-quality product. Demand for a low-quality, mass-produced wine is much less significant. These observations then reinforce Adam Smith's conclusion in *The Wealth of Nations* that the "division of labor [that is, economies of scale] is limited by the extent of the market."[1]

TO THINK ABOUT

1. How do transportation costs affect attaining economies of scale in brewing? How might a large beer producer decide on the optimal number of breweries to operate?
2. Laws that limit interstate sale of wine over the Internet were relaxed significantly as a result of a Supreme Court decision in 2005. How would you expect this to affect the scale of production in the wine industry?

[1]For more on the technology of beer and wine production (together with information on other alcoholic beverages), see Y. Xia and S. Buccola, "Factor Use and Productivity Change in the Alcoholic Beverage Industries," *Southern Economic Journal* (July 2003): 93–109.

returns-to-scale concept can be captured with the Cobb-Douglas production function. This form of the production function (or a simple generalization of it) has been used to study production in a wide variety of industries.

6-5 Input Substitution

Another important characteristic of a production function is how "easily" capital can be substituted for labor, or, more generally, how any one input can be substituted for another. This characteristic depends primarily on the shape of a single isoquant. So far, we have assumed that a given output level can be produced with a variety of different input mixes—that is, we assumed firms could substitute labor for capital while keeping output constant. How easily that substitution can be accomplished may, of course, vary. In some cases, the substitution can be made easily and quickly in response to changing economic circumstances. Mine owners found it relatively easy to automate in response to rising wages for miners, for example. In other cases, firms may have little choice about the input combination they must use. Producers of operas have little chance to substitute capital (scenery) for labor (singers). Economists can measure this degree of substitution very technically, but for us to do so here would take us too far afield.[4] We can look at one special case in which input substitution is impossible. This example illustrates some of the difficulties in input substitution that economists have explored.

Fixed-Proportions Production Function

Figure 6.4 demonstrates a case where no substitution is possible. This case is rather different from the ones we have looked at so far. Here, the isoquants are L-shaped, indicating that

Figure 6.4 Isoquant Map with Fixed Proportions

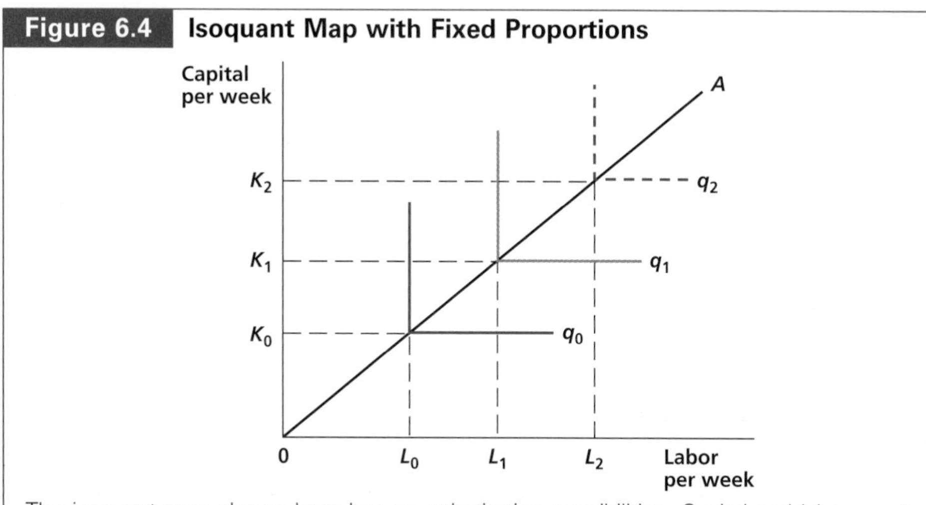

The isoquant map shown here has no substitution possibilities. Capital and labor must be used in fixed proportions if neither is to be redundant. For example, if K_1 machines are available, L_1 units of labor should be used. If L_2 units of labor are used, there will be excess labor since no more than q_1 can be produced from the given machines. Alternatively, if L_0 laborers were hired, machines would be in excess to the extent $K_1 - K_0$.

[4]Formally, the case of input substitution is measured by the *elasticity of substitution,* which is defined as the ratio of the percentage change in *K/L* to the percentage change in the RTS along an isoquant. For the fixed-proportions case, this elasticity is zero because *K/L* does not change at the isoquant's vertex.

machines and labor must be used in absolutely fixed proportions. Every machine has a fixed complement of workers that cannot be varied. For example, if K_1 machines are in use, L_1 workers are required to produce output level q_1. Employing more workers than L_1 will not increase output with K_1 machines. This is shown by the fact that the q_1 isoquant is horizontal beyond the point K_1, L_1. In other words, the marginal productivity of labor is zero beyond L_1. On the other hand, using fewer workers would result in excess machines. If only L_0 workers were hired, for instance, only q_0 units could be produced, but these units could be produced with only K_0 machines. When L_0 workers are hired, there is an excess of machines of an amount given by $K_1 - K_0$.

Fixed-proportions production function
A production function in which the inputs must be used in a fixed ratio to one another.

The production function whose isoquant map is shown in Figure 6.4 is called a **fixed-proportions production function**. Both inputs are fully employed only if a combination of K and L that lies along the ray A, which passes through the vertices of the isoquants, is chosen. Otherwise, one input will be excessive in the sense that it could be cut back without reducing output. If a firm with such a production function wishes to expand, it must increase all inputs simultaneously so that none of the inputs is redundant.

The fixed-proportions production function has a wide variety of applications to the study of real-world production techniques. Many machines do require a fixed complement of workers; more than these would be redundant. For example, consider the combination of capital and labor required to mow a lawn. The lawn mower needs one person for its operation, and a worker needs one lawn mower to produce any output. Output can be expanded (that is, more grass can be mowed at the same time) only by adding capital and labor to the productive process in fixed proportions. Many production functions may be of this type, and the fixed-proportions model is in many ways appropriate for production planning.[5]

Relevance of Input Substitutability

The ease with which one input can be substituted for another is of considerable interest to economists. They can use the shape of an isoquant map to see the relative ease with which different industries can adapt to the changing availability of productive inputs. For example, rapidly rising energy prices during the late 1970s caused many industries to adopt energy-saving capital equipment. For these firms, their costs did not rise very rapidly because they were able to adapt to new circumstances. Firms that could not make such substitutions had large increases in costs and may have become noncompetitive. Another example of input substitutability is found in the huge changes in agricultural production that have occurred during the past 100 years. As farmers gained access to better farm equipment, they discovered that it was very possible to substitute capital for labor while continuing to harvest about the same number of acres. Employment in agriculture declined from about half the labor force to fewer than 3 percent of workers today. The fact that the workers who left farms found employment in other industries also shows that these other industries were able to make substitutions in how they produce their goods.

MICRO QUIZ 6.3

Suppose that artichokes are produced according to the production function $q = 100K + 50L$, where q represents pounds of artichokes produced per hour, K is the number of acres of land devoted to artichoke production, and L represents the number of workers hired each hour to pick artichokes.

1. Does this production function exhibit increasing, constant, or decreasing returns to scale?
2. What does the form of this production function assume about the substitutability of L for K?
3. Give one reason why this production function is probably not a very reasonable one.

[5]The lawn mower example points up another important possibility. Presumably there is some leeway in choosing what size and type of lawn mower to buy. Any device, from a pair of clippers to a gang mower, might be chosen. Prior to the actual purchase, the capital-labor ratio in lawn mowing can be considered variable. Once the mower is purchased, however, the capital-labor ratio becomes fixed.

6-6 Changes in Technology

A production function reflects firms' technical knowledge about how to use inputs to produce outputs. When firms learn new ways to operate, the production function changes. This kind of technical advancement occurs constantly as older, outmoded machines are replaced by more efficient ones that embody state-of-the-art techniques. Workers too are part of this technical progress as they become better educated and learn special skills for doing their jobs. Today, for example, steel is made far more efficiently than in the nineteenth century both because blast furnaces and rolling mills are better and because workers are better trained to use these facilities.

The production function concept and its related isoquant map are important tools for understanding the effect of technical change. Formally, technical progress represents a shift in the production function, such as that illustrated in Figure 6.5. In this figure, the isoquant q_0 summarizes the initial state of technical knowledge. That level of output can be produced using K_0, L_0, or any of a number of input combinations. With the discovery of new production techniques, the q_0 isoquant shifts toward the origin—the same output level can now be produced using smaller quantities of inputs. If, for example, the q_0 isoquant shifts inward to q_0', it is now possible to produce q_0 with the same amount of capital as before (K_0) but with much less labor (L_1). It is even possible to produce q_0 using both less capital and less labor than previously by choosing a point such as A. **Technical progress** represents a real saving on inputs and (as we see in the next chapter) a reduction in the costs of production.

Technical progress
A shift in the production function that allows a given output level to be produced using fewer inputs.

Figure 6.5 Technical Change

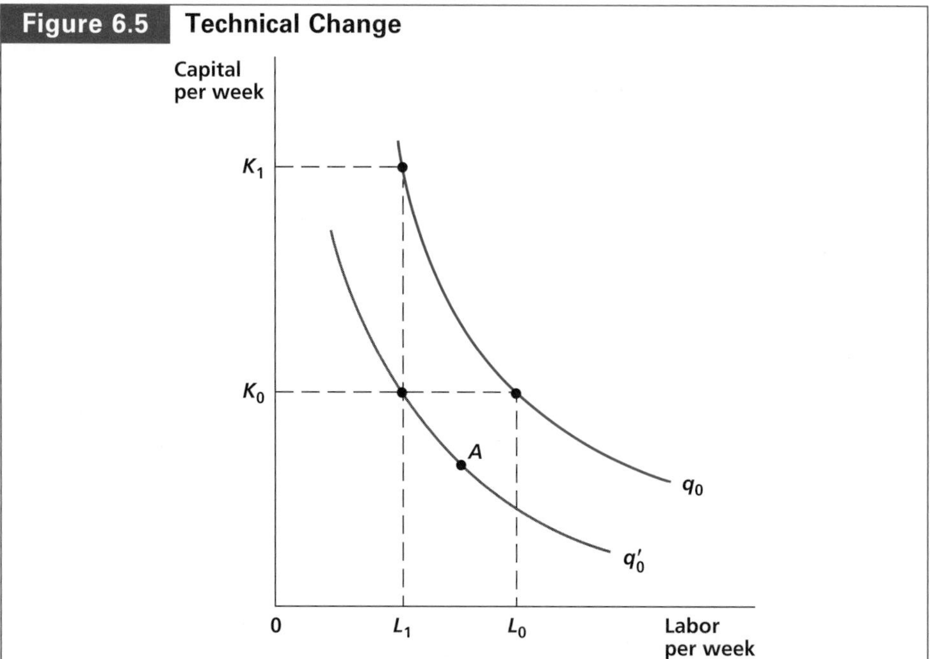

Technical progress shifts the q_0 isoquant to q_0'. Whereas previously it required K_0, L_0 to produce q_0 now, with the same amount of capital, only L_1 units of labor are required. This result can be contrasted to capital-labor substitution, in which the required labor input for q_0 also declines to L_1 and more capital (K_1) is used.

Technical Progress versus Input Substitution

We can use Figure 6.5 to show an important distinction between true technical advancement and simple capital-labor substitution. With technical progress, the firm can continue to use K_0, but it produces q_0 with less labor (L_1). The output per unit of labor input rises from q_0/L_0 to q_0/L_1. Even in the absence of technical improvements, the firm could have achieved such an increase by choosing to use K_1 units of capital. This substitution of capital for labor would also have caused the average productivity of labor to rise from q_0/L_0 to q_0/L_1. This rise would not mean any real improvement in the way goods are made, however. In studying productivity data, especially data on output per worker, we must be careful that the changes being observed represent true technical improvements rather than capital-for-labor substitution.

Multifactor Productivity

Measuring technical change correctly therefore requires that we pay attention to all inputs that enter into the production function. As Figure 6.5 makes it clear, to do this we need to know the form of the production function. Using that knowledge, here is how we might proceed. Suppose that we knew how much capital and labor a firm used in, say, 2005 and 2010. Denote these by $K^{05}, L^{05}, K^{10}, L^{10}$, and let f be the 2005 production function. Now, the change in output that would have been predicted by this production function is

$$\Delta q^{\text{predicted}} = f(K^{10}, L^{10}) - f(K^{05}, L^{05}). \tag{6.5}$$

If the actual change in output between 2005 and 2010 is given by $\Delta q^{\text{actual}} = q^{10} - q^{05}$, we can now define multifactor productivity change as follows:

$$\text{Technical change} = \Delta q^{\text{actual}} - \Delta q^{\text{predicted}}. \tag{6.6}$$

For example, suppose that actual output increased from 100 in 2005 to 120 in 2010, but that using actual input levels would have predicted an increase from 100 to only 110. Then we would say that multifactor productivity gain must have amounted to 10 extra units of output. Putting this on an annual, percentage basis, the figures would suggest that multifactor productivity increased at a rate of about 2 percent per year over this period.

In recent years, governmental statistical agencies have made significant progress in measuring such "multifactor" productivity, mainly because they have become better at measuring capital inputs in production. The results show that the distinction between labor productivity and multifactor productivity can be quite important. For example, between 1990 and 2010, output per hour in U.S. manufacturing rose at the impressive rate of nearly 4 percent per year,[6] whereas estimates of multifactor productivity put the gain at less than 2 percent per year. Similar differences have been found for most developed economies. The mathematics used in making such calculations for the Cobb-Douglas production function is described in Problem 6.10. Application 6.5: Finding the Computer Revolution shows how being careful about measuring productivity changes can help to illuminate the impact that the adoption of new technology is having on the economy.

---

[6]The severe economic downturn associated with the Great Recession of 2007–09 makes these productivity statistics somewhat difficult to interpret. Economic downturns can distort productivity figures because output and the utilization of capital fall reapidly at the start of a recession and rise rapidly once recovery begins. Measuring changes over a period as long as 20 years helps smooth out business-cycle fluctuations to some extent.

APPLICATION 6.5

Finding the Computer Revolution

Economists have intensively studied productivity trends during the past 50 years in an effort to identify factors that may have contributed to improvements. One of the major puzzles in this research is that productivity growth seems to have slowed down just as computers were coming into more widespread usage in the U.S. economy. Table 1 illustrates this paradox. From 1959 to 1973, average labor productivity increased at an annual rate of nearly 3 percent per year and total factor productivity growth was more than 1 percent per year. During the following two decades, however, both rates of productivity increase slowed dramatically. What is odd about this finding is that these two decades were characterized by the rapid introduction of computers into practically all areas of the economy. Presumably these actions should have increased productivity. The inability to detect any such effect caused famous growth theorist Robert Solow to quip that "you can see the computer age everywhere but in the productivity statistics."[1]

Finally, Computers Appear

After 1995, productivity performance in the U.S. economy improved dramatically, and this is where the effect of computers began to appear. As Table 1 shows, during 1995–2000, average labor productivity grew at 2.7 percent per year, and total factor productivity growth returned to its earlier levels. One major reason for this improvement is suggested by the final line in the table, which indicates the importance of total factor productivity gains in information technology producing industries (computers, telecommunications, and software). Before 1995, these industries contributed, at most, one-quarter of one percentage point to annual productivity growth. But that figure more than doubled after 1995. Two related factors seem to have accounted for the increase: (1) a rapid decline in the price of computer-related equipment, and (2) major investments in such equipment by the information technology industries. It was not until the late 1990s that such trends were large enough to appear in the overall statistics.

Will the Trend Continue?

Table 1 also suggests that the contribution of computer technology to productivity growth may have declined in the new century. There is considerable disagreement among economists about whether this decline is just a "blip" in a long-term uptrend or a significant sign that the productivity impact of computers in the workplace has largely ended. Of course, it would not be surprising if computer inputs eventually experienced diminishing returns in production. Whether major new technical improvements will reverse such declines is uncertain at this time.

TO THINK ABOUT

1. Exactly how does computer technology increase productivity? How would you show this with a production function?
2. Who experiences the gains in productivity growth spawned by computers? How would you measure such gains?

[1]In *The New York Times Book Review*, July 12, 1987, p. 36.

Table 1 U.S. Productivity Growth 1959–2006 (average annual rates)

	1959–1973	1973–1995	1995–2000	2000–2006
Average labor productivity	2.82	1.49	2.70	2.50
Total factor productivity	1.14	0.39	1.00	0.92
Total factor productivity from information technology	0.09	0.25	0.58	0.38

Source: Dale W. Jorgenson, Mun S. Ho, and Kevin J. Stiroh, "A Retrospective Look at the U.S. Productivity Growth Resurgence." *Journal of Economic Perspectives* (Winter 2008): 3–24.

Table 6.1 Hamburger Production Exhibits Constant Returns to Scale

GRILLS (K)	WORKERS (L)	HAMBURGERS PER HOUR
1	1	10
2	2	20
3	3	30
4	4	40
5	5	50
6	6	60
7	7	70
8	8	80
9	9	90
10	10	100

Source: Equation 6.7.

6-7 A Numerical Example of Production

Additional insights about the nature of production functions can be obtained by looking at a numerical example. Although this example is obviously unrealistic (and, we hope, a bit amusing), it does reflect the way production is studied in the real world.

The Production Function

Suppose we looked in detail at the production process used by the fast-food chain Hamburger Heaven (HH). The production function for each outlet in the chain is

$$\text{Hamburgers per hour} = q = 10\sqrt{KL}, \tag{6.7}$$

where K represents the number of grills used and L represents the number of workers employed during an hour of production. One aspect of this function is that it exhibits constant returns to scale.[7] Table 6.1 shows this fact by looking at input levels for K and L ranging from 1 to 10. As both workers and grills are increased together, hourly hamburger output rises proportionally. To increase the number of hamburgers it serves, HH must simply duplicate its kitchen technology over and over again.

Average and Marginal Productivities

To show labor productivity for HH, we must hold capital constant and vary only labor. Suppose that HH has four grills ($K = 4$, a particularly easy number of which to take a square root). In this case,

$$q = 10\sqrt{4 \cdot L} = 20\sqrt{L}, \tag{6.8}$$

providing a simple relationship between output and labor input. Table 6.2 shows this relationship. Notice two things about the table. First, output per worker declines as more hamburger flippers are employed. Because K is fixed, this occurs because the flippers get in each other's way as they become increasingly crowded around the four grills. Second, notice that the productivity of each additional worker hired also declines. Hiring more workers drags down output per worker because of the diminishing marginal productivity arising from the fixed number of grills. Even though HH's production exhibits constant returns to scale when both K and L can change, holding one input constant yields the expected declining average and marginal productivities.

The Isoquant Map

The overall production technology for HH is best illustrated by its isoquant map. Here, we show how to get one isoquant, but any others desired could be computed in exactly

[7]Because this production function can be written $q = 10K^{1/2}L^{1/2}$, it is a Cobb-Douglas function with constant returns to scale (since the exponents sum to 1.0). See Problem 6.7.

Table 6.2 Total Output, Average Productivity, and Marginal Productivity with Four Grills

GRILLS (K)	WORKERS (L)	HAMBURGERS PER HOUR (Q)	Q/L	MP_L
4	1	20.0	20.0	—
4	2	28.3	14.1	8.3
4	3	34.6	11.5	6.3
4	4	40.0	10.0	5.4
4	5	44.7	8.9	4.7
4	6	49.0	8.2	4.3
4	7	52.9	7.6	3.9
4	8	56.6	7.1	3.7
4	9	60.0	6.7	3.4
4	10	63.2	6.3	3.2

Source: Equation 6.7.

the same way. Suppose HH wants to produce 40 hamburgers per hour. Then its production function becomes

$$q = 40 \text{ hamburgers per hour} = 10\sqrt{KL} \quad \textbf{(6.9)}$$

or

$$4 = \sqrt{KL} \quad \textbf{(6.10)}$$

or

$$16 = K \cdot L. \quad \textbf{(6.11)}$$

Table 6.3 shows a few of the K, L combinations that satisfy this equation. Clearly, there are many ways to produce 40 hamburgers, ranging from using a lot of grills with workers dashing among them to using many workers gathered around a few grills. All possible combinations are reflected in the "$q = 40$" isoquant in Figure 6.6. Other isoquants would have exactly the same shape, showing that HH has many substitution possibilities in the ways it actually chooses to produce its heavenly burgers.

Table 6.3 Construction of the $q = 40$ Isoquant

HAMBURGERS PER HOUR (Q)	GRILLS (K)	WORKERS (L)
40	16.0	1
40	8.0	2
40	5.3	3
40	4.0	4
40	3.2	5
40	2.7	6
40	2.3	7
40	2.0	8
40	1.8	9
40	1.6	10

Source: Equation 6.11.

Rate of Technical Substitution

The RTS (of L for K) along the $q = 40$ isoquant can also be read directly from Table 6.3. For example, in moving from 3 to 4 workers, HH can reduce its grill needs from 5.3 to 4.0. Hence, the RTS here is given by

$$\text{RTS} = -\frac{\text{Change in } K}{\text{Change in } L} = -\frac{(4 - 5.3)}{(4 - 3)} = \frac{1.3}{1} = 1.3. \quad \textbf{(6.12)}$$

Figure 6.6 Technical Progress in Hamburger Production

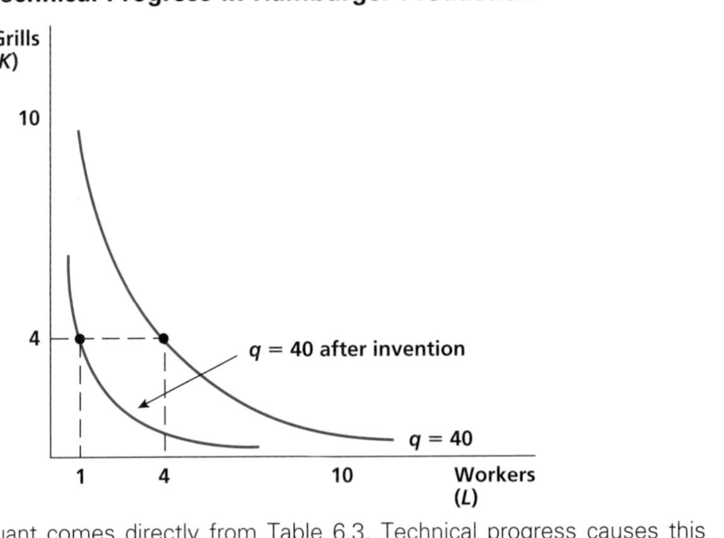

The $q = 40$ isoquant comes directly from Table 6.3. Technical progress causes this isoquant to shift inward. Previously it took four workers with four grills to produce 40 hamburgers per hour. With the invention, it takes only one worker working with four grills to achieve the same output.

This slope then tells the firm that it can reduce grill usage by 1.3 if it hires another worker and it might use such information in its hiring decisions. The calculation is quite different, however, if the firm already hires many workers to produce its 40 burgers. With eight workers, for example, hiring the ninth allows this firm to reduce grill usage by only 0.2 grills. As we shall see in the next chapter, this is a choice that the firm would make only if grills were much less expensive than workers.

KEEP *in* MIND

RTS Is a Slope

Students sometimes confuse the *slope* of an isoquant with the *amounts* of inputs being used. The reason we look at the RTS is to study the wisdom of *changing* input levels (while holding output constant). One way to keep a focus on this question is to always think about moving counterclockwise along an isoquant, adding one unit of labor input (shown on the horizontal axis) at a time. As we do this, the slope of the isoquant will change, and it is this changing rate of trade-off that is directly relevant to the firm's hiring decision.

Technical Progress

The possibility for scientific advancement in the art of hamburger production can also be shown in this simple case. Suppose that genetic engineering leads to the invention of self-flipping burgers so that the production function becomes

$$q = 20\sqrt{K \cdot L}. \tag{6.13}$$

We can compare this new technology to that which prevailed previously by recalculating the $q = 40$ isoquant:

$$q = 40 = 20\sqrt{KL} \tag{6.14}$$

or

$$2 = \sqrt{KL} \tag{6.15}$$

or

$$4 = KL. \tag{6.16}$$

The combinations of K and L that satisfy this equation are shown by the "$q = 40$ after invention" isoquant in Figure 6.6. One way to see the overall effect of the invention is to calculate output per worker-hour in these two cases. With four grills, Figure 6.6 shows that it took four workers using the old technology to produce 40 hamburgers per hour. Average productivity was 10 hamburgers per hour per worker. Now a single worker can produce 40 hamburgers per hour because each burger flips itself. Average productivity is 40 hamburgers per hour per worker. This level of output per worker hour could have been attained using the old technology, but that would have required 16 grills and would have been considerably more costly.

MICRO QUIZ 6.4

Consider the following historical changes in labor productivity. Which of these were "technical progress"? Which were primarily substitution of capital for labor? If the case seems ambiguous, explain why.

1. The increase in coal output per worker when open-pit mining began
2. The increase in auto output per worker with the introduction of the assembly line
3. The increase in electricity output per worker with larger power stations
4. The increase in computer-power output per worker with the availability of better microchips

SUMMARY

Chapter 6 shows how economists conceptualize the process of production. We introduce the notion of a production function, which records the relationship between input use and output, and we show how this function can be illustrated with an isoquant map. Several features of the production function are analyzed in the chapter:

- The marginal product of any input is the extra output that can be produced by adding one more unit of that input while holding all other inputs constant. The marginal product of an input declines as more of that input is used.
- The possible input combinations that a firm might use to produce a given level of output are shown on an isoquant. The (negative of the) slope of the isoquant is called the rate of technical substitution (RTS)—it shows how one input can be substituted for another while holding output constant.
- "Returns to scale" refers to the way in which a firm's output responds to proportionate increases in all inputs. If a doubling of all inputs causes output to more than double, there are increasing returns to scale. If such a doubling of inputs causes output to less than double, returns to scale are decreasing. The middle case, when output exactly doubles, reflects constant returns to scale.
- In some cases, it may not be possible for the firm to substitute one input for another. In these cases, the inputs must be used in fixed proportions. Such production functions have L-shaped isoquants.
- Technical progress shifts the firm's entire isoquant map. A given output level can be produced with fewer inputs.

REVIEW QUESTIONS

1. Provide a brief description of the production function for each of the following firms. What is the firm's output? What inputs does it use? Can you think of any special features of the way production takes place in the firm?
    a. An Iowa wheat farm
    b. An Arizona vegetable farm
    c. U.S. Steel Corporation
    d. A local arc-welding firm
    e. Sears

f. Joe's Hot Dog Stand
g. The Metropolitan Opera
h. The Metropolitan Museum of Art
i. The National Institutes of Health
j. Dr. Smith's private practice
k. Paul's lemonade stand

2. In what ways are firms' isoquant maps and individuals' indifference curve maps based on the same idea? What are the most important ways in which these concepts differ?

3. Roy Dingbat is the manager of a hot dog stand that uses only labor and capital to produce hot dogs. The firm usually produces 1,000 hot dogs a day with five workers and four grills. One day a worker is absent but the stand still produces 1,000 hot dogs. What does this imply about the 1,000 hot dog isoquant? Why do Roy's management skills justify his name?

4. A 2011 news headline read, "Stalled Recovery Hits Productivity." Assuming that the "productivity" referred to in this headline is the customary "average output per worker hour" that is usually reported, how would you evaluate whether this decrease really is a decrease in workers' marginal products?

5. Marjorie Cplus wrote the following answer on her micro examination: "Virtually every production function exhibits diminishing returns to scale because my professor said that all inputs have diminishing marginal productivities. So when all inputs are doubled, output must be less than double." How would you grade Marjorie's answer?

6. Answer question 5 using two specific production functions as examples:
a. A fixed-proportions production function
b. A Cobb-Douglas production function of the form

$$q = \sqrt{K \cdot L}.$$

(See Problems 6.4, 6.7, and 6.8 for a discussion of this case.)

7. Universal Gizmo (UG) operates a large number of plants that produce gizmos using a special technology. Each plant produces exactly 100 gizmos per day using 5 gizmo presses and 15 workers. Explain why the production function for the entire UG firm exhibits constant returns to scale.

8. Continuing the prior question, suppose that Universal Gizmo devises a new plant design that uses 15 gizmo presses and 5 workers also to produce 100 gizmos per day. How would you construct an isoquant for the firm for 100,000 gizmos per day based on the following assumptions:
a. The firm uses plants only of the type specified in question 7.
b. The firm uses plants only of its new type.
c. The firm uses 500 plants of the type in question 7 and 500 plants of the new type.

What do you conclude about the ability of UG to substitute workers for gizmo presses in its production?

9. Can a fixed-proportions production function exhibit increasing or decreasing returns to scale? What would its isoquant map look like in each case?

10. Capital and labor are used in fixed proportions to produce an airline flight. It takes two workers (pilots) and one plane to produce a trip. Safety concerns require that every plane has two pilots.
a. Describe the isoquant map for the production of air trips.
b. Suppose an airline rented 10 planes and hired 30 pilots. Explain both graphically and in words why this would be a foolish thing to do.
c. Suppose technical progress in avionic equipment made it possible for a single pilot to handle a plane safely. How would this shift the isoquant map described in part a? How would this affect the average productivity of labor in this industry? How would this affect the average productivity of capital (planes) in this industry?

PROBLEMS

6.1. Imagine that the production function for tuna cans is given by

$$q = 6K + 4L,$$

where
q = Output of tuna cans per hour
K = Capital input per hour
L = Labor input per hour

a. Assuming capital is fixed at $K = 6$, how much L is required to produce 60 tuna cans per hour? To produce 100 per hour?
b. Now assume that capital input is fixed at $K = 8$; what L is required to produce 60 tuna cans per hour? To produce 100 per hour?

c. Graph the $q = 60$ and $q = 100$ isoquants. Indicate the points found in part a and part b. What is the RTS along the isoquants?

6.2. Frisbees are produced according to the production function

$$q = 2K + L,$$

where

q = Output of Frisbees per hour
K = Capital input per hour
L = Labor input per hour

a. If $K = 10$, how much L is needed to produce 100 Frisbees per hour?
b. If $K = 25$, how much L is needed to produce 100 Frisbees per hour?
c. Graph the $q = 100$ isoquant. Indicate the points on that isoquant defined in part a and part b. What is the RTS along this isoquant? Explain why the RTS is the same at every point on the isoquant.
d. Graph the $q = 50$ and $q = 200$ isoquants for this production function also. Describe the shape of the entire isoquant map.
e. Suppose technical progress resulted in the production function for Frisbees becoming

$$q = 3K + 1.5L.$$

Answer part a through part d for this new production function and discuss how it compares to the previous case.

6.3. Digging clams by hand in Sunset Bay requires only labor input. The total number of clams obtained per hour (q) is given by

$$q = 100\sqrt{L},$$

where L is labor input per hour.

a. Graph the relationship between q and L.
b. What is the average productivity of labor (out put per unit of labor input) in Sunset Bay? Graph this relationship and show that output per unit of labor input diminishes for increases in labor input.
c. The marginal productivity of labor in Sunset Bay is given by

$$MP_L = \frac{50}{\sqrt{L}}.$$

Graph this relationship and show that labor's marginal productivity is less than average productivity for all values of L. Explain why this is so.

6.4. Suppose that the hourly output of chili at a barbecue (q, measured in pounds) is characterized by

$$q = 20\sqrt{KL},$$

where K is the number of large pots used each hour and L is the number of worker hours employed.

a. Graph the $q = 2{,}000$ pounds per hour isoquant.
b. The point $K = 100$, $L = 100$ is one point on the $q = 2{,}000$ isoquant. What value of K corresponds to $L = 101$ on that isoquant? What is the approximate value for the RTS at $K = 100$, $L = 100$?
c. The point $K = 25$, $L = 400$ also lies on the $q = 2{,}000$ isoquant. If $L = 401$, what must K be for this input combination to lie on the $q = 2{,}000$ isoquant? What is the approximate value of the RTS at $K = 25$, $L = 400$?
d. For this production function, the RTS is

$$\text{RTS} = K/L.$$

Compare the results from applying this formula to those you calculated in part b and part c. To convince yourself further, perform a similar calculation for the point $K = 200$, $L = 50$.
e. If technical progress shifted the production function to

$$q = 40\sqrt{KL},$$

all of the input combinations identified earlier can now produce $q = 4{,}000$ pounds per hour. Would the various values calculated for the RTS be changed as a result of this technical progress, assuming now that the RTS is measured along the $q = 4{,}000$ isoquant?

6.5. Grapes must be harvested by hand. This production function is characterized by fixed proportions—each worker must have one pair of stem clippers to produce any output. A skilled worker with clippers can harvest 50 pounds of grapes per hour.

a. Sketch the grape production isoquants for $q = 500$, $q = 1{,}000$, and $q = 1{,}500$ and indicate where on these isoquants firms are likely to operate.
b. Suppose a vineyard owner currently has 20 clippers. If the owner wishes to utilize fully these clippers, how many workers should be hired? What should grape output be?
c. Do you think the choices described in part b are necessarily profit-maximizing? Why might the owner hire fewer workers than indicated in this part?
d. Ambidextrous harvesters can use two clippers—one in each hand—to produce 75 pounds of grapes per hour. Draw an isoquant map (for $q = 500$, 1,000, and 1,500) for ambidextrous harvesters. Describe in general terms the considerations that would enter into an owner's decision to hire such harvesters.

6.6. Power Goat Lawn Company uses two sizes of mowers to cut lawns. The smaller mowers have a 22-inch deck. The larger ones combine two of the 22-inch decks in a single mower. For each size of mower, Power Goat has a different production function, given by the rows of the following table.

	OUTPUT PER HOUR (SQUARE FEET)	CAPITAL INPUT (NO. OF 22″ DECKS)	LABOR INPUT
Small mowers	5,000	1	1
Large mowers	8,000	2	1

a. Graph the $q = 40{,}000$ square feet isoquant for the first production function. How much K and L would be used if these factors were combined without waste?
b. Answer part a for the second function.
c. How much K and L would be used without waste if half of the 40,000-square-foot lawn were cut by the method of the first production function and half by the method of the second? How much K and L would be used if one-fourth of the lawn were cut by the first method and three-fourths by the second? What does it mean to speak of fractions of K and L?
d. In Application 6.3, we showed how firms might use engineering data on production techniques to construct isoquants. How would you draw the $q = 40{,}000$ isoquant for this lawn mowing company? How would you draw the isoquant for some other level of output (say $q = 80{,}000$)?

6.7. The production function

$$q = AK^aL^b,$$

(where $A, a, b \geq 0$) is called a Cobb-Douglas production function. This function is widely used in economic research. Using the function, show the following:
a. The production function in Equation 6.7 is a special case of the Cobb-Douglas.
b. If $a + b = 1$, a doubling of K and L will double q.
c. If $a + b < 1$, a doubling of K and L will less than double q.
d. If $a + b > 1$, a doubling of K and L will more than double q.
e. Using the results from part b through part d, what can you say about the returns to scale exhibited by the Cobb-Douglas function?

6.8. For the Cobb-Douglas production function in Problem 6.7, it can be shown (using calculus) that

$$MP_K = aAK^{a-1}L^b$$
$$MP_L = bAK^aL^{b-1}.$$

If the Cobb-Douglas exhibits constant returns to scale ($a + b = 1$), show that
a. Both marginal productivities are diminishing.
b. The RTS for this function is given by

$$\text{RTS} = \frac{bK}{aL}.$$

c. The function exhibits a diminishing RTS.

6.9. The production function for puffed rice is given by

$$q = 100\sqrt{KL},$$

where q is the number of boxes produced per hour, K is the number of puffing guns used each hour, and L is the number of workers hired each hour.
a. Calculate the $q = 1{,}000$ isoquant for this production function and show it on a graph.
b. If $K = 10$, how many workers are required to produce $q = 1{,}000$? What is the average productivity of puffed-rice workers?
c. Suppose technical progress shifts the production function to $q = 200\sqrt{KL}$. Answer parts a and b for this new situation.
d. Suppose technical progress proceeds continuously at a rate of 5 percent per year. Now the production function is given by

$$q = (1.05)^t 100\sqrt{KL},$$

where t is the number of years that have elapsed into the future. Now answer parts a and b for this production function.
(Note: Your answers should include terms in $(1.05)^t$. Explain the meaning of these terms.)

6.10. One way economists measure total factor productivity is to use a Cobb-Douglas production function of the form $q = A(t)K^aL^{1-a}$, where $A(t)$ is a term representing technical change and a is a positive fraction representing the relative importance of capital input.
a. Describe why this production function exhibits constant returns to scale (see Problem 6.7)
b. Taking natural logarithms of this production function yields

$$\ln q = \ln A(t) + a \ln K + (1-a) \ln L.$$

One useful property of natural logarithms is that the change in the natural logarithm of some variable X is approximately equal to the percentage change in X itself. Explain how this would allow you to calculate annual changes in the technical change factor from knowledge of changes in q, K, and L and of the parameter a.
c. Use the results from part b to calculate an expression for the annual change in labor productivity (q/L) as a function of changes in $A(t)$ and in the capital-labor ratio (K/L). Under what conditions would changes in labor productivity be a good measure of changes in total factor productivity? When would the two measures differ greatly?

7 Costs

Production costs are a crucial determinant of firms' supply decisions. There might be tremendous demand for an advanced robot that cooks, cleans, and does other household chores, but if is exorbitantly expensive to produce, then none may end up being supplied, or at best only a few to rich technology enthusiasts. In this chapter, we will develop some ways of thinking about costs that will help in explaining such decisions. We begin by showing how any firm will choose the inputs it uses to produce a given level of output as cheaply as possible. We then proceed to use this information on input choices to derive the complete relationship between how much a firm produces and what that output costs. Possible reasons why this relationship might change are also examined. By the end of this chapter, you should have a good understanding of all the factors that go into determining the cost structure of any firm. These concepts are central to the study of supply and will be useful throughout the remainder of this book.

7-1 Basic Cost Concepts

Most readers will be at least somewhat familiar with the notion of costs, drawing on their everyday experience answering questions such as "How much will the planned beach vacation cost me?" "How much will I spend to obtain a college degree?" The idea is to add up the expenditures on all the necessary inputs—among other things lodging, airfare, and meals for the vacation; tuition, room, board, and books for the college degree—and the total is the cost. This chapter mostly deals with costs in relation to production by firms, but the basic ideas are similar, so the familiarity should be a virtue in getting the concepts in this chapter across. That said, there are some identifiable cases in which the way people typically think about costs diverges from how economists say one ought to think about them. Roughly speaking, the typical person thinks about costs as accountants, not economists, do. It is worth spending a little time up front learning how to think more like economists and less like accountants.

Economic versus Accounting Costs

Economic costs are all costs that are relevant for an economic decision under consideration. This definition seems tautological, but further parsing of the words will show it is not. First, economic costs include only "relevant" costs. The firm may have receipts for inputs purchased long ago, but what was spent back then may not be relevant for decisions going forward. Rather than keeping track of a whole list of **sunk costs** that cannot be recovered no matter what decisions the firm goes on to make, it is easier to ignore any such sunk costs by excluding them from economic costs. Second, economic costs include "all" the relevant costs. What is meant here is that economic costs include not only those that are easy to measure because the firm has receipts for them, but also those that are more difficult to measure because they are only implicit. Even if no cash was paid for an input, it could have

Economic costs
All costs relevant to an economic decision

Sunk cost
Expenditure that once made cannot be recovered.

been used by the firm for some other purpose or could have been rented or sold to some other firm. Whether the firm buys an input it needs or forgoes selling an input it already has, either way these are **opportunity costs** of using the input in production.

Opportunity cost
Amount inputs used one way would be worth in their best alternative uses.

Accounting costs
Recorded amount paid for inputs.

Accounting costs stress what was actually paid for inputs, even if those amounts were paid long ago. Accounting costs have the advantage of being easier to measure than economic costs. All that is needed is the drawer full of receipts and a calculator to add them up. One does not have to imagine how much an input that was not actually sold might have been sold for. The disadvantage is they may not provide exactly what the firm's manager needs to know to make the right production decision (or what decision maker needs to know to make the right economic decision in more general contexts). An economist would rather have the right cost information even if this is difficult to measure precisely.

The best way to see the difference between the cost concepts is with an example. Suppose you are deciding whether to take a week-long vacation at a beach house that has been in your family for generations. The house is usually rented out, but from time to time you use it for yourself. An accountant might add the cost of your airfare, say \$500, other miscellaneous expenses, say another \$500, and conclude the cost of the vacation is \$1,000. Importantly, the accountant does not include lodging expenses in the total because you got the house for free and do not have to pay anyone to use it for the week. Allowing a dollar value to be put on your benefit from the vacation, using the accounting view of costs would lead you to the rule that any benefit greater than \$1,000 and you would take the vacation and not if the benefit is less than \$1,000.

An economist would disagree with this rule. Although you do not have to pay anyone to use your own house, using the house yourself means you cannot rent it out to someone else. This lost rent is an opportunity cost that has to be considered as part of the total economic cost of the vacation. If the house typically rents for \$1,000, then the total economic cost of the vacation would be \$2,000 not \$1,000. This higher cost leads to a higher threshold on the benefit needed for the vacation to be a good idea. If the dollar value on your benefit is say \$1,500, then since this is less than economic costs, you would be better off not taking the vacation and enjoying the proceeds from renting the house.

Instead of inheriting the house, suppose you bought it some years ago. This would give an accountant an explicit transaction on which to base a cost measure. One possibility is to take the purchase price and divide over some number of years according to a **depreciation schedule**. Then the week's lodging cost could be measured as some fraction of the purchase price. This is a standard method to derive an accounting cost for a house or other long-lived asset. The trouble with this measure of cost is it still may not match the true opportunity cost of using the house rather than renting it out. For example, the house may have been purchased before a subsequent hurricane hit, ruining the beach, reducing house prices and rents. What you forgo when you use the house yourself, rather than renting is the current rent in the area, not some fraction of high pre-hurricane prices that no one would pay now. If house prices and rents fall, accounting costs based on historical expenditures will end up overstating economic costs.[1]

Depreciation schedule
A formula for dividing the up-front payment for a durable asset across periods. The formula can range from the simple (equal installments) to the complicated (matching the rate at which the asset wears out or minimizing tax liability).

[1]In defense of accountants, accounting costs must have their uses—how else to explain the emergence of the whole accounting profession? Return to the case in which you inherited your house but suppose that instead of a vacation, the trip is for business purposes, reimbursed by your employer. If your employer allowed you to submit claims for economic rather than accounting costs, you might have an incentive to overstate the rental rate on your house, \$1,500 rather than \$1,000. Because no explicit rent is paid that week, it would be hard to disprove that you couldn't have rented it out for the higher amount. Your employer could see what you rented the house for in other weeks, but you could always argue that that particular week happens to be the peak of the season, which generates higher rents. Your employer could ask you to quote rents for comparable houses that week, but you could slip in quotes for nicer properties. Reimbursing accounting costs avoids problems of estimating costs for transactions that are not actually observed, avoiding fraud, a key point of accounting systems.

Economic versus Opportunity Costs

Although we have thrown around a lot of different cost concepts, it should be starting to be clear how they differ from each other. This is true except perhaps for the difference between economic and opportunity costs. Are opportunity costs the only ones relevant for economic decisions? If not, what other costs are relevant?

If inputs are sold on competitive markets, as we will assume throughout most of this book, then economic costs and opportunity costs are the same thing. The market price of the input is what is relevant to the economic decision marker (the input buyer). The market price is the opportunity cost of the input because the input seller could always turn around and sell to a different buyer around that price. Assuming competitive input markets, the relationship among cost concepts can be crystallized as follows:

economic costs = opportunity costs = market values
accounting costs = explicit payments = historical values.

When are the concepts of economic costs and opportunity costs different? A wedge can be driven between them if the input market is not competitive. The market price for the input is an economic cost for the input buyer but may be above the input seller's opportunity cost. For example, a couple who wants to celebrate their 25th wedding anniversary in the same beach house where they spent their honeymoon may be willing to pay much more than the market rent to stay there for the week. If the realtor gets wind of the special occasion, he or she may ask the couple to pay $2,000 rather than $1,000, what typical vacationers would be willing to pay. Then $2,000 represents the economic cost to the couple, $1,000 represents the realtor's opportunity cost of renting to them rather than some other vacationer, and the difference, $1,000, is the markup over the competitive price.

Taxes and license fees can also drive a wedge between economic and opportunity costs. For example, the fee for a liquor license is nearly $30,000 in New York State. This would be an economic cost for anyone wanting to open a restaurant in the state serving alcohol. The opportunity cost of the license to the state may be close to zero because there is no limit to the number of licenses it can choose to issue. (If the state expects more vandalism or other damage to the "fabric of society" caused by overindulging restaurant patrons, this might be counted as an opportunity cost to the state, but such costs may be overblown.) In a sense, the license is an essential input into restaurant operation that the state can sell for a nearly $30,000 markup over what a piece of paper with some writing on it would sell for on a competitive market.

To get a better sense of the meaning of the different cost concepts, let's see how they play out for three specific inputs that a productive firm needs to produce outputs: labor, capital, and the services of entrepreneurs (owners).

Labor Costs

Economists and accountants view labor costs in much the same way. To the accountant, firms' spending on wages and salaries is a current expense and therefore is a cost of production. Economists regard wage payments as an *explicit cost*: labor services (worker-hours) are purchased at some hourly **wage rate** (which we denote by w), and we presume that this rate is the amount that workers would earn in their next best alternative employment. If a firm hires a worker at, say, $20 per hour, this figure probably represents about what the worker would earn elsewhere. Therefore, the $20 per hour is an economic cost to the firm and the opportunity cost of the worker's time. Of course, there are cases in the real world where a worker's wage does not fairly reflect economic or opportunity costs. The wages of the dunderhead son of the boss exceed his

Wage rate (w)
The cost of hiring one worker for one hour.

opportunity cost because no one else would be willing to pay him very much; or, prisoners who are paid $.50/hour to make license plates probably could earn much more were they out of jail. Noticing such differences between wages paid and workers' opportunity costs can provide an interesting start to an economic investigation; but, for now, it seems most useful to begin with the presumption that the market wage equals economic cost and opportunity cost, so there is no discrepancy among any of the cost concepts.

Capital Costs

In the case of capital services (machine-hours), accounting and economic definitions of costs differ greatly. Accountants, in calculating capital costs, use the historical price of a particular machine and apply a depreciation rule to determine how much of that machine's original price to charge to current costs. For example, a machine purchased for $1,000 and expected to last 10 years might be said to "cost" $100 per year, in the accountant's view. Economists, on the other hand, regard the amount paid for a machine as a sunk cost. Once such a cost has been incurred, there is no way to get it back. Because sunk costs do not reflect forgone opportunities, economists instead focus on the *implicit cost* of a machine as being what someone else would be willing to pay to use it. Thus, the cost of one machine-hour is the **rental rate** for that machine in the best alternative use. By continuing to employ the machine, the firm is implicitly forgoing the rent someone else would be willing to pay for its use. We use v to denote this rental rate for one machine-hour. This is the rate that the firm must pay for the use of the machine for one hour, regardless of whether the firm owns the machine and implicitly rents it from itself or if it rents the machine from someone else such as Hertz Rent-a-Car. In Chapter 14, we examine the determinants of capital rental rates in more detail. For now, Application 7.1: Stranded Costs and Deregulation looks at a current controversy over costs that has important implications for people's electric and phone bills.

Rental rate (v)
The cost of hiring one machine for one hour.

Entrepreneurial Costs

The owner of a firm is entitled to whatever is left from the firm's revenues after all costs have been paid. To an accountant, all of this excess would be called "profits" (or "losses" if costs exceed revenues). Economists, however, ask whether owners (or entrepreneurs) also encounter opportunity costs by being engaged in a particular business. If so, their entrepreneurial services should be considered an input to the firm, and economic costs should be imputed to that input. For example, suppose a highly skilled computer programmer starts a software firm with the idea of keeping any (accounting) profits that might be generated. The programmer's time is clearly an input to the firm, and a cost should be imputed to it. Perhaps the wage that the programmer might command if he or she worked for someone else could be used for that purpose. Hence, some part of the accounting profits generated by the firm would be categorized as entrepreneurial costs by economists. Residual economic profits would be smaller than accounting profits. They might even be negative if the programmer's opportunity costs exceeded the accounting profits being earned by the business.

MICRO QUIZ 7.1

Young homeowners often get bad advice that confuses accounting and economic costs. What is the fallacy in each of the following pieces of advice? Can you alter the advice so that it makes sense?

1. Owning is always better than renting. Rent payments are just money down a "rat hole"—making house payments as an owner means that you are accumulating a real asset.
2. One should pay off a mortgage as soon as possible. Being able to close out your mortgage and burn the papers is one of the great economic joys of your life!

APPLICATION 7.1

Stranded Costs and Deregulation

For many years, the electric power, natural gas, and telecommunications industries in the United States were heavily regulated. The prices for electricity or phone service were set by public regulatory commissions in such a way as to allow each firm a "fair" return on its investment. This regulatory structure began to crumble after 1980 as both states and the federal government began to introduce competition into the pricing of electricity, natural gas, and long-distance telephone service. Declining prices for all of these goods raised panic among many tradition-bound utilities. The resulting debate over "stranded costs" will continue to plague consumers of all of these goods for many years to come.

The Nature of Stranded Costs

The fundamental problem for the regulated firms is that some of their production facilities became "uneconomic" with deregulation because their average costs exceeded the lower prices for their outputs in newly deregulated markets. In electricity production, that was especially true for nuclear power plants and for generating facilities that use alternative energy sources such as solar or wind power. For long-distance telephone calls, introduction of high-capacity fiber-optic cables meant that older cables and some satellite systems were no longer viable. The historical costs of these facilities had therefore been "stranded" by deregulation, and the utilities believed that their "regulatory contracts" had promised them the ability to recover these costs, primarily through surcharges on consumers.

From an economist's perspective, of course, this plea rings a bit hollow. The historical costs of electricity-generating plants, natural gas transmission pipelines, or telephone cables are sunk costs. The fact that these facilities are currently uneconomic to operate implies that their market values are zero because no buyer would pay anything for them. Such a decline in the value of productive equipment is common in many industries—machinery for making slide rules, 78 rpm recordings, or high-button shoes is also worthless now (though sometimes collected as an antique). But no one suggests that the owners of this equipment should be compensated for these losses. Indeed, the economic historian Joseph Schumpeter coined the term "creative destruction" to refer to this dynamic hallmark of the capitalist system. Why should regulated firms be any different?

Socking It to the Consumer

The utility industry argues that its regulated status does indeed make it different. Because regulators promised them a "fair" return on their investments, they argue, the firms have the right to some sort of compensation for the impact of deregulation. This argument has had a major impact in some instances. In California, for example, electric utilities were awarded more than $28 billion in compensation for their stranded costs—a figure that will eventually show up on every electricity customer's bill. Natural gas customers have had to pay similar charges as they attempt to bypass local delivery systems to buy lower-priced gas. And everyone has become familiar with the bewildering array of special charges and taxes on their telephone bills, all with the intention of cross-subsidizing formerly regulated firms.

The Future of Deregulation

Allowing firms to charge customers for their stranded costs has reduced the move toward deregulation in many markets because paying such costs reduces the incentives that consumers have to use alternative suppliers. Other factors slowing deregulation include the following: (1) the Enron scandal in 2001, which gave electricity deregulation a bad name; (2) special interests have pushed the Federal Communications Commission to adopt a number of measures to protect incumbent firms; and (3) the financial crisis of 2008 has been (perhaps incorrectly) blamed on banking deregulation, so some re-regulation is likely.

TO THINK ABOUT

1. Many regulated firms believe that they had an "implicit contract" with state regulators to ensure a fair return on their investments. What kind of incentives would such a contract provide to the firms in their decisions about what types of equipment to buy?
2. How would the possibility that equipment may become obsolete be handled in unregulated markets? That is, how could this possibility be reflected in an unregulated firm's economic costs?

Just as what the entrepreneur could earn working somewhere else is an economic cost that needs to be weighed in the decision to start a new firm, what a student could earn working rather than going to school is an economic cost that needs to be weighed in the decision to go to college, as discussed right in Chapter 1 of the text, in Application 1.2: Is It Worth Your Time to Be Here? This application is well worth reading again because it contains many insights about the measurement of economic costs in a setting quite familiar to students.

The Two-Input Case

We will make two simplifying assumptions about the costs of inputs a firm uses. First, we can assume, as before, that there are only two inputs: labor (L, measured in labor-hours) and capital (K, measured in machine-hours). Entrepreneurial services are assumed to be included in capital input. That is, we assume that the primary opportunity costs faced by a firm's owner are those associated with the capital the owner provides.

A second assumption we make is that inputs are hired in perfectly competitive markets. Firms can buy (or sell) all the labor or capital services they want at the prevailing rental rates (w and v). In graphic terms, the supply curve for these resources that the firm faces is horizontal at the prevailing input prices.

Economic Profits and Cost Minimization

Given these simplifying assumptions, total costs for the firm during a period are

$$\text{Total costs} = TC = wL + vK, \tag{7.1}$$

where, as before, L and K represent input usage during the period. If the firm sells one product on a competitive market, its total revenues are given by the price of its product (P) times its total output [$q = f(K, L)$, where $f(K, L)$ is the firm's production function]. **Economic profits** (π) are then the difference between total revenues and total economic costs:

Economic profits (π)
The difference between a firm's total revenues and its total economic costs.

$$\begin{aligned}\pi &= \text{Total revenues} - \text{Total costs} = pq - wL - vK \\ &= Pf(K, L) - wL - vK.\end{aligned} \tag{7.2}$$

Equation 7.2 makes the important point that the economic profits obtained by a firm depend only on the amount of capital and labor it hires. If, as we assume in many places in this book, the firm seeks maximum profits, we might study its behavior by examining how it chooses K and L. This would, in turn, lead to a theory of the "derived demand" for capital and labor inputs—a topic we explore in detail in Chapter 13.

Here, however, we wish to develop a theory of costs that is somewhat more general and might apply to firms in markets that may not be perfectly competitive (monopolies or oligopolies) or firms whose objectives are not necessarily to maximize profits (as with a charitable organization supplying a social service). To do that, we begin our study of costs by finessing a discussion of output choice for the moment. That is, we assume that for some reason the firm has decided to produce a particular output level (say, q_1). If this happens to be a competitive firm, its revenues would be fixed at Pq_1. Now we want to show how the firm might choose to produce q_1 at minimal costs. Because revenues are fixed, minimizing costs will make profits as large as possible for this particular level of output. The details of how a firm chooses its actual level of output are taken up in the next chapter.

7-2 Cost-Minimizing Input Choice

To minimize the cost of producing q_1, a firm should choose that point on the q_1 isoquant that has the lowest cost. That is, it should explore all feasible input combinations to find the cheapest one. This will require the firm to choose that input combination for which the marginal rate of technical substitution (RTS) of L for K is equal to the ratio of the inputs' costs, w/v. To see why this is so intuitively, let's ask what would happen if a firm chose an input combination for which this were not true. Suppose the firm is producing output level q_1 using $K = 10$, $L = 10$, and the RTS is 2 at this point. Assume also that $w = \$1$, $v = \$1$, and hence that $w/v = 1$, which is unequal to the RTS of 2. At this input combination, the cost of producing q_1 is \$20, which is not the minimal input cost. Output q_1 can also be produced using $K = 8$ and $L = 11$; the firm can give up 2 units of K and keep output constant at q_1 by adding 1 unit of L. At this input combination, the cost of producing q_1 is only \$19. So, the original input combination of $K = 10$, $L = 10$ was not the cheapest way to make q_1. A similar result would hold any time the RTS and the ratio of the input costs differ. Therefore, we have shown that to minimize total cost, the firm should produce where the RTS is equal to the ratio of the prices of the 2 inputs. Now, let's look at the proof in more detail.

Graphic Presentation

This cost-minimization principle is demonstrated graphically in Figure 7.1. The isoquant q_1 shows all the combinations of K and L that are needed to produce q_1. We wish to find the least costly point on this isoquant. Equation 7.1 shows that those combinations of K and L that keep total costs constant lie along a straight line with slope $-w/v$.[2] Consequently, all lines of equal total cost can be shown in Figure 7.1 as a series of parallel straight lines with slopes $-w/v$. Three lines of equal total cost are shown in Figure 7.1: $TC_1 < TC_2 < TC_3$.

Figure 7.1 Minimizing the Costs of Producing q_1

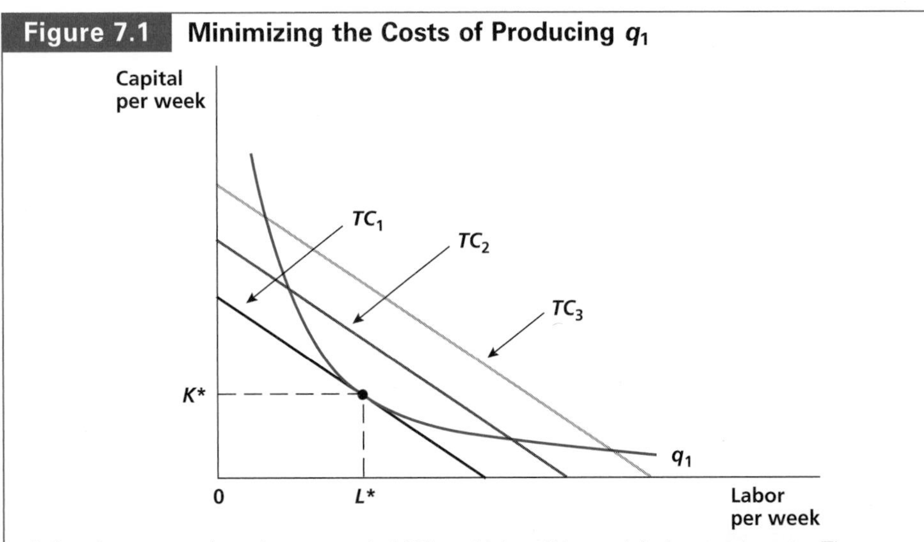

A firm is assumed to choose capital (K) and labor (L) to minimize total costs. The condition for this minimization is that the rate at which L can be substituted for K (while keeping $q = q_1$) should be equal to the rate at which these inputs can be traded in the market. In other words, the RTS (of L for K) should be set equal to the price ratio w/v. This tangency is shown here in that costs are minimized at TC_1 by choosing inputs K^* and L^*.

[2]For example, if $TC = \$100$, Equation 7.1 would read $100 = wL + vK$. Solving for K gives $K = -w/vL + 100/v$. Hence, the slope of this total cost line is $-w/v$, and the intercept is $100/v$ (which is the amount of capital that can be purchased with \$100).

It is clear from the figure that the minimum total cost for producing q_1 is given by TC_1 where the total cost curve is just tangent to the isoquant. The cost-minimizing input combination is L^*, K^*.

You should notice the similarity between this result and the conditions for utility maximization that we developed in Part 2. In both cases, the conditions for an optimum require that decision makers focus on relative prices from the market. These prices provide a precise measure of how one good or productive input can be traded for another through market transactions. To maximize utility or minimize costs, decision makers must adjust their choices until their own trade-off rates are brought into line with those being objectively quoted by the market. In this way, the market conveys information to all participants about the relative scarcity of goods or productive inputs and encourages them to use them appropriately. In later chapters (especially Chapter 10), we will see how this informational property of prices provides a powerful force in directing the overall allocation of resources.

An Alternative Interpretation

Another way of looking at the result pictured in Figure 7.1 may provide more intuition about the cost-minimization process. In Chapter 6, we showed that the absolute value of the slope of an isoquant (the RTS) is equal to the ratio of the two inputs' marginal productivities:

$$\text{RTS}(L \text{ for } K) = \frac{MP_L}{MP_K}. \tag{7.3}$$

The cost-minimization procedure shown in Figure 7.1 requires that this ratio also equal the ratio of the inputs' prices:

$$\text{RTS}(L \text{ for } K) = \frac{MP_L}{MP_K} = \frac{w}{v}. \tag{7.4}$$

Some minor manipulation of this equation yields

$$\frac{MP_L}{w} = \frac{MP_K}{v}. \tag{7.5}$$

This condition for cost minimization says that the firm should employ its inputs so that, at the margin, it gets the same "bang for the buck" from each kind of input hired. For example, consider the owner of an orange grove. If MP_L is 20 crates of oranges per hour and the wage is \$10 per hour, the owner is getting two crates of oranges for each dollar he or she spends on labor input. If tree-shaking machinery would provide a better return on dollars spent, the firm would not be minimizing costs. Suppose that MP_K is 300 crates per hour from hiring another tree shaker and that these wondrous machines rent for \$100 per hour. Then each dollar spent on machinery yields three crates of oranges and the firm could reduce its costs by using fewer workers and more machinery. Only if Equation 7.5 holds will each input provide the same marginal output per dollar spent, and only then will costs be truly minimized. Application 7.2: Is Social Responsibility Costly? looks at some situations where firms may depart from cost-minimizing input choices.

Suppose a firm faces a wage rate of 10 and a capital rental rate of 4. In the following two situations, how much of each input should this firm hire to minimize the cost of producing an output of 100 units? What are the firm's total costs? How would the firm's total costs change if capital rental rates rose to 10?

1. The firm produces with a fixed-proportions production function that requires 0.1 labor hours and 0.2 machine hours for each unit of output.
2. The firm's production function is given by $Q = 10L + 5K$.

APPLICATION 7.2

Is Social Responsibility Costly?

In recent years, there have been increasing calls for firms to behave in a "socially responsible" manner with respect to their hiring, marketing, and environmental activities. The claim is that firms should go beyond simply obeying the law—they should be willing to incur additional costs to achieve a wide variety of desirable social goals. One way of conceptualizing such actions is illustrated in Figure 1. Here, the socially responsible firm opts to produce q_0 using input combination *A*, which differs from the cost-minimizing combination B both because it uses "too many" inputs (compare *A* and *C*) and because it uses them in the wrong proportions (compare *C* and *B*). Whether this actually happens has been a subject of several empirical studies.

Figure 1 Possible Extra Costs of Corporate Social Responsibility

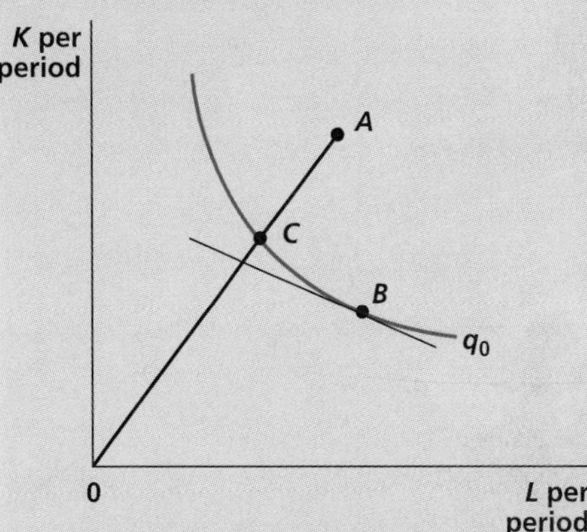

A firm pursuing socially responsible goals might opt to produce q_0 using input combination *A*. This would involve more of both inputs than necessary (compare *A* to *C*) and use of an input combination that was not cost minimizing (compare *C* to *B*).

Waste Minimization in the United Kingdom

Chapple, Paul, and Harris[1] examine voluntary decisions by firms in the United Kingdom to attempt to minimize the environmental wastes they generate from their production. Overall, the authors find that waste reduction activities are costly, primarily because achieving them requires firms to alter their input mixes. Specifically, firms' chief method for reducing waste is to use more thoroughly processed and costly types of material inputs. They may also use more labor input but whether that happens seems to depend on the nature of the industry being examined. In some cases, the use of more refined material inputs may reduce the need for labor (and capital, too), whereas in other cases, using such inputs may require more special equipment and the labor force to operate it.

The Community Reinvestment Act

The Community Reinvestment Act (CRA) of 1977 requires banking institutions to meet certain targets in lending to low- and moderate-income neighborhoods. Banks can voluntarily exceed these targets if they wish, and some observers believe that doing so is a socially responsible thing to do. A 2006 study by Vitaliano and Stella[2] finds that savings and loan institutions that achieve an "outstanding" score on CRA criteria incur about $6.5 million per year in added costs relative to institutions with a "satisfactory" rating. Although the authors' data do not permit them to make a precise statement about the source of these extra costs, they mention the possibility that the particular loans mandated under the CRA may require more labor input to originate and may require closer monitoring during their existence. Interestingly, however, the authors do not find that institutions with higher CRA scores are less profitable, so the higher costs may be balanced by some gains in revenues as well.

TO THINK ABOUT

1. Explain how different types of social responsibility policies might cause firms to opt for input choices such as *A* or *C* in Figure 1.
2. Would a firm that followed socially responsible policies be violating its duty to its shareholders? Under what conditions might this be the case? When might it not be the case?

[1]Wendy Chapple, Catherine Paul, and Richard Harris, "Manufacturing and corporate responsibility: cost implications of voluntary waste minimisation," *Structural Change and Economic Dynamics* 16 (2005): 347–373.

[2]Donald F. Vitaliano and Gregory P. Stella, "The Cost of Corporate Social Responsibility: the case of the Community Reinvestment Act," *Journal of Productivity Analysis.* 26 (2006): 235–244.

Figure 7.2 Firm's Expansion Path

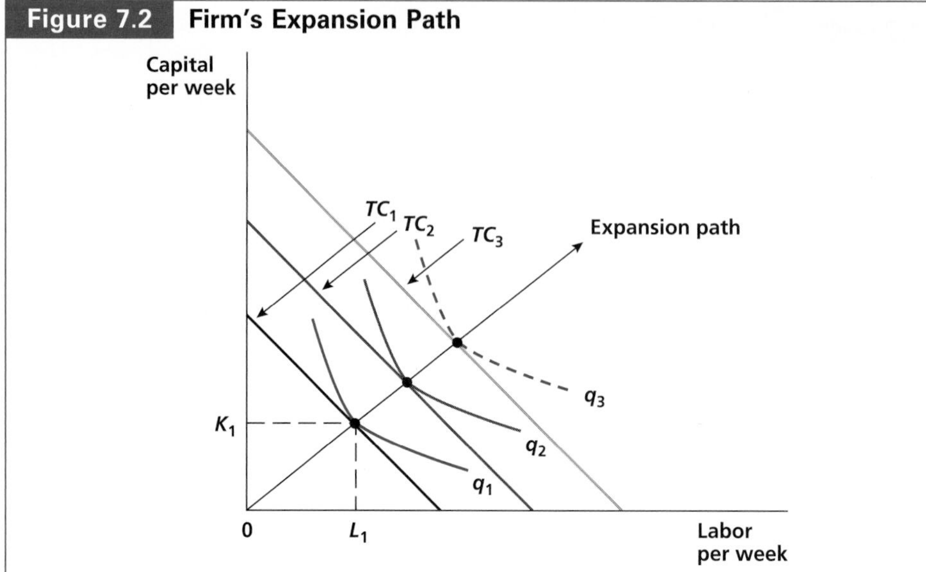

The firm's expansion path is the locus of cost-minimizing tangencies. On the assumption of fixed input prices, the curve shows how input use increases as output increases.

The Firm's Expansion Path

Expansion path The set of cost-minimizing input combinations a firm will choose to produce various levels of output (when the prices of inputs are held constant).

Any firm can perform an analysis such as the one we just performed for every level of output. For each possible output level (q), it would find that input combination that minimizes the cost of producing it. If input prices (w and v) remain constant for all amounts the firm chooses to use, we can easily trace out this set of cost-minimizing choices, as shown in Figure 7.2. This ray records the cost-minimizing tangencies for successively higher levels of output. For example, the minimum cost for producing output level q_1 is given by TC_1, and inputs K_1 and L_1 are used. Other tangencies in the figure can be interpreted in a similar way. The set of all of these tangencies is called the firm's **expansion path** because it records how input use expands as output expands while holding the per-unit prices of the inputs constant. The expansion path need not necessarily be a straight line. The use of some inputs may increase faster than others as output expands. Which inputs expand more rapidly will depend on the precise nature of production.

7-3 Cost Curves

The firm's expansion path shows how minimum-cost input use increases when the level of output expands. The path allows us to develop the relationship between output levels and total input costs. Cost curves that reflect this relationship are fundamental to the theory of supply. Figure 7.3 illustrates four possible shapes for this cost relationship. Panel a reflects a situation of constant returns to scale. In this case, as Figure 6.3 showed, output and required input use are proportional to one another. A doubling of output requires a doubling of inputs. Because input prices do not change, the relationship between output and total input costs is also directly proportional—the

Figure 7.3 Possible Shapes of the Total Cost Curve

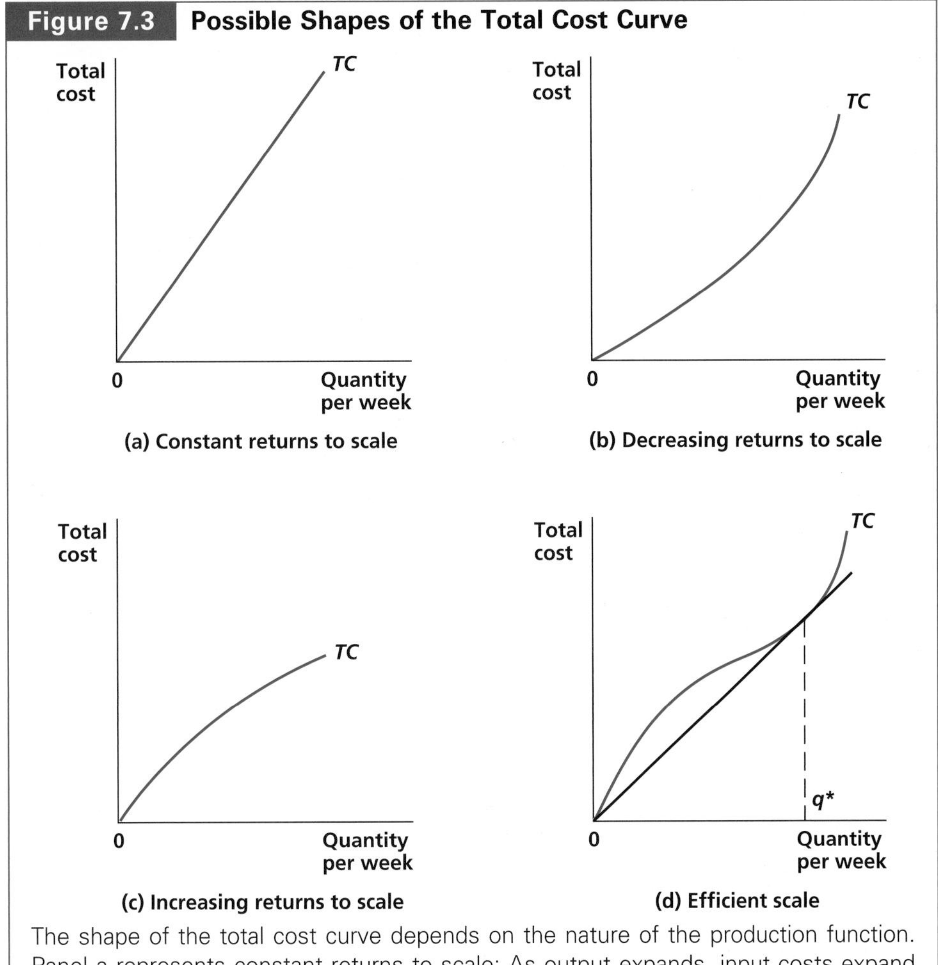

The shape of the total cost curve depends on the nature of the production function. Panel a represents constant returns to scale: As output expands, input costs expand proportionately. Panel b and panel c show decreasing returns to scale and increasing returns to scale, respectively. Panel d represents costs where the firm has an "efficient scale" of operations.

total cost curve is simply a straight line that passes through the origin (since no inputs are required if $q = 0$).[3]

Panel b and panel c in Figure 7.3 reflect the cases of decreasing returns to scale and increasing returns to scale, respectively. With decreasing returns to scale, successively larger quantities of inputs are required to increase output and input costs rise rapidly as output expands. This possibility is shown by the convex total cost curve in panel b.[4] In this case, costs expand more rapidly than output. With increasing returns to scale, on the other hand, successive input requirements decline as output expands. In that case,

[3]A technical property of constant returns to scale production functions is that the RTS depends only on the ratio of K to L, not on the scale of production. For given input prices, the expansion path is a straight line, and cost-minimizing inputs expand proportionally along with output. For an illustration, see the numerical example at the end of this chapter.

[4]One way to remember how to use the terms "convex" and "concave" is to note that the curve in Figure 7.3(c) resembles (part of) a cave entrance and is therefore "concave."

the total cost curve is concave, as shown in panel c. In this case, considerable cost advantages result from large-scale operations.

Finally, panel d in Figure 7.3 demonstrates a situation in which the firm experiences ranges of both increasing and decreasing returns to scale. This situation might arise if the firm's production process required a certain "efficient" level of internal coordination and control by its managers. For low levels of output, this control structure is underutilized and expansion in output is easily accomplished. At these levels, the firm would experience increasing returns to scale—the total cost curve is concave in its initial section. As output expands, however, the firm must add additional workers and capital equipment, which perhaps need entirely separate buildings or other production facilities. The coordination and control of this larger-scale organization may be successively more difficult, and diminishing returns to scale may set in. The convex section of the total cost curve in panel d reflects that possibility.

The four possibilities in Figure 7.3 illustrate the most common types of relationships between a firm's output and its input costs. This cost information can also be depicted on a per-unit-of-output basis. Although this depiction adds no new details to the information already shown in the total cost curves, per-unit curves will be quite useful when we analyze the supply decision in the next chapter.

Average and Marginal Costs

Average cost
Total cost divided by output; a common measure of cost per unit.

Two per-unit-of-output cost concepts are average and marginal costs. **Average cost** (AC) measures total costs per unit. Mathematically,

$$\text{Average Cost} = AC = \frac{TC}{q}. \tag{7.6}$$

This is the per-unit-of-cost concept with which people are most familiar. If a firm has total costs of \$100 in producing 25 units of output, it is natural to consider the cost per unit to be \$4. Equation 7.6 reflects this common averaging process.

For economists, however, average cost is not the most meaningful cost-per-unit figure. In Chapter 1, we introduced Marshall's analysis of demand and supply. In his model of price determination, Marshall focused on the cost of the last unit produced because it is that cost that influences the supply decision for that unit. To reflect this notion of incremental cost, economists use the concept of **marginal cost** (MC). By definition, then,

Marginal cost
The additional cost of producing one more unit of output.

$$\text{Marginal Cost} = MC = \frac{\text{Change in } TC}{\text{Change in } q}. \tag{7.7}$$

That is, as output expands, total costs increase, and the marginal cost concept measures this increase only *at the margin*. For example, if producing 24 units costs the firm \$98 but producing 25 units costs it \$100, the marginal cost of the 25th unit is \$2: To produce that unit, the firm incurs an increase in cost of only \$2. This example shows that the average cost of a good (\$4) and its marginal cost (\$2) may be quite different. This possibility has a number of important implications for pricing and overall resource allocation.

Marginal Cost Curves

Figure 7.4 compares average and marginal costs for the four total cost relationships shown in Figure 7.3. As our definition makes clear, marginal costs are reflected by the slope of the total cost curve since (as discussed in Appendix to Chapter 1) the slope of any curve shows how the variable on the vertical axis (here, total cost) changes for a unit

Figure 7.4 Average and Marginal Cost Curves

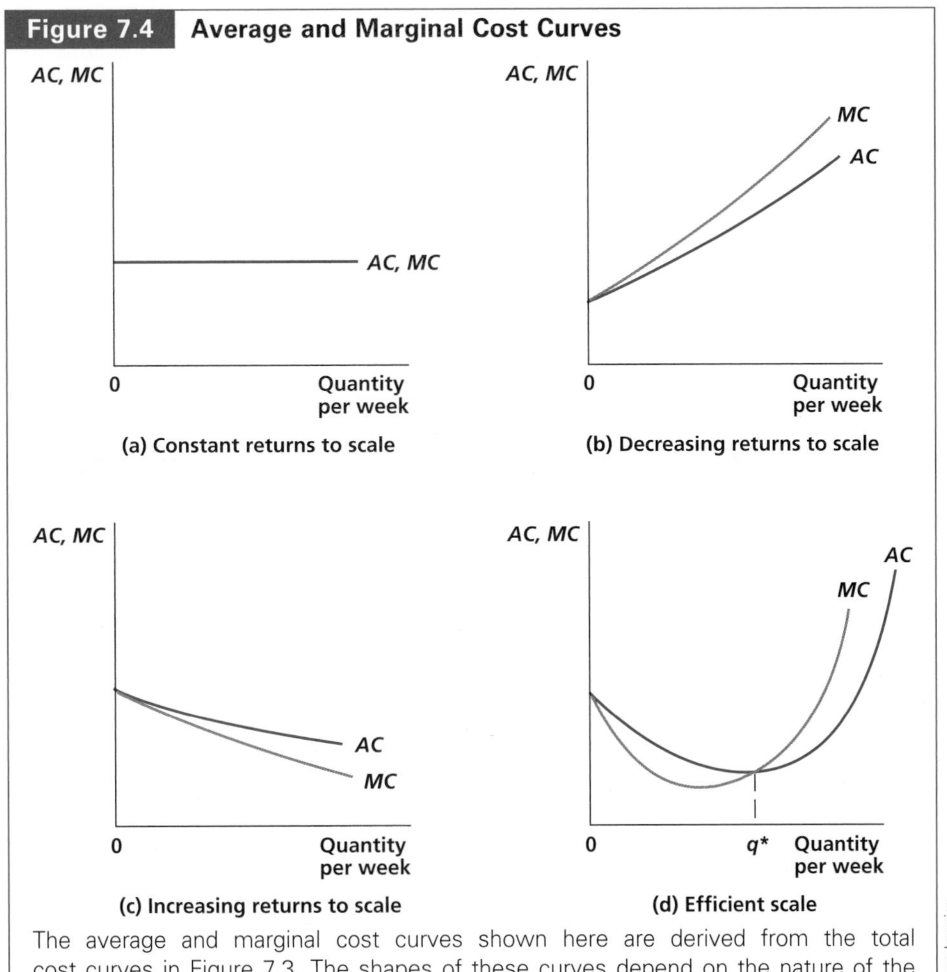

The average and marginal cost curves shown here are derived from the total cost curves in Figure 7.3. The shapes of these curves depend on the nature of the production function.

change in the variable on the horizontal axis (here, quantity).[5] In panel a of Figure 7.3, the total cost curve is a straight line—it has the same slope throughout. In this case, marginal cost (*MC*) is constant. No matter how much is produced, it will always cost the same to produce *one more unit.* The horizontal *MC* curve in panel a of Figure 7.4 reflects this fact.

In the case of decreasing returns to scale (panel b in Figure 7.3), marginal costs are increasing. The total cost curve becomes steeper as output expands, so, at the margin, the cost of one more unit is becoming greater. The *MC* curve in panel b in Figure 7.4 is positively sloped, reflecting these increasing marginal costs.

For the case of increasing returns to scale (panel c in Figure 7.3), this situation is reversed. Because the total cost curve becomes flatter as output expands, marginal costs fall. The marginal cost curve in panel c in Figure 7.4 has a negative slope.

Finally, the case of first concave, then convex, total costs (panel d in Figure 7.3) yields a U-shaped marginal cost curve in panel d in Figure 7.4. Initially, marginal costs fall because the coordination and control mechanism of the firm is being utilized more

[5]If total costs are given by $TC(q)$, then mathematically marginal cost is given by the derivative function $MC(q) = dTC/dq$.

efficiently. Decreasing returns eventually appear, however, and the marginal cost curve turns upward. The *MC* curve in panel d in Figure 7.4 reflects the general idea that there is some optimal level of operation for the firm—if production is pushed too far, very high marginal costs will be the result. We can make this idea of optimal scale more precise by looking at average costs.

Average Cost Curves

Developing average cost (*AC*) curves for each of the cases in Figure 7.4 is also relatively simple. The average and marginal cost concepts are identical for the very first unit produced. If the firm produced only one unit, both average and marginal cost would be the cost of that one unit. Graphing the *AC* relationship begins at the point where the marginal cost curve intersects the vertical axis. For panel a in Figure 7.4, marginal cost never varies from its initial level. It always costs the same amount to produce one more unit, and *AC* must also reflect this amount. If it always costs a firm $4 to produce one more unit, both average and marginal costs are $4. Both the *AC* and the *MC* curves are the same horizontal line in panel a in Figure 7.4.

In the case of decreasing returns to scale, rising marginal costs also result in rising average costs. Because the last unit produced is becoming more and more costly as output expands, the overall average of such costs must be rising. Because the first few units are produced at low marginal costs, however, the overall average will always lag behind the high marginal cost of the last unit produced. In panel b in Figure 7.4, the *AC* curve is upward sloping, but it is always below the *MC* curve.

In the case of increasing returns to scale, the opposite situation prevails. Falling marginal costs cause average costs to fall as output expands, but the overall average also reflects the high marginal costs involved in producing the first few units. As a consequence, the *AC* curve in panel c in Figure 7.4 is negatively sloped and always lies above the *MC* curve. Falling average cost in this case is, as we shall see in Chapter 11, a principal force leading to the creation of monopoly power for firms with such increasing-returns-to-scale technologies.

The case of a U-shaped marginal cost curve represents a combination of the two preceding situations. Initially, falling marginal costs cause average costs to decline also. For low levels of output, the configuration of average and marginal cost curves in panel d in Figure 7.4 resembles that in panel c. Once the marginal costs turn up, however, the situation begins to change. As long as marginal cost is below average cost, average cost will continue to decline because the last unit produced is still less expensive than the prior average. When $MC < AC$, producing one more unit pulls *AC* down. Once the rising segment of the marginal cost curve cuts the average cost curve from below, however, average costs begin to rise. Beyond point q^* in panel d in Figure 7.4, *MC* exceeds *AC*. The situation now resembles that in panel b, and *AC* must rise. Average costs are being pulled up by the high cost of producing one more unit. Because *AC* is falling to the left of q^* and rising to the right of q^*, average costs of production are lowest at q^*. In this sense, q^* represents an "efficient scale" for a firm whose costs are represented in panel d in Figure 7.4. Later chapters show that this output level plays an important role in the theory of price determination. Application 7.3: Findings on Firms' Average Costs looks at how average cost curves can be used to determine which industries might find large-scale firms more appropriate.

MICRO QUIZ 7.3

Suppose that there are to be 10 quizzes in your economics course. You have scored 80 on every one of the first 5 quizzes.

1. What will happen to your average for the course if your grade falls to 60 on each of the next 2 quizzes?
2. What will you have to score on the final 3 quizzes in the course to get your average back to 80?
3. Explain how this example illustrates the relationship between average and marginal costs studied in this section.

APPLICATION 7.3

Findings on Firms' Average Costs

Most studies of firms' long-run costs have found that average-cost curves have a modified *L*-shape, such as the one shown in Figure 1. Average costs tend to decline as larger output levels are examined until some minimum efficient scale, q^*, is reached. Above that output, average costs tend to flatten out as larger scales of output are about equally efficient. Knowing about such cost patterns can often go a long way in explaining how industries evolve over time.

Some Empirical Evidence

Table 1 reports the results of representative studies of long-run average-cost curves for a variety of industries. Entries in the table represent the long-run average cost for a firm of a particular size (small, medium, or large) as a percentage of the minimal average-cost firm in the industry. For example, the data for hospitals indicate that small hospitals have average costs that are about 29.6 percent greater than average costs for large ones. This cost disadvantage of small hospitals can go a long way toward explaining the decline in rural hospitals in the United States in recent years. The large hospitals in the study appear to be large enough to exhaust available efficiencies.

Diseconomies of Scale

The only industry in Table 1 that appears to suffer cost disadvantages of large-scale operations is trucking. Higher costs for large trucking firms may arise because they are more likely to be unionized or because it is harder to monitor many drivers' activities. In order to control their costs, many large trucking firms (especially package delivery firms like UPS or Federal Express) have adopted a number of efficiency-enhancing incentives for their drivers.

Table 1 Long-Run Average-Cost Estimates

INDUSTRY	FIRM SIZE SMALL	MEDIUM	LARGE
Aluminum	167	131	100
Automobiles	145	123	100
Electric power	113	101	102
Farms	134	111	100
Hospitals	130	111	100
Trucking	100	102	106

Sources: Aluminum: J. C. Clark and M. C. Fleming, "Advanced Materials and the Economy," *Scientific American* (October 1986): 51–56. Automobiles: M. A. Fuss and L. Waverman, *Costs and Productivity Differences in Automobile Production* (Cambridge, UK: Cambridge University Press, 1992). Electric power: L. H. Christensen and W. H. Greene, "Economics of Scale in U.S. Power Generation," *Journal of Political Economy* (August 1976): 655–676. Farms: C. J. M. Paul and R. Nehring, "Product Diversification, Production Systems and Economic Performance in U.S. Agricultural Production," *Journal of Econometrics* (June 2005): 525–548. Hospitals: T. W. Granneman, R. S. Brown, and M. V. Pauly, "Estimating Hospital Costs," *Journal of Health Economics* (March 1986): 107–127; Trucking: R. Koenka, "Optimal Scale and the Size Distribution of American Trucking Firms," *Journal of Transport Economics and Policy* (January 1977): 54–67.

Figure 1 Long-Run Average-Cost Curve Found in Many Empirical Studies

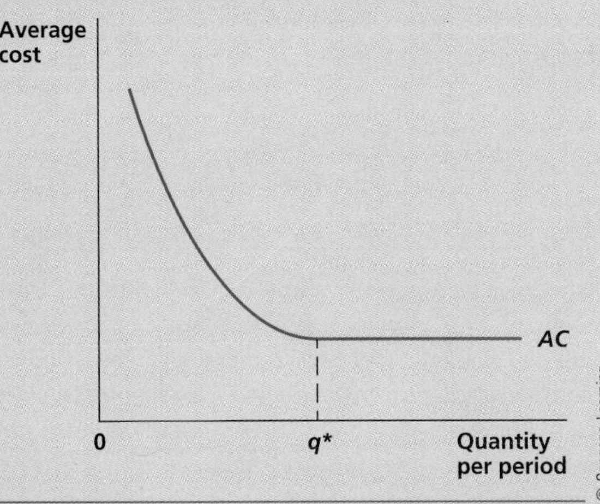

TO THINK ABOUT

1. Is the minimum efficient scale for an industry constant over time? Choose one industry from the table and speculate on how technology may increase or decrease the minimum efficient scale in the future.
2. If small farms are inefficient, why haven't these disappeared? Could the localvore movement or the lure of the traditional farming lifestyle provide explanations?

Economies of Scale

Diseconomies of scale
Average cost rises as output increases.

Economies of scale
Average cost falls as output increases.

To avoid putting off the layperson with talk of slopes and averages, economists have developed some simple terms for the pattern of per-unit cost curves shown in Figure 7.4. A rising *AC* curve as in panel b is referred to as revealing **diseconomies of scale**. In this case, expanding output entails higher average costs. The opposite case—falling *AC* as in panel c—is referred to as revealing **economies of scale**. In this case, expanding output entails lower average costs. Panel d shows the case in which the firm has economies of scale up to output q^* and diseconomies of scale above this level.

You may be forgiven for being initially confused between this new set of concepts and the set of returns to scale concepts (whether constant, decreasing, or increasing) introduced in the previous chapter and used throughout this one. Let's sort things out. The sets of concepts refer to different functions. Returns to scale refers to a property of the *production* function, namely how production scales up as all inputs are scaled up in the same proportion. Economies of scale refers to a property of the *cost* function, namely whether *AC* rises or falls as more output is produced. The additional output may be produced by increasing inputs proportionately but not necessarily. The minimization process underlying the cost function (which underlies *AC*) may involve changing proportions, perhaps adding capital faster than labor.

Fortunately, the sets of concepts are related, and this is why we were able to label Figure 7.4 the way we did. If the production function exhibits constant returns to scale everywhere, *AC* will be flat as in panel a, showing neither economies nor diseconomies of scale. If the production function exhibits decreasing returns to scale everywhere, *AC* slopes up as in panel b, showing diseconomies of scale. If the production function exhibits increasing returns to scale everywhere, *AC* slopes down as in panel c, showing positive economies of scale. It takes some work to see these relationships. In retrospect, that was what much of the discussion over the last several pages was devoted to, arguing informally why these relationships should hold. (If you want formal proofs, you should think about applying to graduate school!)

Production functions can exhibit a mixture of returns to scale, increasing in some places and decreasing in others. Mixed returns to scale can result in a variety of shapes for *AC*, including any of the panels in Figure 7.4. For certain production functions, keeping track of what sort of returns to scale hold for which input combinations can become quite complex, yet identifying whether there are diseconomies or economies of scale remains the simple matter of seeing whether *AC* slopes up or down.

7-4 Distinction between the Short Run and the Long Run

Short run
The period of time in which a firm must consider some inputs to be fixed in making its decisions.

Long run
The period of time in which a firm may consider all of its inputs to be variable in making its decisions.

Economists sometimes wish to distinguish between the **short run** and the **long run** for firms. These terms denote the length of time over which a firm may make decisions. This distinction is useful for studying market responses to changed conditions. For example, if only the short run is considered, a firm may need to treat some of its inputs as fixed because it may be technically impossible to change those inputs on short notice. If a time interval of only one week is involved, the size of a Honda assembly plant would have to be treated as fixed. Similarly, an entrepreneur who is committed to an Internet start-up firm would find it impossible (or extremely costly) to change jobs quickly—in the short run, the entrepreneur's input to his or her firm is essentially fixed. Over the long run, however, neither of those inputs needs to be considered fixed because Honda's factory size can be changed and the entrepreneur can indeed quit the business.

Holding Capital Input Constant

Probably the easiest way to introduce the distinction between the short run and the long run into the analysis of a firm's costs is to assume that one of the inputs is held constant in the short run. Specifically, we assume that capital input is held constant at a level of K_1 and that (in the short run) the firm is free to vary only its labor input. For example, a trucking firm with a fixed number of trucks and loading facilities can still hire and fire workers to change its output. We already studied this possibility in Chapter 6, when we examined the marginal productivity of labor. Here, we are interested in analyzing how changes in a firm's output level in the short run are related to changes in total costs. We can then contrast this relationship to the cost relationships studied earlier, in which both inputs could be changed. We will see that the diminishing marginal productivity that results from the fixed nature of capital input causes costs to rise rapidly as output expands.

Of course, any firm obviously uses far more than two inputs in its production process. The level of some of these inputs may be changed on rather short notice. Firms may ask workers to work overtime, hire part-time replacements from an employment agency, or rent equipment (such as power tools or automobiles) from some other firm. Other types of inputs may take somewhat longer to be adjusted; for example, to hire new, full-time workers is a relatively time-consuming (and costly) process, and ordering new machines designed to unique specifications may involve a considerable time lag. Still, most of the important insights from making the short-run/long-run distinction can be obtained from the simple two-input model by holding capital input constant.

Types of Short-Run Costs

Because capital input is held fixed in the short run, the costs associated with that input are also fixed. That is, the amount of capital costs that the firm incurs is the same no matter how much the firm produces—it must pay the rent on its fixed number of machines even if it chooses to produce nothing. Such **fixed costs** play an important role in determining the firm's profitability in the short run, but (as we shall see) they play no role in determining how firms will react to changing prices because they must pay the same amount in capital costs no matter what they do.[6]

Fixed costs
Costs associated with inputs that are fixed in the short run.

Short-run costs associated with inputs that can be changed (labor in our simple case) are called **variable costs.** The amount of these costs obviously will change as the firm changes its labor input so as to bring about changes in output. For example, although a Honda assembly plant may be of fixed size in the short run (and the rental costs of the plant are the same no matter how many cars are made), the firm can still vary the number of cars produced by varying the number of workers employed. By adding a third shift, for example, the firm may be able to expand output significantly. Costs involved in paying these extra workers would be variable costs.

Variable costs
Costs associated with inputs that can be varied in the short run.

[6]The astute reader may wonder why these fixed costs are included in short-run costs at all. Aren't they sunk and thus irrelevant for economic decisions in the short run? The answer is that we are adopting the perspective of the point in time when the firm invests in the fixed capital. At that point, for example, the extra cost of a larger Honda assembly plant will be an important factor in the decision whether to build that or a smaller plant. Therefore, it is correct to consider the cost of the plant an economic cost. It is also correct to say the cost of the plant is fixed—fixed with respect to the economic conditions that will materialize after the plant is built. Honda cannot predict exactly how much it will want to produce under these conditions, and so the plant it builds may end up being too big or too small. If these conditions persist, Honda will eventually be able to adjust the size of the plant to suit them in the long run.

There is a good reason for adopting the perspective of the construction of the plant (or more generally investment in the fixed cost). This is the only perspective allowing an "apples to apples" comparison of the firm's costs when it is not allowed to adjust some inputs to suit economic conditions (short-run costs) to those when it is allowed to adjust inputs freely (long-run costs).

Input Inflexibility and Cost Minimization

The total costs that firms experience in the short run may not be the lowest possible for some output levels. Because we are holding capital fixed in the short run, the firm does not have the flexibility in input choice that was assumed when we discussed cost minimization and the related (long-run) cost curves earlier in this chapter. Rather, to vary its output level in the short run, the firm will be forced to use "nonoptimal" input combinations.

This is shown in Figure 7.5. In the short run, the firm can use only K_1 units of capital. To produce output level q_0, it must use L_0 units of labor, L_1 units of labor to produce q_1, and L_2 units to produce q_2. The total costs of these input combinations are given by STC_0, STC_1, and STC_2, respectively. Only for the input combination K_1, L_1 is output being produced at minimal cost. Only at that point is the RTS equal to the ratio of the input prices. From Figure 7.5, it is clear that q_0 is being produced with "too much" capital in this short-run situation. Cost minimization should suggest a southeasterly movement along the q_0 isoquant, indicating a substitution of labor for capital in production. On the other hand, q_2 is being produced with "too little" capital, and costs could be reduced by substituting capital for labor. Neither of these substitutions is possible in the short run. However, over the long run, the firm will be able to change its level of capital input and will adjust its input usage to the cost-minimizing combinations.

Figure 7.5 **"Nonoptimal" Input Choices Must Be Made in the Short Run**

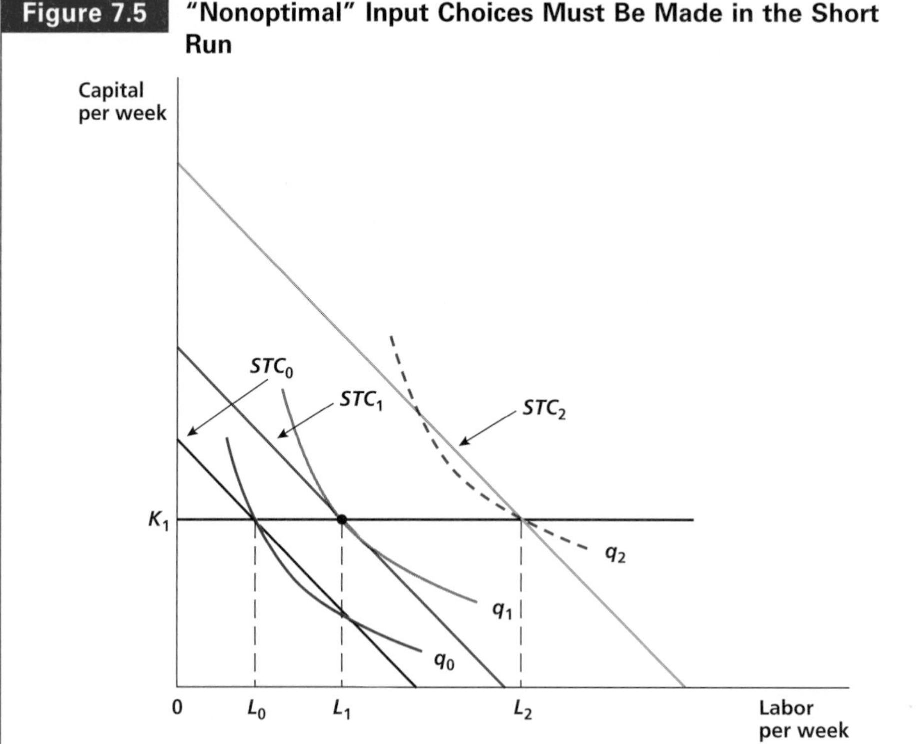

Because capital input is fixed at K_1 in the short run, the firm cannot bring its RTS into equality with the ratio of input prices. Given the input prices, q_0 should be produced with more labor and less capital than it will be in the short run, whereas q_2 should be produced with more capital and less labor than it will be.

7-5 Per-Unit Short-Run Cost Curves

The relationship between output and short-run total costs shown in Figure 7.5 can be used in a way similar to what we did earlier in this chapter to define a number of per-unit notions of short-run costs. Specifically, short-run average cost can be defined as the ratio of short-run total cost to output. Similarly, short-run marginal cost is the change in short-run total cost for a one-unit increase in output. Because we do not use the short-run/long-run distinction extensively in this book, it is unnecessary to pursue the construction of all of these cost curves in detail. Rather, our earlier discussion of the relationship between the shapes of total cost curves and their related per-unit curves will usually suffice.

One particular set of short-run cost curves is especially instructive, however. Figure 7.6 shows the case of a firm with a U-shaped (long-run) average cost curve. For this firm, long-run average costs reach a minimum at output level q^*, and, as we have noted in several places, at this output level, $MC = AC$. Also associated with q^* is a certain level of capital usage, K^*. What we wish to do now is to examine the short-run average and marginal cost curves (denoted by SAC and SMC, respectively) based on this level of capital input. We now look at the costs of a firm whose level of capital input is fixed at K^* to see how costs vary in the short run as output departs from its optimal level of q^*.

Our discussion about the total cost curves in Figure 7.5 shows that when the firm's short-run decision causes it to use the cost-minimizing amount of capital input, short-run and long-run total costs are equal. Average costs then are equal also. At q^*, AC is equal to SAC. This means that at q^*, MC and SMC are also equal, since both of the average cost curves are at their lowest points. At q^* in Figure 7.6, the following equality holds:

$$AC = MC = SAC(K^*) = SMC(K^*). \tag{7.8}$$

For increases in q above q^*, short-run costs are greater than long-run costs. These higher per-unit costs reflect the firm's inflexibility in the short run because some inputs are fixed. This inflexibility has important consequences for firms' short-run supply responses and for price changes in the short run. In Application 7.4: Congestion Costs, we look at some cases where short-run costs rise rapidly as output increases.

Figure 7.6 Short-Run and Long-Run Average and Marginal Cost Curves at Optimal Output Level

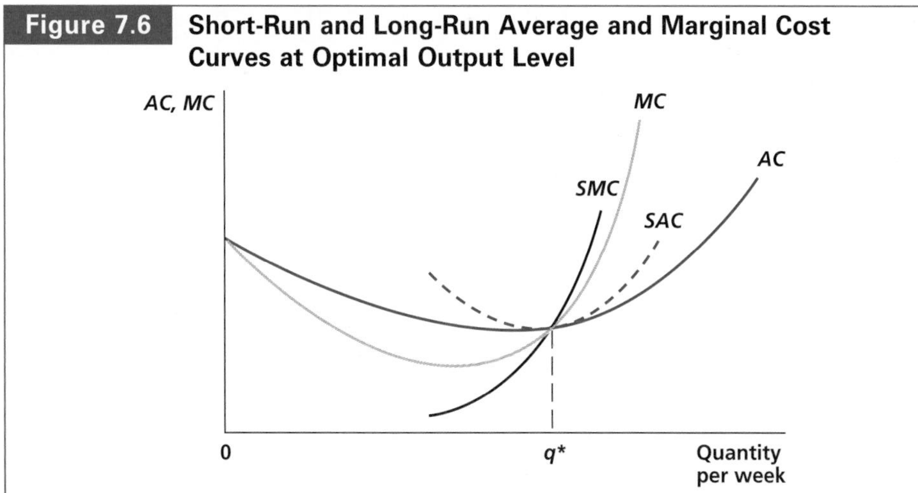

When long-run average cost is U-shaped and reaches a minimum at q^*, SAC and SMC will also pass through this point. For increases in output above q^*, short-run costs are higher than long-run costs.

APPLICATION 7.4

Congestion Costs

One of the clearest examples of rapidly increasing short-run marginal costs is provided by the study of costs associated with crowding. For many facilities such as roads, airports, or tourist attractions, "output" is measured by the number of people that are served during a specified period of time (say, per hour). Because capital (that is roads, terminals, or buildings) is fixed in the short run, the variable costs associated with serving more people primarily consist of the time costs these people incur. In many cases, the increase in these time costs with increasing output can be quite large.

Automobile Congestion

Automobile traffic congestion is a major problem in most cities. Indeed, transportation economists have estimated that each year traffic delays cost U.S. motorists about $50 billion in lost time. Drivers in practically every other country also experience significant costs from traffic problems. One reason that traffic congestion occurs is that the high marginal costs associated with adding an extra automobile to an already crowded highway are not directly experienced by the motorist driving that car. Rather, his or her decision to enter the highway imposes costs on all other motorists. Hence, there is a divergence between the private costs that enter into a motorist's decision to use a particular traffic facility and the total social costs that this decision entails. It is this divergence that leads motorists to opt for driving patterns that overutilize some roads.

Congestion Tolls

The standard answer given by economists to this problem is to urge the adoption of highway, bridge, or tunnel tolls that accurately reflect the social costs that the users of these facilities cause. Because these costs vary by time of day (being highest during morning and evening rush hours), tolls should also vary over the day. With the invention of electronic toll collection technology, toll billing can now be done by mail, with different charges depending on the time of day travel occurs. As more drivers use toll transponders (such as E-ZPass in New York and New Jersey), implementing congestion tolls will become less costly and probably more widespread.

Airport Congestion

Congestion at major airports poses similar problems. Because most travelers want to depart in the early morning or late afternoon, airport runways and approach paths can be especially crowded at those times. The marginal costs associated with the arrival of another plane can be quite high because this can impose delays on many other passengers. Again, economists who have looked at this issue have tended to favor the imposition of some sort of congestion tolls so that peak-time travelers incur the costs they cause. Airports have been relatively slow to adopt such pricing, however, in large part because of political opposition.

Congestion at Tourist Attractions

Tourist attractions such as museums, amusement parks, zoos, and ski areas also experience congestion costs. Not only does the arrival of one more tourist cause others to experience delays, but the added crowding may also diminish the enjoyment of everyone. For example, one study of attendance at the British Museum found that, during periods of heavy use, the arrival of one more visitor reduced everyone else's enjoyment by about £8.05, primarily because views of the most popular exhibits were obscured.[1] The British Museum has a long-standing policy of free admissions, however, so it seems there is little willingness to impose this high marginal cost on peak-time tourists.

TO THINK ABOUT

1. Some commuter groups argue that congestion tolls are unfair because they hit workers who have to commute at certain hours rather than those who drive off-peak in their spare time. Wouldn't a system of uniform (by time of day) tolls be fairer? Regardless of toll schedules, how should toll revenues be used?
2. Standing in line at a theme park can certainly reduce the enjoyment of your visit. What are some of the ways that theme park operators have created incentives to use popular attractions at off-peak hours?

[1]D. Maddison and T. Foster, "Valuing Congestion Costs at the British Museum," *Oxford Economic Papers* (January 2003): 173–190. The authors' use of survey data featuring photos of various levels of crowding at the museum is especially innovative.

7-6 Shifts in Cost Curves

MICRO QUIZ 7.4

Give an intuitive explanation for the following questions about Figure 7.6:

1. Why does *SAC* exceed *AC* for every level of output except q^*?
2. Why does *SMC* exceed *MC* for output levels greater than q^*?
3. What would happen to this figure if the firm increased its short-run level of capital beyond K^*?

MICRO QUIZ 7.5

An increase in the wages of fast-food workers will increase McDonald's costs.

1. How will the extent of the increase in McDonald's costs depend on whether labor costs account for a large or a small fraction of the firm's total costs?
2. How will the extent of the increase in McDonald's costs depend on whether the firm is able to substitute capital for labor?

We have shown how any firm's cost curves are derived from its cost-minimizing expansion path. Any change in economic conditions that affects firms' cost-minimizing decisions will also affect the shape and position of their cost curves. Three kinds of economic changes are likely to have such effects: changes in input prices, technological innovations, and economies of scope.

Changes in Input Prices

A change in the price of an input tilts the firm's total cost lines and alters its expansion path. A rise in wage rates, for example, causes firms to produce any output level using relatively more capital and relatively less labor. To the extent that a substitution of capital for labor is possible (remember that substitution possibilities depend on the shape of the isoquant map), the entire expansion path of the firm rotates toward the capital axis. This movement in turn implies a new set of cost curves for the firm. A rise in the price of labor input causes the entire relationship between output levels and costs to change. Presumably, all cost curves are shifted upward, and the extent of the shift depends both on how "important" labor is in production and on how successful the firm is in substituting other inputs for labor. If labor is relatively unimportant or if the firm can readily shift to more mechanized methods of production, increases in costs resulting from a rise in wages may be rather small. Wage costs have relatively little impact on the costs of oil refineries because labor constitutes a small fraction of total cost. On the other hand, if labor is a very important part of a firm's costs and input substitution is difficult (remember the case of lawn mowers), production costs may rise significantly. A rise in carpenters' wages raises homebuilding costs significantly.

Technological Innovation

In a dynamic economy, technology is constantly changing. Firms discover better production methods, workers learn how to do their jobs better, and the tools of managerial control may improve. Because such technical advances alter a firm's production function, isoquant maps—as well as the firm's expansion path—shift when technology changes. For example, an advance in knowledge may simply shift each isoquant toward the origin, with the result that any output level can then be produced with a lower level of input use and a lower cost. Alternatively, technical change may be "biased" in that it may save only on the use of one input—if workers become more skilled, for instance, this saves only on labor input. Again, the result would be to alter isoquant maps, shift expansion paths, and finally affect the shape and location of a firm's cost curves. In recent years, some of the most important technical changes have been related to the revolution in microelectronics. Costs of computer processing have been halved every 2 years or so for the past 20 years. Such cost changes have had major impacts on many of the markets we study in this book.

Economies of Scope

A third factor that may cause cost curves to shift arises in the case of firms that produce several different kinds of output. In such multiproduct firms, expansion in the output of one good may improve the ability to produce some other good. For example, the experience of the Apple Corporation in producing mobile phones (iPhone) undoubtedly gave it a cost advantage in producing the iPad tablet because the electronics, screen, and software were quite similar between the two products. Or, hospitals that do many surgeries of one type may have a cost advantage in doing other types because of the similarities in equipment and operating personnel used. Such cost effects are called **economies of scope** because they arise out of the expanding scope of operations of multiproduct firms. Application 7.5: Are Economies of Scope in Banking a Bad Thing? looks at one recent controversy in this area.

Economies of scope Reductions in the costs of one product of a multiproduct firm when the output of another product is increased.

Economies of scope or scale may lead to the construction of large factories. Foxconn Technology, which manufactures many of Apple's products under contract, exhibits both. One of its factories in China assembles several different products (iPod, iPad, etc.), and millions of units of each yearly. The complex resembles a small city, employing nearly half a million workers.

7-7 A Numerical Example

If you have the stomach for it, we can continue the numerical example we began in Chapter 6 to derive cost curves for Hamburger Heaven (HH). To do so, let's assume that HH can hire workers at \$5 per hour and that it rents all of its grills from the Hertz Grill Rental Company for \$5 per hour. Hence, total costs for HH during one hour are

$$TC = 5K + 5L, \tag{7.9}$$

where K and L are the number of grills and the number of workers hired during that hour, respectively. To begin our study of HH's cost-minimization process, suppose the firm wishes to produce 40 hamburgers per hour. Table 7.1 repeats the various ways HH can produce 40 hamburgers per hour and uses Equation 7.9 to compute the total cost of each method. It is clear in Table 7.1 that total costs are minimized when K and L are each 4. With this employment of inputs, total cost is \$40, with half being spent on grills (\$20 = \$5 · 4 grills) and the other half being spent on workers. Figure 7.7 shows this cost-minimizing tangency.

Table 7.1 Total Costs of Producing 40 Hamburgers per Hour

OUTPUT (q)	WORKERS (L)	GRILLS (K)	TOTAL COST (TC)
40	1	16.0	\$85.00
40	2	8.0	50.00
40	3	5.3	41.50
40	4	4.0	40.00
40	5	3.2	41.00
40	6	2.7	43.50
40	7	2.3	46.50
40	8	2.0	50.00
40	9	1.8	54.00
40	10	1.6	58.00

Source: Table 6.2 and Equation 7.9.

APPLICATION 7.5

Are Economies of Scope in Banking a Bad Thing?

Banks are financial intermediaries. They collect deposits from a group of depositors and lend them to borrowers, hoping to make profits on the spread between what they charge borrowers and pay to lenders. Banks incur costs in this intermediation, so their net profits depend on how efficiently they conduct these activities. Indeed, because both the costs of banks' funds and the interest rates they receive are largely determined by market forces, variations in operating costs are a major determinant of overall profitability and of the structure of the banking industry.

The Importance of Economies of Scope

Economies of scope can reduce banks' costs if the costs associated with any one particular financial product fall when the bank expands its offerings of other products. For example, a bank may find that its costs of making loans to consumers falls when it also makes loans to retailers because it can economize on transactions costs in dealing with its customers. On a more sophisticated level, banks that operate in many markets simultaneously may find that their costs are lower because they have greater opportunities to diversify risks and can seek out lower cost funds and higher yielding assets.

The Demise of Glass-Steagall

The Glass-Steagall Act of 1933 created a sharp distinction in U.S. banking between "commercial banks" (who take deposits and make loans) and investment banks (who deal in corporate securities). This Act, passed in the midst of the Great Depression, was intended to separate "secure" depository institutions from their "riskier" investment-banking counterparts. Implicitly, the Act ruled out any economies of scope that might have existed by combining the two types of institutions. During the 1990s, it seemed increasingly clear that the distinction between these institutions served no useful role, and in 1999, this part of the Glass-Steagall Act was repealed. Other aspects were also deregulated (for example, restrictions on intestate banking). Most European and Asian countries made similar deregulatory moves.

As banks were deregulated throughout the world, mergers increased dramatically. Apparently, bank managers thought that there were significant economies of scale and scope available to larger institutions. Academic research on the topic was somewhat less sanguine, however. A recent review of many international studies concludes that there may have been some cost savings from economies of scale experienced by smaller institutions but that economies of scope from the offering of multiple banking services were difficult to detect.[1] Nevertheless, banking institutions continued to grow significantly in the new century, and financial connections among them expanded at a rapid pace.

The Consequences of Interconnections

Having banks whose activities are broad-based is in many ways a good thing. When banks invest in many places, they are able to diversify their assets and thereby reduce risk (see Chapter 4). Globalization of banking may open investment opportunities that were previously unavailable, possibly increasing profitability. In addition, by participating in many markets simultaneously, banks may be able to gain better market information with which to make decisions.

But the expanding scope of banks also poses dangers. Because large banks from many countries are dealing with each other at many levels, risks can become more correlated across banks. Hence, the benefits of cross-country diversification can become more apparent than real. In the language of finance, "systemic risks" may be increased. The financial crisis of 2008 exhibited such risks in many stark and unexpected ways. For example, Icelandic banks (which previously had been small-scale, local institutions) experienced widespread failures as their worldwide investments posted losses. A major Irish bank lost heavily on loans to U.S. municipalities and had to be bailed out by a German bank. And one large U.S. investment bank (Lehman Brothers) failed, whereas two others (Goldman, Sachs and Morgan, Stanley) converted to commercial bank status, mainly because they had lost heavily on a variety of new and complex financial instruments. There is no agreement on the role that banks' expanded lists of activities played in initiating the 2008 crisis. But it seems clear that this did contribute to the widespread propagation of the crisis around the world.

POLICY CHALLENGE

What is so "special" about banks and their connection to the financial system? Should banks be subject to more regulations than should be applied to firms in other industries? What would be the underlying reason for such regulation and how might an efficient regulatory regime be designed? How does the global reach of banks complicate the regulatory problem?

[1]See Dean Amel, Colleen Barnes, Fabio Panetta, and Carmelo Sal-leo, "Consolidation and Efficiency in the Financial Sector: A Review of the International Evidence." *Journal of Banking and Finance* 28 (2004): 2493–2519.

Figure 7.7 Cost-Minimizing Input Choice for 40 Hamburgers per Hour

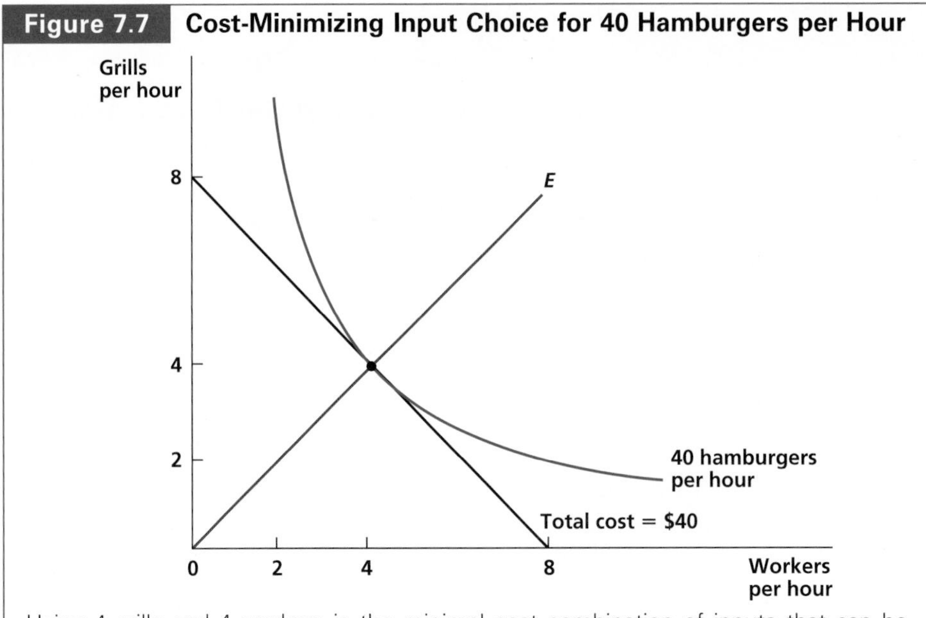

Using 4 grills and 4 workers is the minimal cost combination of inputs that can be used to produce 40 hamburgers per hour. Total costs are $40.

Long-Run Cost Curves

Because HH's production function has constant returns to scale, computing its expansion path is a simple matter; all of the cost-minimizing tangencies will resemble the one shown in Figure 7.7. As long as $w = v = \$5$, long-run cost minimization will require $K = L$ and each hamburger will cost exactly \$1. This result is shown graphically in Figure 7.8.

Figure 7.8 Total, Average, and Marginal Cost Curves

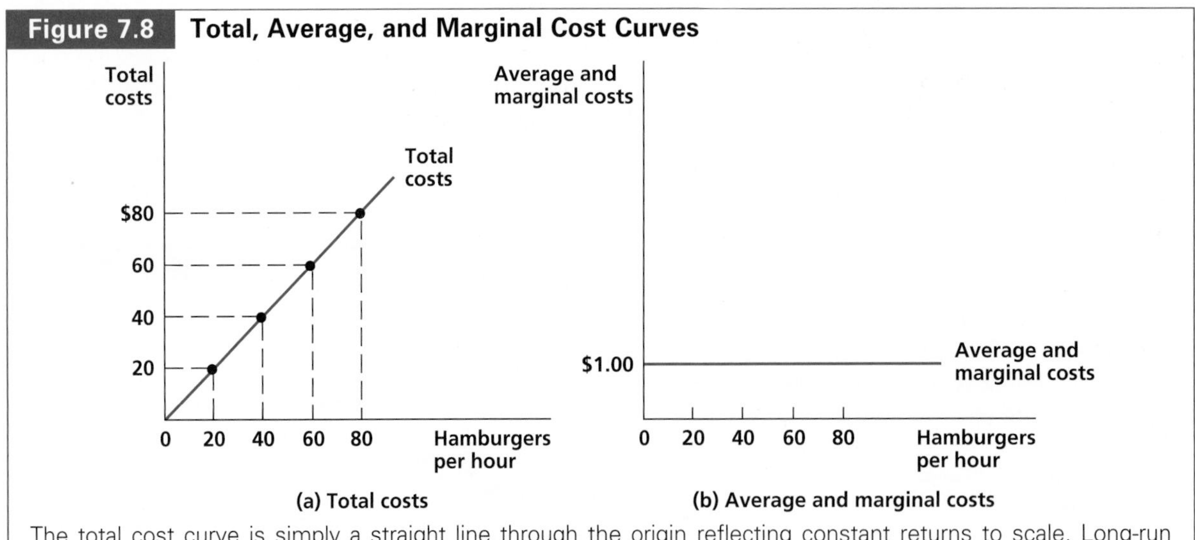

The total cost curve is simply a straight line through the origin reflecting constant returns to scale. Long-run average and marginal costs are constant at \$1 per hamburger.

Table 7.2 Short-Run Costs of Hamburger Production

OUTPUT (q)	WORKERS (L)	GRILLS (K)	TOTAL COST (STC)	AVERAGE COST (SAC)	MARGINAL COST (SMC)
10	0.25	4	$21.25	$2.125	—
20	1.00	4	25.00	1.250	$0.50
30	2.25	4	31.25	1.040	0.75
40	4.00	4	40.00	1.000	1.00
50	6.25	4	51.25	1.025	1.25
60	9.00	4	65.00	1.085	1.50
70	12.25	4	81.25	1.160	1.75
80	16.00	4	100.00	1.250	2.00
90	20.25	4	121.25	1.345	2.25
100	25.00	4	145.00	1.450	2.50

Source: Table 7.3 and Equation 7.9. Marginal costs have been computed using calculus.

HH's long-run total cost curve is a straight line through the origin, and its long-run average and marginal costs are constant at $1 per burger. The very simple shapes shown in Figure 7.8 are a direct result of the constant-returns-to-scale production function HH has.

Short-Run Costs

If we hold one of HH's inputs constant, its cost curves have a more interesting shape. For example, if we fix the number of grills at 4, Table 7.2 repeats the labor input required to produce various output levels (see Table 6.2). Total costs of these input combinations are also shown in the table. Notice how the diminishing marginal productivity of labor for HH causes its costs to rise rapidly as output expands. This is shown even more clearly by computing the short-run average and marginal costs implied by those total cost figures. The marginal cost of the 100th hamburger amounts to a whopping $2.50 because of the 4-grill limitation in the production process.

Finally, Figure 7.9 shows the short-run average and marginal cost curves for HH. Notice that *SAC* reaches its minimum value of $1 per hamburger at an output of 40 burgers per hour because that is the optimal output level for 4 grills. For increases in output above 40 hamburgers per hour, both *SAC* and *SMC* increase rapidly.[7]

KEEP *in* MIND

Production Functions Determine the Shape of Cost Curves

The shapes of a firm's cost curves are not arbitrary. They relate in very specific ways to the firm's underlying production function. For example, if the production function exhibits constant returns to scale, both long-run average and long-run marginal costs will be constant no matter what output is. Similarly, if some inputs are held constant in the short run, diminishing returns to those inputs that are variable will results in average and marginal costs increasing as output expands. Too often, students rush to draw a set of cost curves without stopping to think about what the production function looks like.

[7]For some examples of how the cost curves for HH might shift, see Problem 7.9 and Problem 7.10.

Figure 7.9 Short-Run and Long-Run Average and Marginal Cost Curves for Hamburger Heaven

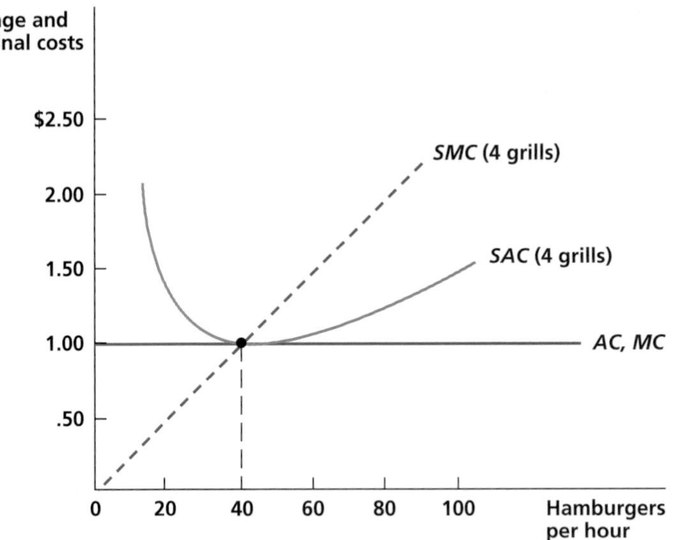

For this constant returns-to-scale production function, *AC* and *MC* are constant over all ranges of output. This constant average cost is $1 per unit. The short-run average cost curve does, however, have a general U-shape since the number of grills is held constant. The *SAC* curve is tangent to the *AC* curve at an output of 40 hamburgers per hour.

SUMMARY

This chapter shows how to construct the firm's cost curves. These curves show the relationship between the amount that a firm produces and the costs of the inputs required for that production. In later chapters, we see how these curves are important building blocks for the theory of supply. The primary results of this chapter are

- To minimize the cost of producing any particular level of output, the firm should choose a point on the isoquant for which the rate of technical substitution (RTS) is equal to the ratio of the inputs' market prices. Alternatively, the firm should choose its inputs so that the ratio of an input's marginal productivity to its price is the same for every input.
- By repeating this cost-minimization process for every possible level of output, the firm's expansion path can be constructed. This shows the minimum-cost way of producing any level of output. The firm's total cost curve can be calculated directly from the expansion path.
- The two most important unit-cost concepts are average cost (that is, cost per unit of output) and marginal cost (that is, the incremental cost of the last unit produced). Average and marginal cost curves can be constructed directly from the total cost curve. The shape of these curves depends on the nature of the firm's production function.
- Short-run cost curves are constructed by holding one (or more) of the firm's inputs constant in the short run. These short-run total costs will not generally be the lowest cost the firm could achieve if all inputs could be adjusted. Short-run costs increase rapidly as output expands because the inputs that can be increased experience diminishing marginal productivities.
- Cost curves shift to a new position whenever the prices of inputs change. Improvements in production techniques also shift cost curves because the same level of output can then be produced with fewer inputs. Expanding one output in a multiproduct firm may reduce costs of some other output when there are economies of scope.

REVIEW QUESTIONS

1. Trump Airlines is thinking of buying a new plane for its shuttle service. Why does the economist's notion of cost suggest that Trump should consider the plane's price in deciding whether it is a profitable investment but that, once bought, the plane's price is not directly relevant to Trump's profit-maximizing decisions? In such a case of "sunk costs," which cost should be used for deciding where to use the plane?

2. Farmer McDonald was heard to complain, "Although my farm is still profitable, I just can't afford to stay in this business any longer. I'm going to sell out and start a fast-food business." In what sense is McDonald using the word *profitable* here? Explain why his statement might be correct if he means profits in the accountant's sense but would be dubious if he is referring to economic profits.

3. Explain why the assumption of cost minimization implies that the total cost curve must have a positive slope: An increase in output must always increase total cost.

4. Suppose a firm had a production function with linear isoquants, implying that its two inputs were perfect substitutes for each other. What would determine the firm's expansion path in this case? For the opposite case of a fixed-portions production function, what would the firm's expansion path be?

5. The distinction between marginal and average cost can be made with some simple algebra. Here are three total cost functions:

   i. $TC = 10q$
   ii. $TC = 40 + 10q$
   iii. $TC = -40 + 10q$.

   a. Explain why all three of these functions have the same marginal cost (10).
   b. How does average cost compare to marginal cost for these three functions? (Note that average cost is only meaningful for $q > 4$ for function iii.)
   c. Explain why average cost approaches marginal cost for large values of q.
   d. Graph the average and marginal cost curves for these three functions. Explain the role of the constant term in the functions.

6. Leonardo is a mechanically minded person who always builds things to help him understand his courses. To help in his understanding of average and marginal cost curves, he draws a TC-q axis pair on a board and attaches a thin wood pointer by a single nail through the origin. He now claims that he can find the level of output for which average cost is a minimum for any cost curve by the following mechanical process: (1) Draw the total cost curve on his graph; (2) rotate his pointer until it is precisely tangent to the total cost curve he has drawn; and (3) find the quantity that corresponds to this tangency. Leonardo claims that this is the quantity where average cost is minimized. Is he right? For which of the total cost curves in Figure 7.3 would this procedure work? When would it not work?

7. Late Bloomer is taking a course in microeconomics. Grading in the course is based on 10 weekly quizzes, each with a 100-point maximum. On the first quiz, Late Bloomer receives a 10. In each succeeding week, he raises his score by 10 points, scoring a 100 on the final quiz of the year.

   a. Calculate Late Bloomer's quiz average for each week of the semester. Why, after the first week, is his average always lower than his current week's quiz?
   b. To help Late Bloomer, his kindly professor has decided to add 40 points to the total of his quiz scores before computing the average. Recompute Late Bloomer's weekly averages given this professorial gift.
   c. Explain why Late Bloomer's weekly quiz averages now have a U-shape. What is his lowest average during the term?
   d. Explain the relevance of this problem to the construction of cost curves. Why does the presence of a "fixed cost" of 40 points result in a U-shaped curve? Are Late Bloomer's average and marginal test scores equal at his minimum average?

8. Beth is a mathematical whiz. She has been reading this chapter and remarks, "All this short-run/long-run stuff is a trivial result of the mathematical fact that the minimum value for any function must be as small as or smaller than the minimum value for the same function when some additional constraints are attached." Use Beth's insight to explain the following:

   a. Why short-run total costs must be equal to or greater than long-run total costs for any given output level
   b. Why short-run average cost must be equal to or greater than long-run average cost for any given output level
   c. That you cannot make a definite statement about the relationship between short-run and long-run marginal cost

9. Taxes can obviously affect firms' costs. Explain how each of the following taxes would affect total, average, and marginal cost. Be sure to consider whether the tax would have a different effect depending on whether one discusses short-run or long-run costs:
   a. A franchise tax of \$10,000 that the firm must pay in order to operate
   b. An output tax of \$2 on each unit of output
   c. An employment tax on each worker's wages
   d. A capital use tax on each machine the firm uses

10. Use Figure 7.1 to explain why a rise in the price of an input must increase the total cost of producing any given output level. What does this result suggest about how such a price increase shifts the *AC* curve? Do you think it is possible to draw any definite conclusion about how the *MC* curve would be affected?

PROBLEMS

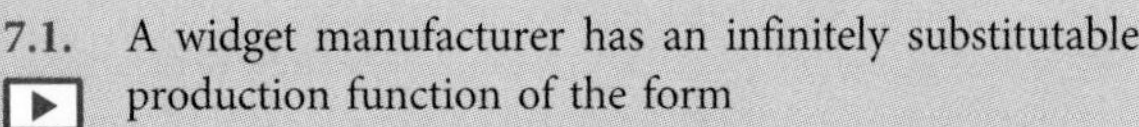

7.1. A widget manufacturer has an infinitely substitutable production function of the form

$$q = 2K + L.$$

a. Graph the isoquant maps for $q = 20$, $q = 40$, and $q = 60$. What is the RTS along these isoquants?
b. If the wage rate (w) is \$1 and the rental rate on capital (v) is \$1, what cost-minimizing combination of K and L will the manufacturer employ for the three different production levels in part a? What is the manufacturer's expansion path?
c. How would your answer to part b change if v rose to \$3 with w remaining at \$1?

7.2. Suppose that the Acme Gumball Company has a fixed proportions production function that requires it to use two gumball presses and one worker to produce 1,000 gumballs per hour.
a. Explain why the cost per hour of producing 1,000 gumballs is $2v + w$ (where v is the hourly rent for gumball presses and w is the hourly wage).
b. Assume Acme can produce any number of gumballs they want using this technology. Explain why the cost function in this case would be $TC = q(2v + w)$, where q is output of gumballs per hour, measured in thousands of gumballs.
c. What is the average and marginal cost of gumball production (again, measure output in thousands of gumballs)?
d. Graph the average and marginal cost curves for gumballs assuming $v = 3$, $w = 5$.
e. Now graph these curves for $v = 6$, $w = 5$. Explain why these curves have shifted.

7.3. The long-run total cost function for a firm producing skateboards is

$$TC = q^3 - 30q^2 + 350q,$$

where q is the number of skateboards per week.
a. What is the general shape of this total cost function?
b. Calculate the average cost function for skateboards. What shape does the graph of this function have? At what level of skateboard output does average cost reach a minimum? What is the average cost at this level of output?
c. The marginal cost function for skateboards is given by

$$MC = 3q^2 - 60q + 350.$$

Show that this marginal cost curve intersects average cost at its minimum value.
d. Graph the average and marginal cost curves for skateboard production.

7.4. Trapper Joe, the fur trader, has found that his production function in acquiring pelts is given by

$$q = 2\sqrt{H},$$

where q = the number of pelts acquired in a day, and H = the number of hours Joe's employees spend hunting and trapping in one day. Joe pays his employees \$8 an hour.
a. Calculate Joe's total and average cost curves (as a function of q).
b. What is Joe's total cost for the day if he acquires four pelts? Six pelts? Eight pelts? What is Joe's average cost per pelt for the day if he acquires four pelts? Six pelts? Eight pelts?
c. Graph the cost curves from part a and indicate the points from part b. Explain why the cost curves have the shape they do.

7.5. A firm producing hockey sticks has a production function given by

$$q = 2\sqrt{K \cdot L}.$$

In the short run, the firm's amount of capital equipment is fixed at $K = 100$. The rental rate for K is $v = \$1$, and the wage rate for L is $w = \$4$.
a. Calculate the firm's short-run total cost function. Calculate the short-run average cost function.

b. The firm's short-run marginal cost function is given by $SMC = q/50$. What are the STC, SAC, and SMC for the firm if it produces 25 hockey sticks? Fifty hockey sticks? One hundred hockey sticks? Two hundred hockey sticks?
c. Graph the SAC and the SMC curves for the firm. Indicate the points found in part b.
d. Where does the SMC curve intersect the SAC curve? Explain why the SMC curve will always intersect the SAC at its lowest point.

7.6. Returning to the gumball producer in Problem 7.2, let's look at the possibility that producing these delectable treats does not necessarily experience constant returns to scale.

a. In Problem 7.2, we showed that the cost function for gumballs was given by $TC = q(2v + w)$, where q is output of gumballs (in thousands), v is the rental rate for gumball presses, and w is the hourly wage. What sort of returns to scale did the underlying production function have? Does the cost function show economies or diseconomies of scale?
b. Suppose instead that the gumball cost function is given by $TC = (2v + w)\sqrt{q}$. Does this function show economies or diseconomies of scale? What does the graph of the total cost curve for this function look like? What do the implies average and marginal cost curves look like?
c. Suppose now that the gumball cost function is $TC = (2v + w)q^2$. Does this function show economies or diseconomies of scale? Illustrate this by graphing the total, average, and marginal cost curves for this function.
d. Economists sometimes measure the degree of economies of scale by $S = AC/MC$. This measure makes sense: if $S < 1$, then $AC < MC$, implying AC slopes up (because MC pulls it up), in which case we have diseconomies of scale. On the other hand, if $S > 1$, then $AC > MC$, implying AC slopes down (because MC pulls it down) and we have (positive) economies of scale. Suppose that the gumball production has associated total and marginal cost functions $TC = (2v + w)q^a$ and $MC = a(2v + w)q^{a-1}$. Compute S in this case, and show how it relates to a. Discuss how the presence of economies or diseconomies of scale relates to a.

7.7. Venture capitalist Sarah purchases two firms to produce widgets. Each firm produces identical products and each has a production function given by

$$q_i = \sqrt{K_i \cdot L_i}$$

where $i = 1, 2$. The firms differ, however, in the amount of capital equipment each has. In particular, firm 1 has $K_1 = 25$, whereas firm 2 has $K_2 = 100$. The marginal product of labor is $MP_L = 5/(2\sqrt{L})$ for firm 1, and $MP_L = 5/\sqrt{L}$ for firm 2. Rental rates for K and L are given by $w = v = \$1$.

a. If Sarah wishes to minimize short-run total costs of widget production, how would output be allocated between the two firms?
b. Given that output is optimally allocated between the two firms, calculate the short-run total and average cost curves. What is the marginal cost of the 100th widget? The 125th widget? The 200th widget?
c. How should Sarah allocate widget production between the two firms in the long run? Calculate the long-run total and average cost curves for widget production.
d. How would your answer to part c change if both firms exhibited decreasing rather than constant returns to scale?

7.8. In Problem 6.7, we introduced the Cobb-Douglas production function of the form $q = K^aL^b$. The cost function that can be derived from this production function is

$$TC = Bq^{1/(a+b)}v^{a/(a+b)}w^{b/(a+b)},$$

where B is a constant, and v and w are the costs of K and L, respectively. The marginal cost function is

$$MC = \left(\frac{B}{a+b}\right)q^{1-1/(a+b)}v^{a/(a+b)}w^{b/(a+b)}.$$

a. To understand these functions, suppose $a = b = 0.5$. Does this function exhibit constant returns to scale? What is the cost function now? Does the cost function exhibit economies or diseconomies of scale? How "important" are each of the input prices in this function?
b. Now return to the Cobb-Douglas cost function in its more general form. Discuss the role of the exponent of q. How does the value of this exponent relate to the returns to scale exhibited by its underlying production function? How do the returns to scale in the production function affect the shape of the firm's total cost curve?
c. Refer to problem 7.6d for a definition of S, a measure of the degree of economies of scale. Compute S for the general Cobb-Douglas form. Relate S to the exponent on q in the cost function and the returns to scale found in the previous part of this question.
d. Discuss how the relative sizes of a and b affect this cost function. Explain how the sizes of these exponents affect the extent to which the total cost function is shifted by changes in each of the input prices.

e. Taking natural logarithms of the Cobb-Douglas cost function yields

$$\ln TC = \ln B + \left(\frac{1}{a+b}\right)\ln q + \left(\frac{a}{a+b}\right)\ln v + \left(\frac{b}{a+b}\right)\ln w.$$

Why might this form of the function be especially useful? What do the coefficients of the log terms in the function tell you?

f. The cost function in part d can be generalized by adding more terms. This new function is called the "Translog Cost Function," and it is used in much empirical research. A nice introduction to the function is provided by the Christenson and Greene paper on electric power generation references in Table 1 of Application 7.3. The paper also contains an estimate of the Cobb-Douglas cost function that is of the general form given in part d. Can you find this in the paper?

7.9. In the numerical example of Hamburger Heaven's production function in Chapter 6, we examined the consequences of the invention of a self-flipping burger that changed the production function to

$$q = 20\sqrt{KL}.$$

a. Assuming this shift does not change the cost-minimizing expansion path (which requires $K = L$), how are long-run total, average, and marginal costs affected? (See the numerical example at the end of Chapter 7.)

b. More generally, technical progress in hamburger production might be reflected by

$$q = (1 + r)\sqrt{KL},$$

where r is the annual rate of technical progress (that is, a rate of increase of 3 percent would have $r = .03$). How will the year-to-year change in the average cost of a hamburger be related to the value of r?

7.10. In our numerical example, Hamburger Heaven's expansion path requires $K = L$ because w (the wage) and v (the rental rate of grills) are equal. More generally, for this type of production function, it can be shown that

$$K/L = w/v$$

for cost minimization. Hence, relative input usage is determined by relative input prices.

a. Suppose both wages and grill rents rise to \$10 per hour. How would this affect the firm's expansion path? How would long-run average and marginal cost be affected? What can you conclude about the effect of uniform inflation of input costs on the costs of hamburger production?

b. Suppose wages rise to \$20 but grill rents stay fixed at \$5. How would this affect the firm's expansion path? How would this affect the long-run average and marginal cost of hamburger production? Why does a multiplication of the wage by four result in a much smaller increase in average costs?

c. In the numerical example in Chapter 6, we explored the consequences of technical progress in hamburger flipping. Specifically, we assumed that the hamburger production function shifted for $q = 10\sqrt{KL}$ to $q = 20\sqrt{KL}$. How would this shift offset the cost increases in part a? That is, what cost curves are implied by this new production function with $v = w = 10$? How do these compare with the original curves shown in Figure 7.8?

d. Answer part c with the input costs in part b of this problem ($v = 5$, $w = 20$). What do you conclude about the ability of technical progress to offset rising input costs?

8 Profit Maximization and Supply

In this chapter, we use the cost curves developed in Chapter 7 to study firms' output decisions. This results in a detailed model of supply. First, however, we briefly look at some conceptual issues about firms.

8-1 The Nature of Firms

Our definition of a firm as any organization that turns inputs into outputs suggests a number of questions about the nature of such organizations. These include the following: (1) Why do we need such firms? (2) How are the relationships among the people in a firm structured? And (3) how can the owners of a firm ensure that their employees perform in ways that are best from an overall perspective? Because firms may involve thousands of owners, employees, and other input providers, these are complicated questions, many of which are at the forefront of current economic research. In this section, we provide a very brief introduction to the current thinking on each of them.

Why Firms Exist

In order to understand why large and complex firms are needed, it is useful to ask first what the alternative might be. If cars were not produced by big enterprises like Toyota, how would peoples' demands for them be met? One conceptual possibility would be for individual workers to specialize in making each car part and in putting various collections of parts together. Coordination of this process could, at least in principle, be accomplished through markets. That is, each person could contract with the suppliers he or she needed and with people who use the parts being produced. Of course, making all of these contracts and moving partly assembled cars from one place to the next would be very costly. Getting the details of each transaction right and establishing procedures on what to do when something goes wrong would involve endless negotiations. Organizing people into firms helps to economize on these costs.

The British-born economist Ronald Coase is usually credited with the idea that firms arise to minimize transactions costs.[1] In the case of automobiles, for example, the scope of auto firms will expand to include parts production and assembly so long as there are gains from handling such operations internally. These gains consist mainly of the ability to invest in machinery uniquely suited to the firm's specific production tasks and to avoid the need to contract with outside suppliers. The fact that such gains exist does not mean that they occur in all cases, however. In some instances, auto firms may find it attractive to contract with outside suppliers for certain parts (such as tires, for example), perhaps because such outsiders are very good at making them. In Coase's

[1] R. Coase, "The Nature of the Firm," *Economica* (November 1937): 386–405.

view, then, a generalized process of seeking the minimum-cost way of making the final output determines the scope of any firm. This insight about transactions costs provides the starting point for much of the modern theory on how complex organizations arise.

Contracts within Firms

The organization of production within firms arises out of an understanding by each supplier of inputs to the firm about what his or her role will be. In some cases, these understandings are explicitly written out in formal contracts. Workers, especially workers who have their contracts negotiated by unions, often arrive at contracts that specify in considerable detail what hours are to be worked, what work rules are to be followed, and what rate of pay can be expected. Similarly, the owners of a firm invest their capital in the enterprise under an explicit set of legal principles about how the capital will be used and how the resulting returns will be shared. In many cases, however, the understandings among the input suppliers in a firm may be less formal. For example, managers and workers may follow largely implicit beliefs about who has the authority to do what in the production process. Or capital owners may delegate most of their authority to a hired manager or to workers themselves. Shareholders in large firms like Microsoft or General Electric do not want to be involved in every detail about how these firms' equipment is used, even though technically they own it. All of these understandings among input suppliers may change over time in response to experiences and to events external to the firm. Much as a basketball or soccer team tries out new offensive plays or defensive strategies in response to the competition they encounter, firms also alter the details of their internal structures in order to obtain better long-term results.

Contract Incentives

Some of the most important questions about a firm's contracts with input suppliers concern the kinds of incentives these contracts provide. Only if these incentives are compatible with the general goals of the firm will operations proceed efficiently. The primary reason that incentives matter is that information about the actual performance of a firm's managers or its employees may be difficult to observe. No boss wants to be constantly looking over the shoulders of all his or her workers to make sure they work effectively. And no shareholder wants to scrutinize managers constantly to make sure they do not waste money. Rather, it may be much less costly to establish the proper incentives in a contract and then leave the individuals involved more or less on their own. For example, a manager who hires a worker to build a brick wall could watch him or her laying each brick to make sure it was placed correctly. A much less costly solution, however, would be to pay the worker on the basis of how well the wall was built and how long it took to do the job. In other cases, measuring a worker's output may not be so easy (How would you assess the productivity of, say, a receptionist in a doctor's office?) and some less direct incentive scheme may be needed. Similarly, a firm's owners will need some way to assess how well their hired manager is doing, even though outside influences may also affect the firm's bottom line. Studying the economics behind such incentive contracts at this stage would take us away from our primary focus on supply, but in Chapter 15 we look in detail at how certain information problems in the management of firms (and in other applications) can be solved through the appropriate specification of contract incentives.

Firms' Goals and Profit Maximization

All of these complexities in how firms are actually organized can pose some problems for economists who wish to make some simple statements about how firms supply economic goods. In demand theory, it made sense to talk about the choices made by a utility-maximizing consumer because we were looking only at the decisions of a single person. But, in the case of firms, many people may be involved in supply decisions, and any detailed study of the process may quickly become too complex for easy generalizations. To avoid this difficulty, economists usually treat the firm as a single decision-making unit. That is, the firm is assumed to have a single owner-manager who makes all decisions in a rather dictatorial way. Usually, we will also assume that this person seeks to maximize the profits that are obtained from the firm's productive activities. Of course, we could assume that the manager seeks some other goal, and in some cases that might make more sense than to assume profit maximization. For example, the manager of a public elementary school would probably not pursue profitability but instead would have some educational goal in mind. Or the manager of the state highway department might seek safe highways (or, more cynically, nice contracts for his or her friends). But for most firms, the profit maximization assumption seems reasonable because it is consistent with the owner doing the best with his or her investment in the firm. In addition, profit maximization may be forced on firms by external market forces—if a manager doesn't make the most profitable use of a firm's assets, someone else may come along who will do better and buy them out. This is a situation we explore briefly in Application 8.1: Corporate Profits Taxes and Firms' Financing Decisions. Hence, assuming profit maximization seems to be a reasonable way to start our study of supply behavior.

8-2 Profit Maximization

If the manager of a firm is to pursue the goal of profit maximization, he or she must, by definition, make the difference between the firm's revenue and its total costs as large as possible. In making such calculations, it is important that the manager use the economist's notion of costs—that is, the cost figure should include allowances for all opportunity costs. With such a definition, economic profits are indeed a residual over and above all costs. For the owner of the firm, profits constitute an above-competitive return of his or her investment because allowance for a "normal" rate of return is already considered as an opportunity cost. Hence, the prospect for economic profits represents a powerful inducement to enter a business. Of course, economic profits may also be negative, in which case the owner's return on investment is lower than he or she could get elsewhere—this would provide an inducement to get out of the business.

Marginalism

If managers are profit maximizers, they will make decisions in a marginal way. They will adjust the things that can be controlled until it is impossible to increase profits further. The manager looks, for example, at the incremental (or marginal) profit from producing one more unit of output or the additional profit from hiring one more employee. As long as this incremental profit is positive, the manager decides to produce the extra output or hire the extra worker. When the incremental profit of an activity becomes zero, the manager has pushed the activity far enough—it would not be profitable to go further.

APPLICATION 8.1

Corporate Profits Taxes and Firms' Financing Decisions

Corporate income taxes were first levied in the United States in 1909, about 4 years before the personal income tax was put into effect. In 2013, corporate income tax revenues amounted to nearly $300 billion, about 10 percent of total federal tax collections. Many people view the tax as a natural complement to the personal income tax. Under U.S. law, corporations share many of the same rights as do people, so it may seem only reasonable that corporations should be taxed in a similar way. Some economists, however, believe that the corporate profits tax seriously distorts the allocation of resources, both because of its failure to use an economic profit concept under the tax law and because a substantial portion of corporate income is taxed twice.

Definition of Profits

A large portion of what are defined as corporate profits under the tax laws is in fact a normal return to shareholders for the equity they have invested in corporations. Shareholders expect a similar return from other investments they might make: if they had deposited their funds in a bank, for instance, they would expect to be paid interest. Hence, some portion of corporate profits should be considered an economic cost of doing business because it reflects what owners have forgone by making an equity investment. Because such costs are not allowable under tax accounting regulations, equity capital is a relatively expensive way to finance a business.

Effects of the Double Tax

The corporate profits tax is not so much a tax on profits as it is a tax on the equity returns of corporate shareholders. Such taxation may have two consequences. First, corporations will find it more attractive to finance new capital investments through loans and bond offerings (whose interest payments are an allowable cost) than through new stock issues (whose implicit costs are not an allowable cost under the tax law). A second effect occurs because a part of corporate income is double taxed—first when it is earned by the corporation and then later when it is paid out to shareholders in the form of dividends. Hence, the total rate of tax applied to corporate equity capital is higher than that applied to other sources of capital.

The Leveraged Buyout Craze

These peculiarities of the corporate income tax are at least partly responsible for the wave of leveraged buyouts (LBOs) that swept financial markets in the late 1980s. Michael Milken and others made vast fortunes by developing this method of corporate financing. The basic principle of an LBO is to use borrowed funds to acquire most of the out standing stock of a corporation. Those involved in such a buyout are substituting a less highly taxed source of capital (debt) for a more highly taxed form (equity). Huge deals such as the $25 billion buyout of RJR Nabisco by the Kohlberg, Kravis, Roberts partnership were an attempt to maximize the true economic profits that can be extracted from a business (some involved in these deals also used questionable financial practices).

Changing Patterns of Leverage

Leverage buyouts declined after 1991 in part because stock prices rose and in part because taxes on dividends and capital gains were reduced. Hence, the advantages of debt-financing over equity financing were diminished. Most buyouts between 1995 and 2005, therefore, were primarily financed by cash purchases of a company's outstanding stock. The low interest rate environment caused by expansionary monetary policy after the Great Recession of 2008–2009, however, changed the calculation once again. The emergence of debt-financing of buyouts was given an added boost when tax rates on capital gains and dividends were raised significantly in early 2013. As a result, many buyout firms used low interest rate loans to pay "dividends" to themselves as a way of reducing their equity stakes. As might have been expected, clever accounting methods made many of these dividends nontaxable to the equity owners. Undoubtedly, the complex structure of the U.S. income tax system will continue to pose such profitable opportunities for changing capital structures in the future.

POLICY CHALLENGE

Does a separate corporate tax make sense when a comprehensive income tax is already in place? Are there advantages in collecting taxes on income from capital at the corporate level rather than at the individual level? Or does the presence of a two-tier tax system just make the tax collection process more complicated and distorting than it needs to be?

The Output Decision

We can show this relationship between profit maximization and marginalism most directly by looking at the output level that a firm chooses to produce. A firm sells some level of output, q, and from these sales the firm receives its revenues, $R(q)$. The amount of revenues received obviously depends on how much output is sold and on what price it is sold for. Similarly, in producing q, certain economic costs are incurred, $TC(q)$, and these also depend on how much is produced. Economic profits (π) are defined as

$$\pi(q) = R(q) - TC(q). \qquad \textbf{(8.1)}$$

Notice that the level of profits depends on how much is produced. In deciding what that output should be, the manager chooses that level for which economic profits are as large as possible. This process is illustrated in Figure 8.1. The top panel of this figure shows rather general revenue and total cost curves. As might be expected, both have positive slopes—producing more causes both the firm's revenues and its costs to increase. For any level of output, the firm's profits are shown by the vertical distance between these two curves. These are shown separately in the lower panel of Figure 8.1. Notice that profits are initially negative. At an output of $q = 0$, the firm obtains no revenue but must pay fixed costs (if there are any). Profits then increase as some output is produced and sold. Profits reach zero at q_1—at that output level revenues and costs are

Figure 8.1 Marginal Revenue Must Equal Marginal Cost for Profit Maximization

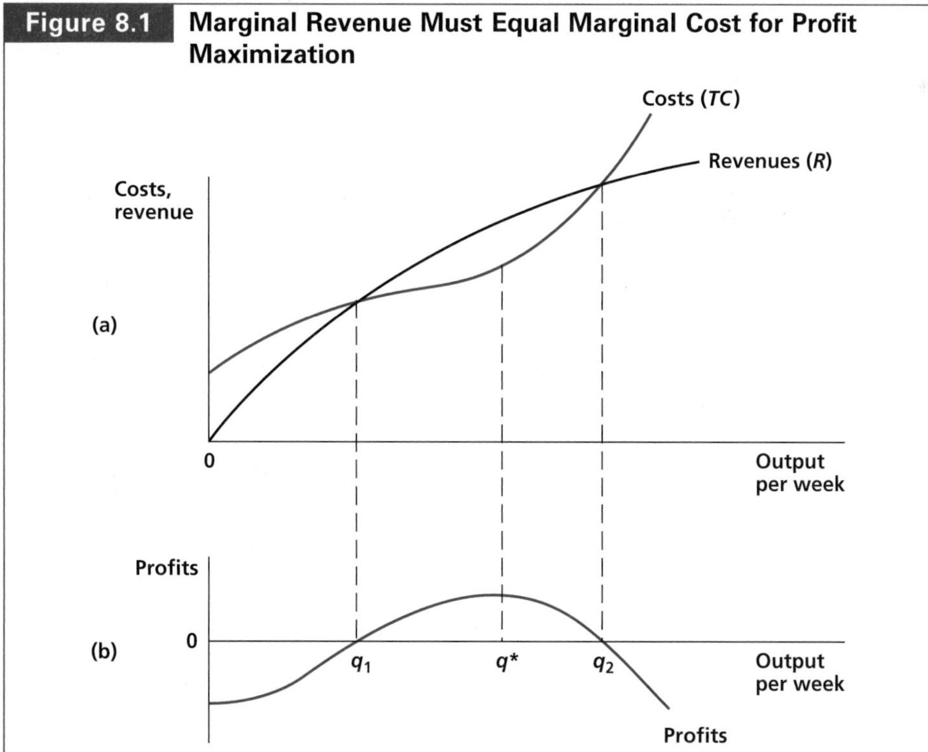

Economic profits are defined as total revenues minus total economic costs and can be measured by the vertical distance between the revenue and cost curves. Profits reach a maximum when the slope of the revenue function (marginal revenue) is equal to the slope of the cost function (marginal cost). In the figure, this occurs at q^*. Profits are zero at both q_1 and q_2.

equal. Beyond q_1, profits increase, reaching their highest level at q^*. At this level of output, the revenue and cost curves are furthest apart. Increasing output even beyond q^* would reduce total profits—in fact, in this case, increasing output enough (to more than q_2) would eventually result in profits becoming negative. Hence, just eyeballing the graph suggests that a manager who pursues the goal of profit maximization would opt to produce output level q^*. Examining the characteristics of both the revenue and cost curves at this output level provides one of the most familiar and important results in all of microeconomics.

The Marginal Revenue/Marginal Cost Rule

Marginal revenue
The extra revenue a firm receives when it sells one more unit of output.

In order to examine the conditions that must hold at q^*, consider a firm that was producing slightly less than this amount. It would find that, if it were to increase its output by one unit, additional revenues would rise faster than would additional costs—so, profits would grow. In economic jargon, a firm that opted to produce less than q^* would find that its **marginal revenue** (*MR*) would be greater than its marginal cost—a sure sign that increasing output will raise profits. Increasing output beyond q^* would, however, cause profits to fall. Beyond q^*, the extra revenue from selling one more unit is not as great as the cost of producing that extra unit, so producing it would cause a drop in profits. Hence, the characteristics of output level q^* are clear—at that output, marginal revenue is precisely equal to marginal cost. More succinctly, at q^*,

$$\text{Marginal revenue} = \text{Marginal cost}, \tag{8.2}$$

or

$$MR = MC. \tag{8.3}$$

Because both marginal revenue and marginal cost are functions of q, Equation 8.3 can usually be solved for q^*. For output levels less than q^*, $MR > MC$, whereas, for output levels greater than q^*, $MR < MC$.

A geometric proof of this key proposition can be developed from Figure 8.1. We are interested in the conditions that must hold if the vertical distance between the revenue and cost curves is to be as large as possible. Clearly this requires that the slopes of the two curves be equal. If the curves had differing slopes, profits could be increased by adjusting output in the direction in which the curves diverged. Only when the two curves are parallel would such a move not raise profits. But the slope of the total cost curve is in fact marginal cost and (as we shall see) the slope of the total revenue curve represents marginal revenue. Hence, the geometric argument also proves the $MR = MC$ output rule for profit maximization.[2]

Marginalism in Input Choices

Similar marginal decision rules apply to firms' input choices as well. Hiring another worker, for example, entails some increase in costs, and a profit-maximizing firm should balance the additional costs against the extra revenue brought in by selling the output

[2]The result can also be derived from calculus. We wish to find the value of q for which $\pi(q) = R(q) - TC(q)$ is as large as possible. The first order condition for a maximum is

$$\frac{d\pi(q)}{dq} = \frac{dR(q)}{dq} - \frac{dTC(q)}{dq} = MR(q) - MC(q) = 0.$$

Hence, the profit-maximizing level for q solves the equation $MR(q) = MC(q)$. To be a true maximum, the second order conditions require that, at the profit maximizing value of q, marginal profits must be decreasing.

produced by this new worker. A similar analysis holds for the firm's decision on the number of machines to rent. Additional machines should be hired only as long as their marginal contributions to profits are positive. As the marginal productivity of machines begins to decline, the ability of machines to yield additional revenue also declines. The firm eventually reaches a point at which the marginal contribution of an additional machine to profits is exactly zero—the extra sales generated precisely match the costs of the extra machines. The firm should not expand the rental of machines beyond this point. In Chapter 13, we look at input hiring decisions in more detail.

8-3 Marginal Revenue

It is the revenue from selling one more unit of output that is relevant to a profit-maximizing firm. If a firm can sell all it wishes without affecting market price—that is, if the firm is a **price taker**—the market price will indeed be the extra revenue obtained from selling one more unit. In other words, if a firm's output decisions do not affect market price, marginal revenue is equal to price. Suppose a firm was selling 50 widgets at \$1 each. Then total revenues would be \$50. If selling one more widget does not affect price, that additional widget will also bring in \$1 and total revenue will rise to \$51. Marginal revenue from the 51st widget will be \$1 (= \$51 – \$50). For a firm whose output decisions do not affect market price, we therefore have

Price taker
A firm or individual whose decisions regarding buying or selling have no effect on the prevailing market price of a good.

$$MR = P. \tag{8.4}$$

Marginal Revenue for a Downward-Sloping Demand Curve

A firm may not always be able to sell all it wants at the prevailing market price. If it faces a downward-sloping demand curve for its product, it can sell more only by reducing its selling price. In this case, marginal revenue will be less than market price. To see why, assume in our prior example that to sell the 51st widget the firm must reduce the price of all its widgets to \$.99. Total revenues are now \$50.49 (= \$.99 × 51), and the marginal revenue from the 51st widget is only \$.49 (= \$50.49 – \$50.00). Even though the 51st widget sells for \$.99, the extra revenue obtained from selling the widget is a net gain of only \$.49 (a \$.99 gain on the 51st widget less a \$.50 reduction in revenue from charging one penny less for each of the first 50). When selling one more unit causes market price to decline, marginal revenue is less than market price:

$$MR < P. \tag{8.5}$$

Firms that must reduce their prices to sell more of their products (that is, firms facing a downward-sloping demand curve) must take this fact into account in deciding how to obtain maximum profits.

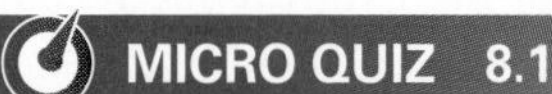

Use the marginal revenue/marginal cost rule to explain why each of the following purported rules for obtaining maximum profits is *incorrect*.

1. Maximum profits can be found by looking for that output for which profit per unit (that is, price minus average cost) is as large as possible.
2. If the firm is a price taker, the scheme outlined in point 1 can be made even more precise—maximum profits may be found by choosing that output level for which average cost is as small as possible. That is, the firm should produce at the low point of its average-cost curve.

A Numerical Example

The result that marginal revenue is less than price for a downward-sloping demand curve is illustrated with a numerical example in Table 8.1. There, we have recorded the quantity of, say, CDs demanded

Table 8.1 Total and Marginal Revenue for CDs ($q = 10 - P$)

PRICE (P)	QUANTITY (q)	TOTAL REVENUE ($P \cdot q$)	MARGINAL REVENUE (MR)
$10	0	$ 0	
9	1	9	$ 9
8	2	16	7
7	3	21	5
6	4	24	3
5	5	25	1
4	6	24	−1
3	7	21	−3
2	8	16	−5
1	9	9	−7
0	10	0	−9

from a particular store per week (q), their price (P), total revenues from CD sales ($P \cdot q$), and marginal revenue (MR) for a simple linear demand curve of the form

$$q = 10 - P. \quad \textbf{(8.6)}$$

Total revenue from CD sales reaches a maximum at $q = 5$, $P = 5$. For $q > 5$, total revenues decline. Increasing sales beyond five per week actually causes marginal revenue to be negative.

In Figure 8.2, we have drawn this hypothetical demand curve and can use the figure to illustrate the marginal revenue concept. Consider, for example, the extra revenue obtained if the firm sells four CDs instead of three. When output is three, the market price per CD is $7 and total revenues ($P \cdot q$) are $21. These revenues are shown by the area of the rectangle P^*Aq^*0. If the firm produces four CDs per week instead, price must be reduced to $6 to sell this increased output level. Now total revenue is $24, illustrated by the area of the rectangle $P^{**}Bq^{**}0$. A comparison of the two revenue rectangles shows why the marginal revenue obtained by producing the fourth CD is less than its price. The sale of this CD does indeed increase revenue by the price at which it sells ($6). Revenue increases by the area of the darkly shaded rectangle in Figure 8.2. But, to sell the fourth CD, the firm must reduce its selling price from $7 to $6 on the first three CDs sold per week. That price reduction causes a fall in revenue of $3, shown as the area of the lightly shaded rectangle in Figure 8.2.

The net result is an increase in revenue of only $3 ($6 − $3), rather than the gain of $6 that would be calculated if only the sale of the fourth CD is considered in isolation. The marginal revenue for other points in this hypothetical demand curve could also be illustrated. In particular, if you draw the case of a firm producing six CDs instead of five, you will see that marginal revenue from the sixth CD is negative. Although the sixth CD itself sells for $4, selling it requires the firm to reduce the price by $1 on the other five CDs it sells. Hence, marginal revenue is −$1 (= $4 − $5).

Figure 8.2 **Illustration of Marginal Revenue for the Demand Curve for CDs ($q = 10 - P$)**

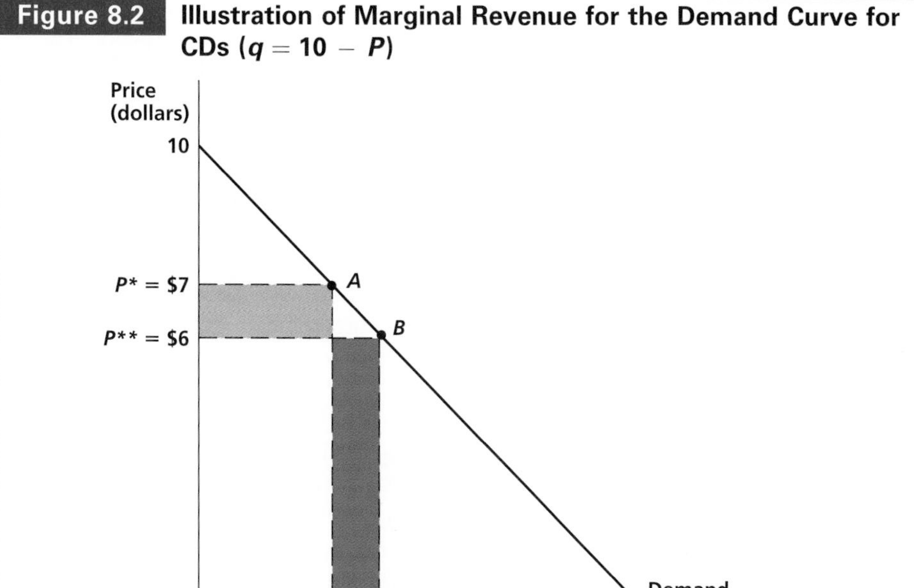

For this hypothetical demand curve, marginal revenue can be calculated as the extra revenue from selling one more CD. If the firm sells four CDs instead of three, for example, revenue will be \$24 rather than \$21. Marginal revenue from the sale of the fourth CD is, therefore, \$3. This represents the gain of \$6 from the sale of the fourth CD *less* the decline in revenue of \$3 as a result of the fall in price for the first three CDs from \$7 to \$6.

Marginal Revenue and Price Elasticity

In Chapter 3, we introduced the concept of the price elasticity of demand ($e_{Q,P}$), which we defined as

$$e_{Q,P} = \frac{\text{Percentage change in } Q}{\text{Percentage change in } P}. \tag{8.7}$$

Although we developed this concept as it relates to the entire market demand for a product (Q), the definition can be readily adapted to the case of the demand curve that faces an individual firm. We define the price elasticity of demand for a single firm's output (q) as

$$e_{q,P} = \frac{\text{Percentage change } q}{\text{Percentage change in } P}, \tag{8.8}$$

where P now refers to the price at which the firm's output sells.[3]

[3]This definition assumes that competitors' prices do not change when the firm varies its own price. Under such a definition, the demand curve facing a single firm may be quite elastic, even if the demand curve for the market as a whole is not. Indeed, if other firms are willing to supply all that consumers want to buy at a particular price, the firm cannot raise its price above that level without losing all its sales. Such behavior by rivals would, therefore, force price-taking behavior on the firm (see the discussion in the next section). For a more complete discussion of interfirm price competition, see Chapter 12.

Table 8.2 Relationship between Marginal Revenue and Elasticity

DEMAND CURVE	MARGINAL REVENUE
Elastic ($e_{q,P} < -1$)	$MR > 0$
Unit elastic ($e_{q,P} = -1$)	$MR = 0$
Inelastic ($e_{q,P} > -1$)	$MR < 0$

Our discussion in Chapter 3 about the relationship between elasticity and total expenditures also carries over to the case of a single firm. Total spending on the good ($P \cdot q$) is now the same as total revenue for the firm. If demand facing the firm is inelastic ($0 \geq e_{q,P} > -1$) a rise in price will cause total revenues to rise. But, if this demand is elastic ($e_{q,P} < -1$), a rise in price will result in smaller total revenues. Clearly, therefore, there is a connection between the price elasticity and marginal revenue concepts. However, because price elasticity concerns reactions to changing prices whereas marginal revenue concerns the effect of changes in quantity sold, we must be careful to clarify exactly what this connection is.

Table 8.2 summarizes the connection between the price elasticity of the demand curve facing a firm and marginal revenue. Let's work through the entries in the table. When demand is elastic ($e_{q,P} < -1$), a fall in price raises quantity sold to such an extent that total revenues rise. Hence, in this case, an increase in quantity sold lowers price and thereby raises total revenue—marginal revenue is positive ($MR > 0$). When demand is inelastic ($0 \geq e_{q,P} > -1$), a fall in price, although it allows a greater quantity to be sold, reduces total revenue. Since an increase in output causes price and total revenue to decline, MR is negative. Finally, if demand is unit elastic ($e_{q,P} = -1$), total revenue remains constant for movements along the demand curve, so MR is zero. More generally, the precise relation between MR and price elasticity is given by[4]

$$MR = P\left(1 + \frac{1}{e_{q,P}}\right), \tag{8.9}$$

and all of the relationships in Table 8.2 can be derived from this basic equation. For example, if demand is elastic ($e_{q,P} < -1$), Equation 8.9 shows that MR is positive. Indeed, if demand is infinitely elastic ($e_{q,P} = -\infty$), MR will equal price since, as we showed before, the firm is a price taker and cannot affect the price it receives.

To see how Equation 8.9 might be used in practice, suppose that a firm knows that the elasticity of demand for its product is −2. It may derive this figure from historical data that show that each 10 percent decline in its price has usually led to an increase in sales of about 20 percent. Now, assume that the price of the firm's output is $10 per unit and the firm wishes to know how much additional

MICRO QUIZ 8.2

How does the relationship between marginal revenue and price elasticity explain the following economic observations?

1. There are five major toll routes for auto mobiles from New Jersey into New York City. Raising the toll on one of them will cause total revenue collected on that route to fall. Raising the tolls on all of the routes will cause total revenue collected on any one route to rise.
2. A doubling of the restaurant tax from 3 percent to 6 percent only in Hanover, New Hampshire, causes meal tax revenues to fall in that town, but a statewide increase of a similar amount causes tax revenues to rise.

[4]A proof of Equation 8.9 proceeds using calculus. Since Total Revenue $= R(q) = Pq$, Marginal Revenue is given by

$$MR = \frac{dTR}{dq} = P + q\frac{dP}{dq} = P\left(1 + \frac{q}{P}\cdot\frac{dP}{dq}\right) = P\left(1 + \frac{1}{e_{q,P}}\right).$$

revenue the sale of one more unit of output will yield. The additional unit of output will not yield \$10 because the firm faces a downward-sloping demand curve: to sell the unit requires a reduction in its overall selling price. The firm can, however, use Equation 8.9 to calculate that the additional revenue yielded by the sale will be $\$5[= \$10 \cdot (1 + 1/-2) = \$10 \cdot 1/2]$. The firm will produce this extra unit if marginal costs are less than \$5; that is, if $MC < \$5$, profits will be increased by the sale of one more unit of output. Although firms in the real world use more complex means to decide on the profitability of changing output or prices, our discussion here illustrates the logic these firms must use. They must recognize how changes in quantity sold affect price (or vice versa) and how these changes affect total revenues. Application 8.2: Maximizing Profits from Bagels and Catalog Sales shows that even for simple products, such decisions may not be straightforward.

8-4 Marginal Revenue Curve

Any demand curve has a **marginal revenue curve** associated with it. It is sometimes convenient to think of a demand curve as an *average revenue curve* because it shows the revenue per unit (in other words, the price) at various output choices the firm might make. The marginal revenue curve, on the other hand, shows the extra revenue provided by the last unit sold. In the usual case of a downward-sloping curve, the marginal revenue curve will lie below the demand curve because, at any level of output, marginal revenue is less than price.[5] In Figure 8.3, we have drawn a marginal revenue curve together with the demand curve from which it was derived. For output levels greater than q_1, marginal revenue is negative. As q increases from 0 to q_1, total revenues $(P \cdot q)$ increase. However, at q_1, total revenues $(P_1 \cdot q_1)$ are as large as possible; beyond this output level, price falls proportionately faster than output rises, so total revenues fall.

Marginal revenue curve
A curve showing the relation between the quantity a firm sells and the revenue yielded by the last unit sold. Derived from the demand curve.

Numerical Example Revisited

Constructing marginal revenue curves from their underlying demand curves is usually rather difficult, primarily because the calculations require calculus. For linear demand curves, however, the process is simple. Consider again the demand for CDs in the previous example. There we assumed that the demand curve had the linear form $q = 10 - P$. The first step in deriving the marginal revenue curve associated with this demand is to solve for P as $P = 10 - q$ and then use the result that the marginal revenue curve is twice as steep as this "willingness-to-pay" curve.[6] That is,

$$MR = 10 - 2q. \tag{8.10}$$

Figure 8.4 illustrates this marginal revenue curve together with the demand curve already shown in Figure 8.2. Notice, as before, marginal revenue is zero when $q = 5$. At this

[5]If the firm is a price taker and can sell all that its owners want at the prevailing market price, the demand curve facing the firm is infinitely elastic (that is, if the demand curve is a horizontal line at the market price) and the average and marginal revenue curves coincide. Selling one more unit has no effect on price; therefore, marginal and average revenue are equal.

[6]Calculus can be used to show this result. If $q = a - bP$, then $P = \frac{a}{b} - \frac{q}{b}$, and total revenue is given by $R(q) = Pq = \frac{aq}{b} - \frac{q^2}{b}$. Hence, marginal revenue is $MR = \frac{dR}{dq} = \frac{a}{b} - \frac{2q}{b}$.

APPLICATION 8.2

Maximizing Profits from Bagels and Catalog Sales

As is usually the case, actual profit-maximizing decisions in the real world are more complicated than economists' theoretical models suggest. Often, firms are uncertain about the demand they face, and they may find that there are constraints on the choices they can actually make. Here, we look at two specific situations where economists have been able to examine such decisions in considerable detail.

Bagels (and Donuts)

Steven Levitt developed a detailed analysis of the delivery of bagels and donuts to Washington, D.C., area businesses over a 15-year period.[1] He was particularly interested in whether the delivery firm seemed to be making profit-maximizing choices with respect to the numbers of bagels and donuts delivered each day and with respect to the prices they were charging. In principle, this should be an easy situation to study because the goods being examined are relatively simple ones and marginal production costs consist mainly of the wholesale price of these goods. Still, Levitt encountered considerable complications. Perhaps the most interesting of these was the fact that bagel sales and donut sales are related. If an office runs out of bagels, some (but not all) disappointed consumers will buy a donut instead and vice versa. An optimal supply policy must take this "cannibalization effect" into account, especially given the fact that during this period Levitt calculated that bagel sales were much more profitable than donut sales. After extensive modeling of profit-maximizing strategies, Levitt concluded that the delivery firm was remarkably good at choosing the proper quantities of bagels and donuts to deliver to a given location. Delivering one more bagel, for example, would have at most yielded about \$.01 in extra profits for the typical location. Having daily sales information clearly helped the firm hone in on the correct delivery strategy.

On the other hand, Levitt concluded that the delivery firm significantly mispriced its products—it could have increased profits by about 50 percent by charging higher prices. There appear to be two reasons why the firm priced in this way. First, payments for bagels and donuts were on the "honor system"—customers simply slipped the money into a lockbox with no one there to check. Hence, the firm may have under-priced to maintain goodwill and the integrity of the honor system. Second, bagel and donut price lists were attached to the lockboxes and were relatively hard to change. So, it may have been less costly to hold prices constant for a time in the face of rising wholesale prices.

Catalog Sales

The notion that prices might be "sticky" (that is, difficult to change) has occupied economists for some time. For example, a 1995 study by Anil Kashyap of prices in the catalogs of L.L.Bean, Orvis, and REI found that these prices were changed infrequently, despite relatively rapid inflation during portions of the periods being examined.[2] Kashyap offered two explanations for this stickiness. First, and most obviously, changing prices was costly for these firms because it meant that they would have to reset the printing for their catalogs. Hence, they were willing to forgo some potential added revenues because it would be too costly to change prices. A second possibility examined by Kashyap is that retail catalogs choose attractive "price points" for their products and are reluctant to change from these for fear consumers will "notice." Of course, everyone is familiar with the fact that firms often charge, say, \$3.99 rather than \$4.00 to make the price seem smaller. Kashyap suggested that this phenomenon is more widespread because consumers have general ideas about what things "should cost." Moving away from such prices, even if justified by cost considerations, could end up hurting sales and profits.

TO THINK ABOUT

1. Because bagels were paid for in a lockbox in Levitt's study, how might considerations of needing the correct change affect pricing?
2. Costs associated with changing prices are sometimes called "menu costs." What are some of the ways that restaurants get around the costs of printing new menus when they wish to change prices?

[1] Steven D. Levitt, "An Economist Sells Bagels: A Case Study on profit-Maximization." *National Bureau of Economic Research Working Paper* 12152. Cambridge, MA. March, 2006.

[2] Anil Kashyap, "Sticky Prices: New Evidence from Retail Catalogues," *The Quarterly Journal of Economics* (February 1995): 245–274.

Figure 8.3 Marginal Revenue Curve Associated with a Demand Curve

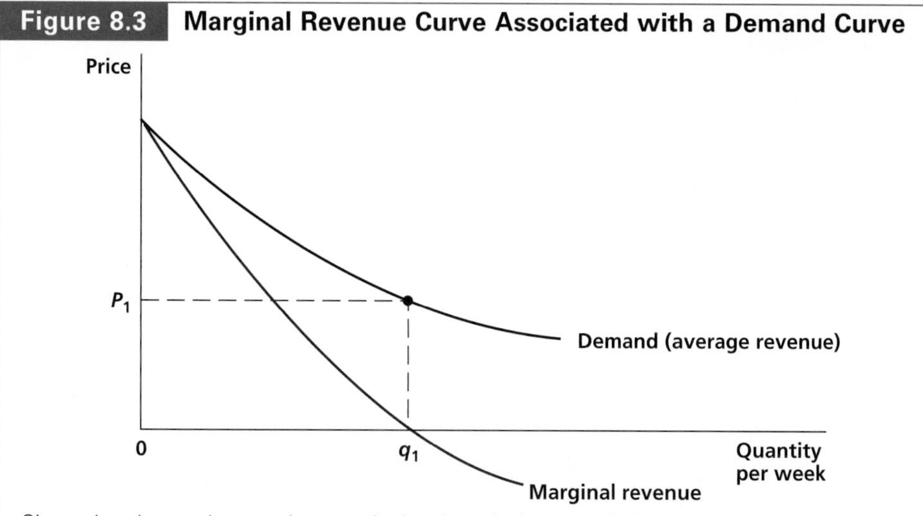

Since the demand curve is negatively sloped, the marginal curve will fall below the demand ("average revenue") curve. For output levels beyond q_1, marginal revenue is negative. At q_1, total revenue ($P_1 \cdot q_1$) is a maximum; beyond this point, additional increases in q actually cause total revenues to fall because of the accompanying decline in price.

Figure 8.4 Marginal Revenue Curve for a Linear Demand Curve

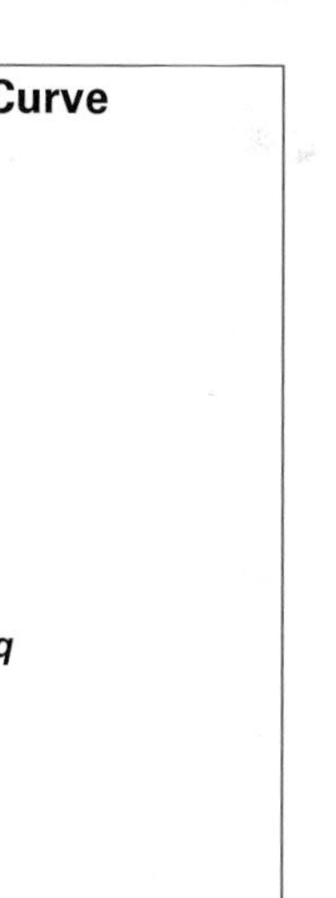

For a linear demand curve, the marginal revenue curve is twice as steep, hitting the horizontal axis at half the quantity at which the demand curve does.

output level,[7] total revenue is at a maximum (25). Any expansion of output beyond $q = 5$ will cause total revenue to fall—that is, marginal revenue is negative. We will use this algebraic approach to calculating marginal revenue in several examples and problems.

[7]The *MR* curve here is calculated using calculus. Hence, the values of *MR* will not agree precisely with those in Table 8.1 because calculus uses small changes in q, whereas the changes shown in the table are "large." Although the figures are close, it will usually be the case that those based on the calculus method used here will be more accurate.

KEEP *in* MIND

Drawing the *MR* Curve Is Simple, but Be Sure Demand Is Linear

The marginal revenue curve shown in Figure 8.4 is twice as steep as the demand curve; therefore, it will have half the q-intercept (that is, 5 instead of 10). Hence, you can always draw a very accurate MR curve by just connecting this point on the q-axis to the P-intercept of the demand curve. But be careful because this approach will only work for a linear demand curve. In other cases (such as shown in Figure 8.3), the relationship between the intercepts of the two curves, if they even exist, may be quite different (see Problem 8.10).

MICRO QUIZ 8.3

Use Equation 8.9 and Figure 8.3 to answer the following questions about the relationship between a demand curve and its associated marginal revenue curve.

1. How does the vertical distance between the demand curve and its marginal revenue curve at a given level of output depend on the price elasticity of demand at that output level?
2. Suppose that an increase in demand leads consumers to be willing to pay 10 percent more for a particular level of output. Will the marginal revenue associated with this level of output increase by more or less than 10 percent? Does your answer depend on whether the elasticity of demand changes as a result of the shift?

Shifts in Demand and Marginal Revenue Curves

In Chapter 3, we talked in detail about the possibility of a demand curve's shifting because of changes in such factors as income, other prices, or preferences. Whenever a demand curve shifts, its associated marginal revenue curve shifts with it. This should be obvious. The marginal revenue curve is always calculated by referring to a specific demand curve. In later analysis, we will have to keep in mind the kinds of shifts that marginal revenue curves might make when we talk about changes in demand. Application 8.3: Evolving Airline Pricing Strategies shows the importance of marginal decisions to the behavior of the airline industry following deregulation.

8-5 Supply Decisions of a Price-Taking Firm

In this section, we look in detail at the supply decisions of a single price-taking firm. This analysis leads directly to the study of market supply curves and price determination—a topic that we take up in the next part. Here, however, we are concerned only with the decisions of a single firm.

Price-Taking Behavior

Before looking at supply decisions, let's briefly explore the price taker assumption. In the theory of demand, the assumption of price-taking behavior seemed to make sense because we all have had the experience of buying something at a fixed price from a vending machine or from a supermarket. Of course, there are situations where you might bargain over price (buying a car or a house), but usually you treat prices as given. The primary reason is that for most of your transactions, there are many other buyers doing the same thing. Whether you buy a Coke from a given vending machine or not will make little difference to the owner of the machine, especially since he or she probably owns many other machines. On the other hand, buying a car or a house is a unique transaction, and you may be able to influence what the seller gets.

APPLICATION 8.3

Evolving Airline Pricing Strategies

Prior to 1978, U.S. airline prices were regulated by the Federal Aviation Administration. The agency also controlled what flights could be offered and constantly debated standards concerning what perks (such as free drinks) could be offered. All of this ended with the Airline Deregulation Act of 1978, which, over time, allowed airlines to follow whatever pricing and marketing strategies they chose. The effects on the nature of air travel have been dramatic.

Discount Pricing

Probably the most obvious effect of airline deregulation was the move toward discount pricing by most carriers. The goal of such airline pricing schemes was to keep prices relatively high for travelers for whom price did not matter very much (business travelers) but gain revenue from those travelers (such as families on vacation) with relatively elastic demands. To accomplish this goal, airlines adopted a wide variety of restrictions on their discount fares, so that they would be unattractive to business travelers. Overall, the advent of discount pricing resulted in a decrease in the average price of airline tickets of about one-third.[1]

Notice how this explanation for discount pricing is consistent with our discussion of marginal revenue, especially with Equation 8.9. If we assume that the marginal costs of flying business travelers and vacation travelers are the same, the profit-maximizing condition $MR = MC$ implies that prices should be lower for those with elastic demands (check this out for yourself). Once freed from price regulation, airlines were able to adopt more flexible pricing schemes that ultimately enhanced consumer welfare.

Adapting Equipment and Routes

Once they were allowed to choose the routes they could fly, airlines also became more cost-conscious in adapting specific planes to their intended routes. Perhaps the greatest success story was Southwest Airlines, which made the decision only to fly Boeing 737 aircraft over medium length routes. Because the airline did not need to service a variety of aircraft types, and because they could adopt innovative loading practices, they were able to keep plane utilization higher (and costs of flying lower) than their competitors. After 2000, a number of new airlines (such as Jet Blue and AirTran) took the Southwest approach one step further by stressing nonstop flights, especially to vacation locales. The cost-savings from avoiding complex interconnections were dramatic.

Unbundling

Although air travel seems a simple matter of moving people from point A to point B, in fact there are a number of different aspects of this travel that people care about. They want comfortable seats, speed in getting through security lines, and access to overhead luggage space. Prior to 2010, most airlines gave customers no choice on these matters—seating, access, and luggage space were primarily bundled together on a first-come, first-served basis. Eventually, the airlines discovered that their customers were willing to pay separately for these items. So, they began offering special options for buying better seats or for gaining early access to a plane (and thereby securing overhead luggage space). In this case, the logic of Equation 8.9 suggests that those customers with the least elastic demand for such flight amenities would pay the most for them. In some cases, the airlines were able to raise the effective price paid by such customers by as much as 25–30 percent.

TO THINK ABOUT

1. Many people are completely bewildered by airline pricing policies—constantly feeling that they are paying more than the person they are sitting next to. Do complicated discount pricing schemes really make airline customers better off, or are these just ways to increase airline profits?
2. Some people view the increasing use of unbundling strategies by airlines to be "unfair." For example, they argue that charging $30 for a better seat ultimately means that higher income people will get better seats than low income people, thereby destroying the "democratic nature" of air travel. Do you agree? Or are better airline seats just like any other good in which the allocation should be determined by willingness and ability to pay?

[1]See C. Winston, "U.S. Industry Adjustment to Economic Deregulation" *Journal of Economic Perspectives* (Summer 1998): 89–110.

The same logic applies to firms. If a firm is producing a good that is just like that produced by many others, it will make little difference how much of it is brought to market because buyers can always buy from another firm. In this case, the firm's only option is to adapt its behavior to the prevailing market price because its decisions won't affect it. On the other hand, if a firm has few competitors, its decisions may affect market price, and it would have to take those effects into account by using the marginal revenue concept. In Part 6, we will look at this situation in detail. But before we get there, we will retain the price-taking assumption.

A Numerical Example Showing Price-Taking Behavior

A numerical example can help illustrate why it may be reasonable for a firm to be a price-taker. Suppose that the demand for, say, corn is given by

$$Q = 16{,}000{,}000{,}000 - 2{,}000{,}000{,}000P, \tag{8.11}$$

where Q is quantity demanded in bushels per year and P is the price per bushel in dollars. Suppose also that there are one million corn growers and that each produces 10,000 bushels a year. In order to see the consequences for price of any one grower's decision, we first solve Equation 8.11 for price:

$$P = 8 - \frac{Q}{2{,}000{,}000{,}000}. \tag{8.12}$$

If $Q = 10{,}000 \times 1{,}000{,}000 = 10{,}000{,}000{,}000$, the price will be $P = \$3.00$. These are the approximate values for long-run U.S. corn production—output is about 10 billion bushels per year, and price is about \$3 per bushel. Now suppose one grower tries to see whether his or her actions might affect price. If he or she produces $q = 0$, total output will be $Q = 10{,}000 \times 999{,}999 = 9{,}999{,}990{,}000$, and the market price will rise to

$$P = 8 - \frac{9{,}999{,}990{,}000}{2{,}000{,}000{,}000} = 3.000005. \tag{8.13}$$

So, for all practical purposes, price is still \$3. In fact, this calculation probably exaggerates the price increase that would be felt if one grower produced nothing because others would surely make up for some of the lost production.

A similar argument applies if a single grower thought about expanding production. If, for example, one very hardworking farmer decided to produce 20,000 bushels in a year, a computation similar to the one we just did would show that price would fall to about $P = \$2.999995$. Again, price would hardly budge. Hence, in situations where there are many suppliers, it appears that it is quite reasonable for any one firm to adopt the position that its decisions cannot affect price. In Application 8.4: Price-Taking Behavior, we look at a few examples where such behavior seems plausible but some complications may arise.

Short-Run Profit Maximization

In Figure 8.5, we look at the supply decision of a single price-taking firm. The figure shows the short-run average and marginal cost curves for a typical firm (see Figure 7.6). We also have drawn a horizontal line at the prevailing price for this firm's product, P^*. This line is also labeled *MR* to show that this is the marginal revenue for this firm—it can sell all it wants and receive this additional revenue from each additional unit sold. Clearly, output level q^* provides maximum profits here—at this output level,

APPLICATION 8.4

Price-Taking Behavior

Finding examples of price-taking behavior by firms in the real world is not easy. Of course, we are all familiar with our roles as price-taking consumers—you either pay the price that the supermarket wants for bread or do without. But for firms, it is sometimes difficult to know how they are actually making production decisions. One approach is to ask where firms get price information. When such information comes from sources that could not reasonably be affected by the firm's output decisions, price-taking behavior seems plausible. Here we look at two examples.

Futures Markets

Futures contracts are agreements to buy or sell a good at a specified date in the future. Such contracts are actively traded for all major crops, for livestock, for energy resources, for precious and industrial metals, and for a variety of financial assets. The prices specified in these contracts are set by the forces of supply and demand on major commodity exchanges and are reported daily in newspapers. This source of price information is widely used both by speculators and by firms for whom the act of production may take some time. For example, your authors both heat their homes with fuel oil. Each heating season, the dealer offers to sell us a predetermined amount of fuel oil at a price determined by the futures price the dealer must pay. Hence, the price we pay and the price the dealer receives is primarily determined in a market that is worldwide.

Similar examples of the importance of futures prices are easy to find. One study of broiler chickens,[1] for example, found that firms based their sales decisions primarily on an index of prices from the broiler futures market. Other researchers have found similar results for such diverse markets as the market for electricity, the market for frozen orange juice, and the market for fresh shrimp. In all of these cases, the firms' primary sources of price information are large, organized markets, results from which can be readily obtained from the media or over the Internet. It seems reasonable that any one firm would assume that its decisions cannot affect the price received.

Market Orders

One reason that price-taking behavior may occur is simply because other ways of proceeding may be too costly. For example, when you wish to buy shares of stock from a broker, there are several ways you can specify what price you are willing to pay. The most common procedure is to place a "market order," which states that you are willing to pay the price that prevails when the order arrives. But you can also place other types of orders featuring various limits on what you are willing to pay. Economists who have looked in detail at these various ways of buying stock generally conclude that it makes little difference what a buyer does.[2] Any gains from using complicated buying strategies are counterbalanced by the extra costs involved in using those strategies.

For some firms, a similar logic may prevail. A soybean farmer, for example, may have two options in selling the crop. He or she may take it to the local dealer and accept the price being offered (which, in turn, is based on what the dealer can sell soybeans for in major markets), or the farmer may set conditions on the sale or try to search out other dealers with better offers. But often it may be the case that the gains of more sophisticated sales methods are simply outweighed by the costs of undertaking them. Costs may be minimized by simply taking the price being offered by the local dealer. The dealer, in turn, is probably determining what to pay based on national information about prices.

TO THINK ABOUT

1. When a firm's production takes some time to accomplish, it may prefer to sell its output in the futures market rather than waiting to see what price prevails when the goods are finally ready for market. Would the same logic apply if the quantity produced could be easily adapted to prevailing market conditions?
2. Under what conditions would a firm spend resources searching for a better price for its output? When would it be content with a readily available offer, even though it is possible there is a better price elsewhere?

[1] L J. Maynard, C. R. Dillon, and J. Carter, "Go Ahead, Count Your Chickens: Cross-Hedging Strategies in the Broiler Industry," *Journal of Agricultural and Applied Economics* (April 2001): 79–90.

[2] See D. P. Brown and Z. M. Zhang, "Market Orders and Market Efficiency," *Journal of Finance* (March 1997): 277–308.

Figure 8.5 Short-Run Supply Curve for a Price-Taking Firm

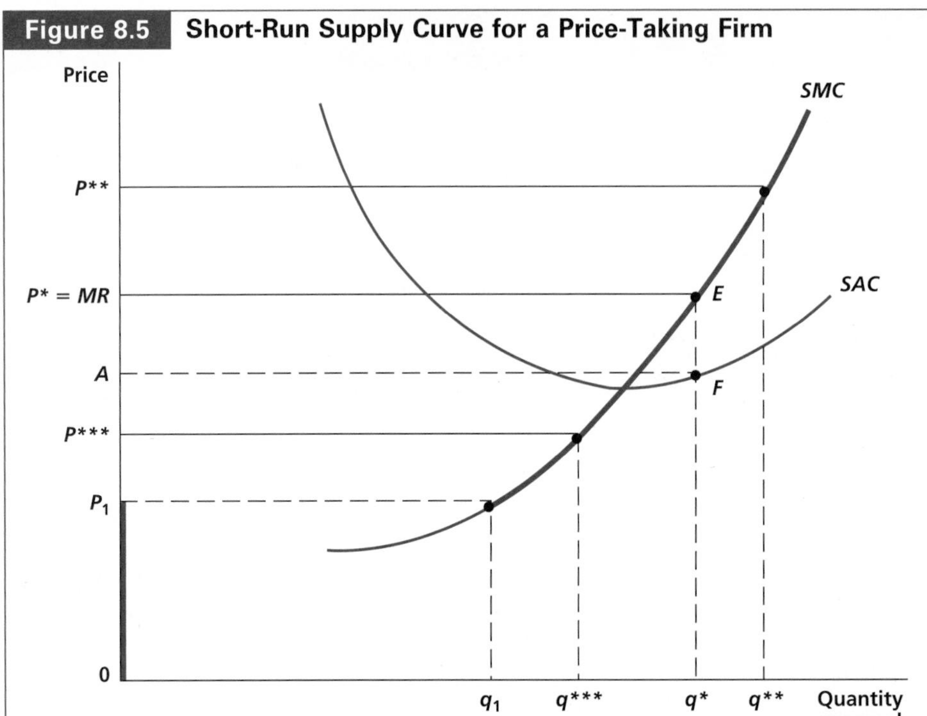

The firm maximizes short-run profits by producing that output for which $P = SMC$. For $P < P_1$ (P_1 = minimum short-run average variable cost), the firm chooses to shut down ($q = 0$). The short-run supply curve is given by the heavy colored lines in the figure.

price (marginal revenue) is indeed equal to marginal cost. You can tell that profits are as large as possible at q^* by simply asking what would happen if the firm produced either slightly more or slightly less. For any q less than q^*, price (P^*) exceeds marginal cost. Hence, an expansion in output would yield more in extra revenues than in extra costs—profits would rise by moving toward q^*. Similarly, if the firm opted for $q > q^*$, now marginal cost would exceed P^*. Cutting back on output would save more in costs than would be lost in sales revenue. Again, profits would rise by moving toward q^*.

Showing Profits

The actual amount of profits being earned by this firm when it decides to produce q^* is easiest to show by using the short-run, average-cost curve. Because profits are given by

$$\text{Profits} = \pi = \text{Total Revenue} - \text{Total Cost} = P^*q^* - STC(q^*), \quad \textbf{(8.14)}$$

we can factor q^* out of this expression to get

$$\text{Profits} = \pi = q^*\left(P^* - \frac{STC}{q^*}\right) = q^*[P^* - SAC(q^*)]. \quad \textbf{(8.15)}$$

So, total profits are given by profits-per-unit (price minus average cost) times the number of units sold. Geometrically, profits per unit are shown in Figure 8.5 by the vertical distance *EF*. Notice that the average cost used to calculate these per-unit profits is the actual average cost experienced when the firm produces q^*. Now, total profits are found by multiplying this vertical distance by the number of units sold, q^*. These are therefore given by the area of the rectangle P^*EFA. In this case, these profits are positive because $P > SAC$. These could be zero if $P = SAC$, or even negative if $P < SAC$. Regardless of whether profits are positive or negative, we know that they are as large as possible because output level q^* obeys the marginal-revenue-equals-marginal-cost rule.[8]

The Firm's Short-Run Supply Curve

Firm's short-run supply curve
The relationship between price and quantity supplied by a firm in the short run.

The positively sloped portion of the short-run marginal cost curve is the **firm's short-run supply curve** for this price-taking firm. That is, the curve shows how much the firm will produce for every possible market price. At a higher price of P^{**}, for example, the firm will produce q^{**} because it will find it in its interest to incur the higher marginal costs q^{**} entails. By considering all possible prices that this firm might face it seems clear that the short-run marginal cost curve will show the quantity they will supply. Hence, that curve is in fact the firm's short-run supply curve.

Negative Profits and the Shutdown Decision

Before fully accepting this conclusion uncritically, we might worry about the possibility that this simple application of the $P = SMC$ rule might yield significant losses for the firm. For example, at a price of P^{***} application of the rule would have the firm produce q^{***} and, because this price falls well below short-run average costs, the firm will have negative profits (that is losses). Would any firm really settle for this dismal outcome?

In order to answer this question, we must ask what other options the firm has. Probably the simplest alternative would be to produce nothing (that is, choose $q = 0$). In the long run this is clearly the best choice. Because, by definition, all production costs can be avoided in the long run, producing nothing will yield a profit of precisely zero—which is much better than a loss. But, in the short run we must consider the fact that the firm will incur fixed costs (for example, heating the factory) no matter how much it produces. It is therefore not so clear that producing nothing (and suffering a loss of all fixed costs) is the best strategy. It may be possible that the firm can do better than this by sticking to the $P = MC$ rule.

Some algebra can help to clarify this situation. In the short run profits are given by:

$$\text{Profits} = \text{Total Revenue} - \text{Total Costs} = Pq - \text{Variable Costs} - \text{Fixed Costs} \quad \textbf{(8.16)}$$

If the firm opts to produce nothing, total revenue is zero as are variable costs. Hence, profits are equal to minus fixed costs—that is, in each period the firm will lose whatever fixed costs it must pay. If the firm is to produce any positive output, it must obtain more profits by doing so than it receives from producing nothing. Hence, it must be the case that:

$$\text{Profits} = Pq - \text{Variable Costs} - \text{Fixed Costs} \geq -\text{Fixed Costs}. \quad \textbf{(8.17)}$$

[8]Technically, the $P = MC$ rule is only a necessary condition for a maximum in profits. The value of q found by applying this rule would not yield maximum profits if the marginal cost curve had a negative slope at q^*. In that case, either increasing or decreasing q slightly would in fact increase profits. For all of our analysis, therefore, we will assume that the short-run marginal cost curve has a positive slope at the output level for which $P = SMC$.

and this implies that

$$Pq - \text{Variable Costs} \geq 0$$
$$\text{or } Pq \geq \text{Variable Costs} \tag{8.18}$$
$$\text{or } P \geq (\text{Variable Costs})/q.$$

So, the firm will produce some positive output, provided that the revenue received from this production exceeds the variable costs incurred. By proceeding in this way, the firm provides some offset to the fixed costs it will incur no matter how much it produces. The final line of Equation 8.18 then tells us how low price can go to achieve this result—that is, price must exceed average variable cost if the firm is to produce anything in the short run. If price falls short of this level, the firm will shut down and produce nothing.

Shutdown price
The price below which the firm will choose to produce no output in the short run. Equal to minimum average variable cost.

This **shutdown price** is shown by the heavy-colored vertical line segment in Figure 8.5. Any price below P_1 will lead the firm to produce no output. But any price above P_1 will cause the firm to produce according to the $P = MC$ rule, even if that decision results in a short-run loss (as it will at a price of P^{***}). Hence our conclusion that the firm's short run supply curve is given by its short run marginal cost curve must be modified a bit to take into account that price might fall below its shutdown level. Should that occur, the firm will simply produce nothing.

Of course, in the long run, no firm can continue to operate at a loss. Hence, in the long run, price must be at least equal to average cost and the analysis of this section applies only to short run situations. Application 8.5: Boom and Bust in the Oil Patch illustrates how the short-run, long-run distinction can play an important role in understanding firms' output decisions. In Chapter 9, we will take up the analysis of how markets operate in the long run in considerably more detail.

A Numerical Illustration

The relationship between market prices and a price-taking firm's supply decision can be illustrated with a simple example. Suppose that a firm's short-run total costs are given by

$$STC = 0.1q^2 + 5q + 300, \tag{8.19}$$

and that short-run marginal costs are

$$SMC = 0.2q + 5. \tag{8.20}$$

If this firm accepts market price (P) as a given, it will maximize profits by setting this price equal to its short-run marginal costs

$$P = SMC = 0.2q + 5. \tag{8.21}$$

Solving for the firm's output (q) yields its short-run supply relationship

$$0.2q = P - 5 \quad \text{or} \quad q = 5P - 25. \tag{8.22}$$

Table 8.3 illustrates the implication of this supply relationship for prices ranging between 10 and 35. Two points are immediately clear from the table. First, as price rises, this firm will produce more (this is obvious because of the positive coefficient for price in Equation 8.22). As the firm produces more, its profits also rise dramatically. This is exactly what we showed in Figure 8.5.

Table 8.3 Supply Behavior for a Firm with costs of STC = $0.1q^2 + 5q + 300$

P	q	Pq	STC	PROFITS
35	150	5250	3300	1950
30	125	3750	2487.5	1262.5
25	100	2500	1800	700
20	75	1500	1237.5	262.5
15	50	750	800	−50
10	25	250	487.5	−237.5

APPLICATION 8.5

Boom and Bust in the Oil Patch

The production of crude oil by both large and small firms provides a number of illustrations of the principles of short-run supply behavior by price-taking firms. Because prices for crude oil are set in international markets, these firms clearly are price takers, responding to the price incentives they face. Drillers face sharply increasing marginal costs as they drill to greater depths or in less accessible areas. Hence, we should expect oil well activity to follow our model of how price-taking firms respond to price changes.

Some Historical Data

Table 1 shows U.S. oil well-drilling activity over the past 4 decades. Here, drilling activity is measured in thousands of feet drilled to measure firms' willingness to drill more wells deeper. The table also shows the average price of crude oil in the various years, adjusted for changing prices of drilling equipment. The tripling of real oil prices between 1970 and 1980 led to a doubling of drilling. In many cases, these additional wells were drilled in high-cost locations (for example, in deep water in the Gulf of Mexico or on the Arctic Slope in Alaska). Clearly, the late 1970s and early 1980s were boom times for oil drillers. As predicted, they responded to price signals being provided through the market.

Price Decline and Supply Behavior

Recessions in 1981 and 1990, combined with vast new supplies of crude oil (from the North Sea and Mexico, for example), put considerable pressure on oil prices. By 1990, real crude oil prices had declined by about 40 percent from their levels of the early 1980s. U.S. drillers were quick to respond to these changing circumstances. As Table 1 shows, less than half the number of feet were drilled in 1990 as in 1980. Many smaller firms ceased production of crude oil entirely during this period because the very low prices did not even cover their variable costs of production such as labor costs and costs of electricity to run their wells.

Price Recovery and the Fracking Revolution

Drilling continued to decline during the 1990s as prices for crude oil stagnated. But, starting after 2000, prices began a major move upward and this increased drilling dramatically. By 2008 (the latest year data are available), real prices had risen dramatically and the number of feet drilled had expanded by more than 250 percent from its low point.

Our model of supply behavior is a relatively static one—it does not allow for technical improvements in production. In later chapters we will seek to remedy this shortcoming. For now, however, we should remark on a major innovation in drilling technology that occurred during the 2000s. With the introduction of hydraulic fracturing ("fracking") and horizontal drilling, oil deposits that could not previously be used profitably became accessible. This revolution in technology in part explains the huge increase in drilling by 2008. More recent data would show an even greater increase. Clearly the high oil prices of the 2000s not only caused firms to drill more, but also led to significant innovations in drilling technology.

POLICY CHALLENGE

Drilling for oil is politically controversial in the United States and much of the rest of the world. Such controversy stems both from the environmental hazards associated with drilling itself and from concerns about climate change that may be induced by using the oil produced. The advent of fracking has exacerbated these disputes with several U.S. states and many European countries banning the practice. Are such outright restrictions the best way to address environmental issues that surround the drilling for oil?

Table 1 World Oil Prices and Oil Well Drilling Activity in the United States

YEAR	WORLD PRICE PER BARREL	REAL PRICE PER BARREL*	THOUSANDS OF FEET DRILLED
1970	$3.18	$7.93	56,860
1980	$21.59	$25.16	125,262
1990	$20.03	$16.30	55,269
2000	$23.00	$16.40	33,777
2008	$95.00	$63.00	88,382

*Nominal price divided by producer price index for capital equipment, 1982 = 1.00.
Source: U.S. Department of Energy, http://www.eia.doe.gov.

MICRO QUIZ 8.4

Use the theory of short-run supply illustrated in Figure 8.5 to answer the following questions:

1. How will an increase in the fixed costs that Burger King must pay to heat its outlets affect the firm's short-run supply curve for Whoppers?
2. How will a $10,000 fine imposed on Burger King for littering by its customers affect the firm's short-run shutdown decision? Would your answer change if the fine were $1,000 per day, to be ended once the littering stopped?

A second observation about the figures in Table 8.3 is that at very low prices this firm makes losses. This suggests we need to check whether the firm would be better off by producing no output when such prices occur. For the prices in the table, this is easily done—since none of the prices yields a loss of greater than the loss of all fixed costs (which here are 300 because those are costs when $q = 0$), it must be the case that production is covering variable costs and to some extent offsetting these fixed costs. In fact, in this example, the firm's shutdown price is given by

$$P_{\text{shutdown}} = \frac{\text{Variable Costs}}{q} = \frac{0.1q^2 + 5q}{q} = 0.1q + 5. \qquad \textbf{(8.23)}$$

Comparing this price to short-run marginal costs (Equation 8.21) shows that this shutdown price is always less than *SMC* (which is set equal to the market price for profit maximization). Hence, in this case, the firm will never shutdown even though it may suffer losses when price is very low. This will not always be the case, however, so you need to check whether shutting down makes sense in every short-run problem.

KEEP *in* MIND

The firm's supply decision is shown by how much they will produce at any given price. To derive this you must first set price equal to marginal cost and then solve for output (as in Equation 8.22) as a function of market price. You do not have a supply relationship until you do so. A final step in finding a solution, then, is to check whether your relationship works for any price, or whether the firm may find it more profitable to produce nothing when price is very low.

SUMMARY

In this chapter, we examined the assumption that firms seek to maximize profits in making their decisions. A number of conclusions follow from this assumption:

- In making output decisions, a firm should produce the output level for which marginal revenue equals marginal cost. Only at this level of production is the cost of extra output, at the margin, exactly balanced by the revenue it yields.
- Similar marginal rules apply to the hiring of inputs by profit-maximizing firms. These are examined in Chapter 13.
- For a firm facing a downward-sloping demand curve, marginal revenue will be less than price. In this case, the marginal revenue curve will lie below the market demand curve.
- When there are many firms producing the same output, it may make sense for any one of them to adopt price-taking behavior. That is, the firm assumes that its actions will not affect market price. So, marginal revenue is given by that market price.
- A price-taking firm will maximize profits by choosing that output level for which price (marginal revenue) is equal to marginal cost. For this reason, the firm's short-run supply curve is its short-run marginal cost curve (which is assumed to be positively sloped).
- If price falls below average variable cost, the profit-maximizing decision for a firm will be to produce no output. That is, it will shut down. The firm will still incur fixed costs in the short run, so its short-run profits will be negative.

REVIEW QUESTIONS

1. Accounting rules determine a firm's "profits" for tax- and dividend-paying purposes. So why should any firm be concerned about its economic profits? Specifically, why should a firm be concerned about the opportunity costs of the people who invest in it when those costs never enter into its accounting statements?
2. "Economic profits are like fly paper—they will attract any capital that happens to be flying nearby." Explain the real world relevance of this colorful statement. Would the statement be correct if "economic profits" were replaced with "accounting profits"? Can you think of any situation where the statement as written might not be true?
3. Explain whether each of the following actions would affect the firm's profit-maximizing decision. (Hint: how would each affect MR and MC?)
   a. An increase in the per unit cost of a variable input such as labor
   b. A decline in the output price for a price-taking firm
   c. Institution of a small fixed fee to be paid to the government for the right of doing business
   d. Institution of a 50 percent tax on the firm's economic profits
   e. Institution of a per-unit tax on each unit the firm produces
   f. Receipt of a no-strings-attached grant from the government
   g. Receipt of a subsidy per unit of output from the government
   h. Receipt of a subsidy per worker hired from the government
4. Sally Greenhorn has just graduated from a noted business school but does not have the foggiest idea about her new job with a firm that sells shrink-wrapped dog biscuits. She has been given responsibility for a new line of turkey-flavored biscuits and must decide how many to produce. She opts for the following strategy: (1) Begin by hiring one worker and one dog biscuit machine (assume workers and machines are used in fixed proportions); (2) if the revenues from this pilot project exceed its costs, add a second worker and machine; (3) if the additional revenues generated from the second worker/machine combination exceed what these cost, add a third; and (4) stop this process when adding a worker/machine combination brings less in revenues than it costs. Answer the following questions about SG's approach:
   a. Is SG using a marginal approach to her hiring of inputs?
   b. Does the approach adopted by SG also imply that she is following a $MR = MC$ rule for finding a profit-maximizing output?
   c. SG's distinguished professor of marketing examines her procedures and suggests she is mistaken in her approach. He insists that she should instead measure the profit on each new worker/machine combination employed and stop adding new output as soon as the last one added earns a lower profit than the previous one. How would you evaluate his distinguished advice?
5. Two students are preparing for their micro exam, but they seem confused:

   Student A: "We learned that demand curves always slope downward. In the case of a competitive firm, this downward-sloping demand curve is also the firm's marginal revenue curve. So that is why marginal revenue is equal to price."

   Student B: "I think you have it wrong. The demand curve facing a competitive firm is horizontal. The marginal revenue curve is also horizontal, but it lies below the demand curve. So marginal revenue is less than price."

   Can you clear up this drivel? Explain why neither student is likely to warrant a grade commensurate with his or her name.
6. Two features of the demand facing a firm will ensure that the firm must act as a price taker:
   a. That other firms be willing to provide all that is demanded at the current price, and
   b. That consumers of the firm's output regard it as identical to that of its competitors.

   Explain why both of these conditions are required if the firm is to treat the price of its output as given. Describe what the demand facing the firm would be like if one of the conditions held but not the other.
7. Two economics professors earn royalties from their textbook that are specified as 12 percent of the book's total revenues. Assuming that the demand curve for this text is a downward-sloping straight line, how many copies of this book would the professors wish their publisher to sell? Is this the same number that the publisher itself would want to sell?
8. Show graphically the price that would yield exactly zero in economic profits to a firm in the short run. With the price, why are profits maximized even though they are zero? Does this zero-profit solution imply that the firm's owners are starving?
9. Why do economists believe short-run marginal cost curves have positive slopes? Why does this belief lead to the notion that short-run supply curves have positive

slopes? What kind of signal does a higher price send to a firm with increasing marginal costs? Would a reduction in output ever be the profit-maximizing response to an increase in price for a price-taking firm?

10. Wildcat John owns a few low-quality oil wells in Hawaii. He was heard complaining recently about the low price of crude oil: "With this \$70 per barrel price, I can't make any money—it costs me \$90 per barrel just to run my oil pumps. Still, I only paid \$1 an acre for my land many years ago, so I think I will just stop pumping for a time and wait for prices to get above \$90." What do you make of John's production decisions?

PROBLEMS

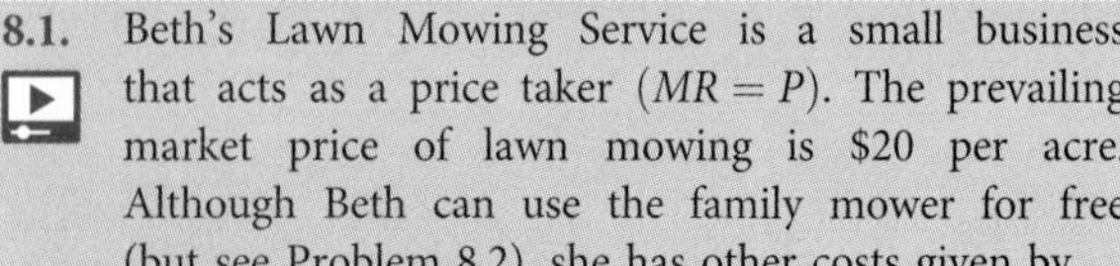

8.1. Beth's Lawn Mowing Service is a small business that acts as a price taker ($MR = P$). The prevailing market price of lawn mowing is \$20 per acre. Although Beth can use the family mower for free (but see Problem 8.2), she has other costs given by

$$\text{Total cost} = 0.1q^2 + 10q + 50,$$
$$\text{Marginal cost} = 0.2q + 10,$$

where q = the number of acres Beth chooses to mow in a week.

a. How many acres should Beth choose to mow in order to maximize profit?
b. Calculate Beth's maximum weekly profit.
c. Graph these results and label Beth's supply curve.

8.2. Consider again the profit-maximizing decision of Beth's Lawn Mowing Service from Problem 8.1. Suppose Beth's greedy father decides to charge for the use of the family lawn mower.

a. If the lawn mower charge is set at \$100 per week, how will this affect the acres of lawns Beth chooses to mow? What will her profits be?
b. Suppose instead that Beth's father requires her to pay 50 percent of weekly profits as a mower charge. How will this affect Beth's profit-maximizing decision?
c. If Beth's greedy father imposes a charge of \$2 per acre for use of the family mower, how will this affect Beth's marginal cost function? How will it affect her profit-maximizing decision? What will her profits be now? How much will Beth's greedy father get?
d. Suppose finally that Beth's father collects his \$2 per acre by collecting 10 percent of the revenues from each acre Beth mows. How will this affect Beth's profit-maximizing decision? Explain why you get the same result here as for part c.

8.3. A number of additional conclusions can be drawn from the fact that the marginal revenue curve associated with a linear demand curve is also linear and has the same price intercept and twice the slope of the original demand curve.

a. Show that the horizontal intercept of the marginal revenue curve (for a linear demand curve) is precisely half of the value of the demand curve's horizontal intercept.
b. Explain why the intercept discussed in part a shows the quantity that maximizes total revenue available from the demand curve.
c. Explain why the price elasticity of demand at this level of output is -1.
d. Illustrate the conclusions of parts a-c with a linear demand curve of the form $q = 96 - 2P$.

8.4. Suppose that a firm faces a demand curve that has a constant elasticity of -2. This demand curve is given by

$$q = 256/P^2.$$

Suppose also that the firm has a marginal cost curve of the form

$$MC = 0.001q$$

a. Graph these demand and marginal cost curves.
b. Calculate the marginal revenue curve associated with the demand curve; graph this curve. (Hint: use Equation 8.9 for this part of the problem.)
c. At what output level does marginal revenue equal marginal cost?

8.5. Although we only discussed profit maximization as a goal of firms in this chapter, many of the tools developed can be used to illustrate other goals as well. To do so, assume a firm faces a downward-sloping, linear-demand curve and has constant average and marginal costs.

a. Suppose this firm wished to maximize the total number of units it sells, subject to the constraint that it cannot operate at a loss. How many units should it produce, and what price should it charge?

b. Suppose this firm wished to maximize the total revenue it collects. How many units should it produce, and what should it charge?
c. Suppose this firm wished to maximize the number of units it sells subject to the constraint that it must earn a profit of 1 percent on its sales. How many units should it produce, and what price should it charge?
d. Suppose this firm wished to maximize its profits per unit. How much should it produce, and what should it charge?
e. Compare the solutions to parts a–d to the output that would be chosen by a profit-maximizing firm. Explain why the results of these goals differ from profit maximization in each case.

8.6. A local pizza shop has hired a consultant to help it compete with national chains in the area. Because most business is handled by these national chains, the local shop operates as a price taker. Using historical data on costs, the consultant finds that short-run total costs each day are given by $STC = 10 + q + 0.1q^2$, where q is daily pizza production. The consultant also reports that short-run marginal costs are given by $SMC = 1 + 0.2q$.

a. What is this price-taking firm's short-run supply curve?
b. Does this firm have a shutdown price? That is, what is the lowest price at which the firm will produce any pizza?
c. The pizza consultant calculates this shop's short-run average costs as

$$SAC = \frac{10}{q} + 1 + 0.1q,$$

and claims that SAC reaches a minimum at $q = 10$. How would you verify this claim without using calculus?
d. The consultant also claims that any price for pizza of less than \$3 will cause this shop to lose money. Is the consultant correct? Explain.
e. Currently the price of pizza is low (\$2) because one major chain is having a sale. Because this price does not cover average costs, the consultant recommends that this shop cease operations until the sale is over. Would you agree with this recommendation? Explain.

8.7. The town where Beth's Lawn Mowing Service is located (see Problems 8.1 and 8.2) is subject to sporadic droughts and monsoons. During periods of drought, the price for mowing lawns drops to \$15 per acre, whereas during monsoons, it rises to \$25 per acre.

a. How will Beth react to these changing prices?
b. Suppose that weeks of drought and weeks of monsoons each occur half the time during a summer. What will Beth's average weekly profit be?
c. Suppose Beth's kindly (but still greedy) father offers to eliminate the uncertainty in Beth's profits by agreeing to trade her the weekly profits based on a stable price of \$20 per acre in exchange for the profits Beth actually makes. Should she take the deal?
d. Graph your results and explain them intuitively.

8.8. In order to break the hold of Beth's greedy father over his struggling daughter (Problems 8.1, 8.2, and 8.7), the government is thinking of instituting an income subsidy plan for the lass. Two plans are under consideration: (1) a flat grant of \$200 per week to Beth, and (2) a grant of \$4 per acre mowed.

a. Which of these plans will Beth prefer?
b. What is the cost of plan (2) to the government?

8.9. Suppose the production function for high-quality brandy is given by

$$q = \sqrt{K \cdot L},$$

where q is the output of brandy per week and L is labor hours per week. In the short run, K is fixed at 100, so the short-run production function is

$$q = 10\sqrt{L}$$

a. If capital rents for \$10 and wages are \$5 per hour, show that short-run total costs are

$$STC = 1{,}000 + 0.05q^2.$$

b. Given the short-run total cost curve in part a, short-run marginal costs are given by

$$SMC = 0.1q.$$

With this short-run marginal cost curve, how much will the firm produce at a price of \$20 per bottle of brandy? How many labor hours will be hired per week?
c. Suppose that, during recessions, the price of brandy falls to \$15 per bottle. With this price, how much would the firm choose to produce, and how many labor hours would be hired?
d. Suppose that the firm believes that the fall in the price of brandy will last for only one week, after which it will wish to return to the level of production in part a. Assume also that, for each hour that the firm reduces its workforce below that described in part a, it incurs a cost of \$1. If it proceeds as in part c, will it earn a profit or incur a loss? Explain.

8.10. Abby is the sole owner of a nail salon. Her costs for any number of manicures (q) are given by

$$TC = 10 + q^2,$$
$$AC = \frac{10}{q} + q,$$
$$MC = 2q.$$

The nail salon is open only 2 days a week—Wednesdays and Saturdays. On both days, Abby acts as a price taker, but price is much higher on the weekend. Specifically, $P = 10$ on Wednesdays and $P = 20$ on Saturdays.

a. Calculate how many manicures Abby will perform on each day.
b. Calculate Abby's profits on each day.
c. The National Association of Nail Salons has proposed a uniform pricing policy for all of its members. They must always charge $P = 15$ to avoid the claim that customers are being "ripped off" on the weekends. Should Abby join the Association and follow its pricing rules?
d. In its brochures, the Association claims that "because salon owners are risk averse (see Chapter 4), they will generally prefer our uniform price policy rather than subjecting themselves to widely fluctuating prices." What do you make of this claim?

PART 5

Perfect Competition

"As every individual endeavours ... to direct industry so that its produce may be of greatest value ... he is led by an invisible hand to promote an end which was no part of his intention. By pursuing his own interest he frequently promotes that of society more effectively than when he really intends to promote it."

—Adam Smith, The Wealth of Nations, 1776

In this part, we look at price determination in markets with large numbers of demanders and suppliers. In such competitive markets, price-taking behavior is followed by all parties. Prices therefore convey important information about the relative scarcity of various goods and, under certain circumstances, help to achieve the sort of efficient overall allocation of resources that Adam Smith had in mind in his famous "invisible hand" analogy.

Chapter 9 develops the theory of perfectly competitive price determination in a single market. By focusing on the role of the entry and exit of firms in response to profitability in a market, the chapter shows that the supply-demand mechanism is considerably more flexible than is often assumed in simpler models. It also permits a more complete study of the relationship between goods' markets and the markets for the inputs that are employed in making these goods. A few applications of these models are also provided.

In Chapter 10, we examine how a complete set of competitive markets operates as a whole. That is, we develop an entire "general equilibrium" model of how a competitive economy operates. Such a model provides a more detailed picture of all of the effects that occur when something in the economy changes.

9 Perfect Competition in a Single Market

This chapter discusses how prices are determined in a single perfectly competitive market. The theory we develop here is an elaboration of Marshall's supply and demand analysis that is at the core of all of economics. We show how equilibrium prices are established and describe some of the factors that cause prices to change. We also look at some of the many applications of this model.

9-1 Timing of a Supply Response

Supply response
The change in quantity of output supplied in response to a change in demand conditions.

In the analysis of price determination, it is important to decide the length of time that is to be allowed for a **supply response** to changing demand conditions. The pattern of equilibrium prices will be different if we are talking about a very short period of time during which supply is essentially fixed and unchanging than if we are envisioning a very long-run process in which it is possible for entirely new firms to enter a market. For this reason, it has been traditional in economics to discuss pricing over three different time frames: (1) the very short run, (2) the short run, and (3) the long run. Although it is not possible to give these terms an exact time length, the essential distinction among them concerns the nature of the supply response that is assumed to be possible. In the *very short run*, there can be no supply response—quantity supplied is absolutely fixed. In the *short run*, existing firms may change the quantity they are supplying but no new firms can enter the market. In the *long run*, firms can further change the quantity supplied and completely new firms may enter a market; this produces a very flexible supply response. This chapter discusses each of these different types of responses.

9-2 Pricing in the Very Short Run

Market period
A short period of time during which quantity supplied is fixed.

In the very short run or **market period**, there is no supply response. The goods are already "in" the marketplace and must be sold for whatever the market will bear. In this situation, price acts only to ration demand. The price will adjust to clear the market of the quantity that must be sold. Although the market price may act as a signal to producers in future periods, it does not perform such a function currently because current period output cannot be changed.

Figure 9.1 illustrates this situation.[1] Market demand is represented by the curve D. Supply is fixed at Q^*, and the price that clears the market is P_1. At P_1, people are willing to take all that is offered in the market. Sellers want to dispose of Q^* without regard to price (for example, the good in question may be perishable and will be worthless if not sold immediately). The price P_1 balances the desires of demanders with the desires of

[1]As in previous chapters, we use Q to represent total quantity bought or sold in a market and q to represent the output of a single firm.

Figure 9.1 Pricing in the Very Short Run

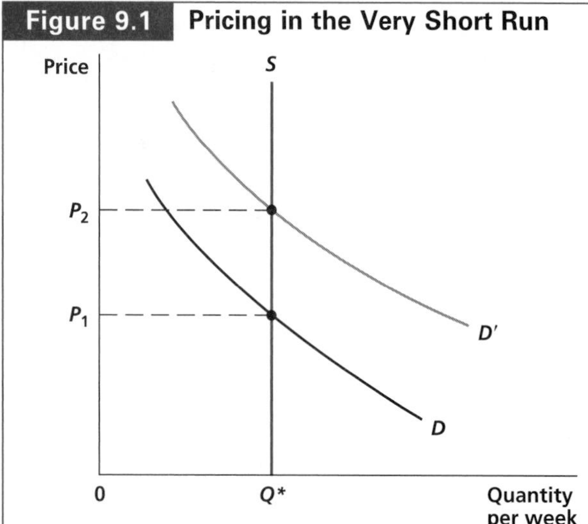

When quantity is absolutely fixed in the very short run, price acts only as a device to ration demand. With quantity fixed at Q^*, price P_1 will prevail in the market-place if D is the market demand curve. At this price, individuals are willing to consume exactly that quantity available. If demand should shift upward to D', the equilibrium price would rise to P_2.

suppliers. For this reason, it is called an **equilibrium price**. In Figure 9.1, a price in excess of P_1 would not be an equilibrium price because people would demand less than Q^* (remember that firms are always willing to supply Q^* no matter what the price). Similarly, a price below P_1 would not be an equilibrium price because people would then demand more than Q^*. P_1 is the only equilibrium price possible when demand conditions are those represented by the curve D.

Shifts in Demand: Price as a Rationing Device

If the demand curve in Figure 9.1 shifted outward to D' (perhaps because incomes increased or because the price of some close substitute increased), P_1 would no longer be an equilibrium price. With the demand curve D', far more than Q^* is demanded at the price P_1. Some people who wish to make purchases at a price of P_1 would find that not enough of the good is now available to meet the increase in demand. In order to ration the available quantity among all demanders, the price would have to rise to P_2. At that new price, demand would again be reduced to Q^* (by a movement along D' in a northwesterly direction as the price rises). The price rise would restore equilibrium to the market. The curve labeled S (for "supply") in Figure 9.1 shows all the equilibrium prices for Q^* for any conceivable shift in demand. The price must always adjust to ration demand to exactly whatever supply is available. In Application 9.1: Internet Auctions, we look at how this price-setting mechanism works in practice.

Equilibrium price
The price at which the quantity demanded by buyers of a good is equal to the quantity supplied by sellers of the good.

Applicability of the Very Short-Run Model

The model of the very short run is not particularly useful for most markets. Although the theory may adequately apply to some situations where goods are perishable, the far more common situation involves some degree of supply response to changing demand. It is usually presumed that a rise in price prompts producers to bring additional quantity into the market. We have already seen why this is true in Chapter 8 and will explore the response in detail in the next section.

Before beginning that analysis, note that increases in quantity supplied in response to higher prices need not come only from increased production. In a world in which some goods are durable (that is, last longer than a single market period), current owners of these goods may supply them in increasing amounts to the market as price rises. For example, even though the supply of Rembrandts is absolutely fixed, we would not draw the market

MICRO QUIZ 9.1

Suppose that a flower grower brings 100 boxes of roses to auction. There are many buyers at the auction; each may either offer to buy one box at the stated price by raising a bid paddle or decline to buy.

1. If the auctioneer starts at zero and calls off successively higher per-box prices, how will he or she know when an equilibrium is reached?
2. If the auctioneer starts off at an implausibly high price ($1,000/box) and successively lowers that price, how will he or she know when an equilibrium is reached?

APPLICATION 9.1

Internet Auctions

Auctions on the Internet have rapidly become one of the most popular ways of selling all manner of goods. Web sites offering auctions range from huge, all-inclusive listings such as those on eBay or Amazon to highbrow specialties (Sotheby's). Virtually every type of good can be found on some Web site. There are sites that specialize in collectibles, industrial equipment, office supplies, and the truly weird (check out Disturbingauctions.com). Occasionally, even human organs have appeared in Internet auctions, though, at least in the United States, selling such items is illegal and this may have been a hoax.

Is Supply Fixed in Internet Auctions?

There is a sense in which Internet auctions resemble the theoretical situation illustrated in Figure 9.1—the goods listed are indeed in fixed supply and will be sold for whatever bidders are willing to pay. But this view of things may be too simple because it ignores dynamic elements that may be present in suppliers' decisions. Suppose, for example, that a supplier has 10 copies of an out-of-print book to sell. Should he or she list all 10 at once? Because buyers may search for what they want only infrequently, such a strategy may not be a good one. Selling all of the books at once may yield rather low prices for the final few sold because, at any one time, there are few demanders who value the books highly. But spreading the sales over several weeks may yield more favorable results.

Special Features of Internet Auctions

A quick examination of auction sites on the Internet suggests that operators employ a variety of features in their auctions. Amazon, for example, has explicitly stated "reserve" prices that must be met before a bid will be considered. eBay does not explicitly report a reserve price, but many items do have reserve prices that can only be discovered through the bidding process. Some auctions provide you with a bidding history, whereas others only tell you the cumulative number of bids. A few auctions offer you the opportunity of buying a good outright at a relatively high price without going through the bidding process. For example, eBay has a "Buy It Now" price on many items. What purposes do these various features of Internet auctions serve? Presumably, an operator will only adopt a feature that promises to yield it better returns in terms of either attracting more buyers or (what may amount to the same thing) obtaining higher prices for sellers. But why do these features promise such higher returns? And why do auctioneers seem to differ in their opinions about what works? Attempts to answer these questions usually focus on the uncertainties inherent in the auction process and how bidders respond to them.[1]

Risks to Participants in Internet Auctions

Because buyers and sellers are total strangers in Internet auctions, a number of special provisions have been developed to mitigate the risks of fraud that the parties might encounter in such situations. The primary problem facing bidders in the auctions is in knowing that the goods being offered meet expected quality standards. An important way that many of the auctions help to reduce such uncertainty is through a grading process for sellers. Previous bidders provide rankings to the auction sites, and these are summarized for potential buyers. A good reputation probably results in a seller receiving higher bids. For sellers, the primary risk is that they will not be paid (or that a check will bounce). Various intermediaries (such as PayPal) have been developed to address this problem.

Penny Auctions

So-called penny auctions (such as Deal Dash) pose added risks to participants. In these auctions bidders must pay for bids that give the auction winner the right to buy items at very low costs. For those who do not win, however, the amounts spent on bids are completely lost. Hence, these activities combine features of auctions and lotteries in which outcomes for participants can be quite variable.

TO THINK ABOUT

1. Do you think that differing internet auction formats yield different final prices? If so, why don't all sellers use only the one that yields the highest price?
2. Why do some sellers on eBay offer "Buy it Now" prices? Doesn't this just put an upper limit on what they might get for their items?

[1]For a discussion of these issues in auction design together with an analysis of various bidding strategies, see P. Bajari and A. Hortacsu, "Economic Insights from Internet Auctions," *Journal of Economic Literature* (June 2004): 457–486.

supply curve for these paintings as a vertical line, such as that shown in Figure 9.1. As the price of Rembrandts rises, people (and museums) become increasingly willing to part with them. From a market point of view, the supply curve for Rembrandts has an upward slope, even though no new production takes place.

9-3 Short-Run Supply

In analysis of the short run, the number of firms in an industry is fixed. There is just not enough time for new firms to enter a market or for existing firms to exit completely. However, the firms currently operating in the market are able to adjust the quantity they are producing in response to changing prices. Because there are a large number of firms each producing the same good, each firm will act as a price taker. The model of short-run supply by a price-taking firm in Chapter 8 is therefore the appropriate one to use here. That is, each firm's short-run supply curve is simply the positively sloped section of its short-run marginal cost curve above the shutdown price. Using this model to record individual firms' supply decisions, we can add up all of these decisions into a single market supply curve.

Construction of a Short-Run Supply Curve

The quantity of a good that is supplied to the market during a period is the sum of the quantities supplied by each of the existing firms. Because each firm faces the same market price in deciding how much to produce, the total supplied to the market also depends on this price. This relationship between market price and quantity supplied is called a **short-run market supply curve.**

Short-run market supply curve
The relationship between market price and quantity supplied of a good in the short run.

Figure 9.2 illustrates the construction of the curve. For simplicity, we assume there are only two firms, A and B. The short-run supply curves for firms A and B (that is, the short-run marginal cost curves for these firms above their shutdown prices) are shown in Figure 9.2(a) and 9.2(b). The market supply curve shown in Figure 9.2(c) is the horizontal sum of these two curves. For example, at a price of P_1, firm A is willing to supply q_1^A and firm B is willing to supply q_1^B. At this price, the total supply in the market is given by Q_1, which is equal to $q_1^A + q_1^B$. The other points on the curve are constructed in an identical way. Because each firm's supply curve slopes upward, the market supply curve will also

Figure 9.2 Short-Run Market Supply Curve

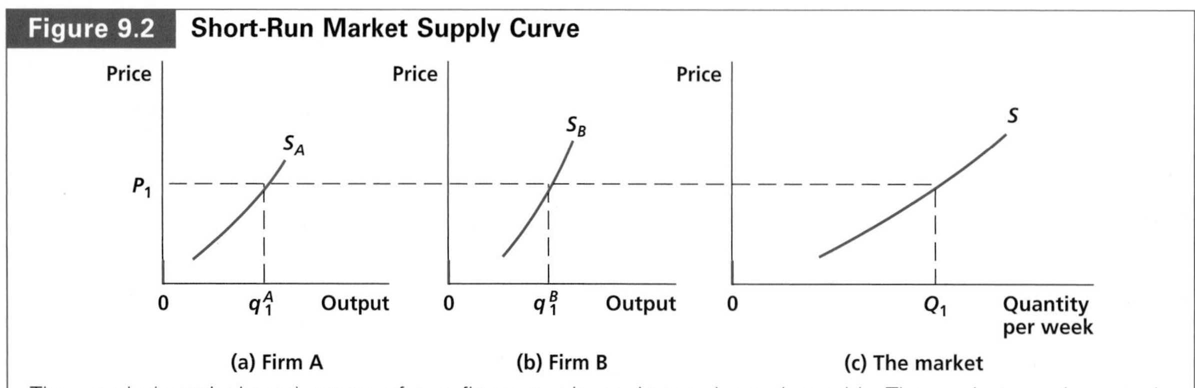

The supply (marginal cost) curves of two firms are shown in panel a and panel b. The market supply curve in panel c is the horizontal sum of these curves. For example, at P_1, firm A supplies q_1^A,—firm B supplies q_1^B, and total market supply is given by $Q_1 = q_1^A + q_1^B$.

slope upward. This upward slope reflects the fact that short-run marginal costs increase as firms attempt to increase their outputs. They are willing to incur these higher marginal costs only at higher market prices.

The construction in Figure 9.2 uses only two firms; actual market supply curves represent the summation of many firms' supply curves. Each firm takes the market price as given and produces where price is equal to marginal cost. Because each firm operates on a positively sloped segment of its own marginal cost curve, the market supply curve will also have a positive slope. All of the information that is relevant to pricing from firms' points of view (such as their input costs, their current technical knowledge, or the nature of the diminishing returns they experience when trying to expand output) is summarized by this market supply curve Should any of these factors change, the short-run supply curve would shift to a new position.

9-4 Short-Run Price Determination

We can now combine demand and supply curves to demonstrate how equilibrium prices are established in the short run. Figure 9.3 shows this process. In Figure 9.3(b), the market demand curve D and the short-run supply curve S intersect at a price of P_1 and a quantity of Q_1. This price-quantity combination represents an equilibrium between the demands of individuals and the supply decisions of firms—the forces of supply and demand are precisely balanced. What firms supply at a price of P_1 is exactly what people want to buy at that price. This equilibrium tends to persist from one period to the next unless one of the factors underlying the supply and demand curves changes.

Functions of the Equilibrium Price

Here, the equilibrium price P_1 serves two important functions. First, this price acts as a signal to producers about how much should be produced. In order to maximize profits, firms produce that output level for which marginal costs are equal to P_1. In the aggregate, then, production is Q_1. A second function of the price is to ration demand. Given the market price of P_1, utility-maximizing consumers decide how much of their limited

Figure 9.3 Interactions of Many Individuals and Firms Determine Market Price in the Short Run

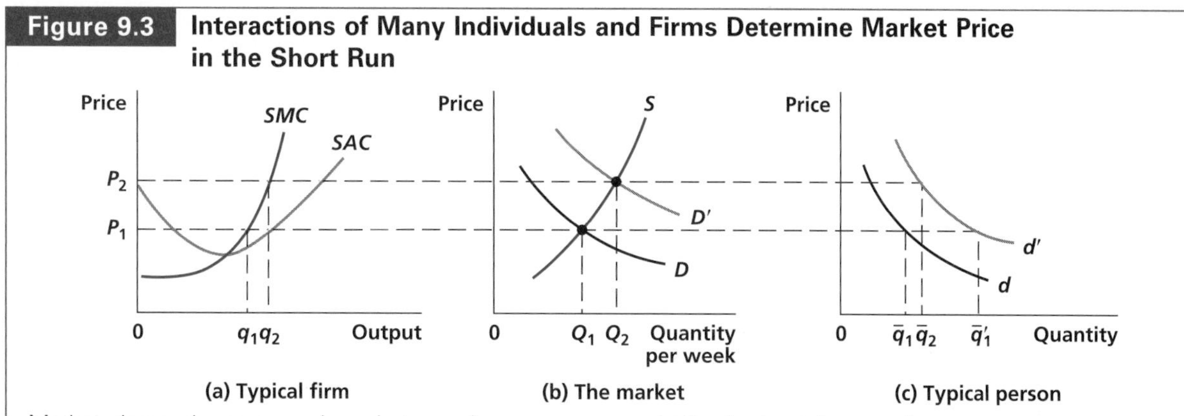

Market demand curves and market supply curves are each the horizontal sum of numerous components. These market curves are shown in panel b. Once price is determined in the market, each firm and each individual treat this price as fixed in their decisions. If the typical person's demand curve shifts to d', market demand will shift to D' in the short run, and price will rise to P_2.

incomes to spend on that particular good. At a price of P_1, total quantity demanded is Q_1, which is precisely the amount that is produced. This is what economists mean by an equilibrium price. At P_1 each economic actor is content with what is transpiring. This is an "equilibrium" because no one has an incentive to change what he or she is doing. Any other price would not have this equilibrium property. A price in excess of P_1, for example, would cause quantity demanded to fall short of what is supplied. Some producers would not be able to sell their output and would therefore be forced to adopt other plans such as reducing production or selling at a cut-rate price. Similarly, at a price lower than P_1, quantity demanded would exceed the supply available and some demanders would be disappointed because they could not buy all they wanted. They might, for example, offer sellers higher prices so they can get the goods they want. Only at a price of P_1 would there be no such incentives to change behavior. This balancing of the forces of supply and demand at P_1 will tend to persist from one period to the next until something happens to change matters.

The implications of the equilibrium price (P_1) for a typical firm and for a typical person are shown in Figure 9.3(a) and 9.3(c), respectively. For the typical firm, the price P_1 causes an output level of q_1 to be produced. The firm earns a profit at this particular price because price exceeds short-run average total cost. The initial demand curve d for a typical person is shown in Figure 9.3(c). At a price of P_1 this person demands $\overline{q}_1$. The market supply and demand curves show the total quantities supplied by all firms and the total quantities demanded by all individuals. P_1 is an equilibrium price because these two totals are equal. Each firm and each individual is content with what they are doing at this price.

MICRO QUIZ 9.2

How does the fact that there are many buyers and sellers in a competitive market enforce price-taking behavior? Specifically, suppose that the equilibrium price of corn is $3 per bushel.

1. The owners of Yellow Ear Farm believe they deserve $3.25 per bushel because the farm has to use more irrigation in growing corn. Can this farm hold out for, and get, the price it wants?
2. United Soup Kitchens believes that it should be able to buy corn for $2.75 because it serves the poor. Can this charity find a place to buy at the price it is willing to pay?

Effect of an Increase in Market Demand

To study a short-run supply response, let's assume that many people decide they want to buy more of the good in Figure 9.3. The typical person's demand curve shifts outward to d', and the entire market demand curve shifts to D'. Figure 9.3(b) shows this new market demand curve. The new equilibrium point is P_2, Q_2: At this point, supply-demand balance is reestablished. Price has now increased from P_1 to P_2 in response to the shift in demand. The quantity traded in the market has also increased from Q_1 to Q_2.

The rise in price in the short run has served two functions. First, as shown in our analysis of the very short run, it has acted to ration demand. Whereas at P_1 a typical individual demanded $\overline{q}_1^1$, now at P_2 only $\overline{q}_2$ is demanded.

The rise in price has also acted as a signal to the typical firm to increase production. In Figure 9.3(a), the typical firm's profit-maximizing output level has increased from q_1 to q_2 in response to the price rise. That is the firm's short-run supply response: An increase in market price acts as an inducement to increase production. Firms are willing to increase production (and to incur higher marginal costs) because price has risen. If market price had not been permitted to rise (suppose, for example, government price controls were in effect), firms would not have increased their outputs. At P_1, there would have been an excess (unfilled) demand for the good in question. If market price is allowed to rise, a supply-demand equilibrium can be reestablished so that what firms produce is again equal to what people demand at the prevailing market price. At the new price P_2, the typical firm has also increased its profits. This increased profitability in response to rising prices is important for our discussion of long-run pricing later in this chapter.

9-5 Shifts in Supply and Demand Curves

In previous chapters, we explored many of the reasons why either demand or supply curves might shift to new positions. Some of these reasons are summarized in Table 9.1. You may wish to review the material in Chapter 3, "Demand Curves," and Chapter 7, "Costs," to see why these changes shift the various curves. These types of shifts in demand and supply occur frequently in real-world markets. When either a supply curve or a demand curve does shift, equilibrium price and quantity change. This section looks briefly at such changes and how the outcome depends on the shapes of the curves.

Short-Run Supply Elasticity

Some terms used by economists to describe the shapes of demand and supply curves need to be understood before we can discuss the likely effects of these shifts. We already introduced the terminology for demand curves in Chapter 3. There, we developed the concept of the price elasticity of demand, which shows how the quantity demanded responds to changes in price. When demand is elastic, changes in price have a major impact on quantity demanded. In the case of inelastic demand, however, a price change does not have very much effect on the quantity that people choose to buy. Firms' short-run supply responses can be described along the same lines. If an increase in price causes firms to supply significantly more output, we say that the supply curve is "elastic" (at least in the range currently being observed). Alternatively, if the price increase has only a minor effect on the quantity firms choose to produce, supply is said to be inelastic. More formally,

$$\text{Short-run supply elasticity} = \frac{\begin{array}{c}\text{Percentage change in quantity}\\ \text{Supplied in short run}\end{array}}{\text{Percentage change in price}} \tag{9.1}$$

For example, if the short-run supply elasticity is 2.0, each 1 percent increase in price results in a 2 percent increase in quantity supplied. Over this range, the short-run supply curve is rather elastic. If, on the other hand, a 1 percent increase in price leads only

Table 9.1 Reasons for a Shift in a Demand or Supply Curve

DEMAND	SUPPLY
Shifts outward (→) because	Shifts outward (→) because
• Income increases	• Input prices fall
• Price of substitute rises	• Technology improves
• Price of complement falls	
• Preferences for good increase	
Shifts inward (←) because	Shifts inward (←) because
• Income falls	• Input prices rise
• Price of substitute falls	
• Price of complement rises	
• Preferences for good diminish	

Short-run elasticity of supply
The percentage change in quantity supplied in the short run in response to a 1 percent change in price while holding other factors that affect supply constant.

to a 0.5 percent increase in quantity supplied, the **short-run elasticity of supply** is 0.5, and we say that supply is inelastic. As we will see, whether short-run supply is elastic or inelastic can have a significant effect on how markets respond to economic events.

Shifts in Supply Curves and the Importance of the Shape of the Demand Curve

A shift inward in the short-run supply curve for a good might result, for example, from an increase in the prices of the inputs used by firms to produce the good. An increase in carpenters' wages raises homebuilders' costs and clearly affects the price they must receive if homebuilding is to be profitable. The effect of such a shift on the equilibrium levels of P and Q depends on the shape of the demand curve for the product. Figure 9.4 illustrates two possible situations. The demand curve in Figure 9.4(a) is relatively price elastic; that is, a change in price substantially affects the quantity demanded. For this case, a shift in the supply curve from S to S' causes equilibrium prices to rise only moderately (from P to P'), whereas quantity is reduced sharply (from Q to Q'). Rather than being "passed on" in higher prices, the increase in the firms' input costs is met primarily by a decrease in quantity produced (a movement down each firm's marginal cost curve) with only a slight increase in price.[2]

This situation is reversed when the market demand curve is inelastic. In Figure 9.4(b), a shift in the supply curve causes equilibrium price to rise substantially, but quantity is little changed because people do not reduce their demands very much if prices rise. Consequently, the shift inward in the supply curve is passed on to demanders almost completely in the form of higher prices. This result is therefore slightly counter-intuitive. Although an increase in the price of an input shifts the *supply* curve, the final effect of this increase on the price and quantity of the good being produced depends on the shape of

Figure 9.4 Effect of a Shift in the Short-Run Supply Curve Depends on the Shape of the Demand Curve

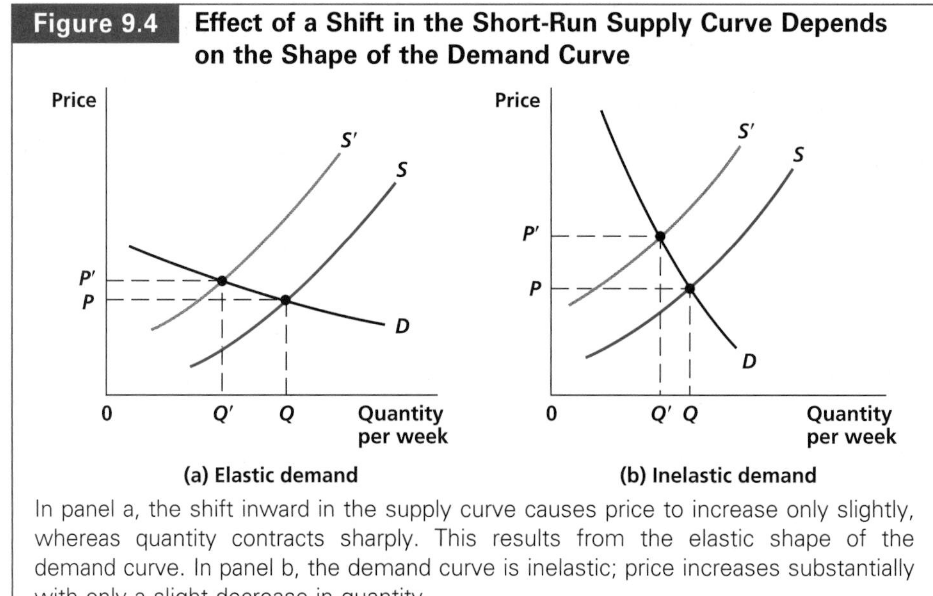

In panel a, the shift inward in the supply curve causes price to increase only slightly, whereas quantity contracts sharply. This results from the elastic shape of the demand curve. In panel b, the demand curve is inelastic; price increases substantially with only a slight decrease in quantity.

[2]Notice, for example, that on the supply curve S', the marginal cost of producing output level Q is considerably higher than the marginal cost of producing Q'.

the *demand* curve. If we focused only on firms' costs, we would not be able to tell what the final outcome would be. Whether increases in costs result primarily in higher prices or in smaller outputs can only be determined with additional information about demand.

Shifts in Demand Curves and the Importance of the Shape of the Supply Curve

For similar reasons, a given shift in a market demand curve will have different implications for P and Q depending on the shape of the short-run supply curve. Two illustrations are shown in Figure 9.5. In Figure 9.5(a), the short-run supply curve for the good in question is relatively inelastic. As quantity expands, firms' marginal costs rise rapidly, giving the supply curve its steep slope. In this situation, a shift outward in the market demand curve (caused, for example, by an increase in consumer income) causes prices to increase substantially. Yet, the quantity supplied increases only slightly. The increase in demand (and in Q) has caused firms to move up their steeply sloped marginal cost curves. The accompanying large increase in price serves to ration demand. There is little response in terms of quantity supplied.

Figure 9.5(b) shows a relatively elastic short-run supply curve. This kind of curve would occur for an industry in which marginal costs do not rise steeply in response to output increases. For this case, an increase in demand produces a substantial increase in Q. However, because of the nature of the supply curve, this increase is not met by great cost increases. Consequently, price rises only moderately.

These examples again demonstrate Marshall's observation that demand and supply together determine price and quantity. Recall from Chapter 1 Marshall's analogy: Just as it is impossible to say which blade of a scissors does the cutting, so too is it impossible to attribute price solely to demand or to supply characteristics. Rather, the effect that shifts in either a demand curve or a supply curve will have depends on the shapes of both of the curves. In predicting the effects of shifting supply or demand conditions on market price and quantity in the real world, this simultaneous relationship must be considered. Application 9.2: Ethanol Subsidies in the United States and Brazil illustrates how this short-run model might be used to examine some of the politics of government price-support schemes.

Figure 9.5 Effect of a Shift in the Demand Curve Depends on the Shape of the Short-Run Supply Curve

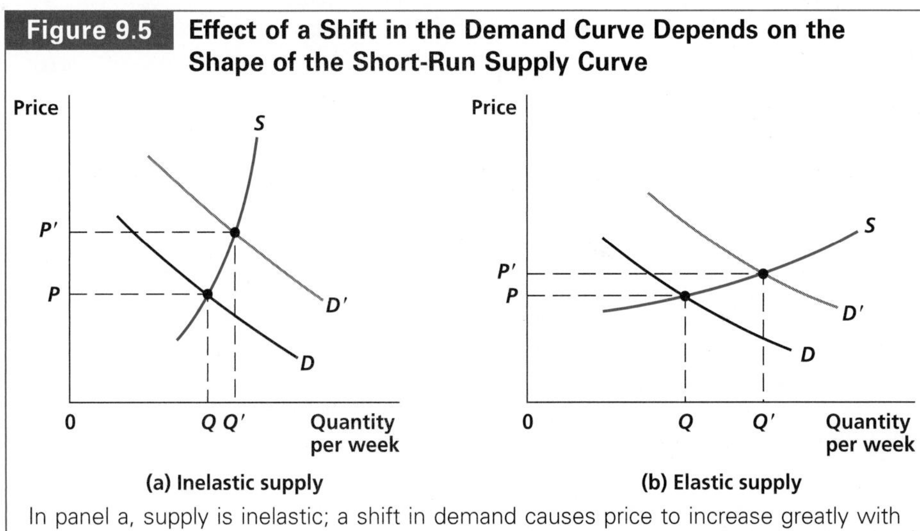

In panel a, supply is inelastic; a shift in demand causes price to increase greatly with only a small increase in quantity. In panel b, on the other hand, supply is elastic; price rises only slightly in response to a demand shift.

APPLICATION 9.2

Ethanol Subsidies in the United States and Brazil

Ethanol is another term for ethyl alcohol. In addition to its role as an intoxicant, the chemical also has potentially desirable properties as a fuel for automobiles because it burns cleanly and can be made from renewable resources such as sugar cane or corn. Ethanol can also be used as an additive to gasoline, and some claim that this oxygenated product reduces air pollution. Indeed, several governments have adopted subsidies for producers of ethanol.

A Diagrammatic Treatment

One way to show the effect of a subsidy in a supply-demand graph is to treat it as a shift in the short-run supply curve.[1] In the United States, for example, producers of ethanol get what amounts to a 54-cents-a-gallon tax credit. As shown in Figure 1, this shifts the supply curve (which is the sum of ethanol producers' marginal cost curves) downward by 54 cents. This leads to an expansion of demand from its presubsidy level of Q_1 to Q_2. The total cost of the subsidy then depends not only on its per-gallon amount but also on the extent of this increase in quantity demanded.

Figure 1 Ethanol Subsidies Shift the Supply Curve

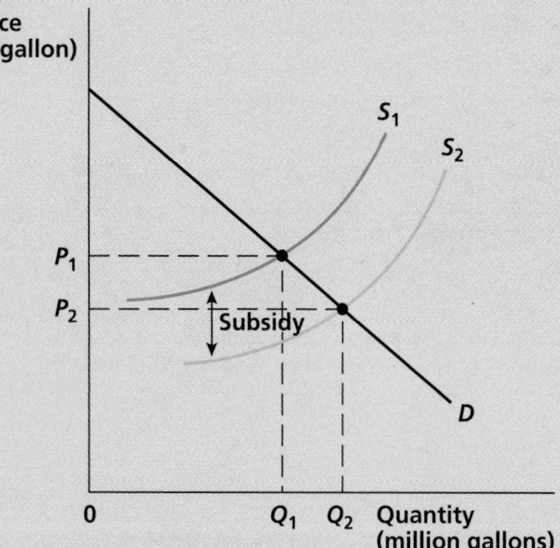

Imposition of a subsidy on ethanol production shifts the short-run supply curve from S_1 to S_2. Quantity expands from Q_1 to Q_2, and the subsidy is paid on this larger quantity.

Ethanol and U.S. Politics

Whether subsidizing ethanol production makes sense in either economic or environmental terms is open to question. But the politics of the ethanol subsidy are clear. The largest corn-producing state, Iowa, is also the site of one of the earliest presidential primaries. And ethanol producers are major donors to many political campaigns. So, for many years, politicians gave overwhelming support to the ethanol subsidy program. In 2013, however, the program was allowed to expire, in part because of its costs. But, because government mandates to use increasing amounts of ethanol in gasoline production remained in effect, things continued as if the subsidy remained by artificially increasing the demand for the additive (how would you show this in Figure 1?). U.S. politicians are probably still happy with this result.

Ethanol and Brazilian Politics

In Brazil, ethanol is made from sugar cane. Although this process is less costly than the corn-based process used in the United States, the urge to subsidize production remains a powerful political force. Although ethanol mandates were reduced in 2000 in response to rising sugar prices, ethanol producers continued to press for additional support. Eventually, in 2013, the Brazilian government announced a new and very large subsidy to all ethanol producers that will last for many years. Brazilian politicians (at least those from sugar-growing regions) are also still happy.

POLICY CHALLENGE

Supporters of ethanol subsidies argue that they meet two important goals: (1) using a renewable source of fuel that is more "environmentally friendly" than oil; and (2) developing a domestic source of fuel that can be substituted for foreign oil imports. How would you assess these arguments? What sort of evidence would support or refute them? Even if the facts tended to support one or both arguments, would a subsidy be the best way to achieve the desired results?

[1]A subsidy can also be shown as a "wedge" between the demand and supply curves—a procedure we use later to study tax incidence.

A Numerical Illustration

Changes in market equilibria can be illustrated with a simple numerical example. Suppose that the quantity of CDs demanded per week (Q) depends on their price (P) according to the simple relation

$$\text{Demand: } Q = 10 - P \tag{9.2}$$

Suppose also that the short-run supply curve for CDs is given by

$$\text{Supply: } Q = P - 2 \text{ or } P = Q + 2 \tag{9.3}$$

Figure 9.6 graphs these equations. As before, the demand curve (labeled D in the figure) intersects the vertical axis at $P = \$10$. At higher prices, no CDs are demanded. The supply curve (labeled S) intersects the vertical axis at $P = 2$. This is the shutdown price for firms in the industry—at a price lower than $2, no CDs will be sold. As Figure 9.6 shows, these supply and demand curves intersect at a price of $6 per CD. At that price, people demand four CDs per week and firms are willing to supply four CDs per week. This equilibrium is also illustrated in Table 9.2, which shows the quantity of CDs demanded and supplied at each price. Only when $P = \$6$ do these amounts agree. At a price of $5 per CD, for example, people want to buy five CDs per week, but only three will be supplied; there is an excess demand of two CDs per week. Similarly, at a price of $7, there is an excess supply of two CDs per week.

If the demand curve for CDs were to shift outward, this equilibrium would change. For example, Figure 9.6 also shows the demand curve D', whose equation is given by

$$Q = 12 - P \tag{9.4}$$

Use the information on Case 1 in Table 9.2 to answer the following questions.

1. Suppose that the government confiscated two CDs per week as being "not suitable for young ears." What would be the equilibrium price of the remaining CDs?
2. Suppose that the government imposed a $4-per-CD tax, resulting in a $4 difference between what consumers pay and what firms receive for each CD. How many CDs would be sold? What price would buyers pay?

Figure 9.6 Demand and Supply Curves for CDs

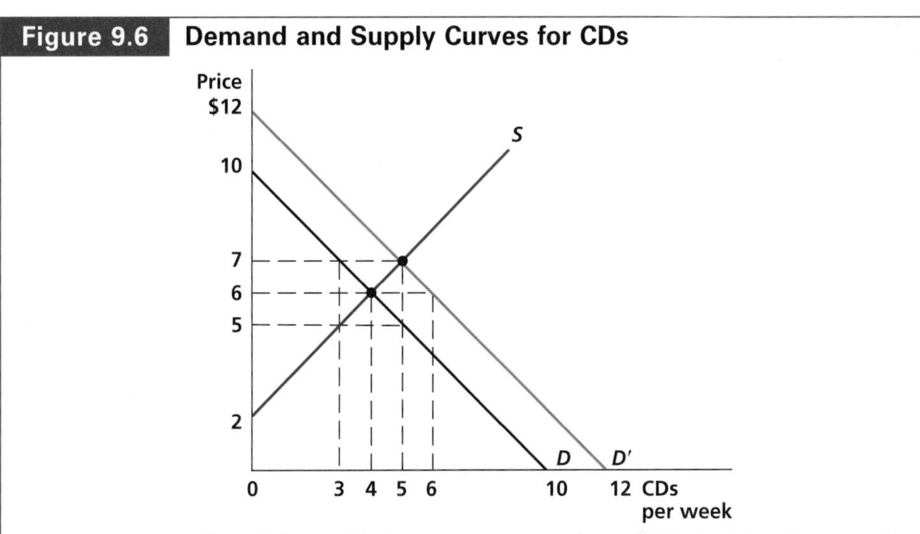

With the curves D and S, equilibrium occurs at a price of $6. At this price, people demand four CDs per week, and that is what firms supply. When demand shifts to D', price will rise to $7 to restore equilibrium.

Table 9.2 Supply and Demand Equilibrium in the Market for CDs

	SUPPLY	DEMAND	
		CASE 1	CASE 2
PRICE	$Q = P - 2$ QUANTITY SUPPLIED (CDS PER WEEK)	$Q = 10 - P$ QUANTITY DEMANDED (CDS PER WEEK)	$Q = 12 - P$ QUANTITY DEMANDED (CDS PER WEEK)
$10	8	0	2
9	7	1	3
8	6	2	4
7	5	3	5
6	4	4	6
5	3	5	7
4	2	6	8
3	1	7	9
2	0	8	10
1	0	9	11
0	0	10	12

New equilibrium. Initial equilibrium.

With this new demand curve, equilibrium price rises to $7 and quantity also rises to five CDs per week. This new equilibrium is confirmed by the entries in Table 9.2, which show that this is the only price that clears the market given the new demand curve. For example, at the old price of $6, there is now an excess demand for CDs because the amount people want ($Q = 6$) exceeds what firms are willing to supply ($Q = 4$). The rise in price from $6 to $7 restores equilibrium both by prompting people to buy fewer CDs and by encouraging firms to produce more.

Algebra is Easier

Finding equilibrium values graphically using supply and demand curves is often time consuming. It is generally much easier to use the algebra of simultaneous equations (as we saw in the Appendix to chapter 1). To do so, however, you must think about the logic of what you are doing. The first step is to solve both the demand and supply relationships for quantity. In our prior example this would result in:

$$\begin{aligned}\text{Quantity Demanded} &= Q = 10 - P \\ \text{Quantity Supplied} &= Q = P - 2\end{aligned} \tag{9.5}$$

Now we can find the equilibrium price by setting quantity demanded equal to quantity supplied:

$$\text{Quantity Demanded} = 10 - P = \text{Quantity Supplied} = P - 2 \tag{9.6}$$

And so the equilibrium price is given by

$$10 - P = P - 2 \text{ or } 2P = 12 \text{ so } P^* = 6 \tag{9.7}$$

And now we can use either function to find equilibrium quantity:

$$Q^* = 10 - P^* = 10 - 6 = 4 = P^* - 2 = 6 - 2. \tag{9.8}$$

If the demand function were to shift to the new position given in Equation 9.4, we would have to derive this solution all over again—there is no shortcut that can be devised using the new demand equation only, since the new equilibrium will depend on both demand and supply factors.

KEEP *in* MIND

Marshall's Scissors

Marshall's scissors analogy is just a folksy way of referring to simultaneous equations. It is a reminder that demand and supply relations must be solved together to arrive at equilibrium price and quantity. One way to do that is by using a graphical approach as in Figure 9.6. A faster way would be to use a purely algebraic method. No matter what approach you take, however, you have not found a market equilibrium until you check that your solution satisfies both the demand equation and the supply equation.

9-6 The Long Run

In perfectly competitive markets, supply responses are more flexible in the long run than in the short run for two reasons. First, firms' long-run cost curves reflect the greater input flexibility that firms have in the long run. Diminishing returns and the associated sharp increases in marginal costs are less important issues in the long run. Second, the long run allows firms to enter and exit a market in response to profit opportunities. These actions have important implications for pricing. We begin our analysis of these various effects with a description of the long-run equilibrium for a competitive industry. Then, as we did for the short run, we show how quantity supplied and prices change when conditions change.

Equilibrium Conditions

A perfectly competitive market is in long-run equilibrium when no firm has an incentive to change its behavior. Such an equilibrium has two components: Firms must be content with their output choices (that is, they must be maximizing profits), and they must be content to stay in (or out of) the market. We discuss each of these components separately.

Profit Maximization

As before, we assume that firms seek maximum profits. Because each firm is a price taker, profit maximization requires that the firm produce where price is equal to (long-run) marginal cost. This first equilibrium condition, $P = MC$, determines both the firm's output choice and its choice of a specific input combination that minimizes these costs in the long run.

Entry and Exit

A second feature of long-run equilibrium concerns the possibility of the entry of entirely new firms into a market or the exit of existing firms from that market. The perfectly competitive model assumes that such entry and exit entail no special costs. Consequently, new firms are lured into any market in which (economic) profits are positive because they can earn more there than they can in other markets. Similarly, firms leave a market when profits are negative. In this case, firms can earn more elsewhere than in a market where they are not covering all opportunity costs.

If profits are positive, the entry of new firms causes the short-run market supply curve to shift outward because more firms are now producing than were in the market previously. Such a shift causes market price (and market profits) to fall. The process continues until no firm contemplating entering the market would be able to earn an economic profit.[3] At that point, entry by new firms ceases and the number of firms has reached an equilibrium. When the firms in a market suffer short-run losses, some firms choose to leave, causing the supply curve to shift to the left. Market price then rises, eliminating losses for those firms remaining in the marketplace.

Long-Run Equilibrium

For our analysis of long-run equilibrium in competitive markets, we initially assume that all the firms producing a particular good have the same cost curves, that is, we assume that no single firm controls any special resources or technologies.[4] Because all firms are identical, the equilibrium long-run position requires every firm to earn exactly zero economic profits. In graphic terms, long-run equilibrium price must settle at the low point of each firm's long-run average total cost curve. Only at this point do the two equilibrium conditions hold: $P = MC$ (which is required for profit maximization) and $P = AC$ (which is the required zero-profit condition).

These two equilibrium conditions have rather different origins. Profit maximization is a goal of firms. The $P = MC$ rule reflects our assumptions about firms' behavior and is identical to the output-decision rule used in the short run. The zero-profit condition is not a goal for firms. Firms' owners would obviously prefer to have large profits. The long-run operations of competitive markets, however, force all firms to accept a level of zero economic profits ($P = AC$) because of the willingness of firms to enter and exit. Although the firms in a perfectly competitive industry may earn either positive or negative profits in the short run, in the long run *only* zero profits prevail. That is, firms' owners earn only normal returns on their investments.

9-7 Long-Run Supply: The Constant Cost Case

The study of long-run supply depends crucially on how the entry of new firms affects the prices of inputs. The simplest assumption one might make is that entry has no effect on these prices. Under this assumption, no matter how many firms enter or leave a market, every firm retains exactly the same set of cost curves with which it started. There are many important cases for which this constant input cost assumption may be unrealistic; we analyze these cases later. For the moment, however, we wish to examine the equilibrium conditions for this **constant cost case**.

Constant cost case
A market in which entry or exit has no effect on the cost curves of firms.

Market Equilibrium

Figure 9.7 demonstrates long-run equilibrium for the constant cost case. For the market as a whole, in Figure 9.7(b), the demand curve is labeled D and the short-run supply curve is labeled S. The short-run equilibrium price is therefore P_1. The typical firm in Figure 9.7(a) produces output level q_1, because at this level of output price is equal to short-run marginal cost (SMC). In addition, with a market price of P_1, output level q_1

[3]Remember, we are using the economic definition of profits here. Profits represent the return to the business owner in excess of that which is strictly necessary to keep him or her in the business. If an owner can earn just what he or she could earn elsewhere, there is no reason to enter a market.

[4]The important case of firms having different costs is discussed later in this chapter. We will see that very low-cost firms can earn positive, long-run profits. These represent a "rent" to whatever input provides the firms' unique low cost (e.g., especially fertile land or a low-cost source of raw materials).

Figure 9.7 **Long-Run Equilibrium for a Perfectly Competitive Market: Constant Cost Case**

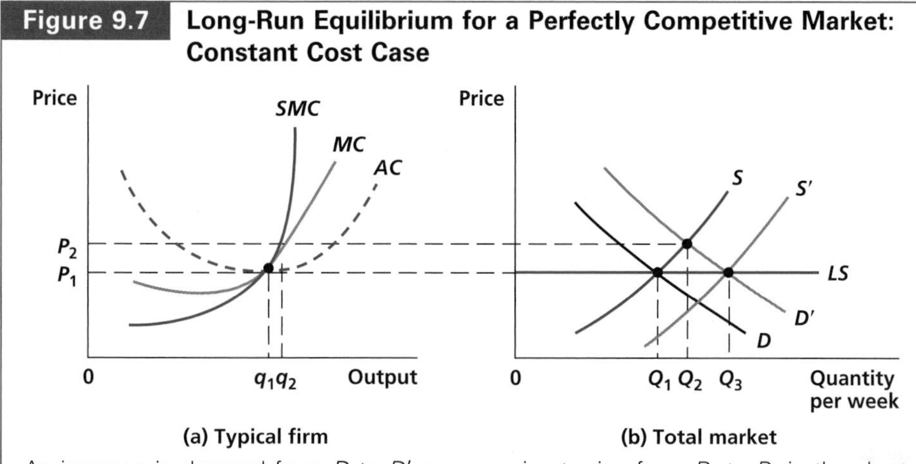

An increase in demand from D to D' causes price to rise from P_1 to P_2 in the short run. This higher price creates profits, and new firms are drawn into the market. If the entry of these new firms has no effect on the cost curves of firms, new firms continue to enter until price is pushed back down to P_1. At this price, economic profits are zero. The long-run supply curve, LS, is therefore a horizontal line at P_1. Along LS, output is increased by increasing the number of firms that each produce q_1.

is also a long-run equilibrium position for the firm. The firm is maximizing profits because price is equal to long-run marginal cost (MC). Figure 9.7(a) also shows a second long-run equilibrium property: Price is equal to long-run average total costs (AC). Consequently, economic profits are zero, and there is no incentive for firms either to enter or to leave this market.

A Shift in Demand

Suppose now that the market demand curve shifts outward to D'. If S is the relevant short-run supply curve, then in the short run, price rises to P_2. The typical firm, in the short run, chooses to produce q_2 and (because $P_2 > AC$) earns profits on this level of output. In the long run, these profits attract new firms into the market.

Because of the constant cost assumption, this entry of new firms has no effect on input prices. Perhaps this industry hires only a small fraction of the workers in an area and raises its capital in national markets. More inputs can therefore be hired without affecting any firms' cost curves. New firms continue to enter the market until price is forced down to the level at which there are again no economic profits being made. The entry of new firms therefore shifts the short-run supply curve to S', where the equilibrium price (P_1) is reestablished. At this new long-run equilibrium, the price-quantity combination P_1, Q_3 prevails in the market. The typical firm again produces at output level q_1, although now there are more firms than there were in the initial situation.

Long-Run Supply Curve

By considering many potential shifts in demand, we can examine long-run pricing in this industry. Our discussion suggests that no matter how demand shifts, economic forces come into play that cause price always to return to P_1. All long-run equilibria occur along a horizontal line at P_1. Connecting these equilibrium points shows the long-run supply response of this industry. This long-run supply curve is labeled *LS* in Figure 9.7. For a constant cost industry of identical firms, the long-run supply curve is a horizontal line at the low point of the firms' long-run average total cost curves. The fact that price cannot depart from P_1 in the long run is a direct consequence of the constancy of input prices as new firms enter.

9-8 Shape of the Long-Run Supply Curve

Contrary to the short-run case, the long-run supply curve does not depend on the shape of firms' marginal cost curves. Rather, the zero-profit condition focuses attention on the low point of the long-run average cost curve as the factor most relevant to long-run price determination. In the constant cost case, the position of this low point does not change as new firms enter or leave a market. Consequently, only one price can prevail in the long run, regardless of how demand shifts, so long as input prices do not change. The long-run supply curve is horizontal at this price.

After the constant cost assumption is abandoned, this need not be the case. If the entry of new firms causes average costs to rise, the long-run supply curve has an upward slope. On the other hand, if entry causes average costs to decline, it is even possible for the long-run supply curve to be negatively sloped. We now discuss these possibilities.

The Increasing Cost Case

The entry of new firms may cause the average cost of all firms to rise for several reasons. Entry of new firms may increase the demand for scarce inputs, driving up their prices. New firms may impose external costs on existing firms (and on themselves) in the form of air or water pollution, and new firms may place strains on public facilities (roads, courts, schools, and so forth), and these may show up as increased costs for all firms.

Increasing cost case
A market in which the entry of firms increases firms' costs.

Figure 9.8 demonstrates market equilibrium for this **increasing cost case**. The initial equilibrium price is P_1. At this price, the typical firm in Figure 9.8(a) produces q_1 and total output, shown in Figure 9.8(c), is Q_1. Suppose that the demand curve for this product shifts outward to D' and that D' and the short-run supply curve (S) intersect at P_2. At this price, the typical firm produces q_2 and earns a substantial profit. This profit attracts new entrants into the market and shifts the short-run supply curve outward.

Suppose that the entry of new firms causes the costs of all firms to rise. The new firms may, for example, increase the demand for a particular type of skilled worker, driving up wages. A typical firm's new (higher) set of cost curves is shown in Figure 9.8(b). The new long-run equilibrium price for the industry is P_3 (here $P = MC = AC$), and at this price Q_3 is demanded. We now have two points (P_1, Q_1 and P_3, Q_3) on the long-run supply curve.[5] All other points on the curve can be found in an analogous way by considering every possible shift in the demand curve. These shifts would trace out the long-run supply curve *LS*. Here, *LS* has a positive slope because of the increasing costs associated with the entry of new firms. This positive slope is caused by whatever causes firms' costs to rise in response to entry. Still, because the supply response is more flexible in the long run, the *LS* curve is somewhat flatter than its short-run counterpart.

[5]Figure 9.8 also shows the short-run supply curve associated with the point P_3, Q_3. This supply curve has shifted to the right because more firms are producing now than were initially.

Figure 9.8 Increasing Costs Result in a Positively Sloped Long-Run Supply Curve

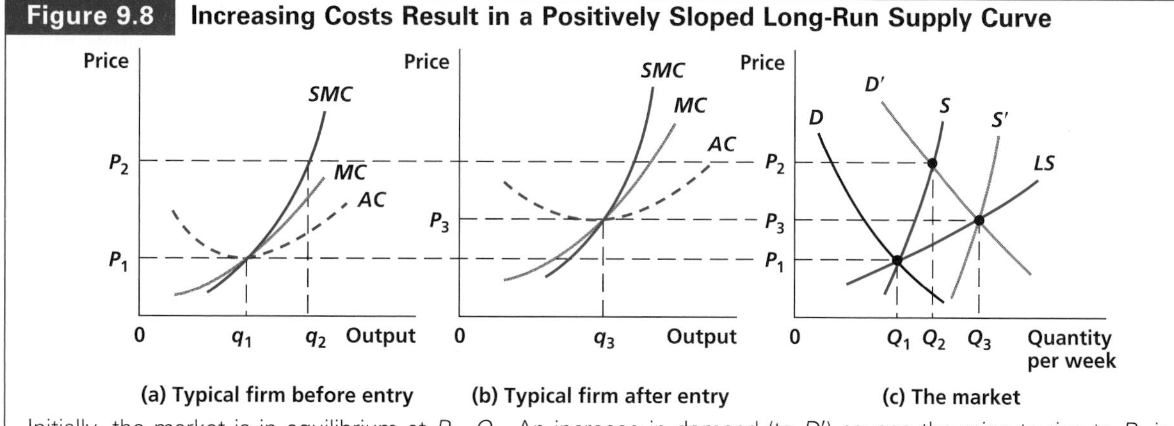

Initially, the market is in equilibrium at P_1, Q_1. An increase in demand (to D') causes the price to rise to P_2 in the short run, and the typical firm produces q_2 at a profit. This profit attracts new firms. The entry of these new firms causes costs to rise to the levels shown in (b). With this new set of curves, equilibrium is reestablished in the market at P_3, Q_3. By considering many possible demand shifts and connecting all the resulting equilibrium points, the long-run supply curve LS is traced out.

Long-Run Supply Elasticity

As we have just shown, the long-run supply curve is constructed by considering all possible shifts in the demand curve for the product. In order to predict the effects that such increases in demand will have on market price, it is important to know something about the shape of the supply curve. A convenient measure for summarizing the shape of long-run supply curves is the **long-run elasticity of supply**. This concept records how proportional changes in price affect the quantity supplied, once all long-run adjustments have taken place. More formally:

Long-run elasticity of supply
The percentage change in quantity supplied in the long run in response to a 1 percent change in price after all adjustments in input prices.

$$\text{Long-run elasticity of supply} = \frac{\begin{array}{c}\text{Percentage change in quantity}\\ \text{Supplied in long run}\end{array}}{\text{Percentage change in price}} \tag{9.9}$$

An elasticity of 10, for example, would show that a 1 percent increase in price would result in a 10 percent increase in the long-run quantity supplied. We would say that long-run supply is very price elastic: The long-run supply curve would be nearly horizontal. A principal implication of such a high price elasticity is that long-run equilibrium prices would not increase very much in response to significant outward shifts in the market demand curve.

A small supply elasticity would have a quite different implication. If the elasticity were only 0.1, for example, a 1 percent increase in price would increase quantity supplied by only 0.1 percent. In other words, the long-run supply curve would be nearly vertical, and shifts outward in demand would result in rapidly rising prices without significant increases in quantity.

Estimating Long-Run Elasticities of Supply

Economists have devoted considerable effort to estimating long-run supply elasticities for competitive industries. Because economic growth leads to increased demands for most products (especially natural resources and other primary products), the reason for this interest is obvious. If long-run supply elasticities are high, real resource prices will not

Table 9.3

INDUSTRY	ELASTICITY ESTIMATE
Corn	+0.27
Soybeans	+0.13
Wheat	+0.03
Aluminum	Nearly infinite
Coal	+15.0
Medical care	+0.15 to +0.60
Natural gas (U.S.)	+0.50
Crude oil (U.S.)	+0.75

Agriculture: J. S. Choi and P. G. Helmberger, "How Sensitive Are Crop Yields to Price Changes and Farm Programs?" *Journal of Agriculture and Applied Economics* (July 1993): 237–244. Aluminum: *Critical Materials Commodity Action Analysis* (Washington, DC: U.S. Department of the Interior, 1975). Coal: M. B. Zimmerman, *The Supply of Coal in the Long Run: The Case of Eastern Deep Coal*, MIT Energy Laboratory Report, September (Cambridge, MA: MIT, 1975). Medical care: L. Paringer and V. Fon, "Price Discrimination in Medicine: The Case of Medicare," *Quarterly Review of Economics and Business* (Spring 1988): 49–68; estimates are based on responsiveness of Medicare services to fees under the program and may overstate elasticities for the entire medical care market. Natural gas: J. D. Khazzoom, "The FPC Staff's Model of Natural Gas Supply in the United States," *The Bell Journal of Economics and Management Science* (Spring 1971). Crude oil: D. N. Epple, *Petroleum Discoveries and Government Policy* (Cambridge, MA: Marc Ballinger, 1984), Chapter 3.

increase rapidly over time. This seems to be the case for relatively abundant resources that can be obtained with only modest increases in costs, such as aluminum or coal. Over time, real prices for these goods have not risen very rapidly in response to increasing demand. Indeed, in some cases, real prices may even have fallen because of technical improvements in production.

On the other hand, cases in which long-run supply curves are inelastic can show sharply escalating real prices in response to increased demand. Again, the ultimate causes for such an outcome relate to conditions in the market for inputs. In cases such as rare minerals (platinum, for example, which is used in automobile exhaust systems), increased demand may require the exploitation of very costly deposits. Perhaps an even more important source of increasing input costs is the market for skilled labor. When expansion of a market, such as that for medical care or computer software, creates new demand for a specialized labor input, wages for these workers may rise sharply, and that gives the long-run supply curve its upward slope.

Table 9.3 summarizes a few studies of long-run supply elasticities. Although there are considerable uncertainties about some of these figures (and, in some cases, the markets may not obey all the assumptions of the perfectly competitive model), they still provide a good indication of the way in which conditions in input markets affect long run supply elasticities. Notice, in particular, that the estimated elasticities for some natural resources are quite high—for these, the constant cost model may be approximately correct. For goods that encounter rising labor costs (medical care) or that require the use of increasingly high-cost locations (oil and farm crops), supply can be rather inelastic.

Can Supply Curves Be Negatively Sloped?

Whether it is possible for long-run supply curves to be negatively sloped has been a subject of debate among economists for decades. Of course, it is well known that supply curves can shift downward if input costs fall. For example, costs of electronic components have fallen dramatically in recent years, shifting down the supply curves for a huge variety of products such as laptop computers and flat-screen televisions. But the declining prices that result from such changes lie on many different supply curves, not on a single, downward-sloping curve. Whether it is possible to devise a reasonable theory to explain why prices might move downward along a single supply curve remains an open question for economists. Application 9.3: How Do Network Externalities Affect Supply Curves? illustrates some of the difficulties that arise in devising such a theory.

MICRO QUIZ 9.4

Table 9.3 reports that the estimated long-run elasticity of supply for natural gas in the United States is about 0.5. Hence, this estimate suggests that the supply of natural gas is fairly inelastic.

1. Is this estimate consistent with the fact that natural gas prices tend to rise rapidly during severe winters?
2. Is this estimate consistent with the fact that natural gas prices have fallen in recent years with the development of new production techniques such as hydraulic fracturing?

APPLICATION 9.3

How Do Network Externalities Affect Supply Curves?

Network externalities arise when adding additional users to a network causes per-unit costs to decline. Such externalities are common in many modern industries in telecommunication and Internet technology. Their presence sets the stage for declining prices as demand expands.

Metcalfe's Law

A basic property of communications networks is that they obey Metcalfe's Law, a principle named for Robert Metcalfe, a pioneer in the development of Ethernet technology. The law states that the usefulness of a given network varies directly with the square of the number of subscribers to that network.[1] This implies that the value of such a network expands much more rapidly than do the costs associated with establishing it. Such increasing returns combined with the impact of rapid change in communications technology itself have led to strong downtrends in the prices of many types of communications networks.

Some Examples

Examples of network externalities occur in the telecommunications, software, and Internet industries:

- **Telecommunications:** The benefits of having a phone or fax machine are greater the larger the number of people with whom one can communicate. Large telephone networks also facilitate other phone applications such as burglar alarm systems and mail-order operations.
- **Applications Software:** The greater the number of users of a given software package, the greater will be the benefits to users in terms of file sharing. For this reason, Microsoft Office has come to dominate the office software business. Microsoft also benefits from network externalities with their Windows operating systems because the large number of Windows installations makes it profitable for others to write applications software only for that system.
- **The Internet:** Network externalities in the Internet are similar to those in telecommunications. The ability of the Internet to carry any sort of digital file enables a much wider range of interactions than is possible with traditional phone networks, however. Especially problematic has been the ability of the Internet to foster piracy of intellectual property such as music or motion pictures.

Network Externalities and Supply Curves

Because prices for telecommunications and Internet services have fallen rapidly, it is tempting to argue that the presence of network externalities in these industries gives their long-run supply curves a negative slope. Falling prices just reflect movement along this supply curve as demand expands. Unfortunately, this analysis is unconvincing because the benefits of network externalities accrue largely to demanders,[2] not to suppliers, in terms of lower input costs. Yes, input prices for telecommunications have also been falling because of technical progress, but this effect is largely independent of network externalities. The prices of computers and digital watches have also been falling without reliance on significant network effects.

Economists remain undecided about the effect of network externalities on markets—especially about their impact on competition. The issue seems to be whether a firm can manage to appropriate some of the benefits of network externalities to itself (as seems to be the case with Microsoft Windows) or whether such externalities open the way for greater competition (as seems to be the case in telephone long-distance service). Developing models that differentiate between these two cases is an important area of economic research.

TO THINK ABOUT

1. Because additional users of a network generate gains to existing users, some economists have argued that new users should be subsidized. Will networks be "too small" without such subsidies?
2. Switching to a new network may pose substantial costs. For example, when a company adopts a new word-processing program, it will often incur large training costs. What economic factors would cause users to shift from an existing network to a new one?

[1]If there are n subscribers in a network, there are n^2-n possible one-way connections among them (because a subscriber cannot connect to himself or herself). This expression may overstate the value of a network, however, because every potential connection is not equally valuable.

[2]For this reason, some authors refer to network externalities as "economies of scale on the demand side of the market."

9-9 Consumer and Producer Surplus

Consumer surplus
The extra value individuals receive from consuming a good over what they pay for it. What people would be willing to pay for the right to consume a good at its current price.

Producer surplus
The extra value producers get for a good in excess of the opportunity costs they incur by producing it. What all producers would pay for the right to sell a good at its current market price.

Supply-demand analysis can often be used to assess the well-being of market participants. For example, in Chapter 3 we introduced the notion of **consumer surplus** as a way of illustrating consumers' gains from market transactions. Figure 9.9 summarizes these ideas by showing the market for, say, fresh tomatoes. At the equilibrium price of P^*, individuals choose to consume Q^* tomatoes. Because the demand curve D shows what people are willing to pay for one more tomato at various levels of Q, the total value of tomato purchases to buyers (relative to a situation where no tomatoes are available) is given by the total area below the demand curve from $Q = 0$ to $Q = Q^*$—that is, by area AEQ^*0. For this value, they pay an amount given by P^*EQ^*0, and hence receive a "surplus" (over what they pay) given by the dark shaded area AEP^*. Possible happenings in the tomato market that change the size of this area clearly affect the well-being of these market participants.

Figure 9.9 also can be used to illustrate the surplus value received by tomato producers relative to a situation where no tomatoes are produced. This measure is based on the intuitive notion that the supply curve S shows the minimum price that producers would accept for each unit produced. At the market equilibrium P^*, Q^*, producers receive total revenue of P^*EQ^*0. But under a scheme of selling one unit at a time at the lowest possible price, producers would have been willing to produce Q^* for a payment of BEQ^*0. At Q^*, therefore, they receive a **producer surplus** given by the light-shaded area P^*EB. To understand the precise nature of this surplus, we must again examine the short-run/long-run distinction in firms' supply decisions.

Figure 9.9 Competitive Equilibrium and Consumer/Producer Surplus

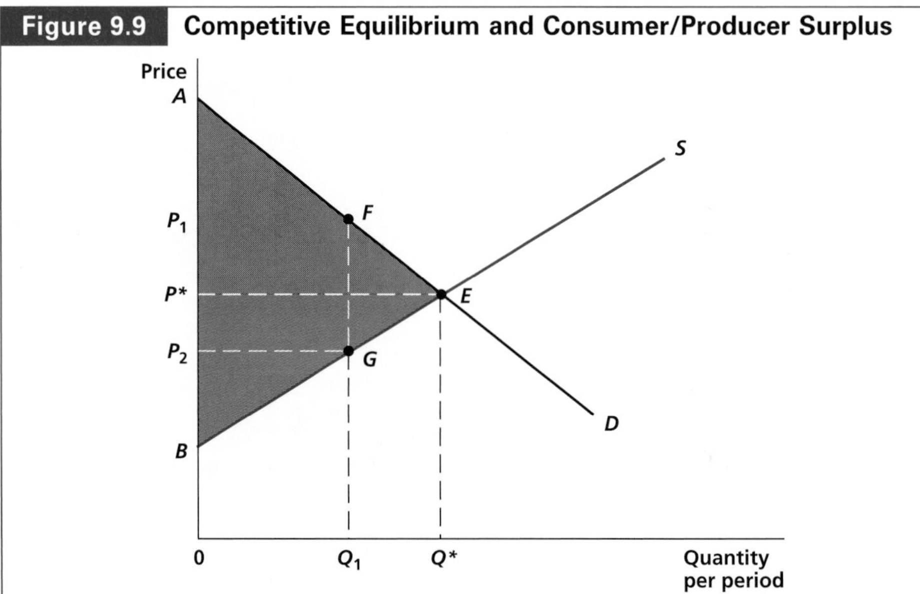

At the competitive equilibrium (Q^*), the sum of consumer surplus (shaded dark) and producer surplus (shaded light) is maximized. For an output level less than Q^*, say Q_1, there is a deadweight loss of consumer and producer surplus given by area FEG.

Short-Run Producer Surplus

The supply curve S in Figure 9.9 could be either a short-run or a long-run supply curve. However, we have shown that the upward slope of S has rather different causes in these two cases. In the short run, the market supply curve is the horizontal summation of all firms' short-run marginal cost curves. The curve's positive slope reflects the diminishing returns to variable inputs that are encountered as output is increased. In this case, price exceeds marginal cost (as reflected by the supply curve) at all output levels, except Q^*. Production of each of these "intramarginal" units of output generates incremental profits for suppliers. Actual short-run profits, then, are given by the sum of all of these profit increments (area P^*EB) plus profits when $Q = 0$. But, by definition, when $Q = 0$, profits are negative—they consist of the loss of all fixed costs. Hence, area P^*EB includes both actual short run profits and all fixed costs. This is an appropriate measure of how much firms that decide to not shut down gain from participating in the market in the short run.[6] In this sense, it is the mirror image of consumer surplus, which measures how much consumers gain by being in the market rather than out of it.

Long-Run Producer Surplus

In the long run, positively sloped supply curves arise because firms experience increasing input costs. When the market is in equilibrium, each firm has zero profits and there are no fixed costs. Short-run producer surplus does not exist in this situation. Instead, long-run producer surplus now reflects the increasing payments being received by the firms' inputs as output expands. The area P^*EB in Figure 9.9 now measures all of these increased payments relative to a situation in which the industry produces no output, in which case these inputs would receive lower prices for their services.

Ricardian Rent

Long-run producer surplus can be most easily illustrated with a situation first described by David Ricardo in the early part of the nineteenth century.[7] Assume there are many parcels of land on which tomatoes might be grown. These range from very fertile land (low costs of production) to very poor, dry land (high costs). The long-run supply curve for tomatoes is constructed as follows. At low prices, only the best land is used to produce tomatoes and few are produced. As output increases, higher-cost plots of land are brought into production because higher prices make it profitable to grow tomatoes on this land. The long-run supply curve for tomatoes is positively sloped because of the increasing costs associated with using less fertile land. Notice that this is a somewhat different reason than we discussed earlier. There, firms had identical cost curves and every firm's costs were affected by rising input prices. In the Ricardian example, firms' costs differ and costs of the last firm to enter the market are higher than all those who entered previously. Still, the situations share many similarities, as we shall see.

---

[6]Some algebra may clarify this. Profits when participating in the market (π_m) at P^* are given by $\pi_m = P^*Q^* - TC$, whereas profits when shut down are given by $\pi_s = -FC$. Hence, the gain from participating in the market is given by $\pi_m - \pi_s = \pi_m - (-FC) = \pi_m + FC$.

[7]See David Ricardo, *The Principles of Political Economy and Taxation* (1817; reprint, London: J. M. Dent and Son, 1965), Chapters 2 and 32.

MICRO QUIZ 9.5

The study of long-run producer surplus is one of the most important ways in which microeconomics ties together effects in various markets. Explain the following scenarios:

1. If the peanut-harvesting industry is a price taker for all of the inputs it hires, there will be no long-run producer surplus in this industry.
2. If the only "scarce" resource in the potato-harvesting industry is land for growing potatoes, total long-run producer surplus in this industry will be measured by total economic rents earned by potato-land owners. How do these rents enter into the pricing of potatoes?

Market equilibrium in this situation is illustrated in Figure 9.10. At an equilibrium price of P^*, both the low-cost and the medium-cost farms earn (long-run) profits. The "marginal farm" earns exactly zero economic profits. Farms with even higher costs stay out of the market because they would incur losses at a price of P^*. Profits earned by the intramarginal farms can persist in the long run, however, because they reflect returns to a rare resource—low-cost land. Free entry cannot erode these profits even over the long term. The sum of these long-run profits constitutes total producer surplus as given by area P^*EB in Figure 9.10(d).

The long-run profits illustrated in Figure 9.10 are sometimes referred to as **Ricardian rent**. They represent the returns obtained by the owners of scarce resources (in this case, fertile tomato-growing land) in a marketplace. Often these rents are "capitalized" into the prices

Ricardian rent
Long-run profits earned by owners of low-cost firms. May be capitalized into the prices of these firms' inputs.

Figure 9.10 Ricardian Rent

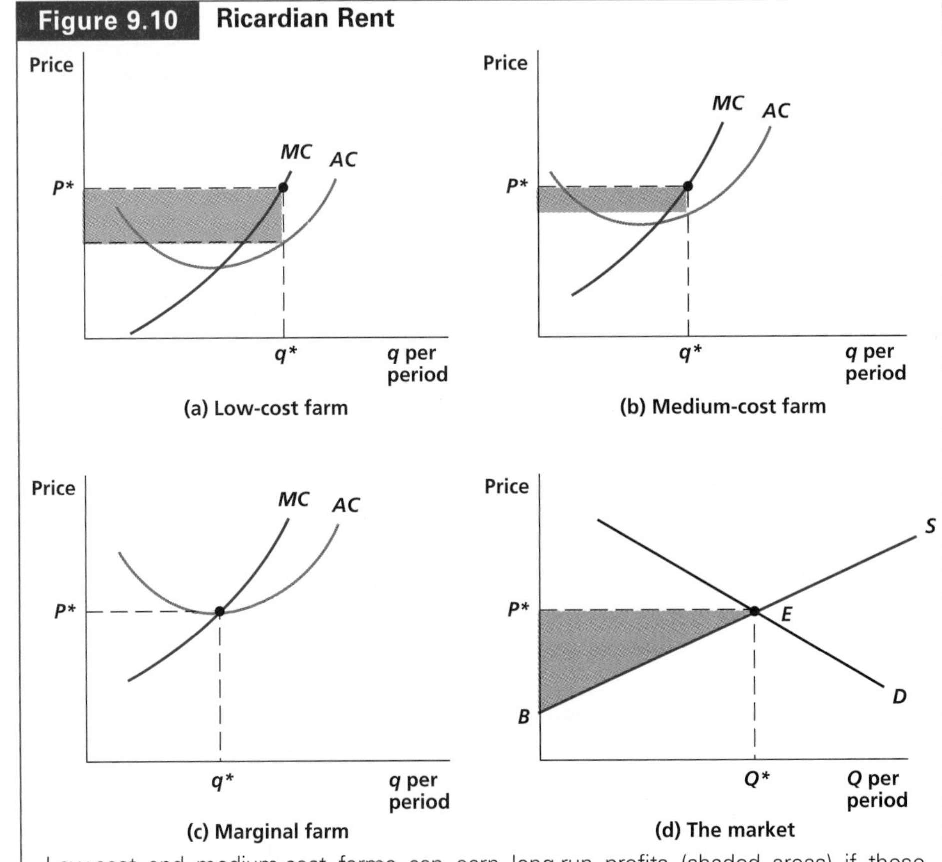

Low-cost and medium-cost farms can earn long-run profits (shaded areas) if these costs reflect ownership of unique resources. Total Ricardian rent represents producer surplus—area P^*EB in (*d*). Ricardian rents are usually capitalized into resource prices.

of these resources; in short, fertile land sells for higher prices than does poor land. Similarly, rich gold mines have higher prices than poor mines, favorably located retail space in malls rents for more than out-of-the-way space, and airport landing slots at Chicago's O'Hare are more valuable than slots at airports in the Yukon.

Economic Efficiency

This description of producer and consumer surplus also provides a simple proof of why economists believe competitive markets produce "efficient" allocations of resources. Although a more detailed examination of that topic requires that we look at many markets (which we do in the next chapter), here we can return to Figure 9.9 as a simple illustration. Any output level for tomatoes other than Q^* in this figure is inefficient in that the sum total of consumer and producer surplus is not as large as possible. If Q_1 tomatoes were produced, for example, a total surplus of area *FEG* would be forgone. At Q_1 demanders are willing to pay P_1 for another tomato, which would cost only P_2 to produce. That gap suggests that there exists a mutually beneficial transaction (such as producing one more tomato at a price of P^*) that could benefit both demanders (who would get the tomato for less than they were willing to pay) and suppliers (who would get more for the tomato than it would cost to produce). Only at Q^* are all such mutually beneficial transactions consummated and only then is the sum of consumer and producer surplus as large as possible.[8] Output level Q^* is said to be an **economically efficient allocation of resources**—a term we explore further in Chapter 10. Application 9.4: Does Buying Things on the Internet Improve Welfare? shows how the extra welfare from expanding markets can be measured. Before turning to a few real-world applications, a numerical example may help illustrate the efficiency concept.

Economically efficient allocation of resources
An allocation of resources in which the sum of consumer and producer surplus is maximized. Reflects the best (utility maximizing) use of scarce resources.

A Numerical Illustration

Consider again a hypothetical market for CDs in which demand is represented by

$$Q = 10 - P \qquad \textbf{(9.10)}$$

and supply by

$$Q = P - 2 \qquad \textbf{(9.11)}$$

We showed that equilibrium in this market occurs at $P^* = 6$ and $Q^* = 4$ CDs per week. Figure 9.11 repeats Figure 9.6 by providing an illustration of this equilibrium. At point E, consumers are spending \$24 ($= 6 \cdot 4$) per week for CDs. Total consumer surplus is given by the dark triangular area in the figure and amounts to \$8 ($= 1/2$ of $4 \cdot 4$) per week. At *E*, producers also receive revenues of \$24 per week and gain a producer surplus of \$8 per week, as reflected by the light triangle. Total consumer and producer surplus is therefore \$16 per week.

The inefficiency of other potential CD output levels can now be illustrated with the help of Figure 9.11. If price remains at \$6 but output is only three tapes per week, for example, consumers and producers each receive \$7.50 per week of surplus in their transactions. Total consumer and producer surplus is \$15 per week—a reduction of \$1 from what it is at *E*. Total surplus would still be \$15 per week with output of three CDs per week at any other price between \$5 and \$7. Once output is specified, the precise price at

[8]Producing more than Q^* would also reduce total producer and consumer surplus since consumers' willingness to pay for extra output would fall short of the costs of producing that output.

APPLICATION 9.4

Does Buying Things on the Internet Improve Welfare?

Technical innovations together with significant network externalities have sharply reduced the transactions costs associated with conducting business over the Internet. These innovations offer the promise of transforming the way selling is done in many industries.

The Gains from Internet Trade

Figure 1 illustrates the nature of the gains from reduced transactions costs of Internet trading. The demand and supply curves in the figure represent consumers' and firms' behavior vis-à-vis any good that might be bought and sold over the Internet. Prior to the decline in Internet costs, per-unit transactions costs exceeded $P_2 - P_1$. Hence, no trading took place; buyers and sellers preferred traditional retail outlets. A fall in these costs increased Internet business. Assuming that the per-unit cost of making transactions fell to zero, the market would show a large increase in Internet trading, settling at the competitive equilibrium, P^*, Q^*. This new equilibrium promises substantial increases in both consumer and producer surplus.

Figure 1 Reduced Transaction Costs Promote Internet Commerce

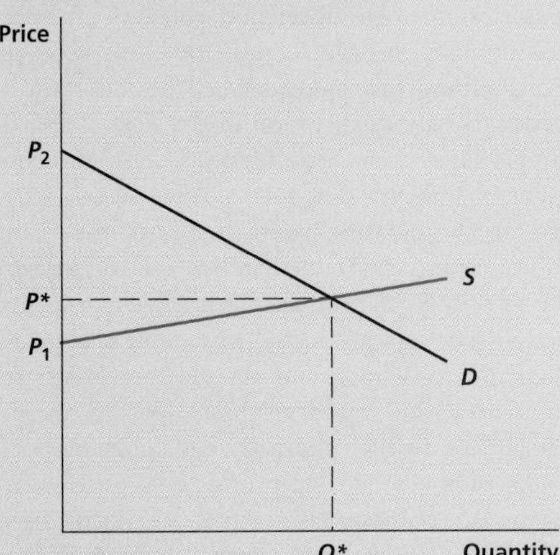

When transaction costs for internet trading exceed $P_2 - P_1$, no transactions occur. As transaction costs decline, equilibrium approaches P^*, Q^*.

The Growth of E-Commerce

Although Internet retailing is relatively new, its growth has been remarkable. In 2013 e-commerce amounted to over $250 billion—nearly six percent of all retail sales. The most important early inroads by Internet sales were in travel-related goods (airline and resort reservations), online financial services, and some narrow categories of consumer goods (for example, books sold by Amazon.com). These are goods for which Internet trading represented some of the largest reductions in transactions costs relative to traditional outlets. More recently, e-commerce has made inroads into many other areas as traditional retailers such as Williams-Sonoma or Home Depot make increasingly large fractions of their sales over the Web, and Amazon has vastly expanded what the firm offers.

The Value Added by Internet Retailers

One question raised by the growth of Internet selling is whether there will remain a separate role for retailers over the long term. If the Internet allows producers to reach customers directly, why would any role for retailing "middlemen" remain? The answer to this query lies in the nature of services that e-retailers can provide. In general, the primary good that such retailers provide is information. For example, Internet automobile sites (such as Edmonds.com or Autobytel.com) not only provide comparative information about the features of various models, but can also point to the dealer that gives the best price. Internet travel services can search for the lowest fare or for the most convenient departure. Many retailing sites make use of customer profiles to suggest items they might like to buy. For example, Amazon.com uses a customer's past book purchases to suggest potential new ones. At LandsEnd.com you can even "try on" clothes. Hence, it appears that Internet retailing is evolving in ways that make the most use of the low cost of providing information to consumers.

TO THINK ABOUT

1. How will the growth of Internet retailing affect traditional "bricks-and-mortar" retailers such as Wal-Mart or Sears? What special services can these retailers offer that the Internet cannot? Are people willing to pay for such services?
2. In recent years there has been much controversy about whether sales taxes should apply to goods sold over the Internet. Local retailers complain that they face unfair competition from on-line stores whose sales incur no sales taxes. On-line retailers reply that collecting sales taxes would be too complicated given the many jurisdictions that impose such taxes. What do you think?

Figure 9.11 Efficiency in CD Sales

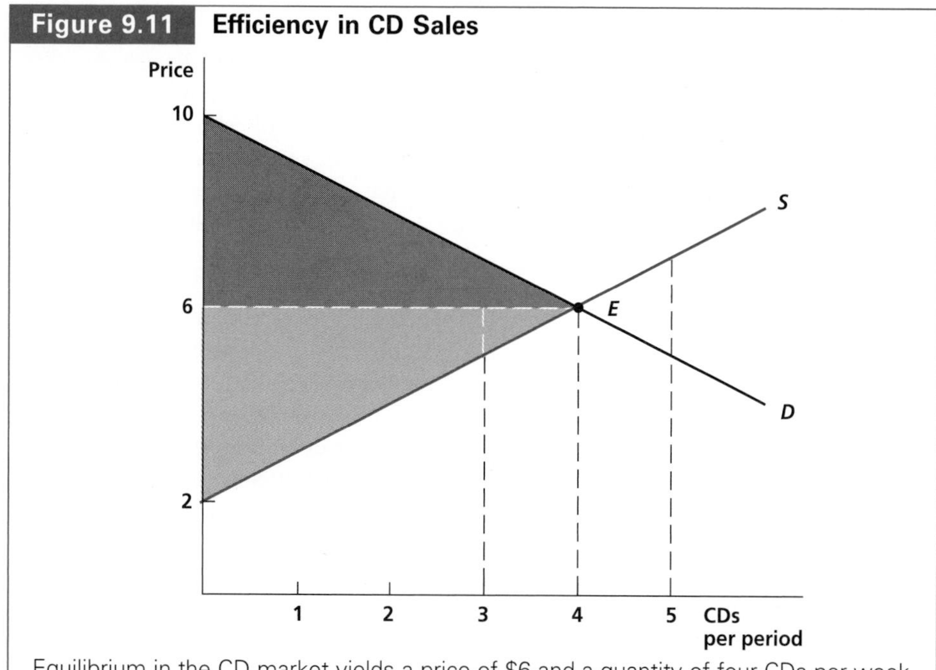

Equilibrium in the CD market yields a price of $6 and a quantity of four CDs per week. Consumer surplus (shaded dark) and producer surplus (shaded light) are each $8. An output of three CDs per week would reduce the sum of consumer and producer surplus from $16 to $15.

which transactions occur affects only the distribution of surplus between consumers and producers. The transaction price does not affect the total amount of surplus, which is always given by the area between the demand curve and the supply curve.

Output levels greater than four CDs per week are also inefficient. For example, production of five CDs per week at a transaction price of $6 would again generate consumer surplus of $7.50 ($8 for the four CDs transaction less a loss of $0.50 on the sale of the fifth CD, since the CD sells for more than people are willing to pay). Similarly, a producer surplus of $7.50 would occur, representing a loss of $0.50 in the production of the fifth CD. Total surplus at this point is now $15 per week, $1 less than at the market equilibrium. Again, the actual price assumed here doesn't matter—it is the fact that costs (reflected by the supply curve *S*) exceed individuals' willingness to pay (reflected by the demand curve *D*) for output levels greater than four CDs per week that results in the loss of total surplus value.

9-10 Some Supply-Demand Applications

The previous discussion shows that the supply-demand model that underlies much of economics not only is good for explaining movements in prices and quantities, but also can be used to assess the welfare of various market participants. In this section, we look at two of the most important such uses: (1) to study the question of who actually pays taxes, and (2) to examine the welfare consequences of expanding international trade.

Tax Incidence

Tax incidence theory
The study of the final burden of a tax after considering all market reactions to it.

An important application of the perfectly competitive model is to the study of the effects of taxes. Not only does the model permit an evaluation of how taxation alters the allocation of resources, but it also highlights the issue of who bears the actual burden of various taxes. By stressing the distinction between the legal obligation to pay a tax and the economic effects that may shift that burden elsewhere, **tax incidence theory** helps to clarify the ways in which taxes actually affect the well-being of market participants.

Figure 9.12 illustrates this approach by considering a "specific tax" of a fixed amount per unit of output that is imposed on all firms in a constant cost industry. Although legally the tax is required to be *paid* by the firm, this view of things is very misleading. To demonstrate this, we begin by showing that the tax can be analyzed as a shift downward in the demand curve facing this industry from D to D'. The vertical distance between the curves measures the amount of the per unit tax, t. For any price that consumers pay (say, P) firms get to keep only $P - t$. It is that after-tax demand curve D', then, that is relevant to firms' behavior. Consumers continue to pay a "gross" price as reflected by the demand curve D. The tax creates a "wedge" between what consumers pay and what firms actually get to keep.

The short-run effect of the tax is to shift the equilibrium from its initial position P_1, Q_1 to the point where the new demand curve D' intersects the short-run supply curve S. That intersection occurs at output level Q_2 at an after-tax price to the firm of P_2. Assuming this price exceeds average variable costs, the typical firm now produces output level q_2 at a loss.

Consumers will pay P_3 for output level Q_2. The graph reveals that $P_3 - P_2 = t$; in the short run, the tax is borne partially by consumers (who see the price they pay rise from P_1 to P_3) and partially by firms, which are now operating at a loss because they are receiving only P_2 (instead of P_1) for their output.

Figure 9.12 Effect of the Imposition of a Specific Tax on a Perfectly Competitive, Constant Cost Industry

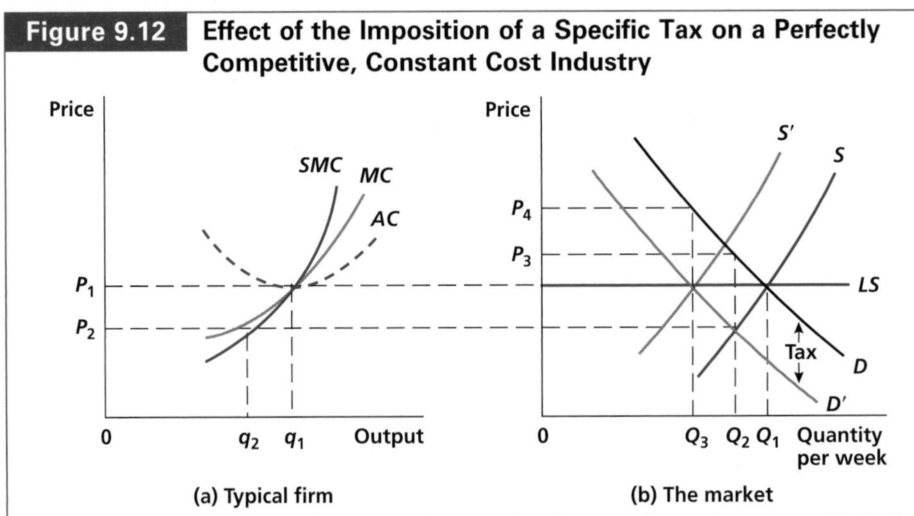

A specific commodity tax of amount t lowers the after-tax demand curve to D'. With this "new" demand curve, Q_2 will be produced in the short run at an after-tax price of P_2. In the long run, firms will leave the industry and the price will return to P_1. The entire amount of the tax is shifted onto consumers in the form of a higher market price (P_4).

Long-Run Shifting of the Tax In the long run, firms do not continue to operate at a loss. Some firms leave the market bemoaning the role of oppressive taxation in bringing about their downfall. The industry short-run supply curve shifts leftward because fewer firms remain in the market. A new long-run equilibrium is established at Q_3 where the after-tax price received by those firms still in the industry enables them to earn exactly zero in economic profits. The firms remaining in the industry return to producing output level q_1. The price paid by buyers in the market is now P_4. In the long run, the entire amount of the tax has been shifted into increased prices. Even though the firm ostensibly *pays* the tax, the long-run burden is borne completely by the consumers of this good.[9]

Long-Run Incidence with Increasing Costs

In the more realistic case of increasing costs, both producers and consumers pay a portion of this tax. Such a possibility is illustrated in Figure 9.13. Here, the long-run supply curve (LS) has a positive slope because the costs of various inputs are bid up as industry output expands. Imposition of the tax, t, shifts the after-tax demand curve inward to D', and this brings about a fall in net price over the long run from P_1 to P_2. Faced with the lower price, P_2, firms leave this industry, which has the effect of reducing some inputs' prices. Long-run equilibrium is reestablished at this lower net price, and consumers now pay a gross price of P_3, which exceeds what they paid previously. Total tax collections are given by the dark area $P_3ABE_2P_2$. These are partly paid by consumers (who pay P_3

Figure 9.13 Tax Incidence in an Increasing Cost Industry

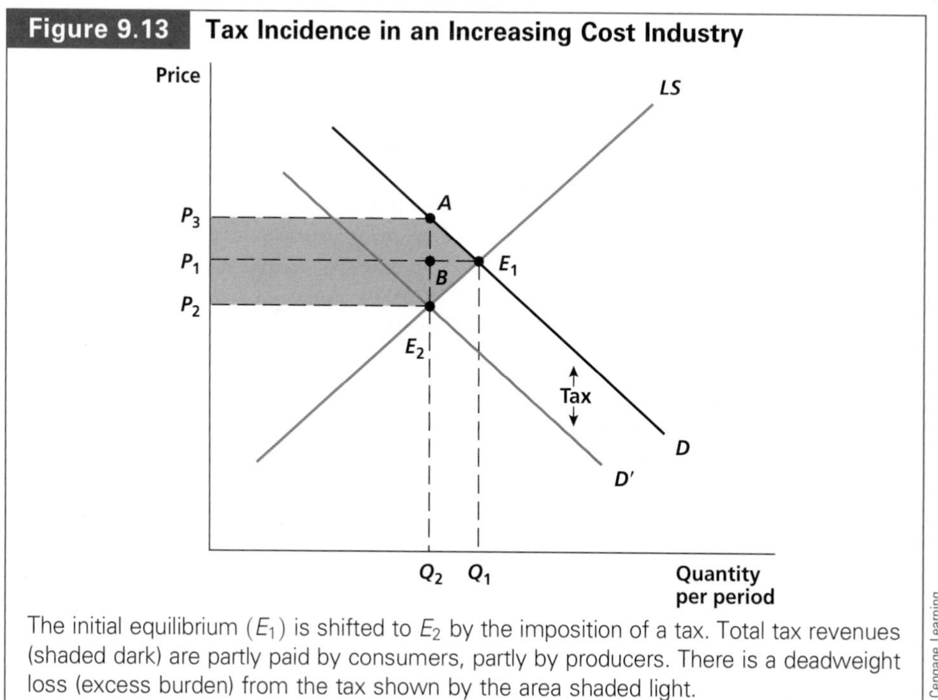

The initial equilibrium (E_1) is shifted to E_2 by the imposition of a tax. Total tax revenues (shaded dark) are partly paid by consumers, partly by producers. There is a deadweight loss (excess burden) from the tax shown by the area shaded light.

[9] Notice that owners of firms leaving the industry incur no long-run burden because they were initially earning zero economic profits, and, by assumption, can earn the same return elsewhere.

instead of P_1) and partly by the owners of firms' inputs who are now paid based on a lower net price, P_2, instead of P_1.[10]

Incidence and Elasticity A bit of geometric intuition suggests that the relative sizes of the price changes shown in Figure 9.13 depend on the elasticities of the demand and supply curves. Intuitively, the market participant with the more-elastic response is able more easily to "get out of the way" of the tax, leaving the one with less elastic response still in place to pay the most. We have already illustrated a special case of this principle in Figure 9.12. In that figure, the long-run elasticity of supply is infinite because of the constant-cost nature of the industry. Because the price received by firms (and by the inputs the firm employs) does not vary as output contracts as a result of the tax, the entire tax burden is shifted onto consumers. This outcome may be quite common in situations of some state or local taxes for which the good being taxed constitutes such a small portion of the national total that local supply is infinitely elastic. For example, a small town that tries to impose a large tax on its restaurants may find that the tax is quickly reflected in the price of restaurant meals. Some restaurant owners can avoid the tax by going elsewhere.

More generally, if demand is relatively inelastic, whereas supply is elastic, demanders pay the bulk of a tax in the form of higher prices. Alternatively, if supply is relatively inelastic but demand is elastic, producers pay most of the tax. Indeed, in this case, we can push the analysis further by noting that the producer's share is paid primarily by those inputs that have inelastic supply curves because it is these inputs that experience the greatest drop in price when demand for their services declines. For example, the producer's share of a tax on gold or silver would be largely paid by mine owners because the supply of mining land to this industry may be very inelastic. The supply of mining machinery or mine workers may be more elastic, however, because these inputs may have good alternative sources of employment. Hence, they would pay little of the tax. Of course, taking account of all of these repercussions of a tax in various markets is sometimes very difficult, and simple models of supply and demand may not be up to the task. Modern analyses of the tax incidence question use computer models of general equilibrium so that effects on many markets can be studied simultaneously. A brief look at these types of models is provided in Chapter 10. Application 9.5: The Tobacco "Settlement" Is Just a Tax looks at the impact of the large liability costs that have ostensibly been imposed on tobacco companies in recent years.

Taxation and Efficiency Because taxation reduces the output of the taxed commodity, there is a reallocation of production to other areas. This reallocation implies that some previously mutually beneficial transactions are forgone and that taxation reduces overall economic welfare. This loss can also be illustrated in Figure 9.13. The total loss in consumer surplus as a result of the tax is given by area $P_3AE_1P_1$. Of this area, P_3ABP_1 is transferred into tax revenues for the government and area AE_1B is simply lost. Similarly, the total loss of producer surplus is given by area $P_1E_1E_2P_2$ with area $P_1BE_2P_2$ being transferred into tax revenues and area BE_1E_2 being lost. By the standard of resource allocation efficiency, the effect of the transfer into tax revenues (which amounts in total to area $P_3AE_2P_2$) is ambiguous. Whether this reduces

MICRO QUIZ 9.6

Suppose that a per-unit tax is imposed on the perfectly competitive golf-tee industry.

1. Why would you expect consumers to pay a larger share of this tax in the long run than in the short run?
2. How would you determine who pays the producer's share of this tax in the long run?

[10]Notice again that the firms' owners, per se, experience no losses here since they earned zero profits before the tax. Rather, the producer's share of the tax burden is borne by the owners of those inputs that have fallen in price.

APPLICATION 9.5

The Tobacco "Settlement" Is Just a Tax

In June 1997, attorneys general from most U.S. states reached an agreement with the largest tobacco companies to settle a series of lawsuits based on the harmful effects of cigarette smoking. That settlement required that the tobacco companies pay about $360 billion to the states over the next 25 years in exchange for limiting future suits against the companies. Because of this limitation on future lawsuits, the settlement required approval by the U.S. Congress—an approval that became embroiled in politics and never happened. Subsequently, in November 1998, the states reached a series of more modest agreements with the tobacco companies that amounted to about $100 billion (in present-value terms) and did not require congressional approval. The economics of this settlement are almost as interesting as the politics.

The Tobacco Settlement as a Tax Increase

Probably the most accurate way to think about this settlement is as an increase in cigarette taxes. The companies play the role of tax collector, but there may be significant shifting of the tax depending on the elasticities involved. Table 3.4 provides an estimate of the price elasticity of demand for cigarettes of −.35. The state settlements added about $.45 per pack, a 20 percent increase on an initial price of about $1.80 per pack. Hence, the quantity of cigarettes sold would be expected to fall by about 7 percent (.20 · [−0.35]) from about 24 billion packs per year to 22.3 billion packs. Total "tax collections" would be $10 billion per year ($0.45 · 22.3 billion packs). Tobacco consumers will pay virtually all of this cost. Assuming that tobacco companies continue to earn about $.25 in profits per pack,[1] the 1.7 billion pack reduction in annual sales will cost them only about $425 million per year. Because tobacco consumers tend to have relatively low incomes, the settlement amounts to a very regressive form of taxation as a way for the states to raise revenue.

Other Effects of the Settlements

A primary goal of the tobacco settlements was to reduce smoking by young people. The resulting price increases may well have that effect. Some empirical evidence suggests that young smokers may have larger price elasticities than adult smokers (perhaps in the −0.5 range), and there is strong evidence that people who do not start smoking as teenagers are much less likely to take it up later. Several other components of the settlements required that tobacco companies sharply restrict marketing practices aimed at young people (Joe Camel was a casualty of the settlement, for example). The overall effectiveness of these measures remains uncertain, however. Still, the price effect alone could have substantial social benefits by eventually reducing the number of smoking-related deaths in the United States.

As for most legislation, several special interests also gained from the tobacco settlement. Many states adopted special programs to aid tobacco farmers and other workers who might be affected by the decline in tobacco sales. The settlement was tailored so that the smallest tobacco company (Liggett) would be rewarded because of the evidence it provided against the other firms in the earlier lawsuits. Because Liggett would benefit from the increase in cigarette prices without having to pay the settlement costs, its profits could easily double. Finally, of course, tort lawyers working on various smoking cases were well rewarded by the settlement. A standard "contingent fee" of 30 percent would have provided them with nearly $3 billion per year, but this unseemly amount was cut to about $750 million per year in the final settlements by the states. Still, the tort lawyers will not go hungry. By some estimates, each will get between $1 million and $2 million per year for the foreseeable future.

TO THINK ABOUT

1. The state settlements actually require tobacco companies to pay a fixed number of dollars each year. How would the analysis of this type of fixed revenue tax differ, if at all, from the approach taken in this application (which treats the settlement as a per-unit tax)?
2. The primary argument of the states in their lawsuits was that smoking was causing them to have to spend more on Medicaid and other health-related expenses. How would you decide whether this is true?

[1]All of the numbers in this example are taken from J. Bulow and P. Klemperer, "The Tobacco Deal," *Brookings Papers on Economic Activity, Microeconomics Annual 1998:* 323–394; and D. M. Cutler et al., "The Economic Impacts of the Tobacco Settlement," *Journal of Policy Analysis and Management* (Winter 2002): 1–19.

the welfare of consumers and producers as a whole depends on how wisely government funds are spent. If the government uses tax revenues to make investments that benefit everyone, the transfer may provide important social benefits to taxpayers. On the other hand, if the tax revenues end up in politicians' pockets or are used for frivolous things (such as palaces), the transfer represents a social loss as well as a personal cost to taxpayers. There is no ambiguity about the loss given by the light area AE_1E_2. This is a **deadweight loss** for which there are no compensating gains. Sometimes this loss is referred to as the "excess burden" of a tax; it represents the additional losses that consumers and producers incur as a result of a tax, over and above the actual tax revenues paid.

Deadweight loss
Losses of consumer and producer surplus that are not transferred to other parties.

A Numerical Illustration

The effects of an excise tax can be illustrated by returning once again to our example of supply-demand equilibrium in the market for CDs. Suppose the government implements a \$2 per CD tax that the retailer adds to the sales price for each tape sold. In this case, the supply function for tapes remains

$$\text{Supply}: Q = P - 2 \tag{9.12}$$

where P is now the net price received by the seller. Demanders, on the other hand, must now pay $P + t$ for each CD, so their demand function becomes

$$\text{Demand}: Q = 10 - (P + t) \tag{9.13}$$

or, since $t = 2$ here,

$$Q = 10 - (P + 2) = 8 - P \tag{9.14}$$

Notice, as we have shown graphically, that the effect of the tax is to shift the net demand curve (that is, quantity demanded as a function of the net price received by firms) downward by the per-unit amount of the tax. Equating supply and demand in this case yields

$$\text{Supply} = P - 2 = \text{Demand} = 8 - P \tag{9.15}$$

or $P^* = 5$, $Q^* = 3$. At this equilibrium, consumers pay \$7 for each CD, and total tax collections are \$6 per week (= \$2 per CD times three CDs per week). As we showed previously, an output of three CDs per week generates a total consumer and producer surplus of \$15 per week, of which \$6 is now transferred into tax revenues. In this particular case, these revenues are half paid by firms (who see the net price fall from \$6 to \$5). The other half of tax revenues are paid by CD consumers who see the price they pay rise from \$6 to \$7. Of course, in other cases the split might not be so even—it would depend on the relative elasticities of supply and demand. Here the excess burden of the tax is \$1 per week. This is a loss in consumer and producer surplus that is not collected in tax revenue. Looked at another way, the excess burden represents about 17 percent (= \$1/\$6) of total taxes collected.

An efficient tax scheme would seek to keep such losses to a minimum.

Graph this numerical illustration of taxation, and use your graph to answer the following questions:

1. What is the value of consumer and producer surplus after the tax is imposed? How do you know that the area of the "deadweight loss triangle" is \$1 here?
2. Suppose that the tax were raised to \$4. How much in extra tax revenue would be collected? How much bigger would the deadweight loss be?
3. How large a tax would foreclose all trading in CDs? What would tax collections be in this case? What would the deadweight loss be?

KEEP *in* MIND

With Taxes, Suppliers and Demanders Pay Different Prices

Taxes create a wedge between the price demanders pay and what suppliers receive. Whenever you are dealing with a tax problem, you must decide whether P will represent the price suppliers receive (as it did in our numerical application where demanders paid $P + t$) or the price demanders pay. If you opt for P to represent the price demanders pay, then suppliers will receive $P - t$. The final conclusions will be the same in either case—it is the size of the tax wedge that matters for the analysis, not the specifics of how it is modeled.

Trade Restrictions

Restrictions on the flow of goods in international commerce have effects similar to those we just examined for taxes. Impediments to free trade may reduce mutually beneficial transactions and cause significant transfers among the parties involved. Once again, the competitive model of supply and demand is frequently used to study these effects.

Gains from International Trade Figure 9.14 illustrates the domestic demand and supply curves for a particular good, say, shoes. In the absence of international trade, the domestic equilibrium price of shoes would be P_D and quantity would be Q_D. Although this equilibrium would exhaust all mutually beneficial transactions between domestic shoe producers and domestic demanders, the opening of international trade presents a number of additional options. If the world shoe price, P_W, is less than the prevailing domestic price, P_D, the opening of trade will cause prices to fall to this world

Figure 9.14 Opening of International Trade Increases Total Welfare

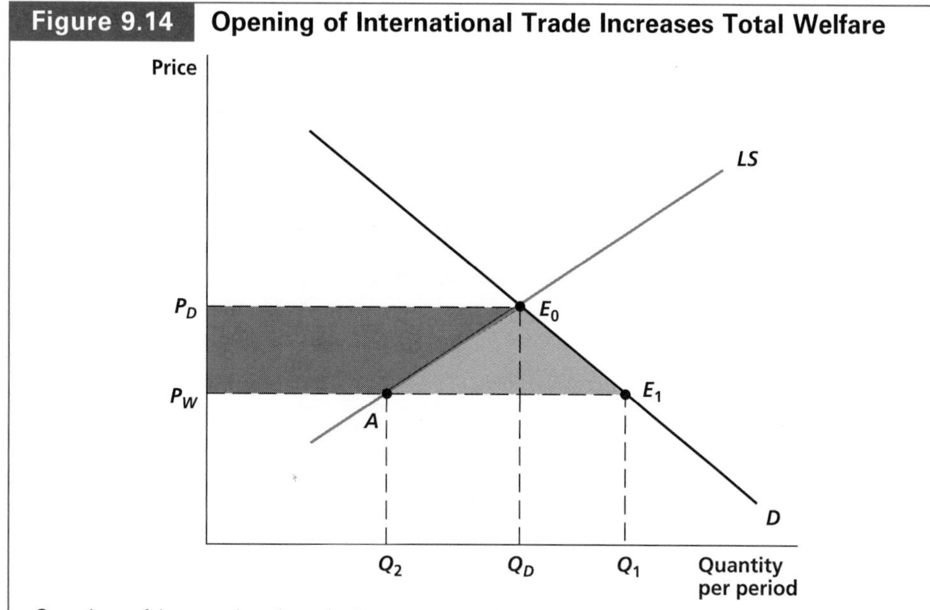

Opening of international trade lowers price from P_D to P_W. At P_W, domestic producers supply Q_2 and demanders want to buy Q_1. Imports amount to $Q_1 - Q_2$. The lower price results in a transfer from domestic producers to consumers (shaded dark) and a net gain of consumer surplus (shaded light).

level.[11] This drop in price will cause quantity demanded to increase to Q_1, whereas quantity supplied by domestic producers will fall to Q_2. Imported shoes will amount to $Q_1 - Q_2$. In short, what domestic producers do not supply at the world price is instead provided by foreign sources.

The shift in the market equilibrium from E_0 to E_1 causes a large increase in consumer surplus given by area $P_DE_0E_1P_W$. Part of this gain reflects a transfer from domestic shoe producers (area $P_DE_0AP_W$, which is shaded dark), and part represents an unambiguous welfare gain (the light area E_0E_1A). The source of consumer gains here is obvious—buyers get shoes at a lower price than was previously available in the domestic market. As in our former analyses, losses of producer surplus are experienced by those inputs that give the domestic long-run supply curve its upward slope. If, for example, the domestic shoe industry experiences increasing costs because shoemaker wages are driven up as industry output expands, then the decline in output from Q_D to Q_2 as a result of trade will reverse this process, causing shoemaker wages to fall.

Tariffs Shoemakers are unlikely to take these wage losses lying down. Instead, they will press the government for protection from the flood of imported footwear. Because the loss of producer surplus is experienced by relatively few individuals whereas consumer gains from trade are spread across many shoe buyers, shoemakers may have considerably greater incentives to organize opposition to imports than consumers would have to organize to keep trade open. The result may be adoption of protectionist measures.

Tariff
A tax on an imported good. May be equivalent to a quota or a nonquantitative restriction on trade.

Historically, the most important type of protection employed has been a **tariff**, that is, a tax on the imported good. Effects of such a tax are shown in Figure 9.15.

Figure 9.15 Effects of a Tariff

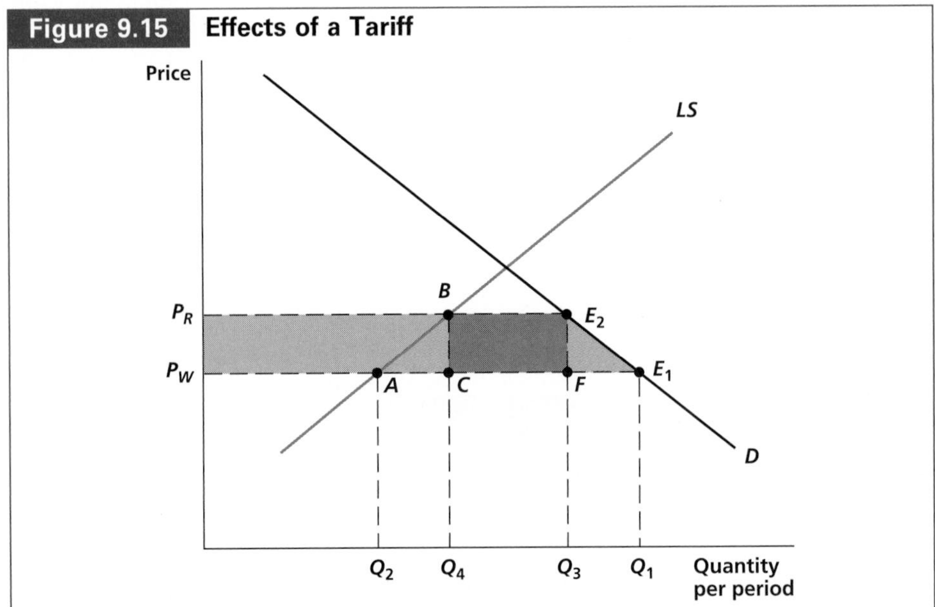

Imposition of a tariff of amount t raises price to $P_R = P_W + t$. This results in collection of tariff revenue (darkest), a transfer from consumers to producers (dark), and two triangles measuring deadweight loss (light). A quota has similar effects, though in this case no revenues are collected.

[11]Throughout our analysis, we assume that this country is a price taker in the world market and can purchase all of the imports it wishes without affecting the price, P_W. That is, the supply curve for the rest of the world is assumed to be infinitely elastic at P_W.

APPLICATION 9.6

The Saga of Steel Tariffs

On June 20, 2008, the U.S. International Trade Commission ruled that China was "dumping" steel products in the United States, thereby paving the way for the imposition of "penalty tariffs" on imported carbon steel pipes and other products. This situation represents just the latest round of protectionist policy for the U.S. steel industry.

Using Every Protectionist Trick

It is hard to find an industry that has had the special protections from imports that have been enjoyed by U.S. steel producers over the past 40 years. Protectionist measures have at various times included (1) import quotas, (2) minimum price agreements with exporters, (3) "voluntary" export restraints from nations that export steel to the United States, (4) a bewildering variety of tariffs, and (5) any number of lawsuits claiming? "unfair" trade practices (the steel pipe case being the latest example). In addition, U.S. steel producers have been the beneficiaries of a number of government loan guarantee and subsidy programs.

Rationale for Protection

The most often heard rationale for protection of the domestic steel industry is that the industry is "vital" to the security and continued strength of the U.S. economy. In wartime, it is claimed, we would not want to be in the position of needing to import all of our steel. More recently, a new twist was added by claiming that U.S. steel producers are at a disadvantage vis-à-vis their foreign rivals because they do not have the newest technology. Temporary tariffs, such as those instituted by the Bush administration in 2002, it was claimed, would give the industry some "breathing room" and a chance to catch up.

Costs of Protection

Whatever the rationale for protection, it is clear that the welfare costs of such programs are high. For example, estimated annual tariff revenues from the 2002 tariffs were about $900 million.[1] Balanced against this was an estimated loss of about $2.5 billion in consumer surplus together with domestic gains in producer surplus of $700 million. Overall, then, there was a net welfare loss of about $900 million per year from the tariff. This amounted to about $180,000 per year for each of the estimated 5,000 jobs "saved" in the domestic steel industry.

Claims and Counter Claims of Dumping

"Dumping" in international trade regulations refers to selling a good at below its costs of production. Goods that are found to have been "dumped" can be subjected to punitive tariffs that can sometimes raise their prices above those charged by domestic producers. In 2008 the United States and the European Union brought dumping charges against China for underpricing some kinds of steel pipe. Tariffs of up to 40 percent were imposed on some items. In a (not unexpected) retaliation, China in 2013 sought to impose similar tariffs on high-performance stainless steel tubes from the European Union (and possibly the United States). Hence, the latest installment of the long-running saga of steel tariffs will now be fought out in a variety of international tribunals that focus on "expert" analysis of dumping claims.

TO THINK ABOUT

1. Why would a firm (or nation) sell a good at below cost? Wouldn't this violate the long-run analysis provided in this chapter? (see Chapter 12 for further insights on this matter)
2. Many different types of imports from China have been subject to "dumping duties" by the U.S. and E.U. in recent years. Such goods include bicycles, yard equipment, and solar panels. Do you think imposition of such duties is good policy? Why shouldn't the U.S. just be happy that China is willing to sell its stuff at low prices?

[1]See G. C. Hufbauer and B. Goodrich, *Time for a Grand Bargain in Steel?* (Washington, DC, Institute for International Economics, 2002).

MICRO QUIZ 9.8

Use Figure 9.15 to answer the following questions about the imposition of a tariff on a competitive industry.

1. Do domestic producers pay any of this tax? Do foreign producers pay any of this tax?
2. Who gains the increase in producer surplus that results from the tariff?
3. Are the sources of the deadweight losses represented by triangles *ABC* and E_2E_1F different? Explain.

Now comparisons begin from the free trade equilibrium E_1. Imposition of a per unit tariff on shoes for domestic buyers of amount t raises the effective price to $P_W + t = P_R$. This price rise causes quantity demanded to fall from Q_1 to Q_3 whereas domestic production expands from Q_2 to Q_4. The total quantity of shoe imports falls from $Q_1 - Q_2$ to $Q_3 - Q_4$. Because each imported pair of shoes is now subject to a tariff, total tariff revenues are given by the darkest area BE_2FC, that is, by $t(Q_3 - Q_4)$.

Imposition of the tariff on imported shoes creates a variety of welfare effects. Total consumer surplus is reduced by area $P_RE_2E_1P_W$. Part of this reduction, as we have seen, is transferred into tariff revenues and part is transferred into increased domestic producer's surplus (area P_RBAP_W, shown in medium blue). The two light blue triangles, *BCA* and E_2E_1F, represent losses of consumer surplus that are not transferred to anyone; these are a deadweight loss from the tariff and are similar to the excess burden imposed by any tax. All of these areas can be measured if reliable empirical estimates of the domestic supply and demand curves for the imported good is available. Application 9.6: The Saga of Steel Tariffs looks at an on-going example.

SUMMARY

The model of perfectly competitive price determination presented in this chapter is probably the most widely used economic model. Even when markets do not meet the strict price-taking assumptions of perfect competition, this model of supply and demand can go a long way toward explaining observed behavior. Details of the model should always be in the back of any economist's mind as he or she thinks about explaining economic data. Some of these key details are as follows:

- The short-run supply curve represents the decisions of a number of price-taking firms. This curve is positively sloped because firms' short-run marginal cost curves are positively sloped.
- An equilibrium price is determined in the short run by the interaction of supply and demand. This price has the property that the quantity that firms are willing to supply is precisely equal to the quantity demanded by individuals.
- The effect of shifts in supply or demand curves on equilibrium price will depend on the shapes of *both* curves.
- Economic profits will attract new entrants and shift the short-run supply curve outward. This process will continue until economic profits are reduced to zero.
- If the entry of new firms has no effect on the prices of the inputs the firm buys, the long-run supply curve will be horizontal. If the entry of new firms raises the prices of firms' inputs, the long-run supply curve will be upward sloping.
- A perfectly competitive market will, in the absence of imperfections such as third-party effects or imperfect information, maximize the sum of producer and consumer surplus. The welfare consequences of various policies can be judged by changes in these surplus measures.
- In the long run, producer surplus represents the extra returns earned by firms' inputs relative to what they would earn if there were no market transactions in the good in question. Ricardian rent is one type of producer surplus that arises because owners of low-cost firms can make economic profits in the long run.
- A supply and demand analysis of taxes can clarify who pays them (the "incidence question") and whether taxes result in deadweight losses ("excess burden").
- The gains from international trade and the welfare effects of trade impediments (such as tariffs) can also be studied with simple supply and demand models.

REVIEW QUESTIONS

1. Each day 1,000 fishing boats return to port with the fish that have been caught. These fish must be sold within a few hours or they will spoil. All of the fish are brought to a single marketplace, and each fisher places a price on the fish he or she has for sale.
   a. How would a fisher know that his or her price was too high?
   b. How would a fisher know that his or her price was too low?
   c. As the day progresses, what would you expect to happen to the prices posted by the fishers?
2. Why is the price for which quantity demanded equals quantity supplied called an "equilibrium price"? Suppose, instead, we viewed a demand curve as showing what price consumers are willing to pay and a supply curve as showing what price firms want to receive. Using this view of demand and supply, how would you define an "equilibrium quantity"?
3. "For markets with inelastic demand and supply curves, most short-run movements will be in prices, not quantity. For markets with elastic demand and supply curves, most movements will be in quantity, not price." Do you agree? Illustrate your answer with a few simple graphs.
4. In long-run equilibrium in a perfectly competitive market, each firm operates at minimum average cost. Do firms also operate at minimum long-run average cost when such markets are out of equilibrium in the short run? Wouldn't firms make more in short-run profits if they opted always to produce that output level for which average costs were as small as possible?
5. Dr. D. is a critic of standard microeconomic analysis. In one of his frequent tirades, he was heard to say, "Take the argument for upward-sloping, long-run supply curves. This is a circular argument if I ever heard one. Long-run supply curves are said to be upward sloping because input prices rise when firms hire more of them. And that occurs because the long-run supply curves for these inputs are upward sloping. Hence, the argument boils down to 'long-run supply curves are upward sloping because other supply curves are upward sloping.' What nonsense!" Does Dr. D. have a point? How would you defend the analysis in this chapter?
6. Dr. E. is an environmentalist and a critic of economics. On *The Charlie Rose Show*, he attacks this book: "That text is typical—it includes all of this nonsense about long-run supply elasticities for natural resources like oil or coal. Any idiot knows that, because the earth has a finite size, all supply curves for natural resources are perfectly inelastic with respect to price. How can a rise in price for, say, oil lead to more oil when all of our oil was created eons ago? Focusing on these ridiculously high elasticity numbers just detracts from studying our real need—the need to conserve." How would you defend the analysis in this book against this tirade?
7. The long-run supply curve for gem diamonds is positively sloped because increases in diamond output increase the wages of diamond cutters. Explain why a decision by people to no longer buy diamond engagement rings would have disastrous consequences for diamond cutters but why such a trend would not really harm the owners of firms in the perfectly competitive gem diamond business.
8. A fledgling microeconomics student is having some trouble grasping the concept of short-run producer surplus. In exasperation, he blurts out, "This is absolute balderdash. I can understand that producer surplus is a good thing for firms because it measures the improvement in their welfare relative to a situation where they cannot participate in the market. But then I'm told that fixed costs are a component of short-run producer surplus. Aren't fixed costs a bad thing? They must be paid! How can they be one component of a good thing?" Can you set this student straight? (*Hint:* When is short-run producer surplus zero?)
9. Suppose that all operators of fast-food restaurants must rent the land for their establishments from other landowners. All other aspects of the costs of fast-food establishments are identical. Why would rents differ among fast-food locations? Would these differences in rents necessarily cause differences in the prices of fast food? What do you make of the claim by Mr. Z that "I simply can't make a go of my McDonald's franchise on the interstate—the landowner just wants too much rent"?
10. "Firms don't pay taxes, only people pay taxes" is a favorite slogan of the *Wall Street Journal*. But our analysis in this chapter shows that in the long run (with an upward-sloping supply curve), at least some portion of a unit tax is paid out of producer surplus. Is the *Wall Street Journal* wrong?

PROBLEMS

9.1. Suppose the daily demand curve for flounder at Cape May is given by $Q_D = 1{,}600 - 600P$, where Q_D is demand in pounds per day and P is price per pound.

a. If fishing boats land 1,000 pounds one day, what will the price be?

b. If the catch were to fall to 400 pounds, what would the price be?

c. Suppose the demand for flounder shifts outward to

$$Q_D = 2{,}200 - 600P$$

How would your answers to part a and part b change?

d. Now assume that Cape May fishermen can, at some cost, choose to sell their catch elsewhere. Specifically, assume that the amount they will sell in Cape May depends on the flounder price and is given by

$$Q_S = -1{,}000 + 2{,}000P \text{ for } Q_S \geq 0$$

where Q_S is the quantity supplied in pounds and P is the price per pound. What is the lowest price at which flounder will be supplied to the Cape May market?

e. Given the demand curve for flounder, what will the equilibrium price be?

f. Suppose now demand shifts to

$$Q_D = 2{,}200 - 600P$$

What will be the new equilibrium price?

g. Explain intuitively why price will rise by less in part f than it did in part c. Graph all your results.

9.2. A perfectly competitive market has 1,000 firms. In the very short run, each of the firms has a fixed supply of 100 units. The market demand is given by

$$Q = 160{,}000 - 10{,}000P$$

a. Calculate the equilibrium price in the very short run.

b. Calculate the demand schedule facing any one firm in the industry. Do this by calculating what the equilibrium price would be if one of the sellers decided to sell nothing or if one seller decided to sell 200 units. What do you conclude about the effect of any one firm on market price?

c. Suppose now that in the short run each firm has a supply curve that shows the quantity the firm will supply (q_i) as a function of market price. The specific form of this supply curve is given by

$$q_i = -200 + 50P$$

Using this short-run supply response, supply new solutions to parts a and b. Why do you get different solutions in this case?

9.3. Suppose there are 100 identical firms in the perfectly competitive notecard industry. Each firm has a short-run total cost curve of the form:

$$STC = \frac{1}{300}q^3 + 0.2q^2 + 4q + 10$$

and marginal cost is given by

$$SMC = .01q^2 + .4q + 4$$

a. Calculate the firm's short-run supply curve with q (the number of crates of notecards) as a function of market price (P).

b. Calculate the industry supply curve for the 100 firms in this industry.

c. Suppose market demand is given by $Q = -200P + 8{,}000$. What will be the shortrun equilibrium price-quantity combination?

d. Suppose everyone starts writing more research papers and the new market demand is given by $Q = -200P + 11{,}200$. What is the new short-run price-quantity equilibrium?

How much profit does each firm make?

9.4. Suppose there are 1,000 identical firms producing diamonds and that the short-run total cost curve for each firm is given by

$$STC = q^2 + wq$$

and short-run marginal cost is given by

$$SMC = 2q + w$$

where q is the firm's output level and w is the wage rate of diamond cutters.

a. If $w = 10$, what will be the firm's (short-run) supply curve? What is the industry's supply curve? How many diamonds will be produced at a price of 20 each? How many more diamonds would be produced at a price of 21?

b. Suppose that the wages of diamond cutters depend on the total quantity of diamonds produced and the form of this relationship is given by

$$w = .002Q$$

where Q represents total industry output, which is 1,000 times the output of the typical firm. In this situation, show that the firm's marginal cost (and short-run supply) curve depends on Q. What is the industry supply curve? How much will be produced at a price of 20? How much more will be produced at a price of 21? What do you conclude about how the shape of the short-run supply curve is affected by this relationship between input prices and output?

9.5. Gasoline is sold through local gasoline stations under perfectly competitive conditions. All gasoline station owners face the same long-run average cost curve given by

$$AC = .01q - 1 + 100/q$$

and the same long-run marginal cost curve given by

$$MC = .02q - 1$$

where q is the number of gallons sold per day.

a. Assuming the market is in long-run equilibrium, how much gasoline will each individual owner sell per day? What are the long-run average cost and marginal cost at this output level?
b. The market demand for gasoline is given by

$$Q_D = 2{,}500{,}000 - 500{,}000P$$

where Q_D is the number of gallons demanded per day and P is the price per gallon. Given your answer to part a, what will be the price of gasoline in long-run equilibrium? How much gasoline will be demanded, and how many gas stations will there be?
c. Suppose that because of the development of solar-powered cars, the market demand for gasoline shifts inward to

$$Q_D = 2{,}000{,}000 - 1{,}000{,}000P$$

In long-run equilibrium, what will be the price of gasoline? How much total gasoline will be demanded, and how many gas stations will there be?
d. Graph your results.

9.6. A perfectly competitive painted necktie industry has a large number of potential entrants. Each firm has an identical cost structure such that long-run average cost is minimized at an output of 20 units ($q_i = 20$). The minimum average cost is \$10 per unit. Total market demand is given by

$$Q = 1{,}500 - 50P$$

a. What is the industry's long-run supply schedule?
b. What is the long-run equilibrium price (P^*) The total industry output (Q^*) The output of each firm (q_i^*)? The number of firms? The profits of each firm?
c. The short-run total cost curve associated with each firm's long-run equilibrium output is given by

$$STC = .5q^2 - 10q + 200$$

where $SMC = q - 10$. Calculate the short-run average and marginal cost curves. At what necktie output level does short-run average cost reach a minimum?
d. Calculate the short-run supply curve for each firm and the industry short-run supply curve.
e. Suppose now painted neckties become more fashionable and the market demand function shifts upward to $Q = 2{,}000 - 50P$. Using this new demand curve, answer part b for the very short run when firms cannot change their outputs.
f. In the short run, use the industry short-run supply curve to recalculate the answers to part b.
g. What is the new long-run equilibrium for the industry?

9.7. Suppose that the demand for broccoli is given by

$$\text{Demand}: Q = 1{,}000 - 5P$$

where Q is quantity per year measured in hundreds of bushels and P is price in dollars per hundred bushels. The long-run supply curve for broccoli is given by

$$\text{Supply}: Q = 4P - 80$$

a. Show that the equilibrium quantity here is $Q = 400$. At this output, what is the equilibrium price? How much in total is spent on broccoli? What is consumer surplus at this equilibrium? What is producer surplus at this equilibrium?
b. How much in total consumer and producer surplus would be lost if $Q = 300$ instead of $Q = 400$?
c. Show how the allocation of the loss of total consumer and producer surplus between suppliers and demanders described in part b depends on the price at which broccoli is sold. How would the loss be shared if $P = 140$? How about if $P = 95$?
d. What would the total loss of consumer and producer surplus be if $Q = 450$ rather than $Q = 400$? Show that the size of this total loss also is independent of the price at which the broccoli is sold.
e. Graph your results.

9.8. The handmade snuffbox industry is composed of 100 identical firms, each having short-run total costs given by

$$STC = 0.5q^2 + 10q + 5$$

and short-run marginal costs given by

$$SMC = q + 10$$

where q is the output of snuffboxes per day.

a. What is the short-run supply curve for each snuffbox maker? What is the short-run supply curve for the market as a whole?
b. Suppose the demand for total snuffbox production is given by

$$Q = 1{,}100 - 50P$$

What is the equilibrium in this marketplace? What is each firm's total short-run profit?
c. Graph the market equilibrium and compute total producer surplus in this case.

d. Show that the total producer surplus you calculated in part c is equal to total industry profits plus industry short-run fixed costs.
e. Suppose now that the government imposed a \$3 tax on snuffboxes. How would this tax change the market equilibrium?
f. How would the burden of this tax be shared between snuffbox buyers and sellers?
g. Calculate the total loss of producer surplus as a result of the taxation of snuffboxes. Show that this loss equals the change in total short-run profits in the snuffbox industry. Why don't fixed costs enter into this computation of the change in short-run producer surplus?

9.9.  The perfectly competitive DVD copying industry is composed of many firms who can copy five DVDs per day at an average cost of \$10 per DVD. Each firm must also pay a royalty to film studios, and the per-film royalty rate (r) is an increasing function of total industry output (Q) given by

$$r = .002Q$$

a. Graph this royalty "supply" curve with r as a function of Q.
b. Suppose the daily demand for copied DVDs is given by

$$\text{Demand: } Q = 1{,}050 - 50P$$

Assuming the industry is in long-run equilibrium, what are the equilibrium price and quantity of copied DVDs? How many DVD firms are there? What is the per-film royalty rate?
(*Hint:* Use $P = AC$. Now $AC = 10 + .002Q$.)
c. Suppose that the demand for copied DVDs increases to

$$\text{Demand: } Q = 1{,}600 - 50P$$

Now, what are the long-run equilibrium price and quantity for copied DVDs? How many DVD firms are there? What is the per-film royalty rate?
d. Graph these long-run equilibria in the DVD market and calculate the increase in producer surplus between the situations described in part b and part c.
e. Use the royalty supply curve graphed in part a to show that the increase in producer surplus is precisely equal to the increase in royalties paid as Q expands incrementally from its level in part b to its level in part c.
f. Suppose that the government institutes a \$5.50-per-film tax on the DVD-copying industry. Assuming that the demand for copied films is that given in part c, how does this tax affect the market equilibrium?
g. How is the burden of this tax allocated between consumers and producers? What is the loss of consumer and producer surplus?
h. Show that the loss of producer surplus as a result of this tax is borne completely by the film studios. Explain your results intuitively.

9.10. The domestic demand for portable radios is given by

$$\text{Demand: } Q = 5{,}000 - 100P$$

where price P is measured in dollars and quantity Q is measured in thousands of radios per year. The domestic supply curve for radios is given by

$$\text{Supply: } Q = 150P$$

a. What is the domestic equilibrium in the portable radio market?
b. Suppose portable radios can be imported at a world price of \$10 per radio. If trade were unencumbered, what would the new market equilibrium be? How many portable radios would be produced domestically? How many portable radios would be imported?
c. If domestic portable radio producers succeeded in getting a \$5 tariff implemented, how would this change the market equilibrium? How much would be collected in tariff revenues? How much consumer surplus would be transferred to domestic producers? What would the deadweight loss from the tariff be?
d. Graph your results.

10 General Equilibrium and Welfare

In Chapter 9, we looked only at a single competitive market in isolation. We were not concerned with how things that happened in that one market might affect other markets. For many economic issues, this narrowing of focus is helpful—we need only look at what really interests us. For other issues, however, any detailed understanding requires that we look at how many related markets work. For example, if we wished to examine the effects of all federal taxes on the economy, we would need to look not only at a number of different product markets but also at markets for workers and for capital.

Economists have developed both theoretical and empirical (computer) models for this purpose. These are called **general equilibrium models** because they seek to study market equilibrium in many markets at once. The models in Chapter 9, on the other hand, are called **partial equilibrium models** because they are concerned with studying equilibrium in only a single market. In this chapter, we take a very brief look at general equilibrium models. One purpose of this examination is to clarify further the concept of economic efficiency that we introduced in Chapter 9.

General equilibrium model
An economic model of a complete system of markets.

Partial equilibrium model
An economic model of a single market.

10-1 A Perfectly Competitive Price System

The most common type of general equilibrium model assumes that the entire economy works through a series of markets like those we studied in Chapter 9. Not only are all goods allocated through millions of competitive markets but also all inputs have prices that are established through the workings of supply and demand. In all of these many markets, a few basic principles are assumed to hold:

- All individuals and firms take prices as given—they are price takers.
- All individuals maximize utility.
- All firms maximize profits.
- All individuals and firms are fully informed; there are no transactions costs, and there is no uncertainty.

These assumptions should be familiar to you. They are ones we have been making in many other places. One consequence of the assumptions (and a few others) is that it can be shown that when all markets work this way they establish equilibrium prices for all goods.[1] At these prices, quantity supplied equals quantity demanded in every market.

[1]Competitive markets can only establish relative, not absolute, prices. That is, these markets can only determine that one apple trades for two oranges, not whether apples and oranges cost \$0.50 and \$0.25 or \$20 and \$10. For this reason, the "price" recorded on the vertical axis of supply and demand curves should always be regarded as a "real" price that shows the price of the good relative to other prices. Absolute ("nominal") prices in an economy are determined by monetary factors, and we look briefly at these factors at the end of this chapter.

Of course not all general equilibrium models incorporate all of the assumptions listed above. In recent years a wide variety of models have been developed that incorporate many different assumptions about how markets work. The tools developed in this chapter should give you a general idea about how all general equilibrium models work.

10-2 Why Is General Equilibrium Necessary?

To see why we need a general model of this type, consider the market for tomatoes that we studied in Chapter 9. Figure 10.1(a) shows equilibrium in this market by the intersection of the demand curve for tomatoes (D) with the supply curve for tomatoes (S). Initially, the price of tomatoes is given by P_1. Figure 10.1 also shows the markets for three other economic activities that are related to the tomato market: 10.1(b) the market for tomato pickers, 10.1(c) the market for cucumbers (a complement to tomatoes in salads), and 10.1(d) the market for cucumber pickers. All of these markets are initially in equilibrium. The prices in these various markets will not change unless something happens to shift one of the curves.

Figure 10.1 **The Market Cost for Tomatoes and Several Related Markets**

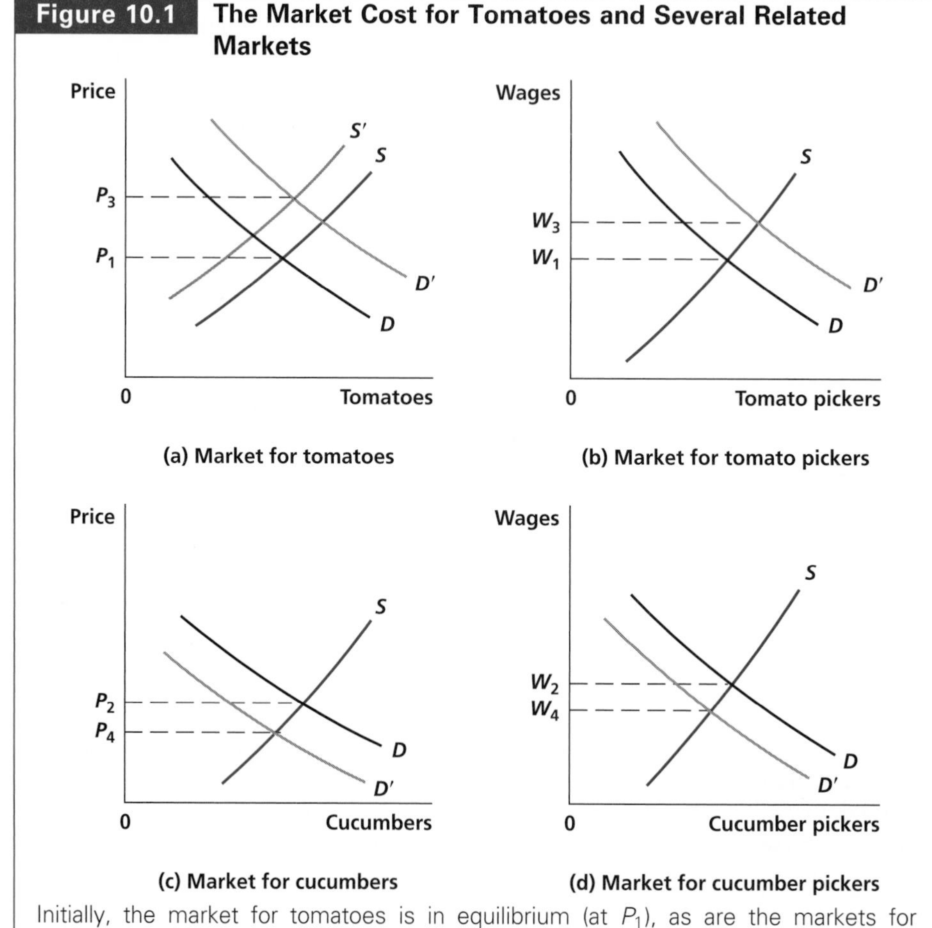

Initially, the market for tomatoes is in equilibrium (at P_1), as are the markets for tomato pickers, cucumbers, and cucumber pickers. An increase in demand for tomatoes disturbs these equilibria. Virtually all the supply and demand curves shift in the process of establishing a new general equilibrium.

Disturbing the Equilibrium

Suppose now that such a change does occur. Imagine a situation where the government announces that tomatoes have been found to cure the common cold, so everyone decides to eat more of them. An initial consequence of this discovery is that the demand for tomatoes shifts outward to. D' In our analysis in Chapter 9, this shift would cause the price of tomatoes to rise and that would be, more or less, the end of the story. Now, however, we wish to follow the repercussions of what has happened in the tomato market into the other markets shown in Figure 10.1. A first possible reaction would be in the market for tomato pickers. Because tomato prices have risen, the demand for labor used to harvest tomatoes increases. The demand curve for labor in Figure 10.1(b) shifts to D'. This tends to raise the wages of tomato pickers, which, in turn, raises the costs of tomato growers. The supply curve for tomatoes (which, under perfect competition, reflects only growers' marginal costs) shifts to S'.

What happens to the market for cucumbers? Because the price of tomatoes has risen and tomatoes and cucumbers are complements, the demand curve for cucumbers shifts inward to D'. This causes cucumber prices to fall. Such a decline in price also reduces the demand for workers to harvest cucumbers. Hence, the wage for these workers falls too.

Reestablishing Equilibrium

We could continue this story indefinitely. We could ask how the lower price of cucumbers affects the tomato market. Or we could ask whether cucumber pickers, discouraged by their falling wages, might consider picking tomatoes, shifting the supply of labor curve in Figure 10.1(b) outward. To follow this chain of events further or to examine even more markets related to tomatoes would add little to our story. Eventually we would expect all four markets in Figure 10.1 (and all the other markets we have not shown) to reach a new equilibrium, such as that illustrated by the lighter supply and demand curves in the figure. Once all the repercussions have been worked out, the final result might be a rise in tomato prices (to P_3), a rise in the wages of tomato pickers (to w_4), a fall in cucumber prices (to P_4), and a fall in the wages of cucumber pickers (to w_4). This is what we mean then by a smoothly working system of perfectly competitive markets. Following any disturbance, all the markets can eventually reestablish a new set of equilibrium prices at which quantity demanded is equal to quantity supplied in each market. In Application 10.1: Modeling Excess Burden with a Computer, we show why using a model that allows for interconnections among markets provides a more realistic and complete picture of how taxes affect the economy than does the single-market approach we took in Chapter 9.

Why are there two supply curves in Figure 10.1(a)? How does this illustrate "feedback" effects? Why would a partial equilibrium analysis of the effect of an increase in demand for tomatoes from D to D' give the wrong answer?

10-3 A Simple General Equilibrium Model

One way to give the flavor of general equilibrium analysis is to look at a simple supply-demand model of two goods together. Ingeniously, we will call these two goods X and Y. The "supply" conditions for the goods are shown by the production possibility frontier

APPLICATION 10.1

Modeling Excess Burden with a Computer

In Chapter 9 we showed that many taxes create "excess burdens" in that they reduce total consumer well-being by more than the amounts collected in tax revenues. A primary shortcoming of our analysis of this issue was that we looked only at a single market—an approach that may significantly understate matters.

Excess Burden in General Equilibrium Models

More precise estimates of the effect of taxation can be obtained from large-scale general equilibrium models. One interesting comparison of excess burden estimates from such models to similar estimates from single-market models found that the simple models may underestimate excess burden by as much as 80 percent.[1] For example, the authors look at a potential 5 percent tax on energy consumption in the United States and find that the excess burden estimated from a simple model is about $0.5 billion per year, whereas it is $2.6 billion per year when studied in a complete model of the economy. The main reason for such large differences is that a single-market analysis fails to consider how an energy tax might affect workers' labor supply decisions.

Some Other Results

Other examples using general equilibrium models to evaluate the excess burden of various tax systems are easy to find. For example, early studies of the entire tax system in the United Kingdom found that the distortions introduced by taxes resulted in a deadweight loss of 6 to 9 percent of total GDP.[2] The tax system imposed particularly heavy costs on British manufacturing industries, perhaps contributing to the country's relatively poor economic performance prior to the Thatcher reforms.

Another set of examples is provided by papers that look at special tax breaks provided to homeowners in the United States. Probably the two most important such breaks are the deductibility of mortgage payments for homeowners and the failure to tax the in-kind services people receive from living in their own homes. This special treatment biases peoples' choices in favor of owning rather than renting and probably causes them to invest more in houses and less in other forms of saving—an effect that was exaggerated by low mortgage rates in 2003–2005. General equilibrium models generally find significant overinvestment in housing, which may impose significant efficiency costs on the U.S. economy.[3]

Tax Progressivity

Finally, a number of authors have been interested in how the progressive income tax affects welfare in the United States (and elsewhere). The advantage of income tax progressivity is that it may reduce inequality in after-tax incomes, thereby providing some implicit "insurance" to low-income people. The disadvantage of such tax schemes is that the high marginal tax rates required may adversely affect the work and savings behavior of high-income people. An interesting paper by Conesa and Krueger uses a computer general equilibrium model to determine whether the degree of progressivity in the U.S. income tax is optimal,[4] or whether some different scheme would provide similar distributional benefits with less overall excess burden. They find that a flat tax (see Application 1A.2) with a large exemption might increase overall welfare by about 1.7 percent relative to the current system.

POLICY CHALLENGE

Discussions of the wisdom of government projects seldom mention the potential costs involved in the taxes needed to finance them. But most of the studies examined here suggest that such costs can be large. Should the announced "costs" of government projects be increased above their actual resource costs to account for the excess burden of the taxes needed to pay for them?

[1] See L. H. Goulder and R. C. Williams III, "The Substantial Bias from Ignoring General Equilibrium Effects in Estimating Excess Burden and a Practical Solution," *Journal of Political Economy* (August 2003): 898–927.

[2] Many of the early uses of general equilibrium models to study tax systems are summarized in J. B. Shoven and J. Whalley, "Applied-General Equilibrium Models of Taxation and International Trade," *Journal of Economic Literature* (September 1985): 1007–1051.

[3] See Y. Nakagami and A. M. Pereira, "Budgetary and Efficiency Effects of Housing Taxation in the United States," *Journal of Urban Economics* (September 1996): 68–86.

[4] J. C. Conesa and D. Kreuger, "On the Optimal Progressivity of the Income Tax Code," National Bureau of Economic Research Working Paper 11044, January (Washington, DC: NBER, 2005).

Figure 10.2 **Efficiency of Output Mix**

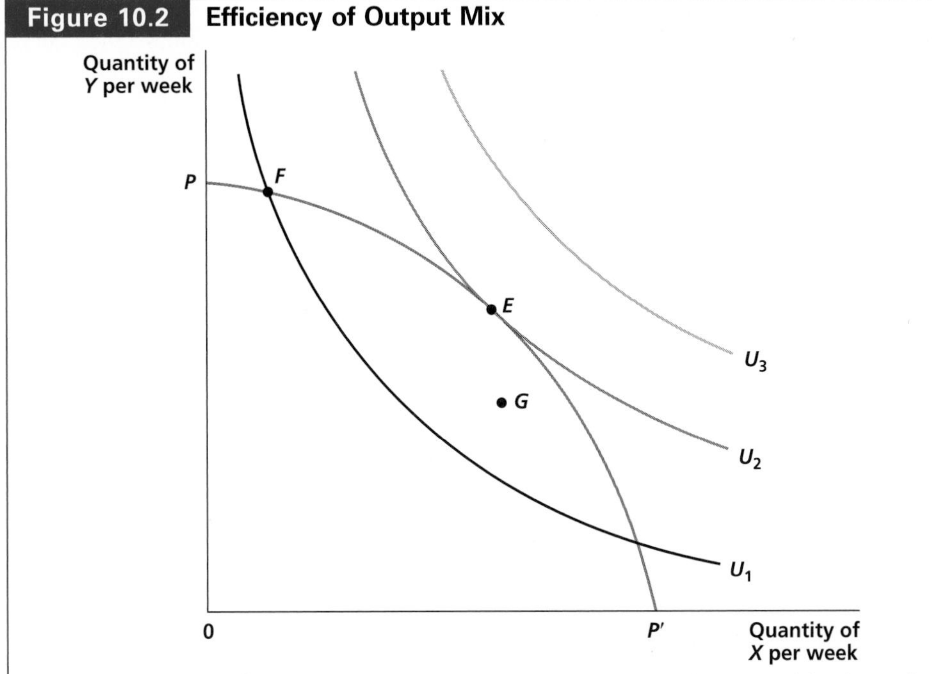

In this economy, the production possibility frontier represents those combinations of *X* and *Y* that can be produced. Every point on the frontier is efficient in a technical sense. However, only the output combination at point *E* is a true utility maximum for the typical person. Only this point represents an economically efficient allocation of resources.

PP′ in Figure 10.2. This curve shows the various combinations of *X* and *Y* that this economy can produce if its resources are employed efficiently.[2] The curve also shows the relative opportunity cost of good *X* in terms of good *Y*. Therefore, it is similar to a "supply curve" for good *X* (or good *Y*).

Figure 10.2 also shows a series of indifference curves representing the preferences of the consumers in this simple economy for the goods *X* and *Y*. These indifference curves represent the "demand" conditions in our model. Clearly, in this model, the best use of resources is achieved at point E where production is X^*, Y^*. This point provides the maximum utility that is available in this economy given the limitations imposed by scarce resources (as represented by the production possibility frontier). As in Chapter 9, we define this to be an economically efficient allocation of resources. Notice that this notion of efficiency really has two components. First, there is a "supply" component—X^*, Y^* is on the production possibility frontier. Any point inside the frontier would be inefficient because it would provide less utility than can potentially be achieved in this situation. The efficiency of X^*, Y^* also has a "demand" component because, from among all those points on *PP′*, this allocation of resources provides greatest utility. This reinforces the notion that the ultimate goal of economic activity is to improve the welfare of people. Here, people decide for themselves which allocation is the best.

[2] All of the points on *PP′* are sometimes referred to as being "technically efficient" in the sense that available inputs are fully employed and are being used in the right combinations by firms. Points inside *PP′* (such as *G*) are technically inefficient because it is possible to produce more of both goods. For an analysis of the relationship between input use and technical efficiency, see Problem 10.9.

The efficient allocation shown at point E in Figure 10.2 is characterized by a tangency between the production possibility frontier and consumer's indifference curve. The increasingly steep slope of the frontier shows that X becomes relatively more costly as its production is increased. On the other hand, the slope of an indifference curve shows how people are willing to trade one good for another in consumption (the marginal rate of substitution). That slope flattens as people consume more X because they seek balance in what they have. The tangency in Figure 10.2 therefore shows that one sign of efficiency is that the relative opportunity costs of goods in production should equal the rate at which people are willing to trade these goods for each other. In that way, an efficient allocation ties together technical information about relative costs from the supply side of the market with information about preferences from the demand side. If these slopes were not equal (say at point F) the allocation of resources would be inefficient (utility would be instead U_1 of U_2).

Notice that the description of economic efficiency in Figure 10.2 is based only on the available resources (as shown by the production possibility frontier) and on the preferences of consumers (as shown by the indifference curves). As the definition of "economics" makes clear, the problem faced by any economy is how to make the best use of its available resources. Here, the term "best use" is synonymous with "utility maximizing." That is, the best use of resources is the one that provides the maximum utility to people. The fact that such an efficient allocation aligns the technical trade-offs that are feasible with the trade-offs people are willing to make (as shown by the tangency at point E in Figure 10.2) also suggests that finding an efficient allocation may have some connection to the correct pricing of goods and resources—a topic to which we now turn.

10-4 The Economic Efficiency of Perfect Competition

First theorem of welfare economics
A perfectly competitive price system will bring about an economically efficient allocation of resources.

In this simple model, the "economic problem" is how to achieve this efficient allocation of resources. One of the most important discoveries of modern welfare economics is to show that, under certain conditions, competitive markets can bring about this result. Because of the importance of this conclusion, it is sometimes called the **first theorem of welfare economics**. This "theorem" is simply a generalization of the efficiency result we described in Chapter 9 to many markets. Although a general proof of the theorem requires a lot of mathematics, we can give a glimpse of that proof by seeing how the efficient allocation shown in Figure 10.2 might be achieved through competitive markets.

In Figure 10.3, we have redrawn the production possibility frontier and indifference curves from Figure 10.2. Now assume that goods X and Y are traded in perfectly competitive markets and that the initial prices of the goods are P_X^1 and P_Y^1, respectively. With these prices, profit-maximizing firms will choose to produce X_1, Y_1 because, from

 MICRO QUIZ 10.2

Suppose that an economy produces only the two goods, left shoes (X) and right shoes (Y). Individuals only want to consume these in combinations for which $X = Y$.

1. Which point (or points) on the production possibility frontier would be economically efficient?
2. Why would a point on the production possibility frontier for which $X = 2Y$ be inefficient?

Figure 10.3 How Perfectly Competitive Prices Bring about Efficiency

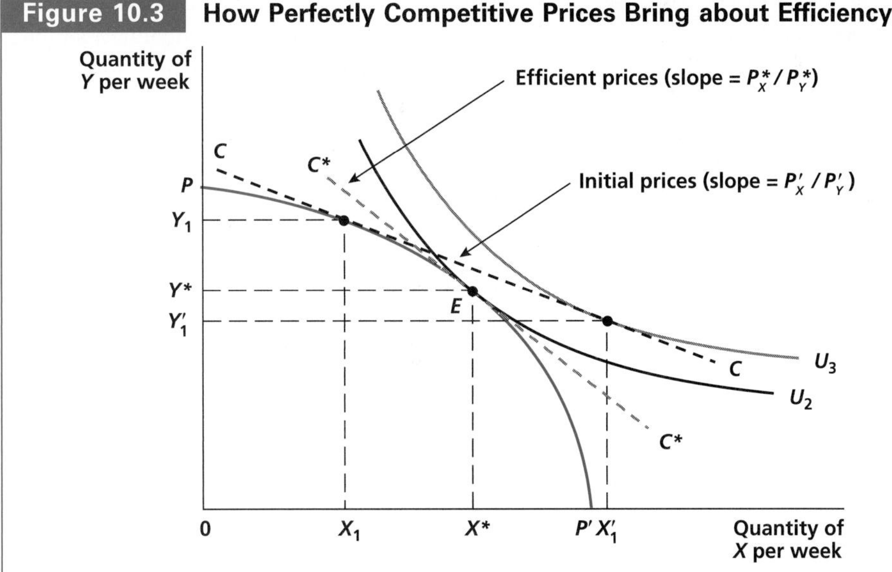

With an arbitrary initial price ratio, firms will produce X_1, Y_1; the economy's budget constraint will be given by line *CC*. With this budget constraint, individuals demand X_1', Y_1', that is, there is an excess demand for good $X(X_1' - X_1)$ and an excess supply of good. $Y(Y_1 - Y_1')$ The workings of the market will move these prices toward their equilibrium levels P_X^*, P_Y^*. At those prices, society's budget constraint will be given by the line C^*C^*, and supply and demand will be in equilibrium. The combination X^*, Y^* of goods will be chosen, and this allocation is efficient.

among all the combinations of *X* and *Y* on the production possibility frontier, this one provides maximum revenue and profits.[3]

On the other hand, given the budget constraint represented by line *CC*, individuals collectively will demand X_1', Y_1'.[4] Consequently, at this price ratio, there is excess demand for good *X* (people want to buy more than is being produced), whereas there is an excess supply of good *Y*. The workings of the marketplace will cause P_X to rise and P_Y to fall. The price ratio P_X/P_Y will rise; the price line will move clockwise along the production possibility frontier. That is, firms will increase their production of good *X* and decrease their production of good *Y*. Similarly, people will respond to the changing prices by

---

[3]The point provides maximum revenue because the price of *X* and *Y* determine the slope of the line *CC*, which represents total revenue for the firm ($P_X^1X + P_Y^1Y$), and this line is as far from the origin as possible given that production must take place on *PP'*. But the production possibility frontier assumes that total input usage is the same everywhere on and inside the frontier. Hence, maximization of revenue also amounts to maximization of profits.

[4]It is important to recognize why the budget constraint has this location. Because P_X^1 and P_Y^1 are given, the value of total production is

$$P_X^1 \times X_1 + P_Y^1 \times Y_1$$

This is the value of total output in the simple economy pictured in the figure. Because of the accounting identity "value of income = value of output," this is also the total income accruing to people in society. Society's budget constraint passes through X_1, Y_1 and has a slope of $-P_X^1/P_Y^1$. This is precisely the line labeled *CC* in the figure.

> **MICRO QUIZ 10.3**
>
> Draw simple supply and demand curve models for determining the prices of X and Y in Figure 10.3. Show the "disequilibrium" points X_1 and X_1' on your diagram for good X and points Y_1 and Y_1' on your diagram for good Y. Describe how both of these markets reach equilibrium simultaneously.

substituting Y for X in their consumption choices. The actions of both firms and individuals simultaneously eliminate the excess demand for X and the excess supply of Y as market prices change.

Equilibrium is reached at X^*, Y^*, with an equilibrium price ratio of P_X^*/P_X^*. With this price ratio, supply and demand are equilibrated for both good X and good Y. Firms, in maximizing their profits, given P_X^* and P_Y^*, will produce X^* and Y^*. Given the income that this level of production provides to people, they will purchase precisely X^* and Y^*. Not only have markets been equilibrated by the operation of the price system, but the resulting equilibrium is also economically efficient. As we showed previously, the equilibrium allocation X^*, Y^* provides the highest level of utility that can be obtained given the existing production possibility frontier. Figure 10.3 provides a simple two-good general equilibrium proof of the first theorem of welfare economics.

Some Numerical Examples

Let's look at a few numerical examples that illustrate the connection between economic efficiency and pricing in a general equilibrium context. In all of these examples, we will assume that there are only two goods (X and Y) and that the production possibility frontier for this economy is a quarter-circle given by the following equation:

$$X^2 + Y^2 = 100, \; X \geq 0, \; Y \geq 0. \quad \textbf{(10.1)}$$

This production possibility frontier is shown in Figure 10.4. Notice that the maximum amount of X that can be produced is 10 (if $Y = 0$) and that the maximum amount of Y that can be produced (if $X = 0$) is also 10.

Figure 10.4 Hypothetical Efficient Allocations

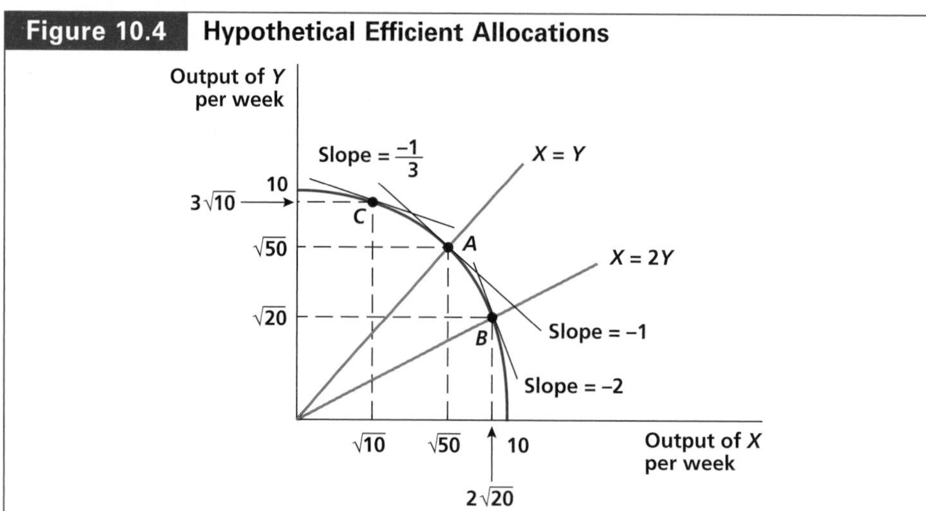

Here, the production possibility frontier is given by $X^2 + Y^2 = 100$. If preferences require $X = Y$, point A will be efficient and $P_X/P_Y = 1$. If preferences require $X = 2Y$, point B will be efficient, $P_X/P_Y = 2$. If preferences require $P_X/P_Y = 1/3$ point C is efficient.

Calculating the slope of this production possibility frontier at any point on it is mainly a problem in calculus; hence, we will show it in a footnote.[5] But the result that the slope is given by the ratio $-X/Y$ will prove useful in working many problems. Now, we must introduce preferences to discover which of the points on the production possibility frontier are economically efficient.

Fixed Proportions Suppose that people wish to consume these two goods in the fixed ratio $X = Y$ (for example, suppose these are left and right shoes). Then, substituting this requirement into the equation for the production possibility frontier would yield

$$X^2 + X^2 = 2X^2 = 100 \quad \text{or} \quad X = Y = \sqrt{50}. \tag{10.2}$$

This efficient allocation is denoted as point A in Figure 10.4. The slope of the production possibility frontier at this point would be $-X/Y = -\sqrt{50}/\sqrt{50} = -1$. Hence, with these preferences, the technical trade-off rate between X and Y is one-for-one; that is, in competitive markets, the goods will have equal prices (and relative opportunity costs).

If peoples' preferences were different, the efficient allocation would also be different. For example, if people wish to consume only combinations of the two goods for which $X = 2Y$, then, substituting into Equation 10.1 yields

$$(2Y)^2 + Y^2 = 5Y^2 = 100, \ Y = \sqrt{20}, \ X = 2\sqrt{20}. \tag{10.3}$$

This is shown by point B in Figure 10.4. At this point, the slope of the production possibility frontier is $-X/Y = -2\sqrt{20}/\sqrt{20} = -2$. So, the price of good X would be twice that of good Y; the fact that more X is demanded in conjunction with the increasing opportunity cost of producing this good (as shown by the concave shape of the production possibility frontier) account for this result.

Perfect Substitutes When goods are perfect substitutes, individual's marginal rates of substitution between the goods will determine relative prices. This is the only price ratio that can prevail in equilibrium because at any other price ratio, individuals would choose to consume only one of the goods. For example, if people view X and Y as perfect substitutes for which they are always willing to trade the goods on a one-for-one basis, then the only price ratio that can prevail in equilibrium is 1.0. If good X were cheaper than good Y, this person would only buy X, and if it were more expensive than good Y, he or she would only buy Y. Therefore, the efficient allocation should be where the slope of the production possibility frontier is -1.0. Using this fact, we have the following Slope $= -X/Y = -1$, so $X = Y$, and equilibrium must again be at point A in Figure 10.4. But notice that the reason for being at A differs from our reason in the fixed proportions case. In that earlier case, the efficient point was at A because people want to consume X and Y in a one-to-one ratio. In this case, people are willing to consume the two goods in any ratio, but, because the goods are perfect substitutes, the slope of the production possibility frontier must be -1.0. Finding where this slope occurs determines the efficient allocation in this case.

To illustrate, suppose people viewed X and Y as perfect substitutes but were always willing to trade 3 units of X for 1 unit of Y. In this case, the price ratio must be $P_X/P_Y = 1/3$. Setting this equal to the slope of the production possibility frontier yields: Slope $= -X/Y = -1/3$ so $Y = 3X$, and the point on the production possibility frontier can be found by

$$\begin{aligned} &X^2 + (3X)^2 = 10X^2 = 100 \text{ so} \\ &X = \sqrt{10} \text{ and } Y = 3\sqrt{10}. \end{aligned} \tag{10.4}$$

[5]Take the total differential of equation 10.1 $2XdX + 2YdY = 0$, and solve for the slope: $dY/dX = -2X/2Y = -X/Y$.

This allocation is shown by point C in Figure 10.4. Because the relative price of X must be low in equilibrium, relatively little of that good will be produced to avoid incurring unwarranted opportunity costs higher than 1/3.

Other Preferences Finding the efficient allocation and associated prices with other kinds of preferences will usually be more complicated than in these simple examples. Still, the basic method of finding the correct tangency on the production possibility frontier continues to apply. This tangency not only indicates which of the allocations on the frontier is efficient (because it meets individual preferences), but it also shows the price ratio that must prevail in order to lead both firms and individuals to this allocation.

KEEP *in* MIND

Slopes and Tangencies Determine Efficient Allocations

Efficiency in economics relates to the trade-offs that firms and individuals make. These trade-offs are captured by the slope of the production possibility frontier and by the slopes of individuals' indifference curves. The efficient points cannot be found by dealing with quantities alone. This is a mistake beginning students often make—they try to find solutions without ever looking at trade-off rates (slopes). This approach "worked" in our first example because you just had to find the point of the production possibility frontier where $X = Y$. But, even in that case, it was impossible to calculate relative prices without knowing the slope of the frontier at this point. In more complicated cases, it will be generally impossible even to find an efficient allocation without carefully considering the trade-off rates involved.

Prices, Efficiency, and Laissez-Faire Economics

We have shown that a perfectly competitive price system, by relying on the self-interest of people and of firms and by utilizing the information carried by equilibrium prices, can arrive at an economically efficient allocation of resources. This finding provides "scientific" support for the laissez-faire position taken by many economists. For example, take Adam Smith's assertion:

> *The natural effort of every individual to better his own condition, when suffered to exert itself with freedom and security, is so powerful a principle that it is alone, and without any assistance, not only capable of carrying on the society to wealth and prosperity, but of surmounting a hundred impertinent obstructions with which the folly of human laws too often encumbers its operations.*[6]

We have seen that this statement has considerable theoretical validity. As Smith noted, it is not the public spirit of the baker that provides bread for people to eat. Rather, bakers (and other producers) operate in their own self-interest in responding to market signals (Smith's invisible hand). In so doing, their actions are coordinated by the market into an efficient, overall pattern. The market system, at least in this simple model, imposes a very strict logic on how resources are used.

That efficiency theorem raises many important questions about the ability of markets to arrive at these perfectly competitive prices and about whether the theorem should act as a guide for government policy (for example, whether governments should avoid interfering in international markets as suggested by Application 10.2: Gains from Free Trade and Free Trade Agreements).

---

[6]Adam Smith, *The Wealth of Nations* (1776; repr., New York: Random House, 1937), 508. Citations are to the Modern Library edition.

10-5 Why Markets Fail to Achieve Economic Efficiency

Showing that perfect competition is economically efficient depends crucially on all of the assumptions that underlie the competitive model. Several conditions may prevent markets from generating such an efficient allocation.

Imperfect Competition

Imperfect competition in a broad sense includes all those situations in which economic actors (that is, buyers or sellers) exert some market power in determining price. The essential aspect of all these situations is that marginal revenue is different from market price since the firm is no longer a price taker. Because of this, relative prices no longer accurately reflect marginal costs, and the price system no longer conveys the information about costs necessary to ensure efficiency. The deadweight loss from monopoly that we will study in Chapter 11 is one example of this inefficiency.

Imperfect competition
A market situation in which buyers or sellers have some influence on the prices of goods or services.

Externalities

A price system can also fail to allocate resources efficiently when there are cost relationships among firms or between firms and people that are not adequately represented by market prices. Examples of these are numerous. Perhaps the most common is the case of a firm that pollutes the air with industrial smoke and other debris. This is called an **externality**. The firm's activities impose costs on other people, and these costs are not taken directly into account through the normal operation of the price system. The basic problem with externalities is that firms' private costs no longer correctly reflect the social costs of production. In the absence of externalities, the costs a firm incurs accurately measure social costs. The prices of the resources the firm uses represent all the opportunity costs involved in production. When a firm creates externalities, however, there are additional costs—those that arise from the external damage. The fact that pollution from burning coal to produce steel causes diseases and general dirt and grime is as much a cost of production as are the wages paid to the firm's workers. However, the firm responds only to private input costs of steel production in deciding how much steel to produce. It disregards the social costs of its pollution. This results in a gap between market price and (social) marginal cost and therefore leads markets to misallocate resources. In Chapter 16, we look at this issue in some detail.

Externality
The effect of one party's economic activities on another party that is not taken into account by the price system.

Public Goods

A third potential failure of the perfectly competitive price system to achieve efficiency stems from the existence of certain types of goods called **public goods**. These goods usually have two characteristics that make them difficult to produce efficiently through private markets. First, the goods can provide benefits to one more person at zero marginal cost. In this sense the goods are "nonrival," in that the cost of producing them cannot necessarily be assigned to any specific user. Second, public goods are "nonexclusive"—no person can be excluded from benefiting from them. That is, people gain from the good being available, whether they actually pay for it or not. To see why public goods pose problems for markets, consider the most important example, national defense. Once a national defense system is in place, one more person can enjoy its protection at zero marginal cost, so this good is nonrival. Similarly, all people in the country benefit from being protected whether they like it or not. It is not possible to exclude people from

Public goods
Goods that are both nonexclusive and nonrival.

APPLICATION 10.2

Gains from Free Trade and Free Trade Agreements

Free trade has been controversial for centuries. One of the most influential debates about trade took place following the Napoleonic Wars in Britain during the 1820s and 1830s. The primary focus of the debate concerned how eliminating high tariffs on imported grain would affect the welfare of various groups in society. Many of the same arguments made in the debate over these "Corn Laws" have reappeared nearly two centuries later in modern debates over free-trade policies.

General Equilibrium Theory of Free Trade

A general equilibrium model is needed to study the impact of free trade on various segments of society. One simple version of such a model is shown in Figure 1. The figure shows those combinations of grain (X) and manufactured goods (Y) that can be produced by, say, British factors of production. If the Corn Laws prevented all trade, point E would represent the domestic equilibrium. Britain would produce and consume quantities X_E and Y_E, and these would yield a utility level of U_2 to the typical British person. Removal of the tariffs would reduce the prevailing domestic price ratio to reflect world prices where grain is cheaper.

Figure 1 Analysis of the Corn Laws Debate

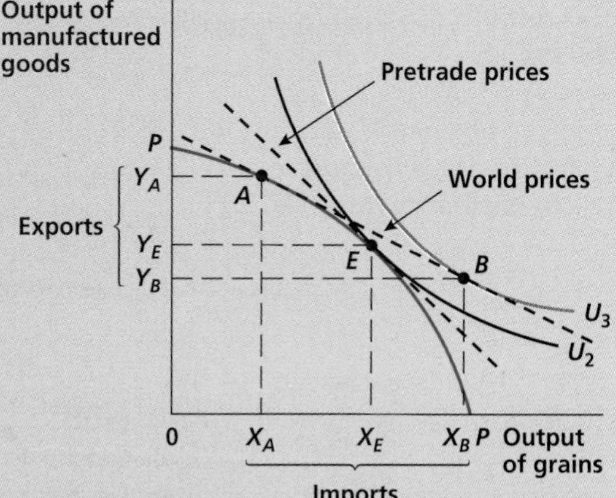

Reduction of tariff barriers on grain would cause production to be reallocated from point E to point A. Consumption would be reallocated from E to B. If grain production were relatively capital intensive, the relative price of capital would fall as a result of these reallocations.

At these world prices, Britain would reduce its production of grain from X_E to X_A and increase its production of manufactured goods from Y_E to Y_A. Trade with the rest of Europe would permit British consumption to move to point B. The country would import grain in amounts $X_B - X_A$ and export manufactured goods $Y_A - Y_B$. The utility of the typical British consumer would rise to U_3. Hence, adoption of free trade can involve substantial welfare gains.

But trade can also affect the prices of various inputs. Because British production has been reallocated from point E to point A, the demand for inputs used in the manufacturing industry will increase, whereas the demand for inputs used to produce grain will fall. In the British case, this was good news for factory workers but bad news for landowners. Not surprisingly, the landowners strenuously fought repeal of the Corn Laws. Ultimately, however, the fact that both workers and typical British consumers gained from trade carried the day, and Britain became a leading proponent of free trade for the remainder of the nineteenth century.

Modern Resistance to Free Trade

Because opening of free trade has the capacity to affect the prices of various inputs, that policy continues to be politically controversial to this day. In the United States and most Western countries, for example, export industries tend to demand skilled workers and significant amounts of high-tech capital equipment. Imports, on the other hand, tend to be produced by less skilled workers. Hence, it might be expected that relaxation of trade barriers would result in rising wages for skilled workers but stagnating or falling wages for workers with fewer skills. This can be seen by the positions that unions take in trade debates—unions representing skilled workers (such as machinists, agricultural equipment workers, or workers in the chemical and petroleum industries) tend to support free trade, whereas those representing less skilled workers (textiles or footwear, for example) tend to oppose it.

A related reason why workers in import-competing industries will oppose free trade initiatives concerns adjustment costs. When production shifts from import to export goods, workers must move out of industries that produce the imported goods. In general, it seems likely that they will eventually be reemployed in other industries, but they may have to learn new skills to get those jobs and the process of doing so may take some time. Many nations offer "trade-adjustment" policies that seek to mitigate the costs involved in such transitions by offering worker training or extra unemployment benefits. The U.S.

Trade Adjustment Assistance (TAA) program, for example, identifies workers for whom international trade was a cause of job loss. If these workers enter a training program (paid for through government vouchers) they may be able to collect unemployment benefits for up to 78 weeks—a full year longer than is provided for under the normal program of unemployment benefits. Workers who need remedial education can collect even more weeks of benefits. In combination with other assistance (such as subsidized health insurance benefits), TAA therefore provides a considerable cushion to workers affected by trade.[1] Whether such assistance can ever fully compensate for the costs individual workers incur from expansion of trade is an open question, however.

The NAFTA Debate

All of these issues were highlighted in the early 1990s debate over the North American Free Trade Agreement (NAFTA). That agreement significantly reduced trade barriers between the United States, Canada, and Mexico. Early computer modeling of the impact of the NAFTA did suggest that the agreement might pose some short-term costs for low-wage workers.[2] But the models also showed that such costs were significantly outweighed by the gains to other workers and to consumers in all of the countries involved. Indeed, some of the more complicated general equilibrium models suggested that low-wage workers in the United States might not be especially harmed by the agreement because it might improve the operations of the labor markets in which they work.

The beneficial outcomes predicted by the general equilibrium modeling of NAFTA largely seem to have materialized. Indeed, trade among the United States, Canada, and Mexico has generally increased during the past decade to a much greater extent than was predicted by the models, especially in areas where goods had not traditionally been traded.[3] The relatively benign effect of this expansion of trade on input markets predicted in the models also seems to be supported by the actual data.

Other Free-Trade Agreements

The apparent success of the NAFTA spawned a number of additional free trade agreements negotiated over the next two decades. Currently the United States has such agreements with twenty countries[4] and a larger "Trans-Pacific" agreement is being developed involving countries in Asia and South America. Although the term "free trade agreement" suggests that these are relatively simple treaties, in fact each agreement has its own peculiarities. Many such features enter the agreements because special interests in the countries involved, bring political pressure to exempt themselves from some treaty provisions. For example, sugar receives special treatment in many U.S. agreements because of the political influence of U.S. sugar producers. Similarly, the political power of rice producers in Japan has made it difficult to reach a broad agreement with that country. In recent years a number of "non-trade" issues have also entered into trade negotiations—especially those related to the environment and to working conditions in the partner countries. Often such "side" issues may be justified—no one wants an agreement with a country that spoils the environment or employs child labor. But, unfortunately, these issues are used by special interest groups to secure gains under the agreements that they would not usually get. Hence, it is important to look at the details of all "free-trade" agreements in order to understand the true economic impacts they will have.

TO THINK ABOUT

1. Figure 1 shows that there are two sources of the utility gains from free trade: (1) a consumption gain because consumers can consume combinations of goods that lie outside a nation's production possibility frontier, and (2) a specialization effect because nations can specialize in producing goods with relatively high world prices. How would you show these effects in Figure 1? What would determine whether the effects were large or small?
2. Figure 1 shows that a nation will export goods that have a lower relative price domestically than they do in international markets (in this case, good *Y*). What factors determine such a nation's "comparative advantage"?

[1]See K. Baicker and M. Rehavi "Policy Watch: Trade Adjustment Assistance" *Journal of Economic Perspectives* (Spring 2004): 239–255.

[2]See N. Lustig, B. Bosworth, and R. Lawrence, eds. *North American Free Trade* (Washington, D.C.: The Brookings Institution, 1992).

[3]T. J. Kehoe, "An Evaluation of the Performance of Applied General Equilibrium Models of the Impact of NAFTA," Research Department Staff Report 320, Federal Reserve Bank of Minneapolis, August (Minneapolis, MN: Federal Reserve Bank of Minneapolis, 2003).

[4]Details of these agreements can be found at the Office of the U.S. Trade Representative: www.ustr.gov/trade-agreements/free-trade-agreements.

such benefits, regardless of what they do. Left to private markets, however, it is extremely unlikely that national defense would be produced at efficient levels. Each person would have an incentive to pay nothing voluntarily for national defense, in the hope that others would pay instead. Everyone would have an incentive to be a "free rider," relying on spending by others (which would never materialize). As a result, resources would then be under-allocated to national defense in a purely market economy. To avoid such misallocations, communities will usually decide to have public goods (other examples are legal systems, traffic control systems, or mosquito control) produced by the government and will finance this production through some form of compulsory taxation. Economic issues posed by this process are also discussed in detail in Chapter 16.

Imperfect Information

Throughout our discussion of the connection between perfect competition and economic efficiency, we have been implicitly assuming that the economic actors involved are fully informed. The most important kind of information they are assumed to have is a knowledge of equilibrium market prices. If for some reason markets are unable to establish these prices or if demanders or suppliers do not know what these prices are, the types of "invisible hand" results we developed may not hold. Consider, for example, the problem that any consumer faces in trying to buy a new television. Not only does he or she have to make some kind of judgment about the quality of various brands (to determine what the available "goods" actually are) but this would-be buyer also faces the problem of finding out what various sellers are charging for a particular set. All of these kinds of problems have been assumed away so far by treating goods as being homogeneous and having a universally known market price. As we will see in Chapter 15, if such assumptions do not hold, the efficiency of perfectly competitive markets is more problematic.

10-6 Efficiency and Equity

Equity
The fairness of the distribution of goods or utility.

So far in this chapter we have discussed the concept of economic efficiency and whether an efficient allocation of resources can be achieved through reliance on market forces. We have not mentioned questions of **equity** or fairness in the way goods are distributed among people. In this section, we briefly take up this question. We show not only that it is very difficult to define what an equitable distribution of resources is but also that there is no reason to expect that allocations that result from a competitive price system (or from practically any other method of allocating resources, for that matter) will be equitable.

Defining and Achieving Equity

A primary problem with developing an accepted definition of "fair" or "unfair" allocations of resources is that not everyone agrees as to what the concept means. Some people might call any allocation "fair" providing no one breaks any laws in arriving at it—these people would call only acquisition of goods by theft "unfair." Others may base their notions of fairness on a dislike for inequality. Only allocations in which people receive about the same levels of utility (assuming these levels could be measured and compared) would be regarded as fair. On a more practical level, some people think the current distribution of income and wealth in the United States is reasonably fair whereas others regard it as drastically unfair. Welfare economists have devised a number of more specific definitions, but these tend to give conflicting conclusions about which resource allocations are or are not equitable. There is simply no agreement on this issue.[7]

Equity and Competitive Markets

Even if everyone agreed on what a fair allocation of resources (and, ultimately, of people's utility) is, there would still be the question of how such a situation should be achieved. Can we rely on voluntary transactions among people to achieve fairness, or will something more be required? Some introspection may suggest why voluntary solutions will not succeed. If people start out with an unequal distribution of goods, voluntary trading cannot necessarily erase that inequality. Those who are initially favored will not voluntarily agree to make themselves worse off. Similar lessons apply to participation in competitive market transactions. Because these are voluntary, they may not be able to erase initial inequalities, even while promoting efficient outcomes.

Adopting coercive methods to achieve equity (such as taxes) may involve problems too. For example, in several places in this book, we have shown how taxes may affect people's behavior and result in efficiency losses that arise from this distortion. Using government's power to transfer income may therefore be a costly activity; achieving equity may involve important losses of efficiency. Making decisions about equity-efficiency trade-offs is a major source of political controversy throughout the world.

10-7 The Edgeworth Box Diagram for Exchange

Issues about equity can best be illustrated with a graphic device called the Edgeworth box diagram. In this diagram, a box is used that has dimensions given by the total quantities of two goods available (we'll call these goods simply X and Y).

The horizontal dimension of the box represents the total quantity of X available, whereas the vertical height of the box is the total quantity of Y. These dimensions are shown in Figure 10.5. The point O_S is considered to be the origin for the first person (call her Smith). Quantities of X are measured along the horizontal axis rightward from O_S; quantities of Y, along the vertical axis upward from O_S. Any point in the box can be regarded as some allocation of X and Y to Smith. For example, at point E, Smith gets X_S^E and Y_S^E. The useful property of the Edge-worth box is that the quantities received by the second person (say, Jones) are also recorded by point E. Jones simply gets that part of the total quantity that is left over. In fact, we can regard Jones's quantities as being measured from the origin O_J. Point E therefore also corresponds to the quantities X_J^E and Y_J^E for Jones. Notice that the quantities assigned to Smith and Jones in this manner exactly exhaust the total quantities of X and Y available.

Mutually Beneficial Trades

Any point in the Edgeworth box represents an allocation of the available goods between Smith and Jones, and all possible allocations are contained somewhere in the box. To discover which of the allocations offer mutually beneficial trades, we must introduce these people's preferences. In Figure 10.6, Smith's indifference curve map is drawn with origin O_S. Movements in a northeasterly direction represent higher levels of utility to

[7]For a discussion of some thinking on this topic, see Amartya Sen's 1998 Nobel Prize speech, reprinted in A. Sen, "The Possibility of Social Choice," *American Economic Review* (June 1999): 349–379.

Figure 10.5 Edgeworth Box Diagram

The Edgeworth box diagram permits all possible allocations of two goods (*X* and *Y*) to be visualized. If we consider the corner O_S to be Smith's "origin" and O_J to be Jones's, then the allocation represented by point *E* would have Smith getting X_S^E and Y_S^E, and Jones would receive what is left over (X_J^E, Y_J^E). One purpose of this diagram is to discover which of the possible locations within the box can be reached through voluntary exchange.

Figure 10.6 Edgeworth Box Diagram of Pareto Efficiency in Exchange

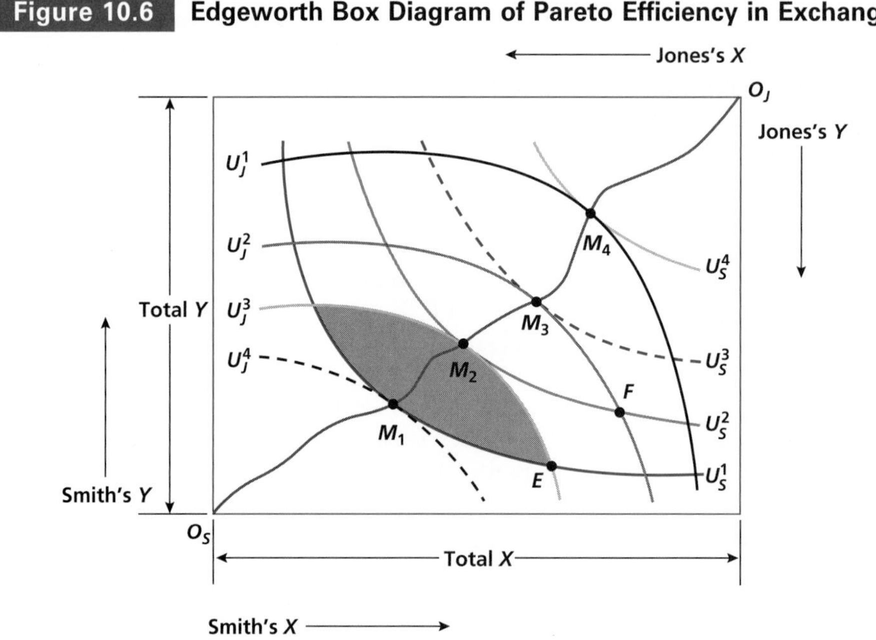

The points on the curve O_S, O_J are efficient in the sense that at these allocations Smith cannot be made better off without making Jones worse off, and vice versa. An allocation such as *E*, on the other hand, is inefficient because both Smith and Jones can be made better off by choosing to move into the dark area. Notice that along O_S, O_J the MRS for Smith is equal to that for Jones. The line O_S, O_J is called the *contract curve*.

Smith. In the same figure, Jones's indifference curve map is drawn with the corner O_J as an origin. We have taken Jones's indifference curve map, rotated it 180 degrees, and fit it into the northeast corner of the Edgeworth box. Movements in a southwesterly direction represent increases in Jones's utility level.

Using these superimposed indifference curve maps, we can identify the allocations from which some mutually beneficial trades might be made. Any point for which the MRS for Smith is unequal to that for Jones represents such an opportunity. Consider an arbitrary initial allocation such as point E in Figure 10.5. This point lies on the point of intersection of Smith's indifference curve U_S^1 and Jones's indifference curve U_J^3. Obviously, the marginal rates of substitution (the slopes of the indifference curves) are not equal at E. Any allocation in the oval-shaped area in Figure 10.6 represents a mutually beneficial trade for these two people—they can both move to a higher level of utility by adopting a trade that gets them into this area.

Pareto efficient allocation
An allocation of available resources in which no mutually beneficial trading opportunities are unexploited. That is, an allocation in which no one person can be made better off without someone else being made worse off.

Efficiency in Exchange

When the marginal rates of substitution of Smith and Jones are equal, however, such mutually beneficial trades are not available. The points M_1, M_2, M_3, and M_4 in Figure 10.6 indicate tangencies of these individuals' indifference curves, and movement away from such points must make at least one of the people worse off. A move from M_2 to E, for example, reduces Smith's utility from U_S^2 to U_S^1, even though Jones is made no worse off by the move. Alternatively, a move from M_2 to F makes Jones worse off but keeps the Smith utility level constant. In general, then, these points of tangency do not offer the promise of additional mutually beneficial trading. Such points are called **Pareto efficient allocations** after the Italian scientist Vilfredo Pareto (1878–1923), who pioneered in the development of the formal theory of exchange. Notice that the Pareto definition of efficiency does not require any interpersonal comparisons of utility; we never have to compare Jones's gains to Smith's losses, or vice versa. Rather, individuals decide for themselves whether particular trades improve utility. For efficient allocations, there are no such additional trades to which both parties would agree.

Contract curve
The set of efficient allocations of the existing goods in an exchange situation. Points off that curve are necessarily inefficient, since individuals can be made unambiguously better off by moving to the curve.

Contract Curve

The set of all the efficient allocations in an Edgeworth box diagram is called the **contract curve**. In Figure 10.6, this set of points is represented by the line running from O_S to O_J and includes the tangencies M_1, M_2, M_3, and M_4 (and many other such tangencies). Points off the contract curve (such as E or F) are inefficient, and mutually beneficial trades are possible. But, as its name implies, moving onto the contract curve exhausts all such mutually beneficial trading opportunities. A move along the contract curve (say, from M_1 to M_2) does not represent a mutually beneficial trade because there will always be a winner (Smith) and a loser (Jones).

MICRO QUIZ 10.4

What would the contract curve look like in the following situations:

1. Smith likes only good X and Jones likes only good Y.
2. Smith and Jones both view X and Y as perfect complements.
3. Smith and Jones are both always willing to substitute one unit of X for one unit of Y and remain equally well-off.

Efficiency and Equity

The Edgeworth box diagram not only allows us to show Pareto efficiency, but also illustrates the problematic relationship between efficiency and equity. Suppose, for example, that everyone agreed that the only fair allocation is one of equal utilities. Perhaps

Figure 10.7 Voluntary Transactions May Not Result in Equitable Allocations

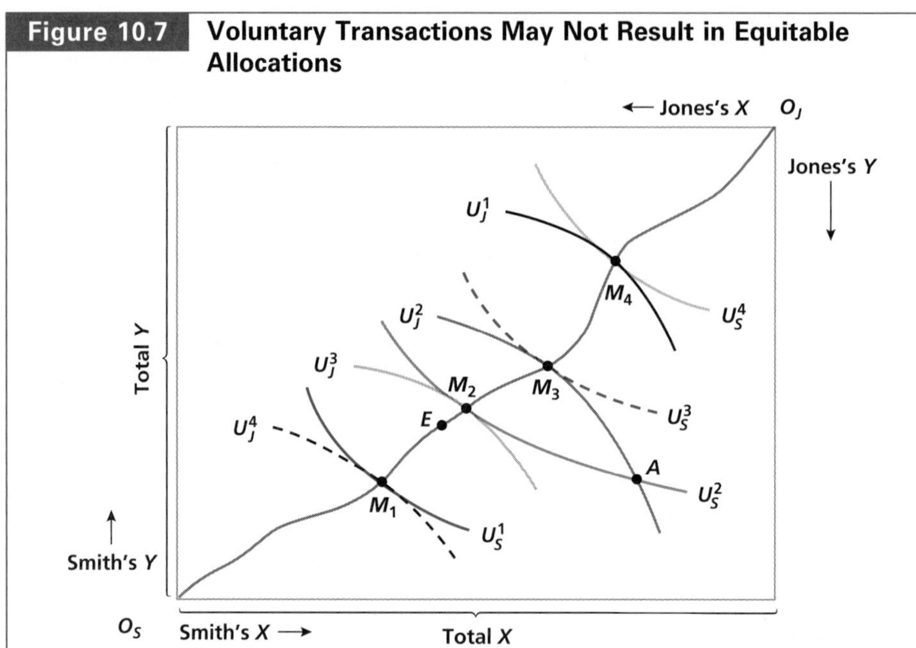

This Edgeworth box diagram for exchange is taken from Figure 10.5. Point E represents a "fair" sharing of the available goods (assuming that can be defined). If individuals' initial endowments are at point *A*, voluntary transactions cannot be relied on to reach point *E* since such an allocation makes Smith worse off than at *A*.

everyone remembers his or her childhood experiences in dividing up a cake or candy bar where equal shares seemed to be the only reasonable solution. This desired allocation might be represented by point *E* in the Edgeworth exchange box in Figure 10.7. On the other hand, suppose Smith and Jones start out at point *A*—at which Smith is in a fairly favorable situation. As we described previously, any allocation between M_2 and M_3 is preferable to point *A* because both people would be better off by voluntarily making such a move. In this case, however, the point of equal utility (*E*) does not fall in this range. Smith would not voluntarily agree to move to point *E* since that would make her worse off than at point *A*. Smith would prefer to refrain from any trading rather than accept the "fair" allocation *E*. In the language of welfare economics, the **initial endowments** (that is, the starting place for trading) of Smith and Jones are so unbalanced that voluntary agreements will not result in the desired equal allocation of utilities. If point *E* is to be achieved, some coercion (such as taxation) must be used to get Smith to accept it. The idea that redistributive taxes might be used together with competitive markets to yield allocations of resources that are both efficient and equitable has proven to be a tantalizing prospect for economists, as Application 10.3: The Second Theorem of Welfare Economics illustrates.

Initial endowments
The initial holdings of goods from which trading begins.

Equity and Efficiency with Production

Examining the relationship between equity and efficiency is more complex in a model in which production occurs. In our discussion so far, the size of the Edgeworth Box has been fixed, and we have only looked at how a given supply of two goods can be allocated between two people. After we allow for production, the size of the Edgeworth Box is no

APPLICATION 10.3

The Second Theorem of Welfare Economics

Zealous students of microeconomics will be happy to know that there is, in fact, a "second" theorem of welfare economics that accompanies the more popular first "invisible hand" theorem. This second theorem focuses on equity and shows how competitive markets might be used to achieve that goal. Specifically, the theorem states that any desired allocation of utility among the members of society can be achieved through the operations of competitive markets, providing initial endowments are set appropriately. Suppose, for example, that equity dictated that the distribution of utility between Smith and Jones in Figure 10.6 must lie between M_2 and M_3 on the contract curve. The second theorem states that this can be achieved by adjusting initial endowments to point F and then allowing competitive trading between these two people. How this state of affairs might be achieved in the real world is the subject of this application.

Lump-Sum Redistribution

Sometimes the second theorem of welfare economics is paraphrased as "social policy should pursue efficiency (competitive pricing), thereby making the 'pie' as big as possible—any resulting undesirable inequalities can be patched up with lump-sum taxes and transfers." It is this vision that provides the impetus to the adherents of many "free-market" policies. But the view is probably too simplistic for at least two reasons. First, most real-world tax and transfer schemes depart significantly from the lump-sum ideal. That is, virtually all such schemes distort people's behavior and therefore cause welfare losses of their own. Second, this approach to achieving equity focuses on patching things up after competitive markets have reached equilibrium, but it is unclear whether any political system would in fact adopt such policies. Still, the lump-sum vision is an attractive one because efficiency gains from competitive markets offer opportunities for Pareto improvements, from which everyone can be made better off. The approach has been widely used in applied economics, especially in the field of law and economics, to evaluate various policy options.[1] For example, in the theory of contracts, a lawyer might argue that all contracts should be kept, regardless of unforeseen factors that may have occurred. Economists, on the other hand, have asked whether breaching some types of contracts might be efficient, creating added utility that could be shared by all parties.

Education and Initial Endowments

Another approach to finding desirable equity-efficiency trade-offs focuses specifically on using general equilibrium models to study the relative merits of various ways of altering initial endowments. Because many people believe that education may be the best route to achieving a more equitable distribution of income, considerable attention has been devoted to looking at the potential effects of large educational subsidies. In one study, for example, the authors use a simple general equilibrium model to study the equity-efficiency trade-offs that arise through the use of subsidies for higher education.[2] They then compare these to what might be obtained through taxes and transfers or through a general program of wage subsidies for low-productivity workers. A key element of their model is that people have differing abilities that affect both their chances for success in school (i.e., graduation) and their future wages. Greater subsidies for higher education help to equalize wages but also involve some deadweight losses because they lure people into higher education that is not a good match for their ability. Perhaps surprisingly, the authors conclude that education may not be an efficient way to alter initial endowments. They find that wage subsidies dominate both education and tax/transfer schemes in that any given level of government spending provides more final utility.

POLICY CHALLENGE

Education or training programs are usually conceived as being better than "welfare" as a way of improving the situation of low-income people because such programs expand production, whereas welfare programs may reduce it. But the evidence of whether education or training programs really add significantly to peoples' earning power is mixed, at best. Can education programs be expanded enough to achieve desired distributional goals? Or will it always be necessary to fall back on some forms of (production-reducing) tax and transfer programs?

[1]A good introductory discussion is in R. Posner, *Economic Analysis of Law*, 6th ed. (New York: Aspen Publishers, 2003), chaps. 1 and 2.

[2]E. A. Hanushek, C. K. Y. Leung, and K. Yilmaz, "Redistribution through Education and Other Transfer Mechanisms," *Journal of Monetary Economics* (November 2003): 1719–1750.

longer given but will depend on how much is actually produced in the economy. Of course, we can still study the utility that people get from various potential ways in which this production might be distributed. But now looking at the effects of redistribution of initial endowments becomes more complicated because such redistribution may actually affect how much is produced. For example, if we were considering a plan that would redistribute income from a person with an "initial endowment" of skills to a person with few skills, we would have to consider whether such a plan would affect the high-skilled person's willingness to work. We should also think about whether receipt of income by a person with few skills might also affect this person's behavior. Although the size of such effects is largely an empirical question, it seems likely that such attempts at redistribution would have some (probably negative) effect on production. On a conceptual level then it is unclear whether such redistribution would actually raise the utility of the low-skilled person—production could decrease by enough that both people could be worse off (for an example, see Problem 10.10). Even if such a large effect would appear to be unlikely, it is still important to know what the effects of redistribution policy on production are so that potential trade-offs between equity and efficiency can be better understood.

10-8 Money in General Equilibrium Models

Thus far in this chapter, we have shown how competitive markets can establish a set of relative prices at which all markets are in equilibrium simultaneously. At several places we stressed that competitive market forces determine only relative, not absolute, prices and that to examine how the absolute price level is determined we must introduce money into our models. Although a complete examination of this topic is more properly studied as part of macroeconomics, here we briefly explore some questions of the role of money in a competitive economy that relate directly to microeconomics.

Nature and Function of Money

Money serves two primary functions in any economy: (1) it facilitates transactions by providing an accepted medium of exchange, and (2) it acts as a store of value so that economic actors can better allocate their spending decisions over time. Any commodity can serve as "money" provided it is generally accepted for exchange purposes and is durable from period to period. Today most economies tend to use government-created (fiat) money because the costs associated with its production (e.g., printing pieces of paper with portraits of past or present rulers or keeping records on computer servers) are very low. In earlier times, however, commodity money was common, with the particular good chosen ranging from the familiar (gold and silver) to the obscure and even bizarre (sharks' teeth or, on the island of Yap, large stone wheels). Societies probably choose the particular form that their money will take as a result of a wide variety of economic, historical, and political forces.

Money as the Accounting Standard

One of the most important functions money usually plays is to act as an accounting standard. All prices can be quoted in terms of this standard. In general, relative prices will be unaffected by which good (or possibly a basket of goods) is chosen as the accounting standard. For example, if one apple (good 1) exchanges for two plums (good 2):

$$\frac{P_1}{P_2} = \frac{2}{1} \tag{10.5}$$

and it makes little difference how those prices are quoted. If, for example, a society chooses clams as its monetary unit of account, an apple might exchange for four clams and a plum for two clams. If we denote clam prices of apples and plums by P_1' and P_2', respectively, we have

$$\frac{P_1'}{P_2'} = \frac{4}{2} = \frac{2}{1} = \frac{P_1}{P_2} \tag{10.6}$$

We could change from counting in clams to counting in sharks' teeth by knowing that 10 sharks' teeth exchange for 1 clam. The price of our goods in sharks' teeth would be

$$P_1'' = 4 \cdot 10 = 40$$

and (10.7)

$$P_2'' = 2 \cdot 10 = 20$$

One apple (which costs 40 teeth) would still exchange for 2 plums that cost 20 teeth each.

Of course, using clams or sharks' teeth is not very common. Instead, societies usually adopt paper money as their accounting standard. An apple might exchange for half a piece of paper picturing George Washington (i.e., \$0.50) and a plum for one-fourth of such a piece of paper (\$0.25). Thus, with this monetary standard, the relative price remains two for one. Choice of an accounting standard does not, however, necessarily dictate any particular absolute price level. An apple might exchange for four clams or four hundred, but, as long as a plum exchanges for half as many clams, relative prices will be unaffected by the absolute level that prevails. Absolute price levels are obviously important, however, especially to people who wish to use money as a store of value. A person with a large investment in clams obviously cares about how many apples he or she can buy with those clams. Although a complete theoretical treatment of the price level issue is beyond the scope of this book, we do offer some brief comments here.

Commodity Money

In an economy where money is produced in a way similar to any other good (gold is mined, clams are dug, or sharks are caught), the relative price of money is determined like any other relative price—by the forces of demand and supply. Economic forces that affect either the demand or supply of money will also affect these relative prices. For example, Spanish importation of gold from the New World during the fifteenth and sixteenth centuries greatly expanded gold supplies and caused the relative price of gold to fall. That is, the prices of all other goods rose relative to that of gold—there was general inflation in the prices of practically everything in terms of gold. Similar effects would arise from changes in any factor that affected the equilibrium price for the good chosen as money. Application 10.4: Commodity Money looks at some current debates about adopting a gold or other commodity standard.

Fiat Money and the Monetary Veil

For the case of fiat money produced by the government, the analysis can be extended a bit. In this situation, the government is the sole supplier of money and can generally choose how much it wishes to produce. What effects will this level of money production have on the real economy? In general, the situation would seem to be identical to that for commodity money.

APPLICATION 10.4

Commodity Money

Throughout history both commodity and fiat money have been widely used. Today we are more accustomed to fiat money—money that is produced by the government at a cost much lower than its exchange value. The ability to control the supply of such money gives governments substantial power to control the general price level and many other macroeconomic variables. In contrast, the use of a particular commodity as money tends to arise by historical accident. Once a social consensus is reached that a certain good will serve as a medium of exchange, the amount of such money in circulation will be determined by the usual laws of supply and demand. Some economists believe this is a desirable feature of using commodity money because it severely limits what governments can do in terms of monetary policy. Regardless of where one comes down on this issue, examining some experiences with commodity money can provide insights about how the monetary and real sectors of any economy are related.

The Gold Standard

Gold has been used as money for thousands of years. In the nineteenth century, this use was formalized under the "gold standard." The process of establishing the standard started in 1821 with the British decision to make the pound freely tradable for gold at a fixed price. Germany and the United States quickly followed the British lead, and by the 1870s most of the world's major economies tied the values of their currencies to gold. This implicitly established an international system of fixed exchange rates. It also limited the power of governments to create fiat money because of the need to maintain a fixed price of their currencies in terms of gold.

Two features of economic life under the gold standard are worth noting. First, because economic output tended to expand more rapidly than the supply of gold during much of the nineteenth century, this was generally a period of falling prices. That is, the price of gold (and currencies tied to gold) increased relative to the price of other goods. Second, any periods of general inflation tended to be associated with new gold discoveries. This was especially true in the United States following gold discoveries in 1848 (in California) and in 1898 (in the Yukon).

Bimetallism

Gold and silver were both used as commodity money in the early history of the United States. The government set the official exchange ratio between the two metals, but that ratio did not always reflect true relative scarcities. Usually gold was defined to have an exchange value higher than its true market value, so gold was used for most monetary transactions. But that meant that money was tight because the gold supply was growing only slowly. William Jennings Bryan's famous "cross of gold" speech in 1896 was essentially a plea to raise the exchange value of silver so that the overall money supply could grow more rapidly. Much of the debate about bimetallism is also reflected in the Frank Baum story *The Wizard of Oz.* For example, the Wicked Witch of the East represents Eastern bankers who wished to maintain a gold-only standard.[1] More generally, experiences with bimetallism show how difficult it is to maintain fixed money prices for two different commodity moneys when the underlying values of the commodities are subject to the laws of supply and demand.

Cigarettes as Money

An interesting example of commodity money arising in strained circumstances is provided by R. A. Radford's famous account of his experiences in a POW camp during World War II.[2] Radford shows that prisoners soon settled on cigarettes as a commodity "money." It was mainly British or French cigarettes that were used as money, because American cigarettes were generally regarded as better for smoking. Arrival of Red Cross packages with fresh cigarette supplies generally led to an overall inflation in the cigarette prices of other goods.

TO THINK ABOUT

1. Suppose you could dictate which commodity would be used as a monetary standard, what criteria would you use in selecting the good to be used?
2. Radford's observation about American cigarettes is an example of Gresham's Law—that "bad" money drives out "good" money. Can you think of other historical examples of this phenomenon?

[1]For a complete discussion, see H. Rockoff, "*The Wizard of Oz* as a Monetary Allegory," *Journal of Political Economy* (August 1990): 739–760.
[2]R. A. Radford, "The Economic Organization of a POW Camp," *Economica* (November 1945): 189–201.

A change in the money supply will disturb the general equilibrium of all relative prices, and, although it seems likely that an expansion in supply will lower the relative price of money (that is, result in an inflation in the money prices of other goods), any more precise prediction would seem to depend on the results of a detailed general equilibrium model of supply and demand in many markets.

Beginning with David Hume, however, classical economists argued that fiat money differs from other economic goods and should be regarded as being outside the real economic system of demand, supply, and relative price determination. In this view, the economy can be dichotomized into a real sector in which relative prices are determined and a monetary sector where the absolute price level (that is, the value of fiat money) is set. Money, therefore, acts only as a "veil" for real economic activity; the quantity of money available has no effect on the real sector.[8] The extent to which this is true is an important unresolved issue in macroeconomics.

MICRO QUIZ 10.5

Sometimes economists are not very careful when they draw supply and demand curves to state clearly whether the price on the vertical axis is a relative (real) price or a nominal price. How would a pure inflation (in which all prices rise together) affect the following:

1. A supply and demand curve diagram that has relative price on the vertical axis?
2. A supply and demand curve diagram that has nominal price on the vertical axis?

SUMMARY

We began this chapter with a description of a general equilibrium model of a perfectly competitive price system. In that model, relative prices are determined by the forces of supply and demand, and everyone takes these prices as given in their economic decisions. We then arrive at the following conclusions about such a method for allocating resources:

- Profit-maximizing firms will use resources efficiently and will therefore operate on the production possibility frontier.
- Profit-maximizing firms will also produce an economically efficient mix of outputs. The workings of supply and demand will ensure that the technical rate at which one good can be transformed into another in production (the rate of product transformation, RPT) is equal to the rate at which people are willing to trade one good for another (the MRS). Adam Smith's invisible hand brings considerable coordination into seemingly chaotic market transactions.
- Factors that interfere with the ability of prices to reflect true marginal costs under perfect competition will prevent an economically efficient allocation of resources. Such factors include imperfect competition, externalities, and public goods. Imperfect information about market prices may also interfere with the efficiency of perfect competition.
- Under perfect competition, there are no forces to ensure that voluntary transactions will result in equitable final allocations. Achieving equity may require some coercion to transfer initial endowments. Such interventions may involve costs in terms of economic efficiency.
- A perfectly competitive price system establishes only relative prices. Introduction of money into the competitive model is needed to show how nominal prices are determined. In some cases, the amount of money (and the absolute price level) will have no effect on the relative prices established in competitive markets.

---

[8]This leads directly to the quantity theory of the demand for money, first suggested by Hume:

$$D_M = \frac{1}{V} \times P \times Q$$

where D_M is the demand for money, V is the velocity of monetary circulation (the number of times a dollar is used each year), P is the overall price level, and Q is a measure of the quantity of transactions (often approximated by real GDP). If V is fixed and Q is determined by real forces of supply and demand, a doubling of the supply of money (together with the requirement that the supply of money equals the demand for money) will result in a doubling of the equilibrium price level.

REVIEW QUESTIONS

1. "An increase in demand will raise a good's price and a fall in demand will lower it. That is all you need to know—general equilibrium analysis is largely unnecessary." Do you agree? How would you use Figure 10.3 to show how changes in demand affect price? Would using this figure tell you more than would using a simple supply-demand diagram?

2. How does the approach to economic efficiency taken in Chapter 9 relate to the one taken here? How is the possible inefficiency in Figure 9.9 related to that in Figure 10.2?

3. Why are allocations on the production possibility frontier technically efficient? What is technically inefficient about allocations inside the frontier? Do inefficient allocations necessarily involve any unemployment of factors of production? In the model introduced in this chapter, would unemployment be technically inefficient?

4. In Chapter 9 we showed that the imposition of a tax involves an "excess burden." How would you show a similar result with a general equilibrium diagram such as Figure 10.3? (Note: With the general equilibrium diagram, you must be more precise about how tax revenue is used.)

5. Suppose two countries had differing production possibility frontiers and were currently producing at points with differing slopes (that is, differing relative opportunity costs). If there were no transportation or other charges associated with international transactions, how might world output be increased by having these firms alter their production plans? Develop a simple numerical example of these gains for the case where both countries have linear production possibility frontiers (with different slopes). Interpret this result in terms of the concept of "comparative advantage" from the theory of international trade.

6. Use a simple two-good model of resource allocation (such as that in Figure 10.2) to explain the difference between technical efficiency and economic (or allocative) efficiency. Would you agree with the statement that "economic efficiency requires technical efficiency, but many technically efficient allocations are not economically efficient"? Explain your reasoning with a graph.

7. In Chapter 9 we showed how a shift in demand could be analyzed using a model of a single market. How would you illustrate an increase in the demand for good X in the general equilibrium model pictured in Figure 10.3? Why would such a shift in preferences cause the relative price of X to rise? What would happen to the market for good Y in this case? Should your discussion here be thought of as "short-run" or "long-run" analysis?

8. Relative prices convey information about both production possibilities and people's preferences. What exactly is that information and how does its availability help attain an efficient allocation of resources? In what ways does the presence of monopoly or externalities result in price information being "inaccurate"?

9. Suppose that the competitive equilibrium shown in Figure 10.3 were regarded as "unfair" because the relative price of X (an important necessity) is "too high." What would be the result of passing a law requiring that P_X/P_Y be lower?

10. In most of the theoretical examples in this book, prices have been quoted in dollars or cents. Is this choice of currency crucial? Would most examples be the same if prices had been stated in pounds, euros, or yen? Or, would it have mattered if the dollars used were "1900 dollars" or "2000 dollars"? How would you change the endless hamburger-soft drink examples, say, to phrase them in some other currency? Would such changes result in any fundamental differences? Or, do most of the examples in this book seem to display the classical dichotomy between real and nominal magnitudes?

PROBLEMS

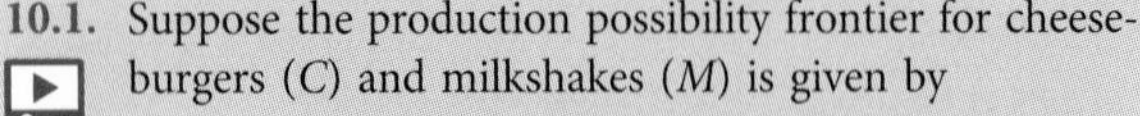

10.1. Suppose the production possibility frontier for cheeseburgers (C) and milkshakes (M) is given by

$$C + 2M = 600$$

a. Graph this frontier.

b. Assuming that people prefer to eat two cheeseburgers with every milkshake, how much of each product will be produced? Indicate this point on your graph.

c. Given that this fast-food economy is operating efficiently, what price ratio (P_C/P_M) must prevail?

10.2. Consider an economy with just one technique available for the production of each good, food and cloth:

GOOD	FOOD	CLOTH
Labor per unit output	1	1
Land per unit output	2	1

a. Supposing land is unlimited but labor equals 100, write and sketch the production possibility frontier.
b. Supposing labor is unlimited but land equals 150, write and sketch the production possibility frontier.
c. Supposing labor equals 100 and land equals 150, write and sketch the production possibility frontier. (Hint: What are the intercepts of the production possibility frontier? When is land fully employed? Labor? Both?)
d. Explain why the production possibility frontier of part c is concave.
e. Sketch the relative price of food as a function of its output in part c.
f. If consumers insist on trading four units of food for five units of cloth, what is the relative price of food? Why?
g. Explain why production is exactly the same at a price ratio of $P_F/P_C = 1.1$ as at $P_F/P_C = 1.9$.
h. Suppose that capital is also required for producing food and cloth and that capital requirements per unit of food are 0.8 and per unit of cloth 0.9. There are 100 units of capital available. What is the production possibility curve in this case? Answer part e for this case.

10.3. Suppose the production possibility frontier for guns (X) and butter (Y) is given by

$$X^2 + 2Y^2 = 900$$

a. Graph this frontier.
b. If individuals always prefer consumption bundles in which $Y = 2X$, how much X and Y will be produced?
c. At the point described in part b, what will be the slope of the production possibility frontier, and what price ratio will cause production to take place at that point? (Hint: By using the approach in the numerical examples in this chapter, show that the slope of this production possibility frontier is $-X/2Y$.)
d. Show your solution on the figure from part a.

10.4. Robinson Crusoe obtains utility from the quantity of fish he consumes in one day (F), the quantity of coconuts he consumes that day (C), and the hours of leisure time he has during the day (H) according to the utility function:

$$\text{Utility} = F^{1/4}C^{1/4}H^{1/2}$$

Robinson's production of fish is given by

$$F = \sqrt{L_F}$$

(where L_F is the hours he spends fishing), and his production of coconuts is determined by

$$C = \sqrt{L_C}$$

(where L_C is the time he spends picking coconuts). Assuming that Robinson decides to work an eight-hour day (that is, $H = 16$), graph his production possibility curve for fish and coconuts. Show his optimal choices of those goods.

10.5. Suppose two individuals (Smith and Jones) each have 10 hours of labor to devote to producing either ice cream (X) or chicken soup (Y). Smith's demand for X and Y is given by

$$X_S = \frac{0.3I_S}{P_X}$$

$$Y_S = \frac{0.7I_S}{P_Y}$$

whereas Jones's demands are given by

$$X_J = \frac{0.5I_J}{P_X}$$

$$Y_J = \frac{0.5I_J}{P_Y}$$

where I_S and I_J represent Smith's and Jones's incomes, respectively (which come only from working).
The individuals do not care whether they produce X or Y and the production function for each good is given by

$$X = 2L$$
$$Y = 3L$$

where L is the total labor devoted to production of each good. Using this information, answer the following:

a. What must the price ratio, P_X/P_Y be?
b. Given this price ratio, how much X and Y will Smith and Jones demand? (Hint: Set the wage equal to 1 here so that each person's income is 10.)
c. How should labor be allocated between X and Y to satisfy the demand calculated in part b?

10.6. In the country of Ruritania there are two regions, A and B. Two goods (X and Y) are produced in both regions. Production functions for region A are given by

$$X_A = \sqrt{L_X}$$
$$Y_A = \sqrt{L_Y}$$

L_X and L_Y are the quantity of labor devoted to X and Y production, respectively. Total labor available in region A is 100 units. That is,

$$L_X + L_Y = 100$$

Using a similar notation for region B, production functions are given by

$$X_B = \frac{1}{2}\sqrt{L_X} \quad Y_B = \frac{1}{2}\sqrt{L_Y}$$

There are also 100 units of labor available in region B:

$$L_X + L_Y = 100$$

a. Calculate the production possibility curves for regions A and B.
b. What condition must hold if production in Ruritania is to be allocated efficiently between regions A and B (assuming that labor cannot move from one region to the other)?
c. Calculate the production possibility curve for Ruritania (again assuming that labor is immobile between regions). How much total Y can Ruritania produce if total X output is 12? (Hint: A graphic analysis may be of some help here.)
d. Without making any explicit calculations, explain how you might develop a production possibility frontier for this whole country.

10.7. There are 200 pounds of food on an island that must be allocated between 2 marooned sailors. The utility function of the first sailor is given by

$$\text{Utility} = \sqrt{F_1}$$

where F_1 is the quantity of food consumed by the first sailor. For the second sailor, utility (as a function of food consumption) is given by

$$\text{Utility} = \frac{1}{2}\sqrt{F_2}$$

a. If the food is allocated equally between the sailors, how much utility will each receive?
b. How should food be allocated between the sailors to ensure equality of utility?
c. Suppose that the second sailor requires a utility level of at least 5 to remain alive. How should food be allocated so as to maximize the sum of utilities subject to the restraint that the second sailor receives that minimum level of utility?
d. What other criteria might you use to allocate the available food between the sailors?

10.8. Return to Problem 10.5 and now assume that Smith and Jones conduct their exchanges in paper money. The total supply of such money is \$60 and each individual wishes to hold a stock of money equal to 1/4 of the value of transactions made per period.

a. What will the money wage rate be in this model? What will the nominal prices of X and Y be?
b. Suppose the money supply increases to \$90, how will your answers to part a change? Does this economy exhibit the classical dichotomy between its real and monetary sectors?

10.9. The Edgeworth box diagram can also be used to show how a production possibility frontier is constructed for an economy as a whole. Suppose there are only two goods that might be produced (X and Y), each using two inputs, capital (K) and labor (L). In order to construct the X–Y production possibility frontier, we must look for efficient allocations of the total capital and labor available.

a. Draw an Edgeworth box with dimensions given by the total quantities of capital and labor available (see Figure 10.4).
b. Consider the lower-left corner of the box to be the origin for the isoquant map for good X. Draw a few of the X isoquants.
c. Now consider the upper-right corner of the box to be the origin for the isoquant map for good Y. Draw a few Y isoquants (as in Figure 10.5) in the Edgeworth box.
d. What are the efficient points in the box you have drawn? What condition must hold for a given allocation of K and L to be efficient?
e. The production possibility frontier for X and Y consists of all the efficient allocations in the Edgeworth box. Explain why this is so. Also explain why inefficient points in the box would be *inside* the production possibility frontier.
f. Use the connection between your box diagram and the production possibility frontier to discuss what the frontier would look like in the following cases:
    i. Production of good X uses only labor, production of good Y uses only capital.
    ii. Both X and Y are produced using K and L in the same fixed proportions as the inputs are available in the economy and both exhibit constant returns to scale.
    iii. Both X and Y have the same production function and both exhibit constant returns to scale.
    iv. Both X and Y are produced using the same production function and both exhibit increasing returns to scale.

10.10. Smith and Jones are stranded on a desert island. Each has in her possession some slices of ham (H) and cheese (C). Smith prefers to consume ham and cheese in the fixed proportions of 2 slices of cheese to each slice of ham. Her utility function is given by $U_S = Min(10H, 5C)$. Jones, on the other hand, regards ham and cheese as perfect substitutes—she is always willing to trade 3 slices of ham for 4 slices of cheese, and her utility function is given by $U_J = 4H + 3C$. Total endowments are 100 slices of ham and 200 slices of cheese.

a. Draw the Edgeworth Box diagram for all possible exchanges in this situation. What is the contract curve for this exchange economy?
b. Suppose Smith's initial endowment is 40 slices of ham and 80 slices of cheese (Jones gets the

remaining ham and cheese as her initial endowment). What mutually beneficial trades are possible in this economy and what utility levels will Smith and Jones enjoy from such trades?

c. Suppose that 20 slices of ham could be transferred without cost from Jones' to Smith's endowment. Now what mutually beneficial trades might occur and what utility levels would be experienced by Smith and Jones?

d. Suppose that Jones objects to the transfer of ham proposed in part c and states, "I'd rather throw the ham away than give it to Smith." If Jones carries through on her threat, what mutually beneficial trades are now possible and what utility levels will be experienced by Smith and Jones?

e. Suppose that Smith expects the ham transfer from Jones and, through carelessness, allows 20 slices of her initial ham endowment to spoil. Assuming the transfer from Jones actually happens, now what mutually beneficial trades are possible, and what are the potential utility levels for Smith and Jones?

f. Suppose now that both of the adverse incentive effects mentioned in parts d and e occur simultaneously. What mutually beneficial trading opportunities remain, and what are the potential utility levels for Smith and Jones?

PART 6

Market Power

"People of the same trade seldom meet together, even for merriment and diversion, but the conversation ends in a conspiracy against the public, or in some contrivance to raise prices."

—Adam Smith, The Wealth of Nations, 1776

In this part we relax the price-taking assumption that we used throughout our study of perfect competition. That is, we look at situations where firms have the power to influence the prices they receive for what they produce.

The study of market power begins in Chapter 11, with the simple case of a single supplier (monopoly). The key point for a monopoly firm is that it can choose to set its price at any level it wishes, but in doing so it must take into account that setting higher prices will cause it to sell less. That is, the firm must be concerned with the fact that the marginal revenue from any sale will fall short of the market price at which a good sells (see Chapter 8). Because the monopoly opts for an output level for which price exceeds marginal cost, this output level will be inefficiently low.

Chapter 12 examines the question of market power in situations where there are two or more suppliers. Such markets are more difficult to study than either perfectly competitive markets or monopoly markets. They are unlike competitive markets because price-taking behavior by firms is unlikely—each firm will recognize that its actions do affect the price it ultimately receives. But the situation is also unlike a monopoly because a firm cannot determine its profit-maximizing decisions in isolation—it must take into account whatever actions its rival(s) will undertake. We will use the tools of game theory developed in Chapter 5 to study a number of increasingly complex types of market interaction.

11 Monopoly

A market is described as a monopoly if it has only one supplier. This single firm faces the entire market demand curve. Using its knowledge of this demand curve, the monopoly makes a decision on how much to produce. Unlike the single competitive firm's output decision (which has no effect on market price), the monopoly output decision will completely determine the good's price.

11-1 Causes of Monopoly

The reason monopoly markets exist is that other firms find it unprofitable or impossible to enter the market. **Barriers to entry** are the source of all monopoly power. If other firms could enter the market, there would, by definition, no longer be a monopoly. There are two general types of barriers to entry: technical barriers and legal barriers.

Barriers to entry
Factors that prevent new firms from entering a market.

Technical Barriers to Entry

A primary technical barrier to entry is that the production of the good in question exhibits decreasing average cost over a wide range of output levels. That is, relatively large-scale firms are more efficient than small ones. In this situation, one firm finds it profitable to drive others out of the industry by price cutting. Similarly, once a monopoly has been established, entry by other firms is difficult because any new firm must produce at low levels of output and therefore at high average costs. Because this barrier to entry arises naturally as a result of the technology of production, the monopoly created is sometimes called a **natural monopoly**.

Natural monopoly
A firm that exhibits diminishing average cost over a broad range of output levels.

The range of declining average costs for a natural monopoly need only be "large" relative to the market in question. Declining costs on some absolute scale are not necessary. For example, the manufacture of concrete does not exhibit declining average costs over a broad range of output when compared to a large national market. In any particular small town, however, declining average costs may permit a concrete monopoly to be established. The high costs of transporting concrete tend to create local monopolies for this good.

Another technical basis of monopoly is special knowledge of a low-cost method of production. In this case, the problem for the monopoly firm fearing entry by other firms is to keep this technique uniquely to itself. When matters of technology are involved, this may be extremely difficult, unless the technology can be protected by a patent (discussed subsequently). Ownership of unique resources (such as mineral deposits or land locations) or the possession of unique managerial talents may also be a lasting basis for maintaining a monopoly.

Legal Barriers to Entry

Many pure monopolies are created as a matter of law rather than as a result of economic conditions. One important example of a government-granted monopoly position is the legal protection provided by a patent. Computer processing chips and prescription drugs are just two notable examples of goods that would-be competitors may be prevented from copying by patent law. Because the basic technology for these products was assigned by the government to only one firm, a monopoly position was established. The rationale of the patent system, originally established in the U.S. Constitution, is that it makes innovation more profitable and therefore encourages technical advancement. Whether or not the benefits of such innovative behavior exceed the cost of creating monopolies is an open question.

A second example of a legally created monopoly is the awarding of an exclusive franchise or license to serve a market. These are awarded in cases of public utility (gas and electric) services, communication services, the post office, some airline routes, some television and radio station markets, and a variety of other businesses. The (often dubious) argument usually put forward in favor of creating these monopolies is that having only one firm in the industry is more desirable than open competition.

In some instances, it is argued that restrictions on entry into certain industries are needed to ensure adequate quality standards (licensing of physicians, for example) or to prevent environmental harm (franchising businesses in the national parks). In many cases, there are sound reasons for such entry restrictions but, in some cases, as Application 11.1: Should You Need a License to Shampoo a Dog? shows, the reasons are obscure. The restrictions act mainly to limit the competition faced by existing firms and seem to make little economic sense.

11-2 Profit Maximization

As in any firm, a profit-maximizing monopoly will choose to produce that output level for which marginal revenue is equal to marginal cost. Because the monopoly, in contrast to a perfectly competitive firm, faces a downward-sloping demand curve for its product, marginal revenue is less than market price. To sell an additional unit, the monopoly must lower its price on all units to be sold in order to generate the extra demand necessary to find a taker for this marginal unit. In equating marginal revenue to marginal cost, the monopoly produces an output level for which price exceeds marginal cost. This feature of monopoly pricing is the primary reason for the negative effect of monopoly on resource allocation.

A Graphic Treatment

The profit-maximizing output level for a monopoly is given by Q^* in Figure 11.1.[1] For that output, marginal revenue is equal to marginal costs, and profits are as large as possible given these demand and cost characteristics. If a firm produced slightly less than

[1]In Figure 11.1 and in the other diagrammatic analyses in this chapter, no distinction is made between the behavior of a monopoly in the short run and in the long run. The analysis is the same in both cases, except that different sets of cost curves would be used depending on the possibilities for adjustment that would be feasible for the firm. In the short run, the monopoly follows the same shutdown rule as does a competitive firm. Notice also that we use "Q" for the monopoly output level because, by definition, this firm serves the entire market.

APPLICATION 11.1

Should You Need a License to Shampoo a Dog?

State governments license many occupations and impose stiff legal penalties on people who run a business without a license. For some of these occupations, licensing is clearly warranted—no one wants to be treated by a quack doctor, for example. However, in other cases, licensing restrictions may go too far. Many states license such occupations as dog groomers and golf-course designers. Here we look in more detail at three specific cases of how such licensing creates monopoly.

Funeral Services[1]

Funeral services are a big business in the United States, with consumers spending as much in this market as on movie tickets. All U.S. states have regulations on funeral services, restricting entry to licensed providers. This may come as no surprise; one shudders at the grim thought of shortcuts taken by fly-by-night embalmers. Some states have gone further, restricting consumers from buying caskets from anywhere but funeral homes. With retailers like Costco retailers touting competitive prices for caskets ordered over the Internet ("starting at $949 delivered,") the consumer benefit from casket regulation is not obvious. A study comparing prices across states found that sales restrictions raised casket prices by a third. However, funeral homes in other states ended up charging more for other funeral services, so that the overall bill for a burial was about the same. Evidently, the entry restrictions are sufficient to enable funeral directors to extract a target sum from each bereaved family, whether the target is achieved by marking up caskets, embalming, or other service.

Liquor Stores and Wine on the Web

Following the repeal of Prohibition, states adopted a variety of restrictions on how alcoholic beverages can be sold. Currently, 18 states operate liquor-store monopolies. In these states, consumers must purchase such beverages from a "state store," and usually they pay extra. In most of the other states, liquor stores are licensed and subject to restrictions on pricing, advertising, and wholesale distribution. There is considerable evidence that alcoholic beverages are more expensive in states with the most restrictive entry laws. Recently, the emergence of Internet sites that sell wine have challenged local liquor monopolies. In 2005 the U.S. Supreme Court ruled that restrictions on interstate sales of wine violated the Commerce Clause of the Constitution, but gave states some leeway in how they might adjust their laws. Some, such as New York, quickly amended their laws to make most Internet wine sales legal. Many other states, however, have continued to make it difficult to buy wine over the Internet. One reason often given for their foot-dragging is to prevent teenagers from buying merlot over the Web. A more likely rationale is simply to protect the profits (and political contributions) of local wine sellers.

Taxicabs

Many cities limit entry of taxicabs just to specially licensed operators. Ostensibly, the purpose of such regulation is to weed out unscrupulous cab drivers who might overcharge passengers new to town. This rationale is not wholly consistent with evidence that tends to show that taxi fares are higher in regulated markets. One study of Toronto, for example, found that prices are about 225 percent higher than would prevail in an unregulated market.[2]

In New York City, the licenses for taxicab operation are medallions, which must be displayed on the outside of the cab. Over 13,000 medallions have been issued, which sounds like a lot, but in the city the size of New York, this represents a tight restriction. Some idea of how tight comes from periodic auctions in which operators sell their medallions to the highest bidder. In a recent auction, the price for a single medallion rose well over $1 million.

TO THINK ABOUT

1. Can you think of good reasons for regulating entry into the businesses described in this application? How would you determine whether these goals are met?
2. Why do you think some states or countries have chosen to license certain occupations while others have not? Who gains and who loses under the current arrangement compared to a competitive market?

[1]The facts and study results are from J. A. Chevalier and F. M. Scott Morton, "State Casket Sales Restrictions: A Pointless Undertaking?" *Journal of Law and Economics* (February 2008): 1–23.

[2]D. W. Taylor, "The Economic Effects of the Direct Regulation of Taxicabs in Metropolitan Toronto," *Logistics and Transportation Review* (June 1989): 169–182.

Figure 11.1 Profit Maximization and Price Determination in a Monopoly Market

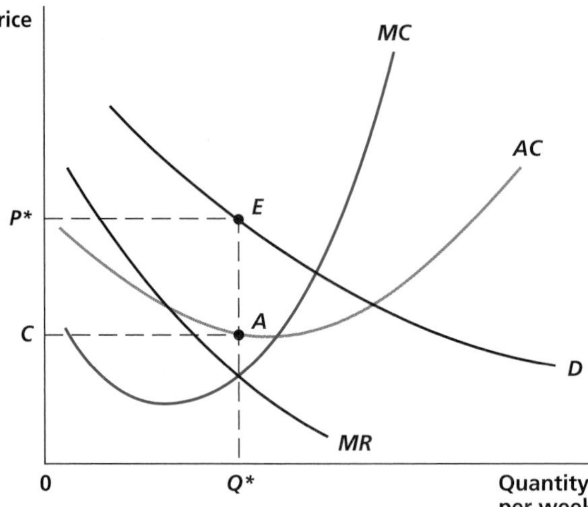

A profit-maximizing monopolist produces that quantity for which marginal revenue is equal to marginal cost. In the diagram, this quantity is given by Q^*, which yields a price of P^* in the market. Monopoly profits can be read as the rectangle P^*EAC.

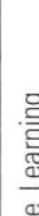

Q^*, profits would fall because the revenue lost from this cutback (MR) would exceed the decline in production costs (MC). A decision to produce more than Q^* would also lower profits since the additional costs from increased production would exceed the extra revenues from selling the extra output. Consequently, profits are at a maximum at Q^*, and a profit-maximizing monopoly will choose this output level.

Given the monopoly's decision to produce Q^*, the demand curve D indicates that a market price of P^* will prevail. This is the price that demanders as a group are willing to pay for the output of the monopoly. In the market, an equilibrium price-quantity combination of P^*, Q^* will be observed.[2] This equilibrium will persist until something happens (such as a shift in demand or a change in costs) to cause the monopoly to alter its output decision.

MICRO QUIZ 11.1

Monopoly behavior can also be modeled as a problem of choosing the profit-maximizing price.

1. Why can a monopoly choose either price or quantity for its output but not both?
2. How should the marginal revenue—marginal cost rule be stated when the monopolist is treated as a price setter?

Monopoly Supply Curve?

In the theory of perfectly competitive markets presented in previous chapters, it was possible to speak of a well-defined industry supply curve. Equilibrium is determined by the single point of intersection between supply and demand. If the demand curve moves in

[2]This combination must be on an elastic section of the demand curve. This is so because MC is positive, so for a profit maximum MR must also be positive. But, if marginal revenue is positive, demand must be elastic, as we showed in Chapter 8. One conclusion to be drawn is that markets that are found to operate along an inelastic portion of the demand curve probably are not characterized by strong monopoly power.

Figure 11.2 Monopoly Does Not Have a Single Supply Curve

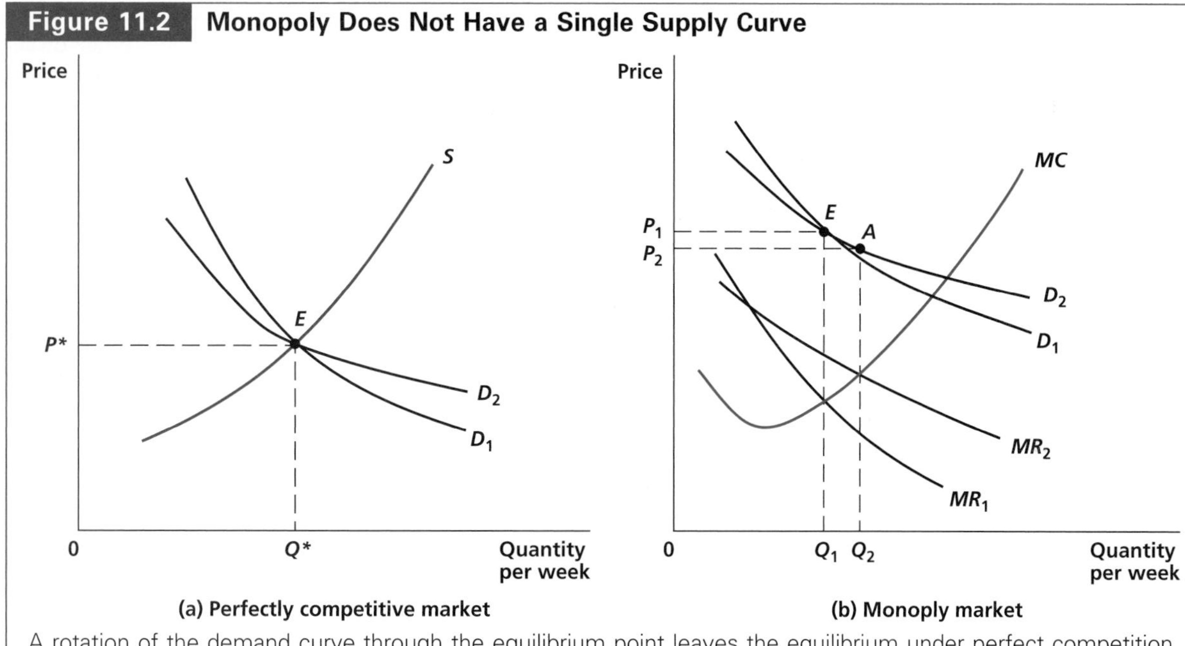

(a) Perfectly competitive market (b) Monoply market

A rotation of the demand curve through the equilibrium point leaves the equilibrium under perfect competition unchanged (graph a) but shifts the equilibrium under monopoly (graph b).

such a way as to leave the point of intersection the same, the perfectly competitive equilibrium stays the same, as in graph (a) in Figure 11.2.

This is no longer true with a monopoly. Consider graph (b) in Figure 11.2. Initially, the demand curve is given by D_1 and the associated marginal revenue curve by MR_1. The initial monopoly equilibrium is given by point *E*. Now, imagine that demand shifts from D_1 to D_2, rotating through the initial equilibrium *E*. If the monopoly had a well-defined supply curve, this demand rotation should not change the equilibrium. However, the figure shows that the equilibrium does change, from *E* to *A*.

No single curve can capture the monopolist's supply decision. The monopolist bases its supply decision on marginal revenue rather than demand directly, and marginal revenue depends on the shape of the demand curve (that is, both the slope of the demand curve as well as its level). Therefore, in the monopoly case, we refer to the firm's supply "decision" rather than supply "curve."

Monopoly rents
The profits that a monopolist earns in the long run.

Monopoly Profits

Economic profits earned by the monopolist can be read directly from Figure 11.1. These are shown by the rectangle P^*EAC and again represent the profit per unit (price minus average cost) times the number of units sold. These profits will be positive when, as in the figure, market price exceeds average total cost. Since no entry is possible into a monopoly market, these profits can exist even in the long run. For this reason, some authors call the profits that a monopolist earns in the long run **monopoly rents**. These

MICRO QUIZ 11.2

Suppose there is an increase in the demand for Jedi light-sabers (a monopoly good):

1. Why might you expect both price and quantity to increase?
2. Could price and quantity move in opposite directions in some cases?

profits can be regarded as a return to the factor that forms the basis of the monopoly (such as a patent, a favorable location, or the only liquor license in town). Some other owner might be willing to pay that amount in rent for the right to operate the monopoly and obtain its profits. The huge prices paid for television stations or baseball franchises reflect the capitalized values of such rents.

11-3 What's Wrong with Monopoly?

Monopolies pose several problems for any economy. Here, we look at two specific complaints: first, monopolies produce too little output; and second, the high prices they charge end up redistributing wealth from consumers to the "fat cat" firm owners.

Our discussion will be illustrated by Figure 11.3, which compares the output produced in a market characterized by perfect competition with the output produced in the same market when it contains only one firm. To make the graph as simple as possible, it has been assumed that the monopoly produces under conditions of constant marginal cost and that the competitive industry also exhibits constant costs with the same minimum long-run average cost as the monopolist.

Figure 11.3 Allocational and Distributional Effects of Monopoly

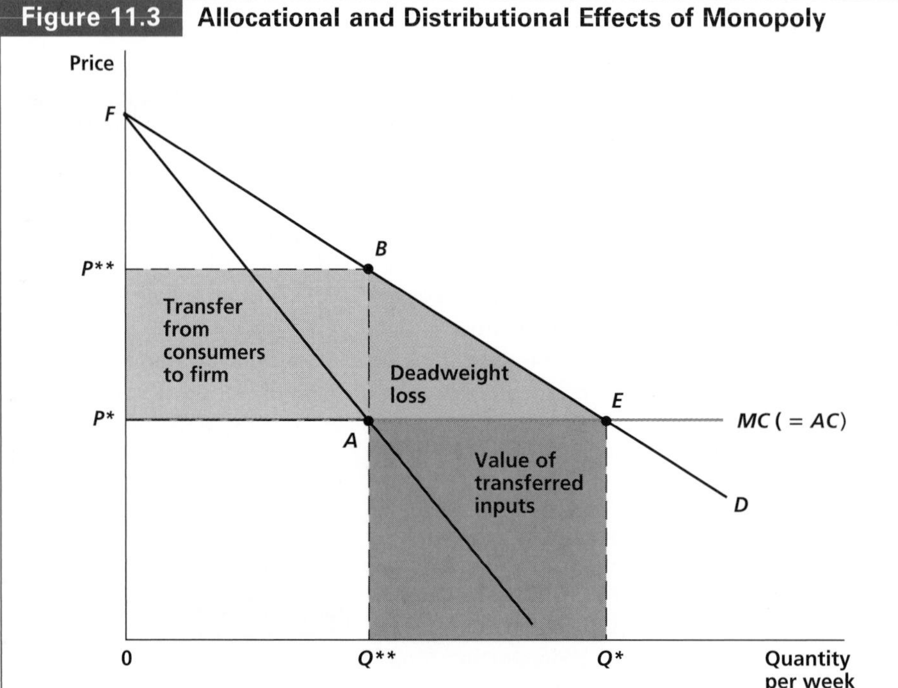

A perfectly competitive industry would produce output level Q^* at a price of P^*. A monopolist would opt for Q^{**} at a price of P^{**}. Consumer expenditures and productive inputs worth AEQ^*Q^{**} are reallocated into the production of other goods. Consumer surplus equal to $P^{**}BAP^*$ is transferred into monopoly profits. There is a deadweight loss given by BEA.

If the market in the figure is competitively organized, Q^* is produced at a price of P^*. The total value of this output to consumers is given by the area under the demand curve (that is, by area FEQ^*0), for which they pay P^*EQ^*0. Consumer surplus is given by the difference between these two areas (the triangle FEP^*). A monopoly would choose output level Q^{**}, for which marginal revenue equals marginal cost. Consumer surplus is FBP^{**}, and consumer spending on the monopoly good is $P^{**}BQ^{**}0$.

Deadweight Loss

As Figure 11.3 shows, if a formerly competitive market is monopolized, output is reduced from Q^* to Q^{**}. This restriction in output is a preliminary indication of the allocational harm done by monopoly. At Q^{**}, unserved consumers would be willing to pay P^{**} for additional output, which would cost only *MC*. However, the monopolist's market control and desire to maximize profits prevent the additional resources from being drawn into the industry to fill this demand.

To get a more precise measure of the inefficiency involved, note that when the formerly competitive market is monopolized, the total value of this good that consumers receive has been reduced by the area BEQ^*Q^{**}. This reduction is not a complete loss, however, because consumers previously had to pay AEQ^*Q^{**} for these goods, and they can now spend this money elsewhere. Because the monopoly produces less, it needs to hire fewer inputs. These released inputs (valued at AEQ^*Q^{**}) will be used to produce those other goods that consumers buy.

The loss of consumer surplus given by the area *BEA* is an unambiguous reduction in welfare as a result of the monopoly. Some authors refer to triangle *BEA* as the "deadweight loss" because it represents losses of mutually beneficial transactions between demanders and the suppliers of inputs (where opportunity costs are measured by *MC*). This loss is similar to the excess burden from a tax, which we illustrated in Chapter 9. It is the best single measure of the allocational harm caused by monopoly.

MICRO QUIZ 11.3

What is lost from the "deadweight loss" that results from the monopolization of a market? Who loses this? Do the monopoly's profits make up for the deadweight loss?

Redistribution from Consumers to the Firm

Figure 11.3 reveals an additional reallocation in the market. At the monopoly's output level Q^{**}, there exist monopoly profits given by the area $P^{**}BAP^*$. In the case of perfect competition, this area was part of the consumer-surplus triangle. If the market is a monopoly, that portion of consumer surplus is transferred into monopoly profits. The area $P^{**}BAP^*$ does not necessarily represent a loss of social welfare. It does measure the redistribution effects of a monopoly from consumers to the firm, and these may or may not be undesirable.

To the casual observer, the redistribution from presumably less well-to-do consumers to presumably wealthier owners would be troubling. A more even distribution of wealth would be preferred so that poorer members of society would not have to do without consumption staples while the rich enjoy frivolous luxuries. However, profits from a monopoly may not always to go the wealthy. For example, consider the decision of Navajo blanket makers to form a monopoly to sell their products to tourists at the Grand Canyon. In this situation, the monopoly profits make the income distribution more equal by transferring income from more wealthy tourists to less wealthy Navajos. Application 11.2: Who Makes Money at Casinos? describes how Native Americans and

APPLICATION 11.2

Who Makes Money at Casinos?

Casino gambling is a big business in many countries. In the United States, casinos take in more than $60 billion each year in gross revenues. In some markets, casinos operate quite competitively. There are so many casinos in Las Vegas, for example, that it is unlikely that any one of them has much power to set prices monopolistically. However, many other locales have adopted entry restrictions on the numbers and sizes of casinos that are permitted. These restrictions provide the possibility for owners who can build casinos to capture substantial monopoly rents. Two illustrations are provided by riverboat casinos and by so-called Indian gaming.

Riverboat Gambling[1]

A number of states along the Mississippi River (Illinois, Iowa, Louisiana, and Mississippi) permit casino gambling only on riverboats. The number of riverboats is strictly regulated, as are many features of their operations. For example, some states have mandatory "cruising" requirements. Under such requirements, the riverboats must actually leave port and cruise along the river. Patrons must participate in the complete cruise, and once the cruise ends they must leave the boat. This might be contrasted to land-based casinos, where patrons can come and go as they like. The purported reason for this cruise requirement (as for many other seemingly odd regulations) is to limit compulsive gambling, but there is little evidence that the regulations have this effect.

One clear impact of the way that riverboat gambling is regulated is monopoly rents for a number of different parties. States are a prime beneficiary—they usually tax net profits from riverboats at more than 30 percent—so obviously they have an incentive to adopt regulations that prevent the outbreak of competition. Some regulations themselves also create monopoly rents. For example, compulsory cruising rules benefit a variety of firms and workers engaged in river transportation who would not earn anything from stationary riverboats. Finally, the owners of the riverboats take in monopoly rents. Riverboat licenses are highly sought after and have sometimes been the fodder for major political scandals when bribes were involved in obtaining them.

Indian Gaming

The Indian Gaming Regulatory Act of 1988 clarified the relationship between states and the Native American tribes living within their borders, making it possible for these tribes to offer casino gambling under certain circumstances. Since the passage of the act, more than 120 tribes have adopted some form of legalized gambling. Revenue from this gambling amounts to nearly $30 billion, approaching half the revenue from all casinos in the United States. Indian gambling establishments range from slot machines in gas stations or card tables in trailers to the luxurious Foxwoods Casino in Connecticut, the largest casino in the nation. Overall, revenues from legalized gambling have become an important source of income for many Indian tribes.

The distributional consequences of Indian gaming are generally beneficial. The tribes offering gambling include some of the poorest people in the United States. A number of studies have documented significant declines in welfare rolls with the introduction of gaming.[2] Still, the income from gambling can be quite unequally distributed, especially in the cases of smaller tribes (interestingly, the largest U.S. tribe, the Navajos in Arizona, does not operate casinos). The very few actual Indian owners of the Foxwoods Casino make many millions of dollars each annually. Assorted lawyers, consultants, and local officials also probably share significantly in the booty.

TO THINK ABOUT

1. Much of the gambling in the United States is illegal. How does the presence of illegal gambling options affect the monopoly power of legalized gambling operations to set prices (that is, to set payouts to winners)? Who benefits from operations to stamp out illegal gambling?
2. How do the details of casino licensing affect which party makes the money from monopoly rents? Could casino workers ever be the primary recipients of casino monopoly rents?

[1]This section is based in part on W. R. Eadington, "The Economics of Casino Gambling," *Journal of Economic Perspectives* (Summer 1999): 173–192.
[2]For a discussion, see G. C. Anders, "Indian Gaming: Financial and Regulatory Issues," *Annals of the American Academy of Political and Social Science* (1998): 98–108.

others have tried to make money from obtaining monopoly rights for gambling. Although rich people still tend to hold more stock than poor, the proportion of the workforce holding stock has gradually increased over time because of the expansion of mutual funds and of retirement accounts invested in the stock market. Therefore, some of the monopoly's owners are average citizens, not all "fat cats."

Because perfectly competitive firms earn no economic profits in the long run, a firm with a monopoly position in a market can earn higher profits than if the market is competitive. This does not imply that monopolist necessarily earn huge profits. Two equally strong monopolies may differ greatly in their profitability. It is the ability of monopolies to raise price above *marginal* cost that reflects their monopoly power. Because profitability reflects the difference between price and *average* cost, profits are not necessarily a definite consequence of monopoly power.

Figure 11.4 exhibits the cost and demand conditions for two firms with essentially the same degree of monopoly power (that is, the divergence between price and marginal cost is the same in both graphs). The monopoly in Figure 11.4(a) earns a high level of profits, whereas the one in Figure 11.4(b) actually earns zero in profits because price equals average cost. Hence, excess profitability is not inevitable, even for a strong monopoly. Indeed, if monopoly rents accrue mainly to the inputs a monopoly uses (for example, rent on a favorably located piece of land), the monopoly itself may appear to make no profits.

A Numerical Illustration of Deadweight Loss

As a numerical illustration of the types of calculations made by economists in studying the effects of monopoly, consider again the example of CD sales introduced in Chapters 8 and 9. Table 11.1 repeats some of the information about this market. Assume now that CDs have a marginal cost of $3. Under a situation of marginal cost pricing, CDs would also sell for $3 each and, as Table 11.1 shows, seven CDs per week would be bought.

Figure 11.4 Monopoly Profits Depend on the Relationship between the Demand and Average Cost Curves

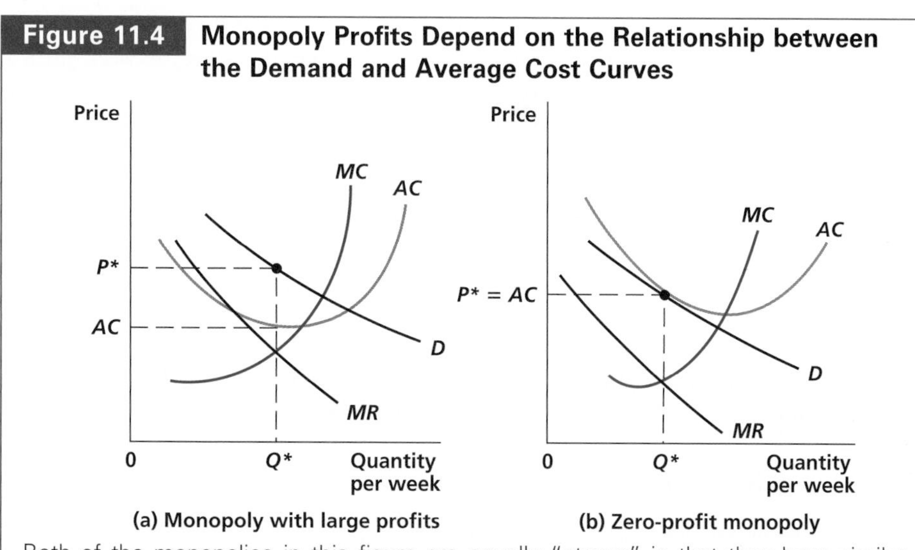

Both of the monopolies in this figure are equally "strong" in that they have similar divergences between market price and marginal cost. Because of the location of the demand and average cost curves, however, it turns out that the monopoly in graph (a) earns high profits, whereas that in graph (b) earns no profits. The size of profits is not a measure of monopoly power.

Table 11.1 Effects of Monopolization on the Market for CDs

	DEMAND CONDITIONS				CONSUMER SURPLUS		
PRICE	QUANTITY (CDS PER WEEK)	TOTAL REVENUE	MARGINAL REVENUE	AVERAGE AND MARGINAL COST	UNDER PERFECT COMPETITION	UNDER MONOPOLY	MONOPOLY PROFITS
$9	1	$9	$9	$3	$6	$3	$3
8	2	16	7	3	5	2	3
7	3	21	5	3	4	1	3
6	4	24	3	3	3	0	3
5	5	25	1	3	2	—	—
4	6	24	−1	3	1	—	—
3	7	21	−3	3	0	—	—
2	8	16	−5	3	—	—	—
1	9	9	−7	3	—	—	—
0	10	0	−9	3	—	—	—
				Totals	$21	$6	$12

Competitive equilibrium: ($P = MC$). Monopoly equilibrium: ($MR = MC$).

Consumer surplus can be computed as the amount people were willing to pay for each CD less what they actually pay ($3). For example, someone who was willing to pay $9 for the first CD sold paid only $3. He or she received a consumer surplus of $6. The sixth column of Table 11.1 makes a similar computation for each level of output from one to seven CDs. As the table shows, total consumer surplus is $21 per week when price is equal to marginal cost.

Suppose now that the CD market is monopolized by a single local merchant with a marginal cost of $3. This profit-maximizing firm will supply four CDs per week since at this level of output marginal revenue equals marginal cost. At this level of sales, price will be $6 per CD, profit per CD will be $3, and the firm will have total profits of $12. These profits represent a transfer of what was previously consumer surplus for the first four buyers of CDs. The seventh column of Table 11.1 computes consumer surplus figures for the monopolized situation. With a price of $6, for example, the buyer of the first CD now receives a consumer surplus of only $3($9 – $6); the other $3 he or she enjoyed under marginal cost pricing has been transferred into $3 of profits for the monopoly. As Table 11.1 shows, total consumer surplus under the monopoly amounts to only $6 per week. When combined with the monopolist's profits of $12 per week, it is easy to see that there is now a deadweight loss of $3 per week ($21 – $18). Some part of what was previously consumer surplus has simply vanished with the monopolizing of the market.

Buying a Monopoly Position

Figure 11.3 assumes that the monopoly's costs are a given and indeed that they are the same as the costs of the competitive firms. Further thought suggests that this may not in fact be the case. Monopoly profits, after all, provide a tantalizing target for firms, and they may spend real resources to achieve those profits. They may, for example, adopt extensive advertising campaigns or invest in ways to erect barriers to entry against other firms and hence obtain monopoly profits. Similarly, firms may seek special favors from the government in the form of tariff protection, restrictions on entry through licensing, or favorable treatment from a regulatory agency. Costs associated with these activities (such as lobbyists' salaries, legal fees, or advertising expenses) may make monopolists' costs exceed those in a competitive industry.

The possibility that costs may be different (and presumably higher) for a monopolist than for a firm in a competitive industry creates some complications for measuring monopolistic distortions to the allocation of resources. Potential monopoly profits may be dissipated into monopoly-creating costs, and it is possible that some of those costs (advertising, for example) may even shift the demand curve facing the producer. Such effects complicate Figure 11.3, and we do not analyze them in detail here.[3] Researchers who have tried to obtain empirical estimates of the dollar value of welfare losses from monopoly have found that these are quite sensitive to the assumptions made about monopolists' costs. Trivial figures of less than 0.5 percent of GDP have been estimated under the assumption that monopolists are not cost increasing. Much more substantial estimates (perhaps 5 percent of GDP) have been derived under rather extreme assumptions about monopolists' higher costs. Despite the variation in these estimates, concern about potential losses from monopolization plays a large role in governments' active enforcement of antitrust laws (to prevent competitive industries from becoming monopolies) and regulations (to mitigate the deadweight loss from existing monopolies).

11-4 Price Discrimination

So far in this chapter we have assumed that a monopoly sells all its output at one price. The firm was assumed to be unwilling or unable to adopt different prices for different buyers of its product. There are two consequences of such a policy. First, as we illustrated in the previous section, the monopoly must forsake some transactions that would in fact be mutually beneficial if they could be conducted at a lower price. The total value of such trades is given by area *BEA* in Figure 11.5 (which repeats Figure 11.3). Second, although the monopoly does succeed in transferring a portion of consumer surplus into monopoly profits, it still leaves some consumer surplus to those individuals who value the output more highly than the price that the monopolist charges (area FBP^{**} in Figure 11.5). The existence of both of these areas of untapped opportunities suggests that a monopoly has the possibility of increasing its profits even more by practicing **price discrimination**—that is, by selling its output at different prices to different buyers. In this section, we examine some of these possibilities.

Price discrimination
Selling identical units of output at different prices.

Perfect Price Discrimination

In theory, one way for a monopoly to practice price discrimination is to sell each unit of its output for the maximum amount that buyers are willing to pay for that particular unit. Under this scheme, a monopoly faced with the situation described in Figure 11.5 would sell the first unit of its output at a price slightly below *F*, the second unit at a slightly lower price, and so forth. When the firm has the ability to sell one unit at a time in this way, there is no reason now to stop at output level Q^{**}. Because it can sell the next unit at a price only slightly below P^{**} (which still exceeds marginal and average cost by a considerable margin), it might as well do so. Indeed, the firm will continue to sell its output one unit at a time until it reaches output level Q^*. For output levels greater than Q^*, the price that buyers are willing to pay falls below marginal cost; hence, these sales would not be profitable.

[3]For a relatively simple treatment, see R. A. Posner, "The Social Costs of Monopoly and Regulation," *Journal of Political Economy* (August 1975): 807–827.

Figure 11.5 Targets for Price Discrimination

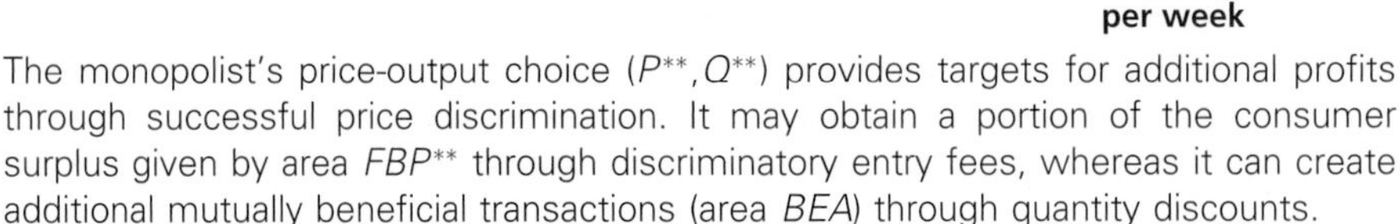

The monopolist's price-output choice (P^{**}, Q^{**}) provides targets for additional profits through successful price discrimination. It may obtain a portion of the consumer surplus given by area FBP^{**} through discriminatory entry fees, whereas it can create additional mutually beneficial transactions (area BEA) through quantity discounts.

Perfect price discrimination
Selling each unit of output for the highest price obtainable. Extracts all of the consumer surplus available in a given market.

The result of this **perfect price discrimination** scheme is the firm's receiving total revenues of $0FEQ^*$,[4] incurring total costs of $0P^*EQ^*$, and, therefore, obtaining total monopoly profits given by area P^*FE. In this case, all of the consumer surplus available in the market has been transferred into monopoly profits. Consumers have had all the extra utility they might have received by consuming this good wrung out of them by the monopolist's price discrimination scheme.

Perhaps somewhat paradoxically, this perfect price discrimination scheme results in an equilibrium that is economically efficient. Because trading proceeds to the point at which price is equal to marginal cost, there are no further unexploited trading opportunities available in this marketplace. Of course, this solution requires that the monopoly knows a great deal about the buyers of its output in order to determine how much each is willing to pay. It also requires that no further trading occur in this good in order to prevent those who buy it at a low price from reselling to those who would have paid the most to the monopoly. The pricing scheme will not work for goods like toasters or concert tickets, which may easily be resold; but, for some services, such as medical office visits or personalized financial or legal planning, providers may have the required monopoly power and may know their buyers well enough to approximate such a scheme. Application 11.3: Financial Aid at Private Colleges looks at another area in which pricing policies are used to extract consumer surplus from unsuspecting students.

[4]Some authors refer to perfect price discrimination as "first-degree price discrimination." In this (relatively unhelpful) terminology, quantity discounts and two-part tariffs where each buyer faces the same pricing menu are referred to as "second-degree price discrimination" and market-separating strategies are referred to as "third-degree price discrimination."

APPLICATION 11.3

Financial Aid at Private Colleges

In recent years, private colleges and universities have adopted increasingly sophisticated methods for allocating financial aid awards. The result of such practices is to charge a wide variety of net prices to students for the same education. Of course, most colleges are not profit-maximizing institutions, and financial aid policies are claimed to have many socially redeeming goals. Still, an investigation of the complexity of this topic can provide useful insights about price discrimination in other markets.

The 1991 Antitrust Case

Prior to the 1990s, most private colleges used a fairly straightforward methodology to determine financial aid awards to their students.[1] The U.S. government proposed a formula to determine a student's need, and schools with sufficient resources would offer such aid. Because specifics of the formula were applied somewhat differently by each school, net prices (that is, the "family contribution") still varied. In order to reduce that variance, 23 of the nation's most prestigious private colleges and universities formed the "Overlap Group" to negotiate the differences. The result was that these schools offered identical net prices (tuition minus scholarship awarded) to individual student applicants. In 1991 the U.S. Justice Department challenged this arrangement as illegal price fixing. In their defense, the schools argued that the overlap arrangement made it possible for them to aid more needy students. The schools settled the case by signing a consent decree in early 1992,[2] though ultimately their conduct was exempted from the antitrust laws under the Higher Education Act passed later that year. However, the turmoil created by the case and increasing competitive pressures in higher education generally led to the proliferation of a vast variety of pricing schemes in the 1990s.

A Different Price for Every Student?

Pricing variants introduced during the 1990s took several forms. Some modest innovations among the most prestigious private schools were focused on the old government methodology for determining aid. Several schools (notably Princeton) unilaterally adopted more generous interpretations of the methodology—essentially cutting prices for certain categories of middle-class students. Other schools adopted "preferential packaging," in which the division of their aid between loans and pure grants was tailored to attract specific kinds of students. And many schools experimented with "merit" aid as they added extra financial support (above that suggested by their formulas) for top students.

Even more innovative pricing strategies began to be adopted during the 1990s by schools that needed to cut the implicit costs of their financial aid operations. Admissions directors frequently gained new job titles ("enrollment managers") and began to worry about decreasing the average "discount rate" that resulted from their financial aid policies. Some schools adopted sophisticated statistical models of applicants' decisions and used them to tailor a pricing policy that minimized the financial aid award necessary to get a particular student to accept an offer of admission. By using information on the student's intended major, whether he or she applied early, and even on whether the student made a visit to the campus, these statistical models try to estimate the student's elasticity of demand for attending the particular institution. Those whose demand is estimated to be less elastic would be charged a higher net price (i.e., offered a smaller scholarship). Schools using this approach, therefore, came very close to employing the kind of information-intensive technology that would be required to practice perfect price discrimination.

TO THINK ABOUT

1. Is the approach to college pricing taken in this application too cynical? After all, these are nonprofit institutions, seeking to do good in the world. Is it fair even to discuss them in a section on monopoly pricing practices?
2. How can the differences in net price that result from financial aid policies persist? Could other industries (say, automobile manufacturing) try the same approach using computer models of prior consumer buying patterns to set individual-specific prices? What would limit this type of price discrimination in other industries?

[1] Of course, athletic scholarships were always a separate category, awarded on the basis of on-the-field promise. And, prior to the 1960s, financial aid was usually based on academic performance and need.

[2] MIT refused to sign the consent decree and went to trial. It was found guilty of price fixing, but that decision was overturned on appeal.

> **MICRO QUIZ 11.4**
>
> Explain why the following versions of a profit-maximizing approach to market separation are not correct.
>
> 1. A firm with a monopoly in two markets and the same costs of serving them should charge a higher price in that market with a higher demand.
> 2. A firm with a monopoly in two markets with different marginal costs should always charge a higher price in the market with the higher marginal costs.

Market Separation

A second way that a monopoly firm may be able to practice price discrimination is to separate its potential customers into two or more categories and to charge different amounts in these markets. If buyers cannot shift their purchasing from one market to another in response to price differences, this practice may increase profits over what is obtainable under a single-price policy.

Such a situation is shown graphically in Figure 11.6. The figure is drawn so that the market demand and marginal revenue curves in the two markets share the same vertical axis, which records the price charged for the good in each market. As before, the figure also assumes that marginal cost is constant over all levels of output. The profit-maximizing decision for the monopoly firm is to produce Q_1^* in the first market and Q_2^* in the second market; these output levels obey the $MR = MC$ rule for each market. The prices in the two markets are then P_1 and P_2, respectively. It is clear from the figure that the market with the less-elastic demand curve has the higher price.[5] The price-discriminating monopolist charges a higher price in that market in which quantity purchased is less responsive to price changes.

Whether a monopoly is successful in this type of price discrimination depends critically on its ability to keep the markets separated. In some cases, that separation may be geographic. For example, book publishers tend to charge higher prices in

Figure 11.6 Separated Markets Raise the Possibility of Price Discrimination

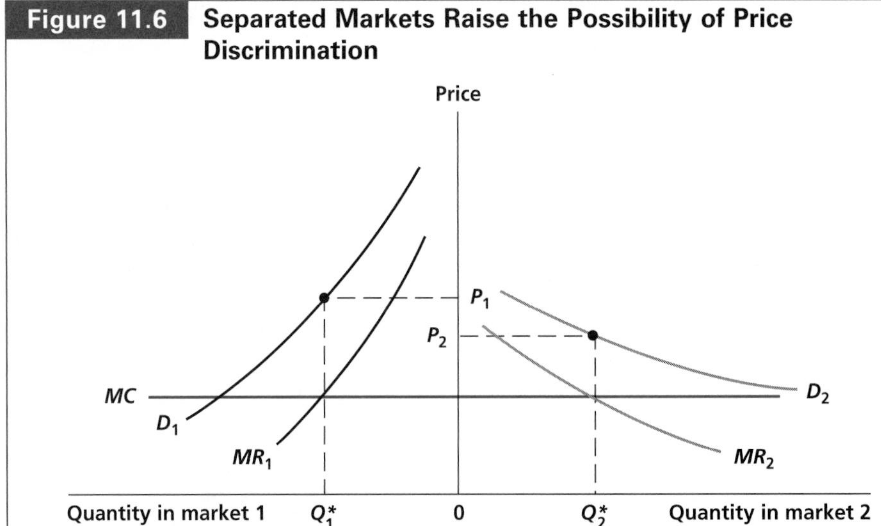

If two markets are separate, a monopolist can maximize profits by selling its product at different prices in the two markets. The firm would choose that output for which $MC = MR$ in each of the markets. The diagram shows that the market that has a less elastic demand curve is charged the higher price by the price discriminator.

[5] *Proof: Since* $MR = P(1 + 1/e)$, $MR_1 = MR_2$ implies that $P_1(1 + 1/e_1) = P_2(1 + 1/e_2)$. If $e_1 > e_2$ (i.e., if the demand in market 1 is less elastic), then P_1 must exceed P_2 for this equality to hold.

the United States than abroad because foreign markets are more competitive and subject to illegal copying. In this case, the oceans enforce market separation; few people travel abroad simply to buy books. Such a discriminatory policy would not work if transportation costs were low, however. As chain stores that charge different prices in different parts of a town have discovered, people flock to where the bargains are.

Price discrimination by time of sale may also be possible. For example, tickets to late-night or afternoon showings of motion pictures are usually cheaper than for evening shows. Discriminating against those who wish to attend prime-time shows succeeds because the good being purchased cannot be resold later. A firm that tried to sell toasters at two different prices during the day might discover itself to be in competition with savvy customers who bought when the price was low and undercut the firm by selling to other customers during high-price periods. If customers themselves can alter when they shop, a discriminatory policy may not work. A firm that offers lower post-Christmas prices may find its pre-Christmas business facing stiff competition from those sales. As always, arrival of competition (even from a monopoly's other activities) makes it impossible to pursue pure monopoly pricing practices.

Nonlinear Pricing

The price discrimination strategy in the previous section requires the monopolist to be able to distinguish the two markets by observation. As long as consumers cannot easily travel between them, different geographic markets are trivial to distinguish by observation. For example, a book producer can sell at higher prices in the United States and abroad simply by knowing the location of the retail store (or the location where the book is being shipped for Internet purchases). A movie theater can observationally distinguish between a student and others by requiring the student to show a current student identification card.

In cases in which the monopolist cannot separate consumers into different markets by observation, it can practice a different form of price discrimination. It can offer different amounts of the good at different per-unit prices. For example, the local coffee shop may sell two cup sizes: an eight-ounce cup for $1.60 and a 16-ounce cup for $2.00. This is not discrimination in the sense of treating different customers differently: all consumers face the same menu. Rather, economists characterize this as a form of discrimination because consumers end up paying different per-unit prices, with those buying the small cup paying 20 cents per ounce and those buying the larger cup paying 12.5 cents per ounce.

The technical term for a schedule of quantities sold at different per-unit prices is **nonlinear pricing**. Nonlinear pricing may be a profitable strategy if each consumer potentially has demand for several units of the good. This is the case with coffee, for example, because consumers typically do not just drink one ounce but may drink a variable amount. (Snow shovels, on the other hand, might make a poor case because the typical consumer may just want to buy one shovel if he or she buys any.) The monopolist can increase profits by fine-tuning the nonlinear pricing scheme to take account of variation in consumer valuations of different units of the good. One source of variation is that an individual consumer may have diminishing value for successive units of the product (presumably the consumer's willingness to pay for additional ounces of coffee diminishes with each additional ounce). Another source of variation is that different consumers may enjoy the good more intensely than others, with

Nonlinear pricing
Schedule of quantities sold at different per-unit prices.

some willing to pay a lot more than others for large quantities (coffee hounds in the coffee example).

The opposite of nonlinear pricing is linear pricing, which in the coffee shop example would allow consumers to fill their cups to whatever level they wanted at a constant price of, say, 15 cents per ounce. Thus far in the text, we have been studying linear pricing without explicitly saying so. In the next few subsections, we will discuss a few of the issues involved in nonlinear pricing.

Two-Part Pricing We begin with the simplest form of nonlinear pricing, two-part pricing, under which consumers must pay an entry fee for the right to purchase however much they want at a constant per-unit price. The classic example is the pricing for amusement rides at some fairs and parks. Consumers are charged an admission fee to get into the park (say, \$40) and then are charged for each ride they go on (say, \$1 per ride). A numerical example can show how adding an admission fee can increase profits for the monopolist over just charging a constant price per ride with no admission fee.

Figure 11.7 shows the demand curve for an individual consumer in our example. Assume this consumer is typical, in that all consumers in the market have roughly the same demands as this one. To further emphasize that this is a single consumer's demand and not the demand of the whole market, we use the lowercase labels *d* and

Figure 11.7 Two-Part Pricing at an Amusement Park

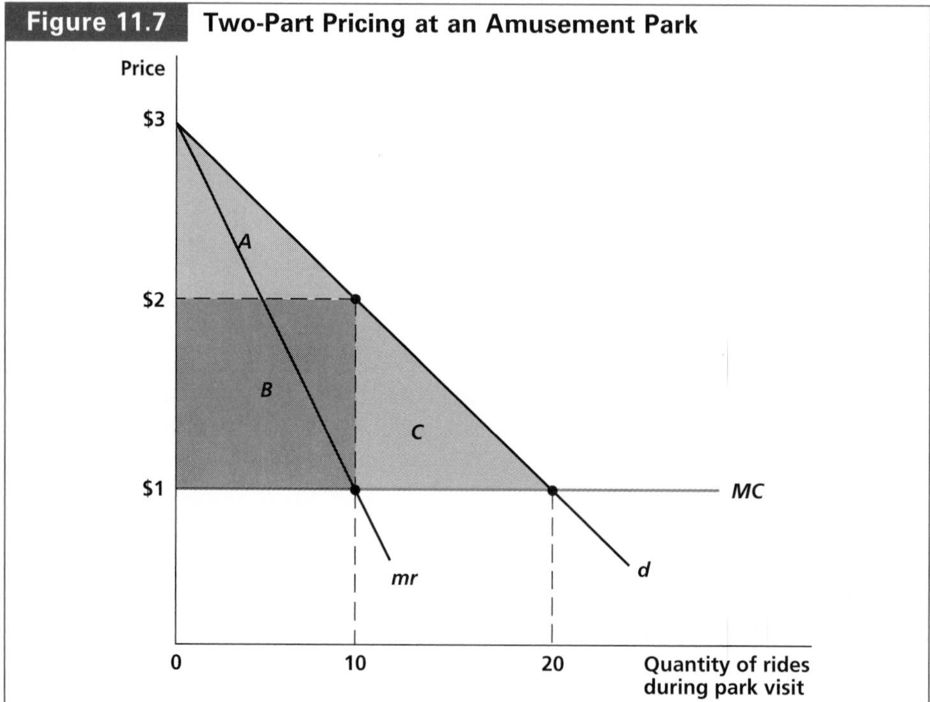

The graph shows the demand curve for a typical individual. With no admission fee, the best the monopoly amusement park can do is to charge \$2 per ride, earning \$10 profit on this consumer. If it can charge an admission fee, it can increase profit to \$20 by dropping the price to \$1 per ride and charging an admission fee equal to the area of *A*, *B*, and *C*.

mr for demand and marginal revenue. Note that the consumer has demand not just for one ride, but also for other numbers. The downward slope of demand curve *d* indicates that the thrill of rides is somewhat satiating, so that the consumer values additional rides less if he or she has already had many. The marginal cost of a ride is $1 in this example. If the monopoly amusement park charges just a price per ride and no admission fee, the best it can do is charge $2 per ride. The consumer ends up taking 10 rides, and the park earns a profit of $10 (given by the area of *B*) from the consumer. The park's overall profit would be $10 times the number of consumers.

Now consider a change in the amusement park's pricing strategy from linear pricing to a two-part scheme by charging an admission fee. The most profitable two-part scheme reduces the price per ride down to marginal cost of $1. The consumer would take 20 rides at this price and would obtain consumer surplus equal to the areas of regions *A*, *B*, and *C*, which works out using the formula for the area of a triangle to $(1/2)(\$3 - \$1)(20) = \$20$. The admission fee to the park can be set to this $20 to extract all of this consumer surplus for the monopolist. Its profits would then be $20 per consumer, or twice what it earns without an admission fee. Now, it is clear why reducing the per-ride price down to the $1 marginal cost is profit-maximizing for the park; this maximizes consumer surplus, which is "soaked up" with the admission fee.

Indeed, the monopolist does so well with two-part-pricing scheme in this example that it earns the same profit as it would under perfect price discrimination. This is an artifact of the simplicity of the example. Among other complications that arise in more realistic settings, consumers are not all identical. Solving for the best two-part pricing scheme when consumers are not all identical is beyond the scope of this chapter. The monopolist would be forced to moderate the admission charge to avoid excluding too many of the lower demand consumers and then would try to make up for this reduced revenue by increasing the per-unit price above marginal cost (but still less than the price would be if there were no admission fee). Application 11.4: Mickey Mouse Monopoly discusses the two-part-pricing scheme and various other nonlinear pricing strategies used at the most famous amusement parks in the world: Disney's.

Quantity Discounts Two-part pricing implicitly involves discounts for larger purchases. Returning to the example in Figure 11.7, if we take account of the $20 admission fee and the $1 price per ride involved in the profit-maximizing two-part scheme, a consumer who takes 10 rides would pay an average price of $3 per ride. At 20 rides, the average price falls to $2. The implicit quantity discount is what makes two-part pricing profitable. It lowers the marginal price facing the consumer, so he or she consumes more of the good, reducing deadweight loss and increasing consumer surplus. Then, the monopolist extracts this extra surplus with the fixed fee (the admission fee).

Two-part pricing is not the only way to generate quantity discounts. Returning to our coffee shop example, the shop does not charge an entry fee but still can offer quantity discounts by offering a menu of different cup sizes with larger cups selling for lower prices per ounce. Quantity discounts are common for many different goods including boxes of ready-to-eat cereal, with large boxes selling for lower unit prices, and frequent-flyer programs, with the airline giving away free travel if the passenger has traveled more than a threshold amount within the year.

APPLICATION 11.4

Mickey Mouse Monopoly[1]

The centerpiece of Disney's Florida theme parks, the Magic Kingdom, is a unique attraction. Amusement park aficionados agree the Magic Kingdom has few substitutes. With this market power, Disney has not been shy about exploring a variety of approaches to price discrimination.

Two-Part Pricing

As of 2014, Disney's pricing scheme for the Magic Kingdom resembles the two-part schemes discussed in the chapter. It charges an admission fee of $95, but then the patron can ride as many rides as he or she wants at no additional charge (only limited by the long lines at popular rides). This is consistent with the best two-part tariff that we found in the numerical example in Figure 11.7. There, we found the profit-maximizing per-ride price is marginal cost. Disney's scheme is profit-maximizing if one thinks that the marginal cost of an additional rider is close to zero. Disney has probably found that the $95 gets the right number of people into the park.

Multiday Tickets

Disney's vast complex of parks could entertain a family for upwards of a week. The value of each successive day diminishes as one spends more time at the amusement parks. Disney has a nonlinear pricing scheme for its multiday tickets that takes account of diminishing values. Figure 1 graphs various measures of price for different packages of days. One can see from the graph that this is a nonlinear pricing scheme. A linear pricing scheme would have a constant per-day price, but in the graph, it is declining. The most striking feature of the graph is that the consumer is charged almost nothing for the fourth and later days. This strategy induces consumers to stay in the park longer to spend money on complementary products.

Multiproduct Monopoly

Disney is not just selling rides at its theme parks. It is also selling complementary goods such as hotel stays, food, and souvenirs. As any park goer will complain, the prices for these complements are well above marginal cost. Still, the prices for these complements are less than one might expect from a stand-alone monopoly hotel, restaurant, or souvenir shop. Disney recognizes that if these prices become too high, they will feed back to reduced park attendance.

Figure 1 Multi-Day Prices at Disney's Theme Parks

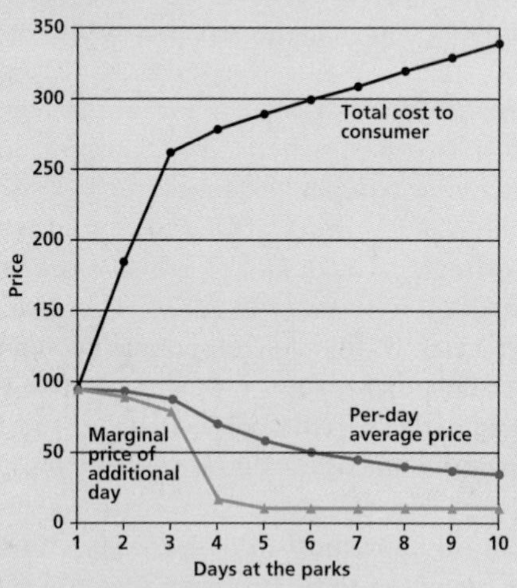

Source: htts://disneyworld.disney.go.com/tickets.

Market Separation

Disney also uses observable consumer characteristics to separate them into different markets. It offers about a 6% price discount for children under 10. It also offers a deal to Florida residents. Floridians may have lower values for Disney theme parks than out-of-staters because they have "been there, done that" or because they can substitute more readily toward competing amusement parks.

TO THINK ABOUT

1. Besides the Magic Kingdom, Disney's theme parks in Florida include Epcot, Animal Kingdom, and Hollywood Studios. While multiday ticket holders already have the option of going to different parks on different days, Disney allows the additional option of "hopping" between theme parks within the same day for a fee. Does this option cost Disney anything to provide? Come up with an economic rationale for the level Disney determined for this fee.
2. Busch owns another complex of amusement parks (including Busch Gardens and Sea-World). Research its pricing schemes, comparing and contrasting them to Disney's.

[1]The title of this application is in homage to the first analytical treatment of two-part pricing, W. Y. Oi, "A Disneyland Dilemma: Two-Part Tariffs for a Mickey Mouse Monopoly," *Quarterly Journal of Economics* (February 1971): 77–96.

If the monopolist serves identical consumers, it would need to offer only one menu item involving the single, profit-maximizing quantity and price combination. However, firms often offer several options, whether small, medium, and large cup sizes at a coffee shop or cereal box sizes at a grocery store. Including several options is a way for a monopolist to deal with the practical reality that it serves not identical consumers but consumers with different valuations for the good. The design of such schemes involves the economics of asymmetric information. Consumers know their individual valuations, but the monopolist may know only market aggregates. The monopolist might be tempted to sell large quantities to high demanders at very high prices. Unfortunately for the monopolist, this price cannot be too high or else the consumers will choose the smaller menu item. We defer a discussion of the subtleties of nonlinear pricing schemes under asymmetric information to Chapter 15.

As with other price discrimination schemes, an important problem for the monopolist is to prevent further transactions between consumers who pay a low price and those who pay a high price. A consumer could buy the 16-ounce coffee cup for $2.00, pour it into two 8-ounce cups, and resell these to other consumers, undercutting the shop's $1.60 price on these smaller cups and making a profit on the transaction. Although it might not be unusual for families and friends to agree to split larger quantities among themselves, we typically do not observe consumers buying goods repackaged by strangers, probably because it is not customary to do so and would lead one to doubt the quality of the good being repackaged and resold. If quantity discounts became especially deep, we might start to see more resale among consumers. Firms are concerned about the possibility of repackaging and resale. For example, some restaurants charge a plate fee to diners who share a meal with someone else in the party rather than ordering for themselves. The requirement that a traveler's identification match the name on the ticket, ostensibly for security reasons, is a useful device for the airlines to prevent consumers from reselling individual legs of round-trip tickets to others.

Pricing for Multiproduct Monopolies If a firm has pricing power in markets for several related products, a number of additional price discrimination strategies become possible. All of these involve coordinating the prices of the goods in ways that convert more of available consumer surplus into profits than would be possible if the goods were priced independently. In some cases, firms can extend monopoly power directly by requiring that users of one product also buy a related, complementary product. For example, some producers of coffee machines require that replacement filters be bought through them and some makers of sophisticated lighting fixtures are the only sources of bulbs for them. Of course, a would-be buyer of such a product usually knows that the firm has a monopoly in replacement parts, so the firm must be careful not to scare off customers with exorbitant prices for those parts. It must also beware of potential entrants who may undersell it on the parts.

Other multiproduct schemes involve the creative pricing of bundles of goods. Automobile producers create various options packages, laptop computer makers configure their machines with specific components, and Chinese restaurants offer combination lunches. The key to the profitability of such bundling arrangements is to take advantage of differences among consumers in their relative preference for various items in the bundle. For example, some buyers of Chinese lunches may have a strong preference for appetizers and never eat dessert, whereas others may skip the appetizers but never skip dessert. But a properly priced "complete lunch" package may tempt appetizer fanciers to buy dessert and vice versa. The restaurant can then obtain higher revenues (and profits) than if it only sold appetizers and desserts separately. Application 11.5: Bundling of Cable and Satellite Television Offerings illustrates how such bundling provisions can be quite intricate in some cases.

Durability

Interesting issues arise when the monopolist sells a durable good, that is, a good that can be used for several periods into the future. Cars last for many years and sometimes hundreds of thousands of miles. Computer software never deteriorates (although even it may become obsolete with the advance of computer hardware and operating systems). The durability of a good is a choice for the monopolist. By spending more on higher quality materials and components, an automobile monopolist could increase the useful life of its cars. A software monopolist can extend the life of version 1.0 of its software by delaying the release of version 2.0, or by allowing consumers to upgrade to intermediate versions (1.1, 1.2 etc.) released at no charge.

A naïve view is that a durable-good monopoly should make a good that wears out as quickly as possible. That way, it can sell to the same consumers more frequently in future periods. In the 1960s, critics of the automobile industry claimed that firms practiced "planned obsolescence" to ensure that there would always be a market for their newer cars. Whether this example is representative of all durable goods monopolies, however, is open to question. The key point is that consumers care about the durability of the goods they buy. They will be less willing to pay high prices for goods that wear out quickly; thus, the monopolist risks losing sales up front if it distorts the durability of its output. It turns out to be rather difficult to generalize about whether a monopoly would produce a less durable good than would firms in a competitive market—it depends on preference for durability on average across consumers compared to that of the marginal consumer (the "last" consumer who is indifferent between buying the good and not).[6]

Another naïve idea regarding a monopolist that sells a good each period for a number of periods into the future can benefit from a form of dynamic price discrimination by which it first sells to the highest demand consumers at the highest prices and gradually lowers the price to serve lower and lower demand consumers. Because the durable good lasts for many periods, when a segment of consumers buys, it is removed from the market for this period of time. The naïve view is that this strategy would allow the monopolist to extract almost all the consumer surplus from each demand segment.

In fact, forward-looking consumers would anticipate the fall in prices in later periods and would not be willing to buy at prices earlier that would extract their entire consumer surplus. Dynamic pricing could then end up harming the monopolist by limiting the prices it charges initially. Ronald Coase argued that consumers

[6]There are cases where competitive firms and monopolies would choose the same level of durability. These were first discussed in P. L. Swan, "Durability of Consumption Goods," *American Economic Review* (December 1970): 884–894.

APPLICATION 11.5

Bundling of Cable and Satellite Television Offerings

The huge expansion in television offerings made possible by improvements in cable and satellite technology has created the possibility for many options for bundling programs to appeal to different categories of consumers.

Theory of Program Bundling

Figure 1 illustrates the theory of program bundling in a very simple case. The figure shows four consumers' willingness to pay for either sports or movie programming. Consumers *A* and *D* are true devotees, willing to pay $20 per month for sports (*A*) or movies (*D*) and nothing for the other option. Consumers *B* and *C* are more diverse in their interests, though their preferences are still rather different from each other. If the firm opts to sell each of the two packages separately, it should charge $15 for each. This will yield $60 to the firm. A bundling scheme, however, that charges $20 for each package if bought individually, but $23 if both are bought,[1] would yield $86. Bundling can offer a substantial increase in revenue to this provider.

Bundling by DIRECTV

These features of bundling are illustrated by DIRECTV's monthly fee schedule for 2014 (see Table 1). DIRECTV limits the ability of subscribers to pick and choose individual channels as they would in a so-called *à la carte* system. Even the lower end Choice package is a bundle—indeed a big bundle—already including 150 channels of news, sports, movies, general interest, and other content. Each step up in package includes a bundle of additional channels, mostly additional sports and movie channels. The monthly fee is higher, but the price per channel drops, at least for the Xtra and Ultimate packages.

Table 1 Sample DIRECTV Channel Bundles

PACKAGE	MONTHLY FEE ($)	CHANNELS	PRICE PER CHANNEL ($)
Choice	34.99	150	0.23
Xtra	39.99	205	0.20
Ultimate	44.99	225	0.20
Premier	91.99	285	0.32

Source: www.directv.com

Figure 1 Consumer Values for Programs

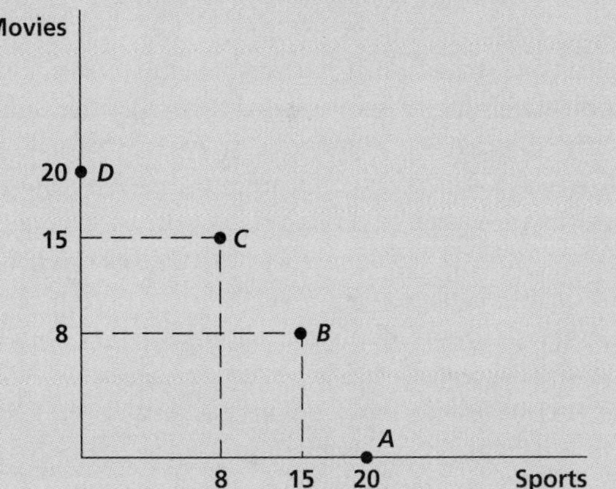

Four consumers have different preferences for movie and sports programming, making bundling profitable.

While you might think there can be nothing beyond Ultimate, in fact there is, Premier, which involves a large jump up in both monthly and per-channel fees. One explanation for the jump in price of the top-end bundle is that it includes premium movie channels such as HBO and Showtime and regional sports networks, all of which are quite costly for DIRECTV to provide. Another explanation is that DIRECTV believes some subscribers will simply opt for "the works" without any careful weighing of marginal benefits and costs.

TO THINK ABOUT

1. Our hypothetical data and the actual data from DIRECTV suggest that bundling is profit maximizing only when consumers have divergent preferences for the items being bundled. Why do you think that is a general result of bundling theory?
2. Why isn't bundling more extensive in retailing? For example, could supermarkets gain by offering shoppers prefilled shopping bags at modestly reduced prices?

[1]With this scheme, *A* and *D* would opt for single packages, and *B* and *C* would buy the combination.

would anticipate that prices would eventually fall all the way to marginal cost.[7] If periods are short enough, this fall could happen quite quickly, so the monopolist would hardly make any profit. In a sense, the monopolist in future periods becomes a sort of competitor with its present-day self. If periods are short, this competition can be intense.

The monopolist would do better by committing not to compete with itself by setting a high price initially and sticking with this price in all future periods. In practice, this commitment is difficult to maintain. After the highest demanders are served and thus no longer "in the market," the firm would have an incentive to renege on its commitment, lowering price to serve lower demand consumers in a subsequent period as long as there were some of these consumers left who are willing to pay more than marginal cost. Here, the monopolist could benefit by distorting the durability of the good. By making the good less durable, the high demanders have to return to the market to buy a replacement more often, and with the high demanders back in the market, the monopolist has less incentive to lower price.

The monopolist could also use other strategies that have a similar effect to reducing durability. An automobile manufacturer could lease the cars instead of selling them. This would force the consumers to return to the car market more often (after the lease is up rather than after the car breaks down). Software firms could come out with more frequent upgrades. In the art market, artists sometimes use the unique strategy of destroying the stone after producing a limited quantity of numbered lithographs, a sure commitment to maintain scarcity and high prices over time.

11-5 Natural Monopolies

There are basically two solutions to minimizing the allocational harm caused by monopolies: (1) make markets more competitive, and (2) regulate price in the monopoly market. In general, economists favor the first of these. Actions that loosen entry barriers (such as eliminating restrictive licensing requirements) can sharply reduce the power of a monopoly to control its prices. Similarly, antitrust laws can be used to reduce the power of monopoly firms to raise entry barriers on their own. Because direct price regulation can be problematic (as we shall see), pro-competitive solutions will generally work better. In the case of a natural monopoly, however, that will not be the case. When average costs fall over the entire range of output, the cost-minimizing solution is to have only a single firm provide the good. Production by several firms would, by definition, be inefficient because it would involve extra costs. Hence, in a natural monopoly situation, direct price regulation may be the only option. How to achieve this regulation is an important subject in applied economics. The utility, communications, and transportation industries are all subject to price regulation in many countries. Although in many cases such regulation may be unwise because the industry is not really a natural monopoly, in other cases price regulation may be the only way to cause these industries to operate in socially desirable ways. Here we look at a few aspects of such price regulation.

[7] R. Coase, "Durability and Monopoly," *Journal of Law and Economics* (April 1972): 143–149.

Marginal Cost Pricing and the Natural Monopoly Dilemma

Does the regulatory pricing dilemma apply to a monopoly with a U-shaped average cost curve? Under what conditions would a regulated policy of marginal cost pricing create losses for the monopoly? Could the policy cause the monopoly to shut down?

By analogy to the perfectly competitive case, many economists believe that it is important for the prices charged by natural monopolies to accurately reflect marginal costs of production. In this way, the deadweight loss from monopolies is minimized. The principal problem raised by a policy of enforced marginal cost pricing is that it may require natural monopolies to operate at a loss.

Natural monopolies, by definition, exhibit decreasing average costs over a broad range of output levels. The cost curves for such a firm might look like those shown in Figure 11.8. In the absence of regulation, the monopoly would produce output level Q_A and receive a price of P_A for its product. Profits in this situation are given by the rectangle P_AABC. A regulatory agency might set a price of P_R for this monopoly. At this price, Q_R is demanded, and the marginal cost of producing this output level is also P_R. Consequently, marginal cost pricing has been achieved. Unfortunately, because of the declining nature of the firm's cost curves, the price P_R (= marginal cost) falls below average costs. With this regulated price, the monopoly must operate at a loss given by area $GFEP_R$. Since no firm can operate indefinitely at a loss, this poses a dilemma for the regulatory agency: either it must abandon its goal of marginal cost pricing, or the government must subsidize the monopoly forever.

Two-Tier Pricing Systems

One way out of the marginal cost pricing dilemma is a two-part pricing system. Under this system, the monopoly is permitted to charge some users a high price while

Figure 11.8 Price Regulation for a Natural Monopoly

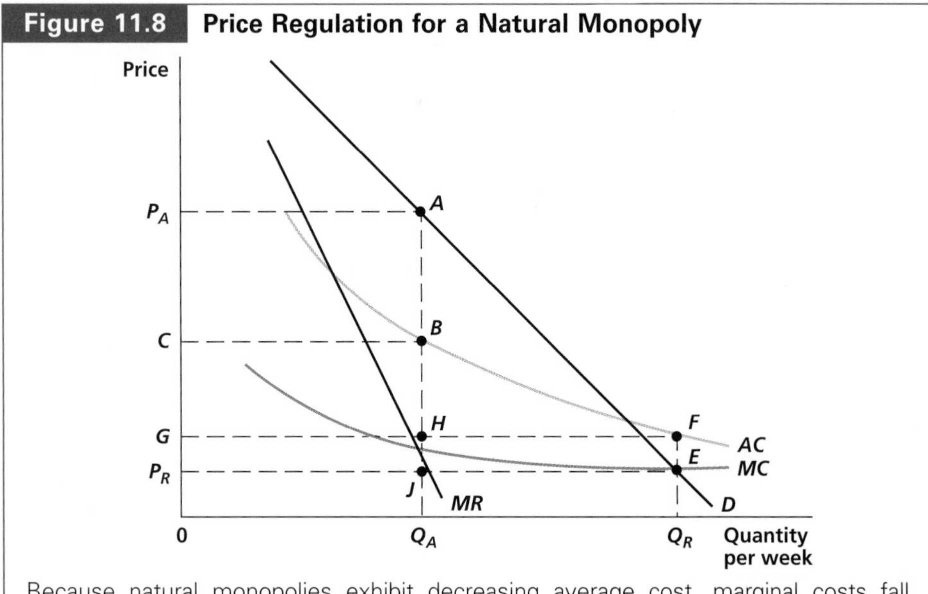

Because natural monopolies exhibit decreasing average cost, marginal costs fall below average cost. Enforcing a policy of marginal cost pricing entails operating at a loss. A price of P_R, for example, achieves the goal of marginal cost pricing but necessitates an operating loss of $GFEP_R$.

APPLICATION 11.6

Does Anyone Understand Telephone Pricing?

In 1974, the Department of Justice filed an antitrust suit against the American Telephone and Telegraph (AT&T) Company, charging unlawful monopolization of the markets for telephone equipment and long-distance service. Filing an antitrust suit against a regulated natural monopoly is rarely done, and legal wrangling over the suit lasted into the 1980s. A settlement was reached in late 1982, and, on January 1, 1984, AT&T formally divested itself of its seven local Bell Operating Companies (Ameritech, Atlantic Bell, Bell South, NYNEX, Pacific Telesis, Southwestern Bell, and U.S. West). AT&T retained its long-distance operations. The goal of this huge restructuring was to improve the performance and competitiveness of the U.S. telephone industry, but lingering effects of regulation have made these gains difficult to obtain.

Subsidization of Local Phone Service

Prior to the breakup, AT&T had been forced by regulators to provide local residential phone service at prices below average cost, making up these losses by charging above-average cost for long-distance calls (similar to the situation shown in Figure 11.6). Over the years immediately prior to the breakup, technical improvements (such as fiber-optics cables) sharply reduced the costs of long-distance service. But regulators chose to keep long-distance rates high and local rates low, increasing the subsidy to local subscribers. By the early 1980s, residential service was estimated to cost about $26 per month, but the typical charge was only $11 per month. Subsidies from long-distance and other sources made up the $15-per-month difference. After the breakup, state regulators were faced with the politically unappealing prospect of implementing huge increases in residential telephone rates. Not surprisingly, local regulators instead opted for a continuation of subsidies from AT&T (and, to a lesser extent, from other long-distance companies such as MCI or Sprint) to the local operators.

The Telecommunications Act of 1996

One promising route to lower costs for local phone service might be provided by increasing competition in these monopoly markets. Under the Telecommunications Act of 1996, the government specified a number of steps that local providers should take to increase such competition.[1]

Not surprisingly, the local firms fought the implementation of many of these provisions in court, thereby making it very costly for any would-be competitor seeking to enter the local marketplace. Local, fixed-line phone service remains very much a monopoly enterprise. Regulators have continued to try to keep local prices low through more direct methods.

Technology Does Not Stand Still

Relentless improvement in telecommunications technology has not permitted phone markets to stand still. After 2000, overcapacity in fiber-optics cable, together with new phone transmission technology, has significantly reduced the prices and profitability of long-distance service. This led to the bankruptcy of some major providers (most notably, the WorldCom Corporation) and continuing troubles for AT&T itself. It also further reduced the ability of regulators to cross-subsidize local service. In addition, the rapid growth of cellular phone networks and the beginning of phone service over the Internet has called into question the continued viability of any sort of fixed-line local phone service. As is the case for any fast-moving market, local phone regulators are having a tough time keeping up with all of this. They have continued to try to practice cross-subsidization, primarily by charging business customers more for local service. But such differential pricing has led many firms to leave local phone networks. Regulators have also added a variety of tax-like charges to phone bills, but these also have proven to be controversial. It seems inevitable that prices of local phone service will increasingly come closer to approximating actual costs.

TO THINK ABOUT

1. Should local phone service be subsidized? Are there socially desirable benefits from ensuring that phone service is available to practically everyone? If so, who should pay the subsidy?
2. The original logic of the AT&T breakup was to treat the long-distance market as potentially competitive and the local exchange as a natural monopoly. Have changes in technology supported that view?

[1]For a discussion of some of these provisions, see R. G. Harris and C. J. Kraft, "Meddling Through: Regulating Local Telephone Competition in the United States," *Journal of Economic Perspectives* (Fall 1997): 93–112.

maintaining a low price for "marginal" users. In this way, the demanders paying the high price in effect subsidize the losses of the low-price customers.

Such a pricing scheme can be illustrated with Figure 11.8. The regulatory commission might decide to permit the firm to charge one class of buyers the monopoly price P_A. At this price, Q_A is demanded. Other users (those who find this good less valuable to them) would be offered a marginal cost price of P_R and would demand $Q_R - Q_A$. With total output of Q_R, average costs are given by $0G$. With this two-tier price schedule, profits earned from those who pay the high price (given by the size of the rectangle P_AAHG) balance the losses incurred on sales to those who pay the low price (these losses are given by the area *HFEJ*). Here, the "marginal user" does indeed pay a price equal to marginal cost and the losses this entails are subsidized by profits from the "intramarginal user."

Although in practice it may not be so simple to establish pricing schemes that maintain marginal cost pricing and cover operating costs, many regulatory commissions do use multipart price schedules that intentionally discriminate against some users to the advantage of others. Application 11.6: Does Anyone Understand Telephone Pricing? illustrates how this was done for many years in the telephone industry and caused major problems in moving to a more competitive situation.

Rate of Return Regulation

Another approach to setting the price charged by a natural monopoly that is followed in many regulatory situations is to permit the monopoly to charge a price above average cost that will earn a "fair" rate of return on investment. Much effort is then spent on defining the "fair" rate and on developing how it might be measured. From an economic point of view, some of the most interesting questions about this procedure concern how rate of return regulation affects the firm's decisions. If, for example, the allowed rate of return exceeds what an owner might earn under competitive circumstances, the firm will have an incentive to use more capital input than needed to truly minimize costs. If regulators typically delay in making rate decisions, firms may be given incentives to minimize costs that would not otherwise exist since they cannot immediately recover their costs through higher rates. Although it is possible to develop formal models of all these possibilities, we will not do so here.

SUMMARY

A market in which there is a single seller is called a monopoly. In a monopoly situation, the firm faces the entire market demand curve. Contrary to the case of perfect competition, the monopolist's output decision completely determines market price. The major conclusions about pricing in monopoly markets are:

- The profit-maximizing monopoly firm will choose an output level for which marginal revenue is equal to marginal cost. Because the firm faces a downward-sloping demand curve, market price will exceed both marginal revenue and marginal cost.
- The divergence between price and marginal cost is a sign that the monopoly causes resources to be allocated inefficiently. Buyers are willing to pay more for one more unit of output than it costs the firm to produce it, but the monopoly prevents this beneficial transaction from occurring. This is the deadweight loss of welfare from a monopoly.
- Because of barriers to entry, a monopoly may earn positive long-run economic profits. These profits may have undesirable distributional effects.
- A monopolist may be able to increase profits further by practicing price discrimination. Adoption of such schemes

depends on the specific nature of demand in the market the monopoly serves.

- If a monopoly produces many different products or if its output is durable, the firm's pricing decisions are more complicated. In some cases, these greater complications will lead to greater monopoly power, whereas in others the potential for monopolistic distortions may be reduced.
- Governments may choose to regulate the prices charged by monopoly firms. In the case of a natural monopoly (for which average costs decline over a broad range of output), this poses a dilemma. The regulatory agency can opt for marginal cost pricing (in which case the monopoly will operate at a loss) or for average cost pricing (in which case an inefficient quantity will be produced).

REVIEW QUESTIONS

1. In everyday discussions, people tend to talk about monopoly firms "setting high prices," but in this chapter we have talked about choosing a profit-maximizing level of output. Are these two approaches saying the same thing? What kind of rule would a monopoly follow if it wished to choose a profit-maximizing price? Why not charge the highest price possible?
2. Why are barriers to entry crucial to the success of a monopoly firm? Explain why all monopoly profits will show up as returns to the factor or factors that provide the barrier to entry.
3. "At a monopoly firm's profit-maximizing output, price will exceed marginal cost simply because price exceeds marginal revenue for a downward-sloping demand curve." Explain why this is so and indicate what factors will affect the size of the price-marginal cost gap.
4. The following conversation was overheard during a microeconomics cram session:

   Student A. "In order to maximize profits, a monopolist should obviously produce where the gap between price and *average* cost is the greatest."

   Student B. "No, that will only maximize profit per unit. To maximize total profits, the firm should produce where the gap between price and *marginal* cost is the greatest since that will maximize monopoly power and hence profits."

   Can you make any sense out of this drivel? Which concepts, if any, have these students not grasped sufficiently?
5. "Monopolies perpetuate inflation. When wages rise, a monopoly simply passes on the increased cost in its price. Competitive firms would not be able to do that." Do you agree? What are the differences between how a monopoly and a competitive firm respond to cost increases?
6. Figure 11.3 illustrates the "deadweight loss" from the monopolization of a market. What is this a loss of?
7. Suppose that the government instituted a per-unit tax on the output of a monopoly firm. How would you graph this situation? What would happen to the market equilibrium after implementation of such a tax? How would you analyze the tax incidence question—that is, how would you show which economic actor pays most of the tax?
8. Describe some of the transactions costs that must be present if a monopoly is to be able to practice price discrimination successfully. Are different types of costs more relevant when the monopolist price discriminates using the strategy of market separation than when using the strategy of nonlinear pricing?
9. Suppose that the Acme manufacturing company has a monopoly position in the market for the two principal types of roadrunner-catching equipment: roller skates and jet-assist backpacks. Describe in general terms how Acme should price both of these products when it knows that the demands for the two goods are related and that the costs of producing the two goods exhibit economies of scope (see Chapter 8).
10. What is a "natural monopoly"? Why does electric power distribution or local telephone service have the characteristics of a natural monopoly? Why might this be less true for electric power generation or long-distance telephone service?

PROBLEMS

11.1.  A monopolist can produce at constant average and marginal costs of $AC = MC = 5$. The firm faces a market demand curve given by $Q = 53 - P$. The monopolist's marginal revenue curve is given by $MR = 53 - 2Q$.

a. Calculate the profit-maximizing price-quantity combination for the monopolist. Also calculate the monopolist's profits and consumer surplus.

b. What output level would be produced by this industry under perfect competition (where price = marginal cost)?
c. Calculate the consumer surplus obtained by consumers in part b. Show that this exceeds the sum of the monopolist's profits and consumer surplus received in part a. What is the value of the "deadweight loss" from monopolization?

11.2. A monopolist faces a market demand curve given by

$$Q = 70 - P.$$

The monopolist's marginal revenue function is given by

$$MR = 70 - 2Q.$$

a. If the monopolist can produce at constant average and marginal costs of $AC = MC = 6$, what out put level will the monopolist choose in order to maximize profits? What is the price at this output level? What are the monopolist's profits?
b. Assume instead that the monopolist has a cost structure where total costs are described by

$$TC = 0.25Q^2 - 5Q + 300$$

and marginal cost is given by

$$MC = 0.5Q - 5.$$

With the monopolist facing the same market demand and marginal revenue, what price-quantity combination will be chosen now to maximize profits? What will profits be?
c. Assume now that a third cost structure explains the monopolist's position, with total costs given by

$$TC = 0.01Q^3 - Q^2 + 45Q + 100$$

and marginal costs given by

$$MC = 0.03Q^2 - 2Q + 45.$$

Again, calculate the monopolist's price-quantity combination that maximizes profits. What will profits be? (Hint: set $MC = MR$ as usual and use the quadratic formula or simple factoring to solve the equation for Q.)
d. Graph the market demand curve, the MR curve, and the three marginal cost curves from part a, part b, and part c. Notice that the monopolist's profit-making ability is constrained by (1) the market demand curve it faces (along with its associated MR curve), and (2) the cost structure underlying its production.

11.3. A single firm monopolizes the entire market for Batman masks and can produce at constant average and marginal costs of

$$AC = MC = 10.$$

Originally, the firm faces a market demand curve given by

$$Q = 60 - P$$

and a marginal revenue function given by

$$MR = 60 - 2Q.$$

a. Calculate the profit-maximizing price-quantity combination for the firm. What are the firm's profits?
b. Now assume that the market demand curve becomes steeper and is given by

$$Q = 45 - 0.5P$$

with the marginal revenue function given by

$$MR = 90 - 4Q.$$

What is the firm's profit-maximizing price-quantity combination now? What are the firm's profits?
c. Instead of the assumptions in part b, assume that the market demand curve becomes flatter and is given by

$$Q = 100 - 2P$$

with the marginal revenue function given by

$$MR = 50 - Q.$$

What is the firm's profit-maximizing price-quantity combination now? What are the firm's profits?
d. Graph the three different situations of part a, part b, and part c. Using your results, explain why there is no meaningful "supply curve" for this firm's mask monopoly.

11.4. Suppose that the market for hula hoops is monopolized by a single firm.
a. Draw the initial equilibrium for such a market.
b. Suppose now that the demand for hula hoops shifts outward slightly. Show that, in general (contrary to the competitive case), it will not be possible to predict the effect of this shift in demand on the market price of hula hoops.
c. Consider three possible ways in which the price elasticity of demand might change as the demand curve shifts outward—it might increase, it might decrease, or it might stay the same. Consider also that marginal costs for the monopolist might be rising, falling, or constant in the range where $MR = MC$. Consequently, there are nine different combinations of types of demand shifts and marginal cost slope configurations. Analyze each of these to determine for which cases it is possible to make a definite prediction about the effect of the shift in demand on the price of hula hoops.

11.5. Suppose a company has a monopoly on a game called Monopoly and faces a demand curve given by

$$Q_T = 100 - P$$

and a marginal revenue function given by

$$MR = 100 - 2Q_T,$$

where Q_T equals the combined total number of games produced per hour in the company's two factories ($Q_T = q_1 + q_2$). If factory 1 has a marginal cost function given by

$$MC_1 = q_1 - 5$$

and factory 2 has a marginal cost function given by

$$MC_2 = 0.5q_2 - 5,$$

how much total output will the company choose to produce and how will it distribute this production between its two factories in order to maximize profits?

11.6. Suppose a textbook monopoly can produce any level of output it wishes at a constant marginal (and average) cost of \$5 per book. Assume that the monopoly sells its books in two different markets that are separated by some distance. The demand curve in the first market is given by

$$Q_1 = 55 - P_1$$

and the curve in the second market is given by

$$Q_2 = 70 - 2P_2.$$

a. This problem is easier to solve if you work out the following preliminary result. Show that for a downward-sloping linear demand curve, profits are maximized when output is set at $Q^*/2$, where Q^* is the output level that would be demanded when $P = MC$.

b. If the monopolist can maintain the separation between the two markets, what level of output should be produced in each market and what price will prevail in each market? What are total profits in this situation?

c. How would your answer change if it cost demanders only \$3 to mail books between the two markets? What would be the monopolist's new profit level in this situation? How would your answer change if mailing costs were 0?

11.7. Suppose a perfectly competitive industry can produce Roman candles at a constant marginal cost of \$10 per unit. Once the industry is monopolized, marginal costs rise to \$12 per unit because \$2 per unit must be paid to politicians to ensure that only this firm receives a Roman candle license. Suppose the market demand for Roman candles is given by

$$Q_D = 1{,}000 - 50P$$

and the marginal revenue function by

$$MR = 20 - Q/25.$$

a. Calculate the perfectly competitive and monopoly outputs and prices.

b. Calculate the total loss of consumer surplus from monopolization of Roman candle production.

c. Graph and discuss your results.

11.8. Consider the following possible schemes for taxing a monopoly:

i. a proportional tax on profits

ii. a tax on each unit produced

iii. a proportional tax on the gap between price and marginal cost.

a. Explain how each of these taxes would affect the monopolist's profit-maximizing output choice. Would the tax increase or decrease the deadweight loss from monopoly?

b. Graph your results for these three cases.

11.9. Bruce runs the only bar in town. An individual consumer's demand for bar drinks is $Q = 8 - P$. The associated marginal revenue curve for this consumer is $MR = 8 - 2Q$. The bar's marginal cost is \$2 per drink.

a. Compute the profit-maximizing monopoly quantity, price, and profit from serving this single consumer if Bruce's Bar charges a constant price per drink rather than using some nonlinear pricing scheme. What would the quantity and profit be if the bar serves 100 consumers identical to this one on a typical night?

b. Suppose Bruce moves to pricing scheme involving an admission fee to the bar but lowers the price per drink to marginal cost (which we showed in the text is the best per-unit price with identical consumers). How should the admission fee be set to maximize profit? How many drinks would the bar sell and how much profit would it earn from this two-part scheme on a typical night when 100 identical consumers show up?

c. Now suppose that, in addition to the 100 consumers mentioned above, an additional 15 show up whose demand for drinks is twice as high as the original consumers (so each has demand $Q = 16 - P$). What profit would Bruce's Bar earn if it continued to use the two-part scheme from b? Show that the bar could earn more profit by moving to a scheme with a \$3 price per drink. (Hint: as a preliminary step, compute the highest admission fee it can charge and still retain the 100 original consumers after increasing the per-drink price to \$3. Then compute profits from both this admission fee charged to all 115 plus the variable sales of drinks to the 100 original and 15 new consumers at a price of $3 per drink.)

11.10. Because of the huge fixed cost of running pipes to everyone's home, natural gas is a natural monopoly. Suppose demand is $Q = 100 - P$ and marginal revenue is $MR = 100 - 2Q$. Suppose marginal cost is $20, and the fixed cost of setting up the natural gas pipelines is $1,000.

a. Compute the industry outcome (quantity, price, profit, consumer surplus, and social welfare) under unregulated monopoly.
b. What regulatory price maximizes social welfare? Compute the industry outcome (quantity, profit, consumer surplus, and social welfare) under this price. Would this policy be sustainable in the long run?
c. Compute the industry outcome with the laxer regulatory policy of constraining price to be no greater than average cost. Would this policy be sustainable in the long run?

12 Imperfect Competition

Many real-world markets fall between the extremes of perfect competition and monopoly. For example, only a handful of airlines may make direct flights between two cities. They may compete to some extent but not dissipate all profits as with perfect competition. Other examples include markets ranging from pharmaceuticals to package delivery. A hallmark of an imperfectly competitive market is the presence of few firms but more than one, in which case the market is called an **oligopoly**.

Oligopoly
A market with few firms but more than one.

Economists have proposed an array of models of imperfectly competitive markets. None has emerged as the "textbook" one, so we will study a variety of the basic models in current use. Several themes will emerge from our study. First, game theory is a valuable tool for studying oligopoly. Throughout this chapter, we will find ourselves applying the concepts of game theory developed in Chapter 5. Second, small changes in details concerning the variables that firms choose, the timing of their moves, or their information about market conditions or rival actions can have a dramatic effect on market outcomes. Last, we may simply have to accept the fact that predicting outcomes in imperfectly competitive industries is difficult based on theory alone; the best way to study real-world markets may involve a combination of theory and empirical evidence. Many of our boxed applications will include empirical evidence relevant to the issue under consideration.

Our analysis will proceed from the short-term decisions firms make (pricing and output decisions) to longer-term decisions (such as advertising, product design, and investment) and to the yet longer-term decisions (entry and exit).

12-1 Overview: Pricing of Homogeneous Goods

This section provides a brief overview of the rest of the chapter. To fix ideas, we will begin by looking at firms' pricing decisions in markets in which relatively few firms each produce the same good. As in previous chapters, we assume that the market is perfectly competitive on the demand side; that is, there are assumed to be many demanders, each of whom is a price taker. We also assume that there are no transactions or informational costs, so that the good in question obeys the law of one price. That is, we can talk accurately about the price of this good. Later in this chapter, we relax this assumption to consider cases where firms sell products that differ slightly from each other and may therefore have different prices.

Competitive Outcome

It is difficult to predict exactly the possible outcomes for prices when there are few firms; prices depend on how aggressively firms compete, which in turn depends on which strategic variables firms choose, how much information firms have about rivals, and how

Figure 12.1 Pricing under Imperfect Competition

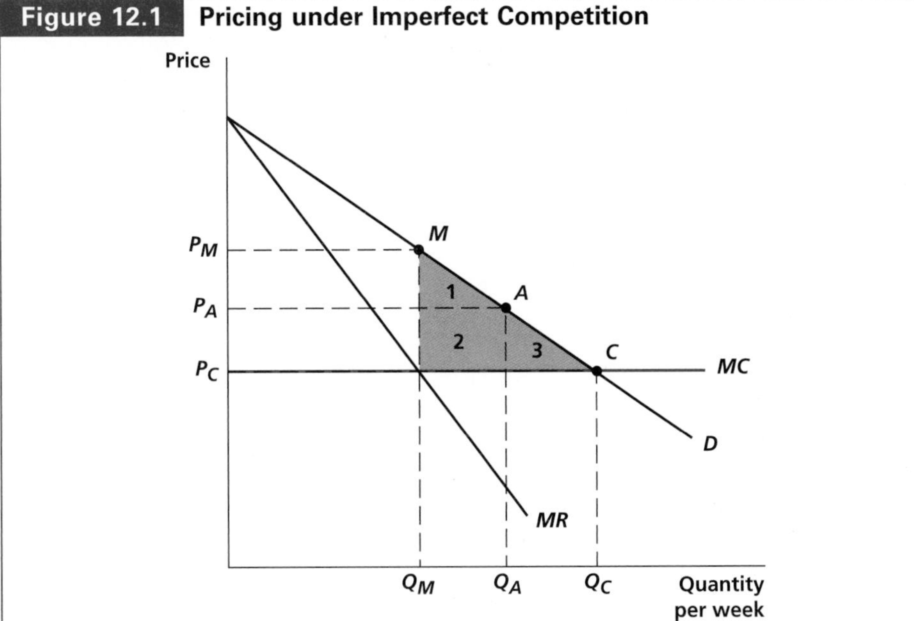

Market equilibrium under imperfect competition can occur at many points on the demand curve. In this figure, which assumes that marginal costs are constant over all output ranges, the equilibrium of the Bertrand game occurs at point *C*, also corresponding to the perfectly competitive outcome. The perfect-cartel outcome occurs at point *M*, also corresponding to the monopoly outcome. Many solutions may occur between points *M* and *C*, depending on the specific assumptions made about how firms compete. For example, the equilibrium of the Cournot game might occur at a point such as *A*. The deadweight loss given by the shaded triangle is increasing as one moves from point *C* to *M*.

often firms interact with each other in the market. The Bertrand model—which we will study in detail later in the chapter—in which identical firms choose prices simultaneously in their one meeting in the market, has a Nash equilibrium at point *C* in Figure 12.1. This figure assumes that marginal cost (and average cost) is constant for all output levels. Even though there may be only two firms in the market, in this equilibrium they behave as if they were perfectly competitive, setting price equal to marginal cost and earning zero profit. We will discuss whether the Bertrand model is a realistic depiction of actual firm behavior, but an analysis of the model shows that it is possible to think up rigorous game-theoretic models in which one extreme—the competitive outcome—can emerge in very concentrated markets with few firms.

Perfect Cartel Outcome

At the other extreme, firms as a group may act as a cartel, recognizing that they can affect price and coordinate their decisions. Indeed, they may be able to act as a perfect cartel, achieving the highest possible profits, namely, the profit a monopoly would earn in the market. Assuming, as before, that these marginal costs are equal and constant for all firms, the output choice is indicated by point *M* in Figure 12.1. Because this coordinated plan would have to specify an output level for each firm, the plan would also dictate how monopoly profits earned by the cartel are to be shared by its members.

One way to maintain a cartel is to bind firms with explicit pricing rules. Such explicit pricing rules are often prohibited by antitrust law. Firms do not need to resort to explicit pricing rules if they interact on the market repeatedly. They can collude tacitly. High collusive prices can be maintained with the tacit threat of a price war if any firm undercuts. We will analyze this game formally and discuss practical difficulties involved with trying to maintain collusion.

Other Possibilities

The Bertrand and cartel models determine the outer limits between which actual prices in an imperfectly competitive market are set (one such intermediate price is represented by point A in Figure 12.1). This band of outcomes may be very wide, and such is the wealth of models available that there may be a model for nearly every point within the band. For example, the Cournot model, in which firms set quantities rather than prices (as in the Bertrand model), leads to an outcome somewhere between C and M in Figure 12.1, such as point A. We will study the Cournot model in detail shortly. For another example, cartel models in which market characteristics make it difficult for firms to sustain a perfect cartel at point M may lead to a point such as A in the figure.

In the end, it may be difficult to predict which outcome between C and M will actually occur. The assumption that firms play a Nash equilibrium in simultaneous games and a subgame-perfect equilibrium in sequential games will help pin down firm behavior, but still the outcome will vary on the game that is being played, and there are many different, plausible ways to specify such a game. In the end, economists turn to data to determine the competitiveness of real-world industries, as discussed in Application 12.1: Measuring Oligopoly Power. It is important to know where the industry is on the line between points C and M because the well-being of society (as measured by the sum of consumer surplus and firms' profits) depends on where this point is. At point C, there is no deadweight loss and society is as well off as possible. At point A, the deadweight loss is given by the area of the shaded triangle 3. At point M, deadweight loss is even greater, given by the area of shaded regions 1, 2, and 3. The closer the imperfectly competitive outcome is to C and the farther it is from M, the better off society will be.

12-2 Cournot Model

Cournot model
An oligopoly model in which firms simultaneously choose quantities.

The first model we will study is the **Cournot model**, named after the French economist who first proposed and analyzed it.[1] Since a formal development of the Cournot model can become quite mathematically complex, a simple numerical example can suffice.

Suppose there are two firms (A and B) that operate costless but healthful springs. Firms simultaneously choose the quantities q_A and q_B of water they will supply (in terms of thousands of gallons) in a single period of competition. We will assume spring water is a homogeneous product, so market price is a function of total quantity $Q = q_A + q_B$ produced. In particular, suppose market demand is given by the equation

$$Q = 120 - P \tag{12.1}$$

and market price by the inverse of Equation 12.1,

[1] A. Cournot, *Researches into Mathematical Principles of the Theory of Wealth*, trans. (New York: Macmillan, 1897). Cournot was one of the first people to use mathematics in economics. Among other advances, he devised the concept of marginal revenue and used this concept both to discuss profit maximization by a monopoly and to develop a model in which two firms compete for the same market.

$$P = 120 - Q. \tag{12.2}$$

We have just defined a game in which the players are the two firms, actions are quantities, and payoffs are profits (which can be computed from our specification of demand and costs). We will look for the Nash equilibrium of this game. Since quantities can be any number greater than or equal to zero, this is a game with continuous actions similar to the Tragedy of the Commons studied in Chapter 5. We will solve for the Nash equilibrium here in a similar way, so it may be helpful for the reader to review the definitions of Nash equilibrium and best-response function, and the analysis of the Tragedy of the Commons, all in Chapter 5, before proceeding.

Nash Equilibrium in the Cournot Model

For a pair of quantities, q_A and q_B, to be a Nash equilibrium, q_A must be a best response to q_B and vice versa. We therefore begin by computing the best-response function for firm *A*. Its best-response function tells us the value of q_A that maximizes *A*'s profit given for each possible choice q_B by firm *B*. In Chapter 8, we presented a rule for the profit-maximizing output choice that applies to any firm ranging from a perfectly competitive firm to a monopoly, namely that profits are maximized by the quantity where marginal revenue equals marginal cost. The same rule applies here.

Computing firm *A*'s marginal cost is easy here: production is costless, so *A*'s marginal cost is 0. Computing *A*'s marginal revenue is a bit more difficult. *A*'s total revenue equals its quantity q_A times market price $P = 120 - Q = 120 - q_A - q_B$:

$$q_A(120 - q_A - q_B). \tag{12.3}$$

Using the expression for total revenue in Equation 12.3, it can be shown,[2] or simply accepted as a fact, that marginal revenue equals

$$120 - 2q_A - q_B. \tag{12.4}$$

Equating marginal revenue in Equation 12.4 with the marginal cost of 0, and solving for q_A gives *A*'s best-response function:

$$q_A = \frac{120 - q_B}{2}. \tag{12.5}$$

We can perform the same analysis for firm *B* and arrive at its best-response function, which expresses the profit-maximizing level of q_B as a function of q_A of the form

$$q_B = \frac{120 - q_A}{2}. \tag{12.6}$$

The best-response functions for both firms are shown in Figure 12.2.

Nash equilibrium requires each firm to play its best response to the other. The only point on Figure 12.2 where both are playing best responses is the intersection between their best-response functions. No other point would be stable because one firm or the other or both would have an incentive to deviate. It is easy to show (either using the graph or solving Equations 12.5 and 12.6 simultaneously) that the point of intersection is given by $q_A = 40$ and $q_B = 40$. In this Nash equilibrium, both firms produce 40, total

[2]Distributing q_A among the terms in parentheses, Equation 12.3 can be rewritten as $120q_A - q_A^2 - q_Aq_B$. Using calculus, one can differentiate this expression for total revenue with respect to q_A to find marginal revenue in Equation 12.4.

APPLICATION 12.1

Measuring Oligopoly Power

As Figure 12.1 shows, the variety of possible models of imperfect competition give a range of possibilities from the perfectly competitive outcome (point *C* in the figure) to the monopoly outcome achieved by a perfect cartel (point *M*). Because theory alone cannot determine where a real-world industry will fall between points *C* and *M*, economists have turned to data to help them answer the question.

Lerner Index

Asking where an industry falls between points *C* and *M* in Figure 12.1 is really just asking how competitive the industry is. The most widely used measure is called the Lerner index (L), which equals the percentage markup of price over marginal cost:

$$L = \frac{P - MC}{P}$$

(the index is expressed as a percentage to remove the units in which the product is measured). If the industry is perfectly competitive, the Lerner index equals zero since price equals marginal cost. For the monopoly/perfect cartel outcome, one can show that the Lerner index is related to the elasticity of market demand;[1] more precisely, the inverse of the absolute value of the elasticity,

$$L = \frac{1}{|e_{Q,P}|},$$

ranging from close to zero for very elastic demand curves to extremely high numbers for very inelastic demand curves.

Problems Measuring Marginal Cost

At first glance, it would seem a simple matter to calculate the Lerner index for an industry. One just needs to plug information on price and marginal cost into the simple formula above. Unfortunately, this is not as easy as it sounds. Price data can be readily obtained just by looking at an advertisement or visiting a store. Unfortunately, data on marginal costs are not readily available. Firms often jealously guard cost information as being competitively sensitive.

Economists have used three tacks to overcome this measurement problem. Up until recently, many utilities (telephone, electricity) were regulated by the government, with firms' prices set to a certain markup over cost. This form of regulation required the government to collect detailed cost information from the regulated firms, which became a data source for economists. A second tack is to look at an industry where the production process is simple enough that one can back marginal cost out using simple facts about the industry. One example is the early history of refined sugar, studied by Genesove and Mullin.[2] The main component of marginal cost is the cost of raw sugar: 108 pounds of raw sugar yields about 100 pounds of refined sugar. Combined with data on the wholesale price of raw sugar, around \$3.30 in 1900, and producers' statements reported in the trade press about the small additional costs of labor and energy to complete the refining process, around 25 cents, the authors came up with a plausible measure of marginal cost of $(108 \times \$3.30) + \$0.25 = \$3.81$ per hundred pounds. For most industries, where there are no direct measures of cost, a third tack is needed, involving estimating a sophisticated econometric model (based on the very same game-theory models studied in this chapter).

Industry Studies

Table 1 presents the estimated Lerner indexes from a number of studies. Note the broad range of possibilities. Rubber, coffee roasting, and sugar, for example, appear to be very competitive, with price being only around 5 percent higher than marginal cost (that is, a Lerner index of around 0.05). Food processing, tobacco, and aluminum appear to be less competitive, with prices estimated to be more than double marginal cost (a Lerner index of more than 0.50). Competitiveness in Uruguayan banking appears to have improved considerably after removal of government entry restrictions.

General Lessons

What makes some of the industries in Table 1 more competitive than others? Unfortunately, there have not yet been enough studies done in a systematic way across industries to make such a comparison. John Sutton has provided perhaps the most extensive synthesis across industries.[3] The clearest determinants of competitiveness appear to be the size of the market relative to fixed costs. Considering a large market such as that for automobiles in the United States, even if fixed costs (including the cost of setting up an assembly plant, the cost of advertising the new product line, and so forth) number in the billions of dollars, the market may be big enough to support a fair number of firms, leading to relatively stiff competition. In a smaller market such as Uruguay, there may be space only for one firm, with the

Table 1 Competitiveness of Various Industries

INDUSTRY	LERNER INDEX
Aluminum	0.59
Autos	
Standard	0.10
Luxury	0.34
Banking (Uruguay)	
Before removing entry restrictions	0.88
After removing entry restrictions	0.44
Coffee roasting	0.06
Electrical machinery	0.20
Food processing	0.50
Gasoline	0.10
Refined sugar	0.05
Textiles	0.07
Tobacco	0.65

Source: Taken from compilations of studies by T. F. Bresnahan, "Empirical Studies of Industries with Market Power," in *Handbook of Industrial Organization*, ed. and (Amsterdam: North-Holland, 1989), Table 17.1 and D. W. Carlton and J. M. Perloff, *Modern Industrial Organization*, 4th ed. (Boston: Pearson, 2005), Table 8.7. Aluminum: V. Suslow, "Estimating Monopoly Behavior with Competitive Recycling: An Application to Alcoa," *RAND Journal of Economics* (Autumn 1986): 389–403. Autos: T. F. Bresnahan, "Departures from Marginal-Cost Pricing in the American Automobile Industry: Estimates for 1977–1978," *Journal of Econometrics* (November 1981): 201–227. Banking: P. Spiller and E. Favaro, "The Effects of Entry Regulation on Oligopolistic Interaction: The Uruguayan Banking Sector," *RAND Journal of Economics* (Summer 1984): 244–254. Coffee roasting: M. J. Roberts, "Testing Oligopolistic Behavior," *International Journal of Industrial Organization* (December 1984): 367–383. Electrical machinery, textiles, tobacco: E. Applebaum, "The Estimation of the Degree of Oligopoly Power," *Journal of Econometrics* (August 1982): 287–299. Food processing: R. E. Lopez, "Measuring Oligopoly Power and Production Responses of the Canadian Food Processing Industry," *Journal of Agricultural Economics* (July 1984): 219–230. Gasoline: M. Slade, "Conjectures, Firm Characteristics, and Market Structure: An Empirical Assessment," *International Journal of Industrial Organization* (December 1986): 347–369. Refined sugar: Genesove and Mullin, cited in footnote 1.

resultant monopoly outcome. The nature of the fixed cost may matter as well. If fixed costs increase in proportion to market size, as, for example, with television advertising expenditures, larger markets may not support any more firms than small, and these large markets may exhibit high price-cost margins. Therefore, whether television and other forms of advertising are important for an industry (yes for autos, no for machine tools) might be an indicator of how competitive that industry is. Other factors that may reduce competitiveness include government restrictions on entry and barriers to international trade.

TO THINK ABOUT

1. Price data may have their own difficulties. Imagine trying to get price data on a new car model. How would you handle the fact that prices are usually set in customer-by-customer negotiations, usually below sticker price? How would you handle the fact that even for a given model there are numerous option packages available, which affect the car price?
2. Are there any surprises in Table 1? Where do you think such industries as home construction, beer, and computers would fit? How about higher education?

[1]Using the fact from Equation 9.3 that $MR = MC$ for a profit-maximizing firm, the fact from Equation 9.9 that $MR = P + P/e_{q,P}$ and the fact that the elasticity of demand facing the firm $e_{q,P}$ equals market demand elasticity $e_{Q,P}$ for a monopoly, yields $P + P/e_{Q,P} = MC$. Rearranging terms, $P - MC = -P/e_{Q,P}$, or $(P - MC)/P = -1/e_{Q,P} = 1/|e_{Q,P}|$.

[2]D. Genesove and W. Mullin, "Testing Static Oligopoly Models: Conduct and Cost in the Sugar Industry, 1890–1914," *RAND Journal of Economics* (Summer 1998): 355–377.

[3]J. Sutton, *Sunk Costs and Market Structure* (Cambridge, MA: MIT Press, 1991).

Figure 12.2 Cournot Best-Response Functions

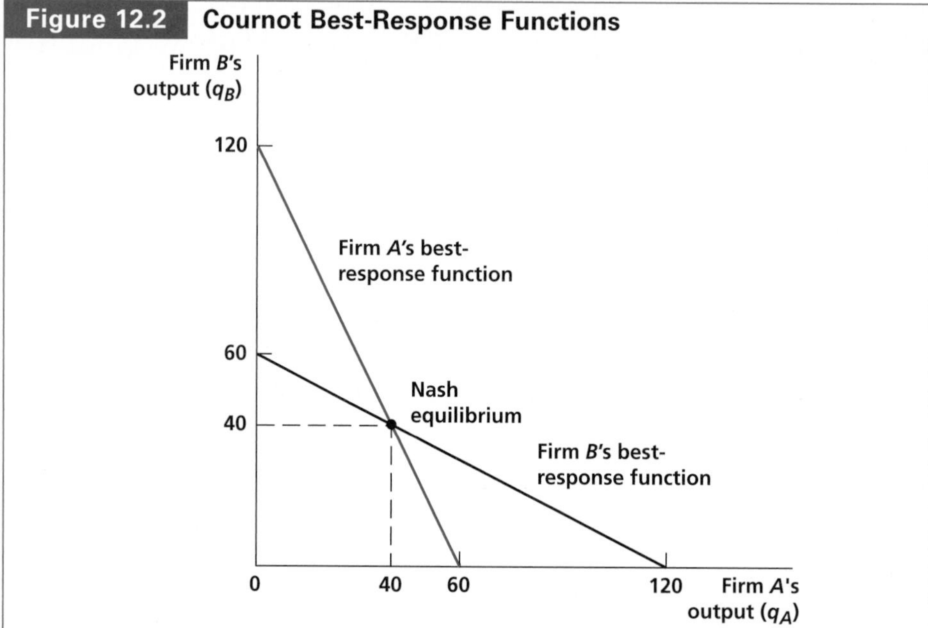

Firm A's best-response function shows the profit-maximizing quantity it would choose for any quantity chosen by firm B. Firm B's best-response function shows the profit-maximizing quantity it would choose for any quantity chosen by firm A. Both firms must play best responses in the Nash equilibrium. The only point on both best-response functions is the point of intersection ($q_A = 40$, $q_B = 40$).

output is 80, and the market price is \$40 (= 120 − 80). Each firm earns revenue and profit equal to \$1,600, and total industry revenue and profit is \$3,200.

Comparisons and Antitrust Considerations

The Nash equilibrium of the Cournot model is somewhere between perfect competition and monopoly. With perfectly competitive firms, the price would be set at marginal cost, \$0. Industry output would be 120, and industry revenue and profit would be \$0. On the other hand, a monopoly's output would be 60, price would be \$60, and revenue and profit would be \$3,600.[3] Putting these results side by side, we see that equilibrium price and industry profit in the Cournot model is above the perfectly competitive level and below the monopoly level; industry output is below the perfectly competitive level and above the monopoly level. The firms manage not to compete away all the profits as in perfect competition. But the firms do not do as well as a monopoly would, either.

The industry does not attain the monopoly profit in the Cournot model because firms do not take into account the fact that an increase in their output lowers price and thus lowers the other firm's revenue. Firms "overproduce" in this sense. According to this model, firms would have an incentive to form a cartel with explicit rules limiting

[3]The monopoly's total revenue is $(120 - Q).Q$ (that is, price $P = 120 - Q$, times quantity, Q). Differentiating total revenue with respect to Q gives marginal revenue $120 - 2Q$. Equating marginal revenue with the marginal cost of 0 shows that the profit-maximizing monopoly output is 60.

output. If such a cartel were illegal, the firms would have a motive to collude tacitly using self-enforcing strategies to reduce output and raise price toward the monopoly levels. With one period of competition, such collusion would be unstable; indeed, we showed that the only stable point is the Nash equilibrium of the Cournot model. Another way to increase profits would be for the firms to merge, essentially turning a Cournot model with two firms into a monopoly model with one firm.

Consumers benefit from the higher output and lower prices in the Cournot model compared to monopoly. Government authorities, through the antitrust laws, often prohibit conspiracies to form cartels and mergers that would increase concentration in the industry (certainly mergers from two firms to one would be examined critically by authorities). Assuming the government authorities act in the interest of consumers, the Cournot model provides some justification for these laws.

MICRO QUIZ 12.1

1. In Figure 12.2, how would an increase in B's marginal cost from zero to a positive number shift its best-response function? Would it shift A's? On a graph, indicate where the new Nash equilibrium would be.
2. On a graph, show how the best-response functions would shift and where the new Nash equilibrium would be if both firms' marginal costs increased by the same amount. What about a cost decrease? What about an increase in the demand intercept above 120?

KEEP *in* MIND

Games with Continuous Actions

The methods used to solve the Cournot model are similar to those used to solve the Tragedy of the Commons from Chapter 5. In fact, except for the interpretation of the players' identities (shepherds versus spring-water producers) and actions (number of sheep versus thousands of gallons of spring water), the two games are exactly the same. The reader can verify that the equilibrium in both involves a choice of 40 units for each player.

Generalizations

The Cournot model can be relatively easily extended to cases involving more complex demand and cost assumptions or to situations involving **three** or more firms. As the number of firms grows large, it can be shown that the Nash equilibrium approaches the competitive case, with price approaching marginal cost. The ease with which the model can be extended, together with the fact that it produces what people think is a realistic outcome for most markets (that is, an outcome between perfect competition and monopoly), has made the Cournot model a work-horse for economists. Application 12.2: Cournot in California provides a good example of its use in economic and policy analysis.

Bertrand Model

We next turn to the **Bertrand model**, named after the economist who first proposed it.[4] Bertrand thought that Cournot's assumption that firms choose quantities was unrealistic, so he developed a model in which firms choose prices. In all other respects the model is the same as Cournot's. We will see that this seemingly small change in the strategic variable from quantities in the Cournot model to prices in the Bertrand model leads to a big change in the equilibrium outcome.

Bertrand model
An oligopoly model in which firms simultaneously choose prices.

[4]J. Bertrand, "Théorie Mathematique de la Richess Sociale," *Journal de Savants* (1883): 499–508.

APPLICATION 12.2

Cournot in California

Wholesale markets for electric power have been increasingly deregulated in many countries. In the United States, the process has evolved rather slowly because each state has a separate regulatory apparatus and moves toward deregulation have generated considerable political controversy. In California, the largest power market in the United States, deregulation of wholesale electricity sales was first authorized in 1996 and actual trading of day-ahead electricity sales began in early 1998. Early attempts to model this process reached cautionary conclusions about the possibilities for market power in this trading. Subsequent events have tended to confirm these predictions.

Modeling Spot Markets in Electricity

Perhaps the most elaborate attempt at modeling the impact of electricity deregulation in California can be found in an important paper by Borenstein and Bushnell.[1] In this paper, the authors focus on the competition between the three major electricity-generating firms in the state (Pacific Gas and Electric, Southern California Edison, and San Diego Gas and Electric) together with a group of smaller in-state and out-of-state suppliers. They argue that the smaller suppliers can be treated as competitive suppliers but that the major in-state producers behave in the way assumed in the Cournot model. That is, each major supplier is assumed to choose its output levels (or, more precisely, its levels of electricity-generating capacity) in a way that treats output by other producers as fixed. The authors then study the resulting Cournot equilibrium under various assumptions about electricity demand and the behavior of out-of-state suppliers.

Results of the Modeling

Borenstein and Bushnell show that under certain circumstances there is substantial market power in California wholesale electricity markets. As we saw in Application 12.1, one way to measure that power is by the Lerner index, the gap between price and marginal cost expressed as a ratio of price. In periods of normal demand, the authors calculate values for this index in the range of 0.10 or less; the gap between price and marginal cost is less than 10 percent of price. However, during peak hours of electric usage or during peak months (i.e., September), the index rises to well over 0.50; the gap between price and marginal cost is more than half of price. Hence, during such peak periods, equilibrium in these markets is far from the competitive ideal. Interestingly, the authors also show that market power can be significantly restrained by larger price elasticities of demand for electricity. But they point out that actual policies in California tend to keep price elasticities small by preventing increases in the wholesale price of electricity from being passed on to consumers.

Actual Price "Spikes" in California

Seldom has an economic model proven to be right so quickly. In the summer of 2000, California experienced a relatively modest shortfall in electric power availability because droughts in the Pacific Northwest reduced the supply of hydroelectric power. The result was a rapid spiking in the wholesale price of electricity in the late summer and fall. From a normal price of perhaps \$50 per megawatt-hour in 1999, peak prices rose to over \$500 per megawatt-hour and sometimes reached over \$1,000. These increases were, more or less, in line with what had been predicted by Borenstein and Bushnell. Because large California electric utilities had not been allowed to sign long-term power contracts, they had little choice but to buy at these prices. But the firms could not pass on these higher prices to their customers, so there were only modest reductions in demand. By 2001, several of California's largest utilities had filed for bankruptcy and had been forced to sell off major portions of their electricity distribution networks to the state.

TO THINK ABOUT

1. The model described in this application assumes that the major suppliers of electricity to California engaged in Cournot-type competition when electricity supplies were tight. Could the large price increases in 2000 also be explained with a competitive model?
2. One result of price spikes in the California electricity market was the filing of many lawsuits against suppliers. Should firms engaged in Cournot-type competition be found guilty of a "conspiracy in restraint of trade"?

[1]S. Borenstein and J. Bushnell, "An Empirical Analysis of the Potential for Market Power in California's Electricity Industry," *Journal of Industrial Economics* (September 1999): 285–323.

To state the model formally, suppose there are two firms in the market, A and B. They produce a homogeneous product at a constant marginal cost (and constant average cost), c. Note that this is a generalization of our assumption in the Cournot model that production was costless. Firms choose prices P_A and P_B simultaneously in a single period of competition. Firms' outputs are perfect substitutes, so all sales go to the firm with the lowest price, and sales are split evenly if $P_A = P_B$. We will generalize the demand curve beyond the particular linear one that we assumed in the Cournot model to be any downward-sloping demand curve.

We will look for the Nash equilibrium of the Bertrand model. It turns out that the marginal analysis (marginal revenue equals marginal cost) we used to derive the best-response functions in the Cournot model will not work here since the profit functions are not smooth. Starting from equal prices, if one firm lowers its price by the smallest amount, its sales and profit would essentially double instantly. The model is simple enough that we will be able to jump to the right answer, and then we will spend some time verifying that our jump was in fact correct.

Nash Equilibrium in the Bertrand Model

The only Nash equilibrium in the Bertrand game is for both firms to charge marginal cost: $P_A = P_B = c$. In saying that this is the only Nash equilibrium, we are really making two statements that both need to be verified: (1) that this outcome is a Nash equilibrium, and (2) that there is no other Nash equilibrium.

To verify that this outcome is a Nash equilibrium, we need to show that both firms are playing a best response to each other or, in other words, that neither firm has an incentive to deviate to some other strategy. In equilibrium, firms charge a price equal to marginal cost, which in turn is equal to average cost. But a price equal to average cost means firms earn zero profit in equilibrium. Can a firm earn more than the zero it earns in equilibrium by deviating to some other price? No. If it deviates to a higher price, it will make no sales and therefore no profit, not strictly more than in equilibrium. If it deviates to a lower price, it will make sales but will earn a negative margin on each unit sold since price will be below marginal cost. So the firm will earn negative profit, less than in equilibrium. Because there is no possible profitable deviation for the firm, we have succeeded in verifying that both firms' charging marginal cost is a Nash equilibrium.

To verify that this outcome is the only Nash equilibrium, there are a number of cases to consider. It cannot be a Nash equilibrium for both firms to price above marginal cost. If the prices were unequal, the higher-pricing firm, which would get no demand and thus would earn no profit, would make positive sales and profit by lowering its price to undercut the other. If the above-marginal-cost prices were equal, either firm would have an incentive to deviate. By undercutting the price ever so slightly, price would hardly fall but sales would essentially double because the firm would no longer need to split sales with the other. A Nash equilibrium cannot involve a price less than marginal cost either because the low-price firm would earn negative profit and could gain by deviating to a higher price. For example, it could deviate by raising price to marginal cost, which, since it also equals average cost, would guarantee the firm zero, rather than negative, profit.

MICRO QUIZ 12.2

In showing that no other outcome but marginal cost pricing for both firms is a Nash equilibrium in the Bertrand game, a case was left out. Argue that it cannot be a Nash equilibrium for one firm to charge marginal cost when the other charges something above marginal cost.

Bertrand Paradox

The Nash equilibrium of the Bertrand model is the same as the perfectly competitive outcome. Price is set to marginal cost, and firms earn zero profit. The result that the Nash equilibrium in the Bertrand model is the same as in perfect competition even though there are only two firms in the market is called the Bertrand Paradox. It is paradoxical that competition would be so tough with as few as two firms in the market. In one sense, the Bertrand Paradox is a general result in that we did not specify the marginal cost c or the demand curve, so the result holds for any c and any downward-sloping demand curve.

In another sense, the Bertrand Paradox is not very general; it can be undone by changing any of a number of the model's assumptions. For example, assuming firms choose quantity rather than price leads to the Cournot game, and we saw from our analysis of the Cournot game that firms do not end up charging marginal cost and earning zero profit. The Bertrand Paradox could also be avoided by making other assumptions, including the assumption that the marginal cost is higher for one firm than another, the assumption that products are slightly differentiated rather than being perfect substitutes, or the assumption that firms engage in repeated interaction rather than one round of competition. In the next section, we will see that the Bertrand Paradox can be avoided by assuming firms have capacity constraints rather than the ability to produce an unlimited amount at constant cost c.

Capacity Choice and Cournot Equilibrium

Capacity constraint
A limit to the quantity a firm can produce given the firm's capital and other available inputs.

The assumption that firms do not have **capacity constraints** is crucial for the stark result in the Bertrand model. Starting from equal prices, if a firm lowers its price slightly, its demand essentially doubles. The firm can satisfy this increased demand because it has no capacity constraints, giving firms a big incentive to undercut. If the undercutting firm could not serve all the demand at its lower price because of capacity constraints, that would leave some residual demand for the higher-priced firm, and would decrease the incentive to undercut.

In many settings, it is unrealistic to suppose that a firm can satisfy any number of customers, even if, say, the number of customers that usually showed up were to suddenly double. Consider a two-stage model in which firms build capacity in the first stage and choose prices in the second stage.[5] Firms cannot sell more in the second stage than the capacity built in the first stage. If the cost of building capacity is sufficiently high, it turns out that the subgame-perfect equilibrium of this sequential game leads to the same outcome as the Nash equilibrium of the Cournot model.

To see this result, we will analyze the game using backward induction. Consider the second-stage pricing game supposing the firms have already built capacities $\overline{q}_A$ and $\overline{q}_B$ in the first stage. Let $\overline{P}$ be the price that would prevail when production is at capacity for both firms. A situation in which

$$P_A = P_B < \overline{P} \tag{12.7}$$

is not a Nash equilibrium. At this price, total quantity demanded exceeds total capacity, so firm A could increase its profits by raising price slightly and still selling $\overline{q}_A$. Similarly,

$$P_A = P_B > \overline{P} \tag{12.8}$$

[5]The model is due to D. Kreps and J. Scheinkman, "Quantity Precommitment and Bertrand Competition Yield Cournot Outcomes," *Bell Journal of Economics* (Autumn 1983): 326–337.

is not a Nash equilibrium because now total sales fall short of capacity. At least one firm (say, firm A) is selling less than its capacity. By cutting price slightly, firm A can increase its profits by selling up to its capacity, $\overline{q}_A$. Hence, the Nash equilibrium of this second-stage game is for firms to choose the price at which quantity demanded exactly equals the total capacity built in the first stage:[6]

$$P_A = P_B = \overline{P}. \qquad \textbf{(12.9)}$$

Anticipating that the price will be set such that firms sell all their capacity, the first-stage capacity-choice game is essentially the same as the Cournot game. The equilibrium quantities, price, and profits will thus be the same as in the Cournot game.

The principal lesson of the two-stage capacity/price game is that, even with Bertrand price competition, decisions made prior to this final (price-setting) stage of a game can have an important impact on market behavior. We will see this theme raised several times later in the chapter.

Comparing the Bertrand and Cournot Results

The contrast between the Bertrand and Cournot models is striking. The Bertrand model predicts competitive outcomes in a duopoly situation, whereas the Cournot model predicts prices above marginal cost and positive profits; that is, an outcome somewhere between competition and monopoly. These results suggest that actual behavior in duopoly markets may exhibit a wide variety of outcomes depending on the precise way in which competition occurs. The range of possibilities expands yet further if we add product differentiation or tacit collusion (issues we will study later in the chapter) to the model. Determining the competitiveness of a particular real-world industry is therefore a matter for careful empirical work, as discussed in Application 12.1.

Despite the differences between the Bertrand and Cournot models, the games offer some common insights. Indeed, the equilibrium outcomes from the two games resemble that from the Prisoners' Dilemma. The Nash equilibrium in all three games is not the best outcome for the players. Players could do better if they could cooperate on an outcome with lower outputs in Cournot, higher prices in Bertrand, or being Silent in the Prisoners' Dilemma. But cooperation is not stable because players have an individual incentive to deviate. In equilibrium of both the Cournot and Bertrand games, firms in a sense compete too hard for their own good (to the benefit of consumers, of course).

12-3 Product Differentiation

Up to this point, we have assumed that firms in an imperfectly competitive market all produce the same good. Demanders are indifferent about which firm's output they buy, and the law of one price holds. These assumptions may not be true in many real-world markets. Firms often devote considerable resources to make their products different from their competitors' through such devices as quality and style variations, warranties and guarantees, special service features, and product advertising. These activities require firms to use additional resources, and firms choose to do so if profits are thereby

[6]For completeness, it should be noted that there is no pure-strategy Nash equilibrium of the second-stage game with unequal prices ($P_A \neq P_B$) The low-price firm would have an incentive to raise its price and/or the high-price firm would have an incentive to lower its price. For large capacities, there may be a complicated mixed-strategy Nash equilibrium, but this can be ruled out by supposing the cost of building capacity is sufficiently high.

increased. Product variation also results in a relaxation of the law of one price, since now the market consists of goods that vary from firm to firm and consumers may have preferences about which supplier to patronize.

Market Definition

That possibility introduces a certain fuzziness into what we mean by the "market for a good," since now there are many closely related, but not identical, products. For example, if toothpaste brands vary somewhat from supplier to supplier, should we consider all these products to be in the same market or should we differentiate among fluoridated products, gels, striped toothpaste, smokers' toothpaste, and so forth? Although this question is of great practical importance in industry studies, we do not pursue it here. Instead, we assume that the market is composed of a few slightly differentiated products that can be usefully grouped together because they are more substitutable for each other than for goods outside the group.

Bertrand Model with Differentiated Products

For the moment, we will take as given the products in the product group under consideration and their characteristics. Later, we will analyze the question of how differentiated a firm might want to make its product, including the nature of the product's design, its quality, and how much it is advertised.

One way to model differentiated products is to specify demand curves that are functions of the product's own price and also of the price of the other good. For example, if there are assumed to be two firms, A and B, each producing a single differentiated product, we might have a demand curve for firm A such as

$$q_A = \frac{1}{2} - P_A + P_B \tag{12.10}$$

and for firm B such as

$$q_B = \frac{1}{2} - P_B + P_A. \tag{12.11}$$

A firm's demand is decreasing in its own price and increasing in the price of the other good. For example, the higher firm B's price, the more of its consumers switch over and buy from A. Demand curves such as in Equation 12.10 and Equation 12.11 can be built up from models of individual consumer behavior, as in Application 12.3: Competition on the Beach.

Given the demand curves in Equation 12.10 and Equation 12.11 and some assumptions about costs, we could solve for the Nash equilibrium of a game in which firms choose price simultaneously, that is, a Bertrand game with differentiated, rather than homogeneous, products. With differentiated products, the profit functions are smooth, so one can use marginal analysis to compute the best-response functions, similar to the analysis of the Cournot model. Rather than working through the details of the computations, see Figure 12.3, which shows what the graphical solution for Nash equilibrium tends to look like in the typical Bertrand game

MICRO QUIZ 12.3

1. In Figure 12.3, how would an increase in B's marginal cost shift its best-response function? Would it shift A's? On a graph, indicate where the new Nash equilibrium might be.
2. On a graph, show how the best-response functions would shift and where the new Nash equilibrium would be if both firms' marginal costs increased by the same amount. What about a cost decrease? What about an increase in the demand intercept above 1/2? What about a decrease in substitutability between the two goods?

APPLICATION 12.3

Competition on the Beach

A simple way to model product differentiation is to assume that firms produce identical products but have different locations. Consumers do not like to travel and would pay a premium to buy from the closest firm.

Hotelling's Line

A widely used model of this type is Hotelling's line, shown in Figure 1.[1] Competition occurs along a linear "beach." The two ice cream stands (*A* and *B*) located on this beach will each draw the nearest customers (because ice cream will melt before a buyer gets back to his or her umbrella). Demand curves such as Equations 12.10 and 12.11 can be generated from this model, assuming that the ice cream stands are located at the ends of the beach and assuming the loss to consumers from melting ice cream is a particular value.

Competition between Politicians

While it is interesting to assume firms' locations are given (at the endpoints of the line or elsewhere) and to use the model to analyze price competition between them, the model can also be used to understand where firms will choose to operate. This can be done in a two-stage model in which firms first choose location then choose price. Assuming that price in the second stage is regulated (say the beach town mandates that ice cream be sold for $2 a cone), the Nash equilibrium of the first-stage location game is for both firms to locate right next to each other in the center. Both firms get half of the demand that way. Neither has an incentive to deviate because it would get less than half the demand if it moved.

Figure 1 Hotelling's Beach

Consumers are located uniformly along the line segment from 0 to 1. Firms *A* and *B* locate somewhere within the line segment. A variety of Nash equilibria are possible for this location game, depending on assumptions about the cost of travel for consumers.

This model has been applied to political campaigns. Citizens locate along an ideological spectrum from the political left to right and prefer to vote for the candidate closest to their ideology. Two candidates choose their positions before the election. The fact that the candidates locate in the center in the Nash equilibrium of this game helps explain the observation that candidates tend to "run to the center" as an election progresses.

Television Scheduling

Models like the Hotelling line have been used to study other markets as well. For example, television networks can be thought of as locating their programs in the spectrum of viewer preferences defined along two dimensions—program content and broadcast timing. The Nash-equilibrium locations tend to be at the center—that is, where there are concentrations of consumers with similar tastes—leading to much duplication of both program types and schedule timing. This has left room for specialized cable channels to pick off viewers with special preferences for programs or viewing times. In many cases (for example, the scheduling of sitcoms), these equilibria tend to be rather stable from season to season. Sometimes scheduling can be quite chaotic, however. For example, the scheduling of local news programs tends to fluctuate greatly, each station jockeying to gain only temporary advantage.[2]

TO THINK ABOUT

1. How does a firm's location give it some pricing power among nearby consumers? Would such power exist if the costs of "traveling" were zero?
2. In 1972, the U.S. Federal Trade Commission brought a complaint against Kellogg, General Foods, and General Mills, claiming that their proliferation of breakfast-cereal varieties left no room for the entry of competitors and allowed them to earn near monopoly profits. How might you think about the characteristics of cereal as belonging on a Hotelling line? Explain how the product-proliferation strategy might work.

[1]H. Hotelling, "Stability in Competition," *Economic Journal* (March 1929): 41–57.

[2]For an analysis of why no pure-strategy Nash equilibrium may exist in this situation, see M. Cancian, A. Bills, and T. Bergstrom, "Hotelling Location Problems with Directional Constraints: An Application to Television News Scheduling," *Journal of Industrial Economics* (March 1995): 121–123.

Figure 12.3 Bertrand Model with Differentiated Products

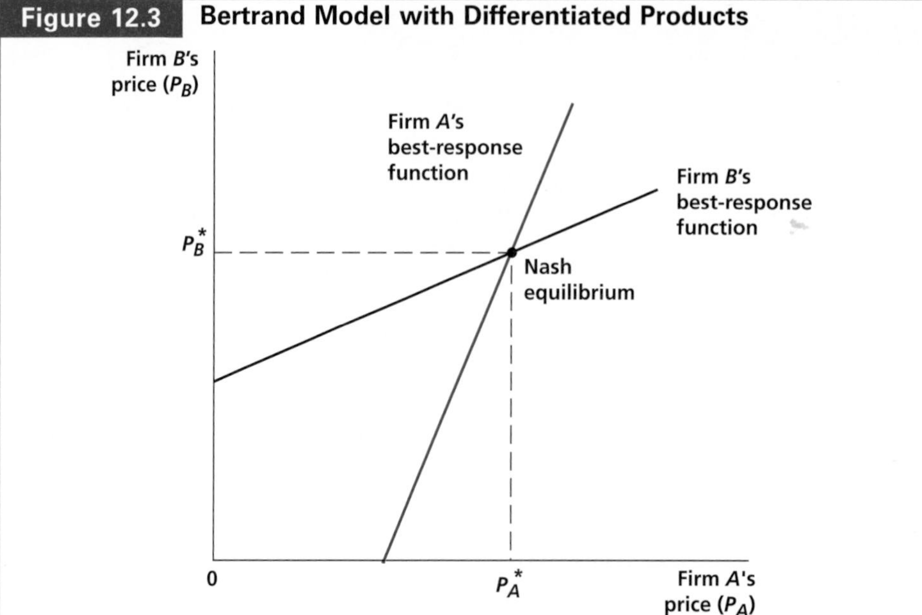

Given demand curves for differentiated products such as Equation 12.10 and Equation 12.11 and given assumptions about costs, one can derive best-response functions such as pictured here. A firm's best-response function gives the profit-maximizing price for a firm given a price charged by its competitor. Best-response functions are upward sloping because *A*, for example, would respond to an increase in *B*'s price, which would raise *A*'s demand, by increasing price. The Nash equilibrium is the point of intersection between the two best-response functions, where *A* sets a price of P_A^* and *B* sets a price of P_B^*.

with differentiated products. The best-response functions show the profit-maximizing price for a firm given a price charged by its competitor. The best-response functions tend to be upward-sloping: an increase in, for example, *B*'s price increases *A*'s demand, which would lead *A* to respond by raising its price. This contrasts with the Cournot case, where the best-response functions were downward sloping (see Figure 12.2). The Nash equilibrium is given by the intersection of the best responses.

Product Selection

The preceding analysis took the products' characteristics as given. But product characteristics—including color, size, functionality, quality of materials, etc.—are strategic choices for the firms just as are price and quantity. Application 12.3: Competition on the Beach suggests one formal way of thinking about a firm's choice of product characteristics. Consider a two-stage game in which firms choose product characteristics in the first stage and price in the second. In the application, a firm's choice of product characteristics is modeled as choosing a location on a Hotelling line (see Figure 1 in the application). Consumers are located along the line. The line can be thought of in the literal sense of differentiation in geographic location. Or it may represent differentiation in product space, for example different points on the color spectrum from red to violet.

There are two offsetting effects at work in the first-stage product-characteristics game. One effect is that firms prefer to locate near the greatest concentration of consumers

Figure 12.4 Increase in Product Differentiation Softens Price Competition

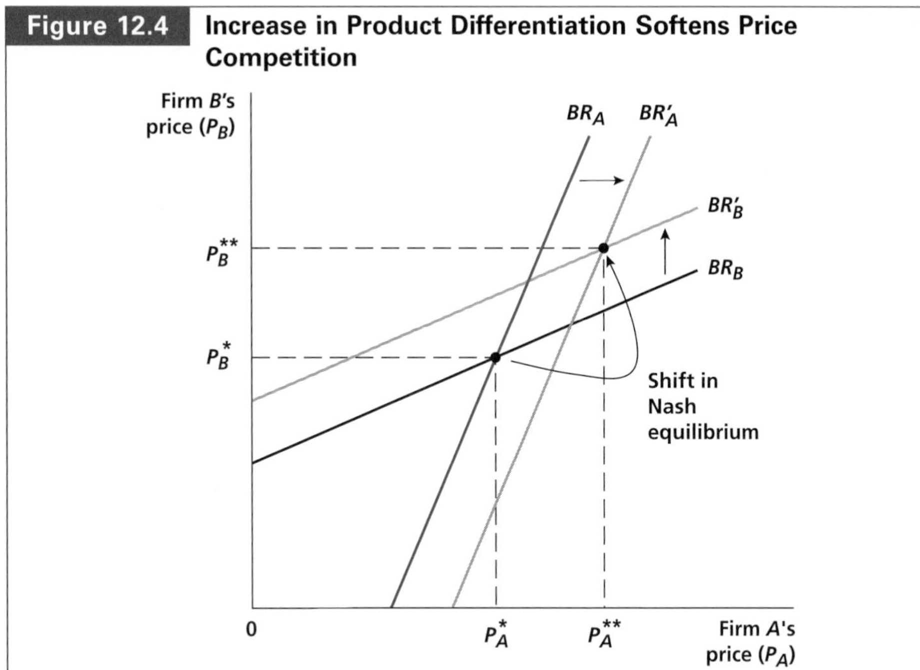

Two firms initially produce moderately differentiated products. The best-response functions for the game involving the simultaneous choice of prices are given by BR_A for A and BR_B for B. If the differentiation between the firms' products is increased, the best-response functions shift out to BR'_A and BR'_B. The Nash equilibrium (bold dot) shifts to one involving higher prices.

because that is where demand is greatest. For example, if consumers' favorite colors are beige and metallic gray automakers will tend to produce beige and metallic-gray cars. This effect leads firms to locate near each other, that is, to produce very similar products. There is an offsetting strategic effect. Firms realize that if their products are close substitutes, they will compete aggressively in the second-stage price game. Locating further apart softens competition, leading to higher prices. This effect is shown in Figure 12.4. An increase in product differentiation between the two firms shifts their best-response functions out and leads to a Nash equilibrium with higher prices for both. Returning to the auto example, if one firm happens to produce mostly sedans, the other might decide to specialize in another niche, say sport-utility vehicles. There may be little substitution between the two auto classes, leaving a firm free to raise prices without fear of losing many customers to its competitor. How the two offsetting effects net out is ambiguous. Depending on the specifics of the market, the subgame-perfect equilibrium of the two-stage game may involve the firms locating close together in some cases and far apart in others.

If firms' products become too specialized, they risk the entry of another firm that might locate in the product space between them. We will take up the question of entry and entry deterrence in a later section.

Search Costs

Prices may differ across goods if products are differentiated. For example, one good may be constructed out of more durable materials than another, and the firm producing the higher-quality good may charge a higher price. Prices may differ even across homogeneous products if consumers are not fully informed about prices. One way to model imperfect price information is to assume that consumers know nothing about the prices any firms charge but can learn about the prices by paying a search cost. A search cost is the cost to the consumer in terms of time, effort, telephone or Internet tolls, and/or fuel costs to contact a store to learn the price it charges for the good. The introduction of search costs is a departure from the analysis in previous chapters, where it was implicitly assumed throughout that all consumers knew the prices for all goods.

There are many possible outcomes, depending on exactly how search costs are specified. An equilibrium that can arise if some consumers have low search costs and others have high search costs is for some firms to specialize in serving the informed (low-search-cost) consumers at low prices and for other firms to specialize in serving the uninformed (high-search-cost) consumers at high prices.[7] The uninformed consumers are "ripped off" in the sense of paying a higher price than they would at another store, but it is simply too costly for them to shop more to learn where the low prices are. Only by luck do some of them end up at a low-price store. How the conclusions of such a model might change with the growing use of the Internet for consumer search is explored in Application 12.4: Searching the Internet.

Advertising

Advertising can be classified into two types. A first type, informative advertising, provides "hard" information about prices, product attributes, and perhaps store locations and hours of operation. Classified ads in newspapers are a good example of this type of advertising. Economists tend to view informative advertising favorably, as a way to lower consumer search costs, increasing transparency and thus firms' competitiveness in the market. A second type of advertising, persuasive advertising, attempts to convince consumers to buy one product rather than another close—perhaps perfect—substitute. Persuasive advertising tends to involve "soft" information, perhaps involving images of attractive people enjoying the product, perhaps leading consumers to make positive associations with the images when they consume the product. Examples include television advertising of lager beers, some of which are chemically almost identical to cheaper, unadvertised beers. Some economists view persuasive advertising less favorably, as a way to soften price competition by increasing apparent rather than real product differentiation. This may provide one rationale for government bans on advertising. However, most studies show that such bans may harm consumers by leading to higher average prices.[8]

One glance at advertising in various media suggests that advertising is an important element of strategic competition between firms. The same strategic effects that arose in our discussion of investments in product differentiation also arise with advertising.

Consider a two-stage model in which firms advertise in the first stage and then compete by choosing prices for differentiated products in the second stage.

1. What strategic effects would come into play if advertising increases the chance that consumers learn about both products rather than just knowing about one or the other?
2. What strategic effects would come into play if advertising persuades consumers that the product occupies a distinct niche?

[7]S. Salop and J. Stiglitz, "Bargains and Ripoffs: A Model of Monopolistically Competitive Price Dispersion," *Review of Economic Studies* (October 1977): 493–510.

[8]See, for example, L. Benham, "The Effects of Advertising on the Price of Eyeglasses," *Journal of Law and Economics* (October 1972): 337–352; and J. Milyo and J. Waldfogel, "The Effect of Price Advertising on Prices: Evidence in the Wake of 44 Liquormart," *American Economic Review* (December 1999): 1081–1096.

APPLICATION 12.4

Searching the Internet

The interplay between the Internet and consumer search costs is complex. On the one hand, the Internet dramatically lowers the cost of getting a price quote. Rather than driving to a store, the consumer can just make a few mouse clicks. In addition, the Internet makes it easier for firms to enter the market, since the cost of setting up a Web site may be lower than a "brick-and-mortar" store. Entry should be expected to increase competitiveness in the market and result in lower prices. There is a wrinkle to this story. Since starting up a store is as easy as setting up a Web site, fly-by-night firms using questionable sales tactics can proliferate because they need to make only a few sales to a few unsuspecting customers to be profitable. Firms can also use Internet technology against consumers to frustrate what should be efficient searches.

Price Dispersion for Books Online

It is hard to imagine a more homogeneous product than a particular book title. Yet studies of Internet bookstores indicate large price differences across retailers. One study found that the difference between the highest and lowest price for *New York Times* bestsellers was around $8, or 65 percent of average price.[1] Large savings were available to consumers who were willing to shop a tone of the alternatives to Amazon and Barnes & Noble, the two largest online bookstores, accounting for 80 percent of online book sales during the period studied (1999–2000). The large price differences may stem from consumers' inability to use price-comparison sites efficiently to find smaller retailers willing to undercut the big bookstores' prices. Or consumers may stick with the large bookstores for fear of being "ripped off" by a retailer with an unknown reputation. As we will see in the discussion of "shady" strategies used by retailers of computer chips, such fears may be well founded.

Bait and Switch for Computer Chips

Ellison and Ellison discuss the example of the sale of computer processors and memory chips sold by retailers listed on various online price-comparison sites.[2] Price was the key advertised element on these sites: firms were listed in order from lowest to highest item price. But other product attributes were not listed there, including shipping costs, warranty and return policies, and product quality. Some retailers were found to have adopted the strategy of listing their low-quality items at very low prices but then trying to get the consumer to trade up to higher-quality substitutes when they clicked through to the retailer's Web site by indicating how lousy the low-quality item was, a sort of bait-and-switch strategy. For those consumers who truly wanted the lowest-quality items, this strategy led to considerable transparency. As a result, these consumers were extremely price sensitive, with estimated price elasticities on the order of −25 or more. Elasticities were less extreme for higher-quality items that required more searching on individual Web sites. Other retailers used the strategy of listing an item for $1 but then adding on a $40 shipping fee. Still other retailers used the strategy of tricking the algorithm used by the price-comparison sites into thinking they had zero prices, thus moving them high up on the list, even though they were actually among the higher-priced retailers.

The strategies for selling computer chips discussed above may be shady but are not illegal. Out-and-out fraud also plagues online shoppers. The most common frauds reported to the U.S. Federal Trade Commission include Internet auction items that are never shipped, "free" Internet access services that lock the consumer into long-term contracts for high fees, and various scams to obtain consumers' credit card and bank account numbers.[3]

TO THINK ABOUT

1. How might a price-comparison Web site earn revenue? What motives would it have to make searches more or less transparent? How could the price-comparison website try to eliminate some of the retailers' obfuscation if it wanted to?
2. Compared to online retailers, "brick-and-mortar" stores have the added expense of the physical space for consumers to see the items sold, but the "touch factor" may be important for consumers' shopping experience. Describe the potential problem raised by cannibalization of sales by online retailers. How might the manufacturer design contracts with online and "brick-and-mortar" retailers to prevent this problem? What are the other relative cost/quality advantages of one form of retailing over the other?

[1]K. Clay, R. Krishnan, and E. Wolff, "Pricing Strategies on the Web: Evidence from the Online Book Industry," *Journal of Industrial Economics* (December 2001): 521–539.
[2]G. Ellison and S. F. Ellison, "Search, Obfuscation and Price Elasticities on the Internet," *Econometrica* (March 2009): 427–452.
[3]U.S. Federal Trade Commission, "*Law Enforcers Target 'Top Ten' Online Scams*," October 31, 2000, http://www.ftc.gov/opa/2000/10/topten.shtm, accessed March 8, 2009.

12-4 Tacit Collusion

We mentioned that the Cournot and Bertrand games bear some resemblance to the Prisoners' Dilemma in that if the firms could cooperate to restrict output or raise prices, they could increase the profits of both, just as the players in the Prisoners' Dilemma would benefit from cooperating on being Silent. In Chapter 5 we concluded that if the Prisoners' Dilemma were repeated an indefinite number of times, the participants can devise ways to adopt more cooperative strategic choices. A similar possibility arises with the Cournot and Bertrand games. Repetition of these games offers a mechanism for the firms to earn higher profits by pursuing a monopoly pricing policy. The reader may want to review the discussion of indefinitely repeated games from Chapter 5 because the following analysis is closely related.

It should be emphasized that here we are adopting a noncooperative approach to the collusion question by exploring models of "tacit" collusion. That is, we use game theory concepts to see whether firms can achieve monopoly profits through *self-enforcing* equilibrium strategies. A contrasting approach would be to assume that firms can form a cartel in which firms are bound to specific outputs and prices by *externally enforced* contracts. Governments have occasionally allowed cartel arrangements to be legally binding, in cases ranging from British shipping cartels in the 1800s to present-day professional sports leagues.[9] Ordinarily, however, such cartels are illegal. In the United States, for example, Section I of the Sherman Act of 1890 outlaws "conspiracies in restraint of trade," so would-be cartel members may expect a visit from law-enforcement officials. Similar laws exist in many other countries. Cartel arrangements may run into the same problems of potential instability as tacitly collusive arrangements, with cartel members secretly trying to chisel on the cartel arrangement when possible. Real-world markets often exhibit aspects of both tacit and explicit collusion, as Application 12.5: The Great Electrical Equipment Conspiracy shows.

To explore the ideas about the stability of collusion more fully (lessons which can be applied to the stability of cartels as well), we will focus on the case of the Bertrand game with homogeneous products (though the Cournot case would provide similar insights). Recall the Nash equilibrium of the game when it was repeated only once was marginal cost pricing for both firms, $P_A = P_B = c$. We will determine the conditions under which the two firms can earn the monopoly profit by tacitly colluding in a repeated game. We will use the subgame-perfect equilibrium concept to make sure collusion is not sustained by threats or promises that are not credible.

Finite Time Horizon

With any definite number of repetitions, the equilibrium is the same as when the game is not repeated. (We found this with the Prisoners' Dilemma in Chapter 5 as well.) Using backward induction to solve for the subgame-perfect Nash equilibrium, no matter how the game was played up to the last period, the players will play the Nash equilibrium $P_A = P_B = c$ in the last period. Promises to play any other way are not credible. Because a similar argument also applies to any period prior to the last one, we can conclude that the only subgame-perfect equilibrium is one in which firms charge the competitive price in every period. The assumptions of the Bertrand model make tacit collusion impossible over any finite period.

---

[9]On shipping cartels, see F. Scott Morton, "Entry and Predation: British Shipping Cartels, 1879–1929," *Journal of Economics and Management Strategy* (Winter 1997): 679–724. Note that even if the cartel arrangements are not legally binding, they may be enforced with threats of violence, as with illegal drug cartels.

APPLICATION 12.5

The Great Electrical Equipment Conspiracy

Even though an industry may be reasonably profitable, the lure of monopoly profits may tempt it to create cartels. The lure is especially strong when there are relatively few firms and when one member of the cartel can easily police what the other members are doing. This was the case with the electrical equipment industry in the early 1950s, when it developed an elaborate price-rigging scheme. However, the scheme came under both increasing internal friction and external legal scrutiny. By the 1960s, the scheme had failed, and executives of several major companies had been imprisoned.[1]

The Markets for Generators and Switch Gear

Electric turbine generators and high-voltage switching units are sold to electric utility companies. Often they are customized to unique specifications and can cost many millions of dollars. With the rapid growth in the use of electricity after World War II, manufacturing this machinery provided a very lucrative business to such major producers as General Electric, Westinghouse, and Federal Pacific Corporations. Although these growth prospects promised good profits for the large firms in the business, the possibility of forming a cartel to raise prices and profits proved to be even more enticing.

The Bid-Rigging Scheme

The principal problem faced by the electrical equipment firms seeking to create a cartel was that most of their sales took place through sealed bidding to large electric utilities. To avoid competition, they therefore had to devise a method for coordinating the bids each firm would make. Through a complex strategy that involved dividing the United States into bidding regions and using the lunar calendar to decide whose turn it was to "win" a bid in a region, the firms were able to overcome the secrecy supposedly guaranteed by submitting sealed bids. The practice worked quite well until the end of the decade. It probably increased total profits of electrical equipment manufacturers by as much as $100 million over the period.

Demise of the Conspiracy

Toward the end of the 1950s, the electrical equipment conspiracy came under increasing internal friction as its leaders (General Electric and Westinghouse) were asked to give a greater share of the business to other firms. New entries into the industry by importers and low-cost domestic producers also caused some problems for the cartel. The final blow to the conspiracy came when a newspaper reporter discovered that some of the bids on Tennessee Valley Authority projects were suspiciously similar. His discovery led to a series of widely publicized hearings led by Senator Estes Kefauver in 1959. These resulted in the federal indictment of 52 executives of the leading generator, switch gear, and transformer companies. Although the government recommended prison sentences for 30 of these defendants, only 7 actually served time in jail. Still, the notoriety of the case and the personal disruption it caused to those involved probably had a chilling effect on the future establishment of other cartels of this type.

Though the electrical equipment manufacturers never again formed an explicit cartel, it appears that they took steps to collude tacitly. Tacit collusion is easier if prices are transparent and goods relatively standardized, for then it is easier for firms to have a common understanding about which prices are acceptable and which are so unacceptably low that should be punished with a price war. To get around the problem that electrical equipment was not standardized and prices were not transparent, General Electric published a simplified formula for calculating the price it would charge as a function of product attributes. Soon after, Westinghouse settled on an identical pricing formula that resulted in identical bids by the two firms for over a decade.[2]

TO THINK ABOUT

1. Why did the electrical equipment manufacturers opt for an illegal bid-rigging scheme rather than settling for some other form of tacit collusion? What about the nature of transactions in this business made the explicit price-fixing solution a necessary one? Would tacit collusion have worked?
2. Prosecution of the electrical equipment conspirators was one of the few cases of a successful "cops and robbers" approach to antitrust law. It involved wire tapping, government informers, and so forth to collect evidence on the illegal behavior of the executives. How would the evidence differ if this had been a case of tacit collusion?

[1]For a popularized and somewhat sensationalized version of this episode, see J. G. Fuller, *The Gentlemen Conspirators* (New York: Grove Press, 1962).
[2]See F. M. Scherer, *Industrial Market Structure and Economic Performance*, 2nd ed. (Boston: Houghton Mifflin, 1980), for a more detailed account.

Indefinite Time Horizon

If firms are viewed as having an indefinite time horizon, matters change significantly. As in Chapter 5, let g be the probability that the game is repeated for another period and $1 - g$ is the probability that the game ends for good after the current period. Thus, the probability that the game lasts at least one period is 1, at least two periods is g, at least three periods is g^2, and so forth.

With an indefinite number of periods, there is no "final" period for backward induction to unravel collusive strategies. Consider the trigger strategies in which each firm sets the monopoly price P_M in every period unless a firm has undercut this price previously. If any firm has undercut, they enter a price-war phase in which they set price to marginal cost c from then on. The threat of charging marginal cost for the rest of the game is credible, since this is equivalent to playing the Nash equilibrium of the one-period game over and over. To show that the proposed trigger strategies constitute a subgame-perfect equilibrium, it remains only to show that no firm has an incentive to undercut the collusive price P_M in a given period. Suppose firm A thinks about cheating in a given period. Knowing that firm B will choose $P_B = P_M$, A can set its price slightly below P_M and, in this period, obtain the entire market for itself. It will thereby earn (almost) the entire monopoly profit (π_M) in this period but will earn nothing in subsequent periods since undercutting will trigger a price war with marginal-cost prices. If instead of deviating firm A continues with the collusive equilibrium, it earns its share of the monopoly profit ($\pi_M/2$) in all future periods. Accounting for the probabilities of reaching these future periods, a firm's expected stream of profits in the collusive equilibrium is

$$\left(\frac{\pi_M}{2}\right)(1 + g + g^2 + \cdots) = \left(\frac{\pi_M}{2}\right)\left(\frac{1}{1-g}\right), \quad \textbf{(12.12)}$$

where the equality holds by a standard result on simplifying infinite series.[10] Undercutting will be unprofitable if

$$\pi_M < \left(\frac{\pi_M}{2}\right)\left(\frac{1}{1-g}\right). \quad \textbf{(12.13)}$$

This condition holds for sufficiently high g, namely $g \geq 1/2$. Another way to see this condition is to think about g as a measure of firms' patience. The more likely the game will continue into the future, the more firms are willing to forgo immediate payoffs for the prospect of future payoffs. The more patient firms are, the more severe is the punishment for undercutting (in the form of lost future profits from cooperating) relative to the short-term gain from undercutting. Condition 12.13 says in effect that firms have to be patient enough to sustain collusion.

In addition to the probability that the market continues into the future, another factor affecting firms' patience is the interest rate. The higher the interest rate, the more valuable are payoffs earned in the current period relative to future periods because current payoffs can be invested, providing a high return. Firms would then be less patient to wait for future payoffs.

The sort of collusion using trigger strategies we have been discussing is tacit: firms never actually have to meet in the proverbial "smoke-filled room." Collusion is also self-enforcing: firms do not need an external authority to enforce the outcome.

[10]Footnote 4 in Chapter 5 showed that $g + g^2 + g^3 + g + \cdots = g/(1-g)$. The series here is 1 more than that series: $1 + g + g^2 + \cdots = 1 + g/(1-g) = 1/(1-g)$.

Generalizations and Limitations

It is straightforward to extend the analysis to allow for any number of firms, N. The profit from deviating would be the same as before, π_M. The present profit from continuing with the collusive equilibrium from Equation 12.12 becomes

$$\left(\frac{\pi_M}{N}\right)\left(\frac{1}{1-g}\right) \quad (12.14)$$

because in equilibrium with N firms, each firm only obtains $1/N$ of the monopoly profit. Thus the new condition for cheating to be unprofitable becomes

$$\pi_M < \left(\frac{\pi_M}{N}\right)\left(\frac{1}{1-g}\right), \quad (12.15)$$

which holds for $g > 1 - 1/N$. The higher N is, the less likely it is for the continuation probability, g, to satisfy the condition (Equation 12.15). Therefore, an increase in the number of firms makes it harder to sustain tacit collusion. What is bad for firms is good for consumers and society, since, if firms cannot tacitly collude, they will charge lower prices, raising consumer surplus and social welfare. This provides additional justification for antitrust authorities to prevent mergers where they think collusion might be a possibility.

The contrast between the competitive results of the Bertrand model and the monopoly results of the tacit-collusion model suggests that the viability of collusion in game-theory models is very sensitive to the particular assumptions made. It was assumed that a firm can easily detect whether another has cheated. In practice, however, the deviator may cut price secretly, and other buyers may not learn about the deviation until much later. In the model, a lag in detection is similar to increasing the period length, which in turn is similar to reducing the probability, g, that the game continues (because the probability that the game ends compounds over time). It is easy to see from the condition in Equation 12.13 that increasing the interest rate reduces the right-hand side and therefore makes collusion harder to sustain. Other firms may only learn about the price cut indirectly, perhaps because they see their own demands have fallen. To deter cheating in this case, firms may have to enter into price wars in demand downturns even if no firm has actually cheated.

If firms compete in quantities as in the Cournot model, or if firms produce differentiated rather than homogeneous products, the equation determining whether collusion can be sustained is slightly different from Equation 12.13. The profit from deviating on the left-hand side of 12.13 may not be as high because the deviator cannot capture the whole market with a tiny price cut. This effect would make collusion easier. The lost profits from punishment on the right-hand side of 12.13 may not be as severe because firms still earn positive profits in the Nash equilibrium they revert to following a deviation. This effect would make collusion harder. The two effects work in opposite directions, so whether collusion is easier or harder to sustain with quantity competition or with differentiated products compared to the basic Bertrand model is ambiguous.

Other categories of models have the two firms competing in several different markets. For example, two airlines might compete on a number of different city-pair routes. If collusion is harder to sustain on some routes than others, say, because there is less information on some routes about competitors' prices, the threat of a price war on all routes for undercutting on one may allow them to leverage the collusion that is easily sustained in some markets to the others.

As might be imagined, results from the wide variety of models of tacit collusion are quite varied.[11] In all such models, the notions of Nash and subgame-perfect equilibria continue to play an important role in identifying whether tacit collusion can arise from strategic choices that appear to be viable.

12-5 Entry and Exit

The possibility of new firms entering an industry plays an important part in the theory of perfectly competitive price determination. Free entry ensures that any long-run profits are eliminated by new entrants and that firms produce at the low points of their long-run average cost curves. With relatively few firms, the first of these forces continues to operate. To the extent that entry is possible, long-run profits are constrained. If entry is completely costless, long-run economic profits are zero (as in the competitive case).

The treatment of entry and exit in earlier chapters left little room for strategic thinking. A potential entrant was concerned only with the relationship between prevailing market price and its own (average or marginal) costs. We assumed that making that comparison involved no special problems. Similarly, we assumed that firms will promptly leave a market they find to be unprofitable. Upon closer inspection, however, the entry and exit issue can become considerably more complex. The fundamental problem is that a firm wishing to enter or exit a market must make some conjecture about how its action will affect market price in subsequent periods. Making these conjectures obviously requires the firm to consider what its rivals will do. What appears to be a relatively straightforward decision, comparing price and average cost, may therefore involve a number of strategic ploys, especially when a firm's information about its rivals is imperfect.

Sunk Costs and Commitment

Many game-theory models of the entry process stress the importance of a firm's commitment to a specific market. If the nature of production requires that firms make specific capital investments in order to operate in a market and if these cannot easily be shifted to other uses, any firm that makes such investments has committed itself to being a market participant. As we saw in Chapter 7, expenditures on such investments are called *sunk costs.* Sunk costs might include expenditures on items such as unique types of equipment (for example, a newsprint-making machine) or on job-specific training for workers (developing the skills to use the newsprint machine). Sunk costs have many characteristics of fixed costs in that these costs are incurred even if no output is produced. Rather than being incurred periodically as are many fixed costs (heating the factory), these costs are incurred only once, as part of the entry process. More generally, any "sunk" decision is a decision that cannot be reversed later. When the firm makes such a decision, it has made a commitment in the market, which may have important consequences for its strategic behavior.

First-Mover Advantages

Although at first glance it might seem that incurring sunk costs by making the commitment to serve a market puts a firm at a disadvantage, in many models that is not the case. Rather, one firm can often stake out a claim to a market by making a commitment to serve it and in the process limit the kinds of actions its rivals find profitable. Many game-theory models, therefore, stress the advantage of moving first.

[11]See J. Tirole, *Theory of Industrial Organization* (Cambridge, MA: MIT Press, 1988), chap. 6.

As a simple numerical example, consider again the Cournot model introduced earlier, wherein two springs can produce water costlessly and face market demand given by $Q = 120 - P$ (see Equation 12.1). We found that the Nash equilibrium quantities were 40 (thousand gallons) each, and firms each earned \$1,600. Suppose now, instead, that firm A has the option of moving first and committing to an output which B observes before B moves. We will use backward induction to solve for the subgame-perfect equilibrium of this sequential game. We thus solve for B's equilibrium strategy first. Firm B will maximize profits given what A has done. We have solved for this best-response function already, in Equation 12.6, repeated here for reference:

$$q_B = \frac{120 - q_A}{2}. \tag{12.16}$$

Firm A can use this to compute the net demand for its own spring's water:

$$q_A = 120 - q_B - P = 120 - \left(\frac{120 - q_A}{2}\right) - P = 60 + \frac{q_A}{2} - P. \tag{12.17}$$

Solving for P gives

$$P = 60 - \frac{q_A}{2}. \tag{12.18}$$

Given this expression for A's inverse demand curve, it can be shown,[12] or taken as given, that A's marginal revenue curve is

$$60 - q_A. \tag{12.19}$$

Firm A maximizes its profit by choosing the quantity at which its marginal revenue in Equation 12.19 equals its marginal cost (recall 0 because production is costless), resulting in an output of $q_A = 60$. Given that firm A's output is 60, firm B chooses to produce

$$q_B = \frac{120 - q_A}{2} = \frac{120 - 60}{2} = 30. \tag{12.20}$$

With total output of 90, spring water sells for \$30, firm A's total profit is \$1,800 ($= 60 \times \$30$)—an improvement over the \$1,600 it earned in the Nash equilibrium of the Cournot model. Firm B's profit has correspondingly been reduced to \$900—a sign of the disadvantage faced by a later mover. Sometimes this solution is referred to as a **Stackelberg equilibrium**, after the economist who first discovered the advantage of moving first in the sequential version of the Cournot model.

Stackelberg Equilibrium
Subgame-perfect equilibrium of the sequential version of the Cournot game.

Consider Figure 12.5, which reproduces the best-response functions from Figure 12.2. If A gets to move first—knowing that B will choose a best response to its output and thus that the equilibrium point will be somewhere on B's best-response function—A chooses the point that maximizes A's profit. This point, the Stackelberg equilibrium, involves higher output for firm A than in the Nash equilibrium of the Cournot game. Firm A's benefit from being the first mover is that by committing to a higher output, A induces B to reduce its output, and a lower output for B benefits A because price will be higher. The Stackelberg equilibrium is only feasible if A's output decision is sunk, that is, irreversibly made, and observable to B before B moves. It is only because A's decision is sunk that it is allowed to commit to an action that is not on its own best-response function. If A could not commit in this way, the outcome would return to the Nash equilibrium from the Cournot game, with both firms producing 40.

---

[12]Firm A's total revenue function is $P \cdot q_A = (60 - q_A/2) \cdot q_A = 60q_A - q_A^2/2$. Differentiating this expression with respect to q_A gives the marginal revenue function $60 - q_A$.

Figure 12.5 Stackelberg Equilibrium and Entry Deterrence

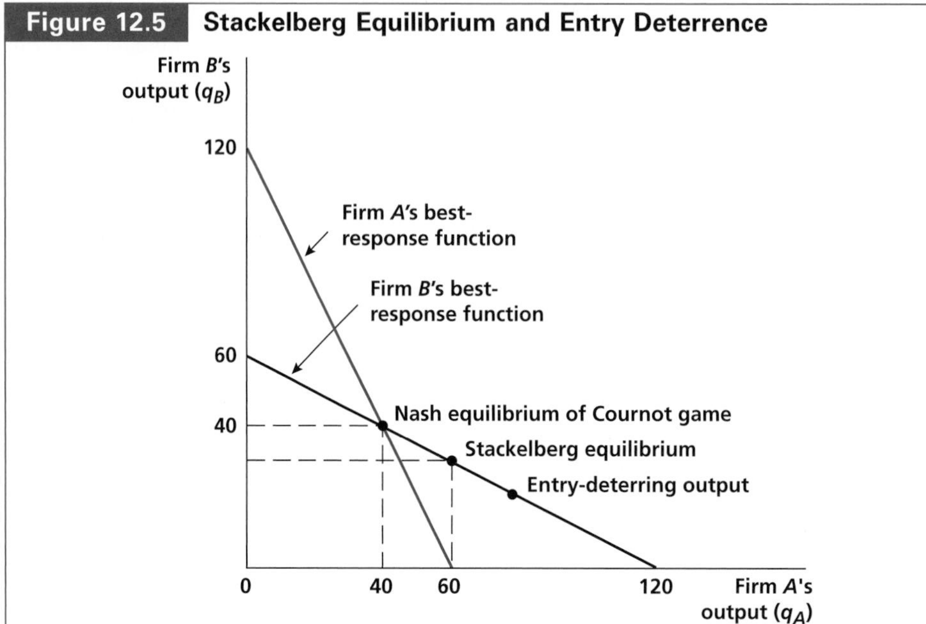

If firm A gets to move first, it effectively gets to choose a point on firm B's best-response function. Firm A will choose the point that maximizes its profit, the point labeled "Stackelberg equilibrium" involving $q_A = 60$. Increasing its output from the Cournot level to the Stackelberg level reduces B's profit. Firm A may wish to commit to an even higher output than in the Stackelberg equilibrium if this reduces B's anticipated profits below its fixed entry cost and thus deters B's entry.

Entry Deterrence

In some cases, first-mover advantages may be large enough to deter all entry by rivals. It seems plausible that the first mover could opt for a very large capacity and thereby discourage all other firms from entering the market. The economic rationality of such a decision is not clear-cut, however. In the Cournot model, for example, the only sure way for one spring owner to deter all entry is to satisfy the total market demand at the firm's marginal and average costs; that is, firm A would have to offer $q_A = 120$, resulting in a price of zero, if it were to have a fully successful entry-deterrence strategy. Obviously, such a choice results in zero profits for the firm and would not be profit maximizing. Instead, it would be better for firm A to accept some entry.

With economies of scale in production, the possibility for profitable entry deterrence is increased. If the firm that is to move first can adopt a large enough scale of operation, it may be able to limit the scale of the potential entrant. The potential entrant will therefore experience such high average costs that there would be no way for it to earn a profit.

A Numerical Example

The simplest way to incorporate economies of scale into the Cournot model is to assume each spring owner must pay a fixed cost of operations. If that fixed cost is given by \$785 (a carefully chosen number!), firm B would still find it attractive to enter if firm A moves first and opts to produce $q_A = 60$. In this case, firm B would earn profits of \$115 (= \$900 − \$785) per period. However, if the first mover opts for $q_A = 64$, this would force firm B to choose

$qB = 28$ [$= (120 - 64) \div 2$]. At this combined output of 92, price would be \$28 and firm *B* would make negative profits [profits $= TR - TC = (28 \cdot 28) - 785 = -1$] and choose not to enter. Firm *A* would now have the market to itself, obtain a price of \$56 ($= 120 - 64$), and earn profits of \$2,799 [$= (56 \cdot 64) - 785$]. Economies of scale, combined with the ability to move first, provide firm *A* with a very profitable entry-deterring strategy. For this strategy to work, *A* must be able to make its sunk output decision before *B* makes its sunk entry decision.

MICRO QUIZ 12.5

1. In the numerical example, suppose *B*'s entry costs were \$700 rather than \$785. How would this affect A's entry-deterring strategy?
2. Suppose *B*'s entry costs were \$910. How would this affect *A*'s entry-deterring strategy?

Limit Pricing

So far, our discussion of strategic considerations in entry decisions has focused on issues of sunk costs and output commitments. A somewhat different approach to the entry-deterrence question concerns the possibility that an incumbent monopoly could deter entry through its pricing policy alone. That is, are there situations where a monopoly might purposely choose a low ("limit") price with the goal of deterring entry into its market?

In most simple cases, the answer is no. The crucial issue is that prices are not usually "sunk." Prices are changed daily or even more frequently in some markets: for example, airlines change their fares on a minute-by-minute basis depending on seat availability. The price charged in one period may have no bearing on the price charged in later periods. If there is no link between the prices charged in different periods, there is no reason for an incumbent monopolist to limit its price before entry since setting a limit price $P_L < P_M$ (where P_M is the monopolist's profit-maximizing price) only reduces its current-period profits without any later strategic benefit.[13]

In richer models, there may be reasons why prices may be related across time. First, if prices are set in a national advertising campaign, it may be difficult to change prices quickly afterward. For example, a camera manufacturer that advertises in a monthly magazine such as *Popular Photography* may find it difficult to change its price and advertise this price change within the month. Second, firms may face a learning curve, whereby costs fall with accumulated production as workers figure out how to produce more efficiently through experience. In the first study to quantify the learning curve, the cost of producing military aircraft during World War II was found to fall by 20 percent for every doubling of output.[14] In the presence of a learning curve, a monopolist can reduce its costs by charging a low price and producing a lot initially, and thus be in a position to be an aggressive, low-cost competitor when potential entrants arrive, making entry for them less appealing. Third, there may be costs for consumers to switch between suppliers.

Consumers having had a good experience with one product may be reluctant to switch to a product of uncertain quality. Consumers may have signed long-term contracts to stay with a certain supplier, as is the case with many cell phone plans. It may

[13]An influential model that can be viewed as an attempt to formalize the limit-pricing story is contestability. According to this model, a market is in equilibrium if incumbents at least break even at the current price and there is no possibility for another firm to make positive profits by entering at a slightly lower price. Incumbents are forced to charge limit prices to prevent entry, sometimes as low as average cost (thus earning zero profit). The implicit assumption that incumbents are forced to maintain the same price before and after entry may be difficult to justify.

[14]T. P. Wright, "Factors Affecting the Cost of Airplanes," *Journal of Aeronautical Sciences* (February 1936): 122–128.

simply be a nuisance to contact the old and new suppliers to make the switch. In the presence of such switching costs, the monopolist may build a large customer base initially through low prices, making entry harder because the entrant may have to offer deep discounts to induce the incumbent's "captive" base of consumers to switch.

Asymmetric Information

A fourth reason why initial prices may have a strategic effect is that a monopolist may know more about a particular market situation than does a potential entrant, and it may be able to take advantage of its superior knowledge to deter entry. As an example, consider the extensive form illustrated in Figure 12.6. Here, firm *A*, the incumbent monopolist, has an equal chance of having high or low production costs as a result of its past investments and luck. Firm *A* knows its own costs but *B* does not. The profitability of *B*'s entry into the market depends on *A*'s costs—with high costs, *B*'s entry is profitable ($\pi_B = 3$); whereas, if *A* has low costs, entry is unprofitable ($\pi_B = -1$). The situation is said to involve **asymmetric information**, that is, at least one of the players is not certain what the payoffs in the game are. We will study games of asymmetric information in more detail in Chapter 15. For now, note that the convention in games of incomplete information is to add a third player, "Nature," who chooses *A*'s costs at random.

Asymmetric information
One player has information about payoffs in the game that another does not.

What is *B* to do? Without any further information, using the formula for expected values from Chapter 5, *B*'s expected profit from entering equals the probability *A*'s costs are high (1/2) times *B*'s profit from entering if *A*'s costs are high (3), plus the probability *A*'s costs are low (1/2) times *B*'s profit from entering if *A*'s costs are low (−1), for a total expected profit of $(1/2)(3) + (1/2)(-1) = 1$. Since 1 exceeds what *B* would earn if it didn't enter (0), *B* will enter if it does not have further information about *A*'s costs.

The particularly intriguing aspects of this game concern whether *A* can influence *B*'s assessment. If *A*'s costs are low, it would like to tell *B* this and have *B* not enter, since

Figure 12.6 Entry Game with Asymmetric Information

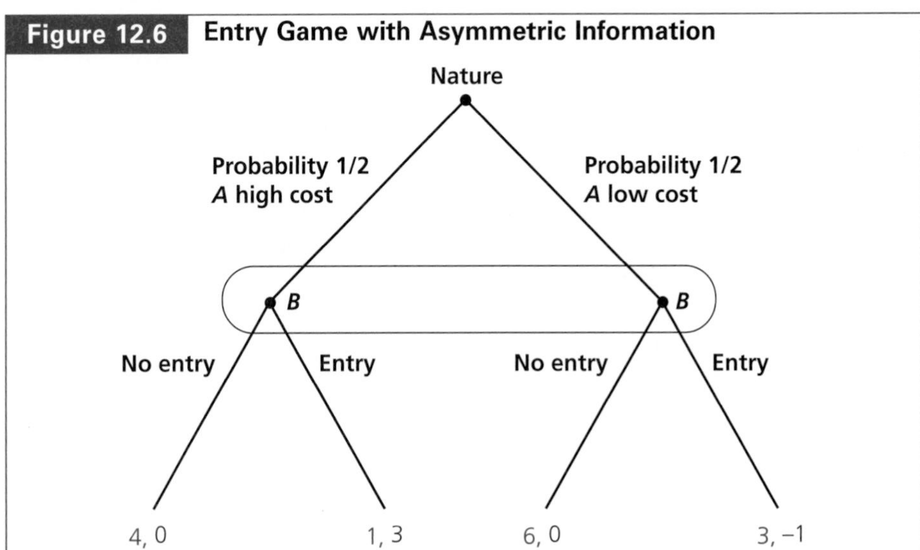

Firm *A* has high or low costs chosen by "Nature" with equal probability. Firm *B* cannot observe *A*'s costs. Firm *B* makes positive profit from entering if *A* is high cost and negative profit if *A* is low cost. Firm *B* will enter if it obtains no further information about *A*'s costs. Firm *A* may try to signal its costs are low by charging a low price to deter *B*'s entry.

A is better off if *B* does not enter. The difficulty is that even when *A*'s costs are high, *A* would like to deter *B*'s entry by lying and saying its costs are low. Firm *B* should not believe *A*'s claim that its costs are low if there is nothing to back the claim up. Charging a low price initially might be a more credible signal. The price would have to be low enough to keep a high-cost *A* from pretending to be low cost. That is, the loss to the high-cost *A* from charging the low price (rather than its monopoly price) would exceed the gain from deterring *B*'s entry by misleading *B* into thinking that its costs were low. Such a signaling strategy would require the low-cost *A* to sacrifice some profits initially, but deterring *B*'s entry may be worth it. This provides a possible rationale for setting a low price as an entry-deterrence strategy.

Predatory Pricing

Predatory pricing
An incumbent's charging a low price in order to induce the exit of a rival.

Tools used to study limit pricing can also shed light on the possibility for **predatory pricing**. The difference between limit pricing and predatory pricing is in a sense semantic: limit pricing is a strategy to deter entry of rivals that have not yet entered, while predatory pricing is a strategy to induce exit of rivals that have already entered. Ever since the formation of the Standard Oil monopoly in the late nineteenth century, part of the mythology of American business is that John D. Rockefeller was able to drive his competitors out of business by charging ruinously low (predatory) prices. Although both the economic logic and the empirical facts behind this version of the Standard Oil story have generally been discounted (see Application 12.6: The Standard Oil Legend), the possibility of encouraging exit through predation continues to provide interesting opportunities for theoretical modeling.

The structure of some models of predatory behavior is similar to that used in limit-pricing models. That is, the incumbent tries to signal its rival that market conditions are unfavorable, deterring entry of a potential competitor in the case of limit pricing and inducing the exit of a rival with predatory pricing. With predatory pricing, the incumbent may, for example, adopt a low-price policy in an attempt to signal to its rival that its costs are low or that market demand is weak. Once the rival is convinced of these market conditions, it may recalculate the expected profitability of continued operations and decide to exit the market.

Such models of predatory pricing may be less plausible than the related limit-pricing models. Predatory pricing requires the rival to have been participating in the market, during which time it could have learned about market conditions and be less subject to incomplete information than an entrant in a limit-pricing model. Another class of models that may be more plausible has firms investing continually to remain in the market. Firms that lack the resources to invest are forced to exit the market. In this setting, the incumbent has an incentive to use low prices to "beat up" its rival in order to exhaust any resources it may have available to invest. As with all predatory strategies, the incumbent sacrifices current profits for long-term gains anticipated when the rival exits. A subtle question is why the rival cannot borrow money from a bank or other financier as a commitment to stay in the market during the predatory episode, deterring predation by convincing the incumbent that predation will not induce the rival's exit. Economists have shown that if there is asymmetric information on the financial market, that is, banks or other financiers do not have perfect information, say about a firm's prospects or effort in turning a profit, the firm may have difficulty borrowing an unlimited amount from a bank or other financier and predation may be a viable strategy. Asymmetric information is a crucial element of most models of predatory pricing, whether the asymmetric information is associated with the market in which the entrant sells the good or the market in which the entrant borrows money.

APPLICATION 12.6

The Standard Oil Legend

The Standard Oil case of 1911 was one of the landmarks of U.S. antitrust law. In that case, John D. Rockefeller's Standard Oil Company was found to have "attempted to monopolize" the production, refining, and distribution of petroleum in the United States, violating the Sherman Act. One of the ways that Standard Oil was found to have established its monopoly was through the use of predatory pricing. The government claimed that the company would cut prices dramatically to drive rivals out of a particular market and then raise prices back to monopoly levels after the rivals had left the market or had sold out to Standard Oil. This view of how Standard Oil operated was promoted by the muckraker author Ida Tarbell and became one of the more durable beliefs about nineteenth-century business practices.[1]

Theory of Predatory Pricing

The economic theory behind the notion that Standard Oil engaged in predatory pricing is much less clear than the muckrakers' strong rhetoric. Economists have offered several rationalizations for predatory pricing, some discussed in the text. First, the predator may wish to signal to rivals that competition will be so tough, say because its costs are so low, that continuing in the market will be unprofitable for them. Such an argument requires rivals to lack knowledge about market conditions that they may reasonably be supposed to have.

Second, a would-be monopolist may wish to force smaller rivals to exit by exhausting their resources. Assuming the predatory firm is not much more efficient than rival firms, in order to cause them to earn negative profits, it must sell its output below average cost, perhaps below marginal cost. It must also be willing to absorb the extra sales that such lowered prices would bring. The predator must, therefore, operate with relatively large losses for some time in the hope that the smaller losses this may cause rivals will eventually prompt them to give up. It is unclear that the predator has longer staying power than its rivals in sticking to a low-price policy—especially since rivals know that price must eventually return to a normal, profitable level. It is also unclear that the predatory firm would prefer to force smaller rivals to exit rather than simply buying them in the marketplace.

Third, the firm may wish to establish a reputation for being a predator. By preying on existing rivals, the firm sacrifices current profits in return for the long-run benefit of scaring off future entrants. This theory requires entrants to believe there is at least a small chance that the predator does not sacrifice current profits when it preys. As above, such an argument requires rivals to lack knowledge about the market that they may reasonably be supposed to have.

Actual Evidence on Standard Oil

Suspicious that the economic arguments were not as strong as the muckraking rhetoric, J. S. McGee reexamined the historical record of what Standard Oil actually did. In a famous 1958 article, McGee concluded that Standard Oil neither tried to use predatory policies nor did its actual price policies have the effect of driving rivals from the oil business.[2] McGee examined over 100 refineries that were bought by Standard Oil between 1871 and 1900. He found no evidence that predatory behavior by Standard Oil caused these firms to sell out. Indeed, in many cases Standard paid quite good prices for these refineries, which themselves were reasonably profitable. McGee also looked in detail at the effect that Standard Oil's retailing activities had on the network of jobbers and small retailers who had grown up around the oil and kerosene business in the late nineteenth century. It seems clear that Standard's retailing methods were superior to those used previously (and were quickly adopted by other firms). The use of local price cutting does not seem to have been practiced by the company, however. Hence, although Standard Oil did eventually obtain an oil-refining monopoly, which probably required some attention by policy makers, it did not appear to attain this position through predatory behavior.

TO THINK ABOUT

1. If the facts do not support the notion of predatory pricing by Standard Oil, why do you think the company is so widely believed to have practiced it? What kinds of market-wide trends were influencing oil pricing during the late nineteenth century? Might these have been mistaken for predatory behavior?
2. Another claim in the Standard Oil case is that Rockefeller obtained preferential rates from railroads to transport oil. Why might railroads have granted such rates to Rockefeller? Would they have an interest in refusing such rates to other shippers?

[1]The antagonistic relationship between Tarbell and Rockefeller had a major impact on the early regulation of American business. For a discussion, see the excellent biography by R. Chernow, *Titan: The Life of John D. Rockefeller* (New York: Random House, 1998).

[2]J. S. McGee, "Predatory Price Cutting: The Standard Oil Case," *Journal of Law and Economics* (October 1958): 137–169.

12-6 Other Models of Imperfect Competition

As should be clear from the analysis so far in this chapter, analyzing a full-blown game-theory model in which prices, output, product characteristics, entry, and exit are all strategic variables can become quite complicated. Economists have tried to simplify the analysis by coming up with shorthand models that focus on some strategic considerations and assume away others. We already studied the most famous shorthand model without thinking of it in these terms: perfect competition. It is not literally true, for example, that firms are price takers. If in an extreme case a firm were to increase its output a millionfold, this output change would probably start to have an impact on market price. A millionfold increase is out of the realm of possibility for small firms in perfectly competitive markets, so the assumption of price-taking behavior is probably not unreasonable. To aid the study of imperfect competition, economists have proposed some shorthand models that combine elements of perfect competition with elements of monopoly and oligopoly. Such models have proved useful in various applications, and so we study them now.

Price Leadership

The first shorthand model of imperfect competition we will study is the **price-leadership model**. This model resembles many real-world situations. In some markets, one firm or group of firms is looked upon as the leader in pricing, and all firms adjust their prices to what this leader does. Historical illustrations of this kind of behavior include the leadership of U.S. Steel Corporation during the early post-World War II period and the pricing "umbrella" of IBM in the formative years of the computer industry.

Price-leadership model
A model with one dominant firm that behaves strategically and a group of small firms that behave as price takers.

A formal model of pricing in a market dominated by a leading firm is presented in Figure 12.7. The industry is assumed to be composed of a single price-setting leader and

Figure 12.7 Formal Model of Price-Leadership Behavior

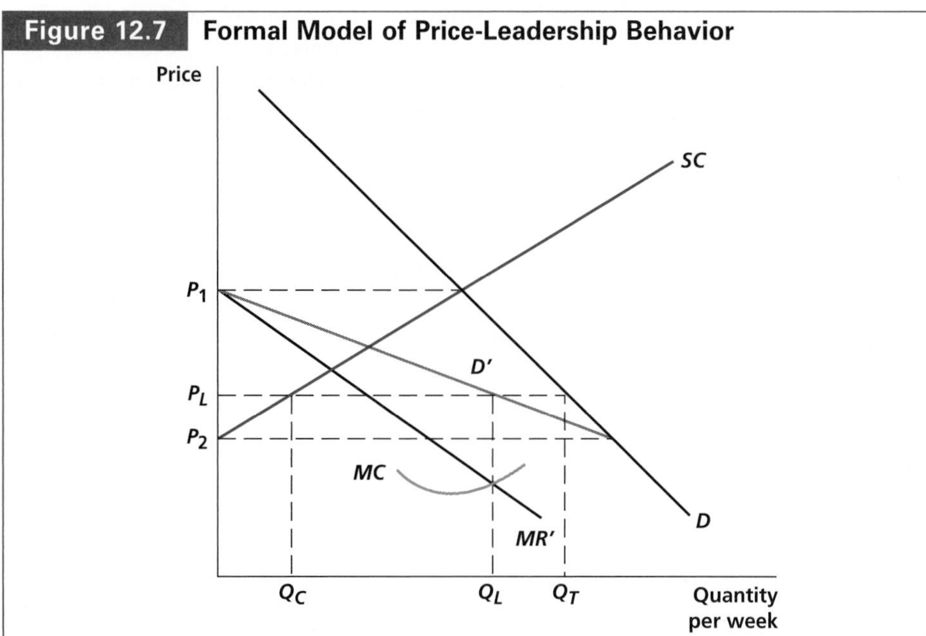

The curve D' shows the residual demand curve facing the price leader. It is derived by subtracting what is produced by the competitive fringe of firms (SC) from market demand (D). Given D', the price leader's profit-maximizing output level is Q_L, and a price of P_L will prevail in the market.

Competitive fringe Group of firms that act as price takers in a market dominated by a price leader.

a **competitive fringe** of firms that take the leader's price as given in their decisions. The demand curve D represents the total market demand curve for the industry's product, and the supply curve SC represents the supply decisions of all the firms in the competitive fringe. Using these two curves, the demand curve (D') facing the industry leader is derived as follows. For a price of P_1 or above, the leader sells nothing since the competitive fringe would be willing to supply all that is demanded. For prices below P_2, the leader has the market to itself since the fringe is not willing to supply anything. Between P_2 and P_1, the curve D' is constructed by subtracting what the fringe will supply from total market demand. That is, the leader gets that portion of demand not taken by the fringe firms. D' is sometimes referred to as the price leader's residual demand curve.

Given the demand curve D', the leader can construct a marginal revenue curve for it (MR') and then refer to its own marginal cost curve (MC) to determine the profit-maximizing output level, Q_L. Market price is then P_L. Given that price, the competitive fringe produces Q_C, and total industry output is Q_T $(= Q_C + Q_L)$.

The price-leadership model takes a shortcut in assuming that the fringe firms are price takers rather than modeling their strategic behavior formally and applying game theory. The shortcut makes the analysis easier and is fitting if the fringe consists of a large number of small firms and if the dominant firm is quite a bit larger than any other firm. Another shortcut is that the model does not deal with how the price leader in an industry is chosen or what happens when a member of the fringe decides to challenge the leader for its position (and profits). Still, the model does show how elements of both the perfect competition and monopoly theories of price determination can be woven together to produce a model of pricing under imperfectly competitive conditions.

Monopolistic Competition

Monopolistic competition Market in which each firm faces a downward-sloping demand curve and there are no barriers to entry.

Another model that weaves together elements of perfect competition and monopoly is **monopolistic competition**, illustrated in Figure 12.8. The monopoly aspect is that firms are assumed to have some control over the price they receive, perhaps because each produces a slightly differentiated product. Firms thus face downward-sloping demand curves, in contrast to the horizontal demand curve of perfect competition. The competitive aspect is that there is free entry. In the free-entry equilibrium, firm's profits are driven to zero, as follows. Initially, the demand curve facing the typical firm is given by d, and economic profits are being earned. New firms are attracted by these profits, and their entry shifts d inward (because now a larger number of substitute products are being sold on a given market). Indeed, entry can reduce profits to zero by shifting the demand curve to d'. The level of output that maximizes profits with this demand curve, q', is not, however, the same as that level at which average costs are minimized, q_{min}. Rather, the firm produces less than that output level and exhibits "excess capacity," given by $q_{min} - q'$.[15]

Monopolistic competition brushes aside strategic considerations. The firm's demand curve is assumed to shift from d to d', without an explicit consideration of the process that leads to the demand shift. In a full-blown game-theory model, it is possible that free entry does not dissipate an

MICRO QUIZ 12.6

1. List the two key features of the model of monopolistic competition.
2. Does the fact that firms have "excess capacity" in the model mean that the government should restrict entry in such a market, or would there be a potential loss from doing so?

[15]This analysis was originally developed by E. H. Chamberlain, *The Theory of Monopolistic Competition* (Cambridge, MA: Harvard University Press, 1950).

Figure 12.8 Monopolistic Competition

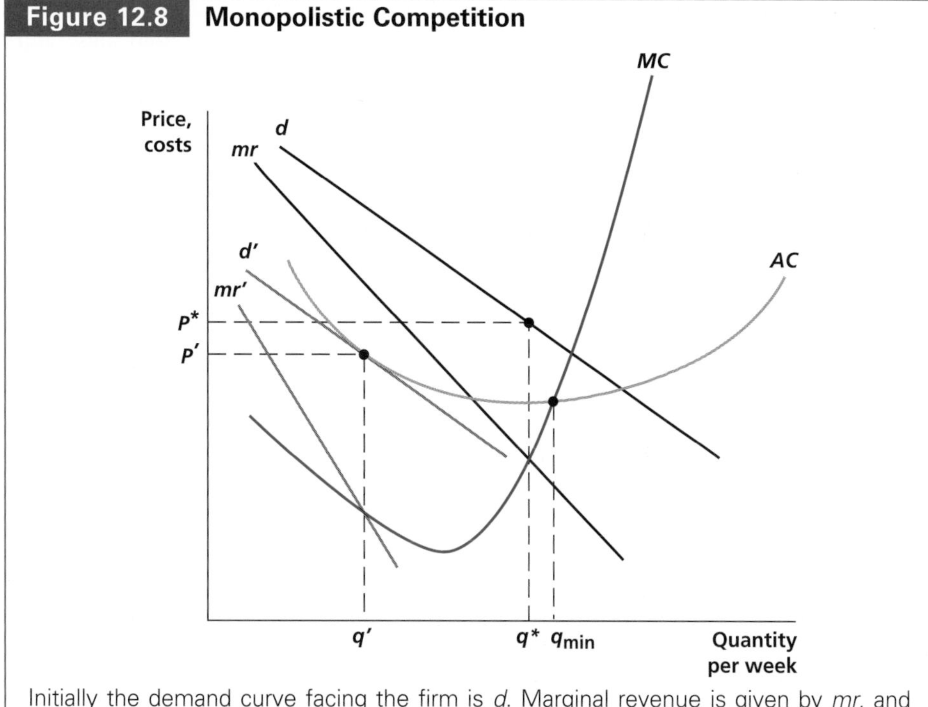

Initially the demand curve facing the firm is *d*. Marginal revenue is given by *mr*, and q^* is the profit-maximizing output level. If entry is costless, new firms attracted by the possibility for profits may shift the firm's demand curve inward to *d'*, where profits are zero. Output level q' is below the level q_{min}, where average costs reach a minimum. The firm exhibits excess capacity, given by $q_{min} - q'$.

incumbent's profits completely. Take the simple case in which firms produce very close substitutes and there is initially a monopoly in the market. Even though the monopolist might be earning lavish profits, other firms would hesitate to enter the market because entry would lead to a situation resembling the Bertrand Paradox (because products are close substitutes). The resulting profits may not be sufficient to cover even a modest fixed cost of entry. Brushing aside strategic considerations is probably only realistic if firms are small enough relative to the market that any given firm's strategic response would have little effect on other firms in the market. Monopolistic competition has thus been applied most successfully to the local competition in industries such as service stations, convenience stores, and restaurants, where there is some product differentiation (in terms of either product characteristics or store location) but entry occurs at a relatively small scale.

12-7 Barriers to Entry

The price-leadership and monopolistic-competition models aside, the rest of the models in this chapter are oligopoly models with only a few firms in the market. For example, there were only two firms in the market in our analysis of the Cournot and Bertrand models. For oligopoly models with few firms to have any applicability, market entry must be somewhat difficult. There might be some of the entry barriers already discussed in connection with monopoly in Chapter 11, which the reader should review again now.

Some new entry barriers arise specifically out of some features of imperfectly competitive markets. Product differentiation and advertising, for example, may raise entry barriers by promoting strong brand loyalty. The possibility of strategic pricing decisions may also deter entry for a number of reasons. Entry tends to make market competition more intense, reducing the profitability of subsequent entry. We saw this in the Cournot model, for example, where the equilibrium output increased from the monopoly to the perfectly competitive level as the number of firms increased. We also saw this in the repeated Bertrand model, where tacit collusion became harder to sustain as the number of firms increased. Incumbents may also manipulate their pricing decisions to convince potential entrants that it would be unprofitable to do so.

Barriers to entry frequently are the central issue when government antitrust authorities decide merger cases. A merger immediately reduces the number of firms in the market (for example, a merger between two firms in a market with four leaves three of them). But the previous paragraph suggests that, according to various models studied so far, reducing the number of firms reduces competition and raises prices. Antitrust authorities, responsible for keeping consumer prices low, should be wary of allowing mergers if they believe the models. Concerns would be lessened if entry barriers were thought to be low enough that any short-term price increase would stimulate entry, and this entry would keep prices low in the long run. Merger cases sometimes hinge on measurements of the cost of entry and the length of time entry might be expected to take (that is, how long the "long run" is), with parties seeking approval for their merger of course arguing that entry will likely be quick and easy.

SUMMARY

In this chapter, we studied models of imperfectly competitive industries, which lie between the extremes of monopoly and perfect competition. Such markets are characterized by relatively few firms that have some effect on market price—they are not price takers—but no single firm exercises complete market control. In these circumstances, there is no generally accepted model of market behavior. We presented a variety of models that economists use to study such industries, often called oligopolies. Some of the main points about the models in this chapter are the following:

- Because there are few firms, the strategic interaction among them becomes an important consideration. The concepts introduced in game theory, in particular Nash and subgame-perfect equilibrium, are useful to develop a formal understanding of this strategic interaction.
- Equilibrium outcomes with few firms may vary greatly from one resembling perfect competition (in the Bertrand model) to one resembling the monopoly outcome (in the model with tacit collusion), and outcomes in between (in the Cournot model).
- Best-response-function diagrams provide a useful tool to analyze oligopoly models such as Cournot and Bertrand with differentiated products.
- Small details about the market—including the strategic variable chosen (prices versus quantities), the nature of product differentiation, the presence of capacity constraints, information about market conditions, and repeated interaction—may have a big impact on the equilibrium.
- Firms may attempt to regain monopoly profits dissipated through imperfect competition by forming a cartel or through tacit collusion. Whether the cartel/collusion is sustainable depends on the trade-off between the short-term gain from cheating and the long-term loss if cheating leads to breakdown of the cartel/collusion. The cartel/collusion is more stable the fewer the number of firms and the more patient they are.
- Two-stage models can be used to understand a broad range of strategic choices beyond standard pricing and output decisions, including advertising, product selection, capacity choice, entry-deterring strategies, and so forth.
- Pricing strategies that deter entry (limit pricing) or induce exit (predatory pricing) are difficult to rationalize without subtle arguments involving asymmetric information about market conditions or about financing opportunities.
- Shorthand models such as monopolistic competition and price-leadership models can be useful for situations in which full-blown game-theoretic models might prove too complicated.

REVIEW QUESTIONS

1. Why is the intersection between firms' best-response functions in Figure 12.2 for the Cournot model or 12.3 for the Bertrand model with differentiated products a graphical illustration of the Nash equilibrium concept?
2. Commercial fishing is an industry that is often given as an example of quantity competition, as in the Cournot model. Can you think of others? Can you give examples of industries in which firms compete in prices? In which of these cases are capacity constraints important, so that the two-stage model of capacity investment and price competition might apply?
3. The Bertrand Paradox relies on the assumption that the demand for any one firm's product is very responsive to pricing by the other firm. Why is this assumption crucial for the competitive results in the Bertrand model? How would those results be affected if consumers were reluctant to shift purchases from one firm to another because of consumer switching costs? What other assumptions are crucial for the Bertrand Paradox?
4. Find examples of informative and of persuasive advertising in your newspaper. Find examples in commercials during your favorite television show. Do the particular ads you picked out persuade you to buy a broad product (orange juice) or a particular brand (Tropicana)?
5. "No cartel in history has ever succeeded for very long. There is just too much opportunity to cheat." What does it mean for a cartel member to "cheat"? What would a member of, say, the OPEC cartel actually do if it were to cheat? Why would this undermine the cartel?
6. Consider a two-stage game in which firms first make a strategic choice such as product design, location on a Hotelling line, capacity, advertising, etc., and, second, compete in prices or quantities. Why is subgame-perfect equilibrium a useful equilibrium concept? What sort of "crazy" Nash equilibria might be ruled out?
7. Consider the market for high-definition televisions, which can be expected to grow in popularity over time as consumers become familiar with it and more programs are developed for it. If there is a first-mover advantage in building capacity, what determines which firm will move first? If firms race to preempt each other to be the first mover, is there some profit-maximizing condition that would determine how long before the anticipated peak in demand firms would start building capacity?
8. Explain the difference between entry deterrence through first-mover investments and entry deterrence through pricing. What assumptions are required for each of these entry-deterrence strategies to be successful? Describe a hypothetical situation under which each strategy might work for an incumbent monopolist.
9. Suppose a firm is considering investing in research that would lead to a cost-saving innovation. Assuming the firm can retain this innovation solely for its own use, will the additional profits from the lower (marginal) cost be greater if the firm is a monopolist or competes against another, say, in a Cournot or Bertrand model?
10. In Figure 12.8, the demand curve facing a firm in a monopolistically competitive industry is shown as being tangent to its average cost curve at q'. Explain why this is a long-run equilibrium position for this firm. That is, why does marginal revenue equal marginal cost, and why are long-run profits zero?

PROBLEMS

12.1. The pricing game between two firms, which can each set either a low or a high price, is given by the following normal form.

		B Low price	*B* High price
A	**Low price**	2, 2	4, 1
	High price	1, 4	3, 3

a. Find the Nash equilibrium or equilibria of the game.

b. How would you label the actions to make this a quantity game like Cournot?

12.2. Refer to Figure 12.1. Suppose demand is

$$Q = 10{,}000 - 1{,}000\,P$$

and marginal cost is constant at $MC = 6$. From the given demand curve, one can compute the following marginal revenue curve:

$$MR = 10 - \frac{Q}{500}.$$

a. Graph the demand, marginal cost, and marginal revenue curves.

b. Calculate the price and quantity associated with point C, the perfectly competitive outcome. Compute industry profit, consumer surplus, and social welfare.

c. Calculate the price and quantity associated with point M, the monopoly/perfect cartel outcome. Compute industry profit, consumer surplus, social welfare, and deadweight loss.
d. Calculate the price and quantity associated with point *A*, a hypothetical imperfectly competitive outcome, assuming that it lies at a price halfway between *C* and *M*. Compute industry profit, consumer surplus, social welfare, and deadweight loss.

12.3. Return to the example used in the text for the Cournot model, where demand was equal to

$$Q = 120 - P.$$

Suppose that instead of costless production, marginal and average costs are constant at

$$MC = AC = 30.$$

Compute the Nash equilibrium quantities, prices, and profits.

12.4. Consider the model of Bertrand competition with differentiated products from the text. Let the demand curves for firms *A* and *B* be given by Equation 12.10 and Equation 12.11, and let the firms' marginal costs be constant, given by c_A and c_B. It can be shown that the best-response function for firm *A* is

$$P_A = \frac{1 + 2P_B + 2c_A}{4}$$

and for firm *B* is

$$P_B = \frac{1 + 2P_A + 2c_B}{4}$$

a. Graph the two best-response functions. Find the Nash equilibrium assuming $c_A = c_B = 0$ algebraically and indicate it on the graph.
b. Indicate on the graph how an increase in c_B would shift the best-response functions and change the equilibrium.
c. Indicate on the graph where analogue to the Stackelberg equilibrium might be, with firm *A* choosing price first and then firm *B*. Is it better to be the first or the second mover when firms choose prices?

12.5. Suppose firms *A* and *B* operate under conditions of constant marginal and average cost but that $MC_A = 10$ and $MC_B = 8$. The demand for the firms' output is given by

$$Q = 500 - 20P.$$

a. If the firms practice Bertrand competition, what will the Nash-equilibrium market price be? (It may help to assume that prices can only be in increments of a penny, so that prices of 9.98, 9.99, and 10 are possible, but not 9.995.)
b. What will the profits be for each firm?
c. Which aspects of the Bertrand Paradox show up in this example, if any?

12.6. Consider the example of the Stackelberg model discussed in the text. Firms choose quantities, with firm *A* moving first, and then firm *B*. As in the text, market demand is given by

$$Q = 120 - P$$

and production is costless.

a. Recall that firm *B*'s best-response function is

$$q_B = \frac{120 - q_A}{2}.$$

Substitute this best-response function into the equation for *A*'s profit, (Equation 12.3), to express *A*'s profit as a function of q_A, labeled π_A. Next, substitute this best-response function into the analogous equation for *B*'s profit to compute *B*'s profit as a function of q_A, labeled π_B. Finally, write the expression for *A's* profit if *B* produces zero as a function of q_A, labeled π_M (where the *M* subscript stands for the fact that *A* is a monopoly if *B* produces zero).

b. Use the formulae from part a to fill in the following table.

q_A	π_A	π_B	π_M
0			
20			
40			
60			
80			
100			
120			

c. Does your table from part b confirm the result from the text that firm *A* would choose $q_A = 60$ in the Stackelberg game? How much would *A* have to produce to deter *B*'s entry if *B* had a fixed cost of entry equal to a bit more than 400? If *B* had a fixed cost of entry a bit more than 100? Would it be worthwhile for *A* to deter *B*'s entry in these cases?

12.7. Using Equation 12.15 from the text, graph the relationship between the number of firms in the market, N, and probability, *g*, that the game continues from one period to the next, needed to sustain collusion in an indefinitely repeated game. What is the greatest number of firms for which collusion would be sustainable if $g = 0.95$?

12.8. Consider a two-period model with two firms, A and B. In the first period, they simultaneously choose one of two actions, Enter or Don't enter. Entry requires the expenditure of a fixed entry cost of 10. In the second period, whichever firms enter play a pricing game as follows. If no firm enters, the pricing game is trivial and profits are zero. If only one firm enters, it earns the monopoly profit of 30. If both firms enter, they engage in competition as in the Bertrand model with homogeneous products.

a. Using backward induction, fold the game back to the first period in which firms make their choice of Enter or Don't enter. Write down the normal form (a 2 by 2 matrix) for this game.
b. Solve for the mixed-strategy Nash equilibrium of this game (see Chapter 6 for a discussion of mixed strategies).
c. Compare the results from the mixed-strategy Nash equilibrium to the Bertrand Paradox.

12.9. The text mentioned a model of predatory pricing in which an incumbent tries to "beat up" a rival, exhausting the resources the rival needs to continue operating in the market, causing it to exit. Consider a specific example of this sort of model given by the extensive form in Figure 12.9. As the figure shows, there are three possible outcomes. If the entrant E does not enter, leaving the incumbent I to operate alone, the incumbent earns 3,600. If the entrant spends fixed entry cost $K < 1{,}600$ and is not preyed upon, each firm earns 1,600 (not including the entry cost). If the entrant comes in and the incumbent preys upon the entrant, it can exhaust the entrant's resources and force it to exit the industry. The period of predation costs the entrant F_E and the incumbent F_I (where F stands for "fighting"). Compute the subgame-perfect equilibrium for $F_I > 2{,}000$ and for $F_I < 2{,}000$. Is predation ever observed in equilibrium? Would a law prohibiting predation affect the equilibrium?

Figure 12.9 Predation Game in Problem 12.9

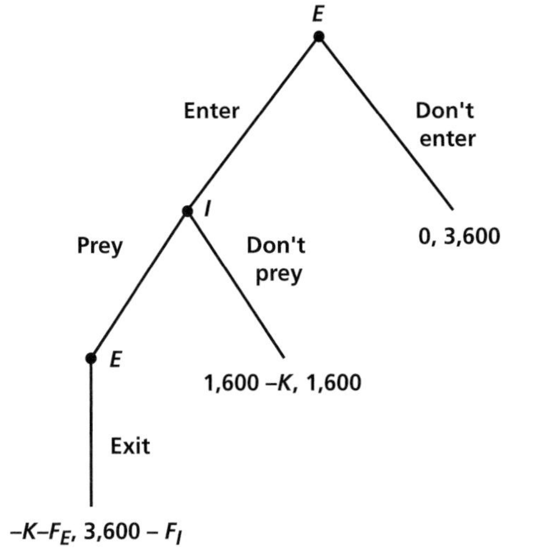

12.10. Suppose that the total market demand for crude oil is given by

$$Q_D = 70{,}000 - 2{,}000\,P,$$

where Q_D is the quantity of oil in thousands of barrels per year and P is the dollar price per barrel. Suppose also that there are 1,000 identical small producers of crude oil, each with marginal costs given by

$$MC = q + 5,$$

where q is the output of the typical firm.

a. Assuming that each small oil producer acts as a price taker, calculate the typical firm's supply curve ($q = \ldots$), the market supply curve ($Q_S = \ldots$), and the market equilibrium price and quantity (where $Q_D = Q_S$).
b. Suppose a practically infinite source of crude oil is discovered in New Jersey by a would-be price leader and that this oil can be produced at a constant average and marginal cost of $AC = MC =$ \$15 per barrel. Assume also that the supply behavior of the competitive fringe described in part a is unchanged by this discovery. Calculate the demand curve facing the price leader.
c. Assuming that the price leader's marginal revenue curve is given by

$$MR = 25 - \frac{Q}{1{,}500},$$

how much should the price leader produce in order to maximize profits? What price and quantity will now prevail in the market?

PART 7

Input Markets

The produce of the earth ... is divided among three classes of the community, namely, the proprietor of land, the owner of the stock of capital necessary for its cultivation, and the laborers by whose industry it is cultivated. To determine the laws which regulate this distribution is the principal problem in Political Economy.

—D. Ricardo, The Principles of Political Economy and Taxation, 1817

Prices for inputs (such as wages for labor or the cost of new equipment) are determined by the same forces of supply and demand that we described for goods' markets in the two previous parts. The main difference is that the roles of supplier and demander are reversed when we consider inputs. The demand for inputs comes from firms that wish to use these inputs to produce goods. Hence, the theory of the demand for inputs is one aspect of firms' profit-maximization decisions. The theory of input supply is more varied. Some inputs such as capital equipment are produced by other firms. This supply process is no different than the process of supply of any other good. In some cases, however, inputs are supplied directly by individuals; most importantly, individuals decide what jobs they will take and what wages they expect. To examine these supply decisions, therefore, we must return to the theory of individual utility maximization.

The study of pricing in input markets is important mainly because individuals get their incomes from these markets. If we are to understand trends in workers' wages, for example, we must understand how the markets that are determining these wages operate. Some of the most important questions in economic policy relate to how to improve the operations of input markets.

Part 7 includes two chapters. Chapter 13 develops some of the general theory of pricing in input markets with special attention to the demand side of the market. We show how the theory of profit maximization leads directly to a theory of the firm's demand for inputs. This theory provides clear predictions about how firms respond to changes in input prices. In the Appendix to Chapter 13, we show how the theory of individual utility maximization can be used to develop a general theory of labor supply.

Chapter 14 examines the ways in which time and interest rates affect input pricing. It begins with a general theory of how interest rates are determined by the supply and demand for loans. The chapter then turns to examine how interest rates affect such important decisions as firms' demands for capital equipment or for finite natural resources.

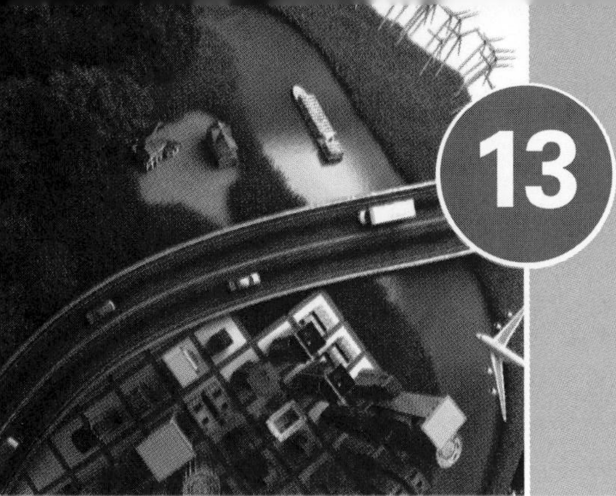

13 Pricing in Input Markets

Input prices are also determined by the forces of demand and supply. In this case, however, market roles are reversed. Now firms are on the demand side of the market, hiring inputs to meet their production needs. These inputs are supplied by individuals through the jobs they take and the capital resources that their savings provide. In this chapter, we will explore some models of how prices are determined in this process. We begin with a fairly extensive discussion of demand, then very briefly summarize the nature of supply decisions. The remainder of the chapter is devoted to examining how demand and supply interact to determine prices. The appendix to this chapter explores questions of labor supply in somewhat more detail. Chapter 14 covers those issues in input pricing that relate mainly to capital such as the role of time and interest rates in economic decisions.

13-1 Marginal Productivity Theory of Input Demand

In Chapter 9, we looked briefly at Ricardo's theory of economic rent. This theory was an important start to the development of marginal economics. Ricardo's notion that price is deter mined by the costs of the "marginal" producer in many ways represents the seed from which modern microeconomics grew. One application of his approach was the development of the "marginal productivity" theory of the demand for inputs. This section investigates that theory in detail.

Profit-Maximizing Behavior and the Hiring of Inputs

The basic concept of the marginal productivity theory of input demand was stated in Chapter 8 when we discussed profit maximization. There we showed that one implication of the profit-maximization hypothesis is that the firm will make marginal input choices. More precisely, we showed that a profit-maximizing firm will hire additional units of any input up to the point at which the additional revenue from hiring one more unit of the input is exactly equal to the cost of hiring that unit. If we use ME_K and ME_L to denote the marginal expense associated with hiring one more unit of capital and labor, respectively and let MR_K and MR_L be the extra revenue that hiring these units of capital and labor allows the firm to bring in, then profit maximization requires that

$$\begin{aligned} ME_K &= MR_K \\ ME_L &= MR_L \end{aligned}. \tag{13.1}$$

Price-Taking Behavior

If the firm is a price taker in the capital and labor markets, we can simplify the marginal expense idea. In this case, the firm can always hire an extra hour of capital input at the prevailing rental rate (v) and an extra hour of labor at the wage rate (w). Therefore, the profit-maximizing requirement reduces to

$$\begin{aligned} v &= ME_K = MR_K \\ w &= ME_L = MR_L \end{aligned} . \tag{13.2}$$

These equations simply say that a profit-maximizing firm that is a price taker for the inputs it buys should hire extra amounts of these inputs up to the point at which their unit cost is equal to the revenue generated by the last one hired. If the firm's hiring decisions affect input prices, it will have to take that into account. We will look at such a situation later in this chapter.

Marginal Revenue Product

To analyze the additional revenue yielded by hiring one more unit of an input is a two-step process. First we must ask how much extra output the additional input can produce. As we discussed in Chapter 6, this magnitude is given by the input's marginal physical productivity. For example, if a firm hires one more worker for an hour to make shoes, the worker's marginal physical productivity (MP_L) is simply the number of additional pairs of shoes per hour that the firm can make.

After the additional output has been produced, it must be sold. Assessing the value of that sale is the second step in analyzing the revenue yielded by hiring one more unit of an input. We have looked at this issue quite extensively in previous chapters—the extra revenue obtained from selling an additional unit of output is, by definition, marginal revenue (MR). So, if an extra worker can produce two pairs of shoes per hour and the firm can take in $4 per pair from selling these shoes, then hiring the worker for an hour has increased the firm's revenues by $8. This is the figure the firm will compare to the worker's hourly wage to decide whether he or she should be hired.

Marginal revenue product (MRP)
The extra revenue obtained from selling the output produced by hiring an extra worker or machine.

The combined effect of the input's marginal productivity and the extra revenue yielded by selling this extra output is called the input's **marginal revenue product (MRP)**. Using this notation, the firm's profit maximizing rules become

$$\begin{aligned} v &= ME_K = MR_K = MP_K \cdot MR = MRP_K \\ w &= ME_L = MR_L = MP_L \cdot MR = MRP_L \end{aligned} \tag{13.3}$$

Hence, the marginal revenue product for any input indicates how much extra revenue will be yielded by hiring one more unit of the input and this is precisely the magnitude that will enter into the profit-maximizing firm's hiring decisions. We can therefore use this concept to study how those decisions change when conditions facing the firm change.

A Special Case—Marginal Value Product

The profit-maximizing rules for input choices are even simpler if we assume that the firm we are examining sells its output in a competitive market. In that case, the firm will also be a price taker in the output market, so that the marginal revenue it takes in from selling one more unit of output is the market price (P) at which the output sells. Using the result that, for a price taker in the goods market, marginal revenue is equal to price, Equation 13.3 becomes

$$v = MP_K \cdot P$$
$$w = MP_L \cdot P \quad (13.4)$$

as the conditions for a profit maximum.[1] We call the terms on the right-hand side of Equation 13.4 the **marginal value product (MVP)** of capital and labor, respectively, since they do indeed put a value on these inputs' marginal physical productivities. The final condition for maximum profits in this simple situation is

$$v = MVP_K$$
$$w = MVP_L \quad (13.5)$$

MICRO QUIZ 13.1

Suppose that a firm has a monopoly in the goods it sells but must hire its two inputs in competitive markets.

1. Will this monopoly hire more or fewer workers than if it sold its output in a competitive market?
2. How will the marginal productivity of workers hired by this monopoly compare to their marginal productivity if the firm were competitive in the output market?

Marginal value product (MVP) A special case of marginal revenue product in which the firm is a price taker for its output.

To see why these are required for profit maximization, consider again our shoe worker example. Suppose the worker can make two pairs of shoes per hour and that shoes sell for $4. The worker's marginal value product is $8 per hour. If the hourly wage is less than this (say, $5 per hour), the firm can increase profits by $3 by employing the worker for one more hour; profits were not at a maximum, so the extra labor should be hired. Similarly, if the wage is $10 per hour, profits would rise by $2 if one less hour of labor were used. Only if the wage and labor's marginal value product are equal will profits truly be as large as possible. Application 13.1: Jet Fuel and Hybrid Seeds looks at profit-maximizing choices for two specific inputs.

13-2 Responses to Changes in Input Prices

Suppose the price of any input (say, labor) were to fall. It seems reasonable that firms might demand more of this input in response to such a change. In this section, we provide a detailed analysis of why the model of a profit-maximizing firm supports this conclusion.

Single Variable Input Case

Let's look first at the case where a firm has fixed capital input and can vary only its labor input in the short run. In this case, labor input will exhibit diminishing marginal physical productivity, so labor's $MVP(= P \cdot MP_L)$ will decline as increasing numbers of labor hours are hired. The downward-sloping MVP_L curve in Figure 13.1 illustrates this possibility. With a wage rate of w_1, a profit-maximizing firm will hire L_1 labor hours.

If the wage rate were to fall to w_2, more labor (L_2) would be demanded. At such a lower wage, more labor can be hired because the firm can "afford" to have a lower marginal physical productivity from the labor it employs. If it continued to hire only L_1, the firm would not be maximizing profits since, at the margin, labor would now be capable of producing more in additional revenue than hiring additional labor would cost. When only one input can be varied, the assumption of a diminishing marginal productivity of

[1] The theory of input demand reflected by Equations 13.3 or 13.4 also implies that firms will minimize costs. To see this, just divide the equations:

$$v/w = MP_K \cdot MR/MP_L \cdot MR = MP_K/MP_L = MP_K \cdot P/MP_L \cdot P.$$

Because the condition $v/w = MP_K/MP_L$ is precisely what is required for cost minimization (see Chapter 7), firms that follow the marginal productivity approach to input demand will also minimize costs. Notice in particular that this is true regardless of whether the firm sells its output in a monopolistic or a competitive market.

APPLICATION 13.1

Jet Fuel and Hybrid Seeds

Although our discussion of input demand uses generic references to "capital" and "labor," the theory applies to any input that firms use. Here we look at two more narrowly defined inputs and show that the marginal productivity theory has relevance to them as well.

Jet Fuel

The price of fuel of jet planes has fluctuated widely over the past 40 years. For example, between 1970 and 1980, prices increased more than sevenfold and fuel costs rose from 13 percent to nearly 30 percent of airline costs. After 1980, however, fuel costs began a slow decline, dropping more than 42 percent by 1999. In 2000, fuel costs made up only about 12 percent of airline costs. After 2002, fuel costs for airlines rose rapidly again, nearly tripling by mid-2008. After a brief period of declining prices in 2009, fuel costs continued their upward trend. By 2013 fuel costs constituted nearly 35 percent of airline operating costs.[1]

Adapting to these trends has posed problems for many airlines. Of course, in the short run, there is very little that the firms can do in response to these changing fuel costs. They must fly the fleets of planes they have and these have relatively fixed demands for fuel. Over the longer term, airline firms can adapt their fleets to prevailing fuel prices, but because bringing on new aircraft takes a long time, it is easy to lag behind market realities. For example, during the early 1980s, airlines improved their fuel economy dramatically as firms responded to the earlier sharp increases in price by purchasing fuel-efficient planes. Passenger miles per gallon of fuel nearly doubled. This trend slowed dramatically in the 1990s, as fuel costs stayed low and airlines paid much more attention to labor and other operating costs. The increases in fuel costs after 2002 therefore caught many airlines by surprise. Although a few (most notably Southwest) had hedged their fuel expenses by purchasing forward contracts, most airlines faced cost increases of as much as 50 percent. Again, in the short run there was little that the airlines could do to economize on fuel other than, for example, shutting off their engines while taxiing. Over the longer run, however, airlines are investing in lighter planes (such as the Boeing 787) and more efficient jet engines that offer significant savings in fuel costs.

Hybrid Seeds

Hybrid seeds for growing corn were developed during the 1930s. In the ensuing decades, the use of this newly invented "input" spread throughout the world. The econometrician Zvi Griliches looked in detail at the decisions by U.S. farmers to adopt these seeds.[2] In this seminal work on the economics of technical change, he showed that such decisions were motivated primarily by farmers' profitability calculations. In states where farmers could expect large increases in yields from adopting hybrids (in Iowa, for example), adoptions came about rapidly. Adoptions proceeded much more slowly in states such as Alabama where weather and soil conditions were not especially favorable for hybrids.

More recent studies of the spread of hybrids throughout the world reach similar conclusions. In nations where the hybrids are highly profitable (India) these seeds have been widely adopted and yields have expanded dramatically. Similar quick adoptions occurred throughout much of Southeast Asia. This "Green Revolution" did not have such a major impact in places such as western Africa, however, where drier climates and rigid price controls on agricultural output sharply reduced the profitability of hybrid adoptions.

TO THINK ABOUT

1. How are airlines' reactions to changing fuel prices affected by the types of planes they own and by the kinds of routes they fly? Would owning a variety of types of planes help to make such adjustments in the short run? What would be the disadvantages of flying many types of aircraft? If you look around an airport, does it seem that different airlines take differing approaches to this question? Can you explain why?
2. The Griliches article was part of a larger debate in economics about the "rationality" of farmers. Some economists argued that farmers should be studied in the way one studies any firm—that is, as a profit-maximizing entity. Others argued that farmers made decisions on "noneconomic" grounds such as tradition or availability of information. Who would you support in this debate? How did the Griliches study contribute to it?

[1]These data come from the U.S. government transportation statistics website: www.transstats.bts.gov.

[2]Z. Griliches, "Hybrid Corn: An Exploration in the Economics of Technical Change," *Econometrica* (October 1957): 501–522.

Figure 13.1 Change in Labor Input When Wage Falls: Single-Variable Input Case

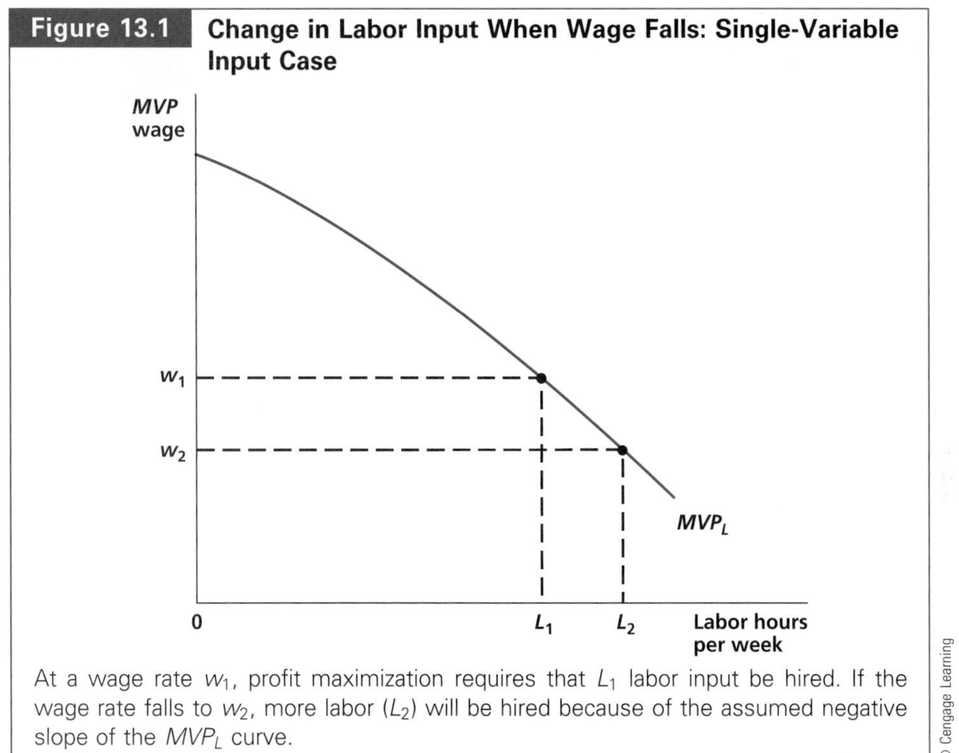

At a wage rate w_1, profit maximization requires that L_1 labor input be hired. If the wage rate falls to w_2, more labor (L_2) will be hired because of the assumed negative slope of the MVP_L curve.

labor ensures that a fall in the price of labor will cause more labor to be hired.[2] The marginal value product curve shows this response.

A Numerical Example

As a numerical example of these input choices, let's look again at the hiring decision for Hamburger Heaven first discussed in Chapter 6. Table 13.1 repeats the productivity information for the case in which Hamburger Heaven uses four grills ($K = 4$). As the table shows, the marginal productivity of labor declines as more workers are assigned to use grills each hour—the first worker hired turns out 20 (heavenly) hamburgers per hour, whereas the 10th hired produces only 3.2 hamburgers per hour. To calculate these workers' marginal value products, we simply multiply these physical productivity figures by the price of hamburgers, which here we assume to be \$1.00. These results appear in the final column of Table 13.1. With a market wage of \$5.00 per hour, Hamburger Heaven should hire four workers. The marginal value product of each of these workers exceeds \$5.00, so the firm earns some incremental profit on each of them. The fifth worker's *MVP* is only \$4.70, however, so it does not make sense to add that worker.

At a wage other than \$5.00 per hour, Hamburger Heaven would hire a different number of workers. At \$6.00 per hour, for example, only three workers would be hired. With wages of \$4.00 per hour, on the other hand, six workers would be employed. The *MVP* calculation provides complete information about Hamburger Heaven's short-run

[2]Because the marginal productivity of labor is positive, hiring more labor also implies that output will increase when *w* declines.

Table 13.1	**Hamburger Heaven's Profit-Maximizing Hiring Decision**		
LABOR INPUT PER HOUR	HAMBURGERS PRODUCED PER HOUR	MARGINAL PRODUCT (HAMBURGERS)	MARGINAL VALUE PRODUCT ($1.00 PER HAMBURGER)
1	20.0	20.0	$20.00
2	28.3	8.3	8.30
3	34.6	6.3	6.30
4	40.0	5.4	5.40
5	44.7	4.7	4.70
6	49.0	4.3	4.30
7	52.9	3.9	3.90
8	56.6	3.7	3.70
9	60.0	3.4	3.40
10	63.2	3.2	3.20

hiring decisions. Of course, a change in the wages of burger flippers might also cause the firm to reconsider how many grills it uses—a subject we now investigate.

Two-Variable Input Case

For the case where the firm can vary two (or more) inputs, the story is more complex. The assumption of a diminishing marginal physical product of labor can be misleading here. If w falls, there will be a change not only in labor input but also in capital input as a new cost-minimizing combination of inputs is chosen (see our analysis in Chapter 7). When capital input changes, the entire MP_L function shifts (workers now have a different amount of capital to work with), and our earlier analysis of how wages affect hiring cannot be made. The remainder of this section presents a series of observations that establish that even with many inputs, a fall in w will lead to an increase in the quantity of labor demanded.

Substitution Effect

In some ways analyzing the two-input case is similar to our analysis of the individual's response to a change in the price of a good in Chapter 3. When w falls, we can decompose the total effect on the quantity of L hired into two components: a substitution effect and an output effect.

Substitution effect (in production)
The substitution of one input for another while holding output constant in response to a change in the input's price.

To study the **substitution effect**, we hold q constant at q_1. With a fall in w, there will be a tendency to substitute labor for capital in the production of q_1. This effect is illustrated in Figure 13.2(a). Because the condition for minimizing the cost of producing q_1 requires that $RTS = w/v$, a fall in w will necessitate a movement from input combination A to combination B. It is clear from the diagram that this substitution effect must cause more labor to be used in response to the fall in w because of the convex shape of the q_1 isoquant. The firm now decides to produce q_1 in a more labor-intensive way.

Output Effect

A firm will usually not hold output constant when w falls, however. The change in w will affect the firm's costs, and this will prompt the firm to alter its output. It is in looking at

Figure 13.2 Substitution and Output Effects of a Decrease in Price of Labor

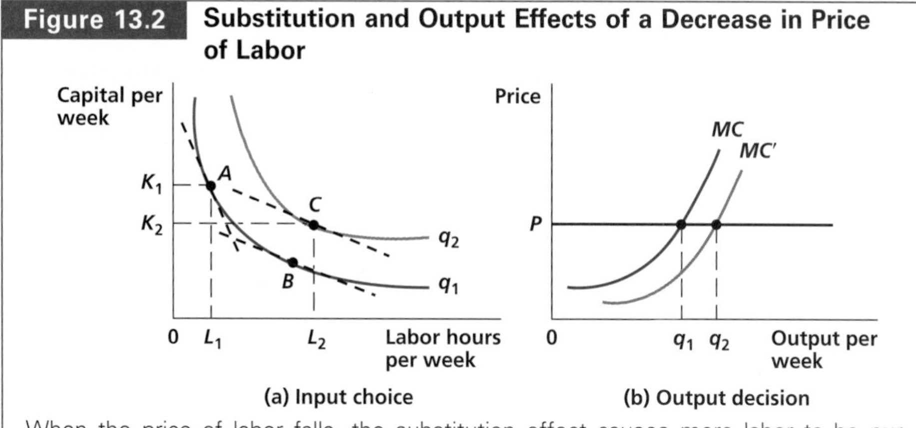

When the price of labor falls, the substitution effect causes more labor to be purchased even if output is held constant. This is shown as a movement from point *A* to point *B* in panel a. The change in *w* will also shift the firm's marginal cost curve. A normal situation might be for the *MC* curve to shift downward in response to a decrease in *w*, as shown in panel b. With this new curve (*MC′*) a higher level of output (q_2) will be chosen. The hiring of labor will increase (to L_2) from this output effect.

this effect—the **output effect**—the analogy to a person's utility-maximization problem breaks down. The reason for this is that consumers have budget constraints, but firms do not. Firms produce as much as profit maximization requires; their need for inputs is derived from these production decisions. In order to investigate what happens to the quantity of output produced, we must therefore investigate the firm's profit-maximizing output decision. A fall in *w*, because it changes relative factor costs, will shift the firm's expansion path. Consequently, all the firm's cost curves will be shifted, and probably some output level other than q_1 will be chosen.

Output effect
The effect of an input price change on the amount of the input that the firm hires that results from a change in the firm's output level.

Figure 13.2(b) illustrates the most common case. As a result of the fall in *w*, the marginal cost curve for the firm has shifted downward to *MC′*. The profit-maximizing level of output rises from q_1 to q_2.[3] The profit-maximizing condition ($P = MC$) is now satisfied at a higher level of output. Returning to Figure 13.2(a), this increase in output will cause even more labor input to be demanded. The combined result of both the substitution and the output effects is to move the input choice to point *C* on the firm's isoquant for output level q_2. Both effects work to increase *L* in response to a decrease in *w*.[4]

Summary of Firm's Demand for Labor

We conclude therefore that a profit-maximizing firm will increase its hiring of labor for two reasons. First, the firm will substitute the now-cheaper labor for other inputs that are now relatively more expensive. This is the substitution effect. Second, the wage

[3]Price (*P*) is assumed to be constant. If all firms in an industry were confronted with a decline in *w*, all would change their output levels; the industry supply curve would shift outward, and consequently *P* would fall. As long as the market demand curve for the firm's output is negatively sloped, however, the analysis in this chapter would not be seriously affected by this observation since the lower *P* will lead to more output being demanded.

[4]No definite statement can be made about how the quantity of capital (or any other input) changes in response to a decline in *w*. The substitution and output effects work in opposite directions (as can be seen in Figure 13.2), and the precise outcome depends on the relative sizes of these effects.

decline will reduce the firm's marginal costs, thereby causing it to increase output and to increase the hiring of all inputs including labor. This is the output effect.

This conclusion holds for any input. Naturally, it can be reversed to show that an increase in the price of an input will cause the firm to hire less of that input. We have shown that the firm's demand curve for an input will be unambiguously downward sloping: the lower a particular input's price, the more of that input will be demanded.[5]

13-3 Responsiveness of Input Demand to Input Price Changes

The notions of substitution and output effects help to explain how responsive to price changes the demand for an input might be. Suppose the wage rate rose. We already know that less labor will be demanded. Now we wish to investigate whether this decrease in quantity demanded by firms will be large or small.

Ease of Substitution

First, consider the substitution effect. The decrease in the hiring of labor from a rise in w will depend on how easy it is for firms to substitute other productive inputs for labor. Some firms may find it relatively simple to substitute machines for workers, and for these firms the quantity of labor demanded will decrease substantially. Other firms may produce with a fixed proportions technology. For them substitution will be impossible. The size of the substitution effect may also depend on the length of time allowed for adjustment. In the short run, a firm may have a stock of machinery that requires a fixed complement of workers. Consequently, the short-run substitution possibilities are slight. Over the long run, however, this firm may be able to adapt its machinery to use less labor per machine; the possibilities of substitution may now be substantial. For example, a rise in the wages of coal miners will have little short-run substitution effect since existing coal-mining equipment requires a certain number of workers to operate it. In the long run, however, there is clear evidence that mining can be made more capital intensive by designing more complex machinery. In the long run, capital has been substituted for labor on a large scale.

Costs and the Output Effect

An increase in the wage rate will also raise firms' costs. In a competitive market, this will cause the price of the good being produced to rise, and people will reduce their purchases of that good. Consequently, firms will lower their levels of production; because less output is being produced, the output effect will cause less labor to be demanded. In this way, the output effect reinforces the substitution effect. The size of this output effect will depend on (1) how large the increase in marginal costs brought about by the wage rate increase is, and (2) how much the quantity demanded will be reduced by a rising price. The size of the first of these components depends on how "important" labor is to

[5]Actually, a proof of this assertion is not as simple as is implied here. The complicating factor arises when the input in question is "inferior," and it is no longer true that the marginal cost curve shifts downward when the price of such an input declines. Nevertheless, as long as the good that is being produced has a downward-sloping demand curve, the firm's demand for the input will also be negatively sloped.

total production costs, whereas the size of the second depends on how price-elastic the demand for the product is.[6]

In industries for which labor costs are a major portion of total costs and for which demand is very elastic, output effects will be large. For example, an increase in wages for restaurant workers is likely to induce a large negative output effect in the demand for such workers, since labor costs are a significant portion of restaurant operating costs and the demand for meals eaten out is relatively price-elastic. An increase in wages will cause a big price rise, and this will cause people to reduce sharply the number of meals they eat out. On the other hand, output effects in the demand for pharmaceutical workers are probably small. Direct labor costs are a small fraction of drug production costs, and the demand for drugs is price-inelastic. Wage increases will have only a small effect on costs, and any increases in price that do result will not reduce demand for drugs significantly. All of these features of labor demand are illustrated by Application 13.2: Controversy over the Minimum Wage.

MICRO QUIZ 13.2

Suppose that state law requires that every gasoline pump have exactly one attendant, and suppose that gasoline pumps are always in use filling motorists' cars.

1. Will a rise in attendants' wages cause fewer to be hired? Explain.
2. Suppose attendants' wages represent one-third of the total cost of gasoline to motorists and that the price elasticity of demand for gasoline is −0.50. What is the elasticity of demand for gasoline pump attendants?

13-4 Input Supply

Firms get their inputs from three primary sources. Labor is provided by individuals who choose among available employment opportunities. Capital equipment is produced primarily by other firms and may be bought outright or rented for a period. Finally, natural resources are extracted from the ground and may be used directly (Exxon produces gasoline from the crude oil it extracts) or sold to other firms (DuPont buys a petroleum feedstock from Exxon). Studying the supply decisions for firms that produce capital equipment and natural resources doesn't require us to develop any new tools. We already know how to model this supply, since nothing in our prior discussion required that firms produce their output only for consumers. Hence, we can safely assume that firms that produce inputs to be sold to other firms have upward-sloping supply curves.[7]

Studying labor supply, however, raises different issues. Labor input (which constitutes the majority of most firms' costs) is supplied by individuals, so our previous models of firms are not much help in analyzing labor supply. Indeed, individuals are also partly involved in the supply of capital. In this case individuals provide the funds (usually channeled through banks or securities) that firms use to finance capital purchases. Again, models of firms' supply behavior do not help us to understand this process. In the appendix to this chapter, we look in detail at models of labor supply. Here we summarize our findings as they relate to drawing labor supply curves. Input supply questions that are related to interest rates (such as the supply of loans for firms or the decision to supply a natural resource) will be taken up in Chapter 14.

[6]Alfred Marshall was the first economist to recognize all of these effects that come into play when an input price changes. He showed that the elasticity of demand for any input (say labor, e_l) is related to: (1) the ease of substituting labor for other inputs (e_s); (2) the share of labor costs in total costs (s); and (3) the elasticity of demand for the product being produced e_D according to the equation $e_l = -(1-s)e_s + se_D$. Because e_s is positive and e_D is negative, both terms in this expression are negative, so the elasticity of demand for labor is definitely negative.

[7]That is, unless these firms are monopolies, in which case our analysis in Chapter 11 would apply.

APPLICATION 13.2

Controversy over the Minimum Wage

The Fair Labor Standards Act of 1938 established a national minimum wage of $0.25 per hour. The Federal minimum wage was raised to $7.25 per hour in 2009 and has remained there since. In 2014 President Obama proposed raising the Federal minimum to $10.10 per hour and several states adopted much higher levels. For example, the Seattle-Tacoma area of Washington state adopted a $15 minimum. Increasing the minimum wage rates is always a contentious political issue, in part because some economists believe that such an increase may be counterproductive.

A Graphic Analysis

Figure 1 illustrates the possible effects of a minimum wage. Figure 1(a) shows the supply and demand curves for labor. Given these curves, an equilibrium wage rate, w_1, is established in the market. At this wage, a typical firm hires l_1 (shown on the firm's isoquant map in Figure 1[b]). Suppose now that a minimum wage of w_2 is imposed by law. This new wage will cause the typical firm to reduce its demand for labor from l_1 to l_2. At the same time, more labor (L_3) will be supplied at the specified minimum wage than was supplied at the lower wage rate. The imposition of the minimum wage will result in an excess of the supply of labor over the demand for labor of $L_3 - L_2$.

Figure 1 Effects of a Minimum Wage in a Perfectly Competitive Labor Market

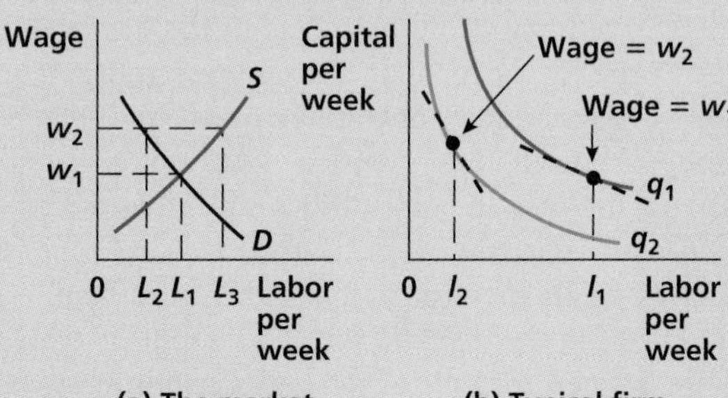

The imposition of a minimum wage (w_2) causes the firm to reduce labor usage to l_2 because it will both substitute capital (and other inputs) for labor and cut back output.

Minimum Wages and Teenage Unemployment

There is some empirical evidence that changes in the minimum wage law have had serious effects in increasing teenage unemployment. Teenagers are the labor-market participants most likely to be affected by minimum wage laws, because their skills usually represent the lower end of the spectrum. Minority group members, for whom unemployment rates often exceed 30 percent, may be especially vulnerable.

Disputes over the Evidence

In an influential 1994 study, David Card and Alan Krueger challenged the belief that minimum wages reduce employment opportunities.[1] In this study, the authors compared employment levels at fast-food restaurants in New Jersey and Pennsylvania following increases in the New Jersey minimum wage. They concluded that there was no negative effect from the increase. That finding has not been universally accepted, however. An analysis of somewhat different data from similar fast-food franchises (Burger King, Wendy's, and KFC) in these states reached the opposite conclusion. More generally, the methods used in the Card-Krueger study have been subject to considerable dispute.[2] Still, although theoretical models provide the clear prediction that higher minimum wages should reduce employment, measuring this effect empirically has proven rather difficult.[3]

POLICY CHALLENGE

As for many economic questions, the minimum wage is controversial because higher minimums represent a trade-off between two desirable goals: (1) The notion that everyone who works full time deserves to make a "living wage"; and (2) The belief that low wages are needed to encourage the hiring of low-skill workers. In such cases making an informed policy choice requires lots of information. You need to know how many people on minimum wage jobs rely on earnings from those jobs as their main source of family income, how earnings of those people would be affected by a higher minimum, and how many jobs might be lost because of the higher minimum. None of these questions is easy to answer definitively, so it not surprising that voters and policymakers are often ambiguous about which position to take on minimum wage legislation.

[1]David Card and Alan Krueger, "Minimum Wages and Employment: A Case Study of the Fast-Food Industry in New Jersey and Pennsylvania," *American Economic Review* (September 1994): 722–793.

[2]The controversy over the Card-Krueger results is summarized in the July 1995 issue of *Industrial and Labor Relations Review.*

[3]For a recent review of the evidence see D. Neumark, J.M.I. Salas and W. Wascher, "Revisiting the Minimum Wage-Employment Debate: Throwing out the Baby with the Bathwater?" NBER Working Paper # 18681. January, 2013. In this paper the authors conclude that each 10 percent increase in the minimum wage is associated with a reduction of 3 percent in teen employment.

Labor Supply and Wages

For individuals, the wages they can earn represent the opportunity cost of not working at a paying job. Of course, no one works 24 hours a day, so individuals incur these opportunity costs regularly. They may refuse jobs with long hours, opt for early retirement, or choose to work in their homes. Presumably, all such decisions will be made to maximize utility. That is, individuals will balance the monetary rewards from working against the psychic benefits of other, nonpaid activities.

A change in the wage rate, because it changes opportunity costs, will alter individuals' decisions. Although, as we show in the appendix to this chapter, the story is relatively complicated, in general we might expect that a rise in the wage would encourage market work. With higher wages, people might voluntarily agree to work overtime or to moonlight, they might retire later, or they might do less at home. In graphical terms, the supply curve for labor is positively sloped—higher wages cause more labor to be supplied.

Two additional observations should be kept in mind about labor supply. First, "wages" should be interpreted broadly to include all forms of compensation. Fringe benefits (such as health insurance), paid vacations, and firm-paid child care are important supplements to cash earnings. When we speak of the market wage w, we include all such returns to workers and these also represent costs to firms.

A second important lesson of labor supply theory is that supply decisions are based on individual preferences. If people prefer some jobs to others, perhaps because some offer a more pleasant work environment, labor supply curves will differ. Similarly, if attitudes toward work change, labor supply curves will shift (as seems to have been the case for married women during the 1960s and 1970s). Hence, a wide variety of "noneconomic" factors may shift labor supply curves.

13-5 Equilibrium Input Price Determination

Bringing the various strands of our analysis together provides a straightforward view of how input prices are determined. This process is illustrated by the familiar demand (D) and supply (S) curves in Figure 13.3. For this figure we have chosen to diagram equilibrium wage determination in the general labor market, but the graph would serve equally well for workers with specific skills or for any other input market. Given this demand-supply configuration, the equilibrium wage is w^*, and L^* units of labor are employed. As for any market, this equilibrium will tend to persist from period to period until demand or supply curves shift. As described earlier, in Application 13.2, government wage regulation also may affect this equilibrium outcome.

Shifts in Demand and Supply

Although you should by now be familiar with analyses in which demand or supply curves shift, the details of input markets are quite different from those for goods markets, so that some review may be in order. Marginal productivity theory provides the guide for understanding shifts in demand. Any factor that shifts a firm's underlying production function (such as the development of labor-saving technologies) will shift its input demand curve. In addition, because the demand for inputs is ultimately derived from the demand for the goods those inputs produce and the prices paid for those goods, happenings in product markets also can shift input demand curves.

Figure 13.3 Equilibrium in an Input Market

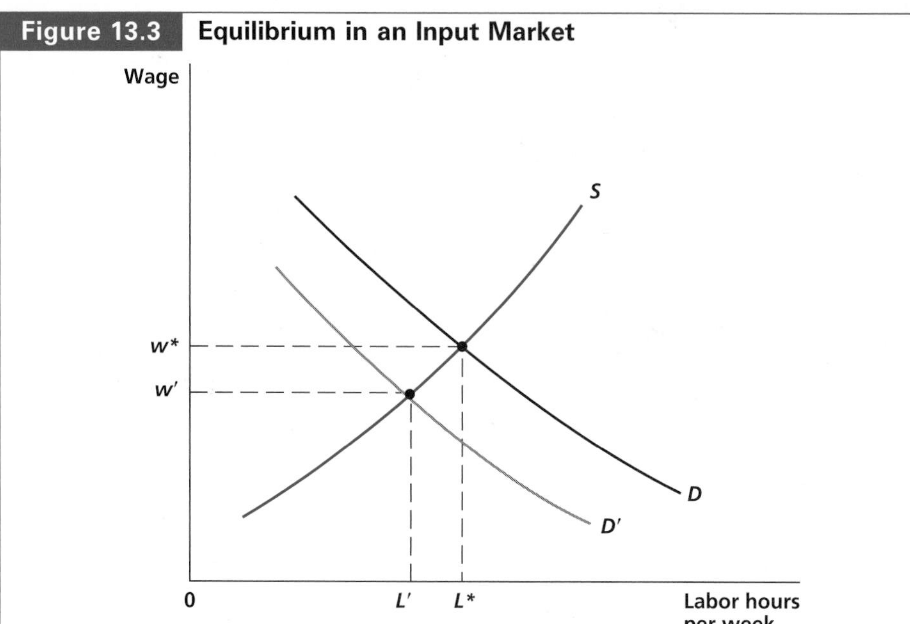

An equilibrium wage (w^*) in the labor market is determined by demand (D) and supply (S). A shift in demand to D' would lower the wage to W' and the quantity of labor demanded to L'. If the wage does not adjust immediately, there may be some unemployment.

MICRO QUIZ 13.3

In the United States, Social Security taxes of about 6 percent are levied on workers, with a matching 6 percent paid by firms. What will determine who *actually pays* these taxes?

An increased demand for four-wheel-drive vehicles raises the price of the vehicles and increases the demand for workers who make them. On the other hand, a decline in the price of clothing brought on, say, by an increase in imports would reduce the demand for apparel workers. This situation can be reflected in Figure 13.3 by the shift in the demand curve to D'. The impact of such a shift would be to reduce equilibrium wages of apparel workers from w^* to w' and equilibrium employment from L^* to L'. If the adjustment in wages does not occur quickly (perhaps because wages are fixed by custom or long-term contract), some unemployment may be experienced in moving to this new equilibrium.

Input supply curves are shifted by a variety of factors. For inputs that are produced by other firms (power tools, railroad locomotives, and so forth), the standard supply analysis applies—supply curves are shifted by anything that affects the input producers' costs. For labor input, changes in individuals' preferences (both for "work" in general and for the characteristics of specific jobs) will shift supply.

All of these various reasons for shifting demand or supply curves for inputs are summarized in Table 13.2. It is important to keep these various factors in mind when you try to understand how the economy as a whole operates. Because people get their incomes from input markets, any investigation of well-being requires an understanding

Table 13.2 Factors That Shift Input Demand and Supply Curves

DEMAND	LABOR SUPPLY	CAPITAL SUPPLY
Demand Shifts Outward	***Supply Shits Outward***	
Rise in output price	Decreased preference for leisure	Fall in input costs of equipment makers
Increase in marginal productivity	Increased desirability of job	Technical progress in making equipment
Demand Shifts Inward	***Supply Shifts Inward***	
Fall in output price	Increased preference for leisure	Rise in input costs of equipment makers
Decrease in marginal productivity	Decreased desirability of job	

of these factors. Application 13.3: Why Is Wage Inequality Increasing? examines some recent trends.

13-6 Monopsony

In some situations, a firm may not be a price taker for the inputs it buys. It may be necessary for the firm to offer a wage above that currently prevailing to attract more employees, or the firm may be able to get a better price on some equipment by restricting its purchases. To explore these situations, it is most convenient to examine the polar case of **monopsony** (a single buyer) in an input market.

Monopsony
Condition in which one firm is the only hirer in a particular input market.

Marginal Expense

If there is only one buyer of an input, that firm faces the entire market supply curve for the input. In order to increase its hiring of labor, say, by one or more units, the firm must move to a higher point on this supply curve. This will involve paying not only a higher wage to the last worker hired but also additional wages to those workers already employed. The extra cost of hiring the added worker therefore exceeds his or her wage rate, and the price-taking assumption we made earlier no longer holds. Instead, for a monopsonist facing an upward-sloping supply curve for an input, the **marginal expense** will exceed the market price of the input. For labor input, for example, the marginal expense (ME_L) of hiring one more worker exceeds the market wage (w).

Marginal expense
The cost of hiring one more unit of an input. Will exceed the price of the input if the firm faces an upward-sloping supply curve for the input.

Notice the similarity between the concept of the marginal expense of an input and the marginal revenue for a monopolist. Both concepts are intended to be used when firms possess market power and their choices have an effect on prices. In such situations, firms are no longer price takers. Instead, firms will recognize that their actions affect prices and will use this information in making profit-maximizing decisions.

A Numerical Illustration

This distinction is easiest to see with a numerical example. Suppose that Yellowstone National Park is the only hirer of bear wardens. Suppose also that the number of

APPLICATION 13.3

Why Is Wage Inequality Increasing?

Wages earned by workers have exhibited a large degree of inequality throughout history. In *The Republic,* for example, Plato laments the fact that some workers make more than 10 times what others make. In recent years, wage inequality seems to have increased throughout the world and especially in the United States.

Measuring Wage Inequality

A first step in understanding the inequality of wages among workers is to think about issues of measurement. One reason earnings differ among workers is that they work differing numbers of hours or may have only seasonal jobs. It is customary, therefore, to look only at full-time, year-round workers in studying inequality. Often researchers look only at men (or women) to try to control for the large changes in the gender composition of the workforce that have occurred in recent years. Finally, it is important to look at total wages (including fringe benefits). Otherwise, changes in the makeup of workers' pay packages can influence trends in inequality.

Studies that address these various issues tend to conclude that wage inequality increased fairly significantly in the United States over the 40 years from 1967 to 2007. One common measure compares the earnings of workers at the 90th percentile of the wage distribution (about $100,000 in 2010) to those of workers at the 10th percentile ($18,000). This 90/10 ratio stood at about 4.2 in 1967 for male, full-time, year-round workers. By 2010, the ratio had risen to 5.5—clearly a significant increase in wage inequality.[1] European countries have also experienced a smaller, but significant increase in inequality over this period.

Supply-Demand Analysis

A careful consideration of demand and supply trends in the labor market is a good starting place for understanding these trends.[2] Any factor that increased the supply of low-wage workers or increased the demand for high-wage workers would be a candidate for explaining the trend. Factors that increased the supply of high-wage workers or increased the demand for low-wage workers would tend to work against the trend.

Researchers have identified two important trends in labor demand that have acted to increase inequality. First, and most important, recent years have seen a sharp increase in the relative demand for technically skilled workers, especially those with computer experience.[3] A second trend affecting labor markets has been a decline in the demand for low-wage workers. Economists have identified two forces behind this trend: (1) a decline in the importance of manufacturing industries in the overall economy, and (2) sustained increases in imports of goods that are produced mainly with unskilled labor. The decline in unionization in the United States may also have exerted some influence by reducing wage premiums earned by union members.

Trends in labor supply have also tended to exacerbate wage inequality. Large (legal and illegal) immigration in the 1990s may have increased the supply of low-wage workers, at least in some areas. Increasing labor supply by women probably has exerted some downward influence on the wages of low-wage men. Overall, however, it appears that these relative supply effects were not as important in affecting inequality as the demand factors.

POLICY CHALLENGE

Many people think that wage inequality is too extreme in the United States (and possibly in other countries). How would you judge whether there is "too much" inequality? If you decided that inequality were too large, what kinds of policies might you propose to change it? For example, what supply- and demand-oriented policies might have a significant impact on wage inequality? What are potential shortcomings of using such a market-based approach? Suppose instead that you opted for a more direct tax/transfer scheme to level wages. What are some of the potential pitfalls to such an approach? More generally, should one focus on wage inequality per se or perhaps on the related problem of poverty and low incomes?

[1]These figures are updated regularly by the U.S. Census Bureau. See http://www.census.gov/hhes/income/data/historical/inequality/.

[2]For a thorough, although a bit out-of-date, econometric investigation, see L F. Katz and K. M. Murphy, "Changes in Relative Wages, 1963–1987: Supply and Demand Factors," *Quarterly Journal of Economics* (February 1992): 35–78.

[3]For a thorough examination of the relation between technical skills and wages see C. Goldin and L.F. Katz, *The Race Between Education and Technology*. Cambridge, MA. Harvard University Press. 2010. A different and somewhat tongue-in-cheek view is provided by J.E. DiNardo and J. Pischke, "The Returns to Computer Use Revisited: Have Pencils Changed the Wage Structure Too?" *Quarterly Journal of Economics* 112(1), February, 1997. Pages 291–303.

people willing to take this job (L) is a simple positive function of the hourly wage (w) given by

$$L = \frac{1}{2}w \tag{13.6}$$

This relationship between the wage and the number of people who offer their services as bear wardens is shown in the first two columns of Table 13.3. Total labor costs ($w \cdot L$) are shown in the third column, and the marginal expense of hiring each warden is shown in the fourth column. The extra expense associated with adding another warden always exceeds the wage rate paid to that person. The reason is clear. Not only does a newly hired warden receive the higher wage, but all previously hired wardens also get a higher wage. A monopsonist will take these extra expenses into account in its hiring decisions.

A graph can be used to help to clarify this relationship. Figure 13.4 shows the supply curve (S) for bear wardens. If Yellowstone wishes to hire three wardens, it must

Table 13.3 Labor Costs of Hiring Bear Wardens in Yellowstone Park

HOURLY WAGE	WORKERS SUPPLIED PER HOUR	TOTAL LABOR COST PER HOUR	MARGINAL EXPENSE
$2	1	$2	$2
4	2	8	6
6	3	18	10
8	4	32	14
10	5	50	18
12	6	72	22
14	7	98	26

Figure 13.4 Marginal Expense of Hiring Bear Wardens

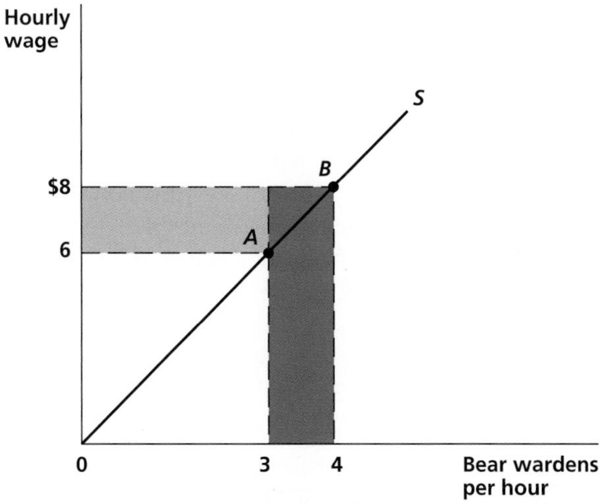

Since Yellowstone Park is (in this example) the only hirer of bear wardens, it must raise the hourly wage offered from \$6 to \$8 if it wishes to hire a fourth warden. The marginal expense of hiring that warden is \$14—his or her wage (\$8, shown in dark blue) plus the extra \$2 per hour that must be paid to the other three wardens (shown in light blue).

pay \$6 per hour, and total outlays will be \$18 per hour. This situation is reflected by point *A* on the supply curve. If Yellowstone tries to hire a fourth warden, it must offer \$8 per hour to everyone—it must move to point *B* on the supply curve. Total outlays are now \$32 per hour, so the marginal expense of hiring the fourth worker is \$14 per hour. By comparing the sizes of the total outlay rectangles, we can see why the marginal expense is higher than the wage paid to the fourth worker. That worker's hourly wage is shown by the dark blue rectangle—it is \$8 per hour. The other three workers, who were previously earning \$6 per hour, now earn \$8. This extra outlay is shown in light blue. Total labor expenses for four wardens exceed those for three by the area of both of the rectangles. In this case, marginal expense exceeds the wage because Yellowstone Park is the sole hirer of people in this unusual occupation.

Monopsonist's Input Choice

As for any profit-maximizing firm, a monopsonist will hire an input up to the point at which the additional revenue and additional cost of hiring one more unit are equal. For the case of labor, this requires

$$ME_L = MVP_L. \tag{13.7}$$

In the special case of a price taker that faces an infinitely elastic labor supply ($ME_L = w$), Equations 13.5 and 13.7 are identical. However, if the firm faces a positively sloped labor supply curve, Equation 13.7 dictates a different level of input choice, as we now show.

A Graphical Demonstration

The monopsonist's choice of labor input is illustrated in Figure 13.5. The firm's demand curve for labor (*D*) is drawn initially on the assumption that the firm is a price taker. The ME_L curve associated with the labor supply curve (*S*) is constructed in much the same way that the marginal revenue curve associated with a demand curve can be constructed. Because *S* is positively sloped, the ME_L curve always lies above *S*. The profit-maximizing level of labor input for the monopsonist is given by L_1. At this level of input use, marginal expense is equal to marginal value product (*MVP*). At L_1 the wage rate in the market is given by w_1. The quantity of labor demanded falls short of that which would be hired in a perfectly competitive market (L^*). The firm has restricted input demand to take advantage of its monopsonistic position in the labor market.

The formal similarities between this analysis and the monopoly analysis we presented in Chapter 11 should be clear. In particular, the actual "demand curve" for a monopsonist consists of a single point. In Figure 13.5 this point is given by L_1, w_1. The monopsonist has chosen this point as the most desirable of all those points on the supply curve *S*. The firm would not choose another point unless some external change (such as a shift in the demand for the firm's output or a change in technology) affects labor's marginal value product.

Numerical Example Revisited

Let's return to the Yellowstone Park Company's decision to hire bear wardens as illustrated in Table 13.3. Suppose careful calculation has suggested to the park's managers that each bear warden has a marginal value product of \$18 per hour in terms of increasing visitors to the park to view the well-tended bears. The figures in Table 13.3 then suggest that the park should hire five workers at an hourly wage of \$10 per hour. If the firm were to

Figure 13.5 **Pricing in a Monopsonistic Labor Market**

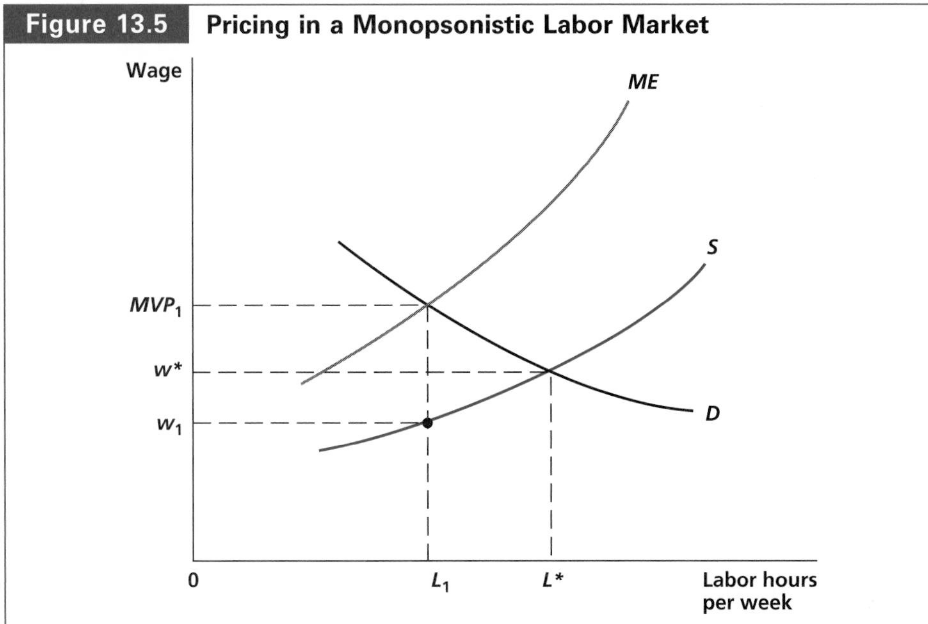

If a firm faces a positively sloped supply curve for labor (S), it will base its decisions on the marginal expense of labor curve (ME_L). Because S is positively sloped, ME_L lies above S. The curve S can be thought of as an average cost of labor curve, and the ME_L curve is marginal to S. At L_1 the equilibrium condition $ME_L = MVP_L$ holds, and this quantity will be hired at a market wage rate w_1.

contemplate hiring a sixth worker, it would have to raise all wages to \$12 per hour, making the marginal expense associated with that hiring \$22—that is \$12 to hire the sixth worker and \$10 to pay each of the previously hired workers \$2 per hour more. Clearly hiring the sixth worker does not make sense because he or she would add only \$18 in added visitor revenue. Notice also that, when the firm hires five workers, each worker only earns \$10 per hour, whereas the worker's value to the firm is \$18 per hour. Such a difference between marginal productivity and the wage paid could not persist in a competitive labor market because other firms would find it profitable to hire the bear wardens away from the Yellowstone Park Company. But the difference might continue to exist in this case because the company is the sole hirer of people with this unusual skill.

KEEP *in* MIND

Calculating Marginal Expense Requires a Supply Curve

The marginal expense concept is based on an upward-sloping supply curve. It is because a firm must pay a higher wage to hire more workers that the marginal expense of hiring exceeds the wage actually paid. This extra expense cannot be calculated without knowledge of the labor supply curve facing the firm. This is precisely the same situation as a monopoly supplier of a good for which marginal revenue cannot be computed without knowledge of the associated demand curve for the good.

Monopsonists and Resource Allocation

In addition to restricting its input demand, the monopsonist pays an input less than its marginal value product. This result is also illustrated in Figure 13.5. At the monopsonist's preferred choice of labor input (L_1), a wage of w_1 prevails in the market. For this level of input demand, the firm is willing to pay an amount equal to MVP_1: This is the amount of extra revenue that hiring another worker would provide to the firm. At L_1 the monopsonist pays workers less than they are "worth" to the firm. This is a clear indication that this firm uses too little labor. Total output could be increased by drawing labor from elsewhere in the economy into this industry. It should be clear from the figure that the extent of this misallocation of resources will be greater the more inelastic the supply of labor is to the monopsonist. The less responsive to low wages the supply of labor is, the more the monopsonist can take advantage of this situation.

Is there a deadweight loss from the monopsony pictured in Figure 13.5? How would this loss be shown graphically? Who would suffer this loss?

Causes of Monopsony

To practice monopsonistic behavior a firm must possess considerable power in the market for a particular input. If the market is reasonably competitive, this cannot occur because other firms will recognize the profit potential reflected in the gap between *MVP*s and input costs. They will therefore bid for these inputs, driving their prices up to equality with marginal value products. Under such conditions the supply of labor to any one firm will be nearly infinitely elastic (because of the alternative employment possibilities available), and monopsonistic behavior will be impossible. Our analysis suggests monopsonistic outcomes will be observed in real-world situations in which, for some reason, effective competition for inputs is lacking. For example, some firms may occupy a monopsonistic position by being the only source of employment in a small town. Because moving costs for workers are high, alternative employment opportunities for local workers are unattractive, and the firm may be able to exert a strong effect on wages paid. Similarly, it may sometimes be the case that only one firm hires a particularly specialized type of input. If the alternative earnings prospects for that input are unattractive, its supply to the firm will be inelastic, presenting the firm with the opportunity for monopsonistic behavior. For example, marine engineers with many years of experience in designing nuclear submarines must work for the one or two companies that produce these vessels. Because other jobs would not make use of these workers' specialized training, alternative employment is not particularly attractive. Since the government occupies a monopoly position in the production of a number of goods requiring specialized inputs (space travel, armed forces, and national political offices, to name a few), it would be expected to be in a position to exercise monopsony power. In other cases a group of firms may combine to form a cartel in their hiring decisions (and, perhaps, in their output decisions too). Application 13.4: Monopsony in the Market for Sports Stars illustrates this relationship in a situation in which it is possible to obtain direct measures of workers' marginal value.

APPLICATION 13.4

Monopsony in the Market for Sports Stars

Occasionally powerful cartels of hirers can achieve a successful monopsony. Professional sports leagues that are able to implement restrictions on competition among teams in hiring players provide several important examples.

Why Study Sports?

Although some economists may indeed be sports fanatics, this is not the primary reason they study the wages of sports stars. Rather, professional athletics represents one of the few industries in which worker productivity is directly observable. Batting averages in baseball, scoring in basketball or hockey, and defensive tackles' "sacks" in football can all be measured and (more importantly) correlated with spectator attendance and television ratings. These provide clear evidence of each person's marginal revenue product—information that is simply not available in most other labor markets.

Monopsony in Major League Baseball

Throughout much of its history, major league baseball limited competition for players among teams with a "reserve clause" that bound players to the teams that first signed them. The monopsony created by this clause was strengthened by a questionable series of court cases that effectively barred the major leagues from prosecution under the U.S. antitrust laws. G. W. Scully constructed numerical estimates of the effects of this monopsony in a famous 1974 article.[1] Scully analyzed which aspects of individual player performance (batting averages, on-base percentages, earned run averages, and so forth) were most closely related to a team's overall performance. His analysis of these data showed that most players' marginal value products exceed their salaries by substantial margins. Major stars were especially underpaid relative to the revenue they generated for their teams. For example, Sandy Koufax (the great Dodger left-hander during the 1950s and 1960s) may have been paid less than 25 percent of what he was "worth."

It was only a matter of time before players came to recognize the effect of the reserve clause and took organized action against it. A players' strike in 1972 (coupled with legal action brought by St. Louis Cardinal outfielder Curt Flood) eventually led to the adoption of a free-agent provision in players' contracts as a partial replacement of the reserve clause. Although the leagues have tried several actions to reestablish their cartel position (such as caps on team salaries and limiting league expansion), they have been unable to return to the powerful position they occupied prior to 1970.

Basketball and Michael Jordan

Similar research on professional basketball players' salaries suggests that the National Basketball Association (NBA) has at times been able to exercise monopsony power. Although the NBA never had the advantage of the reserve clause (because, unlike baseball, it is not exempt from antitrust laws), various draft limitations and salary-cap provisions have served to restrain salaries to some extent. Stars from the 1950s and 1960s such as Wilt Chamberlain, Bill Russell, and Oscar Robertson were probably the most affected by such limits. But it appears that even Michael Jordan (undoubtedly the most famous sports figure of the 1990s) may have been underpaid. Of course, it is hard to feel sorry for Jordan, who was still earning over $10 million a year (as well as getting income from Nike and MCI endorsements) after returning from his brief, mediocre career as a minor league baseball player. But empirical research suggests that he may have been worth over $70 million per year to the NBA as a whole in terms of the higher television ratings they enjoyed when he played.[2]

TO THINK ABOUT

1. Professional leagues argue that they need to constrain competition in players' salaries to ensure some "competitive balance" in league play. Why might this argument have some plausibility? Do teams need to have monopsony power to deal with this problem?
2. The National Collegiate Athletic Association (NCAA) currently forbids student-athletes from obtaining any form of compensation for their performance. Given the huge revenues that schools receive from sports (especially football and basketball), should the NCAA be regarded as a monopsonistic cartel? In practice how does competition for the best players manifest itself in college sports? How does the possibility of playing at the professional level affect schools' and athletes' decisions?

[1] G. W. Scully, "Pay and Performance in Major League Baseball," *American Economic Review* (December 1974): 915–930. For more detail on the status of the players' labor market, see *Scully's The Business of Major League Baseball* (Chicago: University of Chicago Press, 1989).

[2] J. A. Hausman and G. K. Leonard, "Superstars in the National Basketball Association: Economic Value and Policy," *Journal of Labor Economics* (October 1997): 586–624.

Bilateral Monopoly

Bilateral monopoly
A market in which both suppliers and demanders have monopoly power. Pricing is indeterminate in such markets.

In some cases there may be monopoly power on both sides of an input market. That is, suppliers of the input may have a monopoly, and the buyer of the input may be a monopsony. In this situation of **bilateral monopoly** the price of the input is indeterminate and will ultimately depend on the bargaining abilities of the parties involved.

Figure 13.6 illustrates this general result. Although the "supply" and "demand" curves in this diagram intersect at P^*, Q^*, this market equilibrium will not occur, because neither the supplier nor the demander of the input is a price taker. Instead, the monopoly supplier of the input will use the marginal revenue curve (MR) associated with the demand curve D to calculate a preferred price-quantity combination of P_1, Q_1. The monopsonistic buyer of this input, on the other hand, will use the marginal expense curve (ME) to calculate a preferred equilibrium of P_2, Q_2. Although both the monopolist and monopsonist here seek to restrict the quantity hired, the two opposing actors in this market differ significantly on what they think the input should be paid. This will lead to some sort of bargaining between the two parties, with suppliers holding out for P_1 and demanders offering only P_2. Protracted labor disputes in major industries and "holdouts" by sports and entertainment celebrities are evidence of this type of market structure. Application 13.5: Superstars looks at various types of imperfect competition in the market for rock stars.

Figure 13.6 Bilateral Monopoly

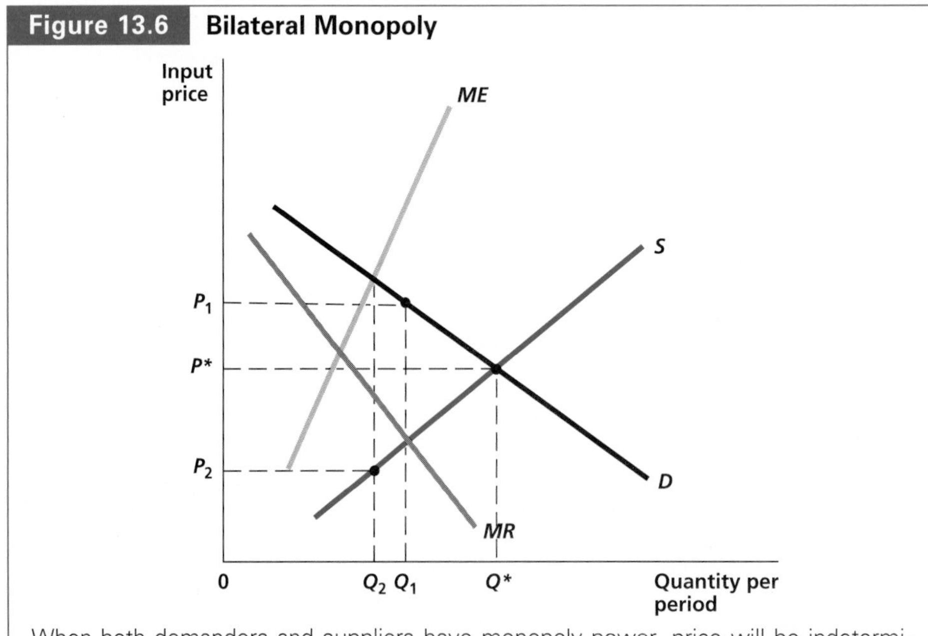

When both demanders and suppliers have monopoly power, price will be indeterminate. Suppliers will want P_1, Q_1, but demanders will want P_2, Q_2.

APPLICATION 13.5

Superstars

There are "superstars" in virtually every walk of life. Top lawyers, physicians, CEOs, golfers, interior decorators, and rock musicians all make extraordinary amounts of money. In this example, we describe the economic theory of superstars generally and then look more specifically at the case of rock musicians.

The Theory of Superstars

Although economists have taken note of superstar salaries for more than a hundred years,[1] the first detailed economic theory was described by Sherwin Rosen in 1981.[2] He explains the extraordinarily large salaries of superstars as stemming from the fact that great talent is scarce. Individuals who possess economically valuable talents will be able to benefit both by charging higher prices for their services and by being able to sell more services. Hence, the total revenue received will increase more rapidly than will actual talent itself. For performance artists, this process will also be aided by the fact that serving increasing numbers of consumers may not involve any substantial increase in costs for the artist—a singer incurs roughly the same cost in performing for 10 people as in performing for 10,000. Artists with great talent will always possess some market power, but they will also face competition from other artists. The actual economic rents that any artist is able to achieve will depend on how many close competitors he or she has.

Evidence from Rock Concerts

The theory of superstars has been applied to a wide variety of pricing situations. In one especially enjoyable application, Alan Krueger used it to explain the rapid increase in the prices for rock concert tickets between 1996 and 2003.[3] According to Krueger's data, the average price for a rock concert ticket increased by more than 80 percent during this 7-year period. Such increases exceeded by a wide margin increases in price for movie or sports tickets during the same period and seem to have occurred for both established stars and new artists. The increases do not seem to be explained by increases in the costs of putting on concerts. Indeed, those costs have probably fallen a bit as new audio technology has been introduced.

Krueger looks at three possible explanations for the increase in rock concert prices. First, he examines the possibility that the trend may reflect an increase in the returns to superstardom. In Rosen's original model, an increase in demand for the services of stars does indeed raise the relative returns of superstars. But, according to Krueger, that was not the case for rock concerts.

Krueger's second potential explanation is that the market for rock concerts may have become more monopolized after 1996. There was a major increase in the fraction of concerts handled by the largest promoters after 1996, so it is possible that the price increase represented an increase in monopoly power. But promotion of rock concerts was more concentrated in a few hands during the 1980s, and Krueger can find little evidence of large profits being made by promoters now.

The author's favorite explanation for the increase in ticket prices concerns the huge increase in illegal copying of music that occurred over the period he examined. Rock artists are in two businesses: performing in concerts and selling their music on CDs or over the Internet. Previously, because people who attended concerts were also likely to buy a group's CDs, performers had an incentive to keep concert prices low in order to expand CD sales. Recently, as CD sales have been eroded through illegal copying, artists may find the low-price strategy less compelling and choose to exercise their market power by raising concert prices. Krueger credits this hypothesis to the singer David Bowie, who warns his fellow performers that they had better get used to touring if they want to make any money in the future.

TO THINK ABOUT

1. Some people argue that super star athletes, musicians, or CEOs don't "deserve" their high rates of pay because in any other occupation they would make far less. Do you agree with this characterization? Are such high rates of pay similar to monopolistic profits that may represent a distortion in resource allocation?
2. Is the "pirating" of music and other copyright material necessarily bad for artists? In what ways might they gain from such activity? How should an artist approach the "optimal" enforcement of his or her copyright?

[1]For example, in his *Principles of Economics, 8th ed.* (London: McMillan and Co., 1920), Alfred Marshall theorizes about the £10,000 earned in a season by the opera star Elizabeth Billington in 1801 (page 686).

[2]S. Rosen, "The Economics of Superstars," *American Economic Review* (December 1981): 845–858.

[3]A. B. Krueger "The Economics of Real Superstars: The Market for Rock Concerts in the Material World," *Journal of Labor Economics* (January 2005): 1–30.

SUMMARY

In this chapter we illustrated some models of markets for inputs. The conclusions of this examination include:

- Firms will hire any input up to the point at which the marginal expense of hiring one more unit is equal to the marginal revenue yielded by selling the extra output that input produces.
- If the firm is a price taker in both the market for its inputs and the market for its output, profit maximization requires that it employ that level of inputs for which the market price of each input (for example, the wage) is equal to the marginal value product of that input (for example, $P \cdot MP_L$).
- If the price of an input rises, the firm will hire less of it for two reasons. First, the higher price will cause the firm to substitute other inputs for the one whose price has risen. Second, the higher price will raise the firm's costs and reduce the amount it is able to sell. This output effect will also cause fewer units of the input to be hired.
- Input supply curves are positively sloped. Capital equipment supply is much like the supply of any good. Labor supply involves individual choices (see the appendix to this chapter).
- Equilibria in input markets resemble those in goods' markets, though reasons for shifts in supply and demand curves are somewhat different.
- If a firm is the sole hirer of an input (a monopsony), its hiring decisions will affect market prices of inputs. The marginal expense associated with hiring an additional unit of an input will exceed that input's price. Firms will take this into account in their hiring decisions—they will restrict hiring below what it would be under competitive conditions.

REVIEW QUESTIONS

1. In the supply-demand model of input pricing, who are the demanders? What type of assumptions would you use to explain their behavior? In this model, who are the suppliers? What types of assumptions would you use to explain their behavior?
2. Profit maximization implies that firms will make input choices in a marginal way. Explain why the following marginal rules found in this chapter are specific applications of this general idea:
   a. $MR_L = ME_L$
   b. $MP_L \cdot MR = ME_L = w$
   c. $MVP_L = ME_L = w$
   d. $MVP_L = w$
   e. $MVP_L = ME_L > w$

   If firms follow these various rules, will they also be producing a profit-maximizing level of output? That is, will they produce that quantity for which $MR = MC$? Will they also be minimizing costs if they use these rules? Explain your answers both intuitively and with algebra.
3. Explain why if a price-taking firm has only one variable input the MVP curve is also its demand curve for that input, but if the firm has two or more variable inputs, its demand curve for one of them reflects a whole family of MVP curves.
4. A fall in the price of an input induces a profit-maximizing firm to experience both substitution and output effects that cause it to hire more of that input. Explain how the profit-maximizing assumption is used in explaining the direction of each of these effects. Did you have to use the assumption that the input is not inferior in your analysis? Do you think a similar statement can be made about inferior inputs?
5. Suppose the price of an input used by firms with fixed-proportions production functions were to fall. Why would such a change not cause any substitution effects for these firms' input demand? Would there, however, be output effects? What would determine the size of these effects?
6. Because input prices are explained by the forces of supply and demand, it is important to understand how various factors may shift these curves. For each of the following factors that may affect market equilibrium in a specific labor market, describe which curve will be shifted and how this shift will affect wage rates:
   - an increase in the price of the output that workers produce
   - an increase in the costs of inputs that substitute for labor
   - an increase in wages being offered in some other market
   - a large influx of new workers into the market
   - regulations requiring that firms provide health insurance for their workers (explain why this may shift both curves)
   - institution of a tax on wages
7. In Chapter 9, we described the notions of consumer and producer surplus as they relate to a competitive equilibrium. How should similar areas be interpreted in a

supply-demand graph of the competitive equilibrium in a factor market?

8. In Chapter 11, we showed the relationship between marginal revenues and market price for a monopoly to be given by

$$MR = P\left(1 + \frac{1}{e}\right),$$

where e is the price elasticity of demand for the product. For a monopsony, a similar relationship holds for the marginal expense associated with hiring more labor:

$$ME = w\left(1 + \frac{1}{e}\right),$$

where e is the elasticity of supply of labor to the firm. Use this equation to show

a. that for a firm that is a price taker in the labor market, $ME = w$;

b. that $ME > w$ for a firm facing a labor supply curve that is not infinitely elastic at the prevailing wage; and

c. that the gap between ME and w is larger the smaller e is.

Explain all of these results intuitively.

9. How would you measure the strength of a monopsonist in an input market? Would a monopsony necessarily be very profitable? What would you need to add to Figure 13.5 in order to show a monopsonist's profit graphically?

10. "In a situation of bilateral monopoly, the two parties are more likely to agree on quantity than on price." Explain why this is the case.

PROBLEMS

13.1. A landowner has three farms (*A*, *B*, and *C*) of differing fertility. The levels of output for the three farms with one, two, and three laborers employed are as follows:

NUMBER OF LABORERS	LEVEL OF OUTPUT		
	FARM *A*	FARM *B*	FARM *C*
1	10	8	5
2	17	11	7
3	21	13	8

For example, if one laborer were hired for each farm, the total output would be $10 + 8 + 5 = 23$. This would represent a poor allocation of labor, since if the farm *C* laborer were assigned to farm *A* the total output would be $17 + 8 = 25$.

a. If market conditions caused the landowner to hire five laborers, what would be the most productive allocation of that labor? How much would be produced? What is the marginal product of the last worker?

b. If we assume that farm output is sold in a perfectly competitive market with one unit of output priced at $1, and we assume that labor market equilibrium occurs when five workers are hired, what wage is paid? How much profit does the landowner receive?

c. Although most of the discussion in this chapter involves marginal ideas, the data in this problem use total output levels. How would you calculate a marginal value product of labor schedule from the data provided? Using this schedule, show how the condition $w = MVP_L$ can be applied for wage rates of $5, $4, and $3.

13.2. Assume that the quantity of envelopes licked per hour by Sticky Gums, Inc., is $q = 10{,}000\sqrt{L}$ where L is the number of laborers hired per hour by the firm. Assume further that the envelope-licking business is perfectly competitive with a market price of $0.01 per envelope. The marginal product of a worker is given by

$$MP_L = 5{,}000/\sqrt{L}.$$

a. How much labor would be hired at a competitive wage of $10? $5? $2? Use your results to sketch a demand curve for labor.

b. Assume that Sticky Gums hires its labor at an hourly wage of $10. What quantity of envelopes will be licked when the price of a licked envelope is $0.10? $0.05? $0.02? Use your results to sketch a supply curve for licked envelopes.

13.3. Suppose there are a fixed number of 1,000 identical firms in the perfectly competitive concrete pipe industry. Each firm produces 1/1,000 of total market output and each firm's production function for pipe is given by

$$q = \sqrt{KL}$$

and for this production function

$$RTS(L \text{ for } K) = K/L.$$

Suppose also that the market demand for concrete pipe is given by

$$Q = 400{,}000 - 100{,}000P,$$

where Q is total concrete pipe.

a. If $w = v = \$1$, in what ratio will the typical firm use K and L? What will be the long-run average and marginal cost of pipe?

b. In the long-run equilibrium, what will be the market equilibrium price and quantity for concrete pipe? How much will each firm produce? How much labor will be hired by each firm and in the market as a whole?
c. Suppose the market wage, w, rose to \$2 while v remained constant at \$1. How will this change the capital-labor ratio for the typical firm, and how will it affect its marginal costs?
d. Under the conditions of part c, what will the long-run market equilibrium be? How much labor will now be hired by the concrete pipe industry?
e. How much of the change in total labor demand from part b to part d represents the substitution effect resulting from the change in wage and how much represents the output effect?

13.4. Suppose the demand for labor is given by

$$L = -50w + 450$$

and the supply is given by

$$L = 100w,$$

where L represents the number of people employed and w is the real wage rate per hour.

a. What will be the equilibrium levels for w and L in this market?
b. Suppose the government wishes to raise the equilibrium wage to \$4 per hour by offering a subsidy to employers for each person hired.
How much will this subsidy have to be? What will the new equilibrium level of employment be? How much total subsidy will be paid?
c. Suppose instead the government declared a minimum wage of \$4 per hour. How much labor would be demanded at this price? How much unemployment would there be?
d. Graph your results.

13.5. Assume that the market for rental cars for business purposes is perfectly competitive, with the demand for this capital input given by

$$K = 1{,}500 - 25v$$

and the supply given by

$$K = 75v - 500,$$

where K represents the number of cars rented by firms and v is the rental rate per day.

a. What will be the equilibrium levels for v and K in this market?
b. Suppose that following an oil embargo gas prices rise so dramatically that now business firms must take account of gas prices in their car rental decisions. Their demand for rental cars is now given by

$$K = 1{,}700 - 25v - 300g,$$

where g is the per-gallon price of gasoline. What will be the equilibrium levels for v and K if $g = \$2$? If $g = \$3$?
c. Graph your results.
d. Suppose that rental car companies complain to the government about the decline in rental rates they receive because of the increase in the gas price from \$2 to \$3 per gallon. What per car subsidy would be needed from the government to restore the higher rental rate firms received when the gas price was \$2 per gallon? How would the benefits of this subsidy be apportioned between the demanders and suppliers of rental cars?

13.6. Suppose that the supply of labor to a firm is given by

$$L = 100w$$

and the marginal expense of labor is given by

$$ME_L = L/50,$$

where w is the market wage. Suppose also that the firm's demand for labor (marginal revenue product) is given by

$$MRP_L = 10 - 0.01L.$$

a. If the firm acts as a monopsonist, how many workers will it hire in order to maximize profits? What wage will it pay? How will this wage compare to the MRP_L at this employment level?
b. Assume now that the firm must hire its workers in a perfectly competitive labor market, but it still acts as a monopoly when selling its output. How many workers will the firm hire now? What wage will it pay?
c. Graph your results.

13.7. Carl the clothier owns a large garment factory on a remote island. Carl's factory is the only source of employment for most of the islanders, and thus Carl acts as a monopsonist. The supply of garment workers is given by

$$L = 80w$$

and the marginal-expense-of-labor is given by

$$ME_L = L/40,$$

where L is the number of workers hired and w is their hourly wage. Assume also that Carl's labor demand (marginal value product) is given by

$$MVP_L = 10 - 0.025L.$$

a. How many workers will Carl hire in order to maximize his profits, and what wage will he pay?

b. Assume now that the government implements a minimum-wage law covering all garment workers. How many workers will Carl now hire, and how much unemployment will there be if the minimum wage is set at \$3 per hour? \$3.33 per hour? \$4.00 per hour?
c. Graph your results.
d. How does the imposition of a minimum wage under monopsony differ in results from a minimum wage imposed under perfect competition (assuming the minimum wage is above the market-determined wage)?

13.8. The Ajax Coal Company is the only employer in its area. It can hire any number of female workers or male workers it wishes. The supply of female workers is given by

$$L_f = 100w_f$$

$$ME_f = L_f/50$$

and of male workers by

$$L_m = 9w_m^2$$

$$ME_m = \frac{1}{2}\sqrt{L_M}$$

where w_f and w_m are, respectively, the hourly wage rate paid to female and male workers. Assume that Ajax sells its coal in a perfectly competitive market at \$5 per ton and that each worker hired (both men and women) can mine two tons per hour. If the firm wishes to maximize profits, how many female and male workers should be hired and what will the wage rates for these two groups be? How much will Ajax earn in profits per hour on its mining machinery? How will that result compare to one in which Ajax was constrained (say, by market forces) to pay all workers the same wage equal to the value of their marginal products?

Note: The following problems involve mainly the material from the Appendix to Chapter 13.

13.9. Mrs. Smith has a guaranteed income of \$10 per day from an inheritance. Her preferences require her always to spend half her potential income on leisure (H) and consumption (C).

a. What is Mrs. Smith's budget constraint in this situation?
b. How many hours will Mrs. Smith devote to work and to leisure in order to maximize her utility, given that her market wage is \$1.25? \$2.50? \$5.00? \$10.00?
c. Graph the four different budget constraints and sketch in Mrs. Smith's utility-maximizing choices. (Hint: When graphing budget constraints, remember that when $H = 24$, $C = 10$, not 0.)
d. Graph Mrs. Smith's supply-of-labor curve.
e. How will Mrs. Smith's supply-of-labor curve (calculated in part d) shift if her inheritance increases to \$20 per day? Graph both supply curves to illustrate this shift.

13.10. A salesperson has a utility function for earnings of the form $Utility = \sqrt{wl}$ where w is the hourly wage received and l is the number of hours worked in a typical day. This person is choosing between two jobs. The first promises a constant workday of 8 hours per day and an hourly wage of \$50 per hour. The second offers a random workday in which he or she sometimes gets only 4 hours of work, whereas other times he or she gets 12 hours of work.

a. If the probability of 4 hour days is 0.5 (and the probability of 12 hour days is also 0.5), how high must the hourly wage rate be on the risky job to get this person to take it?
b. Assuming that the wage for the risky job is that described in part a, will a proportional tax on daily earnings affect this person's choice of job?
c. How would your answer to part b change if daily earnings were subject to a progressive tax rate in which the first \$300 of daily earnings is not taxed and daily earnings over \$300 are taxed at a rate of 50 percent?
d. What proportional tax rate would yield the same tax revenue as the progressive tax, but not affect this person's choices among jobs?

APPENDIX 13A

Labor Supply

In this appendix, we use the utility-maximization model to study individual labor-supply decisions. The ultimate goal of this discussion is to provide additional details about the labor supply curves that we used to study how wages are determined in Chapter 13.

A13-1 Allocation of Time

Part 2 studied how an individual chooses to allocate a fixed amount of income among a variety of available goods. People must make similar choices in deciding how they will spend their time. The number of hours in a day (or in a year) is absolutely fixed, and time must be used as it passes by. Given this fixed amount of time, any person must decide how many hours to work; how many hours to spend consuming a wide variety of goods, ranging from cars and television sets to operas; how many hours to devote to self-maintenance; and how many hours to sleep. Table 13A.1 shows that there is considerable variation in time use between men and women and among various countries around the world. By studying the division of time people choose to make among their activities, economists are able to under stand labor-supply decisions. Viewing work as only one of a number of choices open to people in the way they spend their time enables us to understand how these decisions may be adjusted in response to changing opportunities.

A Simple Model of Time Use

Leisure
Time spent in any activity other than market work.

We assume that there are only two uses to which any person may devote his or her time: either engaging in market work at a wage rate of w per hour or not working. We refer to nonwork time as **leisure**, but to economists this word does not mean idleness. Time that is not spent in market work can be used in many productive ways: for work in the home, for self-improvement, or for consumption (it takes time to use a television set or a bowling ball).[8] All of these activities contribute to a person's well-being, and time will be allocated to them in a utility-maximizing way.

More specifically, assume that utility depends on consumption of market goods (C) and on the amount of leisure time (H) used. Figure 13A.1 shows an indifference curve map for this utility function. The diagram has the familiar shape introduced in Chapter 2. It shows those combinations of C and H that yield an individual various levels of utility.

Now we must describe the budget constraint that faces this person. If the period we are studying is one day, the individual will work $(24 - H)$ hours. That is, he or she will work all of the hours not devoted to leisure. For this work, she or he will earn w per hour and will use this to buy consumption goods.

[8]For the classic treatment of the allocation of time, See G.S. Becker, "A Theory of the Allocation of Time," *The Economic Journal* (September 1965): 493–517.

Table 13A.1 Time Allocation (Percentage of Time during Typical Week)

	MEN U.S.	MEN JAPAN	MEN RUSSIA	WOMEN U.S.	WOMEN JAPAN	WOMEN RUSSIA
Market work	28.3%	33.6%	35.1%	15.4%	15.3%	25.4%
Housework	8.2	2.1	7.1	18.2	18.5	16.1
Personal care and sleep	40.6	43.1	40.4	42.6	42.9	41.6
Leisure and other	22.9	21.2	17.4	23.8	23.3	16.9

Source: Adapted from F. T. Juster and F. P. Stafford, "The Allocation of Time: Empirical Findings, Behavioral Models and Problems and Measurement," *Journal of Economic Literature* (June 1991), Table 13A.1.

Figure 13A.1 Utility-Maximizing Choice of Hours of Leisure and Work

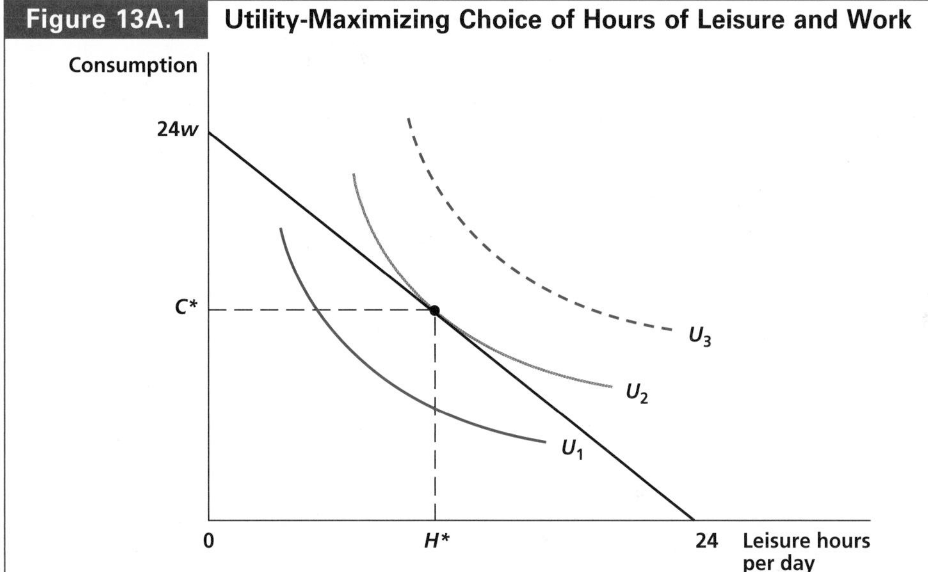

Given his or her budget constraint, this person maximizes utility by choosing H^* hours of leisure and consumption of C^*. At this point, the rate at which he or she is willing to trade H for C (the *MRS*) is equal to the rate at which he or she is able to trade these in the market (the real hourly wage, w).

The Opportunity Cost of Leisure

Each extra hour of leisure this person takes reduces his or her income (and consumption) by w dollars. The hourly wage therefore reflects the opportunity cost of leisure. People have to "pay" this cost for each hour they do not work. The wage rate used to make these calculations should be a real wage in that it should represent how workers can turn their earnings into actual consumer goods. A nominal wage of $1 per hour provides the same purchasing power when the typical item costs $0.25 as does a wage of $100 per hour when that item sells for $25. In either case, the person must work 15 minutes to buy the item. Alternately, in both cases, the opportunity cost of taking one more hour of leisure is to do without four consumption items. In Application 13A.1: The Opportunity Cost of Time, we look at some cases of competing uses of time and illustrate how the notion of opportunity cost can explain the choices people make.

APPLICATION 13A.1

The Opportunity Cost of Time

When people make choices about various ways they might use their time, they take opportunity costs into account. Recognizing this fact leads to some important insights about behavior that might not be understood otherwise.

Travel Choices

In choosing among alternative ways to get to work, people will take both out-of-pocket costs and time costs into account. Studies have found that commuters are quite sensitive to time costs, especially those associated with waiting for a bus or train.[1] People appear to choose between alternative modes of transport in ways that imply the cost of their time is approximately one-half their market wage. Research conducted in connection with the Bay Area Rapid Transit (BART) system in San Francisco, for example, found that fares constituted only about one-fourth of the total costs to passengers. Far more important were time costs involved in getting to the BART stations, parking, waiting for trains, travel, and getting from downtown stations to their final destinations. It is these costs that motivate most commuters in urban areas to continue to use their own cars, even when major investments are made in mass transit systems.

Childbearing

Although the approach seems odd to noneconomists, many economists have studied peoples' decisions to have children by focusing on the costs of children relative to other goods. One of the most important such costs is the opportunity cost of foregone wages for parents who choose to raise children rather than pursue market employment. Not only does this cost amount to more than half of the overall cost of a child, but it also varies significantly among families, depending on the potential wage rate that caregivers might earn. Many economists believe that rising real wage rates for women following World War II is a major reason for the significant decline in birth rates in most Western countries. For example, the birth rate (that is, births per 1,000 people) declined in the United States from 24.1 in 1950 to 13.8 in 2009. Declines in Germany, France, and Japan were even larger. Similarly, lower birth rates in Western countries in relationship to those in developing countries can in part be explained because children are "cheaper" (that is, caregivers have lower wages) in developing countries.[2]

Job Search

When people look for new jobs, they face considerable uncertainty about what openings are available. They must often invest time and other resources in searching for a suitable job match. Again, the opportunity cost of time can play a major role in determining how people look for work. For example, an employed person may undertake only those job interviews that promise significant advancement because he or she may have to take time off from work to make such meetings. On the other hand, an unemployed person may explore a wide variety of approaches to finding a job, some of which (such as checking directly with employers) can be quite time-consuming. The urgency with which an unemployed person looks for work may also be affected by whether he or she is eligible for unemployment benefits because such benefits provide a significant subsidy to further search. Indeed, econometric estimates suggest that each 10 percent increase in weekly unemployment benefits is associated with about half a week's extra unemployment.[3]

TO THINK ABOUT

1. Why do studies of urban transit choices find that people value their time at only about half their potential wage rates? Doesn't the theory of choice imply that the marginal rate of substitution between work and leisure should be given by the full wage rate?
2. Studies of childbearing show that higher-income families tend to have fewer children than lower-income families. Is this finding consistent with a theory that has people choosing the number of children they will have on the basis of their incomes and on the relative price of children?

[1]The classic reference is T. A. Domencich and D. McFadden, *Urban Travel Demand* (Amsterdam: North Holland Press, 1973).
[2]For a discussion that uses economic theory to explain a number of regularities about birth rates, see G. Becker, "On the Interaction between Quantity and Quality of Children," *Journal of Political Economy* (March/April 1973): S279–S288.
[3]For a summary, see P. M. Decker, "Incentive Effects of Unemployment Insurance," in *Unemployment Insurance in the United States*, ed. C. O'Leary and S. Wandner (Kalamazoo, MI: Upjohn Institute, 1999).

Utility Maximization

To show the utility-maximizing choices of consumption and leisure, we must first graph the budget constraint. This is done in Figure 13A.1. If this person doesn't work at all, he or she can enjoy 24 hours of leisure. This is shown as the horizontal intercept of the budget constraint. If, on the other hand, this person works 24 hours per day, he or she will be able to buy $(24 \cdot w)$ in consumption goods. This establishes the vertical intercept in the figure. The slope of the budget constraint is $-w$. This reflects opportunity costs—each added hour of leisure must be "purchased" by doing without w worth of consumption items. For example, if $w = \$10$, this person will earn \$240 if he or she works 24 hours per day. Each hour not worked has an opportunity cost of \$10.

> **MICRO QUIZ 13A.1**
>
> How would you graph the utility-maximizing choices for individuals with the following preferences?
>
> 1. Ms. Steady always works exactly seven hours each day no matter what wage is offered to her.
> 2. Mr. Mellow currently doesn't work, but might if the right wage were offered.

Given this budget constraint, this person will maximize utility by choosing to take H^* hours of leisure and to work the remaining time. With the income earned from this work, he or she will be able to buy C^* units of consumption goods. At the utility-maximizing point, the slope of the budget $(-w)$ is equal to the slope of indifference curve U_2. In other words, the person's real wage is equal to the marginal rate of substitution of leisure hours for consumption.

If this were not true, utility would not be as large as possible. For example, suppose a person's *MRS* were equal to 5, indicating a willingness to give up 5 units of consumption to get an additional hour of leisure. Suppose also that the real wage is \$10. By working one more hour, he or she is able to earn enough to buy 10 units (that is, \$10 worth) of consumption. This is clearly an inefficient situation. By working one hour more, this person can buy 10 extra units of consumption; but he or she required only 5 units of consumption to be as well-off as before. By working the extra hour, this person earns $5(= 10 - 5)$ more units of consumption than required. Consequently he or she could not have been maximizing utility in the first place. A similar proof can be constructed for any case in which the *MRS* differs from the market wage, which proves that the two trade-off rates must be equal for a true utility maximum.

A13-2 Income and Substitution Effects of a Change in the Real Wage Rate

A change in the real wage rate can be analyzed the same way we studied a price change in Chapter 3. When w rises, the price of leisure becomes higher—people must give up more in lost wages for each hour of leisure consumed. The **substitution effect** of an increase in w on the hours of leisure is therefore to reduce them. As leisure becomes more expensive, there is reason to consume less of it. However, the **income effect** of a rise in the wage tends to increase leisure. Because leisure is a normal good, the higher income resulting from a higher w increases the demand for it. Hence income and substitution effects work in the opposite direction. It is impossible to predict whether an increase in w will increase or decrease the demand for leisure time. Because leisure and work are mutually exclusive ways to use time, this also shows that it is impossible to predict what will happen to the number of hours worked when wages change.

Substitution effect of a change in w
Movement along an indifference curve in response to a change in the real wage. A rise in w causes an individual to work more.

Income effect of a change in w
Movement to a higher indifference curve in response to a rise in the real wage rate. If leisure is a normal good, a rise in w causes an individual to work less.

A Graphical Analysis

Figure 13A.2 illustrates two different reactions to an increase in w. In both graphs, the initial wage rate is w_0, and the optimal choices of consumption and leisure are given by C_0 and H_0. When the wage rate increases to w_1, the utility-maximizing combination moves to C_1, H_1. This movement can be divided into two effects. The substitution effect is represented by the movement along the indifference curve U_0 from H_0 to S. This effect works to reduce the number of hours of leisure in both parts of Figure 13A.2. People substitute consumption for leisure since the relative price of leisure has increased.

The movement from S to C_1, H_1 represents the income effect of a higher real wage. Because leisure time is a normal good, increases in income cause more leisure to be demanded. Consequently, the income and substitution effects induced by the increase in w work in opposite directions. In Figure 13A.2(a) the demand for leisure is reduced by the rise in w; that is, the substitution effect outweighs the income effect. On the other hand, in Figure 13A.2(b) the income effect is stronger and the demand for leisure increases in response to an increase in w. This person actually chooses to work fewer hours when w increases. In the analysis of demand, we would have considered this result unusual—when the price of leisure rises, this person demands more of it. For the case of normal consumption goods, income and substitution effects work in the same direction, and both cause quantity to decline when price increases. In the case of leisure, however, income and substitution effects work in opposite directions. An increase in w makes a person better off because he or she is a *supplier* of labor. In the case of a consumption good, an individual is made worse off by a rise in price because he or she is a *consumer* of that good. Consequently, it is not possible to predict exactly how a person will respond to a wage increase—he or she may work more or fewer hours depending on his or her preferences. Application 13A.2: The Earned Income Tax Credit shows that predicting how a wage subsidy will affect labor supply can be tricky indeed.

MICRO QUIZ 13A.2

Suppose the government is choosing between two types of income tax: (1) a proportional tax on wages and (2) a lump-sum tax of a fixed-dollar amount. How would each of these taxes be expected to affect the labor supply of a typical person?

A13-3 Market Supply Curve for Labor

If we are willing to assume that in most cases substitution effects of wage changes outweigh income effects, individual labor supply curves will have positive slopes. We can construct a market-supply-of-labor curve from these individual supply curves by "adding" them up. At each possible wage rate, we add together the quantity of labor offered by each person in order to arrive at a market total. One particularly interesting aspect of this procedure is that, as the wage rate rises, more people may be induced to enter the labor force. That is, rising wages may induce some people who were not previously employed to take jobs. Figure 13A.3 illustrates this possibility for a simple case of two individuals. For a real wage below w_1, neither person chooses to work in the market. Consequently, the market supply curve of labor (Figure 13A.3[c]) shows that no labor is supplied at real wages below w_1. A wage in excess of w_1 causes person 1 to enter the labor market. However, as long as wages fall short of w_2, person 2 will not work. Only at a wage rate above w_2 will both people choose to take a job. As Figure 13A.3(c) shows, the possibility of the entry of these new workers makes the market supply of labor

Figure 13A.2 **Income and Substitution Effects of a Change in the Real Wage Rate**

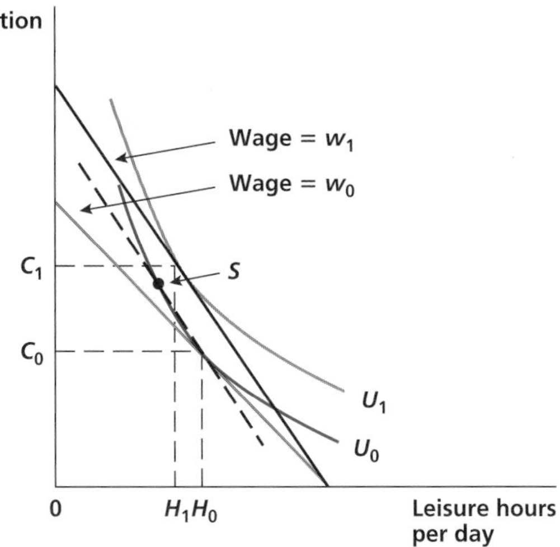

(a) Rise in wage increases work

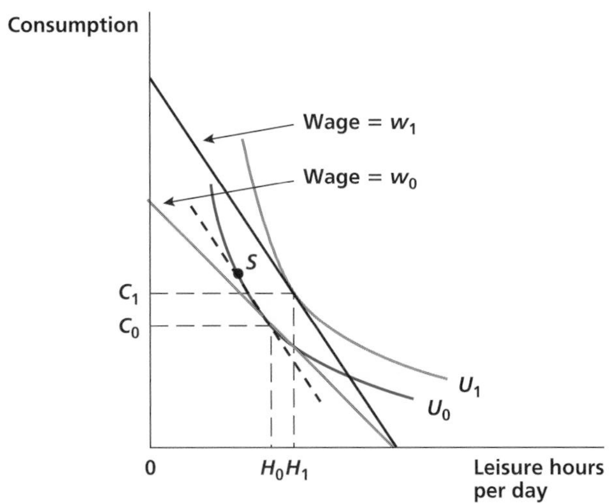

(b) Rise in wage decreases work

Because the individual is a supplier of labor, the income and substitution effects of an increase in the real wage rate affect the hours of leisure demanded (or hours of work) in opposite directions. In panel a, the substitution effect (movement to point *S*) outweighs the income effect and a higher wage causes hours of leisure to decline to H_1. Hours of work, therefore, increase. In panel b, the income effect is stronger than the substitution effect and *H* increases to H_1. Hours of work in this case fall.

APPLICATION 13A.2

The Earned Income Tax Credit

The Earned Income Tax Credit (EITC) was first enacted in the United States in 1975 as a way of increasing the return from working for low-wage people.[1] The size of the credit has been expanded many times during the ensuing decades, most recently in connection with the Obama administration's economic stimulus package of 2009. Our model of labor supply can be used to illustrate the complex incentives that the EITC poses for workers.

Design of the EITC

Figure 1 illustrates the EITC (for a family with two or more children) that was in effect in 2007. For annual earnings less than about \$12,000, the EITC pays 40 percent of those earnings.[2] The maximum credit of \$4,800 is then paid for earnings between \$12,000 and \$15,400. For earnings greater than \$15,400, the credit phases out at a rate of 21 percent—that is, the size of the credit is given by $EITC = \$4{,}800 - 0.21 \cdot (Earnings - \$15{,}400)$. A bit of algebra can be used to show that the EITC reaches zero at earnings of \$38,257.

Incentives in the EITC

One way to study the incentives contained in this complex scheme is to examine how it affects the net wage received by low income workers. For workers with annual wages of less than \$12,000, the EITC represents a 40 percent increase in wages. Once the credit reaches its \$4,800 "plateau," it has no effect on marginal wages received between \$12,000 and \$15,400—it is simply a cash grant. For wages over \$15,400, the EITC imposes an implicit "tax" of 21 percent on wages—at the margin, workers take in only \$0.79 for each dollar they earn. Therefore, our discussion of income and substitution effects suggests that the EITC would have fairly strong positive work incentive effects for the lowest wage workers but that it might pose negative work incentives for workers with modestly higher wages.

Figure 1 EITC schedule in 2007

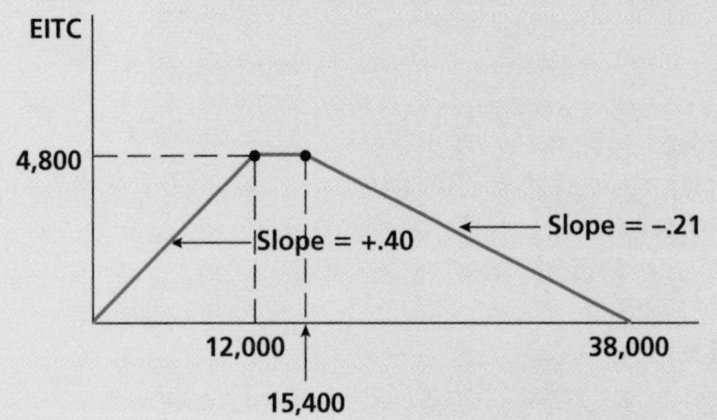

The EITC poses both positive and negative incentives to work.

Research on the Effects of the EITC

Research on the labor supply effect of the EITC is largely consistent with these expectations. For example, Bruce Meyer finds that institution of the EITC clearly increased labor market participation by low-wage single parents—the higher net wage offered caused those who were not working to enter the labor force.[3] However, Meyer finds little support for the possibility that the negative incentives inherent in the EITC design caused modestly higher wage workers to work less. For this group, it appears that hours of work are relatively fixed and cannot be reduced despite the incentives to do so.

POLICY CHALLENGE

Almost all welfare-type programs must have phase-out designs similar to those in the EITC to prevent everyone from being eligible. Keeping phase-out rates low can reduce their negative incentive effects, but lower rates necessarily mean that more people become eligible for welfare subsidies. With multiple programs (for example, the EITC in combination with food stamps and housing assistance subsidies), the combined phase-out rates can create a "welfare wall" that provides severe negative incentives to increase work. Is there any way around this problem? How should programs be integrated to prevent the creation of severe disincentives?

[1]Although the EITC is technically a tax credit that offsets the earner's federal income taxes, the fact that the credit is "refundable" means that it is received even by people whose incomes are so low that they do not pay income taxes. The EITC discussed in this application is received only by people with dependent children although there is a smaller EITC for people without children.

[2]This fraction was raised to 45 percent in the economic stimulus package of 2009.

[3]Bruce D. Meyer, "Labor Supply at the Extensive and Intensive Margins: The EITC, Welfare, and Hours Worked," *American Economic Association Papers and Proceedings* (May 2002): 373–379.

Figure 13A.3 Construction of the Market Supply Curve for Labor

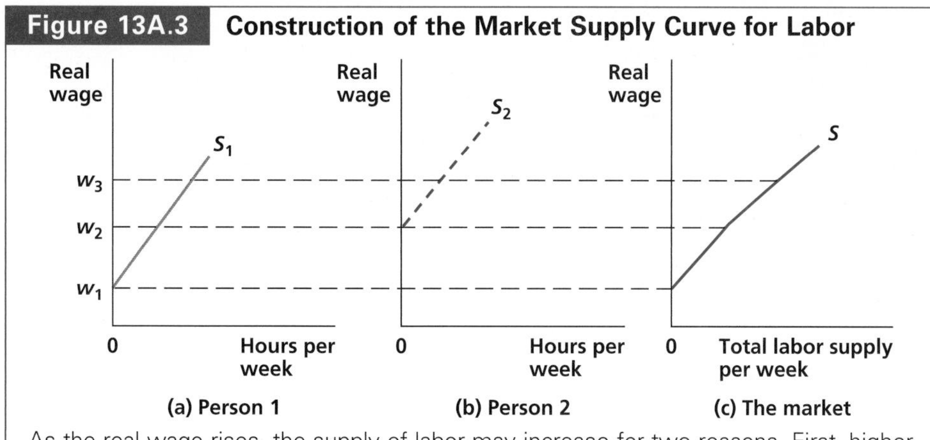

As the real wage rises, the supply of labor may increase for two reasons. First, higher real wages may cause each person to work more hours. Second, higher wages may induce more people (for example, person 2) to enter the labor market.

somewhat more responsive to wage rate increases than would be the case if we assumed that the number of workers was fixed. Changing wage rates not only may induce current workers to alter their hours of work but also, perhaps more importantly, may change the composition of the workforce.

SUMMARY

In this appendix, we have examined the utility-maximizing model of labor supply. This model is another application of the economic theory of choice that we described earlier in this textbook. Although the results are quite similar to those we derived before, the focus here on labor supply provides a number of new insights, including:

- Labor supply decisions by individuals can be studied as one aspect of their allocation of time. The market wage represents an opportunity cost for individuals if they choose not to engage in market work.
- A rise in the market wage induces income and substitution effects into individuals' labor supply decisions. These effects operate in opposite directions. A higher wage causes a substitution effect favoring more market work but an income effect favoring more leisure.
- Construction of the labor supply curve also requires the consideration of labor force participation decisions by individuals.

14

Capital and Time

In this chapter, we look at capital markets. In some respects, this material is not very different from the discussion of general input markets in the previous chapter. Firms acquire capital equipment for the same reason that they hire any input—to maximize profits. Hence, the general rule of hiring an input up to the point at which its marginal revenue product is equal to its market rental rate continues to apply. The main new dimension added in the study of capital markets is the need to explicitly consider questions of time. Because machinery may produce valuable output for many years into the future, we need to take account of the fact that values that occur in different time periods can be compared only after taking account of the potential interest payments that might have been earned. A primary purpose of this chapter then is to show clearly how interest rates affect the rental rates on capital equipment and thereby determine how much capital is hired.

14-1 Time Periods and the Flow of Economic Transactions

Before starting our investigation, it may be best to get some conceptual issues out of the way. As everyone knows, time is continuous—it just keeps passing by, much like a river. Often, however, it is useful to divide time up into discrete intervals such as days, months, or years. This is true also for economic activity. Although economic activity (such as producing and selling cars) proceeds more or less continuously, it is often convenient to divide up this activity into discrete intervals and speak of markets as reaching an equilibrium on a per-day, per-month, or per-year basis. This is how we have proceeded in this book by, for example, noting on most graphs that they refer to "Quantity per period" Hence, these magnitudes are a "flow" per period. Just as one might measure the flow of a river on the basis of gallons per hour, so too economic transactions are usually measured as a per-period flow. For example, gross domestic product (GDP) is measured as total output per year, and total peanut output is measured in bushels per year.

There are two important ways in which transactions can occur across periods. First, some goods may be "durable" in that they last more than one period. Most relevant to this chapter, firms buy machinery and hope to be able to use it for many periods into the future. In deciding whether to make such a purchase, firms must think about the future. Economic models that take account of these decisions are usually fairly straightforward generalizations of the models we have already studied. Still, many new and interesting issues do arise when such future expectations are taken into account.

A second way that transactions can occur across periods is through borrowing and lending. An individual can borrow to increase his or her spending in one period but knows that the loan must be repaid (by spending less) in the next period. Similarly, a firm may borrow in one period to buy equipment that then generates future returns with which to repay the loan. In the next section, we see how this demand and supply for loans determines the interest rate to be paid. Then we show how this interest rate becomes the primary "price" that ties together all transactions that take place over time—especially firms' investment decisions. The appendix to this chapter examines some of the mathematical concepts that relate to interest rates.

14-2 Individual Savings—The Supply of Loans

When individuals save out of their current incomes, these savings have two important economic effects. First, they free up some resources that might otherwise have been devoted to produce goods for consumption. These resources can be used to produce the kinds of investment goods (buildings and equipment) that firms need. Second, savings also provide the funds that firms can use to finance the purchase of these investment goods. Usually, individuals "lend" their funds, not directly to firms, but indirectly through financial intermediaries such as banks or the stock market. In the study of how interest rates are determined, however, it is easiest to think of individuals' savings decisions as directly providing the supply of loans to firms.

Two-Period Model of Saving

Individual savings decisions can be illustrated with a simple utility-maximization model. Suppose that we are concerned only with two periods—this year and next year. Consumption this year 0 is denoted by C_0 and consumption next year 1 is denoted by C_1, and these are the only items that provide utility to this individual. He or she has a current income of Y dollars that can either be spent now on C_0 or saved to buy C_1 next year. Any income saved this year earns interest (at a real interest rate of r[1]) before it is used to buy C_1. The individual's problem then is to maximize utility given this budget constraint.

A Graphical Analysis

Figure 14.1 shows this utility-maximization process. The indifference curves show the utility obtainable from various combinations of C_0 and C_1. To understand the (intertemporal) budget constraint in this problem, consider first the case where $C_1 = 0$. Then $C_0 = Y$, and no income is saved for use in period 1. On the other hand, if all income is saved, $C_0 = 0$ and $C_1 = (1 + r)Y$. In year 1, this person can consume all of his or her income plus the interest earned on that income. For example, if $r = 0.05$ (that is, 5 percent), C_1 will be $1.05Y$. Waiting for the interest to be earned has made it possible for this person to have relatively more consumption in period 1 than in period 0.

Given the two intercepts in Figure 14.1, the entire budget constraint can be constructed as the straight line joining them. Utility maximization is achieved at C_0^*, C_1^* at which point the marginal rate of substitution (MRS) is equal to $(1 + r)$. That is, utility maximization requires equating the rate at which this person is willing to trade C_0 for C_1 to the rate at which he or she is able to trade these goods for each other in the market through saving. The interest rate is clearly an important part of this story because it measures the opportunity cost that the individual incurs when he or she chooses to consume now rather than in the future.

[1]That is, the interest rate is adjusted for any possible change in purchasing power between the two periods. Hence, this real interest rate provides information to the consumer about how *real* consumption this year can be traded for *real* consumption next year. In the appendix to this chapter, we explore the relationship between nominal and real interest rates. All of the analysis in this chapter is based on real interest rates, however.

Figure 14.1 The Savings Decision

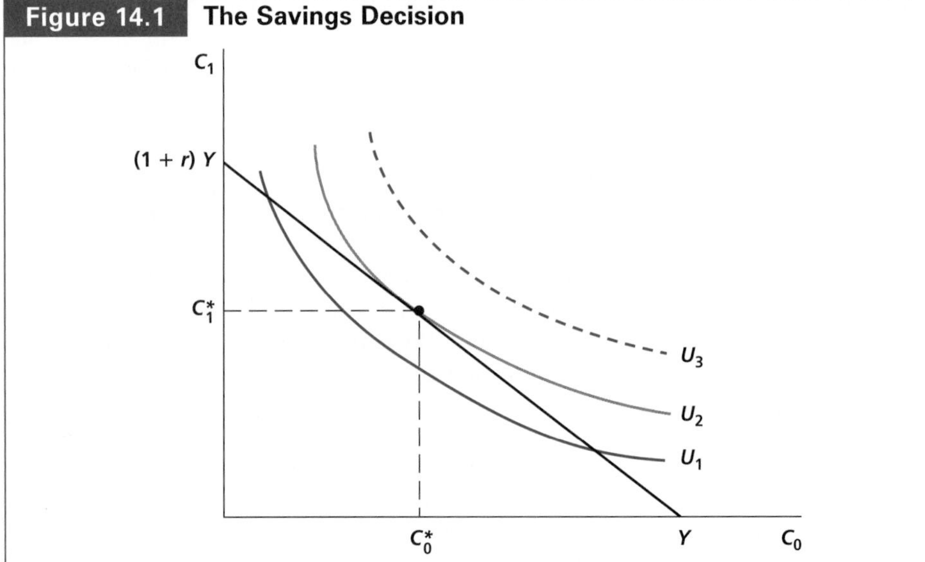

A person with a current income of Y can either spend this on current consumption, C_0, or save it (at an interest rate of r) to buy consumption next year, C_1. Here, the person's utility-maximizing choice is C_0^*, C_1^*. Current savings are $Y - C_0^*$.

A Numerical Example

To provide a numerical example of the type of intertemporal utility maximization shown in Figure 14.1, we must assume a particular form for the utility function. Suppose, for example, utility took a logarithmic form: $U(C_0, C_1) = \ln C_0 + \ln C_1$. In this case, the Marginal Rate of Substitution[2] is given by $MRS = C_1/C_0$, so utility maximization requires

$$MRS = C_1/C_0 = 1 + r \quad \text{or} \quad C_1 = (1 + r)C_0 \tag{14.1}$$

That is, with this simple utility function, consumption should be larger in period 1 than in period 0 because period 1 consumption is "cheaper" since it offers the possibility for earning interest on funds intended for period 1. If, for example, $r = .05$, period 1 consumption should be 5 percent larger than period 0 consumption. With a fixed initial income of, say, \$100, this can be achieved by spending \$50 on period 0 consumption and investing \$50 at 5 percent interest so that period 1 consumption can amount to \$52.50. Notice that, even though this consumer initially splits his or her \$100 evenly, consumption in period 1 ends up being larger because interest earned is spent in period 1 also. Problem 14.2 and 14.3 look at the implications of somewhat different utility functions for such savings behavior. And, in Application 14.4, we will expand substantially on the implications of the type of utility function used here.

KEEP *in* MIND

Intertemporal Choices Must Also Obey a Budget Constraint

As in all of our consumer choice problems, the tangency condition shown in Figure 14.1 and in Equation 14.1 is not enough to solve the problem. Rather, the tangency condition must also be combined with a budget constraint to determine what the final choices are.

---

[2]Here, $MU(C_0) = 1/C_0$, $MU(C_1) = 1/C_1$, so, $MRS = MU(C_0)/MU(C_1) = C_1/C_0$.

Figure 14.2 Effect of an Increase in r on Savings Is Ambiguous

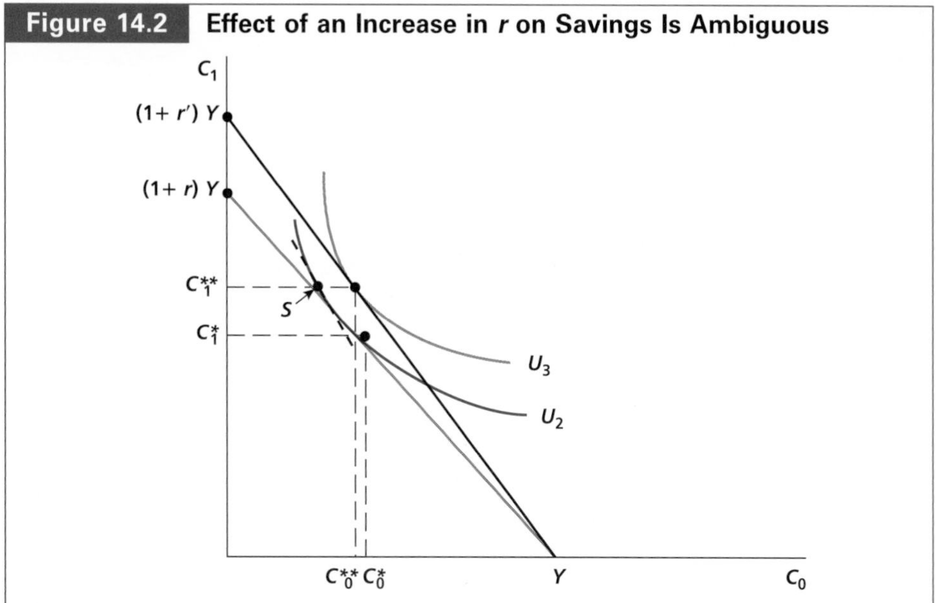

An increase in r to r' causes a substitution effect that reduces C_0 from C_0^* to S (an increase in savings) and an income effect that raises C_0 from S to C_0^{**} (a decrease in savings). In the figure, the rise in r results in a net increase in savings.

Substitution and Income Effects of a Change in *r*

A change in the real interest rate, r, changes the "price" of future versus current consumption. The substitution and income effects of this price change are illustrated in Figure 14.2 for an increase in r. In this case, the rise in r to r' causes this individual to move along the U_2 indifference curve to point S—this is the substitution effect. With a higher r, the opportunity cost of C_0 rises and this person substitutes C_1 for C_0—that is, he or she saves more. But the rise in r also shifts this person's budget constraint outward because he or she is made better off by this rise. This income effect causes the preferred consumption point to move from S to C_0^{**}, C_1^{**}. Assuming that both C_0 and C_1 are normal goods, they should both be increased by this move. The final effect of an increase in r on C_0 (and hence on savings) is indeterminate—the substitution effect increases savings (C_0 falls) whereas the income effect decreases savings (C_0 rises). The net effect depends on the relative sizes of these two effects.[3] In general, economists believe that the substitution effect is probably the stronger of the two effects so that a rise in r encourages savings. This is the final result pictured in Figure 14.2. But there is considerable disagreement about the actual size of this effect, as Application 14.1: Do We Need Tax Breaks for Savers? illustrates.

14-3 Firms' Demand for Capital and Loans

In Chapter 13, we saw that profit-maximizing firms rent additional capital equipment up to the point at which the marginal revenue product of the equipment is equal to the rental rate on the equipment, v. To understand the connections between this demand

[3]This ambiguity is identical to that encountered in looking at the effect on labor supply of an increase in the real wage—see the appendix to Chapter 13 for a discussion.

APPLICATION 14.1

Do We Need Tax Breaks for Savers?

Personal savings rates in the United States are relatively low by international standards. In 2012 total personal savings amounted to about 5.6 percent of personal disposable income. This figure is lower than the one that existed through much of U.S. history and a markedly lower rate than exists in many other countries[1] (where rates above 10 percent are common). Such low savings rates have prompted a variety of concerns. Some observers worry about whether individuals will have adequate savings for their own retirement or for various emergencies. Others worry that inadequate savings will fail to provide sufficient capital accumulation for future generations. As a result, many tax-favored plans for savings have been introduced in recent years.

Recent Savings Incentive Plans

Many savings incentive plans have a similar structure. All of them allow a tax deduction for contributions to the plans[2]. Savings in the plans are then not subject to the federal income tax until benefits are paid out at retirement. The three principal types of such plans are

- Individual Retirement Accounts (IRAs), which are set up by individuals acting on their own. Only low-income individuals receive an income tax deduction for IRA contributions, but everyone can avoid taxation of returns from assets in the plans until they retire.
- 401(k) plans are set up by employers who sometimes make matching contributions to their workers' plans. Both contributions and asset returns are tax-exempt until retirement.
- Keogh plans are similar to IRAs and 401(k) plans, but the plans are intended for self-employed individuals. They generally have higher contribution limits than the other plans do.

Theoretical Effects on Savings

The effect of these various tax benefits on total personal savings is ambiguous. Although special tax treatment does raise the after-tax interest rate for savers, our discussion of Figure 14.2 showed that the effect of such a change on savings is uncertain—income and substitution effects of increases in the effective interest rate work in opposite directions. In addition, the fact that the special tax treatment does not apply to all savings but only to contributions to specific plans gives individuals an incentive to shift their assets into the tax-favored plans without actually changing the total amount of their savings. Hence, the rapid growth of the plans should not be taken as an indication of the plans' ability to stimulate savings.

Research on Savers and Spenders

Because savings incentive plans involve significant losses in tax revenues, much research has been undertaken to determine whether the plans are achieving their goal of increasing savings. Most studies use data on individual savings behavior to detect such influences. Unfortunately, this research has been plagued by one serious problem: it appears that different people have very different attitudes toward saving. Some people are serious savers who will accumulate assets in many forms. Other people are only spenders who never put anything aside. Individuals who participate in one of the special saving plans have shown that they fit into the "saver" category. But to compare their savings behavior to the behavior of those individuals without the plans runs the danger of concluding that the plans themselves increase savings. A more correct interpretation is that plan participation acts only to identify savers who are predisposed to save more. Researchers have been unable to resolve this sample selection problem and the true impact of the special savings plans remains largely unknown.

POLICY CHALLENGE

Low personal savings rates in the United States pose a policy problem because it is more difficult to generate adequate funds for investment than it would be if savings rates were higher. As shown in this example, however, trying to generate more savings through special tax breaks poses difficulties both because such incentives may not work very well and because most of the tax benefits may go to those people who would save a lot anyway. A somewhat different approach would be to "penalize" current consumption through, say, a general sales tax, but this approach would also pose difficulties for lower income people unless some major categories of goods were exempted from such a tax. Other approaches, such as limiting consumer credit or conducting pro-savings advertising campaigns, seem equally problematic. Hence, it appears that no one has a very promising plan for increasing savings. In fact, many government policies (such as Social Security or Medicare) seem to work against that goal.

[1]To some extent, the low savings rate in the United States may reflect faulty measurement. See W. G. Gale and J. Sabelhaus, "Perspectives on the Household Savings Rate," *Brookings Papers on Economic Activity*, no. 1 (1999): 181–224.

[2]Roth IRAs, which became available in 1998, do not allow current deductibility, but all retirement benefits are nontaxable when received.

and the demand for loans, we need to understand the nature of the determinants of this rental rate. We begin by assuming that firms rent all of the capital that they use from other firms. Cases in which firms directly own their own equipment are then easy to explain.

> **MICRO QUIZ 14.1**
>
> One way to study the results of Figure 14.1 and Figure 14.2 is by thinking about the "relative price" of C_1 in terms of C_0.
>
> 1. Explain why the relative price of C_1 is given by $1/(1 + r)$. If $r = 0.10$, what is the relative price of C_1? Explain the meaning of this "price."
> 2. Explain why an increase in r increases the relative price of C_0. Why is the individual's reaction to such a price increase ambiguous here, whereas that was not the case in Chapter 3?

Rental Rates and Interest Rates

Many types of capital equipment are in fact rented in the real world. Hertz rents millions of cars each year to other firms; banks and insurance companies actually own many commercial planes that they rent to airlines; and construction firms rent specialized equipment (for example, heavy-lifting cranes) when they need it. In these cases, the per-period rate that firms have to pay to rent this equipment (v) is determined by the average costs that the rental firms (for example, Hertz) incur. Two such costs are especially important: depreciation costs and borrowing costs. Depreciation costs reflect the physical wear and tear on equipment that occurs during each period that it is used. Borrowing costs may be either explicit or implicit for the firm providing the equipment. If they have financed the purchase of their equipment with a loan, interest payments on that loan are an explicit cost. If, on the other hand, they have bought equipment with internal funds, interest payments are an implicit or opportunity cost. By having the funds tied up in the equipment, the firm is forgoing what it could have earned by putting them in the bank. Hence, interest costs are always relevant to the firm that supplies the rented equipment, no matter how they have actually financed the equipment purchase.

In general, it might be expected that both depreciation and borrowing costs are proportional to the market price of the equipment being rented. If P represents that price, d is the per-period rate of depreciation, and r is the interest rate, we have the following expression for the per-period rental rate (v):

$$\begin{aligned} \text{Rental rate} = v &= \text{Depreciation} + \text{Borrowing costs} \\ &= dP + rP = (d + r)P. \end{aligned} \tag{14.2}$$

For example, suppose an insurance company owns a Boeing 777 that it leases to United Airlines. Suppose also that the current value of the plane is \$50 million, that the plane is expected to deteriorate at a rate of 10 percent each year, and that the real interest rate is 5 percent. Then the insurance company's total annual costs of owning the plane are \$7.5 million (\$5 million in depreciation and \$2.5 million in interest costs). If it is to break even in its plane rental business, that is the rate it must charge United each year for the plane.

Equation 14.2 clearly shows why firms' demand for equipment is negatively related to the interest rate. When the interest rate is high, rental rates on equipment are high and firms try to substitute toward cheaper inputs. When interest rates are low, rental rates are low and firms opt to rent more equipment. Such changes in equipment rentals also bring about accompanying changes in the demand for loans with which to finance the equipment. When interest rates are high, the demand for loans contracts because there is little need to finance equipment purchases. With low interest rates, loan volume picks up as a consequence of the rental firms' needs to add to their available equipment.

Ownership of Capital Equipment

Of course, most capital equipment is owned by the firms that use it; only a relatively small portion is rented. But that distinction does not affect the validity of Equation 14.2. Firms that own equipment are really in two businesses—they produce goods and they lease capital equipment to themselves. In their role as equipment lessors, firms are affected by the same economic considerations as are firms whose primary business is leasing. The implicit rental rates that they pay are the same regardless of who owns the equipment.[4] Application 14.2: Do Taxes Affect Investment? shows how Equation 14.2 can be used to study the ways in which government tax policy can be used to influence firms' decisions to purchase capital equipment.

14-4 Determination of the Real Interest Rate

Now that we have described the two sides of the market for loans, we are ready to describe how the real interest rate is determined. Figure 14.3 shows that the supply of loans is an upward-sloping function of the real interest rate, r. This slope reflects our assumption that individuals increase their savings (and loans to firms) as the interest rate rises. The demand for loans is negatively sloped because higher interest rates cause firms to take out fewer loans to finance investment. Equilibrium then occurs at r^*, Q^*, where the quantity of loans demanded is equal to the quantity supplied. This equilibrium real interest rate provides the price that links economic periods together.

 **MICRO QUIZ 14.2**

A "pure" inflation (in which all prices change by the same amount) should not have any real effect on firms' decisions. Use Equation 14.2 together with the theory of input demand from Chapter 13 to explain why this is so for firms' decisions about how much capital to use.

Because charging of interest on loans has been controversial throughout history (see Application 14.3: Usury), it may be useful to explore the nature of the equilibrium pictured in Figure 14.3 more fully. There are two reasons why we might expect the equilibrium real interest rate (r^*) shown in the figure to be positive. From the perspective of the individuals providing loans, they will expect some return for this. Borrowers, after all, are asking savers to defer some of their possible consumption into the future. Our observations of a natural degree of "impatience" in people would suggest that they seek some sort of compensation for delaying consumption. From the point of view of borrowers, firms will be willing to pay something to lenders because they find that buying capital equipment is profitable. Take the simple case where machines do not depreciate. Then Equation 14.2 shows that firms will employ additional capital equipment up to the point at which $r = v/P$—that is, up to the point at which the interest rate they must pay is equal to the rate of return they earn by buying the machine (at the price P) and thereby save the cost of renting the machine from someone else (v). Hence, in a market economy, interest rates are jointly determined by the willingness of people to lend and the productivity of capital investments made by borrowers.

[4]The mathematical relationship between the present-value calculations that owners must make in deciding whether to purchase new equipment and the rental rate they implicitly pay on the equipment is examined in the appendix to this chapter.

APPLICATION 14.2

Do Taxes Affect Investment?

Although a tax on pure economic profits would not affect firms' input choices, the actual U.S. corporate income tax departs in several ways from such a pure tax. Most important, opportunity costs of equity capital are not deductible under U.S. tax law and allowable depreciation charges for tax purposes often fall short of true economic depreciation. Equation 14.2 should therefore be modified to take into account how the corporate income tax actually affects the rental rate for capital input. This can be done by writing

$$v = (r + d)P\,(1 + t) \qquad \{\text{i}\}$$

where t is the effective tax rate per unit of capital. In the usual case, t is positive. But in some cases, the government may subsidize certain types of capital input, so t then would be negative. Because taxes change the rental rate that firms must pay for their capital, they can obviously affect input choices.

Elements of Tax Policy

Federal tax policy toward investment has undergone many changes in recent years. Three specific elements of tax policy have been frequently adjusted:

- The corporate tax rate has been reduced on several occasions though it is currently one of the highest in the world.
- "Accelerated" depreciation schedules have been adopted to bring depreciation allowances more into line with actual economic depreciation that machines experience.
- Investment tax credits for certain types of capital purchases have been enacted and then abolished.

Brief History of Tax Policy

Major reductions in rates of capital taxation were implemented in 1962 during the Kennedy administration. At that time, depreciation schedules, especially for producers' equipment, were made much more generous. A temporary 7 percent tax credit on all new investment was also enacted. According to some estimates, these changes may have increased total purchases of capital equipment by as much as 20 percent.[1]

Similar changes were instituted early in the Reagan administration (1981). Especially important was the adoption of more generous depreciation schedules for buildings and longer-lived equipment. In some cases, these allowances may have resulted in a subsidy for these investments. But the initial Reagan policies were significantly modified in 1982, so the most generous of the policies had little time to influence investment behavior, which remained sluggish through much of the 1980s.

Policy changes instituted during the Clinton administration primarily involved investment tax credits. Such credits were adopted for research and development expenditures and for smaller firms' new investments. Tax incentives under the second Bush administration were rather narrowly focused (such as credits on investments in ethanol production). Under the 2009 Obama stimulus tax plans, credits focused mainly on generating employment and promoting "green" technologies rather than increasing investment generally.

Effects of Tax Policies

Although it seems clear in principle that changes in tax policies can affect rental rates on capital, the evidence about whether tax changes have had important effects on firms' input choices is quite ambiguous. One reason is that tax benefits for investment may also raise the price of capital equipment, thereby largely offsetting their direct effect on lowering rental rates (see Equation i).[2] Another possibility is that the highly selective (and political) nature of investment incentives may have caused firms to change only what they buy, but not their overall level of investment.

POLICY CHALLENGE

Because firms' demands for structures and capital equipment are fairly elastic, it seems clear that tax policy can be effective in spurring demand for such investment. The policy problem in designing such policies is to avoid providing firms with artificial incentives to invest in the wrong thing. Probably the most significant example, of course, is private housing, where favorable tax treatment leads people to buy far larger houses than they would without such a subsidy. However, there are many other examples where tax policy has been designed to favor only certain (politically popular) types of investment. Some examples include tax breaks for historical restorations, for "green" investments, and for certain types of farming (even Christmas tree farms). It is unclear whether it is possible to develop tax incentives for investment that avoid such political targeting.

[1] R. E. Hall and D. W. Jorgenson, "Tax Policy and Investment Behavior," *American Economic Review* (June 1967): 391–414. Hall and Jorgenson show precisely how various elements of tax policy affect the rental rate on capital.

[2] See A. Goolsbee, "Investment Tax Incentives, Prices, and the Supply of Capital Goods," *Quarterly Journal of Economics* (February 1999): 121–149.

APPLICATION 14.3

Usury

Although the equilibrium pictured in Figure 14.3 seems reasonable, probably no price has been as controversial over many centuries as has the interest rate on loans. Most major religions have, at one time or another, condemned interest payments as being exploitive. Many philosophers, especially those who take a Marxist perspective, have come to similar conclusions. To this day, many nations sharply restrict interest rates, and most U.S. states have "usury laws" that limit what consumers can be charged for credit. In this application, we look briefly at the controversy over interest, with the primary goal of differentiating between positive and normative (see Chapter 1) views of the issue.

Religious and Literary Views

Opposition to the payment of interest on loans dates back at least to the Greek philosophers. Alfred Marshall reports that Aristotle viewed money as "barren" and deriving interest from it as "unnatural"[1] In the Old Testament of the Bible, Moses states, "If you lend money to any of my people with you who is poor, you shall not be to him as a creditor, and you shall not exact interest from him." Later biblical references clarify the nature of this prohibition somewhat by implying that interest is barred only in transactions in which "brothers" lend to "brothers" (usually taken to mean Jews lending to Jews). Interest on loans to "foreigners" is permissible. Other religions that have taken a negative view of interest payments include the Hindu religion in India and most sects of the Muslim religion (to be examined shortly).[2]

World literature has sometimes reflected these religious views. For example, Dante reserved a special place in hell for usurers. In probably the most famous case, Shakespeare's play *The Merchant of Venice* focused on the moneylender Shylock and on his lending contract that demanded a "pound of flesh" if the merchant Antonio was unable to repay his loan. Other literary references can be found in such diverse works as the writings of St. Thomas Aquinas and Mahatma Gandhi.

Normative Basis for Usury Restrictions

Most usury restrictions are derived from two related notions: (1) that borrowers are usually in need and requiring interest payments worsens their situation and (2) that lenders incur no real costs when they provide loans. These beliefs then lead to the conclusion that interest should not be charged. Notice that this is a normative statement about how the economy *should* operate (a normative conclusion about which people may differ). The equilibrium shown in Figure 14.3 makes a positive prediction about how interest rates arise in the real world. Reconciling this prediction with individuals' normative views can sometimes be quite difficult.

Muslim Mortgages

The difficulties are clearly illustrated in the problems faced by some American Muslims who wish to take out mortgages to buy homes. The Koran generally forbids paying or receiving interest, so Muslims who both wish to obey their religious heritage and to purchase good houses face the prospect of having to save for many years before getting a house. Recently U.S. financial institutions have developed a variety of special types of mortgages that Islamic scholars have deemed consistent with the Koran. The general idea of these loans (sometimes called *Murabaha* loans) is to have the financial institution buy a house and lease it back to the resident. The resident then pays the going rental rate for the house plus an extra amount that allows him or her slowly to buy the house. Because the financial institution has an equity investment in the house and therefore incurs risk on the resident's behalf, earning a "profit" is viewed as being consistent with Islamic law.

TO THINK ABOUT

1. In the New Testament Jesus expels "moneychangers" from his local temple. According to some research, these people were involved in lending. Other research indicates they may have been foreign exchange traders. Do you think Jesus should have behaved differently with respect to these two professions?
2. Most states require that lenders publish the "true annual interest charge" on any loans they make. How should this law be interpreted in the case of Muslim mortgages?

[1]A. Marshall, *Principles of Economics*, 8th ed. (London: Macmillan & Co., 1950), 585.

[2]A good summary of religious views is provided in E. L. Glaeser and J. Scheinkman, "Neither Borrower nor a Lender Be: An Economic Analysis of Interest Restrictions and Usury Laws," *Journal of Law and Economics* (April 1998): 1–36.

Figure 14.3 The Real Interest Rate Is Determined in the Market for Loans

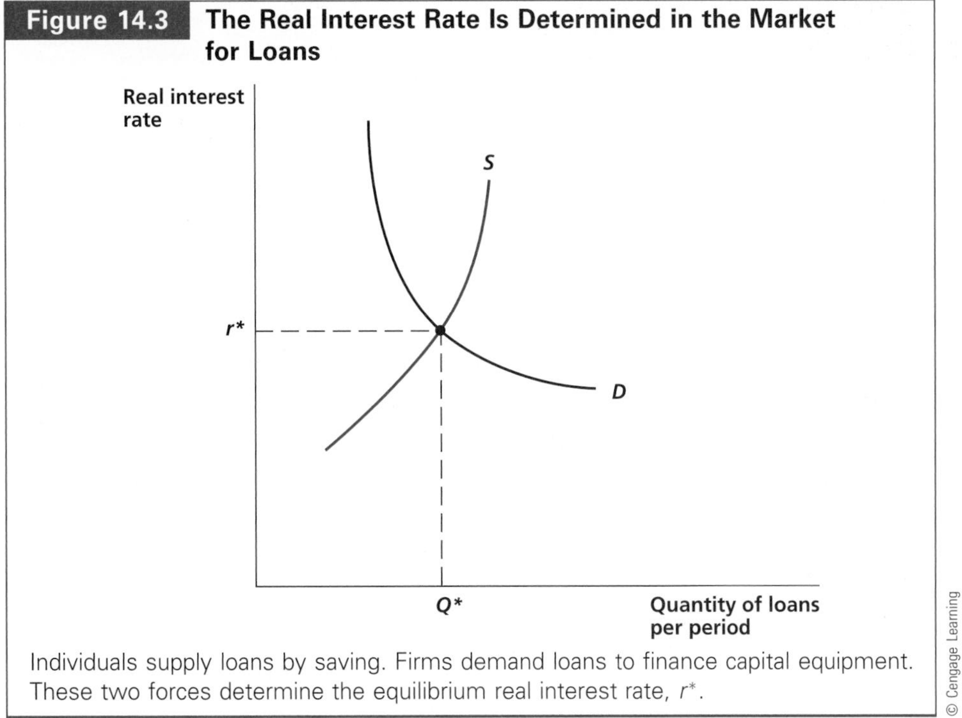

Individuals supply loans by saving. Firms demand loans to finance capital equipment. These two forces determine the equilibrium real interest rate, r^*.

Changes in the Real Interest Rate

This simple theory of how the real interest rate is determined also provides insights about why that interest rate might change. On one hand, any factor that increases firms' demand for capital equipment also increases the demand for loans. Such factors include technical progress that makes equipment more productive, declines in the actual market prices of such equipment, or more optimistic views by firms about the strength of demand for their products in the future. All such effects shift the demand for loans outward, increasing the real interest rate. On the other hand, any factor that affects individual savings affects the supply of loans. For example, availability of government-provided pension benefits in the future may reduce individuals' current savings, thereby raising real interest rates. Similarly, reductions in taxes on savings may increase the supply of loans and reduce the real interest rate. Application 14.4: The Real Interest Rate Paradox looks at some questions about the level of interest rates observed in the economy.

14-5 Present Discounted Value

Probably the most important lesson from studying the economics of decision making over time is that interest rates must be taken into account. Transactions that take place at different times cannot be compared directly because of interest that was or might have been earned (or paid) between the two dates. For example, a promise to pay a dollar today is not the same as a promise to pay a dollar in one year. The dollar today is more valuable because it can be invested at interest for the year. In order to bring comparability to transactions that occur over time, actual dollar amounts must always be adjusted for the effects of potential interest payments.

APPLICATION 14.4

The Real Interest Rate Paradox

Historical data over the past 100 years show that the real interest rate on relatively risk-free investments has averaged about 1–2 percent per year. Most financial economists believe this rate is "too low" to be consistent with standard theories of the supply and demand for loans; hence, the low rates constitute a "paradox." In this application, we explore this paradox and offer a few explanations for it.

Fruit Tree Economics

One way economists have conceptualized the real interest rate determination process is to assume that the consumption growth in the economy is generated by real forces that are beyond the control of individual savers. It is as if the real economy were a fruit tree that yields more fruit each year to consumers. The role of the real interest rate, therefore, is to create an equilibrium at which consumers are happy with this rate of growth. For example, real, per capita consumption has grown at a rate of about 1.8 percent per year during the past 100 years, so a real interest rate will reflect an equilibrium only if this rate of consumption growth rate is what people want. Interestingly, the 1.8 percent consumption growth rate is quite consistent with a real interest rate of 1–2 percent if consumers' preferences are those used in our numerical example earlier in this chapter. There we showed that if $U(C_0, C_1) = \ln C_0 + \ln C_1$, utility maximization requires $C_1/C_0 = 1 + r$, so a real interest rate of 1.8 percent would indeed be consistent with a consumption growth rate of 1.8 percent also. Unfortunately, most economists do not believe that peoples' preferences are of this simple form, however.

Reasons Why the Real Interest Rate Should Be Higher

There are two reasons why economists believe people need a greater interest rate incentive to have consumption grow at 1.8 percent per year:

- **Impatience:** Most economists believe that people discount the utility from future consumption. Our numerical example assumes consumption this year and next year is valued equally. However, if people discount next year's consumption (following the principle that "a bird in the hand…") they will require a higher real interest rate to get them to accept more consumption in the future.
- **Fluctuation Aversion:** Many economists also believe that people are averse to fluctuations in the levels of their consumption. They would rather have an equal consumption stream rather than one that keeps growing (for example, young people borrow so that they can consume more today than is permitted by their incomes). This is another reason favoring higher real interest rates—to get people to accept changing levels of consumption.

Economists who have studied these two factors conclude that they should add about 3–4 percentage points to the real interest rate of 1.8 percent from our simple example.[1] So, we should expect a real interest rate of 5–6 percent rather than the 1–2 percent actually observed.

Possible Explanations

Of course, the facts are what they are, so economists have looked for possible explanations for the low historical levels of real interest rates. Two explanations seem especially appealing. First, it may be the case that consumption is habit forming. Consuming in one year generates a taste for more consumption in the next one. If this is the case, people would indeed want consumption to grow over time, so the factors favoring a higher real interest rate would play a reduced role. A second possibility is that people face constraints on their ability to borrow to finance consumption. For example, firms may be unwilling to lend to people with little credit history. Because such constraints reduce the demand side of the loan market, clearing of the loan market requires a lower real interest rate (see Figure 14.3). In general, then, the "low" real interest rate may not be such a paradox after all.

TO THINK ABOUT

1. Does a real interest rate of 1 or 2 percent seem low to you? Would you be willing to buy an investment that promised such a return? If not, how can the historical returns be so low given that the market for, say, government bonds must be in equilibrium?
2. Doesn't our "fruit tree" model of consumption growth seem rather contrived? What factors do you believe contribute to the actual growth in consumption over time? How do such factors affect the real interest rate determination process?

[1]See, for example, N. R. Kocherlakota, "The Equity Premium: It's Still a Puzzle," *Journal of Economic Literature* (March 1996): 42–71.

Table 14.1 Present Discounted Value of $1 For Various Time Periods and Interest Rates

YEARS UNTIL PAYMENT IS RECEIVED	INTEREST RATE			
	1 PERCENT	3 PERCENT	5 PERCENT	10 PERCENT
1	$0.99010	$0.97087	$0.95238	$0.90909
2	0.98030	0.94260	0.90703	0.82645
3	0.97059	0.91516	0.86386	0.75131
5	0.95147	0.86281	0.78351	0.62093
10	0.90531	0.74405	0.61391	0.38555
25	0.78003	0.47755	0.29531	0.09230
50	0.60790	0.22810	0.08720	0.00852
100	0.36969	0.05203	0.00760	0.00007

Single-Period Discounting

With only two periods, this process is very simple. Because any dollar invested today grows by a factor of $(1 + r)$ next year, the present value of a dollar that is not received until next year is $1/(1 + r)$ dollars. For example, if $r = 0.05$, an investment of $1 today will grow to $1.05 next year. Hence, the promise of $1 next year is worth about $0.95 today.[5] That is, investing $0.95 today will yield $1 in one year. The discount factor $1/(1 + r)$ must always be applied to calculate the **present value** of funds to be paid one year in the future. The first row of Table 14.1 illustrates this discount factor for various interest rates—clearly, the higher the interest rate, the smaller the discount factor.

Present value
Discounting the value of future transactions back to the present day to take account of the effect of potential interest payments.

Multiperiod Discounting

Generalizing the discounting concept to any number of periods is easy. As we show in the appendix to this chapter, the present value of $1 that is not to be paid until n years in the future is given by

$$\text{Present value of \$1 in } n \text{ years} = \$1/(1 + r)^n. \qquad (14.3)$$

This discounting factor allows the user to take into account the compound interest that is forgone by waiting for n years to obtain funds, rather than obtaining them immediately. The entries in Table 14.1 show how this discount term depends both on the interest rate (r) and on the number of years until payment is received (n). For high values of r and/or high values of n, this factor can be very small. For example, the promise of $1 in 10 years with an interest rate of 10 percent is worth only $0.39 today. If payment is delayed for 100 years (again with a 10 percent interest rate), its present value is worth less than one hundredth of a cent! Such calculations make clear that the present value of payments long into the future may be very low, so we should not be surprised that such distant payments play a rather small part in most economic decisions.

MICRO QUIZ 14.3

A state lottery is currently offering a Power Ball payoff of $20 million, which it will pay to the lucky winner in 20 annual $1 million installments. Is this really a $20 million prize? How would you decide its actual value?

[5]To be precise, $1/(1.05) = 0.95238$.

Present Value and Economic Decisions

When looking at economic decisions over time, the concepts of utility maximization by individuals and profit maximization by firms continue to be relevant. But they must be restated to allow for the discounting that should be done in all multiperiod situations. For firms, this reformulation is easy to understand. Instead of assuming that firms "maximize profits," we now assume that they "maximize the present value of all future profits." Virtually all of the results of the theory of profit maximization continue to hold under this revised formulation.[6] For example, profit maximization requires that firms whose revenues and costs may not occur at the same time choose that output level for which the *present value* of marginal revenue equals the *present value* of marginal cost. Similarly, such firms should hire inputs up to the point at which the *present value* of the marginal revenue product is equal to the *present value* of the input's cost. Sometimes economists state the profit-maximization assumption a little differently when speaking about decisions over time—they assume that firms make decisions that seek to "maximize the present value of the firm" But this amounts to just another version of profit maximization, because a firm is worth only the future profits that it generates.

Present-value concepts are also important to your own decisions. Although we do not explore these connections here, problems 14.8 and 14.9 provide you with some practice in avoiding common deceptive sales practices that are based on a failure of consumers to understand how interest rates work. Application 14.5: Discounting Cash Flows and Derivative Securities shows a few more complicated illustrations of present-value calculations that can confuse even the most astute investor.

14-6 Pricing of Exhaustible Resources

One important way in which considerations of time and interest rates enter into economics is in the pricing of natural resources—especially those that are in fixed supply. Ever since Robert Malthus started worrying about population growth in nineteenth-century England, there have been recurrent concerns that we are "running out" of such resources and that market pressures may be accelerating that process. In this section, we try to shed some light on this important issue by focusing on the ways in which resource scarcity might be expected to affect the current pricing of those resources.

Scarcity Costs

Scarcity costs
The opportunity costs of future production forgone because current production depletes exhaustible resources.

What makes the production of nonrenewable resources different from the production of other types of economic goods is that the current production from a fixed stock of the resource reduces the amount that is available in the future. This contrasts with the usual case in which firms' production decisions during one year have no effect on the next year's production. Firms involved in the production of an exhaustible resource must therefore take an additional cost into account: the opportunity cost of not being able to make some sales in the future. These extra costs are defined as the **scarcity costs**. Of course, recognition of these costs does not mean that a firm thinking about producing from a fixed resource stock always opts to produce nothing, constantly hoarding its resource holdings for sale at some future date. But the firm must be careful to incorporate all opportunity costs into its decisions.

[6]For some illustrations, see review question 8 of this chapter. In the theory of corporate finance, some issues do arise in choosing which interest rate to use to compute the present value of future profits, but we do not pursue those issues here.

APPLICATION 14.5

Discounting Cash Flows and Derivative Securities

The concept of present value can be applied to any pattern of cash inflows or outflows. This provides a general way to think about transactions that are really quite complex. Here, we look at two examples.

Mortgage-Backed Securities

Mortgages on houses are the most prevalent type of loan individuals make. These loans commit homeowners to pay a fixed monthly charge, typically for 30 years. Most mortgages also permit early repayments with no penalties. Because mortgages are so long-lived, an active secondary market in them has been developed that permits the initial lender to sell the mortgage to someone else. Often, many mortgages are bundled together in order to achieve economies of scale in buying and selling. Recent innovations in financial markets have carried this process one step further by creating new securities that represent only one portion of the cash flow from a pool of mortgages. These new securities are called "collateralized mortgage obligations" (CMOs). For example, one CMO might promise only the monthly interest payments from a given pool of mortgages. Another might promise all of the actual mortgage repayments from the same pool.

Calculation of the present value of a CMO is in principle a straightforward application of Equation 14A.25 in the appendix 14 to this chapter. Each expected cash flow must be appropriately discounted to the present day. Unfortunately, the fact that people can change their mortgage payoff practices rather sharply as conditions change makes the actual calculation subject to considerable uncertainty in practice.

The Fannie Mae Fiasco

Fannie Mae was the largest dealer in mortgage-backed securities in the United States. Its quasi-governmental status permitted it to borrow at fairly low rates and use the proceeds to invest in a wide variety of mortgage products. The firm's troubles began in 2002, when it encountered a "mismatch" between the timing of its mortgage receipts and the time pattern of payments on the loans it had. The situation was significantly worsened during 2008 as many of the mortgages that Fannie Mae held fell behind on their payments. Ultimately, the government took over the company, posing major potential costs to taxpayers.

Hedging Risks with Credit Default Swaps

Any buyer of a stream of payments faces the possibility that the borrower will default on these payments. A form of insurance against this is provided by credit default swaps (CDSs). These securities represent a promise to duplicate the proposed stream of payments if the borrower does default. Firms that offer such products receive an "insurance premium" for doing so. Pricing this premium for credit default swaps is difficult, however, both because the underlying probability of default can only be guessed at, and the (unknown) timing of a default also affects pricing.

The AIG Fiasco

Although buying CDSs can make considerable sense for risk-averse lenders, selling this derivative product can itself pose special risks, as the insurance firm AIG discovered in 2008. AIG was the largest seller of CDSs in the world. As credit conditions worsened early in 2008, the firm's potential exposure to defaults expanded significantly. Because most CDS contracts required that AIG post collateral to ensure that they could pay off on their CDS contracts, the firm rapidly discovered that it did not have enough collateral for this purpose. Ultimately, it turned to the U.S. government for emergency loans to satisfy the demands of its CDS buyers. Through a series of transactions, the Federal government loaned about $182 billion to AIG over a short period of time. By the end of 2012, however, virtually all of those funds had been repaid.

TO THINK ABOUT

1. Although the derivative securities described in this example sometimes turned out badly, the underlying rationale for them seems reasonable. Why do you think CMOs and CDSs were invented? What goals do they serve? Can you think of other derivative securities that serve other goals?
2. Should the development of derivative securities be subject to extensive regulation? Or should we just rely on the market to develop and price such financial innovations? Should the government provide temporary aid to firms when things turn out badly?

Figure 14.4 **Scarcity Costs Associated with Exhaustible Resources**

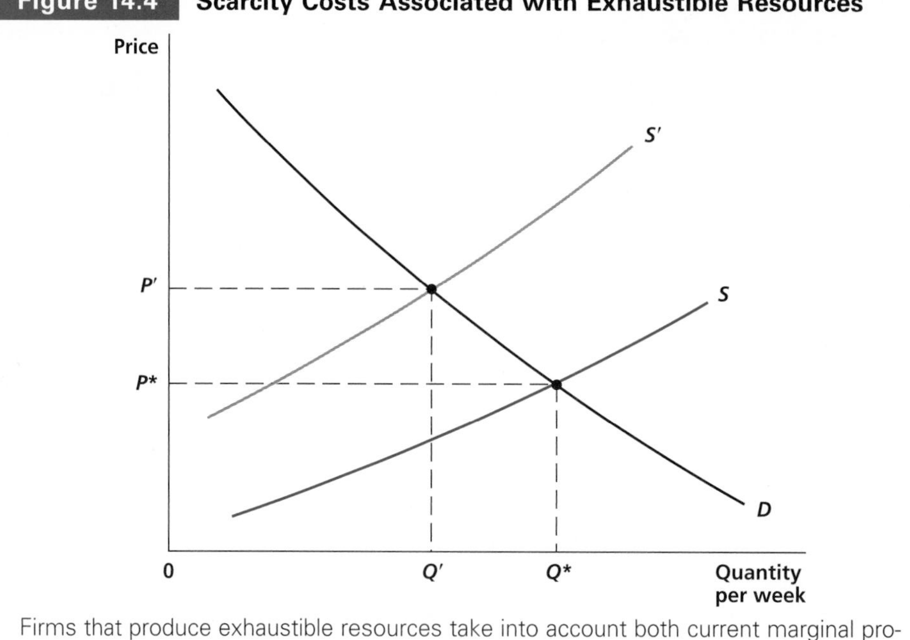

Firms that produce exhaustible resources take into account both current marginal production costs and the opportunity costs of forgone future production. The market supply curve for such firms (S') is above their marginal cost curves to the extent of those scarcity costs.

The implications of scarcity costs are illustrated in Figure 14.4. In the absence of scarcity costs, the industry supply curve for the resource would be given by S. This curve reflects the marginal costs of actually producing the resource (that is, the costs of drilling, mining, and/or refining). Scarcity costs shift firms' marginal cost curves upward because of the extra opportunity cost of forgone future sales that they represent. The new market supply curve is therefore S' and the gap between S and S' represents scarcity costs. Current output falls from Q^* to Q' and market price rises from P^* to P' once these costs are taken into account. These changes effectively encourage "conservation" of the resource—firms withhold some extra resources from the market, intending to sell them sometime in the future.

MICRO QUIZ 14.4

Suppose that kryptonite is discovered on Earth and that one firm owns the entire world supply.

1. Should the monopoly firm take scarcity costs into account?
2. Will the monopoly produce less kryptonite currently than would a competitive industry?

The Size of Scarcity Costs

The actual value of scarcity costs depends on firms' views about what prices for the resource will be in the future. Knowledge of these prices is required if resource owners are to be able to calculate correctly the present value of revenues that will be forgone by producing the resource now out of their currently available stock.[7] As a simple example, suppose that the owner of a copper mine believes that copper will sell for $1 per pound in 10 years. Hence, selling a pound today means forgoing a $1 sale in

[7]If the firm does not actually own the resource (suppose it is mining on public land, for example), it may not take scarcity costs into account because it may believe that it will not have access to the resource in the future. In Chapter 16, we explicitly consider the externalities created when resources are "owned" in common.

APPLICATION 14.6

Are Any Resources Scarce?

The question "Are any resources scarce?" is, of course, intentionally provocative. After all, Earth is of finite size, so (barring mining in space) the total quantity of natural resources is ultimately fixed. Any production today necessarily reduces the amount that can be produced tomorrow. By this test, all natural resources are scarce. The economic consequences of this scarcity, however, are not obvious.

Resource Price Trends

During the past century, the primary trend for natural resource prices has been downward in real terms. As Table 1 shows, annual rates of decline between 1 and 2 percent characterize the price histories for such diverse resources as petroleum, coal, and aluminum. Similarly, farmland prices seem to have declined in real terms, though at a slower rate than natural resources. It is difficult to infer actual scarcity values from these figures because declining relative costs of extraction and development may have masked rising scarcity costs. Since 1970, the decline in real resource prices appears to have slowed and this may indeed indicate an increasing relevance of scarcity costs. Nevertheless, the prospect of rising real resource prices driven by scarcity is not yet a forgone conclusion.

Implications of Scarcity

Even if real prices of natural resources were to follow a rising path indicating their scarcity, market reactions to the trend could be quite complex. The ultimate effect on overall output (GDP) would depend on such factors as the ability of firms to substitute inputs that have stable prices for those that were rising in price, the tendency of rising resource prices to induce various types of resource-saving technical innovations, and the willingness of consumers to reduce their consumption of resource-intensive goods. Modeling all of these various reactions is a formidable undertaking. One fairly careful estimate suggests that resource scarcity might reduce real economic growth rates by about 0.3 percent by the year 2050, with more than half of the decline being attributed to the increasing scarcity of energy resources.[1] Whether this relatively modest estimate will prove accurate is, of course, anyone's guess.

TO THINK ABOUT

1. How should changing costs of resource extraction be factored into an explanation of market prices? In what way might such changes mask changing scarcity values? What is the maximum effect that changing relative extraction costs might be expected to have?
2. Why do economists and environmentalists have such different views on resource scarcity? Don't environmentalists understand that the price system works to mitigate the effects of scarcity? Or is it economists who mistakenly assume that markets will work efficiently when the environment is threatened?

Table 1 Real Prices for Natural Resources (1990 = 100)

RESOURCE	1870	1910	1950	1970	1990
Petroleum	700	250	150	80	100
Coal	550	350	200	110	100
Copper	1,000	500	250	160	100
Iron ore	1,000	750	200	120	100
Aluminum	—	800	180	110	100
Farmland	200	375	80	105	100

Source: Adapted from W. D. Nordhaus, "Lethal Model 2: Limits to Growth Revisited," *Brookings Papers on Economic Activity*, no. 2 (1992): 24–26.

[1]W. D. Nordhaus, "Lethal Model 2: Limits to Growth Revisited," *Brookings Papers on Economic Activity*, no. 2 (1992): 1–43.

10 years because the supply of copper in the mine is fixed. With a real interest rate of, say, 5 percent, Table 14.1 shows that the present value of this opportunity cost is about \$0.61. Assuming that the owner of the mine is indifferent about whether the copper is sold today or in 10 years, the current market price should be about \$0.61 because that is the only price that reflects an equilibrium between present and future sales. If the actual marginal cost of copper production is, say, \$0.35 per pound, then scarcity costs would be \$0.26 per pound. Price would exceed the actual marginal cost of production by this \$0.26 per pound. In this case, the fact that price exceeds marginal cost is not a sign of inefficiency as it has been in several other situations we've looked at. Instead, the price here reflects efficiency in resource use in that consumers are paying all of the costs associated with the current production of the resource.

Time Pattern of Resource Prices

An important implication of this discussion is that, in the absence of any change in real production costs or in firms' expectations about future prices, the relative price of resources should be expected to rise over time at the real rate of interest. In our previous example, because the real rate of interest was assumed to be 5 percent, real copper prices would be expected to rise at 5 percent per year. Only by following that time path would prices always be equal to the present value of \$1 in 10 years.

This result can be shown intuitively from another perspective. Any firm that owns a quantity of a finite natural resource evaluates that holding in the way it evaluates any other investment. Since the real interest rate represents the rate of return on such alternative investments, only if resource prices rise at this rate do they provide a competitive return to the owner. If prices were rising more slowly than the real rate of interest, natural resources would be an inferior investment and firms should put their funds elsewhere. A rate of increase in prices faster than the real interest rate is also unsustainable because investors would quickly bid up the current price of resources to attempt to capture those desirable returns. This important result about resource pricing can be used to study a variety of important economic issues, as Application 14.6: Are Any Resources Scarce? shows.

SUMMARY

In this chapter, we have examined economic issues associated with decisions that are made over time in capital markets. The discussion focused primarily on the role of the real interest rate (r) in providing a "price" that connects one period to the next. Some of the important results of this examination included the following:

- Real interest rates affect individuals' savings decisions. Although income and substitution effects of a change in the real interest rate work in opposite directions in affecting current savings, it is generally believed that the (intertemporal) substitution effect is stronger. Hence, an increase in r causes savings (and loans) to increase.
- The real interest rate represents a cost of capital to firms regardless of whether they rent or own their equipment. An increase in r raises the rental rate on capital equipment and reduces its usage. This also reduces the demand for loans.
- Real interest rates are determined by the supply and demand for loans. Loans are supplied by individuals through their savings decisions. Loans are demanded by firms to finance their purchases of capital equipment.
- Expenditures or receipts in different periods cannot be compared directly because of the opportunity cost of interest payments. Such flows must be discounted so that they can be compared on a common, present-value basis. Investment decisions are an especially important situation where discounting is required.
- Production of finite resources involves additional costs reflecting scarcity. These costs arise because current production involves an opportunity cost in terms of forgone future sales.

REVIEW QUESTIONS

1. Some economic variables are "stocks" in that they represent the total value of something at a point in time, rather than a per-period "flow." Explain the connection between the following flow and stock variables:

FLOW	STOCK
Individual savings	Individual wealth
Firm investment	Firm capital
Education	Human capital
Gold production	Gold

2. Explain why the intertemporal budget constraint pictured in Figure 14.1 can be interpreted as requiring that individuals choose C_0 and C_1 so that the present value of this consumption is equal to their current income.

3. Suppose that an individual obtains the same utility from a given level of consumption regardless of whether it is consumed now or next period. Suppose also that the marginal utility of consumption is diminishing. Why would you expect this person to be "impatient," that is, always choosing C_0 to be greater than C_1? (Hint: What is the relative "price" of C_1 in terms of C_0?)

4. Sometimes retirement planners suggest that people set a "target" for retirement income. For example, the advice might be "Be sure to have accumulated $1,000,000 by the time you are 60." Assuming that the target remains unchanged, how would an increase in the real interest rate affect a person's level of savings to reach this target? Is it appropriate to hold the target constant when the real interest rate changes?

5. P. T. Blowhard is the CEO of Ditch Industries. He was heard to make the following statement about his choice of inputs for digging ditches: "We borrowed $100,000 to buy this Ditch Witch, and we're still paying $8,000 per year in interest on that loan even though the machine is now essentially worthless to any other firm. We could save money by borrowing $70,000 to buy a new DitchKing machine that would do the same job with only $5,600 in interest." What do you make of this argument? Assuming the machines are perfect substitutes, costs would be minimized by using the one with the lower rental rate. Which one has the lower rental rate?

6. CEO Blowhard continues his economic wisdom by discussing his rationale for calculating the present value of the rents he might save by purchasing a building to house his firm: "We could save $25,000 per year in rent by purchasing our own building. Over a 25-year horizon, Nicholson and Snyder's Table 14A.3 (see Appendix 14 to Chapter 14) tells me that the present value of these savings is about $350,000 using a real interest rate of 5 percent. But that is clearly an understatement since our rents are bound to rise because of general inflation. Hence, I'm sure it would be worthwhile for us to purchase a building costing up to at least $500,000." Has the CEO got it right now? How should he take into account the expected inflationary increases in rent in the future?

7. Figure 14.3 shows how the real interest rate is determined by the supply and demand for loans. Explain why this process also determines the rate of return that any capital owner should expect to earn on investments in physical capital. That is, how do you reconcile a "loanable funds" theory of interest rates with a "return on capital" theory of interest rates? If you are adventuresome, you might also seek to reconcile these theories with whatever theory of interest rates you learned in macroeconomics.

8. Suppose that a monopoly farmer of Wonder Grain must pay all of its costs of production in this year but that it must wait until next year to sell its output. Why would the farm's profit-maximizing output be the level for which $MR = MC(1 + r)$? Explain why this profit-maximizing condition takes *all* costs into account. How would this farmer change his or her output decision if the interest rate rose? Explain your result intuitively. Explain also why the firm should also hire any input, such as labor, up to the point at which $MRP_L = w(1 + r)$.

9. Why do scarcity costs occur only in the case of finite resources? Do producers of renewable resources such as fish or trees also incur scarcity costs? Explain the differences between these cases.

10. Our theory of the pricing of exhaustible resources concludes that the prices of such resources should increase (relative to prices of other goods) at a rate equal to the real rate of interest. What does this conclusion assume about the costs involved in actually producing natural resources?
    a. That they are constant
    b. That they increase at the overall rate of inflation
    c. That they also increase relative to prices of other goods at the real rate of interest

    Explain your answer and discuss how resource prices would be expected to move if your assumption were not true.

PROBLEMS

14.1. The budget constraint facing an individual planning his or her consumption over two periods is an intertemporal one in which the present value of consumption expenditures must equal the present value of incomes in the two periods:

$$C_0 + C_1/(1+r) = Y_0 + Y_1/(1+r)$$

where Y and C represent income and consumption respectively and the subscripts represent the two time periods.

a. Explain the meaning of this constraint.
b. If $Y_0 > C_0$, this individual is saving in period 0. Why does this imply that $Y_1 < C_1$?
c. If this individual is saving in period 0, why is $Y_0 - C_0$ less than $C_1 - Y_1$?

14.2. Flexible Felix views present and future consumption as perfect substitutes. He does, however, discount future consumption by a bit to reflect the uncertainties of his life. His utility function is therefore given by

$$U(C_0, C_1) = C_0 + C_1/(1+\delta)$$

where δ (which is a small positive number, such as .03) is the "discount rate" he applies to C_1.

a. Graph Felix's indifference curve map.
b. Show that if r (the real interest rate) exceeds δ, then $C_0 = 0$.
c. Show that if $r < \delta$, then $C_1 = 0$.
d. What do you conclude about the relationship between a person's saving behavior and his or her "impatience"?

14.3. Two roommates, Prudence and Glitter, graduate from college and get identical jobs that pay them \$50,000 this year and \$55,000 next year. The roommates have different utility functions so that the marginal rates of substitution are given by

$$\text{MRS for Prudence} = C_1/3C_0$$
$$\text{MRS for Glitter} = 3C_1/C_0$$

Assume that the real interest rate is 10 percent.

a. What is the present value of each student's income?
b. Focusing first on Prudence, what is her condition for utility maximization?
c. How should Prudence choose C_0 and C_1 so as to satisfy the condition for utility maximization subject to her two-period budget constraint? How much will Prudence borrow or save in period 0?
d. Answer part c for Glitter and discuss whether these two consumers' names are justified.

14.4. The Robotics Corporation produces cuddly toys using only computer-driven robots. The quantity of toys (T) produced per year is given by $T = 10\sqrt{R}$ where R is the number of robots used during each year of production.

a. If the market price of robots is \$2,000, the real interest rate is 0.05, and the depreciation rate on robots is 0.10, what is the firm's implicit rental rate for robot use?
b. What is the firm's total cost function for production of T?
c. If cuddly toys sell for \$60, how many will this firm choose to produce? (Hint: If Total Cost = kT^2, then calculus shows that Marginal Cost = $2kT$.)
d. How many robots will the firm employ for the year?

14.5. Acme Landfill Company is considering the purchase of 10 better trash collection trucks. Each truck costs \$50,000 and will last 7 years. The firm estimates that the purchase will increase its annual revenues by \$100,000 per year for as long as the trucks last. If the real interest rate is 10 percent, should the firm buy the 10 trucks? Would your answer change if the real interest rate fell to 8 percent?

14.6. Scotch whisky increases in value as it ages, at least up to a point. For any period of time, t, the value of a barrel is given by $V = 100t - 6t^2$. This function implies that the proportional rate of growth of the value of the scotch is $(100 - 12t)/V$.

a. Graph this scotch value function.
b. At what value of t is the barrel of scotch most valuable?
c. If the real interest rate is 5 percent, when should this distiller bottle the scotch for immediate sale?
d. How would the distiller's decision change if the real interest rate were 10 percent? (Hint: You will have to use the quadratic equation to solve part d here.)

14.7. To calculate scarcity costs for any finite resource, a price at some future date must be assumed. Suppose, for example, that the real price of platinum will be \$4,000 per ounce in 25 years.

a. If the real interest rate is 5 percent and no change is expected in the real costs of producing platinum over the next 25 years, what should the equilibrium price be today?
b. If the current cost of producing platinum is \$100 per ounce, what are current scarcity costs?
c. What will scarcity costs be in 25 years?

d. Assuming that resource markets are in equilibrium and that real production costs for platinum continue to remain constant, what is the real equilibrium price of the metal in 50 years?

Note: Problems 14.8–14.10 make use of the material on compound interest that is in the appendix to this chapter.

14.8. A persistent life insurance salesman makes the following pitch: "At your age (40) a $100,000 whole life policy is a much better buy than a term policy. The whole life policy requires you to pay $2,000 per year for the next 4 years but nothing after that. A term policy will cost you $400 per year for as long as you own it. Let's assume you live 35 more years—that means you'll end up paying $8,000 for the whole life policy and $14,000 for the term policy. The choice is obvious!"

a. Is the choice so obvious? How does the best buy depend on the interest rate?

b. If the interest rate is 10 percent, which policy is the best buy?

14.9. A car salesman once made the following pitch to one of your authors: "If you buy this $10,000 car with cash you will lose at least $1,500 over the next 3 years in forgone interest (assumed to be 5 percent per year). If you take one of our low-cost auto loans you have to pay only $315 per month for the next 3 years. That amounts to $11,340—$10,000 for the car and $1,340 in interest. With our car loan you will actually save $160 in interest." What do you make of this argument?

14.10. Although perpetual bonds are illegal in the United States, sometimes it is easiest to assume that interest payments last forever to show some simple results based on Equation 14A.24. Use that equation to show the following:

a. Assuming no inflation, the value of a bond that pays $10 per year is $200 with a real rate of interest of 5 percent.

b. If inflation is 3 percent per year and interest payments rise at that rate, the current value of the perpetual bond is still $200.

c. If inflation is 3 percent per year and the bond's payments are fixed at $10, that the current value of the perpetual bond is $125 can be shown in two ways:

i. By assuming that the nominal rate of interest is 8 percent and using that rate for discounting

ii. By adjusting the $10 payment for inflation in each period and using a real discount rate of 5 percent (Hint: This latter proof is easiest if you use the approximation $[1+r][1+p^e] \approx 1+r+p^e$ for small values of r [the real interest rate] and p^e [the expected inflation rate].)

APPENDIX 14A

Compound Interest

People encounter compound interest concepts almost every day. Calculating returns on bank accounts, deciding on the true cost of an automobile loan, and buying a home with a mortgage all involve the use of interest rate computations. This appendix shows how some of those computations are made. The methods introduced are useful not only in economics classes but in many personal financial decisions too.

A14-1 Interest

Interest
Payment for the current use of funds.

Interest is payment for the time value of money. A borrower gets to use funds for his or her own purposes for a time and in return pays the lender some compensation. Interest rates are usually stated as some percentage of the amount borrowed (the principal). For example, an annual interest rate of 5 percent would require someone who borrowed \$100 to pay \$5 per year in interest.

Throughout this appendix, we assume that the market has established an annual interest rate, i, and that this interest rate will persist from one year to the next. It is a relatively simple matter to deal with interest rates that change from one period to another, but we do not consider them here. We are also not particularly interested in whether i is a "nominal" interest rate (such as a rate quoted by a bank) or a "real" interest rate that has been adjusted for any inflation that may occur over time.[8] The mathematics of compound interest is the same for both nominal and real interest rates.

A14-2 Compound Interest

Compound interest
Interest paid on prior interest earned.

If you hold funds in a bank for more than one period, you receive **compound interest**—that is, you receive interest not only on your original principal but also on the interest that you earned in prior periods and left in the bank. Compounding is relatively complicated and results in rather dramatic growth over long periods.

Interest for One Year

If you invest \$1 at the interest rate of i, at the end of one year you will have

$$\$1 + \$1 \cdot i = \$1 \cdot (1 + i) \tag{14A.1}$$

For example, if i is 5 percent, at the end of one year, you will have

$$\$1 + \$1 \cdot (0.05) = \$1 \cdot (1.05) = \$1.05 \tag{14A.2}$$

[8]Later in this appendix, we look at the mathematical relationship between nominal and real interest rates.

Interest for Two Years

If at the end of the first year, you leave your money in the bank, you will now earn interest on both the original \$1 and on your first year's interest. At the end of two years, you will therefore have

$$\$1 \cdot (1+i) + \$1 \cdot (1+i) \cdot i = \$1 \cdot (1+i)(1+i) = \$1 \cdot (1+i)^2 \quad \textbf{(14A.3)}$$

To understand this equation, it is helpful to expand the term $(1+i)^2$. Remember from algebra that

$$(1+i)^2 = 1 + 2i + i^2 \quad \textbf{(14A.4)}$$

At the end of two years, \$1 will grow to

$$\$1 \cdot (1+i)^2 = \$1 \cdot (1 + 2i + i^2) = \$1 + \$1 \cdot (2i) + \$1 \cdot i^2 \quad \textbf{(14A.5)}$$

At the end of two years, you will have the sum of three amounts:

1. Your original \$1
2. Two years' simple interest on your original \$1, that is, $\$1 \cdot 2i$
3. Interest on your first year's interest, that is, $[(\$1 \cdot i) \cdot i] = \$1 \cdot i^2$

If the interest rate is 5 percent, at the end of two years you will have

$$\$1 \cdot (1.05)^2 = \$1 \cdot (1.1025) = \$1.1025 \quad \textbf{(14A.6)}$$

This represents the sum of your original \$1, two years' interest on the \$1 (that is, \$0.10), and interest on the first year's interest (5 percent of \$0.05, which is \$0.0025). The fact that you will have more than \$1.10 is a reflection of compounding (that is, earning interest on past interest). As we look at longer and longer periods of time, the effects of this compounding become much more pronounced.

Interest for Three Years

If you now leave these funds, which after two years amount to $\$1 \cdot (1+i)^2$, in the bank for another year, at the end of this third year you will have

$$\$1 \cdot (1+i)^2 + \$1 \cdot (1+i)^2 \cdot i = \$1 \cdot (1+i)^2(1+i) = \$1 \cdot (1+i)^3 \quad \textbf{(14A.7)}$$

For an interest rate of 5 percent, this amounts to

$$\$1 \cdot (1+0.05)^3 = \$1 \cdot 1.157625 = \$1.157625 \quad \textbf{(14A.8)}$$

The fact that you get more than your original \$1 and three years' simple interest (\$0.15) again reflects the effects of compounding.

A General Formula

By now the pattern should be clear. If you leave your \$1 in the bank for any number of years, n, you will have, at the end of that period,

$$\text{Value of \$1 compounded for } n \text{ years} = \$1 \cdot (1+i)^n \quad \textbf{(14A.9)}$$

With a 5 percent interest rate and a period of 10 years, you would have

$$\$1 \cdot (1.05)^{10} = \$1 \cdot 1.62889 \ldots = \$1.62889 \quad \textbf{(14A.10)}$$

MICRO QUIZ 14A.1

The term $(1+i)^3$ can be expanded to be $1+3i+3i^2+i^3$. Carefully explain why each of these terms is required in order to reflect the complete effects of compounding. You may have to do some factoring to make your explanation clear.

Without compounding you would have had \$1.50—your original \$1 plus 10 years' interest at \$0.05 per year. The extra \$0.12889 comes about through compounding.

To illustrate the effects of compounding further, Table 14A.1 shows the value of \$1 compounded for various time periods and interest rates.[9] Notice how compounding becomes very important for long periods. For instance, the table shows that, at a 5 percent interest rate, \$1 grows to be \$131.50 over 100 years. This represents the original \$1, simple interest of \$5 (\$0.05 per year for 100 years), and a massive \$125.50 in interest earned on prior interest. At higher interest rates, the effect of compounding is even more pronounced because there is even more prior interest on which to earn interest. At a 1 percent interest rate, only about 26 percent of the funds accumulated over 100 years represents the effects of compounding. At a 10 percent interest rate, more than 99.9 percent of the huge amount accumulated represents the effects of compounding.

Compounding with Any Dollar Amount

The use of \$1 in all of the computations we have made so far was for convenience only. Any other amount of money grows in exactly the same way. Investing \$1,000 is just the same as investing a thousand one-dollar bills—at an interest rate of 5 percent this amount would grow to \$1,050 at the end of 1 year $[\$1{,}000 \cdot (1.05)]$; it would grow to \$1,629 at the end of 10 years $[\$1{,}000 \cdot (1.629)]$; and to \$131,501 at the end of 100 years $[\$1{,}000 \cdot 131.501]$.

Algebraically, D dollars invested for n years at an interest rate of i will grow to

$$\text{Value of } \$D \text{ invested for } n \text{ years} = \$D \cdot (1+i)^n. \quad \textbf{(14A.11)}$$

Application 14A.1: Compound Interest Gone Berserk illustrates some particularly extreme examples of using this formula.

Table 14A.1 Effects of Compound Interest for Various Interest Rates and Time Periods with an Initial Investment of \$1

	INTEREST RATE			
YEARS	1 PERCENT	3 PERCENT	5 PERCENT	10 PERCENT
1	\$1.01	\$1.03	\$1.05	\$1.10
2	1.0201	1.0609	1.1025	1.2100
3	1.0303	1.0927	1.1576	1.3310
5	1.051	1.159	1.2763	1.6105
10	1.1046	1.344	1.6289	2.5937
25	1.282	2.094	3.3863	10.8347
50	1.645	4.384	11.4674	117.3909
100	2.705	19.219	131.5013	13,780.6123

[9]All calculations in this appendix were done on a Hewlett-Packard financial calculator—a device that is highly recommended. Some versions of Texas Instruments calculators also have nice financial options.

APPLICATION 14A.1

Compound Interest Gone Berserk

The effect of compounding can be gigantic if a sufficiently long period is used. Here are three of your authors' favorite examples.

Manhattan Island

Legend has it that in 1623 Dutch settlers "purchased" Manhattan Island from Native Americans living there for trinkets worth about \$24. The usual version of the story claims that the sellers were robbed in this transaction. But suppose they had invested the money? Real returns on stocks have averaged about 7 percent, so let's calculate how the \$24 invested in stocks would have grown during the 390 years since the sale.

$$\begin{aligned}\text{Value of \$24 in 2013} &= 24 \cdot (1.07)^{390} \\ &= 24 \cdot (288{,}000{,}000{,}000) \\ &= \$6{,}912{,}000{,}000{,}000\end{aligned}$$

That is, the funds would have grown to be nearly \$7 trillion—a value that is probably greater than the land on Manhattan Island is worth today.

Horse Manure in Philadelphia

In the 1840s the horse population of Philadelphia was growing at 10 percent per year. The city fathers, fearing excessive crowding, decided to restrict the number of horses in the city. It's a good thing! If the horse population of 50,000 in 1845 had continued to grow at 10 percent per year, there would have been quite a few of them in 2013.

$$\begin{aligned}\text{Number of Horses in 2013} &= 50{,}000 \cdot (1.10)^{168} \\ &= 50{,}000 \cdot (8{,}994{,}000) \\ &= 449{,}720{,}000{,}000\end{aligned}$$

Nearly 450 billion horses would have posed some problems for the city. Assuming each horse produces 0.25 cubic feet of manure per day, there would be about 3,000 feet of manure per year covering each square foot of Philadelphia today. Luckily, the City of Brotherly Love (author Nicholson's hometown) was spared this fate through timely government action.

Rabbits in Australia

Rabbits were first introduced into Australia in 1860. They found a country relatively free of natural predators and multiplied rapidly. If we assume that two rabbits started this process and that the population was growing at 100 percent per year, in only 20 years there were

$$\begin{aligned}\text{Number of rabbits in 1880} &= 2 \cdot (1+1)^{20} \\ &= 2^{21} \\ &= 2{,}097{,}152\end{aligned}$$

If the growth continued for the next 133 years, by 2013 there would have been 2^{154} rabbits, amounting to many trillions of rabbits per square foot of Australia. Clearly they built the "rabbit-proof fence" for a reason.

TO THINK ABOUT

1. The preposterous numbers in these examples suggest there is something wrong with the calculations. Can you put your finger on precisely why each is pure nonsense?
2. Compounding with high interest rates can produce astounding results. Often people look at very high interest rates (50 percent or more) in some developing countries and calculate how rich they will be in only a few years. What are they forgetting?

A14-3 Present Discounted Value

Because interest is paid on invested dollars, a dollar you get today is more valuable than one you won't receive until next year. You could put a dollar you receive today in a bank and have more than a dollar in one year. If you wait a year for the dollar, you will do without this interest that you could have earned.

Present value
Discounting the value of future transactions back to the present day to take account of the effect of potential interest payments.

Economists use the concept of present discounted value—or, more simply, **present value**—to reflect this opportunity cost notion. The present discounted value of the dollar you will not get for one year is simply the amount you would have to put in a bank now to have \$1 at the end of one year. If the interest rate is 5 percent, for example, the present value of \$1 to be obtained in one year is about \$0.95—if you invest \$0.95 today, you will have \$1 in one year, so \$0.95 accurately reflects the present value of \$1 in one year.

An Algebraic Definition

More formally, if the interest rate is i, the present discounted value of \$1 in one year is $\$1/(1+i)$ since

$$\frac{\$1}{1+i}\cdot(1+i)=\$1. \tag{14A.12}$$

If $i = 5$ percent, the present discounted value (PDV) of \$1 in one year is

$$PDV=\frac{\$1}{1.05}=\$0.9524 \tag{14A.13}$$

and

$$\$0.9524\cdot 1.05=\$1. \tag{14A.14}$$

A similar computation would result for any other interest rate. For example, the *PDV* of \$1 payable in one year is \$0.971 if the interest rate is 3 percent, but \$0.909 when the interest rate is 10 percent. With a higher interest rate, the PDV is lower because the opportunity costs involved in waiting to get the dollar are greater.

Waiting two years to get paid involves even greater opportunity costs than waiting one year since now you forgo two years' interest. At an interest rate of 5 percent, \$0.907 will grow to be \$1 in two years—that is, $\$1=\$0.907\cdot(1.05)^2$. Consequently, the present value of \$1 payable in two years is only \$0.907. More generally, for any interest rate, i, the present value of \$1 payable in two years is

$$PDV \text{ of } \$1 \text{ payable in two years} = \$1/(1+i)^2 \tag{14A.15}$$

and, for the case of a 5 percent interest rate,

$$\begin{aligned} PDV \text{ of } \$1 \text{ payable in two years} &= \$1/(1.05)^2 \\ &= \$1/1.1025 \\ &= \$0.907. \end{aligned} \tag{14A.16}$$

General *PDV* Formulas

The pattern again should be obvious. With an interest rate of i, the present value of \$1 payable after any number of years, n, is simply

$$PDV \text{ of } \$1 \text{ payable in } n \text{ years} = \$1/(1+i)^n. \tag{14A.17}$$

Calculating present values is the reverse of computing compound interest. In the compound interest case (Equation 14A.9), the calculation requires multiplying by the interest factor $(1+i)^n$, whereas in the present discounted value case (Equation 14A.17) the calculation proceeds by dividing by that factor. Similarly, the present value of any number of dollars (\$$D$) payable in n years is given by

$$PDV \text{ of } \$D \text{ payable in } n \text{ years} = \$D/(1+i)^n. \tag{14A.18}$$

Again, by comparing Equation 14A.11 and Equation 14A.18, you can see the different ways that the interest factor $(1+i)^n$ enters into the calculations.

Table 14A.2 **Present Discounted Value of $1 for Various Time Periods and Interest Rates**

YEARS UNTIL PAYMENT IS RECEIVED	INTEREST RATE			
	1 PERCENT	3 PERCENT	5 PERCENT	10 PERCENT
1	$0.99010	$0.97087	$0.95238	$0.90909
2	0.98030	0.94260	0.90703	0.82645
3	0.97059	0.91516	0.86386	0.75131
5	0.95147	0.86281	0.78351	0.62093
10	0.90531	0.74405	0.61391	0.38555
25	0.78003	0.47755	0.29531	0.09230
50	0.60790	0.22810	0.08720	0.00852
100	0.36969	0.05203	0.00760	0.00007

Note: These amounts are the reciprocals of those in Table 14A.1.

In Table 14A.2, your authors have again put their calculators to work to compute the present discounted value of $1 payable at various times and for various interest rates. The entries in this table are the reciprocals of the entries in Table 14A.1 because compounding and taking present values are different ways of looking at the same process. In Table 14A.2, the PDV of $1 payable in some particular year is smaller the higher the interest rate. Similarly, for a given interest rate, the PDV of $1 is smaller the longer it is until the $1 will be paid. With a 10 percent interest rate, for example, a dollar that will not be paid for 50 years is worth less than 1 cent ($0.00852) today. Application 14A.2: Zero-Coupon Bonds shows how such PDV calculations apply to a popular type of financial asset.

A14-4 Discounting Payment Streams

Dollars payable at different points of time have different present values. One must be careful in calculating the true worth of streams of payments that occur at various times into the future—simply adding them up is not appropriate. Consider a situation that has irritated your authors for some time. Many state lotteries promise grand prizes of $1 million (or, sometimes, much more) that they pay to the winners over 25 years. But $40,000 per year for 25 years is not "worth" $1 million. Indeed, at a 10 percent interest rate, the present value of such a stream is only $363,200—much less than half the amount falsely advertised by the state. This section describes how such a calculation can be made. There is really nothing new to learn about discounting streams of payments—performing the calculations always involves making careful use of the general discounting formula. However, repeated use of that formula may be very time consuming (if a stream of income is paid, say, at 100 different times in the future), and our main purpose here is to present a few shortcuts?

If the interest rate is 5 percent, would you rather have $1,000 in 5 years or $3,000 in 25 years? Would your answer change if the interest rate were 10 percent?

APPLICATION 14A.2

Zero-Coupon Bonds

U.S. Treasury notes pay their interest semiannually. In the past, each bond had a series of coupons for these interest payments. An owner would clip off a payment coupon and turn it in to the Treasury for payment. This is the origin of the term "coupon clipper" for elderly Scrooge-type characters living off their bond holdings. Today, of course, coupons are a thing of the past. Bond owners are recorded on computer files, and checks are routinely sent out to them when interest payments are due. Still, the idea that bonds are nothing more than a big coupon book of interest payments to be made at specific dates has spawned a variety of innovations.

Invention of Zero-Coupon Bonds

One of the most important such innovations occurred in the late 1970s when large financial institutions started buying large numbers of Treasury bonds and "stripping" off the interest (and principal) payments into separate financial assets. For example, consider a 10-year treasury note that promises 20 semiannual interest payments of \$20 on each \$1,000 bond together with a return of the \$1,000 principal in 10 years. A large financial institution can buy \$100 million of such bonds and sell off \$2 million worth of interest payments for each of the 20 semiannual interest payment dates into the future. The firm can also sell \$100 million of principal payments due in 10 years. Hence it has created 21 new financial assets based on its underlying bond holdings. Because the payments promised by these assets are supported by actual bond holdings of the financial institution, they are a low-risk investment for people who will need their funds at specific dates in the future.

Applying the *PDV* Formula

Because the interest and principal payments will not be received until some date in the future, we must use present-value calculations to determine what they are worth today. For example, a promised interest payment of \$20 in, say, six years with an interest rate of 5 percent would be worth $\$20/(1+i)^6 = \$20/(1.05)^6 = \$14.92$ today. A buyer that paid \$14.92 for the promise of \$20 in six years would achieve a return of 5 percent on his or her funds and would avoid the hassle of having to deal with periodic interest payments.

Yields on Zeros

Zero-coupon bonds trade regularly in the open market. The price of this promise to pay a set amount in the future is determined by the forces of supply and demand, just like any other good. Using this market price it is then possible to calculate the implicit yield (that is the effective interest rate) being promised by using the present value-formula. For example, in late 2013, a 10-year "strip" that promised to pay \$100 in 10 years was priced at about \$72. The yield on this investment can be calculated by solving the following equation for *i*:

$$72 = \frac{100}{(1+i)^{10}} \text{ or}$$
$$(1+i)^{10} = \frac{100}{72} = 1.3889 \text{ so}$$
$$1+i = (1.3889)^{0.1} = 1.0334.$$

So, the implicit rate of interest being promised on this zero-coupon bond is about 3.34 percent.[1] A person who buys the zero at \$72 will receive the equivalent of an interest rate of 3.34 percent on his or her investment after 10 years.

TO THINK ABOUT

1. Does an investor who buys a zero-coupon bond have to hold onto the asset until it comes due? Suppose that a person who bought the 10-year strip described above decided to sell it after four years. What would determine the yield he or she actually received on the investment? What would determine the yield this seller could get if he or she wanted to invest the proceeds for a new 10-year period?
2. U.S. Treasury "bills" operate much like strips. Bills with a maturity value of, say, \$1,000 are sold on a discount basis and the buyer receives an implicit yield by holding to maturity. For example, a 65-day Treasury bill with a maturity value of \$1,000 currently might sell for \$997. What is the annual yield on this investment? (Hint: You must first compute the daily yield on this investment. Then you must compound this daily yield over 365 days to get an effective annual yield.)

[1]The true rate is a bit lower than this because interest should be considered to be paid on a daily basis rather than annually as is assumed in the calculation (see Application 14A.3). The daily yield on this strip is about 3.29 percent.

An Algebraic Presentation

Consider a stream of payments that promises \$1 per year starting next year and continuing for three years. By applying Equation 14A.18, it is easy to see that the present value of this stream is

$$\text{PDV} = \frac{\$1}{1+i} + \frac{\$1}{(1+i)^2} + \frac{\$1}{(1+i)^3}. \qquad \textbf{(14A.19)}$$

If the interest rate is 5 percent, this value would be

$$\begin{aligned}\frac{\$1}{1.05} + \frac{\$1}{(1.05)^2} + \frac{\$1}{(1.05)^3} &= \$0.9523 + \$0.9070 + \$0.8639 \\ &= \$2.7232.\end{aligned} \qquad \textbf{(14A.20)}$$

Consequently, just as for the lottery, \$1 a year for three years is not worth \$3 but quite a bit less because of the need to take forgone interest into account in making present-value calculations. If the promised stream of payments extends for longer than three years, additional terms should be added to Equation 14A.19. The present value of \$1 per year for five years is

$$\text{PDV} = \frac{\$1}{1+i} + \frac{\$1}{(1+i)^2} + \frac{\$1}{(1+i)^3} + \frac{\$1}{(1+i)^4} + \frac{\$1}{(1+i)^5}, \qquad \textbf{(14A.21)}$$

which amounts to about \$4.33 at a 5 percent interest rate. Again, \$1 per year for five years is not worth \$5.

The *PDV* equation can be generalized to any number of years (n) by just adding the correct number of terms:

$$\text{PDV} = \frac{\$1}{1+i} + \frac{\$1}{(1+i)^2} + \cdots + \frac{\$1}{(1+i)^n}. \qquad \textbf{(14A.22)}$$

Table 14A.3 uses this formula to compute the value of \$1 per year for various numbers of years and interest rates. Several features of the numbers in this table are important to keep in mind when discussing present values. As noted previously, none of the streams is worth in present-value terms the actual number of dollars paid. The figures are always less than the number of years for which \$1 will be paid. Even for low interest rates, the

Table 14A.3 **Present Value of \$1 per Year for Various Time Periods and Interest Rates**

	INTEREST RATE			
YEARS OF PAYMENT	1 PERCENT	3 PERCENT	5 PERCENT	10 PERCENT
1	\$.99	\$.97	\$.95	\$.91
2	1.97	1.91	1.86	1.74
3	2.94	2.83	2.72	2.49
5	4.85	4.58	4.33	3.79
10	9.47	8.53	7.72	6.14
25	22.02	17.41	14.09	9.08
50	39.20	25.73	18.26	9.91
100	63.02	31.60	19.85	9.99
Forever	100.00	33.33	20.00	10.00

difference is substantial. With a 3 percent interest rate, \$1 per year for 100 years is worth only \$31 in present value. At higher interest rates, the effect of discounting is even more pronounced. A dollar each year for 100 years is worth (slightly) less than \$10 in present-value terms with an interest rate of 10 percent.

Perpetual Payments

The value of a stream of payments that goes on "forever" at \$1 per year is reported as the final entry in each column of Table 14A.3. To understand how this is calculated, we can pose the question in a slightly different way. How much (\$X) would you have to invest at an interest rate of i to yield \$1 a year forever? That is, we wish to find \$X that satisfies the equation

$$\$1 = i \cdot \$X. \qquad \textbf{(14A.23)}$$

But this just means that

$$\$X = \$1/i. \qquad \textbf{(14A.24)}$$

Perpetuity
A promise of a certain number of dollars each year, forever.

which is the way the entries in the table were computed. For example, the present value of \$1 per year forever with an interest rate of 5 percent is \$20 ($= \$1 \neq 0.05$). With an interest rate of 10 percent, the figure would be \$10($= \$1/0.10$). Such a permanent payment stream is called a **perpetuity**. Although these are technically illegal in the United States (however, many people set up "permanent" endowments for cemetery plots, scholarships, and prize funds), other countries do permit such limitless contracts to be written. In the United Kingdom, for example, perpetuities originally written in the 1600s are still bought and sold. Equation 14A.24 shows that, even though such perpetuities in effect promise an infinite number of dollars (since the payments never cease), in present-value terms they have quite modest values. Indeed, for relatively high interest rates, there isn't much difference between getting \$1 a year for 25 or 50 years and getting it forever. At an interest rate of 10 percent, for example, the present value of a perpetuity (which promises an infinite number of dollars) is only \$0.92 greater than a promise of a dollar a year for only 25 years. The infinite number of dollars to be received after year 25 are only worth \$0.92 today.[10]

[10]Using the formula for perpetuities provides a simple way of computing streams that run for only a limited number of years. Suppose we wished to evaluate a stream of \$1 per year for 25 years at a 10 percent interest rate. If we used Equation 14A.22, we would need to evaluate 25 terms. Instead, we could note that a 25-year stream is an infinite stream less all payments for year 26 and beyond. The present value of a perpetual stream is

$$\frac{\$1}{i} = \frac{\$1}{0.10} = \$10.$$

whereas the present value of a perpetual stream that starts in year 25 is

$$\frac{\$10}{(1+i)^{25}} = \frac{\$10}{(1+0.10)^{25}} = \frac{\$10}{10.83} = \$0.92.$$

The value of a 25-year stream is

$$\$10 - \$0.92 = \$9.08.$$

which is the figure given in Table 14A.3.

More generally, a stream of \$1 per year for n years at the interest rate i has a present value of

$$PDV = \frac{\$1}{i} - \frac{\$1/i}{(1+i)^n} = \frac{\$1}{i}\left(1 - \frac{1}{(1+i)^n}\right).$$

Varying Payment Streams

The present value of a payment stream that consists of the same number of dollars each year can be calculated by multiplying the value of $1 per year by that amount. In the lottery illustration with which we began this section, for example, we calculated the present value of $40,000 per year for 25 years. This is 40,000 times the entry for $1 per year for 25 years at 10 percent from Table 14A.3 (40,000 · $9.08 = $363,200). The present value of any other constant stream of dollar payments can be calculated in a similar fashion.

When payments vary from year to year, the computation can become more cumbersome. Each payment must be discounted separately using the correct discount factor from Equation 14A.18. We can show this computation in its most general form by letting D_i represent the amount to be paid in any year i. Then the present value of this stream would be

$$\text{PDV} = \frac{D_1}{1+i} + \frac{D_2}{(1+i)^2} + \frac{D_3}{(1+i)^3} + \cdots + \frac{D_n}{(1+i)^n}. \quad \textbf{(14A.25)}$$

Here, each D could be either positive or negative depending on whether funds are to be received or paid out. In some cases, the computations may be very complicated, as we saw in Application 14.5. Still, Equation 14A.25 provides a uniform way to approach all present-value problems.

Calculating Yields

Yield
The effective (internal) rate of return promised by a payment stream that can be purchased at a certain price.

Equation 14A.25 can also be used to compute the **yield** promised by any payment stream. That is, we can use the equation to compute the implied interest rate that discounts any payment stream to the present price that a buyer must pay for the rights to the stream. If we let P be the price of the payment stream and if we know the periodic payments to be made ($D_1 \ldots D_n$), then Equation 14A.25 becomes

$$P = \text{PDV} = \frac{D_1}{1+i} + \frac{D_2}{(1+i)^2} + \cdots + \frac{D_n}{(1+i)^n}, \quad \textbf{(14A.26)}$$

where now i is an unknown to be computed. Solving this equation can be clarified if we let $\delta = 1/(1 + i)$. Then Equation 14A.26 can be written as

$$P = \delta D_1 + \delta^2 D_2 + \cdots + \delta^n D_n, \quad \textbf{(14A.27)}$$

which is an n-degree polynomial in the unknown δ. This polynomial equation can usually be solved for d and hence for the yield (or "internal rate of return") on the flow of payments.

Reading Bond Tables

One of the most common applications of this type of calculation is the computation of yields on bonds. Most ordinary bonds promise to pay a stream of annual interest payments for a given number of years and to make a final repayment of principal when the bond matures. For example, suppose a bond broker lists a "6.25% bond maturing in May 2038," which currently sells for $1,260. This bond is simply a promise to pay 6.25 percent of its initial face amount ($1,000) each year and then to repay the $1,000 principal when interest payments end, 25 years from 2013. The yield on this bond is found by solving the following equation for δ [and also for $i = (1 - \delta)/\delta$]:[11]

$$1{,}260 = 62.5\delta + 62.5\delta^2 + \cdots + 62.5\delta^{25} + 1{,}000\delta^{25} \qquad \textbf{(14A.28)}$$

The result of this calculation amounts to 4.46 percent—that is the yield on this particular bond. Notice that in this case the yield is less than the interest rate quoted on the bond, in part because the bond's current price is greater than $1,000.

MICRO QUIZ 14A.3

For the bond described in the text, how would the yield be affected by

1. Increasing the annual interest payment from $62.50 to $65?
2. Increasing the repayment amount from $1,000 to $1,100?
3. Shortening the maturity date from 2038 to 2028?

A14-5 Frequency of Compounding

So far we have talked only about interest payments that are compounded once a year. That is, interest is paid at the end of each year and does not itself start to earn interest until the next year begins. In the past, that was how banks worked. Every January, depositors were expected to bring in their bank books so that the past year's interest could be added. People who withdrew money from the bank prior to January 1 often lost all the interest they had earned so far in the year.

Since the 1960s, however, banks and all other financial institutions have started to use more frequent, usually daily, compounding. This has provided some extra interest payments to investors, because more frequent compounding means that prior interest earned begins itself to earn interest more quickly. In this section, we use the tools we have developed so far to explore this issue.

Semiannual Compounding

As before, assume the annual interest rate is given by i (or in some of our examples 5 percent). But now suppose the bank agrees to pay interest two times a year—on January 1 and on July 1. If you deposit $1 on January 1, by July 1 it will have grown to be $\$1 \cdot (1 + i/2)$ since you will have earned half a year's interest. With an interest rate of 5 percent, you will have $1.025 on July 1. For the second half of the year, you will earn interest on $1.025, not just on $1. At the end of the year, you will have $\$1.025 \cdot 1.025 = \$1.05063$, which is slightly larger than the $1.05 you would have with annual compounding. More generally, with an interest rate of i, semiannual compounding would yield

$$\$1(1 + i/2)(1 + i/2) = \$1(1 + i/2)^2 \qquad \textbf{(14A.29)}$$

at the end of one year. That this is superior to annual compounding can be shown with simple algebra:

$$\$1 \cdot (1 + i/2)^2 = \$1(1 + i + i^2/4) = \$1 \cdot (1 + i) + \$1 \cdot i^2/4. \qquad \textbf{(14A.30)}$$

which is clearly greater than $\$1 \cdot (1 + i)$. The final term in Equation 14A.30 reflects the interest earned in the first half of the year, $\$1 \cdot (i/2)$, times the interest rate in the second half of the year $(i/2)$. This is the bonus earned by semiannual compounding.

[11]The actual calculation is a bit more complicated than described here because adjustments have to be made for the actual dates at which interest and principal payments are to be made. Typically, interest payments are made semiannually.

Table 14A.4 Value of $1 at a 5 Percent Annual Interest Rate Compounded with Different Frequencies and Terms

	FREQUENCY			
YEARS ON DEPOSIT	ANNUAL	SEMIANNUAL	MONTHLY	DAILY
1	$1.0500	$1.0506	$1.0512	$1.0513
2	1.1025	1.1038	1.1049	1.1052
3	1.1576	1.1596	1.1615	1.1618
5	1.2763	1.2801	1.2834	1.2840
10	1.6289	1.6386	1.6471	1.6487
25	3.3863	3.4371	3.4816	3.4900
50	11.4674	11.8137	12.1218	12.1803
100	131.5013	139.5639	146.9380	148.3607

A General Treatment

We could extend this algebraic discussion to more frequent compounding—quarterly, monthly, or daily—but little new information would be added. More frequent compounding would continue to increase the effective yield that the 5 percent annual interest rate actually provides. Table 14A.4 shows how the frequency of compounding has this effect over time periods of various durations. The gains of using monthly rather than annual compounding are relatively large, especially over long periods of time when small differences in effective yields can make a big difference. Gains in going from monthly to daily compounding are fairly small, however. The extra yield from compounding even more frequently (every second?) is even smaller. Application 14A.3: Continuous Compounding shows that, for some purposes, using such frequent compounding can make calculations much easier.

Real versus Nominal Interest Rates

Although we have made no distinction between real and nominal interest rates in our discussion of compound interest in this appendix, the analysis in Chapter 14 itself made clear that it is the real (inflation-adjusted) interest rate that matters for most economic decisions. In this section, we explore the relationship between the more common concept of a "nominal" interest rate and its real counterpart.

Suppose that you are thinking about making a one period loan of $1. The borrower agrees to pay you a nominal interest rate of i for this one period. Hence, he or she promises to return $\$1(1+i)$ to you next period, but this promise is purely in nominal terms—it disregards any possible inflation between the two periods. Because you as the lender ultimately care about how the money you receive from your loan can be used to buy things next year, you need to discount the value to be received for expected inflation. If the expected proportional change in the overall price level is given by p^e, the real value of your loan repayment is

$$\text{Real Value of Repayment} = \frac{(1+i)}{(1+p^e)} \qquad \textbf{(14A.31)}$$

Now, we can use this expression to define the "real" interest rate (r) being paid on this loan as

APPLICATION 14A.3

Continuous Compounding

Perhaps surprisingly, the mathematics involved with "continuous" compounding (that is, compounding that occurs every instant of time) is really quite simple. A familiarity with continuous compounding can allow you to make very good approximations to interest calculations that would otherwise be very cumbersome.

The Amazing *e*

One of the most important constants[1] in mathematics is the number "*e*," which takes a value of approximately 2.718281828. The mathematician Euler discovered the constant in 1727, thereby explaining why this letter was chosen. The constant seems to turn up everywhere in mathematics. For us, the most important property of *e* is that it is used in continuous compounding. Consider an annual interest rate of i that will be compounded n times in one year. The result of this compounding will be

$$\left(1+\frac{i}{n}\right)^{n}.$$

If n approaches infinity, the value of this expression is precisely e^{i}. For example, if $i = 0.05$, $e^{i} = e^{.05} = 1.05127$. So an annual interest rate of 5 percent that is continuously compounded has an effective annual yield of 5.13 percent. If compounding extends for t years, \$1 becomes $\$1 \cdot (e^{i})^{t} = \$1 \cdot e^{it}$.

The Rule of 70

A simple application of continuous compounding is to provide a rule of thumb for calculating doubling time for any given interest rate. To find the time anything doubles we wish to solve the equation $e^{it} = 2$ for t. Taking natural logarithms yields

$$t^{*} = \frac{ln2}{i} = \frac{0.6913}{i}.$$

If we approximate 0.6913 as 0.7, this is the "rule of 70." To find any doubling time, just divide the interest rate into 0.70. For example, anything growing at 5 percent per year will double in about 14 (= 0.7/0.05) years.

Growth Rates of Products and Ratios

When economic magnitudes follow exponential growth rates, calculations combining two or more series can be especially simple. For example, suppose we have two series, x and y growing at rates of r_1 and r_2 respectively. Then the product $x \cdot y$ is growing like

$$z = x \cdot y = e^{r_1 t} \cdot e^{r_2 t} = e^{(r_1+r_2)t} \qquad \{i\}$$

That is, the product of the two variables is growing at a rate that equals the *sum* of the individual growth rates. If, for example, real GDP is growing at 3 percent per year and inflation is 2 percent per year, nominal GDP is growing at 5 percent per year. A similar result works for growth rates in the ratio of two variables. That is, the ratio of two variables grows at a rate that equals the *difference* in their growth rates. For example, if real GDP is growing at 3 percent per year and population growth is 1 percent per year, per capita GDP is growing at 2 percent per year.

Discounting

With continuous compounding, the appropriate discount factor is e^{-it}, which plays the same role that $1/(1+i)^{t}$ does in discrete discounting. Any continuous stream of payments can be discounted to the present day by using this factor. As a simple example, the value of payments of \$1 per year for 25 years discounted at an interest rate of 5 percent is given by

$$\begin{aligned} PDV &= \int_{0}^{25} \$1 \cdot e^{-.05t}dt = \$1 \cdot \frac{e^{-.05t}}{-.05}\Big|_{0}^{25} \\ &= \$1\left(\frac{e^{-1.25}}{-.05} - \frac{1}{-.05}\right) \qquad \{ii\} \\ &= \$20(1 - e^{-1.25}) = \$14.27. \end{aligned}$$

TO THINK ABOUT

1. The U.S. consumer price index was 152 in 1995 and 233 in 2013. How would you use continuous compounding formulas to calculate the annual rate of change during this 18-year period?
2. How would you change equation (ii) to calculate the value of a dollar per year forever?

[1]One indication of the significance of e is that Google in its initial stock offering in 2004 sold precisely \$2,718,281,828 worth of stuck. That is, it sold "e billion" worth of shares. The firm's 2005 stock offering was based on π.

$$1 + r = \frac{1+i}{1+p^e} \quad \text{or} \quad (1+r)\cdot(1+p^e) = 1+i. \tag{14A.32}$$

If we now expand the left side of Equation 14A.32, we get

$$(1+r)(1+p^e) = 1 + r + p^e + rp^e = 1 + i. \tag{14A.33}$$

Finally, because both r and p^e are small, we can use the approximation that $rp^e \approx 0$ so Equation 14A.33 can be written as

$$i = r + p^e \quad \text{or} \quad r = i - p^e. \tag{14A.34}$$

That is, we can always compute a real interest rate from a nominal one by subtracting the expected proportional change in prices. For example, if a loan promised a nominal interest rate of 5 percent (that is, 0.05), and prices were expected to rise by 2 percent over the period (that is, by 0.02), the real interest rate promised by the loan is 3 percent $(0.03 = 0.05 - 0.02)$. In most economic problems, this is precisely the sort of adjustment you should make when presented with a nominal interest rate in a situation where a real interest rate is required. Although we would usually expect the nominal interest rate to be positive (no one would lend money in the expectation that less would be returned in the future), Equation 14A.34 shows that real interest rates could easily turn negative. For example, if the nominal interest rate on a loan is 4 percent, and the expected inflation rate is 7 percent, the implied real interest rate is -3 percent. Surely any would-be borrower would be foolish not to borrow at such a favorable real rate. Indeed, this appears to be one explanation for the housing bubble in the United States (and elsewhere) during the years 2001–2005 when (given high rates of expected price appreciation for houses) real interest rates on mortgages were indeed negative for many borrowers.

A14-6 The Present Discounted Value Approach to Investment Decisions

The present discounted value concept provides an alternative way of approaching the theory of capital demand that we discussed in Chapter 14. When a firm buys a machine, it is in effect buying a stream of net revenues in future periods. In order to decide whether to purchase the machine, the firm must assign some value to this stream. Because the revenues will accrue to the firm in many future periods, the logic of the preceding pages suggests that the firm should compute the present discounted value of this stream. Only by doing so will the firm have taken adequate account of the opportunity costs associated with alternative assets it might have bought.

Consider a firm in the process of deciding whether to buy a particular machine. The machine is expected to last n years and will give its owner a stream of real returns (that is, marginal value products) in each of the n years. Let the return in year i be represented by R_i. If r is the real interest rate on alternative investments, and if this rate is expected to prevail for the next n years, the present discounted value (*PDV*) of the machine to its owner is given by

$$PDV = \frac{R_1}{1+r} + \frac{R_2}{(1+r)^2} + \cdots + \frac{R_n}{(1+r)^n}. \tag{14A.35}$$

This represents the total value of the stream of payments that is provided by the machine, once adequate account is taken of the fact that these payments occur in

> **MICRO QUIZ 14A.4**
>
> Equation 14A.33 assumes that machines do not depreciate. How should the equation be changed if the machine deteriorates at the rate of d per year? If the machine still lasts forever (even though it will be very deteriorated), will its rental rate be given by the formula in Chapter 14—that is, $v = (r + d)P$?

different years. If the PDV of this stream of payments exceeds the price (P) of the machine, the firm should make the purchase. Even when opportunity costs are taken into account, the machine promises to return more than it will cost to buy and firms would rush out to buy machines. On the other hand, if P exceeds the machine's PDV, the firm would be better off investing its funds in some alternative that promises a rate of return of r. When account is taken of forgone returns, the machine does not pay for itself. No profit-maximizing firm would buy such a machine.

In a competitive market, the only equilibrium that can persist is one where the price of a machine is exactly equal to the present discounted value of the net revenues it provides. Only in this situation will there be neither an excess demand for machines nor an excess supply of machines. Hence, market equilibrium requires that

$$P = \text{PDV} = \frac{R_1}{1+r} + \frac{R_2}{(1+r)^2} + \cdots + \frac{R_n}{(1+r)^n}. \quad \textbf{(14A.36)}$$

Present Discounted Value and the Rental Rate

For simplicity, assume now that machines do not depreciate and that the marginal value product is the same in every year. This uniform return will then also equal the rental rate for machines (v), since that is what another firm would be willing to pay for the machine's use during each period. With these simplifying assumptions, we may write the present discounted value from machine ownership as

$$\text{PDV} = \frac{v}{1+r} + \frac{v}{(1+r)^2} + \cdots + \frac{v}{(1+r)^n} + \cdots \quad \textbf{(14A.37)}$$

where the dots (...) indicate that payments go on forever. But because in equilibrium $P = \text{PDV}$, our earlier discussion of perpetuities gives

$$P = \frac{v}{r} \quad \textbf{(14A.38)}$$

or

$$v = rP. \quad \textbf{(14A.39)}$$

which is the same as Equation 14.1 when $d = 0$. For this case, the present discounted value criterion gives results identical to those outlined earlier using the rental rate approach. In equilibrium, a machine must promise owners the prevailing rate of return.

SUMMARY

This appendix surveys mathematical calculations involving compound interest concepts. Dollars payable at different points in time are not equally valuable (because those payable in the distant future require the sacrifice of some potential interest), and it is important to be careful in making comparisons among alternative payment schedules. Discussing this issue we show:

- In making compound interest calculations, it is necessary to take account of interest that is paid on prior interest earned. The interest factor $1 + (i)^n$—where n is the number of years over which interest is compounded—reflects this compounding.
- Dollars payable in the future are worth less than dollars payable currently. To compare dollars that are payable at

different dates requires using present discounted value computations to allow for the opportunity costs associated with forgone interest.

- Evaluating payment streams requires that each individual payment be discounted by the appropriate interest factor. It is incorrect simply to add together dollars payable at different times.
- More frequent compounding leads to higher effective returns because prior interest paid begins to earn interest more quickly. There is an upper limit to the increased yield provided, however.
- Nominal and real interest rates are related by the equation $1 = r + p^e$ (where p^e is the expected proportional change in prices during the period).
- The present discounted value formula provides an alternative approach to investment decisions that reaches the same result already derived in Chapter 14.

PART 8

Market Failures

The marginal private net product ... accrues to the person responsible for investing resources. In some conditions this is equal to, in some it is greater than, in others it is less than the marginal social net product.

—Arthur C. Pigou, The Economics of Welfare, 1920

In Part 5 we saw that competitive markets can in some circumstances lead to an efficient allocation of resources. One major reason that this efficiency may fail to materialize is when firms have market power—a situation we studied in Part 6. In this final part of the book we look more broadly at additional reasons why the beneficial outcomes from competitive markets may not occur. We also examine potential ways of fixing such "failures" of competitive markets to make them work better.

There are three chapters in Part 8. In Chapter 15, we look in detail at the role of information in economic activity. We are especially concerned with situations in which economic actors may have differing information about a potential market transaction. We show why markets may perform poorly in these cases of "asymmetric information."

Chapter 16 explores situations in which market transactions affect third parties not directly involved in these transactions. Two general types of such "externalities" provide the focus for this chapter. First we look at environmental externalities—that is, situations where market transactions benefit or harm third parties. We show that in some cases there are effective, market-based solutions to such problems. A second type of externalities examined in Chapter 16 is "public good" externalities. These arise in situations where people cannot be excluded from benefiting from certain kinds of goods and, therefore, have an incentive to avoid paying for them. The solution to such problems is usually compulsory taxation, although the economic efficiency of that solution may often be open to question as well.

Finally, Chapter 17 takes a brief look at the rapidly expanding field of behavioral economics. We are especially concerned with situations where market participants may make mistakes or have other limits on their rationality. We show that if people make bad decisions, it is possible (though by no means certain) that a paternalistic government can make them better off by suggesting better decisions or prohibiting bad options.

15 Asymmetric Information

In previous chapters, we have seen how markets can allocate goods efficiently and examined some of the factors (such as monopoly) that can prevent such a result. In this chapter, we will see that another factor, participants' lack of full information about the market, can also lead markets to be inefficient. Using game theory, we will analyze a series of models in which one player has better information about the uncertain economic environment than others. This extra information is variously referred to as hidden, private, or **asymmetric information**. Game theory will enable us to better understand the range of clever strategies that might be used to cope with asymmetric information. Even if market participants can resort to such clever strategies, the market will be less efficient than if all participants had full information.

Asymmetric information
In a game with uncertainty, information that one player has but the other does not.

The tools developed in this chapter will allow us to analyze an array of important and interesting economic situations. How does a boss ensure that an employee is working hard when the boss cannot observe every move the employee makes? How does the firm ensure it hires talented employees when such talent is difficult to measure? Can the employer use a person's education as a signal of talent? How should a coffee shop set its menu of prices and cup sizes to extract the most money from coffee drinkers, whose demands might be unknown to the shop? Will used-car markets consist of mostly lemons if buyers cannot judge quality? Will high-risk consumers, the most expensive to insure, be the only ones to buy health insurance? When should a player bluff in poker?

Games of asymmetric information are the focus of much recent research in economics. Given the complexity of the subject, we will only provide a brief overview in this chapter, but it should be sufficient to give you a taste of the exciting developments in this area. We begin with perhaps the simplest setting in which to study asymmetric information, contracts between just two parties where one or the other has better information. Even in this simple setting, called the principal-agent model, a large number of interesting applications can be studied. Then we will move on to more complicated settings.

15-1 Principal-Agent Model

We will begin our study of games of asymmetric information by focusing on a simple but influential game, called the principal-agent model. The game involves a contract signed between two players in an environment involving uncertainty. The player making the contract offer is called the **principal**. The player who decides whether to accept the contract or not and then performs under the terms of the contract is called the **agent**. The agent is typically the party with the private information.

Principal
Player offering the contract in a principal-agent model.

Agent
Player who performs under the terms of the contract in a principal-agent model.

The principal-agent model encompasses a wide variety of applications as shown in Table 15.1. Note that the same party might be a principal in one setting and an agent in another. For example, a company's CEO is the principal in dealings with the company's

Table 15.1 Applications of the Principal-Agent Model

		AGENT'S PRIVATE INFORMATION	
PRINCIPAL	AGENT	HIDDEN ACTION	HIDDEN TYPE
Patient	Doctor	Effort, unnecessary procedures	Medical knowledge, severity of condition
Manager	Employee	Effort	Job skill
Shareholders	Manager	Effort, executive decisions	Managerial skill
Student	Tutor	Preparation, patience	Subject knowledge
Monopoly	Customers	Abuse product	Valuation for good
Health insurer	Insurance purchaser	Risky activity	Preexisting condition
Parent	Child	Delinquency	Moral fiber

employees but is the agent of the firm's owners, the shareholders. We will study a number of the applications from Table 15.1 in detail throughout the remainder of the chapter, beginning with two that will help introduce some of the chapter's main ideas in Application 15.1: Principals and Agents in Franchising and Medicine.

The analysis is somewhat different depending on whether the agent has private information about an action under his or her control or about an innate characteristic outside his or her control (the agent's "type"). See Table 15.1 for some examples of each case. We will study each in turn, beginning with the case of hidden action.

15-2 Worker Moral Hazard

Moral-hazard problem The best hidden action for the agent may not be good for the principal.

The version of the principal-agent model in which the agent has private information about his or her action has been colorfully labeled the **moral-hazard problem**. The agent may end up choosing an action that is good for him or herself but bad for the principal. If the action is hidden, there may be no way for the principal to prevent this outcome. We will avoid judgments ourselves here, but one could forgive the principal for thinking that such an agent was not being moral, hence the label, coined by insurers in the early history of that industry.

To be concrete, we will base the entire discussion of the moral-hazard problem in this section on the first entry from Table 15.1 in which the principal is a manager and the agent is a worker. Perhaps as an antidote to the underrepresentation of females in management,[1] economists often take the manager to be female and the worker to be male, and we will follow this convention. To make the example even more concrete, suppose that the worker's job is to assemble electronic devices. By putting in more effort, which may not be easy for the manager to observe, the worker can increase salable output by reducing the number of defective units.

The setting can be modeled as a sequential game in which the manager moves first, offering an employment contract to the worker, who moves second, deciding whether to

[1]Women occupied 40% of management positions but only 23% in manufacturing industries according to a U.S. General Accounting Office report, *Women in Management: Analysis of Female Managers' Representation, Characteristics, and Pay*, GAO-10-892R, Washington DC: September 20, 2010.

APPLICATION 15.1

Principals and Agents in Franchising and Medicine

Problems in principal-agent relationships arise in economic situations as diverse as fast-food operations and the provision of medical care. A closer examination shows that these two situations have much in common.

Franchising

Many large businesses operate their local retail outlets through franchise contracts. The McDonald's Corporation, for example, does not actually own every place that displays the golden arches. Instead, local restaurants are usually owned by small groups of investors who have bought a franchise from the parent company. The widespread use of franchise contracts by McDonald's and other retailers suggests that they are very useful in solving the principal-agent problems that arise in the industry.[1]

One problem that has to be solved is to get retail outlets to operate at the lowest cost possible. Fast food restaurants operate on thin margins; a small cost increase may turn a very profitable outlet into an unprofitable one. Keeping costs low and operations running smoothly requires constant attention by the manager. It seems impossible for central headquarters to monitor the daily operation of thousands of far-flung restaurants. Franchise contracts offer a solution. The franchisee gets to keep a large share of the profits generated by the local restaurant, thereby providing significant incentives to manage it efficiently without direct monitoring.

In solving one problem, franchise contracts raise another. McDonald's success depends on consistency across restaurants. A customer knows exactly what a McDonald's hamburger will taste like from Maine to California. A franchisee who only keeps a share of local profits may be inclined to cut costs by cutting quality since the loss of consistency across franchises matters less to the local restaurant than the parent company. Franchise contracts contain additional provisions to help maintain consistent quality. McDonald's franchisees, for example, must meet certain food-quality and service standards, and they must purchase their supplies (hamburgers, frozen fries, buns, napkins, and so forth) from firms that also meet standards set by the parent company. In return, the franchisee gets some management assistance and enjoys the reputation of the McDonald's trademark (together with its national advertising).

Doctors and Patients

A similar set of problems occurs between physicians and their patients. When people are sick, they often have very little idea of what is wrong or what the most promising treatment is. They place themselves under a physician's care in the belief that the physician has better information on which to base decisions about the proper course of action. The physician then acts as an agent for the patient. But there are several reasons why a physician might not choose exactly what a fully informed patient would choose. The physician generally pays none of the patient's bills; to the physician, the price of anything prescribed is essentially zero. Indeed, since the physician may in many instances also be the provider of care, he or she may even benefit financially from the services prescribed. A number of studies have gathered evidence on such physician-induced demand, and most have reported relatively small but significant effects.

Physicians as Double Agents

Most medical care consumers have insurance. Because insurance companies must rely on physicians to deliver care, this raises a second principal-agent situation in which the companies need some way to ensure that physicians will not overprescribe care. With traditional fee-for-service insurance, providing such incentives to physicians is very difficult because the company cannot monitor every physician decision. This is one reason that many health care plans have adopted "prepaid" features such as those found in health maintenance organizations (HMOs). Under these plans, insured patients pay an annual fee covering all of their medical needs. That annual fee then becomes a budget constraint for physicians, who now may more carefully consider the costs of the care they deliver.

TO THINK ABOUT

1. Many states have enacted laws that protect franchisees from their larger parent firms. For example, some states do not allow the establishment of new franchises from the same parent if that would be "unfair" to existing firms. How would such restrictions affect the efficiency of franchise contracts?
2. Why do many medical care consumers hate their HMOs? Do we need an HMO patients' "Bill of Rights" to ensure that such consumers are fairly treated?

[1]For a summary of empirical evidence, see F. Lafontaine and M. E. Slade, "Retail Contracting: Theory and Practice," *Journal of Industrial Economics* (March 1997): 1–25.

accept the contract, and if so, how much effort to expend. We will use the subgame-perfect equilibrium concept, which in this context ensures the following:

1. The worker accepts the contract if it provides him with at least as high a payoff as the best alternative if he rejected it.
2. The worker chooses effort to maximize his utility taking into account contractual pay and effort costs.

In other words, the worker acts in his self-interest, not in the interest of the manager directly. The worker only acts in the manager's interest indirectly if incentives are provided in the contract.

The last point is central to our analysis of the moral-hazard problem. When an organization involves more than one individual (here a firm involving a manager and a worker), it cannot simply be assumed that they act together in concert. Such an assumption would be inconsistent with everything we have assumed about the behavior of microeconomic agents. Throughout the text we have assumed that agents act in their own best interest, whether consumers maximizing utility, firms maximizing profit, or players playing best-responses in games. Our analysis of the principal-agent problem can be thought of as the natural extension of maximizing behavior to organizations involving more than one person.

Full Information about Effort

Suppose first that the manager can observe the worker's effort perfectly. In this case, effort can be viewed as an input into the production process much like capital or labor. Denoting the level of effort by E, the profit-maximizing level of E can be found in much the same way as the profit-maximizing level of K or L in Chapter 13. Let's start then by reviewing some key results from that chapter. We saw that the profit-maximizing level of an input equalizes the marginal expense of hiring an additional unit and the marginal revenue generated by that unit. For example, in the case of the labor input, if the firm is a price taker on the labor market, the marginal expense of labor is the wage rate w. If the firm sells its output competitively at market price P, the marginal revenue generated by an additional unit of labor is the marginal value product $MVP_L = MP_L \cdot P$. That is, an additional unit of labor produces MP_L more units of output, which are sold at a price of P each. The profit-maximizing level of labor satisfies

$$w = MVP_L = MP_L \cdot P. \qquad \textbf{(15.1)}$$

We can borrow some of these ideas to compute the profit-maximizing level of effort. Figure 15.1 illustrates the computation. The horizontal line is the marginal cost of effort to the worker, labeled MC_E, the additional pay needed to exactly compensate him for the disutility of working slightly harder. While obviously a measure of the cost of effort from the worker's perspective; it also becomes an economic cost to the firm: if the firm tries to get away with paying less, the worker will either refuse to work as hard as specified or, if necessary, quit his job. Effort is a fairly nebulous variable to quantify. The figure scales effort in such a way that a unit is that amount of effort that would require a \$1 of compensation to offset. This allows MC_E as a horizontal line with a height of \$1. (This scaling is convenient, but the analysis would be similar if MC_E were, say, an upward-sloping curve.) The marginal value product of effort, $MVP_E = MP_E \cdot P$, is shown by the downward-sloping curve. It slopes down because, holding other inputs constant, effort exhibits diminishing marginal productivity. There are only so many additional defects that the worker can prevent by concentrating harder on the job. The profit-maximizing effort level E^* is given by the intersection between the MC_E and MVP_E curves, or in other words the level of effort for which the marginal value product of effort is \$1.

Figure 15.1 Effort Choice under Full Information

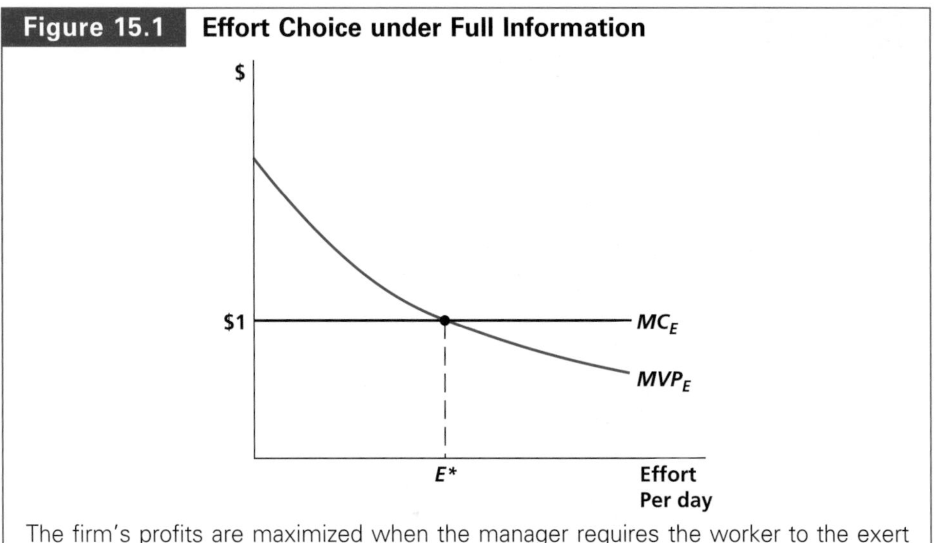

The firm's profits are maximized when the manager requires the worker to the exert effort E^* given by the intersection of the marginal cost of effort to the worker and its marginal value product to the firm.

What contract can the manager offer the worker to implement the outcome in the figure? One possibility is a contract that says "in order to receive any pay you need to exert E^* units of effort." The pay would have to be set so that, subtracting the disutility of effort, which according to our scaling is $\$E^*$, the result is no lower than the worker could get at some other firm. Presumably the worker would not just look at the wage offered by alternative jobs but also the effort they would require. Because effort is observable, the manager can watch to make sure the worker exerts the target level E^*.

Unobservable Effort

More realistic is the case in which the manager does not observe the worker's effort perfectly. After all, the manager cannot always be looking over the worker's shoulder every minute of the day, making sure he is on task rather than wandering around the factory or checking e-mail. Even if the manager were right at the worker's side, it would be difficult for her to gauge how intensely he is concentrating.

While the manager may not be able to observe the worker's effort, she may be able to observe the number q of non-defective devices that he assembles and may be able to get the worker to exert effort with an incentive scheme S that conditions his pay on q. For example, a linear incentive scheme would have the form

$$S = a + bq, \tag{15.2}$$

where a is the fixed payment which the worker receives regardless of output and b is the "power" of the scheme, measuring how closely the worker's pay is tied to his performance.

Figure 15.2 depicts some example incentive schemes. Line S_1 corresponds to constant pay that does not depend on performance at all (zero power). With lines S_2 and S_3, the worker's pay does depend on his performance. Line S_2 has a moderate slope and thus is a moderate-powered incentive scheme. The worker's pay increases with q, but not so quickly. Line S_3 is a high-powered incentive scheme. The worker receives no fixed pay; instead he receives the sales price P for each non-defective unit produced.

Figure 15.3 graphs the effort levels induced by the incentive schemes from Figure 15.2. The worker chooses the effort given by the intersection of the marginal

Figure 15.2 **Power of Incentive Schemes**

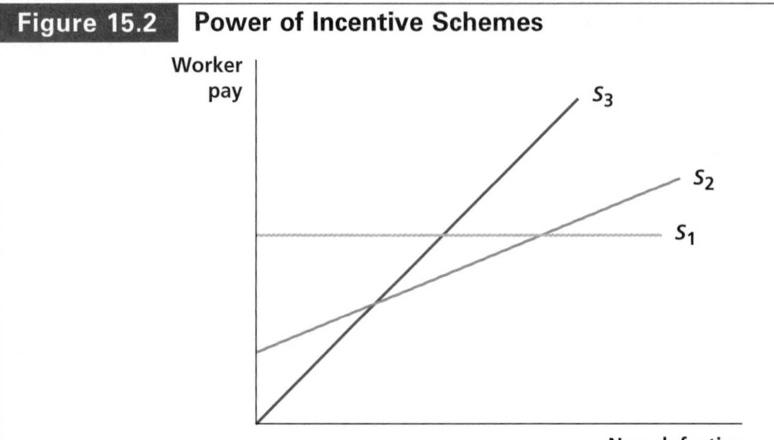

Lines S_1, S_2, and S_3 correspond to different incentive schemes, which ink the worker's pay to his performance (here, non-defective devices produced, q). The slope of the incentive scheme, also called its "power," measures how tightly the worker's pay is linked to his performance, ranging from the case in which there is no linkage (constant pay, S_1) to the case in which the manager lets the worker keep the revenue from sales of the assembled devices (line S_3).

Figure 15.3 **Worker's Induced Effort**

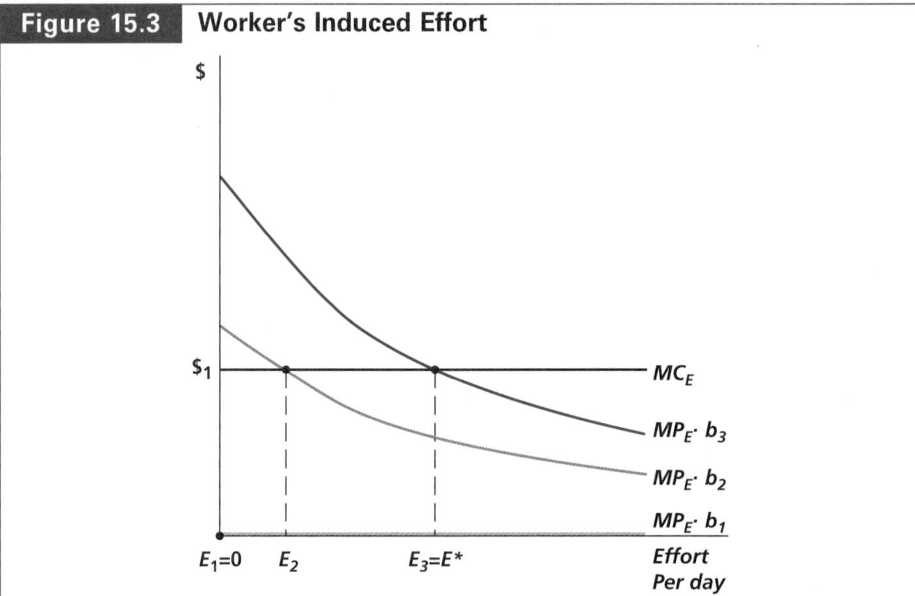

The worker chooses the effort given by the intersection of marginal cost ($1) and marginal value. His marginal value of effort depends on the power of his incentive scheme. Scheme S_1 has no power ($b_1 = 0$), so the worker's effort has no marginal value to him, leading him to undertake no effort ($E_1 = 0$). The worker exerts more effort the more powerful is the incentive scheme. Scheme S_3, which lets the worker keep all the revenue from devices he assembles ($b_3 = P$) yields the same marginal value of effort to the worker as the MVP_E curve from Figure 15.1, leading him to undertake efficient effort ($E_3 = E^*$).

cost and the marginal value *to him* of additional effort. The marginal value of effort *to him* depends on the power of his incentive scheme. Incentive scheme S_1 has no power. Since the worker's pay does not depend on his effort, he would choose not to exert any. The medium-powered incentive scheme S_2 results in moderate effort (E_2), and the high-powered incentive scheme S_3 results in the highest effort of the three (E_3).

MICRO QUIZ 15.1

Figure 15.1 shows why E^* is the effort level that is best from the joint perspective of worker, manager, and firm. Explain why the firm wouldn't prefer to induce yet higher effort than E^* even though the marginal value product is still positive for higher effort levels.

We can say more about the equilibrium effort induced by incentive scheme S_3. Because S_3 transfers all the proceeds from the sales of each unit to the worker, keeping none for the firm, marginal value of effort to the worker is the same as the firm's MVP_E curve from Figure 15.1. The worker would choose the same effort as in the full-information case, E^*. This is a general result: the worker can be induced to exert the efficient level of effort even in the presence of asymmetric information by letting the worker keep all the proceeds from his effort.

While S_3 induces efficient effort, no sensible manager would offer workers precisely this scheme. It gives away all the revenue to workers, leaving nothing for the firm. One possibility is to charge the worker up-front for the privilege of being part of the firm, which then entitles him to some of the proceeds from his output. Such a scheme is illustrated as line S_5 in Figure 15.4. This scheme isn't as crazy as it first sounds: in some stadiums, program vendors pay for the right to sell during games but then keep a large share of program sales. Amway (a company that makes health and beauty products) sellers also have similar compensation schemes. However, such schemes are rare, and the next subsection provides some reasons.

Figure 15.4 Worker Participation Decision

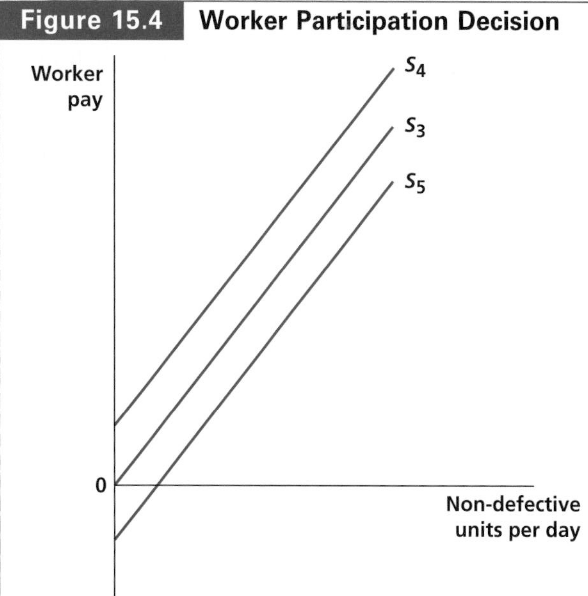

Fixing the slope of the incentive scheme, its intercept determines the worker's participation decision. Depending on his best alternative if he does not sign the contract, the intercept could be at 0 as with line S_3, could involve some fixed salary as with S_4, or could require the worker to pay to join the firm as with S_5. The best scheme for the firm is the lowest line that still induces the worker to participate.

Problems with High-Powered Incentives

High-powered incentives would seem to solve the moral-hazard problem. Unfortunately, there are factors outside our simple model that lead to problems with them.

The problem that has received the greatest attention in the economics literature is risk aversion on the part of workers. Suppose there is uncertainty whether an assembled device is defective. While care in assembly may decrease the chance of a defect, it may be due in part to a random mechanical or electronic failure outside the worker's control. Tying the worker's pay to the number of non-defective units will introduce uncertainty into his compensation. The higher the power of the incentive scheme, the greater is the uncertainty introduced. Of course a constant wage has no uncertainty. On the other hand a high-powered incentive scheme such as S_3 in Figure 15.2 might lead to large fluctuations. Indeed, schemes that charge workers an up-front fee in return for a claim on the proceeds from his output leave open the possibility that an unlucky worker may bring home less money at the end of the day than he started with. As discussed in Chapter 5, risk-averse individuals dislike uncertainty; they need to be paid to accept even fair gambles. Introducing uncertainty in the worker's pay by tying it to uncertain outcomes exposes the worker to risk. Exposing the worker to risk is costly for the firm because an individual is much less capable of bearing risk than a sizable company, which can diversify the risk of defects across many workers (see the discussion of the benefits of diversification in Chapter 5). A publicly held firm usually has many shareholders who only hold a tiny fraction of its stock, thus further diversifying any risks in the firm's operations. An individual worker may require a significant risk premium to be added to his incentive scheme to compensate for risk. In the end, the manager may decide to lower the power of the incentive schemes offered to workers, accepting the fact that effort will be lower, but feeling that the savings on risk premia may be worth it.

Risk aversion would not prevent the manager and worker from attaining the efficient outcome if effort were observable. The worker's pay could be conditioned directly on his effort, which would be fully under his control and about which he would have no uncertainty. Asymmetric information about effort forces the incentive scheme to be conditioned on something uncertain like non-defective output, which then exposes the worker to risk.

Hence, there is a trade-off between effort incentives and risk. High-powered incentive schemes induce a lot of effort, but expose risk-averse workers to a lot of risk and may require a high risk premium to get the worker to accept the risk. At the other extreme, a constant wage induces no effort, but does not expose the worker to any risk. The optimal scheme offered to risk-averse workers may involve some compromise between the two extremes.

There are other problems with high-powered incentives besides risk aversion. First, the worker may not be able to afford a large up-front payment to join the firm. Second, if the worker gets most of the benefit from increasing output, his manager may not do her part to increase output. For example, whether the factory has a reliable source of electricity to run the machines that the worker uses is an open question in many developing countries. Frequent power outages may make it impossible for workers to produce anything during large stretches of the workday. But if workers rather than the manager obtain the high-powered incentive schemes, the manager may have little incentive to acquire generators or negotiate with utilities for more reliable electricity supply. Third, a worker hired from outside the firm may have little information about operations inside the company. The manager might try to recruit workers by exaggerating how much they can expect to produce and earn, making a high-powered incentive scheme seem more lucrative than it actually is. The skeptical worker might instead insist on a constant wage that would be the same whether or not the manager was honest about how difficult the job actually is.

Substitutes for High-Powered Incentives

If the manager cannot offer the worker high-powered incentives for the reasons mentioned above, she may have to resort to other strategies to get the worker to work hard. One possibility is to have the employee monitored. Unfortunately, monitoring may not be a perfect solution. Measuring something as nebulous as "effort" might be prohibitively difficult. Even if it were possible to measure effort, what would guarantee that the person hired to do the monitoring would do a careful job? The same moral-hazard problems may confront the monitor as the worker. In addition, there might be an incentive for the worker to bribe the monitor to issue a good report about his or her efforts.

The possibility of firing the worker may provide crude incentives. The manager may have a general impression of which workers are productive and which are not and may periodically cull those that are not. The threat of firing may not be a big penalty for workers who can easily find another job at a similar wage. However, if the firm pays an **efficiency wage**, a higher wage than what its workers would typically earn elsewhere, the threat of losing this premium can induce them to work hard.

Efficiency wage
Wage set higher than market rate leading workers to fear firing.

Another possibility is that workers like to look good for internal promotions or to get a higher paying job elsewhere. Some have suggested that such situations may lead workers to overwork, as might be the case with new associates at law firms or investment banks, or with assistant professors, working in some cases 100 hours in a week. Workers may try to convince potential employers that they are more talented than they really are by substituting hard work for any shortcomings in talent. Potential employers may not be fooled, but in the "rat race" that is the job market, one may have to overwork just to avoid being mistaken for someone less talented.

A Numerical Example

As a numerical example of the moral-hazard problem, consider the firm that was called Hamburger Heaven in a number of previous chapters but which will now be called Handheld Heaven to reflect the type of product assembled by the worker in this chapter. Table 15.2 shows the output of working electronic devices for various levels of the worker's effort. For convenience, the unit of effort has been set so that each one involves a marginal cost to the worker of 175.

The efficient level of effort under full information is $E = 4$. This level of effort generates the greatest difference between the revenue from the output and the total effort cost to the worker (1,400 − 700 = 700). The marginal value product of this fourth unit of effort, 200, exceeds the marginal cost of this unit of effort to the worker, 175, so the manager should require the worker to work at least this hard. It would be inefficient to require the worker to work harder (that is, require $E = 5$) because the 100 marginal value product of the fifth unit of effort is less than the 175 marginal cost to the worker. The contract that implements this full-information solution depends on what the worker can earn (net of effort costs) in his next best employment. Suppose this is 300. Then the manager can implement the full-information solution by offering to pay the worker 1,000 if he exerts effort $E = 4$ and nothing otherwise. This would cover the worker's 700 total cost of effort and provide enough in addition (300) to match the worker's best outside option to make sure he accepts the contract.

Table 15.2 How Worker Effort Affects Handheld Heaven's Operations

WORKER EFFORT PER DAY	WORKING DEVICES PRODUCED PER DAY	MARGINAL PRODUCT OF EFFORT	REVENUE ($100 PER DEVICE, IN $)	MARGINAL VALUE PRODUCT OF EFFORT (IN $)	WORKER'S TOTAL COST OF EFFORT (IN $)	WORKER'S MARGINAL COST OF EFFORT (IN $)
1	5	5	500	500	175	175
2	9	4	900	400	350	175
3	12	3	1,200	300	525	175
4	14	2	1,400	200	700	175
5	15	1	1,500	100	875	175

Table 15.3 Various Incentive Schemes at Handheld Heaven

		INCENTIVE SCHEME S_2 ($a = 200, b = 50$)			INCENTIVE SCHEME S_5 ($a = -400, b = 100$)		
WORKER EFFORT PER DAY	WORKING DEVICES PRODUCED PER DAY	TOTAL PAY (IN $)	MARGINAL PAY (IN $)	FIRM PROFIT (IN $)	TOTAL PAY (IN $)	MARGINAL PAY (IN $)	FIRM PROFIT (IN $)
1	5	450	250	50	100	500	400
2	9	650	200	250	550	400	400
3	12	800	150	400	800	300	400
4	14	900	100	500	1,000	200	400
5	15	950	50	550	1,100	100	400

Equilibrium with incentive scheme S_5 Equilibrium with incentive scheme S_2

If effort is not observable, the manager can think about offering different incentive schemes to try to induce effort. Two examples are shown in Table 15.3.

The subscripts have been chosen so you can match the schemes to their illustrations in the figures. Incentive scheme S_2 offers 200 of fixed pay and 50 per unit of incentive pay. If offered this scheme, the worker would choose to exert effort $E = 2$. An additional unit of effort produces three more working devices, resulting in additional pay of 150. This does not cover his 175 marginal cost of the additional unit of effort. After subtracting off the total paid to the worker from total revenue, the firm's equilibrium profit from S_2 is 250. Incentive scheme S_5 is higher powered than S_2, offering 100 per unit of incentive pay. Essentially this scheme turns the marginal value product from sales of the device over to the worker but requires the worker to make a fixed payment of 400 to the firm. This scheme induces greater effort from the worker, in fact the same effort as with full information, $E = 4$. The firm's profit under this scheme is 400 (the firm earns the same 400 fixed payment from the worker regardless of the worker's effort).

MICRO QUIZ 15.2

Suppose the manager offered the worker an incentive scheme with $b = 75$, so its power is between the two schemes in the numerical example.

1. What effort level would this scheme induce from the worker?
2. Assume the worker can earn 300 (net of effort costs) in his best alternative job. What level of fixed payment a can the manager offer to make sure the worker accepts the contract?

Based just on the information in the table, the manager should offer scheme S_5 rather than S_2. The firm earns more profit in equilibrium 400 rather than 200. However, there might be additional reasons why scheme S_5 would not work well in practice—all the reasons mentioned under the heading of problems with high-powered incentives. For example, if the number of working devices produced in a day has some randomness to it, and the worker is risk averse, he may need to receive a premium to compensate him for the risk. He might be unwilling to accept a contract requiring him to pay 400 to the firm; he may be willing to participate only if the firm makes a fixed payment to him. If so, a lower-powered incentive scheme like S_2 might end up being more profitable for the firm than S_5.

Executives in the Firm

The analysis of the moral-hazard problem so far took the agent to be a line worker, at the bottom of the firm's hierarchy. The analysis applies as well to executives at the top of the hierarchy. In this new setting, which corresponds to the second row in Table 15.1, we have a slight role reversal, where the top executive plays the role of the agent and the shareholders play the role of the principal. Shareholders (or the compensation committee acting on the shareholders' behalf) try to design an incentive scheme to induce the executive to work hard on behalf of the firm. Rather than resulting in a few more non-defective units, executive effort may result in billions of dollars of additional revenue to the firm, so carefully designing the executive incentive's scheme provides big payoffs.[2]

As we saw earlier, an incentive scheme such as S_4 in Figure 15.4 provides the agent with powerful incentives while ensuring the principal gets something out of the deal. In the present setting, S_4 turns out to be equivalent to having the shareholders sell the firm to the executive. The executive captures the entire marginal value product from an increase in her effort. Of course, the shareholders would not turn all of the firm's revenues over to the executive for nothing; they would require her to pay them for their shares. While having the executive buy out the firm may seem outlandish, it happens from time to time. In 2013, for example, Michael Dell orchestrated a $25 billion buyout of the computer company (Dell) that he founded and ran.

There are other practical ways of increasing the power of the executive's incentive scheme besides selling her the firm. She can be offered a bonus tied to the performance of the firm. She can receive shares of the firm's stock, the value of which automatically fluctuates with the fortunes of the firm. Stock options, analyzed in Application 15.2: The Good and Bad Effects of Stock Options, are a form of executive incentive pay that governments cannot seem to make up their minds whether to favor or not.

Summing Up

To sum up, it is natural to ask how the results in the presence of the moral-hazard problem accord with the results from the standard model of a perfectly-competitive market with no private information. First, the presence of moral hazard raises the possibility of slack and inefficiency completely absent in the standard model. Returning to the version of the moral-hazard problem in which the agent is a worker and principal the manager, the worker does not exert as much effort as he would if effort were observable. Even if the manager does the best she can in the presence of asymmetric information to provide incentives for effort, she must balance the benefits of incentives against the cost of exposing the worker to too much risk.

Second, while the worker can be regarded as an input like any other (capital, labor, materials, and so forth) in the standard model, in the presence of the moral-hazard problem the worker becomes a unique sort of input. It is not enough to pay a fixed amount for this input as a firm does when it rents capital. How productive the worker is depends on the structure of his compensation.

The term moral hazard has been showing up recently in the news, in particular in reports on the global financial crisis and subsequent government bailouts. Application 15.3: Moral Hazard in the Financial Crisis discusses how the concepts from this chapter can help make some sense of these news reports.

---

[2]Some economists believe that, far from being lazy, executives have the opposite problem: they enjoy the prestige of running the biggest firm possible. Executives may try to "build empires," authorizing investment projects without regard to their profitability. It would be difficult for shareholders to second guess which investments were profitable, given the expertise to make such decisions may have been the reason for hiring the executive to begin with.

APPLICATION 15.2

The Good and Bad Effects of Stock Options

Stock options grant to the holder the ability to buy shares at a fixed price. If the market price of these shares rises, option holders will benefit because they can buy the stock at less than the market price (and perhaps resell it, making a quick profit). Options are usually granted by firms to their executives as one way of providing incentives to manage the firm in a way that will increase the price of its shares.

The Explosion in Stock Options

Use of stock options as a form of executive compensation has grown rapidly in recent years. In 1980, most firms did not offer options to their executives and, in those that did, the value of options constituted a fairly small percentage of total compensation. By 2000, top executives of the largest companies received more than half their total compensation in the form of stock options, sometimes amounting to options worth hundreds of millions of dollars. There are many reasons for the increased popularity of stock options as a form of compensation. Rising stock prices throughout the decade of the 1990s undoubtedly made this form of compensation more attractive to executives. From the perspective of firms, the accounting treatment of options (which are often assigned a zero cost to the firm granting them) made them a low-cost way to pay their executives. A special provision in the tax laws enacted in 1993 specified that firms could not deduct executive pay of more than $1 million per year unless that pay was tied to company performance—a further spur to the use of options.

Incentive Effects of Options

Stock options clearly do succeed in tying an executive's compensation to the performance of a company's stock. By one estimate, stock options provide more than 50 times the pay-to-performance ratio provided by conventional pay packages.[1] Dollar for dollar, options also provide more pay-to-performance incentives than would a simple grant of shares to the executive. For example, it would cost the firm $1 million to grant 10,000 shares of $100 stock to an executive. The executive would gain $100,000 from a 10 percent increase in firm value. If the executive were instead given 100,000 options to buy the stock at $100, the executive would gain ten times more ($1 million) from a 10 percent increase in firm value.

But the exact incentive effects of stock options are complex, depending on precisely how the options are granted and the ways in which the stock price for the firm performs. For example, options are less valuable when the firm pays large dividends to its shareholders, so the executive may have an incentive to hold back on dividend increases. For another example, options are more valuable when the price of a company's stock is more volatile. This is because the option holder's gain from stock price increases is unbounded above but is bounded below by zero for falls in the stock price (the option is simply "out of the money"). Options may therefore induce executives to make more risky investments than they ordinarily would.

Unanticipated Incentive Effects: Accounting Fraud

Executives with significant holdings of stock options can make huge amounts of money if the values of their shares rise. In recent years, it has been common to see executives making hundreds of millions of dollars on such stock price movements. One unintended effect of giving CEOs such a large stake in seeing a higher stock price has been to encourage them to seek to manipulate information that can affect the price of their shares. Executives of the WorldCom Corporation, for example, hid nearly $4 billion in corporate expenses in 2001 so that their company would look more profitable. The firm's CEO benefited handsomely when he bailed out of the firm's stock. Accounting fiascos such as those at Enron and Tyco also seem to have been motivated in part by the desire to keep stock prices up so options holders could benefit. Whether stock-option contracts can be adjusted to reduce the incentives for such actions remains an open question.

TO THINK ABOUT

1. Michael Eisner, CEO of the Walt Disney Corporation, once received over $500 million in stock options. Do you think he managed the company better than if he had been awarded only $50 million's worth?
2. If the price of a company's stock declines, stock options may become worthless. What would be the effect of a policy that promised to adjust the purchase price specified in the option contract downward when this happens?

[1] B. J. Hall and J. B. Liebman, "Are CEOs Really Paid Like Bureaucrats?" *Quarterly Journal of Economics* (August 1998): 653–691.

APPLICATION 15.3

Moral Hazard in the Financial Crisis

The term "moral hazard" has been used over and over again in the context of news stories about the recent financial crisis,[1] a crisis some commentators think may send the global economy into a severe and prolonged recession. In this application, we will try to understand the use of the term in this context and connect it to the concepts introduced in this chapter.

Scope of the Crisis

As of this writing, the global economy is experiencing a severe financial crisis. All the major U.S. investment banks have failed, been taken over, or changed their status to commercial banks. Numerous commercial banks have experienced "runs" (races by depositors to withdraw funds before the bank runs out of reserves) or have failed. Access to credit for banks, firms, and consumers has essentially frozen. Global stock markets have experienced precipitous declines.

Although all the causes of the crisis are not yet fully understood, an important contributing factor seems to have been the bursting of the housing bubble. The sharp fall in house prices reduced the value of the mortgage loans and derivative securities held by investment and commercial banks. Banks' losses were magnified because they borrowed to buy more of these securities, effectively "doubling down" on their housing market bet, a bet that promised huge gains if the housing market remained strong, but huge losses if not. The complexity of the securities combined with the uncertain direction of the global economy makes it difficult to have a clear forecast of banks' and other firms' solvency. In the face of this uncertainty, investors are reluctant to invest in anything other than government bonds, causing private credit markets to freeze up.

Government Bailouts

The U.S. and other governments have pursued radical policies to prevent further unraveling of the financial system, fearing that large bank failures and frozen credit markets would spread like a contagious disease, causing other bank failures and worsen the forecast economic recession. The U.S. Treasury facilitated the takeover of the investment bank Bear Stearns by lending the purchaser, J.P. Morgan, nearly $30 billion on favorable terms (taking Bear Stearns' risky investments as collateral). Congress passed a $700 billion plan to bail out banks by having the government buy their troublesome mortgage and derivative securities, presumably at above-market prices. Most recently, governments around the world have begun supplying banks with additional capital by purchasing shares of bank stock.

Moral Hazard

Think of the government as the principal and a bank as an agent. The government/principal would like the bank/agent to behave in a prudent way ("effort" in this context) so that it does not have to be bailed out and so that it does not harm other banks that are interconnected with it in the financial system. The government tries to encourage prudent behavior through regulation and through the terms of the bailout. However, bailout policies such as buying up a bank's bad securities at above-market prices or supplying capital to poorly performing banks have the same effect as reducing the power (slope) of the incentive scheme in Figure 15.2. Insulating the bank from some of the losses from its imprudent behavior provides the bank with less incentive to behave prudently.

The U.S. government took some measures to avoid setting a precedent that would encourage imprudent behavior. With the Bear Stearns merger, it initially only agreed to facilitate the deal if the price offered to Bear shareholders was sufficiently low to serve as a punishment ($2, down from an historical high of $172). It refused to bail out another huge investment bank, Lehman Brothers. Provisions were added to the $700 billion bailout plan to punish participating CEOs by eliminating "excessive" pay, bonuses, and severance packages.

TO THINK ABOUT

1. What bailout policies seem to be working to calm financial markets? Now that governments are engaged in bailouts, is the media continuing to report on moral hazard as a significant problem in the financial markets?
2. In the absence of legally binding contracts, a principal can still mitigate agent moral hazard by maintaining a reputation that it will let the agent suffer for its actions even if this harms the principal in the short run, too. What other areas of life besides bank regulation do we observe principals trying to build such reputations?

[1]See, for example, D. Henninger, "Welcome to 'Moral Hazard'," *Wall Street Journal* (October 2, 2008): A17

15-3 Private Information about Consumer Type

Next we turn to the other main variant of the principal-agent model. In contrast to the moral-hazard problem, in which the agent has private information about an action he or she chooses *after* the contract is signed, the information problem studied in this section involves private information the agent has about his or her type (an innate characteristic) *before* the contract is signed.

To make the analysis concrete, we will consider the application in which the principal is a monopoly firm and the agent is a customer. Consumers differ in how much they value the good, but these valuations are not observable to the monopolist. The monopolist offers the customer a menu of different-sized bundles at different prices. This setup is identical to the model of second-degree price discrimination studied in Chapter 11. With second-degree price discrimination, the monopolist is not restricted to a constant price per unit but rather offers a menu of bundles at different prices, perhaps involving price discounts for large purchases, and has the consumers select bundles from the menu themselves. We will build on the earlier analysis by being slightly more detailed here and highlighting the important features of the principal-agent problem when the agent has private information about his or her type.

Examples of this sort of second-degree include a coffee shop's offering a 12-ounce cup at \$1.50 and a 24-ounce cup at \$2.50. Bundles can be distinguished by quality instead of quantity as well. Airlines' first class has plusher seats, more leg room, and better meals than coach class, comforts that may cost three or four times the coach fare. How does the monopolist decide on such a menu of quantity/price bundles or quality/price bundles, which constitutes, in effect, the contract offered to the customer? We will investigate this question carefully in the next several subsections.

Figure 15.5 Profit-Maximizing Bundle with One Consumer Type

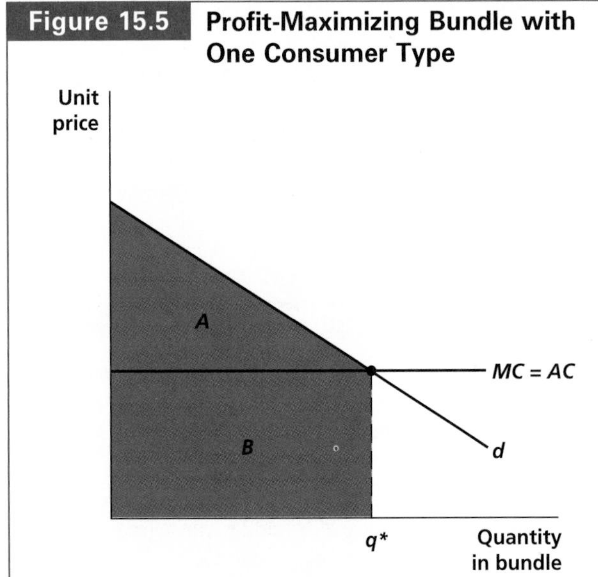

Facing an individual, representative consumer, the monopolist chooses a bundle q^* maximizing combined surplus, given by the intersection between its marginal cost *MC* and the individual's demand *d*. The monopolist charges a bundle price equal to the shaded area (*A* and *B*) and earns profit equal to the area of *A*.

One Consumer Type

In this subsection we examine the monopolist's problem of selling to consumers who all have the same value for the good—in other words, there is a single consumer type. To simplify the analysis, we will consider an individual, representative consumer and suppose the monopolist has constant marginal and average costs. Figure 15.5 presents the solution to the problem. As shown in the figure, q^* is given by the intersection of the individual's demand and marginal cost, the same quantity as would arise under perfect competition. This result is no surprise. We saw in Chapter 9 that perfect competition under these conditions results in an economically efficient allocation of resources. The idea here is for the monopolist to generate an efficient allocation but then "soak up" all the surplus for itself with the price it sets for the whole bundle. The consumer would be willing to pay as much as the entire shaded area (A and B) for the bundle. This is what the monopolist charges. After subtracting off total cost (equal to the area of B), the monopolist is left with profit given by the area of A.

Two Consumer Types, Full Information

If the monopolist has full information about types and can act on this information (that is, can require a consumer to buy only the bundle directed at his or her particular type and not some other bundle, and can prevent consumers from selling repackaged bundles among themselves), the analysis of two consumer types adds nothing new to the analysis of one type. Figure 15.6 illustrates this case. One group of consumers ("high types") has a high value for the product and the other group ("low types") has a lower value.

If the monopolist sees that a particular consumer is a low type, it maximizes profit by offering a bundle with q_L units, given by the intersection between marginal cost and the low type's demand curve. The bundle price equals the area of the dark-shaded region (A and B), and the monopolist's profit from that consumer equals the area of region A. Similarly, if the consumer turns out to be the high type, the profit-maximizing bundle involves q_H units given by the intersection between the high type's marginal consumer surplus and the monopolist's marginal cost. The bundle price equals the area of the entire shaded region A, B, C, and D, and the monopolist's profit from that consumer equals the area of A and C.

Two Consumer Types: Asymmetric Information

The menu of bundles that maximized profit in the full-information case will not work if the monopolist cannot observe the consumer's types. The q_H-unit bundle meant for the

Figure 15.6 Profit-Maximizing Bundles with Full Information About Two Consumer Types

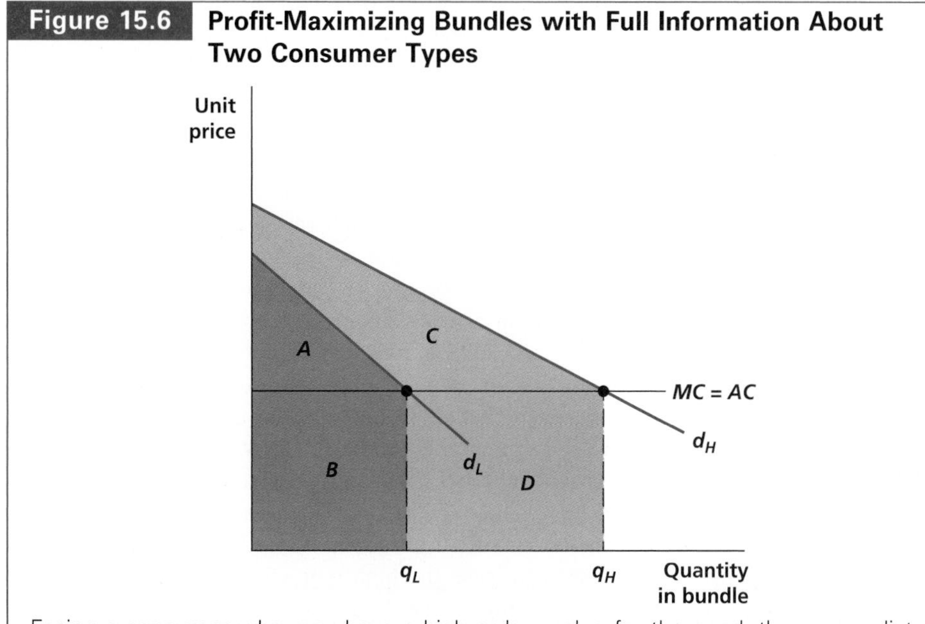

Facing a consumer who may have a high or low value for the good, the monopolist chooses bundles given by the intersection between its marginal cost and each type's demand. The high type receives the larger bundle, q_H, and the low type receives the smaller bundle, q_L.

Figure 15.7 Full-Information Solution Is Not Incentive-Compatible

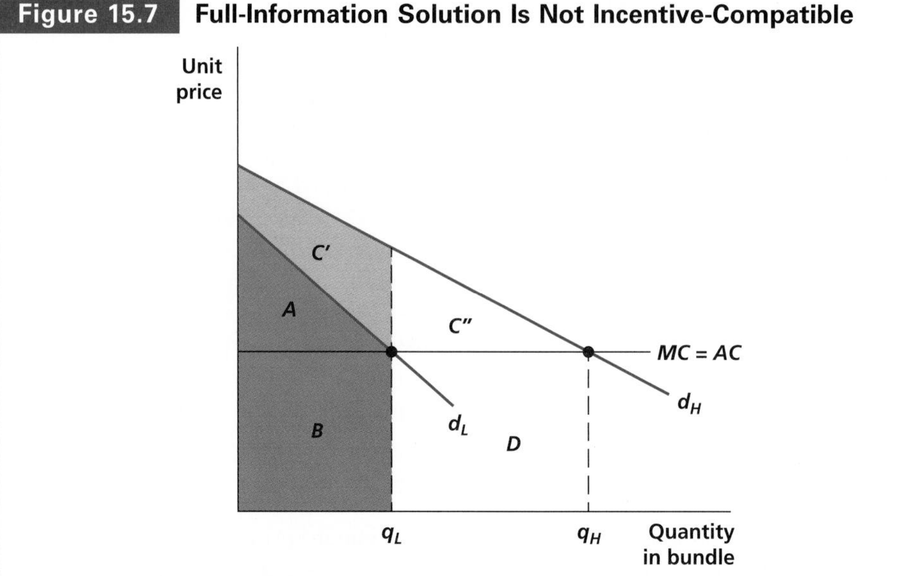

The bundles from Figure 15.6, reproduced here, would not be incentive-compatible. The high type would gain surplus equal to the area of region C' by purchasing the bundle meant for the low type.

high-value type is priced to extract all of his or her consumer surplus. The high type would obtain positive surplus from instead purchasing the q_L-unit bundle meant for the low-value type. Figure 15.7 shows why. The high type would be willing to pay up to the area of the shaded regions A, B, and C' for the q_L-unit bundle. After subtracting off the bundle's price (the dark-shaded areas A and B), the high-value type is left with positive surplus equal to the area of the light-shaded region C'. This is better than purchasing the q_H-unit bundle and getting no surplus.

Incentive-compatible Describes contract that gets the agent to make the intended choice.

The q_H-unit bundle sold at a price that extracts all of the high type's consumer surplus is not **incentive-compatible**. Left the choice between the two bundles, the high type would have an incentive to choose the bundle meant for the other type. The q_H-unit bundle could be made incentive-compatible for the high type by reducing its price so that the high type would be left with at least as much surplus as if he or she bought the q_L-unit bundle. In particular, the price for the q_H-unit bundle would have to be reduced by the area of region C' (and so equal the combined area of regions A, B, C'', and D).

The monopolist can do even better than this. The monopolist can reduce the quantity associated with the bundle meant for the low-value type. On the one hand, reducing quantity reduces the profit from the sale of the bundle to low-value consumers. But a bigger effect is that the bundle meant for the low-value type becomes much less attractive to the high-value type. The high-value type places a high value on quantity, and a reduction in quantity "scares him or her off" from choosing the low-value bundle. As a result, the monopolist does not need to leave the high type with as much surplus, and can raise the price charged for the q_H-unit bundle.

The profit-maximizing bundles are shown in Figure 15.8. Reducing the quantity in the low type's bundle from q_L to q_L' does reduce the profit from sales to low-value consumers, by an amount equal to the area of triangle E. But this reduction in quantity makes the low type's bundle much less attractive to the high type. The price at which

Figure 15.8 Profit-Maximizing Bundles Under Asymmetric Information

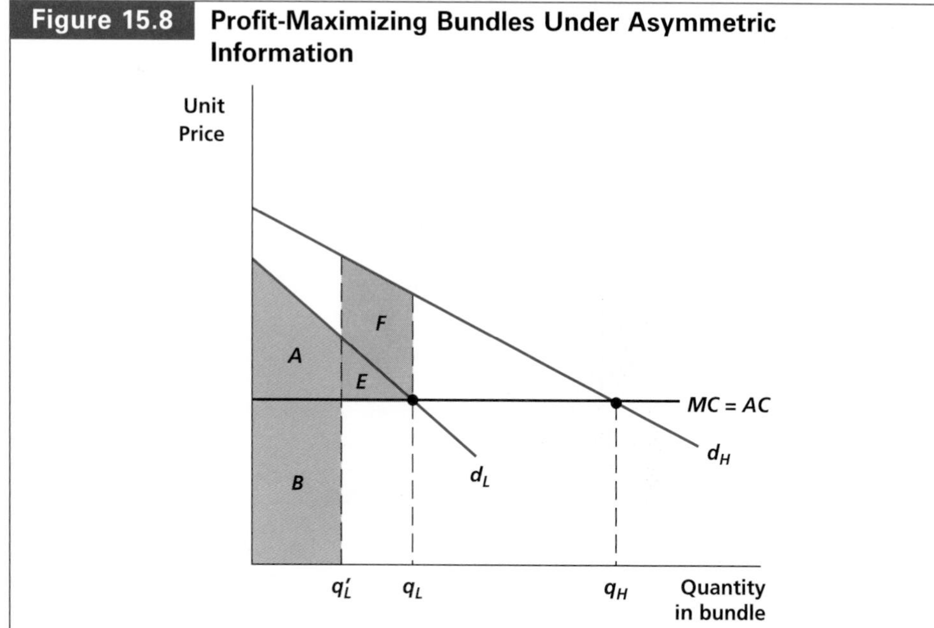

By reducing the quantity in the low-type's bundle, the monopolist reduces the profit from sales to low types by the area of E. This loss is more than offset by the amount that the price of the high-type's bundle can be increased while maintaining incentive-compatibility (equal to the area of F).

the q_H-unit bundle is sold can be increased by the area of F and still ensure that the high type buys this rather than the bundle meant for the low type.

By distorting the low type's quantity, the monopolist sacrifices efficiency. The low type would be willing to pay more than what it costs to increase the size of his or her bundle. The monopolist's gain is that it can squeeze more revenue out of the high type. As shown in Figure 15.8, the revenue squeezed from the high type (the area of region F) can be much larger than the loss from selling an inefficiently small bundle to the low type (the area of triangle E).

How much the monopolist distorts the low type's quantity downward depends on how many consumers are of each type. If there are a lot of low-value consumers, the monopolist would not be willing to distort the quantity in their bundle very much, since the loss from this distortion would be substantial and there would not be many high-value consumers from whom to squeeze additional revenue. The more high-value consumers, the more the monopolist is willing to distort the quantity in the low type's bundle downward. Indeed, if there are enough high-value consumers, the monopolist may decide not to serve the low-value consumers at all and just offer one bundle that would be purchased by the high types. This would allow the monopolist to squeeze all of the surplus from the high types, because they would have no other option left.

Examples

Consider the example of a coffee shop that caters to 200 consumers, 100 of whom are typical coffee drinkers (low types), 100 of whom are coffee hounds (high types). The shop can put one, two, or three espresso shots in a single cup of coffee; even coffee

Figure 15.9 Coffee Shop Example

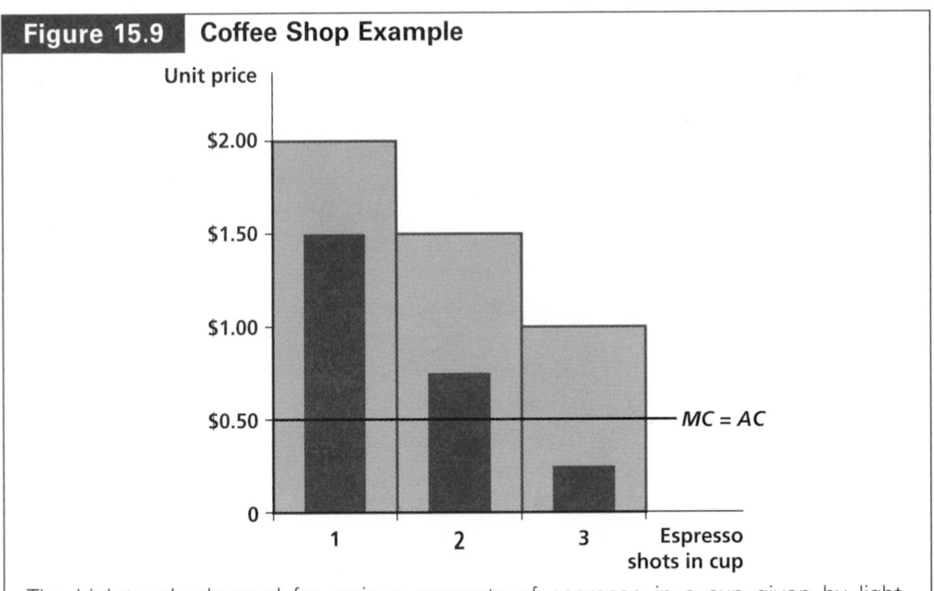

The high-type's demand for various amounts of espresso in a cup given by light-shaded bars and the low-type's demand by dark-shaded bars.

hounds have their limit, as they consider four shots as too many. Consumer demands—which given the discrete nature of shots appear as step functions rather than lines—are shown in Figure 15.9. Looking at the demand curve of the high types, given by the light-shaded bars, we see that their marginal value for the first shot is $2.00, for the second shot is $1.50, and for the third shot is $1.00. The demand curve of the low types, given by the dark-shaded bars, indicates that their marginal values are $1.50, $0.75, and $0.25 for the first, second, and third shots. The shop has a constant average and marginal cost of $0.50 per shot.

As a thought experiment, suppose the shop can identify the consumer's type and force the consumer to buy the cup meant for him or her. The profit-maximizing menu would involve putting three shots in a large coffee sold to high types for $2.00 + 1.50 + 1.00 = \$4.50$ and putting two shots in a small coffee sold to low types for $1.50 + 0.75 = \$2.25$. This menu extracts all the surplus from both types. The low type's marginal value for the third shot does not justify the marginal cost of brewing it, so it would be inefficient to sell them a larger cup.

Now put the thought experiment aside and suppose, more realistically, that there is asymmetric information about types. The shop would not know which consumers are high types, and so will not be able to forbid them from buying a small coffee with only two shots. To induce high types to buy the larger cup, its price has to be reduced to $3.25. This new, lower price yields each high type the same $1.25 consumer surplus he or she gets from buying the two-shot coffee at its $2.25 price. The shop's profit from the 100 high types would be $100(3.25 - 1.50) = \$175$ and from the 100 low types would be $100(2.25 - 1.00) = \$125$, for a total of $300.

The coffee shop could do even better by reducing the number of shots in the small coffee from two to one and reducing its price to $1.50. This would make the small cup less attractive to high types, allowing the shop to increase the price for the large cup to $4.00. The shop's profit from the 100 high types is $100(4.00 - 1.50) = \$250$ and from the 100 low types is 100(1.50 – 0.50) = \$100, for a total of \$350, a \$50 increase in total profit compared to the menu in which there were two shots in a small coffee.

Notice that the shop is not squeezing all of the profit out of the low types that it could. Low types would each be willing to pay \$0.75 for another shot, more than the \$0.50 marginal cost of brewing it. But including two shots in the small cup makes it more attractive for high types, possibly more attractive than paying \$4.00 for the triple shot. The size of the small cup is reduced—not to harm low types—but to reduce the small cup's appeal to coffee hounds, thereby allowing the shop to charge more for the large cup. For this way of adjusting the menu to work, removing a shot from the small cup must reduce its appeal for high types at a greater rate than for low types. But indeed this is the case because high types value each shot more than low types do. Reducing the size of the small cup from a double to a single-shot allows the shop to charge \$0.75 more for the large cup and still get high types to buy it. On the other hand, the shop only loses \$0.25 profit from each small cup sold because low types' marginal value for the second shot is not much greater than marginal cost.

If enough consumers are high types, the shop may decide only to offer the triple shot at the price of \$4.50 that, as seen in the thought experiment with full information, extracts all of surplus of high types. The shop would effectively have full information about consumers' types because only coffee hounds would show up to buy at such a high price.

The numerical coffee shop example assumed 100 consumers of each type. Suppose instead there are only 40 low-type consumers.

1. Show that the shop's total profits under asymmetric information when it sells a triple-shot cup to high types and a single-shot cup to low types is at best \$290.
2. Show that the shop can earn more if it removes the small cup from the menu entirely and just serves high types with a large cup.

The same logic holds for airplane fares, reinterpreting q to be the quality rather than the quantity in a bundle. Consumers only demand one flight at any one time, but the quality of that flight may vary depending on the size of the seat, the quality of the meal, and other amenities together represented by q. The airline might offer different classes of travel on one flight, say coach and business class. The typical coach-class passenger may be willing to pay more than the marginal cost of increasing the comfort of the seat and improving the meal service: it may only cost, say, \$30 (in terms of extra seat cushioning, more fuel, and better meals) to make the coach-class flight reasonably comfortable. But the airline may still keep coach seats small and limit meals. If coach class is too comfortable, there may be little reason for business-class passengers to pay the exorbitant prices for those seats. Some discomfort in coach class "scares" business-class passengers off from buying coach tickets.

Inefficiency with Hidden Types

Because this chapter is in the part of the book on market failures, it is worth going back over the example and identifying the inefficiency that arises in the presence of hidden types. In an effort to extract more revenue from the high type, the principal distorts the quantity or quality in the low type's offering, below what would be efficient under full information. In the numerical example of the coffee shop, the cup sold to low types has two shots under full information but only one under asymmetric information. This reduction in quantity is profitable for the coffee shop but results in a loss of social welfare. In the airline example, the quality of seats or meal service in coach class may be inefficiently low compared to the full-information case.

Adverse Selection in Warranties and Insurance

The inefficiencies can be even worse when the firm sells not a simple good such as coffee or an airplane trip but a more complicated contract such as a warranty or insurance to the consumer. Whereas a cup of coffee costs the same to brew regardless of to whom it is sold, the cost of fulfilling a contract may depend on the consumer's type.

Consider a warranty promising to replace a lawn mower if it breaks down. Whether it breaks down depends on the quality of its construction—presumably the warranty was offered in the first place to provide some assurance to the consumer about its quality—but also depends on the consumer's hidden type. A mower is more likely to break down if operated by a consumer with a large yard filled with roots and stones than with a small, smooth yard. However, it is the first type of consumer that will be most attracted to mowers carrying full warranties because these contracts shift the high cost of likely replacement from them to the firm. An increase in the percentage of these high-cost consumers will force the firm to raise price in equilibrium, leading other consumers to substitute toward less-expensive mowers with limited or no warranties. These effects may spiral until only the costliest consumers almost certain to wreck their mowers buy models with full warranties. That warranties tend to attract consumers who are the costliest to serve is such a concern to firms that it has received a special name: the **adverse-selection problem**. Application 15.4: Adverse Selection in Insurance provides more detail on this problem as it arises in that important market context.

Adverse-selection problem
Worst agent types are the ones most eager to transact with the principal.

A firm's attempt to deal with the adverse-selection problem can lead to inefficiencies. It would be efficient for a risk-neutral company to provide full warranty or insurance coverage to risk-averse consumers. But this may not happen in equilibrium with hidden types. The firm may only offer partial coverage, perhaps charging a return fee for warranties or imposing deductibles or copayments on insurance. Consumer types that are less likely to make a claim may be priced out of the market entirely.

15-4 Asymmetric Information in Competitive Markets

The principal-agent model studied so far is a very simple setting since it involved just a single principal and a single agent. (In the few cases involving several agents, for example several coffee shop customers, this did not complicate the analysis since the agents did not directly compete.) In this section, we will see how the results change in a market setting, with competing agents, or competing principals, or both.

Moral Hazard with Several Agents

Adding agents to the basic principal-agent model can make the moral-hazard problem better or worse, depending on the details of the setting. Suppose first that a single principal needs to hire a team of several agents to perform a task. The moral-hazard problem may be more severe in this setting. Each of the agents may slack off, relying on the efforts of the others. In large teams, it may be difficult to identify who is working hard and who is not, possibly leading all of them to slack. It is hard to provide a large number of agents with high-powered incentives because even if the firm is sold to the team of them, each would only obtain a small fraction of the firm's gross profit.

On the other hand, if there are many agents in the market, but each works for a separate firm/principal, moral hazard may be less of a problem than it would be with

APPLICATION 15.4

Adverse Selection in Insurance

The earliest application of the idea of adverse selection, and indeed the genesis of the term itself, was in the study of insurance markets. As we saw in Chapter 5, actuarially fair insurance can increase the utility of risk-averse individuals, implying that individuals who face very different probabilities of loss should pay different insurance premiums. The difficulty faced by insurers in this situation is in estimating an individual's probability of loss so that insurance can be correctly priced. When insurers possess less information than do insurance buyers, adverse selection may undermine the entire insurance market.

A Theoretical Model

This possibility is illustrated in Figure 1, which assumes that two individuals initially face identical consumption prospects represented by point *A*. If person 1 has a relatively low risk of incurring state 2, costs of insurance will be low and this individual's budget constraint is given by *AE*. If insurance is fairly priced, this risk-averse individual would choose to fully insure by moving to point *E* on the certainty line. For person 2, losses are more likely. Fair insurance costs are represented by *AF*. This person, too, might choose to be fully insured by moving to point *F*. If the insurance company cannot tell how risky a particular customer is, however, this twin solution is unstable. Person 2 will recognize that he or she can gain utility by purchasing a policy intended for person 1. The additional losses this implies means that the insurer will lose money on policy *AE* and will have to increase its price, thereby reducing person 1's utility. Whether there is a final solution to this type of adverse selection is a complex question. It is possible that person 1 may choose to face the world uninsured rather than buy an unfairly priced policy.[1]

Figure 1 Adverse Selection in Insurance Markets

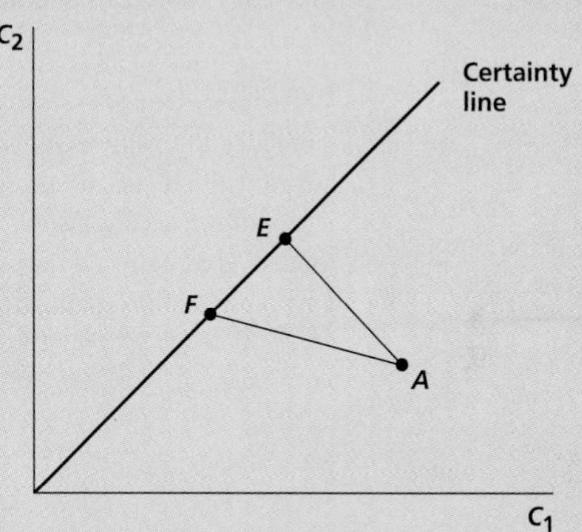

Two individuals face identical consumption prospects at *A*. Low-risk individuals can buy insurance at a rate reflected by *AE*; high-risk individuals must pay the rate reflected by *AF*. If insurers cannot distinguish among individuals, high-risk people will choose *AE*-type policies and cause them to be unprofitable. Low-risk individuals will be made worse off by the absence of such policies.

Safe-Driver Policies

Adverse selection arises in all sorts of insurance, ranging from life insurance to health insurance to flood insurance to automobile insurance. Consider the case of automobile insurance. Traditionally, insurers have used accident data to devise group rating factors that assign higher premium costs to groups such as young males and urban dwellers, who tend to be more likely to have accidents. Such rate-setting procedures sometimes come under political attack as unfairly lumping both safe and unsafe drivers together. A 1989 ballot initiative in California, for example, sharply limited the use of rating factors by requiring them to be primarily individual-based rather than group-based. Because data on individuals are hard to obtain and are not very good at predicting accidents, the main result has been to force rates together for all groups. The main beneficiary of the law seems to have been young male drivers in Los Angeles. Figure 1 suggests that individuals in safer groups (females and rural California residents) may have been the losers.

POLICY CHALLENGE

The U.S. Affordable Care Act (commonly called "Obamacare") contains a number of provisions that can be viewed as addressing adverse-selection problem. Explain the adverse-selection problem in the specific context of health insurance. Research the Affordable Care Act and identify the provisions that target the adverse-selection problem. Explain how those provisions would help.

[1]For one of the original discussions of this issue, see M. Rothschild and J. Stiglitz, "Equilibrium in Competitive Insurance Markets: An Essay on the Economics of Imperfect Information," *Quarterly Journal of Economics* (November 1976): 629–650.

one agent. By comparing the performance of their own firms with that of others', uncertainty about agents' efforts can be reduced. If a firm's gross profit is low, but so are the gross profits of similar firms, it can be inferred that the poor performance was due to random market forces rather than the agent's slacking off. On the other hand, if all firms but one perform well, it becomes increasingly clear that the one agent had slacked off. Such comparisons are most useful when firms operate in similar lines of business that are exposed to similar market forces.

Auctions

Consider the monopoly-consumer model, but suppose the monopoly has a limited number of units to sell to several competing consumers (if the monopoly produced an unlimited amount at a constant marginal cost, consumers would not end up competing even if there were many of them, so nothing would change from our previous analysis of the adverse-selection problem). The result would be an auction setting. Auctions have received a great deal of attention in the economics literature since William Vickery's foundational work for which he won the Nobel Prize in economics.[3] Auctions continue to grow in significance as a market mechanism, used for selling goods ranging from airwave spectrums, to Treasury bills, to foreclosed houses, to collectibles on the Internet auction site eBay (discussed in Application 9.1: Internet Auctions).

Competition among consumers in an auction can help the monopolist solve the hidden-type problem. High-value consumers are pushed to bid high to avoid losing the good to another bidder. The exact outcome of the auction depends on the nature of the economic environment (which consumers know what information when) and the auction format.

There are a host of different auction formats. Auctions can involve sealed bids or open outcries. Sealed-bid auctions can be first price (the highest bidder wins the object and has to pay his or her bid) or second price (the highest bidder still wins but only has to pay the next-highest bid). Open-outcry auctions can be ascending, as in the so-called English auction when buyers yell out successively higher bids until no one is willing to top the last, or descending, as in the so-called Dutch auction when the auctioneer starts with a very high price and lowers it continuously until one of the participants stops the auction by accepting the price at that point. The monopolist can decide whether or not to set a "reserve clause," which requires bids to be over a certain threshold or else the object will not be sold. Even more exotic auction formats are possible. In an "all-pay" auction, for example, losers as well as winners are required to pay their bids. The penny auctions described in Application 9.1: Internet Auctions use this format.

A powerful and somewhat surprising result due to Vickery is that in simple settings (risk-neutral bidders who each know their valuation for the good perfectly, no collusion, and so forth), the different auction formats listed previously (and many more besides) provide the monopolist with the same expected revenue in equilibrium. To see why this result is surprising, consider two formats in more detail, a first-price, sealed-bid auction and a second-price, sealed-bid auction. Suppose that a single object is to be auctioned. In the first-price, sealed-bid auction, all bidders simultaneously submit secret bids. The auctioneer unseals the bids and awards the object to the highest bidder, who pays his or her bid. In equilibrium, each bidder bids strictly less than what the object is worth to him or her (we will call this his or her "valuation" for short). A bidder receives zero surplus

[3]W. Vickery, "Counterspeculation, Auctions, and Competitive Sealed Tenders," *Journal of Finance* (March 1961): 8–37.

Table 15.4 Bidding Valuation 50 is Player 1's Dominant Strategy in a Second-Price Auction

		Player 2		
		$b_2 < 30$	$30 < b_2 < 50$	$b_2 > 50$
Player 1	$b_1 = 30$	$50 - b_2$	0	0
	$b_1 = 50$	$50 - b_2$	$50 - b_2$	0

from bidding his or her valuation (losing bidders get no surplus; the winning bidder transfers his or her entire valuation to the monopolist and again gets no surplus). By bidding less than his or her valuation, there is a chance that others' valuations, and thus bids, are low enough so that the bidder wins the object and makes a positive surplus.

In a second-price, sealed-bid auction, the highest bidder pays the next-highest bid rather than his or her own. In this auction format, a bidder's dominant strategy is to bid his or her valuation. This is an interesting result in its own right and worth analyzing in some detail. Let b_1 be player 1's bid and b_2 be player 2's. Table 15.4 presents the normal form for the game. It is partial in that it only shows player 1's payoffs and only shows two strategies for player 1, bidding his or her valuation ($b_1 = 50$) and bidding less ($b_1 = 30$). Looking at the first column of the matrix, if $b_2 < 30$, player 1 wins the object, pays b_2, and obtains payoff $50 - b_2$ whether he or she bids 30 or 50. The payoffs from the two strategies tie. Looking at the last column, if $b_2 > 50$, player 1 loses the object and gets payoff 0 whether he or she bids 30 or 50. Again, the payoffs from the two strategies tie. Looking at the middle column, however, if b_2 is between 30 and 50, then bidding 50 is better than 30 for player 1 because he or she loses the object and earns a payoff of 0 by bidding 30 but wins the object and earns payoff $50 - b_2 > 0$ by bidding 50. As the underlined payoffs indicate, bidding 50 is always at least as good for player 1 as bidding 30 and is strictly better against some of player 2's strategies. Similar arguments can be used to show that bidding 50 dominates any of player 1's alternatives, implying that bidding 50 is a dominant strategy for player 1.

With an understanding of equilibrium bidding in second-price auctions, we can compare first-and second-price, sealed-bid auctions. Each format has plusses and minuses regarding the revenue the monopolist earns from it. On one hand, bidders shade their bids below their valuations in the first-price auction but not in the second-price auction, a "plus" for second-price auctions. On the other hand, the winning bidder pays the highest bid in the first-price auction but only the second-highest bid in the second-price auction, a "plus" for first-price auctions. The surprising result is that these plusses and minuses balance perfectly, so that they both provide the monopolist with the same expected revenue.

In more complicated settings, the long list of different auction formats do not necessarily yield

The analysis in Table 15.4 shows that player 1 prefers to bid 50 (his or her valuation) rather than 30 (a lower bid than his or her valuation). Use a similar analysis to show that player 1 would prefer to bid 50 than 70 (a higher bid than his or her valuation).

the same revenue. One complication that is frequently considered is to suppose that the good has the same value to all the bidders but they do not know exactly what that value is. Each bidder only has an imprecise estimate of what that value might be. For example, bidders for oil tracts may have each conducted their own surveys of the likelihood that there is oil below the surface. All bidders' surveys taken together may give a clear picture of the likelihood of oil, but each one separately may only give a rough idea. For another example, the value of a piece of art depends in part on its resale value (unless the bidder plans on keeping it in the family forever), which in turn depends on others' valuations; each bidder knows his or her own valuation but perhaps not others'. Such a setting is called a **common-values setting**.

Common-values setting
Object has the same value to all bidders, but each only has an imprecise estimate of that value.

The most interesting new issue that arises in a common-values setting is the **winner's curse**. The winning bidder realizes that every other bidder probably thought the good was worth less than he or she did, meaning that he or she probably overestimated the value of the good. The winner's curse sometimes leads inexperienced bidders to regret having won the auction. Sophisticated bidders take account of the winner's curse by shading down their bids below their imprecise estimates of the value of the good, so that they never regret having won the auction in equilibrium.

Winner's curse
Winning reveals that all other bidders thought the good was worth less than the highest bidder did.

Analysis of the common-values setting becomes complicated, and the different auction formats listed here no longer yield equivalent revenue. Roughly speaking, auctions that incorporate other bidders' information in the price paid tend to provide the monopolist with more revenue. For example, a second-price auction tends to be better than a first-price auction because the price paid in a second-price auction depends on what other bidders think the object is worth. If other bidders thought the object was not worth much, the second-highest bid will be low and the price paid by the winning bidder will be low, helping to solve the winner's curse problem.

The Market for Lemons

Whereas in the auction setting we supposed there was a single seller who was matched with several potential buyers, we could imagine markets in which many buyers and many sellers are matched. A particularly intriguing problem may arise in such markets if each seller has private information about the quality of the good he or she is selling. As George Akerlof showed in the article for which he won the Nobel Prize in economics, in equilibrium sometimes only the lowest-quality goods, the "lemons," get sold.[4]

To gain more insight about this result, consider the used-car market. Suppose used cars are of two types (good cars and lemons) and only the owner of a car knows which type his or her car is. Since buyers cannot differentiate between good cars and lemons, all used cars of a particular type will sell for the same price—somewhere between the true worth of the two types. The owner of a car will choose to keep his or her car if it is a good one (since a good car is worth more than the prevailing market price) but will sell the car if it is a lemon (since a lemon is worth less than the market price). Consequently, only lemons will be brought to the used-car market, and the quality of cars traded will be less than expected.

The lemons problem leads the market for used cars to be much less efficient than it would be in the standard competitive model in which quality is known (indeed, in the standard model, there is no issue about knowing the quality of different goods, since typically they all are assumed to be of the same quality). Whole segments of the market

[4]G. A. Akerlof, "The Market for 'Lemons': Quality Uncertainty and the Market Mechanism," *Quarterly Journal of Economics* (August 1970): 488–500.

disappear—along with the gains from trade in these segments—because higher-quality items are no longer traded. In the extreme, the market can simply break down with nothing being sold (or perhaps just a few of the worst items).

The lemons problem can be mitigated by trustworthy used-car dealers, by development of car-buying expertise by the general public, by sellers providing proof that their cars are trouble-free, or by sellers offering money-back guarantees.

But anyone who has ever shopped for a used car knows the problem of potential lemons is a very real one. Application 15.5: Looking for Lemons discusses the evidence for the lemons problem in markets ranging from trucks to baseball free agents.

Consider the market for used cars.

1. What information about the car might an owner know better than a prospective buyer, and so be a source of private information?
2. Whose interest is it in to "solve" the lemons problem, the seller, the buyer, or both? What measures can each side take to solve the problem?

15-5 Signaling

Our analysis of the hidden-type problem so far has mainly focused on the case in which the uninformed party makes the first move, offering a contract to the party with private information. For example, the monopolist made the first move by offering a menu of different bundles to consumers, who had private information about their valuations (their types); consumers moved next by choosing which bundle to purchase.

The reverse is also possible. The player with private information can take the first action and thereby signal something about his or her type. Examples abound. A student may seek additional education as a signal that he or she is unusually talented to prospective employers. A person may drive a fancy car as a signal of wealth to prospective spouses or buy large diamond rings as a signal of his or her affection. A professional-looking Web site may signal to customers that the business is not a fly-by-night operation. An incumbent firm may price low to convince future entrants that it is a "tough" competitor. A high bet may signal that a poker player has a good hand (though the player may be bluffing).[5]

In formal terms, such settings are known as signaling games. In a signaling game, Nature moves first, choosing the first player's type at random from a number of possibilities. The first player's type is private information, unknown to the second player, who only knows the probabilities that Nature might choose one type or the other. The first player makes a move called a signal since it is observed by the second player. Based on the information provided by the signal, the second player updates his or her beliefs about the first player's type. Then the second player chooses his or her move and the game ends.

Spence Education Model

We will analyze signaling games in terms of a single application, Spence's education model,[6] named after Michael Spence, who received the Nobel Prize in economics for

[5]The lemons problem can be thought of as a version of a signaling model. By offering a car for sale, the seller is signaling something about the quality of the car, namely, that the car is not so high quality that the seller is willing to keep it rather than selling it at the going market price. Of course, this is a signal that the seller would rather not send.

[6]A. M. Spence, "Job Market Signaling," *Quarterly Journal of Economics* (August 1973): 355–377.

APPLICATION 15.5

Looking for Lemons

Economists have spent some time trying to find markets in which the quality deterioration predicted by the lemons model is apparent. Here, we look at three such investigations.

Pickup Trucks

Although used pickup trucks might be expected to exhibit quality deterioration because of asymmetric information between buyers and sellers, that does not appear to be the case. A 1982 study of pickup purchases during the 1970s found that about 60 percent of such trucks were bought used.[1] After controlling for the mileage that trucks had traveled, the author found no difference in the repair records for trucks purchased new versus those purchased used. The author offered two explanations for the relatively good quality of used pickups. First, pickup buyers may have some expertise in truck repair or can gain that expertise by looking at several pickups before buying. Second, it seems possible that, in some cases, sellers provide repair records in order to get good prices for their trucks.

Free Agents in Baseball

Professional baseball players become "free agents" after playing a certain number of years with the teams that initially sign them. Because a player's present team may know much more about his physical conditions and general skills than does a would-be hirer, the market for "used players" may provide another case where asymmetric information leads to quality deterioration. Consistent with this idea, one study found that free agents hired by a new team spent almost twice as many days on baseball's disabled list as did those who were re-signed by their own teams.[2] Of course, teams undoubtedly recognize the adverse incentives inherent in the trading of free agents. So, detailed physical examinations and other kinds of tryouts have become commonplace in recent years. No team wants to be saddled with a multimillion-dollar "dud" if that can be avoided.

Thoroughbreds

Many racehorse "yearlings" are sold at auction. One of the largest of these is the Keeneland auction that is held in September near Lexington, Kentucky. An article examining the sale prices from this auction in 1994 found evidence that lemons may appear among the thoroughbreds.[3] The authors divided sellers at the auction into two groups—those stables that both breed and race horses and those that are only in the breeding business. They reasoned that breeder-only stables would bring all of their yearlings to the auction but that those stables that also raced would have an incentive to keep the best horses for themselves. Although a would-be buyer has relatively little information about the racing quality of any yearling, he or she does know the nature of the stable from which it comes and therefore is in a position to suspect that the racers' offerings will contain relatively more lemons.

Evidence on auction prices tended to confirm these expectations. The authors found that, after holding constant such factors as the quality of the yearlings' parents, yearlings from stables that are heavily involved in racing tended to have lower prices than did those from breeder-only stables. Specifically, the authors estimated that each race that a stable entered in 1993 tended to reduce the price of its 1994 yearlings by nearly one percentage point. Apparently, buyers at the Keeneland auction were cautious about buying yearlings from breeders who may have incentives to take the best horses out of their offerings.

TO THINK ABOUT

1. Each of these examples suggests that buyers may take steps to address problems raised by asymmetric information. Do sellers have similar incentives to provide information to buyers?
2. The late 1990s saw a huge number of initial offerings of common stock by Internet start-up companies. How might the lemons model be applied to these initial offerings? Did subsequent events bear out the model?

[1] E. W. Bond, "A Direct Test of the 'Lemons' Model: The Market for Used Pickup Trucks," *American Economic Review* (September 1982): 836–840.
[2] K. Lehn, "Information Asymmetries in Baseball's Free Agent Market," *Economic Inquiry* (January 1984): 37–44.
[3] B. Chezum and D. Wimmer, "Roses or Lemons: Adverse Selection in the Market for Thoroughbred Yearlings," *Review of Economics and Statistics* (August 1997): 521–526.

developing it (a prize shared with George Akerlof and Joseph Stiglitz, both of whose work was encountered earlier in the chapter). Workers have an equal chance of being one of two types, high skill or low skill. A low-skill worker generates no marginal revenue product for the firm, and a high-skill worker generates marginal revenue product r. The firm bases its hiring decision on the profit from hiring the worker, equal to his marginal revenue product minus his wage, which will be computed and subtracted off later. Skill is private information for workers and cannot be observed by employers. Before the hiring decision, workers can obtain education. We will make the extreme assumption that education does nothing to enhance a worker's productivity directly. Rather, it may provide a signal of skill to future employers because high-skill workers find it easier to obtain more education. Let c be the cost of obtaining an education, where $c = c_L$ for a low-skill worker, $c = c_H$ for a high-skill worker, and $c_L > c_H$. The assumption that it is easier for high-skill workers to obtain education is crucial in the signaling model. If education were as costly or more costly for the high-skill workers to obtain, education could not provide a signal of skill.

The game tree for the Spence signaling game is shown in Figure 15.10. Nature moves first, choosing the worker's skill, low or high, with probability 1/2 each. The worker observes his or her skill and then makes the decision to get an education or not (this could be thought of as additional education beyond high school or an advanced degree beyond college, such as an MBA). The firm observes the education decision but not the worker's type. Assume the firm is representative of a large number of firms that compete for the worker. The worker's wage is set competitively; that is, the expected

Figure 15.10 Spence Signaling Game in Extensive Form

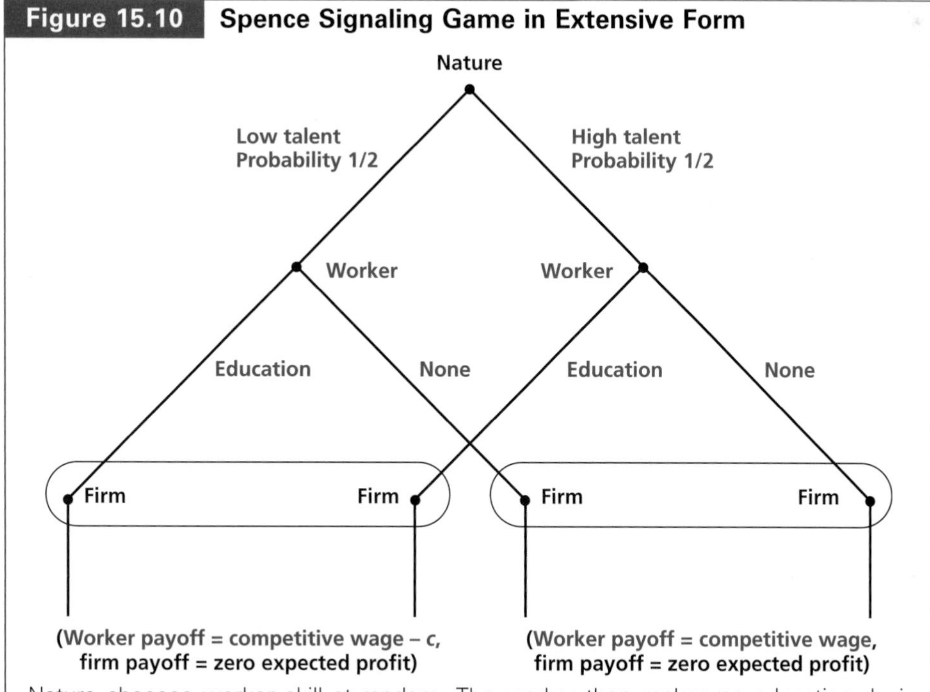

Nature chooses worker skill at random. The worker then makes an education decision. The ovals around selected decision points for the firm indicate that the firm observes the worker's education decision but not skill. The payoffs, calculated in the text, provide the worker with a competitive wage based on the representative firm's beliefs about the worker's skill.

marginal revenue product is incorporated into the wage, so the firm earns zero expected profit after subtracting off the wage.

Signaling games often have multiple equilibria, and that is true in this game. In searching for these equilibria, it often helps to look for two different kinds, separating equilibria and pooling equilibria. In a **separating equilibrium,** each different type of worker chooses a different action, so the action is a perfect signal of the worker's skill. In a **pooling equilibrium**, all types choose the same action, so the equilibrium action is an uninformative signal. The uninformed player knows nothing beyond the initial probabilities Nature used to draw the first player's type.

Separating equilibrium Each type chooses a different action in a signaling game.

Pooling equilibrium All types choose the same action in a signaling game.

Separating Equilibrium

Let's begin by looking for a separating equilibrium. There is only one sensible possibility for a separating equilibrium: the high-skill type chooses to get an education and the low-skill type does not. (The other possibility is that the low-skill type obtains an education and the high-skill type does not, but this outcome does not make sense.) How would the competitive wage be set in this equilibrium? If the firm sees the worker get an education, it knows the worker must be high skill and would generate marginal revenue product r. Competition among firms for the worker would drive the wage up to r and the firm would earn zero profit net of the wage. If the firm sees that the worker did not get an education, it knows the worker must be low skill and would generate no marginal revenue product. The firm would pay the worker a wage of zero. To summarize the strategies in this separating equilibrium, the high-skill type gets an education and the low-skill type does not. The firm pays wage r to an educated worker and zero to an uneducated worker.

Recall that to check for a Nash equilibrium in the simple games in Chapter 5, we needed to check whether any player would want to deviate. In signaling games, the equilibrium check is a bit more involved. We need to check whether *any type* of any player would want to deviate. In our education game, let's check first that the firm would not want to deviate from the proposed separating equilibrium. There is no reason for the firm to offer higher wages, since it is able to hire the worker at the present wages. If the firm offers a lower wage, it will lose the worker to some other firm on the competitive market and will earn zero profit, which is not strictly more than it earns in equilibrium (also zero profit). Next we need to check whether either type of worker would want to deviate. In equilibrium, the high-skill worker earns the wage r minus the cost of education c_H. If the high-skill worker deviates by choosing no education, the firm would believe the worker is low skill and pay a zero wage, and the worker would earn nothing (though he or she would save the cost of getting an education). For the high-skill worker not to want to deviate,

$$r - c_H > 0. \tag{15.3}$$

In equilibrium, the low-skill worker's payoff is zero. If the low-skill worker deviates by pretending to be high skill and obtaining an education, he or she would earn the high-skill wage r minus the cost of education c_L. For the low-skill worker not to want to deviate in this way,

$$r - c_L < 0. \tag{15.4}$$

Putting conditions 15.3 and 15.4 together, a separating equilibrium requires $c_H < r < c_L$. In other words, for the separating equilibrium to work, the gap between the high- and low-skill workers' cost of obtaining an education must be large enough that the return to education, r, falls somewhere in between the two types' costs of obtaining an education.

In the separating equilibrium, each worker is paid according to his or her productivity. There is some deadweight loss in that the high type has to pay the cost of getting an education, which is socially wasteful since it does not add to productivity. An education is still a worthwhile investment for the high type because it results in a better wage.

Pooling Equilibria

Next we will look for a pooling equilibrium, in particular, the pooling equilibrium in which both types of worker obtain an education. The idea is that the low-skill worker chooses the same action as the high-skill worker to prevent being distinguished from the high-skill types and paid a lower wage. In equilibrium, the firm learns nothing about the worker's skill from seeing the fact that the worker is educated. The firm's best guess is that the worker is high or low skill with equal probability 1/2, the same probabilities that Nature used to choose the worker type initially. The firm's expected marginal revenue product from the worker equals the probability of high skill, 1/2, times the marginal revenue product r of a high-skill worker, plus the probability of low skill, 1/2, times the marginal revenue product, 0, of a low-skill worker: that is, $(1/2)(r) + (1/2)(0) = r/2$. Thus the competitive wage is $r/2$.

We need to check whether any type of any player would want to deviate from the proposed pooling equilibrium. As with the separating equilibrium, here the competitive wage is set so that the firm earns zero expected profit and would not gain from deviating. The question remains whether either type of worker would want to deviate by choosing not to get an education. Since education is costliest for the low-skill worker, it is this type's deviation we have to worry about. In equilibrium, the low-skill worker earns the wage $r/2$ minus the cost of education c_L. What it earns by deviating to "no education" depends on the competitive wage paid to uneducated workers, which in turn depends on what the firm believes about an uneducated worker's skill. The rules of probability provide little guidance as to what this belief should be because seeing an uneducated worker is a totally unexpected event for the firm; the firm never encounters such a worker in equilibrium. Game theorists have devoted considerable attention to this thorny question of what might be sensible beliefs after something unexpected happens, and there is unfortunately no settled answer. In the present application, it is plausible to assume that the firm has pessimistic beliefs about an uneducated worker's skill, that is, the firm believes that if the worker chooses not to get an education, he or she is certainly a low-skill worker.[7] If so, by deviating to "no education," a low-skill worker would save the cost of education but would get a wage of zero for a total payoff of zero. The low-skill worker would choose not to deviate if $r/2 - c_L > 0$. For the proposed pooling equilibrium to work, the low-skill worker's cost of pooling with the high-skill type by obtaining an education cannot be too high relative to the expected wage.

Suppose it is more expensive for the high-skill worker to get an education: $c_L < c_H$.

1. Will there be a separating equilibrium?
2. Can there be pooling equilibria?

---

[7]Alternatively, it is also plausible to assume that the firm learns nothing about the worker's type if it observes an uneducated worker. Given this belief, there is no reason for workers to obtain an education, and the pooling equilibrium, in which both types obtain an education, would not exist.

We could also look for a pooling equilibrium in which both types choose not to get an education. Whether or not such an equilibrium exists again depends on the firm's beliefs following an unexpected event, this time, the unexpected event of seeing an educated worker. As long as the firm is not too confident that an educated worker is high skill, there will exist a pooling equilibrium in which both types of worker do not get an education.

Predatory Pricing and Other Signaling Games

The Spence model is but one application of signaling games. Another important application, alluded to in Chapter 12 on imperfect competition, is predatory pricing, where an incumbent firm prices low for a sufficient time to induce the exit of a rival. As noted in Chapter 12, it is difficult to rationalize predatory pricing as an equilibrium strategy unless there is some private information in the game.

One possibility is that the incumbent has private information about its cost. The lower the incumbent's cost, the lower the prices it would charge, whether it is a monopolist or competes against an entrant. The lower the incumbent's prices, the less an entrant would earn in competition with the incumbent. The incumbent's cost may be so low that the entrant would be unprofitable in competition with it. If the entrant knew the incumbent's costs were this low, it would not enter the market or would exit if it had entered. Such a low-cost incumbent may gain from signaling its costs are low to separate itself from a higher-cost one against which entry might be profitable. The low-cost incumbent could try to signal its type by pricing low during an initial period, low enough that a high-cost type would rather have the entrant in the market rather than charge such a low price during the initial period. The predation game may also have equilibria in which the high-cost type of incumbent pools with the low-cost type by pricing low during the initial period, if by doing so it would prevent entry by preventing the entrant from learning its type.

As mentioned previously, there are a wide variety of other applications of signaling games. Poker can be analyzed as a signaling game. An interesting feature of poker is that extreme types on both ends, players with very good hands as well as players with very bad hands, gain from pooling with other types. A player with a very good hand would like opponents to believe his or her hand is not so good so that they continue betting; a player with a bad hand would like to bluff that his or her hand is good so that others fold.

Inefficiency in Signaling Games

The presence of private information typically leads to inefficiency in signaling games. In the Spence education model, depending on the equilibrium, one or the other type of worker, or even sometimes both, obtained an education even though education had no social benefit in terms of raising productivity. If firms had full information about worker productivity, there would be no need for workers to seek wasteful education. This is a typical finding in signaling games. Players with private information may depart from the efficient action to manipulate the information received by other players.[8]

[8]The need to signal private information can increase efficiency in rare cases. Paradoxically, if the market is already inefficient, say because of monopoly or externalities, adding another source of inefficiency in the form of private information can improve matters. For example, in the predation model with a monopoly incumbent firm, lowering its price to signal low cost leads to higher consumer surplus and perhaps higher social welfare, at least in the initial period.

SUMMARY

In this chapter, we extended our analysis of game theory to situations in which one player has private information. Some of the main points in this chapter are the following:

- Compared to the standard competitive model in which there is full information, private information typically leads markets to operate inefficiently. Depending on the model, private information (also called asymmetric information) can lead to slack, undersupply, or distortion of other economic decisions. In the extreme, asymmetric information can lead the entire market to break down.
- Inefficiency does not stem from a failure of firms to maximize profit or consumers to maximize utility. Players are still assumed to maximize their payoffs, but maximizing payoffs in the presence of asymmetric information leads to inefficiency.
- The principal-agent model is a simple starting point to study games with asymmetric information. The principal must design the contract it offers to the agent carefully, recognizing that the contract must give the agent the incentives to make the right choices and must be attractive enough to get the agent to accept the contract in the first place.
- In one version of the principal-agent model, the agent takes a hidden action. In the other version, the agent's type is hidden.
- We studied the hidden-action problem (also called the moral-hazard problem) in an application in which worker effort boosts firm output. The worker only exerts effort if given an incentive contract tying pay to performance. But tying pay to performance has the drawback of exposing the worker to risk for which he has to be compensated.
- We studied the hidden-type problem in an application in which a monopoly sells to consumers with different values for the good. The monopoly may distort the low type's contract option in order to make it less attractive to the high type. This allows the monopoly to increase the price charged for high type's contract option.
- Asymmetric information problems are particularly severe with contracts like warranties and insurance. An adverse-selection problem may arise whereby the most costly consumers to serve end up being the ones most drawn to the contracts.
- Having consumers compete in an auction helps the monopolist solve the hidden-type problem. In simple settings, many different auction formats produce equivalent revenues, but this no longer holds in more complicated settings.
- In a "lemons" market, sellers have private information about their own good's quality. The market may unravel as no seller with a quality good would be willing to sell at the prevailing price.
- In a signaling game, the player with private information about its type makes the first move. Signaling games often have multiple equilibria, including separating equilibria, in which the first mover's action perfectly identifies its type, and pooling equilibria, in which all types choose the same action.

REVIEW QUESTIONS

1. Consider the moral-hazard problem that arises when a risk-averse manager, whose effort is unobservable, runs a firm on behalf of shareholders. Explain how the trade-off between incentives and risk prevents the firm from obtaining the fully efficient outcome. How can the moral-hazard problem be eliminated if effort is observable? How can the moral-hazard problem be eliminated if effort is unobservable but the manager is risk neutral?
2. Many contracts between professional athletes and the teams on which they play involve incentive provisions. Can you provide some examples? Do you think moral hazard is a serious problem for professional athletes? Why or why not? Discuss the problem of using incentive contracts for unproven rookies, whose playing time may depend on the discretion of the coach. How might incentive contracts worsen the problem with performance-enhancing drugs such as steroids?
3. For each of the following types of insurance, explain how the moral-hazard problem might arise. Explain how the adverse selection problem might arise.
   a. Life insurance
   b. Health insurance
   c. Homeowners' insurance
   d. Automobile insurance
   e. Unemployment insurance

   How might an insurance company adjust the insurance contract to mitigate the moral-hazard and adverse-selection problems?
4. A computer manufacturer offers an optional extended warranty on the laptops it sells. What signal does the fact that the manufacturer offers this warranty send to potential consumers about laptop quality? Does this reduce consumers' incentives to purchase the extended warranty? Suppose consumers are of two types, heavy

users who travel with laptops, exposing them to the risk of accidental damage, and light users. Explain how market forces may lead the price of the extended warranty to reflect the heavy users' risk of damage rather than the average consumers'.

5. Consider the problem of a monopolist setting a menu of price/quantity bundles when there are two types of consumer and types are unobservable. The source of inefficiency in this setting is that the monopolist distorts the quantity in the low demanders' bundle. Why does the monopolist do this? Explain with reference to Figure 15.9. Why isn't the quantity in the high demanders' bundle also distorted?

6. The famous comedian Groucho Marx once quipped that "I would never join a club that would have me as a member." Modified to apply to market settings, the quote might be rewritten, "I would never buy from a seller who was willing to sell to me." Under what sort of market conditions would this quote apply? Connect this quote to Akerlof's lemons model. Among other things, use this quote to help identify the source of inefficiency in the lemons model.

7. Why is it a good idea to bid your (known) valuation in a second-price, sealed-bid auction? Why is it a bad idea to bid your (known) valuation in a first-price, sealed-bid auction? Explain, with reference to the "winner's curse," why it is an even worse idea to bid what you think your valuation is when you are not exactly sure of its value.

8. Consider a signaling model in which the first player may be one of two types. What determines the other player's beliefs about the first player's type before observing the first-player's signal? After observing the first player's signal, what beliefs must the second player have about the first player's type in a separating equilibrium? What beliefs must the second player have in a pooling equilibrium?

9. In the Spence model of education signaling we studied, what was inefficient about the equilibria? Why did the presence of asymmetric information (the fact that firms do not know the workers' productivities, but the workers themselves do) lead to this inefficiency? We saw that there were at least three possible equilibria that arose under certain conditions: a pooling equilibrium in which both types (high and low productivity) obtained an education, a pooling equilibrium in which neither type did, and a separating equilibrium in which only the high-productivity worker obtained an education. Are any of these equilibria more efficient than the others? Do workers enjoy having private information, or does your answer depend on the worker's type?

10. Suppose you invented a test that can easily measure worker productivity in Spence's signaling model. Who would be interested in paying for the test? Would workers pay to take it? Would firms pay to be able to administer it? One way for the firm to "test" workers is to have an initial probationary period during which it observes workers' productivity and fires them or adjusts their wages according to how the workers perform. What affect would this strategy have on the return to education? Can you think of real-world markets in which firms use such strategies?

PROBLEMS

15.1. Ben assembles units of the iSpy, a surveillance device remotely controlled from an app on customers' mobile phones. By exerting effort E, he produces $q = \sqrt{E}$ devices, implying that the marginal product of his effort is

$$MP_E = \frac{1}{2\sqrt{E}}.$$

The iSpy sells for \$100 each. Ben's marginal cost of a unit of effort is \$1. His manager, Sarah, considers three different incentive schemes she might offer him:

- Scheme 1 pays him a constant \$750.
- Scheme 2 pays him \$500 plus a 40% share of the revenue from sales of the iSpys he assembles that week.
- Scheme 3 gives him a 60% share of the revenue from sales of the iSpys he assembles but no fixed compensation.

Complete the following tasks for each incentive scheme.

a. Represent each incentive contract on the same graph, with quantity (non-defective units per week) on the horizontal axis and pay (dollars per week) on the vertical axis as in Figure 15.2.
b. Determine how many iSpys Ben assembles under each scheme.
c. Determine which scheme Sarah should offer him.

15.2. Clare manages a piano store. Her utility function is given by

$$\text{Utility} = w - 100,$$

where w is the total of all monetary payments to her and 100 represents the cost to her of the effort of running the store. Clare's next best alternative to managing the store provides her with zero utility. The store's revenue depends on random factors. There is a 50% chance it earns $1,000 and a 50% chance it earns only $400.

a. If shareholders offered to share half of the store's revenue, what would her expected utility be? Would she accept such a contract? What if she were only given a quarter share? What would be the lowest share she would accept to manage the firm?
b. What is the most Clare would pay to buy out the store if shareholders decided to sell it to her?
c. Suppose instead that shareholders decided to offer her a $100 bonus if the store earns $1,000. What fixed salary would Clare need to be paid in addition to get her to accept the contract?

15.3. Return to problem 15.2. Suppose that Clare can still choose to exert effort, as in the previous problem, but that she can also choose not to exert effort. If she does not exert effort, she has no effort cost, so her utility is just the wage, w; the shop's revenue is $400 for certain.

a. If shareholders offered to share half of the store's revenue, what effort would Clare choose? Would she accept such a contract? What if she were only given a quarter share? What would be the lowest share that would get her to exert effort?
b. Suppose instead that shareholders decided to offer her a $100 bonus if the store earns $1,000. Show that this would not get her to work hard. What is the minimum bonus that she would need to be paid? What fixed salary would she need to be paid in addition to get her to accept the contract?

15.4. A ready-to-eat cereal manufacturer faces two types of consumers, adults and children, having the following demand schedules.

OUNCE OF CEREAL	MARGINAL VALUE THIS OUNCE PROVIDES ADULTS IN CENTS	MARGINAL VALUE THIS OUNCE PROVIDES CHILDREN IN CENTS
First	20	40
Second	16	32
Third	12	24
Fourth	8	16
Fifth	4	8
Sixth	0	0

Cereal costs $0.15 per ounce to produce. The manufacturer has full information about types because adults hate sweet children's cereal and children hate the fiber-filled adult cereal. What is the optimal bundle to offer adults and to children in this full-information setting?

15.5.  Ahab's Coffee has 150 customers. Fifty of them are small and 100 are big, with appetites for coffee matching their size. Small people value coffee at $0.10 per ounce for the first 8 ounces and nothing for more than that. Large people value coffee at $0.15 per ounce for the first 10 ounces and nothing for more than that. Coffee costs $0.05 per ounce to produce.

a. What is Ahab's profit-maximizing strategy if it can sell a small cup to small people and a large cup to large people and prevent anyone from buying one or more of the other sized cups (either for their own consumption or to resell to other people). How much profit does Ahab's earn, and how much surplus does each type of consumer obtain?
b. For the rest of the question, suppose it is illegal for Ahab's to charge prices based on people's size. Show that the strategy from part a would not work now by computing the surplus big customers would get from buying a small cup and showing this is more than their surplus from buying a large cup.
c. What is the most Ahab's can charge for a 10-ounce cup and an 8-ounce cup and still have some customers buy each sized cup? Calculate the profit Ahab's can earn from such a pricing strategy.
d. Show that Ahab's can do better than in part c by reducing the size of the small cup from 8 ounces to 6 ounces.
e. Show that Ahab's does even better than in part c or part d if it ignores small customers and just sells one size of cup, which big customers end up buying.

15.6. L. L. Bean, among other stores, has a policy of replacing shoes that wear out with new ones. Suppose there are two types of shoe buyers. Half of them have desk jobs and only have a 20 percent chance of wearing out their shoes. The other half have active jobs (construction, nursing) and have a 60 percent chance of wearing out their shoes. A pair of shoes costs $25 to produce.

a. If the store cannot distinguish between the two types, what is the lowest price it can charge for shoes and still break even on average? (This is the price that would prevail in a competitive market.)
b. What would happen to the equilibrium if the desk workers' valuation for shoes was less than the market price in part a? What is a possible source of inefficiency in this new equilibrium?
c. Compute the competitive equilibrium if shoe manufacturers can charge an extra price for shoes with a replacement guarantee, assuming that only the active workers purchase the guarantee.

15.7. Tess and Meg are the only two bidders in an auction for a van Gogh painting. Each can be one of two types with equal probability: a low-value consumer with valuation $1 million or a high-value consumer with valuation \$2 million. Each knows her own type but only knows the probabilities of the other's type.

a. Suppose they compete in a sealed-bid, second-price auction. What are the equilibrium bidding strategies? Compute the seller's expected revenue.
b. Repeat part a supposing there are three identical bidders. What if there are N bidders?
c. Explain how your answer from parts a and b can be used to compute the seller's expected revenue from a first-price, sealed-bid auction.

15.8. Suppose 100 cars will be offered on the used-car market, 50 of them good cars, each worth \$10,000 to a buyer, and 50 of them lemons, each worth \$2,000.

a. Compute a buyer's maximum willingness to pay for a car if he or she cannot observe the car's type.
b. Suppose that there are enough buyers that competition among them leads cars to be sold at their maximum willingness to pay. What would the market equilibrium be if sellers value good cars at \$8,000? At \$6,000?

15.9. A firm earns marginal revenue product of 100 from a low-ability worker and 200 from a high-ability worker. A quarter of the workers are low-ability and the rest are high-ability.

a. If competitive firms have no signals available, what is the equilibrium wage they would pay?
b. Under what conditions on the cost of getting an education for each type, c_L and c_H, is there a separating equilibrium?
c. Suppose $c_L = 50$ and $c_H = 0$. Outline a pooling equilibrium in which both types get an education. Be sure to specify the firm's out-of-equilibrium beliefs if it were to meet an uneducated worker. Similarly, outline a pooling equilibrium in which neither type gets an education.

15.10. An incumbent firm may be a low-cost type, with constant marginal cost of production 10, or a high-cost type, with marginal cost of production 20, with probabilities t and $1 - t$, respectively. The incumbent's type is private information. The incumbent produces as a monopolist in the first period. An entrant who has marginal cost 15 may enter the market between periods. Entry requires at least a small fixed investment. If the entrant comes in the market, it learns what the incumbent's marginal cost is, and firms engage in Bertrand competition in homogeneous products in the second period (see Chapter 12 for a discussion of Bertrand competition). Consumer demand is the same in each period. Suppose there is no discounting between periods, so the incumbent's objective is to maximize the sum of first- plus second-period profit.

a. What is the Nash equilibrium of the second-stage game if the entrant enters? Solve the game for each type of incumbent.
b. Argue that the entrant would not enter if it believes the incumbent is certainly low cost but would enter if it believes the incumbent is certainly high cost.
c. Assume that the low-cost type's monopoly price is greater than 20. Use your answer from part b to argue that 20 is the highest possible price that the low-cost type of incumbent can charge in a separating equilibrium.

16 Externalities and Public Goods

In Chapter 10, we encountered the "First Theorem of Welfare Economics," which stated that, under certain conditions, reliance on competitive markets will yield an economically efficient allocation of resources. We also noted that there are a variety of situations that may cause competitive markets to fail to achieve such an outcome. In this chapter, we explore two of the most important examples of such "market failure." We begin by describing the general problem of "externalities"—that is, situations where the production or consumption of a good affects third parties not actually involved in the transaction. We also look at various ways that problems raised by externalities in private markets might be addressed. The concluding sections of the chapter then focus on a specific type of externality—the benefits that individuals receive from public goods. Our particular interest there is on asking how well various methods of public decision making (for example, voting) allocate resources to this kind of good.

16-1 Defining Externalities

An **externality** is an effect of one economic actor's activities on another actor's well-being that is not taken into account by the normal operations of the price system. This definition stresses the direct, nonmarket effect of one actor on another, such as soot falling out of the air or toxic chemicals appearing in drinking water. The definition does not include effects that take place through the market. If I buy a shirt that is on sale before you get there, I may keep you from getting it and thereby affect your well-being. That is not an externality in our sense because the effect took place in a market setting.[1] Its occurrence does not affect the ability of markets to allocate resources efficiently since whether you or I get the shirt is only a distributional question. Real externalities can occur between any two economic actors. Here, we first illustrate negative (harmful) and positive (beneficial) externalities between firms. We then consider externalities between people and firms and conclude with a few externalities between people.

Externality
The effect of one party's economic activities on another party that is not taken into account by the price system.

Externalities between Firms

Consider two firms—one producing eyeglasses, another producing charcoal (this is an actual example from nineteenth-century English law). The production of charcoal is said to have an external effect on the production of eyeglasses if the output of eyeglasses depends not only on the amount of inputs chosen by the eyeglass firm but also on the level at which the production of charcoal is carried on. Suppose these two firms are located near each other, and the eyeglass firm is downwind from the charcoal firm. In this case, the output of eyeglasses may depend not only on the level of inputs the

[1]Sometimes such effects are called "pecuniary" externalities to distinguish them from the "technological" externalities we will be discussing.

eyeglass firm uses itself but also on the amount of charcoal in the air, which affects its precision grinding wheels. The level of pollutants, in turn, is determined by the output of the charcoal firm. Increases in charcoal output would cause fewer high-quality eyeglasses to be produced even though the eyeglass firm has no control over this negative effect.[2]

The relationship between two firms may also be beneficial. Most examples of positive externalities are rather bucolic in nature. Perhaps the most famous, proposed by James Meade, involves two firms, one producing honey by raising bees and the other producing apples.[3] Because the bees feed on apple blossoms, an increase in apple production will improve productivity in the honey industry. The beneficial effects of having well-fed bees is a positive externality to the beekeeper. Similarly, bees pollinate apple crops and the beekeeper provides an external benefit to the orchard owner. Later in this chapter, we examine this situation in greater detail because, surprisingly enough, the beekeeper–apple grower relationship has played an important role in economic research on the significance of externalities.

Externalities between Firms and People

Firms may impact directly on people's well-being. A cement firm that spews dust into the air imposes costs on people living near the plant in the form of ill health and increased dirt and grime. Similar effects arise from firms' pollution of water (for example, mining firms that dump their waste into Lake Superior, reducing the lake's recreational value to people who wish to fish there), misuse of land (strip mining that is an eyesore and may interfere with water supplies), and production of noise (airports that are located near major cities). In all of these cases, at least on first inspection, it seems that firms will not take any of these external costs into account when deciding how much to produce.

Of course, people may also have external effects on firms. Drivers' auto pollution harms the productivity of citrus growers, cleaning up litter and graffiti is a major expense for shopping centers, and the noise of Saturday night rock concerts on college campuses probably affects motel rentals. In these cases, there may be no simple way for the affected parties to force the people who generate the externalities to take the full costs of their actions into account.

Externalities between People

Finally, the activity of one person may affect the well-being of someone else. Playing a radio too loud, smoking cigars, or driving during peak hours are all consumption activities that may negatively affect the utility of others. Planting an attractive garden or shoveling the snow off one's sidewalk may, on the other hand, provide beneficial externalities. In many cases, such externalities are resolved by bargaining between the affected parties, not through market transactions.

Reciprocal Nature of Externalities

Although these examples of externalities picture one actor as the cause of the problem and some other actor as the helpless victim (or beneficiary), that is not a very useful

[2]We will find it necessary to redefine the assumption of "no control" considerably as the analysis of this chapter proceeds.

[3]James Meade, "External Economies and Diseconomies in a Competitive Situation," *Economic Journal* (March 1952): 54–67.

way of looking at the problem. By definition, externalities require (at least) two parties, and in a sense each should be regarded as the "cause." If the producer of eyeglasses had not located its factory near the charcoal furnace, it would not have suffered any negative effects on its grinding wheels; if individuals didn't live below airport flight paths, noise would only be a minor problem; and if you were out of earshot, it wouldn't matter that someone else had the radio's volume turned up. Recognizing these reciprocal relationships is not intended to exonerate polluters, only to clarify the nature of the problem. In all of these cases, two economic actors are seeking to use the same resource, and (as we illustrate in Application 16.1: Secondhand Smoke) there are no unambiguous economic principles for deciding whose claim is stronger.

16-2 Externalities and Allocational Efficiency

In many cases, the presence of externalities such as those we have just described can cause a market to operate inefficiently. We discussed the reasons for this briefly in Chapter 10 and repeat these reasons here using the example of eyeglass and charcoal producers. Production of eyeglasses yields no externalities but is negatively affected by the level of charcoal output. We now show that resources may be allocated inefficiently in this situation. Remember that for an allocation of resources to be efficient price must be equal to true social marginal cost in each market. If the market for eyeglasses is perfectly competitive (as we assume both markets to be), price will indeed be equal to this good's private marginal cost. Since there are no externalities in eyeglass production, there is no need to make a distinction between private and social marginal cost in this case.

For charcoal production, the story is more complex. The producer of charcoal will still produce that output for which price is equal to private marginal cost. This is a direct result of the profit-maximization assumption. However, because of the negative effect that production of charcoal has on eyeglass production, it will not be true that private and social marginal costs of charcoal production are equal. Rather, the **social cost** of charcoal production is equal to the private cost *plus* the cost that charcoal production imposes on eyeglass firms in terms of reduced or inferior output. The charcoal-producing firm does not recognize this effect and produces too much charcoal. Society would be made better off by reallocating resources away from charcoal production and toward the production of other goods.

Social costs
Costs of production that include both input costs and costs of the externalities that production may cause.

A Graphical Demonstration

Figure 16.1 illustrates the misallocation of resources that results from the externality in charcoal production. Assuming that the charcoal producer is a price taker, the demand curve for its output is a horizontal line at the prevailing market price (say, P^*). Profits are maximized at q^*, where price is equal to the private marginal cost of producing charcoal (MC). Because of the externality that charcoal production imposes on eyeglass makers, however, the social marginal cost of this production (MCS) exceeds MC as shown in Figure 16.1. The vertical gap between the MCS and the MC curves measures the harm that producing an extra unit of charcoal imposes on eyeglass makers. At q^*, the social marginal cost of producing charcoal exceeds the price people are willing to pay for this output (P^*). Resources are misallocated, and production should be reduced to q' where social marginal cost and price are equal. In making this reduction, the reduction in total social costs (area ABq^*q') exceeds the reduction in total spending on charcoal (given by area AEq^*q'). This comparison shows that the allocation of resources is improved by a reduction in charcoal output because social costs are reduced to a greater

APPLICATION 16.1

Secondhand Smoke

Many of the economic issues that arise in cases of externalities are illustrated by controversies over secondhand smoke. The term secondhand smoke (or, more formally, environmental tobacco smoke, or ETS) refers to the effects of smokers' consumption of cigarettes and other tobacco products on third-party bystanders. This is a separate issue from the harmful effects of smoking on smokers themselves—an activity that generally does not involve externalities, strictly defined.

Health Effects of Secondhand Smoke

Although few doubt that secondhand smoke is annoying, the question of whether ETS has serious health consequences is controversial. The Environmental Protection Agency estimates that approximately 2,200 people die annually as a result of the increased incidence of lung cancer among those exposed to ETS. The agency suggests that the figure could be much higher if possible effects of ETS on heart disease were also taken into account. But these estimates, as is the case for many such epidemiological calculations, are based on relatively simple comparisons between individuals who live or work in proximity to smokers and those who do not. It is possible that other factors may explain such correlations. Regardless of the scientific evidence, however, many people believe that secondhand smoke is very harmful and a variety of private and public actions have been taken to mitigate this externality.

Reciprocal Nature of the ETS Externality

As for all externalities, the ETS externality involves reciprocal effects. Smokers harm bystanders with their smoke, but attempts to limit the "rights" of smokers impose inconveniences that need not arise if the bystanders were not present. Although the costs of inconvenience to smokers are seldom mentioned, they are not necessarily trivial. For example, one study of the potential impact of workplace restrictions on smoking calculates a loss in smokers' consumer surplus of approximately $20 billion per year.[1] Of course, such estimates may be far off the mark. But the fact that any specification of rights to use a "free" resource (here, air) will significantly affect the welfare of the parties involved makes the issue a controversial one.

Private Actions

For many years, decisions regarding secondhand smoke were handled through private transactions. People decided when and where to smoke in their homes or in homes they were visiting. Railroads designated smoking cars; airlines and restaurants had smoking sections, and workers would negotiate among themselves over whether smoking on the job would be permitted. Such private restrictions on smoking have been tightened in recent years, mainly in response to market pressures. For example, all airlines have banned smoking from all flights, and many restaurants have gone smoke free. Most hotel chains now offer nonsmoking rooms, and some have begun segregating smokers and nonsmokers by floors. Smoking has also been banned from most public venues such as movie theaters or sports arenas.

Public Actions

Concern about ETS has also been reflected in the demand for government regulation. The Occupational Safety and Health Administration has proposed banning virtually all workplace smoking, and recent polls suggest that many people would support a broader ban on smoking in all public places. Some economists have asked whether such additional restrictions (beyond those adopted privately) are really efficient. They ask for clear evidence that private choices by smokers and nonsmokers have not been adequate for ameliorating most of the adverse effects of smoking externalities. Given the declining number of smokers and the increasing aggressiveness with which nonsmokers pursue their rights, however, it seems likely that smoking regulations will become increasingly restrictive.

TO THINK ABOUT

1. Some people argue that smokers create additional "externalities" in their behavior by driving up healthcare and insurance costs for nonsmokers. Are such effects "externalities"? How, if at all, do they distort the allocation of resources? How would an efficient market handle smoking risks in, say, health insurance premiums?
2. Nonsmokers can often avoid ETS through their own behavior (for example, by refusing to patronize establishments that permit smoking). How, if at all, should the costs that nonsmokers incur by taking such actions be taken into account in defining an optimal policy toward ETS?

[1]W. K. Viscusi, "Secondhand Smoke: Facts and Fantasy," *Regulation*, no. 3 (1995): 42–49.

Figure 16.1 An Externality in Charcoal Production Causes an Inefficient Allocation of Resources

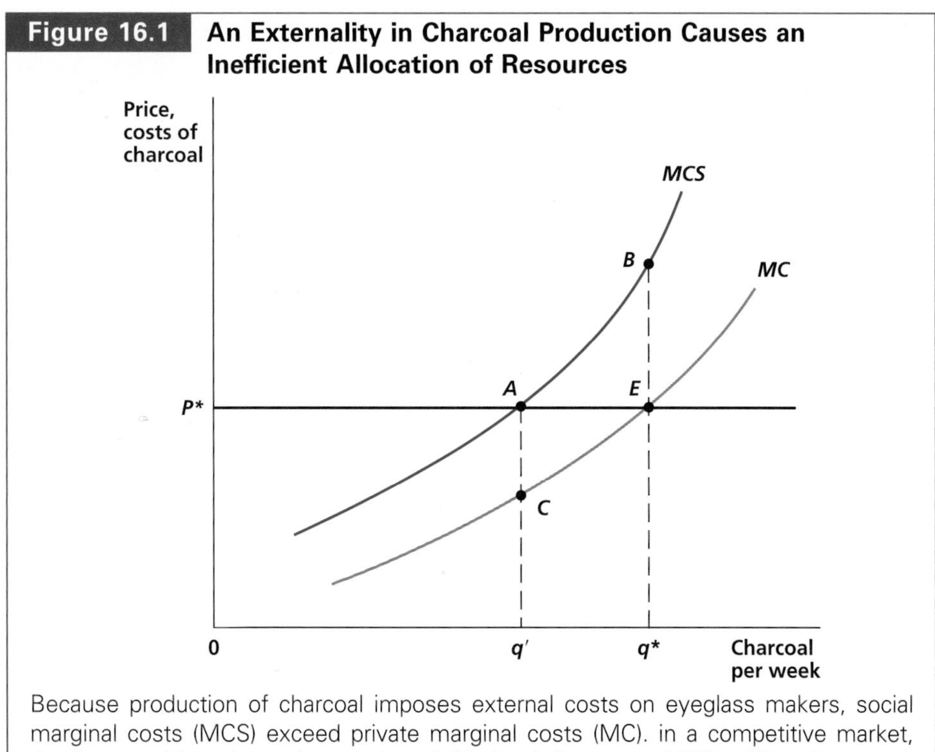

Because production of charcoal imposes external costs on eyeglass makers, social marginal costs (MCS) exceed private marginal costs (MC). in a competitive market, the firm would produce q^* at a price of P^*. At q^*, however, $MCS > P^*$ and resource allocation could be improved by reducing output to q'. With bargaining among the parties, however, output level q' may be arrived at voluntarily.

Property rights
The legal specification of who owns a good and the trades the owner is allowed to make with it.

extent than are consumers' expenditures on charcoal. Consumers can reallocate their spending toward something else that involves lower social costs than charcoal does.

MICRO QUIZ 16.1

At several places in previous chapters, we have illustrated "deadweight loss" triangles. Explain why the triangle *ABE* in Figure 16.1 represents exactly the same kind of deadweight loss as in the monopoly case.

16-3 Property Rights, Bargaining, and the Coase Theorem

The conclusion that externalities always distort the allocation of resources should not be accepted uncritically, however. To explore the issue further, we need to introduce the concept of property rights to show how these rights might be traded voluntarily between the two firms. Simply put, **property rights** are the legal specification of who owns a good and of the types of trades that this current owner is allowed to make. Some goods may be defined as **common property** that is owned by society at large and may be used by anyone; others may be defined as **private property** that is owned by specific people. Private property may either be *exchangeable* or *nonexchangeable*, depending on whether the good in question may or may not be traded to someone else. In this book, we have been primarily concerned with exchangeable private property, and we consider these types of property rights here.

Common property
Property that may be used by anyone without cost.

Private property
Property that is owned by specific people who may prevent others from using it.

Costless Bargaining and Competitive Markets

For the purposes of the charcoal-eyeglass externality, it is interesting to consider the nature of the property right that might be attached to the air shared by the charcoal and eyeglass firms. Suppose property rights were defined so as to give sole rights to use of the air to one of the firms, but that the firms were free to bargain over exactly how the air might be used. At first, you might think that if rights to the air were given to the charcoal producer, pollution would result; whereas if rights were given to the eyeglass firm, the air would remain pure and grinding machines would work properly. This might not be the case, because your snap conclusion disregards the bargains that might be reached by the two parties. Indeed, some economists have argued that if there are no transactions (bargaining) costs, the two parties left on their own will arrive at the efficient output (q'), and this will occur regardless of who "owns" the rights to use the air.

Ownership by the Polluting Firm

Suppose the charcoal firm owns the right to use the air as it wishes. It must then add the costs (if any) related to this ownership into its total costs. What are the costs associated with air ownership? Again, the opportunity cost notion provides the answer. For the charcoal firm, the costs of using the air as a dumping place for its dust are what someone else is willing to pay for this resource in its best alternative use. In our example, only the eyeglass maker has some alternative uses for the air (to keep it clean), and the amount that this firm would be willing to pay for clean air is precisely equal to the external damage done by charcoal pollution. If the charcoal firm calculates its costs correctly, its marginal cost curve (including the implicit cost of air use rights) becomes MCS in Figure 16.1. The firm will therefore produce q' and sell the remaining air use rights to the eyeglass maker for a fee of some amount between AEC (the lost profits from producing q' rather than q^* tons of charcoal) and ABEC (the maximum amount the eyeglass maker would pay to avoid having charcoal output increased from q' to q^*—that is, the total social cost of expanding charcoal output).

Ownership by the Injured Firm

A similar result would occur if eyeglass makers owned the rights to use the air as they pleased. In this case, the charcoal producer would be willing to pay up to the amount of profits it earns on each unit of output for the right to produce that unit (again, we are assuming that there is no less damaging way to produce charcoal). The eyeglass maker will accept the payment so long as it covers the costs being imposed on it by the added output of the charcoal firm. For output levels less than q' it is clear that what the charcoal firm is willing to pay (which is given by $P^* - MC$) exceeds the cost being incurred by the eyeglass firm ($MCS - MC$). For output levels greater than q', however, the profits that the charcoal firm earns from producing one more unit are smaller than the added cost imposed on the eyeglass firm. Hence, bargaining between the firms will arrive at a charcoal output level of q'. Again, as when the charcoal firm had the property rights for air usage, an efficient allocation can be reached by relying on voluntary bargaining between the two firms. In both situations, some production of charcoal takes place, and there will therefore be some air pollution. Having no charcoal output (and no pollution) would be inefficient in the same sense that producing q^* is inefficient—scarce resources would not be efficiently allocated. In this case, there is some "optimal level" of charcoal output, eyeglass output, and air pollution that may be achieved through bargains between the firms involved.

The Coase Theorem

We have shown that the two firms left on their own can arrive at the efficient output level (q'). Assuming that making such transactions is costless, both parties will recognize the advantages of striking a deal. Each will be led by the "invisible hand" to the same output level that would be achieved through an ideal merger. That solution will be reached no matter how the property rights associated with air use are assigned. The pollution-producing firm has exactly the same incentives to choose an efficient output level as does the injured firm. The ability of the two firms to bargain freely causes the true social costs of the externality to be recognized by each in its decisions. This result is sometimes referred to as the **Coase theorem** after the economist Ronald Coase, who first proposed it in this form.[4] Application 16.2: Property Rights and Nature looks at some examples of how a proper definition of property rights can often improve the allocation of resources in the presence of externalities.

Coase theorem
If bargaining is costless, the social cost of an externality will be taken into account by the parties, and the allocation of resources will be the same no matter how property rights are assigned.

Distributional Effects

There are distributional effects that do depend on who is assigned the property rights to use the air. If the charcoal firm is given the air rights, it will get the fee paid by the eyeglass maker, which will make the charcoal producer at least as well off as it was producing q^*. If the eyeglass firm gets the rights, it will receive a fee for air use that at least covers the damage the air pollution does. Because, according to the Coase result, the final allocation of resources will be unaffected by the way in which property rights are assigned,[5] any assessment of the desirability of the various possibilities might be made on equity grounds. For example, if the owners of the charcoal firm were very wealthy and those who make eyeglasses were poor, we might argue that ownership of the air use rights should be given to eyeglass makers on the basis of distributional equity. If the situation were reversed, one could argue for giving the charcoal firm the rights. The price system may sometimes be capable of solving problems in the allocation of resources caused by externalities, but, as always, it will not necessarily achieve equitable solutions. Such issues of equity in the assignment of property rights arise in every allocational decision, not only in the study of externalities, however.

MICRO QUIZ 16.2

The Coase theorem requires both that property rights be fully specified and that there be no transactions costs.

1. Would efficiency be achieved if transactions costs were zero but property rights did not exist?
2. Would efficiency be achieved if transactions costs were high but property rights were fully defined? Would your answer to this question depend on which party was assigned the property rights?

The Role of Transactions Costs

The result of the Coase theorem depends crucially on the assumption of zero transactions costs. If the costs of striking bargains were high, the workings of this voluntary exchange system might not be capable of achieving an efficient result. In the next section, we examine situations where transactions costs are high and show that competitive markets will need some help if they are to achieve efficient results.

[4]See Ronald Coase, "The Problem of Social Cost," *Journal of Law and Economics* (October 1960): 1–44.

[5]Assuming that the wealth effects of how property rights are assigned do not affect demand and cost relationships in the charcoal market.

APPLICATION 16.2

Property Rights and Nature

The notion that the specification and enforcement of property rights may aid in coping with externalities has provided a number of surprising insights. Some of the most picturesque of these involve natural surroundings.

Bees and Apples

Bees pollinate apple trees, and apple blossoms provide nectar with which bees produce honey. Despite the seeming complexity of these externalities, it appears that markets function quite well in this situation. In many locales, contractual bargaining between beekeepers and orchard owners is well developed. Standard contracts provide for the renting of bees for the pollination of many crops. Research has shown that the rents paid in these contracts accurately reflect the value of honey that is yielded from the rentals. Apple growers, for example, must pay higher rents than clover growers because apple blossoms yield considerably less honey.[1] Because bargaining among those affected by these externalities is relatively costless, this seems to be a situation where the Coase theorem applies directly.

Shellfish

Overfishing results from an externality—no single fisher takes into account the fact that his or her catch will reduce the amounts that others can catch. In the open seas, there is no easy solution to this sort of externality—costs of enforcing property rights are just too high. But in coastal situations, where property can be effectively policed, the harmful effects of overfishing can be ameliorated. When these rights are defined and enforced, private owners will recognize how their harvesting practices affect their own fish stocks.

This possibility has been especially well documented for coastal shellfish, such as oysters and lobsters. In cases where property rights to specific fishing grounds are well defined, average catches are much higher over the long run. For example, one comparison of oyster yields in Virginia and Maryland during the 1960s found that catches were nearly 60 percent higher in Virginia. The authors attributed this finding to the fact that Virginia state law made it much easier to enforce private coastal fishing rights than did Maryland law.[2] Similar results have been found by comparing harvest yields between family-owned and communal lobster beds on the Maine coast.

Elephants

The potential conservationist value of property rights enforcement has also been discovered by African nations who are seeking to preserve their elephant herds. In the past, ivory hunters have been ruthless in their killing of elephants. Strong international sanctions have been largely ineffective in preventing the carnage. During the 1980s, for example, elephant populations declined by more than 50 percent in east African countries, such as Kenya.

Several southern African nations, most notably Botswana, have taken a different approach to elephant preservation. These countries have allowed villages to capitalize on their local elephant herds by giving them the right to sell a limited number of elephant hunting permits and by encouraging them to develop tourism in protected elephant areas. Essentially, the elephants have been converted into the private property of villages, which now have an incentive to maximize the value of this asset. Elephant herds have more than doubled in Botswana.

TO THINK ABOUT

1. In the bees-apples case, considerable bargaining may be required to reach a satisfactory contract, and, in some instances, the bees may wander out of their contracted areas. What factors would determine whether it will be cost effective to develop private property contracts in such situations?
2. Isn't the notion of "privatizing wildlife" (as Botswana has done for elephants) crass commercialism? Wouldn't a better solution be to develop a conservationist ethic under which everyone agreed to nurture the planet's wild heritage?

[1]The classic examination of this question is S. N. S. Cheung, "The Fable of the Bees: An Economic Investigation," *Journal of Law and Economics* (April 1973): 11–33.

[2]R. J. Agnello and L. P. Donnelly, "Property Rights and Efficiency in the Oyster Industry," *Journal of Law and Economics* (October 1975): 521–533.

16-4 Externalities with High Transactions Costs

When transactions costs are high, externalities may cause real losses in economic welfare. The fundamental problem is that, with high transactions costs, economic actors face no pressure to take into account the externalities they cause. All solutions to externality problems in these cases must therefore find some way to get the actors to "internalize" these effects. In this section, we look at three such methods, each of which has both advantages and disadvantages.

Legal Redress

The operation of the law may sometimes provide a way for taking externalities into account. If those who are injured by an externality have the right to sue for damages in a court of law, the possibility of such suits may lead to internalization. For example, if the charcoal producer shown in Figure 16.1 can be sued for the harm that it does to eyeglass makers, payment of damages will increase the costs associated with charcoal production. Hence, the charcoal marginal cost curve will shift upward to MCS and an efficient allocation of resources will be achieved.

This discussion suggests that different types of law might be applied in cases of externalities, depending on whether transactions costs are high or low. When transactions costs are low, careful specification of rights under property law can be used to achieve efficient results because the Coase theorem applies. When transactions costs are high, the law of "torts" (harms) should be used because lawsuits can get those who create externalities to recognize the damage that they do. Hence, the possibility of legal redress provides an important complement to the Coase theorem.[6]

Of course, using the legal system requires real resources. Lawyers, judges, and expert witnesses do not come cheap. These costs may multiply rapidly as the number of injured parties increases. Hence, any full assessment of the desirability of using the law to obtain market-like solutions to the externality problem must take the costs of using the law into account. Still, it seems clear that in many cases of externalities, such as automobile accidents or other types of personal injuries, use of the legal system may prove to be expeditious. Application 16.3: Product Liability looks at some advantages and disadvantages of using legal approaches to issues of product safety.

Taxation

A second way to achieve internalization is through taxation. This remedy was first suggested by the welfare economist A. C. Pigou in the 1920s,[7] and it remains the standard economists' solution for many types of externalities.

The taxation solution is illustrated in Figure 16.2. Again, MC and MCS represent the private and social marginal costs of charcoal production, and the market price of charcoal is given by P^*. An excise tax of amount t would reduce the net price received by the

[6]These insights were first noted in G. Calabresi and A. D. Melamed, "Property Rules, Liability Rules, and Inalienability," *Harvard Law Review* (March 1972): 1089–1128. Notice that the lawsuits described here are intended only to recover "Compensatory damages" that compensate for the harm that externalities do. See Application 16.3 for a discussion of "punitive" damages.

[7]A. C. Pigou, *The Economics of Welfare*, 4th ed. (London: Macmillan, 1946); Pigou also stressed the desirability of providing subsidies to firms that produce beneficial externalities.

APPLICATION 16.3

Product Liability

Concerns about product safety have multiplied significantly in recent years. Here we look at some of the law and economics behind this trend.

A Coase Theorem

Situations in which products cause injuries are not necessarily externalities under our definition because the product supplier and the consumer have a market relationship between one another. With perfect information and low transactions costs, the Coase theorem suggests that it may be possible to achieve an efficient allocation even when products are dangerous. A simple illustration is provided in Figure 1 for the case of, say, chainsaws. Use of chainsaws provides utility to people (try cutting up a fallen tree without one) but also causes injuries. Under a legal specification of caveat emptor (let the buyer beware), consumers would be responsible for all injuries caused. The demand curve for saws would be given by D. The supply curve for chainsaws would reflect only production costs and would be given by S. Market equilibrium occurs at P^*, Q^*. Suppose instead that suppliers are liable for all injuries that chainsaws cause. Costs of these injuries (c) would shift the supply curve upward to S'. Demanders would now know that they would be compensated for the injuries they sustain from chainsaw operation, so they would be willing to pay c more for any output level—demand would shift upward by c. The new market equilibrium would be given by $P^* + c$, Q^*. That is, quantity produced would remain the same, but the price would now explicitly reflect injury costs. Regardless of the legal regime that is in place, the efficient quantity of chainsaws will be produced.

Figure 1 Coase Theorem for Product Safety

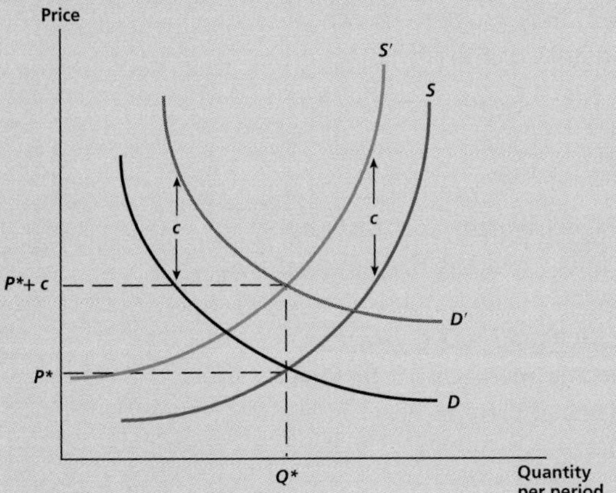

If demanders bear liability for injuries, market equilibrium will be at P^*, Q^*. If suppliers bear liability, equilibrium will be at $P^* + c$, Q^*. The same quantity is produced under both legal regimes.

Imperfect Information

Outcomes under the two legal regimes will differ if the parties to chainsaw transactions are not perfectly informed. In this case, attaining an efficient solution will require that the liability be placed on the best-informed party. For example, suppose that most chainsaw injuries occur because, unknown to consumers, firms produce mechanically defective saws. Placing the legal liability on the firms will ensure that they take injury costs into account. On the other hand, if most injuries occur because people do dumb things with their chainsaws, efficiency can be obtained by opting for caveat emptor in order to give users an incentive to be careful.

Punitive Damages

Efficiency is achieved in Figure 1 under the various legal regimes because the parties are made to internalize the costs of injuries into their decisions. In legal jargon, payment of these costs is called "compensatory damages" because such payments accurately compensate for injuries incurred. In the U.S. legal system (though not in some other countries' systems), parties injured by a product can also sue for "punitive damages." These damages are intended to "send a message" rather than compensate for actual physical harm. In general, economists doubt the wisdom of such damages because they may overdeter valuable production and cause firms to adopt excessive safety features that would not meet a cost-benefit test.

POLICY CHALLENGE

This example shows that product liability law has a potentially beneficial role to play in improving the allocation of resources to risky products, especially when those risks are not understood by consumers. In actual practice, however, product liability cases have been criticized for yielding wildly differing results and for imposing unrealistic damage assessments on firms. Many observers have suggested that product liability law (and its close relative medical malpractice law) needs to be reformed by tightening up standards of scientific proof and by putting caps on certain types of claims. Achieving the right balance between such restrictions and helping markets to internalize harms is no easy task.

Figure 16.2 Taxation Solution to the Externality Problem

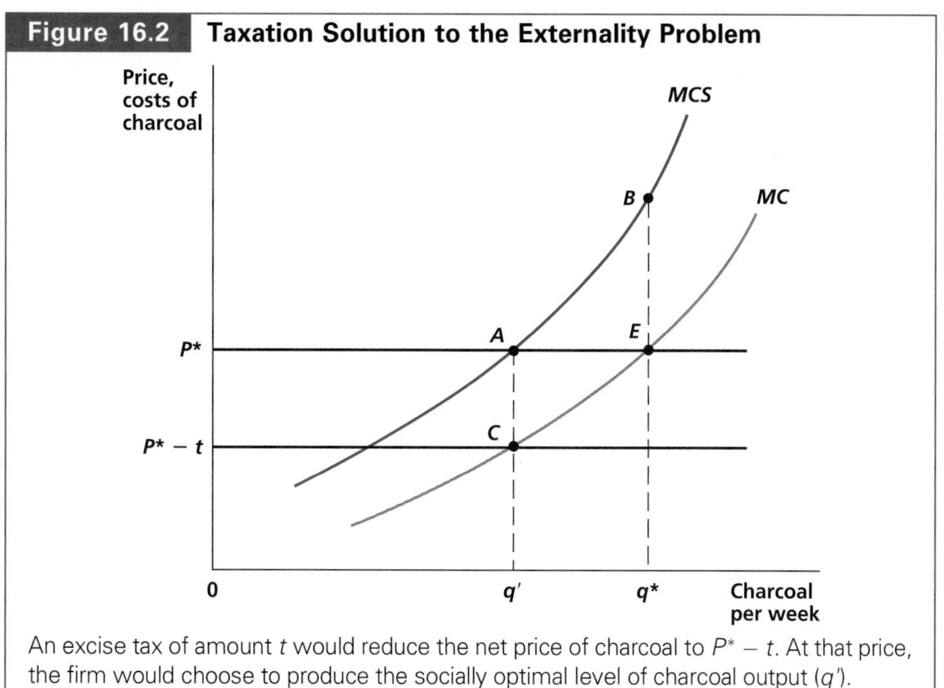

An excise tax of amount t would reduce the net price of charcoal to $P^* - t$. At that price, the firm would choose to produce the socially optimal level of charcoal output (q').

firm to $P^* - t$, and at that price the firm would choose to produce q'. The tax causes the firm to reduce its output to the socially optimal amount. At q', the firm incurs private marginal costs of $P^* - t$ and imposes external costs on eyeglass makers of t per unit. The per-unit tax is therefore exactly equal to the extra costs that charcoal producers impose on eyeglass producers.[8] The problem then for government regulators is to decide on the proper level for such a **Pigovian tax**.

Pigovian tax
A tax or subsidy on an externality that brings about an equality of private and social marginal costs.

Regulation of Externalities

A third way to control externalities in situations of high transactions costs is through regulation. In order to look at some of the issues that arise in regulation, let's consider the case of policy toward environmental pollution. The horizontal axis in Figure 16.3 shows percentage reductions in environmental pollution from some source below what would occur in the absence of any regulation. The curve MB in the figure shows the additional social benefits obtained by reducing such pollution by one more unit. These benefits consist of possibly improved health, the availability of additional recreational or aesthetic benefits, and improved production opportunities for other firms. As for most economic activities, this provision of benefits is assumed to exhibit diminishing returns—the curve MB slopes downward to reflect the fact that the marginal benefits from additional reductions in pollution decline as stricter controls are implemented.

The curve MC in Figure 16.3 represents the marginal costs incurred in reducing environmental emissions. The positive slope of this curve reflects our usual assumptions of increasing marginal costs. Controlling the first 50 or 60 percent of pollutants is a relatively low-cost activity, but controlling the last few percentage points is rather costly. As reductions in emissions approach 100 percent, marginal costs rise very rapidly.

[8]Notice that the Pigovian tax equals the harm of the externality at output q' (distance AC). A tax equal to the harm at ouput level q^* (distance BE) would be too large.

Figure 16.3 Optimal Pollution Abatement

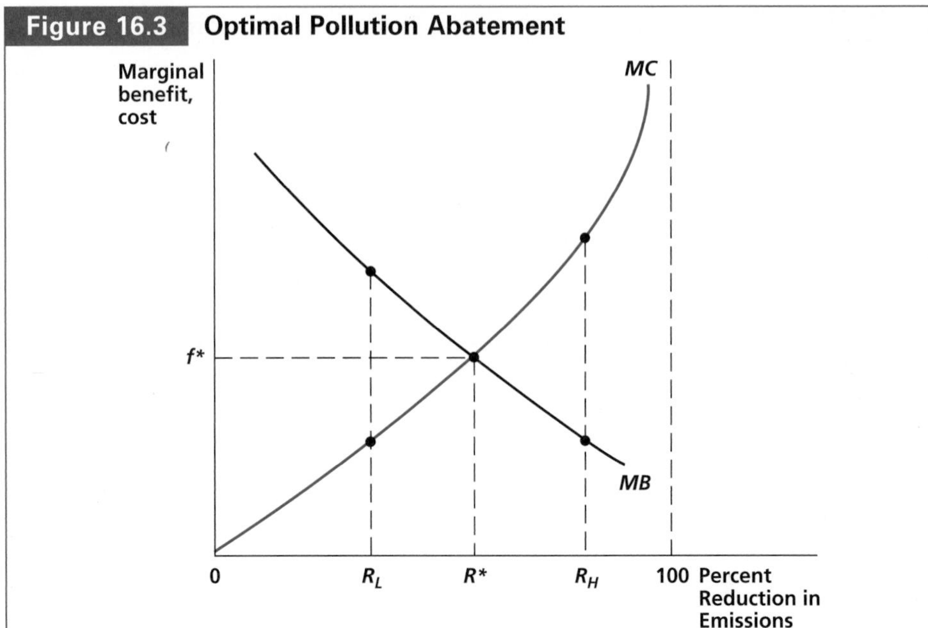

The *MB* and *MC* curves show the marginal benefits and marginal costs, respectively, of pollution abatement. R^* represents an optimal allocation of resources to this purpose. Such an outcome may be attained through the imposition of an effluent fee of f^*, through the sale of marketable pollution permits, or through direct controls.

Optimal Regulation

Given this configuration, it is clear that R^* is the optimal level of pollution reduction. For reductions less than R^* (say, R_L), the marginal benefits associated with further tightening of environmental controls exceed the marginal cost of achieving lower pollution levels, so emissions should be reduced further. Reductions in excess of R^* are also inefficient—environmental control can be pushed too far. At R_H, the marginal cost of emissions control exceeds the marginal benefits obtained, so less-strict regulation may be desirable. To noneconomists, the notion that there is an optimal level of pollution (that R^* is less than 100 percent) may sound strange, but this result reflects the general principles of efficient resource allocation we have been studying throughout this book.

Fees, Permits, and Direct Controls

There are three general ways that emissions reductions of R^* might be attained through regulatory policy. First, the government may adopt a Pigovian-type "effluent fee" of f^* for each percent that pollution is not reduced. Faced with such a charge, the polluting firm will choose the optimal emissions reduction level, R^*. For reductions less than R^*, the fee exceeds the marginal cost of pollution abatement, so a profit-maximizing firm will opt for abatement. Reductions in emissions of more than R^* would be unprofitable, however, so the firm will opt to pay the fee on $(100 - R^*)$ of its pollutants. One important feature of the fee approach is that the firm itself is free to choose whatever combination of output reduction and adoption of pollution control technology achieves R^* at minimal cost.

A similar allocational result would be attained if governmental regulators issued permits that allow firms to "produce" $(100 - R^*)$ percent of their unregulated emissions levels. Figure 16.3 implies that, if such permits were freely tradable, they would sell for a price of f^*. In this case, a competitive market for pollution permits ensures that the optimal level of emissions reductions will be attained at minimal social cost.

A third regulatory strategy would be simply to implement reductions of R^* through direct controls. In this case, which tends to be the one most often followed in the United States, firms would be told the level of emissions they would be allowed. Such a direct approach can, in principle, duplicate the allocations provided by lawsuits, Pigovian taxation, or marketable permits. If, as is often the case, direct control is also accompanied by specification of the precise mechanism by which R^* is to be achieved (for example, through the installation of a special kind of pollution-control equipment) the cost-minimization incentives incorporated in the other approaches may be lost. Application 16.4: Power Plant Emissions and the Global Warming Debate looks at the principal current issue in environmental policy.

Suppose that the government does not have detailed information about the costs of the firms that produce pollution.

1. Why are the three methods described here for attaining R^* superior to a regulatory strategy that requires firms to install a specific technology that would allow them to attain R^*?
2. How well do the three strategies minimize the information that the government needs?

16-5 Public Goods

The activities of governments can have important externalities. For many of the goods that governments provide, the benefits are shared by all citizens. For example, one of the primary functions of all governments is the provision of a common defense. All citizens benefit from this whether or not they pay taxes for it. More generally, the government establishes such things as property rights and laws of contract that create a legal environment in which economic transactions occur. Benefits arising from this environment are, again, shared by all citizens.

One way of summarizing these observations is to conclude that the government provides many *public goods* to its citizens. In a sense, governments are not very different from other organizations such as labor unions, professional associations, or even fraternities and sororities. They provide benefits to, and impose obligations on, their members. Governments differ primarily because they may be able to achieve economies of scale because they provide benefits to everyone and because they have the ability to finance their activities through compulsory taxation.

Attributes of Public Goods

The preceding discussion of public goods is circular—governments are defined as producers of public goods, and public goods are defined as the stuff governments produce. Many economists (starting with Paul Samuelson) have tried to attach a more specific, technical definition to the term *public good*.[9] The purpose of such a definition is to differentiate those goods that are public by nature from those that are suitable for private

[9]See Paul A. Samuelson, "The Pure Theory of Public Expenditure," *Review of Economics and Statistics* (November 1954): 387–389. Usually the implication is that governments should not produce private goods because competitive markets will do a better job.

APPLICATION 16.4

Power Plant Emissions and the Global Warming Debate

Electric power represents as much as 50 percent of the energy used in most industrial economies, and most electric power is produced from burning fossil fuels. This burning yields a variety of unhealthy byproducts, including sulfuric acid, nitric acid, and mercury. Most regulation of electric power production has traditionally focused on these pollutants. More recently, however, the focus has shifted onto regulating carbon dioxide, a product of burning fossil fuels previously thought to be "harmless." In this application, we first look at efforts to control sulfuric acid from power plants. Then, we take up the issue of global warming and proposals seeking to control carbon dioxide emissions.

Regulating Sulfuric Acid

Emissions of sulfuric acid from power plants produces "acid rain," a process that harms lakes and forests. Most attempts to control such emissions have followed a "command-and-control" (CAC) approach. Under this approach, air-quality standards are defined by law, and plants are required to install specific equipment that enables them to meet the standards. To achieve the defined goal, most large power plants must install "scrubbers" that clean the exhaust fumes in their stacks. A variety of studies have found that these regulations are not especially cost-effective. A primary reason for the extra costs is the inflexibility of the regulations—plants are not free to adapt the required technology to prevailing meteorological or geographical realities. Studies of cost-effectiveness conclude that, in the United States, costs may have exceeded a least-cost ideal by a factor of two or more.

Emission Charges

An alternative, more efficient approach favored by many economists would follow Pigou's proposal by imposing a tax on power plants for their harmful emissions. With such a charge, utility owners would be free to choose any technology that promised emissions reductions at a marginal cost that is equal to or less than this charge. Computer simulations of the effect suggest that it would be considerably more cost-effective. Both Japan and France have made significant use of the emissions-charge approach.

Emissions Trading

The Clean Air Act amendments of 1990 incorporated an innovation in regulatory procedures that was expected to improve the cost-effectiveness of the CAC procedures used in the United States. Under this plan, power plants that reduced their levels of certain pollutants (mainly sulfur dioxide) below those specified by the air-quality standards achieve "credits" for doing so. They are then permitted to sell those credits to other firms. The purchasing firm can exceed air-quality standards by the extent of its credits. In principle, this can reduce the overall costs associated with achieving any particular air-quality standards, because those firms that can achieve additional reductions at the lowest marginal cost will do so. Results from studies of such emissions trading suggest that cost savings of approximately 50 percent have been achieved over what would prevail under a pure CAC framework.[1]

The Global Warming Controversy

Recent years have seen increasing concerns about the carbon dioxide (CO_2) emissions from power plants (and other burning of fossil fuel), mainly because of the possibility that such emissions may contribute to global warming. Although the scientific evidence is not perfect, there is some consensus that allowing CO_2 to build up in the atmosphere may raise temperatures by about 2–3 degrees Celsius over the next 100 years, leading to potential losses of GDP in the range of 5 percent or more. Under the Kyoto Protocol, nations would be required to meet this threat by reducing their carbon dioxide emissions significantly to well below 1990 levels. Many nations (including the United States) have not explicitly signed onto this agenda, however, in part because of lingering questions about whether immediate action is required and about what the payoff to restrictions on CO_2 emissions might be.

A bit of mathematics from Chapter 14 may help to clarify why reaching a consensus on global warming policy is difficult. Suppose that GDP is expected to grow at a rate of g over the next 100 years. If we let current GDP be represented by Y, then GDP in 100 years will be $Y(1+g)^{100}$. If timely CO_2 policy will save 5 percent of this GDP, the benefits of such a policy would be $B = .05Y(1+g)^{100}$, but now these benefits must be discounted to allow for the opportunity cost of capital (r) over this 100-year period. So, our final value for the estimated benefits of a major anti-global-warming initiative is

$$B = \frac{.05Y(1+g)^{100}}{(1+r)^{100}}. \quad \textbf{(1)}$$

Clearly, the value of this expression depends on the values of g and r. If we were to use what might be considered consensus values of $g = .03$, $r = .05$, the value for this expression becomes $B = .0073Y$. That is, the present value of saving 5 percent of GDP in 100 years is somewhat less than 1 percent of current GDP. According to this calculation, then, one should be willing to spend a modest amount on reducing CO_2 emissions but not enough to severely hamper the economy. Of course, assuming alternative values for g or r would change these calculations significantly—and that is another reason that policy is so controversial. Only modest changes in assumptions can lead to vast differences in the overall assessment of the policy because the consequences occur so far in the future.[2]

Obama's Cap-and-Trade Policy

Because experiences with CAC environmental policies have proven so costly, many economists support an alternative emissions trading approach for dealing with the CO_2 problem. Under such a plan, CO_2 emissions would be "capped" at a certain level, and permits would be issued by the government for achieving that level. These permits would be tradable in an open market, thereby establishing a "price" for carbon emissions. Power plants (and others required to have permits) would then choose cost-minimizing techniques given these prices. The "cap" for emissions could then be progressively lowered over time to achieve whatever goals were decided to be optimal, given the evolving scientific evidence.

This is precisely the proposal made by the Obama Administration early in 2009. Under this plan, CO_2 emissions in the United States would be gradually reduced to 14 percent below 2005 levels by 2020 and to 83 percent below those levels by 2050. Carbon permits would be auctioned off by the government and would be expected to raise about $700 billion over a 10-year period. Of course, such a cost will ultimately be passed on to consumers of electricity. By some estimates, electricity costs would rise about 7–10 percent over what they would have been. Such cost increases would not be uniform across the country, however.[3] They would be largest where electricity is generated by high-CO_2 methods, especially the burning of coal.

POLICY CHALLENGE

Developing an efficient approach to regulating CO_2 emissions is perhaps the greatest policy challenge facing many nations over the next decade. Not only will policy responses have to be flexible enough to adapt to emerging scientific evidence, but they must also be robust to the variety of political attempts to manipulate them to special interest advantages that are sure to arise. A few of the questions that will need to be addressed include

- **How stringent should CO_2 caps be?** Answering this question will implicitly show how much we are willing to spend to achieve CO_2 reductions.
- **Whose emissions should be capped?** Operating a cap-and-trade policy for power plants is relatively easy because there are few of them, but designing CO_2 reduction policy for other emitters is much more difficult and vulnerable to political pressures. For example, in principle, reducing automobile emissions might be obtained through a higher gasoline tax, but such a tax would not directly tax CO_2 emissions, so its incentive effects are more complex than in the power plant case.
- **What to do with emission permit revenues?** A large-scale cap-and-trade program will generate significant revenues. These may be used to finance other forms of government spending or to reduce other taxes. Views on the desirability of these different approaches will (obviously) vary widely.

[1]R. Rico, "The U.S. Allowance Trading System for Sulfur Dioxide: An Update on Market Experience," *Energy and Resource Economics* (March 1995): 115–129.
[2]For an extended discussion of these issues, see Martin L. Weitzman, "A Review of the Stern Review on the Economics of Climate Change," *Journal of Economic Literature* (September 2007): 703–724.
[3]For a discussion of many of the issues that arise in adoption of a cap and trade policy, see Congressional Budget Office, *An Evaluation of Cap-and-Trade Programs for Reducing U.S. Carbon Emissions*, June (Washington, DC: Congressional Budget Office, 2001).

markets. The most common definitions of public goods stress two attributes that seem to characterize many of the goods governments produce: nonexclusivity and nonrivalry.

Nonexclusivity

One property that distinguishes many public goods is whether people may be excluded from the benefits the goods provide. For most private goods, exclusion is indeed possible. I can easily be excluded from consuming a hamburger if I don't pay for it. In some cases, exclusion is either very costly or impossible. National defense is the standard example. Once an army or navy is established, everyone in a country benefits from its protection whether they pay for it or not. Similar comments apply on a local level to such goods as mosquito control or inoculation programs against disease. In these cases, once the programs are implemented, all of the residents of a community benefit from them and no one can be excluded from those benefits, regardless of whether he or she pays for them. These **nonexclusive goods** pose problems for markets because people are tempted to "let the other guy do it" and benefit from this person's spending.

Nonexclusive goods
Goods that provide benefits that no one can be excluded from enjoying.

Nonrivalry

A second property that characterizes many public goods is nonrivalry. **Nonrival goods** are goods for which benefits can be provided to additional users at zero marginal social cost. For most goods, consumption of additional amounts involves some marginal costs of production. Consumption of one more hot dog, for example, requires that various resources be devoted to its production. For some goods, however, this is not the case. Consider one more automobile crossing a highway bridge during an off-peak period. Because the bridge is already there anyway, one more vehicle crossing it requires no additional resources and does not reduce consumption of anything else. One more viewer tuning into a television channel involves no additional cost, even though this action would result in additional consumption taking place. Consumption by additional users of such a good is nonrival in that this additional consumption involves zero marginal social costs of production; such consumption does not reduce other people's ability to consume. Again, goods with the nonrival property pose problems for markets because the efficient price (=marginal cost) for such a good is zero.

Nonrival goods
Goods that additional consumers may use at zero marginal costs.

Categories of Public Goods

The concepts of nonexclusivity and nonrivalry are in some ways related. Many goods that are nonexclusive are also nonrival. National defense and mosquito control are two examples of goods for which exclusion is not possible and for which additional consumption takes place at zero marginal cost. Many other instances might be suggested.

These concepts are not identical. Some goods may possess one property but not the other. It is, for example, impossible (or at least very costly) to exclude some fishing boats from ocean fisheries, yet one more boat imposes social costs in the form of a reduced catch for all concerned. Similarly, use of a bridge during off-peak hours may be nonrival, but it is possible to exclude potential users by erecting toll booths. Table 16.1 presents a cross-classification of goods by their possibilities for exclusion and their rivalry. Several examples of goods that fit into each of the categories are provided. Many of the examples in boxes other than the upper left corner in the table are often produced by the government. Nonrival goods are sometimes privately produced—there are private bridges, swimming pools, and highways that consumers must pay to use even though this use involves zero marginal cost. Nonpayers can be excluded from consuming these goods,

Table 16.1 Types of Public and Private Goods

		Exclusive: Yes	Exclusive: No
Rival	Yes	Hot dogs Automobiles Houses	Fishing ground Public grazing land Clean air
	No	Bridges Swimming pools Scrambled satellite television signal	National defence Mosquito Control Justice Ideas

so a private firm may be able to cover its costs.[10] Still, even in this case, the resulting allocation of resources will be inefficient because price will exceed marginal cost.

For simplicity we define **public goods** as having both of the properties listed in Table 16.1. That is, such goods provide nonexclusive benefits and can be provided to one more user at zero marginal cost. Public goods are both nonexclusive and nonrival.

Public goods
Goods that are both nonexclusive and nonrival.

16-6 Public Goods and Market Failure

The definition of public goods suggests why private markets may not produce them in adequate amounts. For exclusive private goods, the purchaser of that good can appropriate the entire benefits of the good. If Smith eats a pork chop, for example, that means the chop yields no benefits to Jones. The resources used to produce the pork chop can be seen as contributing only to Smith's welfare, and he or she is willing to pay whatever this is worth.

For a public good, this will not be the case. In buying a public good, any one person will not be able to appropriate to himself or herself all the benefits the good offers. Because others cannot be excluded from benefiting from the good and because others can use the good at no cost, society's potential benefits from the public good will exceed the benefits that accrue to any single buyer. However, the purchaser will not take the potential benefits of this purchase to others into account in his or her expenditure decisions. Consequently, private markets will tend to underallocate resources to public goods. Before starting our general treatment of the topic, it may be useful to look at one type of public good, ideas, that can be produced privately with a little help, as Application 16.5: Ideas as Public Goods shows.

A Graphical Demonstration

One way to show why markets underallocate resources to public goods is by looking at the demand curve associated with such goods. In the case of a private good, we found the

[10]Nonrival goods that permit imposition of an exclusion mechanism are sometimes referred to as *club goods* since provision of such goods might be organized along the lines of private clubs. Such clubs might then charge a "membership" fee and permit unlimited use by members. The optimal size of a club is determined by the economies of scale present in the production process for the club good. For an analysis, see R. Cornes and T. Sandler, *The Theory of Externalities, Public Goods, and Club Goods* (Cambridge: Cambridge University Press, 1986).

APPLICATION 16.5

Ideas as Public Goods

Ideas for new products or artistic creations have both of the properties that define public goods. Ideas are nonexclusive because no one can be prevented from using them. They are also nonrival because additional people may use ideas at zero marginal cost. Because of these properties, it seems likely that valuable ideas will be underproduced in a market economy. People will be reluctant to invest time in thinking up new inventions or in developing works of art and literature when they know that others can easily copy their work. This fact is recognized in the U.S. Constitution, where Congress is given the power "to promote the progress of science and useful arts, by securing for limited times to authors and inventors the exclusive right to their respective writings and discoveries." That is, the Congress is empowered to convert what would normally be public goods into a private property right that authors and inventors have exclusive control over for a time. The benefit of such a provision is that it provides incentives for creation of new "intellectual property." The disadvantage is that the owner of this property is given what may result in a temporary monopoly in its use. Finding a proper trade-off between these effects has proven to be elusive both in the United States and internationally.[1] Here we look at two examples.

Drug Patents

Development of a new drug is an expensive process—some estimates put the cost as high as $1 billion for each successful new drug. Once developed, however, others can copy a drug at a very low marginal cost. Hence, it is likely that free riders can undermine the incentives to discover new pharmaceuticals. Awarding of patents creates a temporary property right that seeks to avoid this problem. Patents are controversial, however, because the monopoly they provide to patent holders can enable the firms to charge prices far above marginal cost for the most in-demand drugs. This issue has become especially salient with respect to drugs for treating AIDS, especially in Africa. A number of proposals have been made for the compulsory licensing of drug patents or for speeding up the time at which "generic" substitutes for various drugs can be introduced. Some have suggested that drug purchasers should form monopsonistic cartels (see Chapter 12) to counteract the power of drug monopolies. For example, it has been proposed that the U.S. Medicare program negotiate prices with drug companies, something that is currently forbidden by law. Of course, it is possible that all such actions could have some effect on incentives to discover new, life-prolonging drugs.

Music and Motion Pictures

Music and motion pictures are protected by copyright laws. These laws are intended to provide an economic incentive to individuals who create such works, by enabling them to capture the fruits of their efforts. Copyright law originated in the early eighteenth century and for most of its existence applied mainly to printed works. The advent of recording technologies, especially those that use digital files, has vastly expanded the problems that arise in seeking to enforce the law. Because digital files can be copied at essentially zero marginal cost, creators can easily lose control of their intellectual property. Illegal copying and distribution of music has probably progressed the most rapidly due in part to success of the MP3 format. By some estimates, less than ten percent of music files that are transferred among listeners result in royalty payments to artists. Digital files of motion pictures have been following a similar route. Often copies of new motion pictures are available before the films ever appear in theaters. Major recording and film firms continue to search for both legal and technological fixes to these problems.

POLICY CHALLENGE

The development of an optimal policy for protection of intellectual property requires a careful consideration of the trade-off between creating incentives for the production of such property and the deadweight losses arising from the monopoly that such property rights provide to their owners. In principle, one would imagine that this trade-off would yield different levels of protection for different types of property. That is, patent or copyright protection could vary in duration or could require various types of rights sharing, depending on these relative costs and benefits. For example, some health care advocates argue that drug patents should allow some creation of generics when the primary beneficiaries are residents of low-income countries (this is the case for AIDS-related drugs). Some creative artists argue that copyright protection should be enforced more rigorously, whereas many digital advocates argue against this view. Clearly, reaching a nuanced policy consensus can be very difficult.

[1]For a complete discussion of the issues raised in this application, see W. M. Landes and R. A. Posner, *The Economic Structure of Intellectual Property Law* (Cambridge, Mass.: Harvard University Press, 2003).

market demand curve (see Chapter 3) by summing people's demands horizontally. At any price, the quantities demanded by each person are summed up to calculate the total quantity demanded in the market. The market demand curve shows the marginal evaluation that people place on an additional unit of output. For a public good (which is provided in about the same quantity to everyone), we must add individual demand curves vertically. To find out how society values some level of public good production, we must ask how each person values this level of output and then add up these valuations.

This idea is represented in Figure 16.4 for a situation with only two people. The total demand curve for the public good is the vertical sum of each person's demand curve. Each point on the curve represents what person 1 and person 2 together are willing to pay for the particular level of public good production. Producing one more unit of the public good would benefit both people because the good is nonexclusive; so, to evaluate this benefit, we must add up what each person would be willing to pay. This is shown in Figure 16.4 by adding what person 1 is willing to pay to what person 2 is willing to pay. In private markets, on the other hand, the production of one more unit benefits only the person who ultimately consumes it. Because each person's demand curve in Figure 16.4 is below the true total demand for the public good, no single buyer is willing to pay what the good is worth to society as a whole. Therefore, in many cases, private markets may undervalue the benefits of public goods because they take no account of the externalities the goods create. Hence, resources will be underallocated to them.

Figure 16.4 Derivation of the Demand for a Public Good

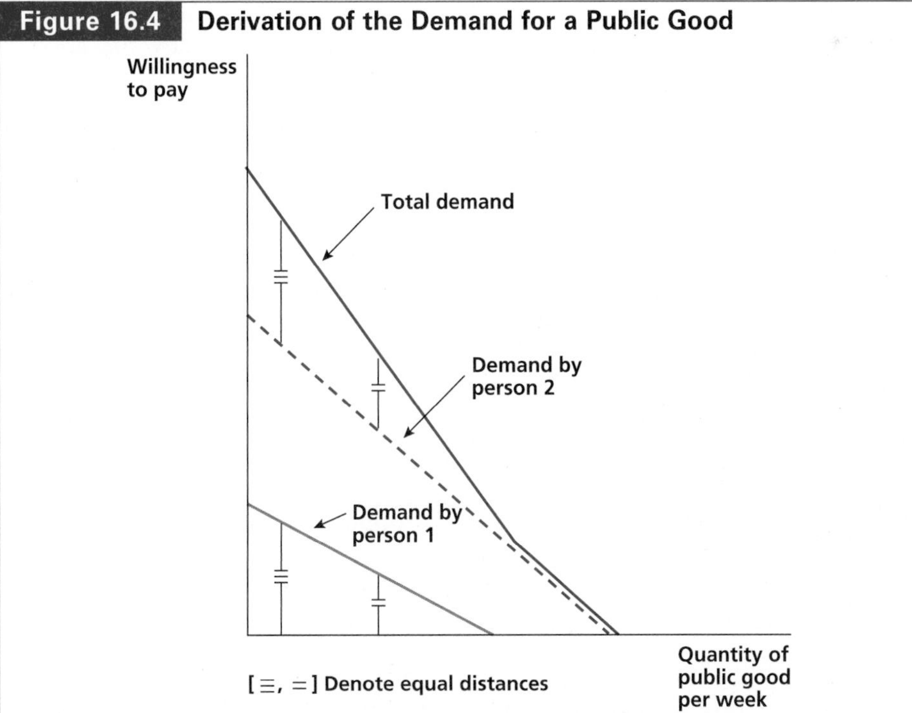

Because a public good is nonexclusive, the price that people are willing to pay for one more unit (their marginal valuations) is equal to the sum of what each individual would pay. Here person 1's willingness to pay is added vertically to person 2's to get the total demand for the public good.

16-7 Solutions to the Public Goods Problem

Free rider
A consumer of a nonexclusive good who does not pay for it in the hope that other consumers will.

Because private markets will not allocate resources efficiently to the production of public goods, some other mechanism must be found. Unfortunately, as anyone who tries to organize a picnic (or get his or her children to clean their rooms) quickly discovers, getting people to provide public goods voluntarily is a difficult task. Because people know that they will benefit from the good regardless of whether or not they contribute to its production, everyone will have an incentive to be a **free rider**. That is, they will refrain from contributing to production in the hope that someone else will. In general, this will result in the underproduction of the public good in question.

Nash Equilibrium and Underproduction

One approach that illustrates this underproduction relies on the concept of Nash equilibrium, first introduced in Chapter 5. Consider the situation of two roommates illustrated in Table 16.2. Each roommate may either clean the room or not. A clean room provides more utility than a dirty room to both of the players in this game. But each player would also prefer to have a clean room cleaned by his or her roommate to one in which the cleaning is shared. On the other hand, each roommate prefers a dirty room to one that he or she has had to clean alone. In this game (which resembles the Prisoner's Dilemma game in Chapter 5), the only Nash equilibrium is for neither player to clean the room. Any choice by one player to clean would induce the other to shirk. But this dirty equilibrium is inferior to a situation where both players clean the room—a Pareto improvement that would require some degree of coercion to enforce.

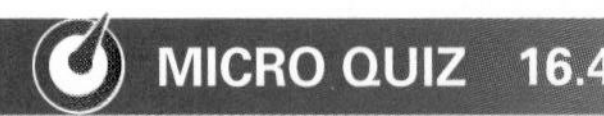
MICRO QUIZ 16.4

1. Explain why a public good must have the nonexclusivity feature if free riding is to occur.
2. Would a public good that had the non-rivalry property but not the nonexclusivity property be subject to free riding? Why might such a good be produced at inefficient levels anyway?

Compulsory Taxation

Although the room-cleaning example is a trivial one in comparison to issues of public goods production that involve national defense or providing for public health, the nature of the problem is the same for any public good. The free-rider problem is inescapable. Hence, some compulsory mechanism must be found to ensure efficient production. Most often, this solution relies on some form of tax-like measure. That is, members of a group

Table 16.2 Nash Equilibrium Under-produces Public Goods in the Room-Cleaning Game

		B Don't clean	*B* Clean
A	Don't clean	1, 1	3, 0
A	Clean	0, 3	2, 2

who are expected to benefit from a public good must in some way be forced to pay for it in the optimal amounts. The fact that there can be an efficient equilibrium with compulsory taxation was first illustrated by the Swedish economist Erik Lindahl in 1919. Lindahl's argument can be shown graphically for a society with only two individuals (again, the ever-popular Smith and Jones). In Figure 16.5, the curve labeled *SS* shows Smith's demand for a particular public good. Rather than using the price of the public good on the vertical axis, we instead record the share of a public good's cost that Smith must pay (which varies from 0 percent to 100 percent). The negative slope of *SS* indicates that, at a higher tax "price" for the public good, Smith will demand a smaller quantity of it.

Jones's demand for the public good is derived in much the same way. Now, however, we record the proportion paid by Jones on the right-hand vertical axis on Figure 16.5 and reverse the scale so that moving up the axis results in a lower tax price paid. Given this convention, Jones's demand for the public good (*JJ*) has a positive slope.

The Lindahl Equilibrium

The two demand curves in Figure 16.5 intersect at *C*, with an output level of 0*E* for the public good. At this output level, Smith is willing to pay, say, 60 percent of the good's cost, whereas Jones pays 40 percent. That point *C* is an equilibrium is suggested by the following argument. For output levels less than 0*E*, the two people combined are willing to pay more than 100 percent of the public good's cost. They will vote to increase its level of production (but see the warnings about this statement in the next section). For output levels greater than 0*E*, the people are not willing to pay the total cost of the public good being produced and may vote for reductions in the amount being provided. Only

Figure 16.5 Lindahl Equilibrium in the Demand for a Public Good

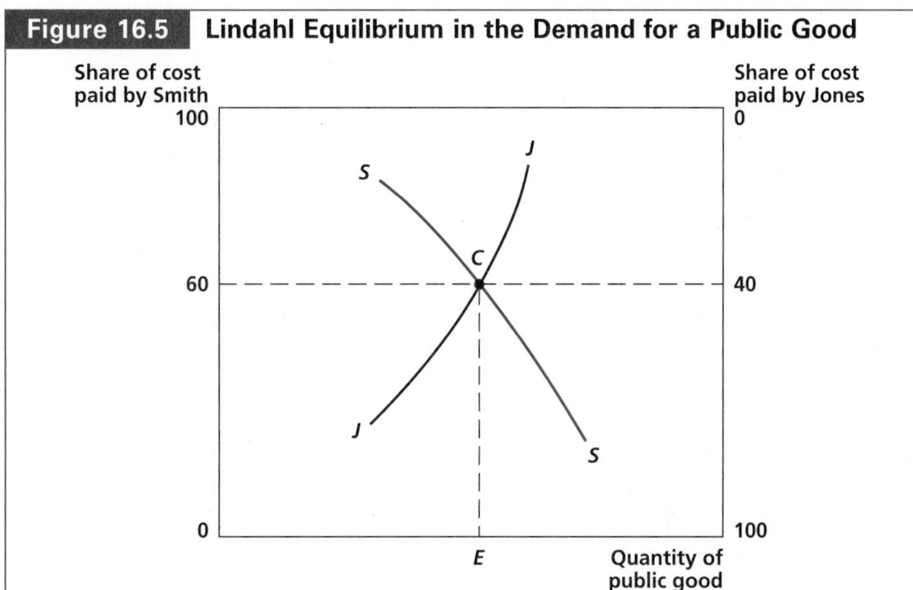

The curve *SS* shows that Smith's demand for a public good increases as the tax share that Smith must pay falls. Jones's demand curve for the public good (*JJ*) is constructed in a similar way. The point *C* represents a Lindahl equilibrium at which 0*E* of the public good is supplied, with Smith paying 60 percent of the cost. Any other quantity of the public good is not an equilibrium since either too much or too little funding would be available.

Lindahl equilibrium Balance between people's demand for public goods and the tax shares that each must pay for them.

for output level $0E$ is there a **Lindahl equilibrium** where the tax shares precisely pay for the level of public good production undertaken by the government.

Not only does this allocation of tax responsibilities result in an equilibrium in people's demands for public goods, but it is also possible to show that this equilibrium is efficient. The tax shares introduced in Lindahl's solution to the public goods problem play the role of "pseudo prices" that mimic the functioning of a competitive price system in achieving efficiency. Unfortunately, for reasons we now examine, this solution is not a particularly practical one.

16-8 Revealing the Demand for Public Goods

Although the Lindahl equilibrium is efficient, computation of the optimal tax shares requires knowledge of individuals' demands for public goods. A major problem is how to get people to reveal those demands. In usual market transactions, people reveal their demands by either choosing to buy or not to buy a given product. If someone really likes Steven Spielberg movies, he or she reveals that by renting them. By declining to rent Oliver Stone films, he or she reveals that they are not worth the price. Getting people to reveal their demands for public goods is much more difficult, however, because of the free-rider problem. If each person knows that his or her tax share will be based on his or her personal demand for public goods, there is a clear incentive to try to hide this true demand. Of course, the government may try any number of clever schemes to try to induce people to show their true preferences; but, often, this proves to be a very frustrating task. Application 16.6: Fund Raising on Public Broadcasting describes one such situation that is probably very familiar to many of you. In the end, any government will probably have to depart from the Lindahl ideal and resort to more pragmatic ways of determining how much will be spent on public goods.

Local Public Goods

Some economists believe that the problem of revealing the demand for public goods may be more tractable on a local than on a national level.[11] Because people are relatively free to move from one locality to another, they may indicate their preferences for local public goods by choosing to live in communities that offer them utility-maximizing public-goods taxation packages. "Voting with one's feet" provides a mechanism for revealing demand for public goods in much the same way that "dollar voting" reveals demand for private goods. People who want high-quality schools or a high level of police protection can "pay" for them by choosing to live in highly taxed communities. Those who prefer not to receive such benefits can choose to live elsewhere. These observations suggest that some decentralization of government functions may be desirable.

16-9 Voting for Public Goods

Voting is used to decide questions about the production and financing of public goods in many institutions. In some instances, people vote directly on policy questions. That is the case in New England town meetings and many statewide referenda (such as those discussed later in Application 16.7) and for many of the public policies adopted in

[11]See C. M. Tiebout, "A Pure Theory of Local Expenditures," *Journal of Political Economy* (October 1956): 416–424.

APPLICATION 16.7

Referenda on Limiting Public Spending

In recent years, many states have passed tax-limitation statutes, and several constitutional amendments have been proposed to serve the same purpose at the federal level. Here we look at the forces behind such laws.

California's Proposition 13

The tax-limitation idea largely originated in California with the passage of Proposition 13 in 1977. This ballot initiative, which passed by a two-to-one margin, required that property in California be taxed at a maximum rate of 1 percent of the 1975 fair-market value and imposed sharp limits on tax increases in future years. It resulted in a decline in local property tax revenues of nearly 60 percent between fiscal 1978 and 1979.

Two hypotheses have been proposed to explain why voters demanded such a drastic change in policy. The first views Proposition 13 as a demand for changing the sources of local tax revenues. Under this view, citizens were largely content with the existing levels of local services but wanted state tax sources (primarily income and sales tax) to take over a larger share of the burden, particularly to finance public schools. A second hypothesis views Proposition 13 as a statement by voters that local government had grown too large and that voters wished to see a cutback. Extensive research on Proposition 13 finds support for both of these propositions.[1] California voters did raise other state taxes after Proposition 13 was passed. But there is also evidence that spending is significantly lower than it would have been in the absence of Proposition 13. Outcomes such as government employment and the wages of government employees also seem to have been curtailed.

Massachusetts and Michigan

Evidence from studies of other tax-limitation initiatives tends to be somewhat contradictory as to voters' motivations. For example, Ladd and Wilson used personal survey data to examine voter patterns in Massachusetts in connection with the 1980 passage of "Proposition 2 1/2"—a proposal very similar to Proposition 13.[2] Consistent with the California studies, they also found evidence to contradict the notion that voters simply wanted to shift the source of local revenues (say, from the property tax to the income tax). But voters feared the loss of "vital" services (especially schools) and did not seem to want large cutbacks. Instead, they preferred "greater efficiency" in government but seemed to be quite vague as to what actual policies that might require. Similar conclusions have been obtained by studying voters' opinions in connection with voting on many other state-tax-limitation referenda. Voters seem quite willing to entertain limits on taxes but seldom have specific suggestions on where spending should be cut. There is some evidence that voters are more willing to limit local and state taxes if expenditures on schools and public safety (typically the largest items in the budget) can be maintained.

Home Rule in Illinois

A study of the decisions of communities in Illinois to adopt "Home Rule," thereby eliminating state-level restrictions on spending, sheds additional light on voters' motivations.[3] In this case, the author shows that more heterogeneous communities seem to prefer to keep restrictions on local spending, whereas those communities with more homogeneous populations are willing to forsake the restrictions. An interpretation of this finding is that, as Tiebout's model of local public goods suggests, members of relatively homogeneous communities may have similar views about the proper size and functions of government. But, in heterogeneous communities, voters fear that those favoring spending will get the upper hand. These voters therefore feel the need for some sort of outside constraint.

TO THINK ABOUT

1. Since World War II, the fraction of GDP devoted to government has risen substantially in virtually every Western country. How do you explain this rise? Is this an accurate reflection of changing demands for public goods, or is it a reflection of a structural tendency toward greater public spending in democracies?
2. Two kinds of tax "limitation" provisions have been proposed at the national level in the United States: (1) a balanced-budget requirement, and (2) a limitation on the fraction of GDP devoted to government spending. Does the analysis of this chapter provide any reasons for thinking that either of these might be a good idea?

[1] See "Forum on Proposition 13," *National Tax Journal* (March 1999): 99–138.

[2] H. Ladd and J. B. Wilson, "Why Voters Support Tax Limitations—Proposition 21/2," *National Tax Journal* (June 1982): 127–148.

[3] J. A. Temple, "Community Composition and Voter Support for Tax Limitations: Evidence from Home-Rule Elections," *Southern Economic Journal* (April 1996): 1002–1016.

people they have chosen to represent them. As was the case in the situations we studied in Chapter 15, agents may be able to take advantage of the informational asymmetries between themselves and the principals they represent (here, the voters) in ways that increase their own utility but distort the allocation of resources away from the voters' true demands for public goods. Hence, just as private markets may fail to provide efficient allocations in the presence of public goods, so too may governments fail in the provision of such goods. For example, many economics actors may find it in their interests to use the government to obtain monopoly gains for themselves that would not otherwise be obtainable without government help. They may, for example, enlist the government's aid in limiting competition in their markets or they may seek spending that benefits them alone. Through such **rent-seeking behavior** they may be able to get governmental agents to distort the allocations of resources away from what the voters would actually prefer if their preferences could be measured directly. To study all of the ways in which this might happen would, however, take us far beyond the intended subject matter of this book.

Rent-seeking behavior
Firms or individuals influencing government policy to increase their own welfare.

SUMMARY

We began this chapter with a demonstration of the misallocation of resources that may be created by an externality. We then proceeded to look at a number of consequences of this observation.

- When transactions costs are low and property rights are fully specified, no governmental intervention may be required to cope with an externality. Private negotiations between the parties may result in an efficient allocation regardless of how the property rights are assigned (the Coase theorem).
- Some externalities, such as those associated with environmental pollution, involve high transactions costs. In this case, legal redress or governmental intervention may be required to achieve an efficient allocation (although intervention does not guarantee such a result).
- The traditional method for correcting the allocational harm of an externality, first proposed by A. C. Pigou, is to impose an optimal tax on the economic agent creating the externality.
- Environmental regulation can proceed through the use of fees, pollution permits, or direct control. In the simplest case, these can have identical out-comes. In actuality, however, the incentives incorporated under each may yield quite different results.
- Pure public goods have the property of nonexclusivity and nonrivalry—once the good is produced, no one can be excluded from receiving the benefits it provides, but additional people may benefit from the good at zero cost. These properties pose a problem for private markets because people will not freely choose to purchase public goods in economically efficient amounts. Resources may be underallocated to public goods.
- In theory, compulsory taxation can be used to provide public goods in efficient quantities by charging taxpayers what the goods are worth to each of them. However, measuring this demand may be very difficult because each person has an incentive to act as a free rider by understating his or her demands.
- Direct voting may produce paradoxical results. However, in some cases, majority rule will result in the choice of policies favored by the median voter.

REVIEW QUESTIONS

1. If one firm raises the costs of another firm by bidding against it for its inputs, that is not an externality by our definition. But, if a firm raises the costs of another firm by polluting the environment, that is an externality. Explain the distinction between these two situations. Why does the second lead to an inefficient allocation of resources but the first does not?
2. Our general definition of economic efficiency focuses on mutually beneficial transactions. Explain why the presence of externalities may result in some mutually beneficial transactions being forgone. Illustrate these using Figure 16.1.
3. The proof of the Coase theorem requires that firms recognize both the explicit and implicit costs of their decision. Explain a situation where a firm's failure to curtail pollution may cause it to incur implicit costs. Why is the assumption of zero bargaining costs crucial if the firm is to take account of these costs?

4. Explain why the level of emissions control R^* in Figure 16.3 is economically efficient. Why would the levels of abatement given by R_L and R_H result in inefficiency? What kinds of inefficient trades would be occurring at these levels of abatement?
5. Figure 16.3 shows that an emissions fee can be chosen that attains the same level of pollution reduction as does direct control. Explain why firms would make the same choices under either control method. Would this equivalence necessarily hold if government regulators did not know the true marginal costs of emissions control?
6. For each of the following goods, explain whether it possesses the nonexclusive property, the nonrival property, or both. If the good does not have the characteristics of a public good but is, nevertheless, produced by the government, can you explain why?
   a. Television receivers
   b. Over-the-air television transmissions
   c. Cable television transmissions
   d. Elementary education
   e. College education
   f. Electric power
   g. Delivery of first-class mail
   h. Low-income housing
7. The Lindahl solution to the public-goods problem promises economic efficiency on a voluntary basis. Why would each person voluntarily agree to the tax assessments determined under the Lindahl solution? What choice is he or she being asked to make?
8. Why is the "paradox of voting" a paradox? What, if anything, is undesirable about a voting scheme that cycles? How will issues be decided in such cases?
9. "Under perfect competition, voting with dollars achieves economic efficiency, but democratic voting (one person–one vote) offers no such promise." Do you agree? Why does the specification of one vote per person interfere with the ability to achieve economic efficiency?
10. Why would individuals or firms engage in rent-seeking behavior? How much will they spend on such behavior? How, specifically, can rent-seeking harm the allocation of resources?

PROBLEMS

16.1. Suppose a firm produces charcoal in a perfectly competitive charcoal industry where the price of charcoal is \$20 per ton. This particular firm, however, enjoys a competitive advantage over other firms because it is located on a scenic river that enables it to have relatively low production costs. Specifically, the firm's Total Costs are given by $TC(q) = 0.2q^2 + 200$ and its marginal costs by $MC(q) = 0.4q$ where q represents the firms charcoal output in tons per day.

a. What will the firm's daily output of charcoal be in this situation and how much will it earn in profits?
b. Suppose there is an eyeglass manufacturer downriver from this firm that incurs extra costs per day of $0.1q$ (where again q is the output of the charcoal firm). What are the social marginal costs of charcoal production and what is the socially optimal output level for this firm?
c. If the government wished to impose a tax on the charcoal firm to cause it to produce at the socially optimal level of output, what should that tax be (per ton of charcoal)?
d. If the government imposes that tax calculated in part c, will the charcoal firm continue to produce in this location?
e. Graph your solutions to this problem.

16.2. On the island of Pago-Pago, there are two lakes and 20 fishers. Each fisher gets to fish on either lake and expects to keep the average catch on that lake. On Lake X, the total number of fish caught is given by

$$F^X = 10L_X - \frac{1}{2}L_X^2,$$

where L_X is the number of fishers on the lake. The amount an additional fisher will catch is $MP_X = 10 - L_X$. For Lake Y, the relationship is

$$F^Y = 5L_Y.$$

a. Under this organization of society, what will the total number of fish caught be? Explain the nature of the externality in this equilibrium.
b. The chief of Pago-Pago, having once read an economics book, believes that she can raise the total number of fish caught by restricting the number of fishers allowed on Lake X. What is the correct number of fishers on Lake X to allow in order to maximize the total catch of fish? What is the number of fish caught in this situation?
c. Being basically opposed to coercion, the chief decides to require a fishing license for Lake X. If the licensing procedure is to bring about the optimal allocation of labor, what should the cost of a license be (in terms of fish)?

16.3. Suppose that the oil industry in Utopia is perfectly competitive and that all firms draw oil from a single (and practically inexhaustible) pool. Each competitor believes that he or she can sell all the oil he or she can produce at a stable world price of \$100 per barrel and that the cost of operating a well for one year is \$10,000.

Total output per year (Q) of the oil field is a function of the number of wells (N) operating in the field. In particular,

$$Q = 500N - N^2$$

and the amount of oil produced by each well (q) is given by

$$q = \frac{Q}{N} = 500 - N.$$

The output from the Nth well is given by

$$MP_N = 500 - 2N.$$

a. Describe the equilibrium output and the equilibrium number of wells in this perfectly competitive case. Is there a divergence between private and social marginal cost in the industry?
b. Suppose that the government nationalizes the oil field. How many oil wells should it operate? What will total output be? What will the output per well be?
c. As an alternative to nationalization, the Utopian government is considering an annual license fee per well to discourage over drilling. How large should this license fee be to prompt the industry to drill the optimal number of wells?

16.4. Mr. Wile E. Coyote purchases a variety of equipment with which to catch roadrunners. Invariably he finds that the equipment fails to work as promised. For example, the Acme Road Runner Rocket he purchased misfired and pushed him backward over a steep cliff, the Acme Flamethrower only singed his whiskers, and the Acme spring-mounted net ended up capturing him instead of the roadrunner.

a. Show how the Coase theorem would apply to transactions between predators and companies manufacturing roadrunner-catching equipment. In the full information case, would the equipment have efficient operating characteristics regardless of how legal liability is defined?
b. Many predators, including Mr. Coyote, are rather careless in how they use their equipment. If this carelessness is not affected by assignment of legal liability and if it is fully understood by producers, would its presence change your answer to part a?
c. Suppose predators became even more careless when they knew manufacturers would have legal liability for any injuries. How would this affect your answer to part a?
d. Assume that a single firm (the Acme Manufacturing Company) has a monopoly in the supply of roadrunner-catching equipment. How, if at all, would this change your answer to part a?

Note: (This question was motivated by the great comic essay by Ian Frazier, *Coyote v. Acme*, New York: Farrar, Straus and Giroux, 1996.)

16.5. As an illustration of the apple-bee externality, suppose that a beekeeper is located next to a 20-acre apple orchard. Each hive of bees is capable of pollinating 1/4 acre of apple trees, thereby raising the value of apple output by \$25.

a. Suppose the market value of the honey from one hive is \$50 and that the beekeeper's marginal costs are given by

$$MC = 30 + .5Q,$$

where Q is the number of hives employed. In the absence of any bargaining, how many hives will the beekeeper have and what portion of the apple orchard will be pollinated?
b. What is the maximum amount per hive the orchard owner would pay as a subsidy to the beekeeper to prompt him or her to install extra hives? Will the owner have to pay this much to prompt the beekeeper to use enough hives to pollinate the entire orchard?

16.6. A government study has concluded that the marginal benefits from controlling cow-induced methane production are given by

$$MB = 100 - R,$$

where R represents the percentage reduction from unregulated levels. The marginal cost to farmers of methane reduction (through better cow feed) is given by

$$MC = 20 + R.$$

a. What is the socially optimal level of methane reduction?
b. If the government were to adopt a methane fee that farmers must pay for each percent of methane they do not reduce, how should this fee be set to achieve the optimal level of R?
c. Suppose there are two farmers in this market with differing costs of methane reduction. The first has marginal costs given by

$$MC_1 = 20 + \frac{2}{3}R_1,$$

whereas the second has marginal costs given by

$$MC_2 = 20 + 2R_2.$$

Total methane reduction is the average from these two farms. If the government mandates that each farm reduce methane by the optimal percentage calculated in part a, what will the overall reduction be and what will this reduction cost (assuming there are no fixed costs to reducing g methane)?

d. Suppose, instead, that the government adopts the methane fee described in part b. What will be the total reduction in methane and what will this reduction cost?

e. Explain why part c and part d yield different results.

16.7. Suppose there are only two people in society. The demand curve for person *A* for mosquito control is given by

$$q_A = 100 - P.$$

For person *B*, the demand curve for mosquito control is given by

$$q_B = 200 - P.$$

a. Suppose mosquito control is a nonexclusive good—that is, once it is produced everyone benefits from it. What would be the optimal level of this activity if it could be produced at a constant marginal cost of \$50 per unit?

b. If mosquito control were left to the private market, how much might be produced? Does your answer depend on what each person assumes the other will do?

c. If the government were to produce the optimal amount of mosquito control, how much would this cost? How should the tax bill for this amount be allocated between the individuals if they are to share it in proportion to benefits received from mosquito control?

16.8. Suppose there are three people in society who vote on whether the government should undertake specific projects. Let the net benefits of a particular project be \$150, \$140, and \$50 for persons *A*, *B*, and *C*, respectively.

a. If the project costs \$300 and these costs are to be shared equally, would a majority vote to undertake the project? What would be the net benefits to each person under such a scheme? Would total net benefits be positive?

b. Suppose the project cost \$375 and again costs were to be shared equally. Now would a majority vote for the project and total net benefits be positive?

c. Suppose (presumably contrary to fact) votes can be bought and sold in a free market. Describe what kinds of results you might expect in part a and part b.

16.9. The town of Pleasantville is thinking of building a swimming pool. Building and operating the pool will cost the town \$5,000 per day. There are three groups of potential pool users in Pleasantville: (1) 1,000 families who are each willing to pay \$3 per day for the pool, (2) 1,000 families who are each willing to pay \$2 per day for the pool, and (3) 1,000 families who are each willing to pay \$1 per day for the pool. Suppose also that the intended pool is large enough so that whatever number of families come on any day will not affect what people are willing to pay for the pool.

a. Which property of public goods does this pool have? Which does it not have?

b. Would building the pool be an efficient use of resources?

c. Consider four possible prices for family admission to the pool: (1) \$3, (2) \$2, (3) \$1, and (4) \$0. Which of these prices would result in covering the cost of the pool? Which of the prices would achieve an efficient allocation of resources?

d. Is there any pricing scheme for admission to this pool that would both cover the pool's cost and achieve an efficient allocation of resources?

e. Suppose that this pool has a capacity of only 2,000 families per day. If more than 2,000 families are admitted, the willingness to pay of any family (with children or not) falls to \$0.50 per day. Now what is the efficient pricing scheme for the pool?

16.10. The demand for gummy bears is given by

$$Q = 200 - 100P$$

and these confections can be produced at a constant marginal cost of \$0.50.

a. How much will Sweettooth, Inc., be willing to pay in bribes to obtain a monopoly concession from the government for gummy bear production?

b. Do the bribes represent a welfare cost from rent seeking?

c. What is the welfare cost of this rent-seeking activity?

17 Behavioral Economics

Neoclassical economics
Assumes fully rational maximizing behavior.

The entire book so far has adopted the perspective of **neoclassical economics**. An economic agent—whether a consumer, firm, or player in a soccer game for that matter—was assumed to make fully rational decisions. To the best of the agent's knowledge, these decisions maximized the agent's payoffs (utility, profit, or goal scoring in different instances). This is not to say that we always assumed agents had perfect information about the economic environment. A homeowner who could foresee that his or her house would not suffer fire, flood, or other damage could have saved money by not purchasing homeowners' insurance, but not knowing in advance whether an accident would occur, the correct decision might have been to buy insurance. In cases involving uncertainty, our previous analysis assumed that agents maximize *expected* payoffs.

Behavioral economics
Study of economic behavior that departs from full rationality.

One of the major areas of active research in economics recognizes that economic agents may not behave as perfectly rational, calculating machines, which maximize payoffs or expected payoffs. They may sometimes make mistakes in their calculations. They may have other psychological biases that may lead them to make decisions that do not maximize their payoffs (at least if measured by monetary payoffs). This new area of research is called **behavioral economics** because, rather than taking fully rational behavior for granted, it tries to measure how rational behavior actually is and why it falls short of full rationality when it does. This branch of research seeks to integrate the insights and methods of psychology into economics. Two of the pioneers in this area of economics, Daniel Kahneman and Amos Tversky, were in fact psychologists by training, although the economics profession claimed them as their own with the awarding of the Nobel Prize in economics in 2002.[1] This chapter will provide an introduction to the work of Kahneman, Tversky, and other contributors to this exploding area of research.

17-1 Should We Abandon Neoclassical Economics?

There is obvious appeal in seeking to understand how agents actually make decisions instead of assuming decisions are made in some idealized, perfectly rational way. Should we abandon the neoclassical economics entirely in favor of a behavioral perspective? Have we then wasted the past 16 chapters studying the rational model? We better have good answers to those questions, and the answers better be "no"!

First, neoclassical models, whether applied to consumers, firms, or soccer players, have provided adequate predictions of behavior, certainly better than no model at all. Of course, these models could always stand to be improved by the addition of realistic psychological elements. In the meantime, as these models are improved and integrated in the standard ones, the standard models will continue to be of value.

[1]Tversky died before receiving the Nobel Prize.

Second, idealized rational behavior may provide a benchmark toward which actual decisions tend as the decision maker experiments over time with different decisions and learns more about the economic environment. The neoclassical model may fare poorly as a predictor of instinctive decisions made in unfamiliar surroundings but may perform better as a predictor of long-run behavior by experienced agents. Market forces may put some discipline on mistakes made by firms: those that make too many mistakes or are run by managers suffering from severe biases may go out of business after a while. However, it is a question for empirical research which models, neoclassical or behavioral, perform better and over what time frame.

Third, even if actual behavior falls short of the ideal in the long run, still the ideal of fully rational behavior can provide a standard against which we can compare actual behavior. It is hard to speak of a "bias" unless one has a standard of comparison.

Fourth, the neoclassical model provides considerable discipline in modeling economic situations. Just as a test question might have a million wrong answers but just one right one, so there may be a million possible biases but just one way to act rationally. Rather than looking for a deep explanation for a particular behavior, the tendency might be to attribute the behavior to a bias that fits that particular circumstance but cannot be generalized beyond. Of course, as behavioral economics continues to mature, this disadvantage will continue to be reduced as the knowledge gained about the psychology of economic decisions continues to be consolidated into a few general propositions with predictive power across different settings.

17-2 Limits to Human Decision Making: An Overview

The general theme that connects the findings in behavioral economics is that the ability of humans to make payoff-maximizing decisions may be limited. These limits fall into three areas:

- limited cognitive ability
- limited willpower
- limited self-interest.[2]

The rest of the chapter will be organized around this classification.

To provide a preview of what will come, the first limit relates to complex decisions or decisions that require some calculations. Decisions involving uncertainty, for example, require the person to be able to work with probabilities and expected values. Decisions about investments may require the person to understand formulas for present discounted values. A perfect calculating machine could quickly perform the required calculations and make the right decisions. A real person may make mistakes in performing complex calculations or may avoid the calculations entirely and instead rely on an educated guess.

[2]This classification of behavioral economics is due to R. Thaler and S. Mullainathan, "Behavioral Economics," in N. Smelser and P. Baltes, eds., *International Encyclopedia of Social Sciences* (New York: Elsevier, 2001): 1094–1100. Other useful surveys include one focusing on the application of behavioral economics to financial markets: N. Barberis and R. Thaler, "A Survey of Behavioral Finance," in G. Constandinides, M. Harris, and R. Stulz, eds., *Handbook of the Economics of Finance* (New York: Elsevier, 2003): 1051–1121; one providing a general overview that highlights evidence from field experiments: S. DellaVigna, "Psychology and Economics: Evidence from the Field," *Journal of Economic Literature* (June 2009): 315–372; and one looking at biological bases for behavioral economics: C. Camerer, G. Loewenstein, and D. Prelec, "Neuroeconomics: How Neuroscience Can Inform Economics," *Journal of Economic Literature* (March 2005): 9–64.

We will study whether the resulting decisions tend to be right on average, involving only infrequent and random mistakes, or whether the decisions are consistently biased in certain directions. Will self-aware people realize their potential for mistakes and take steps to reduce problems arising from them? Will market forces tend to amplify or reduce the consequences of cognitive mistakes?

We will then go on to study the second limitation: limits to human willpower. These limits are important for dynamic decisions, that is, decisions involving some sort of timing element where actions taken up front may have longer term implications. For example, at the beginning of the week, a student may make plans for how much he or she will study for a test at the end of the week. When the time comes, the lure of television or video games may be too strong, and he or she may abandon the plans to study. After, the student may even regret having not studied. Such self-control problems may arise in many contexts including diet, exercise, smoking, saving, and so forth. We present one model of self-control problems in which people weigh their well-being more when they are living in the moment than when they were planning ahead for it.

Finally, we will turn to the third human limitation: limits to human self-interest. Humans may not just care about their own payoffs, income, or consumption; they may care about others as well. Certainly, this is not a completely foreign concept for standard economics to handle. Economists have long been modeling and studying altruistic behavior, for example, the sacrifices that a parent may make for a child or other family member or acts of charity. This simple form of altruism is fairly easy to capture in standard models. Others' well-being may be just another good that a consumer can purchase along with hamburgers, televisions, etc. There are more complex interpersonal values that may be difficult for standard models to capture, and here is where behavioral economics comes in. People may care not just about the income or consumption levels that they and others end up with. They may get direct utility from broader social goals such as fairness and justice. Whether you want to be kind or nasty to someone else may not be predetermined but might depend on whether they were kind or nasty to you previously. We will try to integrate these interpersonal values into our model of decision making. These values matter most in strategic settings—the purview of game theory. We will see at the end of the chapter then how these broader concerns might lead us to modify the game-theoretic analysis from Chapter 5.

17-3 Limited Cognitive Power

An old story tells of a queen who wanted to reward a hero for slaying a dragon. Reflecting her interest in puzzles, the queen offers him the choice of one of two prizes. The first is to receive \$100,000 each day for a month. The second is to receive an amount of money that doubles in size each day starting from a penny, so it is worth one penny the first day, two pennies the second, four the next, and so on for a month. Which should the hero choose? In one sense, this is a simple economic choice. There are no tradeoffs involved; the hero should opt for whichever prize involves more money. However, the underlying math problem is somewhat difficult. Assuming the month has 31 days, the first prize is worth $31 \times \$100{,}000 = \$3.1$ million. The hero chooses

1. Use a calculator to verify the value of the second prize offered by the queen.
2. Suppose the queen offers a third prize. This prize starts at \$10,000 on the first day, doubling every other day over a 31-day month. Before doing any calculations, guess whether the hero should choose this prize. Check your guess by calculating the exact prize value.

this because the second prize, involving only pennies at first, does not seem like it will amount to much. The hero has been tricked, though. The formula for the value of the second prize is $2^{30}/100$, which one can show with a calculator is over $10 million. Therefore, the second prize would be the rational choice. The hero ends up giving up millions of dollars by making the wrong choice. (He still comes away with more than $3 million, so don't feel too bad for him.)

The queen was able to play a trick on the hero because she realized that most people are unfamiliar with **exponential growth** processes, such as doubling each day.[3] They are more familiar with simple linear trends that grow much more slowly. Without calculators, which presumably were not around in the hero's time, the rules of thumb that people use lead them to underestimate the rate of exponential growth. Although the story of the queen and hero is fictional, as noted in Application 17.1: Household Finance, the trick is used today by financial companies to get consumers to borrow at above-market rates and save at below-market rates.

Exponential growth
A doubling or other proportionate increase each period.

Humans are not computers. Limited cognition impairs people's ability to make the "right" economic decision, whether choosing the biggest prize in the queen's puzzle or making the other economic decisions we will go on to study. Limited cognitive powers will be increasingly strained the more complex the decision. Any of the following factors could add to this complexity:

- complicated formulas involved such as exponential growth
- uncertainty
- overwhelming number of choices
- multiple steps of reasoning required.

Faced with decisions requiring high levels of cognition but unable to perform these exercises with computer-like accuracy, humans will necessarily resort to short cuts and rules of thumb. These might be accurate in some settings and inaccurate in others. Behavioral economists have worked hard to uncover what these rules of thumb are and to determine when they produce poor decisions and when they do not. The next few sections will study each of the complicating factors on bulleted list in more detail.

Uncertainty

Decisions made under uncertainty involve many complications. In the famous example of the Allais Paradox, the following choices between gambles are offered:

> **Allais Scenario 1:** Choose between the following two gambles. Gamble *A* offers an 89% chance of winning $1,000, a 10% chance of winning $5,000, and a 1% chance of winning nothing. Gamble *B* provides $1,000 with certainty.
>
> **Allais Scenario 2:** Choose between the following two gambles. Gamble *C* offers an 89% chance of winning nothing and an 11% chance of winning $1,000. Gamble *D* offers a 90% chance of winning nothing and a 10% chance of winning $5,000.

Before doing any math, which choice would you make in each scenario? Maurice Allais, the economist after whom the paradox is named, posited (and subsequent

[3]The Appendix to Chapter 14 contains an extensive discussion of exponential growth as it applies to interest-rate calculations.

APPLICATION 17.1

Household Finance

Managing a household's finances seems like a simple task at first glance, but a closer look reveals substantial complexity. How much should parents save each year for their children's future college expenses? How much should they save for retirement and where should they invest the savings—a bank certificate of deposit, the stock market, or gold? Economists have investigated whether the average person is equipped with the basic math skills to answer such questions, whether people use those skills to plan for the future, and how close those plans come to what an expert financial advisor would suggest.

Financial Literacy

To test whether people have the basic math skills to make simple financial decisions, a survey asked questions such as the following: A bank account that pays 10% interest is opened with $200. How much would you have in the account after two years? Although readers of this book wouldn't have much difficulty with this question, the study found less than one fifth of the respondents answered it correctly.[1] Without outside help (learning from smart neighbors, hiring expert financial planners, or reading good books on the subject), these results suggest that the average household may have trouble making the right financial decisions.

Retirement Planning

Further evidence from this study suggests that rather than seeking outside help for financial decisions, most people just throw up their hands. Among older respondents for whom retirement is a more salient issue, only a third had considered how much money they would need for retirement, and less than a fifth had come up with a savings plan. Financially literate respondents were better planners, and the better planners had accumulated more retirement wealth, even accounting for all the other characteristics (education, income, etc.) that might affect planning and wealth. Financial literacy appears to be a useful life skill that is perhaps too rare in the population.

Car Loans

There is a common thread linking the difficulty the hero had in selecting the right prize offered by the queen in the text and the difficulty four fifths of the respondents had in answering the bank-account question above. Both calculations deal with compound growth, which is badly underestimated by the linear approximations people tend to use.

Victor Stango and Jonathan Zinman show that for any given stream of loan repayments, this bias in people's thinking leads them to underestimate the implied annual percentage interest rate (APR).[2] Lenders have an incentive to fool consumers into taking high-interest rate loans for automobiles and other purchases by advertising low monthly payments. This strategy works because the same bias that makes the hero underestimate compound growth also makes borrowers underestimate how quickly loan principal balances decline. For example, for a five-year loan of $10,000, the average principal balance over the life of the loan is only about $5,000 because some principal is paid back with each monthly installment. The authors found that consumers who underestimated interest rates in hypothetical questions the most carried loans with worse terms (higher APRs) than others. What is more interesting is that they received the relatively higher APRs exactly when the government's enforcement of truth-in-lending regulations (requiring lenders to quote APRs in advertisements) was lax. One might think competition would drive high-interest lenders out of the market, but the complexity of loans (specifying monthly payments, interest rates, and repayment periods) may allow lenders to shroud high rates, making it hard for consumers to comparison shop.

POLICY CHALLENGE

One symptom of the recent U.S. economic crisis is the growing number of late mortgage payments and home foreclosures. Some blame predatory lenders, who induced naïve consumers to sign complicated contracts (involving adjustable rates, balloon payments, and other features) with unfavorable terms that the consumers did not understand. Read some newspaper accounts of the Mortgage Reform and Anti–Predatory Lending Act, introduced into the U.S. House of Representatives in March 2009. What are potential costs and benefits of this bill? How much of the foreclosure problem can be attributed to consumer naiveté versus an unexpected decline in economic conditions?

[1] A. Lusardi and O. S. Mitchell, "Baby Boomer Retirement Security: The Roles of Planning, Financial Literacy, and Housing Wealth," *Journal of Monetary Economics* (January 2007): 205–224.

[2] V. Stango and J. Zinman, "Fuzzy Math, Disclosure Regulation, and Market Outcomes: Evidence from Truth-in-Lending Reform," *Review of Financial Studies* (February 2011): 506–534.

experiments have shown) that most people would choose gamble B over A and D over C.[4] In the first scenario, people seem to prefer the sure thing; in the second scenario, since there is no sure thing and the probabilities are fairly close, people seem to go for the higher amount.

In fact, this set of responses involves an inconsistency. The subject prefers B to A if the expected utility from B exceeds that from A:

$$U(1{,}000) > .89\,U(1{,}000) + .1\,U(5{,}000) + .01\,U(0), \tag{17.1}$$

where we have used the formula for expected values reviewed in Chapter 4. For D to be preferred to C,

$$.9\,U(0) + .1\,U(5{,}000) > .89\,U(0) + .11\,U(1{,}000). \tag{17.2}$$

However, Equation 17.1 reduces to $.11\,U(1{,}000) > .1\,U(5{,}000) + .01\,U(0)$, whereas (17.2) leads to the reverse inequality, so the two conditions are inconsistent.

One explanation offered by behavioral economics for this inconsistency is that people find it difficult to think through the expected-value formula. In particular, they have trouble when small probabilities are involved, tending to overweight them, perhaps because they are more used to using the formula for a simple average in which all numbers receive equal weight. This might explain why people tend not to like gamble A if they mistakenly put too much weight on the very slim (1%) chance of getting nothing.

In a set of experiments run by Kahneman and Tversky, different groups of subjects were presented with one of the following two scenarios.[5]

> **Kahneman and Tversky Scenario 1:** In addition to \$1,000 up front, the subject must choose between two gambles. Gamble A offers an even chance of winning \$1,000 or nothing. Gamble B provides \$500 with certainty.
>
> **Kahneman and Tversky Scenario 2:** In addition to \$2,000 up front, the subject must choose between two gambles. Gamble C offers an even chance of losing \$1,000 or nothing. Gamble D results in the loss of \$500 with certainty.

The authors found 16% of subjects chose A in the first scenario, and 68% chose C in the second scenario. Although the two scenarios are framed in different ways (the first specifying winnings added to a smaller initial payment, the second losses relative to a larger initial payment), the allocations are identical across them. A and C both involve an even chance of gaining \$1,000 or \$2,000, and B and D both involve a certain total payment of \$1,500. Simply changing the way the choices are framed, which should be irrelevant from an economic standpoint, leads people to change their decisions.

One explanation is, again, that subjects make mistakes in the difficult calculations involved in decisions under uncertainty. All four gambles A through D provide

[4]M. Allais, "Le Comportement de l'Homme Rationnel devant le Risque: Critique des Postulats et Axiomes de l'École Américaine," *Econometrica* (October 1953): 503–546.

[5]D. Kahneman and A. Tversky, "Prospect Theory: An Analysis of Decision under Risk," *Econometrica* (March 1979): 263–291.

> **MICRO QUIZ 17.2**
>
> On a graph similar to Figure 17.1, demonstrate that the person with standard, risk-averse preferences would choose *B* or *D* over the other gambles in the two Kahneman and Tversky scenarios.

the same expected return ($1,500). A risk-averse subject should then choose the one with no risk (*B* or *D*). The people who chose *C* over *D* might have been confused by how the choice was framed and perhaps may not have computed final allocations correctly or at all.

Prospect Theory

Prospect theory Theory that people are very sensitive to small losses from current wealth.

Kahneman and Tversky took a different view. Rather than mistakes, the choices in the experiments reflected subjects' legitimate preferences, but preferences that do not fit the standard model. They proposed a new model, called **prospect theory**, the key ingredient of which is that people are very sensitive to small declines in their current wealth.

These preferences cannot arise with the standard utility functions we saw in Chapter 4, drawn again in (a) in Figure 17.1. People with standard preferences are essentially risk neutral for very small gambles and only become worried about risk for gambles involving big fluctuations in wealth.

Aversion to small gambles can be modeled by putting a kink in the utility function at the current wealth level (called the reference point *R*), as in (b) of Figure 17.1. The function's has a steeper slope to the left of *R* than to the right, so that small gains cannot compensate for small losses. The utility function flattens out moving further to the left of *R*, implying that people become less sensitive to large losses. When wealth changes, the utility function shifts, so that a new kink forms at the new level of wealth. The new wealth level establishes a new reference point. A person's utility is no longer just a function of final wealth, as with standard utility functions, but a function of the path (of gains and losses) by which he or she arrived at that final

Figure 17.1 Standard Preferences versus Prospect Theory

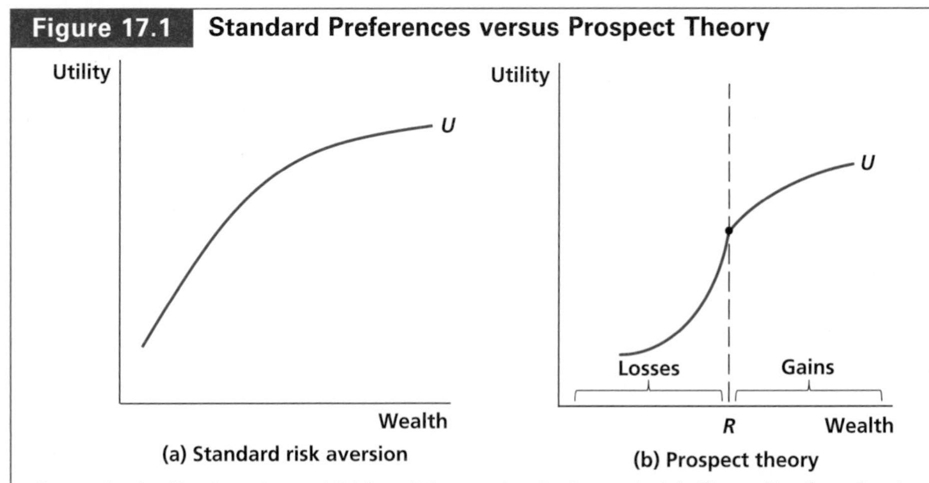

A standard utility function exhibiting risk-aversion is drawn in (a). The utility function in (b) illustrates prospect theory. The kink at *R* means that the person suffers more harm from small losses than benefits from small gains, although the sensitivity to larger losses diminishes as the curve becomes flatter as one moves left from *R*.

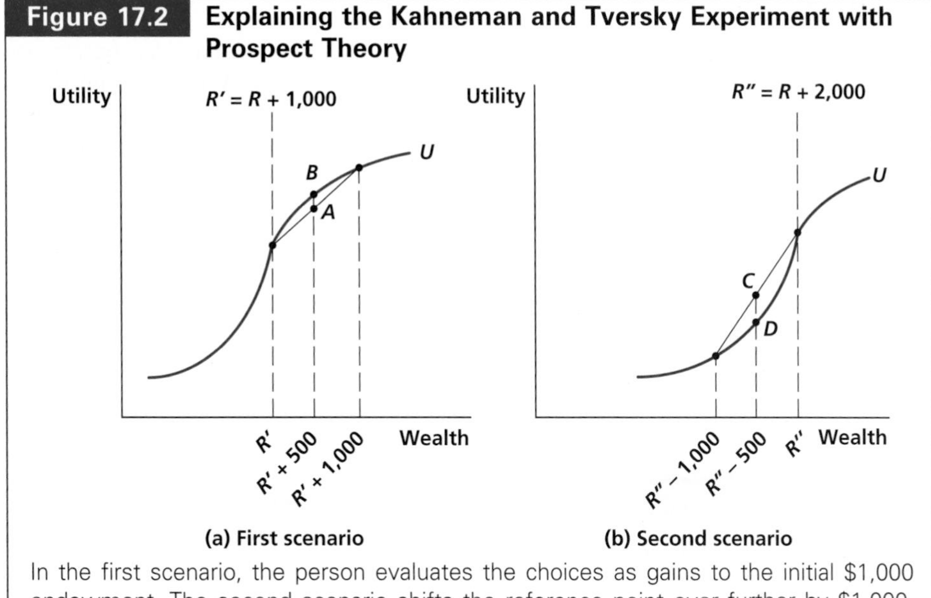

Figure 17.2 Explaining the Kahneman and Tversky Experiment with Prospect Theory

In the first scenario, the person evaluates the choices as gains to the initial \$1,000 endowment. The second scenario shifts the reference point over further by \$1,000, and now the changes are regarded as losses. The person prefers *B* to *A* in panel (a) and *C* to *D* in panel (b), even though *A* provides the same final allocation as *C*, and *B* provides the same final allocation as *D*.

wealth. Figure 17.2 shows how such a utility function can capture the results of Kahneman and Tversky's experiment. In the first scenario, drawn in (a), the initial payment of \$1,000 shifts the reference point to R'. The additional payments (\$1,000 with probability 1/2 with A and \$500 for certain with B) are perceived as gains. The person has standard preferences over gains. Given that both outcomes provide the same expected payment, the subject prefers the sure outcome (*B*) over the risky one (*A*). In the second scenario, shown in (b), the larger initial payment of \$2,000 shifts the reference point over even further to the right, so that the additional transfers are now perceived as losses. The certain prospect of losing \$500 is so painful to subjects that they would trade this for a smaller chance of losing a larger amount. This shows up on the graph as point *C*'s lying above point *D*.

There is a big debate in the economics literature about how best to approach choice anomalies such as revealed in the experiments of Allais or Kahneman and Tversky. Are these better modeled as mistakes, or are they legitimate, rational preferences that simply require us to rethink what it means to be rational? One empirical test is to see how subjects behave when they are allowed more time to become familiar with the choice setting, perhaps try out different choices, and learn with experience. If the subjects continue to exhibit the anomalous choices, then they are probably legitimate preferences. If they change to the rational choice, then the anomaly might have been a mistake.[6]

---

[6]We will say more about whether learning reduces behavioral biases later in the text. Regarding prospect theory, in experiments testing whether endowing a subject with a mug or a candy bar made them unwilling to give it up, John List found that only inexperienced market participants tended to behave according to prospect theory; experienced ones (in this case, dealers at card shows) had standard preferences. See John List, "Neoclassical Theory Versus Prospect Theory: Evidence from the Marketplace," *Econometrica* (March 2004): 615–625.

Framing

Kahneman and Tversky's experiment revealed that subjects' decisions can be affected simply by restating the same choice in two different ways. When a choice was expressed as a gain to a small initial endowment, people tended to make different decisions than when the same choice was expressed as a loss from a larger initial endowment. The phenomenon that small changes in the wording of choices can affect decisions, labeled a **framing effect**, has been found by psychologists and behavioral economists to apply very generally to many different areas of human decision making. Beef labeled 80% lean is preferred to that labeled 20% fat. Basketball players who make 52% of their shots are judged to be better than those missing 48%. Patients may opt for surgery with a 95% survival rate while avoiding a procedure with 5% chance of death.[7]

Framing effect
The same choice, presented in two different ways, leads to different decisions.

Overall, it appears that framing a choice around a positive attribute tends to bias people toward preferring that choice. The existence of framing effects poses a problem in economics because the theory tends to focus on real outcomes and does not have much to say about wording. Here is certainly an area where psychology can contribute to economics. Economists need to better understand such questions as when framing effects are strongest, whether people can be trained through experience to see through framing, and how framing effects can best be integrated into standard economic models.

According to a recent poll, 61% of citizens approve of an elected official's performance, and 39% disapprove.

1. How would a political supporter like to see these poll results reported?
2. How would a political enemy like to see these poll results reported?

Paradox of Choice

Let us turn to the next item on our list of factors complicating decision making. Economists tend to believe that more choices always make a person better off. The person is free to ignore choices he or she does not like, and some of the additional choices may end up being preferred.

Psychologists have pointed out that there may be an exception to this argument. If people are confronted by too many choices, they may simply shut down and not make any decision. The idea that more choices may make people worse off has been called the "paradox of choice."[8] One experiment that clearly illustrated the paradox was conducted in a grocery store. In one treatment, a table was set up with six different jars of jam to sample; in another, twenty-four jars. The experimenters found that consumers were more likely to purchase jam in the first treatment when only six were displayed. The experiment has been repeated in various settings, consistently showing that consumers enjoy the shopping experience less and purchase less when too many choices are offered.

Of course, it is tedious and complicated to sample and compare twenty-four different jars of jam. It is quite reasonable to think that one would be better off not buying jam than to sample each of twenty-four kinds. A better shopping strategy might be to

[7]For a survey of experiments on framing effects, see I. P. Levin, S. L. Schneider, and G. J. Gaeth, "All Frames Are Not Created Equal: A Typology and Critical Analysis of Framing Effects," *Organizational Behavior and Human Decision Processes* (November 1998): 149–188.

[8]B. Schwartz, *The Paradox of Choice: Why More Is Less* (New York: HarperCollins 2004).

Figure 17.3 Classifying Jams to Solve the Paradox of Choice

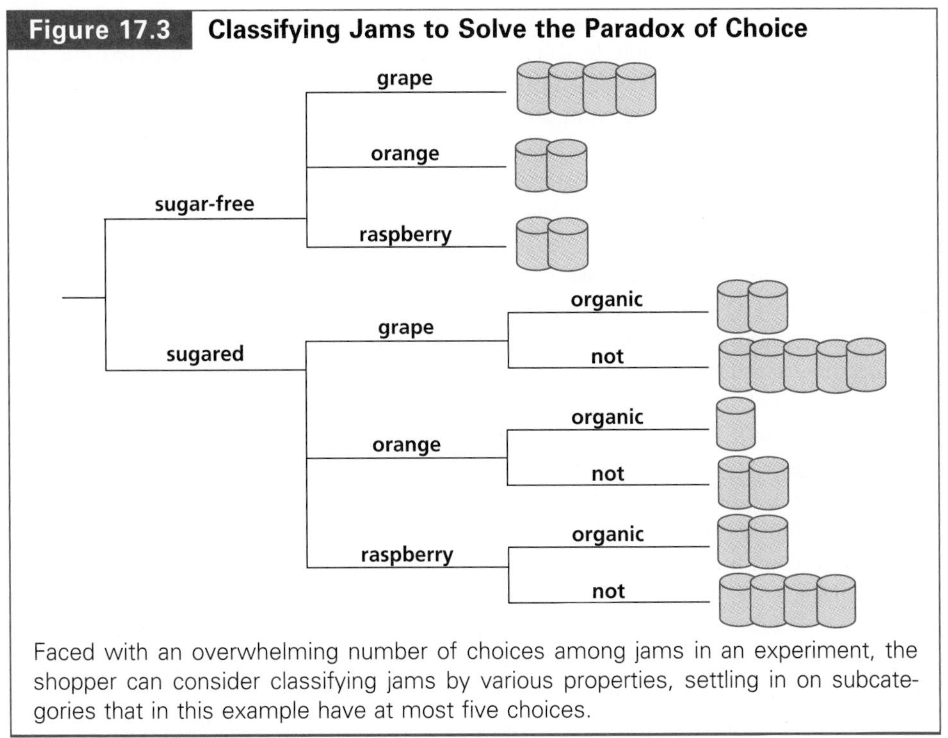

Faced with an overwhelming number of choices among jams in an experiment, the shopper can consider classifying jams by various properties, settling in on subcategories that in this example have at most five choices.

limit one's sampling to a manageable subset, perhaps as few as six as in the first treatment. This would keep the shopper from being worse off when offered more choices. However, selecting six jams to sample at random from twenty-four is not the same thing as being offered the original six to sample. The store might have chosen the best six to highlight, whereas a random six from twenty-four might not represent the best choices for consumers. Another strategy might be to categorize the jams, perhaps dividing the twenty-four jams into sugared and sugar-free categories, then into fruit subcategories, and so forth, finally sampling only among the small number that fall into the most promising subcategory as shown in Figure 17.3. Forming such a classification might take experience which shoppers might have for some products but not for others. For example, wine enthusiasts may be able to narrow down a choice among hundreds of bottles to two or three very quickly but may be at a loss when choosing among jams.

Multiple Steps in Reasoning

The final item on our list of possible limits to cognitive ability is the difficulty in thinking through many steps of reasoning involved in some complicated problems. This issue often comes up in games and other strategic situations.[9] Take the game of chess. If chess

[9]Multiple steps in reasoning may also be required for decision problems that are not strategic. In X. Gabaix, D. Laibson, G. Moloche, and S. Weinberg, "Costly Information Acquisition: Experimental Analysis of a Boundedly Rational Model," *American Economic Review* (September 2006): 1043–1068, experimental subjects were given a choice among gambles and allowed to learn, for a fee, whether or not each gamble was a "winner" in whatever order they liked. Figuring out the best order to learn about the gambles required subjects to think ahead several steps. Most subjects chose an order that was efficient when learning about just one gamble but inefficient if learning about several, suggesting that subjects were good at thinking ahead one step but not more.

were played by two supercomputers with limitless calculating power, it would not be much fun. Both would be able to think through all the possibilities and determine that the first mover would win, the second mover would win, or the game would end in a tie. Of course, such limitless supercomputers do not exist, and chess is complicated enough that our existing computers have not yet been able to "solve" it to find out how it should always play out. Chess is fun precisely because our cognitive limitations do not allow us to think through all the way to the end.

In Chapter 5 on game theory, the ability of players to think through a long chain of reasoning was important when we came to sequential games. Players who act first in such games need to anticipate how later movers would respond to their actions. Our assumption, implicit in the equilibrium concept we assumed—subgame-perfect equilibrium—was that players are perfectly able to think through how the game will play out. Everyone expects everyone else to play rationally whenever given the chance to move. For simple games such as the sequential Battle of the Sexes (see Figure 5.3), in which only two sequential decisions are made, and each only involves two actions (ballet or boxing), it is not unreasonable that the cognitive ability of players would not be strained by thinking through the game. More complicated games like chess obviously would strain cognition.

Although it is not as complicated as chess, the Centipede Game, shown in Figure 17.4, requires many steps of reasoning. The game has one hundred small stages (hence the name). At each stage, the player can choose to end the game (E) or allow it to continue (C). Players benefit from letting the game continue because payoffs for both players then accumulate. However, if a player is set to end the game in a given stage, the other has an incentive to preempt this by ending the game a stage before. For example, if player 2 ends the game in the second stage, player 1 earns 0, but would gain 1 by preempting and ending the game right at the start.

If players think to the end of the game, they will realize that player 2 should end the game before it reaches (100, 100) to get an extra bonus in the last stage. But then player 1 should end the game in the next-to-last stage. Continuing to extend this reason from the end to the beginning of the game shows that the outcome should be (this is the subgame-perfect

MICRO QUIZ 17.4

Instead of playing an equilibrium, suppose player 1 believes that 2 chooses C in the last stage with a certain probability. What would this probability have to be for 1 to choose C rather than E in the next-to-last stage?

Figure 17.4 Centipede Game

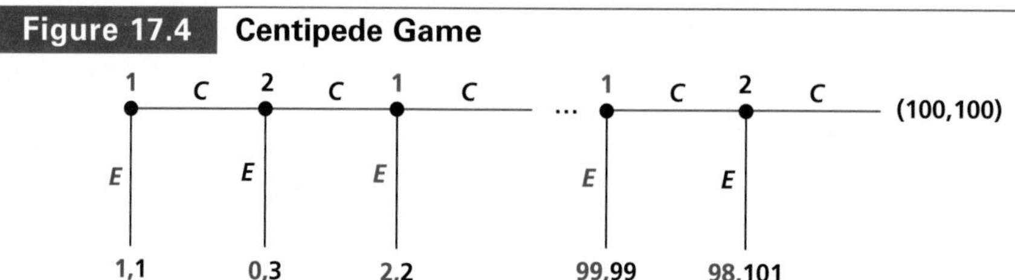

Players 1 and 2 alternative moves one hundred times, each time either ending the game with E or allowing it to continue with C. Payoffs in parentheses list player 1's first and then player 2's. In theory, each player should reason that the other will end the game, so they should end it themselves one step before. In the subgame-perfect equilibrium, player 1 ends the game with E immediately, and players earn very little. In experiments, subjects allow the game to go on for a while, allowing payoffs to accumulate.

equilibrium) for player 1 to end the game immediately, giving both a much lower payoff (1 each) than if the game ran to the end (100 each).

It might start to strain realism to think that the average player would be willing or able to think through the hundred steps of logic required to unravel the game, but this is to the benefit of the players because if the game does not end immediately but goes on for a while, payoffs for both accumulate. Even if one of the players, say player 1, is sophisticated enough to think it through perfectly, if he or she believes there is even a slight chance that the other is not so sophisticated to realize the game should end immediately, it may be worth the risk to let the game go on for a while. The risk is the small loss of 1 if player 2 chooses E immediately, but potential gains from letting the game continue can be quite large (as much as 100). In experimental play, the game (or some variant of it) continues longer—and players earn more—than what theory would predict.[10]

In the Centipede Game, sophisticated players do not really have an advantage over unsophisticated ones. They may gain one or two additional points by ending the game slightly before the bitter end, but not much more. In other settings, sophisticated players can have a big advantage over unsophisticated ones. In chess, for example, a grand master could beat a novice in short order. Another example is provided by Application 17.2: Cold Movie Openings, which suggests that sophisticated movie studios, who are in the business of marketing movies—the bad as well as the good—may try to pass off bad movies on unsuspecting moviegoers by keeping critics from being able to review them in advance.

Evolution and Learning

From an evolutionary perspective, it is not surprising that humans cannot calculate as well as a supercomputer. Human's cognitive abilities were shaped by the problems faced by the hunter-gatherers who were our evolutionary ancestors. From this perspective, what is remarkable is not that we may have difficulty in, for example, evaluating a complex mathematical formula in our heads. What is remarkable is that we can calculate and perform higher math at all! After all, it is not clear what evolutionary advantages are directly provided by these cognitive abilities. Perhaps they were the by-product of being able to make decisions about whether to risk moving to a new territory or being able to understand social hierarchies within a tribe, either of which might have required surprisingly complex lines of thought.

Human cognitive abilities are not fully determined at birth by nature. These abilities continued to be developed throughout our schooling and beyond. We are able to learn. Often, a particular new subject or problem seems difficult at first but with study and practice becomes more familiar and easier to understand. For example, intermediate microeconomics may have seemed like a daunting subject at the start of this term, but perhaps having read to this point in the book, the core concepts are second nature to you now (the authors hope anyway).

A learning perspective suggests that people are most likely to make mistakes with complex decisions in unfamiliar settings. The abstract choices among gambles associated with the experiments of Allais and Kahneman and Tversky and others may have been

[10] R. McKelvey and T. Palfrey, "An Experimental Study of the Centipede Game," *Econometrica* (July 1992): 803–836.

APPLICATION 17.2

Cold Movie Openings

In the summer of 2004, 20th Century Fox released *Alien vs. Predator*. Unlike the vast majority of movies, the distributor did not allow critics to screen it before its opening weekend, so moviegoers had to make their decision to see the movie without seeing a review first. The movie was the top box office draw that weekend, with a U.S. gross of $38 million. However, once the negative critical reviews came out, the movie's revenue dropped like a lead balloon.[1]

The strategy of having the movie open without critical reviews is called a "cold opening." Presumably, movie studios pursue this strategy when they have a bad movie that they expect to be panned by critics. If moviegoers do not see bad reviews, perhaps they will believe the movie is of average quality.

Rational Moviegoers

If moviegoers use all available information to make rational decisions about which movie to see, they should not be fooled by the cold-opening strategy. They should take the absence of any critical reviews as a very bad sign of quality. In an academic study of cold openings, Brown, Camerer, and Lovallo found that that the critical reviews for cold-opened movies—when they were finally reviewed—were only half as good as the average movie (a rating of 25 compared to about 50 for the average movie using a measure that combines a large number of critics' reviews on a 100-point scale).[2]

If moviegoers applied this expected quality discount to movies that are cold opened, cold opening would unravel as a profitable strategy. The unraveling would work as follows. All the movies that, although mediocre, are still better than the average cold-opened movie would have their films screened to distinguish themselves from the average cold-opened movie. This would make cold opening an even worse signal of quality. Of the remaining movies, again, those that are better than average would have their movies screened and so on until all but the very worst movie would seek reviews. Such a process is called an "information cascade," fully revealing the quality of all products despite a desire to hide it from the market.

Fooling Some of the People Some of the Time

The market does not work this way in practice. The authors show that, holding constant quality (by accounting for the review score the movie eventually gets) and many other factors, cold opening turns out to be a profitable strategy, boosting overall box office revenue by about 15%. This provides evidence that the average consumer does not think through the studio's strategy enough to take cold opening as a bad sign but rather just infers that the movie is of average quality across all movies.

The studios have a higher level of strategic thinking. The fact that they use the cold-opening strategy at all suggests they realize that at least some moviegoers can be fooled. What is surprising is not that studios use the cold-opening strategy but that they use the strategy so rarely. It seems that many more bad movies should follow the example of *Alien vs. Predator*, which, although it flopped after the opening weekend, made enough money initially up front so that, when combined with international and DVD revenues, it managed to earn a profit. Perhaps studios are afraid that consumers will learn the secret of cold opening if they use the strategy too often. The number of cold-opened movies has been increasing over the past several years, suggesting that studios are gradually learning that the strategy is profitable. Twenty-nine movies were cold-opened in 2008, including *Rambo, Meet the Spartans, and Saw V*.[3]

TO THINK ABOUT

1. Consider the fact that cold openings are becoming more common recently. Would this fact affect the signal you, as a fully rational and fully informed consumer, would take from cold opening now, compared to the past?
2. There are a few cases in which movie studios cold open movies that go on to get fairly good reviews (for example, *Snakes on a Plane*, which opened in 2006). What do you think explain these cases?

[1] G. Snyder, "Inside Move: Cold Shoulder? Genre Pix Nix Crix but Generate B.O. Heat," *Variety International* (September 5, 2005). Available at http://www.variety.com/article/VR1117909980.html.

[2] A. L. Brown, C. Camerer, and D. Lovallo, "To Review or Not to Review? Limited Strategic Thinking at the Movie Box Office," *American Economic Journal: Microeconomics* (May 2012): 1–26.

[3] P. Chattaway, "This Movie Was not Screened for Critics, 2008," *Filmchat Blog* (original post January 1, 2008). Available at http://filmchatblog.blogspot.com/2008/01/this-movie-was-not-screened-for-critics.html. The author maintains lists of movies that are not prescreened dating back to 2006.

quite unfamiliar to subjects. If the subjects encountered such gambles more frequently as part of the routine of daily life, they might learn which is the right choice to make through trial and error.

Thus, if this learning perspective is correct, behavioral economics may be a good approximation to short-run behavior. Neoclassical economics, with its assumption of fully rational decision making, may be a good approximation to long-run behavior when situations become familiar. Application 17.3: Going for It on Fourth Down, provides evidence against this view. Professional football coaches, who are among the world's best at their jobs and who have faced almost every game situation over and over again, seem to be making mistakes regarding a decision that should be familiar to them. The controlled lab experiment in Application 17.4: Let's Make a Deal, suggests the opposite. At first, most subjects make the wrong decision about whether to stay with their initial choice (of a door behind which a prize may lie) or to switch after some new information is revealed. If given the chance to learn, by the end of the experiment, many subjects come to realize that switching is better.

A learning perspective does not make firm predictions about high-stakes decisions that are made infrequently. Which college should I attend? Whom should I marry? Which mortgage should I choose? On the one hand, the decision maker has little opportunity to learn given the one-time nature of the decisions. On the other hand, the high-stakes nature of the choice may lead him or her to take extra time to deliberate to make the right choice. Understanding the extent of behavioral biases in these sorts of decisions is an extremely important research question.

Self-Awareness

A person with limited cognitive abilities who is aware of his or her limitations may be in a much better position than one who is not. The person may avoid accepting gambles and other offers unless he or she is quite sure that there is no possibility of loss. After all, what appears to be a good deal may just be due to a misperception. The person will appear to the outside to be averse to small risks and to be excessively cautious, but both may be a natural response to mistakes in decision making, especially regarding decisions made in unfamiliar situations. When confronted by an overwhelming number of choices that the person's limited cognitive abilities would have difficulty sorting through, again, the person would be inclined to take the cautious approach and refuse to consider the choice at all, as did the subjects in the experiment with dozens of jam varieties in the Paradox of Choice section.

17-4 Limited Willpower

A second limitation to full rationality shows up when people face decisions with a short-term cost that will have a long-run payoff. Consider the decision facing a student every day: the decision regarding whether or not to study. Studying requires strenuous mental exertion. Watching television, playing sports, or socializing with friends is often more enjoyable at any given moment. On the other hand, studying provides the long-run rewards of increased knowledge, better grades, and better future career prospects. At the start of the week, when sitting down to come up with a study plan, a fully rational student would weigh the short-run costs of studying against the long-term rewards and

APPLICATION 17.3

Going for It on Fourth Down

In the sport of American football, a team has a series of chances (called downs) to move the ball a total of ten yards. If it has not gained ten yards by the fourth and last down, it can do one of two things: kick the ball away or "go for it." There are two types of kicks depending on how far away the team is from the goal line; if it is relatively close it can kick a field goal through the goal posts, worth three points; if it is far away, it can punt the ball to the opponent, pushing them back toward the end zone they are defending. "Going for it" means trying to make up the remainder of the ten yards on the last play. If unsuccessful, the ball is turned over to the other team at that field position. If successful, the team retains the ball for at least another series of downs, allowing it the possibility of finally carrying the ball into the opponent's end zone for a touchdown worth seven points (actually six points plus an extra-point kick that is seldom missed).

Pressure on the Coach

Whether to kick or "go for it" on fourth down is one of the most difficult a team's coach has to make. There are many factors to consider, not just the points that might be produced by the different strategies, but the probabilities of success and also the resulting field position for the opponent in each case. Field position matters because it affects the chances of both teams to score as the game continues. The coach has only an instant to make the decision. The game, and perhaps the team's season, may turn on this one decision. Adding to the pressure are the screaming fans and the anticipated second-guessing in the media the next day if the strategy turns out to be unsuccessful.

On the other hand, if anyone can make the right decision, it should be coaches in the National Football League (NFL). With team budgets reaching into the hundreds of millions of dollars a year, they can hire the best and most experienced coaches in the world. These coaches have presumably established a track record of winning, based in part on making the right decision on fourth down.

Too Conservative?

Using data on all NFL football plays from 1998 to 2000, an economist, David Romer, applied sophisticated statistical techniques to compute the difference in the number of points earned over the course of the game from kicking versus "going for it" on fourth down in every different situation (including the team's current field position and the number of yards it needs when "going for it."[1] What he found overturned conventional wisdom. Teams within 10 yards of the end zone should "go for it" even if they need as many as five yards to be successful. Even when backed up against one's own end zone, a team should "go for it" if they only need a few yards.

Actual NFL coaching decisions are much more conservative. Within ten yards of the end zone, needing to gain more than two yards was enough to deter most teams from "going for it," opting to kick instead. Romer's results suggest that coaches were "leaving points on the table" by not adopting a more aggressive strategy.

Michael Lewis, author of widely read books that suggest how economics and statistics can be used to improve the performance of baseball and other professional sports teams, reported on the angry reaction that Romer's study elicited among some coaches. Said one, "If we all listened to the professor, we may be all looking for professor jobs."[2] Lewis suggested several reasons why coaches did not follow Romer's prescriptions. They may be making a strategic mistake. Perhaps they do not take full account of the value of leaving the opponent in poor field position if they are unsuccessful in "going for it" close to the end zone. Another possibility is that coaches have prospect-theory preferences. They may count the three points from a field goal (which close to the end zone is almost automatic) as part of their current point total and be very averse to any risk of losing these points by "going for it." Even if they themselves do not have these sorts of preferences, they may be acting in the interest of others (the team owner, fans, or the media) who do.

TO THINK ABOUT

1. Do you think NFL coaching strategy will eventually change as a result of Romer's work? Does your prediction depend on the underlying reason why coaches were not following this strategy (mistakes versus preferences)?
2. Imagine you are the coach of an NFL team that is playing a much better opponent. How might this affect your decision to kick or "go for it"?

[1]D. Romer, "Do Firms Maximize? Evidence from Professional Football," *Journal of Political Economy* (April 2006): 340–365.
[2]M. Lewis, "If I Only Had the Nerve," *ESPN Magazine* (December 18, 2006).

APPLICATION 17.4

Let's Make a Deal

Let's Make a Deal, a game show that debuted on television some decades ago, has proved to be so popular that reruns are still being shown today. In one part of the show, Monty Hall offered the contestant a choice of three doors. Behind one of the doors was a valuable prize, perhaps $1,000 or a new car. Behind the other two were booby prizes (pieces of junk or other worthless items). The contestant picked one of the three doors. Monty Hall would reveal the booby prize behind one of the other two doors. The contestant was then given the choice of whether to stay with his or her initial choice or switch to the remaining door.

In fact, there is some controversy over whether this exact choice was offered to contestants on *Let's Make a Deal.* Daniel Friedman's review of old show transcripts questions suggests it may not have been.[1] Still, the legend of the "three-door problem" (also called the "Monty Hall problem") has taken on a life of its own, spawning an ongoing debate about whether the contestant should stand pat or switch in these sorts of situations.

A Tough Decision

The decision to stand pat or switch is difficult. One's first thought might be that Monty Hall revealing a booby prize does not change the fact that every door had an equal chance of having the valuable prize behind it. According to this line of thinking, one should be indifferent between standing pat or switching: both doors should still have an equal chance of having the prize.

Further thought indicates that the correct choice is to switch. One way to see this is to note that chance that the contestant chose the correct door initially was 1/3, so that the chance they chose the wrong door was 2/3. The chance the contestant was wrong is still 2/3 after Monty reveals the booby prize behind one of the other doors, but now the contestant knows exactly which of the other doors to switch to and have a 2/3 chance of now being right.[2] That is, the contestant is twice as likely to win the prize if he or she switches.

Lab Experiments

Friedman simulated the game show decision in the lab but with much smaller prizes (a 30-cent gain if one chose correctly). Subjects switched (the rational choice) less than one third of the time.

Friedman then went on to variants of the experiment in which subjects were allowed to learn. In one variant, he informed subjects about the payoffs generated by their choice and the payoffs they would have earned from the other choice. Over repeated play, subjects who stood pat learned that switching tended to win more often. More than half ended up deciding to switch. Projecting the rate of learning out, the author suggested that over 90% would end up switching if they were allowed to observe enough repeated trials.

Game Shows as Experiments

Game shows make nice testing grounds for economic theory. Like the lab, they often provide simple settings in which contestants decisions can easily be seen to be in or out of line with theory. Unlike the lab, the stakes can be extraordinarily high. Stakes in the lab are limited by the researcher's budget. In Friedman's experiments, for example, the gain for making the correct decision amounted to a few pennies. Critics wonder whether such low stakes are large enough to get people to think seriously about the choices involved. The stakes in a game show—amounting to thousands or in some cases hundreds of thousands of dollars—should be enough to get contestants to think hard. There are now scores of economics articles that use game shows as testing grounds, including a study of whether contestants seem to have preferences that accord with prospect theory in *Card Sharks* to a study of whether contestants are making sensible strategic decisions in *Jeopardy!*[3]

TO THINK ABOUT

1. If you were designing a new lab experiment in economics, how many trials would you have subjects play to allow them to become familiar with the setting? On what factors would this depend? How could you determine what the "right" number of trials is?
2. In the Oscar-winning movie *Slumdog Millionaire*, the hero of the movie, a contestant on a game show, is fed the wrong answer by the host to try to get him to lose.[4] (The hero wisely chooses to ignore the host's "hint.") If Monty Hall has this same animosity toward contestants on *Let's Make a Deal,* how might this show up in when and whom to selects to offer the chance of switching? Would switching remain the correct decision for contestants? What if Monty is known instead to have a benevolent attitude toward contestants?

[1]D. Friedman, "Monty Hall's Three Doors: Construction and Deconstruction of a Choice Anomaly," *American Economic Review* (September 1998): 933–946.
[2]The Bayes Rule is a statistical formula that can be used to prove this result formally.
[3]The studies are R. Gertner, "Game Shows and Economic Behavior: Risk-Taking on 'Card Sharks'," *Quarterly Journal of Economics* (May 1993): 507–521; and A. Metrick, "A Natural Experiment in 'Jeopardy!'," *American Economic Review* (March 1995): 240–253.
[4]*Slumdog Millionaire* (Fox Searchlight, 2008).

come up with a plan of action, setting aside some time for studying and some time for leisure. He or she would have no trouble sticking with the plan because at every instant he or she would weigh the costs and benefits the same as when the plan was made at the start of the week.

In reality, it is not always so easy to stick with the plan. When the time comes to study, the pleasures of leisure activities sometimes lure the student away. The student ends up studying less than he or she intended and at the end may even regret having studied so little. The trouble is that one's perspective seems to change over time. When one is "in the moment," the pain of studying and the pleasure of leisure seem to weigh very heavily. When one is outside the moment (either beforehand when planning or afterward when reflecting back), the long-run benefits of studying seem to grow in importance. One's preferences are not necessarily consistent over time. Sticking with an initial, rational plan of action requires willpower to ignore short-run temptations. Sometimes, willpower fails, and the person deviates from the plan.

Behavioral economics seeks to incorporate the very real possibility of self-control problems absent from the standard model. Perhaps the simplest model that has been developed involves hyperbolic discounting, which we will discuss next.

Hyperbolic Discounting

To model choices with long-term consequences, we will imagine that people experience a flow of utilities (which can be positive for benefits or negative for losses) over time from each choice. The choice that generates the highest total sum across all periods is the best one for the individual. For example, suppose two decisions have consequences over the horizon of a week. The first provides utility -10 on the first day and 2 each day for the rest of the week; the second provides -5 on the first day and 1 each day for the rest of the week. The total for the first decision is

$$-10 + 2 + 2 + 2 + 2 + 2 + 2 = 2$$

and for the second is

$$-5 + 1 + 1 + 1 + 1 + 1 + 1 = 1$$

so the person would prefer the first decision.

Willpower problems can be captured by allowing the person to weigh utility experienced in different periods differently. In particular, assume that utility earned in the current period receives full weight (weight 1), but utility earned in any later period only receives weight w, where w is some number between 0 and 1. A person with $w < 1$ is said to exhibit **hyperbolic discounting**. The word "discounting" relates to the fact that a lower value is placed on future compared with current utility. The word "hyperbolic" relates to the immediate, steep drop in the value of utility followed by a leveling off after the current period, much like a hyperbola drops rapidly as one moves away from the origin before flattening out. As we will see, hyperbolic discounting will lead to preferences that are inconsistent over time and to willpower problems. A person with $w = 1$ does not exhibit hyperbolic discounting and will turn out to have no willpower problems.

Hyperbolic discounting
Steep drop in weight on utility earned after the current period.

Numerical Example

Return to the case of a student who is making a study plan on Sunday for the rest of the week. The person is deciding whether or not to study on Monday for an exam on Friday. Suppose that the student has other activities on Tuesday, Wednesday, and Thursday, so the only day available to study is Monday. Studying is less pleasurable than the alternative of leisure and so provides a flow utility of −20 on Monday. Studying leads to a higher grade on the exam, providing a flow utility of 30 on Friday. (These utility numbers are relative to the utility from not studying, taken to be 0 each day.) Should the student plan to study, and if so, will this plan be carried out?

First, take the case in which the student does not exhibit hyperbolic discounting. In coming up with a study plan on Sunday, he or she will make the decision to study or not so that the sum of utilities from Sunday's perspective is highest. Panel (a) of Figure 17.5 shows the weights he or she puts on the flow utilities each day from Sunday's perspective. As panel (a) shows, the student puts a consistent weight 1 on the utility earned on any day during the week. Studying provides a total weighted sum of utilities equal to $-20 + 30 = 10$. Because this weighted sum is greater than the weighted sum from not studying (0), the student would plan to study. When Monday arrives, the student's weights on flow utilities are the same as before, 1 each day, shown in panel (c) of the figure. The weighted sum of utilities from studying and not studying would be the

Figure 17.5 Hyperbolic Discounting in the Student Example

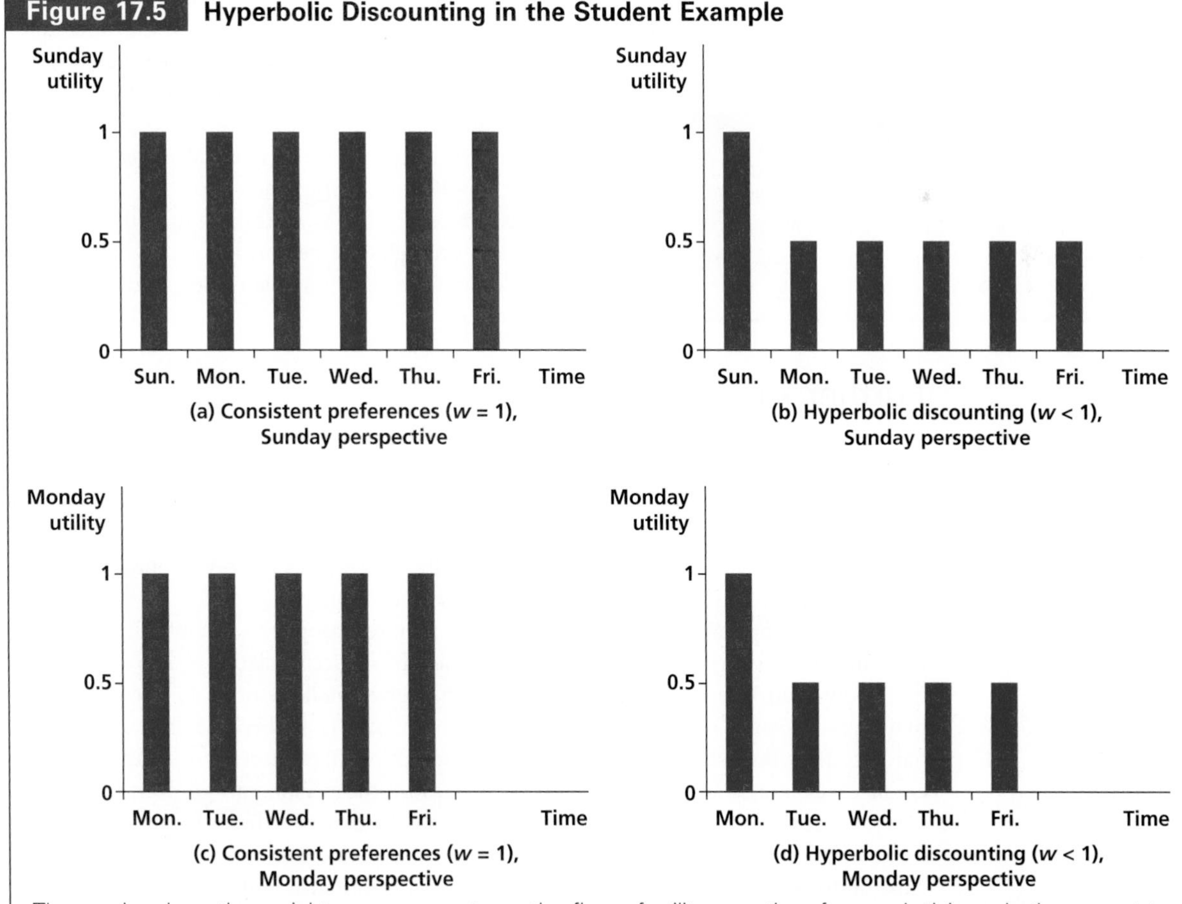

The graphs show the weights a person puts on the flow of utility over time from a decision whether or not to study. Panels (a) and (c) show the weights that a person who is not a hyperbolic discounter would put on utilities, either from the perspective of Sunday, panel (a), or Monday, panel (c). Panels (b) and (d) show the weights for a hyperbolic discounter, from his or her perspective on Sunday in panel (b) and Monday in panel (d).

same from Monday's as from Sunday's perspective, and the student would end up carrying out Sunday's plan by studying on Monday.

Now take the case in which the student exhibits hyperbolic discounting. To use a round number, suppose that $w = 1/2$, meaning that utility later in the week is only worth half of today's utility. The weights on utility he or she uses at the planning stage on Sunday are shown in panel (b) of Figure 17.5. The weighted sum of utilities from Sunday's perspective is $(1/2)(-20) + (1/2)(30) = 5$. Because this weighted sum is greater than the 0 earned for not studying, the student would plan to study. Even though this student discounts future utility more than the student who was not a hyperbolic discounter, from Sunday's perspective, both types of students have the same *relative* valuation for Monday utility compared with Friday utility.

When Monday arrives, things change for the hyperbolic discounter. The student's weights on utility flows are now given by panel (d) of Figure 17.5. Because Monday is now the current day, the student puts full weight on utility earned on Monday. Later days receive half weight. The weighted sum of utilities from studying is now $-20 + (1/2)(30) = -5$. Since the weighted sum is negative, the student chooses not to study, abandoning the plan from the day before.

The hyperbolic discounter is inconsistent over time. He or she would like to study and plans to do so ahead of time, but when the time to study comes, the immediate pain is too great, and the student pursues leisure instead. It is easy to see that whether the student follows through on the plan to study depends on the value of w. Given a w, the weighted sum of utilities from Monday's perspective is $-20 + (w)(30)$, which is positive if $w > 2/3$. We can think of w as a measure of willpower: if w is high enough, the person has enough willpower to carry through on plans to study and not otherwise.

MICRO QUIZ 17.5

The example shows that the hyperbolic discounter does not carry through on a plan to study when studying costs 20 utils. For what cost level would this same person carry through on a study plan?

Further Applications

We have focused on how limited willpower might affect a student's studying behavior. Limited willpower may affect many other spheres of life—any decision with long-term consequences. The decisions to diet and exercise are perfect examples. People may have good intentions to maintain a healthy diet and a regular exercise routine because these both have long-term health benefits, but when the time comes to do without a treat or to endure the pain of a work out, one's willpower often flags.

Another application is to saving. Saving requires people to put off the short-run pleasure of consumption for the long-term benefit of accumulating a store of savings that grows with accumulated interest and other investment returns. Limited willpower may prevent some people from reaching their savings goals because they may find it hard to deny themselves the pleasure of consumption. Easy access to credit, say using credit cards, may make the problem worse because the person can go even beyond his current means and spend him or herself into a debt that is difficult to get out of later. Large balances on credit cards may be a signal of someone who is making a rational calculation to borrow in this way but may be a signal of impulsive spending when the long-run interest of the person may be to reduce spending and to save.

Perhaps the most severe example of a willpower problem is addiction to drugs or alcohol. The addict may realize that the habit is ruining his or her life but may still be powerless to fight the urge for a "fix" in the short term.

Commitment Strategies

If people suffer from self-control problems, they may be in a better position if they are self-aware enough to realize they have such problems. Then they can try to come up with strategies that somehow help them commit to the original plan. Homer's epic, *The Odyssey*, provides a memorable example of such commitment strategies. The ship captained by the epic's hero, Odysseus, is about to encounter the sirens, mythical creatures whose irresistible appearance and singing lure sailors to dive off their ships into the foaming ocean to their deaths. Odysseus (known for his cleverness) has all the sailors cover their eyes and ears and has himself tied to the mast to prevent him from jumping off while piloting the ship. Using this strategy, the ship sails past the danger without losing any of the crew.

Commitment strategies work by either raising the cost of actions one wishes to avoid or by lowering the cost of actions one would like to commit to. In the case of Odysseus, his option of jumping off the ship was closed off by having him tied to the mast, which we can think of equivalently as increasing the cost of this action to a prohibitive level. Examples of commitment strategies outside of mythology include a student's removing distractions, such as television and video games from his or her room to better stick to plan to study. Throwing out electronics seems like an odd strategy at first, disposing of goods that we imagine should provide utility. True, a fully rational person with no self-control problem would be worse off without goods such as a television or a video game console. However, once we allow for the possibility of self-control problems, that person may be better off (at least from the perspective of the planning stage) throwing out goods because this removes possible temptations that may lead one to break from one's studying plans.

The analysis here runs counter to the discussion of option value in Chapter 4. In that chapter, we found that options were valuable in the presence of uncertainty because the option in question may turn out to be the best choice in certain circumstances, and the person would only take the option if it is better than other choices. In this chapter, where we have moved from fully rational decision makers to ones with limitations, options may not always be good. At the planning stage, the person may prefer to cut off options to prevent him or herself from taking an action that is appealing in the short run but disadvantageous in the long run.

Other examples of commitment strategies include a dieter's throwing high-fat foods in the garbage. Of course, the person can always replace the food by going shopping again, but throwing out the food raises the cost of eating high-fat food a bit because it requires the person to go through extra shopping effort. The extra cost and delay might be enough to allow the person to overcome the temptation. Another commitment strategy is to enlist the support of peers who will reward one with praise for sticking with the plan and penalize with scorn when one does not. Programs for overcoming addiction, such as Alcoholics Anonymous, provide support for addicts by matching them with sponsors (former addicts who may provide praise and helpful advice).

Application 17.5: "Put a Contract Out on Yourself" describes a novel commitment strategy that has people pledge a certain amount of money that is forfeited if they break their commitments. The higher the amount of money put at stake, the more costly is the action that the person wants to avoid (overeating, not exercising, not studying), and the more commitment power the person has to avoid the action. The application describes a Web site that two behavioral economics scholars have set up to facilitate such commitments.

APPLICATION 17.5

"Put a Contract Out on Yourself"[1]

Professors who study behavioral economics are not themselves immune from willpower problems. Two Yale professors, Dean Karlan and Ian Ayres, who found it difficult to maintain their ideal weights, hit upon a brilliant strategy to do so. The strategy, which relies on economic incentives, works as follows. Promise a friend to reach a target weight by a certain date and then maintain this weight. Put up an amount of money, say \$100, that is forfeited if the goal is not reached or maintained. The threat of losing \$100 may allow the person to resist the short-run temptation of breaking with a diet or exercise plan. If the commitment works, the money need never be paid, just promised.

The professors claim to personally have much more at stake than \$100—more on the order of \$5,000. Both claim to have maintained their goals without having to pay anything out.

Savings Schemes in the Philippines

The idea of using contracts with economic incentives to solve self-control problems was supported by Karlan's earlier research on increasing savings through the use of savings accounts with commitment features.[2] The study offered savers the possibility of opening an account that limited withdrawals until a certain target date or savings amount was reached. Subjects who were more likely to suffer self-control problems (based on responses to hypothetical questions about delaying gratification) more often chose to participate in these new savings accounts when offered the chance. Access to these new savings accounts almost doubled savings for the subjects.

Back to the Numerical Example

To see how putting money behind one's commitments can help with self-control problems, return to the example in the text of a student who plans on Sunday to study on Monday (at a cost of 20 that day) for a test on Friday (gaining 30 that day if well prepared) but who discounts utility everyday after the present by half. Without any payments, we saw that the student did not carry out Sunday's plan to study because on Monday the weighted sum of utilities from studying was negative: $-20 + 30/2 = -5$, but if the student promises on Sunday to pay more than 5 (in utility terms) if he or she does not study on Monday, this will induce the student to study because now the loss from studying exceeds that from not studying (-5 or more) from Monday's perspective.

stickK.com

The Yale professors have developed a Web site, http://www.stickK.com that facilitates commitment contracts by having people fill out a form, set a pledge amount, provide a payment card that will be charged if the commitment is not met, and select someone to serve as a "referee" to verify whether or not the pledge is met. As of this writing, over a quarter of a million contracts involving \$17 million in pledges have been signed for commitments ranging from quitting smoking, to stopping nail biting, to finishing a screenplay. To further enhance commitment value, one can choose to forfeit the money to an enemy or to a charity that supports causes one strongly opposes (such as an opposing political party).

Numerous other applications have been developed to help combat self-control problems. Anti-Social, SelfControl, and StayFocused block access to social-networking websites, email, and other computer distractions for a specified period of time. Social-networking websites can themselves be a positive force for self control through virtual fitness groups allowing members to keep track of each others' progress in achieving exercise goals.

TO THINK ABOUT

1. Whom would you select to "referee" your commitment contract? What would be the drawbacks of selecting a friend to "referee" the commitment contract? What about an enemy?
2. Which self-control problems would be easiest to specify in a contract and have a "referee" monitor? Which problems would be difficult to monitor?

[1]Tag line from the Web site http://www.stickK.com, accessed March 17, 2009.

[2]N. Ashraf, D. Karlan, and W. Yin, "Tying Odysseus to the Mast: Evidence from a Commitment Savings Product in the Philippines," *Quarterly Journal of Economics* (May 2006): 635–672.

17-5 Limited Self-Interest

In this section, we will study the third of the limits on a decision maker who, at least in economists' simplest models, perfectly maximizes his or her own payoff. There are limits to people's self-interest in that they do not just care about their own material well-being. They also care about interpersonal values such as prestige, fairness, and justice. For example, it is hard to argue that people do not care about how they are perceived by others. Considerable money and effort are spent on choosing the right clothing, not just because of the warmth or comfort it provides—people often change into other clothes as soon as they reach the privacy of their own homes—but because of how attractive it makes them to others. People may be willing to make considerable sacrifices not just for their social standing but for fairness, justice, or many other interpersonal values.

These interpersonal values may have been instilled in us by our upbringing, or they may be more instinctual, perhaps programmed into us by evolutionary forces acting on our distant hunter-gatherer ancestors. For example, driving seems to bring out some our innate sense of justice. Many of us have experienced our "blood boiling" after being cut off by another driver (or some other action interpreted as being aggressive). For some people, the emotion is so intense that they respond physically, gesturing at the bad driver or driving aggressively toward them. These responses are costly because they increase the risk of accident or retaliation by the bad driver. A rational driver interested only in maximizing monetary payoffs would never choose these costly physical responses because there is no offsetting monetary benefit. It must be the case that responding to the other person provides nonmonetary payoffs. Administering justice to the bad driver may provide its own reward.

In this section, we will study behavioral economists' attempts to integrate interpersonal values into the standard model. Some interpersonal values, such as altruism, can be captured without much change to standard models. Some, such as fairness and justice, will require a deeper inquiry into interpersonal interactions and thus into the realm of game theory. We will see how the analysis from Chapter 5 on game theory can be modified to capture these other interpersonal values.

Altruism

Charitable giving amounted to over $300 billion in the United States in 2012.[11] Parents pay considerably more than that feeding, clothing, and entertaining their children (even leaving aside the enormous bills for college tuition). These large expenditures reflect **altruism**, a concern for the well-being of others beyond oneself, whether others in need or one's family members.

Altruism
Regard for others' well-being.

Altruism is not hard to capture in the standard model. Figure 17.6 shows a utility function for an individual, (called person 1) who cares about the well-being of another (called person 2). Rather than corresponding to person 1's own consumption of goods, such as soft drinks or hamburgers, here the axes correspond to each person's overall consumption. In a sense, more consumption for person 2 (indicated on the vertical axis) is regarded as a "good" for person 1. Just as in Chapter 2, the utility-maximizing choice is given by point of tangency between the budget constraint and an indifference curve, point *A* in the figure. The altruistic person 1 ends up giving some income to 2. If 1 were completely selfish, he or she would not give any income away and instead be at point *S*.

[11] *Giving USA 2013: The Annual Report on Philanthropy for the Year 2012* (Giving USA Foundation, 2013).

Figure 17.6 Altruism

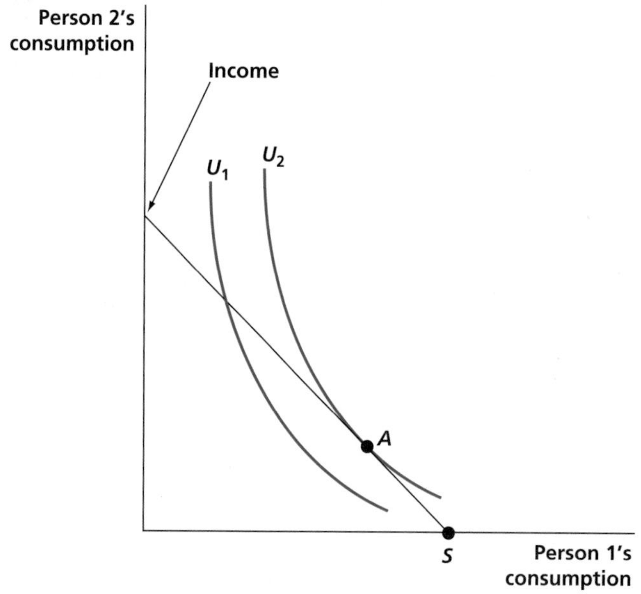

Person 2's consumption

Income

U_1 U_2

A

S

Person 1's consumption

A selfish person would keep all income for his or her own consumption (point *S*). If person 1 is altruistic toward person 2, then 1 may prefer to give some money to 2 to raise 2's consumption (point *A*).

Fairness

Other interpersonal values take a bit more work to model. Behavioral economists have noticed that subjects in lab experiments depart from the predictions of standard game theory in that they seem to have a preference for fairness, willing to give up some amount of money to select an outcome with a more even distribution of payoffs between players. This is seen most clearly in experiments with the Ultimatum Game, described in Application 5.4 in the earlier chapter on game theory. A simplified version of the game is given in Figure 17.7. In this sequential game, player 1 moves first, proposing a split of a total pot of $10 between him or herself and the second player. The second player then chooses whether or not to accept the proposal. If the proposal is rejected, both get nothing. In this simplified version, player 1 can only make one of two possible proposals, a low one (giving $1 to player 2 and keeping $9 for 1) and an even one (dividing the $10 pot equally between the two players). As can be shown by backward induction, in the subgame-perfect equilibrium, the proposer chooses low, and the responder accepts (choice *A*). Player 2 accepts all offers, even the low one, because rejecting reduces his or her monetary payoff. Knowing 2 accepts all offers, 1 makes the least generous offer.

Figure 17.7 Ultimatum Game

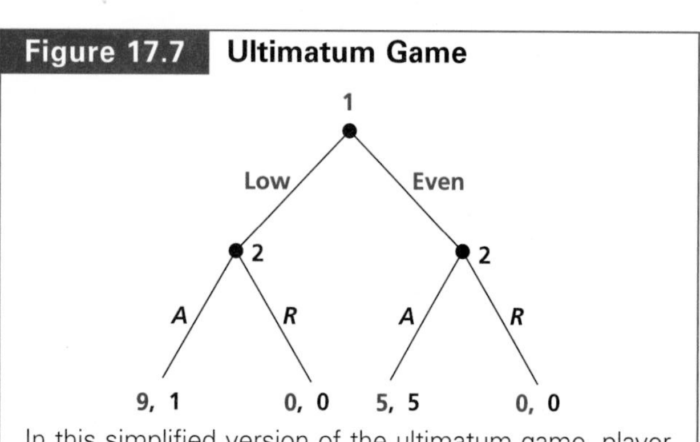

In this simplified version of the ultimatum game, player 1 moves first, offering either a low ($1) or even ($5) share of $10 total. Player 2 then decides whether to accept the offer (*A*) or reject it (*R*).

That is the theory. As noted in Application 5.4, experimental results differ markedly. In most cases, player 1 proposes an even split of the total pot. When a low offer is made, the responder often rejects it. Behavioral economists have explained the divergence between theory and experiment by suggesting that subjects do not just care about maximizing monetary payoffs but also have a preference for fairness. Subjects lose utility if there is a big gap between what they and other players earn in the game. Note the difference from altruism: an altruistic subject benefits if the other gains regardless of their relative positions; a subject with a preference for fairness likes the other to gain only if that makes their positions more even.

Return to the Centipede Game (Figure 17.4). Assume now that in addition to caring about monetary payoffs, both players have a preference for fairness in that they lose 1 util for each dollar gap between the their payoffs (in absolute value).

1. Write down the extensive form for this new game.
2. Find the equilibrium. Can fairness provide another explanation of the experimental behavior in the Centipede Game cited earlier in the chapter?

Figure 17.8 shows how the game changes if we add a preference for fairness. In panel (a), both players are assumed to gain 1 util for every dollar they earn, but they lose utility (1 util per dollar) if there is a gap between the two player's earnings. Player 1's payoff if a low offer is accepted falls from 9 to 1 because it has to be adjusted by the \$8 gap between the players' monetary payoffs in that even. Player 2's payoff falls from 1 to −7. With these new payoffs, 2 would prefer to reject a low offer. Player 1 ends up making an even offer in the subgame-perfect equilibrium. Panel (b) provides an alternative model in which the player that ends up ahead does not care about fairness; only the player who earns less does. This can be thought of as a model of envy. In this alternative, if a low offer is accepted, player 1's utility is 9, and player 2's utility is –7.

The subgame-perfect equilibrium is the same in panel (b) as in (a), both involving an even offer that is accepted. The logic behind the equilibrium is different. With both players having a preference for fairness in panel (a), player 1 prefers making the even offer because he or she does not like to be too far ahead of 2. With only player 2 having preferences for fairness as in panel (b), player 1 makes an even offer, but only because he or she is afraid that player 2 would reject a low offer out of envy.

Behavioral economists have tried to sort out which of these subtly different models of fairness seems to be operating in the real world. One way to do so is to run

Figure 17.8 Ultimatum Game with Different Fairness Preferences

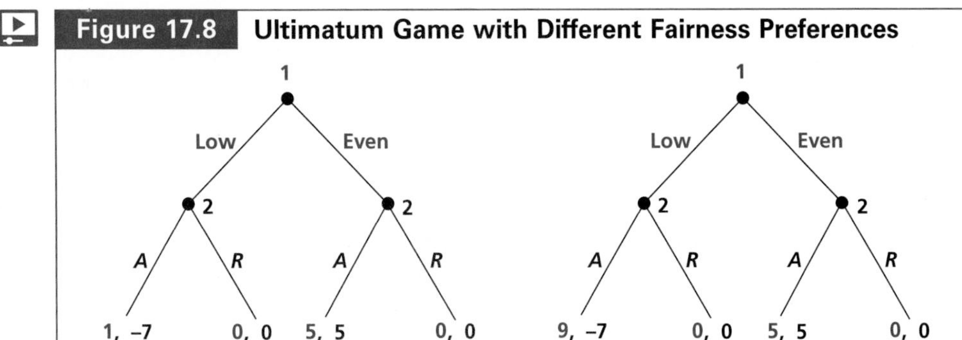

The purely monetary payoffs from the previous figure have been modified to reflect fairness preferences. In panel (a), increasing the gap between their monetary payoffs is costly to both players. In panel (b), a gap in monetary payoffs only harms the player who earns less.

Figure 17.9 Dictator Game

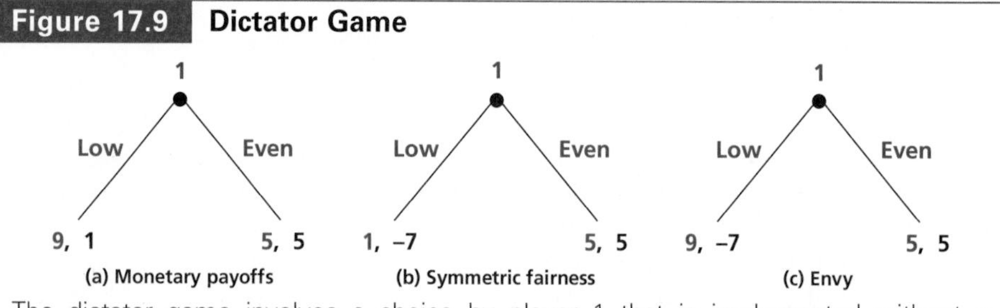

The dictator game involves a choice by player 1 that is implemented without a response from player 2. The three panels show how the payoffs change as one changes players' preferences. In panel (a), they care only about monetary payoffs. In (b) both players have additional preferences for fairness. In (c), only the player who earns less cares about the gap in payoffs.

experiments with a new game such as the Dictator Game, shown in Figure 17.9. The Dictator Game is related to the Ultimatum Game except that there is no second stage after the initial proposal. Player 1's proposal is directly implemented without a response from player 2. Panel (a) gives the monetary payoffs in this game (which is actually just a simple decision for player 1 rather than a full-fledged game). Panel (b) shows how the payoffs would be adjusted if player 1 has a concern for fairness, even if he or she ends up ahead of the other player. Panel (c) shows the payoffs in the case in which only the player who earns less cares about fairness. The two games in (b) and (c) have different predictions; player 1 should make the even offer in (b) and the low offer in (c). As noted in Application 5.4, which discusses the Dictator Game further, the experimental results are somewhat mixed. Moving from the Ultimatum to the Dictator Game increases the number of low offers subjects make, but some subjects continue to make even offers in the Dictator Game. While we await further experimental evidence, perhaps the best operating assumption is that some people care more about fairness than others.

The two panels in Figure 17.8 do not exhaust the different models of fairness that behavioral economists have proposed and tested. Some suggest that people are less concerned with fairness than with rewarding the good behavior of others and punishing their bad behavior. This sort of behavior is called **reciprocity**. Others suggest that people are more concerned that they appear to be fair rather than actually be fair. People behave differently if they are sure no one is watching. Application 5.4 discusses some of the experiments used to test these other theories of fairness, including detailed procedures ensuring that the subject cannot be observed by the person carrying out the experiments.

Reciprocity
Rewarding good behavior and punishing bad behavior.

Market versus Personal Dealings

One's interpersonal values may depend on with whom one is interacting. A person might be very altruistic toward family, friends, and perhaps community members, but less so to strangers. This might explain why charitable giving tends to be concentrated within communities than might be expected if one had a general altruism toward everyone around the globe. This may also explain some of the variance in interpersonal values shown in lab experiments. Subjects who regard those they are matched against as fellow community members involved in a common enterprise may show strong interpersonal values toward them. Subjects who regard those they are matched against as "anonymous others" may pay less attention to interpersonal values and instead maximize monetary payoffs. Exactly what frame of reference one player uses to view another in an experiment may be quite unstable because it may depend on minute details.

One detail that seems to have an important effect on behavior is the distinction between commercial and personal transactions. In commercial dealings, people tend to behave as rational payoff maximizers. They try to extract as much for themselves as possible. In personal dealings, other values begin to matter, leading people, for example, to behave more altruistically or fairly. Introducing money into a personal relationship can have perverse consequences because it can lead people to reframe the dealing as commercial. The consequences can be quite unexpected, as they were when a daycare center imposed fines for being late to pick up children in Application 17.6: Late for Daycare Pickup.

17-6 Policy Implications

In the other chapters in this last part of the book on market failures, we encountered two possible sources of inefficiency in markets. One was asymmetric information (Chapter 15) and the other was externalities (Chapter 16). In yet earlier chapters we saw that market power can be a source of inefficiency, for example when the monopolist in Chapter 11 restricted output in order to raise price above marginal cost, leading to a deadweight loss.

Behavioral economics offers yet another source of market failures: limits to cognitive ability and willpower may lead participants to make the "wrong" decisions in the market. Moreover, sophisticated firms may understand consumer biases and may try to exploit these biases for their own profit. Some behavioral economists use this line of reasoning to argue that the government should play a paternalistic role, intervening in markets to fix participants' mistakes and overcome other limits to rationality. Some neoclassical economists counter that participants have the strongest incentives and best information to make the right decisions for themselves. They argue that government paternalism has a good chance of increasing rather than decreasing market failures. This is a controversial question in economics, so we will try to present ideas from both sides below.

Borrowing and Savings Decisions

To take a concrete example, consider decisions to borrow or save. As discussed in Application 17.1, the decision can involve complicated interest calculations and other hard math, which often lead to mistakes. Therefore, limits to cognitive ability may lead to the wrong savings decision, perhaps biasing people to save too little. Limits to willpower also may lead people to save too little because there are tempted by the lure of immediate consumption.

Possible government interventions that might help people make the "right" savings decision would be to mandate a savings plan, say requiring people to save a minimum of 15% of their income, or it could subsidize savings, say by exempting interest earnings from income tax, as is done with Individual Retirement Accounts (IRAs) in the United States, discussed in Application 14.1. The government could leave it to people to invest the savings in their own way (stocks, bonds, bank accounts) or could tax them directly and invest the money for them. Governments in effect do this through their retirement programs, including Social Security in the United States. One argument for government interventions such as IRAs and Social Security programs is that behavioral biases lead people to save too little and are better off if forced to save above a certain minimum or have their savings subsidized. On the borrowing side, if people are thought to be led to

APPLICATION 17.6

Late for Daycare Pickup

People seem to behave differently in market transactions as opposed to personal dealings. When the Ultimatum Game is run in the lab with the usual framing, as we have seen, people exhibit a preference for fairness, offering even divisions of the pot of money and rejecting low offers. Dressing the exact same game up as a market transaction between buyers and sellers, experimental behavior turned out to exhibit much less fairness, with lower offers being made and accepted.[1] A unique field experiment sheds more light on the effect of framing transactions as either commercial or personal.

Late Fines

The experiment involved daycare centers.[2] A perennial problem at daycare centers is that an absent-minded or overworked parent can sometimes show up late to pick up his or her child at the end of the day. Having to keep the center open late is expensive for the center because it must pay its workers overtime and may be burdensome for the workers.

To study the effect of monetary incentives on this lateness problem, researchers conducted an experiment in which they approached a number of daycare centers within the same city. They randomly selected a sample of the centers to impose a monetary fine (amounting to about $5 for being 10 or more minutes late). The effect of the fines was surprising. Instead of reducing the lateness problem, the number of parents who showed up late doubled.

One explanation is that, prior to the fine being imposed, parents put considerable weight on the well-being of the center and the workers and tried very hard to show up on time. When a fine was imposed, the transaction stopped being personal and became commercial. Parents just compared the small, $5 cost with the benefit of staying a bit later at work and often found it worthwhile to be late.

Persistence

After allowing parents time to adjust to the fine, the researchers introduced another twist into the experiment: they went back to the status quo by removing the fines at all the centers. Removing the fines had no effect. Centers that had fines continued to have twice as many late parents as centers that never had a fine. Apparently, a temporary fine was enough to adjust parents' attitudes toward the center and its workers, and this attitude persisted regardless of the level of the actual fine.

Don't Mix Business and Pleasure

The daycare experiment suggests why people may be very reluctant to introduce money into personal relationships. People tend to "lend" flour and eggs to neighbors who run out and also perform other favors without any cash changing hands. Wouldn't it be more efficient just to pay for these things rather than keeping track of who owes what favors to whom? At work, colleagues help each other out all the time without exchanging money for it, and the same often happens within the family. It might be puzzling at first to a student of economics who has learned about all the advantages of the market that so much activity is effectively placed outside of the market by removing consideration of money and prices. The results from the field experiment suggest that this may be a way to encourage people to act according to their interpersonal values.

Society seems to find certain transactions acceptable when done on a voluntary basis, but repugnant when money is involved. Sex provides one example: most states continue to enforce laws against prostitution while striking down laws against adultery. Human organs provide another: paying for kidneys might increase supply and save the lives of some of those waiting for a transplant, the idea of an kidney or other organ market seems too distasteful for policymakers to contemplate.[3]

TO THINK ABOUT

1. What would happen to the number of late pickups if the fine were increased from $5 to $6? What if it were increased to $50 or even $500? How might the graph look if average number of late pickups (on the vertical axis) were plotted against the level of the late fine (on the horizontal axis).
2. Think of some examples from your personal experience of situations where small fines were applied for "bad" behavior or small bonuses for "good" behavior. Did the prices have the anticipated effect or a perverse effect on behavior in these situations?

[1]E. Hoffman, K. McCabe, K. Shachat, and V. Smith, "Preferences, Property Rights, and Anonymity in Bargaining Experiments," *Games and Economic Behavior* (November 1994): 346–380.
[2]U. Gneezy and A. Rustichini, "A Fine is a Price," *Journal of Legal Studies* (January 2000): 1–17.
[3]A. Roth, "Repugnance as a Constraint on Markets," *Journal of Economic Perspectives* (Summer 2007): 37–58.

borrow too much because of calculation mistakes or willpower problems, the government might regulate credit cards, perhaps putting a cap on the number of cards a person can have or the credit limit for each card or requiring a waiting period after applying for a card before it can be used. The government might regulate the level of interest rates or how they are advertised (truth-in-lending laws in the United States.) if people tend to miscalculate interest rates from information on loan amounts and periods as suggested in Application 17.1.

Other Goods and Services

Government interventions in other areas could address the problems raised by behavioral economics. If consumers are thought to be overwhelmed by choices at retail outlets, the government could restrict stores' offerings or perhaps tax overall shelf space. If irrational choices are leading to overeating, the government could ban or tax high-calorie or high-fat foods. Of course many governments around the world already ban certain narcotics and restrict or heavily tax tobacco and alcohol. Many of the arguments for the government interventions here are paternalistic in nature, based again on the problems identified by behavioral economics.

Market Solutions

Some neoclassical economists are not completely convinced that research in behavioral economics has proved the existence of limits to rationality. They are not so sure people's decisions are mistaken in systematic ways that can be improved by government intervention. If one takes this view, then government interventions to influence choices that are not in fact mistakes will lead to deadweight losses, just as price controls and taxes were shown to do in Chapter 9.

A less extreme view would be that although people undoubtedly make mistakes, the consequences of these mistakes may lessen over time. People may learn to make better decisions with experience or may seek advice from experienced friends, colleagues, or professionals. People may learn to avoid offers that are "too good to be true," sticking with the status quo unless one is sure the new opportunity will be a good one or to recognize especially difficult decisions and take special care in making those. Although a bias toward the status quo may not be perfectly efficient, it may provide a fairly satisfactory level of well-being. The market may recognize a profitable opportunity in providing products and solutions that solve behavioral biases. Any of these mechanisms could, over the long term, mitigate the problems suggested by behavioral economics.

Whether competition by itself can eventually overcome any behavioral bias or limit to rationality is a matter of recent interest in economics. The model of perfect competition might suggest that products and services that are best for consumers will be produced in the long run, and these will be sold at marginal cost. Good firms will drive out bad firms, and good choices will drive out bad ones. However, there are limits to what competition can do. Different consumers like different things, and a whole range of products and choices may persist in the long run to serve each niche rather than the market converging to one "right" product or choice. In addition, people's cognitive limitations may make them imperfect shoppers, so firms that offer bad or expensive choices may persist in the market in the long run.[12]

[12]See X. Gabaix and D. Laibson, "Shrouded Attributes, Consumer Myopia, and Information Suppression in Competitive Markets," *Quarterly Journal of Economics* (May 2006): 505–540.

"Nudging" the Market

If the government intervenes in the market with regulations, taxes, or subsidies for paternalistic reasons, it risks being wrong about the underlying behavioral problem and introducing deadweight loss where there was none before. Milder interventions that preserve voluntary choice may help solve behavioral problems with less risk. The government can try to increase the availability of simple information that helps consumers make complicated choices. The government can do this either by supplying the information itself or by mandating that firms provide such information usually in some standard format. This was done in the United States with the truth-in-lending laws mentioned above, one provision of which required lenders to quote annual percentage rates for loans, a simple number that can be used to compare the relative attractiveness of two loans with very different and very complicated terms. Another example is the requirement to display nutritional information in a standard format on the back of food packages.

Another mild intervention that can address behavioral problems while still retaining the best features of voluntary transactions is to provide a default choice that is good for most consumers but to allow them to opt for some different option if they so choose. Choice is not restricted, so any deadweight loss from distorting free decisions should be minimized, but consumers who may otherwise have made a bad decision, if they stick with the default option, will end up not doing too badly in the default.

An example is provided by defined-contribution retirement plans, 401(k) plans, which firms offer to their employees. When the default was nonparticipation, requiring an active decision to opt into the plans, less than half of employees were found to enroll in a 401(k). When the default was switched to participation, almost all of the employees enrolled.[13] If firms are concerned that their employees save too little for retirement, a natural policy response would be to set the default at some moderate level of participation. Those employees with special reasons for saving less can still choose to do so.

A recent popular book by two leading behavioral economists suggests that firms and governments should apply the same idea—of "nudging" how choices are presented to highlight ones that might be best for people—in many other spheres besides retirement savings, ranging from offering sensible defaults health plans to arranging food in a cafeteria line so that healthy items are encountered first.[14]

SUMMARY

This chapter provided an introduction to behavioral economics. By integrating the fields of psychology and economics, this growing research area seeks to understand whether and why actual decisions depart from idealized, fully rational ones. Some of the broad insights discussed in the chapter include the following.

- Departures from full rationality can be classified in three ways: limits to cognitive ability, limits to willpower, and limits to self-interest.
- Cognitive ability may be especially strained when making decisions that involve complicated formulas, uncertainty, an overwhelming number of choices, or multiple steps of reasoning. Experiments have uncovered some systematic biases in these sorts of decisions.
- An early, influential behavioral model is prospect theory. According to this theory, people take their current wealth as a reference point and dislike small losses from this point (contrasting the standard theory, which suggests

[13]B. Madrian and D. F. Shea, "The Power of Suggestion: Inertia in 401(k) Participation and Savings Behavior," *Quarterly Journal of Economics* (November 2001): 1149–1187.

[14]R. H. Thaler and C. R. Sunstein, *Nudge: Improving Decisions about Health, Wealth, and Happiness* (Yale University Press, 2008).

people should be risk neutral regarding small gambles). People with these preferences may make different decisions in equivalent settings when only the framing of the situation is changed.

- People with limited willpower may behave inconsistently over time, for example, planning to exercise, study, or quit smoking, but then being unable to stick with the plan when the time comes. We studied the model of hyperbolic discounting, in which people change the relative weights that they put on present versus future well-being as plans are put into action.
- In strategic settings, people may not act to maximize their monetary payoffs because they may have other interpersonal values such as altruism, fairness, and justice. We studied ways to model these interpersonal values.
- Behavioral economics provides a further rationale for government intervention in markets to correct the irrational decisions of participants. Such interventions may harm social welfare if the government misconstrues rational decisions as mistakes. A compromise may be for policy makers to highlight choices that they judge to be good for people but still allow people to freely choose other options.

REVIEW QUESTIONS

1. Describe the three limits to rational decision making identified in this chapter.

2. Distinguish between behavioral and neoclassical economics. What are the relative merits of each approach? Would you expect the relative merits to change as knowledge advances?

3. One oddity often observed in the market is that stores charge prices ending in 99 (so we see prices of $1.99, $5.99, and so forth). Explain why this sort of pricing might be puzzling to economists. Some have suggested that this is due to stores trying to exploit a cognitive limitation of shoppers. What sort of cognitive limitation might this be? Would you expect market forces to prevent firms from exploiting consumers in this or other ways?

4. Behavioral economists have different views of the anomalies uncovered by experiments. Some view the anomalies as evidence of mistakes in decision making. Others view the anomalies as providing a new understanding of people's true preferences. What difference does it make for policy which theory is right? How could the theories be tested apart using experiments?

5. According to prospect theory, people are very averse to small risks. How is this captured on a utility function? How is this different from the standard theory about choice under uncertainty discussed in Chapter 4?

6. Argue that in the Centipede Game, a player is better off being known to be short-sighted. Are there any other settings in which it would be useful to be known to have behavioral biases?

7. What did Odysseus's having himself tied to the mast indicate about the level of his rationality? Provide three other examples of commitment devices used in the real world.

8. Distinguish between altruism, fairness, and reciprocity. Suggest experiments related to the Ultimatum Game that could sort out how much each of these interpersonal values matter to subjects.

9. A vast amount of information is available on Internet Web sites free of charge. The Website author may just be altruistic. Give at least two other motives for Websites to give away information. Which motives seem to best fit some of your favorite Web sites that give away free information?

10. "Behavioral economics justifies intervention in the market by a paternalistic government." Explain the pros and cons of this view. What other market failures were identified in the book where government intervention might have been called for? Is the argument for intervening to solve behavioral problems stronger or weaker than the argument for intervening to solve these other market failures?

PROBLEMS

17.1. A queen gives a dragon-slaying hero a choice between two prizes. The first provides $100,000 a day for d days; the second provides an amount of money that doubles in size each day for d days starting from a penny (so one penny the first day, two pennies the second, four pennies the next, etc.).

a. Provide the formula for the amount of money after d days provided by each prize.

b. Graph your results for values of d ranging from 0 to 31 days.

c. Using your graph, advise the hero on which prize he should choose depending on the number of days d involved in the queen's offer.

17.2. Imagine that you are a subject in one of Maurice Allais lab experiments involving the same four gambles as in the chapter. Gamble A provides an 89% chance of winning \$1,000, a 10% chance of winning \$5,000, and a 1% chance of winning nothing. Gamble B provides a 100% chance of winning \$1,000. Gamble C provides an 11% chance of winning \$1,000 and an 89% chance of winning nothing. Finally, gamble D provides a 10% chance of winning \$5,000 and a 90% chance of winning nothing. Your utility function over money is $U(x) = \sqrt{x}$.

a. Compute your expected utility from each of the four gambles.
b. In the first scenario, you are given a choice between gambles A and B. Which would you choose given your utility function?
c. In the second scenario, you are given a choice between gambles C and D. Which would you choose given your utility function?
d. Compare your choices in the two scenarios, and compare them to the actual experimental results reported in the text.

17.3. Refer back to Chapter 5, in particular to the Prisoners' Dilemma in Figure 5.1. Imagine that these payoffs are monetary payoffs.

a. Suppose that players only care about monetary payoffs, with \$1 = 1 util. Find the pure-strategy Nash equilibria.
b. Suppose that players have a preference for fairness. Each player loses 1 util for each dollar difference (in absolute value) between their payoffs. Show how the Prisoners' Dilemma payoffs would change by writing down a new normal form. Find the pure-strategy Nash equilibria.
c. Suppose that players have different fairness preferences than in part b. Suppose that only the player who earns less money cares about fairness. That player loses 1 util for each dollar less he or she earns than the other player. Write down the normal form of the Prisoners' Dilemma reflecting these new preferences. Find the pure-strategy Nash equilibria.

17.4. Refer back to Chapter 5, in particular to the Battle of the Sexes in Table 5.5. Imagine that these payoffs are monetary payoffs.

a. Suppose that players only care about monetary payoffs, with \$1 = 1 util. What are the pure-strategy Nash equilibria?
b. Suppose that players have extreme preferences for fairness. Each player loses 10 utils for each dollar difference (in absolute value) between their payoffs. Show how the payoffs in the Battle of the Sexes would change by writing down a new normal form. Find the pure-strategy Nash equilibria.
c. Suppose that players have different fairness preferences than in part b. Now only the player who earns *more* money cares about fairness. This player feels guilty about earning more, losing 10 utils for each dollar advantage. Write down the normal form of the Battle of the Sexes reflecting these new preferences. Find the pure-strategy Nash equilibria.

17.5.  Refer to the Ultimatum Game in Figure 17.7. Recall that the payoffs are monetary payoffs.

a. Suppose that players only care about monetary payoffs, with \$1 = 1 util. Find the subgame-perfect equilibrium.
b. Suppose that players are imperfectly altruistic. They receive 1 util for each dollar they earn but 1/2 for each dollar the other player earns. Write down the extensive form reflecting the new payoffs. Find the subgame-perfect equilibrium.
c. Suppose that players are perfectly altruistic, receiving 1 util for each dollar in the sum of their earnings. Write down the extensive form reflecting the new payoffs. Find the subgame-perfect equilibrium.
d. Suppose that players are perfectly selfless, getting 1 util for each dollar the other player earns but no utility for their own earnings. Write down the extensive form reflecting the new payoffs. Find the subgame-perfect equilibrium. Does player 1 end up choosing the outcome that player 2 prefers?

17.6. Julia visits her local grocery store to buy a jar of jam. She is overwhelmed to see the twenty-four varieties shown in Figure 17.3 there.

a. Suppose she makes her decision by evaluating every pairwise comparison among the twenty-four varieties. How many comparisons does she have to make, and how long will it take her if she requires 1 second for each comparison?
b. Suppose she uses a different system for making her decision. First, she considers each of the separate categories separately and m the pair-wise comparisons just within the category to find the best. Then, she takes the best from each category and makes all the pairwise comparisons among them. Has she reduced the number of comparisons and total decision time using this system?

17.7. Will and Becky are two college students who are planning on Sunday how much they will study on Monday for a test on Tuesday. Will weighs future utility the same as current utility. Becky is more impulsive. She puts weight 1 on current period utility but only weight w on utility earned in future periods where $0 < w < 1$. Let s be the cost in terms of utility on Monday from studying. Let b be the benefit in terms of utility on Tuesday from studying and thus performing well on the test.

a. Under what condition on s and b would Will plan to study for the test? What condition is required for him to carry through on his plan?
b. Under what conditions on s and b would Becky plan to study for the test? What condition is required for her to carry through on her plan?

17.8. In period 1, Mr. Consistent and Mr. Hyperbolic are each trying to come up with a plan for how much they will exercise in period 2. Exercise is less enjoyable than other leisure activities, leading to a loss of 100 in terms of period 2 utils. Exercise provides health benefits, realized in period 3, leading to a gain of 250 in terms of period 3 utils. They put the following weights on utilities each period:

	CURRENT PERIOD	PERIOD AFTER CURRENT ONE	TWO PERIODS AFTER CURRENT ONE
Mr. Consistent	1	0.5	0.25
Mr. Hyperbolic	1	0.35	0.175

According to this table, Mr. Consistent's weight on future utility falls by half each period. Mr. Hyperbolic's weights are related to Mr. Consistent's; the difference is that Mr. Hyperbolic's are reduced a further 30% for periods after the current one.

a. Would Mr. Consistent plan to exercise in period 1? Would he follow through on this plan in period 2?
b. Show that Mr. Hyperbolic would not follow through on his exercise plan.
c. Suppose Mr. Hyperbolic could sign a contract in period 1 that forced him to give up an amount of money valued at x utils in period 2 if he does not stick with his exercise plan. How high would x have to be to help him commit to his plan?

17.9. Prospect Pete's preferences are given by the following utility function. His wealth prior to taking a gamble serves as a reference point. He gains 1 util for each dollar of wealth in the reference point. A gain beyond this reference point is worth 1 util per dollar. A loss below this reference point subtracts off 2 utils per dollar. Faced with the choice between gambles, he will choose the one giving the highest expected utility. He has signed up to be a subject in an experiment. Before starting the experiment, his wealth is $10,000.

a. In a first experiment, he is given a choice between two gambles. Gamble A offers an even chance of winning $250 or losing $100. Gamble B provides $30 with certainty. Which gamble would he choose?
b. In a second experiment, he is given a $100 starting bonus. Then, he is given the choice between two different gambles. Gamble C offers an even chance of winning $150 or losing $200. Gamble D results in a loss of $70 with certainty. What choice would he make if he calculates his reference point including the $100 starting bonus? Would his choice change his reference point is his initial $10,000 wealth, meaning that he considers the $100 starting bonus as part of the amount he gets from the gambles?
c. Are Pete's choices in parts a and b the same as he would make if he only cared about the final wealth level he ends up with after the experiment?

17.10. Trans-fatty potato chips are competitively supplied. The supply curve is

$$Q_S = \frac{P}{2}.$$

Demand for these potato chips is

$$Q_D = 100 - 2P.$$

a. Compute the equilibrium price, quantity, consumer surplus, producer surplus, and social welfare.
b. Suppose that consumers make irrational decisions either because of cognitive or willpower limitations, leading them to buy too many bags of potato chips. Although their true demand if they made rational decisions is as given already, their perceived or "mistaken" demand is

$$Q_D = 200 - 2P.$$

Compute the equilibrium price and quantity now. Demonstrate the deadweight loss triangle on a diagram of the market and compute the deadweight loss.
c. What per-unit tax could the government impose to correct this deadweight loss problem?
d. Suppose instead the government made a mistake and the second demand is actually the true demand stemming from rational decisions. What deadweight loss has the government introduced with the tax?

Glossary

A

Accounting costs Recorded amount paid for inputs. (p. 220)

Adverse-selection problem Worst agent types are the ones most eager to transact with the principal. (p. 504)

Agent Player who performs under the terms of the contract in a principal-agent model. (p. 485)

Altruism Regard for others' well-being. (p. 571)

Asymmetric information In a game with uncertainty, information that one player has but the other does not. (pp. 400, 485)

Average cost Total cost divided by output; a common measure of cost per unit. (p. 230)

Average effect The ratio of Y to X at a particular value of X (also the slope of the ray from the origin to the function). (p. 32)

B

Backward induction Solving for equilibrium by working backward from the end of the game to the beginning. (p. 180)

Barriers to entry Factors that prevent new firms from entering a market. (p. 345)

Behavioral economics Study of economic behavior that departs from full rationality. (p. 550)

Bertrand model An oligopoly model in which firms simultaneously choose prices. (p. 381)

Best response A strategy that produces the highest payoff among all possible strategies for a player given what the other player is doing. (p. 161)

Best-response function Function giving the payoff-maximizing choice for one player for each of a continuum of strategies of the other player. (p. 172)

Bilateral monopoly A market in which both suppliers and demanders have monopoly power. Pricing is indeterminate in such markets. (p. 432)

Budget constraint The limit that income places on the combinations of goods that an individual can buy. (p. 61)

C

Capacity constraint A limit to the quantity a firm can produce given the firm's capital and other available inputs. (p. 384)

***Ceteris paribus* assumption** In economic analysis, holding all other factors constant so that only the factor being studied is allowed to change. (p. 47)

Coase theorem If bargaining is costless, the social cost of an externality will be taken into account by the parties, and the allocation of resources will be the same no matter how property rights are assigned. (p. 525)

Common property Property that may be used by anyone without cost. (p. 523)

Common-values setting Object has the same value to all bidders, but each only has an imprecise estimate of that value. (p. 508)

Competitive fringe Group of firms that act as price takers in a market dominated by a price leader. (p. 404)

Complements Two goods such that when the price of one increases, the quantity demanded of the other falls. (p. 94)

Complete preferences The assumption that an individual is able to state which of any two options is preferred. (p. 50)

Composite good Combining expenditures on several different goods whose relative prices do not change into a single good for convenience in analysis. (p. 73)

Compound interest Interest paid on prior interest earned. (p. 446)

Constant cost case A market in which entry or exit has no effect on the cost curves of firms. (p. 290)

Consumer surplus The extra value individuals receive from consuming a good over what they pay for it. What people would be willing to pay for the right to consume a good at its current price. (pp. 100, 296)

Contour lines Lines in two dimensions that show the sets of values of the independent variables that yield the same value for the dependent variable. (p. 35)

Contract curve The set of efficient allocations of the existing goods in an exchange situation. Points off that curve are necessarily inefficient, since individuals can be made unambiguously better off by moving to the curve. (p. 331)

Cournot model An oligopoly model in which firms simultaneously choose quantities. (p. 376)

Cross-price elasticity of demand The percentage change in the quantity demanded of a good in response to a 1 percent change in the price of another good holding other determinants of demand constant. (p. 117)

D

Deadweight loss Losses of consumer and producer surplus that are not transferred to other parties. (p. 306)

Demand function A representation of how quantity demanded depends on prices, income, and preferences. (p. 79)

Dependent variable In algebra, a variable whose value is determined by another variable or set of variables. (p. 23)

Depreciation schedule A formula for dividing the up-front payment for a durable asset across periods. The formula can range from the simple (equal installments) to the complicated (matching the rate at which the asset wears out or minimizing tax liability). (p. 220)

Diminishing returns Hypothesis that the cost associated with producing one more unit of a good rises as more of that good is produced. (p. 12)

Diseconomies of scale Average cost rises as output increases. (p. 234)

Diversification The spreading of risk among several alternatives rather than choosing only one. (p. 134)

Dominant strategy Best response to all of the other player's strategies. (p. 165)

E

Economic costs All costs relevant to an economic decision. (p. 219)

Economic profits (π) The difference between a firm's total revenues and its total economic costs. (p. 224)

Economically efficient allocation of resources An allocation of resources in which the sum of consumer and producer surplus is maximized. Reflects the best (utility maximizing) use of scarce resources. (p. 299)

Economics The study of the allocation of scarce resources among alternative uses. (p. 3)

Economies of scale Average cost falls as output increases. (p. 234)

Economies of scope Reductions in the costs of one product of a multiproduct firm when the output of another product is increased. (p. 240)

Efficiency wage Wage set higher than market rate leading workers to fear firing. (p. 493)

Elasticity The measure of the percentage change in one variable brought about by a 1 percent change in some other variable. (p. 106)

Equilibrium price The price at which the quantity demanded by buyers of a good is equal to the quantity supplied by sellers of the good. (pp. 13, 278)

Equity The fairness of the distribution of goods or utility. (p. 328)

Expansion path The set of cost-minimizing input combinations a firm will choose to produce various levels of output (when the prices of inputs are held constant). (p. 228)

Expected value The average outcome from an uncertain gamble. (p. 125)

Exponential growth A doubling or other proportionate increase each period. (p. 553)

Extensive form Representation of a game as a tree. (p. 163)

Externality The effect of one party's economic activities on another party that is not taken into account by the price system. (pp. 325, 519)

F

Fair gamble Gamble with an expected value of zero. (p. 126)

Fair insurance Insurance for which the premium is equal to the expected value of the loss. (p. 130)

Firm Any organization that turns inputs into outputs. (p. 195)

Firm's short-run supply curve The relationship between price and quantity supplied by a firm in the short run. (p. 267)

First theorem of welfare economics A perfectly competitive price system will bring about an economically efficient allocation of resources. (p. 320)

Fixed costs Costs associated with inputs that are fixed in the short run. (p. 235)

Fixed-proportions production function A production function in which the inputs must be used in a fixed ratio to one another. (p. 208)

Focal point Logical outcome on which to coordinate, based on information outside of the game. (p. 174)

Framing effect The same choice, presented in two different ways, leads to different decisions. (p. 558)

Free rider A consumer of a nonexclusive good who does not pay for it in the hope that other consumers will. (p. 538)

Functional notation A way of denoting the fact that the value taken on by one variable (Y) depends on the value taken on by some other variable (X) or set of variables. (p. 23)

G

General equilibrium model An economic model of a complete system of markets. (p. 315)

Giffen's paradox A situation in which an increase in a good's price leads people to consume more of the good. (p. 90)

H

Homogeneous demand function Quantity demanded does not change when prices and income increase in the same proportion. (p. 80)

Hyperbolic discounting Steep drop in weight on utility earned after the current period. (p. 566)

I

Imperfect competition A market situation in which buyers or sellers have some influence on the prices of goods or services. (p. 325)

Incentive-compatible Describes contract that gets the agent to make the intended choice. (p. 500)

Income effect The part of the change in quantity demanded that is caused by a change in real income. A movement to a new indifference curve. (p. 83)

Income effect of a change in w Movement to a higher indifference curve in response to a rise in the real wage rate. If leisure is a normal good, a rise in w causes an individual to work less. (p. 441)

Income elasticity of demand The percentage change in the quantity demanded of a good in response to a 1 percent change in income holding other determinants of demand constant. (p. 115)

Incomplete information Some players have information about the game that others do not. (p. 187)

Increase or decrease in demand The change in demand for a good caused by changes in the price of another good, in income, or in preferences. Graphically represented by a shift of the entire demand curve. (p. 98)

Increase or decrease in quantity demanded The increase or decrease in quantity demanded caused by a change in the good's price. Graphically represented by the movement along a demand curve. (p. 98)

Increasing cost case A market in which the entry of firms increases firms' costs. (p. 292)

Independent variable In an algebraic equation, a variable that is unaffected by the action of another variable and may be assigned any value. (p. 23)

Indifference curve A curve that shows all the combinations of goods or services that provide the same level of utility. (p. 53)

Indifference curve map A contour map that shows the utility an individual obtains from all possible consumption options. (p. 56)

Individual demand curve A graphic representation of the relationship between the price of a good and the quantity of it demanded by a person, holding all other factors constant. (p. 95)

Inferior good A good that is bought in smaller quantities as income increases. (p. 81)

Initial endowments The initial holdings of goods from which trading begins. (p. 332)

Intercept The value of *Y* when *X* equals zero. (p. 25)

Interest Payment for the current use of funds. (p. 466)

Isoquant A curve that shows the various combinations of inputs that will produce the same amount of output. (p. 199)

Isoquant map A contour map of a firm's production function. (p. 199)

L

Leisure Time spent in any activity other than market work. (p. 438)

Lindahl equilibrium Balance between people's demand for public goods and the tax shares that each must pay for them. (p. 540)

Linear function An equation that is represented by a straight-line graph. (p. 25)

Long run The period of time in which a firm may consider all of its inputs to be variable in making its decisions. (p. 234)

Long-run elasticity of supply The percentage change in quantity supplied in the long run in response to a 1 percent change in price after all adjustments in input prices. (p. 293)

M

Marginal cost The additional cost of producing one more unit of output. (p. 230)

Marginal effect The change in *Y* brought about by a one unit change in *X* at a particular value of *X* (also the slope of the function). (p. 31)

Marginal expense The cost of hiring one more unit of an input. Will exceed the price of the input if the firm faces an upward-sloping supply curve for the input. (p. 425)

Marginal product The additional output that can be produced by adding one more unit of a particular input while holding all other inputs constant. (p. 196)

Marginal rate of substitution (MRS) The rate at which an individual is willing to reduce consumption of one good when he or she gets one more unit of another good. The absolute value of the slope of an indifference curve. (p. 54)

Marginal revenue The extra revenue a firm receives when it sells one more unit of output. (p. 254)

Marginal revenue curve A curve showing the relation between the quantity a firm sells and the revenue yielded by the last unit sold. Derived from the demand curve. (p. 259)

Marginal revenue product (MRP) The extra revenue obtained from selling the output produced by hiring an extra worker or machine. (p. 414)

Marginal value product (MVP) A special case of marginal revenue product in which the firm is a price taker for its output. (p. 415)

Market demand The total quantity of a good or service demanded by all potential buyers. (p. 102)

Market demand curve The relationship between the total quantity demanded of a good or service and its price, holding all other factors constant. (p. 102)

Market line A line showing the relationship between risk and annual returns that an investor can achieve by mixing financial assets. (p. 145)

Market period A short period of time during which quantity supplied is fixed. (p. 277)

Median voter A voter whose preferences for a public good represent the middle point of all voters' preferences for the good. (p. 544)

Microeconomics The study of the economic choices individuals and firms make and of how these choices create markets and affect welfare. (p. 4)

Mixed strategy Randomly selecting from several possible actions. (p. 167)

Models Simple theoretical descriptions that capture the essentials of how the economy work. (p. 4)

Monopolistic competition Market in which each firm faces a downward-sloping demand curve and there are no barriers to entry. (p. 404)

Monopoly rents The profits that a monopolist earns in the long run. (p. 349)

Monopsony Condition in which one firm is the only hirer in a particular input market. (p. 425)

Moral-hazard problem The best hidden action for the agent may not be good for the principal. (p. 486)

N

Nash equilibrium A set of strategies, one for each player, that are each best responses against one another. (p. 161)

Natural monopoly A firm that exhibits diminishing average cost over a broad range of output levels. (p. 345)

Neoclassical economics Assumes fully rational maximizing behavior. (p. 550)

Nonexclusive goods Goods that provide benefits that no one can be excluded from enjoying. (p. 534)

Nonlinear pricing Schedule of quantities sold at different per-unit prices. (p. 359)

Nonrival goods Goods that additional consumers may use at zero marginal costs. (p. 534)

Normal form Representation of a game using a payoff matrix. (p. 163)

Normal good A good that is bought in greater quantities as income increases. (p. 81)

O

Oligopoly A market with few firms but more than one. (p. 374)

Opportunity cost The cost of a good as measured by the alternative uses that are foregone by producing it. (pp. 5, 220)

Option contract Financial contract offering the right, but not the obligation, to buy or sell an asset over a specified period. (p. 137)

Output effect The effect of an input price change on the amount of the input that the firm hires that results from a change in the firm's output level. (p. 419)

P

Pareto efficient allocation An allocation of available resources in which no mutually beneficial trading opportunities are unexploited. That is, an allocation in which no one person can be made better off without someone else being made worse off. (p. 311)

Partial equilibrium model An economic model of a single market. (p. 315)

Perfect price discrimination Selling each unit of output for the highest price obtainable. Extracts all of the consumer surplus available in a given market. (p. 356)

Perpetuity A promise of a certain number of dollars each year, forever. (p. 474)

Pigovian tax A tax or subsidy on an externality that brings about an equality of private and social marginal costs. (p. 529)

Pooling equilibrium All types choose the same action in a signaling game. (p. 512)

Positive-normative distinction Distinction between theories that seek to explain the world as it is and theories that postulate the way the world should be. (p. 17)

Predatory pricing An incumbent's charging a low price in order to induce the exit of a rival. (p. 401)

Present value Discounting the value of future transactions back to the present day to take account of the effect of potential interest payments. (pp. 457, 469)

Price discrimination Selling identical units of output at different prices. (p. 355)

Price elasticity of demand The percentage change in the quantity demanded of a good in response to a 1 percent change in its price while holding other determinants of demand constant. (p. 106)

Price taker A firm or individual whose decisions regarding buying or selling have no effect on the prevailing market price of a good. (p. 255)

Price-leadership model A model with one dominant firm that behaves strategically and a group of small firms that behave as price takers. (p. 403)

Principal Player offering the contract in a principal-agent model. (p. 485)

Private property Property that is owned by specific people who may prevent others from using it. (p. 523)

Probability The relative frequency with which an event occurs. (p. 125)

Producer surplus The extra value producers get for a good in excess of the opportunity costs they incur by producing it. What all producers would pay for the right to sell a good at its current market price. (p. 296)

Production function The mathematical relationship between inputs and outputs. (p. 195)

Production possibility frontier A graph showing all possible combinations of goods that can be produced with a fixed amount of resources. (p. 4)

Proper subgame Part of the game tree including an initial decision not connected to another in an oval and everything branching out below it. (p. 179)

Property rights The legal specification of who owns a good and the trades the owner is allowed to make with it. (p. 523)

Prospect theory Theory that people are very sensitive to small losses from current wealth. (p. 556)

Public goods Goods that are both nonexclusive and nonrival. (pp. 325, 535)

Pure strategy A single action played with certainty. (p. 167)

R

Rate of technical substitution (RTS) The amount by which one input can be reduced when one more unit of another input is added while holding output constant. The negative of the slope of an isoquant. (p. 201)

Real option Option arising in a setting outside of finance. (p. 137)

Reciprocity Rewarding good behavior and punishing bad behavior. (p. 574)

Rental rate (v) The cost of hiring one machine for one hour. (p. 222)

Rent-seeking behavior Firms or individuals influencing government policy to increase their own welfare. (p. 546)

Returns to scale The rate at which output increases in response to proportional increases in all inputs. (p. 204)

Ricardian rent Long-run profits earned by owners of low-cost firms. May be capitalized into the prices of these firms' inputs. (p. 298)

Risk aversion The tendency of people to refuse to accept fair gambles. (p. 126)

Risk neutral Willing to accept any fair gamble. (p. 129)

S

Scarcity costs The opportunity costs of future production forgone because current production depletes exhaustible resources. (p. 458)

Separating equilibrium Each type chooses a different action in a signaling game. (p. 512)

Short run The period of time in which a firm must consider some inputs to be fixed in making its decisions. (p. 234)

Short-run elasticity of supply The percentage change in quantity supplied in the short run in response to a 1 percent change in price while holding other factors that affect supply constant. (p. 284)

Short-run market supply curve The relationship between market price and quantity supplied of a good in the short run. (p. 280)

Shutdown price The price below which the firm will choose to produce no output in the short run. Equal to minimum average variable cost. (p. 268)

Simultaneous equations A set of equations with more than one variable that must be solved together for a particular solution. (p. 36)

Slope The direction of a line on a graph; shows the change in Y that results from a unit change in X. (p. 26)

Social costs Costs of production that include both input costs and costs of the externalities that production may cause. (p. 521)

Stackelberg equilibrium Subgame-perfect equilibrium of the sequential version of the Cournot game. (p. 397)

Stage game Simple game that is played repeatedly. (p. 182)

Statistical inference Use of actual data and statistical techniques to determine quantitative economic relationships. (p. 39)

Subgame-perfect equilibrium Strategies that form a Nash equilibrium on every proper subgame. (p. 180)

Substitutes Two goods such that if the price of one increases, the quantity demanded of the other rises. (p. 94)

Substitution effect (in consumption) The part of the change in quantity demanded that is caused by substitution of one good for another. A movement along an indifference curve. (p. 81)

Substitution effect (in production) The substitution of one input for another while holding output constant in response to a change in the input's price. (p. 418)

Substitution effect of a change in w Movement along an indifference curve in response to a change in the real wage. A rise in w causes an individual to work more. (p. 441)

Sunk cost Expenditure that once made cannot be recovered. (p. 219)

Supply response The change in quantity of output supplied in response to a change in demand conditions. (p. 277)

Supply-demand model A model describing how a good's price is determined by the behavior of the individuals who buy the good and of the firms that sell it. (p. 8)

T

Tariff A tax on an imported good. May be equivalent to a quota or a nonquantitative restriction on trade. (p. 308)

Tax incidence theory The study of the final burden of a tax after considering all market reactions to it. (p. 302)

Technical progress A shift in the production function that allows a given output level to be produced using fewer inputs. (p. 209)

Testing assumptions Verifying economic models by examining the validity of the assumptions on which they are based. (p. 15)

Testing predictions Verifying economic models by asking if they can accurately predict real-world events. (p. 15)

Theory of choice The interaction of preferences and constraints that causes people to make the choices they do. (p. 47)

Transitivity of preferences The property that if A is preferred to B, and B is preferred to C, then A must be preferred to C. (p. 50)

Trigger strategy Strategy in a repeated game where the player stops cooperating to punish another player's break with cooperation. (p. 182)

U

Utility The pleasure or satisfaction that people get from their economic activity. (p. 47)

V

Variable costs Costs associated with inputs that can be varied in the short run. (p. 235)

Variables The basic elements of algebra, usually called X, Y, and so on, that may be given any numerical value in an equation. (p. 23)

W

Wage rate (w) The cost of hiring one worker for one hour. (p. 221)

Winner's curse Winning reveals that all other bidders thought the good was worth less than the highest bidder did. (p. 508)

Y

Yield The effective (internal) rate of return promised by a payment stream that can be purchased at a certain price. (p. 475)

Solutions

To Odd-Numbered Problems

This section contains solutions to all of the odd-numbered problems in the text. Solutions to all of the text problems are contained in the *Instructor's Manual.*

Chapter 1

1.1 a.

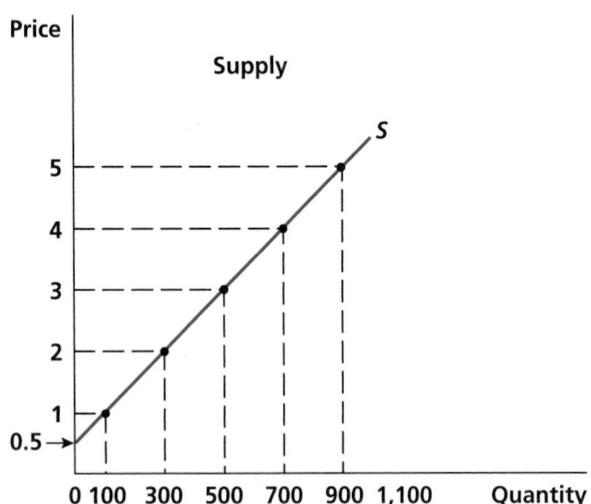

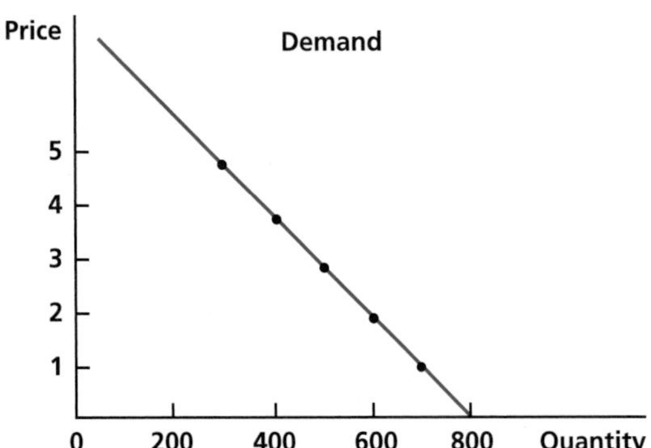

b. The supply points seem to be on a straight line. Use $\frac{\Delta Q}{\Delta P} = 200$. So, $Q = a + 200P$.
At $P = 1$, $Q = 100$ this implies $a = -100$. So the final supply equation is $Q_S = -100 + 200P$
Applying the same logic to the demand data yields $Q_D = 800 - 100P$.

c. If $P = 0$, $Q_S = -100$ (= 0 because can't have negative supply), $Q_D = 800$, $ED = 800$.

d. If $P = 6$, $Q_S = 1100$, $Q_D = 200$, $ES = 900$.

1.3 a. Excess Demand is the following at the various prices

$$P = 1\ ED = 700 - 100 = 600$$
$$P = 2\ ED = 600 - 300 = 300$$
$$P = 3\ ED = 500 - 500 = 0$$
$$P = 4\ ED = 400 - 700 = -300$$
$$P = 5\ ED = 300 - 900 = -600$$

The auctioneer found the equilibrium price where $ED = 0$.

b. Here is the information the auctioneer gathers from calling quantities:

$$Q = 300\ PS = 2\ PD = 5$$
$$Q = 500\ PS = 3\ PD = 3$$
$$Q = 700\ PS = 4\ PD = 1$$

So, the auctioneer knows that $Q = 500$ is an equilibrium.

c. Many callout auctions operate this way – though usually quantity supplied is a fixed amount. Many financial markets operate with "bid" and "asked" prices which approximate the procedure in part b

1.5

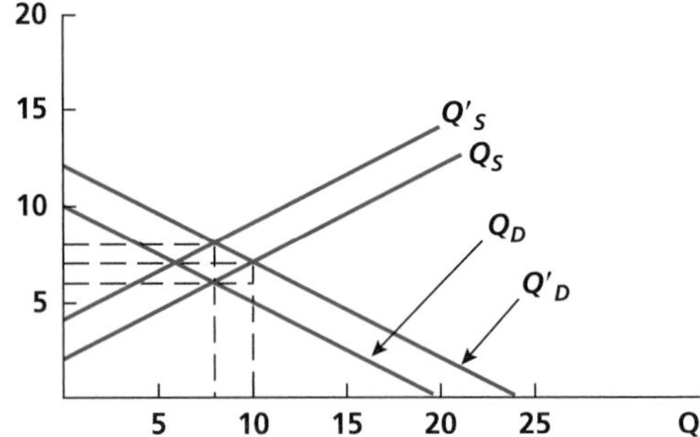

The algebraic solution proceeds as follows:

a. $Q_D = -2P + 20$.
$Q_S = 2P - 4$.
Set $Q_D = Q_S$: $-2P + 20 = 2P - 4$
$$24 = 4P$$
$$P = 6.$$
Substituting for P gives: $Q_D = Q_S = 8$.

b. Now $Q_D' = -2P + 24$.
Set $Q_D = Q_S$: $-2P + 24 = 2P - 4$
$28 = 4P$
$P = 7$.
Substituting gives: $Q_D = Q_S = 10$.
c. $P = 8$, $Q = 8$ (see graph).

1.7 a.

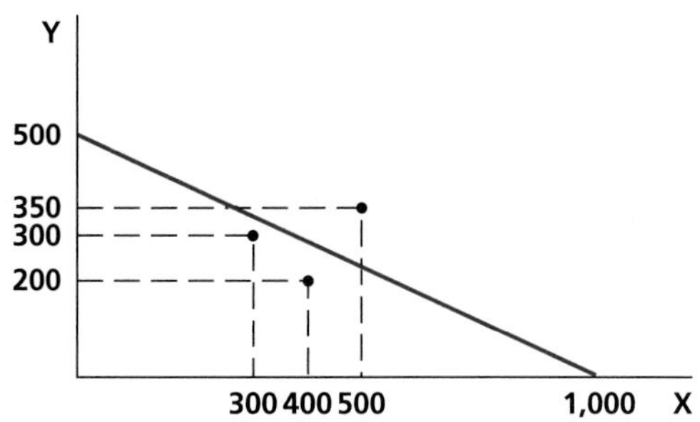

b. Both these points lie below the frontier.
c. This point lies beyond the frontier.
d. Opportunity cost of $1Y$ is $2X$ no matter how much is produced.

1.9 a. $X^2 + 4Y^2 = 100$.
If $X = Y$, then $5X^2 = 100$, and $X = \sqrt{20}$ and $Y = \sqrt{20}$.

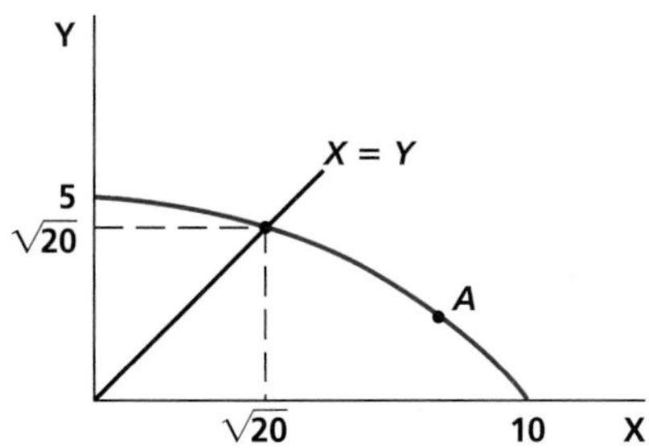

b. If only X is produced, $X = 10$. So can trade any combination for which $X + Y = 10$.
c. Because consumers wish X and Y in equal amounts, should have $X = Y = 5$.
d. Costs of forgone trade would be a loss of X of $5 - \sqrt{20} \approx 0.53$. Loss in Y would be the same.

Chapter 2

2.1 a. $\dfrac{\$8.00}{\$.40/\text{apple}} = 20$ apples can be bought.

b. $\dfrac{\$8.00}{\$.10/\text{banana}} = 80$ bananas can be bought.

c. 10 apples cost:
10 apples $\cdot$ \$.40/apple = \$4.00, so there is \$8.00 − \$4.00 = \$4.00 left to spend on bananas, which means $\dfrac{\$4.00}{\$.10/\text{banana}} = 40$ banana can be bought.

d. One less apple frees \$.40 to be spent on bananas, so $\dfrac{\$4.00}{\$.10/\text{banana}} = 4$ more bananas can be bought

e. $\$8.00 = \$.40 \cdot$ number of apples $+\$.10 \cdot$ number of bananas $= .40A + .10B$.

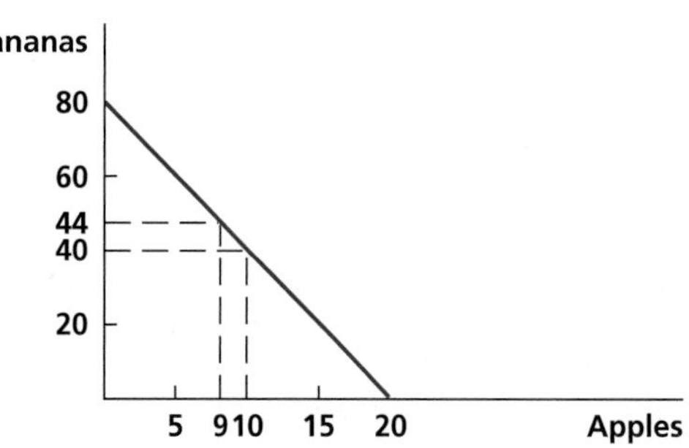

2.3 a. If $U = \sqrt{C \cdot D}$ indifference curves are hyperbolas

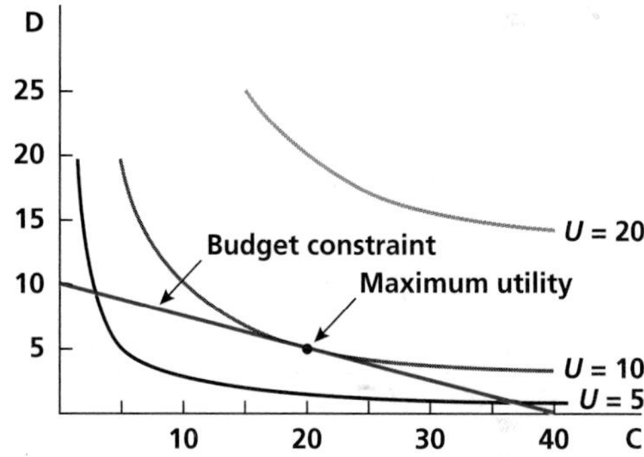

b. Budget constraint is $200 = 5C + 20D$ shown on graph
c. With 200 can buy $10D$. With $D = 10$, $C = 0$, and $U = 0$
d. See graph. If, say, spend 100 on C and 100 on D can only buy $C = 20$, $D = 5$. Well below $U = 20$.
e. With $C = 20$, $D = 5$, $U = 10$
f. To show solution in e is highest, try

$C = 40, D = 0, U = 0$
$C = 24, D = 4, U = \sqrt{96} < 10$
$C = 16, D = 6, U = \sqrt{96} < 10$
$C = 0, D = 10, U = 0$

so $C = 20$, $D = 5$, looks like maximum

2.5

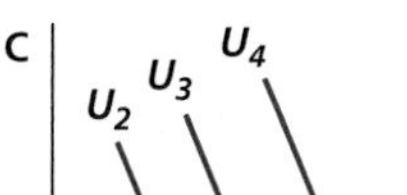
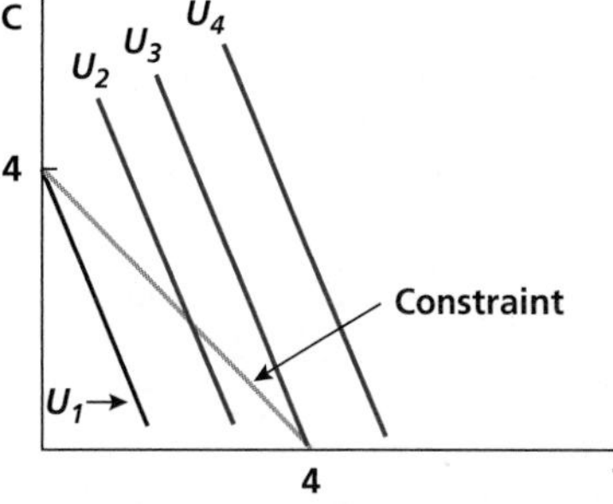

a. The indifference curves here are straight lines with a slope $-4/3$. The MRS is therefore $4/3$.

b. Because a unit of tea provides more additional utility than does a unit of coffee, she will spend all of her funds on tea when the prices of the two goods are equal. Therefore: $T = 4$, $C = 0$.
c. The graph shows that the indifference curves are steeper than the budget constraint, so the maximum occurs on the T axis.
d. With more income she would continue to buy only tea. If coffee price falls to \$2, now coffee is a cheaper way to obtain utility – one unit of coffee yields 3 units of utility at a cost of \$2, so with coffee utility costs \$2/3 per unit. With tea, utility costs \$3/4 per unit.

2.7

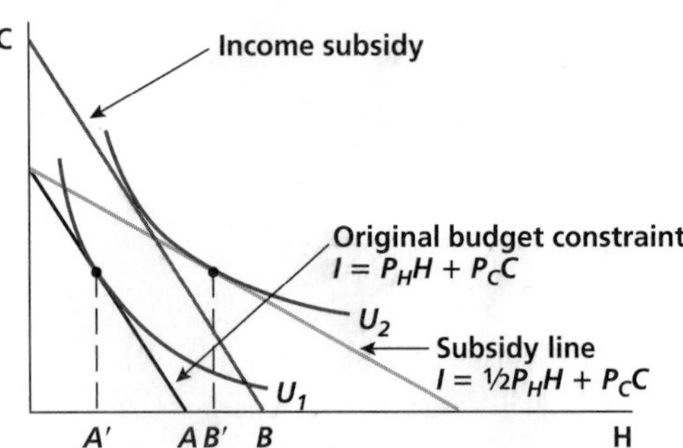

Income subsidy is cheaper since $AB < A'B'$. The income grant is smaller because it does not distort market prices. The subsidy is more costly because it encourages people to buy more of the subsidized even though it is not really cheaper.

2.9

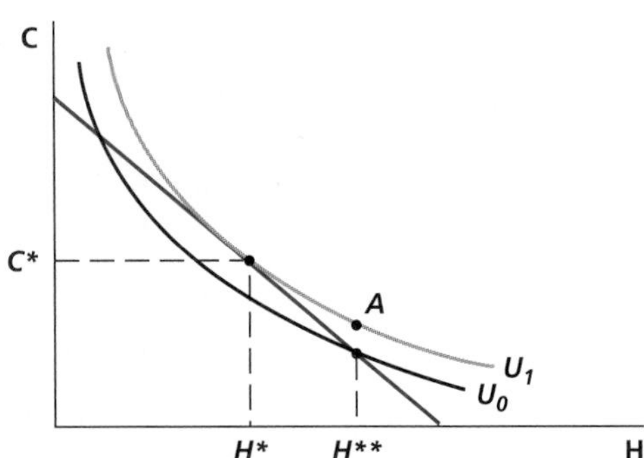

a. The figure shows that an unconstrained choice will yield utility level U_1 with choices of C^*, H^*.
b. If the government requires purchase of H^{**}, utility would fall to U_0. Low-income consumers are most likely to be constrained by $H \geq H^{**}$.
c. To return to U_1, budget constraint must allow this person to reach point A. Income must be increased so part budget constraint passes through A.
d. New budget must have same C-intercept and pass through A.

Chapter 3

3.1 a. $I = \$200$; $S = J$.
$P_S S + P_J J = 20S + 20S = 200$; $40S = 200, S = 5, J = 5$
b. $P_S S + P_J J = I$; $20S + 30S + 200$; $50S = 200$.
$S = 4, J = 4$
c.

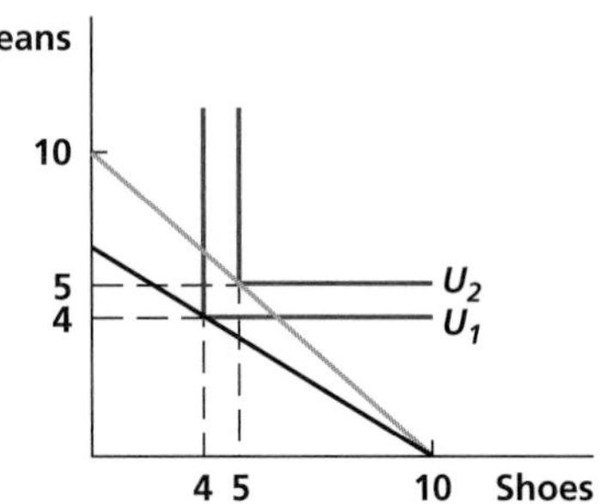

Elizabeth's indifference curves are L-shaped since she only gains utility when shoes and jeans are purchased in a one-to-one proportion. Ten pairs of shoes and five pairs of jeans yield the same utility as five pairs of shoes and five pairs of jeans.
d. The change from U_2 to U_1 is entirely attributable to the income effect. There is no substitution effect due to Elizabeth's insistence on a fixed proportion of jeans and shoes.

3.3 a. He must spend \$.10 per sandwich on each sandwich ingredient. So, with \$3, he can buy 15 sandwiches. These will require 15 ounces of jelly and 30 ounces of peanut butter.
b. Now he must spend \$.15 on jelly and \$.10 on peanut butter for each sandwich. Hence he can now buy only 12 sandwiches – 12 ounces of jelly (costing \$1.80) and 24 ounces of peanut putter (costing \$1.20).
c. In order to return to buying 15 sandwiches, he will need an income of \$3.75. Hence he needs a compensation of \$.75.
d. The graph shows that the sandwich inputs are consumed in fixed proportions:

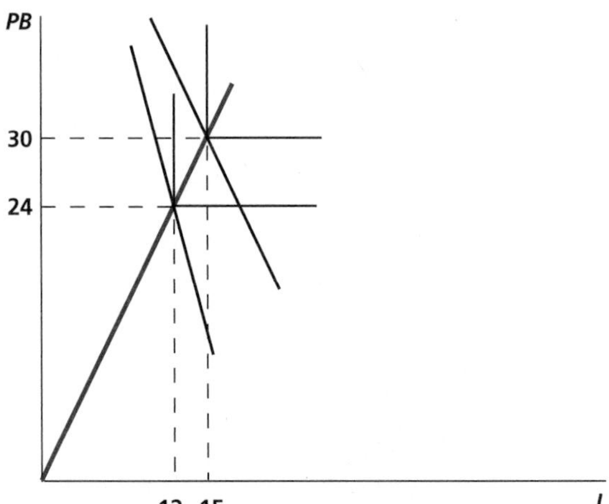

e. This is really a problem in the demand for peanut butter and jelly sandwiches. He will spend all of his income on this one item. The demand curve is given by $Q = 3/P$ (where P is the price of a peanut butter and jelly sandwich.

f. There are no substitution effects here. The reason jelly purchases decline in part b is due solely to an income effect.

3.5 a. This is simply a matter of definition—starting from a specific utility-maximizing point, the regular demand curve examines the consequence of changing price, holding income and other prices constant. The compensated demand curve examines the consequences of changing price, holding utility and other prices constant.

b. The compensated demand curve does not incorporate income effects. Therefore, the impact of a given price change is smaller than would be the case with a regular demand curve (assuming the good is a normal good).

c. Because the construction of a compensated demand curve can be based on any utility level and because utility levels vary along the regular demand curve, any point on the regular demand curve can be a basis for constructing a unique compensated demand curve.

d. There are no substitution effects in Irving's demand for chianti. His compensated demand curve is perfectly inelastic at the prevailing level of chianti consumption. A change in chianti consumption would change utility and represent a different compensated demand curve. Irving's regular demand curve for chianti is not perfectly inelastic because it also involves income effects when the price of this wine changes.

3.7 a. $P = 0,\ Q = 20.$

b. $Q = 0,\ P = 20.$

c. $P \cdot Q = 20P - P^2$ Here are a few values:

$P = 2,\ PQ = 36;\ P = 4,\ PQ = 64;\ P = 6,$
$PQ = 84;\ P = 8,\ PQ = 96;\ P = 10,\ PQ = 100;$
$P = 12,\ PQ = 96;\ P = 14,\ PQ = 84;\ P = 16,$
$PQ = 64;\ P = 18,\ PQ = 36.$

d. From this calculation is seems that $P = 10$ provides maximum expenditures here. That this is indeed the case can be shown with calculus by differentiating the expression for total spending with respect to price.

e. With this new demand curve, both the price and quantity intercepts are doubled. Total spending is now given by $PQ = 40P - 2P^2 = 2(20P - P^2)$ so, for each price, total spending is twice what it was in part c. Again, total expenditures are maximized when $P = 10,\ PQ = 200.$

3.9 a. Because the market demand curve is the horizontal sum of each individual's demand curve, the total consumer surplus area will just be the sum of each individual's consumer surplus area.

b. The graph shows that with a perfectly inelastic demand curve, the loss in consumer surplus is largest because there is no reduction in quantity demanded. When demand is more elastic the loss is smaller because demanders reduce the quantity of the good they demand (and spend the funds elsewhere). Intuitively, with elastic demand people can get away from a price rise whereas with inelastic demand they cannot.

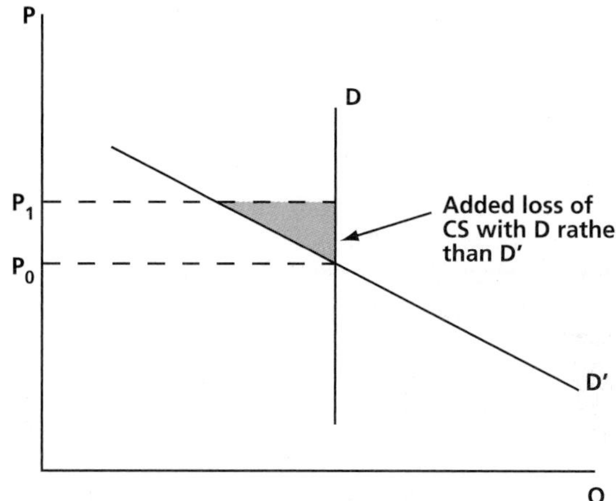

c. The above figure shows that, if demand is perfectly inelastic, the statement is true. But, if demand is less than perfectly inelastic, the reduction in quantity purchased in response to the price rise will make the change in total spending less than the loss of consumer surplus. Indeed, if demand is elastic, the price rise will actually cause total spending to fall even though there will still be a loss of consumer surplus.

Chapter 4

4.1 a. The expected payoffs from gambles 1 and 2 are, respectively,

$$\left(\frac{18}{38}\right)(+1{,}000) + \left(\frac{20}{38}\right)(-1{,}000) \approx -52.6$$

$$\left(\frac{1}{38}\right)(17{,}500) + \left(\frac{37}{38}\right)(-500) \approx -26.3.$$

They are both negative, not zero as required of fair gambles.

b. The expected utility from gambles 1 and 2 are, respectively,

$$\left(\frac{18}{38}\right)\sqrt{11{,}000} + \left(\frac{20}{38}\right)\sqrt{9{,}000} \approx 99.61$$

$$\left(\frac{1}{38}\right)\sqrt{27{,}500} + \left(\frac{37}{38}\right)\sqrt{9{,}500} \approx 99.27.$$

The first is higher, so Wen should choose gamble 1.

c. The expected utility from not taking a gamble is $\sqrt{10{,}000} = 100$, higher than the expected utility from gambles 1 or 2.

4.3 a. $E(U) = .75 \log(10{,}000) + .25 \log(9{,}000) = 3.9886$.
b. $E(U)$ with insurance $= \log(9{,}750) = 3.9890$. Hence $U_w > U_{w.o}$.
c. Will pay up to point where $U_w = U_{w.o}$. So want $3.9886 = \log(10{,}000 - P)$, where P is the premium cost. $10^{3.9886} = 10{,}000 - P = 9.741$. $P_{\max} = \$259$.
d. Fair insurance: $E(L) = .30 \cdot 1{,}000 = \$300$. Since $\$300 > \$259$, she will not buy this insurance even though this is fair insurance. This is an example of moral hazard.

4.5 a. $U = \ln(\$18{,}000) = 9.798$
b. $U = \ln(\$18{,}300) = 9.815$
c. If Molly invests \$100 in the trip, she will have a wealth of \$17,900 if Crazy Eddie does not have the set and \$18,200 if he does. $E(U) = .5\ln(17{,}900) + .5\ln(18{,}200) = 9.801$. Since this exceeds the utility from part a, it is worth the trip.

4.7 a. The expected value of the prize is \$7,500. The value of the option is $(.5 \times \$0) + (.5 \times \$8{,}000) = \$4{,}000$. So the option is not worth what is being asked.
b. The variability of income is lower with the option (ranging only between 3,500 and 10,500 rather than between 0 and 15,000), so a particularly risk-averse contestant may choose the option even at an actuarially unfair price.

4.9 a. With the first utility function, $\sqrt{I} = 0.5\sqrt{116{,}000} + 0.5\sqrt{98{,}000}$, implying $I = 106{,}800$, for a certainty equivalent yield of 6.8%. Similar calculations show the certainty equivalent yield is 6.6% with the second utility function and 6.2% with the third. With any of these utility functions, stocks offer a much higher certainty equivalent yield than do bonds.
b. This extreme utility function entails a certainty equivalent yield of 3.2% for stocks, still higher than bonds.

Chapter 5

5.1 a. A plays Up; B plays Left.
b. A's dominant strategy is Up. B does not have a dominant strategy.

5.3 a.

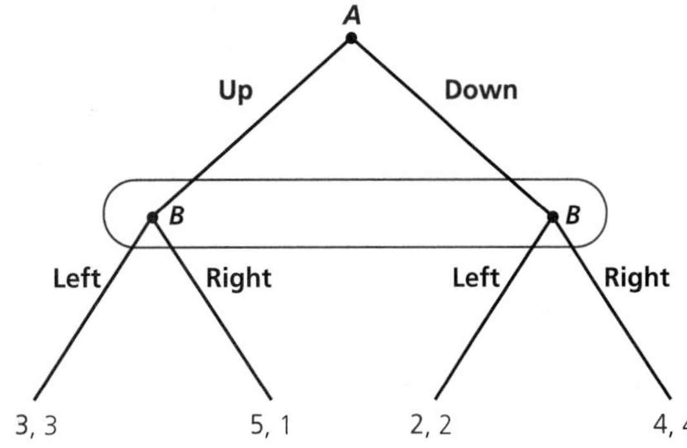

b.

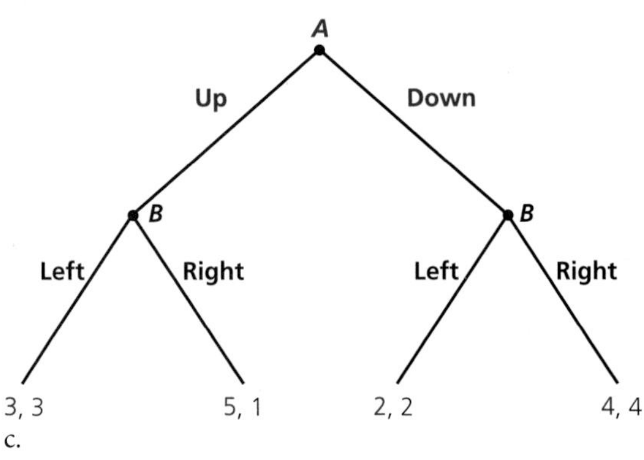

c.

		B: Left | Up, Left | Down	Left | Up, Right | Down	Right | Up, Left | Down	Right | Up, Right | Down
A	Up	3, 3	3, 3	5, 1	5, 1
	Down	2, 2	4, 4	2, 2	4, 4

There are two Nash equilibria: first, A plays Up, and B plays "Left | Up, Left | Down"; second, A plays Down, and B plays "Left | Up, Right | Down." The second is a subgame-perfect equilibrium.

5.5 a.

		B: Shirk	Work
A	Shirk	0, 0	4, −2
	Work	−2, 4	1, 1

b. Both shirk.
c. Shirking is a dominant strategy for both. Game resembles the Prisoners' Dilemma.

5.7 a. Using the underlining method shows that Rat is a dominant strategy for both and that both choosing Rat is a Nash equilibrium.
b. Expected payoff in equilibrium is

$$\begin{aligned} & 1 + (g)(1) + (g^2)(1) + (g^3)(1) + \cdots \\ &= (1)(1 + g + g^2 + g^3 + \cdots) \\ &= 1/(1 - g). \end{aligned}$$

If a player deviates to Rat in the first period, his or her payoff is 3 in the first period and 0 from then on. For the trigger strategies to be an equilibrium, $1/(1 - g) \geq 3$, implying $g \geq 2/3$.
c. The expected equilibrium payoff is the same as in part b, $1/(1 - g)$. If a player deviates from tit-for-tat, he or she earns 3 in the first period, 0 in the second,

and then the players return to the original equilibrium for an expected payoff of

$$\begin{aligned} &3 + (g)(0) + (g^2)(1) + (g^3)(1) + \cdots \\ &= 2 + 1 + (g)(1 - 1) + (1)(g^2 + g^3 + \cdots) \\ &= 2 - g + (1)(1 + g + g^2 + g^3 + \cdots) \\ &= 2 - g + 1/(1 - g). \end{aligned}$$

For this payoff from deviating to be less than the equilibrium payoff, $2 - g \leq 0$, implying $g \geq 2$. This is impossible since g is a probability. So players cannot sustain cooperation on Silent using tit-for-tat.

5.9 a. There are four pure-strategy Nash equilibria, one in which none of the three locate in the mall and three different ones in which two locate in the mall and the third does not (so three different ones, one for each different left-out store *A*, *B*, and C).

b. Playing cooperatively, they might reach one of the three outcomes in which two of the stores locate in the mall and the third does not. The sum of the payoffs is the highest in these outcomes, 4. The stores locating in the mall may pay the left-out one for not locating there, perhaps each paying 2/3 so that total surplus is split evenly.

Chapter 6

6.1 a. $K = 6$, $q = 6K + 4L = 6(6) + 4L = 36 + 4L$.

If $q = 60$, $4L = 60 - 36 = 24$, $L = 6$.

If $q = 100$, $4L = 100 - 36 = 64$, $L = 16$.

b. $K = 8$, $q = 6K + 4L = 6(8) + 4L = 48 + 4L$.

If $q = 60$, $4L = 60–48 = 12$, $L = 3$.

If $q = 100$, $4L = 100–48 = 52$, $L = 13$.

c. RTS = 2/3. If L increases by 1 unit, q can remain constant by decreasing K by 2/3 units.

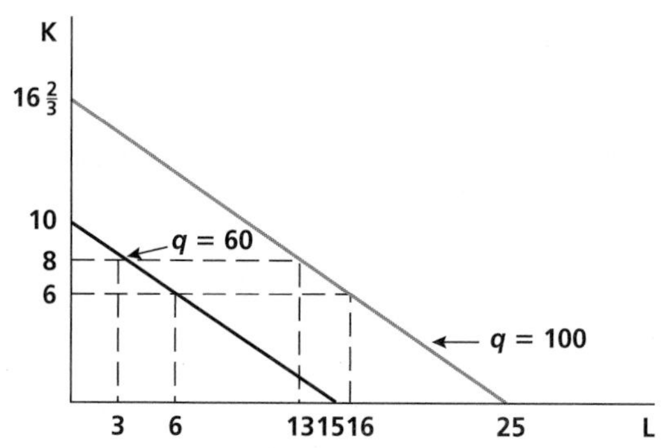

6.3 a.

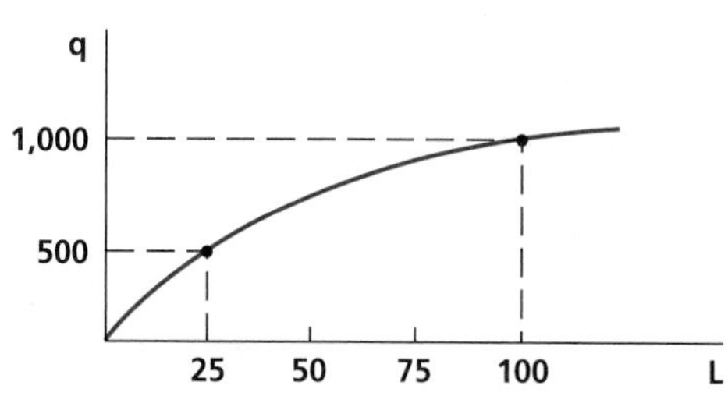

b. $AP_L = \dfrac{q}{L} = \dfrac{100}{\sqrt{L}}$.

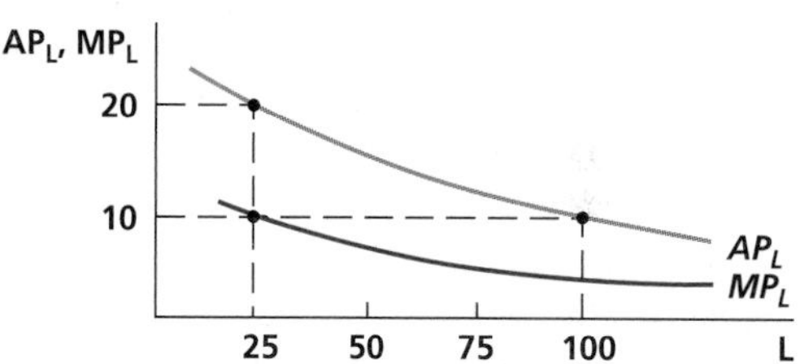

c. Graph above. Since the AP_L is everywhere decreasing, then each additional worker must be contributing less than the average of the existing workers, bringing the average down. Therefore, the marginal productivity must be lower than the average.
Here $MP_L = (1/2)AP_L$.

6.5 a.

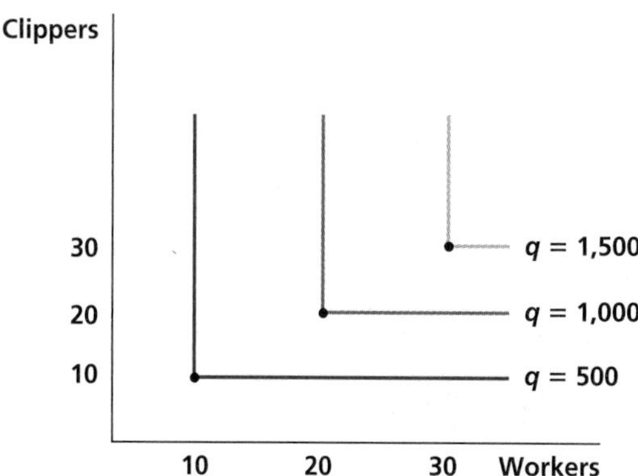

Will operate at the vertex of the isoquants.

b. Hire 20 workers, $q = 1{,}000$.

c. Depends on whether grapes can be sold for a price exceeding average cost.

d.

Clippers

40 $q = 1{,}500$

26⅔ $q = 1{,}000$

13⅓ $q = 500$

6⅔ 13⅓ 20 Workers

Choice would depend on clipper costs and wages for ambidextrous workers.

6.7 a. In 6.7, $A = 10$, $a = b = 1/2$.
b. If we use $2K$, $2L$, have $q = A(2K)^a(2L)^b = 2^{a+b}AK^aL^b$, and if $a + b = 1$, this is twice AK^aL^b.
c. From b, it follows that output will less than double or more than double if $a + b < 1$ or $a + b > 1$.
d. Function can exhibit any returns to scale desired depending on the values of a and b.

6.9 a. $q = 100\sqrt{K \cdot L} = 1{,}000$, so $\sqrt{K \cdot L} = 10$, or $K \cdot L = 100$.

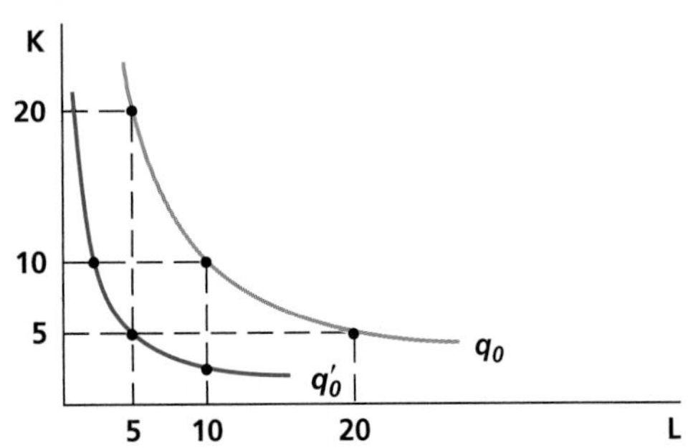

b. $K = 10$, $L = 10$. $AP_L = q/L = 1{,}000/10 = 100$ boxes per hour per worker.
c. If $q = 200\sqrt{KL} = 1{,}000$; $\sqrt{KL} = 5$, or $KL = 25$. Isoquant shifts to q_0' Now, if $K = 10$, $L = 2.5$. $AP_L = q/L = 1{,}000/2.5 = 400$ boxes per hour per worker.
d. $q = (1.05)^t 100\sqrt{KL} = 1{,}000$, so $\sqrt{KL} = 10/(1.05)^t$ or $KL = 100/(1.05)^{2t}$. Hence, the amounts of capital and labor required to produce 1,000 units of output fall over time. If $K = 10$, $L = 10$, $AP_L = 1{,}000(1.05)^t/10 = 100(1.05)^t$. Therefore the average product of labor grows over time at 5 percent per year.

Chapter 7

7.1 a.

K

30

20 $q = 60$

10 $q = 40$ $q = 20$

20 40 60 L

RTS = 1/2 since, if L is increased by one, K can be reduced by 1/2 while holding q constant.
b. Since RTS $= 1/2 < w/v = 1$, the manufacturer will use only K. For $q = 20$, $K = 10$; $q = 40$, $K = 20$; $q = 60$, $K = 30$. The manufacturer's expansion path is simply the K-axis.
c. If $v = \$3$, RTS $= 1/2 > w/v = 1/3$, the manufacturer will use only L. For $q = 20$, $L = 20$; $q = 40$, $L = 40$; $q = 60$, $L = 60$. Now the manufacturer's expansion path is the L-axis.

7.3 a. This is a cubic cost curve. It resembles Chapter 7.3 (d).
b. $AC = TC/q = q^2 - 30q + 350$.
This is a parabola. It reaches a minimum at the axis of symmetry:
$q = -(-30)/2 = 15$.
At $q = 15$, $AC = 225 - 450 + 350 = 125$.
c. At $q = 15$, $MC = 3(225) - 900 + 350 = 125$.
d.

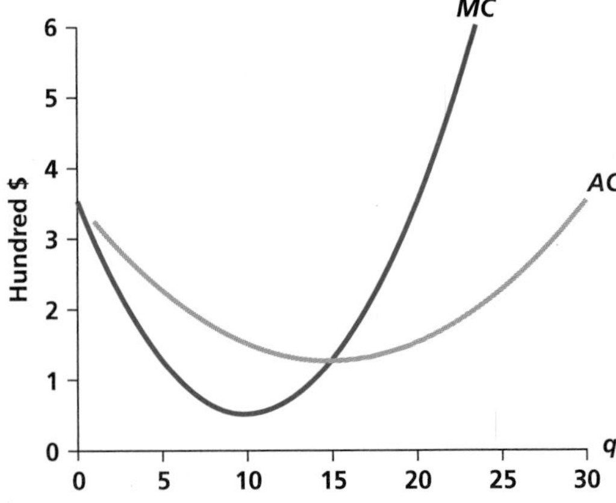

7.5 a. $q = 2\sqrt{K \cdot L}$. $K = 100$, $q = 2\sqrt{100 \cdot L}$.

$q = 20\sqrt{L}$. $\sqrt{L} = \dfrac{q}{20}$. $L = \dfrac{q^2}{400}$.

$$STC = vK + wL = 1(100) + \frac{(q^2)}{100}$$

$$= 100 + \frac{(q^2)}{100}.$$

$$SAC = \frac{STC}{q} = \frac{100}{q} + \frac{q}{100}.$$

b. $SMC = \dfrac{q}{50}$.

If $q = 25$, $STC = 100 + \dfrac{(25)^2}{100} = 106.25$.

$SAC = \dfrac{100}{25} + \dfrac{25}{100} = 4.25$.

$SMC = \dfrac{25}{50} = 5$.

If $q = 50$, $STC = 100 + \dfrac{(50)^2}{100} = 125$.

$SAC = \dfrac{100}{50} + \dfrac{50}{100} = 2.50$.

$SMC = \dfrac{50}{50} = 1$.

If $q = 100$, $STC = 100 + \dfrac{(100)^2}{100} = 200$.

$SAC = \dfrac{100}{100} + \dfrac{100}{100} = 2$.

$SMC = \dfrac{100}{50} = 2$.

If $q = 200$, $STC = 100 + \dfrac{(200)^2}{100} = 500$.

$SAC = \dfrac{100}{200} + \dfrac{200}{100} = 2.50$.

$SMC = \dfrac{200}{50} = 4$.

c.

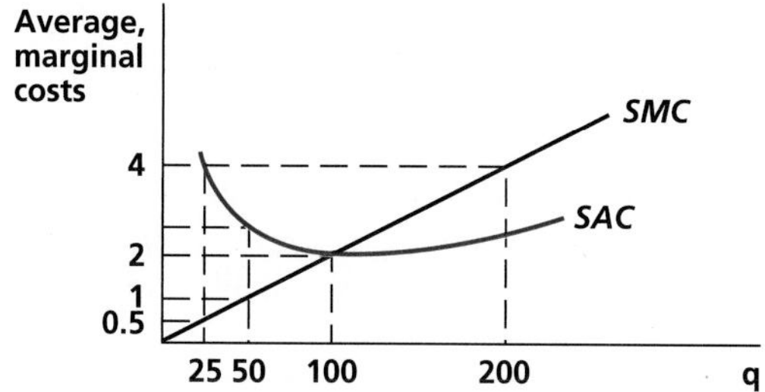

d. As long as the marginal cost of producing one more unit is below the average cost curve, average costs will be falling. Similarly, if the marginal cost of producing one more unit is higher than the average cost, then average costs will be rising. Therefore, the *SMC* curve must intersect the *SAC* curve at its lowest point.

7.7 Minimizing costs requires equal marginal productivities of labor in each plant. If labor were more productive in one plant than another, costs could be lowered by moving workers.

a. $MP_{L_1} = MP_{L_2}$. $5/2\sqrt{L_1} = 5/\sqrt{L_2}$.

$2\sqrt{L_1} = \sqrt{L_2}$. $L_2 = 4L_1$.

$q_1 = 5\sqrt{L_1}$; $q_2 = 10\sqrt{L_2} = 10\sqrt{4L_1} = 20\sqrt{L_1}$.

Hence $q_2 = 4q_1$

b. $4q_1 = q_2$, so $q_1 = q/5$, $q_2 = 4q/5$, where q is total output.

STC (Plant 1) $= 25 + wL_1 = 25 + \dfrac{q_1^2}{25}$.

STC (Plant 2) $= 100 + wL_2 = 100 + \dfrac{q_2^2}{100}$.

$$STC = STC\ (\text{Plant } 1) + STC\ (\text{Plant } 2)$$

$$= 25 + \frac{q_1^2}{25} + 100 + \frac{q_2^2}{100}$$

$$= 125 + \frac{(q/5)^2}{25} + \frac{(4q/5)^2}{100}$$

$$= 125 + \frac{q^2/25}{25} + \frac{16q^2/25}{100}$$

$$= 125 + \frac{q^2}{125}.$$

$MC = \dfrac{2q}{125}$. $AC = \dfrac{125}{q} + \dfrac{q}{125}$.

$MC\ (100) = \dfrac{200}{125} = \$1.60$.

$MC\ (125) = \$2.00$ $MC\ (200) = \$3.20$.

c. Because of constant returns to scale, in the long run one can change K. It is really not important where production occurs. Production could be split evenly or produced all in one plant.

$TC = K + L = 2q$. $AC = 2 = MC$.

d. If there were decreasing returns to scale, then each firm should have equal share of production. *AC* and *MC* are no longer constant. They are increasing functions of q preventing either plant from being too large.

7.9 a. Now $K = L$, so $q = 20L$.

$TC = vK + wL = 5K + 5L = 10L$, so

$TC = 0.5q$. $AC = TC/q = 0.5$.

$MC = \Delta TC/\Delta q = 0.5$.

These costs are half what they were before.

b. All costs will fall at the rate of r per year.

Chapter 8

8.1 a. Set $P = MC$, $20 = .2q + 10$. $q = 50$.

b. $$\text{Maximum profits} = TR - TC$$
$$= (50 \cdot 20) - [.1(50)^2 + 10(50) + 50]$$
$$= 1000 - 800 = 200.$$

c.

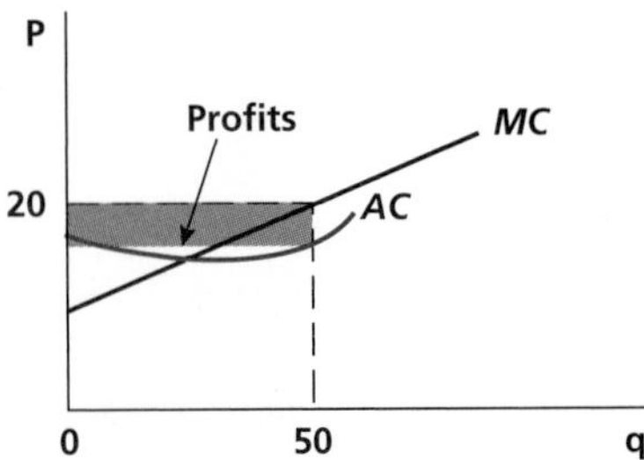

8.3 a. Assume that the demand curve has the linear form $P = c - dQ$. Then marginal revenue is given by $MR = c - 2dQ$. Solving for the Q-intercept of the demand curve yields $Q = 0 \Rightarrow c = dQ^* \Rightarrow Q^* = c/d$. Making the same calculations for MR yields: $MR = 0 = c - 2dQ^{**} \Rightarrow Q^{**} = c/2d$ as was to be shown.

b. Total spending is maximized when $MR = 0$.

c. If demand were inelastic raising price would increase spending, if demand were elastic lowering price would increase spending. Neither of these can happen because total spending is at a maximum.

d. First, solve for P: $P = 48 - Q/2 \Rightarrow MR = 48 - Q$. If $P = 0$, $Q^* = 96$. $MR = 0$ when $Q^{**} = 48$. With $Q = 48$, $P = 24$ and total spending is 1152. This is the maximum spending with this demand curve.

8.5 a. Let $AC = MC = c$ and suppose demand is given by $Q = a - bP$. The firm should now charge $P = c$ and total quantity sold will be $Q = a - bc$.

b. Since $MR = \frac{a}{b} - \frac{2Q}{b}$. So, $MR = 0$ when $Q = \frac{a}{2}$ hence, $P = \frac{a}{2b}$.

c. This is the same analysis as in case a except now it must be the case that $PQ - cQ = .01PQ$. Hence $\frac{P-c}{P} = .01$.

d. It should sell just one unit. Price would be $\frac{a-1}{b}$ and unit profits would be $\frac{a-1-bc}{b}$.

e. The solution in part a is the competitive solution and profits will be zero. Profits are not maximized in part b because $MR = 0 < c$. In part c profits are also probably not at a maximum because $MR < c$. In part d profits are clearly not at a maximum because the firm could profitably produce a second unit at a lower per-unit profit.

8.7 a. Beth's supply function is $q = 5P - 50$.
If $P = 15$, $q = 25$.
If $P = 25$, $q = 75$.

b. When $P = 15$, $\pi = 15 \cdot 25 - 362.5 = 375 - 362.5 = 12.5$.
When $P = 25$, $\pi = 25 \cdot 75 - 1{,}362.5 = 1{,}875 - 1{,}362.5 = 512.5$.
Average $\pi = (512.5 + 12.5) \div 2 = 262.5$.

c. If $P = 20$, $q = 50$, $\pi = 1{,}000 - 800 = 200$. The father's deal makes Beth worse off.

d.

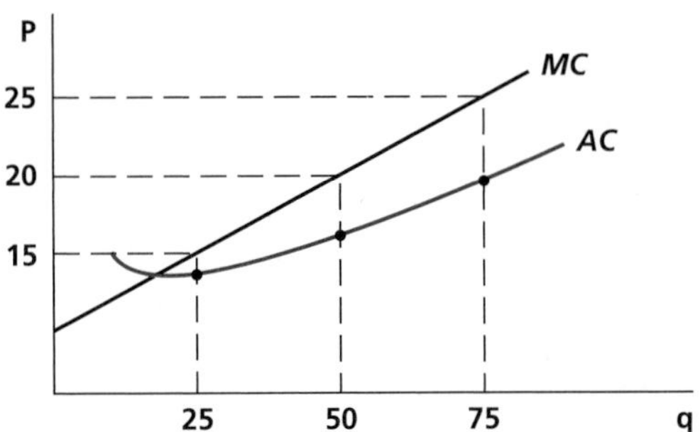

Since high profits are associated with high P, q combination, it's more profitable to let price fluctuate.

8.9 a.
$$STC = vK + wL$$
$$= 10 \cdot 100 + wL$$
$$= 1{,}000 + 5L$$
but $q = 10\sqrt{L}$, so $L = \dfrac{q^2}{100}$.

Hence, $STC = 1{,}000 + q^2/20$.

b. Use $P = MC$.
$20 = .1q$, so $q = 200$. $L = q^2/100$, so $L = 400$.

c. If $P = 15$, $P = MC$ implies $15 = .1q$ or $q = 150$, $L = 225$.

d. Cost will be 175 to reduce L from 400 to 225. With $q = 150$, Profits $= TR - TC = 15(150) - (1{,}000 + .05q^2) = 2{,}250 - (1{,}000 + 1{,}125) = 125$. After paying severance cost of 175, the firm will incur a loss of 50. Note that if the firm continues to hire 400 workers it will have no severance costs and profits of $TR - TC = 15(200) - [1{,}000 + .05(200)^2] = 3{,}000 - (1{,}000 + 2{,}000) = 0$, which is better than in part d. An output level of $180 (L = 324)$ would yield an overall profit for the firm.

Chapter 9

9.1 a. Set supply equal to demand to find equilibrium price:
$$Q_S = 1{,}000 = Q_D = 1{,}600 - 600P.$$
$$1{,}000 = 1{,}600 - 600P.$$
$$600 = 600P$$
$$P = 1/\text{pound}$$

b. $$Q_S = 400 = 1{,}600 - 600P.$$
$$600P = 1{,}200.$$
$$P = 2/\text{pound}$$

c. $Q_S = 1{,}000 = 2{,}200 - 600P.$

$$1{,}200 = 600P.$$
$$P = 2/\text{pound}$$
$$Q_S = 400 = 2{,}200 - 600P.$$
$$600P = 1{,}800.$$
$$P = 3/\text{pound}$$

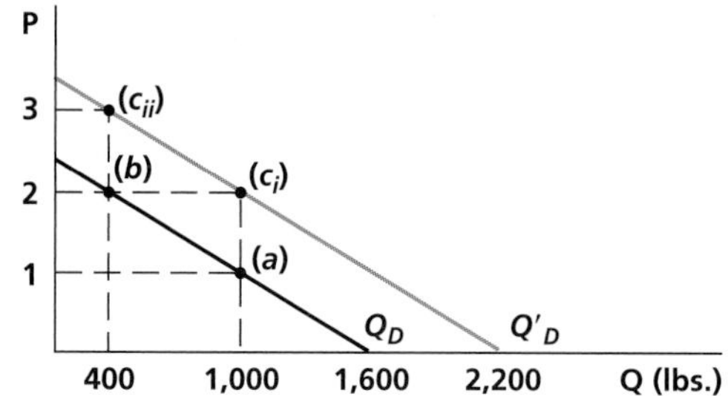

d. Quantity supplied is positive only for $P \geq 0.5$.

e. Set Quantity demanded equal to Quantity supplied:

$$1600 - 600P = -1000 + 2000P \Rightarrow P = 1,\ Q = 1000.$$

f. Now $2200 - 600P = -1000 + 2000P \Rightarrow 3200 = 2600P \Rightarrow P = 32/26 = 1.23$.

g. The price rise here is smaller because the rise in price induces added supply to meet the added demand whereas previously supply was unaffected by price.

9.3 a. Profit maximization requires $P = SMC = .01q^2 + .4q + 4 = (.1q + 2)^2$. Solving for P yields: $.1q + 2 = \sqrt{P} \Rightarrow q = 10\sqrt{P} - 20$.

b. With 100 firms, supply is given by $Q = 100q = 1000\sqrt{P} - 2000$.

c. Set supply equal to demand: $1000\sqrt{P} - 2000 = -200P + 8000 \Rightarrow P = 25,\ Q = 3000$.

d. Now $1000\sqrt{P} - 2000 = -200P + 11{,}200 \Rightarrow P = 36$, $Q = 4{,}000$. Since each firm now produces 40, total revenue is 1,440. $STC = 703$, so short run profits are 737.

9.5 a. In long-run equilibrium, $AC = P$ and $MC = P$, so $AC = MC$.

$$.01q - 1 + \frac{100}{q} = 0.02q - 1$$
$$\frac{100}{q} = 0.01q.$$
$$\frac{10{,}000}{q} = q, \text{ so } q^2 = 10{,}000$$
$$q = 100 \text{ gallons}$$
$$AC = .01(100) - 1 + \frac{100}{100} = 1 - 1 + 1 = 1.$$
$$MC = .02(100) - 1 = 2 - 1 = 1.$$

b. In the long run, $P = MC$; $P = \$1$.
$Q_D = 2{,}500{,}000 - 500{,}000(1) = 2{,}000{,}000$ gallons. The market supplies 2,000,000 gallons, so

$$\frac{2{,}000{,}000 \text{ gallons}}{100 \text{ gallons/station}} = 20{,}000 \text{ gas stations}$$

c. In the long run, $P = \$1$ still since the AC curve has not changed. Q_D

$$= 2{,}000{,}000 - 1{,}000{,}000(1)$$
$$= 1{,}000{,}000 \text{ gallons.}$$
$$\frac{1{,}000{,}000 \text{ gallons}}{100 \text{ gallons/station}} = 10{,}000 \text{ gas stations.}$$

9.7 a. With $Q = 400$, demand curve yields $400 = 1{,}000 - 5P$, or $P = 120$. For supply, $400 = 4P - 80$, or $P = 120$. Hence, P is an equilibrium price. Total spending on broccoli is $400 \cdot 120 = 48{,}000$. On the demand curve when $Q = 0$, $P = 200$. Hence, area of the consumer surplus triangle is $.5(200 - 120)\ (400) = 16{,}000$. On the supply curve, $P = 20$ when $Q = 0$. Producer surplus is then $.5(120 - 20)\ (400) = 20{,}000$.

b. With $Q = 300$, the total loss of surplus would be given by the area of the triangle between the demand and supply curves, which is $.5(140 - 95)\ (100) = 2{,}250$.

c. With $P = 140$, consumer surplus is $.5(200 - 140)\ (300) = 9{,}000$. Producer surplus is $.5(95 - 20)(300) + 45(300) = 24{,}750$. Consumers lose 7,000, producers gain 4,750, net loss is 2,250. With $P = 95$, consumer surplus is $.5(200 - 140)\ (300) + 45(300) = 22{,}500$. Producer surplus is $.5(95 - 20)(300) = 11{,}250$. Consumers gain 6,500, producers lose 8,750; again net loss is 2,250.

d. With $Q = 450$, demand price would be 110, supply price is 132.50. Total loss of surplus is $.5(132.5 - 110)(5) - 562.50$. Net loss is shared depending on where price falls between 110 and 132.5.

e. 

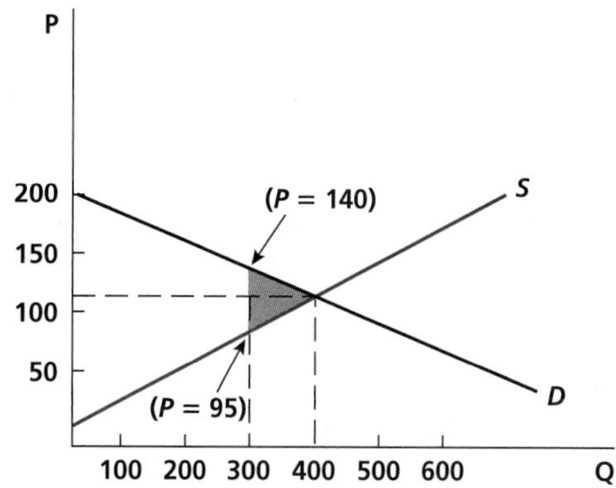

9.9 a.

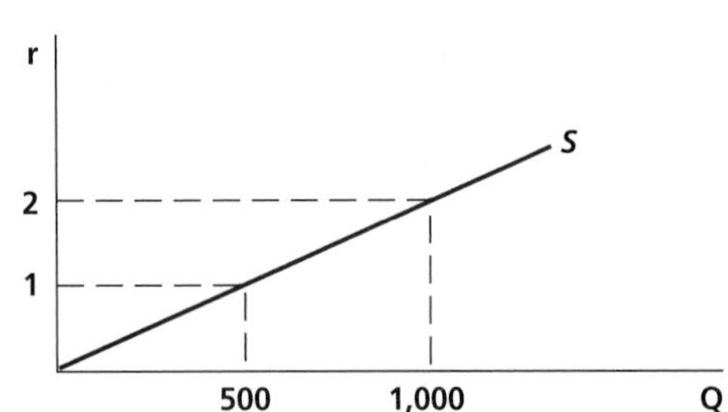

b. Since $P = AC = 10 + r = 10 + .002Q$, substitute this into demand: $Q = 1{,}050 = 50P = 1{,}050 - 500 - .1Q$, or $1.1Q = 550$, $Q = 500$.
Since each firm produces 5 DVDs, there will be 100 firms. Royalty is $r = .002(500) = 1$, so $P = 11$.

c. With $Q = 1{,}600 = 50P$, same substitution gives $Q = 1{,}600 - 500 - .1Q$ or $1.1Q = 1{,}100$, $Q = 1{,}000$. So now there are 200 firms and $r = .002(1{,}000) = 2$, so $P = 12$.

d.

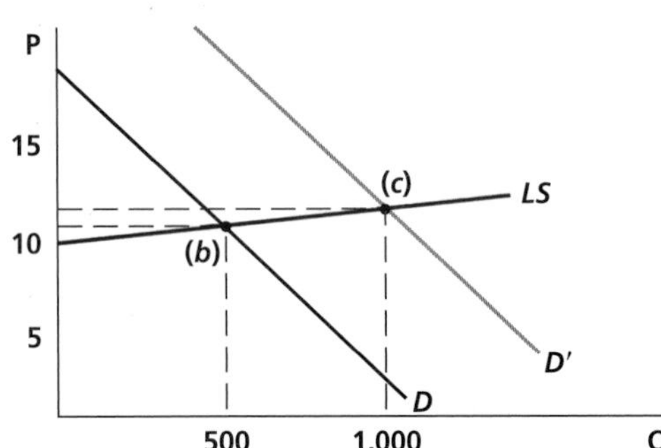

Producer surplus when $P = 11$ is $.5(11 - 10)(500) = 250$. When $P = 12$, it is $.5(12 - 10)(1{,}000) = 1{,}000$.

e. Royalties when $Q = 500$ are 500. Increment when Q rises from 500 to 1,000 is $(2 - 1)(500) + .5(2 - 1)(1{,}000 - 500) = 500 + 250 = 750$, which is precisely the increase in producer surplus in part d.

f. With the tax demand is now

$$Q = 1{,}600 - 50(P + 5.5).$$

Since $P = 10 + .002Q$, this means

$$Q = 1{,}600 - 500 - .1Q - 275$$

or

$$1.1Q = 825,\ Q = 750,\ P = 11.5.$$

Price to consumers is 17.

g. Total tax collections are

$$5.5(750) = 4{,}125.$$

Consumers pay $(17 - 12)(750) = 3{,}750$ Producers pay $(12 - 11.5)(750) = 375$. Consumer surplus is now $.5(32 - 17)(750) = 5{,}625$ whereas previously it was $.5(32 - 12)(1{,}000) = 10{,}000$, so the loss is 4,375: 3,750 of tax revenue and 625 from foregone transactions. Producer surplus was 1,000; now it is $.5(11.5 - 10)(750) = 562.5$ a loss of 437.5.

h. All of the lost producer surplus is a loss of royalties. Now $r = .002(750) = 1.5$ whereas previously $r = 2$. Loss is $(2 - 1.5)(750) + .5(2 - 1.5)(250) = 375 + 62.5 = 437.5$.

Chapter 10

10.1 a. The production possibility frontier for M and C is shown as:

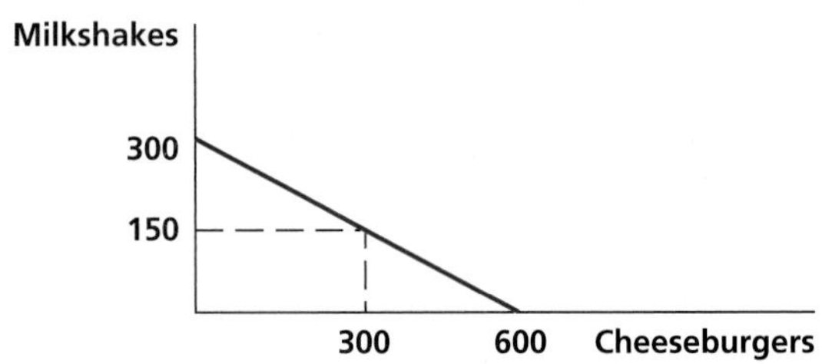

b. If people want $M = \frac{1}{2}C$ and technology requires $C + 2M = 600$, then $C + 2\left(\frac{1}{2}C\right) = 600.2C = 600$, or $C = 300$. $M = 150$.

c. Negative slope $= RPT = \frac{1}{2}$. If efficiency holds, $RPT = MRS = P_C/P_M$, so $P_C/P_M = \frac{1}{2}$

10.3 a. The frontier is a quarter ellipse:

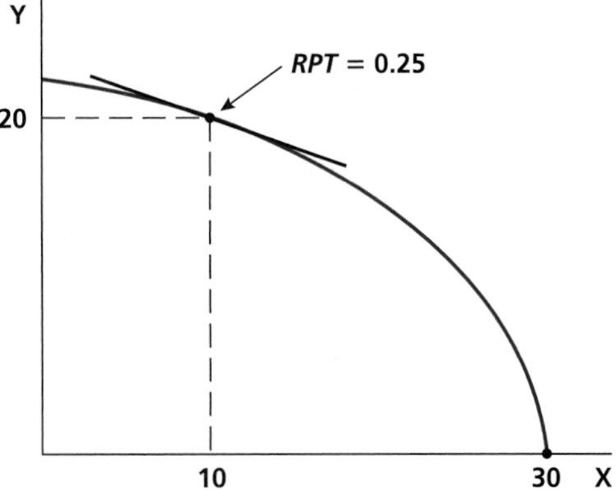

b. If $Y = 2X$, $X^2 + 2(2X)^2 = 900$.
$9X^2 = 900$; $X = 10$, $Y = 20$. This point is shown on the frontier in part a.

c. If $X = 9$ on the production possibility frontier, $Y = \sqrt{819} = 20.25$.

If $X = 11$ on the frontier, $Y = \sqrt{779} = 19.75$.

Hence, the RPT is $-\frac{\Delta Y}{\Delta X} = \frac{.50}{2} = 0.25$.

10.5 a. $P_X P_Y = 3/2$, since $RPT = -\frac{\Delta Y}{\Delta X} = -\frac{(-3)}{2}$ from the production technology which depends on labor only.

b. If wage = 1, Smith spends 3 on X, 7 on Y, Jones spends 5 on X, 5 on Y Total spent on X is 8, total on Y is 12. Total spending equals total income (20). Since $w = 1$, average cost of X is 1/2, of Y is 1/3 So, $P_X = 1/2$, $P_Y = 1/3$. With these prices, Smith demands $6X$, $21Y$ and Jones demands $10X$, $15Y$

c. Production is $X = 16$, $Y = 36$ 20 hours of labor are allocated: 8 to X production, 12 to Y production.

10.7 200 total pounds of food, $U_1 = \sqrt{F_1}$, $U_2 = \frac{1}{2}\sqrt{F_2}$.

a. With 100 pounds each $U_1 = 10$, $U_2 = 5$.

b. Equal utilities require $\sqrt{F_1} = \frac{1}{2}\sqrt{F_2}$,

$$F_1 = 1/4F_2:$$
$$F_1 = 40,\ F_2 = 160$$

c. With $U_2 \geq 5$, best choice is $U_2 = 5$, since extra food yields more utility to person 1. Hence, $F_2 = 100$, $F_1 = 100$.

d. Perhaps one might opt for maximizing the sum of utilities. This yields the very unequal result of $F_1 = 160$, $F_2 = 40$, $U_1 = 4\sqrt{10}$, $U_2 = \sqrt{10}$. But $U_1 + U_2 = 5\sqrt{10} = 15.8$, which exceeds value in the other parts.

10.9 a-d. Construction closely follows that used for the Edgeworth Exchange diagram.

e. The inefficient points in the Edgeworth Box are allocations where it is possible to increase output of both goods. Points inside the production possibility frontier have this same feature.

f. i. The axes of the Edgeworth Box are the efficient allocations.

ii. Efficient allocations lie along the main diagonal of the Box. The production possibility frontier is a straight line.

iii. In this case too the production possibility frontier is a straight line. Only with differing input intensities would the frontier have a concave shape.

iv. The frontier would be convex.

Chapter 11

11.1 a. For maximum profits, set $MR = MC$.

$MR = 53 - 2Q = MC - 5$.

$Q = 24$, $P = 29$.

$\pi = TR - TC = 24 \cdot 29 - 24 \cdot 5 = 696 - 120 = 576$.

$$\text{Consumer surplus} = \frac{1}{2}(53 - 29) \cdot 24 = 288.$$

b. $MC = P = 5$, $Q = 48$.

c. Consumer surplus $= \frac{1}{2}(48)^2 = 1{,}152$.

$1{,}152 >$ Profits + consumer surplus $= 576 + 288 = 864$.

Deadweight loss $= 1{,}152 - 864 = 288$.

Also $(1/2)\Delta Q \cdot \Delta P = (1/2)(24)(24)$.

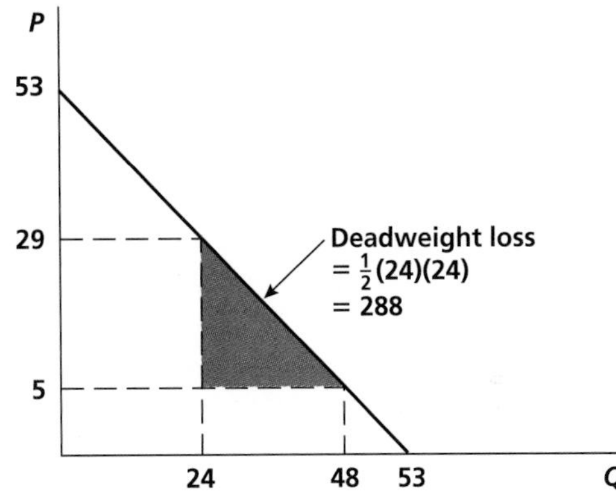

11.3 a. $AC = MC = 10$, $Q = 60 - P$, $MR = 60 - 2Q$.

For profit maximization, $MC = MR$.

$$10 = 60 - 2Q,\ 2Q = 50,\ Q = 25,$$
$$P = 35.$$
$$\pi = TR - C = (25)(35) - (25)(10)$$
$$= 625.$$

b. $AC = MC = 10$, $Q = 45 - .5P$. $MR = 90 - 4Q$.

For profit maximization, $MC = MR$, $10 = 90 - 4Q$, $80 = 4Q$, $Q = 20$, $P = 50$.

$$\pi = (20)(50) - (20)(10) = 800.$$

c. $AC = MC = 10$, $Q = 100 - 2P$, $MR = 50 - Q$

For profit maximization, $MC = MR$, $10 = 50 - Q$, $Q = 40$, $P = 30$.

$$\pi = (40)(30) - (40)(10) = 800.$$

d.

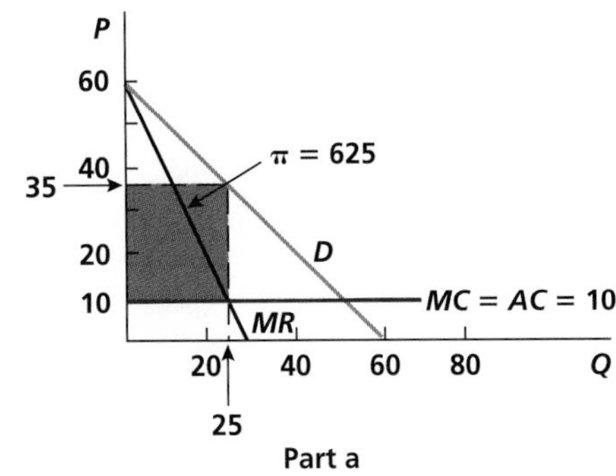

Part a

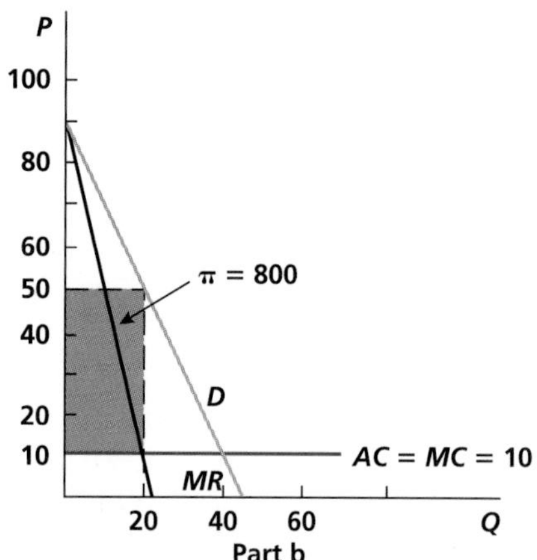

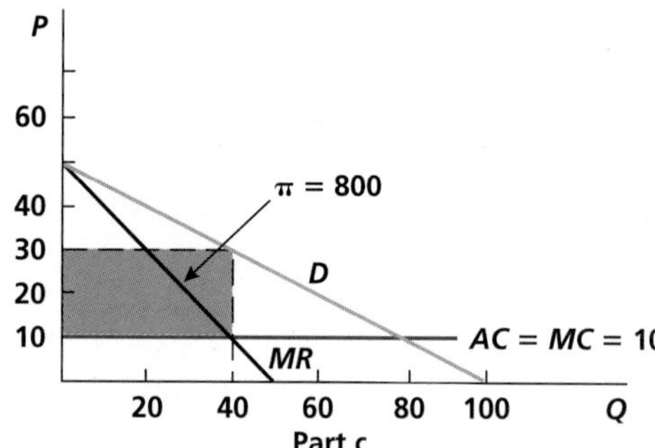

The supply curve for a monopoly is the single point on the demand curve that corresponds to profit maximization. Any attempt to connect equilibrium points (price/quantity points) on the market demand curves has little meaning and brings about a strange shape. One reason for this is that as the demand curve shifts, its elasticity (and its MR curve) often changes, bringing about widely varying price and quantity combinations.

11.5 A multiplant monopolist will still produce where $MR = MC$ and will equalize MC among factories.

$$MR = 100 - 2(q_1 + q_2) \text{ and } MC_1 = MC_2.$$
$$q_1 - 5 = .5q_2 - 5.\ q_1 = .5q_2.$$
$$MR = 100 - 2(.5q_2 + q_2).$$
$$MR = MC_2,\ 100 - 2(1.5q_2) = .5q_2 - 5.$$
$$3.5q_2 = 105.$$
$$q_2 = 30 \text{ and } q_1 = 15, \text{ so } Q_T = 45.$$

11.7 $Q_D = 1{,}000 - 50P$; $MR = 20 - Q/25$; $MC = 10$ under PC; $MC = 12$ under monopoly.

a. *Perfect competition:*

$$P = MC = 10.$$
$$Q_D = 1{,}000 - 50(10) = 500 = Q_S.$$

Monopoly:

$$MC = MR$$
$$12 = 20 - Q/25$$
$$300 = 500 - Q$$
$$Q = 200;$$
$$200 = 1{,}000 - 50P;$$
$$50P = 800;$$
$$P = 16.$$

b. Loss of consumer surplus due to monopolization can easily be obtained from the graph (shaded portion). Area of shaded portion $= (16 - 10)(200) + (1/2)(16 - 10)(500 - 200) = 1{,}200 + 900 = 2{,}100$. This area is much larger than loss of consumer surplus if monopolist's $MC = 10$.

c.

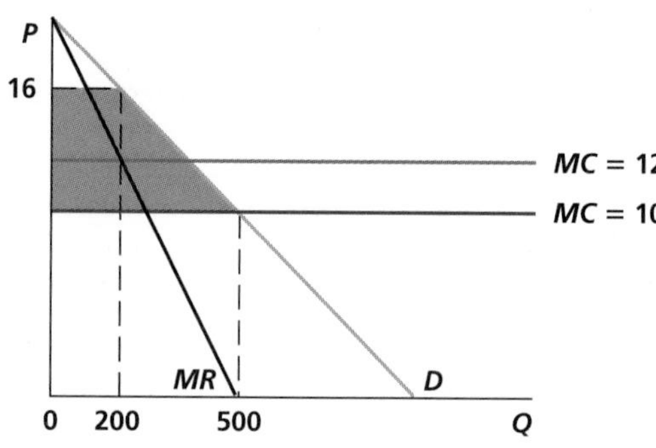

11.9 a. Equating MR and MC yields $Q^* = 3$. Thus $P^* = 5$ and profit is 9. The profit from 100 such consumers is 900.

b. An individual's consumer surplus at a price of 2 is 18, the highest admission fee that can be charged. With 100 such consumers, profit is $100 \times 18 = 1{,}800$ (all profit comes from the admission fee because there is no profit margin on drinks).

c. With the pricing scheme from part b, profit is $115 \times 18 = 2{,}070$ with 15 new consumers. With a \$3 drink price, each original consumer buys 5 drinks and each new one 13 drinks. A total of $(100)(5) + (15)(13) = 695$ drinks are sold at a profit margin of \$1 each. The admission fee has to be lowered to 12.50 not to deter original consumers (this is an original consumer's surplus at the \$3 price). Total profit from admission fees and drinks is $695 + (155)(12.50) = 2{,}132.50$.

Chapter 12

12.1 a. The Nash equilibrium is for both to price low.

b. You could relabel "Low Price" as "High Output" and "High Price" as "Low Output."

12.3 Equation (14.4) states the marginal revenue for Cournot firm A with the given demand curve is

$$120 - 2q_A - q_B.$$

Equating this marginal revenue with marginal cost 30 yields

$$120 - 2q_A - q_B = 30$$

implying

$$90 - 2q_A - q_B = 0.$$

Similarly, for firm B,

$$90 - 2q_B - q_A = 0.$$

Solving the two preceding equations simultaneously gives

$$q_A^* = q_B^* = 30.$$

Industry output $= 30 + 30 = 60$.
To find P, solve $60 = 120 - P$, implying $P = 60$.
Firm profit $= (60 - 30)(30) = 900$. Industry profit $= 2 \times 900 = 1{,}800$.

12.5 a. There are many Nash equilibria. Firm A charges any price along the one-cent-increment grid from \$8.02 to \$10.01 (inclusive). Firm B undercuts A by one cent. All of these involve weakly dominated actions for firm A except the highest price one, in which it charges \$10.01 and B charges \$10. Firm B gets all the demand. Assume through out the remainder of the answer that this is the Nash equilibrium that is played. Leaving the complications associated with the large number of equilibria aside, it is sufficient that students realize that prices will be around \$10 and the low-cost firm will make all the sales.

b. A earns zero profit. B earns

$$10 - 6 = 4$$

per unit and sells

$$Q = 500 - 20 \times 10 = 300$$

units for a profit of

$$4 \times 300 = 1{,}200.$$

c. Price equals marginal cost as in the Bertrand Paradox, though the price is equal to the high-cost firm's marginal cost. One of the firms earns zero profit as in the Bertrand Paradox, but unlike in the Bertrand Paradox one of the firms earns positive profit.

12.7 Dividing both sides of Equation (12.15) by π_M and rearranging shows that collusion is sustainable for $N \leq 1/(1-g)$. The graph of the upper bound is below.

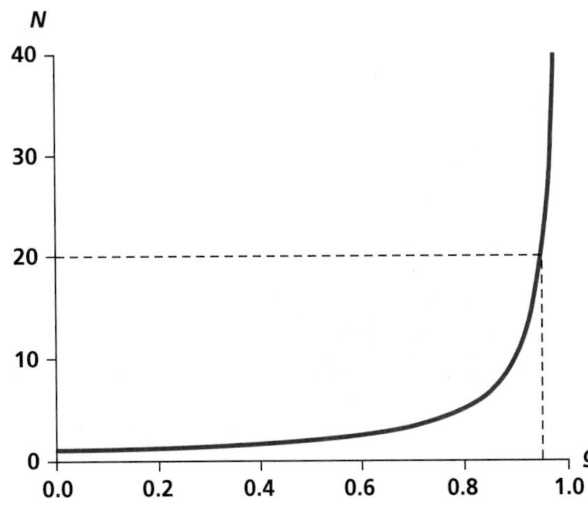

As indicated by the dotted line, for $g = 0.95$, collusion is sustainable with 20 or fewer firms.

12.9 First suppose $F_I > 2{,}000$. Then I will not prey. E earns $1{,}600 - K > 0$ if it enters, and so will enter. Next suppose $F_I < 2{,}000$. Then I would prey if E entered. E would earn $-K - F_E < 0$ if it entered, and so would choose not to. Predation would not be observed in either case. The only case in which I would be inclined to prey (if $F_I < 2{,}000$), E does not enter and so there is no firm to prey upon.

Chapter 13

13.1 a. With five workers, put each successively where its MP_L is greatest. First worker goes to A, second goes to B, third goes to A, fourth goes to C, fifth goes to A. Output $= 21 + 8 + 5 = 34$. MP of last worker is 4.

b. $P \cdot MP_L = \$1.00 \cdot 4 = \$4.00 = w$. With five workers, the wage bill is $wL = \$20$. Profits are $\pi = TR - TC = PQ - wL = \$34 - \$20 = \$14$.

c. MVP of first worker (farm A) is \$10, the second worker (Farm B) is \$8, the third worker (Farm A again) is \$7, the fourth worker (Farm C) is \$5 and the fifth worker (Farm A once again) is \$4. At a wage of \$5, 4 workers are hired. At a wage of \$4, 5 workers are hired. At a wage of \$3, a second worker is hired on Farm B.

13.3 a. $w = v = \$1$, so K and L will be used in a one-to-one ratio.

$$TC = w \cdot L + vK = L + K = 2L, \text{ so}$$

$$AC = \frac{2L}{q} = \frac{2L}{\sqrt{KL}} = \frac{2L}{\sqrt{LL}} = 2 \text{ and}$$

$$MC = 2.$$

b. Since $P = 2$, quantity demanded is $Q = 400{,}000 - 100{,}000(2) = 200{,}000$ pipe.

$$q = \frac{200{,}000 \text{ pipe}}{1{,}000 \text{ firms}} = 200 \text{ pipe/firm}.$$

$q = 200 = \sqrt{L \cdot K} = L$ so 200 workers are hired per firm, 200,000 by the industry.

c. When $w = \$2$ and $v = \$1$, cost minimization requires $K/L = 2$.
$TC = wL + vK$, so $= 2L + K = 4L = 2\sqrt{2}q$ so $AC = MC = 2\sqrt{2}$.

d. $P = 2\sqrt{2}$, $Q = 400{,}000 - 100{,}000(2\sqrt{2}) = 117{,}157$.
$q = 117.2$
$L = 117.2/\sqrt{2} = 83$
Total hiring is 83,000 workers.

e. If $Q = 200{,}000$ at the new wage, $L = \frac{200{,}000}{\sqrt{2}} = 141{,}000$ workers would have been hired by the industry. So if Q were unchanged, 59,000 fewer workers would have been hired = substitution effect. The remaining 58,000 fewer workers $(141{,}000 - 83{,}000)$ are the result of the lower output; that is, the output effect.

13.5 a. Demand. $K = 1{,}500 - 25v$
Supply. $K = 75v - 500$
Equilibrium is found by setting quantity supplied equal to quantity demanded.

$$75v - 500 = 1{,}500 - 25v$$
$$100v = 2{,}000$$
$$v = 20,\ K = 1{,}000.$$

b. Now demand is $K = 1{,}700 - 25v - 300g$.
If $g = 2$, $K = 1{,}700 - 25v - 600 = 1{,}100 - 25v$.
The new equilibrium is

$$75v - 500 = 1{,}100 - 25v.$$
$$100v = 1{,}600$$
$$v = 16,$$
$$K = 700.$$

If $g = 3$, demand is $K = 1{,}700 - 25v - 900 = 800 - 25v$, and the equilibrium is

$$75v - 500 = 800 - 25v.$$
$$100v = 1{,}300$$
$$v = 13,\ K = 475.$$

c. The graph shows these changing equilibria as demand shifts in along a stationary supply curve.

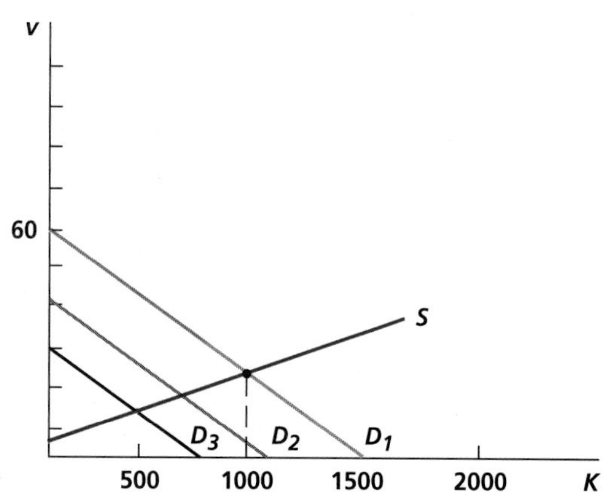

13.7 Supply. $L = 80w$. $ME_L = \frac{L}{40}$.
Demand: $L = 400 - 40MVP_L$.

a.
$$40MVP_L = 400 - L$$
$$MVP_L = 10 - \frac{L}{40}$$

Using the profit maximizing condition,

$$\frac{L}{40} = 10 - \frac{L}{40} \cdot \frac{2L}{40} = 10$$
$$L = 200.$$

Get w from supply curve.

$$w = \frac{L}{80} = \frac{200}{80} = \$2.50$$

b. For Carl, the marginal expense of labor now equals the minimum wage, and, in equilibrium, the marginal expense of labor will equal the marginal revenue product of labor.

$$w_m = ME_L = MVP_L.$$
$$w_m = \$3.00.$$

Carl's Demand	***Supply***
$L = 400 - 40MVP_L$	$L = 80w$
$L = 400 - 40(3)$	$L = 80(3)$
$L = 280.$	$L = 240.$

Demand > supply. Carl will hire 240 workers, with no unemployment. To study effects of minimum, try \$3.33 and \$4.00.

$w_m = \$3.33$
$L = 400 - 40(3.33) = 267.$ $\quad L = 80(3.33) = 267.$

Demand = supply, Carl will hire 267 workers, with no unemployment.

$w_m = \$4.00$
$L = 400 - 40(4.00) = 240.$ $\quad L = 80(4.00) = 320.$

Supply > demand, Carl will hire 240 workers, unemployment = 80.

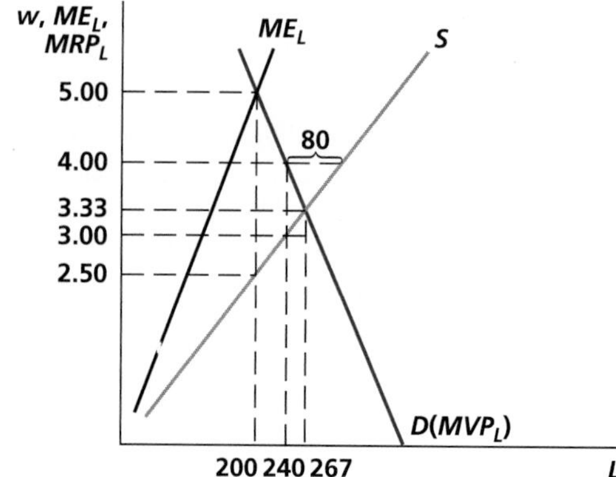

c. Under perfect competition, a minimum wage means higher wages but fewer workers employed. Under monopsony, a minimum wage may result in higher wages and more workers employed as shown by some of the cases studied in part b.

13.9 a. Budget constraint. $C = w(24 - H) + 10$.

b. Due to Mrs. Smith's preferences, she insists on spending half of potential income $(w \cdot 24 + 10)$ on consumption and half on leisure. This means value of consumption = value of leisure (i.e., $w \cdot H$) for all wage rates.

$$C = wH$$

Substituting for C.

$$\begin{aligned} w(24 - H) + 10 &= wH \\ 24 - H + 10/w &= H \\ 2H &= 24 + 10/w \\ H &= 12 + 5/w \end{aligned}$$

For $w = \$1.25$; $H = 16$; $C = 1.25(24 - 16) + 10 = 20$.

For $w = \$2.50$; $H = 14$; $C = 2.50(24 - 14) + 10 = 35$.

For $w = \$5.00$; $H = 13$; $C = 5.00(24 - 13) + 10 = 65$.

For $w = \$10.00$; $H = 12.5$; $C = 10.00(24 - 12.5) + 10 = 125$.

c. The graph shows Mrs. Smith's changing choices as the wage rises. Hours of leisure H fall toward 12 as w rises.

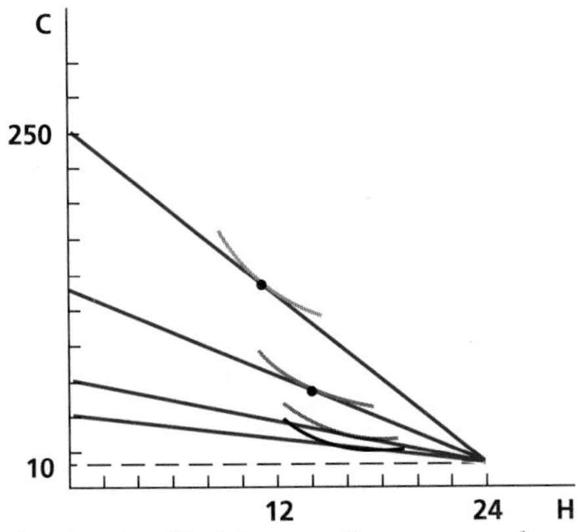

d. Mrs. Smith's labor supply curve can be constructed directly from the data in part b. It is upward sloping, being asymptotic to 12 hours as w rises.

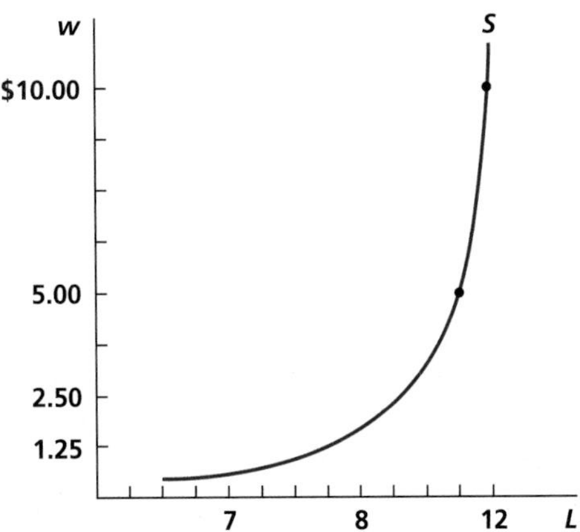

e. Algebra as in part b shows that the demand for leisure is now

$$\begin{aligned} H &= 12 + 10/w \\ L &= 24 - H = 12 - 10/w. \end{aligned}$$

Hence, at each wage less labor will be supplied with this higher level of income guarantee.

Chapter 14

14.1 a. The budget constraint shows that spending must equal income in present-value terms, but income and consumption are not constrained to be equal in either period.

b. If this individual saves in period zero, consumption will of necessity exceed income in period 1.

c. Because period 0 savings $(= Y_0 - C_0)$ earn interest, more can be spent in terms of dissaving $(= C_1 - Y_1)$ in period 1.

14.3 a. Present value of income is $50{,}000 + 55{,}000/(1 + r) = 50{,}000 + 55{,}000/1.1 = 100{,}000$

b. Prudence has $MRS = 1 + r$, or $C_1/3\ C_0 = 1.1$.

c. Budget constraint in present value terms is $100{,}000 = C_0 + C_1/1.1$. Using the utility maximizing condition from part b gives $100{,}000 = C_0 + 3.3\ C_0/1.1$. Hence $C_0 = 25{,}000$. Savings in period 0 are 25,000. With these savings $C_1 = 55{,}000 + 25{,}000(1.1) = 82{,}500$.

d. For Glitter, $MRS = 3\ C_1/C_0 = 1.1$. Substitution into budget constraint (Prudence and Glitter have the same budget constraint) yields $100{,}000 = C_0 + 1.1\ C_0/3.3 = 4\ C_0/3$. Hence, for her, $C_0 = 75{,}000$. Savings in period 0 are $-$ 25,000. Glitter borrows 25,000 and repays $25{,}000(1.1) = 27{,}500$. Hence $C_1 = 55{,}000 - 27{,}500 = 27{,}500$.

14.5 a. Assuming revenues are received at the end of each year gives a present value of \$486,841 when $r = 0.1$. This falls short of the current purchase price of \$500,000 for the ten trucks. When $r = 0.08$, the present value of future revenue is \$520,637, which means that the investment would be profitable.

14.7 a. Price should be $4{,}000/(1.05)^{25} = 4{,}000/3.3864 = 1{,}181$.
b. Scarcity costs $= 1{,}181 - 100 = 1{,}081$
c. Assuming real production costs stay at \$100, scarcity costs in 25 years are \$3,900.
d. In 50 years price is $1{,}181(1.05)^{50} = 4{,}000(1.05)^{25} = 13{,}545$.

14.9 The fallacy here is that the calculation assumes that you have borrowed \$10,000 for all 3 years. Since the repayment plan includes some repayment of the \$10,000 too, the effective amount borrowed is only about half that amount. The actual effective interest rate on the loan, assuming that the \$315 payments are made at the start of each month, is about 8.7 percent, well above the 5 percent opportunity cost.

Chapter 15

15.1 a. The equations for the graphs are $S_1 = 750$, $S_2 = 500 + 40q$, and $S_3 = 60q$, which look as follows:

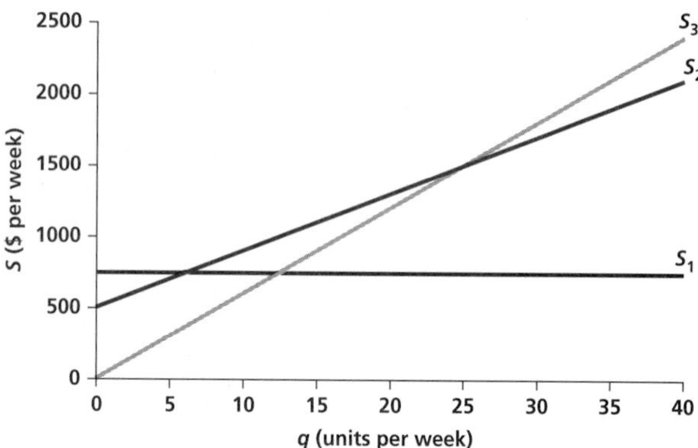

b. Equating Ben's marginal cost of effort (\$1) with his marginal benefit, $1 = MP_E \cdot b = \frac{b}{2\sqrt{E}}$, implying $\sqrt{E} = b/2$. Substitute into the output function: $q = \sqrt{E} = b/2$. Ben's output is half of the b term with each incentive scheme: 0 with the first scheme, 20 with the second, and 30 with the third.
c. Sarah's profit is -750 from the first scheme,

$$100 \cdot 20 - (500 + 40 \cdot 20) = 700$$

from the second, and

$$100 \cdot 30 - (60 \cdot 30) = 1{,}200$$

from the third, her best choice.

15.3 a. From part a of problem 15.2, if she receives half of a firm's return, Clare's expected utility from exerting effort is 250. If she does not exert effort, her utility is $400/2 = 200 < 250$. So she will exert effort. We saw in problem 15.2 that she would accept the contract. With a quarter share of revenue, by part a of problem 15.2 her expected utility from working is 75. Her expected utility from not working is $400/4 = 100 > 75$. Clare would accept the contract and not exert effort. For Clare to exert effort, her revenue share must solve

$$(0.5)(1{,}000\,s) + (0.5)(400s) - 100 \geq 400s, \text{ or } s \geq 1/3.$$

b. If she works hard, her expected utility with the bonus is

$$(0.5)(100s) - 100 = -50.$$

If she does not work hard, her utility is 0. So she would not work hard. (Adding a fixed part to the wage would not change the answer.) The bonus b that would induce her to work hard solves

$$(0.5)b - 100 \geq 0;$$

that is, $b \geq 200$. She would not need an additional fixed wage since the bonus also would give her at least as much expected utility as her outside option.

15.5 a. Small cup: 8 ounces sold at 80 cents.
Large cup: 10 ounces sold at \$1.50.
Consumers obtain no net surplus. Ahab earns

$$(50)[0.80 - (8)(0.05)] = \$20$$

profit from small consumers and

$$(100)[1.50 - (10)(0.05)] = \$100$$

profit from large consumers for a total of \$120.
b. Big consumers would obtain

$$(8)(0.15) - (0.80) = 0.40 > 0$$

net surplus.
c. The 8-ounce cup sells for 0.80. The price for the 10-ounce cup satisfies

$$(0.5)(10) - p \geq 0.40,$$

where the right-hand side, 0.40, is the large consumer's net surplus from buying the 8-ounce cup (see part b). The highest such price is $p = 1.10$. Ahab's profit is \$20 from sales of the 8-ounce cup (see part a) and

$$(100)(1.10 - 0.50) = \$60$$

from large consumers for a total profit of \$80.
d. The 6-ounce cup is sold for 60 cents to small consumers for a profit of

$$(50)(0.60 - 0.30) = \$15.$$

Large consumers would obtain a net surplus of

$$(6)(0.15) - 0.60 = 0.30$$

from consuming the 6-ounce cup. The large cup must be sold at a price satisfying

$$(10)(0.15) - p \geq 0.30.$$

The highest such price is $p = 1.20$. Profit from the large consumers is

$$(100)(1.20 - 0.50) = \$70.$$

Total profit is \$85, greater than the profit in part c.

15.7 a. The equilibrium is for each to bid her valuation. The price paid will be \$1 million unless both have high values, in which case the price will be \$2 million. Expected revenue thus is

$$(3/4)(1 \text{ million}) + (1/4)(2 \text{ million}) = \$1.25 \text{ million}.$$

b. With three bidders, the price paid will be \$2 million if at least two have high valuations and \$1 million otherwise. The probability of at least two having high valuations is 1/2. You can see this by listing the $2^3 = 8$ equally likely permutations of valuations (*LHL*, *HHL*, and so forth) and noting that half of them involve two or more high valuations *H*. Expected revenue equals

$$(1/2)(2 \text{ million}) + (1/2)(1 \text{ million}) = \$1.5 \text{ million}.$$

With N bidders, expected revenue increases in N. Computing the probability of at least two high valuations is a difficult mathematical exercise that students are not expected to be able to solve. For the record, expected revenue can be shown to be

$$\left[1 - (N+1)\left(\frac{1}{2}\right)^N\right](2 \text{ million}) + (N+1)\left(\frac{1}{2}\right)^N (1 \text{ million}).$$

c. Expected revenue is the same for a first-price as from a second-price auction by the revenue-equivalence theorem.

15.9 a. $(1/4)(100) + (3/4)(200) = 175.$

b.

$$200 - c_L \geq 100$$

and

$$200 - c_H < 100$$

or together,

$$c_L \leq 100 < c_H.$$

c. There is a pooling equilibrium in which both get an education. This is an equilibrium as long as the firm's beliefs are that an uneducated worker is unproductive. By obtaining an education in this equilibrium, low-productivity workers obtain payoff

$$175 - c_L = 175 - 50 = 125.$$

If a low-productivity worker does not get an education, his or her payoff is $100 < 125$. So the low-productivity worker would indeed prefer to get an education. Of course a high-productivity worker would as well since he or she has a lower cost of obtaining an education.

There is also a pooling equilibrium in which neither type gets an education. This is an equilibrium if the firm believes an educated worker is equally likely to be high- or low-ability. There would be no return to education, and so both types would not get an education in equilibrium.

Chapter 16

16.1 a. $MC = .4q$. $P = \$20$. Set $P = MC$. $20 = .4q$, $q = 50$.

b. $MCS = .5q$. Set $P = MCS$. $20 = .5q$. $q = 40$.
At optimal production level of $q = 40$, the marginal cost of production is $MC = .4q. = .4(40) = 16$, so the excise tax $t = 20 - 16 = \$4$.

c.

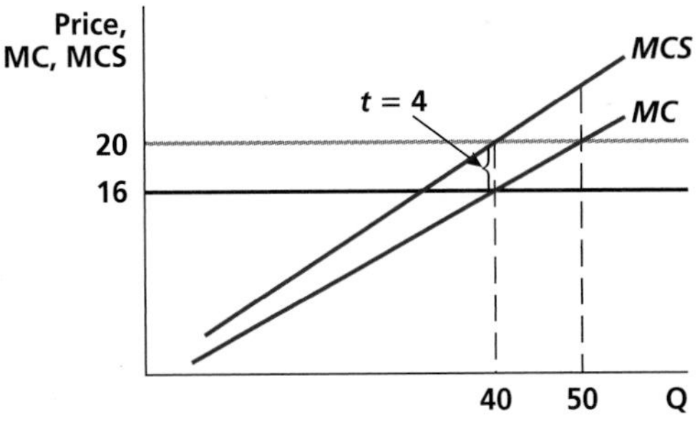

Price, MC, MCS
MCS
MC
t = 4
20
16
40 50 Q

16.3 $AC = MC = 10{,}000$/well.

a. Produce where revenue/well $= 10{,}000 = 100q = 50{,}000 - 100N$. $N = 400$. There is an externality here because drilling another well reduces output in *all* wells. Total output is 40,000.

b. Produce where $MVP = MC$ of well.
$MVP = 50{,}000 - 200N = 10{,}000$. $N = 200$. Now total output would be 60,000.

c. Let Tax $= X$. Want revenue/well $- X = 10{,}000$ when $N = 200$. At $N = 200$, average revenue per well $= 30{,}000$. Charge $X = 20{,}000$.

16.5 a. For profit maximization, set $P = MC$, $50 = 30 + .5Q$. Hence $Q = 40$ hives. There will be enough bees to pollinate only 10 acres.

b. Orchard owner would pay up to \$25 per hive. A \$20 subsidy would result in total receipts per hive of 70, and profit maximization would dictate $70 = 30 + .5Q$ or $Q = 80$—enough hives to pollinate the entire 20 acres.

16.7 a. Marginal valuation for person $A = P = 100 - q_A$; for B, Marginal valuation $= P = 200 - q_B$. Because of the public good nature of mosquito control, these should be added "vertically."
Marginal value $= 300 - 2q$ (since $q_A = q_B$). Set this equal to marginal cost of 50, which gives $q = 125$.
b. Free-rider problem could result in having no production. Each person would let the other do it.
c. Total cost $= 50 \cdot 125 = \$6{,}250$. Area under demand curve for $A = \$5{,}000$, for $B = \$17{,}188$. One solution would be to share costs in proportion to these values.

16.9 a. This pool is excludable, unlike many public goods. It is nonrival, however, because there is a zero marginal cost for one more user.
b. Families as a whole are willing to pay \$6,000 per day for the pool, which would cost only \$5,000 per day. Building the pool would improve the allocation of resources.
c. None of these prices would cover the cost of the pool. A price of either \$1 or \$0 would be efficient but would require the pool to operate at a loss.
d. An efficient pricing scheme would require those who value the pool most to pay more. There is no single price policy that both covers the pool's cost and yields an efficient allocation.
e. The economic value of the pool is maximized when it is used by 2,000 families. To avoid operating at a loss, however, it still will be necessary for those who value the pool at \$3 to pay that amount.

Chapter 17

17.1 a. The first prize is $100{,}000d$, and the second is $2^{d-1}/100$ (in dollars).
b.

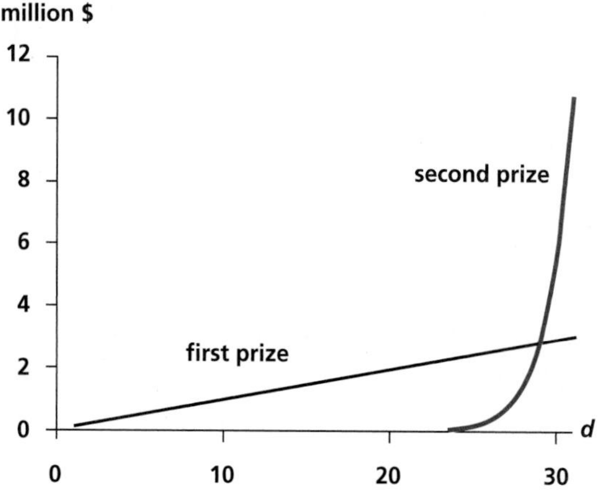

c. The curves cross between day 29 and 30. The first prize is better for shorter time spans and the second prize for longer time spans.

17.3 a. Both play Rat.
b.

		B: Rat	B: Silent
A	Rat	1, 1	0, −3
A	Silent	−3, 0	2, 2

Now there are two equilibria: both play Rat and both play Silent.

c.

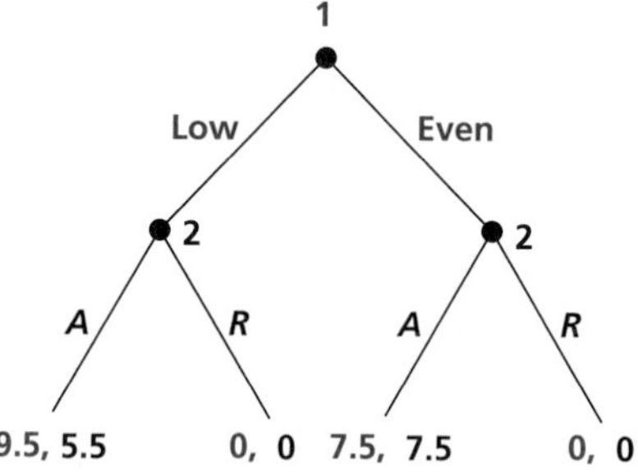

		B: Rat	B: Silent
A	Rat	1, 1	3, −3
A	Silent	−3, 3	2, 2

Both play Rat, as in part a again.

17.5 a. Player 1 makes a low offer; player 2 accepts either offer.
b.

The equilibrium is the same as in part a.

c.

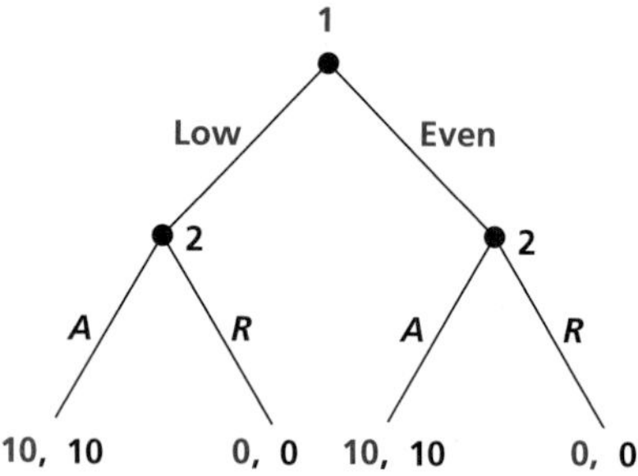

Now, besides the equilibrium in part a, there is another one in which player 1 makes an even offer and 2 accepts either offer.

d.

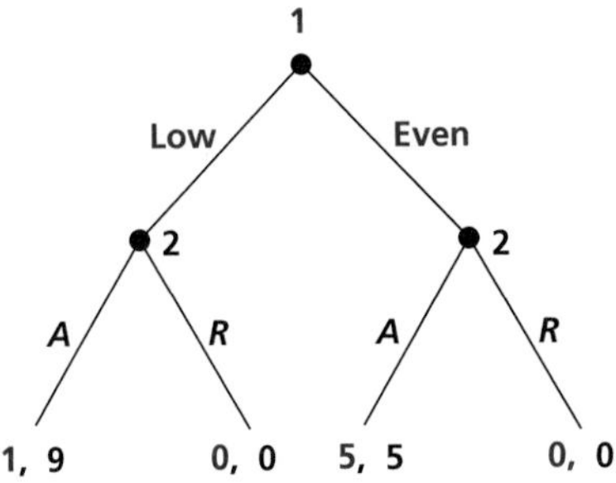

In equilibrium, 1 offers an even split and 2 accepts any offer. Paradoxically, 2 gains a higher monetary payoff but lower utility than if he or she received the low offer.

17.7 a. Will plans to study, and also carries out his plan, if $s < b$.

b. Becky plans to study if $s < b$, but she only follows through if $s < wb$.

17.9 a. Pete's expected utility from gamble A is $10{,}000 + (1/2)(250) - (1/2)(2)(100) = 10{,}025$ and from gamble B is 10,030, so he chooses B.

b. Pete's expected utility from gamble C is $10{,}100 + (1/2)(150) - (1/2)(2)(200) = 9{,}975$ and from gamble D is $10{,}100 - (2)(70) = 9{,}960$, so he chooses C.

c. A yields the same wealth levels as C. B yields the same as D.

Brief Answers

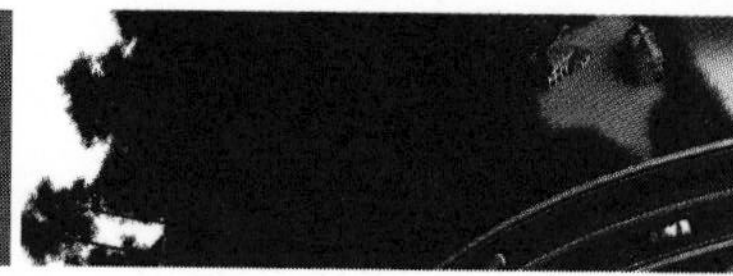

To Micro Quizzes

1.1 The curve is a "frontier" because it shows *the most* of one good that can be produced if the output of the other good is held fixed (assuming that resource availability is also held constant). With a *concave* shape, the opportunity cost of producing, say, X increases as X output increases. If the frontier were *convex,* the opportunity cost of producing more X would fall as X output expanded. That might happen, for example, if X production exhibited major economies of scale.

1.2 Supply and demand curves show economic actors' voluntary reactions to alternative prices. At the intersection of these curves, therefore, both parties to the transaction are satisfied. Any other P, Q combination would not lie at the intersection, so at least one party would not be at a position voluntarily chosen.

1.3 Consumer income, the prices of goods related to computers, or people's preferences for computing could all shift the demand. Supply would be shifted by anything that affects the costs of making computers. The price of computers *does not* shift either curve because the curves themselves reflect demanders' and suppliers' reactions to all possible prices.

1A.1 The intercept is in the same units as the dependent variable—100,000 pounds per week. The slope is the change in the dependent variable for a unit change in the independent variable—5,000 pounds per week for each one dollar per pound increase in the price. If flounder were measured in pounds and price in cents, the equation would be: $Q = 100{,}000 + 50P$.

1A.2 If $Y = -5X/6 + 10$, $Y = 0$ when $X = 12$. Comparison of the graphs shows that the same change in X-intercept can come about through parallel shifts by suitably changing the Y-intercept.

1A.3 Here, each extra worker hour increases the grape harvest by 20 pounds per hour. The average productivity is given by $Q/L = 100/L + 20$. The value of this expression is 30 for $L = 10$, 25 for $L = 20$, and 22 for $L = 50$.

1A.4 A reduction in Z from 9 to 3 would require X to increase from 1 to 3 to keep Y at 3. If Z is further reduced to 1, X would have to increase to 9 to keep Y at 3. More generally, if Y = 3, X must equal 9/Z.

1A.5 The shift outward in Figure 1A.6 comes about because the intercept in the equation $X + Y = 3$ changes to 5. This is a change in one of the factors held constant under *ceteris paribus.* Figure 1A.6 resembles a market in which there has been an increase in demand, perhaps from an increase in consumers' incomes.

1A.6 With approach 1 it is likely that many other factors that affect broccoli demand change over time. Hence the points will not lie along a single demand curve. The averaging process suggested in approach 2 may improve matters, but it is still unlikely that the unmeasured factors that affect broccoli demand will cancel out across cities through this process.

2.1 Completeness implies that all of the points in the positive quadrant of the graph can be ranked. If, say, point X_1, Y_1 is preferred to X^*, Y^*, then any other point in the "?" areas for which $X \geq X_1$ and $Y \geq Y_1$ will also be preferred to X^*, Y^*.

2.2 Positively sloped indifference curves would imply that an increase in the amount of X consumed would have to be met by an *increase* in the amount of Y consumed to keep the individual equally well-off. But this would imply that an increase in either X or Y alone would diminish utility—a contradiction to the definition of economic "goods." The MRS cannot be computed at E or F because the indifference curve is not known at those points. All that is known is that E lies above U_I, F below it.

2.3 The budget constraint in this case would be a straight line with intercepts of 5 on the Frisbee axis and 10 on the beach ball axis. A doubling of income would double both of these intercepts. A doubling of the goods' prices also would bring the budget constraint back to its original position.

2.4 With these prices, an individual can forgo one movie DVD and buy an additional 1.7 music CDs or give up 1.7 CDs to get a DVD. If the MRS is 2 CDs for 1 DVD, he or she is willing to give up more CDs than required to get a DVD. Hence, he or she should buy fewer CDs and more DVDs in order to maximize utility.

2.5 1. In Figure 2–8(c), utility maximization requires that if $MRS > P_X/P_Y$ even when $Y = 0$, then $Y = 0$ is the best choice. In Figure 2.9(c), the MRS is 1 since these are identical goods, so if $P_X/P_Y > 1$ should choose $X = 0$. Your authors never eat lima beans because $P_{limas}/P_Y > MRS$ even when limas = 0. Because limas sell at a positive price, however, someone must like these dreadful vegetables.

2. The equilibrium in Figure 2.9(d) will exist at the vertex of the indifference curves for any price ratio. No matter what the separate prices are of left and right shoes, this person will always consume them in pairs (unless he or she cannot afford a single pair).

3.1 In the first case, housing and other goods will both increase directly in proportion to income. In the second, the goods will increase in proportion to income until housing reaches an "adequate" level; then, no more will be bought, and all extra income will be used to purchase other goods.

3.2 1. Brands of gasoline are perfect substitutes so any significant variation in price would cause most demanders to switch to the lower cost brand.

2. Big box retailers sell many of the same products sold by local retailers, at a lower price. Because the goods themselves are perfect substitutes, demanders will patronize the lower price retailer.

3.3 A decrease in the price of tea will have a substitution effect that reduces coffee purchases but an income effect that increases coffee purchases (assuming coffee is a normal good). A decrease in the price of cream will increase coffee purchases because the goods are complementary. It will also increase coffee purchases because of a positive income effect (again, assuming that coffee is a normal good). The income effects are in the same direction in both of these cases, but the substitution effects are in different directions.

3.4 Reporter 1 confuses a movement along the demand curve for oranges caused by a shift in the supply curve (the freeze raises costs causing such a move) and a shift of a the demand curve. The curve does not shift, so there are no "lower prices" as a result. Reporter 2 also makes the confusion by implying that demand falls and remains low. The freeze-induced movement along the demand curve can be reversed by a more normal cropsupply. Notice how all of this could be clarified by graphing the events described.

3.5 Consumer surplus is measured on a demand curve for which the axes are price (in dollars, say, per unit) and quantity (units). Therefore, areas are measured in \$/unit · units = \$—consumer surplus is a monetary measure that can be compared to other monetary figures. If price rose by 10 percent the decline in consumer surplus would be greater than 10 percent because quantity falls also.

3.6 Case 1 would shift the demand for nutmeg *outward* so that at each price quantity demanded would increase by 2 million pounds per year. That is, the curve would be shifted to the right by an amount of 2 million pounds measured horizontally. Case 2 would shift the demand for nutmeg *upward* by \$1 at each quantity. That is, the curve would shift upward in a vertical direction by \$1.

3.7 1. In the left hand panel, a fall in price would cause total spending to fall—demand is inelastic. In the right hand panel such a decline would cause total spending to rise—demand is elastic.

2. The percent change in total spending for a one percent change in market price is given by $1 + e_{Q,P}$ as can be shown by $\frac{\Delta PQ/PQ}{\Delta P/P} = \frac{(\Delta P \cdot Q + \Delta Q \cdot P)/PQ}{\Delta P/P} = 1 + \frac{\Delta Q/Q}{\Delta P/P}.$ Hence, this information would also yield a precise estimate of the price elasticity of demand.

3.8 If every good had an income elasticity of demand greater than 1, then a 1 percent increase in income would cause total spending to rise by more than 1 percent—an impossibility given the budget constraint. If every income elasticity of demand were less than 1, then a 1 percent increase in income would increase total spending by less than 1 percent—leaving some income unspent (which would not maximize utility in a one-period model). If 95 percent of income were spent on housing, a high income elasticity of demand would result in housing expenditures quickly exhausting income when income rises. For example, suppose a consumer had an income of \$100, spending \$95 on housing. If the income elasticity of demand for housing were 2, then a 10 percent increase in income (to \$110) would cause a 20 percent increase in spending on housing (to \$114). Hence, housing spending would now exceed income, an impossibility.

3.9 A fall in the price of beer will cause consumers to substitute beer for pizza. But it will also increase overall purchasing power, which will tend to increase pizza purchases. The substitution and income effects work in opposite directions. Because a 10 percent increase in all prices and income must leave demand unchanged, the sum of these three elasticities must be zero.

4.1 1. 0.

2. \$200.

3. \$100.

4.2 The person would prefer risk if the function were convex (rather than concave as shown in Figure 4-1).

4.3 1. The expected value of the bet is zero in either case, but the variability of outcomes is much higher with the single flip.

2. The expected time to be served is the same under either approach, but the variability is higher with lines for each teller (the feeling that one has chosen the wrong line is universal).

3. Your authors feel that any scoring in sports involves some randomness. Hence, sports in which many goals are scored will be more likely to reveal the best team than sports where only a few goals are scored (true, soccer fans will probably disagree).

4.4 1. The proposed transaction is to buy the film at \$100 million. The expected value of this transaction depends on the expected film revenue and on the probability Lucas will make the movie. Both of these features add variability to the transaction's value. Presumably the duration of the option is infinite.

2. The value of the option is expected film revenue minus \$100 million discounted to the present day and by the probability the film will be made.

4A.1 1. There is no risk because C is the same in both states of the world.

2. The actuarially fair slope is $-0.6/0.4 = -1.5$. This person should be able to trade 1 unit of C_1 for 1.5 units of C_2 because state 1 is more likely to occur.

3. To find the slope of the indifference curve, start with the *MRS* between C_1 and C_2 that would be observed in a world of certainty. Then account for uncertainty by adjusting this MRS by the ratio of the probabilities 0.6/0.4 of the states occurring.

4. At point E, $C_1 = C_2$, so the MRS between them under certainty is –1. By part 3, the slope of the indifference curve is just –1 times the ratio of the probabilities, 0.6/0.4, leaving us with the actuarially fair slope of –1.5 from part 2.

5.1 1. $(1/2)(1) + (1/2)(-1) = 0$.

2. $(1/2)(-1) + (1/2)(1) = 0$.

3. Parts 1 and 2 showed that *A's* expected payoff from playing either heads or tails is 0. Therefore, *A's* expected payoff from the indicated mixed strategy is $(1/2)(0) + (1/2)(0) = 0$.

5.2 1. No.

2. No. If a player has a dominant strategy, he or she would obtain a higher expected surplus from playing it than any other strategy and so would play the dominant strategy with probability one.

5.3 1. The payoff vector (2,1) is associated with two different Nash equilibria. In the first one, B always plays ballet no matter what *A* does. In the second, *B* always follows *A*. These are two very different strategies.

2. There are three different ways *B* could end up playing Ballet. He could play the strategy of always choosing Ballet. He could play the strategy of following *A*, and *A* could have played Ballet. Or he could play the strategy of doing the opposite of *A*, and *A* could have chosen Boxing. To be clear about which strategy *B* is actually playing, one needs to specify a complete contingent plan following any action by *A*.

5.4 1. $g = 0$.

2. Relenting would make sustaining cooperation more difficult. Only the threat of punishment deters deviation from cooperation. Relenting reduces the severity of the punishment, and less severe punishments have less deterrence value.

5.5 1. The three equations, found by equating marginal benefits with marginal costs (zero) are $120 - 2s_A - s_B - s_C = 0$, $120 - s_A - 2s_B - s_C = 0$, and $120 - s_A - s_B - 2s_C = 0$. Solving them simultaneously, $s_A^* = s_B^* = s_C^* = 30$.

6.1 In Case 1, the marginal product of labor is 50 apples per hour. The average productivity of labor declines as L increases because the fixed term, "10," is divided by progressively larger amounts of labor. In Case 2, the marginal product of labor is five books dusted per minute. The average productivity of labor increases as L increases because the "-10" term is divided by progressively larger amounts of labor input.

6.2 The RTS here: 1/2 hour of labor time can be substituted for an increase in shovel size. The one-hole isoquant is two points: (a) 1 hour, small shovel; (b) 1/2 hour, large shovel. A worker using a small shovel can dig 1/2 the hole in 1/2 an hour. If he or she then switches to the large shovel, the hole can be completed in 1/4 an hour. Hence, this production technique would use 3/4 an hour of labor time.

6.3 1. Clearly a doubling of K and L would double output here. So the function exhibits constant returns to scale.

2. The function assumes that K and L are perfect substitutes. The RTS for this function is a constant—it does not diminish as L increases.

3. The function implies that q can be produced without using any labor input—a situation that is unlikely.

6.4 1. At least in part technical progress, though some substitution also.

2. At least in part technical progress, though some substitution also.

3. Almost exclusively substitution of capital for labor.
4. Almost entirely technical progress.

7.1 Rent payments are for housing services. Someone who lives in his or her own house similarly pays for such services in the form of forgone earnings on the funds invested. So, the key question is which form of housing consumption provides the services at lower costs (including opportunity costs). Paying off the mortgage converts explicit interest costs into implicit ones (the forgone earnings one could obtain by investing funds tied up in the house). If opportunity costs are the same as mortgage costs, burning the mortgage has no significance.

7.2 1. With fixed proportions, it will take 10 labor hours and 20 hours of capital services to produce 100 units of output. Total cost will be $10 \cdot 10 + 20 \cdot 4 = 180$. If capital rental rates rise to 10, the firm will continue to use the same fixed proportions but its total costs will increase to 300.
2. With this production function, the RTS (L for K) is 2. That is, an extra unit of labor can substitute for two units of capital. With $w = 10$ and $v = 4$, cost minimization requires that the firm use only capital: if it hires 20 units to produce 100 units of output, total costs are 80 (they would be 100 if only labor were used). If v increases to 10, labor becomes the less expensive input. The firm will use $L = 10$ and incur total costs of 100.

7.3 1. Average will be $(80.5 + 60.2)/7 = 520/7 = 74.3$.
2. Need $(520 + 3x)/10 = 80$, $3x = 280$, $x = 93.3$
3. When the marginal score falls below the average, the average falls. When the marginal score exceeds the average, the average rises.

7.4 1. SAC exceeds AC for every output level except q^*, because at all other output levels the firm is using a level of capital input that is not cost minimizing.
2. SMC exceeds MC for $q > q^*$, because there are more significant diminishing returns to variable inputs in the short run (when some inputs are fixed) than in the long run.
3. An increase in K above K^* would shift the SAC and SMC rightward along the AC curve.

7.5 The larger the fraction of total costs that are attributable to labor, the greater will be the effect of the increase in wages on total costs. If the firm is able to substitute capital for labor, the extent of this cost increase may be ameliorated.

8.1 1. Profit per unit is greatest when the gap between average revenue and average cost is greatest. That may not be where marginal revenue and marginal costs are equal. Even if application of the $MR = MC$ rule reduces profit per unit, it will increase *total* profits.
2. Since price is equal to "average revenue," the proposed rule would indeed maximize profit per unit. When average revenue is fixed, minimizing average cost would achieve this goal. For the reasons listed in 1, however, this would not maximize *total* profits.

8.2 1. The demand for any one crossing is elastic. When all crossings are taken together, however, the demand is inelastic.
2. The same argument applies here. The demand for meals in any one town may be elastic, but, if the tax increase is statewide, consumers cannot so easily escape it.

8.3 1. Equation 8.9 implies that $MR/P = 1 + 1/e$. Hence, the less elastic is the demand (assuming $e < -1$), the smaller will be the ratio MR/P
2. Equation 8.9 implies that the *percentage* change in P will be the same as the *percentage* change in MR if e does not change. If e changes, the two percentages may differ.

8.4 1. An increase in fixed costs will affect neither the SMC curve nor the shutdown point.
2. The fine could be treated as a fixed cost and therefore would have no effect on supply decisions. A daily fine would still be treated as a fixed cost in Whopper supply decisions. But it might provide an incentive to the firm to adopt new, less littering packaging materials.

9.1 1. When only 100 paddles are in the air
2. When paddles in the air increase to 100 (Are these two prices the same?)

9.2 1. The farmer cannot get the \$3.25, even though his or her costs may require that, because any buyer can get all the corn desired at \$3.
2. No seller will sell to the soup kitchen at \$2.75 if he or she can make \$3 elsewhere (unless the seller derives utility from helping the poor).

9.3 1. The price would rise to \$7. Demand would be 3 and supply would be $5 - 2 = 3$.
2. Trial and error using Table 9-2 suggests that a price to buyers of \$8 and to sellers of \$4 would create the necessary tax "wedge." In this case, the quantity demanded and supplied would be 2.

9.4 1. Yes, the outward shift in demand would cause movement along the (inelastic) supply curve, raising price substantially.
2. Yes, fracking shifts the supply curve outward, causing a movement along an inelastic demand curve and lower prices.

9.5 1. If expansion of the industry does not lead to increases in the prices of any inputs, the long-run supply curve will be perfectly elastic.
2. As the demand for potato land increases, its price will rise. This will be the sole reason for rising potato prices. Producer surplus will be the extra rents earned by potato landowners. The rents do not "cause" the price increase—rather, they are a result of it.

9.6 1. Because short-run supply is less elastic than long-run supply
2. One would need to examine the reasons for the upward slope in the long-run supply curve. Owners of inputs that cause the upward slope would pay the producer's share of the tax.

9.7 1. Consumer surplus is $\frac{1}{2}(10-7)(3)=4.5$. Producer surplus is $\frac{1}{2}(5-2)(3)=4.5$. Taxes are 6. Hence, total surplus plus taxes amount to 15. Prior to the tax, consumer surplus was 8 and producer surplus was 8. With the tax, there is a deadweight loss of 1. That can also be computed as $\frac{1}{2}(t)(\Delta Q)=\frac{1}{2}(2)(1)=1$
2. With a tax of 4, $P-2=10-(P+4)$ or $P=4$; $P+t=8$ and $Q=2$. Deadweight loss is $\frac{1}{2}(t)(\Delta Q)=\frac{1}{2}(4)(2)=4$ Consumer surplus $=\frac{1}{2}(10-8)(2)=2$, producer surplus $=\frac{1}{2}(4-2)(2)=2$, and tax collections are 8. Adding the three gives 12, a loss of 4 from total surplus when there are no taxes.
3. With a tax of, say, 8, $Q=0$. All producer and consumer surplus would be lost. There would be no tax collected.

9.8 1. Relative to a situation of free trade, domestic producers pay none of this tax. Assuming that the foreign supply curve is infinitely elastic, foreign producers pay none of the tax either. The tariff is paid solely by domestic consumers.
2. The increase in producer surplus from the tariff goes to those inputs that give rise to the positively sloped long-run supply curve.
3. Both areas are losses of consumer surplus that are not captured by firms nor by the government.

10.1 The primary reason for the second supply curve is to allow for repercussions in labor markets that serve the tomato industry. The rise in tomato pickers' wages shifts the supply curve. A model that looked at the effect of the shift in demand without considering these labor market effects would underpredict the impact of the increase in demand on tomato prices.

10.2 1. Only the point for which $X=Y$ on the frontier would be economically efficient.
2. A point for which $X=2Y$ on the frontier is inefficient because utility can be improved by producing more Y and less X until a point where $X=Y$ is reached.

10.3 The initial price of X would be below equilibrium. The initial price for Y would be above equilibrium. Raising P_X and lowering P_Y would restore equilibrium in both markets simultaneously.

10.4 1. The only efficient point is where Smith gets all the X and Jones gets all the Y.
2. In this case, only the points on the diagonal of the box would be efficient.
3. In this case, all of the points in the box would be efficient.

10.5 a. A pure inflation would have no effect on relative prices, hence, with a correctly drawn supply-demand diagram, neither the demand curve nor the supply curve should shift.
b. If the supply-demand curve (incorrectly) shows nominal price on the vertical axis, a pure inflation would shift both demand and supply curves up by precisely the same amounts. Equilibrium quantity would remain unchanged.

11.1 1. The monopoly is constrained by the demand curve for its product. That curve provides a menu of price-quantity combinations—once one variable is chosen, the other is defined as well.
2. The profit maximization rule for price setting must still focus on the $MR=MC$ idea. The price should be chosen so that the extra revenue from lowering the price slightly (this amount must be positive because the monopoly will operate only where demand is elastic) is just equal to the extra costs involved in producing the extra output that is sold.

11.2 1. The increase in demand will shift the marginal revenue curve outward. If MC is positively sloped, quantity will increase. Since MR has also increased, P will increase unless the elasticity of demand changes greatly (see part 2).
2. Although quantity will always rise when MR shifts outward along a positively sloped MC curve, price itself could fall if demand became much more elastic. Since $MR=P(1+1/e)$, a large enough increase in $(1+1/e)$ could allow P to fall even though MR increases.

11.3 The deadweight loss of consumer surplus is fundamentally a loss of utility to consumers—they receive less utility than they would if the market were competitive. Monopoly profits are a transfer from consumer surplus to the monopoly. They are not part of the deadweight loss.

11.4 1. The price in each market depends on the slope of the demand curve as well as the level.

2. The monopoly should set $MR = MC$ in both markets. If the elasticities in the markets differ, this need not imply that the market with higher MC will have a higher price.

11.5 With U-shaped average costs, there is no regulatory dilemma—the regulator can set $P = MC =$ minimum AC and achieve efficiency with zero economic profits. If P is set below AC, losses will result. Clearly, P could also be set below the shutdown price.

12.1 1. B's best-response function would shift in toward the origin. A's would not shift. The new Nash equilibrium would be at the point of intersection between B's new best-response function and A's unchanged one. The new Nash equilibrium would involve higher output for A and lower for B.

2. If costs for both increased, both best-response functions would shift in toward the origin. The Nash equilibrium would involve lower output for both. If costs decreased, the opposite would happen. An increase in the demand intercept would cause both best-response functions to shift out from the original and the Nash equilibrium quantities to increase.

12.2 It cannot be a Nash equilibrium because the firm that charges marginal cost earns zero profit in the outcome but could earn positive profit by deviating to a price slightly higher than marginal cost and less than the other firm's price.

12.3 1. B's best-response function would shift up. A's would not shift. The new Nash equilibrium would involve higher prices for both.

2. Both firms' best-response functions would shift away from the origin. The new Nash equilibrium would involve higher prices for both. A cost decrease would have the opposite effect. An increase in the demand intercept would shift the best-response functions away from the origin and result in higher Nash equilibrium prices. A decrease in sub-stitutability is tricky to formalize. Thought about the right way, it would probably result in best-response functions shifting out and increasing Nash equilibrium prices.

12.4 1. An increase in this sort of advertising would make the products closer substitutes and intensify second-stage price competition between them. Recognizing this effect, firms may cut back on advertising to keep competition softer and prices higher.

2. This sort of advertising would have the opposite effect as in part 1.

12.5 1. A would have to produce more to deter B's entry (complicated calculations show that A would be required to produce about 67 to deter B's entry).

2. A can deter B's entry simply producing the Stackelberg output of 60. This also happens to be the monopoly output. The implication is that A's simply operating as a monopolist ignoring B is sufficient to deter B's entry.

12.6 1. Downward-sloping demand and free entry (so zero profits).

2. The potential loss would be a loss of product diversity. The fact that demand curves facing individual firms are assumed to be downward-sloping in the monopolistic-competition model is often justified by the assumption that firms' products are at least slightly differentiated. If a firm exits, consumers lose the variety of the good it offers and thus lose some consumer surplus.

13.1 1. The monopoly will hire labor up to the point at which $w = MR \cdot MP_L$ and capital up to the point at which $v = MR \cdot MP_K$. Because $MR < P$, MP_K and MP_L must be higher than in the competitive case. Hence the firm must hire less of these inputs.

2. The marginal productivity of both inputs must be higher.

13.2 1. There will be no substitution effects from the wage increase. But the wage increase may cause a rise in gasoline prices and therefore a fall in the demand for gasoline and for attendants to pump it.

2. Because of the fixed-proportions nature of production, again there is no need to worry about substitution effects. A 10 percent rise in wages will raise gasoline prices by 3.33 percent. That will result in a decline in purchases of 1.67 percent and a similar decline in hiring of attendants. Hence, the elasticity of demand is -0.167 $(= -1.67/10)$.

13.3 As for any tax, the actual incidence of the 12 percent total tax depends on the elasticities of supply and demand.

13.4 Yes, there is a deadweight loss triangle in Figure 13.5 that is similar to the deadweight loss from monopoly. Part of the loss is suffered by suppliers who receive lower wages than they would under competition; part is suffered by demanders who cannot convert all of the surplus they would enjoy under competition into monopsony profits.

13A.1 1. The indifference curves have income and substitution effects of increases in w always precisely balanced at 7 hours of work.

2. The indifference curve map intersects the leisure axis with a slope steeper than the prevailing wage rate.

13A.2 The proportional tax on wages effectively reduces the wage rate, inducing income and substitution effects in labor supply—the substitution effect would favor less work, the income effect more work. A lump-sum tax would have no substitution effect, only an income effect favoring more work.

14.1 1. C_1 is effectively "cheaper" than C_0 because interest can be earned before C_1 is purchased. If $r = 0.10$, the relative price of C_1 is $1/1.1 = 0.909$. Refraining from buying 0.909 units of C_0 permits this person to buy one unit of C_1.

2. An increase in r reduces $1/(1 + r)$. For example, if $r = 0.15$, the relative price of C_1 is 0.870, a reduction from 0.909. This price decline has both income and substitution effects that favor consuming more C_1. The ambiguity is in the effect on C_0: a higher relative price of C_0 creates substitution effects causing C_0 to fall but income effects causing C_0 to rise (because the higher interest rate increases the person's purchasing power in this case).

14.2 A pure inflation would not affect the real interest rate nor the depreciation rate in Equation 14.1. It would raise the price of machinery, P, and the price of the firm's output, P^*, both by the same amount. Hence, in the equation $MVP_K = v = P(r + d)$, the effects of inflation would appear on both sides and would cancel out, leaving the firm's capital use decision unchanged.

14.3 Clearly, the present value of the payments is not $20 million. To calculate the present value, one would need to assume a specific nominal interest rate (nominal because the lottery payments are nominal). At 5 percent, for example, $1 million per year for 20 years has a present value of $12.5 million, significantly less than $20 million. At a 10 percent interest rate, the present value is only $8.5 million.

14.4 1. The finite nature of the resource poses the same sort of opportunity cost for the monopoly as for a competitive firm.

2. If the future price is assumed to be the same for the monopoly and the competitive firm, the result that the resource price must rise at the rate of interest implies that the monopoly price will be identical to the competitive price in all time periods. The firm cannot exercise its monopoly power.

14A.1 If $1 is invested for 3 years, the terms in the expansion have the following meanings:

a. 1—the original dollar is returned.

b. $3i$—interest is earned on the original dollar in each year.

c. $3i^2$—interest earned on Year 1's interest in Year 2 (i^2) plus interest on Year 1's interest in Year 3 (i^2) plus interest on Year 2's interest in Year 3 (i^2), which equals $3i^2$ in all.

d. i^3—interest earned in Year 3 on the interest earned in Year 2 on Year 1's interest.

14A.2 With a 5 percent interest rate, the present value of $1,000 in 5 years is $784 (see Table 14A-2). The value of $3,000 in 25 years is 3(295) = $885, so it is worth the wait. If the interest rate is 10 percent, the $1,000 has a present value of $621, and the $3,000 has a present value of $277: With the higher interest rate, the wait is clearly not worthwhile.

14A.3 1. Increasing the annual payment to $65 would raise the yield to 4.97 percent.

2. Increasing the maturity value to $1,100 would raise the yield to 4.76 percent.

3. Reducing the maturity to 15 years would lower the yield to 4.50 percent (because fewer payments are received and the $1000 face value of the bond is returned sooner).

14A.4 Depreciation can be handled by assuming that the machine's rental rate deteriorates at the rate d per period. Hence, in period n, the numerator to Equation 14A.37 should be $v/(1 + d)^n$. The equation therefore becomes $\sum_1^n v/(1 + r)^i(1 + d)^i$. Because $= (1 + r)(1 + d) \approx (1 + r + d)$, this can be approximated by $\sum_1^n = v/(1 + r + d)^i$, and taking n to infinity yields $P = v/(r + d)$, which is Equation 14.2.

15.1 The manager has to be paid enough to get him or her to work at the firm rather than somewhere else. The more effort the firm tries to induce from the manager, the more the manager has to be paid to compensate. So while marginal value product may be increasing in E above E^*, profit (marginal value product minus manager pay) is not.

15.2 1. His payoff (total pay minus total effort cost) is highest for three units of effort: 900 – 525 – 375. This is the last unit for which his marginal pay is greater than his marginal cost of effort.

2. In the absence of a fixed fee, the worker's payoff was $375 in part 1. The manager can charge the worker $75 for the privilege of working there and still match the alternative.

15.3 1. The shop can charge $1.50 for the one-shot cup and have low types buy. This provides $0.50 consumer surplus to high types, so the most a three-shot cup can be sold for and have high types buy is $4. Profit per high type is 4 – (3)(0.50) = $2.50 and per low type is 1.50 – 0.50 = $1, for total profit of $290.

2. The shop can charge $4.50 to high types for the three-shot cup and earn 4.50 – (3)(0.50) = $3 per high type for total profit of $300.

15.4 There are three ranges for player 2's bid: first, 2 could bid below 50; second, between 50 and 70; and third, above 70. First, if 2 bids below 50, player 1 would win the object whether he or she bid 50 or 70 and would pay the other player's bid regardless. Second, if 2 bids between 50 and 70, 1 would win the object and earn a negative surplus (equal to the difference between his or her valuation 50 and player 2's bid) if it bid 70; if it bid 50 it would lose the object and earn zero surplus. Third, if 2 bids above 70, 1 loses the object and pays nothing whether its bid is 50 or 70.

15.5
1. The seller may know how diligently the car was maintained, whether the car had sustained an accident, whether the car is prone to breakdown, how the car handles in different driving conditions, and so forth.
2. Sellers of higher-quality cars and buyers would benefit from solving the lemons problem. The lemons problem results in mutually advantageous trades not being executed. Some solutions were offered in the text: seller reputation, buyer knowledge about quality indicators, certification by an independent repair shop (hired by either the buyer or the seller), money-back guarantees offered by the seller, seller-provided repair histories, and so forth.

15.6
1. No. If there were, high types would have to prefer to separate than pool. The higher wage must compensate them for any higher education cost. But then a low type would benefit from mimicking the high-type's education level. It would get the same wage as a high type but would have to pay a lower education cost.
2. Yes. For example, there is a pooling equilibrium in which no one gets an education. This equilibrium could be supported by out-of-equilibrium beliefs that an educated worker has an equal chance of being a high or low type (so education does not change the firm's initial beliefs).

16.1 These deadweight losses are losses of utility that would have gone to consumers under an efficient market equilibrium, just as in the monopoly case.

16.2
1. In the absence of enforceable property rights, Coase-type exchanges would not occur because neither party could be sure that the other would stick to the agreement.
2. With high transactions costs, property rights' assignments matter. The rights should be assigned to the party most likely to internalize the externality. This observation is crucial to the study of law and economics.

16.3
1. Under all three strategies, firms are left on their own to choose cost-minimizing control strategies. The requirement of specific technologies for all firms would not be likely to result in cost minimization.
2. The government does not need to know anything about the specific cost functions of firms under any of the three market-based strategies.

16.4
1. Free riding arises because individuals obtain benefits from the public good without paying for them. That requires nonexclusion. If exclusion were possible (even if the good were nonrival), production could take place in "clubs."
2. To achieve efficiency with nonrival goods requires that the price for each use be zero. With such a price there would be no way to pay the production costs of the good unless the provision of the good could be organized as a club with an entry fee.

17.1 The exact prize is $10{,}000 \times 2^{(31-1)/2}$, nearly \$328 million.

17.2 A is a gamble with the same expected payoff as the certain outcome B. A risk-averse person with a standard concave utility function would prefer B to A (see Figure 4.1 for a representative diagram). The same comparison holds for C relative to D.

17.3
1. To take advantage of framing effects, a supporter would cite the 61% approval number.
2. The detractor would cite 39% disapproval number.

17.4 Player 1's payoff for E is 99. Player 1's expected payoff for C is $(1-p)(98)+(p)(100)$, where p is player 2's probability of continuing. Player 1 chooses C if $p > 1/2$.

17.5 The cost of studying would have to be less than 15.

17.6
1. The payoffs when player 1 chooses E in Figure 17.4 would remain the same. The payoffs when player 2 chooses E need to be adjusted by subtracting 3 from both players' payoffs.
2. Now, players prefer C to E whenever they are given the chance to move. The game continues all the way to the end, and each player earns 100. A preference for fairness could explain why the game does not end immediately in Centipede experiments.

Index

D

E

J

K

L

M

N

O

P

Q

R

S